HUMAN RESOURCE MANAGEMENT: GAINING A COMPETITIVE ADVANTAGE

HUMAN RESOURCE MANAGEMENT: GAINING A COMPETITIVE ADVANTAGE

Raymond A. Noe
UNIVERSITY OF MINNESOTA

John R. Hollenbeck
MICHIGAN STATE UNIVERSITY

Barry Gerhart
CORNELL UNIVERSITY

Patrick M. Wright
TEXAS A & M UNIVERSITY

AUSTEN
PRESS

IRWIN

BURR RIDGE, ILLINOIS
BOSTON, MASSACHUSETTS
SYDNEY, AUSTRALIA

Publisher: William Schoof
Acquisitions Editor: John Weimeister
Production Manager: Bob Lange

Development, design, and production provided by
Elm Street Publishing Services, Inc.
Developmental Editor: Karen Hill
Project Editor: Phyllis Crittenden
Production Manager: Kelly Spiller
Text and Cover Design: Rebecca Lemna, Lloyd–Lemna Design
Electronic Text Manager: Kathy Harsch
Permissions Editor: Abby Westapher

Compositor: Elm Street Publishing Services, Inc.
Typeface: 10/12 Palatino
Printer: Von Hoffmann Press, Inc.

Library of Congress Cataloging-in-Publication Data

Human resource management: gaining a competitive advantage
/ Raymond A. Noe…[et al.]
p. cm.
Includes bibliographical references and indexes.
ISBN 0–256–11349–1
1. Personnel management—United States.   I. Noe, Raymond A.
HF5549.2.U5H8   1994
658.3—dc20   93–26120

Printed in the United States of America
    4 5 6 7 8 9 0 VH 9 8 7 6 5

Address editorial correspondence:
Austen Press
18141 Dixie Highway
Suite 111
Homewood, IL 60430

Address orders:
Richard D. Irwin, Inc.
1333 Burr Ridge Parkway
Burr Ridge, IL 60521

Austen Press
Richard D. Irwin, Inc.

PREFACE

To grow and thrive in today's competitive environment, organizations must deal with several major challenges. First, they must provide "value." Traditionally, the concept of value has been considered a function of finance or accounting. However, we believe that how human resources are managed is crucial to the long-term value of a company and ultimately to its survival. Our definition of value includes not only profits but employee growth and satisfaction, additional employment opportunities, protection of the environment, and contributions to community programs.

Second, organizations must be competitive. We believe that all aspects of human resource management—including how companies interact with the environment; acquire, develop, and compensate human resources; and design and measure work—can help companies meet their competitive challenges and create value. Meeting challenges is necessary to create value and to gain a competitive advantage.

The challenges organizations face today can be grouped into four categories:

- **The global challenge.** Increasingly, companies are finding that to survive they must compete with companies around the world. Companies must both defend their domestic markets from foreign competitors and broaden their scope to encompass global markets. Recent threats to and successes of U.S. business have proven that globalization is a continuing challenge.

- **The quality challenge.** Key to success in today's world is providing customers with high-quality products and services. Companies that cannot give customers quality at a reasonable cost risk losing out to competitors.

- **The social challenge.** The two components of the social challenge are understanding and utilizing a diverse work force and operating in an ethical and legal manner. As we approach the 21st century, the U.S. work force is becoming increasingly diverse. Women and minorities are entering the work force in record numbers. Forward-looking businesses are coming to terms with this fact and capitalizing on the strengths of diversity. Ethics and legal issues are also receiving greater attention in today's business environment. More and more, businesses are realizing the benefits of behaving ethically and responsibly.

- **The technology and structure challenge.**   Using technological advances effectively can provide companies with an edge. Also, structuring work efficiently reduces costs and time. Working smarter is the idea behind the use of teams and human resource information systems.

We believe that organizations must successfully deal with these challenges to create and maintain value, and the key to facing these challenges is a motivated, well-trained, and committed work force.

The major theme of *Human Resource Management: Gaining a Competitive Advantage* is how the management of human resources can help companies meet their competitive challenges. We begin the book with a discussion of the global, quality, social, and technological challenges facing U.S. businesses and the role of human resource management in helping companies meet these challenges. Topics such as managing a diverse work force, total quality management, and work teams are discussed in detail in the first chapter and throughout the text as they relate to human resource management practices.

Each chapter discusses current best practice and research. Boxed examples within each chapter illustrate how human resource practices have helped companies meet global, quality, social, and technological and structural challenges and gain a competitive advantage. To be successful, managers must effectively motivate, train, and support their people. Each chapter emphasizes what managers can do to effectively manage human resources.

We think this book represents a new and valuable approach to teaching human resource management for several reasons:

- The text draws from the diverse research, teaching, and consulting experiences of four authors. The teamwork approach gives a depth and breadth to the coverage that is not found in other texts.

- Human resource management is viewed as critical to the success of a business. The text emphasizes how the human resource function, as well as the management of human resources, can help companies gain a competitive advantage.

- The book discusses current issues such as work-force diversity, the quality movement, work teams, and technology, all of which have a major impact on business and human resource practice.

- Chapters related to global human resource management and strategic human resource management are introduced early in the book, and these issues are integrated throughout the text. These are key topics in human resource management today.

- A complete chapter is provided on human resource information systems, which are becoming increasingly popular to cut costs, increase efficiency, and improve the quality of decision making in human resource management.

ORGANIZATION

Human Resource Management: Gaining a Competitive Advantage includes an introductory chapter (Chapter 1) and six parts.

Chapter 1 provides a detailed discussion of the global, quality, social, and technology and structure challenges that influence U.S. companies' abilities to successfully meet the needs of shareholders, customers, employees, and other stakeholders. We discuss how the management of human resources can help companies meet the competitive challenges.

Part I includes a discussion of the environmental forces that companies face in attempting to capitalize on their human resources as a means to gain competitive advantage. The environmental forces include the strategic direction of the business, global issues in the management of human resources, the legal environment, and employee relations.

A key focus of the strategic human resource management chapter is highlighting the role that staffing, performance management, training and development, and compensation play in different types of business strategies. Social and political changes, such as the formation of the European Economic Community and the proposed North American Free Trade Agreement, are discussed in the chapter on global human resource management. Issues related to how to select, prepare, and reward employees for foreign assignments, given the country's cultural, educational, political, and economic environment, are also discussed. A key focus of the legal chapter is enhancing managers' understanding of laws related to sexual harassment, affirmative action, and accommodations for disabled employees. The various types of discrimination and ways they have been interpreted by the courts are discussed. The chapter on employee relations emphasizes how practices and policies related to employee safety, health, job security, and working conditions can improve company competitiveness by alleviating health care costs and job stress, which can result from an unfair and unsafe work environment.

Part II deals with work design, employee performance, and work attitudes. Here we explore how work can be designed to improve productivity and efficiency, employee safety, and job satisfaction. The performance management chapter examines the strengths and weaknesses of performance management methods that use ratings, objectives, or behaviors. The influence of total quality management on performance management systems is also examined. The chapter on work attitudes identifies work attitudes (e.g., job satisfaction) that can influence company productivity and competitiveness. Interventions that can help managers maximize employee productivity and satisfaction to avoid withdrawal behaviors such as absenteeism are discussed.

Part III explores how companies can determine their human resource needs and recruit and select employees who will contribute to company productivity. The recruitment chapter illustrates the process by which individuals choose jobs and the role of the manager in shaping job choices. The chapter emphasizes the actions that employers can take during the recruitment process to ensure that job candidates make choices that further the company's goals as well as their own. The human resource planning chapter illustrates the process of developing a human resource plan. Also, the role of human resource planning in companies and its link to the business strategy, as well as staffing, training, and compensation strategies, are emphasized. The selection chapter emphasizes ways to minimize errors in employee selection and placement to improve the company's competitive position. Selection method standards such as validity and reliability are discussed in easily understandable terms without compromising the technical complexity of these issues. The chapter discusses selection methods such as interviews and various types of tests (including personality, honesty, and drug tests) and compares them on measures of validity, reliability, utility, and legality.

Part IV focuses on the development of human resources: training, employee development, and career management are each discussed in separate chapters. We discuss the components of effective training systems and the manager's role in determining employees' readiness for training, creating a positive learning environment, and ensuring training is used on the job. The advantages of different training methods are described, including discussion of adventure learning and interactive video.

Current issues in employee development, including managing workforce diversity, managing work teams, and cross-cultural preparation are emphasized. The use of assessment, job experiences, formal courses, and mentoring relationships to develop employees is discussed. The career management chapter begins with a discussion of the development needs of employees at different career stages. Several issues related to the competitive challenges are discussed, including work and family conflict, plateauing, career planning, and effective outplacement and management of survivors.

Part V covers rewarding and compensating human resources, including designing pay structures, recognizing individual contributions, and providing benefits. Here we explore how managers should decide the pay rate for different jobs, given the company's compensation strategy and the worth of jobs. The advantages and disadvantages of merit pay, gainsharing, and skill-based pay are discussed. The benefits chapter highlights the different types of employer-provided benefits and discusses how benefit costs can be contained. International comparisons of compensation and benefit practices are provided.

Part VI covers special topics in human resource management including labor-employee relations and human resource information systems. Union structure and memberships, the organizing process, contract negotiations, and the relationship between labor relations and competitiveness are discussed. The human resource information systems chapter provides an easy-to-understand, up-to-date overview of hardware and databases used to manage human resources. The steps that are necessary for the successful development, implementation, and purchase of human resource information systems or software are highlighted. A key emphasis of the chapter is discussing available software applications that can help managers improve their effectiveness and efficiency in managing human resources.

Video Cases at the end of each part integrate the concepts presented. These cases are intended to give students practice in real-life situations by allowing them to consider a variety of human resource issues simultaneously.

FEATURES DESIGNED TO AID LEARNING

Human Resource Management provides several features designed to aid learning:

- Learning objectives at the beginning of each chapter inform students about what they should know about managing human resources when they read the chapter.
- A chapter-opening vignette presents a real business problem or issue that provides background for the issues discussed in the chapter.
- Competing through Globalization, Competing through Quality, Competing through Social Responsibility, and Competing through Technology & Structure boxes in the chapters highlight how companies have gained a competitive advantage through effective human resource management practices designed to meet global, quality, social, and technology and structure challenges. The examples are drawn from a wide spectrum of businesses in different sectors of the economy, such as manufacturing, health care, service, and sales.

  For example, the "Competing through Social Responsibility" box in Chapter 2, "Strategic Human Resource Management," discusses how two small businesses, Kingston Technology and Pacer Technologies, derive their success from offering specialized products and recognizing the role of human resources in providing competitive advantage. For example, based on Kingston Technology founder's beliefs that the company's employees are the most valuable asset, Kingston only promotes from within even if technical knowledge might be acquired more quickly by hiring from the external labor market.

  In Chapter 11, "Personnel Selection and Placement," the "Competing through Technology & Structure" box shows how Carrier Corporation designed a new selection system to choose employees for its new high-technology air compressor assembly plant. The new selection system has helped the company save over $25 million a year.

  The "Competing through Globalization" box in Chapter 13, "Employee Development," discusses how General Electric Medical Systems in Milwaukee increased non-U.S. business revenue from 13 percent in 1985 to 40 percent in 1992. Their success in the global marketplace is a direct result of the company's multifaceted approach to cross-cultural preparation, which involves employees who have overseas assignments and employees who have daily contact with employees from foreign subsidiaries in Tokyo and Paris.

In Chapter 17, "Employee Benefits," the "Competing through Quality" box illustrates how Xerox has controlled the growth of health care costs through managing competition of health care providers. Xerox has reduced health care costs by identifying the most efficient and effective health maintenance organizations through benchmarking.

- Important terms used in human resource management are boldfaced in each chapter.

- In-text examples feature companies from the service, retail, and manufacturing sectors of the economy.

- Discussion questions at the end of each chapter help students learn the concepts presented in the chapter and understand potential applications of the chapter material.

- End-of-chapter cases present business problems related to the management of human resources. The cases give students the opportunity to immediately apply what they have learned in the chapter.

- End-of-part video cases provide examples of companies that have used human resource management practices to gain a competitive advantage. The 12- to 15-minute videos contain conversations with managers and employees and footage of the operations of the business. The video cases and accompanying questions challenge students to view human resource issues and problems from multiple perspectives.

- An end-of-book glossary defines key terms used in human resource management.

- Name and subject indexes at the end of the book aid in finding topics and key people and companies.

- State-of-the-art use of design and color make the book more readable for students and enhance learning.

READINGS BOOK

Readings in Human Resource Management, a companion publication to *Human Resource Management,* provides up to three current articles for each of the chapters covered in this text. These articles discuss important techniques, trends, issues, and research findings related to the management of human resources. The articles are appropriate for undergraduate and graduate students in human resource management courses in masters of business administration, industrial relations, and human resource management curricula.

INSTRUCTOR MATERIALS

- **Instructor's Manual and Transparency Masters.**   Authored by Denise Tanguay Hoyer, Fraya Wagner, and Jean McEnery of Eastern Michigan University, the *Instructor's Manual* contains a lecture outline and notes, answers to the discussion questions, additional discussion questions and exercises, teaching suggestions, term paper and project topics, and answers to the end-of-chapter cases and video cases. Included at the end of the *Instructor's Manual* are 75 transparency masters, some completely new material, some drawn from key figures and tables in the text. Also included in the package are 25 color transparency acetates.

- **Test Bank.** The *Test Bank* contains 25 true/false, 50 multiple-choice, and 10 essay questions per chapter, for a total of more than 1,600 questions. Questions are graded by level of difficulty, and text page references where answers can be found are provided.

- **Computerized Testing Program.** Available through Richard D. Irwin, this test generator allows instructors to add and edit questions, create up to 99 different versions of the test, and more.

- **Videos.** Each instructor who adopts *Human Resource Management* receives a free copy of the end-of-part videos. The videos can be used to generate in-class discussion and draw students' interest. A wide variety of company settings give the videos broad appeal.

ACKNOWLEDGMENTS

Several people have provided valuable assistance that made this book possible. Bill Schoof, president of Austen Press, gave us the opportunity to provide a new perspective for teaching human resource management. John Weimeister, Austen Press editor, gave us useful information about the human resource textbook market, coordinated all book reviews, helped us in making all of the major decisions regarding the book, and helped make writing this book an enjoyable experience. Bill and John's expertise, patience, and humor helped us produce a high-quality product, yet enjoy the process. Denise Tanguay Hoyer and Jean McEnery of Eastern Michigan University developed the end-of-part video cases and discussion questions and provided help with scripting the videos. Denise Tanguay Hoyer, Fraya Wagner, and Jean McEnery of Eastern Michigan University wrote the *Instructor's Manual*. Also, many thanks to the students who helped class-test the *Test Bank* questions; and to Allan Cohen's Consultation Services at the University of Wisconsin, who reviewed the *Test Bank* and helped us develop quality questions.

Thanks to the development and production staff at Elm Street Publishing Services. Karen Hill, our developmental editor, provided valuable suggestions for improving our writing style and helped us understand how to present our ideas and concepts to maximize students' learning. Phyllis Crittenden, Kathy Harsch, Sue Langguth, Ted Murach, and Kelly Spiller made sure that the production of the text went smoothly. Also, thanks to Bruce MacLean of MacLean Video Productions for shooting the custom video footage for the text.

Finally, we would like to thank the more than 250 respondents to the human resource management questionnaire, whose comments provided insight for the initial draft of the text. Also, Susan Raynis, Clarkson University, took the time to give us helpful suggestions early in the project. And special thanks to the focus group members and manuscript reviewers, who provided us with valuable feedback:

Allison Barber
Michigan State University

Ron Beaulieu
Central Michigan University

Chris Berger
Purdue University

Sarah Bowman
Idaho State University

Charles Braun
University of Kentucky

Georgia Chao
Michigan State University

Michael Crant
University of Notre Dame

John Delery
Texas A & M University

Tom Dougherty
University of Missouri

Cynthia Fukami
University of Denver

Dan Gallagher
James Madison University

Terri Griffith
University of Arizona

Bob Hatfield
Indiana University

Rob Heneman
Ohio State University

Wayne Hockwater
Florida State University

Denise Tanguay Hoyer
Eastern Michigan University

Gwen Jones
State University of New York at Albany

Tom Kolenko
Kennesaw State College

Larry Mainstone
Valparaiso University

Nicholas Mathys
DePaul University

Robert Paul
Kansas State University

Sam Rabinowitz
Rutgers University

Katherine Ready
University of Wisconsin

Mike Ritchie
University of South Carolina

Josh Schwarz
Miami University, Ohio

Christina Shalley
University of Arizona

Richard Simpson
University of Utah

Scott Snell
Pennsylvania State University

Charles Vance
Loyola Marymount University

Raymond A. Noe
John R. Hollenbeck
Barry Gerhart
Patrick M. Wright

October 1993

ABOUT THE AUTHORS

Raymond A. Noe is Associate Professor in the Industrial Relations Center, Carlson School of Management, University of Minnesota. He received his BS in psychology from The Ohio State University and his MA and PhD in psychology from Michigan State University. Professor Noe conducts research and teaches undergraduate, graduate, and practitioner classes in human resource management, quantitative methods, human resource information systems, training, employee development, and organizational behavior. He has published articles in the *Academy of Management Journal, Academy of Management Review, Journal of Applied Psychology, Journal of Vocational Behavior,* and *Personnel Psychology*. Professor Noe is currently on the editorial board of several journals including *Personnel Psychology, Journal of Business and Psychology,* and the *Journal of Training Research*. Professor Noe has received awards for his teaching and research excellence, including the Herbert G. Heneman Distinguished Teaching Award in 1991 and the Ernest J. McCormick Award for Distinguished Early Career Contribution from the Society for Industrial and Organizational Psychology in 1993.

John R. Hollenbeck is Professor of Management at the Eli Broad Graduate School of Business Administration at Michigan State University. He received his PhD in management and organizational behavior from New York University in 1984. Professor Hollenbeck currently serves on the editorial boards of several journals, including *Personnel Psychology, Academy of Management Journal, Organizational Behavior and Human Decision Processes,* and the *Journal of Management*. Professor Hollenbeck has been recognized for both his research and teaching. He was the first recipient of the Ernest J. McCormick Award for Distinguished Early Career Contributions to the field of Industrial and Organizational Psychology in 1992 and was the 1987 Teacher-Scholar Award winner at Michigan State University. Dr. Hollenbeck's research focuses on self-regulation theories of work motivation, employee separation and acquisition processes, and team decision making and performance.

Barry Gerhart is Associate Professor at the Center for Advanced Human Resource Studies and Chair of the Department of Personnel and Human Resource Studies, School of Industrial and Labor Relations at Cornell University. He received his BS in psychology from Bowling Green State University in 1979 and his PhD in industrial relations from the University of Wisconsin-Madison in 1985. His research is in the areas of compensation/rewards, staffing, and employee attitudes. Professor Gerhart has worked with a variety of organizations, including GE, TRW, Corning, Bausch & Lomb, and Blue Cross/Blue Shield of Maryland. His work has appeared in the *Academy of Management Journal, Industrial Relations, Industrial and Labor Relations Review, Journal of Applied Psychology, Personnel Psychology,* and *Handbook of Industrial and Organizational Psychology,* and he serves on the editorial board of the *Academy of Management Journal.* He was a corecipient of the 1991 Scholarly Achievement Award, Human Resources Division, Academy of Management.

Patrick M. Wright is Assistant Professor of Management and Coordinator of the Master of Science in Human Resource Management program in the College of Business Administration and Graduate School of Business at Texas A&M University. He holds a BA in psychology from Wheaton College and an MBA and a PhD in organizational behavior/human resource management from Michigan State University. He teaches, conducts research, and consults in the areas of personnel selection, employee motivation, and strategic and international human resource management. His research articles have appeared in journals such as the *Journal of Applied Psychology, Organizational Behavior and Human Decision Processes, Journal of Management,* and *Human Resource Management Review.* He also serves as an ad hoc reviewer for the *Journal of Applied Psychology, Organizational Behavior and Human Decision Processes, Academy of Management Journal,* and *Journal of Management.* In addition, he has consulted for a number of organizations, including Whirlpool Corporation, Amoco Oil Company, and the North Carolina State Government.

BRIEF CONTENTS

1   Human Resource Management: Gaining a Competitive Advantage 1

I   MANAGING THE INTERNAL AND EXTERNAL ENVIRONMENTS 41

2   Strategic Human Resource Management 43
3   Global Issues in Human Resource Management 79
4   The Legal Environment and Equal Employment Opportunity 117
5   Employee Relations 157
VIDEO CASE   Southwest Airlines: Competing through People 187

II   ASSESSING WORK AND WORK OUTCOMES 193

6   The Analysis and Design of Work 195
7   Performance Management 233
8   Work Attitudes and Job Withdrawal 279
VIDEO CASE   Detroit Diesel Corporation: An Evolution of Tasks and Attitudes 308

III   ACQUIRING HUMAN RESOURCES 313

9   Human Resource Planning 315
10   Job Choice and the Recruitment of Human Resources 341
11   Personnel Selection and Placement 375
VIDEO CASE   Nucor: Selecting High Performers 409

IV   DEVELOPING HUMAN RESOURCES 415

12   Training 417
13   Employee Development 459
14   Career Management 501
VIDEO CASE   Training Is Our Competitive Advantage: Arthur Andersen and Andersen Consulting 536

V   COMPENSATING HUMAN RESOURCES 541

15   Pay Structure Decisions 543
16   Recognizing Individual Contributions with Pay 581
17   Employee Benefits 617
VIDEO CASE   Budget Rent-a-Car and International Compensation 658

VI   SPECIAL TOPICS IN HUMAN RESOURCE MANAGEMENT 663

18   Collective Bargaining and Labor Relations 665
19   Human Resource Information Systems 715
VIDEO CASE   Saturn Corporation and the UAW: A Test of Labor's Partnership with Management 748

GLOSSARY 755

NAME INDEX 765

SUBJECT INDEX 779

CONTENTS

1 **Human Resource Management: Gaining a Competitive Advantage 1**
Chaparral Steel: Improving Company Performance through Human Resource Management 1

Introduction 2

A Historical View of Human Resource Management Practices 3

Competitive Challenges Influencing Human Resource Management 6
  The Global Challenge 6
  The Quality Challenge 8
  The Social Challenge 14
  The Technology and Structure Challenge 26

Meeting the Competitive Challenges through HRM Practices 31
  Managing the Internal and External Environments 32
  Assessing Work and Work Outcomes 33
  Acquiring Human Resources 33
  Developing Human Resources 34
  Compensating Human Resources 34
  Special Issues 34
  Organization of This Book 35

COMPETING THROUGH GLOBALIZATION:
Preparing International Management Talent at Gillette Company 8

COMPETING THROUGH QUALITY:
Zytec Corporation: A Baldrige Award Winner 13

COMPETING THROUGH SOCIAL RESPONSIBILITY:
Managing Customer and Employee Diversity 22

COMPETING THROUGH TECHNOLOGY & STRUCTURE:
Team-based Manufacturing at Levi Strauss & Company 28

Case: Meeting Competitive Challenges 39

I   MANAGING THE INTERNAL AND EXTERNAL ENVIRONMENTS   41

2   Strategic Human Resource Management   43

Human Resources—A Source of Competitive Advantage   43

Introduction   44

What Is Strategic Management?   45

Components of the Strategic Management Process   46

Strategy Formulation   48

The Role of HR in Strategy Formulation   49

Example: People Express   53

Strategy Implementation   55

HR Practices   56

Strategic Types   61

HR Needs in Strategic Types   63

Directional Strategies   64

The Role of Human Resources in Providing Strategic Competitive Advantage   67

Strategic Management for the HR Function: A Customer Orientation   69

Strategic Human Resource Executives   72

Summary   74

COMPETING THROUGH GLOBALIZATION:

Global View of the Human Capital Shortage   51

COMPETING THROUGH QUALITY:

Total Quality Management at Allied Signal   60

COMPETING THROUGH SOCIAL RESPONSIBILITY:

Putting Employees First: Lessons from Small Business   69

COMPETING THROUGH TECHNOLOGY & STRUCTURE:

Restructuring Human Resources: Workforce Solutions   73

Case: A New Strategic Direction   77

3   Global Issues in Human Resource Management   79

When Play Can Pay   79

Introduction   80

Current Global Changes   82

European Economic Community   82

German Unification   82

Disintegration of the Soviet Union   83

North American Free Trade Agreement (NAFTA)   83

Factors Affecting HRM in Global Markets   84

Culture   84

Education/Human Capital   90
Political/Legal System   92
Economic System   93

Managing Employees in a Global Context   96
Types of International Employees   96
Levels of Global Participation   98
Managing Expatriates in Global Markets   102

Summary   112

COMPETING THROUGH GLOBALIZATION:
Japanese Managers Adopt American Management Practices   90

COMPETING THROUGH SOCIAL RESPONSIBILITY:
The Fundamental Social Rights of Workers in the EEC   94

COMPETING THROUGH TECHNOLOGY & STRUCTURE:
Socialist HRM Practices in the Former Soviet Bloc Countries   95

COMPETING THROUGH QUALITY:
Labor Costs Are Not Everything: Productivity
Increases Make Companies Competitive   103

Case: Managing an Israeli Subsidiary   115

4   The Legal Environment and Equal Employment Opportunity   117
Discrimination in the News   117

Introduction   118
The Regulatory Model   119

The Legal System in the United States   119
Legislative Branch   121
Executive Branch   121
Judicial Branch   122

Equal Employment Opportunity   123
Constitutional Amendments   123
Congressional Legislation   123
Executive Orders   130

Enforcement of Equal Employment Opportunity   131
Equal Employment Opportunity Commission (EEOC)   131
Office of Federal Contract Compliance Procedures (OFCCP)   133

Types of Discrimination   135
Disparate Treatment   135
Disparate Impact   138
Pattern or Practice   143
Retaliation for Participation and Opposition   144

Current Issues Regarding Diversity and Equal Employment Opportunity   145

   Sexual Harassment   145

   Affirmative Action and Reverse Discrimination   148

   Reasonable Accommodation for Disabled Americans   149

Summary   152

COMPETING THROUGH TECHNOLOGY & STRUCTURE:

Technological Solutions to Disparate Impact at Carrier   140

COMPETING THROUGH GLOBALIZATION:

Sexual Harassment Overseas   146

COMPETING THROUGH SOCIAL RESPONSIBILITY:

Social Concern Translates to Profitability at the Principal Financial Group   151

Case: A Discriminatory Culture at Shoney's   155

5   Employee Relations   157

Did She Know the Job Was Dangerous when She Took It?   157

Introduction   158

Employee Safety   159

   The Occupational Safety and Health Act   159

   Safety Awareness Programs   163

Employee Health   165

   Employee Assistance Programs   168

   Employee Wellness Programs   170

Employee Security and Working Conditions   172

   Discipline, Due Process, and Discharge   172

   Plant-Closing Legislation   175

   Nontraditional Work Schedules   176

   Job Sharing and Part-Time Work   178

   Family-Friendly Policies   180

Summary   182

COMPETING THROUGH TECHNOLOGY & STRUCTURE:

New Keyboard Designs Reduce CTDs   165

COMPETING THROUGH GLOBALIZATION:

Are American Companies Importing Japanese-Style Occupational Stress?   171

COMPETING THROUGH SOCIAL RESPONSIBILITY:

Care for Children and Elders   181

Case: Easing the Physician Shortage   185

VIDEO CASE   Southwest Airlines: Competing through People   187

II   ASSESSING WORK AND WORK OUTCOMES   193

6   The Analysis and Design of Work   195

Redesigning Work for Today's Marketplace   195

Introduction   197

Work-Flow Analysis   199

Analyzing Work Outputs   199
Analyzing Work Processes   202
Analyzing Work Inputs   202

Job Analysis   204

The Importance of Job Analysis to HR Managers   205
The Importance of Job Analysis to Line Managers   206
Job-Analysis Information   207
Job Analysis Methods   210
A Manager's Guide to Performing Job Analysis   216

Job Design   220

Motivational Approach   220
Mechanistic Approach   225
Biological Approach   225
Perceptual/Motor Approach   226
Implications of Different Approaches for Job Design   227

Summary   228

COMPETING THROUGH QUALITY:
Total Quality Management and Work-Flow Design at Carrier   204

COMPETING THROUGH TECHNOLOGY & STRUCTURE:
Technological Solutions to HR Problems: Ergonomics at Toyota   226

Case: Whirlpool's Automated Parts Distribution Center   232

7   Performance Management   233

Former Coach Cries Foul on Firing   233

Introduction   234

An Organizational Model of Performance Management   235

Purposes of Performance Management   237

Strategic Purpose   237
Administrative Purpose   237
Developmental Purpose   238

Performance Measures Criteria   238

Strategic Congruence   239
Validity   239
Reliability   240

Acceptability   241
Specificity   241

Approaches to Measuring Performance   241
The Comparative Approach   241
The Attribute Approach   244
The Behavioral Approach   248
The Total Quality Approach   256

Choosing a Source for Performance Information   265
Supervisors   265
Peers   265
Subordinates   266
Self   266
Customers   267

Errors in Performance Measurement   267
Rater Errors   267
Reducing Rater Errors   269

Performance Feedback   270
Ways to Improve the Performance Feedback Process   270

Developing and Implementing a System that Follows Legal Guidelines   272

Summary   273

COMPETING THROUGH QUALITY:
The TQM Approach to Performance Measurement at Ensoniq Corporation   263

COMPETING THROUGH TECHNOLOGY & STRUCTURE:
Team Appraisals at Digital   269

Case: Managing Employee Performance   278

8   **Work Attitudes and Job Withdrawal   279**
Violence and the U.S. Postal Service   279

Introduction   280

Job Satisfaction   281
Defining Job Satisfaction   281
Measures of Job Satisfaction   282

Job Withdrawal   284
Behavior Change   286
Physical Job Withdrawal   286
Psychological Withdrawal   287
Health Problems   289

Sources of Job Dissatisfaction   291
Physical and Technological Environment   293
Social Environment   294

Behavior Settings   295
Person   295
Organizational Tasks   297
Organizational Roles   300

Summary   302

COMPETING THROUGH GLOBALIZATION:
The Link between Employee Commitment and Company Success   291

COMPETING THROUGH TECHNOLOGY & STRUCTURE:
Ethical Issues with E-mail   296

COMPETING THROUGH SOCIAL RESPONSIBILITY:
Coping with the Results of Corporate Downsizing   303

**Case: The Broken Link: Decentralized Authority
and Employee Satisfaction   307**

VIDEO CASE   Detroit Diesel Corporation: An Evolution of Tasks and Attitudes   308

III   ACQUIRING HUMAN RESOURCES   313

9   Human Resource Planning   315

A Tale of Two Labor Shortages   315

Introduction   317

The Role of Human Resource Planning in Organizations   317
Relationship to Overall Business Strategy   318
Relationship to Human Resource Subfunctions   318

The Human Resource Planning Process   319
Forecasting   319
Goal Setting   331
Strategic Choice   331
Program Implementation   335
Program Evaluation   335

The Special Case of Affirmative Action Planning   336

Summary   338

COMPETING THROUGH GLOBALIZATION:
Prestige, Productivity, and Ethics Figure into the Equation   327

COMPETING THROUGH QUALITY:
A Permanent Solution to a Temporary Problem   333

COMPETING THROUGH SOCIAL RESPONSIBILITY:
Breaking Down Barriers in the Workplace   337

Case: Corporate Strategy and Human Resource Planning   340

10   Job Choice and the Recruitment of Human Resources   341

Urban Unemployment and Minority Teenagers   341

Introduction   342

Factors That Influence Job Choice   343

Vacancy Characteristics   343

Characteristics of Individuals   346

The Role of Human Resource Recruitment   355

Personnel Policies   356

Recruitment Sources   359

Recruiters   366

Summary   370

COMPETING THROUGH GLOBALIZATION:

Recruiting Japanese Managers: If You Can't Beat Them, Have Them Join You   347

COMPETING THROUGH SOCIAL RESPONSIBILITY:

Small Business Reaps Benefits of Company Layoffs   363

COMPETING THROUGH TECHNOLOGY & STRUCTURE:

Databases Pool Available Talent   365

Case: Can Small Be Better for Recruiting?   374

11   Personnel Selection and Placement   375

Feeling Insecure in the Security Industry   375

Introduction   376

Selection Method Standards   377

Reliability   377

Validity   380

Generalizability   384

Utility   385

Legality   387

Types of Selection Methods   392

Interviews   392

References and Biographical Data   394

Physical Ability Tests   395

Cognitive Ability Tests   395

Personality Inventories   398

Work Samples   398

Honesty and Drug Tests   400

Summary   403

COMPETING THROUGH TECHNOLOGY & STRUCTURE:

High Selection Standards Lower Costs at Carrier Corporation   389

COMPETING THROUGH SOCIAL RESPONSIBILITY:
The Controversy Surrounding Race Norming 391

COMPETING THROUGH GLOBALIZATION:
Personnel Selection and Cross-Cultural Barriers in Russia 401

Case: Personnel Selection in Team Environments 408

VIDEO CASE   Nucor: Selecting High Performers 409

IV   **DEVELOPING HUMAN RESOURCES 415**

12   **Training 417**
Using Training to Gain a Competitive Advantage 417

Introduction 418
High-Leverage Training Strategy: A Systematic Approach 419
Designing Effective Training Systems 420
Needs Assessment 420
Ensuring Employees' Readiness for Training 428
Create a Learning Environment 433
Ensure Transfer of Training 436
Training Methods 437
Evaluating Training Programs 445

Special Issues 451
Legal Issues 451
Training and Pay Systems 453

Summary 453

COMPETING THROUGH TECHNOLOGY & STRUCTURE:
Training versus Learning at Esso 421

COMPETING THROUGH SOCIAL RESPONSIBILITY:
Basic Skills Receive Boost from Concerned Companies 434

COMPETING THROUGH QUALITY:
Training Is the Key to Customer Service at Revco 438

COMPETING THROUGH GLOBALIZATION:
Companies Take Global View of Training 439

Case: Maintenance Training at General Mills 458

13   **Employee Development 459**
Management Development Continues at GTE Despite Restructuring 459
Introduction 460

The Work Roles of Employees, Managers, and Executives 461

Employees' Work Roles   461

Managers' Work Roles   463

Executives' Work Roles   464

Organizational Characteristics That Influence Employee Development 466

Integration of Business Units   467

Global Presence   467

Business Conditions   467

Staffing Strategy   468

Human Resource Planning   470

Unionization   470

Manager, Employee, and Human Resource Staff
Involvement in Development   470

Approaches to Employee Development 471

Formal Education   471

Assessment   472

Job Experiences   477

Interpersonal Relationships   481

Current Issues in Employee Development 484

Cross-Cultural Preparation   484

Managing Work-Force Diversity   486

Joint Union-Management Programs   490

Succession Planning   492

Developing Managers with Dysfunctional Behaviors   493

Summary 494

COMPETING THROUGH QUALITY:

Baptist Memorial Hospital Develops Total Quality Council—
and Its Employees   462

COMPETING THROUGH TECHNOLOGY & STRUCTURE:

Employee Skills Benefit Both Southwest Industries and Its Workers   464

COMPETING THROUGH GLOBALIZATION:

GE Medical Systems Help Employees "Go Global"   487

COMPETING THROUGH SOCIAL RESPONSIBILITY:

UPS Carries Diversity Training to Great Lengths   491

Case: Keeping Pace with Work-Force Diversity   499

14   Career Management   501

Three Employees' Career Concerns   501

Introduction   503

The Career Concept   504

What Is a Career?   504
A Model of Career Development   505

Career-Planning Systems   509
Components of Career-Planning Systems   509
Role of Employees, Managers, and Company in Career Planning   510

Career Development Issues   514
Socialization and Orientation   514
Career Plateauing   516
Dual Career Paths   517
Skills Obsolescence   520
Balancing Work and Family   521
Company Policies to Accommodate Work and Family   522
Job Loss   525
Retirement   528

Summary   530

COMPETING THROUGH GLOBALIZATION:
Ex-Professor Learns Japanese and Manufacturing at Fujitsu   507

COMPETING THROUGH TECHNOLOGY & STRUCTURE:
British Petroleum Discovers the Benefits of a Dual Career-Path System   520

COMPETING THROUGH SOCIAL RESPONSIBILITY:
Older Workers' Career Possibilities Expand   529

Case: Career Opportunities Affect Morale and Performance   535

VIDEO CASE   Training Is Our Competitive Advantage:
Arthur Andersen and Andersen Consulting   536

V   COMPENSATING HUMAN RESOURCES   541

15   Pay Structure Decisions   543
Reducing Employment to Cut Labor Costs   543
Introduction   544
Equity Theory and Fairness   545
Developing Pay Levels   547
Market Pressures   547
Employees as a Resource   549
Deciding What to Pay   549
Market Pay Surveys   549
Developing a Job Structure   552
Job Evaluation   552
Developing a Pay Structure   553

Conflicts between Market Pay Surveys and Job Evaluation   558
Monitoring Compensation Costs   559

The Importance of Process: Communication and Participation Issues   559
Participation   559
Communication   560

Current Challenges   561
Problems with Job-based Pay Structures   561
Responses to Problems with Job-based Pay Structures   562
Can the U.S. Labor Force Compete?   564
Executive Pay   568

Government Regulation of Employee Compensation   570
Equal Employment Opportunity   570
Minimum Wage, Overtime, and Prevailing Wage Laws   574

Summary   575

COMPETING THROUGH TECHNOLOGY & STRUCTURE:
Skill-based Pay and Empowerment at General Electric Appliances   563

COMPETING THROUGH GLOBALIZATION:
Quality and Market Proximity Also Affect Plant Locations in
Global Car Industry   567

COMPETING THROUGH SOCIAL RESPONSIBILITY:
Executive Pay at Ben & Jerry's Ice Cream   571

Case: Rewarding Employees on the Slow Track   579

16   **Recognizing Individual Contributions with Pay   581**
Sears Discontinues Incentive Pay in Auto Centers   581

Introduction   582
How Does Pay Influence Individual Employees?   583
Influences on Labor-Force Composition   586

Programs   586
Merit Pay   588
Individual Incentives   592
Profit Sharing and Ownership   593
Gainsharing, Group Incentives, and Team Awards   598
Mixed Plans and Strategy Examples   600

Managerial and Executive Pay   601

Process and Context Issues   604
Employee Participation in Decision Making   605
Communication   605
Pay and Process: Intertwined Effects   606

Organization Strategy and Compensation Strategy: A Question of Fit   607

International Comparisons 608

Summary 610

COMPETING THROUGH TECHNOLOGY & STRUCTURE:
Stock Options and Silicon Valley 596

COMPETING THROUGH QUALITY:
Bonuses and Communications at Herman Miller 601

COMPETING THROUGH SOCIAL RESPONSIBILITY:
Empowering Employees to Design Their Own Incentive Programs 606

Case: Incentive Pay for Doctors 615

17   **Employee Benefits 617**

Social Responsibility or Financial Solvency? 617

Introduction 618

Reasons for Benefits Growth 619

Benefits Programs 622

Social Insurance (Legally Required) 622
Private Group Insurance 627
Retirement 628
Pay for Time Not Worked 634

Managing Benefits: Employer Objectives and Strategies 636

Surveys/Benchmarking 636
Cost Control 637
Nature of the Work Force 645
Communicating with Employees 647
Flexible, or Cafeteria-Style, Benefit Plans 648

General Regulatory Issues 650

Nondiscrimination Rules and Qualified Plans 650
Sex, Age, and Disability 651
Retiree Health-Care Accounting Changes 652

Summary 653

COMPETING THROUGH SOCIAL RESPONSIBILITY:
General Electric's 401(k) Retirement Plan 631

COMPETING THROUGH QUALITY:
Managed Competition at Xerox 644

COMPETING THROUGH TECHNOLOGY & STRUCTURE:
Benefits for Part-Timers at Starbucks Coffee Company 646

Case: Are the Retirement Years the Golden Years? 657

VIDEO CASE   Budget Rent-a-Car and International Compensation 658

VI   SPECIAL TOPICS IN HUMAN RESOURCE MANAGEMENT   663

18   Collective Bargaining and Labor Relations   665

Conflict and Cooperation: GM and the UAW   665

Introduction   666

The Labor Relations Framework   667

Goals and Strategies   669
Society   669
Management   671
Labor Unions   671

Union Structure, Administration, and Membership   673
National and International Unions   673
Local Unions   675
American Federation of Labor and Congress of Industrial
Organizations (AFL-CIO)   675
Union Security   675
Union Membership and Bargaining Power   677

Legal Framework   681
Unfair Labor Practices—Employers   682
Unfair Labor Practices—Labor Unions   683
Enforcement   684

Union and Management Interactions: Organizing   685
Why Do Employees Join Unions?   685
The Process and Legal Framework of Organizing   685
Representation Elections: Management and Union
Strategies and Tactics   686

Union and Management Interaction: Contract Negotiations   690
The Negotiation Process   690
Management's Preparation for Negotiations   691
Negotiation Stages and Tactics   693
Bargaining Power, Impasses, and Impasse Resolution   693
Management's Willingness to Take a Strike   694
Impasse-Resolution Procedures: Alternatives to Strikes   695

Union and Management Interactions: Contract Administration   696
Grievance Procedure   696
New Labor-Management Strategies   699

Labor Relations Outcomes   700
Strikes   701
Wages and Benefits   703
Productivity   704
Profits and Stock Performance   706

The International Context   706

The Public Sector   708

Summary   708

COMPETING THROUGH TECHNOLOGY & STRUCTURE:
Proactive Changes at Union Camp Paper   669

COMPETING THROUGH SOCIAL RESPONSIBILITY:
A New Model of Union-Management Cooperation at Magma Copper   702

COMPETING THROUGH GLOBALIZATION:
Labor-Management Cooperation at Ford Motor Company   705

Case: United Airlines Gets Tough on Unions   712

19   Human Resource Information Systems   715

Tellabs, Inc.   715

Introduction   716

Historical Evolution of HRISs   717

Types of Computer Applications in Human Resource Management   718
  Transaction Processing, Reporting, and Tracking   718
  Decision Support Systems   718
  Expert Systems   718

Databases and Hardware for HRISs   719
  What Is a Database?   719
  Choosing Hardware   721
  Mainframe Computers   722
  Personal Computers   722
  Security and Privacy Issues: Databases, Hardware, and Software   725

Steps in the Development of an HRIS   727
  Analysis   727
  System Design   728
  Implementation   730
  Evaluation   731

HRIS Applications   732
  Staffing Applications   732
  Human Resource Planning Applications   735
  Performance-Management Applications   738
  Training and Career Development Applications   738
  Compensation and Benefits Applications   740

Summary   744

COMPETING THROUGH TECHNOLOGY & STRUCTURE:
Succession Planning at AT&T   736

COMPETING THROUGH QUALITY:
Technology Meets Total Quality Management at TRW   744

Case: The Search for a New Payroll System at Medtronic, Inc.   747

VIDEO CASE   Saturn Corporation and the UAW: A Test of Labor's
Partnership with Management   748

Glossary   755

Name Index   765

Subject Index   779

NOTE TO THE INSTRUCTOR

Austen Press texts are marketed and distributed by Richard D. Irwin, Inc. For assistance in obtaining supplementary material for this and other Austen Press titles, please contact your Irwin sales representative or the customer service division of Richard D. Irwin at (800) 323–4560.

HUMAN RESOURCE MANAGEMENT: GAINING A COMPETITIVE ADVANTAGE

Objectives

After reading this chapter, you should be able to:

1. Discuss the competitive challenges influencing U.S. companies.
2. Discuss what companies should do to be competitive in the global marketplace.
3. Outline the basic principles of total quality management.
4. Identify the similarities and differences between the current and future work force.
5. Propose several actions companies should take to successfully manage a diverse work force.
6. Discuss how technology is affecting company and work design and managers' and employees' work responsibilities.
7. Recommend human resource management practices that can help companies successfully deal with global, quality, technological, and social challenges.

Chaparral Steel: Improving Company Performance through Human Resource Management

A Texas steel company, Chaparral Steel, produces steel products used in the construction of mobile homes, automobiles, and appliances. Chaparral Steel has been able to increase sales, profit margins, and labor productivity. For example, labor productivity is over two times that of other U.S. steel-making firms. How has Chaparral Steel achieved such success in an industry dominated by Japanese and German steel companies? Chaparral's success is the result both of technological innovativeness and of the way the company has used its human resources to meet competitive challenges.

Chaparral Steel's human resource policies and managerial practices motivate employees to use their talents to design and implement equipment and process improvements. One such practice is the company's compensation policy. Every employee is salaried and shares in the profits. A participative approach to performance management gives employees the opportunity to increase their levels of knowledge and expertise.

Performance is measured against the employee's goals and objectives rather than job requirements or a job description. The goals and objectives are established jointly between supervisors and employees. Employees are free to use whatever means possible to reach their goals.

The company also uses training and education to gain a competitive advantage. To ensure that employees are prepared to deal with advances in steel-producing technology, each employee receives approximately 120 hours of classroom training each year. The company encourages employees to become familiar with other operations through cross-training. Cross-training develops a work force that has multiple skills. This provides the company with the ability to quickly change manufacturing processes and adopt new technology to meet customer needs.

SOURCE: G. E. Forward, D. E. Beach, D. A. Gray, and J. C. Quick, "Mentofacturing: A Vision for American Industrial Excellence," *Academy of Management Executive 5,* no. 3 (1991): 32–44.

INTRODUCTION

Chaparral Steel's success illustrates that the management of human resources plays a key role in determining the effectiveness and competitiveness of U.S. businesses in the next decade. **Competitiveness** refers to the company's ability to maintain and gain market share in its industry. Chaparral Steel's human resource practices have helped the company gain a **competitive advantage** over U.S. and foreign competitors. That is, Chaparral Steel's human resource practices have helped the company create products that are valued by their customers. The value of a product is determined by its quality and how closely the product fits customer needs.

Competitiveness is related to company effectiveness. Effectiveness is determined by whether the company satisfies the needs of groups within and outside the company (stakeholders). For example, important stakeholders include stockholders, who want a return on their investment; customers, who want a high-quality product or service; and employees, who desire interesting work and reasonable compensation for their services. The community, which wants the company to contribute to activities and projects and minimize pollution of the environment, is also an important stakeholder. Companies that do not meet stakeholders' needs are unlikely to have a competitive advantage over other firms in their industry.

Human resource practices contribute to companies' competitiveness in many ways. For example, human resource management (HRM) practices contribute to delivery of the organization's products and services through (1) selecting employees who will be innovative, creative, and successful in performing their jobs, (2) preparing employees to work with new manufacturing and service technologies, and (3) rewarding good performance.[1] Effective HRM practices also contribute to both customer and employee satisfaction and retention, and the development of a favorable reputation in the community in which the firm is located. However, the potential role of HRM in company effectiveness has only recently been recognized.

Before we address how human resources can be managed to gain a competitive advantage, it is important to understand how the role of HRM as a contributor to company effectiveness has evolved over time. Also, it is important to understand the types of competitive challenges that U.S. companies are facing in the next decade. We begin the chapter with a historical overview of the role of HRM. The second section of the chapter identifies competitive challenges that U.S. companies will face in the next decade that influence their ability to successfully meet the needs of shareholders, customers, employees, and other stakeholders. We discuss how these competitive challenges are influencing HRM practices. The chapter concludes by highlighting the HRM practices covered in this book and the ways they can help companies deal with the competitive challenges.

A HISTORICAL VIEW OF HUMAN RESOURCE MANAGEMENT PRACTICES

Human resource management practices have been shaped by many historical forces.[2] During the 1800s, the U.S. economy depended primarily on agriculture and small family businesses. Human resource management practices were conducted by the most senior employees of the business. New employees learned their jobs through serving as an apprentice to a more experienced employee. Relatives and friends of the senior members of the companies or farm were given priority for new jobs. Compensation often included a small wage and food and housing.

The first formal HRM practices developed as a result of the Industrial Revolution. Factories required large numbers of employees with specific skills to operate machines that performed specialized operations. As a result, managers who specialized in human resources were needed to train and schedule workers. The development of **Scientific Management** in 1911 emphasized the importance of identifying employees who had the appropriate skills and abilities for performing each job, providing wage incentives to employees for increased productivity, providing employees with rest breaks, and carefully studying jobs to identify the best method for performing the job. Most companies were bureaucratic organizations. That is, positions were organized into a hierarchy of authority, with each position given specific responsibilities. Employees made decisions about how work was to be done and provided suggestions to improve products only if management assigned these responsibilities to them. From 1911 to 1930, human resource practices were primarily conducted by what was known as the "personnel department." The personnel department's major role was to keep track of employee records. These records included basic information about employees such as the date of their hire, their position, health information, and performance reviews. The personnel department also administered payroll and interviewed job applicants, as well as terminated poorly performing employees.

Between 1930 and 1970, companies began to recognize the relationship between employee participation in decision making, employee job satisfaction, and employee absenteeism, turnover, and unionization efforts. This was the result of a new management philosophy that suggested that employees will contribute to company goals if they are given the opportunity to participate in decisions concerning their job and to take responsibility for their work **(Theory Y management)**. The **Hawthorne studies** conducted at a Western Electric plant in 1927 also suggested that increases in employee productivity can be realized if employees are treated in a positive manner.

During this time major advances in employee selection techniques were made. World War II sparked the development of psychological tests that could quickly and accurately identify individuals' interests, skills, and abilities. Following the war, these tests were increasingly used for selecting new employees and placing them in appropriate jobs.

Personnel departments also became responsible for ensuring that companies' human resource practices were in compliance with legislation such as the Civil Rights Act of 1964, which made it illegal for employment decisions to be made on the basis of gender, religion, race, color, or national origin.

As a result of these developments, the responsibilities of personnel departments (now called "employee relations" or "human resource departments") expanded beyond the administrative role to include testing, negotiating labor contracts, conducting attitude surveys, and complying with expanding employment legislation. Although the relationship between human resource practices and productivity was beginning to be recognized, the major role of employee relations departments was to ensure that employee-related issues did not interfere with the manufacturing, selling, or development of goods and services. HRM tended to be reactive–that is, it occurred in response to a business problem or need. HRM was not part of the strategic business plans of the company. Line managers usually referred human resource problems to a specialist in the employee relations department rather than attempting to solve the problem themselves.

It has only been in the last ten years that companies have viewed HRM practices as a means to enhance the operations of the other functions of the business and contribute directly to the firm's profitability. This has occurred because chief executive officers, line managers, and human resource managers increasingly recognize that HRM practices play a key role in determining companies' success in gaining a competitive advantage.

One of the most comprehensive studies ever conducted regarding HRM was done by IBM and Towers Perrin consulting firm. They solicited the opinions of approximately 3,000 human resource professionals, managers, and consultants from 12 countries. The goals of this project were to determine HRM's role in gaining a competitive advantage and to identify the key priorities of company decision makers (HR executives, consultants, chief operating officers) who influence human resource management practices. The study found that:

- Globalization of businesses, a reduction in the number of persons entering the work force, and changing characteristics of the work force were the environmental factors most likely to influence the competitiveness of American companies from 1991 to 2000.

- Line managers and HR managers agreed that high productivity, quality, customer satisfaction, and linking HRM to the company's business strategy were the most important goals for both 1991 and the year 2000.

- The single biggest challenge for HR managers is to shift their focus from current operation to strategies for the future.

- HRM should focus on quality, customer service, productivity, employee involvement, teamwork, and creating a flexible work force.

- HRM needs to be responsive to the competitive marketplace.

- HRM practices should be jointly developed and implemented by human resource and line managers.[3]

The report concludes that "human resources is being transformed from a specialized, stand-alone function to a broad corporate competency in which human resources and line managers build partnerships to gain competitive advantage and achieve overall business goals."[4]

In addition to opinions and beliefs, changes in the reporting relationships of human resource managers emphasize the increased importance and greater role that HRM is beginning to play in many companies. Managers in charge of the human resource function sit on high-level committees that are given the task of shaping the strategic direction of the company; they report directly to the CEO, president, or board of directors; and they are being asked to propose solutions to the challenges that the firm is facing.[5]

Why has the importance of human resource management recently increased over the last ten years? HRM is seen by managers as the most important lever for companies to gain a competitive advantage over both domestic and foreign competitors. We believe this is because HRM practices are directly related to companies' success in meeting competitive challenges. In the next section we discuss each of these challenges and their implications for HRM.

COMPETITIVE CHALLENGES INFLUENCING HUMAN RESOURCE MANAGEMENT

Four competitive challenges that companies will face in the next decade will increase the importance of human resource management practices: the global challenge, the quality challenge, the social challenge, and the technology and structure challenge. These four challenges are shown in Figure 1.1.

The Global Challenge

We are in the midst of a global restructuring of the world's markets. Companies are finding that to survive they must compete for foreign markets abroad, as well as fend off foreign corporations' attempts to gain ground at home. To meet these challenges, U.S. business must expand into foreign markets and do a better job of preparing employees for international assignments.

Development of Global Markets.   Statistics suggest that U.S. companies are not currently meeting the challenge of global competition. The United States ranks first in productivity. However, it has not kept pace with gains in productivity, the standard of living, trade, and investment made by Japan, Canada, France, Italy, the United Kingdom, and Germany.[6] For example, the U.S. share of world exports dropped from 25 percent in 1960 to 13 percent in 1985.[7]

One of the ways to increase company profits and competitiveness is to move into international markets. Opportunities for U.S. business are available as a result of the reunification of Germany, the restructuring of the former Soviet Union, and the formation of the European Economic Community. Also, the provisions of the North American Free Trade Agreement attempt to eliminate all trade barriers between Mexico, the United States, and Canada. Some forecasters predict that by the end of the 1990s, the European Common Market and markets of countries in the Pacific Rim will be equal to the North American market.[8]

Many U.S. companies already have substantial foreign operations. Of the 50 largest multinational companies, 21 received at least 40 percent of their total operating profits from foreign operations.[9] For example, to gain access to European markets, General Electric recently purchased Tungsram, a Budapest, Hungary, light bulb maker.[10] Tungsram factories make automotive lamps and fluorescent bulbs sold in U.S., Japanese, and European consumer and industrial markets. Other U.S. companies are just beginning to penetrate foreign markets. For example, Ferro Corporation, a $1 billion manufacturer of coatings, plastics, and specialty chemicals, has recently reorganized its corporate structure to focus its products and businesses toward overseas markets.[11]

FIGURE 1.1   Competitive Challenges Influencing U.S. Companies

The following figure illustrates the four challenges facing U.S. companies today.

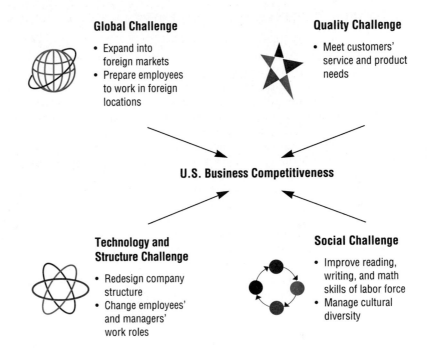

Although U.S. business's problems in gaining access to foreign markets relate to differences in economic, structural, historic, and cultural differences between countries, a major factor may also be U.S. companies' lack of investment in human resources. Traditionally, U.S. business has attempted to improve productivity by cutting costs related to human resources, while Japanese, German, and other competitors have invested heavily in employee training and new work designs. To compete in the world economy, U.S. companies need to put greater effort into selecting and retraining talented employees, employee training and development, and dismantling the traditional company structure, which limits employees' ability to be innovative and creative.[12]

Preparing Employees for International Assignments.   Besides taking steps to ensure that employees are better used, U.S. companies must do a better job of preparing employees and their families for overseas

Globalization

PREPARING INTERNATIONAL MANAGEMENT TALENT AT GILLETTE COMPANY

To ensure that the Gillette Company can capitalize on talent from throughout the world for its goal of international management, the company develops employees with potential through its International Graduate Trainee Program. Gillette chooses students graduating from universities in Mexico, Japan, Colombia, and the other 56 countries in which it has facilities. Students who accept traineeships are given a six-month assignment in their home country. After completing this assignment, the trainees travel to company headquarters in Boston for a one-year program. In Boston, trainees are paired with an executive mentor. They work in two of the company's five business areas (marketing, finance, manufacturing, personnel, sales) to gain a broad perspective of the company's operations.

A total of 113 trainees have graduated from the program since 1987. Approximately half of the graduates are still employed by Gillette in their home countries. They hold positions such as general manager, controller, and production manager. The value of the program is recognized by foreign companies, which try to entice program graduates to leave Gillette. The program costs between $20,000 and $25,000 per trainee each year. However, it is less expensive for the company to develop managers through this program than to recruit managers with international experience. The cost of recruiting managers with international experience ranges from $100,000 to $200,000.

SOURCE: J. J. Laabs, "Optimas Award Winners Chart New Frontiers in HR," *Personnel Journal*, January 1993, 49–64.

assignments. The failure rate for expatriates (U.S. employees sent to work abroad) is higher than that for European and Japanese expatriates.[13] U.S. companies must carefully select employees to work abroad based on their ability to understand and respect the cultural and business norms of the host country, their language skills, and their technical ability. (In Chapter 13, "Employee Development," we discuss effective cross-cultural training practices.) Additionally, U.S. companies must be willing to train and develop foreign employees. The "Competing through Globalization" box discusses one company's trainee program.

The Quality Challenge

Japan, Korea, and the Pacific Rim countries have taken over many product markets previously dominated by the United States, including automobiles, tires, electronics, and steel. Studies comparing U.S. competitiveness with other countries suggest that the United States is no longer leading the world in wealth and technology.[14] During the 1980s, the United States imported $920 billion more products than it exported. U.S. automobile companies supply only 60 percent of the U.S. market from factories based in the United

States. American factories' share of the semiconductor market has slipped from 57 to 36 percent.

One of the major reasons U.S. companies have failed to maintain their leadership in these industries has been the decline in customers' perceptions of the quality of U.S. products. Quality is defined as the extent to which a product or service satisfies the customer's requirements.[15] The "customer" can be the general public, vendors, or suppliers outside the company (external customers), as well as employees and departments within the company who share information or jointly assemble a product or perform a service (internal customers). Traditionally, U.S. companies have attempted to ensure quality by inspecting products following their production, a "fix it if it's wrong" approach. However, the Japanese and other world competitors have taken a different approach. They emphasize designing quality into a product as it is produced rather than relying on the inspection process to spot defects. This can be considered a "get it right the first time" approach.

One result of the loss of world market share has been an increased emphasis by U.S. companies on quality management. One survey found that over half of the companies surveyed reported that they have total quality as a strategic goal or policy.[16] **Total quality management (TQM)** can be defined as "a cooperative form of doing business that relies on the talents and capabilities of both labor and management to continually improve quality and productivity using work teams."[17] The strategies that companies may use to improve quality vary depending on which quality expert's philosophy the company chooses to follow (see Table 1.1).[18]

The major difference between the experts' definitions of quality is whether customer, product, or manufacturing process is emphasized. For example, Deming emphasizes how well a product or service meets the customer's needs, and Crosby's approach to quality emphasizes how well the service or manufacturing process meets engineering standards.

The experts' approaches to improving quality share several common principles. Benchmarking is the foundation of a quality improvement program. **Benchmarking** is the process of finding examples of excellent products, services, or systems.[19] These examples serve as the quality standard or goal for the company. The company redesigns products and services to meet or exceed the standard. For example, before designing the Taurus and Sable automobiles, engineers at Ford Motor Company disassembled Toyotas and Hondas to identify the most desirable features of these automobiles. The engineers then designed many of these features into the Taurus and Sable.

Although there are various approaches to TQM (e.g., Deming, Juran, Crosby), these approaches share several common principles. Table 1.2 illustrates the six basic principles of total quality management. The total quality movement has caused a shift in management philosophy: How human resource issues are handled plays a key role in whether quality is achieved and, ultimately, in the success of the company.[20] For example, conditions

TABLE 1.1   Summary of Experts' Approaches to Quality

Expert	Definition of Quality	Emphasis
W. Edwards Deming	How well a product or service meets customers' needs	Customer
Joseph Juran	How well a product or service meets customers' needs	Customer
	Company willingness to service product after sale	
Philip Crosby	Product conforms to engineering standards zero defects	Manufacturing
Genichi Taguchi	Product operates without unintended variability	Value of Product
	Product does not harm customer	

SOURCE: Based on L. B. Forker, "Quality: American, Japanese, and Soviet Perspectives," *Academy of Management Executive* 5 (1991):63–74; B. Brocka and M. Z. Brocka, *Quality Management* (Homewood, Ill.: Business One Irwin, 1992).

TABLE 1.2   Principles of Total Quality Management

1. Customer focus
2. Focus on process as well as results
3. Prevention versus inspection
4. Use employees' expertise
5. Fact-based decision making
6. Feedback

SOURCE: Adapted from J. R. Jablonski, *Implementing Total Quality Management: An Overview* (San Diego: Pfeiffer & Company, 1991).

need to be created for employees to be innovative, creative, and take risks to meet customer demands. Participative problem-solving approaches should be used, involving managers, employees, and customers. Communications between managers and employees concerning customer needs, development opportunities, and resources need to be enhanced.

Rewarding U.S. Firms for Quality.   The Malcolm Baldrige National Quality Award and ISO 9000 have been established to recognize companies that have high-quality products, services, and management practices. **ISO 9000** quality standards were developed by the International Organization for Standardization, an organization in Geneva,

Switzerland.[21] ISO 9000 standards were developed initially for companies in the European Community, but they have been adopted by other countries and regions throughout the world, including Austria, Switzerland, Norway, Japan, Australia, South America, and Africa. The ISO 9000 quality standards include 20 requirements dealing with issues such as how to document quality-improvement efforts and handle poor products. U.S. companies hoping to win contracts from European Community customers need to have ISO 9000 certification.

The **Malcolm Baldrige National Quality Award** was established in 1987 by President Ronald Reagan to promote quality awareness, to recognize quality achievements of U.S. companies, and to publicize successful quality strategies.[22] To become eligible for the Baldrige award, companies must complete a detailed application that consists of basic information about the company, such as location, markets, and products, as well as an in-depth presentation of how the firm addresses specific criteria related to quality improvement. The ISO 9000 standards are similar to those for the Baldrige award. The Baldrige award criteria are shown in Table 1.3. A board of examiners composed of quality experts from industry, academia, and professional societies evaluates the company's application and also conducts site visits. All Baldrige award applicants receive written feedback summarizing the company's strengths and needs for improvement. A maximum of two awards per year are given to firms in three categories—manufacturing companies, service companies, and small businesses.

Examining the criteria listed in Table 1.3, we see a recognition of the increasing importance of the role that human resources can play in improving companies' competitiveness. The weight given to how they use human resources (150 points) is exceeded only by the importance of quality and operational results and customer satisfaction. To attain total quality, managers must ensure that technological innovations are made and adopted, but more critical is how the people who are responsible for quality are managed.[23] Clearly, to be a recognized as a leader in product or service quality, U.S. companies must effectively use their human resources.

One example of the important role that human resource management plays in improving quality is Xerox Corporation.[24] During the 1980s Xerox lost photocopy market share to competing Japanese and American firms. Through sweeping changes initiated by then-CEO David Kearns, Xerox was able to recapture and improve on lost market share. Xerox's commitment to quality was recognized through receiving the Baldrige award in 1989. What did Xerox management do differently? Its new quality policy had two aspects: satisfy customers and make quality improvement the job of every Xerox employee. Xerox studied companies that were recognized for quality. Comprehensive training was undertaken with all employees to explain their role in the quality effort. Xerox's quality focus consisted of emphasizing teamwork and giving employees the skills necessary to work with others in order to get work accomplished. Employees were provided with universal ways to solve problems (identifying and analyzing problems, generating solutions, implementing and evaluating solutions) and to ensure

TABLE 1.3   Categories and Point Values for the Malcolm Baldrige
National Quality Award Examination

Category	Points
Leadership	*90*
How senior executives create and sustain a visible quality value system to guide activities toward quality	
Customer Focus and Satisfaction	*300*
Company's knowledge of the customer, customer service systems, responsiveness to customer, customer satisfaction	
Human Resource Development and Management	*150*
Company's efforts to develop and utilize the work force and to maintain an environment conducive to full participation, continuous improvement, and personal and organizational growth	
Information and Analysis	*80*
Scope, validity, use and management of data and information that underlies the firm's quality system	
Strategic Quality Planning	*60*
Company's planning process for retaining or achieving quality leadership and integration of quality improvement into business plans	
Management of Process Quality	*140*
Process design and control, company's approaches to total quality control of goods and services	
Quality and Operational Results	*180*
Quality levels and quality improvement using objective measures derived from analysis of customer requirements. Quality levels compared with competing companies	
Total Points	*1,000*

SOURCE: Adapted from Bureau of Business Practices, *Profiles of Malcolm Baldrige Award Winners* (Boston: Allyn & Bacon, 1992), 27.

that customer requirements for products were being maintained. On-the-job application of problem solving and quality approaches were emphasized. Groups of employees selected projects that would benefit from problem solving or quality improvement. Existing training programs were evaluated to make sure that they included an emphasis on meeting customer, not company, requirements for product quality and service.

Some argue that the popularity of the Baldrige award has caused managers to devote too much time to completing the rigorous evaluation

Quality

ZYTEC CORPORATION: A BALDRIGE AWARD WINNER

Zytec Corporation, a 1991 winner of the Baldrige Award, is a leading manufacturer of power supplies for computers and other electronic equipment. Zytec employs approximately 750 employees. One example of how Zytec empowered employees in order to improve quality is the firm's management by planning strategy. All levels of employees are involved in setting long-term and annual improvement goals. Six cross-functional teams create a five-year plan, which was reviewed by employees from all areas of the company. The plan is then incorporated into corporate objectives and departmental guidelines. Each department uses these guidelines to create departmental goals and action plans, which are reviewed with the company's CEO. Selected customers and suppliers are also invited to review the long-range plan before it is finalized. This process assures responsiveness to customer needs, as well as ensuring that all parts of the organization are working together to achieve the company's goals.

The focus on quality is also apparent in other aspects of Zytec's human resource management policies. Employees are extensively trained in analytical and problem-solving skills and are expected to use these skills to assure production of a quality product. Zytec also created a multifunctional employee program which rewards employees for the number of job skills they acquire. This program has led to a flexible and knowledgeable work force. The design and development of new products is carried out from start to finish by interdepartmental teams. What benefits have resulted from the quality movement at Zytec? Since 1988 Zytec has enjoyed a 50 percent improvement in manufacturing yields, a 26 percent reduction in cycle time, a 50 percent reduction in the design cycle, and a 40 percent decrease in product costs.

SOURCE: Bureau of Business Practice, *Profiles of Malcolm Baldrige Award Winners* (Boston: Allyn & Bacon, 1992), 90–94.

process and too little time concentrating on promoting quality within the company.[25] Also, along with the recognition of winning the award comes the need to devote time speaking to companies in the United States and abroad about the organization's quality-improvement process. However, many companies use the Baldrige application process as a guide for managers to evaluate their own operations rather than a strict set of rules to follow. For example, managers at IBM's Rochester, Minnesota, plant are required to score their operation every 90 days on the basis of the Baldrige criteria. One Baldrige award winner is profiled in the "Competing through Quality" box.

The Baldrige award appears to be having a positive impact on the quality of products and services produced by U.S. companies. A study of 20 companies that were among the highest-scoring applicants for the Baldrige award suggests that total quality management results in overall improvement in corporate performance (including better employer relations and increased productivity, customer satisfaction, and market share).[26] One important finding of the study was that none of the companies included in the study realized positive benefits immediately. Those companies that realized benefits from total quality management took a well-planned approach in implementing the program. Increasing employee participation in improving product and service quality takes time.

The Social Challenge

Companies face several challenges as a result of changes in the work force and employment rates in different sectors of the economy (e.g., manufacturing, service, health care). The composition of the labor market, projected changes in the structure of the economy, skill deficits in the labor force, and employee values will have a significant influence on human resource practices and company competitiveness in the next decade.[27] U.S. companies will also be faced with the challenge of ensuring that human resource practices are ethical and do not contradict federal or state laws.

Composition of the Labor Force.   The U.S. labor force of the next decade will be older, more culturally diverse, and growing at a slower rate than at any time in the last 40 years. According to government statistics, labor force growth has slowed considerably in comparison with the 1960s and 1970s. The largest growth of the labor force is expected to be in the 35- to 54-year-old age groups, as the "baby-boom" generation advances in age. Figure 1.2 shows the changing age distribution of the work force. One of the challenges that the aging labor force creates for companies is how to create career-development systems that utilize and reward older employees' talents.[28] For example, in most companies, managerial positions provide the greatest salary and promotion opportunities. However, the number of employees desiring managerial positions is expected to far exceed the number of available positions.

As Figure 1.3 shows, the fastest-growing segment of the U.S. labor force is women, Hispanics, blacks, and Asians. The twentieth century work force will include greater proportions of women and minorities than ever before in the history of the United States.[29] Through HRM practices, companies have the opportunity to ensure that the talents, skills, and values of women and minorities are fully utilized to help develop high-quality products and services.

Structure of the Economy.   Employment in manufacturing is expected to shrink slightly. However, manufacturing will still account for one-third of the total dollar output of all industries. Health, business, personal, and recreational services will be the largest-growing sector of the economy. Jobs in these areas are expected to increase almost one-third over their current level in the next decade. The number of retail trade jobs is expected to reach almost 23 million by the year 2000, accounting for almost 20 percent of wage and salary jobs in the U.S. economy.

In Table 1.4 industries with the fastest-growing and most rapidly declining employment rates are presented. The data presented in this table

FIGURE 1.2   Changing Distribution of Age in the Labor Force

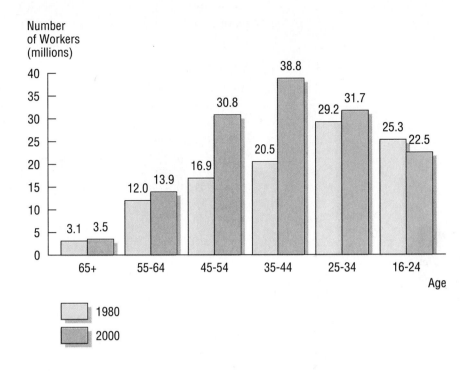

SOURCE: IFTF; derived from historical data from the U.S. Bureau of Labor Statistics; Labor force statistics derived from the Current Population Survey, 1948–87, Table A-9, Employment and Earnings, January 1990, Table A-3, and *Monthly Labor Review,* November 1989, Table 4.

highlight the point that employment is projected to increase faster in indus-tries that include occupational groups requiring the most education, such as health care and computer and data-processing services, than basic indus-tries such as textiles, automobiles, and coal mining, which traditionally have not placed a premium on employees' education level. The introduc-tion of new computer-based technology into the manufacturing sector will require employees to learn skills related to using technology to collect, retrieve, and analyze production data. Retail jobs will be the last source of jobs for unskilled workers.[30] Technology has made it possible for employees with low reading and math skills to record transactions with customers by replacing numerical key pads on point-of-sale terminals with pictures of products and menu items.

Skill Deficiencies.   It is expected that the supply of individuals with the necessary education and training will not meet the demands of jobs in the U.S. economy.[31] For example, as shown in Figure 1.4, most new jobs created in the next decade will require higher levels of reading and writing skills

FIGURE 1.3   Projected Increase of New Entrants to the Labor Force, 1985–2000

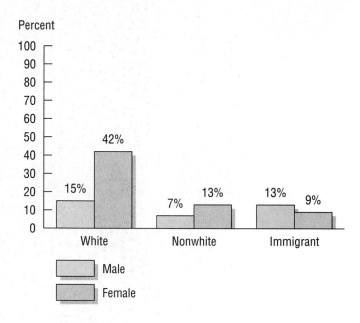

SOURCE: Adapted from W. B. Johnston and A. Packer, *Workforce 2000: Work and Workers for the Twenty-first Century.* (New York: Hudson Institute, 1987).

than new employees will bring to the job. Also, projections of the Bureau of Labor Statistics suggest that the most rapid rate of growth is among jobs requiring technical skills. These occupations and craft jobs often do not require a four-year college degree but instead rely on postsecondary education, such as that obtained from technical schools.

There are two different aspects of this problem. One involves new entrants to the labor force. In the United States, a large population of individuals have only fourth to eighth grade literacy levels. The low level of educational attainment is especially a problem for Hispanics and African Americans, who have low high school completion rates. Persons with only fourth to eighth grade literacy levels may make up as much as 65 percent of the entry-level work force over the next fifteen years.[32] This means that many new entrants to the labor market will not have the education needed to qualify for on-the-job or postsecondary training needed for the available jobs.

A second aspect of the skills problem involves the current labor force. One estimate is that 27 million adults in the United States lack the basic writing, reading, and computational skills needed to perform well in the workplace.[33] A 1990 survey on workplace literacy and basic skills conducted by the Commerce Clearing House and Society for Human Resource Management found that nearly two-thirds of the companies surveyed currently employ

TABLE 1.4   Employment Change in Selected Industries, 1988–2000

Industry[a]	1988 Level (Thousands)	Annual Rate of Change, 1988–2000
Fastest Growing		
Computer and data processing services	678	4.9
Outpatient facilities and health services, n.e.c.[b]	675	4.7
Personnel supply services	1,369	4.1
Water and sanitation including combined services	152	3.9
Residential care	391	3.8
Offices of health practitioners	1,850	3.5
Arrangement of passenger transportation	175	3.4
Research, management, and consulting services	811	3.2
Individual and miscellaneous social services	571	3.2
Personal services, n.e.c.	294	3.2
Nursing and personal care facilities	1,319	3.1
Credit reporting and business services, n.e.c.	776	3.1
Miscellaneous publishing	79	3.1
Security and commodity brokers and exchanges	449	3.0
Advertising	237	2.8
Legal services	852	2.8
Automotive rentals, without drivers	164	2.7
Accounting, auditing, and services, n.e.c.	530	2.7
Miscellaneous transportation services	141	2.7
Detective and protective services	464	2.6

continued

SOURCE: Bureau of Labor Statistics, *Outlook 2000* (Washington, D.C.: U.S. Government Printing Office, 1990), p. 30.

[a] Ranking is based on industries with employment levels of more than 50,000 in 1988.

[b] n.e.c. = not elsewhere classified

people who lack basic skills.[34] Basic skills were defined as the ability to use printed and written information to function effectively on the job. Approximately half of the survey respondents felt that job applicants with a high school diploma were insufficiently literate for employment. Companies report that employee skill deficiencies in reading, math, and problem solving limit their ability to upgrade technology, redesign work, and upgrade the quality of their products and services.[35] Employees fail to enroll in training

TABLE 1.4   *continued*

Industry	1988 Level (Thousands)	Annual Rate of Change, 1988–2000
Most Rapidly Declining		
Tobacco manufactures	56	–2.8
Telephone and telegraph apparatus	111	–2.3
Miscellaneous textile goods	56	–2.3
Alcoholic beverages	72	–2.2
Office and accounting machines	56	–2.2
Footwear, except rubber and plastic	90	–2.1
Railroad transportation	299	–2.1
Tires and inner tubes	84	–2.0
Photographic equipment and supplies	112	–1.8
Coal mining	151	–1.8
Luggage, handbags, and leather products, n.e.c.	54	–1.8
Miscellaneous transportation equipment	62	–1.7
Engines and turbines	94	–1.6
Electronic home entertainment equipment	85	–1.6
Sugar and confectionery products	98	–1.6
Apparel	893	–1.6
Knitting mills	211	–1.5
Sawmills and planing mills	206	–1.5
Automotive stampings	102	–1.5
Metal cans and shipping containers	53	–1.5

programs and engage in unsafe work practices because they cannot read well enough to understand written memos and instructions.

Besides academic skills (reading, writing, arithmetic), a joint research project between the American Society for Training and Development and the U.S. Department of Labor identified seven other types of skills that U.S. employers say are basic to success in the workplace.[36] The seven basic skills are listed in Table 1.5. This study found that knowing how to learn served as the foundation for the other skills. Knowing how to learn is critical because the workplace demands that employees understand their work and the way it fits into the mission of the entire organization, that employees be able to innovate to improve product and service quality, and that they stay up-to-date with advances in technology.

FIGURE 1.4   Mismatch between Employees' Reading Skill Level and Job Demands

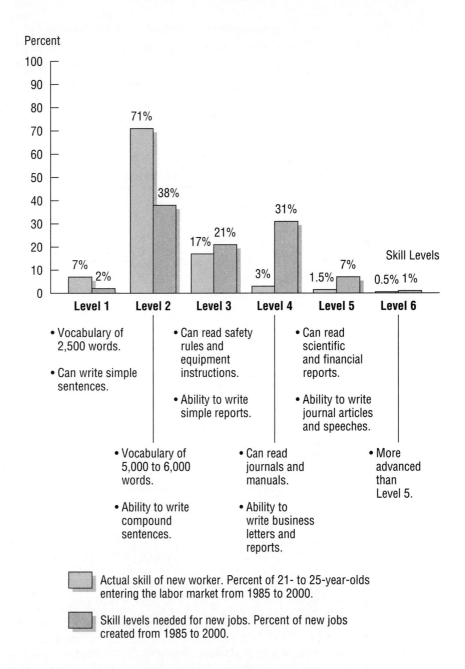

Actual skill of new worker. Percent of 21- to 25-year-olds entering the labor market from 1985 to 2000.

Skill levels needed for new jobs. Percent of new jobs created from 1985 to 2000.

SOURCE: Adapted from W. B. Johnston, *Workforce 2000* (Indianapolis: Hudson Institute, 1987); U.S. Department of Labor, *Opportunity 2000* (Washington, D.C.: U.S. Government Printing Office, 1987).

TABLE 1.5   The Skills Employers Want

- Influence: organizational effectiveness and leadership
- Group effectiveness: interpersonal skills, negotiations
- Personal management: self-esteem, goal setting, and personal career development
- Adaptability: creativity and problem solving
- Communications: listening and oral communications
- Competence: reading, writing, and computation
- Knowing how to learn

SOURCE: Adapted from A. P. Carnevale, L. J. Gainer, and A. S. Meltzer, *Workplace Basics: The Essential Skills Employers Want* (San Francisco: Jossey-Bass, 1990).

The implications of the changing labor market for managing human resources are far-reaching. Because labor market growth will be primarily in female and minority populations, U.S. companies will have to ensure that employees and human resource management systems are free of bias to capitalize on the perspectives and values that women and minorities can contribute to improving product quality, customer service, product development, and market share. Increasing levels of employment in the service sector of the economy suggest that HRM practices in these companies need to ensure that customer service is rewarded and improved. Finally, governments of global competitors (such as Denmark, France, Ireland, and Japan) are actively supporting the education and training of their work forces through payroll taxes and laws requiring companies to invest at least 1 percent of their payroll into company-provided or government-sponsored training.[37]

Because the U.S. government has yet to develop a comprehensive basic-skills policy, the burden falls on employers to invest in basic-skills training and joint training ventures with universities, community colleges, and high schools. A *Fortune* magazine poll of service and industrial 500 companies found that nearly 25 percent of the companies reported spending $1 million or more on educational programs and school reform.[38] Many more were directing money to preschool and elementary school programs, from 27 percent in 1990 to 64 percent in 1991, based on the belief that to influence future employees' work values and interest in education, you have to reach them at an early age.

Employee Values.   Because the work force is predicted to become more diverse in terms of age, ethnicity, and racial background, it is unlikely that one set of values will characterize all employees.[39] For example, "baby busters" (employees born between 1965 and 1975) value unexpected rewards for work accomplishments, opportunities to learn new things, praise, recognition, and time with the manager. "Traditionalists," employees born between 1925 and 1945, tend to be uncomfortable challenging the status quo and authority. They value income and employment security.

There are several aspects of work that all employees will value regardless of their background. Employees will view work as a means to self-fulfillment, that is, a means to more fully use their skills and abilities, meet their interests, and allow them to live a desirable life-style.[40] A recent report indicated that employees who are given opportunities to fully use their skills, opportunities for greater responsibilities, opportunities to develop skills, a fair promotion system, and a manager who can be counted on to represent the employee's best interests are more committed to their companies.[41] The new employee values will require that companies develop human resource management practices that provide more opportunity for individual contribution and entrepreneurship.[42] Because employees place more value on the quality of nonwork and family life, employees will demand more flexible work policies that allow them to choose work hours and locations where work is performed.

Using the Talents of a Diverse Work Force.   As we mentioned in our discussion of the composition of the work force, the ethnic and cultural diversity of the work force is increasing. For several reasons, work force diversity will be a major human resource challenge in the next decade. Companies will be challenged to ensure that the talents, experiences, values, and perspectives of all employees are utilized in pursuit of increased productivity and product quality. The lack of employees who possess the basic reading, writing, and math skills required to be successful in many jobs means that companies will have to invest in basic skills training. Also, companies will have to create conditions to ensure that skilled employees remain with the organization. Finally, increased government attention regarding the treatment of employees (pay, training, advancement opportunities) will continue and may eventually result in new legislation. For example, the Equal Employment Opportunity Commission recently completed a study comparing women and minorities' and white males' development opportunities involving nine Fortune 500 companies.[43] This study found that women and people of color often do not receive management development and training programs and career advancement assignments. In order to avoid the threat of potential litigation, it is important for companies to take steps to ensure that all employees are treated fairly in terms of development opportunities, salary, and opportunities for advancement. The "Competing through Social Responsibility" box presents one company's efforts to manage diversity.

Managing cultural diversity involves many different activities, including creating an organizational culture that values diversity, ensuring that human resource management systems are bias-free, facilitating higher career involvement of women, promoting knowledge and acceptance of cultural differences, ensuring involvement in education both within and outside the company, and dealing with employees' resistance to diversity.[44] Table 1.6 presents ways that managing cultural diversity can provide com-

COMPETING THROUGH Social Responsibility

MANAGING CUSTOMER AND EMPLOYEE DIVERSITY

Pacific Gas and Electric (PG&E) has taken steps to manage diversity in order to meet business needs. To serve gas and electric customers in Northern California, a geographic area characterized by diverse ethnic groups, PG&E developed customer service programs to help eliminate language barriers. PG&E is providing multilingual telephone service and developing service information brochures in several different languages to provide better service to its diverse customer base.

PG&E is also proactive in managing diversity within its work force. PG&E has a certification program that prepares line and staff employees to provide diversity training to other employees. PG&E provides scholarships,

counseling, work-study programs, and training programs to help women and minorities prepare for jobs in all levels of the company. PG&E is also working with managers to improve interpersonal skills (e.g., conflict resolution, team building, coaching, and counseling) that are useful in dealing with a diverse work force. Through group workshops, PG&E encourages their employees to understand their stereotypes and assumptions about ethnic and racial groups.

PG&E efforts to manage diversity have been rewarded. In 1989 the company received the U.S. Department of Labor's Opportunity 2000 Award, which recognizes companies who proactively engage in efforts to deal with the changing characteristics of the work force.

SOURCE: R. B. Johnson and J. O'Mara, "Shedding New Light on Diversity Training," *Training and Development,* May 1992, 45–52.

petitive advantage. Traditionally, in many U.S. companies, the costs of poorly managing cultural diversity were viewed as mainly increased legal fees associated with discrimination cases. However, as Table 1.6 illustrates, the implications of successfully managing the diverse work force of the next decade go beyond legal concerns. How diversity issues are managed has implications for creativity, problem solving, retaining good employees, and developing markets for the firm's products and services. In order to successfully manage a diverse work force, managers must develop a new set of skills. These skills include:

1. Communicating effectively with employees from a wide variety of cultural backgrounds.

2. Coaching and developing employees of different ages, educational backgrounds, ethnicity, physical ability, and race.

3. Providing performance feedback that is based on objective outcomes rather than values and stereotypes that work against women, minorities, and handicapped persons by prejudging these persons' abilities and talents.

4. Creating a work environment that makes it comfortable for employees of all backgrounds to be creative and innovative.[45]

TABLE 1.6   How Managing Cultural Diversity Can Provide Competitive Advantage

1. Cost Argument	As organizations become more diverse, the cost of a poor job in integrating workers will increase. Those who handle this well will thus create cost advantages over those who don't.
2. Resource-Acquisition Argument	Companies develop reputations on favorability as prospective employers for women and ethnic minorities. Those with the best reputations for managing diversity will win the competition for the best personnel. As the labor pool shrinks and changes composition, this edge will become increasingly important.
3. Marketing Argument	For multinational organizations, the insight and cultural sensitivity that members with roots in other countries bring to the marketing effort should improve these efforts in important ways. The same rationale applies to marketing to subpopulations within domestic operations.
4. Creativity Argument	Diversity of perspectives and less emphasis on conformity to norms of the past (which characterize the modern approach to management of diversity) should improve the level of creativity.
5. Problem-solving Argument	Heterogeneity in decisions and problem-solving groups potentially produces better decisions through a wider range of perspectives and more thorough critical analysis of issues.
6. System Flexibility Argument	An implication of the multicultural model for managing diversity is that the system will become less determinant, less standardized, and therefore more fluid. The increased fluidity should create greater flexibility to react to environmental changes (i.e., reactions should be faster and at less cost).

SOURCE: T. H. Cox and S. Blake, "Managing Cultural Diversity: Implications for Organizational Competitiveness," *Academy of Management Executive* 5 (1991): 47.

Many U.S. companies have already made a commitment to ensuring that diversity in their work force is recognized and effectively used for competitive advantage. For example, Digital Equipment Corporation wanted to move beyond affirmative action and equal employment opportunity as the sole means for supporting a diverse work force. Its goal was to create a workplace where employees' individual differences were not only tolerated but valued and celebrated. As a result, the company developed programs that focused on helping employees become aware of their cultural, and physical and racial stereotypes. Also, they actively sponsored celebrations of racial, ethnic, and cultural differences.[46]

Avon Products Incorporated has used employee networks to help faci‑ tate the development of minorities and to understand their concern‑

perspectives. Each Avon network, which represents a different minority employee group within the company, holds quarterly meetings and has a budget, a mission statement, and a member who is a senior officer in the company. The senior management members bring management's viewpoint to the network and inform the network of the direction of the company. These senior members also keep management apprised of employees' reactions to policies, particularly in regard to diversity issues.[47]

Avon once had a similar network for women but disbanded it after the program achieved its objective—an increase in the number of women holding management positions. At Avon, the goal is to create an organization where employees do not feel a need for a network based on their nationality, race, or gender. That is, Avon wants all employees to feel they are recognized, informed, rewarded, and developed by the company.

At Motorola, diversity issues are dealt with from four perspectives. First, awareness training is used to get the current work force to appreciate individual differences. Second, a task force to deal with issues such as child and elder care was established. Third, a work-styles task force examines the feasibility of job sharing and flextime. Finally, to help improve the work force preparedness of potential employees, a committee looks at ways the company can help schools to better prepare future employees.[48]

Many companies (e.g., Honeywell, Procter & Gamble, Wang) are currently involved in diversity training efforts using role plays, videotapes, and experiential exercises, which focus on understanding cultural differences, communication styles, and the ways stereotypes influence behavior toward persons with different characteristics.

The bottom line is that in order to gain a competitive advantage in the next decade, companies must harness the power of the diverse work force. The implication of diversity for human resource practices will be highlighted throughout this book. For example, from a staffing perspective, it is important to ensure that tests used to select employees are not biased against minority groups. From a training perspective, it is clear that all employees need to be made aware of the potential damaging effects of stereotypes. From a compensation perspective, new benefits such as elder care and daycare need to be included in reward systems to accommodate the needs of a diverse work force.

Legislation and Litigation.   Five main areas of the legal environment have influenced human resource management over the past 20 years.[49] These areas include equal employment opportunity legislation, employee safety and health, employee pay and benefits, employee privacy, and job security.

Legislation in these areas will continue to have a major impact on human resource management practices. For example, in 1991 the Equal Employment Opportunity Commission finalized regulations that implement provisions of the Americans with Disabilities Act (ADA).[50] As a result of the ADA, employers are required to accommodate known mental or physical limitations of otherwise qualified employees, unless it would result in undue expense. As a result of the ADA, employers are reevaluating their hiring and training practices, benefit plans, job design, and physical facilities.

Similarly, employers have to ensure that their human resource practices comply with the Civil Rights Act of 1991. The Civil Rights Act of 1991 addresses issues related to who (employee or employer) bears the burden of proof in employment discrimination cases, what types of tests qualify as a "business necessity," whether test scores can be adjusted to meet affirmative action requirements, and how much compensation can be awarded for discrimination.[51] Some employment practices that were acceptable under the Civil Rights Act of 1964 (such as adjusting selection test scores on the basis of race, sex, or national origin) are unlawful under the new act.

A final area of litigation that will have a major influence on HRM practices involves job security. As companies are forced to close plants and lay off employees because of restructuring, technology changes, or financial crisis, the number of cases dealing with the illegal discharge of employees has increased. The issue of what constitutes employment at will, that is, employment that can be terminated at any time without notice, will be debated. Employers' work rules, recruitment practices, and performance evaluation systems will need to be revised to ensure that these systems do not falsely communicate employment agreements the company does not intend to honor (e.g., lifetime employment).

Ethical Considerations. Many decisions related to the management of human resources are characterized by uncertainty. Ethics can be considered the fundamental principles by which employees and companies interact.[52] These principles should be considered in making business decisions and interacting with clients and customers. Recent surveys suggest that the general public and managers do not have positive perceptions of the ethical conduct of U.S. businesses. For example, in a survey conducted by *The Wall Street Journal*, four out of ten executives reported they were asked to behave unethically.[53] Approximately one-half of *Harvard Business Review* readers polled between 1960 and 1976 believed that managers do not live up to ethical standards.

As a result of unfavorable perceptions of U.S. business practices and an increased concern for better serving the customer, U.S. companies are becoming more aware of the need for all representatives of the company to act responsibly.[54] They have an interest in the way their employees behave because customer, government agencies, and vendor perceptions of the company play an important role in maintaining the relationships necessary to sell products and services.

Ethical, successful companies can be characterized by four principles.[55] First, in their relationship with customers, vendors, and clients, these companies emphasize mutual benefits. Second, employees assume responsibility for the actions of the company. Third, they have a sense of purpose or vision the employees value and use in their day-to-day work. Finally, they emphasize fairness; that is, another person's interests count as much as their own.

A good example of the behavior of a profitable company that is characterized by a high level of ethical behavior is Johnson & Johnson.[56] As a result of illegal tampering with Tylenol on grocery store shelves by a distraught individual, seven people died from ingesting contaminated Tylenol capsules. Johnson & Johnson's management pulled all Tylenol off the shelves at a cost of more than $10 million. They took this action based on their corporate vision, which requires the company to always honor its obligations to consumers. In the short term, $10 million seems like a large amount of money. However, in the long term, Johnson & Johnson's action increased the firm's integrity in consumers' eyes, resulting in Tylenol's nearly recapturing its market share after the incident.

There are basically three standards that human resource managers must satisfy for these practices to be considered ethical.[57] First, human resource practices must result in the greatest good for the largest number of people. Second, employment practices must respect basic human rights of privacy, due process, consent, and free speech. Third, managers must treat employees and customers equitably and fairly. Throughout the book we will highlight ethical dilemmas in human resource management practices.

The Technology and Structure Challenge

Technological advances in manufacturing, transportation, telecommunications, and microprocessors are expected to have a major impact on work design, company structure, and the skills that employees need to be successful. Over half of the employees currently working in the United States have already experienced major technological changes in their jobs.[58]

It is anticipated that technological advances will result in five major changes in U.S. companies in the next decade:

1. Employees will be given more responsibility for work and use a wider variety of skills.
2. There will be an increased use of teams to perform work.
3. Managers' role as coaches and resource persons will increase.
4. Company structure will continue to flatten.
5. Human resource information bases will be increasingly available.

Change in Employees' Work Roles and Skill Requirements.   New technology causes changes in basic skill requirements and work roles and often results in combining jobs.[59] For example, computer-integrated manufacturing uses robots and computers to automate the manufacturing process. The computer allows the production of different products that meet market demands simply by reprogramming the computer. As a result, laborer, material handler, operator/assembler, and maintenance jobs may be merged into one position. Computer-integrated manufacturing requires employees to monitor equipment and troubleshoot problems with sophisticated equipment, share information with other employees, and understand the interaction between components of the manufacturing process.[60]

Technology is often a means to achieve product diversification and customization. As a result, employees need job-specific product knowledge and basic learning skills to keep up with product development and design improvements. The ability to customize products and services demands that employees have the ability to listen and communicate with customers. Interpersonal skills, such as negotiation and conflict management, and problem-solving skills are more important than physical strength, coordination, and fine-motor skills, which were previously required for many manufacturing and service jobs.

Increase in the Use of Teams to Perform Work.   As the information needed to improve product quality and customer service becomes more available to employees at the point of sale or point of production because of advances in microprocessing systems, employees will be expected to make more decisions concerning how their jobs are performed. One of the most popular methods of increasing employee responsibility and control are work teams. Work teams involve employees with various skills, who together interact to assemble a product or provide a service. Work teams frequently assume many of the activities usually reserved for managers, such as selecting new team members, planning work schedules, and coordinating activities with customers and other units within the firm. Work teams also perform inspection and quality-control activities while the product or service is being completed, an important component for achieving total quality. Advanced manufacturing technology and teamwork play an important role at Levi Strauss & Company, which is discussed in the "Competing through Technology and Structure" box.

Another example of teamwork is Rubbermaid's development of a plastic portable storage bin that holds pens and files and provides a writing surface.[61] A cross-functional team of engineers, designers, and marketing personnel worked jointly with customers to determine the features they wanted in the new product. Typically, each functional area is concerned more with issues related to the function rather than with customer concerns (for example, marketing personnel are more concerned with price than design issues). Use of the team approach permitted simultaneous discussion of price and design features, which resulted in the best possible product for the customer. Satisfying the customer through the team approach resulted in sales that were 50 percent above projections.

Changes in the Nature of Managerial Work.   To gain the maximum benefit from the introduction of new technology in the workplace, managers must be able to move away from the "military model" of management, which emphasizes controlling, planning, and coordinating activities, and instead focus on creating work conditions that facilitate employee creativity and innovation. Because of advances in technology, information is more readily accessible to employees at all levels of the company, and decision

Technology & Structure

COMPETING THROUGH

TEAM-BASED MANUFACTURING AT LEVI STRAUSS & COMPANY

Employees at Levi Strauss & Company Blue Ridge, Georgia, plant who make Levis and Dockers, are participating in a new manufacturing process. This team-based approach, known as Alternative Manufacturing System (AMS), ties compensation and incentives to team goals. In the previous manufacturing system, employees worked on small parts of the garment (such as sewing pockets), then passed the garment to another employee who added another part (such as rivets). Employees did not see the end product. In the AMS system, employees work in a horseshoe configuration, which provide each team member with the opportunity to see others work. Team members have to work together to solve problems, such as unfinished work piling up. In the AMS, managers serve coaching and facilitating roles. Each manager is responsible for training team members. Teams receive over 80 hours of training to increase their understanding of production, budgeting, workflow, and product mix. This training is needed because teams are involved with the entire garment manufacturing process.

The results of the AMS have been encouraging. The AMS has resulted in lower plant inventories, shorter lead times, better garment quality, and less absenteeism, turnover, and injuries.

SOURCE: J. J. Laabs, "HR's Vital Role at Levi Strauss," *Personnel Journal,* December 1992, 35–46.

making increasingly is decentralized. As a result, it is difficult, and certainly not effective, for managers to attempt to directly control interactions between work teams or between work teams and customers.

The manager's job will increasingly be to empower employees. **Empowerment** means giving employees responsibility and authority to make decisions regarding all aspects of product development or customer service.[62] Employees are then held accountable for products and services and, in return, share the rewards and failures that result. For empowerment to be successful, managers must serve in a linking and coordinating role.[63] The linking role involves representing employees (or teams) by ensuring that adequate resources are provided to perform the work (external linking), facilitating interactions across departments (informal linking), and ensuring that employees are updated on important issues and cooperate with each other through sharing of information and resources (internal linking). In addition, managers who successfully perform the internal linking role must be available and willing to help employees deal with problems daily.

Although strong interpersonal skills and communications skills are required by both managers and employees, managers either have to be able to provide answers to technical issues or, more likely, be able to refer employees to persons within or outside the firm who can provide insight into technical problems. This means that managers have to be more aware of various resources available within the company and the community.

Changes in Company Structure.   The traditional design of U.S. companies emphasizes efficiency, decision making by managers, and dissemination of information from the top of the company to lower levels. However, this structure will not be effective in the work environment of the next decade, in which personal computers will give employees immediate access to information needed to complete customer orders or modify product lines. Many companies such as Xerox, Apple Computer, and Levi Strauss have recognized the need to move to an adaptive, high-involvement organizational structure.[64] In the adaptive organizational structure (see Figure 1.5), employees are in a constant state of learning and performance improvement. Employees are free to move wherever they are needed in the company. The adaptive organization is characterized by a core set of values or vital vision that drives all organizational efforts.[65] Previously established boundaries between managers and employees, employees and customers, employees and vendors, and the various functions within the company are abandoned. Employees, managers, vendors, customers, and suppliers work together to improve service and product quality and to create new products and services. Line employees are trained in multiple jobs, communicate directly with suppliers and customers, and interact frequently with engineers, quality experts, and employees from other functions. For example, at Becton Dickinson, makers of high-tech diagnostic systems such as blood analyzers, the company's vision is to develop ideas and beat the competition to market. Divisions are allowed to develop their own business strategies in order to meet this vision. Each division can structure their businesses to meet their needs. Cross-functional teams that include vendors, suppliers, and marketing, engineering, and manufacturing employees are used. The organization redesign resulted in the development of new instruments designed to process blood in 25 percent less time than previous development efforts.

Increased Availability of Information Bases Related to the Company's Human Resources.   Improvements in technology related to microcomputers and software have also had a major impact on the use of information for managing human resources. Traditionally, computers had been used in human resources only for compensation and benefits, for example, administering payroll. However, new advances in microchips have made it possible to store large quantities of data on personal computers and to perform statistical analyses that were once only possible with large mainframe computers. A human resource information system (HRIS) is a system used to acquire, store, manipulate, analyze, retrieve, and distribute information related to the company's human resources.[66] From the manager's perspective, an HRIS can be used to support strategic decision making, to avoid litigation, to evaluate programs or policies, or to support daily operating concerns.

Traditionally, HR software applications have been developed in response to record-keeping requirements dictated by legislation. As a result, most companies have HRISs that track payroll and benefits informa-

FIGURE 1.5   The Adaptive Organization

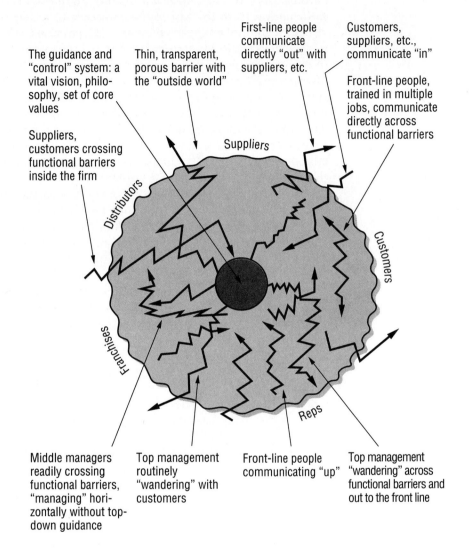

The guidance and "control" system: a vital vision, philosophy, set of core values

Thin, transparent, porous barrier with the "outside world"

First-line people communicate directly "out" with suppliers, etc.

Customers, suppliers, etc., communicate "in"

Front-line people, trained in multiple jobs, communicate directly across functional barriers

Suppliers, customers crossing functional barriers inside the firm

Suppliers

Distributors

Customers

Franchises

Reps

Middle managers readily crossing functional barriers, "managing" horizontally without top-down guidance

Top management routinely "wandering" with customers

Front-line people communicating "up"

Top management "wandering" across functional barriers and out to the front line

SOURCE: T. Peters, "Restoring American Competitiveness: Looking for New Models of Organizations," *Academy of Management Executive* 2 (1988): 104.

tion in response to compliance requirements of legislation such as the Comprehensive Omnibus Budget Reconciliation Act, which requires group health plans to offer health benefits to former employees who have either retired or been terminated. Similarly, the large majority of companies also have HRIS applications related to applicant tracking and adverse impact analysis in response to Title VII of the Civil Rights Act.[67]

However, a number of trends suggest that performance management, succession planning, and training and employee-development applications are becoming increasingly important. For example, future projections of the level of skills that will be available in the future work force suggest that math and reading competencies will be below the level required by new jobs. Changing technology can easily make the skills of technical employees obsolete. To meet internal and external customers' demands, work teams consisting of employees from different functional areas with different skills will have to be assembled. These trends demand that employees' skills and competencies will need to be monitored carefully. In response to this trend, several companies have already implemented training and development applications. For example, in 1984, Chevron did not have an easy and efficient way to get information to management regarding employees' skills and competencies needed to make training decisions and succession planning. To deal with the introduction of new technologies, customer demands, and employee attrition, Chevron needed immediate access to skill information on almost 300,000 employees located in various geographic locations. In response to this need, Chevron developed an HRIS known as EPIC (Emphasizing People in Chevron). The new system is invaluable for individual career planning, tracking the education needs of technical employees to combat obsolescence, and identifying employees to fill permanent positions or special assignments.[68]

MEETING THE COMPETITIVE CHALLENGES THROUGH HRM PRACTICES

We have discussed the global, quality, social, and technology and structure challenges U.S. companies are facing. We have emphasized that the management of human resources plays a critical role in determining companies' success in meeting the challenges. HRM practices have not traditionally been seen as providing economic value to the company. Economic value is usually associated with equipment, technology, and facilities. However, HRM practices have been shown to have economic value.[69] Compensation, staffing, training and development, performance management, and other HRM practices are investments. These investments directly affect employees' motivation and ability to provide products and services that are valued by customers. Research has shown that companies that attempt to increase their competitiveness by investing in new technology and becoming involved in the quality movement also make investments in state-of-the-art staffing, training, and compensation practices.[70] Figure 1.6 shows examples of human resource practices that help companies deal with the four challenges. For example, to meet the quality challenge, companies need to identify through their selection processes whether prospective employees value customer relations and have the levels of interpersonal skills necessary to work with fellow employees in teams. To meet social, technological, and

FIGURE 1.6   Examples of How HR Practices Can Help Companies
Meet the Competitive Challenges

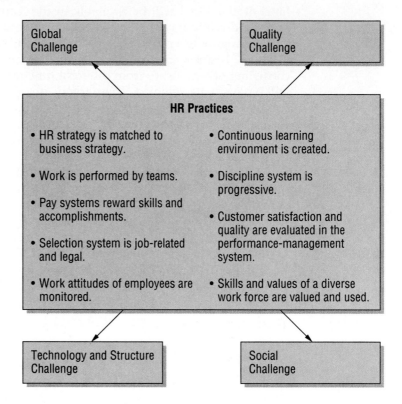

quality challenges companies need to capitalize on the diversity of values, abilities, and perspectives that employees bring to the workplace through the use of work teams.

Human resource management practices that help companies deal with the four competitive challenges can be grouped into the five dimensions shown in Figure 1.7. The five HRM areas include managing the internal and external environments, assessing work and work outcomes, acquiring human resources, developing human resources, and compensating human resources. In addition, some organizations have special issues relating to labor management relations and human resource information systems.

Managing the Internal and External Environments

Managing internal and external environmental factors allows employees to make the greatest possible contribution to company productivity and competitiveness. Creating a positive environment involves:

FIGURE 1.7 Major Dimensions of HRM Practices Contributing
to Company Competitiveness

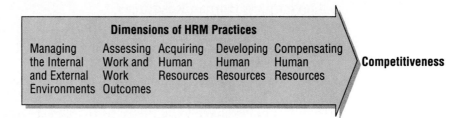

- Linking HRM practices to the company's business objectives, that is, strategic human resource management.
- Understanding international HRM issues.
- Ensuring that HRM practices comply with federal, state, and local laws.
- Creating an employment relationship that benefits both the company and the employee, that is, ethical employee relations.

Assessing Work and Work Outcomes

Because HRM practices affect employee productivity, it is important to design work to maximize productivity. It is also important to identify the quantity and quality of services, behaviors, or products that employees are providing. This area of human resource management deals with:

- Designing work to maximize employees' innovation, creativity, product quality, and customer service.
- Determining employees' productivity and quality of their work.
- Measuring employees' attitudes about the work and work environment.

Acquiring Human Resources

Customer needs for new products or services influence the number and type of employees businesses need to be successful. Terminations, promotions, and retirements also influence human resource requirements. Managers need to predict the number and type of employees who are needed to meet customer demands for products and services. Managers must also identify current or potential employees who can successfully deliver products and services. This area of human resource management deals with:

- Determining human resource requirements, that is, human resource planning.

- Recruiting employees and placing them in jobs that best use their skills.
- Selecting employees.

Developing Human Resources

Managers need to insure that employees have the necessary skills to perform current and future jobs. As we discussed earlier, because of new technology and the quality movement many companies are redesigning work so that it is performed by teams. As a result, managers and employees may need to develop new skills to be successful in a team environment. Employees also have to be prepared to interact with employees who have different values and ethnic and racial backgrounds. Because many employees value work that is personally rewarding and does not interfere with nonwork activities, managers also need to help employees identify their work interests and goals and cope with issues such as balancing work and family roles. This area of human resource management deals with:

- Ensuring employees have the skills needed to perform their current job.
- Preparing employees for future work roles and dealing with a more diverse gender, racial, and ethnic work force.
- Identifying employees work interests, goals, and values, and other career issues.

Compensating Human Resources

Besides interesting work, pay and benefits are the most important incentives that companies can offer employees in exchange for contributing to productivity, quality, and customer service. Also, pay and benefits are used to reward employees membership in the company and attract new employees. The positive influence of new work designs, new technology, and the quality movement on productivity can be damaged if employees are not satisfied with the level of pay and benefits or believe pay and benefits are unfairly distributed. This area of human resource management deals with:

- Creating pay systems.
- Rewarding employee contributions.
- Providing employees with benefits.

Special Issues

In some companies, employees are represented by a labor union. Managing human resources in a union environment requires knowledge of specific laws, contract administration, and the collective bargaining process.

Human resource information systems use computer hardware and software to assist in the human resource management process. Computer applications in human resource management represent new innovations in the

TABLE 1.7   Topics Covered in This Book

I.   *Managing the Internal and External Environments*
2   Strategic Human Resource Management
3   Global Issues in Human Resource Management
4   The Legal Environment and Equal Employment Opportunity
5   Employee Relations

II. *Assessing Work and Work Outcomes*
6   The Analysis and Design of Work
7   Performance Management
8   Work Attitudes and Job Withdrawal

III. *Acquiring Human Resources*
9   Human Resource Planning
10   Job Choice and the Recruitment of Human Resources
11   Personnel Selection and Placement

IV. *Developing Human Resources*
12   Training
13   Employee Development
14   Career Management

V.   *Compensating Human Resources*
15   Pay Structure Decisions
16   Recognizing Individual Contributions with Pay
17   Employee Benefits

VI. *Special Topics in Human Resource Management*
18   Collective Bargaining and Labor Relations
19   Human Resource Information Systems

---

field that many companies are just beginning to implement. Managers in companies that plan to have or currently do have human resource information systems need to be aware of the types of computer hardware and software, how to design and develop systems and choose software, and the current human resource management applications.

Organization of This Book

The topics to be covered in this book are organized according to the five areas of human resource management and special issues. Table 1.7 shows the chapters covered in the book.

The content of each chapter in the book is based on academic research and examples of effective company practices. Each chapter includes examples of how the human resource management practice covered in the chapter helps a company gain a competitive advantage by addressing global, social, quality, or technology and structure challenges.

Discussion Questions

1. Traditional human resource management practices were developed and administered by the company's human resource department. A recent study of HRM practices by IBM and Towers Perrin consulting firm suggested that line managers are likely to play a major role in developing and implementing HR practices. Why do you think line managers are becoming more involved in developing and implementing HR practices?

2. Staffing, training, compensation, and performance management are important HRM functions. How can each of these functions help companies deal with quality challenges? technology challenges? social challenges? global challenges?

3. This book covers five human resource management practice areas: managing the internal and external environment for human resources, assessing work and work outcomes, acquiring human resources, developing human resources, and compensating human resources. Which area do you believe contributes most to helping the company gain a competitive advantage? Which area do you believe contributes the least? Why?

4. If you were asked to draw a historical time line from 1900 to 1993 identifying the events that have shaped HRM, what would you include?

Notes

1. A. S. Tsui and L. R. Gomez-Mejia, "Evaluating Human Resource Effectiveness," in *Human Resource Management Evolving Rules and Responsibilities,* ed. L. Dyer (Washington, DC: BNA Books, 1988), pp. 1187–1227.

2. F. W. Taylor, *The Principles of Scientific Management* (New York: Harper & Row, 1911); R. L. Daft, *Management,* 2nd ed. (Chicago: Dryden Press, 1991); F. J. Landy, *The Psychology of Work Behavior,* 4th ed. (Pacific Grove, CA: Brooks/Cole, 1989).

3. Towers Perrin, *Priorities for Competitive Advantage: An IBM Study Conducted by Towers Perrin,* 1992.

4. Towers Perrin, *Priorities for Competitive Advantage,* p. 6.

5. B. Bailey, "Ask What HR Can Do for Itself," *Personnel Journal* 70, no. 7 (1991): 35–39; D. Filipowski, "Life after HR," *Personnel Journal,* (June 1991): 64–71.

6. L. Kraar, "The Rising Power of the Pacific," *Fortune* Fall 1990: 8–14; M. A. Hitt, R. E. Hoskisson, and J. S. Harrison, "Strategic Competitiveness in the 1990's: Challenges and Opportunities for U.S. Executives." *Academy of Management Executive* 5, no. 2 (1991): 7–22; T. A. Stewart, "U.S. Productivity: First but Fading," *Fortune,* October 19, 1992, 54–57.

7. D. Ulrich and M. F. Wiersema, "Gaining Strategic and Organizational Capability in a Turbulent Business Environment," *The Academy of Management Executive* 3, no. 2 (1989): 115–122.

8. J. A. Marciariello, J. W. Burke, and D. Tilley, "Improving American Competitiveness: A Management Systems Perspective," *Academy of Management Executive* 3, no. 4 (1989): 294–303.

9. *Forbes,* July 27, 1987, 152–154.

10. B. O'Reilly, "Your New Global Workforce," *Fortune,* December 14, 1992, 52–60.

11. E. Brandt, "Global HR," *Personnel Journal* 70 (1991): 38–44.

12. M. A. Hitt, R. E. Hoskisson, and J. S. Harrison, *Academy of Management Executive* 5, no. 2 (1991): 7–22.

13. R. L. Tung, "Expatriate Assignments: Enhancing Success and Minimizing Failure," *Academy of Management Executive* 1 (1987): 117–126.

14. T. A. Stewart, "The New American Century: Where We Stand," *Fortune,* Spring/Summer 1991, 12–23.

15. L. B. Forker, "Quality: American, Japanese, and Soviet Perspectives," *The Executive* 5, no. 4 (1991): 63–74.

16. J. R. Jablonski, *Implementing Total Quality Management: An Overview* (San Diego: Pfeiffer & Company, 1991).

17. J.R. Jablonski, *Implementing Total Quality Management.*

18. Forker, "Quality: American, Japanese, and Soviet Perspectives," 63–74.

19. B. Gerber, "Benchmarking," *Training,* November 1990, 36–44.

20. R. L. Dodson, "Speeding the Way to Total Quality," *Training and Development Journal* 45, no. 6 (1991): 35–42.

21. S. L. Jackson, "What You Should Know about ISO 9000," *Training,* May 1992, 48–52; Bureau of Business Practices, *Profile of ISO 9000* (Boston: Allyn & Bacon, 1992).

22. United States Department of Commerce. *1991 Application Guidelines: Malcolm Baldrige National Quality Award.* (Gaithersburg, MD: National Institute of Science and Technology, 1991).

23. K. F. Fisher and J. F. Spillane, "Quality and Competitiveness," *Training and Development Journal* 45 (1991): 19–22, 24.

24. S. Caudron, "Xerox Won the Baldrige," *Personnel Journal,* April 1991, 98–102.

25. J. Main, "Is the Baldrige Overblown?" *Fortune,* July 1, 1991, 62–64.

26. General Accounting Office, *Management Practices: U.S. Companies Improve Performance through Quality Efforts* (GAO/NSIAD–91–190)(Washington, DC: U.S. General Accounting Office, 1991).

27. Bureau of Labor Statistics, *Outlook 2000* (Bulletin 2352)(Washington, DC: U.S. Government Printing Office, 1990).

28. A. Saveri, "The Realignment of Workers and Work in the 1990s," *New Directions in Career Planning and the Workplace,* ed. J. M. Kummerow (Palo Alto, Cal.: Consulting Psychologists Press, 1991), 117–153.

29. Bureau of Labor Statistics, *Occupational Outlook Handbook* (Washington DC: U.S. Government Printing Office, May 1992).

30. A. Saveri, "The Realignment of Workers."

31. A. P. Carnevale, L. J. Gainer, and A. S. Meltzer, *Workplace Basics: The Essential Skills Employers Want* (San Francisco: Jossey-Bass, 1990).

32. I. S. Kirsch and A. Junglebutt, *Literacy: Profiles of America's National Assessment of Educational Process* (Princeton, N.J.: Educational Testing Service, 1991).

33. E. E. Gordon, J. Ponitcell, and R. R. Morgan, "Back to Basics," *Training and Development Journal,* August 1989, 73–76.

34. Commerce Clearinghouse, *1990 SHRM/CCH Survey* (Chicago, Ill.: Commerce Clearing House, Inc., 1990).

35. The National Association of Manufacturers/Towers Perrin Company, *Today's Dilemma: Tomorrow's Competitive Edge* (Washington, DC: The National Association of Manufacturers, 1991); Center for Public Resources, *Basic Skills in the U.S. Workforce* (Washington, DC: Center for Public Resources, 1983).

36. A. P. Carnevale, L. J. Gainer, and A. S. Meltzer, *Workplace Basics.*

37. National Center on Education and the Economy, *America's Choice: High Skills or Low Wages,* (Rochester, N.Y.: National Center on Education and the Economy, 1990).

38. J. Keehn, "How Business Helps the Schools," *Fortune,* October 21, 1991, 161–180.

39. C. M. Solomon, "Managing the Baby Busters," *Personnel Journal,* March 1992, 52–59.

40. B. Wooldridge and J. Wester, "The Turbulent Environment of Public Personnel Administration: Responding to the Challenge of the Changing Workplace of the Twenty-First Century," *Public Personnel Management* 20 (1991): 207–224.

41. "Employee Dissatisfaction on Rise in Last 10 Years, New Report Says," *Employee Relations Weekly* (Washington DC: Bureau of National Affairs, 1986).

42. D. T. Hall and J. Richter, "Career Gridlock: Baby Boomers Hit the Wall," *The Executive* 4 (1990): 7–22.

43. U.S. Department of Labor, *A Report on the Glass Ceiling Initiative* (Washington, DC: U.S. Department of Labor, 1991).

44. T. H. Cox and S. Blake, "Managing Cultural Diversity: Implications for Organizational Competitiveness," *The Executive* 5 (1991): 45–56.

45. M. Loden and J. B. Rosener, *Workforce America!* (Homewood, Ill.: Business One Irwin, 1991).

46. B. A. Walker and W. C. Hanson, "Valuing Differences at Digital Equipment Corporation," *Diversity in the Workplace* (New York, NY, Guilford Press, 1992): 119–137.

47. C. M. Solomon, "The Corporate Response to Work Force Diversity," *Personnel Journal* 68, no. 8 (1989): 42–53.

48. B. Gerber, "Managing Diversity," *Training* 27, no. 7 (1990): 23–30.

49. J. Ledvinka and V. G. Scarpello, *Federal Regulation of Personnel and Human Resource Management,* 2nd ed. (Boston: PWS-Kent, 1991).

50. EEOC Regulations on the Americans with Disabilities Act, 56 Federal Register 35, 1991, 736.

51. Civil Rights Act of 1991 Public law 102-166, November 21, 1991. 105 STAT 1071. *Congressional Record,* 137.

52. M. Pastin, *The Hard Problems of Management: Gaining the Ethics Edge* (San Francisco: Jossey-Bass, 1986).

53. R. Ricklees, "Ethics in America," *The Wall Street Journal,* October 31–November 3, 1983, 33.

54. C. Lee, "Ethics Training: Facing the Tough Questions," *Training,* March 31, 1986, 33, 38–41.

55. Pastin, *The Hard Problems of Management.*

56. Lee, "Ethics Training."

57. G. F. Cavanaugh, D. Moberg, and M. Velasquez, "The Ethics of Organizational Politics," *Academy of Management Review* 6 (1981): 363–374.

58. P. Choate and P. Linger, *The High-Flex Society* (New York: Knopf, 1986); P. B. Doeringer, *Turbulence in the American Workplace* (New York: Oxford University Press, 1991).

59. Choate and Linger, (1986).

60. K. Miller, *Retraining the American Work Force* (Reading, Mass.: Addison-Wesley, 1989).

61. B. Dumaine, "Who Needs a Boss?" *Fortune,* May 7, 1990, 52–59.

62. T. J. Atchison, "The Employment Relationship: Untied or Re-tied," *Academy of Management Executive* 5 (1991): 52–62.

63. D. McCann and C. Margerison, "Managing High Performance Teams," *Training and Development Journal,* November 1989, 52–60.

64. B. D. Dumaine, "The Bureaucracy Busters," *Fortune,* 1991, 36–50.

65. T. Peters, "Restoring American Competitiveness: Looking for New Models of Organizations," *The Executive* 2 (1988): 103–110.

66. M. J. Kavanaugh, H. G. Guetal, and S. I. Tannenbaum, *Human Resource Information Systems: Development and Application* (Boston, Mass.: PWS-Kent, 1990).

67. S. E. Forrer and Z. B. Leibowitz, *Using Computers in Human Resources* (San Francisco: Jossey-Bass, 1991).

68. J. F. Stright, "Managing a Culture of Change," *The Review,* February/March, 1991, 16–22.

69. W. F. Cascio, *Costing Human Resources: The Financial Impact of Behavior in Organizations,* 3rd ed. (Boston: PWS-Kent, 1991).

70. S. A. Snell and J. W. Dean, "Integrated Manufacturing and Human Resource Management: A Human Capital Perspective," *Academy of Management Journal* 35 (1992): 467–504.

MEETING COMPETITIVE CHALLENGES

Recently Postage Meter Inc. faced serious competition in its postage meter business. From 1920 to 1990 Postage Meter Inc. had the largest market share in the postage meter business. But by 1990, European firms had trimmed its market share to 75 percent. Postage Meter Inc. continues to use an assembly line to manufacture its postage meters, although computer-based technology used to manufacture the postage meter is available from several vendors. Employees are paid on the basis of seniority. Many employees lack basic math and communications skills. Recent reports from sales managers indicate that customers are complaining that the most popular postage meter that the company manufactures is slower and more difficult to maintain than postage meters produced by European competitors. Just recently, Postage Meter Inc. has expanded its sales operations to Japan and Europe. The salespersons have had difficulty dealing with Japanese customers. The Japanese seem to resent it when the salespeople praise the company's product and they resist pressure to set delivery dates for the postage meters they are interested in purchasing.

QUESTIONS

1. What competitive challenges is Postage Meter Inc. facing?

2. What can be done to help Postage Meter Inc. regain its market share?

3. What role could human resource management practices play in helping Postage Meter Inc. deal with its foreign competition?

I

MANAGING THE INTERNAL AND EXTERNAL ENVIRONMENTS

Chapter 1 discussed the global, quality, social, and technological and structural challenges U.S. companies are facing. The chapter emphasized that the management of human resources will determine companies' success in meeting these challenges. Human resources must be acquired, developed, and compensated in ways that ensure that customers receive high-quality products and services. Work must be designed to take advantage of new information, manufacturing, and service technologies. Employees need to learn to work with others from different ethnic, racial, gender, and cultural backgrounds, both in the United States and abroad.

To effectively manage human resources, a company must consider the context in which it oper-

ates. The management of human resources must support the strategic direction of the company. Human resource management practices should be congruent with the cultural, legal, and political systems of the countries in which the company operates. To maximize employee productivity and satisfaction, companies need to create an employment relationship that is fair and ensures the health, safety, and well-being of all employees.

Chapter 2, "Strategic Human Resource Management," discusses the strategic management process and common business strategies that companies adopt. The chapter highlights the role that staffing, performance management, training and development, and compensation play in each type of business strategy. The chapter emphasizes that the human resource function must adopt a customer orientation to help the company successfully execute its business strategy.

Chapter 3, "Global Issues in Human Resource Management," discusses the important social and political changes (such as the formation of the European Economic Community and the proposed North American Free Trade Agreement) that have increased the need for U.S. companies to move into foreign markets. The cultural, educational, political, and economic factors that affect the appropriateness of human resource management practices in different countries are emphasized. Important issues related to selecting, preparing, and rewarding U.S. employees in foreign assignments are highlighted.

Chapter 4, "The Legal Environment and Equal Employment Opportunity," presents the major laws that influence the management of human resources. An overview of the legal system and enforcement agencies is also provided. The various types of discrimination and the ways they have been interpreted in the courts is discussed. A key focus of the chapter is understanding the implications of laws related to sexual harassment, affirmative action, and accommodations for disabled employees.

Chapter 5, "Employee Relations," discusses the policies and practices that can establish good relations between companies and their employees. These policies and practices are related to employee safety, health, job security, and working conditions. The chapter discusses employee assistance programs and wellness programs that can help lower companies' health care costs and help employees effectively manage job stress and their physical well-being. A key focus of the chapter is how to create a fair and productive work environment through the use of alternative work schedules, work arrangements, and progressive discipline systems. The implications of the employment-at-will doctrine for job security and termination are highlighted.

STRATEGIC HUMAN RESOURCE MANAGEMENT

Objectives   *After reading this chapter, you should be able to:*

1. Describe the differences between strategy formulation and strategy implementation.
2. List the components of the strategic management process.
3. Discuss the role of the HR function in strategy formulation.
4. Describe the linkages between HR and strategy formulation.
5. Discuss the more popular typologies of generic strategies and the various HR practices associated with each.
6. Describe the different HR issues and practices associated with various directional strategies.
7. Discuss the role of HR as a customer service business.
8. List the competencies the HR executive needs to become a strategic partner in the company.

Human Resources—A Source of Competitive Advantage

In the late 1970s the American automobile industry was reeling from the effects of increased competition from Japanese auto manufacturers. Ford and General Motors made different strategic decisions about how they would respond to this competition. GM decided to devote substantial capital investments to robotics, based partly on the assumption that *people were the problem.* Many of GM's managers believed that the autoworkers performed shoddy work, were not motivated or skilled, and had no commitment to the company. Thus, robotics would allow them to reduce the people-related problems by minimizing the human input required in the manufacturing and assembly process.

Ford's managers, on the other hand, believed that *people were the solution.* Thus, they decided to devote investments (approximately $200,000 per plant) to people through the Employee Involvement (EI) programs. The program required training employees, cooperating with them, and allowing them more influence in decision making. Don Peterson, Ford's CEO during most of the 1980s, stated that "you should adopt the philosophy that people—not the technology, not profits—are the key to your success."

How did these different strategic decisions work out? During the 1980s, GM invested $90 billion in new plants, equipment, and acqui-sitions. In spite of the fact that this amount would have been enough to buy competing firms Toyota and Nissan (which would have increased their market share), GM lost 12 market share points (to 35%) and lost large amounts of money. Ford, on the other hand, in 1983 made the greatest turnaround in U.S. corporate history. During the mid- to late-eighties, Ford's profits exceeded GM's every quarter, and by 1990, it held 22.3 percent of the U.S. market. In fact, in 1992, Ford's Taurus replaced Honda's Accord as the best selling car in the United States.

SOURCES: A. Taylor, "U.S. Cars Come Back," Fortune 126, no. 11, Nov. 16, 1992, 52–85; J. Mitchell and N. Templin, Ford's Taurus Passes Honda Accord as Bestselling Car in a Lackluster Year. *The Wall Street Journal,* January 7, 1993, B1.

INTRODUCTION

Business organizations have a number of resources at their disposal that they can use to compete with other companies. These resources are physical (e.g., plant, equipment, technology, and geographical location), organizational (e.g., the structure, planning, controlling, and coordinating systems, and group relations), and human (e.g., the experience, skill, and intelligence of employees). It is these resources under the control of the company that provide it with competitive advantage.[1]

The goal of strategic management in an organization is to deploy and allocate resources in a way that provides it with a competitive advantage. As you can see, two of the three classes of resources (organizational and human) are directly tied to the human resource function. As Chapter 1 pointed out, the role of human resource management is to ensure that a company's human resources provide it with a competitive advantage. Chapter 1 also pointed out some of the major competitive challenges that companies face today. These challenges require companies to take a proactive, strategic approach in the marketplace.

To be maximally effective, the HRM function must be integrally involved in the company's strategic management process. This means that human resource managers should (1) have input into the strategic plan, both in terms of people-related issues and in terms of directing the human resource pool toward particular strategic alternatives; (2) have specific knowledge of the organization's strategic goals; (3) know what types of employee skills, behaviors, and attitudes are needed to support the strategic plan; and (4) develop programs to ensure that employees have those skills, behaviors, and attitudes.

We begin this chapter by discussing the concept of strategy and by depicting the strategic management process. Then we discuss the levels of integration between the HRM function and the strategic management process in strategy formulation. Then we will review some of the more common strategic models and, within the context of these models, discuss the various types of employee skills, behaviors, and attitudes, and the ways human resource practices aid in implementing the strategic plan. Finally, we present a model that views the HR function as a separate business within a company, which makes it easier to promote strategic thinking within the HR department.

WHAT IS STRATEGIC MANAGEMENT?

Many authors have noted that, in today's competitive market, organizations must engage in strategic planning in order to survive and prosper. *Strategy* comes from the Greek word *strategos,* which has its roots in military language. It refers to a general's grand design behind a war or battle. In fact, the *Webster's New American Dictionary* defines strategy as the "skillful employment and coordination of tactics," and as "artful planning and management."

Strategic management is a *process,* an approach to addressing the competitive challenges an organization faces. It can be thought of as managing the "pattern or plan that integrates an organization's major goals, policies, and action sequences into a cohesive whole."[2] These strategies can be either the generic approach to competing or the specific adjustments and actions taken to deal with a particular situation.

First, business organizations engage in generic strategies that often fit into some strategic type. One example is "cost, differentiation, or focus."[3] Another is "defender, analyzer, prospector, or reactor."[4] Different organizations within the same industry often have different generic strategies. These generic strategy types describe the consistent way the company attempts to position itself relative to competitors.

However, a generic strategy is only a small part of the strategic management process. Thus, the second aspect of strategic management is the process of developing strategies for achieving the company's goals in light of its current environment. Thus, business organizations engage in generic strategies, but they also make choices about such things as how to scare off competitors, how to keep competitors weaker, how to react to and influence pending legislation, how to deal with various stakeholders and special-interest groups, how to lower production costs, how to raise revenues, what technology to implement, and how many and what types of people to employ. Each of these decisions may present competitive challenges that have to be considered.

Thus, strategic management is more than a collection of strategic types. It is a process for analyzing a company's competitive situation, developing the company's strategic goals, and devising a plan of action and allocation of resources (human, organizational, and physical) that will increase the likelihood of achieving those goals. This kind of strategic approach should be emphasized in human resource management. Thus, HR managers should be trained to identify the competitive issues the company faces with regard to human resources and think strategically about how to respond.

Strategic human resource management (SHRM) can be thought of as "the pattern of planned human resource deployments and activities intended to enable an organization to achieve its goals."[5] For example, many firms have developed integrated manufacturing systems such as advanced manufacturing technology, just-in-time inventory control, and total quality management in an effort to increase their competitive position. However, these systems must be run by people. SHRM in these cases entails assessing the employee skills required to run these systems and engaging in HR practices, such as selection and training, that develop these skills in employees.[6] To take a strategic approach to HRM, we must first have an understanding of the role of HRM in the strategic management process.

Components of the Strategic Management Process

The strategic management process has two distinct yet interdependent phases: strategy formulation and strategy implementation. During **strategy formulation** the strategic planning groups decide on a strategic direction by defining the company's mission and goals, its external opportunities and threats, and its internal strengths and weaknesses. They then generate various strategic alternatives and compare those alternatives' ability to achieve the company's mission and goals. During **strategy implementation**, the organization follows through on the strategy that has been chosen. This consists of structuring the organization, allocating resources, ensuring that the firm has skilled employees in place, and developing reward systems that align employee behavior with the organization's strategic goals. Both of these strategic management phases must be performed effectively. It is important to note that this process does not happen sequentially. As we will discuss later with regard to emergent strategies, this process entails a constant cycling of information and decision making. Figure 2.1 presents the strategic management process.

In recent years organizations have recognized that the success of the strategic management process depends largely on the extent to which the HR function is involved. Thus, in strategic HRM, the HR function is involved in both strategy formulation and strategy implementation. The HR executive provides the strategic planners with information about the company's human resource capabilities, and these capabilities are usually a

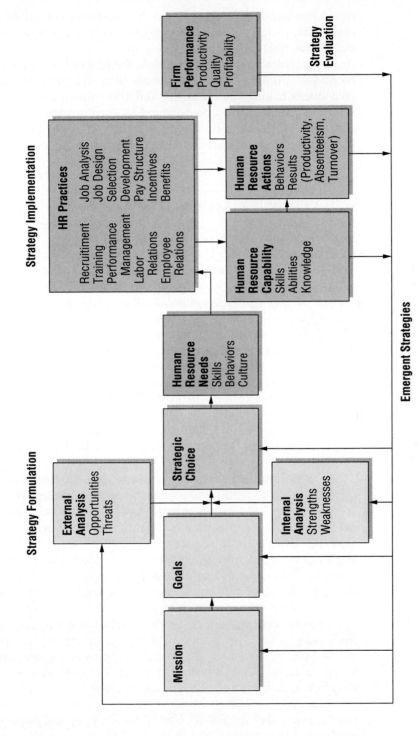

FIGURE 2.1 A Model of the Strategic Management Process

47

direct function of the HR practices. This information about human resource capabilities helps top managers choose the best strategy, since they can consider how well each strategic alternative would be implemented. Once the strategic choice has been determined, the role of HR changes to the development and alignment of HR practices that will provide the company with employees having the necessary skills to implement the strategy. In addition, HR practices must be designed to elicit actions from employees in the company. In the next two sections of this chapter, we show how HR can provide a competitive advantage in the strategic management process.

STRATEGY FORMULATION

Five major components of the strategic management process are relevant to strategy formulation.[7] These components are depicted in Figure 2.2. The first component is the organization's **mission**. The mission is a statement of the organization's reason for being; it usually specifies the customers served, the needs satisfied and/or the values received by the customers, and the technology used. The mission statement is often accompanied by a statement of a company's vision and/or values. For example, Table 2.1 illustrates the mission, vision, and values of Amoco Corporation.

An organization's **goals** are what it hopes to achieve in the medium- to long-term future; they reflect how the mission will be operationalized. The overarching goal of most profit-making companies in the United States is to maximize stockholder wealth. But companies have to set other long-term goals in order to maximize stockholder wealth. For example, one of Digital Equipment Corporation's goals is to be one of the leading personal computer makers.

External analysis consists of examining the organization's operating environment to identify the strategic *opportunities* and *threats*. Examples of "opportunities" are customer markets that are not being served, technological advances that can aid the company, and labor pools that have not been tapped. "Threats" include potential labor shortages, new competitors entering the market, pending legislation that might adversely affect the company, and competitors' technological innovations. In fact, the "Competing through Globalization" box shows one example of how labor shortages are affecting companies' decisions to set up global operations.

Internal analysis attempts to identify the organization's *strengths* and *weaknesses*. It focuses on the quantity and quality of resources available to the organization—financial, capital, technological, and human resources. Organizations have to honestly and accurately assess each resource to decide whether it is a strength or a weakness.

External analysis and internal analysis combined constitute what has come to be called the SWOT (strengths, weaknesses, opportunities, threats) analysis. After going through the SWOT analysis, the strategic planning team has at its disposal all the information it needs to generate a number of

FIGURE 2.2   Strategy Formulation

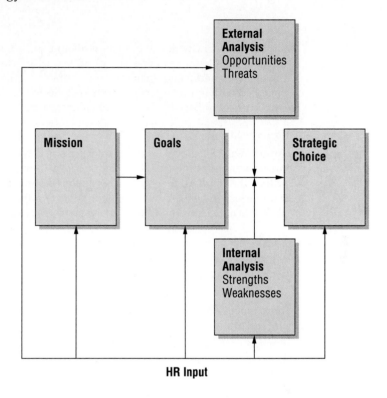

strategic alternatives. The strategic managers compare these alternatives' ability to attain the organization's strategic goals; then they make their **strategic choice**. The strategic choice is the organization's strategy; it describes the ways the organization will attempt to fulfill its mission and achieve its long-term goals.

The Role of HR in Strategy Formulation

A firm's strategy formulation process usually takes place at its top levels, with a strategic planning group consisting of the chief executive officer, the chief financial officer, the president, and various divisional vice-presidents. However, each component of the strategy formulation process involves people-related business issues. Therefore, the HR function needs to be involved in each of those components.

Four levels of integration seem to exist between the HR function and the strategic management function: administrative linkage, one-way linkage, two-way linkage, and integrative linkage.[8] These levels of linkage will be discussed in relation to the different components of strategic management. The linkages are illustrated by Figure 2.3.

TABLE 2.1   Amoco Corporation's Mission, Vision, and Values

Our Mission

Amoco is a worldwide integrated petroleum and chemical company. We find and develop petroleum resources and provide quality products and services for our customers. We conduct our business responsibly to achieve a superior financial return, balanced with our long-term growth, benefiting shareholders and fulfilling our commitment to the community and environment.

Our Vision

Amoco will be a global business enterprise, recognized throughout the world as preeminent by employees, customers, competitors, investors, and the public. We will be the standard by which other businesses measure their performance. Our hallmarks will be the innovation, initiative, and teamwork of our people and our ability to anticipate and effectively respond to change and to create opportunity.

Our Values

Integrity—We insist on honest, fair and trustworthy behavior in all our activities.

People—We respect the individual rights and dignity of all people. Our individual and collective actions and talents create our competitive advantage.

Technology—We believe that technology is a key to the future success of our organization.

Environment, Health, and Safety—We pledge to protect the environment and the health and safety of employees, the users of our products and the communities in which we operate.

Business Relationships—We are committed to customer satisfaction and mutually beneficial business relationships.

Progress—We challenge ourselves to continually improve.

SOURCE: Amoco Corporation, Annual Report, 1990.

Administrative Linkage.   In administrative linkage, the lowest level of integration, the HR function's attention is focused on day-to-day activities. The HR executive has no time or opportunity to take a strategic outlook toward HR issues. The company's strategic business planning function exists without any input from the HR department. Thus, in this level of integration, the HR department is completely divorced from any component of the strategic management process, both in strategy formulation and strategy implementation. The department simply engages in administrative work unrelated to the company's core business needs.

One-Way Linkage.   In one-way linkage, the firm's strategic business planning function develops the strategic plan and then informs the HR function of the plan. Many believe this level of integration constitutes strategic HRM—that is, the role of the HR function is to design systems and/or programs that implement the strategic plan. Although one-way

Globalization

GLOBAL VIEW OF THE HUMAN CAPITAL SHORTAGE

In the United States we often hear the warning of the impending "human capital shortage." Projections are that until the year 2000, the entrants into the work force will have skills that are far below the skill level required for the jobs that are being created. This predicted shortage has a number of companies worried about their ability to attract and retain the skilled employees they need to gain or maintain competitive advantage.

However, this human capital shortage is almost nonexistent for companies that look beyond the borders of the United States. They are discovering that many countries have a surplus of skilled employees. For example, in Ireland, over 25 percent of 18-year-olds go off to college, far more than most European countries, and Irish colleges turn out an impressive number of technically trained graduates. The country has only 1.1 million jobs for a popula-

tion of 3.5 million. Thus, Irish workers consider themselves lucky to have jobs, resulting in an annual turnover rate of about 1 percent nationwide. In addition, the Irish government provides tax and other incentives (as much as a year's pay per job) for foreign companies to create jobs in Ireland. The result of all of this is that operating costs can be 30 to 35 percent lower in Ireland than in the United States. Quarterdeck Office Systems (a software company) and Metropolitan Life (insurance) are just two companies that have availed themselves of the abundant Irish labor supply.

Although many companies' strategies require setting up international operations because of the desire to penetrate foreign markets, in the future it is highly likely that it will be the abundance of skilled human resources that drive foreign expansion.

SOURCE: J. Martin, "Your New Global Work Force," *Fortune,* December 14, 1992, 52–66.

FIGURE 2.3 Linkages of Strategic Planning and HRM

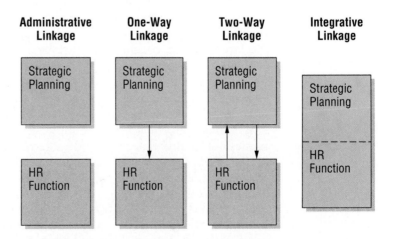

SOURCE: Adapted from K. Golden and V. Ramanujam, 1985.

linkage does recognize the importance of human resources in implementing the strategic plan, it precludes the company from considering human resource issues while formulating the strategic plan. This level of integration often leads to strategic plans that the company cannot successfully implement.

Two-Way Linkage.   Two-way linkage *does* allow for consideration of human resource issues during the strategy formulation process. This integration occurs in three sequential steps. First, the strategic planning team informs the HR function of the various strategies the company is considering. Then, HR executives analyze the human resource implications of the various strategies, presenting the results of this analysis to the strategic planning team. Finally, after the strategic decision has been made, the strategic plan is passed on to the HR executive, who develops programs to implement it. The strategic planning function and the HR function are interdependent in two-way linkage.

Integrative Linkage.   Integrative linkage is dynamic and multifaceted, based on continuing rather than sequential interaction. In most cases, the HR executive is an integral member of the senior management team. Rather than an iterative process of information exchange, companies with integrative linkage have their HR functions built right into the strategy formulation and implementation processes.

What kinds of input would be evidenced in this level of integration? First, in helping define the firm's mission and goals, the HR executive needs to remember that these statements can be used to get employees to support the company wholeheartedly. The statements need to be worded in such a way that the employees direct their behavior toward the achievement of the company's mission and goals. A mission statement that very mechanically describes the company's products and customers will not inspire employees to go beyond their formal job duties to help the company succeed.

Many of the opportunities and threats in the external environment are people related. With fewer and fewer highly qualified individuals entering the labor market, organizations are beginning to compete not just for customers but for employees. It is the HR's role to keep close tabs on the external environment for human resource–related opportunities and threats, especially for those that are directly related to the HR function: potential labor shortages, competitor wage rates, government regulations affecting employment, and so on. For example, as discussed in Chapter 1, U.S. companies are finding that more and more high school graduates lack the basic skills needed to work, one source of the "human capital shortage."[9] However, not recognizing this environmental threat, many companies have encouraged the exit of older, more skilled workers while hiring less skilled younger workers who require basic skills training.[10]

An analysis of a company's internal strengths and weaknesses also requires input from the HR function. Today, companies are increasingly realizing that their human resources are one of their most important assets.

In fact, one estimate is that over one-third of the total growth in U.S. GNP between 1943 and 1990 was the result of increases in human capital. Failure to consider the strengths and weaknesses of the company's work force may result in its choosing strategies it is not capable of pursuing. For example, one company chose a strategy of cost reduction through technological improvements. It built a plant designed around a computer-integrated manufacturing system with statistical process controls. Though this choice may seem like a good one, the company soon learned otherwise. It discovered that its employees could not operate the new equipment because 25 percent of the work force was functionally illiterate.[11]

Thus, with an integrative linkage, strategic planners consider all the people-related business issues before making a strategic choice. These issues are identified with regard to the mission, goals, opportunities, threats, strengths, and weaknesses, leading the strategic planning team to make a more intelligent strategic choice. While this process does not guarantee success, companies that address these issues are more likely to make a choice that will ultimately succeed. Some examples of the role of HR in strategic planning are provided in Table 2.2.

Example: People Express

People Express is an example of the people-related business issues involved in strategic management. People Express, founded in the early 1970s, entered the market as a low-cost airline. It had phenomenal early success, attributable in no small measure to the way it used its human resources. Using a very intense hiring process—applicants had to pass a number of interviews and assessments before being hired—the company made sure it had extremely high-quality employees who fit the "People Express" mold. In addition, the high productivity coupled with relatively low wages provided People Express with a competitive cost advantage over the major airline carriers.

During its growth period, however, People Express rapidly increased its number of flights, which meant a corresponding increase in the number of employees. The company was unable to hire enough highly qualified employees to maintain its level of service quality. This was partly because of the extensiveness of its hiring and training processes and partly because there simply were not enough individuals in the labor market who met the company's qualifications. As a result, the existing labor force was required to work long overtime hours under very stressful conditions. As one might expect, customer service suffered immensely, with negative outcomes—such as increased baggage loss and theft—until, ultimately, People Express filed for bankruptcy.[12]

If HR at People Express had taken a strategic perspective, would things have been different? The employees agreed with the company's mission and goals, but the company simply did not have the internal strengths (enough high-quality employees) to implement the expansion strategy. Neither did the external environment offer the necessary opportunities

TABLE 2.2

Examples of the Role of HR in Strategic Management

Philip Morris Companies Inc: Hamish Maxwell, Chairman and CEO

"At Philip Morris, we are a results-oriented and a people-sensitive company. Our senior human resource executive reports to me, is a member of the Corporate Planning Committee, and is actively involved in setting the strategic direction of the business. With the size and complexity of the company increased as a result of the recent acquisition of Kraft, strategic planning has and must continue to take the impact of people management issues into account. I expect that this role will strengthen."

AT&T: Robert E. Allen, Chief Executive Officer

"At the time of the government break-up, AT&T had a domestic work force, a reputation for lifelong employment and a history of predictability. Since 1984, however, we have trimmed about 70,000 jobs in the U.S., increased our presence overseas while at the same time enlightened our people about topsy-turvy, unpredicted global marketplace. Throughout the past five years, the human resource department at AT&T has been a lynch pin."

Dow Chemical U.S.A.: Keith R. McKennon, President

"To succeed in today's dynamic environment, we must be good at preparing our people for change—in the marketplace and in the work force. A diverse team of Dow people must be recruited, trained and mobilized to assure those skills that will best meet customer needs. To do this, we will tie our human resource plans ever more closely to capital planning and the strategic thrusts of our businesses."

Shell Oil Company: F. H. Richardson, President and CEO

"The process of human resources management is an integral part of our company's strategic planning efforts. Key business plans, as well as the external environment, are considered in light of human resource implications. The process includes strategic evaluation sessions focusing on human resource issues."

Amoco Corporation: Richard M. Morrow, Chairman

"Amoco's strategic planning process focuses primarily on the financial and operating information required to meet the corporation's short- and long-term goals. The human resource function utilizes this data and the established goals to assess the people needs of the organization and develop appropriate plans to recruit, develop, motivate and retain the people required. The final process is the integration of the operating, financial and human resources components into the corporation's strategic plan."

Chrysler Motors Corporation: Robert A. Lutz, President

"At Chrysler, we see the role of human resources as twofold—to provide leadership and programs that contribute importantly to the direction and performance of the corporation, and to promote a participative work environment that results in enhanced employee job satisfaction and the production of quality goods and services."

SOURCE: Reprinted with permission of *HRMagazine* (formerly Personnel Administrator). Published by the Society for Human Resource Management, Alexandria, VA.

(access to highly qualified employees) to implement the strategy. If the HR function had raised these issues *prior* to the decision to rapidly expand operations, it might have encouraged People Express to delay the expansion, or at least to expand at a rate that would have allowed the company to attract, select, and train employees to maintain its high level of customer service.

Thus, the strategic choice might have been one that would have kept People Express in business.

Research has indicated that most companies exist at either the one-way or two-way linkage levels, with few companies existing at either the administrative or integrative level.[13] As we've mentioned before, companies are beginning to recognize that in an intensely competitive environment, managing human resources strategically can provide a competitive advantage. Thus, companies at the administrative linkage level will either become more integrated or face extinction. In addition, companies will move toward becoming integratively linked in an effort to manage human resources strategically.

It is of utmost importance that all people-related business issues be considered during the strategy formulation process. These issues are identified in the HR function. Mechanisms or structures for integrating the HR function into strategy formulation may help the strategic planning team make the most effective strategic choice. Once that strategic choice is determined, HR must take an active role in implementing it. This role will be discussed in the next section.

STRATEGY IMPLEMENTATION

Once an organization has gone through the process of strategy formulation and made its strategic choice, it has to execute that strategy—make it come to life in its day-to-day workings. The strategy a company pursues dictates certain HR needs. The foundation of any strategy is that certain tasks must be accomplished in pursuit of the company's goals, that individuals must possess certain skills to perform those tasks, and that these individuals must be motivated to perform them effectively.

The basic premise behind strategy implementation is that "an organization has a variety of structural forms and organizational processes to choose from when implementing a given strategy," and these choices make an economic difference.[14] Five important variables determine success in strategy implementation: organizational structure; task design; the selection, training, and development of people; reward systems; and types of information and information systems (see Figure 2.4).

As can be seen in Figure 2.4, HR has primary responsibility for three of the five implementation variables: task, people, and reward systems. In addition, HR can also directly impact the two remaining variables: structure and information and decision processes. First, for the strategy to be successfully implemented, the tasks must be designed and grouped into jobs in a way that is efficient and effective.[15] In Chapter 6 we will examine how this can be done through the processes of job analysis and job design. Second, the HR function must ensure that the organization is staffed with people who have the necessary knowledge, skill, and ability to perform their part in implementing the strategy. This goal is achieved primarily through recruitment, selection and placement, training, development, and

FIGURE 2.4   Variables to be Considered in Strategy Implementation

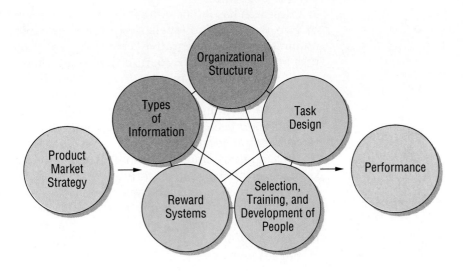

career management, topics covered in Chapters 10 through 14. In addition, the HR function must develop performance management and reward systems that lead employees to work for and support the strategic plan. The specific types of performance management systems are covered in Chapter 7, and the many issues involved in developing reward systems are discussed in Chapters 15 through 17. In other words, the role of the HR function becomes one of (1) ensuring that the company has the proper number of employees with the levels and types of skills required by the strategic plan,[16] and (2) developing "control" systems that ensure that those employees are acting in ways that promote the achievement of the goals specified in the strategic plan. [17]

How does the HR function do this? As Figure 2.5 shows, it is through administering HR practices: job analysis/design, recruitment, selection systems, training and development programs, performance management systems, reward systems, and labor relations programs. The details of each of these HR practices are the focus of the rest of this book. However, at this point it is important to present a general overview of the HR practices and their role in strategy implementation. We will then discuss the various strategies companies pursue and the types of HR systems congruent with those strategies. First, we focus on how the strategic types are implemented; then we discuss the HR practices associated with various directional strategies.

HR Practices

The HR function could be thought of as having six menus of HR practices from which companies can choose the ones that are most appropriate to implementing the strategy. Each of these menus refers to a particular func-

FIGURE 2.5   Strategy Implementation

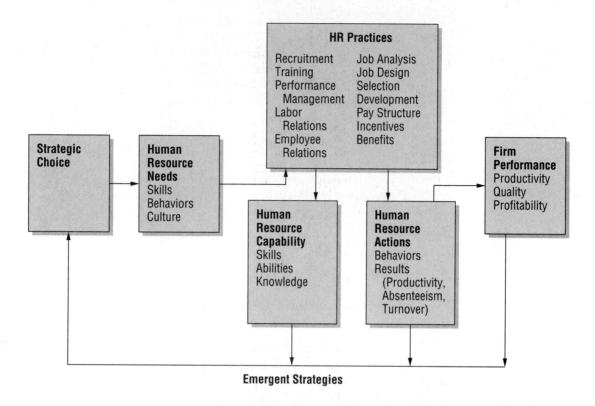

tional area of HRM: job analysis/design, recruitment/selection, training and development, performance management, pay structure/incentives/benefits, and labor/employee relations.[18] These menus are presented in Table 2.3.

Job Analysis and Design.   Companies produce a given product or service (or set of products or services), and the manufacture of these products requires that a number of tasks be performed. These tasks are grouped together to form jobs. **Job analysis** is the process of getting detailed information about jobs. **Job design** deals with making decisions about what tasks should be grouped into a particular job. The way that jobs are designed should have an important tie to the strategy of an organization, because the strategy requires either new and different tasks, or different ways of performing the same tasks. In addition, because many strategies entail the introduction of new technologies, this has an impact on the way that work is performed.[19]

In general, jobs can range from having a narrow range of tasks, most of which are simplified and require a limited range of skills, to having a broad array of complex tasks requiring multiple skills. In the past, the narrow

TABLE 2.3   Menu of HR Practice Options

Job Analysis/Design

Few tasks ⟷ Many tasks
Simple tasks ⟷ Complex tasks
Few skills required ⟷ Many skills required
Specific job descriptions ⟷ General job descriptions

Recruitment/Selection

External sources ⟷ Internal sources
Limited socialization ⟷ Extensive socialization
Assessment of specific skills ⟷ Assessment of general skills
Narrow career paths ⟷ Broad career paths

Training and Development

Focus on current job skills ⟷ Focus on future job skills
Individual orientation ⟷ Group orientation
Train few employees ⟷ Train all employees
Spontaneous, unplanned ⟷ Planned, systematic

Performance Management

Behavioral criteria ⟷ Results criteria
Developmental orientation ⟷ Administrative orientation
Short-term criteria ⟷ Long-term criteria
Individual orientation ⟷ Group orientation

Pay Structure/Incentives/Benefits

Pay weighted toward salary/benefits ⟷ Pay weighted toward incentives
Short-term incentives ⟷ Long-term incentives
Emphasis on internal equity ⟷ Emphasis on external equity
Individual incentives ⟷ Group incentives

Labor/Employee Relations

Collective bargaining ⟷ Individual bargaining
Top-down decision making ⟷ Participation in decision making
Formal due process ⟷ No due process
View employees as expense ⟷ View employees as assets

SOURCES: Adapted from Randall S. Schuler and Susan F. Jackson, "Linking Competitive Strategies with Human Resource Management Practices," *Academy of Management Executive* 1 (1987): 207–219, and Cynthia Fisher, Lyle Schoenfeldt, and Ben Shaw, *Human Resource Management,* 2d ed. (Boston: Houghton, Mifflin, 1992).

design of jobs has been used to increase efficiency, while the broad design of jobs has been associated with efforts to increase innovation. However, with the advent of total quality management methods and a variety of employee involvement programs such as quality circles, many jobs are moving toward the broader end of the spectrum.

Employee Recruitment and Selection.   **Recruitment** is the process through which the organization seeks applicants for potential employment. **Selection** refers to the process by which it attempts to identify applicants with the necessary knowledge, skills, abilities, and other characteristics that will help the company achieve its goals. Companies engaging in different strategies need different types and numbers of employees. Thus, the strategy a company is pursuing will have a direct impact on the types of employees that it seeks to recruit and select.[20]

Employee Training and Development.   A number of skills are instilled in employees through training and development. **Training** refers to a planned effort to facilitate the learning of job-related knowledge, skills, and behavior by employees. **Development** involves acquiring knowledge, skills, and behavior that improve employees' ability to meet the challenges of a variety of existing jobs or jobs that do not yet exist. Changes in strategies often require changes in the types, levels, and mixes of skills. Thus, the acquisition of strategy-related skills is an essential element of the implementation of strategy.

For example, many companies have recently emphasized quality in their products, engaging in total quality management (TQM) programs. These programs require extensive training of all employees in the TQM philosophy, methods, and often other skills that ensure quality.[21]

Through recruitment, selection, training, and development, companies can obtain a pool of human resources capable of implementing a given strategy.[22] The "Competing through Quality" box shows the importance Allied Signal places on developing a pool of human capital as a means of increasing its competitive advantage.

Performance Management.   **Performance management** is used to ensure that employees' activities and outcomes are congruent with the organization's objectives. It entails specifying those activities and results that will result in the firm successfully implementing the strategy. For example, companies that are "steady state" (i.e., not diversified), tend to have evaluation systems that call for subjective performance assessments of managers. This stems from the fact that those above the focal managers in the hierarchy have extensive knowledge about how the work should be performed. On the other hand, diversified companies are more likely to use quantitative measures of performance to evaluate managers because top managers have less knowledge about how work should be performed by those below them in the hierarchy.[23]

COMPETING THROUGH

Quality

TOTAL QUALITY MANAGEMENT AT ALLIED SIGNAL

Since Lawrence Bossidy took over as chief executive at Allied Signal, operating profits have increased by 28.5 percent, return on shareholder's equity jumped from 8.9 percent to 17 percent, and the stock price has risen from 29 3/8s to 55 1/2. How did this turnaround take place? Bossidy has implemented a total housecleaning and culture change, in which HR has played an important role.

First, Bossidy developed a statement of corporate vision ("One of the world's premier companies, distinctive and successful") and values (e.g., customer satisfaction, integrity, teamwork, and speed). Although this statement seems to be standard fare for corporate vision/ value statements, it has galvanized people.

Second, he immersed the company in total quality management as a means of turning the vision and values into reality. For example, to implement the total quality management program, all 90,000 employees will attend a four-day course in total quality management concepts, procedures, and applications.

Finally, he implemented a top-to-bottom change in human resource management. In the quest to increase the quality of their human resource pool, teams of top managers developed detailed plans for revamping college recruiting, staffing, career development, and training and education. These teams studied top companies such as Corning, Bechtel, Hewlett-Packard, and Johnson & Johnson, using them as benchmarks. In addition, they held focus groups with employees to identify how HR could better serve the needs of employees. Their master plan is to develop a deeper pool of human capital through career pathing, rotating managers across businesses, and management education. Bossidy believes that this investment in people will help Allied Signal achieve its ambitious growth goals.

SOURCE: T. Stewart, "Allied Signal's Turnaround Blitz," *Fortune*, November 30, 1992, 72–76.

Similarly, executives who have extensive knowledge of the behaviors that lead to effective performance use performance management systems that focus on the behaviors of their subordinate managers. However, when executives are unclear about the specific behaviors that lead to effective performance, they tend to focus on evaluating the objective performance results of their subordinate managers.[24]

Pay Structure, Incentives, and Benefits. The pay system has an important role in implementing strategies. First, a high level of pay and/or benefits relative to competitors can ensure that the company attracts and retains high-quality employees, but this might have a negative impact on the company's overall labor costs.[25] Second, by tying pay to performance, the company can elicit specific activities and levels of performance from employees.

In a study of how compensation practices are tied to strategies, researchers examined 33 high-tech and 72 traditional companies. They classified them by whether they were in a growth stage (greater than 20 percent inflation-adjusted increases in annual sales) or a maturity stage. They found that high-tech companies in the growth stage used compensation systems that were highly geared toward incentive pay, with a lower percentage of total pay devoted to salary and benefits. On the other hand, compensation systems among mature companies (both high-tech and traditional) devoted a lower percentage of total pay to incentives and a high percentage to benefits.[26]

Labor and Employee Relations.   Whether companies are unionized or not, the general approach to relations with employees can strongly impact its potential for gaining competitive advantage. In the late 1970s Chrysler Corporation was faced with bankruptcy. Lee Iacocca, the new president of Chrysler, asked the union for wage and work-rule concessions in an effort to turn the company around. The union agreed to the concessions, in return receiving profit sharing and a representative on the board. Within only a few years, the relationship with and support from the union allowed Chrysler to pull itself out of bankruptcy to record profitability.[27]

Companies can choose to treat employees as an asset that requires investment of resources, or as an expense to be minimized.[28] They have to make choices about how much employees can and should participate in decision making, what rights employees have, and what the company's responsibility is to them. The approach it takes in making these decisions can result in it either successfully achieving its short- and long-term goals or ceasing to exist.

Strategic Types

As we previously discussed, companies can be classified by the generic strategies they pursue. It is important to note that these generic "strategies" are not what we mean by a strategic plan. They are merely similarities in the ways companies seek to compete in their industries. A number of typologies have been offered, but we will focus on two related ones: Porter's typology of cost, differentiation, and focus,[29] and Miles and Snow's typology of defenders, analyzers, prospectors, and reactors.

Porter's Generic Strategies.   According to Michael Porter of Harvard, competitive advantage stems from a company being able to create value in its production process. Value can be created in one of two ways. First, value can be created by reducing costs. Second, value can be created by differentiating a product or service in such a way that it allows the company to charge a premium price relative to its competitors. Thus, this leads to two basic strategies. According to Porter, the "overall cost leadership" strategy focuses on becoming the lowest-cost producer in an industry. This strategy is achieved by constructing efficient large-scale facilities, by reducing costs through capitalizing on the experience curve, and by controlling overhead costs and costs in such areas as R&D, service, sales force, and advertising. This strategy provides above-average returns within an industry, and it tends to bar other firms' entry into the industry, since the firm can lower its prices below competitors' costs. For example, IBM-clone computer manufacturers like AST and Dell have captured an increased share of the personal computer market by offering personal computers at lower cost than IBM, Apple, and Compaq.

The "differentiation" strategy, according to Porter, attempts to create the impression that the company's product or service is different from that of others in the industry. The perceived differentiation can come from creating a brand image, from technology, from offering unique features, or from unique customer service. If a company succeeds in differentiating its product, it will achieve above-average returns, and the differentiation may protect it from price sensitivity. For example, IBM has consistently emphasized its brand image and its reputation for superior service while charging a higher price for its computers.

A focus strategy generally consists of either reducing costs or differentiating a product in order to meet the needs of a particular market niche. A company with a focus strategy tries to serve a particular target segment better than any of its competitors. The way this is done depends on the target group. For example, Cray remains focused on providing high-performance mainframe computer systems and avoids entry in the PC market.

Miles and Snow's Strategic Types.   In Miles and Snow's typology, "defenders" are companies that have relatively narrow and stable product-market domains. These companies make few major adjustments in their structures, technologies, strategies, and methods or operations. Defender companies try to increase efficiency so that they can compete on the basis of low cost and make additional profits in the absence of significant competition. "Prospectors" are firms that constantly search for new product and market opportunities. These companies experiment and try to create uncertainty among their competitors through diverse product lines, multiple technologies, product development, and market research. "Analyzers" are companies that seek to integrate aspects of defenders and prospectors. They operate in both stable and unstable domains and watch competitors closely for new ideas, only adopting those that seem most promising. Analyzers have a limited basic product line with a number of related products, focusing on production efficiency, process engineering, and marketing. Finally, "reactors" are companies that seem to have no consistent strategy other than responding to what their competitors do.

Although these two typologies differ somewhat, they share certain themes. Both the defender and the cost strategies focus on minimizing production costs in order to produce the lowest-cost (although not necessarily the lowest-price) product or service in the industry. Both the differentiation and the prospector strategies emphasize constantly developing new products or innovations so that the company's products will be perceived as unique by consumers. Finally, both the focus and the analyzer strategies combine aspects of other strategies by competing on a cost basis in some markets while competing by differentiation in others.

HR Needs in Strategic Types

While all of the strategic types require competent people in a generic sense, each of the strategies also requires different types of employees with different types of behaviors and attitudes. As we noted earlier in Figure 2.1, different strategies require employees with specific skills and also require these employees to exhibit different "role behaviors."[30] **Role behaviors** are the behaviors that are required of an individual in his or her role as a job holder in a social work environment. These role behaviors vary on a number of dimensions, as depicted in Table 2.3. Additionally, different role behaviors are required by the different strategies. For example, companies engaged in a cost/defender strategy require employees to have a high concern for quantity and a short-term focus, to be comfortable with stability, and to be risk averse. These employees are expected to exhibit role behaviors that are relatively repetitive and performed independently or autonomously.

Thus, companies engaged in cost/defender strategies, because of the focus on efficient production, tend to specifically define the skills they require and invest in training employees in these skill areas. They also rely on behavioral performance management systems with a large performance-based compensation component. These companies promote internally and develop internally consistent pay systems with high pay differentials between superiors and subordinates. They seek efficiency through worker participation, soliciting from employees ideas on how to achieve more efficient production.

On the other hand, employees in companies with a differentiation/prospector strategy need to be highly creative and cooperative; to have only a moderate concern for quantity, a long-term focus, and a tolerance for ambiguity; and to be risk takers. Employees in these companies are expected to exhibit role behaviors that include cooperating with others, taking risks, developing new ideas, and taking a balanced approach to process and results.

Thus, differentiation/prospector companies will seek to generate more creativity through broadly defined jobs with general job descriptions. They may recruit more from outside, engage in limited socialization of newcomers, and provide broader career paths. Training and development activities focus on cooperation. The compensation system is geared toward external equity, as it is heavily driven by recruiting needs. These companies develop results-based performance management system and divisional/corporate performance evaluations to encourage risk taking on the part of managers.[31]

Finally, as was already discussed, the focus/analyzer strategy is a combination of the other two strategies. These companies have the human resource needs of cost/defenders in the markets where they seek to compete on the basis of cost, and the needs of differentiation/prospectors in the markets where they wish to compete through innovation.

Thus, focus/analyzers require decentralized HR practices. These companies frequently switch their HR practices to correspond with the particular product-market demands. They attempt to develop new markets like differentiation/prospectors and then compete like cost/defenders once these markets have matured. This requires that in some markets they focus on results-based appraisals, emphasize selecting competent individuals, and have compensation systems that promote risk taking. However, over time their HR practices come to resemble those of the cost/defender strategy by shifting to greater investments in training, pay, and promotion systems with high pay and status differentials and appraisal systems that emphasize behaviors.

Directional Strategies

As discussed earlier in this chapter, strategic typologies are useful for classifying the way in which different organizations seek to compete within an industry. However, it is very seldom that a company's strategic planning team sits down and makes a strategic choice to be a "defender," "prospector," "analyzer," or "reactor." Instead, these groups usually decide that they need to invest more in product development or to diversify as a means for growth. With these types of strategies it is more useful for the HR function to aid in evaluating the feasibility of the various alternatives and to develop programs that support the strategic choice.

Companies have used four possible categories of directional strategies to meet objectives.[32] Strategies emphasizing market share or operating costs are considered "concentration" strategies. With this type of strategy a company is attempting to focus on what it does best within its established markets and can be thought of as "sticking to its knitting." Strategies focusing on market development, product development, innovation, or joint ventures make up the "internal growth" strategy. Companies with an internal growth strategy are channeling their resources toward building upon existing strengths. Those attempting to integrate vertically, horizontally, or to diversify are exhibiting an "external growth" strategy. This strategy attempts to expand a company's resources or to strengthen its market position through acquiring or creating new businesses. Finally, a "divestment" strategy is one made up of retrenchment, divestitures, or liquidation. These strategies are observed among companies facing serious economic difficulties and seeking to pare down their operations.

Implications for Human Resources. The human resource implications of each of these strategies are quite different. Concentration strategies require that the company maintain the current skills that exist in the organization. This requires that training programs provide a means of keeping those skills sharp among people in the organization and that compensation programs focus on retaining people who have those skills. Appraisals in this strategy tend to be more behavioral because the environment is more certain, and the behaviors necessary for effective performance tend to be established through extensive experience.

Internal growth strategies present unique staffing problems. Growth requires that a company constantly hire, transfer, and promote individuals, and expansion into different markets may change the necessary skills that prospective employees must have. In addition, appraisals often consist of a combination of behaviors and results. The behavioral appraisal emphasis stems from the knowledge of effective behaviors in a particular product market, and the results appraisals focus on achieving growth goals. Compensation packages will be heavily weighted toward incentives for achieving growth goals. Training needs will differ depending on the way the company attempts to grow internally. For example, if the organization seeks to expand its markets, training will focus on knowledge of each market, particularly when the company is expanding into international markets. On the other hand, when the company is seeking innovation or product development, training will be of a more technical nature, as well as focusing on interpersonal skills such as team building. Joint ventures require extensive training in conflict-resolution techniques because of the problems associated with combining people from two distinct organizational cultures.

Training in conflict resolution is also necessary when companies engage in an external growth strategy. All the options for external growth (with the exception of conglomerate diversification) consist of acquiring or developing new businesses, and these businesses will often have distinct cultures. Thus, many HR programs will face problems in integrating and standardizing practices across the company's businesses. The relative value of standardized practices versus diverse practices across businesses must be weighed against the environmental requirements of each distinct business. For example, with regard to pay practices, a company may desire a consistent internal wage structure across diverse businesses to maintain employee perceptions of internal equity in the larger organization. For example, in a recent new business developed by IBM, the company was pressured by the new business's employees to maintain the same wage structure as IBM's main operation. However, some businesses may be functioning in environments where pay practices are driven heavily by market wages. To require these businesses to adhere to the pay practices of businesses in other environments may result in an ineffective wage structure.

In these cases, the role of HR may be broken up between corporate and business-level needs. The corporate HR function provides services such as legal advice and consulting in developing particular HR practices for business-level HR functions. The business-level HR function, on the other hand, may have the responsibility of developing HR programs and practices that support the particular business's needs.

Retrenchment.   Finally, of increasing importance to organizations in today's times of recession and global competition is HR's role in a retrenchment strategy. Retrenchment requires downsizing, or what is now called "rightsizing," and this almost always requires reducing the work force. This presents a number of challenges and opportunities for HR. In terms of challenges, the HR function must "surgically" reduce the work force by cutting only the workers who are less valuable in terms of their performance. This is difficult because the best workers are most able (and often willing) to find alternative employment and may leave voluntarily prior to any layoff. For example, General Motors and the United Auto Workers recently agreed to an early retirement program for individuals between the ages of 51 and 65 who have been employed for ten or more years. The program entails providing those who agree to retire with their full pension benefits, even if they obtain employment elsewhere, and as much as $13,000 toward the purchase of a GM car.[33]

Early retirement programs, although humane, essentially reduce the work force with a "grenade" approach. This means that the work force reduction does not distinguish between good and poor performers, as if one simply threw a hand grenade into a room full of employees. In fact, recent research is pointing to the fact that when companies downsize by offering early retirement programs, they usually end up rehiring to replace essential talent within a year. This often means that the company does not achieve its cost-cutting goals because it spends between one-half and one and one-half of the departing employee's salary in hiring and retraining costs.[34]

Another challenge is to boost the morale of employees who remain after the reduction. Survivors may feel guilt over keeping their jobs when their friends have been laid off, or they may feel envy for having to work when their friends have retired with attractive severance and pension benefits. Their reduced satisfaction with and commitment to the organization may interfere with work performance. Thus, the HR function has to maintain open communication channels with remaining employees to build their trust and commitment. In addition, companies going through downsizing often develop compensation programs that tie the individual's compensation to the company's success. Employee ownership programs often result from downsizing, and gainsharing plans such as the Scanlon Plan were originated in companies facing economic difficulties.

In spite of these challenges, retrenchment provides exciting opportunities for HR. First, downsizing often allows the company to "get rid of dead wood" and make way for fresh ideas. If done effectively, it can evolve from retrenchment into a much leaner and stronger entity. In addition, downsizing is often a unique opportunity to change an organization's culture. In firms characterized by antagonistic labor-management relations, downsizing can force the parties to cooperate and to develop new, positive relationships.[35] Finally, retrenchment can demonstrate to top-management decision makers the value of the company's human resources to its ultimate success. The role of HR is to effectively manage the process in a way that makes this value undeniable.

Strategy Evaluation and Control. A final component to the strategic management process is that of strategy evaluation and control. Thus far we have focused on the planning and implementation of strategy. However, it is extremely important for the firm to constantly monitor the effectiveness of both the strategy and the implementation process. This monitoring makes it possible for the company to identify problem areas and either revise existing new structures and/or strategies or devise new ones. It is in this process that we see emergent strategies appear as well as the critical nature of human resources in competitive advantage.

The Role of Human Resources in Providing Strategic Competitive Advantage

Thus far we have presented the strategic management process as including a step-by-step procedure by which HR issues are raised prior to deciding on a strategy and then HR practices are developed to implement that strategy. However, we must note that human resources can provide a strategic competitive advantage in two additional ways: through emergent strategies and through enhancing competitiveness.

Emergent Strategies. Having discussed the process of strategic management, we also must distinguish between intended strategies and emergent strategies. Most people think of strategies as being proactive, rational decisions aimed toward some predetermined goal. The view of strategy we have presented thus far in the chapter focuses on intended strategies. Intended strategies are the result of the rational decision-making process used by top-level managers as they develop a strategic plan. This is consistent with definition of strategy as "the pattern or plan that integrates an organization's major goals, policies, and action sequences into a cohesive whole."[36] The idea of emergent strategies is evidenced by the feedback loop in Figure 2.1.

Most strategies that companies espouse are intended strategies. For example, when Compaq was founded, the company had its strategy summarized in its name, an amalgam of the words *computer, compact,* and *quality.* Thus, the intended strategy was to build compact portable computers that were completely free of any defect, and all of the company's efforts were directed toward implementing that strategy. Following that strategy allowed Compaq to become one of the fastest-growing companies in the world, commanding 20 percent of the world market in 1991.[37]

Emergent strategies, on the other hand, consist of the strategies that evolve from the grass roots of the organization and can be thought of as what organizations actually do, as opposed to what they intend to do. Strategy can also be thought of as "a pattern in a stream of decisions or actions."[38] For example, when Honda Motor Company first entered the U.S. market with its 250 cc and 305 cc motorcycles in 1959, it believed that no market existed for its smaller 50 cc bike. However, the sales on the larger motorcycles were sluggish, and Japanese executives riding the Honda 50s running errands around Los Angeles attracted a lot of attention, including that of a buyer with Sears, Roebuck. Honda discovered a previously undiscovered market as well as a new distribution outlet (general retailers) that it had not planned on. This emergent strategy resulted in Honda having a 50 percent market share by 1964.[39]

The distinction between intended and emergent strategies has important implications for human resource management. The new focus on strategic HR has tended to focus primarily on intended strategies. Thus, HR's role has been seen as identifying for top management the people-related business issues relevant to strategy formulation, and then developing HR systems that aid in the implementation of the strategic plan.

However, most emergent strategies are identified by those lower in the organizational hierarchy. It is often the rank-and-file employees who provide ideas for new markets, new products, and new strategies. HR plays an important role in facilitating communication throughout the organization, and it is this communication that allows for effective emergent strategies to make their way up to top management. This fact led Philip Caldwell, Ford's chairman in the early 1980s to state, "It's stupid to deny yourself the intellectual capability and constructive attitude of tens of thousands of workers."[40]

Enhancing Firm Competitiveness.   A related way in which HR can be a source of competitive advantage is through developing a human capital pool that provides the company with the unique ability to adapt to an ever-changing environment. Recently, managers have become interested in the idea of a "learning organization."[41] The learning organization is one in which people continually expand their capacity to achieve the results they desire. This requires the company to be in a constant state of learning through monitoring the environment, assimilating information, making decisions, and flexibly restructuring in order to compete in that environment. Companies that develop such learning capability have a competitive advantage. Although certain organizational information-processing systems can be an aid, ultimately the people (human capital) who make up the company provide the raw materials in a learning organization.

Thus, the role of HR in competitive advantage should continue to increase because of the fast-paced change characterizing today's business environment. It is becoming increasingly clear that even as American automakers have increased the quality of their cars to compete with the Japanese, these competitors have now developed such flexible and adaptable manufacturing systems that they can respond to customer needs more quickly.[42] This flexibility of the manufacturing process allows the emergent strategy to come directly from the marketplace by determining and responding to the exact mix of customer desires. It requires, however, that the company have people in place who have the skills to similarly adapt quickly.[43] As George Walker, president of Delta Wire, stated, "Anyone can come in and buy machines like I have. The difference is the knowledge of your workers."[44] This statement exemplifies the increasing importance of human resources in developing and maintaining competitive advantage.[45] The "Competing through Social Responsibility" box illustrates the importance of people in companies' economic success.

Social Responsibility

PUTTING EMPLOYEES FIRST: LESSONS FROM SMALL BUSINESS

Often we think that prosperous small businesses derive their success from offering a specialized product or finding a way to meet the needs of a certain market niche. Although there is truth in the view that both of these are pathways to success, it is important to realize that products must be produced by people, and the only way that market needs can be met is through what employees do. In fact, most successful small businesses put people first.

For example, Kingston Technology, a company that produces components for upgrading computer memory and processors, has seen its sales increase 368 percent compounded annually to $251 million between 1987 and 1992. To what do the founders attribute their success? Listen to vice-president of engineering, David Sun. "We feel obligated to the employee. Don't ever say the customer comes first. Your employee is your most valuable asset, and your vendor is your second most valuable asset. Take care of the first two, and the customer is taken care of."

Kingston only promotes from within, even if it means training someone to gain specialized technical knowledge that might be more quickly acquired by hiring from the outside. As Sun says, "We can always learn, as long as we are patient. We have good people." And what happens when

they make mistakes? According to Sun, "As long as the people are good, if you make a mistake you can always recover, because they **care**— they care about failure. When you cannot recover is when you have the wrong people."

Another example is Pacer Systems, a defense industry supplier with $28 million a year in revenues. Pacer views its employees as assets that the company invests in and pays 35 cents in benefits for every dollar in salary. The company offers a stock option plan for managers and is currently developing an employee stock ownership plan (ESOP) for employees. In addition, most employees are in a plan that pays bonuses based on profitability of the company as well as their particular work group. The lowest paid employees receive spot bonuses of $400.

Again, Pacer attempts to invest in its people as a means of attaining organizational success. Jack Rennie, founder of the firm, believes that treating employees well is not only socially desirable but necessary to remain competitive. Thus, Pacer engaged in participative management long before it became trendy. He says, "If you try to run a company as a disciplinarian, you're not going to last long in this environment. Business is too complex for you to handle everything yourself."

SOURCE: C. Burck, "The Real World of the Entrepreneur," *Fortune*, April 5, 1993, 62–81.

STRATEGIC MANAGEMENT FOR THE HR FUNCTION: A CUSTOMER ORIENTATION

This chapter has focused on explaining the strategic management process that takes place at the organization level and discussing the role of HR in this process. HR has been seen as a strategic partner that has input into the formulation of the company's strategy and develops and aligns HR programs to help implement the strategy. However, for the HR function to become truly strategic in its orientation, it must view itself as being a sepa-

FIGURE 2.6   Customer-Oriented Perspective of the HR Function

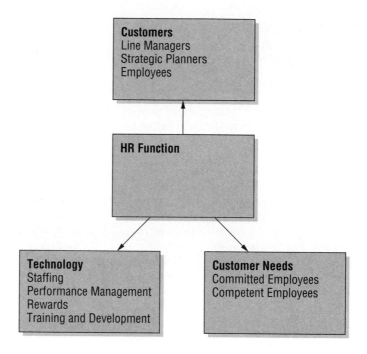

rate business entity and engage in strategic management in an effort to effectively serve the various internal customers.

In this respect, one recent trend within the field of HRM, consistent with the total quality management philosophy, is for the HR executive to take a customer-oriented approach to implementing the function. In other words, the strategic planning process that takes place at the level of the business can also be performed with the HR function. HR executives in more progressive American companies have begun to view the HR function as a strategic business unit and have tried to define that business in terms of their customer base, their customers' needs, and the technologies required to satisfy customers' needs (Figure 2.6). For example, Weyerhauser Corporation's human resources department identified 11 characteristics that would describe a quality human resource organization; these are presented in Table 2.4.

A customer orientation is one of the most important changes in the HR function's attempts to become strategic. It entails first identifying customers. The most obvious example of HR customers are the line managers who require HR services. In addition, the strategic planning team is a customer in the sense that it requires the identification, analysis, and recommendations regarding people-oriented business problems. Employees are also HR customers because the rewards they receive from the employment relationship are determined and/or administered by the HR department.

TABLE 2.4 Characteristics of HR Quality at Weyerhauser Corporation

- Human resources products and service are linked to customer requirements.
- Customer requirements are translated into internal service applications.
- Processes for producing products and services are documented with cost/value relationships understood.
- Reliable methods and standardized processes are in place.
- Waste and inefficiency is eliminated.
- Problem solving and decision making are based on facts and data.
- Critical success variables are tracked, displayed, and maintained.
- Human resources employees are trained and educated in total quality tools and principles.
- Human resource systems have been aligned to total quality implementation strategies.
- Human resource managers provide leadership and support to organizations on large-scale organizational change.
- Human resource professionals function as "strategic partners" in managing the business and implementing total quality principles.

In addition, the products of the HR department must be identified. Line managers want to have high-quality employees committed to the organization. The strategic planning team requires information and recommendations for the planning process as well as programs that support the strategic plan once it has been identified. Employees want compensation and benefit programs that are consistent, adequate, and equitable, and they want fair promotion decisions. At Southwest Airlines, the "People" department administers customer surveys to all clients as they leave the department to measure how well their needs have been satisfied.

Finally, the technologies through which HR meets customer needs vary depending on the need being satisfied. Selection systems ensure that applicants selected for employment have the necessary knowledge, skills, and abilities to provide value to the organization. Training and development systems meet the needs of both line managers and employees by providing employees with development opportunities to ensure they are constantly increasing their human capital and, thus, providing increased value to the company. Performance management systems make clear to employees what is expected of them and ensure line managers and strategic planners that employee behavior will be in line with the company's goals. Finally, reward systems similarly benefit all customers (line managers, strategic planners, and employees). These systems ensure line managers that employees will use their skills for organizational benefit, and they provide strategic planners with ways to ensure that all employees are acting in ways that will support the strategic plan. Obviously, reward systems provide employees with an equitable return for their investment of skills and effort.

For example, Whirlpool Corporation's HR managers go through a formalized process of identifying their customer, the need/value they satisfy, and the technology used to satisfy the customer. As Whirlpool planned for start-up of a centralized service "supercenter," the plan called for hiring between 100 and 150 employees to serve as call takers who receive service requests from Whirlpool appliance owners and set up service appointments from these calls. The HR manager in charge of developing a selection system for hiring these call takers identified the operations manager in charge of phone service as the HR department's customer, the delivery of qualified phone call takers as the need satisfied, and the use of a structured interview and paper-and-pencil tests as the technologies employed.

This customer-service orientation may be the trend of the future. It provides a means for the HR function to specifically identify who its customers are, what customers' needs are being met, and how well those needs are being met. In fact, as the "Competing through Technology and Structure" box shows, IBM's HR function has actually become a business and may provide an example for what the future holds for HR departments. This is a mind-set that will have to become instilled in future HR managers who hope to demonstrate the value that the function adds to the company.

Strategic Human Resource Executives

As this chapter has demonstrated, HR is becoming an important part of the strategic management process. Successful companies increasingly recognize this importance. This is evidenced by the fact that between 1984 and 1989, salaries of HR executives rose 69 percent, compared with only 56 percent for other top executives. In fact, among the Fortune 500 companies, median cash compensation for top HR people was $175,000, with over 100 making in excess of $250,000.[46] This increased role and importance for HR executives will require different skills than were possessed by those in earlier times.

In the future, HR professionals will need four basic competencies to become partners in the strategic management process (see Figure 2.7).[47] First, they will need to have "business competencies," knowing the company's business and understanding its economic financial capabilities. This calls for making logical decisions that support the company's strategic plan based on the most accurate information possible. Because in almost all companies the effectiveness of decisions must be evaluated in terms of dollar values, the HR executive must be able to calculate the costs and benefits of each alternative in terms of its dollar impact.[48] In addition, it requires that the nonmonetary impact must be considered. The HR executive must be fully capable of identifying the social and ethical issues attached to its HR practices.

Second, HR professionals will have to have "professional/technical knowledge" of state-of-the-art HR practices in areas such as staffing, development, rewards, organizational design, and communication. New selection techniques, performance appraisal methods, training programs, and

Technology & Structure

RESTRUCTURING HUMAN RESOURCES: WORKFORCE SOLUTIONS

When work units seek to implement total quality management (TQM) in their function, these efforts require that the unit begin to think of itself as a business. The entails defining who the customers are, what the customers' needs are, and what products the unit is producing to meet those needs. When the work unit is a staff function, this process presents some problems because it is sometimes difficult to treat the unit as a business itself. However, IBM's HR department has gone beyond thinking about the function as a business to actually making it one.

IBM is developing a subsidiary company called Workforce Solutions that is made up of much of what used to be known as IBM's personnel function. The division is now a professional services firm that provides what amounts to human resource consulting services to line managers. This new expanded role presents a unique set of problems and issues.

First, Workforce Solutions, in line with TQM principle, must identify its customers,

recognize its customers' needs, and define the product and service offerings to meet those needs. Because the new division will be a profit center within the organization, increased attention must be paid to (1) identifying the costs of the various products and services and (2) developing systems for billing clients within IBM. These needs have repercussions on the appraisal and training systems within the division. Workforce Solutions employees will be appraised by how well they obtain certain profit figures. This new appraisal requires training the traditional HR managers in accounting and financial techniques.

Because Workforce Solutions is in its infant stages, it is too early to tell how effective this new structure is. If it turns out to be successful, the subsidiary may begin to offer its products and services to firms other than IBM. Thus, this extensive restructuring consistent with the principles of TQM may turn out to be the model for the HR organization of the future.

SOURCE: L. Thornburg, "IBM's Agents of Influence," *HR Magazine*, February 1993, 80–84.

incentive plans are constantly being developed. Some of these programs can provide value, while others may be no more than the products of today's HR equivalent of "snake oil." The HR executive must be able to critically evaluate the new techniques offered as state-of-the-art HR programs and use only those that will benefit the company.

Third, they must be skilled in the "management of change processes," such as diagnosing problems, implementing organizational changes, and evaluating results. Every time a company changes its strategy even in a minor way, the entire company has to change. These changes result in conflict, resistance, and confusion among the people who must implement the new plans or programs. The HR executive must have the skills to oversee the change in a way that ensures its success. In fact, one recent survey of Fortune 500 companies found that 87 percent of the companies had their organization development/change function as part of the HR department.[49]

Finally, these professionals must also have "integration competencies," meaning the ability to integrate the three other competencies to increase the

FIGURE 2.7   Human Resource Competencies

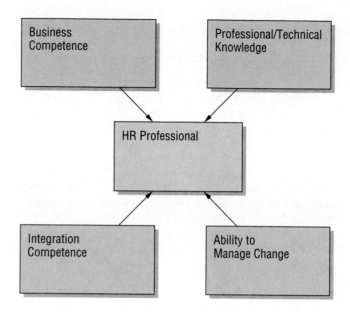

company's value. This requires that, although specialist knowledge is necessary, a generalist perspective must be taken in making decisions. This entails seeing how all the functions within the HR area fit together to be effective and recognizing that changes in any one part of the HR package are likely to require changes in other parts of the package. For example, a health-care company in central Texas was attempting to fill a position in the X-ray department. It was able to identify qualified candidates for the position, but none of the candidates accepted the offer. It was not until the company examined its total package (i.e., pay, benefits, promotion opportunities, etc.) and changed the composition of the package that it was able to fill the position.

SUMMARY

A strategic approach to human resource management seeks to proactively provide a competitive advantage through the company's most important asset: its human resources. The HR function needs to be integrally involved in the formulation of strategy in order to identify the people-related business issues the company faces.[50] Once the strategy has been determined, HRM has a profound impact on the implementation of the plan by developing and aligning HR practices that ensure that the company has motivated employees with the necessary skills. In addition, the strategic role of the HR function is enhanced by the HR department's own strategic planning, particularly by identifying its customers and the needs the department meets. Finally, the emerging strategic role of the HR function requires that HR professionals in the future develop business, professional/technical, change management, and integration competencies. As you will see more clearly in later chapters, this strategic approach requires more than simply developing a valid selection procedure, or state-of-the-art performance management systems. Only through these competencies can the HR professional take a strategic approach to human resource management.

Discussion Questions

1. Pick one of your university's major sports teams (e.g., football or basketball). How would you characterize that team's generic strategy? How does the composition of the team members (in terms of size, speed, ability, etc.) relate to that strategy? What are the strengths and weaknesses of the team? How do those dictate the team's generic strategy and its approach to a particular game?

2. Do you think that it is easier to tie human resources to the strategic management process in large or in small organizations? Why?

3. Consider some of the organizations you have been affiliated with. What are some examples of human resource practices that were consistent with that organization's strategy? What are examples of practices that were inconsistent with its strategy?

4. How can strategic management within the HR department ensure that HR plays an effective role in the company's strategic management process?

5. What types of specific skills (e.g., knowledge of financial accounting methods) do you think HR professionals will need in order to have the business, professional/technical, change management, and integrative competencies necessary in the future? Where can you seek to develop each of these skills?

6. What are some of the key environmental variables that you see changing in the business world today? What impact will those changes have on the HR function in organizations?

Notes

1. J. Barney, "Firm Resources and Sustained Competitive Advantage," *Journal of Management* 17 (1991): 99–120.

2. J. Quinn, *Strategies for Change: Logical Incrementalism* (Homewood, Ill.: Richard D. Irwin, 1980).

3. M. Porter, *Competitive Strategy: Techniques for Analyzing Industries and Competitors* (New York: Free Press, 1980).

4. R. Miles and C. Snow, *Organizational Strategy, Structure, and Process* (New York: McGraw-Hill, 1978).

5. P. Wright and G. McMahan, "Theoretical Perspectives for Strategic Human Resource Management," *Journal of Management* 18 (1992): 295–320.

6. S. Snell and J. Dean, "Integrated Manufacturing and Human Resource Management: A Human Capital Perspective," *Academy of Management Journal* 35 (1992): 467–504.

7. C. Hill and G. Jones, *Strategic Management Theory: An Integrated Approach* (Boston: Houghton Mifflin, 1989).

8. K. Golden and V. Ramanujam, "Between a Dream and a Nightmare: On the Integration of the Human Resource Function and the Strategic Business Planning Process," *Human Resource Management* 24 (1985): 429–451.

9. W. Johnston and A. Packer, *Workforce 2000: Work and Workers for the Twenty-first Century* (Indianapolis, Ind.: Hudson Institute, 1987).

10. "Labor Letter," *The Wall Street Journal*, December 15, 1992, A1.

11. M. Hitt, R. Hoskisson, and J. Harrison, "Strategic Competitiveness in the 1990s: Challenges and Opportunities for U.S. Executives," *The Executive* 5 (May, 1991): 7–22.

12. D. Whitestone and L. Schlesinger, *People Express,* Harvard Business School Case 9-483-103.

13. Golden and Ramanujam, "Between a Dream and a Nightmare."

14. J. Galbraith and R. Kazanjian, *Strategy Implementation: Structure, Systems, and Process* (St. Paul, Minn.: West Publishing, 1986).

15. B. Schneider and A. Konz, "Strategic Job Analysis," *Human Resource Management* 27 (1989): 51–64.

16. P. Wright and S. Snell, "Toward an Integrative View of Strategic Human Resource Management," *Human Resource Management Review* 1 (1991): 203–225.

17. S. Snell, "Control Theory in Strategic Human Resource Management: The Mediating Effect of Administrative Information," *Academy of Management Journal* 35 (1992): 292–327.

18. R. Schuler, "Personnel and Human Resource Management Choices and Organizational Strategy," In *Readings in Personnel and Human Resource Management* 3rd ed., eds. R. Schuler, S. Youngblood, and V. Huber (St. Paul, Minn.: West Publishing, 1988).

19. J. Dean and S. Snell, "Integrated Manufacturing and Job Design: Moderating Effects of Organizational Inertia," *Academy of Management Journal* 34 (1991): 776–804.

20. J. Olian and S. Rynes, "Organizational Staffing: Integrating Practice with Strategy," *Industrial Relations* 23 (1984): 170–183.

21. G. Smith, "Quality: Small and Midsize Companies Seize the Challenge—Not a Moment Too Soon," *Business Week*, November 30, 1992, 66–75.

22. J. Kerr and E. Jackofsky, "Aligning Managers with Strategies: Management Development versus Selection," *Strategic Management Journal* 10 (1989): 157–170.

23. J. Kerr, "Strategic Control through Performance Appraisal and Rewards," *Human Resource Planning* 11 (1988): 215–223.

24. S. Snell, "Control Theory in Strategic Human Resource Management: The Mediating Effect of Administrative Information," *Academy of Management Journal* 35 (1992): 292–327.

25. G. Milkovich, "A Strategic Perspective on Compensation Management," In *Research in Personnel and Human Resource Management*, K. Rowland and G. Ferris, eds., 6 (1988): 263–288.

26. D. Balkin and L. Gomez-Mejia, "Toward a Contingency Theory of Compensation Strategy," *Strategic Management Journal* 8 (1987): 169–182.

27. A. Taylor, "U.S. Cars Come Back," *Fortune*, November 16, 1992, 52, 85.

28. S. Cronshaw and R. Alexander, "One Answer to the Demand for Accountability: Selection Utility as an Investment Decision," *Organizational Behavior and Human Decision Processes* 35 (1986): 102–118.

29. M. Porter, *Competitive Advantage* (New York: Free Press, 1985).

30. R. Schuler and S. Jackson, "Linking Competitive Strategies with Human Resource Management Practices," *Academy of Management Executive* 1 (1987): 207–219.

31. R. Miles and C. Snow, "Designing Strategic Human Resource Management Systems," *Organizational Dynamics* 13, no. 1 (1984): 36–52.

32. A. Thompson and A. Strickland, *Strategy Formulation and Implementation: Tasks of the General Manager*, 3rd ed. (Plano, Texas: BPI, 1986).

33. N. Templin, "UAW to Unveil Pact on Slashing GM's Payroll," *The Wall Street Journal*, December 15, 1992, A3.

34. J. Lopez, "Managing: Early-Retirement Offers Lead to Renewed Hiring," *The Wall Street Journal*, January 26, 1993, B1.

35. N. Templin, "A Decisive Response to Crisis Brought Ford Enhanced Productivity," *The Wall Street Journal*, December 15, 1992, A1.

36. J. Quinn, *Strategies for Change: Logical Incrementalism* (Homewood, Ill: Richard D. Irwin, 1980).

37. E. Calonius, "Smart Moves by Quality Champs," *Fortune*, (1991): 24–28.

38. H. Mintzberg, "Patterns in Strategy Formulation," *Management Science* 24 (1978): 934–948.

39. R. Pascale, "Perspectives on Strategy: The Real Story behind Honda's Success," *California Management Review* 26 (1984): 47–72.

40. N. Templin, "A Decisive Response to Crisis Brought Ford Enhanced Productivity," *The Wall Street Journal*, December 15, 1992, A1.

41. P. Senge, *The Fifth Discipline* (New York: Doubleday, 1990).

42. T. Stewart, "Brace for Japan's Hot New Strategy," *Fortune*, September 21, 1992, 62–76.

43. C. Snow and S. Snell, *Staffing as Strategy*, vol. 4 of *Personnel Selection* (San Francisco: Jossey-Bass, 1992).

44. T. Batten, "Education Key to Prosperity—Report," *Houston Chronicle*, September 7, 1992, 1B.

45. P. Wright, "Human Resources as a Competitive Weapon," *Applied Advances in Strategic Management* 2 (1991): 91–122.

46. J. Solomon, "People Power," *The Wall Street Journal*, March 9, 1990, R33.

47. D. Ulrich and A. Yeung, "A Shared Mindset," *Personnel Administrator*, March 1989, 38–45.

48. G. Jones and P. Wright, "An Economic Approach to Conceptualizing the Utility of Human Resource Management Practices," *Research in Personnel/Human Resources* 10 (1992): 271–299.

49. G. McMahan and R. Woodman, "The Current Practice of Organization Development within the Firm: A Survey of Large Industrial Corporations," *Group and Organization Studies* 17 (1992): 117–134.

50. R. Schuler and J. Walker, "Human Resources Strategy: Focusing on Issues and Actions," *Organizational Dynamics*, Summer 1990, 5–19.

A NEW STRATEGIC DIRECTION

Compaq was founded on the strategy of developing a compact computer of high-quality that would compete with IBM. The essence of the strategy was to offer consumers a high-performance computer at a premium price, sold and serviced only through authorized computer dealers. The engineering-oriented culture stressed innovation and bringing products to market quickly without regard to cost. This strategy served the company well, resulting in it becoming one of the fastest-growing companies in the history of U.S. business.

C A S E

However, as a number of smaller companies such as Dell and AST entered the industry by selling computers at a substantially lower cost, Compaq's market share and profits plunged, and in 1991 its stock price dropped from $75 per share in February to less than $25 per share in November. In October 1991, Compaq announced two firsts for the company: a quarterly loss, amounting to approximately $70 million; and plans to lay off 1,700 employees.

In November 1991, Eckhard Pfeiffer was named to replace company cofounder Rod Canion as chief executive officer in an effort to reverse this downward performance spiral. Nine hours after being appointed CEO, Pfeiffer called a meeting to start planning the company's new strategy. Compaq's new strategy was to introduce low-price, high-quality PCs. To do this, the company had to focus on shorter product-development cycles and lower manufacturing, material, and overhead costs; expand field customer service and support organizations by 50 percent; and identify new markets, including home, educational, and small-business segments.

QUESTIONS

1. If you were the corporate vice-president of human resources at Compaq, what would be the issues that you would want to examine regarding the viability of this strategy prior to the company's decision to adopt it?

2. Given that the decision has been made, what will be the new HR needs in implementing the strategy, and what specific HR practices do you think will be necessary to meet these needs?

3

GLOBAL ISSUES IN HUMAN RESOURCE MANAGEMENT

Objectives

After reading this chapter, you should be able to:

1. Identify the recent changes that have caused companies to expand into international markets.
2. Discuss the four factors that most strongly influence HRM in international markets.
3. List the different categories of international employees.
4. Identify the four levels of global participation and the HRM issues faced within each level.
5. Discuss the ways companies attempt to select, train, compensate, and reintegrate expatriate managers.

When Play Can Pay

What does it take to make managers understand other cultures? If you ask senior managers at South Korea's largest company, Samsung Group, they might answer, "Goofing off."

Samsung was recently introduced to the need to understand other cultures when they sent a calendar to its major customers that depicted fashion models holding various Samsung appliances. Managers were unaware that the calendar might offend some customers because of the way some of the models were dressed.

This faux pas led the managers to see the need for some type of training to get in touch with the cultures of their customers, primarily those in the United States. Their internationalization campaign has many parts. Cards with Japanese or

American phrases are taped up in bathrooms each day. Managers who will be sent overseas attend a boot camp for a month. At the boot camp they are awakened each day at 5:15 AM for a jog, meditation, and lessons on table manners, dancing, and avoiding sexual harassment.

In addition, the brightest junior executives are being sent overseas for a year to simply goof off. The company believes that the best way to understand the culture is to immerse oneself in it by engaging in simple activities like hanging out at the mall. The program will cost $80,000 for each of the 400 future stars, but the company is convinced that it will be worth it.

SOURCE: "Korea's Biggest Firm Teaches Junior Execs Strange Foreign Ways," *The Wall Street Journal*, December 30, 1992.

INTRODUCTION

The environment in which business competes is rapidly becoming globalized. More and more companies are entering international markets by exporting their products overseas, building plants in other countries, and entering into alliances with foreign companies. Of the world's 50 largest organizations, 31 have their headquarters outside the United States. Of the top 100 organizations, 39 have their headquarters in the United States, followed by Japan with 15 and Germany with 12. Japan is currently home to 23 of the 50 largest banks in the world, whereas the United States is home to only four (Citicorp, Chase Manhattan, J.P. Morgan, and Bank of America).[1]

A recent survey of 12,000 managers from 25 different countries indicates how common international expansion has become, both in the United States and in other countries.[2] Of the U.S. managers surveyed, 26 percent indicated that their companies had recently expanded internationally. Among the larger companies (10,000 or more employees), 45 percent had expanded internationally during the previous two years. Currently, exports account for 11 percent of the gross domestic product in the United States, and they have been growing at a rate of 12 percent a year since 1987.[3]

Indeed, most organizations now function in the global economy. Thus, American businesses are entering international markets at the same time foreign companies are entering the U.S. market. Table 3.1 displays the number of workers employed by U.S. companies in some selected countries.

What is behind the trend toward expansion into global markets? Companies are attempting to gain a competitive advantage, and this advantage can be provided by international expansion in a number of ways. First, these countries are new markets with large numbers of potential customers. For companies that are producing below their capacity, they provide a means of increasing sales and profits. Second, many companies are building production facilities in other countries as a means of capitalizing on those

TABLE 3.1 Employees of U.S. Multinationals (in thousands)

	1977	1982	1985	1990
Britain	1,069.3	830.7	809.5	846.7
China	N.A.	N.A.	N.A.	14.4
Germany[a]	587.4	541.3	541.1	590.5
India	94.6	75.2	71.8	38.3
Ireland	27.6	38.4	35.2	45.5
Jamaica	N.A.	8.8	6.2	8.7
Japan	389.1	302.0	331.0	407.8
Mexico	370.1	470.3	466.0	551.6
Singapore	44.2	46.1	49.0	85.8
Thailand	27.3	29.4	29.1	64.4

SOURCES: The U.S. Commerce Department Organization for Economic Cooperation and Development. Courtesy of B. O'Reilly, "Your New Global Workforce." Used with permission of *Fortune*, © 1992, Time Inc. All rights reserved.
[a] East and West Germany combined for 1990.

countries' lower labor costs for relatively unskilled jobs. For example, many of the *maquiladora* plants (foreign-owned plants located in Mexico that employ Mexican laborers) provide low-skilled labor at considerably lower cost than in the United States. In 1988, the average industrial monthly wage in Mexico was $109.[4]

According to a recent survey of almost 3,000 line executives and HR executives from 12 countries, international competition is the number one factor affecting HRM. Those surveyed indicated they expect it to remain the most important factor in the year 2000. The globalization of business structures and globalization of the economy ranked fourth and fifth, respectively.[5] Deciding whether to enter foreign markets and whether to develop plants or other facilities in other countries, however, is no simple matter, and many human resource issues surface.

This chapter discusses the human resource issues that must be addressed in order to gain competitive advantage in a world of global competition. This is not a chapter on international human resource management (i.e., the specific HRM policies and programs companies use to manage human resources across international boundaries).[6] The chapter focuses instead on the key factors that must be addressed in order to strategically manage human resources in an international context. We discuss some of the important events that have increased the global nature of business over the past few years. We then identify some of the factors that are most important to HRM in global environments. Finally, we examine particular issues related to managing expatriate managers. These issues present unique opportunities for firms to gain competitive advantage.

CURRENT GLOBAL CHANGES

A number of recent social and political changes have accelerated the movement toward international competition. The effects of these changes have been profound and far-reaching. Many are still evolving. In this section, we discuss the major developments that have accentuated the need for organizations to gain a competitive advantage through effectively managing human resources in a global economy.

European Economic Community

European countries have managed their economies individually for years. Because of the countries' close geographic proximity, their economies have become intertwined. This created a number of problems for international businesses; for example, the regulations of one country, such as France, might be completely different from those of another country, such as Germany. In response, most of the European countries agreed to participate in the European Economic Community, which began in 1992. The EEC is a confederation of most of the European nations that agree to engage in free trade with one another, with commerce regulated by an overseeing body called the European Commission (EC). Under the EEC, legal regulation in the participating countries has become more, although not completely, uniform. Assuming the EEC's trend toward free trade among members continues, Europe has become the largest free market in the world.

German Unification

From the end of World War II until 1989, what had formerly been Germany was divided into two countries: East Germany, controlled by the Soviet Union and existing under a socialist economic system, and West Germany, allied to the Western industrial democracies. Not long before the collapse of the Soviet Union in 1989, the Berlin Wall, which had divided the countries for nearly half a century, fell. By 1990, steps were being taken to reunify East and West Germany. Thus, East Germany, which was previously not engaging in international commerce, has now entered the global market.

With reunification, the movement toward capitalism in East Germany has caused tremendous human resource problems. In East Germany, the socialist government guaranteed every citizen a job. Thus, there had been tremendous overstaffing and little motivation to maximize performance. With the integration into a capitalist economy, East German companies were forced to compete with leaner firms, leading them to lay off large numbers of managers and workers. This created further problems because many of the managers had not achieved their positions through managerial skill but by being loyal members of the Communist party.[7] East Germany's lack of state-of-the-art technology and infrastructure coupled with its overstaffing problem have made the companies based in that part of Germany uncompetitive. The relatively low wage rates and high skills of East German workers, however, make it an attractive site for foreign direct investment.

Disintegration of the Soviet Union

Soon after the Berlin Wall fell, the Soviet Union collapsed. Countries that were once controlled by the Soviet Union are now in the process of converting their Communist economic systems to a capitalist system. These countries have become attractive markets to companies in other countries.

Many of these countries have had little or no private investment in over 40 years. Almost all their industrial facilities were controlled by the government and run extremely inefficiently. In addition, the poor quality and lack of availability of goods in the former Soviet Union had created pent-up demand. However, as these countries move toward democratic political systems and free-market economic systems, they are privatizing government-owned businesses. In 1992, Hungary alone sold off 400 large state companies and 16,000 state-owned shops and restaurants.[8] These countries offer existing facilities, abundant supplies of trained labor, and a central location for shipping products throughout Europe. No wonder they are attractive to international firms.

North American Free Trade Agreement (NAFTA)

NAFTA is an agreement between Canada, the United States, and Mexico that will, if ratified by Congress under the Clinton administration, create a free market even larger than the European Economic Community. The United States and Canada have already had a free trade agreement since 1989, but NAFTA will bring Mexico into the consortium. The agreement has been prompted by Mexico's increasing willingness to open its markets and facilities in an effort to promote economic growth.[9] As previously discussed, the *maquiladora* plants exemplify this trend.

NAFTA should increase U.S. investment in Mexico because of Mexico's substantially lower labor costs for low-skilled employees. This should have two effects on employment in the United States. First, many low-skilled jobs will head south, decreasing employment opportunities for U.S. citizens who lack higher-level skills. Second, it will increase the employment opportunities for Americans with higher-level skills beyond those which are already being observed.[10]

These changes—the European Economic Community, German reunification, the disintegration of the socialist Soviet Union, and NAFTA—all exemplify events that are pushing companies to compete in a global economy. These developments are opening new markets and new sources of technology and labor in a way that has never been seen in history. However, this era of increasing international competition accentuates the need to manage human resources effectively to gain competitive advantage in a global marketplace. This requires understanding the effects of some of the factors that can determine the effectiveness of various HRM practices and approaches.

FACTORS AFFECTING HRM IN GLOBAL MARKETS

Companies that enter global markets must recognize that these markets are not simply mirror images of their home country. Countries differ along a number of dimensions that influence the attractiveness of direct foreign investment in each country. These differences determine the economic viability of building an operation in a foreign location, and they have a particularly strong impact on HRM in that operation. Although researchers in international management have identified a number of factors that can affect HRM in global markets, we focus on four factors, as depicted in Figure 3.1: culture, education/human capital, the political/legal system, and the economic system.[11]

Culture

By far the most important factor influencing international HRM is the culture of the country in which a facility is located. Culture is defined as "the set of important assumptions (often unstated) that members of a community share."[12]. These assumptions consist of beliefs about the world and how it works and the ideals that are worth striving for.[13]

Culture is important to HRM for two reasons. First, it often determines the other three factors. Culture can greatly affect a country's laws, in that laws are often the codification of right and wrong as defined by the culture. Culture also affects human capital, because if education is greatly valued by the culture, then members of the community try to increase their human capital. Finally, as we will discuss later, cultures and economic systems are closely intertwined.[14]

However, the most important reason that culture is important to HRM is that it often determines the effectiveness of various HRM practices. Practices found to be effective in the United States, for example, may not be effective in a culture that has different beliefs and values.[15] For example, U.S. companies rely heavily on individual performance appraisal, and rewards are tied to individual performance. In Japan, however, individuals are expected to subordinate their wishes and desires to those of the larger group. Thus, individual-based evaluation and incentives are not nearly as effective there and, in fact, are seldom observed among Japanese organizations.[16]

In this section we will examine two models that attempt to characterize different cultures. These models illustrate why culture can have a profound influence on HRM.

Hofstede's Cultural Dimensions.   In a classic study of culture, Geert Hofstede identified four dimensions on which various cultures could be classified.[17] In a later study, he added a fifth dimension that aids in

FIGURE 3.1   Factors Affecting Human Resource Management in International Markets

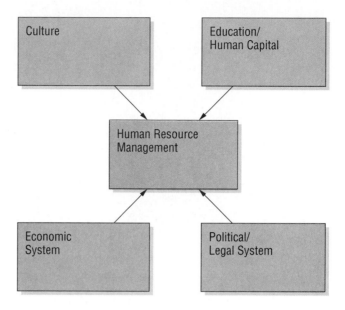

characterizing cultures.[18] The relative scores for ten major countries are provided in Table 3.2. **Individualism/collectivism** describes the strength of the relation between an individual and other individuals in the society, that is, the degree to which people act as individuals rather than as members of a group. In individualist cultures, such as the United States, Great Britain, and the Netherlands, people are expected to look after their own interests and the interests of their immediate families. The individual is expected to stand on his or her own two feet rather than be protected by the group. In collectivist cultures, such as Colombia, Pakistan, and Taiwan, people are expected to look after the interest of the larger community, which is expected to protect people when they are in trouble.

The second dimension, **power distance,** concerns how a culture deals with hierarchical power relationships and, particularly, the unequal distribution of power. It describes the degree of inequality among people that is considered to be normal. Cultures with small power distance, such as those of Denmark and Israel, seek to eliminate inequalities in power and wealth as much as possible, whereas countries with large power distances, such as India and the Philippines, seek to maintain those differences.

Differences in power distance often result in miscommunication and conflicts between people from different cultures. For example, in Mexico and Japan, individuals are always addressed by their titles (e.g., Señor Smith or Smith-san, respectively). Individuals from the United States, however, often believe in minimizing power distances by using first names.

TABLE 3.2   Culture Dimension Scores for Ten Countries

	PD[a]	ID	MA	UA	LT
USA	40 L[b]	91 H	62 H	46 L	29 L
Germany	35 L	67 H	66 H	65 M	31 M
Japan	54 M	45 M	95 H	92 H	80 H
France	68 H	71 H	43 M	86 H	30[c] L
Netherlands	38 L	80 H	14 L	53 M	44 M
Hong Kong	68 H	25 L	57 H	29 L	96 H
Indonesia	78 H	14 L	46 M	48 L	25[c] L
West Africa	77 H	20 L	46 M	54 M	16 L
Russia	95[c] H	50[c] M	40[c] L	90[c] H	10[c] L
China	80[c] H	20[c] L	50[c] M	60[c] M	118 H

SOURCE: Reprinted with permission of G. Hofstede, "Cultural Constraints in Management Theories," *Academy of Management Executive* 7 (1993): 91.
[a] PD = Power Distance; ID = Individualism; MA = Masculinity; UA = Uncertainty Avoidance; LT = Long-Term Orientation
[b] H = top third, M = medium third, L = bottom third (among 53 countries and regions for the first four dimensions; among 23 countries for the fifth)
[c] estimated

Although this is perfectly normal, and possibly even advisable in the United States, it can be offensive and a sign of disrespect in other cultures.

The third dimension, **uncertainty avoidance,** describes how cultures seek to deal with the fact that the future is not perfectly predictable. It is defined as the degree to which people in a culture prefer structured over unstructured situations. Some cultures, such as those of Singapore and Jamaica, have weak uncertainty avoidance. They socialize individuals to accept this uncertainty and take each day as it comes. People from these cultures tend to be rather easygoing and flexible regarding different views. Other cultures, such as those of Greece and Portugal, socialize their people to seek security through technology, law, and religion. Thus, these cultures provide clear rules as to how one should behave.

Fourth, the **masculinity-femininity** dimension describes the division of roles between the sexes within a society. In "masculine" cultures, such as those of Germany and Japan, what are considered traditionally masculine values—showing off, achieving something visible, and making money—permeate the society. These societies stress assertiveness, performance, success, and competition. "Feminine" cultures, such as those of Sweden and Norway, promote values that have been traditionally regarded as feminine, such as putting relationships before money, helping others, and preserving the environment. These cultures stress service, care for the weak, and solidarity.

Finally, the fifth dimension comes from the philosophy of the Far East and is referred to as the **long-term-short-term orientation**. Cultures high on the long-term orientation focus on the future and hold values in the present that will not necessarily provide an immediate benefit such as thrift (saving) and persistence. Hofstede found that many Far Eastern countries such as Japan and China have a long-term orientation. Short-term orientations, on the other hand, are found in the United States, Russia, and West Africa. These cultures are oriented toward the past and present and promote respect for tradition and for fulfilling social obligations.

The current Japanese criticism of management practices in the United States illustrates the differences in long/short-term orientation. Japanese managers, traditionally exhibiting a long-term orientation, engage in five- to ten-year planning. This leads them to criticize U.S. managers, who are traditionally much more short term in orientation because their planning often consists of quarterly to yearly time horizons.

These five dimensions help us understand the potential problems of managing employees from different cultures. Later in this chapter we will explore how these cultural dimensions affect the acceptability and utility of various HRM practices. However, it is important to note that these differences can have a profound influence on whether a company chooses to enter a given country. One interesting finding of Hofstede's research was the impact of culture on a country's economic health. He found that countries with individualist cultures were more wealthy. Collectivist cultures with high power distance were all poor.[19] Cultures seem to affect a country's economy through their promotion of individual work ethics and incentives for individuals to increase their human capital. Figure 3.2 maps the countries Hofstede studied on the two characteristics of individualism/collectivism and economic success.

Harrison's Cultural Factors. More recently, Lawrence Harrison has illustrated the importance of culture to HRM.[20] He identified four fundamental cultural factors that determine a country's economic success. **Radius of trust** refers to the identification that individuals feel with others in society—in other words, the sense of community. When trust is high, societies concern themselves with the progress of the masses through investment in education and public health. **Rigor of the ethical system** often derives from religion. It can affect the degree of social justice in the culture and the extent to which there is an independent judiciary and due process. A third factor, **exercising of authority**, can stifle risk taking, innovation, and entrepreneurship by penalizing initiative. If the culture promotes an authoritarian value system, economic success is less likely. Finally, **work, innovation, saving, and profit** incorporate "(1) the belief that rationality presents a tool with which the world can be manipulated and wealth increased, (2) a consequent high emphasis on education, and (3) an orientation toward the future that encourages planning and saving."[21]

FIGURE 3.2 The Position of the 50 Countries on Their Individualism Index (IDV) versus Their 1970 National Wealth

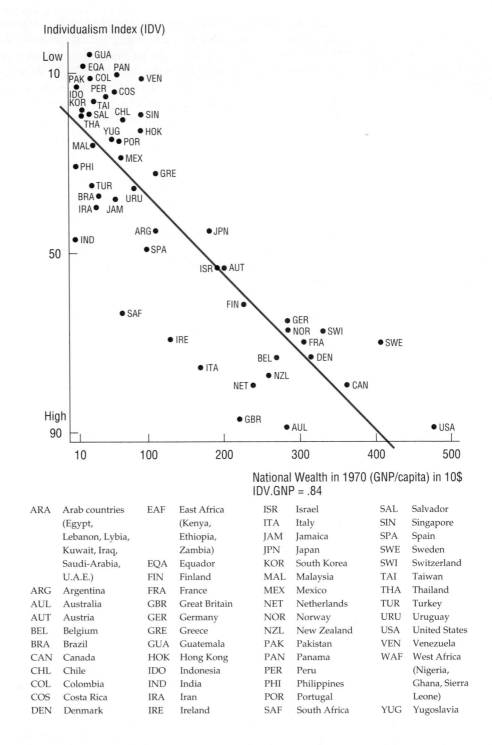

ARA	Arab countries (Egypt, Lebanon, Lybia, Kuwait, Iraq, Saudi-Arabia, U.A.E.)	EAF	East Africa (Kenya, Ethiopia, Zambia)	ISR	Israel	SAL	Salvador
				ITA	Italy	SIN	Singapore
				JAM	Jamaica	SPA	Spain
				JPN	Japan	SWE	Sweden
		EQA	Equador	KOR	South Korea	SWI	Switzerland
		FIN	Finland	MAL	Malaysia	TAI	Taiwan
ARG	Argentina	FRA	France	MEX	Mexico	THA	Thailand
AUL	Australia	GBR	Great Britain	NET	Netherlands	TUR	Turkey
AUT	Austria	GER	Germany	NOR	Norway	URU	Uruguay
BEL	Belgium	GRE	Greece	NZL	New Zealand	USA	United States
BRA	Brazil	GUA	Guatemala	PAK	Pakistan	VEN	Venezuela
CAN	Canada	HOK	Hong Kong	PAN	Panama	WAF	West Africa (Nigeria, Ghana, Sierra Leone)
CHL	Chile	IDO	Indonesia	PER	Peru		
COL	Colombia	IND	India	PHI	Philippines		
COS	Costa Rica	IRA	Iran	POR	Portugal		
DEN	Denmark	IRE	Ireland	SAF	South Africa	YUG	Yugoslavia

SOURCE: G. Hofstede, "The Cultural Relativity of Organizational Theories," *Journal of International Business Studies* 14, no. 2 (1983): 75–90.

Harrison compares the economic success of a number of countries according to their levels of these cultural factors. He cites the economic success of cultures such as Taiwan, Korea, and Brazil that have higher levels of trust, ethics, and savings and low levels of authoritarianism. These are contrasted with less economically successful cultures such as Haiti, Nicaragua, and the former Soviet bloc countries, which have the opposite types of cultures. Both Hofstede's and Harrison's research point to the fact that certain characteristics of culture are related to the economic success of that culture, again highlighting the important role that culture plays in a company's success.

Implications of Culture for HRM.   Cultures have an important impact on approaches to managing people. As we discuss later, the culture can strongly impact the education/human capital of a country, the political/legal system, and the economic system. As both Hofstede and Harrison found, culture also has a profound impact on a country's economic health by promoting certain values that either aid or inhibit economic growth.

More important to this discussion, however, is that cultural characteristics influence the ways managers behave in relation to subordinates as well as the perceptions of the appropriateness of various HRM practices. First, cultures differ strongly on such things as how subordinates expect leaders to lead, how decisions are handled within the hierarchy, and (most importantly) what motivates individuals. For example, in Germany, managers achieve their status by demonstrating technical skills, and thus, employees look to them to assign their tasks and resolve technical problems. In the Netherlands, on the other hand, managers focus on seeking consensus among all parties and must engage in an open-ended exchange of views and balancing of interests.[22] Clearly, these have different implications for selecting and training managers in the different countries.

Second, cultures strongly influence the appropriateness of HRM practices. For example, as previously discussed, the extent to which a culture promotes an individualistic versus collectivist orientation will affect the effectiveness of individually oriented human resource systems. In the United States companies often focus selection systems on assessing an individual's technical skill and, to a lesser extent, social skills. In collectivist cultures, on the other hand, companies focus more on assessing how well an individual will perform as a member of the work group.

Similarly, cultures can influence compensation systems. Individualistic cultures such as those found in the United States often exhibit great differences between the highest- and lowest-paid individuals in an organization, with the highest-paid individual often receiving 200 times the salary of the lowest. Collectivist cultures, on the other hand tend to have much flatter salary structures, with the top-paid individual receiving only about 20 times the overall pay of the lowest-paid one.

Cultural differences can affect the communication and coordination processes in organizations. Collectivist cultures, as well as those with less of an authoritarian orientation, more highly value group decision making and participative management practices. When a person raised in an individual-

Globalization

JAPANESE MANAGERS ADOPT AMERICAN MANAGEMENT PRACTICES

A common theme among American management thought is that U.S. companies need to look to Japan to find the proper ways to manage people. People point to the participative management styles, quality circles, and employee loyalty to the company as practices that should be replicated in American companies. However, people seldom discuss the American practices that the Japanese admire.

A recent survey of over 400 senior Japanese executives working in America revealed that these managers admire a number of management practices and characteristics about workers in the United States. For example, one manager said that the United States has given much more attention than Japan to equal opportunity for women and minorities. He stated, "Today more and more women are working in Japan, but they don't have enough opportunity there to climb the corporate ladder."

In addition, although Americans admire the group decision-making processes of Japanese organizations, Japanese managers admire the assertiveness and individuality they observe among Americans. Said one manager, "I like the U.S. system of a more decentralized form of management. I like the idea of giving more power to individuals to make key decisions, rather than making those decisions in a group, which is the way it is done in Japan."

Thus, it appears that as international commerce continues to expand into a global economy, managers from different cultures will look to the most effective aspects of other cultures to help them manage human resources more effectively. Just as U.S. managers will continue to learn from their international counterparts, so these counterparts seem to be learning from the United States.

SOURCE: R. Yates, "Japanese Managers Say They're Adopting Some U.S. Ways," *Chicago Tribune*, February 29, 1992, b1.

istic culture must work closely with those from a collectivist culture, communication problems and conflicts will often appear. Much of the emphasis on "cultural diversity" programs in organizations focuses on understanding the cultures of others in order to better communicate with them.

Although cultures are quite diverse and are likely to always remain so, as interactions across cultures become more common, the management practices of one culture are being assimilated by others. The "Competing through Globalization" box illustrates how the management practices associated with different cultures are becoming more integrated.

Education/Human Capital

A company's potential to find and maintain a qualified work force is an important consideration in any decision to expand into a foreign market. Thus, a country's human capital resources can be an important HR issue. Human capital refers to the productive capabilities of individuals—that is, the knowledge, skills, and experience that have economic value.[23]

Countries differ in their levels of human capital. For example, as discussed in Chapter 1, the United States suffers from a human capital shortage because the jobs being created require skills beyond those of most of the new entrants into the work force.[24] In former East Germany, there is an excess of human capital in terms of technical knowledge and skill because of that country's large investment in education. However, East Germany's business schools did not teach management development, so there is a human capital shortage for managerial jobs.[25] Similarly, companies in what used to be West Germany have shifted toward types of production and service that require high-skilled workers; this is creating a human capital shortage for high-skill jobs, yet the unemployment rate remains high because of a large number of low-skilled workers.[26]

A country's human capital is determined by a number of variables. A major variable is the educational opportunities available to the labor force. In the Netherlands, for instance, government funding of school systems allows students to go all the way through graduate school without paying.[27] Similarly, the free education provided to citizens in the former Soviet bloc resulted in high levels of human capital, in spite of the poor infrastructure and economy that resulted from the socialist economic systems. In contrast, some Third World countries such as Nicaragua or Haiti have relatively low levels of human capital because of a lack of investment in education.

A country's human capital may profoundly affect a foreign company's desire to locate there or enter that country's market. Countries with low human capital attract facilities that require low skills and low wage levels. This explains why U.S. companies desire to locate their currently unionized low-skill–high-wage manufacturing and assembly jobs to Mexico, where they can obtain low-skilled workers for substantially lower wages. Similarly, Japan ships its messy, low-skill work to neighboring countries while maintaining its high-skill work at home.[28] Countries like Mexico, with relatively low levels of human capital, might not be as attractive for operations that consist of more high-skill jobs.

Countries with high human capital are attractive sites for direct foreign investment that creates high-skill jobs. In Ireland, for example, over 25 percent of 18-year-olds attend college, a rate much higher than other European countries. In addition, Ireland's economy supports only 1.1 million jobs for a population of 3.5 million. The combination of high education levels, a strong work ethic, and high unemployment make the country attractive for foreign firms because of the resulting high productivity and low turnover. The Met Life insurance company set up a facility for Irish workers to analyze medical insurance claims. It has found the high levels of human capital and the high work ethic to provide such a competitive advantage that the company is currently looking for other work performed in the United States to be shipped to Ireland. Similarly, for this reason, many believe that NAFTA will result in a loss of low-skill jobs in the United States but also in an increased number of high-skill jobs in the United States. The increase in high-skill jobs would result from increased commerce between the two nations combined with the higher levels of human capital available in the United States versus Mexico.[29]

Recent changes in the former Soviet bloc countries, however, point to the fact that human capital and labor costs are not always negatively related. For example, when Daniel Industries was considering establishing a factory in West Germany, it found high costs of land, labor, and buildings. Instead, it bought the assets of a measuring instruments company in East Germany that was formerly run by the state. Daniel Industries has found that East German workers have high levels of engineering skills stemming from the demanding apprenticeship training required before they entered the work force. In addition to the impressive skills of these workers, they cost about half as much as West German workers.[30]

Political/Legal System

The regulations imposed by a country's legal system can strongly affect HRM. The political/legal system often dictates the requirements of certain HRM practices, such as training, compensation, hiring, firing, and layoffs. In large part, the legal system is an outgrowth of the culture in which it exists. Thus, the laws of a particular country often reflect societal norms about what constitutes legitimate behavior.[31]

For example, the United States has led the world in eliminating discrimination in the workplace. Because of the importance this has in our culture, we also have legal safeguards such as equal employment opportunity laws (to be discussed in the following chapter) that strongly affect the hiring and firing practices of firms. As a society, we also have strong beliefs regarding the equity of pay systems, and thus, the Fair Labor Standards Act (to be discussed in Chapter 16), among other laws and regulations, sets the minimum wage for a variety of jobs. We have regulations that dictate much of the process for negotiation between unions and management. These regulations profoundly affect the ways in which human resources are managed in the United States.

Similarly, the legal regulations regarding HRM in other countries reflect their societal norms. For example, in Germany employees have a legal right to "codetermination" at the company, plant, and individual level. At the company level, a firm's employees have direct influence on the important decisions that affect them, such as large investments or new strategies. This is brought about through having employee representatives on the supervisory council *(Aufsichtsrat).* At the plant level, codetermination exists through works councils. These councils have no rights in the economic management of the company, but they can influence HRM policies on such issues as working hours, payment methods, hirings, and transfers. Finally, at the individual level, employees have contractual rights, such as the right to read their personnel files and the right to be informed about how their pay is calculated.[32]

The EEC provides another example of the effects of the political/legal system on HRM. The EEC's Community Charter of December 9, 1989, provides for the fundamental social rights of workers. These rights include freedom of movement, freedom to chose one's occupation and be fairly compensated, guarantee of social protection via social security benefits, freedom of association and collective bargaining, equal treatment for men and women, and a safe and healthy work environment, among others. These rights are summarized in the "Competing through Social Responsibility" box.

Economic System

A country's economic system influences HRM in a number of ways. As previously discussed, a country's culture is integrally tied to its economic system, and these systems provide many of the incentives for developing their human capital. In socialist economic systems, there are ample opportunities for developing human capital because the education system is free. However, under these systems, there is little economic incentive to develop human capital because there are no monetary rewards for increasing human capital. In addition, as the "Competing through Technology and Structure" box notes, in former Soviet bloc countries, an individual's investment in human capital did not always result in a promotion. Rather, it was investment in the Socialist party that led to career advancements.

In capitalist systems, the opposite situation exists. There is less opportunity to develop human capital without higher costs (you have probably observed the tuition increases at U.S. universities). However, those who do invest in their individual human capital, particularly through education, are more able to reap monetary rewards, thus providing more incentive for such investment. In the United States, individuals' salaries usually reflect differences in human capital (i.e., high-skill workers receive higher compensation than low-skill workers). In fact, the most recent research estimates that individual's wages increase by between 10 percent and 16 percent for each additional year of schooling.[33]

In addition to the effects of an economic system on HRM, the health of the system can have an important impact. For example, we referred earlier to lower labor costs in Mexico. In developed countries with a high level of wealth, labor costs tend to be quite high relative to those in developing countries. While labor costs are related to the human capital of a country, they are not perfectly related, as shown by Table 3.3. This table provides a good example of the different hourly labor costs for manufacturing jobs in various countries.

An economic system also affects HRM directly through its taxes on compensation packages. Thus, the differential labor costs shown in Table 3.3 do not always reflect the actual take-home pay of employees. Socialist systems are characterized by tax systems that redistribute wealth by taking a higher

Social Responsibility

THE FUNDAMENTAL SOCIAL RIGHTS OF WORKERS IN THE EEC

The charter of the European community guarantees the fundamental social rights of workers. These rights might seem to be familiar to American workers because many of them have been guaranteed already or are issues of continuing debate in the United States. Some of these rights are discussed below.

Freedom of Movement.   Articles, 7, 48, and 51 provide for the free movement of workers throughout the territory of the EEC. This enables workers to engage in any occupation or profession and to receive equal treatment with regard to access to employment, working conditions, and social protection in the host country.

Improvement of Living and Working Conditions.   Workers also have the right to a weekly rest period (weekend) and to a paid annual leave (vacation). These must be stipulated in laws, a collective agreement, or a contract of employment, depending upon the country.

Social Protection.   Every worker in the EEC has a right to adequate social protection and to receive an adequate level of social security benefits, regardless of the job or the size of the employing firm. In addition, persons who have been unable to enter or reenter the work force have a right to some social assistance to meet their subsistence needs.

Freedom of Association and Collective Bargaining.   Workers (through trade unions) and employers (through trade associations) have the right to negotiate and conclude collective bargaining agreements under the conditions laid down by the host country's laws. This includes the right to strike, again, subject to the laws of the host country.

Vocational Training.   Every worker in the EEC is guaranteed access to vocational training and to receive additional training throughout his or her working life.

Equal Treatment for Men and Women.   The agreement guarantees both equal opportunities and equal treatment for men and women.

Information, Consultation, and Participation for Workers.   Workers have the right to be given relevant company information, to be consulted regarding company decisions, and to participate in the management of work enterprises.

Health and Safety at the Workplace.   Every worker is guaranteed a safe and healthful working environment.

Protection of Children and Young People. The minimum age of employment must not be lower than the minimum age at which young people can leave school and can be no lower than 15 years of age. Night work is prohibited for workers under the age of 18. Young people must receive equitable pay in accordance with national practice.

Elderly Persons.   Every worker in the EEC, at the time of retirement, must be able to enjoy resources that afford him or her a decent standard of living. Retired individuals without pensions must be afforded medical and social assistance suited to his or her needs.

Disabled Persons.   All disabled persons are entitled to concrete measures aimed at improving their social and professional integration.

SOURCE: Commission of the European Communities, *The European Community 1992 and Beyond* (Luxembourg: Office for Official Publications of the European Communities, 1991).

Technology & Structure

COMPETING THROUGH

SOCIALIST HRM PRACTICES IN THE FORMER SOVIET BLOC COUNTRIES

Americans tend to take an extremely ethnocentric view of HRM practices, assuming to some extent that all cultures seek to maximize productivity and, thus, use HRM practices similar to those found in the United States. However, an analysis of the HRM practices in the former Soviet bloc countries reveals the effects of a cultural/political/legal system on HR.

In socialist countries such as East Germany and Russia, motivation was considered to be a social, rather than individual, phenomenon. In the socialist personality, the human being was seen as *homo politicus* (political man) for whom socialist consciousness was sufficient motivation. Seeking this idealistic consciousness was the goal of all education and training, even taking precedence over technical training. In addition, the social relationship within the work collective was assumed to be an important motivator, rather than things such as pay.

All managerial career planning was founded on this socialist ideal and was referred to as *cadre work*. This was performed to define the leadership and next-generation leaders for each company as well as nationwide. The central nomenclature served as a societywide employment plan for all leadership positions. Managers were selected using political criteria such as "dedication to the working class, to its Marxist-Leninist party and to the socialist state, "developed socialist consciousness," and faithful cooperation with the party."

This system has resulted in tremendous challenges for these countries as they move to market economies. Primarily, it created a system of managers who were promoted based on political rather than technical skills. Thus, one important issue companies face in these countries is to develop elaborate assessment systems to identify those managers who possess adequate managerial skills as opposed to those who gained their positions based on socialist party loyalty.

SOURCE: R. Pieper, "Socialist HRM: An Analysis of HRM Theory and Practice in the Former Socialist Countries in Eastern Europe," *The International Executive* 34, no. 6 (1992): 499–516.

percentage of a person's income as he or she moves up the economic ladder. Capitalist systems attempt to reward individuals for their efforts by allowing them to keep more of their earnings. Table 3.4 shows that a manager being paid $100,000 would take home vastly different amounts in different countries because of the varying tax rates. Companies that do business in other countries have to present compensation packages to expatriate managers that are competitive in take-home, rather than gross, pay. HRM responses to these issues affecting expatriate managers will be discussed in more detail later in this chapter.

In conclusion, every country varies in terms of its culture, human capital, legal system, and economic systems. These variations directly influence the types of HRM systems that must be developed to accommodate the particular situation. The extent to which these differences affect a company depends on how involved the company is in global markets. In the next sec-

TABLE 3.3   Labor Costs in Several Countries

	Gross Hourly Compensation	Hourly Wage	Benefits[a]
Western Germany	$24.39	$13.09	$11.30
Switzerland	23.39	15.51	7.88
Sweden	22.30	12.72	9.58
Italy	19.51	9.52	9.99
Netherlands	19.35	10.66	8.69
Austria	18.73	9.49	9.24
Japan	17.85	13.60	4.25
France	16.10	8.49	7.61
United States	15.40	11.18	4.22
Britain	13.71	9.59	4.12
Greece	6.71	4.08	2.63
Portugal	4.75	2.70	2.05

SOURCE: Reprinted with permission of *The Wall Street Journal,* © 1993 Dow Jones & Company, Inc. All rights reserved.
[a] Includes: Health care, pensions, workers' compensation and other insurance

tions we discuss important concepts of global business and various levels of global participation, particularly noting how these factors come into play.

MANAGING EMPLOYEES IN A GLOBAL CONTEXT

Types of International Employees

Before discussing the levels of global participation, we need to distinguish between parent countries, host countries, and third countries. A **parent country** is the country in which the company's corporate headquarters is located. For example, the United States is the parent country of General Motors. A **host country** is the country in which the parent country organization seeks to locate (or has already located), a facility. Thus, Great Britain is a host country for General Motors, because GM has operations there. A **third country** is a country other than the host country or parent country, and a company may or may not have a facility there.

There are also different categories of employees. **Expatriate** is the term generally used for employees sent by a company in one country to manage operations in a different country. With the increasing globalization of business, it is now important to distinguish among different types of expatri-

TABLE 3.4   Maximum Marginal Federal Tax Rates[a]

Country	1985 Maximum Marginal Rate	1988 Maximum Marginal Rate	Income Level at which Reached	
			In Local Currency	In U.S. Dollars[b]
Argentina	45%	38.25%	A416,500	$119,000
Australia	49	49	A$35,001	25,894
Belgium	72	70.8	BFr4,202,000	121,235
Brazil	60	50	Cz$2,784,600	38,536
Canada	34	29.87	Can$55,000	44,571
France	65	56.8	FFr720,000	128,251
Germany	56	56	DM260,000	157,100
Hong Kong	17.5	16.5	HK$300,000	38,462
Italy	65	62	Lit600,000,000	488,599
Japan	70	60	¥50,000,000	403,714
Korea	55	55	W60,000,000	79,915
Mexico	55	50	Ps45,063,804	20,484
Netherlands	72	72	Fi229,625	123,521
Singapore	40	33	S$400,000	200,100
Spain	66	56	Pta8,000,000	72,483
Sweden	50	45	SKr190,000	32,418
Switzerland	13.75	11.5	SFr423,600	310,557
United Kingdom	60	40	£19,300	36,415
United States	50	33	US$71,900	71,900
Venezuela	45	45	Bs8,000,000	271,647

SOURCE: Used with permission of P. Dowling and R. Schuler, *International Dimensions of Human Resource Management,* (Boston: PWS-Kent, 1990).

[a]Maximum marginal rates are those applicable to resident citizens as of January 1, 1988, with one exception: the rate for the U.K. reflects April 1988 changes. Where different rates apply to married and single employees, the married employee rate is shown. Social security taxes are excluded.

[b]Based on April 1, 1988 exchange rates, adjusted for high inflation countries.

ates. **Parent-country nationals (PCNs)** are employees who were born and live in the parent country. **Host-country nationals (HCNs)** are those employees who were born and raised in the host, as opposed to the parent, country. Finally, **third-country nationals (TCNs)** are employees born in a country other than the parent country or host country but who work in the host country. Thus, a manager born and raised in Brazil employed by an organization located in the United States and assigned to manage an operation in Thailand would be considered a TCN.

Levels of Global Participation

We often hear companies referred to as "multinational" or "international." However, it is important to understand the different levels of participation in international markets. This is especially important because as a company becomes more involved in international trade, different types of HRM problems arise. In this section, we examine Nancy Adler's categorization of the various levels of international participation from which a company may choose.[34] Figure 3.3 depicts these levels of involvement.

Domestic.   Most companies begin by operating within a domestic marketplace. For example, an entrepreneur may have an idea for a product that meets a need in the U.S. marketplace. This individual then obtains capital to build a facility that allows the product or service to be produced in a quantity that meets the needs of a small market niche. This requires recruiting, hiring, training, and compensating a number of individuals who will be involved in the production process, and these individuals are usually drawn from the local labor market. The focus of the selection and training programs are often on the employees' technical competence to perform job-related duties and to some extent on interpersonal skills. In addition, because the company is usually involved in only one labor market, determining the market rate of pay for various jobs is relatively easy.

As the product grows in popularity, the owner might choose to build additional facilities in different parts of the country to reduce the costs of transporting the product over large distances. In making the decision where to locate these facilities, the owner must consider the attractiveness of the local labor markets. Various parts of the country may have different cultures that make those areas more or less attractive according to the work ethics of the potential employees. Similarly, the human capital in the different areas may vary greatly because of differences in educational systems. Finally, the local pay rates may differ. It is for these reasons that the U.S. economy in the past ten years has experienced a movement of jobs from northern states, which are characterized by strong unions and high labor costs, to the Sun Belt states, which have lower labor costs and are less unionized.

Incidentally, even domestic companies face problems with cultural diversity. In the United States, for example, the representation of women and minorities is increasing within the work force. These groups come to the workplace with worldviews that differ from those of the traditional white male. Thus, we are seeing more and more emphasis on developing systems for managing cultural diversity within single-country organizations, even though the diversity might be on a somewhat smaller scale than the diversity of cultures across national boundaries.[35]

It is important to note that companies functioning at the domestic level face an environment with very similar cultural, human capital, political/legal systems, and economic systems, although some variation might be observed across states and geographical areas.

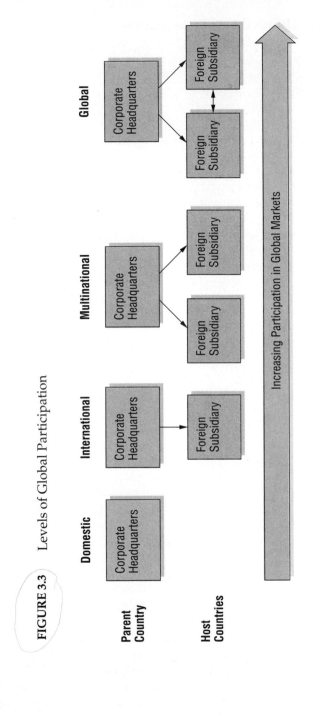

FIGURE 3.3 Levels of Global Participation

International.   As more competitors enter the domestic market, companies face the possibility of losing market share; thus, they often seek other markets for their products. This usually requires entering international markets, initially by exporting products, but ultimately by building production facilities in other countries. The decision to participate in international competition raises a host of human resource issues. All the problems regarding locating facilities are magnified. One must consider whether a particular location provides an environment where human resources can be successfully acquired and managed.

Now the company faces an entirely different situation with regard to culture, human capital, the political/legal system, and the economic system. For example, the availability of human capital is of utmost importance, and there is a substantially greater variability in human capital between the United States and other countries than there is among the various states in the United States.

A country's legal system may also present HR problems. For example, France has a relatively high minimum wage, which drives labor costs up. In Germany, companies are legally required to offer employees influence in the management of the firm. Companies that develop facilities in other countries have to adapt their HR practices to conform to the host country's laws. This requires the company to gain expertise in the country's HRM legal requirements and knowledge about how to deal with the country's legal system, and it often requires the company to hire one or more HCNs. In fact, some countries legally require companies to hire a certain percentage of HCNs for any foreign-owned subsidiary.

Finally, cultures have to be considered. To the extent that the country's culture is vastly different from that of the parent organization, conflicts, communication problems, and morale problems may occur. Expatriate managers must be trained to identify these cultural differences, and they must be flexible enough to adapt their styles to those of their host country. This requires an extensive selection effort to identify individuals who are capable of adapting to new environments and an extensive training program to ensure that the culture shock is not devastating.

Multinational.   Whereas international companies build one or a few facilities in another country, they become multinational when they build facilities in a number of different countries, attempting to capitalize on lower production and distribution costs in different locations. The lower production costs are gained by shifting production from higher-cost locations to lower-cost locations. For example, some of the major U.S. automakers have plants all over the world. They continue to shift their production from the United States, where labor unions have gained high wages for their members, to maquiladora facilities in Mexico, where the wages are substantially lower. Similarly, these companies minimize distribution costs by locating facilities in Europe for manufacturing and assembling automobiles to sell in the European market. They are also now expanding into some of the former Soviet bloc countries to produce automobiles for the European market.

The HRM problems multinational companies face are similar to those international companies face, only magnified. Instead of having to consider only one or two countries' cultural, human capital, legal, and economic systems, the multinational company must address these differences for a large number of countries. This accentuates the need to select managers capable of functioning in a variety of settings, provide them with necessary training, and provide for flexible compensation systems that take into account the different market pay rates, tax systems, and costs of living.

Multinational companies now employ many "inpatriates"—managers from different countries who become part of the corporate headquarters staff. This creates a need to integrate managers from different cultures into the culture of the parent company. In addition, multinational companies now take more expatriates from countries other than the parent country and place them in facilities of other countries. For example, a manager from Scotland, working for a U.S. company, might be assigned to run an operation in South Africa. This practice accentuates the need for cross-cultural training to provide managerial skills for interaction with individuals from different cultures.

Global.   Many researchers now propose a fourth level of integration: global organizations. Global organizations compete on state-of-the-art, top-quality products and services and do so with the lowest costs possible. Whereas multinational companies attempt to develop identical products distributed worldwide, global companies increasingly emphasize flexibility and mass customization of products to meet the needs of particular clients. Multinational companies are usually driven to locate facilities in a country as a means of reaching that country's market or lowering production costs, and the company must deal with the differences across the countries. Global firms, on the other hand, choose to locate a facility based on the ability to effectively, efficiently, and flexibly produce a product or service and attempts to create synergy through the cultural differences.

This creates the need for HRM systems that encourage flexible production (thus presenting a host of HRM issues). These companies proactively consider the cultures, human capital, political/legal systems, and economic systems to determine where production facilities can be located to provide a competitive advantage. Global companies have multiple headquarters spread across the globe, resulting in less hierarchically structured organizations that emphasize decentralized decision making. This results in the need for human resource systems that recruit, develop, retain, and use managers and executives who are competent transnationally.

A transnational HR system is characterized by three attributes.[36] **Transnational scope** refers to the fact that HR decisions must be made from a global rather than a national or regional perspective. This creates the need to make decisions that balance the need for uniformity (to ensure fair treatment of all employees) with the need for flexibility (to meet the needs of employees in different countries). **Transnational representation** reflects the multinational composition of a company's managers. Global participation does not necessarily ensure that each country is providing managers to the company's ranks. This is a prerequisite if the company is to achieve the next attribute. **Transnational process** refers to the extent to which the company's planning and decision-making processes include representatives and ideas from a variety of cultures. This attribute allows for diverse viewpoints and knowledge associated with different cultures, increasing the quality of decision making.

These three characteristics are necessary for global companies to achieve cultural synergy. Rather than simply integrating foreigners into the domestic organization, a successful transnational company needs managers who will treat managers from other cultures as equals. This synergy can only be accomplished by combining selection, training, appraisal, and compensation systems in such a way that managers have a transnational rather than a parochial orientation. However, a survey of 50 companies in the United States and Canada found that global companies' HR systems are far less transnational in scope, representation, and process than the companies' strategic planning systems and organizational structures.[37]

In conclusion, the entry into international markets creates a host of HRM issues that must be addressed if the company is to gain competitive advantage. The "Competing through Quality" box describes some of these issues in detail. Once the choice has been made to compete in a global arena, companies must seek to manage employees who are sent to foreign countries (expatriates and third-country nationals.)

This causes the need to shift from focusing only on the culture, human capital, political/legal and economic influences of the host country to examining the ways to manage the expatriate managers who must be located there. Selection systems must be developed that allow the company to identify managers capable of functioning in a new culture. These managers must be trained to identify the important aspects of the new culture in which they will live as well as the relevant legal/political and economic systems. Finally, these managers must be compensated to offset the costs of uprooting oneself and one's family to move to a new situation vastly different from their previous lives. In the next section, we address the issues regarding the management of expatriates.

Managing Expatriates in Global Markets

We have outlined the major macrolevel factors that influence HR in global markets. These factors can affect a company's decision whether to build facilities in a given country. In addition, if a company does develop such facilities, these factors strongly affect the HR practices used. However, one important issue that has been recognized over the past few years is the set of problems inherent in selecting, training, compensating, and reintegrating expatriate managers.

Quality

LABOR COSTS ARE NOT EVERYTHING: PRODUCTIVITY INCREASES MAKE COMPANIES COMPETITIVE

To hear most people discuss the strategic location of manufacturing facilities, one would think that labor costs are the only variable considered. As important as low labor costs are, however, additional considerations often offset lower labor costs.

For example, Cle. de Saint-Gobain, a giant French glass and building products maker had a very labor-intensive production plant in Malaysia. The low labor costs in Malaysia provided some incentive to stay. However, the firm discovered that it could locate an automated plant in the United States, and lower quality-control and transport costs would more than offset the labor cost advantage.

Similarly, when BMW was looking to locate an assembly plant in North America, it considered Mexico because of lower labor costs. However, relative to its home country, the United States was considered a low-cost location (the total costs in the South Carolina site are expected to be 20 percent below those in Bavaria). In addition, BMW feared that customers might perceive the quality of a Mexican-built luxury automobile as being inferior to one built in the United States, prompting BMW to stay out of Mexico.

While transport costs and image problems often affect the decision where to locate a plant, existing facilities are finding that they can maintain their competitive stance through increasing productivity to offset the labor-cost advantages offered by foreign countries. For example, Alcan Aluminum Ltd.'s aluminum smelter in Sebree, Kentucky, was unable to compete with the lower overall costs of facilities in Canada and the Middle East because of their brand new smelters and cheaper power supplies. However, the company decided to increase productivity enough to offset the cost disadvantage. The strategy was successful, for the plant doubled its production volume with 10 percent fewer employees. The plant now matches competitors' costs at home and has even begun exporting to Mexico.

SOURCE: R. Keatley, "Luxury-Automakers Consider Mexico: Its Low-Cost Labor versus Image Perceptions," *The Wall Street Journal*, November 27, 1992, p. A4; and D. Milbank, "U.S. Productivity Gains Cut Costs, Close Gap with Low-Wage Overseas Firms," *The Wall Street Journal*, A2.

The importance to the company's profitability of making the right expatriate assignments should not be underestimated. Expatriate managers' average compensation package is approximately $250,000,[38] and the cost of an unsuccessful expatriate assignment (i.e., one who returns early) is approximately $100,000.[39] In spite of the importance of these assignments, U.S. organizations have been astoundingly unsuccessful in their use of expatriates. Between 16 and 40 percent of all American employees sent on expatriate assignments overseas return early, a rate almost two to three times that of foreign nationals.[40] In addition, of those expatriates who remain on assignment, many are ineffective, resulting in a loss of productivity. In fact, 30 to 50 percent of American expatriates are evaluated by their firms as either ineffective or marginally effective in their performance.[41]

In this final section of the chapter, we discuss the major issues relevant to the management of expatriate managers. These issues cover the selection, training, compensation, and reacculturation of expatriates.

Selection of Expatriate Managers.   One of the major problems in managing expatriate managers is determining which individuals in the organization are most capable of handling an assignment in a different culture. Expatriate managers must have technical competence in the area of operations; otherwise, they will be unable to earn the respect of subordinates. However, technical competence has been almost the sole variable used in deciding whom to send on overseas assignments, despite the fact that multiple skills are necessary for successful performance in these assignments.[42]

A successful expatriate manager must also be sensitive to the country's cultural norms, flexible enough to adapt to those norms, and strong enough to make it through the inevitable culture shock. In addition, the manager's family must be similarly capable of adapting to the new culture. These adaptive skills have been categorized into three dimensions:[43] (1) the self dimension (the skills that enable a manager to maintain a positive self-image and psychological well-being); (2) the relationship dimension (the skills required to foster relationships with the host-country nationals); and (3) the perception dimension (those skills that enable a manager to accurately perceive and evaluate the host environment). Table 3.5 presents a series of considerations and questions to ask potential expatriate managers to assess their ability to adapt to a new cultural environment.

Little evidence suggests that U.S. companies have invested much effort in attempting to make correct expatriate selections. One researcher found that only 5 percent of the firms she surveyed administered any tests to determine the degree to which expatriate candidates possessed cross-cultural skills.[44] More recent research reveals that only 35 percent of firms choose expatriates from multiple candidates and that those firms emphasize only technical job-related experience and skills in making these decisions.[45]

These findings glaringly demonstrate that U.S. organizations need to improve their success rate in overseas assignments. As we will show in Chapter 11, the technology for assessing individuals' knowledge, skills, and abilities has advanced. The potential for selection testing to decrease the failure rate and productivity problems of U.S. expatriate managers seems promising.

Training and Development of Expatriates.   Once an expatriate manager has been selected, it is necessary to prepare that manager for the upcoming assignment. Because these individuals already have job-related skills, some firms have focused development efforts on cross-cultural training. A review of the cross-cultural training literature found support for the belief that cross-cultural training has an impact on effectiveness.[46]

What exactly is emphasized in cross-cultural training programs? The details regarding these programs will be discussed in Chapter 12. However,

TABLE 3.5

Interview Worksheet for International Candidates

Motivation

- Investigate reasons and degree of interest in wanting to be considered.
- Determine desire to work abroad, verified by previous concerns such as personal travel, language training, reading, and association with foreign employees or students.
- Determine whether the candidate has a realistic understanding of what working and living abroad requires.
- Determine the basic attitudes of the spouse toward an overseas assignment.

Health

- Determine whether any medical problems of the candidate or his or her family might be critical to the success of the assignment.
- Determine whether he or she is in good physical and mental health, without any foreseeable change.

Language Ability

- Determine potential for learning a new language.
- Determine any previous language(s) studied or oral ability (judge against language needed on the overseas assignment).
- Determine the ability of the spouse to meet the language requirements.

Family Considerations

- How many moves has the family made in the past among different cities or parts of the United States?
- What problems were encountered?
- How recent was the last move?
- What is the spouse's goal in this move?
- What are the number of children and the ages of each?
- Has divorce or its potential, death of a family member, etc., weakened family solidarity?
- Will all the children move? Why or why not?
- What are the location, health, and living arrangements of grandparents and the number of trips normally made to their home each year?
- Are there any special adjustment problems that you would expect?
- How is each member of the family reacting to this possible move?
- Do special educational problems exist within the family?

continued

SOURCE: Reprinted with permission, pp. 55–57 from *Multinational People Management*, by D. M. Noer. Copyright © 1989 by the Bureau of National Affairs, Inc., Washington D.C. 20037.

for now, most attempt to create an appreciation of the host country's culture so that expatriates can behave appropriately.[47] This entails emphasizing a few aspects of cultural sensitivity. First, expatriates must be clear about

TABLE 3.5

continued

Resourcefulness and Initiative

- Is the candidate independent; can he or she make and stand by his or her decisions and judgments?
- Does he or she have the intellectual capacity to deal with several dimensions simultaneously?
- Is he or she able to reach objectives and produce results with whatever personnel and facilities are available, regardless of the limitations and barriers that might arise?
- Can the candidate operate without a clear definition of responsibility and authority on a foreign assignment?
- Will the candidate be able to explain the aims and company philosophy to the local managers and workers?
- Does he or she possess sufficient self-discipline, and self-confidence to overcome difficulties or handle complex problems?
- Can the candidate work without supervision?
- Can the candidate operate effectively in a foreign environment without normal communications and supporting services?

Adaptability

- Is the candidate sensitive to others, open to the opinions of others, cooperative, and able to compromise?
- What are his or her reactions to new situations, and efforts to understand and appreciate differences?
- Is he or she culturally sensitive, aware, and able to relate across the culture?
- Does the candidate understand his or her own culturally derived values?
- How does the candidate react to criticism?
- What is his or her understanding of the U.S. government system?
- Will he or she be able to make and develop contacts with his or her peers in the foreign country?
- Does he or she have patience when dealing with problems?
- Is he or she resilient; can he or she bounce back after setbacks?

Career Planning

- Does the candidate consider the assignment anything other than a temporary overseas trip?
- Is the move consistent with his or her progression and that planned by the company?
- Is his or her career planning realistic?
- What is the candidate's basic attitude toward the company?
- Is there any history or indication of interpersonal problems with this employee?

Financial

- Are there any current financial and/or legal considerations that might affect the assignment, e.g., house purchase, children and college expenses, car purchases?
- Are financial considerations negative factors, i.e., will undue pressures be brought to bear on the employee or his or her family as a result of the assignment?

their own cultural background, particularly as it is perceived by the host nationals. With an accurate cultural self-awareness, managers can modify their behavior to accentuate the effective characteristics while minimizing

TABLE 3.6   Americans as Others See Them

People from other countries are often puzzles and intrigued by the intricacies and enigmas of American culture. Below is a selection of actual observations by foreigners visiting the United States. As you read them, ask yourself in each case if the observer is accurate, and how you would explain the trait in question.

India

"Americans seem to be in a perpetual hurry. Just watch the way they walk down the street. They never allow themselves the leisure to enjoy life; there are too many things to do."

Kenya

"Americans appear to us rather distant. They are not really as close to other people —even fellow Americans—as Americans overseas tend to portray. It's almost as if an American says, "I won't let you get too close to me.' It's like building a wall."

Turkey

"Once we were out in a rural area in the middle of nowhere and saw an American come to a stop sign. Though he could see in both directions for miles and no traffic was coming, he still stopped!"

Colombia

"The tendency in the United States to think that life is only work hits you in the face. Work seems to be the one type of motivation."

Indonesia

"In the United States everything has to be talked about and analyzed. Even the littlest thing has to be 'Why, Why, Why?' I get a headache from such persistent questions."

Ethiopia

"The American is very explicit; he wants a 'yes' or 'no.' If someone tries to speak figuratively, the American is confused."

Iran

"The first time…my [American] professor told me, 'I don't know the answer, I will have to look it up,' I was shocked. I asked myself, 'Why is he teaching me?' In my country, a professor would give the wrong answer rather than admit ignorance."

SOURCE: J. Feig and G. Blair, *There is a Difference*, 2nd ed (Washington, DC: Meridian House International, 1980).

those that are dysfunctional.[48] Table 3.6 displays the ways Americans tend to be perceived by those in other countries.

Second, expatriates must understand the particular aspects of culture in the new work environment. Although culture is an elusive, almost invisible phenomenon, astute expatriate managers must perceive the culture and adapt their behavior to it. This entails identifying the types of behaviors and

interpersonal styles that are considered acceptable, both in business meetings and social gatherings. For example, Germans value promptness for
meetings to a much greater extent than Latin Americans.

Finally, expatriates must learn to communicate accurately in the new
culture. Some firms attempt to use expatriates who speak the language of
the host country, and a few provide language training. However, most
companies simply assume that the host-country nationals all speak the parent country's language. Although this assumption might be true, seldom
do these nationals speak the parent country language fluently. Thus, expatriate managers must be trained to communicate with others when language barriers exist. Table 3.7 offers some tips for communicating across
language barriers.

Effective cross-cultural training helps ease an expatriate's transition to
the new work environment. It can also help avoid costly mistakes, such as
the expatriate who attempted to bring two bottles of brandy into the Muslim
country of Qatar. The brandy was discovered by customs; not only was the
expatriate deported, the company was also "disinvited" from the country.[49]

Compensation of Expatriates.   One of the more troublesome aspects of
managing expatriates is determining the compensation package. As
previously discussed, these packages average $250,000, but it is necessary to
examine the exact breakdown of these packages. Most use a balance sheet
approach to determine the total package level. This approach entails
developing a total compensation package that equalizes the purchasing
power of the expatriate manager with that of employees in similar positions
in the home country and provides incentives to offset the inconveniences
incurred in the location. Purchasing power includes all of the expenses
associated with the expatriate assignment. Expenses include *goods and
services* (e.g., food, personal care, clothing, recreation, and transportation),
housing (for a principal residence), *income taxes* (paid to federal and local
governments), *reserve* (e.g., savings, payments for benefits, pension
contributions), and *shipment and storage* (costs associated with moving
and/or storing personal belongings). A typical balance sheet is shown in
Figure 3.4.

As you can see from this figure, the employee starts with a set of costs
for taxes, housing, goods and services, and reserve. However, in the host
country, these costs are significantly higher. Thus, the company must make
up the difference between costs in the home and those in the host country,
then provide a premium and/or incentive for the employee to go through
the trouble of living in a different environment.

Total pay packages have four components. First, there is the *base salary*.
Determining the base salary is not a simple matter, however. Fluctuating
exchange rates between countries may make an offered salary a raise some
of the time, a pay cut at other times. In addition, the base salary may be
based on comparable pay in the parent country or it may be based on the
prevailing market rates for the job in the host country. Expatriates are often

TABLE 3.7   Communicating across Language Barriers

Verbal Behavior

- *Clear, slow speech.* Enunciate each word. Do not use colloquial expressions.
- *Repetition.* Repeat each important idea using different words to explain the same concept.
- *Simple sentences.* Avoid compound, long sentences.
- *Active verbs.* Avoid passive verbs.

Nonverbal Behavior

- *Visual Restatements.* Use as many visual restatements as possible, such as pictures, graphs, tables, and slides.
- *Gestures.* Use more facial and hand gestures to emphasize the meaning of words.
- *Demonstration.* Act out as many themes as possible.
- *Pauses.* Pause more frequently.
- *Summaries.* Hand out written summaries of your verbal presentation.

Attribution

- *Silence.* When there is a silence, wait. Do not jump in to fill the silence. The other person is probably just thinking more slowly in the non-native language or translating.
- *Intelligence.* Do not equate poor grammar and mispronunciation with lack of intelligence; it is usually a sign of second language use.
- *Differences.* If unsure, assume difference, not similarity.

Comprehension

- *Understanding.* Do not just assume that they understand; assume that they do not understand.
- *Checking comprehension.* Have colleagues repeat their understanding of the material back to you. Do not simply ask if they understand or not. Let them explain what they understand to you.

Design

- *Breaks.* Take more frequent breaks. Second language comprehension is exhausting.
- *Small modules.* Divide the material into smaller modules.
- *Longer time frame.* Allocate more time for each module than usual in a monolingual program.

Motivation

- *Encouragement.* Verbally and nonverbally encourage and reinforce speaking by non-native language participants.
- *Drawing out.* Explicitly draw out marginal and passive participants.
- *Reinforcement.* Do not embarrass novice speakers.

SOURCE: Used with permission of N. Adler, *International Dimensions of Organization Behavior*, 2nd ed. (Boston: PWS-Kent, 1991).

FIGURE 3.4   The Balance Sheet

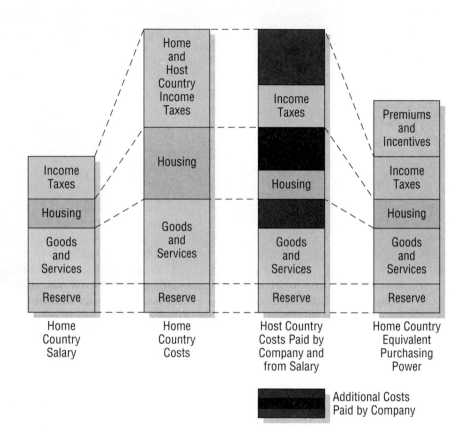

SOURCE: C. Reynolds, "Compensation of Overseas Personnel," in *Handbook of Human Resource Administration,* 2nd ed., J. J. Famularo, ed. (New York: McGraw-Hill, 1986), p. 51. Reprinted with permission.

offered a salary premium beyond that of their present salary as an inducement to accept the expatriate assignment.

Tax equalization allowances are a second component. They are necessary because of countries' different taxation systems in high-tax countries. For example, a senior executive earning $100,000 in Belgium (with a maximum marginal tax rate of 70.8 percent) could cost a company almost $1 million in taxes over five to seven years.[50] Under most tax equalization plans, the company withholds the amount of tax to be paid in the home country, then pays all of the taxes accrued in the host country.

A third component, *benefits,* presents additional compensation problems. Most of the problems have to do with the transportability of the benefits. For example, if an expatriate contributing to a pension plan in the United States is moved to a different country, does the individual have a new pension in the host country, or should the individual be allowed to contribute to the existing pension in his or her home country? What about health-care systems located in the United States? How does the company ensure that expatriate employees have equal health-care coverage? For example, in one company, the different health-care plans available resulted in situations where it might cost significantly less to have the employee fly to the United States to have a procedure performed rather than have it done in the host country. However, the health plans did not allow this alternative.

Finally, *allowances* are often offered to make the expatriate assignment less unattractive. Cost-of-living allowances are payments that offset the differences in expenditures on day-to-day necessities between the host country and the parent country. Housing allowances ensure that the expatriate can maintain the same home-country living standard. Education allowances reimburse expatriates for the expense of placing their children in private English-speaking schools. Relocation allowances cover all the expenses of making the actual move to a new country, including transportation to and from the new location, temporary living expenses, and shipping and/or storage of personal possessions.

Reacculturation of Expatriates A final issue of importance to managing expatriates is dealing with the reacculturation process when these managers reenter their home country. It has recently been recognized that reentry is no simple feat. Culture shock takes place in reverse. The individual has changed, the company has changed, and the culture has changed while the expatriate was overseas. Twenty percent of workers want to leave the company when they return from an overseas assignment, and this presents potentially serious morale and productivity problems.[51] In fact, the most recent estimates are that 25 percent of expatriate managers leave the company within one year of returning from their expatriate assignments.[52] If these repatriates leave, the company has virtually no way to recoup its substantial investment in human capital.[53]

Companies are increasingly making efforts to help expatriates ease through this transition. Two characteristics help in this transition process.[54] *Communication* refers to the extent to which the expatriate receives information and recognizes changes while abroad. The closer the contact with the home organization while abroad, the more proactive, effective, and satisfied the expatriate will be upon reentry. *Validation* refers to the amount of recognition received by the expatriate upon return home. Expatriates who receive recognition from their peers and their bosses for their foreign work and their future potential contribution to the company have fewer troubles with reentry compared with those who are treated as if they were "out of the loop."

Finally, one research study noted the role of an expatriate manager's expectations about the expatriate assignment in determining repatriation adjustment and job performance. This study found that managers whose job expectations (constraints and demands in terms of volume and performance standards) and nonwork expectations (living and housing conditions) were met exhibited a greater degree of repatriation adjustment and higher levels of job performance.[55]

SUMMARY

Today's organizations are more involved in international commerce than ever before, and the trend will continue. Recent historic events such as the development of the EEC, the reunification of Germany, the disintegration of the Soviet Union, and NAFTA have accelerated the movement toward a global market. Companies competing in the global marketplace require top-quality people in order to compete successfully. This requires that managers be aware of the many factors that significantly affect HRM in a global environment such as the culture, human capital, political/legal system, and economic system, and that they understand how these factors come into play in the various levels of global participation. Finally, it requires that they be adept at developing HR systems that maximize the effectiveness of all human resources, particularly with regard to expatriate managers. One cannot overestimate the importance of effectively managing human resources in order to gain competitive advantage in today's global marketplace.

Discussion Questions

1. What current trends and/or events (besides those mentioned at the outset of the chapter) are responsible for the increased internationalization of the marketplace?

2. According to Hofstede (in Table 3.2), the United States is low on power distance, high on individuality, high on masculinity, low on uncertainty avoidance, and low on long-term orientation. Russia, on the other hand, is high on power distance, moderate on individuality, low on masculinity, high on uncertainty avoidance, and low on long-term orientation. Many American managers are transplanting their own HRM practices into Russia while companies seek to develop operations there. How acceptable/effective do you think the following practices will be and why? (a) Extensive assessments of individual abilities for selection; (b) Individually based appraisal systems; (c) Suggestion systems; (d) Self-managing work teams?

3. The chapter notes that political/legal and economic systems can reflect a country's culture. The former Eastern bloc countries seem to be changing their political/legal and economic systems. Is this change brought on by their cultures, or will culture have an impact on the ability to change these systems? Why?

4. Think of the different levels of global participation. What companies that you are familiar with exhibit the different levels of participation?

5. Think of a time when you had to function in another culture (e.g., on a vacation, job, etc.). What were the major obstacles you faced, and how did you deal with them? Was this a stressful experience? Why? How can companies help expatriate employees deal with the stress?

6. What types of skills do you need to be able to manage in today's global marketplace? Where do you expect to get those skills? What classes/experiences will you need?

Notes

1. P. J. Dowling, "Human Resource Issues in International Business," *Syracuse Journal of International Law and Commerce* 13, no. 2 (1986): 255–271.

2. R. M. Kanter, "Transcending Business Boundaries: 12,000 World Managers View Change," *Harvard Business Review,* May–June 1991, 151–164.

3. R. Norton, "Will a Global Slump Hurt the U.S.?" *Fortune,* February 22, 1993, 63–64.

4. M. B. Teagarden, M. C. Butler, and M. A. Von Glinow, "Mexico's Maquiladora Industry: Where Strategic Human Resource Management Makes a Difference," *Organizational Dynamics* 21 (1992): 34–47.

5. Towers Perrin, *Priorities for Competitive Advantage: A Worldwide Human Resource Study* (Valhalla, N.Y.: Towers Perrin, 1991).

6. R. Schuler, "An Integrative Framework of Strategic International Human Resource Management," *Journal of Management,* in press.

7. R. Pieper, "Socialist HRM: An Analysis of HRM Theory and Practice in the Former Socialist Countries of Eastern Europe," *The International Executive* 34, no. 6 (1992): 499–516.

8. G. Schares and K. Olsen, "Hungary: A Giant Step Ahead," *Business Week,* April 15, 1991, p. 58.

9. L. Rubio, "The Rationale for NAFTA: Mexico's New "Outward Looking" Strategy," *Business Economics* (1991): 12–16.

10. Towers Perrin and Hudson Institute, *Workforce 2000: Competing in a Seller's Market* (Valhalla, N.Y.: Towers Perrin, 1990).

11. R. Peiper, *Human Resource Management: An International Comparison* (Berlin: Walter de Gruyter, 1990).

12. V. Sathe, *Culture and Related Corporate Realities* (Homewood, Ill.: Richard D. Irwin, 1985).

13. M. Rokeach, *Beliefs, Attitudes, and Values* (San Francisco: Jossey-Bass, 1968).

14. L. Harrison, *Who Prospers? How Cultural Values Shape Economic and Political Success* (New York, N.Y.: Free Press, 1992).

15. N. Adler, *International Dimensions of Organizational Behavior,* 2nd ed. (Boston: PWS-Kent, 1991).

16. R. Yates, "Japanese Managers Say They're Adopting Some U.S. Ways," *Chicago Tribune,* February 29, 1992, B1.

17. G. Hofstede, "Dimensions of National Cultures in Fifty Counties and Three Regions," In *Expectations in Cross-Cultural Psychology,* ed. J. Deregowski, S. Dziurawiec, and R. C. Annis (Lisse, Netherlands: Swets and Zeitlinger, 1983).

18. G. Hofstede, "Cultural Constraints in Management Theories," *Academy of Management Executive* 7 (1993): 81–90.

19. G. Hofstede, "The Cultural Relativity of Organizational Theories," *Journal of International Business Studies* 14, (1983): 75–90.

20. L. Harrison, *Who Prospers: How Cultural Values Shape Economic and Political Success* (New York: Basic Books, 1992).

21. Ibid.

22. G. Hofstede, "Cultural Constraints in Management Theories."

23. S. Snell and J. Dean, "Integrated Manufacturing and Human Resource Management: A Human Capital Perspective," *Academy of Management Journal* 35 (1992): 467–504.

24. W. Johnston and A. Packer, *Workforce 2000: Work and Workers for the Twenty-first Century* (Indianapolis, Ind.: Hudson Institute, 1988).

25. H. Meyer, "Human Resource Management in the German Democratic Republic: Problems of Availability and the Use of Manpower Potential in the Sphere of the High-Qualification Spectrum in a Retrospective View," *Human Resource Management: An International Comparison,* ed. R. Peiper (Berlin: Walter de Gruyter, 1990).

26. P. Conrad and R. Peiper, "Human Resource Management in the Federal Republic of Germany," in *Human Resource Management: An International Comparison,* ed. R. Peiper (Berlin: Walter de Gruyter, 1990).

27. N. Adler and S. Bartholomew, "Managing Globally Competent People," *The Executive* 6, (1992): 52–65.

28. B. O'Reilly, "Your New Global Workforce," *Fortune,* December 14, 1992, 52–66.

29. Ibid.

30. Ibid.

31. J. Ledvinka and V. Scardello, *Federal Employment Regulation in Human Resource Management* (Boston: PWS–Kent, 1991).

32. Conrad and Peiper, "Human Resource Management in the Federal Republic of Germany."

33. R. Solow, "Growth with Equity through Investment in Human Capital," The George Seltzer Distinguished Lecture, University of Minnesota.

34. Adler, *International Dimensions of Organizational Behavior.*

35. S. Jackson & Associates, *Diversity in the Workplace: Human Resource Initiatives* (New York: The Guilford Press, 1991).

36. Adler & Bartholomew, "Managing Globally Competent People."

37. Ibid.

38. L. Copeland and L. Griggs, *Going International* (New York: Random House, 1985).

39. K. F. Misa and J. M. Fabriacatore, "Return on Investments of Overseas Personnel," *Financial Executive* 47 (April 1979): 42–46.

40. R. Tung, "Selection and Training Procedures of U.S., European, and Japanese Multinational Corporations," *California Management Review* 25, no. 1 (1982): 57–71.

41. Copeland and Griggs, *Going International.*

42. M. Mendenhall, E. Dunbar, and G. R. Oddou, "Expatriate Selection, Training, and Career-Pathing: A Review and Critique," *Human Resource Management* 26 (1987): 331–345.

43. M. Mendenhall and G. Oddou, "The Dimensions of Expatriate Acculturation," *Academy of Management Review* 10 (1985): 39–47.

44. R. Tung, "Selecting and Training of Personnel for Overseas Assignments," *Columbia Journal of World Business* 16, no. 2 (1981): 68–78.

45. Moran, Stahl, & Boyer, Inc., *International Human Resource Management* (Boulder, Colo.: Moran, Stahl, & Boyer, Inc., 1987).

46. J. S. Black and M. Mendenhall, "Cross-Cultural Training Effectiveness: A Review and Theoretical Framework for Future Research," *Academy of Management Review* 15 (1990): 113–136.

47. P. Dowling and R. Schuler, *International Dimensions of Human Resource Management* (Boston: PWS-Kent, 1990).

48. Adler, *International Dimensions.*

49. Dowling and Schuler, *International Dimensions.*

50. R. Schuler and P. Dowling, *Survey of ASPA/I Members* (New York: Stern School of Business, New York University, 1988).

51. "Workers Sent Overseas Have Adjustment Problems, a New Study Shows," *The Wall Street Journal,* June 19, 1984, 1.

52. J. S. Black, "Repatriation: A Comparison of Japanese and American Practices and Results," *Proceedings of the Eastern Academy of Management Bi-annual International Conference,* Hong Kong (1989): 45–49.

53. J. S. Black, "Coming Home: The Relationship of Expatriate Expectations with Repatriation Adjustment and Job Performance," *Human Relations* 45 (1992): 177–192.

54. Adler, *International Dimensions.*

55. Black, "Coming Home."

MANAGING AN ISRAELI SUBSIDIARY

National Semiconductor is a high-tech American-owned company located in Santa Clara, California. The firm is also the parent company of National Semiconductor, Israel. Although general values and goals are shared by both organizations, one of the major challenges of National Semiconductor was to manage the differences in cultures of American versus Israeli workers.

For example, workers in the United States are used to a culture that emphasizes the individual. U.S. workers tend to work alone, have a high need for privacy, have high mobility across organizations, go about problem solving in a systematic, organized way, feel high levels of personal responsibility, try to avoid conflict, are risk averse, and are quite accepting of hierarchical authority. Israeli workers, on the other hand, live in a culture where individuals are socialized to identify primarily with groups. Thus, they are more used to working as a group, have low mobility, are more spontaneous and improvisational in solving problems, tend toward conflict, and tend to question authority.

This presents a difficult managerial situation. The decision-making system at National Semiconductor, Israel must accentuate the strengths and minimize the weaknesses of both cultures. Thus, on one hand, the system must capitalize on the high technical skills and personal integrity of Israeli workers. At the same time, it must elicit the positive aspects of the American culture, such as taking a more systematic approach to problem solving. This was the problem faced by the Research and Development Center, which employed 150 engineers responsible for the design and development of integrated circuits, software, modems, fax machines, and other technologies.

QUESTIONS

1. What should the decision-making system at National Semiconductor, Israel look like?
2. How would you go about implementing this decision-making system?
3. What aspects of the Israeli culture might work against the system's implementation?

SOURCE: E. Lazar, "Values Must Blend in Overseas Operations," *Personnel Journal,* February 1993, 67–70.

4

THE LEGAL ENVIRONMENT AND EQUAL EMPLOYMENT OPPORTUNITY

Objectives   *After reading this chapter, you should be able to:*

1. Identify the three branches of government and the role each plays in influencing the legal environment of human resources management.
2. List the major federal laws that require equal employment opportunity and the protections provided by each of these laws.
3. Discuss the roles, responsibilities, and requirements of the federal agencies responsible for enforcing equal employment opportunity laws.
4. Identify the four theories of discrimination under Title VII of the Civil Rights Act and apply these theories to different discrimination situations.
5. Identify behavior that constitutes sexual harassment and list things that an organization can do to eliminate or minimize it.
6. Discuss the legal issues involved with preferential treatment programs.
7. Identify the types of reasonable accommodation required under the Americans with Disabilities Act.

Discrimination in the News

After writing three trial columns for *Scientific American's* "Amateur Scientist" column, which deals primarily with physics and tinkering, Forrest Mims III was not hired by the magazine's editor, Jonathon Piel. Former editors Timothy Appenzeller and Armand Schwab, Jr., believed that Piel didn't hire Mims because of Mims's creationist views, which might damage the magazine's credibility among mainstream biologists, who believe the world has evolved over billions of years. Some of Mims's colleagues came to his defense. Alcestis Oberg, an internationally recognized technical writer, said, "The nation was founded on the belief that nobody should be discriminated against on the basis of the race, creed, or color. That should be applied in journalism as it is in life." Harry Helms, an editor of a number of Mims's books, added, "It's like asking is Forrest black, or is Forrest a Jew?"

In another case, USX Corporation recently agreed to pay $42 million to resolve a class-action suit alleging that its hiring practices at its Fairless Works, near Philadelphia, discriminated against black applicants. The company said that during the period in question, 17 percent of the applicants it hired at the plant were black, whereas the labor market in the area was 11.5 percent black. However, the court ruled that the company had discriminated because blacks had made up 26 percent of the applicants at the plant. USX responded that quota hiring would have been the only way to avoid the court's finding of discrimination.

Finally, in an ironic example of the pervasiveness of discrimination lawsuits, an Hispanic civil rights group recently sued the Houston Equal Employment Opportunity Office, which is in charge of enforcing EEO regulations for the Houston area. The suit alleges patterns and practices of discrimination against women and Hispanics with regard to promotions, as well as retaliation against employees who allege these discriminatory practices. The suit deals with a specific management job category, Government Manager–13, which has a gross annual pay of $47,920. The suit notes that of the 12 Hispanic females in the local EEOC office staff, none of them has reached the GM-13 status.

SOURCE: J. Abernathy, "Journal's Firing of Creationist Draws Fire," *Houston Chronicle,* date unknown; P. Zengerle, "USX to Pay $42 Million in Suit over Hiring Bias," *Houston Chronicle,* 1991; J. Urban and J. Zuniga, "LULAC Complaint Filed Against EEOC," *Houston Chronicle,* February 19, 1993, 22A.

INTRODUCTION

In the opening chapter, we discussed the environment of the HR function, and we noted that a number of different environmental factors affect an organization's HRM function. One such is the legal environment, particularly the laws affecting the management of people. As could be seen in the two cases we just described, almost any employment decision can be made in such a way that it illegally discriminates against individuals or groups of individuals. In this chapter, we first present an overview of the U.S. legal system, noting the different legislative bodies, regulatory agencies, and judicial bodies that determine the legality of certain HRM practices. We then discuss the major laws and executive orders that govern these practices.

One point to make clear at the outset is that managers often want a list of "dos and don'ts" that will keep them out of legal trouble. They rely on rules such as "Don't ever ask a female applicant if she is married" without understanding the "why" behind these rules. Clearly, there are certain practices that are illegal or inadvisable, and this chapter will provide some valuable tips for avoiding discrimination lawsuits. However, such lists are not compatible with a strategic approach to HRM and are certainly not the route to developing a competitive advantage. They are simply mechanical reactions to the situations. Our goal is to provide an understanding of how the legislative, regulatory, and judicial systems work to define equal employment opportunity law. Armed with this understanding, a manager is better prepared to manage people within the limits imposed by the legal system. Doing so effectively is a source of competitive advantage.

The Regulatory Model

How does the regulatory system affect management decisions regarding human resource management? Figure 4.1 presents James Ledvinka's model for the legal environment of HR.[1] We will now discuss this model and the responsibilities of the various branches of government.

The first component of Ledvinka's model is "societal problems." When the public (or a special-interest group) perceives that a situation is not fair and that it can be rectified through government intervention, it exerts pressure on the government to act. The pressure is aimed at enacting legislation that addresses the problem. These laws can be written by Congress or the president, but they must be passed by both houses of Congress and signed into law by the president.

Once the laws are written and passed, they must be enforced. This comes about two ways. First, federal agencies, such as the Equal Employment Opportunity Commission (EEOC), enforce some laws, either by bringing lawsuits or by issuing regulatory rulings and conducting investigations. Second, the federal court system enforces laws by determining the outcomes of lawsuits that allege the laws have been broken. Court opinions also serve as regulatory actions in that they provide some direction for employers.

Finally, in response to these regulatory actions, management must respond by developing human resource policies and programs that ensure the company's compliance with the existing legal requirements. Given this overview of how regulations affect management decisions, let's look more deeply into this country's legal framework.

THE LEGAL SYSTEM IN THE UNITED STATES

The foundation for the U.S. legal system is set forth in the U.S. Constitution, which affects HR in two ways. First, it delineates a citizen's constitutional rights, on which the government cannot impinge.[2] Most individuals are aware of the "Bill of Rights," the first ten amendments to the Constitution, but other amendments, such as the Fourteenth Amendment, also influence

FIGURE 4.1   Regulatory Model of Equal Employment Opportunity

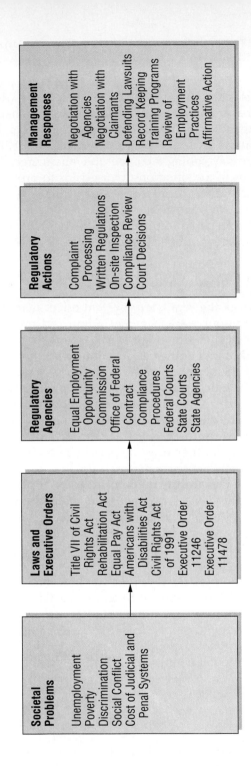

Societal Problems

Unemployment
Poverty
Discrimination
Social Conflict
Cost of Judicial and
    Penal Systems

Laws and Executive Orders

Title VII of Civil
    Rights Act
Rehabilitation Act
Equal Pay Act
Americans with
    Disabilities Act
Civil Rights Act
    of 1991
Executive Order
    11246
Executive Order
    11478

Regulatory Agencies

Equal Employment
    Opportunity
    Commission
Office of Federal
    Contract
    Compliance
    Procedures
Federal Courts
State Courts
State Agencies

Regulatory Actions

Complaint
    Processing
Written Regulations
On-site Inspection
Compliance Review
Court Decisions

Management Responses

Negotiation with
    Agencies
Negotiation with
    Claimants
Defending Lawsuits
Record Keeping
Training Programs
Review of
    Employment
    Practices
Affirmative Action

SOURCE: Adapted from James Ledvinka, *Federal Regulation of Personnel and Human Resource Management* (Boston: Kent Publishing, 1982), p. 23.

HR. The Fourteenth Amendment, also called the "equal protection clause," states that all individuals are entitled to equal protection under the law.

Second, the Constitution established three major governing bodies: the legislative, executive, and judicial branches. The Constitution explicitly defines the roles and responsibilities of each of these branches. Each branch has its own areas of authority, but these areas have often overlapped, and the borders between the branches are often blurred.

Legislative Branch

The legislative branch of the federal government consists of the House of Representatives and the Senate. These bodies develop laws that govern many HR activities. Most of the laws stem from a perceived societal need. For example, during the civil rights movement of the early 1960s, the legislative branch moved to ensure that various minority groups received equal opportunities in many areas of life. One of these areas was employment, and thus Congress enacted Title VII of the Civil Rights Act. Similar perceived societal needs have brought about labor laws such as the Occupational Safety and Health Act, the Employee Retirement Income Security Act, the Age Discrimination in Employment Act, and, more recently, the Americans with Disabilities Act (ADA) and the Civil Rights Act (CRA) of 1991.

Executive Branch

The executive branch consists of the president of the United States and the many regulatory agencies the president oversees. Although the legislative branch passes the laws, the executive branch affects these laws in many ways. First, the president can propose bills to Congress that, if passed, would become laws. Second, the president has the power to veto any law passed by Congress, thus ensuring that few laws are passed without presidential approval—which allows the president to influence how laws are written.

Third, the regulatory agencies, under the authority of the president, have responsibility for enforcing the laws. Thus, a president can influence what types of violations are pursued. For example, many laws affecting employment discrimination are enforced by the EEOC under the Department of Justice. During President Jimmy Carter's administration, the Department of Justice brought a lawsuit against Birmingham, Alabama's fire department for not having enough black firefighters. This suit resulted in a consent decree that required blacks to receive preferential treatment in hiring and promotion decisions. Two years later, during Ronald Reagan's administration, the Justice Department sided with white firefighters in a lawsuit against the city of Birmingham, alleging that the preferential treatment required by the consent decree discriminated against white firefighters.[3]

Fourth, the president can issue executive orders, which regulate the activities of organizations that have contracts with the federal government.

For example, Executive Order 11246, signed by President Lyndon Johnson, required all federal contractors and subcontractors to engage in affirmative action programs designed to hire and promote women and minorities within their organizations. Fifth, the president can influence the Supreme Court to interpret laws in certain ways. When particularly sensitive cases come before the Court, the attorney general, representing the executive branch, argues for certain preferred outcomes. Finally, the president appoints all the judges in the federal judicial system, subject to approval from the legislative branch. This affects the interpretation of many laws. In recent years, conservative federal judges appointed by Ronald Reagan and George Bush have been less prone to broad interpretations of federal laws. However, this might soon change as President Clinton has vowed to appoint judges with different judicial philosophies.

Judicial Branch

The judicial branch consists of the federal court system, which is made up of three levels. The first level consists of the U.S. District Courts and quasi-judicial administrative agencies. The district courts hear cases involving alleged violations of federal laws. The quasi-judicial agencies, such as the National Labor Relations Board (actually an arm of the executive branch, but serving a judicial function), hear cases regarding their particular jurisdictions (in this case, disputes between unions and management). If neither party to a suit is satisfied with the decision of the court at this level, the parties can appeal the decision to the U.S. Courts of Appeals. These courts were originally set up to ease the Supreme Court's case load, so appeals generally go from the federal trial level to one of the 13 appellate courts before they can be heard by the highest level, the Supreme Court. The Supreme Court must grant *certiorari* before hearing an appealed case. However, this is not usually granted unless two appellate courts have come to differing decisions on the same point of law or if the case deals with an important interpretation of constitutional law.

The Supreme Court serves as the court of final appeal. Decisions made by the Supreme Court are binding; they can be overturned only through legislation. For example, Congress, dissatisfied with the Supreme Court's decisions in certain cases such as *Wards Cove Packing v. Antonio*, overturned those decisions through the Civil Rights Act of 1991.[4]

Having described the legal system that affects the management of HR, we now explore some major laws that currently regulate HR activities, particularly equal employment opportunity laws. We first discuss the major laws that mandate equal employment opportunity in the United States. Then we examine the agencies involved in enforcing these laws. This leads us into an examination of the four theories of discrimination, with a discussion of some relevant court cases. Finally, we explore some equal employment opportunity issues facing today's managers.

EQUAL EMPLOYMENT OPPORTUNITY

Equal employment opportunity refers to the government's attempt to ensure that all individuals have an equal chance for employment, regardless of race, color, religion, sex, or national origin. To accomplish this, the federal government has used constitutional amendments, legislation, and executive orders as well as the court decisions that interpret these laws. The major EEO laws we discuss are summarized in Table 4.1.

Constitutional Amendments

Thirteenth Amendment.   The Thirteenth Amendment of the Constitution abolished slavery in the United States. Though one might be hard-pressed to cite an example of race-based slavery today, the thirteenth amendment has been applied in cases where the discrimination involved the "badges" (symbols) and "incidents" of slavery.

Fourteenth Amendment.   The Fourteenth Amendment forbids the state from taking life, liberty, or property without due process of law and prevents the states from denying the equal protection of the laws. Passed immediately after the Civil War, this amendment originally applied only to discrimination against blacks. It was soon broadened to protect other groups such as aliens and Orientals, and more recently it has been applied to the protection of whites in allegations of reverse discrimination. In *Bakke v. California Board of Regents*, David Bakke alleged that he had been discriminated against in the selection of entrants to the University of California at Davis medical school.[5] The university had set aside 16 of the available 100 places for "disadvantaged" applicants who were members of racial minority groups. Under this quota system, Bakke was able to compete for only 84 positions, whereas a minority applicant was able to compete for all 100. The court ruled in favor of Bakke, noting that this quota system had violated white individuals' right to equal protection under the law.

One important point regarding the Fourteenth Amendment is that it is applicable only to "state actions." This means that only the decisions or actions of the government or of private groups whose activities are deemed state actions can be construed as violations of the Fourteenth Amendment. Thus, one could file a claim under the Fourteenth Amendment if one were fired from a state university (a government organization), but not if one were fired by a private employer.

Congressional Legislation

The Reconstruction Civil Rights Acts (1866 and 1871).   The Thirteenth Amendment eradicated slavery in the United States, and the Reconstruction Civil Rights Acts were attempts to further this goal. The Civil Rights Act

TABLE 4.1

Summary of Major EEO Laws and Regulations

Act	Requirements	Covers	Enforcement Agency
Thirteenth Amendment	Abolished slavery	All individuals	Court system
Fourteenth Amendment	Provides equal protection for all citizens and requires due process in state action	State actions (e.g., decisions of governmental organizations)	Court system
Civil Rights Acts of 1866 and 1871 (as amended)	Grant all citizens the right to make, perform, modify, and terminate contracts and enjoy all benefits, terms, and conditions of the contractual relationship	All individuals	Court system
Equal Pay Act of 1963	Requires that men and women performing equal jobs receive equal pay	Employers engaged in interstate commerce	EEOC
Title VII of CRA	Forbids discrimination based on race, color, religion, sex, or national origin	Employers with 15 or more employees working 20 or more weeks per year; labor unions; and employment agencies	EEOC
Age Discrimination in Employment Act of 1967	Prohibits discrimination in employment against individuals between 40 and 70 years of age	Employers with 15 or more employees working 20 or more weeks per year; labor unions; employment agencies; federal government	EEOC
Rehabilitation Act of 1973	Requires affirmative action in the employment of handicapped individuals	Government agencies, federal contractors and subcontractors with contracts greater than $2,500	OFCCP
Pregnancy Discrimination Act	Prohibits discrimination in employment on the basis of pregnancy	Same as Title VII	EEOC
Americans with Disabilities Act	Prohibits discrimination against disabled individuals	Employers with more than 25 employees (until July, 1994, when it will cover employers with more than 15 employees)	EEOC
Executive Order 11246	Requires affirmative action in hiring women and minorities	Federal contractors and subcontractors with contracts greater than $10,000	OFCCP
Civil Rights Act of 1991	Prohibits discrimination (same as Title VII)	Same as Title VII, plus applies Section 1981 to employment discrimination cases	EEOC
Family and Medical Leave Act	Requires employers to provide 12 weeks of unpaid leave for family and medical emergencies	Employers with more than 50 employees	

passed in 1866 was later broken into two statutes. Section 1982 granted all persons the same property rights as white citizens. Section 1981 granted other rights, including the right to enter into and enforce contracts. Courts have interpreted Section 1981 as granting individuals the right to make and enforce *employment* contracts. The Civil Rights Act of 1871 granted all citizens the right to sue in federal court if they felt they had been deprived of some civil right. Although these laws might seem outdated, they are still used because they allow the plaintiff to recover both compensatory and punitive damages.

In fact, these laws came to the forefront in a recent Supreme Court case: *Patterson v. McClean Credit Union*.[6] The plaintiff had filed a discrimination complaint under Section 1981 for racial harassment. After being hired by McClean Credit Union, Patterson failed to receive any promotions or pay raises while she was employed there. She was also told that "blacks work slower than whites." Thus, she had grounds for discrimination and filed suit under Section 1981, arguing that she had been discriminated against in the making and enforcement of an employment contract. The Supreme Court ruled that this situation did not fall under Section 1981 because it did not involve the making and enforcement of contracts. However, the Civil Rights Act of 1991 amended this act to include the making, performance, modification, and termination of contracts, as well as all benefits, privileges, terms, and conditions of the contractual relationship.

The Equal Pay Act of 1963.   The Equal Pay Act, an amendment to the Fair Labor Standards Act, requires that men and women in the same organization who are doing equal work must be paid equally. The act defines *equal* in terms of skill, effort, responsibility, and working conditions. However, the act allows for reasons why men and women performing the same job might be paid differently. If the pay differences are the result of differences in seniority, merit, quantity or quality of production, or any factor other than sex (e.g., shift differentials or training programs), then differences are legally allowable.

Title VII of the Civil Rights Act of 1964.   This is the major legislation regulating equal employment opportunity in the United States. It was a direct result of the civil rights movement of the early 1960s, led by such individuals as Dr. Martin Luther King, Jr. It was Dr. King's philosophy that people should be "judged by the content of their character, and not the color of their skin." To ensure that employment opportunities would be based on one's character or ability rather than on their race, Congress wrote and passed Title VII, which President Lyndon Johnson signed into law.

Title VII states that it is illegal for an employer to "(1) fail or refuse to hire or discharge any individual, or otherwise discriminate against any individual with respect to his compensation, terms, conditions, or privileges of employment because of such individual's race, color, religion, sex, or national origin, or (2) to limit, segregate, or classify his employees or applicants for employment in any way that would deprive or tend to deprive any individual of employment opportunities or otherwise adversely affect his status as an employee because of such individual's race, color, religion, sex, or national origin." The act applies to organizations with 15 or more employees working 20 or more weeks a year that are involved in interstate commerce, as well as state and local governments, employment agencies, and labor organizations.

One interesting note is that the act originally excluded sex as a protected classification. Congress did not add sex because of a strong perceived need among the civil rights community to protect women from discrimination. Instead, a group of southern Democrats in Congress who vehemently opposed the act amended it to include sex in order to make it harder to pass. They perceived (wrongly) that, if the act included sex as a protected category, it could not garner enough votes for passage.

Age Discrimination in Employment Act (ADEA).   Passed in 1967 and amended in 1986, this act prohibits discrimination against employees over the age of 40. The act almost exactly mirrors Title VII in terms of its substantive provisions and the procedures to be followed in pursuing a case.[7] As with Title VII, the EEOC is responsible for enforcing this act.

The ADEA was designed to protect older employees when a firm reduces its work force through layoffs. By targeting older employees, who tend to have higher pay, a firm can substantially cut their labor costs. Recently, firms have often offered early retirement incentives, a possible violation of the act because of the focus on older employees. Early retirement incentives require employees to sign an agreement waiving their rights to sue under the ADEA. Courts have tended to uphold the use of early retirement incentives and waivers as long as the individuals were not coerced into signing the agreements, the agreements were presented in a way that the employees could understand, and the employees were given enough time to make a decision.[8]

However, age-discrimination complaints make up a large percentage of those filed with the EEOC, and the number of complaints continues to grow. In all of 1985, approximately 22,800 age-discrimination complaints were filed with the federal and state EEO agencies, but over 31,000 were filed in 1991. In addition, these cases can be costly. Most of the cases are settled out of court, but these settlements run from between $50,000 to $400,000 per employee.[9] In one recent case, Hazen Paper Company fired an employee after a disagreement regarding whether or not the employee deserved a raise. The employee claimed that Hazen willfully discriminated against him because of his age. Hazen has already paid $600,000 in damages and $500,000 in legal fees, and, pending the decision of an appeal, may be liable for an additional $560,000 in damages.[10]

The Vocational Rehabilitation Act of 1973.   This act covers executive agencies and contractors and subcontractors that receive more than $2,500 annually from the federal government. It requires them to engage in affirmative action for disabled individuals. Congress designed this act to encourage employers to actively recruit qualified disabled individuals and to make reasonable accommodations to allow them to become active members of the labor market. The Employment Standards Administration of the Department of Labor enforces this act.

Vietnam Era Veteran's Readjustment Act of 1974. Similar to the Rehabilitation Act, this act requires federal contractors and subcontractors to take affirmative action toward employing Vietnam veterans (those serving between August 5, 1964, and May 7, 1975). The OFCCP has authority to enforce this act.

Civil Rights Act of 1991. The Civil Rights Act of 1991 (CRA 1991) amends Title VII of the Civil Rights Act of 1964, Section 1981 of the Civil Rights Act of 1866, the Americans with Disabilities Act, and the Age Discrimination in Employment Act of 1967. Congress wrote this act in response to five 1989 Supreme Court case decisions. The *Wards Cove v. Antonio* decision dealt with the role of statistical disparities in proving discrimination.[11] The *Martin v. Wilks* case dealt with the right of nonminorities to contest consent decrees requiring affirmative action.[12] *Hopkins v. Price Waterhouse* was a case of sex discrimination, and the decision addressed which side has the burden of proof when a discriminatory motive is admitted, but defendant claims that the same decision would have been made without it.[13] *Patterson v. McClean Credit Union* addressed the applicability of Section 1981 to cases of employment discrimination.[14] Finally, *Lorance v. AT&T Technologies* was over defining the specific date of a discriminatory act when a seniority system is changed.[15] These decisions prompted civil rights activists to argue that the court was throwing the civil rights movement back 30 years.

We will discuss the specific amendments of CRA 1991 when they are applicable, particularly in our discussion of the different theories of discrimination. However, we would like to point out now that one of the major changes in EEO law under CRA 1991 has been the addition of compensatory and punitive damages in cases of discrimination under Title VII and the Americans with Disabilities Act. Before CRA 1991, Title VII limited damage claims to equitable relief such as back pay, lost benefits, front pay in some cases, and attorney's fees and costs. CRA 1991 allows compensatory and punitive damages when intentional or reckless discrimination is proven. Compensatory damages include such things as future pecuniary loss, emotional pain, suffering, and loss of enjoyment of life. Punitive damages are meant to discourage employers from discriminating by providing for payments to the plaintiff beyond the actual damages suffered.

Recognizing that one or a few discrimination cases could put an organization out of business, thus adversely affecting many innocent employees, Congress has put limits on the amount of punitive damages. Table 4.2 depicts these limits. As can be seen, damages range from $50,000 to $300,000 per violation, depending upon the size of the organization. Punitive damages are only available if the employer intentionally discriminated against the plaintiff(s) or if the employer discriminated with malice

TABLE 4.2   Maximum Punitive Damages Allowed under the Civil Rights Act of 1991

Employer Size	Damage Limit
14 to 100 employees	$50,000
101 to 200 employees	$100,000
201 to 500 employees	$200,000
More than 500 employees	$300,000

or reckless indifference to the employee's federally protected rights. These damages are excluded for an employment practice held to be unlawful because of its disparate impact.[16]

The addition of damages to CRA 1991 has had two immediate effects. First, by increasing the potential payoff for a successful discrimination suit, it has increased the number of suits filed against businesses. Second, organizations are now more likely to grant all employees an equal opportunity for employment, regardless of their race, gender, religion, or national origin. Many organizations have felt the need to make the composition of their work force mirror the general population to avoid costly lawsuits. This act adds a financial incentive for doing so.

Americans with Disabilities Act (ADA) of 1990.   According to the Census Bureau, the National Center for Medical Rehabilitation Research, and the National Center for Health Statistics:

- 22 million Americans have hearing impairments.
- 2 million have epilepsy.
- 16.4 million have heart disease.
- 1.2 million are partially or completely paralyzed.
- 6 million have missing extremities or parts of extremities.
- 18.4 have orthopedic impairments or deformities.
- 2.1 million have speech impairments.
- 645,000 use wheelchairs.

A 1986 Harris survey found that of the 18.3 million disabled Americans between the ages of 16 and 64, 12.2 million were not working. Yet, 8.2 million of those not working expressed that they would like to have a job. A 1987 Harris survey found that almost 80 percent of the managers surveyed rated the overall job performance of their disabled employees as good to excellent.

One of the most far-reaching acts concerning the management of human resources is the Americans with Disabilities Act. This act protects individuals with disabilities from being discriminated against in the workplace. It prohibits discrimination based on disability in all employment practices such as job application procedures, hiring, firing, promotions, compensation, and training—in addition to other employment activities such as advertising, recruitment, tenure, layoff, leave, and fringe benefits. It also requires that employers make "reasonable accommodations" for disabled employees, as long as the accommodations do not present an "undue burden." The specific issues regarding reasonable accommodation and undue burden will be discussed later in this chapter. The act covers employers with 25 or more employees starting July 26, 1992, and will be expanded to cover employers with 15 or more employees as of July 26, 1994. Because this act is so new, we will cover its various stipulations individually.

ADA defines a disability as a physical or mental impairment that substantially limits one or more major life activities, a record of having such an impairment, or being regarded as having such an impairment. The first part of the definition refers to individuals who have serious disabilities—such as epilepsy, blindness, deafness, or paralysis—that affect their ability to perform major life activities such as walking, seeing, performing manual tasks, learning, caring for oneself, and working. The second part refers to an individual who has a history of disability, such as someone who has had cancer but is currently in remission, someone with a history of mental illness, or someone with a history of heart disease. The third part of the definition, "being regarded as having a disability," refers, for example, to an individual who is severely disfigured and is denied employment because an employer fears negative reactions from others.[17]

Thus, ADA covers specific physiological disabilities such as cosmetic disfigurement, or anatomical loss affecting the neurological, musculoskeletal, sensory, respiratory, cardiovascular, reproductive, digestive, genitourinary, hemic, or lymphatic systems. In addition, it covers mental and psychological disorders such as mental retardation, organic brain syndrome, emotional or mental illness, and learning disabilities. However, conditions such as obesity, substance abuse, eye and hair color, and left-handedness are not covered.[18]

Pregnancy Discrimination Act of 1979.   This act protects pregnant women from discrimination. The act requires that pregnant women be treated as any other employees, based on their ability or inability to work. A woman cannot be refused a job or promotion, be fired, or otherwise discriminated against merely because she is pregnant or has had an abortion. She also cannot be forced to take a leave as long as she is able to work. Finally, if other employees are entitled to receive their jobs back after a leave, then this benefit must be offered to pregnant women.

It was believed that this act would provide the necessary opportunities for women to hold a job and have a family. However, because of the perception that this was not completely effective, as well as additional concerns regarding the impact of family emergencies on employment opportunities, the Family and Medical Leave Act was passed.

Family and Medical Leave Act of 1993.   This act was signed by President Bill Clinton on February 5, 1993. Although the act does not fall exactly under the rubric of EEO legislation, it does have a profound impact on the employment relationship and is particularly relevant to women in the work force. The act requires employers having more than 50 employees to provide 12 weeks of unpaid leave for employees after the birth or adoption of a child, to care for a seriously ill child, spouse, or parent, or in the case of the employee's own serious illness. The employer must guarantee the employee the same or a comparable job upon the employee's return. The act also requires the employer to pay the health-care coverage for the employee during the 12-week leave, but the employer can require the employee to reimburse these premiums if the employee fails to return to work. Employers are allowed to exempt "key" employees—defined as the highest-paid 10 percent of their work force—whose leave would cause substantial economic harm to the employer. Also exempt are employees who have not worked at least 1,250 hours (25 hours a week) in the previous 12 months.[19]

Executive Orders

Executive orders are directives issued and amended unilaterally by the president. These orders do not require congressional approval, yet they have the force of law. Three executive orders directly affect HRM.

Executive Order 11246.   President Johnson issued this executive order, which prohibits discrimination based on race, color, religion, sex, and national origin. Unlike Title VII, this order applies only to federal contractors and subcontractors. Employers receiving more than $10,000 from the federal government must take affirmative action to ensure against discrimination, and those with contracts greater than $50,000 must develop a written affirmative action plan for each of their establishments within 120 days of the beginning of the contract. The Office of Federal Contract Compliance, discussed later in this chapter, enforces this executive order.

Executive Order 11478.   President Richard M. Nixon issued this order, which requires the federal government to base all its employment policies on merit and fitness, and specifies that race, color, sex, religion, and national origin should not be considered. (The U. S. Office of Personnel Management is in charge of this.) The order also extends to all contractors and subcontractors doing $10,000 worth of business with the federal government. (The relevant government agencies have the responsibility to ensure that the contractors and subcontractors comply with the order.)

ENFORCEMENT OF EQUAL EMPLOYMENT OPPORTUNITY

As discussed previously, the executive branch of the federal government bears most of the responsibility for enforcing the laws passed by the legislative branch. In addition, the executive branch must enforce the executive orders issued by the president. The two agencies responsible for the enforcement of the laws and executive orders are the Equal Employment Opportunity Commission (EEOC) and the Office of Federal Contract Compliance Procedures (OFCCP), respectively.

Equal Employment Opportunity Commission (EEOC)

A division of the Department of Justice, the EEOC is responsible for enforcing most of the EEO laws, such as Title VII, the Equal Pay Act, and the Americans with Disabilities Act. The EEOC has three major responsibilities: investigating and resolving discrimination complaints, gathering information, and issuing guidelines.

Investigation and Resolution.   Table 4.3 depicts the deadlines for investigating and resolving a discrimination complaint. Individuals who feel they have been discriminated against must file a complaint with the EEOC or a similar state agency within 180 days of the incident. Failure to file a complaint within the 180 days results in the case's being dismissed immediately, with certain exceptions, such as the enactment of a seniority system that has an intentionally discriminatory purpose.

Once the complaint is filed, the EEOC takes responsibility for investigating the claim of discrimination. The complainant must give the EEOC 60 days to investigate the complaint. If the EEOC either does not believe the complaint to be valid or fails to complete the investigation, the complainant may sue in federal court. If the EEOC determines that discrimination has taken place, its representatives will attempt to provide a reconciliation between the two parties without burdening the court system with a lawsuit. Sometimes, the EEOC enters into a consent decree with the discriminating organization. This decree is an agreement between the agency and the organization that the organization will cease certain discriminatory practices and possibly institute additional affirmative action practices to rectify its history of discrimination.

If the EEOC cannot come to an agreement with the organization, there are two options. First, it can issue a "right to sue" letter to the alleged victim, which certifies that the agency has investigated and found validity in the victim's allegations. Second, although less likely, the agency may aid the alleged victim in bringing suit in federal court. In either case, the lawsuit must be filed in federal court within 300 days of the alleged discriminatory

TABLE 4.3   Deadlines for Filing a Discrimination Suit under Title VII

Deadlines	Example
Day	**Day**
0 ─┐ Date of alleged discriminatory act	┌ 0
	Employee files a complaint with the state Civil Rights Commission ─ 95
	Investigation takes place (60 days)
	Employee is now eligible to file suit in federal court ─155
180 ─ Final day to file a complaint with the EEOC or state agency in charge of enforcing EEO	
	Employee has until Day 300 to file the suit. After Day 300, the suit cannot be heard (unless it dealt with an intentionally discriminatory change in a seniority system) └─300
300 ─┘ Final day to file suit in federal court	

act. This cannot be overemphasized; many valid complaints lose their standing in court because of the failure to file the lawsuit on time.

Under former EEOC Chair Eleanor Norton-Holmes and into the term of her successor, Clarence Thomas, so many complaints were filed (particularly age-discrimination complaints) that EEOC investigators couldn't get to them all. Many cases were still being investigated after the 300-day deadline, nullifying the complainant's chances in court. The complainants assumed that once they had filed their claims with the EEOC, the agency would take complete control of the process, but this is not the case. The complainant has the sole responsibility for ensuring that all the deadlines provided in Title VII are met. Many valid cases of discrimination were lost simply because of the failure to meet the required deadlines.

However, thanks to the *Lorance v. AT&T Technologies* case, CRA 1991 now allows for exceptions to the 300-day deadline. In this case, the union voted to change its seniority system from a plantwide system to a departmentwide system. This meant that whenever individuals were transferred, or promoted to another department, they lost their seniority and were vulnerable to layoffs. The change was favored by the men in the union, opposed by the women. A few years later, when layoffs occurred, the women filed a lawsuit that claimed that the departmentwide seniority system discriminated against them. The Supreme Court ruled that the allegedly discriminatory act occurred on the date of the change in seniority systems; thus the case had been filed long past the 300-day deadline. CRA 1991 amended Title VII to provide exceptions to the 300-day deadline for filing lawsuits in cases where intentionally discriminatory seniority systems are being contested.

Information Gathering.   The EEOC also plays a role in monitoring the hiring practices of organizations. Each year, organizations with 100 or more employees must file a report (EEO-1) with the EEOC that provides the number of women and minorities employed in nine different job categories. The EEOC computer analyzes these reports to identify patterns of discrimination that can then be attacked through class-action suits.

Issuance of Guidelines.   A third responsibility of the EEOC is to issue guidelines that help employers determine when their decisions are violations of the laws enforced by the EEOC. These guidelines are not laws themselves, but the courts give great "deference" to them when hearing employment discrimination cases.

For example, the *Uniform Guidelines on Employee Selection Procedures* is a set of guidelines issued by the EEOC, the Department of Labor, the Department of Justice, and the U.S. Civil Service Commission.[20] This document provides guidance on the ways an organization should develop and administer selection systems so as not to violate Title VII. The courts often refer to the *Uniform Guidelines* to determine whether a company has engaged in discriminatory conduct or to determine the validity of the procedures it used to validate a selection system. Another example: Since the recent passage of the ADA, employers have been somewhat confused about the act's implications for their hiring procedures. Therefore, the EEOC issued guidelines in the *Federal Register* that provided more detailed information regarding what the agency will consider legal and illegal employment practices concerning disabled individuals. Although companies are well advised to follow these guidelines, it is possible that courts will interpret the ADA differently from the EEOC. Thus, through the issuance of guidelines the EEOC provides employers with directions for making employment decisions that do not conflict with existing laws.

Office of Federal Contract Compliance Procedures (OFCCP)

The OFCCP is the agency responsible for enforcing the executive orders that cover companies doing business with the federal government. Businesses with contracts for more than $50,000 cannot discriminate in employment based on race, color, religion, national origin, or sex, and they must have a written affirmative action plan on file.

These plans have three basic components.[21] First, the **utilization analysis** is a comparison of the race, sex, and ethnic composition of the employer's work force with that of the available labor supply. For each job group, the employer must identify the percentage of its work force with that characteristic (e.g., female) and identify the percentage of workers in the relevant labor market with that characteristic. If the percentage in the employer's work force is much less than the percentage in the comparison group, then that minority group is considered to be "underutilized."

Second, the employer must develop specific **goals and timetables** for achieving balance in the work force concerning these characteristics (particularly where underutilization exists). Goals and timetables specify the percentage of women and minorities that the employer seeks to have in each job group and the date by which that percentage is to be attained. These are not to be viewed as quotas. Quotas entail setting aside a specific number of positions to be filled only by members of the protected class. Goals and timetables are much more flexible, requiring only that the employer have specific goals and take steps toward the achievement of those goals. In fact, one study that examined companies with the goal of increasing black employment found that only 10 percent of them actually achieved their goals. Although this may sound discouragingly low, it is important to note that these companies increased their black employment more than companies that set no such goals.[22]

Third, employers with federal contracts must develop a list of **action steps** they will take toward attaining their goals to reduce underutilization. The company's CEO must make it clear to the entire organization that the company is committed to reducing underutilization, and all management levels must be involved in the planning process. Some steps that organizations can take is to communicate job openings to women and minorities through publishing the company's affirmative action policy, recruiting at predominantly female or minority schools, participating in programs designed to increase employment opportunities for underemployed groups, and taking steps to remove unnecessary barriers to employment. Organizations must also take affirmative steps toward hiring Vietnam veterans and disabled individuals.

The OFCCP annually audits government contractors to ensure that they have been actively pursuing the goals in their plans. These audits consist of (1) examining the company's affirmative action plan and (2) conducting on-site visits to examine how individual employees perceive the company's affirmative action policies. If the OFCCP finds that the contractors or subcontractors are not complying with the executive order, then its representatives may notify the EEOC (if there is evidence that Title VII has been violated), advise the Department of Justice to institute criminal proceedings, request that the Secretary of Labor cancel or suspend any current contracts, and forbid the firm from bidding on future contracts. This last penalty, called *debarment*, is the OFCCP's most potent weapon.

Having discussed the major laws defining equal employment opportunity and the agencies that enforce these laws, we now discuss the various types of discrimination and how these forms of discrimination have been interpreted by the courts in a number of cases.

TYPES OF DISCRIMINATION

How would you know if you had been discriminated against? Assume that you have applied for a job and were not hired. How do you know if the organization decided not to hire you because you are unqualified, because you are less qualified than the individual ultimately hired, or simply because the person in charge of the hiring decision "didn't like your type"? Discrimination is a multifaceted issue. It is often not easy to determine the extent to which unfair discrimination affects an employer's decisions.

Title VII of the Civil Rights Act provides three theories of discrimination: disparate treatment, disparate impact, and pattern or practice. In addition, there is protection for those participating in discrimination cases or opposing discriminatory actions. In the act, these theories are stated in very general terms. However, the court system has defined and delineated these theories through the cases brought before it. A comparison of the theories of discrimination is given in Table 4.4.

Disparate Treatment

Disparate treatment exists when individuals in similar situations are treated differently, and the different treatment is based on the individual's race, color, religion, sex, national origin, age, or disability status. If two people with the same qualifications apply for a job and the employer decides whom to hire based on one individual's race, the individual not hired is a victim of disparate treatment. Under the disparate treatment the plaintiff must prove that there was a discriminatory motive—that is, that the employer *intended* to discriminate.

Whenever individuals are treated differently because of their race, sex, and so on, there is disparate treatment. For example, if a company fails to hire women with school-age children (assuming the women will be frequently absent) but hires men with school-age children, the applicants are being treated differently based on sex. Another example would be an employer who checks the references and investigates the conviction records of minority applicants but does not do so for white applicants. Why are managers advised not to ask about marital status? Because in most cases, a manager will either ask only the female applicants, or, if the manager asks both males and females, he or she will make different assumptions about females ("She will have to move if her husband gets a job elsewhere") and the males ("He's very stable"). In all these examples, notice that (1) people are being treated differently, and (2) there is an actual intent to treat them differently.[23]

To understand how disparate treatment is applied in the law, let's look at how an actual court case, filed under disparate treatment, would proceed.

The Plaintiff's Burden.   As in any legal case, the plaintiff has the burden of proving that the defendant has committed an illegal act. This is the idea of a "prima facie" case. In a disparate treatment case, the plaintiff meets the prima facie burden by showing four things:

TABLE 4.4

Comparison of Discrimination Theories

Types of Discrimination	Disparate Treatment	Disparate Impact	Pattern and Practice
Show Intent?	Yes	No	Yes
Prima facie case	Individual is member of a protected group, was qualified for the job, was turned down for the job, and the job remained open	Statistical disparity in the effects of a facially neutral employment practice	Statistical disparity in the composition of a work force, and individual cases of discrimination
Employer's defense	Produce a legitimate, non-discriminatory reason for the employment decision or show BFOQ	Prove that the employment practice bears a manifest relationship with job performance	Cite Title VII's statement that the act does not require a firm's work force to mirror that of the population
Defendant's rebuttal	Reason offered was merely a "pretext" for discrimination	Alternative procedures exist which meet the employer's goal without having disparate impact	
Monetary Damages	Compensatory and punitive damages	Equitable relief (e.g., back pay)	Compensatory and punitive damages

1. The plaintiff belongs to a protected group.
2. The plaintiff applied for and was qualified for the job.
3. Despite possessing the qualifications, the plaintiff was rejected.
4. After the plaintiff was rejected, the position remained open and the employer continued to seek applicants with similar qualifications, or the position was filled by someone with similar qualifications.

Although these four things may seem easy to prove, it is important to note that what the court is trying to do is rule out the most obvious reasons for rejecting the plaintiff's claim (i.e., the plaintiff did not apply or was not qualified, or the position was already filled or had been eliminated). If these alternative explanations are ruled out, the court assumes that the hiring decision was based on a discriminatory motive.

The Defendant's Rebuttal.   Once the plaintiff has made the prima facie case for discrimination, the burden shifts to the defendant to produce some legitimate, nondiscriminatory reason for not hiring the plaintiff. One legitimate nondiscriminatory reason would be that, though the plaintiff was qualified, the defendant hired an individual with even better qualifications. Another possible defense would be that, for this job, race, sex, religion, and so on, was a **bona fide occupational qualification (BFOQ)**. For example, if one were hiring an individual to hand out towels in a women's locker room, being a woman might be a BFOQ. However, there are very few cases in which race or sex qualify as a BFOQ, and in these cases it must be a *necessary*, rather than simply a preferred, characteristic of the job.

UAW v. Johnson Controls, Inc., illustrates the difficulty in using a BFOQ as a defense.[24] Johnson Controls, a manufacturer of car batteries, had instituted a "fetal protection" policy that excluded women of childbearing age from a number of jobs in which they would be exposed to lead, which can cause birth defects in children. The company argued that sex was a BFOQ, essential to maintaining a safe workplace. The Supreme Court did not uphold the company's policy, arguing that BFOQs are limited to policies that are directly related to a worker's ability to do the job.

The Plaintiff's Rebuttal. If the defendant provides a legitimate, nondiscriminatory reason for its employment decision, the burden shifts back to the plaintiff. The plaintiff must now show that the reason offered by the defendant was not in fact the reason for its decision but merely a "pretext" or excuse for its actual discriminatory decision. This could entail providing evidence that white applicants with very similar qualifications to the plaintiff have often been hired while black applicants with very similar qualifications were all rejected. To illustrate disparate treatment, let's look at the first major case dealing with disparate treatment, *McDonnell Douglas Corp. v. Green.*

McDonnell Douglas Corp. v. Green. This Supreme Court case was the first to delineate the four criteria for a prima facie case of discrimination. From 1956 to 1964, Green had been an employee at McDonnell Douglas, a manufacturing plant in St. Louis, Missouri, that employed about 30,000 people. In 1964, he was laid off during a general work force reduction. While unemployed, he participated in some activities that the company undoubtedly frowned upon: a "lock-in," where he and others placed a chain and padlock on the front door of a building to prevent the employees from leaving; and a "stall-in," where a group of employees stalled their cars at the gates of the plant so that no one could enter or leave the parking lot. About three weeks after the lock-in, McDonnell Douglas advertised for qualified mechanics, Green's trade, and he reapplied. When the company rejected his application, he sued, arguing that the company didn't hire him because of his race and because of his persistent involvement in the civil rights movement.

In making his prima facie case, Green had no problem showing that he was a member of a protected group, that he had applied for and was qualified for the job (having already worked in the job), that he was rejected, and that the company continued to advertise the position. The company's defense was that the plaintiff was not hired because he participated in the lock-in and the stall-in. In other words, the company was merely refusing to hire a troublemaker.

The plaintiff responded that the company's stated reason for not hiring him was a pretext for discrimination. He pointed out the fact that white employees who had participated in the same activities (the lock-in and stall-in) were rehired, whereas he was not. The court found in favor of the plaintiff.

This case illustrates how similarly situated individuals (white and black) can be treated differently (whites hired back while blacks were not) and the differences in treatment can be based on race. As we discuss later, most plaintiffs bring cases of sexual harassment under this theory of discrimination, sexual harassment being a situation where individuals are treated differently because of their sex.

Mixed-Motive Cases.   In a mixed-motive case, the defendant acknowledges that some discriminatory motive existed but argues that the same hiring decision would have been reached even without the discriminatory motive. In *Hopkins v. Price Waterhouse,* Elizabeth Hopkins was an accountant who had applied for partnership in her firm. Although she had brought in a large amount of business and had received high praise from her clients, she was turned down for a partnership on two separate occasions. In her performance reviews, she had been told to adopt more feminine dress and speech and received many other comments that suggested gender-based stereotypes. In court, the company admitted that a sex-based stereotype existed but argued that it would have come to the same decision (i.e., not promoted Hopkins) even if the stereotype had not existed.

One of the main questions that came out of this case was, Who has the burden of proof? Does the plaintiff have to prove that a different decision would have been made (i.e., that Hopkins would have been promoted) in the absence of the discriminatory motive? Or does the defendant have to prove that the same decision would have been made?

According to CRA 1991, if the plaintiff demonstrates that race, sex, color, religion, or national origin was a motivating factor for any employment practice, the prima facie burden has been met, and the burden of proof is on the employer to demonstrate that the same decision would have been made even if the discriminatory motive had not been present. If the employer can do this, the plaintiff cannot collect compensatory or punitive damages. However, the court may order the employer to quit using the discriminatory motive in its future employment decisions.

Disparate Impact

The second type of discrimination is called **disparate impact**. It occurs when a facially neutral employment practice disproportionately excludes a protected group from employment opportunities. A facially neutral employment practice is one that lacks obvious discriminatory content yet affects one group to a greater extent than other groups, such as an employment test. Although the Supreme Court inferred disparate impact from Title VII in the *Griggs v. Duke Power* case, it has since been codified into the Civil Rights Act of 1991.

There is an important distinction between disparate impact and disparate treatment discrimination. For there to be discrimination under disparate treatment, there has to be intentional discrimination. Under disparate impact, intent is irrelevant. The important criterion is that the consequences of the employment practice are discriminatory.

For example, if, for some practical reason, you hired individuals based on their height, you may not have intended to discriminate against anyone, and yet using height would have a disproportionate impact on certain protected groups. Women tend to be shorter than men, so fewer women will be hired. Certain ethnic groups, such as Orientals, also tend to be shorter than those of European ancestry. Thus, your facially neutral employment practice will have a disparate impact on certain protected groups. The "Competing through Technology and Structure" box explains how one company has tried to eliminate disparate impact.

This is not to imply that simply because a selection practice has disparate impact it is necessarily illegal. Some characteristics (such as height) are not equally distributed across race and gender groups, and in some jobs, these characteristics may be related to successful performance in the job. However, the important question is whether the characteristic is related to successful performance on the job. To help you understand how disparate impact works, let's look at a court proceeding involving a disparate impact claim.

The Plaintiff's Burden.   In a disparate impact case, the plaintiff must make the prima facie case by showing that the employment practice in question disproportionately affects a protected group relative to the majority group. To illustrate this theory, let's assume that you are a manager who has 60 positions to fill. Your applicant pool has 80 white and 40 black applicants. You use a test that selects 48 of the white and 12 of the black applicants. Is this a disparate impact? Two alternative quantitative analyses are often used to determine whether a test has adverse impact.

The **four-fifth's rule** states that a test has disparate impact if the hiring rate for the minority group is less than four–fifths (or 80%) of the hiring rate for the majority group. Applying this analysis to the example above, we would first calculate the hiring rates for each group:

$$\text{Whites} = 48/80 = 60\%$$

$$\text{Blacks} = 12/40 = 30\%$$

Then we would compare the hiring rate of the minority group (30%) with that of the majority group (60%). Using the four-fifth's rule, we would determine that the test has adverse impact if the hiring rate of the minority group is less than 80 percent of the hiring rate of the majority group. Because it is less (i.e., 30%/60% = 50%, which is less than 80%), we would conclude that the test has adverse impact. The four-fifth's rule is used as a "rule of thumb" by the EEOC in determining adverse impact.

The **standard deviation rule** uses actual probability distributions to determine adverse impact. This analysis uses the difference between the expected representation (or hiring rates) for minority groups and the actual

Technology & Structure

TECHNOLOGICAL SOLUTIONS TO DISPARATE IMPACT AT CARRIER

One of the major problems with many manufacturing and assembly jobs is that the job requirements tend to favor men over women. Many jobs require substantial levels of physical strength because of the need to lift or move heavy objects. Companies that hope to hire the best employees for these jobs tend to use some type of test of physical abilities to ensure that employees possess the necessary strength to perform the job. However, because women are, on average, somewhat weaker physically than men, these tests tend to have disparate impact against females.

However, a few companies are increasingly attempting to provide technological solutions to problems such as this. Carrier Corporation, a manufacturer of air-conditioning systems, has found one technological solution. In an effort to remain competitive, Carrier determined that it would have to assemble the compressors for their air-conditioning units, and this required building a new plant. In designing the plant, the company attempted to consider how physical abilities might limit the labor pool.

The answer was to build the plant with highly automated technology that would minimize the physical ability requirements. Thus, through technological innovation, Carrier designed the workplace so that women are capable of performing any job. The plant is designed so that no employee ever has to lift an object heavier than 12 pounds. This has allowed Carrier to have women and men working side-by-side in every work unit, something unheard of in most manufacturing plants. Carrier exemplifies a concern for promoting diversity in employment and using creative solutions to problems that tend to stifle diversity.

SOURCE: E. Norton, "Small Flexible Plants May Play Crucial Role in U.S. Manufacturing," *The Wall Street Journal,* January 13, 1993, A1–2.

representation (or hiring rate) to determine whether the difference between these two values is greater than would occur by chance. Thus, in our example, 33 percent (40 of 120) of the applicants were blacks, so one would expect 33 percent (20 of 60) of those hired to be black. However, only 12 black applicants were hired. To determine if the difference between the expected representation and the actual representation is greater than we would expect by chance, we calculate the standard deviation (which, you might remember from your statistics class, is the standard deviation in a binomial distribution):

$$\sqrt{\text{Number Hired} \times \frac{\text{Number of Minority Applicants}}{\text{Number of Total Applicants}}}$$

$$\times \frac{\text{Number of Nonminority Applicants}}{\text{Number of Total Applicants}}$$

or, in this case:

$$\sqrt{60 \times \frac{40}{120} \times \frac{80}{120}} = 3.6$$

If the difference between the actual representation and the expected representation (eight in this case) of blacks is greater than 2 standard deviations (2 × 3.6, or 7.2 in this case), we would conclude that the test had adverse impact against blacks, because we would expect this result less than 1 time in 20 if the test were equally difficult for both whites and blacks.

The *Wards Cove Packing Co. v. Antonio* case involved an interesting use of statistics. The plaintiffs showed that the jobs in the cannery (lower-paying jobs) were filled primarily with minority applicants (in this case, American Eskimos). However, only a small percentage of the noncannery jobs (those with higher pay) were filled by nonminorities. The plaintiffs argued that this statistical disparity in the racial makeup of the cannery and noncannery jobs was proof of discrimination. The federal district, appellate, and Supreme Courts all found for the defendant, stating that this disparity was not proof of discrimination. However, the Supreme Court went further and stated that the burden of proof always lies with the plaintiff.

One of the major issues in the debate over CRA 1991 was deciding who has the burden of proof in disparate impact cases. In *Griggs v. Duke Power*, the court found that once the plaintiff had made the prima facie case (i.e., established statistical disparities in hiring), the burden of proof shifted to the defendant. In the *Wards Cove* case, the Supreme Court ruled that the burden of proof always lies with the plaintiff, which means that the defendant merely has to "produce" a legitimate nondiscriminatory goal that it hoped to achieve with the employment practice—thus lessening the defendant's burden (although it is the same burden required under disparate treatment). CRA 1991 changed disparate impact theory by (1) codifying the theory of disparate impact (previously only inferred from the *Griggs* decision) and (2) requiring that, once the prima facie case has been met by showing a statistical disparity, the burden of proof falls on the defendant. To sustain a business-necessity defense, the defendant must prove that the employment practice bears a relationship to the employment practice in question. Thus, the law mandates the same burdens required under the *Griggs* decision.[25]

Once the plaintiff has demonstrated adverse impact, he or she has met the burden of a prima facie case of discrimination.

Defendant's Rebuttal.   According to CRA 1991, once the plaintiff has made a prima facie case, the burden of proof shifts to the defendant, who must show that the employment practice is a "business necessity." This is accomplished by showing that the practice bears a relationship with some legitimate employer goal. With respect to job selection, this relationship is demonstrated by showing the job relatedness of the test, usually by reporting a validity study of some type (to be discussed in Chapter 11). For now suffice it to say that the employer shows that the test scores are significantly correlated with measures of job performance.

Measures of job performance used in validation studies can include such things as objective measures of output, supervisor ratings of job performance, and success in training.[26] Normally, performance-appraisal ratings are used, but these ratings must be valid for the court to accept the validation results. For example, in *Albermarle Paper v. Moody,* the employer demonstrated that the selection battery predicted performance (measured with supervisors' overall rankings of employees) in only some of the 13 occupational groups in which it was used. In this case, the court was especially critical of the supervisory ratings used as the measure of job performance. The court stated, "There is no way of knowing precisely what criterion of job performance the supervisors were considering."[27]

Plaintiff's Rebuttal.   If the employer shows that the employment practice is the result of some business necessity, the plaintiff's last resort is to argue that there are other employment practices that could sufficiently meet the employer's goal, practices that would not have adverse impact. Thus, if a plaintiff can demonstrate that selection tests other than the one used by the employer exist, that they do not have adverse impact, and that they correlate with job performance as highly as the employer's test, then the defendant can be found guilty of discrimination. Many cases deal with standardized tests of cognitive ability, and it is important to examine alternatives to these tests that have less adverse impact while still meeting the employer's goal. At least two separate studies reviewing alternative selection devices such as interviews, biographical data, assessment centers, and work sample tests have concluded that none of them met both criteria.[28] Thus, it seems that when the employment practice in question is a standardized test of cognitive ability, plaintiffs will have a difficult time rebutting the defendant's rebuttal.

Griggs v. Duke Power.   To illustrate how this process works, let's look at the *Griggs v. Duke Power* case.[29] Following the passage of Title VII, Duke Power instituted a new system for making selection and promotion decisions. The system required either a high school diploma or a passing score on two professionally developed tests (the Wonderlic Personnel Test and the Bennett Mechanical Comprehension Test). A passing score was set so that it would be equal to the national median for high school graduates who had taken the tests.

The plaintiffs met their prima facie burden showing that both the high school diploma requirement and the test battery had adverse impacts on blacks. According to the 1960 census, 34 percent of white males had high school diplomas, compared with only 12 percent of black males. Similarly, 58 percent of white males passed the test battery, whereas only 6 percent of blacks passed.

Duke Power was unable to defend its use of these employment practices. A company vice-president testified that the company had not studied the relationship between these employment practices and the employees' ability to perform the job. In addition, employees already on the job who did not have high school diplomas and had never taken the tests were performing satisfactorily. Thus, Duke Power lost the case.

It is interesting to note that the court recognized that the company had not intended to discriminate, mentioning the fact that the company was making special efforts to help undereducated employees through financing two-thirds of the cost of tuition for high school training. This illustrates the importance of the *consequences,* as opposed to the *motivation,* in determining discrimination under the disparate impact theory.

Pattern or Practice

The third kind of discrimination is called **pattern or practice**. Title VII allows for special discrimination lawsuits that are brought by the attorney general. According to Section 707 of the act, if there is reasonable cause to believe that a person or a group is engaging in a "pattern or practice" that denies the rights provided by Title VII, the attorney general may bring a lawsuit against them. This kind of lawsuit can be thought of as classwide disparate treatment. As with the disparate treatment theory, it must be proven that the employer *intended* to discriminate against a particular class of individuals. However, plaintiffs can usually demonstrate this by showing a statistical disparity between the work force and a relevant comparison group and by showing that this disparity is the result of some discriminatory motive.

In pattern-or-practice suits, the major debate is usually over what constitutes a statistical comparison group or what the relevant labor market is. A relevant labor market consists of those workers who have the skills needed to perform the job and who are within reasonable commuting distance to that job. Often, the definition of the relevant labor market (i.e., what constitutes having the skills and/or what is a reasonable commuting distance) determines whether a protected group is underrepresented in an organization.

In *Hazelwood School District v. United States*, the attorney general had brought a lawsuit against a suburban St. Louis school district for allegedly engaging in a "pattern or practice" of employment discrimination.[30] The focus of the case was a comparison between the percentage of blacks on the school district's work force and the percentage of blacks in other comparison groups. According to the 1970 census, 5.7 percent of the nation's teachers were black, 15.4 percent of the teachers in the St. Louis area were black, and 42 percent of the teachers in the city of St. Louis were black. But the Hazelwood school district had only hired its first black school teacher in 1969, and between 1972 and 1974, only 3.7 percent of the teachers it hired were black.

The plaintiff argued that the relevant comparison groups should be the teachers in the St. Louis area and the teachers in the city of St. Louis, which resulted in large disparities (3.7 percent compared with either 15.4 percent or 42 percent). In addition, the plaintiffs cited instances of individual discrimination, such as the fact the 16 black applicants who were turned down for jobs met the criteria set forth in *McDonnell Douglas v. Green* for a prima facie case of disparate treatment discrimination. However, the school district argued that these comparisons were unfair, because the city of St. Louis had an affirmative action hiring plan that was (1) inflating the percentages of black teachers in the area and (2) stealing potential black teachers from their recruiting pool.

The Supreme Court remanded the case to the district court to consider such issues as whether the racially based hiring policies of the St. Louis School District were in effect as far back as 1970, the extent to which these policies changed the district's racial composition, the extent to which they diverted to the city teachers who might otherwise have been recruited by Hazelwood, and the extent to which teachers employed by the city would prefer to be employed by other districts such as Hazelwood. As you can see, lawsuits brought under the theory of pattern-or-practice discrimination tend to focus on comparative statistics, and much of the argument centers on what constitutes the relevant comparison group.

Notice that the plaintiff had to show a statistical disparity between the organization's work force and the relevant labor market. However, the plaintiff also had to demonstrate that there was some discriminatory intent, which was shown by citing the number of individuals who would have met the prima facie burden in a disparate treatment cast. The prospect of pattern-or-practice lawsuits often prompts companies to keep an eye on how close their minority representation compares with that of the relevant work force.

Retaliation for Participation and Opposition

Suppose that you overhear a supervisor in your workplace telling someone that he refuses to hire women because he knows they are just not cut out for the job. Believing this to be illegal discrimination, you face a dilemma. Should you come forward and report this statement? Or, if someone else files a lawsuit for gender discrimination, should you testify on behalf of the plaintiff? What happens if your employer threatens to fire you if you do anything?

Title VII of the Civil Rights Act of 1964 provides you with some protection. It states that employers cannot retaliate against employees for either "opposing" a perceived illegal employment practice or "participating in a proceeding" related to an alleged illegal employment practice. *Opposition* refers to expressing to someone through proper channels that you believe that an illegal employment act has taken place or is taking place. *Participation* refers to actually testifying in an investigation, hearing, or court proceeding regarding an illegal employment act. Clearly, the purpose of this provision is to protect employees from employers' threats and other forms of intimidation aimed at discouraging the employees from bringing to light acts they believe to be illegal.

These cases can be extremely costly for companies because they are alleging acts of intentional discrimination, and therefore plaintiffs are entitled to punitive damages. For example, one 41-year-old former Allstate employee who claimed that a company official told her that the company wanted a "younger and cuter" image recently was awarded $2.8 million in damages from an Oregon jury. The jury concluded that she was forced out of the company for opposing age discrimination against other employees.[31]

This does not mean that employees have an unlimited right to talk about how racist or sexist their employers are. The courts tend to frown on employees whose activities result in a poor public image for the company unless those employees had attempted to use the organization's internal channels—approaching one's manager, raising the issue with the HR department, and so on—before going public.

CURRENT ISSUES REGARDING DIVERSITY AND EQUAL EMPLOYMENT OPPORTUNITY

Because of recent changes in the labor market, most organizations' demographic compositions are becoming increasingly diverse. A study by the Hudson Institute projected that 85 percent of the new entrants in to the U.S. labor force over the next decade will be females and minorities.[32] Integrating these groups into organizations made up predominantly of white males will bring attention to important issues like sexual harassment, affirmative action, and the "reasonable accommodation" of disabled employees.

Sexual Harassment

The Clarence Thomas Supreme Court confirmation hearings in 1992 brought the issue of sexual harassment into increased prominence. Anita Hill, one of Thomas's former employees, alleged that he had sexually harassed her while she was working under him at the Department of Education and the Equal Employment Opportunity Commission. Although the allegations were never substantiated, the hearing made many people more aware of how often people are sexually harassed in the workplace. The "Competing through Globalization" box demonstrates that sexual harassment is a worldwide problem as well.

Sexual harassment refers to unwelcome sexual advances (See Table 4.5). It can take place in two basic ways. "Quid pro quo" harassment occurs when some kind of benefit or punishment is made contingent upon the employee submitting to sexual advances. For example, a male manager tells his female secretary that if she submits to sex with him, he will help her get promoted, or he threatens to fire her if she fails to do so; these are clearly cases of quid pro quo sexual harassment.

The *Bundy v. Jackson* case illustrates a case of quid pro quo sexual harassment.[35] Sandra Bundy was a personnel clerk with the District of Columbia Department of Corrections. She received repeated sexual propositions from Delbert Jackson, who was at the time a fellow employee (although he later became the director of the agency). She later began to

Globalization

COMPETING THROUGH

SEXUAL HARASSMENT OVERSEAS

Sexual harassment problems are not limited to the United States, and therefore companies that operate in other nations need to be aware of international differences in the prevalence of this problem. Companies also need to be familiar with the protections that are available to their workers who are living and working in different countries.

A recent survey of 23 nations conducted by the International Labor Office (ILO), for example, indicates that between 15 percent and 30 percent of the women surveyed in these countries have experienced sexual harassment from supervisors or coworkers. One major trouble spot is Spain, for example, where 84 percent of women workers reported that sexual remarks or jokes were directed toward them while on the job. Seventy-seven percent were inappropriately touched by male supervisors or coworkers. Japan can also be problematic in that 82 percent of women surveyed said they were subject to *seku hara,* the Japanese term for sexual harassment. This was particularly problematic when working after hours and serving alcohol to male colleagues (a practice that is obligatory in the job description of many of these workers).

Harassment of one employee by another is not the only form that this problem can take. In many international locations, sexual harassment of employees by "third parties" (e.g., clients) is much more of a problem than employee–employee harassment. Even though control over third parties is somewhat limited, as a recent case involving Trans World Airlines indicates, employers can still be held liable for such harassment if it can be proven that the employer was knowledgeable of the problem and did nothing to stop it.

Fortunately, other countries are now cracking down on sexual harassment. Seven nations, including France, Belgium, Australia, Canada, New Zealand, Spain, and Sweden have laws similar to those in the United States. Still others such as Japan cover such matters with legislation dealing with "unfair firing." Yet, there are still countries such as the Netherlands and Russia where there isn't even a parallel translation for the phrase "sexual harassment" (although both Russian and Dutch women immediately recognized the concept when explained by ILO surveyors). Clearly, if a company wants to be able to compete by sending its best personnel into international locales, it must recognize that these people need to be protected from harassment, and this may be trickier in some places than in others.

SOURCES: A. Karr, "Issue of Sex Harassment at Workplace Is Gaining More Attention Worldwide," *The Wall Street Journal,* December 1, 1992, A16; L.A. Winokur, "Harassment of Workers by 'Third Parties' Can Lead to Maze of Legal, Moral Issues," *The Wall Street Journal,* October 26, 1992, B1-B4.

receive propositions from two of her supervisors, Arthur Burton and James Gainey. When she raised the issue to their supervisor, Lawrence Swain, he dismissed her complaints, told her that "any man in his right mind would want to rape you," and asked her to begin a sexual relationship with him. When Bundy became eligible for a promotion, she was passed over because of her "inadequate work performance," although she had never been told that her work performance was unsatisfactory. The U.S. Court of Appeals found that Bundy had been discriminated against because of her sex, thereby extending the idea of discrimination to sexual harassment.

TABLE 4.5   EEOC Definition of Sexual Harassment

Unwelcome sexual advances, requests for sexual favors and other verbal or physical contact of a sexual nature constitute sexual harassment when

1. submission to such conduct is made either explicitly or implicitly a term of condition of an individual's employment,

2. submission to or rejection of such conduct by an individual is used as the basis for employment decisions affecting such individual, or

3. such conduct has the purpose or effect of unreasonably interfering with an individual's work performance or creating an intimidating, hostile or offensive working environment.

SOURCE: EEOC Guideline based on the Civil Rights Act of 1964, Title VII.

A more subtle, and possibly more pervasive form of sexual harassment is "hostile working environment". This occurs when someone's behavior in the workplace creates an environment that makes it difficult for someone of a particular sex to work. Many plaintiffs in sexual harassment lawsuits have alleged that men ran their fingers through the plaintiffs' hair, made suggestive remarks, and physically assaulted them by touching their intimate body parts. Other examples include: having pictures of naked women posted in the workplace, using offensive sexually explicit language, or using sexual innuendo in conversations.

It is important to note that these types of behaviors are actionable under Title VII because they treat individuals differently based on their sex. The courts have tended to define a prima facie case of sexual harassment as consisting of the following five things:

1. The plaintiff was a member of a protected class.

2. The plaintiff was subject to unwelcome sexual advances.

3. The harassment was based on sex.

4. The harassment was sufficiently severe or pervasive to alter the terms, conditions, or privileges of employment.

5. The employer was liable for the actions of its employees.[36]

There are three critical issues in these cases. First, the plaintiff cannot have "invited or incited" the advances. Often, the plaintiff's sexual history, whether she or he wears provocative clothing, and whether she or he engages in sexually explicit conversations are used to prove or disprove that the advance was unwelcome. However, in the absence of substantial evidence that the plaintiff invited the behavior, courts usually lean toward assuming that sexual advances do not belong in the workplace and thus are unwelcome. In *Meritor Savings Bank v. Vinson*, Michelle Vinson claimed that during the four years she worked at a bank she was continually harassed by the bank's vice-president, who repeatedly asked her to have sex (she eventually agreed) and sexually assaulted her.[37] The Supreme Court ruled that the victim's voluntary participation in sexual relations was not the major issue, that the focus of the case was on whether or not the vice-president's advances were unwelcome.

A second critical issue is that the harassment must have been severe enough to alter the terms, conditions, and privileges of employment. Although it has not yet been consistently applied, many courts have used the "reasonable woman" standard in determining the severity or pervasiveness of the harassment. This consists of assessing whether a reasonable woman, faced with the same situation, would have reacted similarly. The reasonable woman standard recognizes that behavior that might be considered appropriate by a man (e.g., off-color jokes) might not be considered appropriate by a woman.

The third issue is that the courts must determine whether the organization is liable for the actions of its employees. In doing so, the court usually examines two things. First, did the employer know about, or should he or she have known about, the harassment? Second, did the employer act to stop the behavior? If the employer knew about it and the behavior did not stop, the court usually decides that the employer did not act appropriately to stop it.

To ensure a workplace free from sexual harassment, there are some important steps that organizations can follow. First, the organization can develop a policy statement that makes it very clear that sexual harassment will not be tolerated in the workplace. Second, all employees, new and old, can be trained to identify inappropriate workplace behavior. Third, the organization can develop a mechanism for reporting sexual harassment that encourages people to speak out. Fourth, management can prepare to take prompt disciplinary action with those who commit sexual harassment as well as appropriate action to protect the victims of sexual harassment.[38]

Affirmative Action and Reverse Discrimination

Few would argue that having a diverse work force in terms of race and gender is a desirable goal, if all individuals have the necessary qualifications. In fact, many organizations today are concerned with developing and managing diversity. To eliminate discrimination in the workplace, many organizations have affirmative action programs to increase minority representation. Affirmative action was originally conceived as a way of taking extra effort to attract and retain minority employees. This was normally done by extensively recruiting minorities on college campuses, advertising in minority-oriented publications, and providing educational and training opportunities to minorities.[39] However, over the years, many organizations have resorted to quotalike hiring to ensure that their work force composition mirrors that of the labor market. Sometimes these organizations act voluntarily; in other cases, the quotas are imposed by the courts or by the EEOC. Whatever the impetus for these hiring practices, many white and/or male individuals have fought against them, alleging what is called "reverse discrimination."

A recent example of an imposed quota program is the one at the fire department in Birmingham, Alabama. Having admitted a history of discriminating against blacks, the department entered into a consent decree with the EEOC to hold a certain number of positions at all levels in the fire department open for minorities. The result was that some white applicants were denied employment or promotion in favor of black applicants who scored lower on a selection battery. The white firefighters sued the department for reverse discrimination, and in *Martin v. Wilks* the court found that the white firefighters had been discriminated against. The court stated in its opinion that individuals cannot be deprived of their rights in proceedings to which they are not a party (i.e., the consent decree). However, this decision was subsequently overturned by a provision in the Civil Rights Act of 1991.

One example of a voluntary effort at ensuring adequate minority representation in the work force is the practice of "race norming." Research on standardized testing has found that black and Hispanic applicants score lower than white or Asian applicants. Thus, to hire based solely on these tests would have an adverse impact on the former groups.[40] To eliminate this, race norming computes each individual's score as a percentile score *within* his or her respective racial group.[41]

The Department of Labor used race norming to test applicants for employment in other organizations by using the validity generalization version of the General Aptitude Test Battery (VG-GATB).[42] The relative scoring for various subgroups is depicted in Table 4.6. As can be seen, white, black and Hispanic applicants who receive the same raw score on the test would receive three different percentile scores, based on their relative ranking in their respective racial groups.[43]

Many felt this scoring scheme was both unfair and inconsistent with Title VII, which prohibits discrimination against individuals based on race—although in this case it was white applicants who felt discriminated against. How much actual discrimination against nonminorities occurs as a result of race norming is discussed in Chapter 10. For now, you should know that Congress prohibited race norming in the Civil Rights Act of 1991.

Reasonable Accommodation for Disabled Americans

According to the Americans with Disability Act (ADA), an organization must make "reasonable accommodation" to the physical or mental limitations of an individual with a disability who is otherwise qualified unless it would impose an "undue hardship" on the organization's operations. "Reasonable accommodation" is broadly defined to include making existing facilities (such as washrooms, cafeterias, and auditoriums) readily accessible to and usable by individuals with disabilities. Such things as restructuring jobs, developing part-time or modified work schedules, reassigning individuals or modifying equipment or devices, adjusting training materials and policies, and providing qualified readers or interpreters for individuals with disabilities are also considered reasonable accommodations.[44] The

TABLE 4.6   Race-Normed Scores for an Individual Scoring 300 on the
VG-GATB for Different Job Families

Race	Family I	Family II	Family III	Family IV	Family V
Black	79	59	87	83	73
Hispanic	62	41	74	67	55
White/Other	39	42	47	45	42

Note: Family I includes jobs such as machinist, cabinetmaker, and toolmaker. Family II includes helpers in many types of agriculture and manufacturing. Family III includes professional jobs such as accountant, chemical engineer, nurse, and editor. Family IV includes jobs such as bus driver, bookkeeper, and carpet layer. Family V includes jobs such as exterminator, butcher, and file clerk.

"Competing through Social Responsibility" box describes one company's efforts to achieve these goals.

In defining reasonable accommodations, it is necessary to distinguish between "essential" and "marginal" job functions. Essential job functions are the fundamental duties of the position. In determining these, it is necessary to perform an extensive job analysis that shows the employer's judgment of what is an essential function, the amount of time spent performing those functions, the consequences of not requiring the jobholder to perform the functions, and the work experience of current or past jobholders. Marginal job functions are those that may be performed in the job but need not be performed by all holders of the job. According to the ADA, individuals with disabilities cannot be denied employment if they cannot perform *marginal* job functions; and to the extent their disability affects their performance of *essential* job functions, the employer must explore whether it is possible to make reasonable accommodations.[45]

Employers are not required to make reasonable accommodations if the applicant or employee does not request the accommodation. Employers are also not required to make reasonable accommodations if applicants do not meet the required qualifications for the job. Similarly, employers are not required to lower their quality standards or provide personal-use items such as glasses or hearing aids to make reasonable accommodation. Finally, employers are not required to make reasonable accommodations if to do so would be an undue hardship. Whether something is an undue hardship is determined by looking at the nature and cost of the accommodation and the overall financial resources of the facility. However, the regulations provide that if a requested accommodation would result in undue hardship and outside funding is not available, the individual with the disability should be given the option of paying the portion of the cost that constitutes an undue hardship.

The issue of reasonable accommodations also comes into play in the application and selection process. Disabled individuals cannot be excluded from jobs they could actually perform merely because their disability pre-

Social Responsibility

COMPETING THROUGH

SOCIAL CONCERN TRANSLATES TO PROFITABILITY AT THE PRINCIPAL FINANCIAL GROUP

With the passage of the Americans with Disabilities Act, many employers are concerned with how compliance will adversely impact their profitability. However, The Principal Financial Group, one of the largest insurance and financial services groups in the United States, has found that finding employment opportunities for the disabled has helped their bottom line.

Feeling that the company was responsible for motivating and guiding capable disabled employees to return to work, The Principal developed the Mainstream Program. The program recognizes that with the proper rehabilitation, many employees who become disabled are fully able to return to some type of work. This rehabilitation comes in the form of a temporary work site evaluation and transitional work environment for employees who are mentally or physically disabled in a way that prevents them from temporarily or permanently being able to perform their jobs. The program has helped employees who had such conditions as carpal tunnel syndrome, chemical dependency, back injuries, diabetes, eating disorders, multiple sclerosis, and mental or nervous disorders.

The Mainstream staff of four full-time employees works with doctors and employees to assess workers' skills, capabilities, and restrictions from the onset of the disability. Once released by the physician, employees can start working as little as two hours a day, increasing the number of hours as they feel more comfortable. The employees are frequently evaluated as to their progress and the areas that they need to improve. The ultimate goal is to return the employees to their original job (with necessary accommodations), but when this is not possible, the program seeks to find jobs in other departments that fit the individual's capabilities.

Managers who use employees from the program note that it not only benefit employees but also benefits the company. From 1990 through 1991, The Principal claims that the Mainstream Program resulted in a total savings of $774,859. In fact, from its inception in 1986, the company has saved over $1 million in disability claims and replacement costs. Thus, The Principal has discovered that keeping employees with disabilities results in increased profits. Says Dorothy Bates, one of the participants in the Mainstream Program, "It's just good business to help people be more productive."

SOURCE: S. Tucker, "Mainstreaming Employees Who Have Disabilities," *Personnel Journal,* August 1992, 43–49.

vents them from taking a test that is a prerequisite for the job. For example, an applicant with a visual disability who is unable to read the fine print on a written employment test cannot be excluded from a job because of the test if he or she possesses the required knowledge being measured by the test.[46] In fact, one recent EEOC decision regarding the interpretation of the ADA required a firm that provides training services to hire sign language translators to translate lectures for deaf students.

ADA increases the physician's role in the selection process for physically demanding jobs. For many jobs, employers try to screen out applicants who have back problems or are prone to back problems. However, according to ADA, inquiries or medical examinations are not allowed before an offer of employment. Although a medical exam can be required after an offer of employment has been made, it is advisable to have a physician view the actual job site and learn what the job entails before making an assertion that a certain physical condition will create a high probability of substantial harm to the individual. Currently back problems account for 14 percent of the ADA claims, the largest single category of disability claims.[47]

While the ADA has laudable goals and will obviously help disabled Americans to become self-sufficient, contributing members to society, the law is having an immediate impact of increased litigation. The EEOC estimates a 30 percent increase in the number of complaints for 1992 because of the ADA and Civil Rights Act of 1991.[48] This estimate is borne out by the fact that ADA claims are averaging over 1,000 a month in the first seven months after the act came into effect. Forty-five percent of the claims deal with firings, 20 percent from harassment, discipline, suspension, or failure to promote, and 20 percent from failure to hire or rehire.[49] These numbers suggest that designing HR systems that are consistent with the provisions of the ADA may be one of the major challenges faced by HR executives in the future.

SUMMARY

Viewing employees as a source of competitive advantage results in dealing with them in ways that are ethical and legal. An organization's legal environment—particularly the laws regarding equal employment opportunity—has a particularly strong effect on its HRM function. HRM is concerned with the management of people, and government is concerned with protecting individuals. One of HRM's major challenges therefore, is to perform its function within the legal constraints imposed by the government. Given the multimillion-dollar settlements resulting from violations of EEO laws (and the moral requirement to treat people fairly regardless of their gender or race) HR and line managers need a good understanding of the legal requirements and prohibitions in order to manage the business in ways that are sound, both financially and ethically. Organizations that do so effectively will definitely have a competitive advantage.

Discussion Questions

1. Disparate impact theory was originally created by the court in the *Griggs* case before finally being codified by Congress 20 years later in the Civil Rights Act of 1991. Given the system of law in the United States, from what branch of government should theories of discrimination develop?

2. Disparate impact analysis (the four-fifths rule, standard deviation analysis) is used in employment discrimination cases. The National Assessment of Education Progress conducted by the U.S. Department of Education found that among 21- to 25-year olds (a) 60 percent of whites, 40 percent of Hispanics, and 25 percent of blacks could locate information in a news article or almanac; (b) 25 percent of whites, 7 percent of Hispanics, and 3 percent of blacks could decipher a bus

schedule; and (c) 44 percent of whites, 20 percent of Hispanics, and 8 percent of blacks could correctly determine the change they were due from the purchase of a two-item restaurant meal. Do these tasks (locating information in a news article, deciphering a bus schedule, or determining correct change) have adverse impact? What are the implications?

3. Many companies have dress codes that require men to wear suits and women to wear dresses. Is this discriminatory according to disparate treatment theory? Why or why not?

4. Cognitive ability tests seem to be the most valid selection devices available for hiring employees, yet they also have adverse impact against blacks and Hispanics. Given the validity and adverse impact, and considering that race norming is illegal under CRA 1991, what would you say in response to a recommendation that such tests be used for hiring?

5. How will the reasonable accommodation requirement of ADA affect jobs such as law enforcement officers and firefighters?

6. The reasonable woman standard recognizes that women have different ideas of what constitutes appropriate behavior than men. What are the implications of this distinction? Do you think it is a good or bad idea to make this distinction?

7. Employers' major complaint about ADA is that the costs of making reasonable accommodations will make them less competitive relative to other businesses (especially foreign ones) that do not face these requirements. Is this a legitimate concern? How should employers and society weigh the costs and benefits of ADA?

Notes

1. J. Ledvinka, *Federal Regulation of Personnel and Human Resource Management* (Boston: Kent, 1982).
2. Ibid.
3. Martin v. Wilks 49 FEP Cases 1641 (1989).
4. Wards Cove Packing Co. v. Antonio FEPC 1519 (1989).
5. Bakke v. Regents of the University of California 17 FEPC 1000 (1978).
6. Patterson v. McLean Credit Union 49 FEPC 1814 (1978).
7. J. Friedman and G. Strickler, *The Law of Employment Discrimination: Cases and Materials,* 2nd ed. (Mineola, N.Y.: The Foundation Press, 1987).
8. "Labor Letter," *The Wall Street Journal,* August 25, 1987, 1.
9. J. Woo, "Ex-workers Hit Back with Age-Bias Suits," *The Wall Street Journal,* December 8, 1992, B1.
10. P. Barrett, "How One Man's Fight for a Raise Became a Major Age Bias Case," *The Wall Street Journal,* January 6, 1993, A1, A8.
11. Wards Cove Packing Co. v. Antonio FEPC 1519 (1989).
12. Ibid.
13. *Price Waterhouse* 49 FEPC 954 (1989).
14. Ibid.
15. Lorance v. AT&T Technologies 49 FEPC 1656 (1989).
16. Special feature issue: "The New Civil Rights Act of 1991 and What It Means to Employers," *Employment Law Update* 6 (December 1991): 1–12.

17. "ADA: The Final Regulations (Title I): A Lawyer's Dream/An Employer's Nightmare," *Employment Law Update* 16, no. 9 (1991): 1.

18. "ADA Supervisor Training Program: A Must for Any Supervisor Conducting a Legal Job Interview," *Employment Law Update* 7, no. 6 (1992): 1–6.

19. T. O'Brien, U. Gupta and B. Marsh, "Most Small Businesses Appear Prepared to Cope with the New Family-Leave Rules," *The Wall Street Journal,* February 8, 1993, B1.

20. Equal Employment Opportunity Commission (1978), "Uniform Guidelines on Employee Selection Procedures," *Federal Register* 43 (1978): 38290–38315.

21. Ledvinka, *Federal Regulation.*

22. R. Pear, "The Cabinet Searches for Consensus on Affirmative Action," *The New York Times,* October 27, 1985, E5.

23. McDonnell-Douglas v. Green, 411 U.S. 972 (1973).

24. UAW v. Johnson Controls, Inc. (1991).

25. Special Feature: The New Civil Rights Act of 1991 and What it Means to Employers. *Employment Law Update* 6, no. 12 (1991): 1–6.

26. Washington v. Davis, 12 FEP 1415 (1976).

27. Albermarle Paper Company v. Moody, 10 FEP 1181 (1975).

28. R. Reilly and G. Chao, "Validity and Fairness of Some Alternative Employee Selection Procedures," *Personnel Psychology* 35 (1982): 1–63; J. Hunter and R. Hunter, "Validity and Utility of Alternative Predictors of Job Performance," *Psychological Bulletin* 96 (1984): 72–98.

29. Griggs v. Duke Power Company, 401 U.S. 424 (1971).

30. Hazelwood School District v. United States, 433 U.S. 299, (1977).

31. Woo, "Ex-workers Hit Back with Age-Bias Suits.

32. *Workforce 2000* (Indianapolis, Ind.: The Hudson Institute, 1987).

33. R. Gray, "How to Deal with Sexual Harassment," *Nation's Business* (December 1991): 28–30.

34. E. Wagner, "A Closer Look at Hostile-Environment Harassment," *Supervisory Management* (April 1992): 1–4.

35. Bundy v. Jackson, 641 F.2d 934, 24 FEP 1155 (D.C. Cir., 1981).

36. R. Paetzold and A. O'Leary-Kelly, "Sexual Harassment and the Law: A Review of Court Cases" (Paper presented at the 1992 National Academy of Management Meeting).

37. Meritor Savings Bank v. Vinson, (1986).

38. Paetzold and O'Leary-Kelly, 1992.

39. C. Murray, "The Legacy of the 60's," *Commentary* (July 1992): 23–30.

40. Hunter and Hunter, "Validity and Utility of Alternative Predictors."

41. L. Wynter and J. Solomon, "A New Push to Break the Glass Ceiling," *The Wall Street Journal,* November 15, 1989, B1.

42. T. Noah, "Job Tests Scored on Racial Curve Stir Controversy," *The Wall Street Journal,* April 26, 1991, B1.

43. R. Holland, "Big Brother's Test Scores," National Review, p. 35–36 (September 3, 1991).

44. Special feature issue: "ADA—Accommodating Disabilities: A Practical Guide for Your Supervisors," *Employment Law Update* 7 (August 1992): 1–6.

45. Holland, *National Review,* September 3, 1991.

46. "Lawyers Disable Disability," *The Wall Street Journal,* January 11, 1993, A14.

47. "Labor Letter," *The Wall Street Journal,* September 8, 1992, A1.
48. J. Lublin, "Disabilities Act Will Compel Business to Change Many Employment Practices," *The Wall Street Journal,* 1992, B1.
49. "Lawyers Disable Disabilities," *The Wall Street Journal.*

C A S E

A DISCRIMINATORY CULTURE AT SHONEY'S

For 30 years, Shoney's Inc., the nation's third largest family restaurant chain, reflected the personality of its founder and major shareholder, Raymond Danner. Danner bought the franchise rights for three Shoney's Big Boy restaurants in 1959 and added Captain D's, and Lee's Famous Recipe restaurants during the 1970s. The chain grew to 1,803 restaurants spread across 36 states.

However, in 1989, nine Shoney's employees brought a lawsuit against the firm, alleging "classwide disparate impact against blacks." Some of the alleged discriminatory incidents were:

1. One executive claimed that in 1982, Mr. Danner had suggested donating money to the Ku Klux Klan, stating, "Those guys are really right."

2. A former Shoney's manager claimed that in 1981 Mr. Danner told an area supervisor at one of the restaurants in Nashville, "You've got too many niggers here…If you don't fire them, I'll fire you."

3. No blacks worked in white-collar, secretarial, or data-processing jobs at the headquarters until the late 1980s, and until 1987, no black had been promoted to division manager.

4. A former assistant manager said that she was told by her supervisor to pencil in the "o" on the Shoney's logo on the application form of black applicants so that they would not be called for a follow-up interview.

In 1989, Danner relinquished the reigns of the chairmanship to CEO David Boyd. In September 1989, at the request of the EEOC, Shoney's agreed to spend $30 million over three years to recruit more minorities, hire more black vendors, and help blacks to acquire franchises. Shortly after, Leonard Roberts took over as chairman and hired Shoney's first black officer, Betty J. Marshall, as vice-president of corporate and community affairs. However, Roberts sensed that discriminatory attitudes still permeated the organization. He stated, "I can fight all sorts of business-related problems, but life is too short to spend so much time trying to buck a system of racism."

QUESTIONS

1. Assume that you were Roberts. What types of changes would you begin to implement to change the culture at Shoney's?

2. What specific changes in HR practices (e.g., hiring, training, appraisal, compensation) would you implement to prevent further discriminatory actions?

SOURCE: B. Pulley, "Culture of Racial Bias at Shoney's Underlines Chairman's Departure," *The Wall Street Journal*, December 21, 1992, A1.

5

EMPLOYEE RELATIONS

Objectives   *After reading this chapter, you should be able to:*

1. Identify the major provisions of the Occupational Safety and Health Act (1970) and the rights of employees that are guaranteed by this act.
2. Develop a safety awareness program focused on either job-specific hazards or on specific injuries.
3. Specify the major components of employee assistance programs and employee wellness programs, as well as the steps involved in creating and maintaining such programs.
4. Design working conditions conducive to maintaining individuals' economic and psychological well-being.

Did She Know the Job Was Dangerous when She Took It?

Susan Harrigan worked at what was traditionally considered one of the safest jobs one could have: a typist. However, after three years of battling deadlines for *Newsday*, her employer, she developed pain in her lower arms and hands that was completely disabling. After developing this pain, Harrigan could not do even the most basic tasks such as turning doorknobs or tying shoelaces.

When one thinks about workers exposed to dangers or health hazards, many occupations spring to mind, such as firefighters, police officers, chemical workers, construction workers, and health-care personnel. Secretaries, typists, cashiers, and data-entry personnel are not usually considered to be at risk. According to the Occupational Safety and Health Administration (OSHA), however, workers in these job categories, and indeed any workers who spend a great deal of time working with computers, are candidates for the "illness of the decade"–cumulative trauma disorders (CTDs). In fact, as computers have spread in the workplace, CTDs and other forms of computer-related injuries and illnesses have become the fastest-growing category of occupational hazard, affecting 185,000 people a year and costing $27 billion a year in lost earnings and medical expenses.

The common symptoms of CTDs include pain or discomfort in the fingers, hands, wrists, arms, shoulders, or neck, caused by performing repetitive tasks in awkward positions. Some data-entry personnel hit keyboard keys 10,000 times an hour. Moreover, today's technology does not require manual carriage return or manual paper removal, which would provide some variety in muscle use. In fact, people can now file and communicate to one another without ever removing their hands from a keyboard. It is little wonder that carpal tunnel syndrome, a neurological problem associated with the wrists and lower arm, is the most prevalent disorder of this kind among clerical workers.

In 1987, OSHA ruled that repetitive motion problems inherent in working with computers should be categorized as occupational hazards. This means that employers can now be prosecuted and fined for failing to protect workers from these conditions, which is precisely what has happened to companies such as Pepperidge Farm, IBP, John Morell, and the manufacturer of Susan Harrigan's word processor.

SOURCES: J. Adler, "Typing without Keys: An Epidemic of Injuries among Office Workers Prompts a Search for a Better Keyboard," *Newsweek,* December 7, 1992, 63–64; M. J. Dainoff, "The Illness of the Decade," *Computerworld* 26 (1992): 27–33; D. S. Jackson, "Crippled by Computers," *Time,* October 11, 1992, 70–72; M. Mallory, "An Invisible Workplace Hazard Gets Harder to Ignore," *Business Week,* January 30, 1989, 92–93; L. Reynolds, "Can You Repeat That?" *Personnel* 68 (1991): 19–20.

INTRODUCTION

Employers and employees each have their own sets of needs and values, requiring some sort of balance to be struck between them. Often they form a kind of "psychological contract" that defines this relationship, and this contract—with or without the support of a formal collective bargaining agreement—influences the outcomes achieved by each side.[1]

In this chapter, we examine some of the areas in which employee relations can vary. In some areas, like employee safety, employers' actions are regulated by federal laws, leaving them less latitude. In others, however, employers have the discretion to choose how benevolent they wish to be in providing for employee health, employment security, working conditions, and assistance with nonwork problems.

Many employers believe they can recruit and retain the best personnel by establishing a strong, positive image in the area of progressive employee relations. Other employers move unilaterally toward progressive employee relations to ward off labor unions. Finally, others believe that good employee relations can reduce costs and lower the potential for costly litigation. In any case, many view employee relations as an area where they can gain competitive advantage over others trying to recruit out of the same labor pool.

This chapter reviews what employers bring to their side of the psychological contract and discusses what effects these programs have on employees, employers, and society as a whole. We group the various programs into three general categories: employee safety, employee health, and employee security and working conditions.

EMPLOYEE SAFETY

Employee safety is regulated both by the federal and state governments. However, to fully maximize the safety and health of workers, employers need to go well beyond the letter of the law and embrace its spirit. With this in mind, we first spell out the specific protections guaranteed by federal legislation then discuss various kinds of safety awareness programs that attempt to reinforce these standards.

The Occupational Safety and Health Act

Although concern for worker safety would seem to be a universal societal goal, the **Occupational Safety and Health Act of 1970 (OSHA)**—the most comprehensive legislation regarding worker safety—did not emerge in this country until the early 1970s. At that time, there were roughly 15,000 work-related fatalities every year.

OSHA authorized the federal government to establish and enforce occupational safety and health standards for all places of employment affecting interstate commerce. The responsibility for inspecting employers, applying the standards, and levying fines was assigned to the Department of Labor. The Department of Health was assigned responsibility for conducting research to determine the criteria for specific operations or occupations and for training employers to comply with the act. Much of this research is conducted by an agency called the National Institute for Occupational Safety and Health (NIOSH).

An important feature of OSHA was the provision that the Department of Labor could authorize individual states to substitute their own standards in their own states. Thus, although we discuss only federal legislation in this book, it is important to remember that some employers may be operating under state-enforced guidelines. This provision of the act has recently led to controversy. Some states are believed to be not as protective or as consistent in their protection as the federal government.[2]

Employee Rights under OSHA.   The main provision of OSHA states that each employer has a general duty to furnish each employee a place of employment free from recognized hazards that cause or are likely to cause death or serious physical harm. This is referred to as the **general duty clause**. The Department of Labor recognizes many specific types of hazards, and employers are required to comply with all of the occupational safety and health standards published by NIOSH.

A recent example is the development of OSHA standards for occupational exposure to blood-borne pathogens such as the AIDS virus. These standards identify 24 affected industrial sectors, encompassing 500,000 establishments and 5.6 million workers. Among other features, these standards require employers to develop an "exposure control plan" (ECP). An ECP must include a list of jobs whose incumbents might be exposed to blood, methods for implementing precautions in these jobs, postexposure follow-up plans, and procedures for evaluating incidents in which workers are accidentally infected.

Although NIOSH publishes numerous standards it is clearly not possible for regulators to anticipate all possible hazards that could occur in the workplace. Thus, the general duty clause requires employers to be constantly alert for potential sources of harm in the workplace (as defined by the standards of a reasonably prudent person) and to correct these. The act also grants several rights to employees, as shown in Table 5.1.

Fines for safety violations are never levied against the employees themselves. The assumption is that safety is primarily the responsibility of the employer, who needs to work with employees to ensure they engage in safe working procedures. Moreover, the organization cannot discharge or discriminate against any worker who requests an OSHA inspection.

OSHA Inspections.   Inspections are not always instigated at the request of employees. An inspection can come about because the Department of Labor has targeted special industries (e.g., transportation) or special hazards (e.g., exposure to AIDS) for close scrutiny. Some firms are also randomly selected out of a nationwide pool. Thus, being inspected is by no means an indication that an employer is engaging in unsafe practices. Inspections typically ensue, however, after a firm has had a fatal accident or other catastrophe.

OSHA inspections are conducted by specially trained agents of the Department of Labor, who are often called "compliance officers." These inspections usually follow a tight "script." Typically, the compliance officer shows up unannounced. For obvious reasons, OSHA's regulations prohibit advance notice of inspections. The officer, after presenting his or her credentials, informs the employer of the reasons for the inspection and describes, in a general way, the procedures necessary to conduct the investigation.

TABLE 5.1 Rights Granted to a Worker under the Occupational Safety and Health Act

The employee has the right to:
1. Request an inspection.
2. Have a representative present at an inspection.
3. Have dangerous substances identified.
4. Be promptly informed about exposure to hazards and be given access to accurate records regarding exposures.
5. Have employer violations posted at the work site.

TABLE 5.2 Components of an OSHA Inspection

The compliance officer:
1. Reviews an employer's records of deaths, injuries and illnesses.
2. Conducts a tour of the premises, usually accompanied by a company representative.
3. Interviews employees.
4. Holds a closing conference to discuss findings and set time frames for correcting any potential violations.

The four major components of an OSHA inspection are shown in Table 5.2. First, the compliance officer reviews the employer's records of deaths, injuries, and illnesses. OSHA requires this kind of record keeping from all firms with 11 or more full- or part-time employees. Second, the officer, typically accompanied by a representative of the employer (and perhaps by a representative of the employees), conducts a "walkaround" tour of the employer's premises. On this tour, the officer makes a note of any conditions that he or she thinks violate specific published standards or the less-specific general duty clause. At this time, the inspector may take pictures or samples of the air or water to provide hard evidence of conditions that employers might otherwise alter shortly after the inspection. The third component of the inspection, employee interviews, may take place during the tour. At this time, any person who is aware of a violation can bring it to the attention of the officer. The representative of the employer cannot interfere with these interviews or with any other aspect of the "walkaround" inspection.

Finally, there is a closing conference. Here, the compliance officer discusses his or her findings with the employer, noting any violations. The employer is given a reasonable time to correct these violations. If any violation represents an imminent danger (i.e., it could cause serious injury or death before being eliminated through the normal enforcement procedures), the officer may, through the Department of Labor, seek a restraining order from a U.S. District Court. Such an order compels the employer to correct the problem immediately.

Citations and Penalties.   If a compliance officer believes that a violation has occurred, he or she issues a citation to the employer that specifies the exact practice or situation that violates the act. In doing so, the inspector must refer to the precise provision of the act that has been violated. The employer is required to post this citation in a prominent place near the location of the violation—even if the employer intends to contest it.

Nonserious violations may be assessed up to $1,000 for each incident, but this may be adjusted downward if the employer has no prior history of violations or if the employer has made a good-faith effort to comply with the act. Serious violations of the act, or willful and repeated violators, may be fined up to $10,000 per incident. These fines can also be adjusted downward for smaller firms.

In addition to these civil penalties, criminal penalties may also be assessed for willful violations that result in the death of an employee. Fines can go as high as $20,000, and the employer or agents of the employer can be imprisoned. Criminal charges can also be brought against anyone who falsifies records that are subject to OSHA inspection or anyone who gives advance notice of an OSHA inspection without permission from the Department of Labor.

The employer has the right to contest the compliance officer's finding but must do so within 15 days of the citation. The employer also has the right to ask for a temporary or permanent exclusion (i.e., variance) from the standard if it can be shown that the current facilities provide as much or more protection to employees than the recommended change.

The Effect of OSHA.   OSHA has been unquestionably successful in raising the level of awareness of occupational safety. Yet, legislation alone cannot solve all the problems of work-site safety. Indeed, the number of occupational illnesses increased fivefold between 1985 and 1990, according to a survey by the Bureau of Labor Statistics.[3]

OSHA has not had a more profound impact on safety outcomes for several reasons. First, many feel that the standards are too restrictive and that they reduce firms' competitiveness—especially in light of less-restrictive policies regulating foreign competitors. For example, the cost per life saved associated with restrictions on workers exposed to formaldehyde has been estimated at $94 billion.[4] Indeed, some people felt that when Ronald Reagan was president, the Department of Labor de-emphasized OSHA enforcement in an effort to increase international price competitiveness and support an expanding economy.[5] Enforcement of the provisions can suffer if they are not supported by either the executive branch of the government, by employers, or by employees themselves.

Second, for all but the smallest companies, OSHA's fines are generally too low to instill true fear in nonenthusiastic employers. Even the criminal penalties, because they do not specify what level of management should be punished, rarely cause concern among top-level executives.[7]

Finally, most industrial accidents are a product of unsafe behaviors, not unsafe working conditions. Since the act does not directly regulate employee behavior (e.g., does not set fines for engaging in unsafe behaviors), little behavior change can be expected unless employees are convinced of the standards' importance.[7] This has been recognized by labor leaders. For example, Lynn Williams, president of the United Steelworkers of America has noted: "We can't count on government. We can't count on employers. We must rely on ourselves to bring about the safety and health of our workers."[8]

Since conforming to the statute alone does not necessarily guarantee safety, many employers go beyond the letter of the law. In the next section, we examine the various kinds of employer-initiated safety awareness programs that both comply with OSHA requirements and, in some cases, exceed them.

Safety Awareness Programs

Safety awareness programs go beyond compliance with OSHA and attempt to instill symbolic and substantive changes in the organization's emphasis on safety. These programs typically focus on either specific jobs and job elements or on specific types of injuries or disabilities. There are three primary components to a safety awareness program: identifying hazards, communicating and educating those at risk, and reinforcing safe practices.

Identifying Specific Job Hazards. Employees, supervisors, and other knowledgeable sources need to sit down and discuss potential problems related to safety. The *Job Hazard Analysis Technique* is one means of accomplishing this.[9] With this technique, each job is broken down into basic elements, and each of these is rated for its potential for harm or injury. If there is consensus that some job element has high hazard potential, this element is isolated and potential technological or behavioral changes are considered.

Another means of isolating unsafe job elements is to study past accidents. *Technic of Operations Review* (TOR) is an analysis methodology that helps managers determine which specific element of a job led to a past incident.[10] The first step in a TOR analysis is to establish the facts surrounding the incident. To accomplish this, all members of the work group involved in the accident give their initial impressions of what happened. The group must then, through group discussion, reach a consensus on the single, systematic failure that most contributed to the incident, as well as two or three major secondary factors that contributed to it.

An analysis of jobs at Burger King, for example, revealed that certain jobs required employees to walk across surfaces that were wet or slippery and that this led to many falls. Specific corrective action was taken based on analysis of where people were falling and what conditions led to these falls. Now Burger King provides mats at critical locations and has generally upgraded its floor maintenance. The company also makes slip-resistant shoes available to employees in certain job categories.[11]

Communicating Specific Job Hazards to Those at Risk.   Communication of an employee's risk should take advantage of several media. Direct verbal supervisory contact is important for its saliency and immediacy. Written memos are important because they help establish a "paper trail" that can later document a history of concern regarding the job hazard. Posters, especially those placed near the hazard, serve as a constant reminder, reinforcing other messages.

In communicating risk, it is important to recognize two distinct audiences. Sometimes there are relatively young or inexperienced workers who need special attention. Research by the National Safety Council indicates that 40 percent of all accidents happen to individuals in the 20 to 29 age group and that 48 percent of all accidents happen to workers during their first year on the job.[12] The employer's primary concern with respect to this group is to *inform* them. However, the employer must not overlook experienced workers. Here the key concern is to *remind* them. Research indicates that long-term exposure and familiarity with a specific threat leads to complacency.[13] Experienced employees need retraining to jar them from complacency about the real dangers associated with their work.

Reinforcing Safe Practices on Specific Jobs.   One common technique for reinforcing safe practices is a safety incentive program. These programs reward workers for their support and commitment to safety goals. Initially, programs are set up to focus on improving short-term monthly or quarterly goals or to encourage safety suggestions. These short-term goals are later expanded to include more wide-ranging long-term goals. Prizes are typically distributed in highly public forums (e.g., annual meetings or events). These prizes usually consist of merchandise rather than cash because merchandise represents a lasting symbol of achievement. A good deal of evidence suggests that such programs are effective in reducing injuries and their cost.[14]

Promoting Safety by Focusing on Specific Injuries.   Whereas the safety awareness programs just described focus primarily on the job, other programs focus on specific injuries or disabilities. This chapter opened by discussing CTDs. As the "Competing through Technology and Structure" box shows, employers can fight this problem in many ways, and increasingly this is being achieved by breakthroughs in computer keyboard design.

Lower back disability (LBD) is another major problem that afflicts many employees. LBD accounts for approximately 25 percent of all workdays lost, costing firms nearly $30 billion a year.[15] Human resource managers can take many steps to prevent LBD and rehabilitate those who are already afflicted. Table 5.3 outlines a typical back-related safety awareness program and high-

Technology & Structure

NEW KEYBOARD DESIGNS REDUCE CTDS

Companies can take many steps to protect their employees from CTDs. The traditional approach to solving this problem has been to give typist and data-entry personnel workers time off task. Some employers, for example, ensure that workers on such jobs take 15 minutes of off-terminal activity for every 90 minutes of exposure. Others use job-rotation programs to provide for even longer periods of time off-screen. Improvements in work-space design can also help reduce CTDs. Adjustable chairs, footrests, and detachable keyboards help minimize unchanging or awkward postures. Finally, stretching exercises for the back, arms, wrists, and fingers can also be beneficial.

Thompson's Computer Electronics of Bloomington, Indiana, incorporated many of these suggestions into its safety programs with remarkable success. The company reduced its CTD cases by 46 percent in one year and total workers' compensation (not including reserves) was 20 percent less than for the previous year.

In the future, however, employers may be able to turn to technological improvements in keyboard design to further alleviate these kinds of problems. For example, a keyboard called MIKey, invented by a Maryland optometrist, splits the traditional keyboard down the middle and angles the two halves inward for a more natural posture. The Kinesis Corporation of Bellevue, Washington, has developed a keyboard that puts the keys into two curved wells that are shoulder distance apart. There are even keyboards that work like accordians, where the keys are placed on two vertical planes so that the operator's hands face each other. Finally, a machine called Datahand eliminates the need for keys altogether. Developed by Industrial Innovations of Scottsdale, Arizona, Datahand consists of two padded handrests with individual finger wells that look like holes in a bowling ball. Operators work the system by moving their fingers around the wells, each of which controls six or seven symbols. Companies that take advantage of these and other technological breakthroughs in computer design may gain competitive advantage by increasing productivity while simultaneously providing a safer job for their employees.

SOURCES: W. Atkinson, "Alleviating CTS and Other Work Problems," *Office* 113 (1991): 42–43; L. Hazzard, J. Mautz, and G. Wrightsman, "Job Rotation Cuts Cumulative Trauma Cases," *Personnel Journal* 71 (1992): 29–32.

lights specific practices in the areas of job design, personnel placement, training, compensation, and supervision that can be taken to ameliorate LBD.

Eye injuries are another target of safety awareness programs. The National Society to Prevent Blindness estimates that 1,000 eye injuries occur every day in occupational settings.[16] A ten-step program to reduce eye injuries is outlined in Table 5.4. Similar guidelines can be found for everything from chemical burns, to electrocution, to boiler explosions.[17]

EMPLOYEE HEALTH

Programs for ensuring employee safety are primarily directed at preventing accidents and injuries that might occur on the work site. However, many employers are expanding their focus to the general level of employee health. There are several reasons for this broader interest.

TABLE 5.3   Outline of a Typical Safety Awareness Program for Minimizing Lower Back Disability

Work-Site Assessment

I. Review jobs for risk factors, lifting techniques, safety equipment, etc.

II. Take slides of employees at work

III. Review injury records

On-Site Education

I. Introduction

   A. Present facts regarding back injury

   B. Overview of general causes of back injury

   C. Outline goals of the session

II. Anatomy

   A. Overview of vertebrae, ligaments, muscles, discs, joints, and nerves

III. Causes of Back Injuries

   A. Poor Posture

   B. Forward bending

   C. Decreased flexibility

   D. Poor physical fitness

   E. Accidents

   F. Poor work habits: Proper/improper standing, sitting, lying, lifting

IV. Basic Body Mechanics

   A. Principles of lifting

   B. Proper sitting, sleeping, standing, driving positions

SOURCE: J. R. Hollenbeck, D. R. Ilgen, and S. M. Crampton, "Lower Back Disability in Occupational Settings: A Review of the Literature from a Human Resource Management View," *Personnel Psychology* 45 (1992): 265.

First, employees who are drug or alcohol dependent or who have emotional or physical health problems often experience difficulties on the job or create difficulties for those who work with them. Supervisors may be able to spot such problems but be reluctant to get involved in what they perceive to be the personal lives of employees. Supervisors may also feel unqualified to handle the complexities of these problems. With an organizationally sanctioned program in place to help these employees, the supervisors can stick to their area of expertise (i.e., monitoring employee performance) and refer any employee whose performance seems to be hindered by health problems to a staff of experts. If these kinds of programs prevent problems that inhibit performance, the payoff in productivity could be substantial.

TABLE 5.3   continued

    V. Health Education

       A. Aerobics

       B. Flexibility and exercises

       C. Strength and exercises

       D. Home program: Daily living and household activities (e.g., getting out of bed, dressing, tooth brushing, vacuuming, dishes, shopping, cooking, etc.)

       E. Nutrition

       F. Weight control

       G. Stress management

       H. Relaxation techniques

    VI. First Aid

       A. What to do for a new injury

    VII. Summary

       A. Summarize anatomy, posture, body mechanics, exercise program

       B. Provide written materials on all topics and exercises presented

       C. Life back care: Practical application of methods

       D. Peer pressure/team effort

On-Site Follow-Up

    I. Monitor safety/injury records

    II. Review injured employees' records

    III. Make further recommendations if needed

A second reason for a broader interest in employee health is that many employers are currently responsible for the health-care costs of their employees (not just the costs of work accidents). Given the rise in these costs relative to labor costs in general, it is fiscally wise to do whatever is possible to hold such costs down.

Third, many organizations simply believe that these kinds of programs create goodwill among employees, which translates into increased job satisfaction and higher retention rates. Employee goodwill also contributes to an organizational image that makes the company more competitive when trying to recruit or retain the best personnel.

This broader interest in employee health has resulted in two general types of programs. First, **employee assistance programs (EAPs)** attempt to ameliorate problems encountered by workers who are drug dependent, alcoholic, or psychologically troubled. These programs are remedial in

TABLE 5.4   A Ten-Step Program for Reducing Eye-related Injuries

1. Conduct an eye-hazard job analysis.
2. Test all employees' vision to establish a baseline.
3. Select protective eyewear designed for specific operations.
4. Establish a 100 percent behavioral compliance program for eyewear.
5. Ensure that eyewear is properly fitted.
6. Train employees in emergency procedures.
7. Conduct ongoing education programs regarding eye care.
8. Continually review accident-prevention strategies.
9. Provide management support.
10. Establish written policies detailing sanctions and rewards for specific results.

SOURCE: T. W. Turrif, "NSPB Suggests 10-Step Program to Prevent Eye Injury," *Occupational Health and Safety* 60 (1991): 62–66.

nature: They try to help employees overcome their problems. Second, **employee wellness programs**, which are preventive in nature, attempt to promote good health among employees who are not necessarily having current health problems. Both types of programs have been identified as essential to managing health-benefits costs in the 1990s.[18] We review both kinds of programs in the next two sections.

Employee Assistance Programs

Drug and alcohol abuse have been estimated to cost U.S. companies nearly $100 billion a year in lost productivity.[19] Although health-care costs in general have risen sharply, the treatment costs for mental and chemical dependency disorders appear to be rising even faster.[20] To lower these costs, many employers are turning to EAPs.

An EAP is basically a referral service that supervisors or employees can use to seek professional treatment for varying kinds of problems. EAPs began in the 1950s with a focus on treating alcoholism, but in the 1980s they expanded into drug treatment as well. EAPs continue to evolve, and many of them are now fully integrated into companies' overall health-benefits plans, serving as gatekeepers for health-care utilization—especially for mental health.[21] When the Campbell Soup Company incorporated mental health treatment into its EAP in 1990, claims costs associated with psychiatrists decreased 28 percent in a single year.[22] This kind of program is frequently referred to as a *carve-out plan*. In carve-out plans, coverage of mental health and chemical dependency benefits is provided by a single vendor that has responsibility for all of the company's health benefits.

EAPs vary widely, but most share some basic elements. First, the programs are usually identified in official documents published by the employer (e.g., employee handbooks). Supervisors (and union representatives, where relevant) are trained to use the referral service for employees whom they suspect of having health-related problems. Employees are also trained to use the system to make self-referrals when necessary. Finally, the costs and benefits of the programs (as measured in positive employee outcomes such as return-to-work rates) are evaluated, typically annually.

Given EAP's wide range of options, relative novelty, and evolving natures, one cannot emphasize enough how important it is to evaluate their success. For example, there is a current debate about the desirability of costly, intensive, inpatient alcoholism and substance abuse services over less costly outpatient care. Some fear that the lower initial costs of outpatient treatment might be offset by higher long-term costs because of relapse or other forms of failure. To settle this question for themselves, General Electric performed an experiment at its plant in Lynn, Massachusetts. To evaluate the relative effectiveness of three possible treatment courses, GE researchers assessed the experiences of 227 workers who were randomly assigned to one of the three treatments: (1) compulsory hospitalization followed by participation in Alcoholics Anonymous (AA), (2) compulsory AA without hospitalization, or (3) the employee's choice of treatments (1) or (2).

The results of this study indicated that after two years, the workers who received hospital care fared the best, despite the fact that this option was chosen less often by the employees themselves.[23] A similar study of drug dependency has shown similar results.[24] The message from these studies is clear: Although both employers (for cost reasons) and employees (for convenience reasons) may be attracted to short-term, low-cost treatments, everyone might be better served by focusing on long-term costs and well-being.

Another controversy surrounding EAPs is whether to establish an in-house EAP staffed with professionals who work for the company or employ an outside agency. The in-house approach is usually more cost-effective and offers employees rapid and convenient access to services. However, in-house plans run the risk of a loss of confidentiality. Indeed, lawsuits have been filed by employees who alleged that they suffered harm in the course of obtaining services from in-house EAPs.[25]

By adhering to certain guidelines, employers can minimize their liability while still benefiting from EAPs. First, the company should retain the services of qualified, experienced professionals and be able to document their qualifications objectively. Second, the company should not use overly coercive tactics in securing employees' participation in the EAP. This is easier said than done, and supervisors will likely require training in how to confront troubled personnel in a manner that makes them willing to seek help rather than become defensive. Third, companies should strive to keep EAP use confidential. For example, it is a good idea to keep EAP records separate from the rest of the human resource database system and strictly limit access to the EAP data. Fourth, employers should ensure that employees have the opportunity to provide feedback on the services received through their EAP. This allows the company to catch any problems while they are still isolated events rather than patterns of abuse.

Finally, it should be noted that underlying most EAP programs is the philosophy that when all is said and done, employees must be willing to help themselves. It is unrealistic to think that employers can solve all their employees' problems if the employees themselves are not interested in changing their behavior. Sometimes nothing less than the threat of termination will arouse action in a troubled employee. The human resource manager—in order to protect the company, other employees, customers, and the individual in question—must be ready to take action if necessary. We discuss the proper means for initiating an employee termination later in this chapter.

Employee Wellness Programs

Employee assistance programs work with specific individuals who have health-related problems that interfere with productive employment. In contrast, employee wellness programs (EWPs) are more generic efforts to raise the overall health levels of all employees. EWPs focus on changing behaviors both on and off work that could eventually lead to future health problems. Stress management, for example, is often a target for EWPs. As the "Competing through Globalization" box indicates, stress management may be more critical in some countries than others.

As we have seen, the short-term gains in controlling health-care costs derived from limiting coverage are usually wiped out by long-term losses caused by treatment failure and relapse. Thus, many organizations have concluded that the only effective means of reducing health-care expenditures is to avoid them in the first place. EWPs are preventive in nature; they attempt to manage health-care costs by decreasing employees' needs for services. Typically, these programs aim at specific health risks such as high blood pressure, high cholesterol levels, smoking, and obesity. They also try to promote positive health influences such as physical exercise and good nutrition.

As with EAPs, there are a variety of EWPs. We distinguish between two broad classes of programs: passive and active. The difference is that passive programs use little or no outreach to individuals, nor do they provide ongoing support to motivate them to avail themselves of the resources. Active wellness centers assume that behavior change requires not only awareness and opportunity but support and reinforcement.

One example of a passive wellness program is a health education program. Health education programs have two central goals: raising awareness levels of health-related issues and informing people on health-related topics. In these kinds of programs, a health educator usually conducts classes or lunchtime lectures (or coordinates outside speakers). The program may also have various promotions (e.g., annual mile run or "smoke-outs") and include a newsletter that reports on current health-related issues. Health education programs are the most common form of employee wellness program.[26]

Another kind of passive employee wellness program is the fitness facility program. In this kind of program, the company sets up a center for physical fitness equipped with aerobic and muscle-building exercise machines

Globalization

ARE AMERICAN COMPANIES IMPORTING JAPANESE-STYLE OCCUPATIONAL STRESS?

In 1993, the Geneva-based International Labor Office gave official recognition to the term *karoshi,* which is the common term in Japan for "death by overwork." On the average, Japanese managers work over 500 more hours a year than those in West Germany and over 250 more hours than American managers. Yet, at a time when American companies are importing more and more types of Japanese management practices, the widespread problems with *karoshi,* the dark side of the Japanese economic miracle, seem to question the wisdom of adopting *all* Japanese business practices.

Is *karoshi* being imported into the United States? Surveys seem to indicate that it might be. In a recent poll of 206 CEOs from the Fortune 500 and Service 500 companies, 77 percent indicated that "large U.S. companies will have to push their managers harder if we are to compete successfully with the Japanese." Moreover, whereas 62 percent of the CEOs agreed that managers are working longer hours today than ten years ago, a whopping 91 percent disagreed with the notion that "compa-

nies are pushing managers too hard." Texaco CEO James Kinnear summed up the feelings of the respondents well when he stated, "Heads of companies must set objectives and monitor employee performance—and if that leads to longer hours, then so be it!"

It is ironic that many U.S. companies are beginning to adopt this strategy just when Japanese firms are starting to back away from it. For example, the Japanese government recently announced a \$2 million study of *karoshi,* and some of the major companies are forcing managers to take time off. The Sony Corporation announced in 1990 that all employees would be required to take a vacation of a week or two, whether they wanted to or not. Moreover, as part of a nationwide drive toward a five-day workweek, Japanese banks all close on Saturdays. If making employees work longer hours is truly going to become a major competitive strategy of U.S. organizations, then the development of employee wellness centers to counter the negative side effects of this strategy should be seriously considered.

SOURCES: K. Smith, "Dying for a Living," *Time Magazine,* May 3, 1993, 19; D. E. Sanger, "Tokyo Tries to Find Out If 'Salarymen' Are Working Themselves to Death," *The New York Times,* March 19, 1990, A-8; S. Solo, "Stop Whining and Get Back to Work," *Fortune* 121 (March 12, 1990): 49–51.

and staffed with certified athletic trainers. The facility is publicized within the organization, and employees are free to use it on their own time. Health education classes related to smoking cessation and weight loss may be offered in addition to the facilities.

Although fitness facility programs are usually more expensive than health education programs—and differ slightly in focus—both kinds of programs are classified as passive. They identify individuals in risk categories, advise them to take action, and provide resources with which to take action (education and/or facilities).

In contrast to passive wellness centers, active wellness centers assume that behavior change requires not only awareness and opportunity but encouragement and assistance. One kind of active wellness center is the outreach and follow-up model. This type of wellness center contains all the features of a passive model (identification, education, and facilities), but it also has counselors who handle one-on-one outreach and provide tailored, individualized programs for employees. Typically, tailored programs obtain baseline measures on various indicators (weight, blood pressure, lung capacity, etc.) and measure individuals' progress relative to these indicators over time. The programs set goals and provide small, symbolic rewards to individuals who meet their goals.

Research on these different types of wellness centers leads to several conclusions.[27] First, the costs of health education programs are significantly less than those associated with either fitness facility programs or the follow-up model. Second, as indicated in Figure 5.1, all three models are effective in reducing the risk factors associated with cardiovascular disease (obesity, high blood pressure, smoking, and lack of exercise). However, the follow-up model is significantly better than the other two in reducing the risk factors.

Whether the added cost of follow-up programs compared with health education programs is warranted is a judgment that only employers, employees, and unions can make. Apparently, as indicated in Table 5.5, many employers believe that incentives are worth the extra cost. There appears to be no such ambiguity associated with the fitness facility model, however. This type of wellness center is as costly as the follow-up model but only as effective as the health education model. Providing a fitness facility that does not include systematic outreach and routine long-term follow-up to assist people with risk factors is not cost-effective in reducing health risks. As some authors have noted, "Attendants may sit in the fitness center like the 'Maytag repairman' waiting for people to come."[28]

EMPLOYEE SECURITY AND WORKING CONDITIONS

Whereas the previous two sections discussed issues of physical safety and physical health, this section focuses on policies directed toward employees' economic and psychological well-being. Many aspects of working conditions within organizations are related to these outcomes, and we examine several.

Discipline, Due Process, and Discharge

Despite a company's best efforts in the area of personnel selection, training, and design of compensation systems, some employees will occasionally fail to meet performance requirements or will violate company policies while on the job. When this happens, organizations need to invoke a discipline program that could ultimately lead to the individual's discharge. Historically, in the absence of a specified contract, either the employer or the employee could sever the employment relationship at any time. The severing of this relationship could be for "good cause," "no cause," or even

FIGURE 5.1 The Cost and Effectiveness of Three Different Types of Employee Wellness Designs

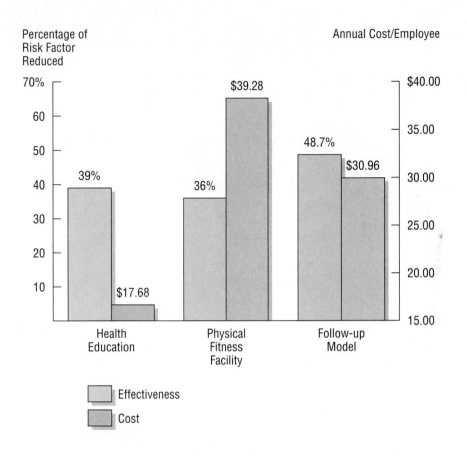

SOURCE: J. C. Erfurt, A. Foote, and M. A. Heirich, "The Cost Effectiveness of Worksite Wellness Programs for Hypertension Control, Weight Loss, Smoking Cessation and Exercise," *Personnel Psychology* 45 (1992): 5–27.

"bad cause." Over time, this policy has been referred to as the **employment-at-will doctrine.**

The employment-at-will doctrine has eroded significantly over time, however, and today employees who are fired sometimes sue their employers for "wrongful discharge." A wrongful discharge suit typically attempts to establish that the discharge either (1) violated an implied contract or covenant (i.e., the employer acted unfairly) or (2) violated public policy (i.e., the employee was terminated because he or she refused to do something illegal, unethical, or unsafe).

Courts have been quite willing to listen to such cases, and employees win settlements over 70 percent of the time. The average award is more than

TABLE 5.5   Examples of Employers and the Incentives Used to Promote Wellness

Employer	Targeted Risk Factors	Examples of Incentives
Hershey Foods	Smoking, seat belt use, weight, blood pressure, and cholesterol levels	$32/mo. surcharge if overweight $35/mo. surcharge for high blood pressure
Sony Corporation	Smoking, annual blood screening, mammograms, children's physicals	$300 if someone stops smoking Full reimbursement for expenses related to risk factors
California Edison	High blood pressure, weight, smoking	$10 rebate on health insurance to those participating in a regular screening program
Johnson & Johnson	High blood pressure cholesterol levels, weight	"Live for Life" dollars that can be used to purchase sweatsuits, cookbooks, and other health-related merchandise
U-Haul International	Smoking, weight	$5 penalty per pay period if one smokes or is overweight
Pacific National Bank	High blood pressure, cholesterol, weight	$120 to those who participate in a series of health screens and pass certain requirements
Champion International	Mammograms, Pap smears, blood screens, and other medical tests	$100 credit toward the companies flexible benefit plan
Control Data Corporation	Smoking	10% surcharge on health insurance premiums
Baker Hughes	Smoking, cholesterol, triglycerides, high blood pressure, weight	$100 deposit in an employee's health-care reimbursement account if employee passes tests on all five risk factors

SOURCES: C. Woolsey, "Linking Wellness to Health-Care Costs," *Business Insurance,* February 17, 1992, 12; J. E. Santora, "Sony Promotes Wellness to Stabilize Health-Care Costs," *Personnel Journal,* September 1992, 40–45; S. Caudron, "Are Health Incentives Disincentives?" *Personnel Journal,* August 1992, 35–39; E. Smith, "Workers Get Incentives to Take Medical Tests," *The Wall Street Journal,* November 11, 1992, B1; L. Bloc, "Employers Monitor Lifestyles: Financial Incentives for Wellness Gain Favor," *Business Insurance,* February 7, 1992, 4–6.

$500,000, and the cost for mounting a defense can be anywhere from $50,000 to $250,000.[29] With these costs at stake, it is easy to see why the development of a standardized, systematic approach to discipline and discharge is critical to all organizations. These decisions should not be left solely to the discretion of individual managers or supervisors.

Effective organizational discipline programs have two central components: documentation (which includes specific publication of work rules and

TABLE 5.6   An Example of a Progressive Discipline Program

Offense Frequency	Organizational Response	Documentation
First offense	Unofficial verbal warning	Witness present
Second offense	Official written warning	Document filed
Third offense	Second official warning, with threat of temporary suspension	Document filed
Fourth offense	Temporary suspension and "last chance notification"	Document filed
Fifth offense	Termination (with right to go to arbitration)	Document filed

job descriptions that should be in place prior to administering discipline) and progressive punitive measures. Except in the most extreme cases, employees should generally not be terminated for first offenses. Rather, as shown in Table 5.6, punitive measures should be taken in incremental steps of increasing magnitude. This may start with an unofficial warning for the first offense, followed by a written reprimand for additional offenses. At some point, later offenses may lead to a temporary suspension (and perhaps referral to an employee assistance program, if it is relevant to the case). Before a company can suspend an employee, it may need to issue a "last chance notification," indicating that the next offense will result in termination. Some firms, such as Illinois trucking company Reliable Cartage, even employ a peer review process for employees who feel they were inappropriately disciplined.[30]

Termination should ensue only after the employer has gone through all these steps and documented the process with written correspondence that was sent to the employee and then kept on file. Such procedures may seem exasperatingly slow, and they may fail to meet the supervisor's emotional need for quick and satisfying retribution. In the end, however, when problem employees are discharged, the chance that they can prove they were discharged for poor cause has been minimized. The organization has a documented record that the employee was treated fairly and, if anything, with leniency. The employee is unable to claim that the discharge was for violation of an implied contract or covenant or a violation of public policy. Thus, although it is slow, the process can save the organization time and money in the long run.

Plant-Closing Legislation

Discharging a single employee is an isolated event affecting that individual's psychological and economic well-being after having failed to conform to an organization's established rules. If this is a troubling event, one can hardly imagine the debilitating economic and psychological effects of a plant closing. Thousands of employees who have done nothing wrong may be discharged. Plant closings may also have ripple effects on other small employers in a geographical area: suppliers, distributors and contractors.[31]

Historically, many plants have closed with no advance warning, leaving individuals and the surrounding community poorly prepared to handle the economic and psychological tragedy. The Plant Closing Act of 1988 was passed to respond to this problem. It requires organizations to give 60-days' written notice to employees and their communities of any closure or layoff affecting 50 or more full-time employees. At the state level Maine, Wisconsin, Massachusetts, and others have similar laws that go beyond the federal laws.

Many speculated that plant-closing legislation would hurt employers' profitability by forcing them to operate unprofitable plants for up to two months longer than warranted. Others contended that such legislation might make the United States (or certain states) less attractive for companies opening new plants. In fact, neither of these potential side effects seems to have resulted from passage of this act.[32]

Nontraditional Work Schedules

It has been projected that in the year 2000, 75 percent of all families will be dual-career families and many more will be single-parent families.[33] When one combines this estimate for the future with past data on the growing number of working mothers shown in Figure 5.2, the need for nontraditional work schedules becomes clear. Changes such as these have prompted many organizations to alter traditional work schedules to schedules that better meet the nonwork needs of employees. Although designed primarily to assist working parents, however, the costs and benefits of such programs are experienced by all employees. Nontraditional work schedules take two forms: compressed workweeks and flextime.

Compressed Workweeks.   The traditional work schedule consists of a 40-hour week with five 8-hour work days. A **compressed workweek** is a 40-hour workweek composed of four 10-hour workdays. Compressed workweeks have several advantages. First, from the employee's perspective, the time it takes to travel to and from work is reduced by 20 percent. In addition, having a nonweekend day off each week makes it easier to schedule nonwork activities such as doctor's appointments and parent-teacher conferences. Finally, having a block of three days off rather than two makes certain leisure activities (e.g., those involving travel) easier to manage.

From the organization's perspective, the compressed workweek is believed to reduce the costs of starting and stopping work (e.g., setup and closedown procedures, daily documentation, etc.), which only have to be performed four times instead of five. In addition, absenteeism and tardiness are lower with compressed workweeks because there is less pressure on employees to schedule important nonwork events during the workweek. For

FIGURE 5.2   The Growing Percentage of Working Mothers in the Work Force

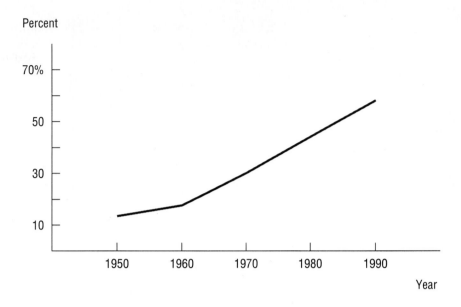

some types of jobs, there may be concerns about fatigue and fatigue-related mistakes or injuries, but little evidence suggests this is a major problem.[34]

Flextime.   Flextime is another form of nontraditional work schedule receiving increasing attention in many organizations. The **flextime** concept was developed in Germany in the late 1960s and was first introduced in the United States by Control Data Corporation in 1972.[35] Although use of flextime varies, most programs contain three primary components: bandwidth, core time, and flexible hours (see Figure 5.3).

First, a specified "bandwith" determines when the work site will be open (e.g., 6:00 AM to 8:00 PM). Second, during "core time" (e.g., 10:00 AM to 2:00 PM), everyone is expected to be at the work site. Third, there is a set of "flexible hours" when someone may or may not be at work (e.g., 6:00 AM to 10:00 AM and 2:00 PM to 8:00 PM). In addition, some programs include a "banking" component, which allows someone to perform the 40-hour workweek by loading up on flexible hours on one day (e.g., working 6:00 AM to 8:00 PM on Monday) and then working only during the core hours on other days.

FIGURE 5.3   A Typical Band Flextime Program

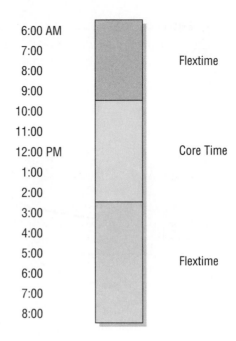

Research on flextime suggests that it has no major consistent effect, good or bad, on employee productivity. However, research consistently indicates that it reduces absenteeism and tardiness and increases employee satisfaction.[36] In addition, many employers believe that this kind of flexibility enhances their ability to compete in the labor market. As James Bosco, a manager at Automatic Data Processing notes, "Hopefully, I'm creating something here that the company down the street doesn't have."[37]

One potential disadvantage is that this type of scheduling can increase the job difficulty of the manager who must coordinate everyone's schedule. Research on managerial attitudes supports this theory, but the same research suggests that the benefits to the manager—through reduced absenteeism and tardiness and increased employee satisfaction—offset these costs. In one study, of the manager surveyed, 97 percent approved of permanent adoption of flextime.[38]

Job Sharing and Part-Time Work

Although the compressed workweek and flextime scheduling both allow greater accommodation of an employee's nonwork needs, they still assume that an individual will work roughly 40 hours a week. Job-sharing programs and part-time work relax that assumption and attempt to accommodate the needs of persons who cannot or do not wish to work that many hours.

Job Sharing.   In a job-sharing arrangement, two qualified employees divide the hours, the responsibilities, and (sometimes) the benefits of one full-time job. Job sharing allows an organization to staff a full-time job with part-time workers who have full-time careers with the organization—rather than using outsiders like temporary workers. For this reason, job sharing is more suitable than traditional part-time employment for higher-level jobs that require continuity and specific, local expertise. Another desirable feature of such arrangements is that the pair of employees often complement each others' strengths and weaknesses; hence, the pair performs better than either individual could have performed alone.[39]

Part-Time Employment.   Part-time employment is another option that organizations use to create more flexible working conditions. It comes in two varieties: permanent and temporary. Permanent part-time employment is similar to job sharing in that the person works solely for one employer. Unlike job sharing, however, the person is not teamed with any other employees. Rather, the person has all the responsibilities for the job but works at it for a reduced number of hours. Part-time workers often have limited or no benefits, which reduces employers' costs significantly compared with using full-time workers.

Temporary part-time workers do not work solely for one employer; they move from employer to employer over relatively short periods of time. Temporaries are often employed by agencies that specialize in providing short-term help for organizations. Although "temporary agencies" have traditionally dealt in clerical support, today many of them are expanding into more complex areas such as accounting.

The number of temporary agencies increased significantly through the 1990s for a number of reasons. First, temporaries receive no benefits; hence, they are cheaper to employ than full-time workers. Second, temporary workers can be used as a buffer to protect full-time workers from the inevitable effects of business cycles. That is, rather than hiring additional full-time workers when cyclical demand for products is up and then have to lay them off when demand is down, employers can hire temporaries to meet their needs on the upside and then cast them off when demand eases. In theory, since these workers see their jobs as only temporary, this should be less disruptive to their lives than laying off full-time workers whose lives are built around different assumptions.

The first two reasons for the expansion of temporary agencies focus on the demand side, but there is also a supply-side reason. Today many more employees are only interested in part-time, temporary jobs, which allow them to take employment when and where they want it (e.g., during the winter) and turn it down when they are not interested (e.g., during the summer). This kind of flexibility is simply unavailable in full-time jobs, and a temporary employee is perceived more favorably than an employee who hops excessively from one full-time job to another.

Family-Friendly Policies

Organizations can take other steps, aside from work schedules and part-time employment, to ease employees' conflicts between work and nonwork. We use the general term "family-friendly policies" to categorize these steps; three specific programs fall under this general heading: child care, elder care, and family-leave policies.

Child Care.   Over 4,000 U.S. companies currently provide some form of child-care support to their employees, and this number is increasing yearly.[40] This support comes in several different forms that vary in their degree of organizational involvement. The least level of involvement is when an organization merely helps employees collect and supply information about the cost and quality of available child care. At the next level, organizations provide vouchers or discounts for employees to use at existing child-care facilities. At the highest level, firms provide on-site child care directly to their employees. The "Competing through Social Responsibility" box shows how employers try to recruit and retain the best personnel by providing for their employees' child-care needs.

An organization's decision to staff its own child-care facility should not be taken lightly. It is typically a costly venture with important liability concerns. Moreover, the results, in terms of reducing absenteeism and enhancing productivity, are often mixed. One reason for this is that many organizations are "jumping on the day-care bandwagon" without giving much thought to the best form of assistance for their specific employees. Research by Ellen Ernst Kossek has shown that employees' child-care needs vary both among and within firms. Not all programs are right for all employers, and certain characteristics of an organization's specific work force (average age of employees, number of single parents, age of children, employment status of employee's spouse) determine the best alternative.[41]

Organizations that fail to do an adequate needs analysis (see Chapter 12) often wind up purchasing the wrong alternative. For example, one Fortune 500 company found that less than 2 percent of its work force used a flexible spending account that had been adopted as the chief company policy on child care. The waste and inefficiency of this practice could have been avoided had a more thorough needs analysis been conducted before the program was implemented.[42]

Elder Care.   In addition to child-care problems, some organizations are confronted with employees who have to care for aging parents. Given this country's aging population, the problem is likely to get even worse. Provision of elder-care support is lagging behind child care. Currently, only 4 percent of U.S. organizations provide elder-care information and referral services, and only 3 percent provide company-sponsored elder-care education.[43]

Social Responsibility

COMPETING THROUGH

CARE FOR CHILDREN AND ELDERS

On September 11, 1992, the Family and Medical Leave Act was sent to the White House, where it was eventually vetoed by then-President George Bush. On the same day, 137 private companies and nonprofit organizations announced they had formed the American Business Collaboration for Quality Dependent Care. This coalition was spearheaded by corporate leaders such as IBM, AT&T, and Johnson & Johnson and shows how many employers are stepping in where the government fears to tread on family-related issues affecting the workplace. This group still survives today, despite the passage of the Family Leave Act that occurred in the first 100 days of Bill Clinton's administration. As noted by Fran Rogers, CEO of Work/Family Directions Inc., "The country is struggling to determine whose responsibility dependent care is," and as this coalition made clear, many private employers were not willing to wait for the government to take this responsibility."

The goal of the coalition was to raise $25 million to fund a variety of child-care and elder-care projects across the United States and is representative of many privately sponsored forays into the day-care/elder-care field. Different employers have tried different methods in the past. For example, AT&T finances off-site child care by giving large donations to local child-care centers. In return for a

$25,000 donation, AT&T asks that local care centers reserve half their places for children of AT&T employees. This is a good solution for AT&T because it is less costly than starting up its own center—which it views as tantamount to getting involved in a business that it knows nothing about.

This solution was not viable for American West Airlines, however. Its employees worked irregular shifts, were widely dispersed geographically, and often needed care for several days. The Phoenix-based carrier instead adopted a plan that centered around private home-care providers who lived in the employees' neighborhoods. The airline developed a staff of eight people who trained and monitored over 50 different individual care providers who worked out of their own homes.

Finally, on top of subsidies, some companies add a safety net for employees whose regular day-care providers fail on any given day. For example, at its New York headquarters, Time-Warner provides a center for employees to turn to if a school is closed or if a regular provider is sick. This kind of "emergency support" is valuable to employees who, for the most part, are happy with their own child-care arrangements. These and other innovative programs will become increasingly important as companies compete for human resources in a tightening labor market.

SOURCES: T. Segal, "Family Care: Tips for Companies that Are Trying to Help," *Business Week,* September 28,

Family Leave. One form of assistance to employees with children or aging parents is employee leave. Helping pass federal legislation mandating parental leave policies was one of Bill Clinton's major accomplishments in his first 100 days in office. Many companies had such policies in place prior to the passage of the Family Leave Act. For example, IBM provides a three-year personal leave of absence for employees who maintain full benefits while away from work. IBM executives believe that these kinds of family-friendly policies enhance employee loyalty as well as the organization's employee-

FIGURE 5.4   How U.S. Policy on Family Leave Compared with Other Industrialized
Nations Prior to Passage of the Family Leave Act

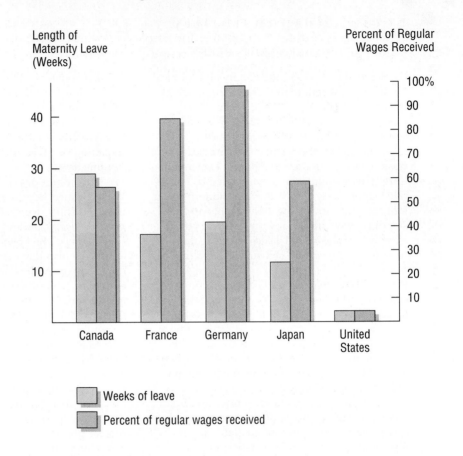

SOURCE: J. Jaben, "Family Leave: National Debate Focuses on Flexibility, Fairness," *Business Marketing,*
November 1992, 36.

recruitment efforts.[44] Figure 5.4 compares U.S. family-leave policies to those
of other industrialized nations prior to passage of the Family Leave Act.

SUMMARY

This chapter has discussed the rights and responsibilities of employees and
employers. Paramount among these rights is the right to a safe workplace.
The federal Occupational Safety and Health Act was discussed, but many
organizations find it beneficial to go beyond these guidelines. Therefore, we
discussed the role of safety awareness programs for various kinds of jobs,
job elements, and specific disabilities. Although no federal legislation cur-

rently compels organizations to offer health-promotion activities for their employees, many organizations, concerned with the rising costs of health care and the loss of productivity associated with an unhealthy work force, do provide such support. Such support can come in the form of employee assistance programs for employees with current physical or psychological problems, or wellness centers, which focus on employees who are currently healthy and desire to stay that way. Finally, we examined many steps that an organization can take to provide better working conditions for its employees. The purpose of these programs is to ensure the work force's economic and psychological well-being. Although they may increase the organization's operating costs, these programs' potential for enhancing productivity, reducing turnover, and making the organization a more competitive recruiter often compensates for these costs.

Discussion Questions

1. Employees have always been central to organizational effectiveness, and yet the concern for establishing good employee–employer relations has never been stronger than today. What are some of the major features of the business environment confronting organizational leaders today that may be responsible for this?

2. Although the computerized word processor was a technological improvement that enhanced productivity, it eventually led to health problems among workers that were not caused by the previous technology (i.e., standard manual typewriters). Can you think of any other technological innovations that enhanced productivity but that might not be improvements in terms of worker health and psychological well-being?

3. Many have suggested that OSHA penalties are too small and misdirected (i.e., aimed at employers rather than employees) to have any significant impact on employee safety. Do you think that OSHA-related sanctions need to be strengthened, or are existing penalties sufficient? Defend your answer.

4. Compare and contrast the underlying philosophies behind employee assistance programs and employee wellness programs. In your opinion, do these types of programs act as substitutes or as complements for each other?

5. The discipline and discharge procedures described in this chapter are systematic but rather slow. In your opinion, are there some offenses that should lead to immediate dismissal, and if so, how would you justify this to a court if you were sued for "wrongful discharge"?

Notes

1. J. G. March and H. A. Simon, *Organizations* (New York: Wiley, 1958).
2. M. E. Personick and E. C. Jackson, "Injuries and Illnesses in the Workplace, 1990," *Monthly Labor Review* 115 (1992): 37–38.
3. R. L. Simison, "Safety Last," *The Wall Street Journal,* March 18, 1986, 1.
4. J. Labate, "Bringing Reason to Regulation," *Fortune,* October 19, 1992.
5. J. V. Grimaldi and R. H. Simonds, *Safety Management* (Homewood, Ill.: Richard D. Irwin, 1989).

6. R. A. Reber, J. A. Wallin, and D. L. Duhon, "Safety Programs that Work," *Personnel Administrator* 34 (1989): 66–69.

7. J. Roughton, "Managing a Safety Program through Job Hazard Analysis," *Professional Safety* 37 (1992): 28–31.

8. M. A. Verespec, "OSHA Reform Fails Again," *Industry Week,* November 2, 1992, 36.

9. R. G. Hallock and D. A. Weaver, "Controlling Losses and Enhancing Management Systems with TOR Analysis," *Professional Safety* 35 (1990): 24–26.

10. H. Herbstman, "Controlling Losses the Burger King Way," *Risk Management* 37 (1990): 22–30.

11. L. Bryan, "An Ounce of Prevention for Workplace Accidents," *Training and Development Journal* 44 (1990): 101–102.

12. J. F. Mangan, "Hazard Communications: Safety in Knowledge," *Best's Review* 92 (1991): 84–88.

13. T. Markus, "How to Set Up a Safety Awareness Program," *Supervision* 51 (1990): 14–16.

14. R. King, "Active Safety Programs, Education Can Help Prevent Back Injuries," *Occupational Health and Safety* 60 (1991): 49–52.

15. J. R. Hollenbeck, D. R. Ilgen and S. M. Crampton, "Lower Back Disability in Occupational Settings: A Review of the Literature from a Human Resource Management View," *Personnel Psychology* 45 (1992): 247–278.

16. T. W. Turriff, "NSPB Suggests 10-Step Program to Prevent Eye Injury," *Occupational Health and Safety* 60 (1991): 62–66.

17. D. Hanson, "Chemical Plant Safety: OSHA Rule Addresses Industry Concerns," *Chemical and Engineering News* 70 (1992): 4–5; K. Broscheit and K. Sawyer, "Safety Exhibit Teaches Customers and Employees about Electricity," *Transmission and Distribution* 43 (1992): 174–179; R. Schuch, "Good Training Is Key to Avoiding Boiler Explosions," *National Underwriter* 95 (1992): 21–22.

18. M. McGarvey, "The Challenge of Containing Health-Care Costs," *Financial Executive* 8 (1992): 34–40.

19. R. Tadjer-Winkler, "How Some Agents Are Winning the Battle against Addiction," *Life Association News* 87 (1992): 88–96.

20. B. B. Pflaum, "Seeking Sane Solutions: Managing Mental Health and Chemical Dependency Costs," *Employee Benefits Journal* 16 (1992): 31–35.

21. J. Smith, "EAPs Evolve to Health Plan Gatekeeper," *Employee Benefit Plan Review* 46 (1992): 18–19.

22. E. Stetzer, "Bringing Sanity to Mental Health," *Business Health* 10 (1992): 72.

23. S. Johnson, "Results, Relapse Rates Add to Cost of Non-Hospital Treatment," *Employee Benefit Plan Review* 46 (1992): 15–16.

24. C. Mulcany, "Experts Eye Perils of Mental Health Cuts," *National Underwriter* 96 (1992): 17–18.

25. G. C. Parliman and E. L. Edwards, "Employee Assistance Programs: An Employer's Guide to Emerging Liability Issues," *Employee Relations Law Journal* 17 (1992): 593–601.

26. J. E. Fielding and P. V. Pirerchia, "Frequency of Worksite Health Promotion Activities," *American Journal of Public Health* 79 (1989): 16–20.

27. J. C. Erfurt, A. Foote, and M. A. Heirich, "The Cost-Effectiveness of Worksite Wellness Programs for Hypertension Control, Weight Loss, Smoking Cessation and Exercise," *Personnel Psychology* 45 (1992): 5–27.

28. Ibid.

29. J. B. Copeland, W. Turque, L. Wright, and D. Shapiro, "The Revenge of the Fired," *Newsweek,* February 16, 1987, 46–47.

30. J. Johnson, "Those Little Things Have to Be Heard," *Nation's Business,* July 1992, 17.

31. D. Collins, "Plant Closings: Establishing Legal Obligations," *Labor Law Journal* 40 (1989): 67–69.

32. M. Cooper and A. Holmes, "The Disaster that Never Happened," *U.S. News and World Report,* February 26, 1990, 47–48.

33. S. L. Guinn, "The Changing Workforce," *Training and Development Journal* 43 (1989): 36–39.

34. *1987 American Society for Personnel Administration and Commerce Clearing House Survey,* June 26, 1987.

35. J. A. Hollingsworth and F. A. Wiebe, "Flextime: An International Innovation with Limited U.S. Acceptance," *Industrial Management* 31 (1989): 22–26.

36. J. L. Pierce, J. W. Newstrom, R. B. Dunham, and A. E. Barber, *Alternative Work Schedules* (Needham Heights, Mass.: Allyn and Bacon, 1989).

37. S. Shellenbarger, "Managers Navigate Uncharted Waters Trying to Resolve Work-Family Conflicts," *The Wall Street Journal,* December 7, 1992, B1, B7.

38. V. A. Schein, E. H. Mauner, and J. F. Novak, "Impact of Flexible Working Hours on Productivity," *Journal of Applied Psychology* 62 (1977): 463–465.

39. Pierce et al., *Alternative Work Schedules.*

40. D. E. Friedman, "Addressing the Supply Problem: The Family Daycare Approach," *Investing in People: A Strategy to Address America's Workforce Crisis* (Washington, D. C.: U.S. Department of Labor, 1989).

41. E. E. Kossek, "Diversity in Child Care Assistance Needs: Employee Problems, Preferences, and Work-Related Outcomes," *Personnel Psychology* 43 (1990): 769–791.

42. E. E. Kossek, *The Acceptance of Human Resource Innovation: Lessons from Management* (Westport, Conn.: Quorum, 1989).

43. S. E. Sullivan and J. B. Gilmore, "Employers Begin to Accept Eldercare as a Business Issue," *Personnel* 68 (1991): 3–4.

44. J. C. Mason, "IBM at the Crossroads," *Management Review* 80 (1991): 10–14.

EASING THE PHYSICIAN SHORTAGE

Because of their small budgets and location, inner-city hospitals, as well as those in remote rural areas, have a very difficult time recruiting physicians. Employers in the health-care industry in such areas have increasingly turned toward nurse practitioners as the solution to this problem. Unlike physician's assistants, who must work under a doctor's supervision, nurse practitioners work independently and can even prescribe certain medications on their own. With an average salary of around $42,000, nurse practitioners are a cost-effective means of supplying quality health care in rural and inner-city locations.

The number of nurse practitioners available, however, is small. The field is still female-dominated, and while more women are becoming physicians, few men have taken up the slack and adopted nurse practitioner careers. Thus, there is currently a labor shortage in this area, with four jobs available for every graduate of a nurse practitioner program.

Assume that you were the human resource director at a rural hospital whose organizational strategy was to reduce costs through the use of nurse practitioners, and then answer the following questions.

QUESTIONS

1. What steps in the area of employee relations would you, as human resource director, take to make your organization more attractive to potential employees with nurse practitioner qualifications? Differentiate short-term and long-term strategies.

2. How would you make the policies discussed above known to potential applicants for these positions? In what ways must employers with progressive employee relations support these practices with aggressive information campaigns?

SOUTHWEST AIRLINES: COMPETING THROUGH PEOPLE

V I D E O   C A S E

For some organizations, the slogan "focus on customers" is merely a slogan. At Southwest Airlines, however, it is a daily goal. For example, Southwest employees responded quickly to a customer complaint: Five students who commuted weekly to an out-of-state medical school notified Southwest that the most convenient flight got them to class 15 minutes late. To accommodate the students, Southwest moved the departure time up by a quarter of an hour.

Southwest Airlines is an organization that has built its business and corporate culture around the tenets of total quality management. Focus on the customer, employee involvement and empowerment, and continuous improvement are not just buzz words to Southwest employees or to Herb Kelleher, CEO of Southwest Airlines in Dallas. In fact, Kelleher has even enlisted passengers in the effort to strengthen the customer-driven culture. Frequent fliers are asked to assist personnel managers in interviewing and selecting prospective flight attendants. Focus groups are used to help measure passenger response to new services and to help generate new ideas for improving current services. Additionally, the roughly 1,000 customers who write to the company every week generally get a personal response within four weeks.

The Airline Industry

Southwest has been posting hefty profits in an industry that expected to lose $2 billion in 1992. Since the 1978 Airline Deregulation Act, constant fare wars and intense competition have contributed to a turbulent environment for the industry. Under deregulation, the government no longer dictates where a given airline will fly and which cities should have service. Rates and service are now determined through competitive forces. The impact on the industry has been tremendous. In 1991 alone, three carriers went through bankruptcy and liquidation, and in early 1992, TWA sought protection from its creditors. Very few airlines, such as Southwest, American, and Delta, have continued to grow during the late 1980s and early 1990s.

Both external factors, such as the price of jet fuel and the strength of the economy, and internal factors, including routing system designs, computerized reservation systems, and motivated, competent employees, help to determine success. The airline industry is capital intensive, with large expenditures for planes. In addition, carriers must provide superior customer service. Delayed flights, lost baggage, over-booked flights, cancellations, and unhelpful airline employees can quickly alienate an airline's passengers.

Southwest's Corporate Strategy

Herb Kelleher has been the primary force in developing and maintaining a vision and strategy which have enabled Southwest Airlines to grow and maintain profitability. Created in the late 1960s as a low-fare, high-frequency, short haul, point-to-point, single-class, noninterlining, fun-loving airline, it expands by "doing the same old thing at each new airport," Kelleher reports.

"Taking a different approach" is the Southwest way, which has allowed the airline to maintain a 15 percent annual growth rate even during a period of drastic change. Although reservations and ticketing are done in advance of a flight, seating occurs on a first-come, first-serve basis and is only one illustration of the company's nonconformist practices. Turnaround times are kept to an industry low of 15 minutes with the help of pilots and crew who clean and restock the planes. Refreshments are limited to soft drinks and peanuts, except on its longer flights when cookies and crackers are added to the menu. Southwest does not exchange tickets or baggage with other carriers. Kelleher has noted that if Southwest adopted an assigned seating and computerized, interlining reservation system, ground time would increase enough to necessitate the purchase of at least seven additional airplanes. At a cost of $25 million a piece, the impact on the fares customers pay would be high. Currently, Southwest charges significantly less than its competitors.

Corporate Philosophy, Culture, and HRM Practices

How does Southwest maintain its unique, cost effective position? In an industry in which antagonistic labor-management relations are common, how does Southwest build cooperation with a work force that is 85 percent unionized? Led by Kelleher, the corporation has developed a culture that treats employees the same way it treats passengers—by paying attention, being responsive, and involving them in decisions.

According to Ann Rhoades, Vice-President of People (the company's top HRM person), the company does not keep employees by paying them at a level higher than other airlines (although average pay is among the highest) but, rather, by treating them as part of the family. As Kelleher has stated, "If you don't treat your own people well, they won't treat other people well." So, Southwest's focus is not only on the customer but on the employees, too.

A positive work environment brings with it high expectations for employee initiative and performance at Southwest, however. Evidence of the company culture can be seen in the recruitment and selection process, which takes place only in the cities to which Southwest flies, "because we think people have to know us to understand us," says Rhoades. "We look for extroverts, people with a sense of humor and who say 'we' rather than 'I,'" she says. Job applications for 2,400 positions in 1993 are expected to reach 90,000. This large labor pool allows the company to hire employees who most closely fit a culture in which they are asked to use their own judgment and to go beyond "the job description."

Kelleher's philosophy of "fun in the workplace" can be seen in a number of company practices. Company parties can be triggered by many events, including the CEO's birthday, when employees dress in black. The annual company chili cook-off, Southwest's annual awards dinner, and the every Friday "Fun Day," when employees wear casual clothes or even costumes to work, illustrate the company credo that a sense of humor is a must and that relaxed people are productive people. Kevin Krone, Area Manager of Marketing in the Detroit office, described efforts by the Detroit area airport employees to set up get-togethers to foster both fun and the commitment to the Southwest family that supports the airline's culture.

Employee involvement in decision making is another key tenet of organizational culture at Southwest. "Everyone affected by a decision is involved in making the decision," Rhoades says. An active, informal suggestion system and all types of incentives (cash, merchandise, and travel passes) serve to reward employees for their ideas. Both teams and individuals are expected, as part of their role at Southwest, to contribute to the development of customer service improvements and cost savings.

Corporate responses to difficult issues are consistently formulated around the company philosophy. As the cost of benefits has risen, cost-conscious Southwest redesigned the employee benefits program into a flexible plan. However, the company went a step further. The director of benefits and compensation, Libby Sartain, believed that for the effort to succeed and satisfy employees, communication was critical. After seeking the advice of more than 700 employees in seven different cities, a promotional program that parodied newspapers and morning news shows was presented. Horoscopes, advice columns, and advertisements all promoted the new program, BenefitsPlus. Employees found this format more fun and less intimidating than the traditional benefits brochure. In fact, the effort won Southwest first place in the 1990 Business Insurance Employee Benefits Communication Awards competition. More importantly, employees understand their benefits options and appreciate the willingness of their organization to communicate openly.

Many human resource practices have been designed to support the company culture. Compensation programs are designed to increase the connections between Southwest and its employees, who enjoy the benefits of a profit-sharing program. Southwest employees own roughly 11 percent of the company's outstanding stock. The company's union contracts have avoided overly restrictive work rules in order to support the efficient operation of the company. Part of the company credo is that employees need to be able (and want to be able) to step in wherever they are needed, regardless of job title or classification. In 1990, a five-year contract with the pilots was negotiated, demonstrating the trust between the employees and the organization. Annual employee turnover, at 7 percent, is the industry's lowest.

The combined focus on customers and employees has led to an increase in the diversity of Southwest's work force. To serve passengers in the southwestern United States more effectively, the company has been recruiting Spanish-speaking employees as well as offering a Spanish Berlitz course at a discount to current employees.

The employees of Southwest are actively involved in numerous community-based service projects at Ronald McDonald house and the Junior Olympics, among others. This commitment to service is encouraged and demonstrated within the organization, too. A catastrophe fund, initiated by employees, supports individual employees during personal crises. Departments frequently show appreciation to other departments by giving awards and parties.

SOURCES:
J. Castelli, "Finding the Right Fit," *HRMagazine,* September 1990, 38–41; D.K. Henderson, "Southwest Luvs Passengers, Employees, Profits," *Air Transport World,* July 1991, 32–41; J.E. Hitchcock, "Southwest Airlines Renovates Benefits System," *HRMagazine,* July 1992, 54–56; C.A. Jaffe, "Moving Fast by Standing Still," *Nation's Business,* October 1991, 57–59; J.C. Quick, "Crafting an Organizational Culture: Herb's Hand at Southwest," *Organizational Dynamics,* 21 (1992): 45–56; R.S. Teitelbaum, "Southwest Airlines: Where Service Flies Right," *Fortune,* August 24, 1992, 115–116.

Kelleher claims that Southwest will not expand through the purchase of other airlines because the difficulty of merging two corporate cultures, particularly when one is so strong, would be too great. "Our people are very proud of what they've created. They look on Southwest Airlines as a crusade, and a crusade is an emotional thing. I don't think you can transfer that.

"We tell our people that we value inconsistency," Kelleher explains. "By that I mean that we're going to carry 20 million passengers this year and that I can't foresee all of the situations that will arise at the stations across our system. So what we tell our people is, 'Hey, we can't anticipate all of these things, **you** handle them the best way possible. **You** make a judgement and use **your** discretion; we trust you'll do the right thing.' If we think you've done something erroneous, we'll let you know—without criticism, without backbiting."

Employees offer a large number of what they consider to be "everyday examples" of ways they provide high-quality service to their customers. When a California customer service agent was approached by a harried man who needed to catch a flight to meet his vacationing family, the man wanted to check his dog onto the flight. Because Southwest does not fly animals, this could have caused him to miss the flight and his family. The service agent involved volunteered to take the dog home, care for it, and bring the dog back to meet the man two weeks later, upon his return. A torn-up back yard and a very appreciative customer were the outcomes.

DISCUSSION QUESTIONS

1. How has Southwest dealt with the competitive challenges in the airline industry today? Rank, in order of importance, the various human resource practices and business practices (such as the low price strategy) that Southwest Airlines has developed to successfully meet its competitive challenges.

2. How might a ground crew supervisor at Southwest describe her job, given the corporate culture and practices of this organization?

3. Which Southwest HRM strategies directly support total quality management?

4. What aspects of work life at Southwest do you think you would most enjoy and least enjoy? Why?

5. Would the HRM practices used at Southwest Airlines work in other organizations? Why or why not?

ASSESSING WORK AND WORK OUTCOMES

We have discussed how companies must consider internal and external environmental characteristics (business strategy, globalization, legal environment, employee relations) to manage human resources to gain a competitive advantage. In addition, to remain competitive, companies must design work processes to maximize the quality of products and services. Also, companies need to determine how employees' contributions to the quality of products or services will be measured.

In Chapter 6, "The Analysis and Design of Work," we examine how work is designed and analyzed. An understanding of the entire process of developing a product or providing a service is essential to meeting total quality goals. Chapter 6 discusses how work-flow processes are analyzed and demonstrates how managers can obtain detailed information about jobs. This information is critical not only for work design but also for employee selection, training, and compensation. The chapter emphasizes how various aspects of work are related to employee satisfaction, productivity, and physical well-being.

Simultaneously with designing work, the company should identify how it will determine employee's effectiveness in providing products and services. In Chapter 7, "Performance Management," we examine the strengths and weaknesses of different approaches to performance management that are based on behavior, bottom-line results, and quality. We discuss how managers can most effectively use performance information to motivate employees to improve their performance.

Chapter 8, "Work Attitudes and Job Withdrawal," discusses the important employee work attitudes that have the potential to affect competitiveness. Job withdrawal and job dissatisfaction have been shown to be related to absenteeism, health problems, and turnover, all of which adversely affect company competitiveness. The chapter identifies company policies and manager actions that can help prevent job dissatisfaction and job withdrawal.

6

THE ANALYSIS AND DESIGN OF WORK

Objectives *After reading this chapter, you should be able to:*

1. Analyze a work-flow process, identifying the output, activities, and inputs in the production of a product or service.
2. Understand the importance of job analysis in strategic and human resource management.
3. Choose the right job-analysis technique for a variety of human resource activities.
4. Identify the tasks performed and the skills required in a given job.
5. Understand the different approaches to job design.
6. Understand the trade-offs among the various approaches to designing jobs.

Redesigning Work for Today's Marketplace

In today's competitive world, organizations are increasingly facing the need to increase productivity via downsizing or "right-sizing." In the past, they sought to increase productivity by producing more units to capitalize on economies of scale. Now, however, the rules have changed, and they must compete by offering a better, higher-quality product, customized to the needs of the customer, at a lower price. This requires a massive redesign or "reengineering" of the way work is performed.

For example, at Duke Power Company in Charlotte, North Carolina, the customer-service function had been decentralized, with 260 customer-service representatives working at 96 separate locations. These employees worked during usual business hours and had little training in the functioning of the utility company or its services. Thus, when customers called, the representatives often had to refer them to another department or to put the customer on hold while the representative sought the relevant information.

Facing deregulation and potential competition in its market, Duke Power had to find innovative ways to more effectively meet its customers' needs. This required a redesign of work in its entire customer-service function. Now, customer-service reps work at one site, and service is available 24 hours a day via an answering service. The reps have been extensively trained and have information at their fingertips so that they can achieve the goal of answering 100 percent of the questions callers ask. They now have more duties and make more decisions and have increased their earnings by 10 percent. The strategy has paid off, as Duke Power has reduced the number of walk-in customers, which are very costly to the company.

Whirlpool Corporation, the world's largest appliance manufacturer, has similarly redesigned its customer-service function.

Historically customer service has been performed by service technicians going to the customer's home, diagnosing the problem, and fixing the appliance. However, in an effort to meet the needs of cost-conscious customers, Whirlpool centralized its customer-service phone center in Knoxville, Tennessee. When customers call the 800 service line, they speak with a customer-service rep, many times a former service technician, who can help to diagnose the problem over the phone. The rep can set up a service appointment with the local Whirlpool service center or can order the parts for those customers who want to do-it-themselves. In addition, these reps can help talk customers through fixing their own appliances over the phone.

These are just two examples of how increasing competition is affecting the way work is performed. However, one thing is certain. In a world of global competition, all companies will have to rethink their traditional view of work and redesign it to meet customers' needs with quick, high-quality products and services.

SOURCE: W. Neikirk, "Wanted: Skilled Jack-of-All-Trades," *Chicago Tribune*, February 22, 1993, sect. 1, p. 1.

INTRODUCTION

In Chapter 2, we discussed the processes of strategy formulation and strategy implementation. Strategy formulation is the process by which the company decides how it will compete in the marketplace; this is often the energizing and guiding force for everything it does. Strategy implementation is the way the strategic plan gets carried out in activities of organizational members. We noted in that chapter that there are five important components in the strategy implementation process, three of which are directly related to the human resource management function and one of which we will discuss in this chapter: the task or job.[1]

One of the first tasks of strategy implementation is to design the tasks that are to be performed. If a company seeks to compete in the automobile market, it will have to define and engage in all the tasks necessary to produce automobiles. These include jobs such as gathering market information, designing the cars, planning production schedules, and actually producing the automobiles. In addition, each of these tasks requires identifying a set of more detailed tasks that have to be performed, down to identifying the specific tasks each individual will perform.

The way in which a firm competes can have a profound impact on the way tasks are organized, and the way the tasks are designed may provide the company with a competitive advantage.[2] For example, if a company wishes to engage in a low-cost strategy, it will often organize into tasks that are very simple and repetitive.[3] General Motors uses an assembly-line work process whereby union employees perform very narrowly defined sets of tasks. In this type of work system, employees can be viewed as a commodity—that is, an input that is easily replaceable because of the low level of skill required. This allows the company to hire individuals who may not have a high level of skill and easily train them how to perform the job.

On the other hand, if a company wishes to compete on the criterion of quality, it may choose to organize its production process quite differently. For example, Volvo, an automobile company known for its high-quality products, organizes its production process around work teams, each of which has a set of responsibilities and the authority to decide how to carry out those responsibilities.[4] Note that the same tasks are performed in both cases (e.g., assembling a wheel to the axle), yet these tasks may be grouped together differently. In the former case, one individual would perform a narrow range of tasks (as in assembly-line production), while in the second case, the team has a broad range of tasks to complete, and the team members have the authority to decide how to complete them.

In addition, the ways in which jobs are designed can in fact affect company work-unit performance. In a study within the automobile industry, researchers noted that one trend in auto plants was toward reducing the number of job classifications, thus allowing or requiring workers to perform a broader range of tasks. They found that reducing the classifications did not affect labor productivity or product quality, but that it did lead to an improvement in economic performance.[5]

TABLE 6.1   Key Terms in the Analysis and Design of Work
(Illustrated by a Professor's Job)

Element

The smallest divisible unit of work, without analyzing distinct motions or mental processes (e.g., "Writes a test question").

Task

A collection of elements performed closely in time having a meaningful and identifiable outcome (e.g., "Constructs examinations for testing student knowledge of material").

Duty

A collection of tasks having a common objective or focus (e.g., teaching).

Position

A collection of tasks, and duties assigned to be performed by a single individual (e.g., the budgeted position that is filled by your professor).

Job

A collection of positions that are similar enough in tasks and duties to share a common job title (e.g., assistant professor of management).

Job Family

A collection of jobs similar enough in tasks and duties to be grouped together for some personnel purpose, e.g., validating a selection system (e.g., assistant professors, associate professors, and full professors in management).

Occupation

A job or collection of jobs found across a number of different organizations (e.g., academic professors in general).

This chapter discusses the design and analysis of work. Table 6.1 presents some of the key terms that are necessary to understand how work is analyzed and designed. The fields of job analysis and job design have extensive overlap, yet in the past they have been treated differently.[6] Job analysis has focused on analyzing existing jobs to gather information for other human resource management practices such as selection, training, performance appraisal, or compensation.[7] Job design, on the other hand, has focused on redesigning existing jobs to make them more efficient or more motivating to jobholders.[8] Thus, job design has had a more proactive orientation toward changing the job, whereas job analysis has had a passive, information-gathering orientation. However, as we will show in this chapter, these two approaches are interrelated.

One of the major problems in the past has been that HR professionals and line managers have examined a particular job in isolation from the larger process of the unit's work flow. Both job analysis and job design are only subsets of the broader topic of work-flow design. **Work-flow design** is the process of analyzing the tasks necessary for the production of a product or service and allocating these tasks to particular work units or individuals. Thus, the first section of this chapter discusses the analysis of work process within a given work unit. This work analysis is strongly tied to the strategic management of an organization and has received increasing attention because of the total quality management (TQM) movement discussed in Chapter 1. Having provided an understanding of the broader context of jobs, the chapter discusses the need for and usefulness of both job analysis and the techniques for performing job analysis. Finally, the chapter concludes by presenting the various approaches to job design to provide managers with an understanding of the costs and benefits of emphasizing different characteristics of jobs when designing or redesigning them.

WORK-FLOW ANALYSIS

To understand adequately any individual job, a manager must first understand the larger context in which the job exists. To view a particular position in isolation from other positions with which it is interdependent will result in a flawed conception of the position. Therefore, effective managers have an accurate picture of the work flow in their departments or work units.

For example, as noted in Chapter 1, the institution of the Malcolm Baldrige National Quality award resulted in the development of many TQM programs in American businesses. A theme common to nearly all quality programs is the need to identify clearly the outputs of work, to specify the quality standards for those outputs, and to analyze the processes and inputs necessary for producing outputs that meet the quality standards.[9] This conception of the work-flow process is useful for TQM because it provides a means for the manager to understand all the tasks required to produce a high-quality product as well as the skills necessary to perform those tasks. This work-flow process is depicted in Figure 6.1. In this section, we present an approach for analyzing the work process of a department as a means of examining jobs in the context of an organization.

Analyzing Work Outputs

Every work unit, whether a department, team, or individual, seeks to produce some output that others can use. An output is the product of a work unit and is often an identifiable thing, such as a completed purchase order, an employment test, or a hot, juicy hamburger. However, an output can also be a service, such as the services provided by an airline that transports you to some destination, a housecleaning service that maintains your house, or a baby-sitter who watches over your children.

We often picture an organization only in terms of the product that it produces and focus on that product as the output. For example, one could

FIGURE 6.1   Developing a Work-Unit Activity Analysis

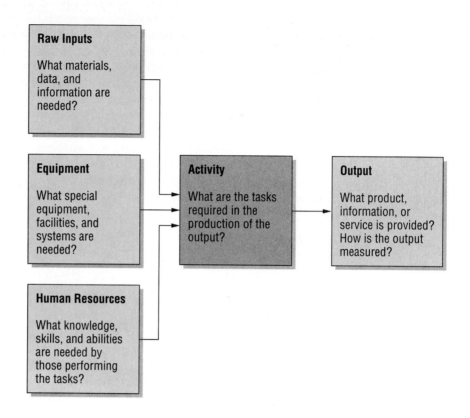

easily identify the output of IBM as computers. However, to produce computers requires many work units, each generating a variety of outputs, and
each of these work units has a number of individuals who generate some
work output. Thus, an important determinant of the effectiveness of any
organization is the efficiency and effectiveness with which it produces the
many products within the various work units.

However, merely identifying an output or set of outputs is not sufficient. Once these outputs have been identified, it is necessary to specify the
standards for the quantity or quality of these outputs. For example, a
recently developed productivity improvement technique known as ProMES
(productivity measurement and evaluation system) focuses attention on
both identifying work-unit outputs and specifying the levels of required
performance for different levels of effectiveness.[10] With ProMES, the members of a work unit identify each of the products (outputs) of the work unit
for the various customers. They then evaluate the effectiveness of each level
of products in the eyes of their customers. For example, ProMES was used
in a military auto-repair shop. As shown in Figure 6.2, members of the work
unit identified four products and the levels of effectiveness associated with
different product levels. This technique provides a means of examining the

FIGURE 6.2 Examples of ProMES Output Effectiveness Functions

Objective performance is shown on the horizontal axes and rated effectiveness on the vertical axes.

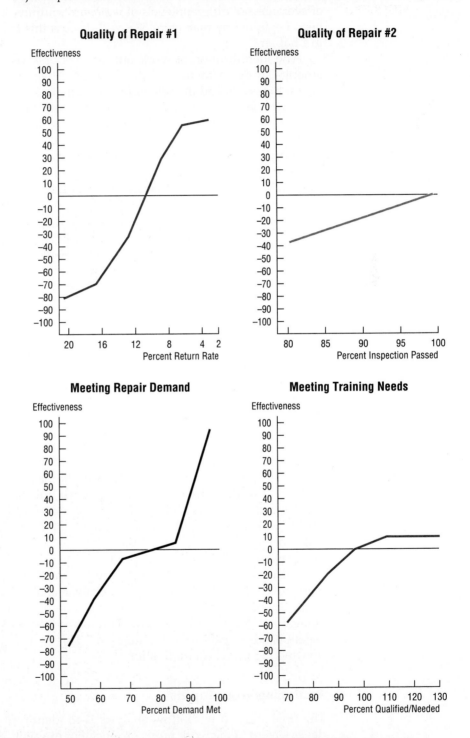

SOURCE: R. Pritchard, S. Jones, P. Roth, K. Stuebing, and S. Ekeberg, (1989) The evaluation of an Integrated Approach to Measuring Organizational Productivity, Vol. 42, No. 1, p. 78. *Personnel Psychology.*

effectiveness of different levels of work-unit outputs, a process that has long been neglected by managers. We will discuss this technique in more detail in Chapter 7.

The identification of work outputs has only recently gained attention among HR departments. As discussed in Chapter 2, HR executives have begun to understand the role of the HR department as they have attempted to analyze their customers inside the company and the products that those customers desire from the HR function.[11] This has resulted in HR managers' having a clearer understanding of the specific products that they supply to the company and allows them to focus on producing high-quality products. Without an understanding of the output of a work unit, any attempt at increasing work-unit effectiveness will be futile.

Analyzing Work Processes

Once one has identified the outputs of the work unit, it is possible to examine the work processes used to generate the output. The work processes are the activities that members of a work unit engage in to produce a given output. Every process consists of operating procedures that specify how things should be done at each stage of the development of the product. These procedures include all the tasks that must be performed in the production of the output. These tasks are usually broken down into those performed by each person in the work unit.

Again, to design work systems that are maximally efficient, a manager needs to understand the processes required in the development of the products for that work unit. Often, as work loads increase within a work group, the group will grow by adding positions to meet these new requirements. However, when the work load lightens, members may take on tasks that do not relate to the work unit's product in an effort to appear busy. Without a clear understanding of the tasks necessary to the production of an output, it is difficult to determine whether the work unit has become overstaffed. Having a clear understanding of the tasks required allows the manager to specify which tasks are to be carried out by which individuals and eliminate tasks that are not necessary for the desired end. This ensures that the work group maintains a high level of productivity.

For example, Microsoft, currently the most successful computer software company in the world, strategically manages the design of the total work-flow process for competitive advantage. To maintain the sense of being an underdog, Microsoft deliberately understaffs its product teams in "small bands of people with a mission." This ensures both a lean organization and high levels of motivation.[12]

Analyzing Work Inputs

The final stage in work-flow analysis is to identify the inputs used in the development of the work unit's product. For example, assume that you were assigned a paper on "The Importance of Human Resources to Organizational

Performance." The output of your work process will be a paper that you will turn in to the professor. To produce this paper, you must perform a number of tasks, such as conducting research, reading articles, and writing the paper. What, however, are the inputs? As shown in Figure 6.1, these inputs can be broken down into the raw materials, equipment, and human skills needed to perform the tasks. *Raw materials* consist of the materials that will be converted into the work unit's product. Thus, for your assignment, the raw materials would be the information available in the library regarding the various effects of human resources on organizational performance.

Equipment refers to the technology and machinery necessary to transform the raw materials into the product. As you attempt to develop your paper, you may go to the library and use the library computer-search system that provides you with a list of recent articles on the relationship between human resources and organizational performance. In addition, once you sit down to write, you will most likely have to use either a typewriter or, more likely in today's high-technology world, a word processor to put your thoughts on paper.

The final inputs in the work-flow process are the *human skills* and efforts necessary to perform the tasks. Many skills are required of you in producing your paper. For example, you need to have some knowledge of how to work the library computer-search facilities, you need to have some typing skill (or know the phone number of a good typist), and you definitely need the ability to reason and write. Again, these skills are much more valuable for producing a high-quality product than are other skills such as being able to play a saxophone.

It is important to note that a flawed product can be caused by deficiencies at any phase in the production process. For example, if you fail to perform the task of spell-checking your paper before turning it in, you may receive a lower grade. Similarly, if you cannot obtain the best raw materials (i.e., you cannot find the right articles), use the proper equipment (e.g., the computer is down), or do not possess the necessary skills (you do not write well), your paper will receive less than the maximum grade.

The same process used to analyze an individual's work assignment can be applied at the work-unit level. Work units consist of people performing certain tasks aimed at producing a specified output. If the work-flow process is to be performed effectively, the individuals in the work unit must first have the skills necessary to perform the required tasks. However, they also must completely understand and be willing to perform the tasks required of them. It is ultimately the manager's responsibility to obtain these inputs—that is, to ensure that the individuals in the work unit have the necessary skills and are motivated to perform these tasks. The "Competing through Quality" box provides an example of how paying careful attention to the entire work-flow process can provide companies with a competitive advantage.

This analysis is often complex. Thus, in carrying out their responsibilities, managers usually seek guidance from the human resource function. The HR department can aid managers by working together to analyze the jobs, that is, by helping them to identify the tasks performed and the skills

Quality

COMPETING THROUGH

TOTAL QUALITY MANAGEMENT AND WORK-FLOW DESIGN AT CARRIER

Work-flow analysis and design is an integral part of TQM efforts. Most TQM approaches emphasize the need to understand the outputs, activities, and inputs to ensure the highest quality. Carrier Corporation exemplifies the value of analyzing work-flow process to maximize both quality and productivity.

At their Arkadelphia, Arkansas, plant, which manufactures compressors, work teams have the authority to make decisions about the workplace, even to the point of rearranging the work-flow process. One work team realized that the machines were laid out so that a compressor would have to skip one machine, only to have to be brought back to that machine later in the production process. Because this process was cumbersome and inefficient, the team made the decision one morning to pull up the machines and

rearrange them. This idea was approved by one supervisor, and the work area was reorganized within four days. In most plants, such a change would have been bogged down in management committees for months.

In addition, the workers are trained to perform a large number of different jobs in the plant. This provides Carrier with two types of flexibility. First, on a daily basis, if one employee is sick, others can fill in quickly. Second, as Thomas Kassouf, president of the compressor division points out, "The whole plant could probably be reconfigured in several weeks' time." The success of the plant is evidenced by the fact that Carrier expects to produce each compressor for $35 less than it would cost to buy them from other producers. This could save the firm as much as $26.3 million a year.

SOURCE: E. Norton, "Small, Flexible Plants May Play Crucial Role in U.S. Manufacturing," *The Wall Street Journal,* January 13, 1993, A1–A2.

required to perform them. This is the process of job analysis, which will be discussed in the next section. Also, sometimes there may be a need to design new jobs or to redesign existing jobs to maximize work-unit performance. The process of job design will be discussed later in this chapter.

As you can see, managers need to understand the production process for their work unit to maximize its efficiency and effectiveness. But how does a manager develop an understanding of the various jobs that make up the work unit? This knowledge is gained through job analysis.

JOB ANALYSIS

Job analysis refers to the process of getting detailed information about jobs.[13] Job analysis has deep historical roots. For example, in his description of the "just" state, Socrates argued that society needed to recognize three things. First, there are individual differences in aptitudes for work, meaning that individuals differ in their abilities. Second, unique aptitude requirements exist for different occupations. Third, to achieve high-quality performance, society must attempt to place people in occupations that best suit their aptitudes. In other words, for society (or an organization) to succeed, it must have detailed information about the requirements of jobs (through job analysis), and it must ensure that a match exists between the job requirements and individuals' aptitudes (through selection).[14]

Whereas Socrates was concerned with the larger society, it is even more important for organizations to understand and match job requirements and people to achieve high-quality performance. This is particularly true in today's competitive marketplace. Thus, the information gained through job analysis is of utmost importance; it has great value to both human resource and line managers.

The Importance of Job Analysis to HR Managers

Job analysis is such an important activity to HR managers that it has been called the building block of everything that personnel does.[15] This statement refers to the fact that almost every human resource program requires some type of information that is gleaned from job analysis: selection, performance appraisal, training and development, job evaluation, career planning, work redesign, and human resource planning.[16]

Selection.   Human resource selection deals with identifying the most qualified applicants for employment. To identify which applicants are most qualified, it is first necessary to determine the tasks that will be performed by the individual hired and the knowledge, skills, and abilities the individual must have to perform the job effectively. This information is gained through job analysis.[17]

Performance Appraisal.   Performance appraisal deals with getting information about how well each employee is performing his or her job in order to reward those who are effective, improve the performance of those who are ineffective, or provide a written justification for why the poor performer should be disciplined. Through job analysis, the organization can identify the behaviors and results that distinguish effective performance from ineffective performance.[18]

Training and Development.   Almost every employee hired by an organization will require some training in his or her job. Some training programs may be more extensive than others, but all require the trainer to have identified the tasks performed in the job to ensure that the training will prepare individuals to perform the job effectively.[19]

Job Evaluation.   The process of job evaluation involves assessing the relative dollar-value worth of each job to the organization to set up internally equitable pay structures. If pay structures are not equitable, employees will be dissatisfied and quit, or they will not see the benefits of striving for promotions. To put dollar values on jobs, it is necessary to get information about different jobs to determine which jobs deserve higher pay than others.[20]

Career Planning.   Career planning entails matching an individual's skills and aspirations with opportunities that are or may become available in the organization. This matching process requires that those in charge of career planning know the skill requirements of the various jobs. This allows them to guide individuals into jobs in which they will succeed and be satisfied.

Work Redesign.   As previously discussed, job analysis and job design are interrelated. Often, a firm will seek to redesign work to make it more efficient or effective. To redesign the work, detailed information about the existing job(s) must be available. In addition, redesigning a job will, in fact, be similar to analyzing a job that does not yet exist.

Human Resource Planning.   In human resource planning, planners analyze an organization's human resource needs in a dynamic environment and develop activities that enable a firm to adapt to change. This planning process requires accurate information about the levels of skill required in various jobs to ensure that enough individuals are available in the organization to meet the human resource needs of the strategic plan.[21]

The Importance of Job Analysis to Line Managers

Job analysis is clearly important to the HR department's various activities, but it may not be as clear why it is important to line managers. There are many reasons. First, managers must have detailed information about all the jobs in their work group to understand the work-flow process. Earlier in this chapter, we noted the importance of understanding the work-flow process, specifically, identifying the tasks performed and the knowledge, skills, and abilities required to perform them. In addition, an understanding of this work-flow process is essential if a manager chooses to redesign certain aspects to increase efficiency or effectiveness.

Second, managers need to understand the job requirements to make intelligent hiring decisions. Very seldom do employees get hired by the human resource department without a manager's input. Managers will often interview prospective applicants and recommend who should receive a job offer. However, if the manager does not have a clear understanding of what tasks are performed on the job and the skills necessary to perform them, then the hiring decision may result in employees whom the manager "likes" but who are not capable of performing the job successfully.

Third, a manager is responsible for ensuring that each individual is performing his or her job satisfactorily (or better). This requires the manager to evaluate how well each person is performing and to provide feedback to those whose performance needs improvement. Again, this requires that the manager clearly understand the tasks required in every job.

Job-Analysis Information

There are a number of methods for analyzing jobs and no "one best way." Each job-analysis method provides a different type of information; thus, the method used will depend on the type of information ultimately needed. In this section, we first discuss the different types of information gleaned from job analysis. Then, we will discuss four different methods for analyzing jobs in the context of those types of information in order to provide an analysis of the different types of job-analysis information provided by particular techniques. Then we present one practical hands-on approach that is most useful for managers who are attempting to get information about jobs for their purposes.

Two types of information are most useful in job analysis: job descriptions and job specifications. A **job description** is a list of the tasks, duties, and responsibilities (TDRs) that the job entails. TDRs are observable actions. For example, a clerical job requires the jobholder to type. If you were to observe someone in that position over the course of a day, you would certainly see him or her typing at one time or another. When a manager attempts to evaluate job performance, it is most important to have detailed information about the work performed in the job (i.e., the TDRs). This makes it possible to determine how well an individual is meeting each job requirement. A sample job description is provided in Table 6.2.

A **job specification** is a list of the knowledge, skills, abilities, and other characteristics (KSAOs) that an individual must have to perform the job. *Knowledge* refers to factual or procedural information that is necessary for successfully performing a task. A *skill* is an individual's level of proficiency at performing a particular task. *Ability* refers to a more general enduring capability that an individual possesses. Finally, other characteristics might be personality traits such as one's achievement motivation or persistence. Thus, KSAOs are characteristics about people that are not directly observable; they are only observable when individuals are carrying out the TDRs of the job. Thus, if someone applied for the clerical job discussed, you could not simply look at the individual to determine whether she or he possessed typing skills. However, if you were to observe that individual type something, you could make an assessment of the level of typing skill the individual had. When a manager is attempting to fill a position, it is important to have accurate information about the characteristics a successful jobholder must have. This requires focusing on the KSAOs of each applicant.

Thus, the type of information gained in job analysis differs in terms of whether it is information about the work performed or about the worker performing it. In addition, job-analysis techniques differ in the specificity of the information they provide.[22] Some job-analysis techniques provide information that is very detailed and specific to a given job or a set of closely related jobs. This information is useful for developing performance-appraisal or selection systems that are closely tailored to a particular job. On the other hand, some job-analysis techniques use a standardized informational frame-

TABLE 6.2   A Sample Job Description

General Description of Job: General maintenance and repair of all equipment used in the operations of a particular district. Includes the servicing of company vehicles, shop equipment, and machinery used on job sites.

1. *Essential Duty (40%): Maintenance of Equipment*

   Tasks: Keep a log of all maintenance performed on equipment. Replace parts and fluids according to maintenance schedule. Regularly check gauges and loads for deviances that may indicate problems with equipment. Perform nonroutine maintenance as required. May involve limited supervision and training of operators performing maintenance.

2. *Essential Duty (40%): Repair of Equipment*

   Tasks: Requires inspection of equipment and a recommendation that a piece be scrapped or repaired. If equipment is to be repaired mechanic will take whatever steps are necessary to return the piece to working order. This may include a partial or total rebuilding of the piece using various hand tools and equipment. Will primarily involve the overhaul and troubleshooting of diesel engines and hydraulic equipment.

3. *Essential Duty (10%): Testing and Approval*

   Tasks: Ensure that all required maintenance and repair has been performed and that it was performed according to manufacturer specifications. Approve or reject equipment, as being ready for use on a job.

4. *Essential Duty (10%): Maintain Stock*

   Tasks: Maintain inventory of parts needed for the maintenance and repair of equipment. Responsible for ordering satisfactory parts and supplies at the lowest possible cost.

Nonessential Functions

   Other duties as assigned.

---

work that is applied to examine all jobs. These techniques provide very general information that enables managers to compare dissimilar jobs. This information is most useful for developing internally equitable compensation systems and for developing effective career plans.

Figure 6.3 shows the four types of information that can be gained from job analysis.[23]

Position-Specific Worker Information.   First, in quadrant 1, job analysis can provide information about the worker (i.e., KSA) that is very specific to the job being analyzed. This might be specific bits of technical knowledge (e.g., knowledge of electrical wiring for microwave ovens) that one would be expected to have or skills in operating a particular piece of equipment. This information is useful in many different human resource activities. Such

FIGURE 6.3   Types of Information That Can Be Gained in Job Analysis

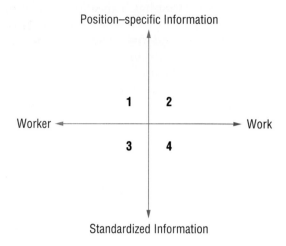

SOURCE: Adapted from P. Wright and K. Wexley, "How to Choose the Job-Analysis Method You Really Need," *Personnel*, May 1985, 51–55.

information is especially useful for developing tests that focus on measuring an applicant's technical knowledge.[24] It is also useful for developing performance-appraisal systems that provide feedback regarding an employee's specific knowledge or skill deficiencies. Finally, it is useful for developing the content of many training programs aimed at increasing employee knowledge and skill in a particular job.

Position-Specific Work Information.   Job analysis may also focus on providing information about the type of work performed. Quadrant 2 represents information about the specific tasks performed in the job, and this information is very detailed. This type of information would be in the form of statements describing the particular task performed with reference to specific tools, machines, or other positions. It is especially useful for selection, performance appraisal, training, and job redesign. Again, work-sample-oriented tests often consist of having employees perform simulations of the actual tasks performed in the job.[25] Behaviorally oriented performance-appraisal systems, such as Behaviorally Anchored Rating Scales (BARS) and Behavioral Observation Scales (BOS),[26] require knowledge of the specific behaviors exhibited on a job that distinguish effective from ineffective performance. Many training programs are geared toward training individuals in specific work procedures, thus requiring knowledge of the actual tasks performed.[27] Finally, when a manager or company is considering redesigning a job or set of jobs, it is important to understand the specific tasks performed to restructure or reallocate those tasks.

Standardized Worker Information.   As shown in quadrant 3, job analysis can provide information about the worker and be presented in a very standardized format. This allows for comparisons across jobs that might not be very similar to one another. More generalized abilities, such as physical strength and cognitive ability, are examples of this type of information, which is extremely useful for many human resource practices such as human resource planning, career planning, compensation, and selection. Human resource planning requires having information about the generic skill requirements of all the jobs in the organization. Such information also provides for more effective career planning by allowing the firm to identify career ladders where employees' skills match the skills required across different jobs. Finally, this type of information is necessary for developing internally equitable compensation systems, where jobs having higher skill requirements have correspondingly higher wage levels.

Standardized Work Information.   Finally, quadrant 4 represents information about the work being performed, where the information is provided in a way that allows for comparisons across dissimilar jobs. This type of information consists of generic task statements such as "managing the work of others" or "working with customers." Such information is particularly relevant to human resource planning, career planning, and compensation. With regard to human resource planning, standardized information allows planners to understand the similarities and dissimilarities among different jobs in order to promote and transfer individuals to fill human resource needs. Similarly, having knowledge of the similarities in the generic types of activities performed in different jobs allows for career planning that meets the needs and desires of individual employees. Finally, job-evaluation systems require information about work activities that allows for making comparisons across different jobs.

We can see that job analysis is important to all human resource management activities and that different types of job-analysis information are most appropriate for different human resource activities. With that in mind, we discuss next a few of the more popular job-analysis methods available to managers. Each of these job-analysis techniques yields different types of information.

Job Analysis Methods

The different types of job-analysis methods are the Job Element Method, the Fleishman Job Analysis System, Task Analysis, and the Position Analysis Questionnaire. Figure 6.4 shows the relationships between job-analysis information and job-analysis methods.

Job Element Method.[28]   The Job Element Method entails asking subject-matter experts (SMEs) to generate a list of the knowledge, skills, abilities, and personal traits (called job elements) that are required to perform a job. A group of SMEs then rates each job element on four scales. The "barely

FIGURE 6.4   Job-Analysis Methods That Provide Different Types of Information

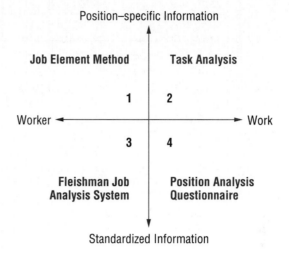

SOURCE: Adapted from P. Wright and K. Wexley, "How to Choose the Job-Analysis Method You Really Need," *Personnel*, May 1985, 51–55.

acceptable" scale is the percentage of barely acceptable employees who have a particular job element. The "superior" scale is the percentage of superior employees who have the job element. "trouble likely" refers to the probability of trouble occurring in an employee who lacks the job element. the "practical" scale is concerned with the practicality of finding people with the job element. An example of these rating scales is provided in Figure 6.5.

As you can see, this method provides position-specific information about the characteristics a worker needs to succeed on the job. As previously discussed, this type of information is most relevant to developing selection, training, and some types of performance-appraisal systems. However, while the job element method may be appropriate for these human resource activities, it is not usually appropriate if the job-analysis information is to be used in human resource planning, career development, or job evaluation.

Fleishman Job Analysis System.[29]   Another job-analysis technique that elicits information about the worker's characteristics is the Fleishman Job Analysis System (FJAS). This approach defines *abilities* as enduring attributes of individuals that account for differences in performance. The system is based on a taxonomy of abilities that adequately represent all the dimensions relevant to work. This taxonomy includes 52 cognitive, psychomotor, physical, and sensory abilities listed in Table 6.3.

FIGURE 6.5
Example of a Job Element Rating Scale

Job:
Grade:

Date:

(col. $\overline{3}$ $\overline{4}$ $\overline{5}$)

Rater No.

Rater Name and Grade:
Title and Location:

Job No.

$\overline{6}$ $\overline{7}$ $\overline{8}$)

Page No. $\overline{}$
(col. $\overline{1}$ $\overline{2}$)

Element No.	Barely acceptable workers	To pick out superior workers	Trouble likely if not considered	Practical. Demanding this element, we can fill	Columns	(These columns for use in hand calculation of values)					
						S X P	T	Item Index	Total Value		Training Value
(Do not Punch)	(B) + all have ✓ some have 0 almost none have	(S) + very important ✓ valuable 0 does not differentiate	(T) + much trouble ✓ some trouble 0 safe to ignore	(P) + all openings ✓ some openings 0 also no openings				(IT)	(TV)	P' (+= 0 ✓ = 1 0 = 2) SP'	(TR)
								SP + T	IT + S – B – P		S + T + SP' – B
					9–12						
					13–16						
					17–20						
					21–24						
					25–28						
					29–32						
					33–36						
					37–40						
					41–44						
					45–48						
					49–52						
					53–56						
					57–60						
					61–64						
					65–68						
					69–72						
					73–76						
					77–80						

Note: for all categories except P', + counts 2, ✓ counts 1, 0 counts 0.
For category P', + counts 0, ✓ counts 1, 0 counts 2.

U.S. Civil Service Commission
Personnel Research and Development Center
Washington, D.C.

SOURCE: E. S. Primoff, *How to Prepare and Conduct Job Element Examinations*, Washington, D.C.: U.S. Government Printing Office, 1975, p. 12.

TABLE 6.3   Abilities Included in the Fleishman Job Analysis System

1.	Oral comprehension	27.	Arm-hand steadiness
2.	Written comprehension	28.	Manual dexterity
3.	Oral expression	29.	Finger dexterity
4.	Written expression	30.	Wrist-finger speed
5.	Fluency of ideas	31.	Speed of limb movement
6.	Originality	32.	Static strength
7.	Memorization	33.	Explosive strength
8.	Problem sensitivity	34.	Dynamic strength
9.	Mathematical reasoning	35.	Trunk strength
10.	Number facility	36.	Extent flexibility
11.	Deductive reasoning	37.	Dynamic flexibility
12.	Inductive reasoning	38.	Gross body coordination
13.	Information ordering	39.	Gross body equilibrium
14.	Category flexibility	40.	Stamina
15.	Speed of closure	41.	Near vision
16.	Flexibility of closure	42.	Far vision
17.	Spatial orientation	43.	Visual color discrimination
18.	Visualization	44.	Night vision
19.	Perceptual speed	45.	Peripheral vision
20.	Selective attention	46.	Depth perception
21.	Time sharing	47.	Glare sensitivity
22.	Control precision	48.	Hearing sensitivity
23.	Multilimb coordination	49.	Auditory attention
24.	Response orientation	50.	Sound localization
25.	Rate control	51.	Speech recognition
26.	Reaction time	52.	Speech clarity

The actual FJAS scales consist of descriptions of the ability, followed by behavioral benchmark examples of the different levels of the ability along a seven-point scale. An example of the written comprehension ability scale from the FJAS is presented in Figure 6.6.

In using the job-analysis technique, SMEs are presented with each of the 52 scales. These experts indicate the point on the scale that best represents the level of that ability required in a particular job. These ratings provide an accurate picture of the ability requirements of the job. Consistent with our matrix of job-analysis information, substantial research has shown the value of this general approach for human resource activities such as career development, selection, and training.[30]

FIGURE 6.6   Example of an Ability from the Fleishman Job Analysis Method

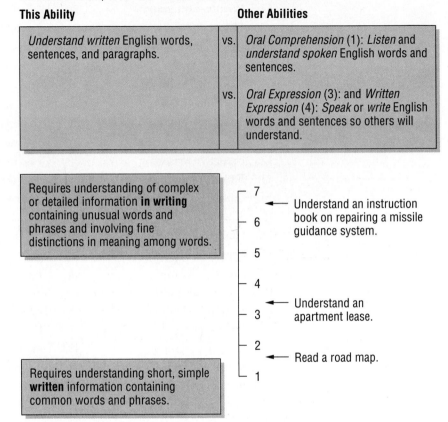

Written Comprehension

This is the ability to understand written sentences and paragraphs.
How written comprehension is different from other abilities:

This Ability		Other Abilities
Understand written English words, sentences, and paragraphs.	vs.	*Oral Comprehension* (1): *Listen* and *understand spoken* English words and sentences.
	vs.	*Oral Expression* (3): and *Written Expression* (4): *Speak* or *write* English words and sentences so others will understand.

Requires understanding of complex or detailed information **in writing** containing unusual words and phrases and involving fine distinctions in meaning among words.

7
— Understand an instruction book on repairing a missile guidance system.
6

5

4

3 — Understand an apartment lease.

2

1 — Read a road map.

Requires understanding short, simple **written** information containing common words and phrases.

SOURCE: E. A. Fleishman and M. D. Mumford, "Evaluating Classifications of Job Behavior: A Construct Validation of the Ability Requirements Scales," *Personnel Psychology* 44 (1991): 523–576. The complete set of ability requirement scales, along with instructions for their use, may be found in Fleishman, E. A. (1992). Fleishman Job Analysis Survey (F-JAS). Palo Alto, CA: Consulting Psychologists Press.

Task Analysis Inventory.   The task analysis inventory method refers to several different methods, each with slight variations. However, common to these approaches is the focus on analyzing all the tasks performed in the focal job. (It is not uncommon to have over 100 tasks.)

For example, the task inventory-CODAP method[31] entails asking subject-matter experts (SMEs) to generate a list of the tasks performed in a job. Once this list has been developed, the SMEs rate each task on dimensions such as the relative amount of time spent on the task, the frequency of task performance, the relative importance of the task, the relative difficulty of

TABLE 6.4   Example of Tasks for Service Technician Job Derived from Task Analysis

- Reads blueprints for appliances
- Questions customer to assess malfunction of machine
- Repairs malfunctioning machine
- Computes cost estimate
- Takes payment from customer and makes change when necessary
- Offers service contracts to customers
- Reads technical manuals to keep updated
- Attends training programs on new machines
- Helps other technicians when needed

the task, and whether the task can be learned on the job relatively quickly. These ratings are then subjected to the CODAP computer program that organizes the tasks into dimensions of similar tasks.

A variation of this method is the "task analysis" method.[32] This method also consists of generating a list of tasks but differs from the task inventory-CODAP method in that, once this list has been developed, SMEs are asked to identify the skills, abilities, and personal characteristics required to perform each task. An example from a task analysis is presented in Table 6.4.

Task inventories focus on providing detailed information about the work performed in a given job, and this kind of information does not allow for easy comparisons of very dissimilar jobs. However, the detail of the information can be helpful in developing both selection exam plans and performance-appraisal criteria.[33]

Position Analysis Questionnaire.   The Position Analysis Questionnaire (PAQ) has both an extensive research base and broad application across many different types of jobs and organizations.[34] The PAQ is a standardized job-analysis questionnaire containing 194 items. These items represent work behaviors, work conditions, or job characteristics that are generalizable across a wide variety of jobs. They are organized into six sections:

1. *Information input*—Where and how a worker gets information needed to perform the job.
2. *Mental processes*—The reasoning, decision-making, planning, and information-processing activities that are involved in performing the job.
3. *Work output*—The physical activities, tools, and devices used by the worker to perform the job.
4. *Relationships with other persons*—The relationship with other people required in performing the job.
5. *Job context*—The physical and social contexts where the work is performed.

6. *Other characteristics*—The activities, conditions, and characteristics other than those previously described that are relevant to the job.

The job analyst is asked to determine whether each item applies to the job being analyzed. The analyst then rates the item on six scales: extent of use, amount of time, importance to the job, possibility of occurrence, applicability, and special code (special rating scales used with a particular item). These ratings are submitted to the PAQ headquarters, where a computer program generates a report regarding the job's scores on the job dimensions.

Research has indicated that the PAQ measures 32 dimensions and 13 overall dimensions of job (listed in Table 6.5) and a given job's scores on these dimensions can be very useful. The significant database has linked scores on certain dimensions to scores on subtests of the General Aptitude Test Battery (GATB). Thus, knowing the dimension scores provides some guidance regarding the types of abilities that are necessary to perform the job. Obviously, this technique provides information about the work performed in a format that allows for comparisons across jobs, whether those jobs are similar or dissimilar.

In spite of its widespread use, the PAQ is not without problems. The most important problem is that to fill out the test, an employee needs the reading level of a college graduate; this often disqualifies some job incumbents from the PAQ. In fact, it is recommended that only job analysts trained in how to use the PAQ should complete the questionnaire, rather than job incumbents or supervisors.[35]

A Manager's Guide to Performing Job Analysis

Although many valid job-analysis techniques exist, each has its own strengths and weaknesses. Most managers cannot afford the time it takes to learn these different techniques, given the purposes they have for job analysis. In this section, we present an easy technique for getting job-analysis information that will be useful to you. You will notice that this technique is simply a brief way of performing the task analysis discussed previously. We first discuss the issues to consider when choosing whom to ask for job-analysis information. Then we provide a framework for eliciting the necessary information.

Sources of Job-Analysis Information.   In performing the job analysis, one question that often arises is, Who should make up the group of incumbents that are responsible for providing the job-analysis information? Whatever job-analysis method you choose, the process of job analysis entails obtaining information from people familiar with the job. We refer to these people as subject-matter experts (SMEs) because they are experts in their knowledge of the job.

In general, it will be useful for you to go to the job incumbent to get the most accurate information about what is actually done on the job. However, particularly when the job analysis will be used for compensation purposes, incumbents might have an incentive to exaggerate their duties. Thus, you

TABLE 6.5   Overall Dimensions of the Position Analysis Questionnaire

Decision/communication/general responsibilities
Clerical/related activities
Technical/related activities
Service/related activities
Regular day schedule versus other work schedules
Routine/repetitive work activities
Environmental awareness
General physical activities
Supervising/coordinating other personnel
Public/customer/related contact activities
Unpleasant/hazardous/demanding environment
Nontypical work schedules

will also want to ask others familiar with the job, such as supervisors, to look over the information generated by the job incumbent. This serves as a check to determine whether what is being done is congruent with what is supposed to be done in the job. Although job incumbents and supervisors are the most obvious and frequently used sources of job-analysis information, other sources can be helpful, particularly for service jobs.

It is important to understand the usefulness of different sources of job-analysis information, because this information is only as good as the source. Research has revealed some interesting findings regarding various sources of job-analysis information, particularly regarding job incumbents and supervisors.

One question is whether supervisors and incumbents agree in their job-analysis ratings. Some research has demonstrated significant differences in the job-analysis ratings provided from these two different sources.[36] However, other research found greater agreement between supervisors and subordinates when rating general job duties than when rating specific tasks.[37] One conclusion that can be drawn from this research is that incumbents may provide the most accurate estimates of the actual time spent performing job tasks. However, supervisors may be a more accurate source of information about the importance of job duties.

Another question is whether a job incumbent's own performance level is related to the job-analysis ratings. Although it is intuitively appealing to think that individuals who perform well in a job might give different ratings than individuals who do not perform well, the research has not borne this out. One frequently cited study compared the job-analysis ratings of effective and ineffective managers and found that they tended to give the same ratings despite their performance level.[38] However, more recent research has also examined the relationship between job analysis and employee performance.

In this research no differences were observed between high and low performers regarding the tasks and KSAs generated, the ratings made regarding the time spent, or importance of the tasks.[39] However, differences have been observed in the types of critical incidents generated[40] and the ratings of the level of effectiveness of various incidents.[41] Thus, research at present seems inconclusive regarding the relationship between the performance level of the job analyst and the job-analysis information he or she provides.

While the relationship between job-analysis ratings and job performance is inconclusive, research has strongly demonstrated some demographic differences in job-analysis information. One study found differences between males and females and between blacks and whites in the importance and time-spent ratings for a variety of tasks.[42] Similarly, another study observed minor differences between males and females and between blacks and whites in job-analysis ratings. However, in this study larger differences in ratings were the result of the experience level of the job incumbent.[43] These research results imply that when conducting a job analysis, you should take steps to ensure that the incumbent group responsible for generating the job-analysis information represents a variety of gender, racial, and experience-level categories.

Gathering the Job Analysis Information.   Having chosen the sources of job-analysis information, it is important to plan the job-analysis meeting to elicit high-quality information. To do this, you can structure the job-analysis meeting in the following ways. These steps help people think through the job in a way that does not overwhelm them with information.

1. *Identify the major job dimensions*—This can be done by drawing a big circle like a pie. Tell the job analysts to think about the job like a pie, where everything they do fits into that pie. Then ask them to cut the pie up into the four to eight major chunks of tasks that tend to be interrelated. For example, as we have depicted in Figure 6.7, if you are analyzing a professor's job, the major dimensions of the job might be teaching, research, advising, service, and consulting.

2. *Identify the tasks*—Once the job is broken into the major dimensions, it is easier to begin brainstorming the various tasks that are part of each dimension. For example, concerning teaching—and much to a student's dismay—a professor must (a) prepare lectures, (b) deliver lectures, (c) hold office hours to answer student questions, (d) develop examinations, (e) grade examinations, and (f) compute final grades.

3. *Identify the KSAs*—Having developed a list of tasks, it is now much easier to go back to each task and think about the KSAs that are necessary to perform those tasks effectively. For example, to deliver a lecture, a professor must possess (a) knowledge of the course material, (b) knowledge of effective teaching techniques, (c) good public-speaking skills, and, one would hope, (d) a good sense of humor.

These steps are useful and necessary for getting a good understanding of the way each job is currently being performed. As we discussed at the outset

FIGURE 6.7   Identifying Job Dimensions and Job Tasks for a University Professor's Job

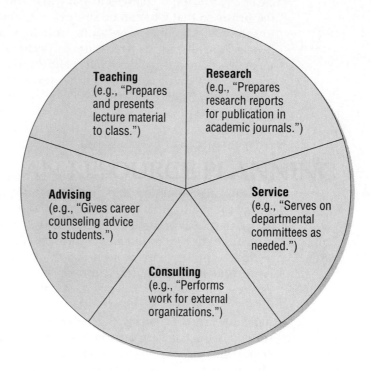

of this chapter and in Chapter 2, strategic implementation requires that jobs are strategically managed. A major portion of implementing a strategy is concerned with designing work units and jobs to achieve the strategic plan. Thus, two additional steps can be added in the job-analysis process.[44]

4. *Identify the potential factors that could change jobs*—This entails having individuals who are part of the strategic planning process brainstorm the environmental, technological, and strategic factors that are likely to change in the next three to five years. For example, is the company planning to expand into international markets? Is it building plants with new and different technologies? These issues might have important implications for the type of work performed as well as the skills necessary for job incumbents to perform them.

5. *Predict the nature of the changing job*—This requires job analysts to predict how the factors identified in step 4 might change the existing structure of jobs. For example, if the company plans to expand internationally, then managers will be required to change the way they do things. It also might require future managers to have international experience or foreign language skills.

Having completed this process, a manager now has a very accurate picture of the tasks performed in the job and the KSAs required of a jobholder to be effective in performing all the major tasks. In addition, it should be clear what types of changes in the work unit are likely to affect the jobs in the future so that jobs can be strategically managed. This allows a manager to effectively manage the work unit through understanding the work process and the skills necessary to perform effectively. However, if the work load changes substantially, either positively or negatively, this may require redesigning the jobs. In the next section, we discuss the process of job design and job redesign.

JOB DESIGN

So far we have approached the issue of managing work in a passive way, focusing only on understanding what gets done, the way it gets done, and the skills required to get it done. While this is necessary, it is a very static view of jobs, in that jobs must already exist and that they are already assumed to be structured in the one best way. However, a manager may often be faced with a situation in which the work unit does not yet exist, requiring jobs within the work unit to be designed from scratch. Sometimes work loads within an existing work unit are increased, or work-group size is decreased while the same work load is required, a trend increasingly observed with the movement toward downsizing.[45] Finally, sometimes the work is not being performed in the most efficient manner. In these cases, a manager may decide to change the way that work is done in order for the work unit to perform more effectively and efficiently. This requires redesigning the existing jobs.

Job design is the process of defining the way work will be performed and the tasks that will be required in a given job. **Job redesign** refers to changing the tasks or the way work is performed in an existing job. To effectively design jobs, one must thoroughly understand the job as it exists (through job analysis) and its place in the larger work unit's work-flow process (work-flow analysis). Having a detailed knowledge of the tasks performed in the work unit and in the job, a manager then has many alternative ways to design a job. This can be done most effectively through understanding the trade-offs between certain design approaches.

Recent research has identified four basic approaches that have been used among the various disciplines (e.g., psychology, management, engineering, ergonomics) that have dealt with job-design issues.[46] All jobs can be characterized in terms of how they fare according to each approach; thus, a manager needs to understand the trade-offs between emphasizing one approach over another. In the next section we discuss each of these approaches and examine the implications of each for the design of jobs. Table 6.6 displays how jobs are characterized along each of these dimensions.

Motivational Approach

The motivational approach to job design has its roots in the organizational psychology and management literatures. It focuses on the job characteristics that affect the psychological meaning and motivational potential, and it

TABLE 6.6   Characterizing Jobs on Different Dimensions of Job Design

The Motivational Job-Design Approach

1. *Autonomy:* Does the job allow freedom, independence, or discretion in work scheduling, sequence, methods, procedures, quality control, or other decisions?
2. *Intrinsic job feedback:* Do the work activities themselves provide direct, clear information about the effectiveness (in terms of quality and quantity) of job performance?
3. *Extrinsic job feedback:* Do other people in the organization (such as managers and coworkers) provide information about the effectiveness (in terms of quality and quantity) of job performance?
4. *Social interaction:* Does the job provide for positive social interaction (such as teamwork or coworker assistance)?
5. *Task/goal clarity:* Are the job duties, requirements, and goals clear and specific?
6. *Task variety:* Does the job have a variety of duties, tasks, and activities?
7. *Task identity:* Does the job require completion of a whole and identifiable piece of work? Does it give the incumbent a chance to do an entire piece of work from beginning to end?
8. *Ability/skill-level requirements:* Does the job require a high level of knowledge, skills, and abilities?
9. *Ability/skill variety:* Does the job require a variety of types of knowledge, skills, and abilities?
10. *Task significance:* Is the job significant and important compared with other jobs in the organization?
11. *Growth/learning:* Does the job allow opportunities for learning and growth in competence and proficiency?

The Mechanistic Job-Design Approach

1. *Job specialization:* Is the job highly specialized in terms of purpose and/or activity?
2. *Specialization of tools and procedures:* Are the tolls, procedures, materials, etc. used on this job highly specialized in terms of purpose?
3. *Task simplification:* Are the tasks simple and uncomplicated?
4. *Single activities:* Does the job require the incumbent to do only one task at a time? Does it not require the incumbent to do multiple activities at one time or in very close succession?
5. *Job simplification:* Does the job require relatively little skill and training time?
6. *Repetition:* Does the job require performing the same activity or activities repeatedly?
7. *Spare time:* Is there very little spare time between activities on this job?
8. *Automation:* Are many of the activities of this job automated or assisted by automation?

continued

SOURCE: Reprinted by permission of publisher, fom *Organizational Dynamics*, Winter/1987 ©1987. American Management Association, New York. All rights reserved.

TABLE 6.6   continued

The Biological Job-Design Approach

1. *Strength:* Does the job require fairly little muscular strength?
2. *Lifting:* Does the job require fairly little lifting, and/or is the lifting of very light weights?
3. *Endurance:* Does the job require fairly little muscular endurance?
4. *Seating:* Are the seating arrangements on the job adequate (with ample opportunities to sit, comfortable chairs, good postural support, etc.)?
5. *Size difference:* Does the workplace allow for all size differences between people in terms of clearance, reach, eye height, leg room, etc.?
6. *Wrist movement:* Does the job allow the wrists to remain straight, without excessive movement?
7. *Noise:* Is the workplace free from excessive noise?
8. *Climate:* Is the climate at the workplace comfortable in terms of temperature and humidity, and is it free of excessive dust and fumes?
9. *Work breaks:* Is there adequate time for work breaks given the demands of the job?
10. *Shift work:* Does the job not require shift work or excessive overtime?

The Perceptual/Motor Job-Design Approach

1. *Lighting:* Is the lighting in the workplace adequate and free from glare?
2. *Displays:* Are the displays, gauges, meters, and computerized equipment used on this job easy to read and understand?
3. *Programs:* Are the programs in the computerized equipment for this job easy to learn and use?
4. *Other equipment:* Is the other equipment (all types) used on this job easy to learn and use?
5. *Printed job materials:* Are the printed materials used on this job easy to read and interpret?
6. *Workplace layout:* Is the workplace laid out so that the employee can see and hear well enough to perform the job?
7. *Information input requirements:* Is the amount of attention needed to perform this job fairly minimal?
8. *Information output requirements:* Is the amount of information that the employee must output on this job, in terms of both action and communication, fairly minimal?
9. *Information processing requirements:* Is the amount of information that must be processed, in terms of thinking and problem solving, fairly minimal?
10. *Memory requirements:* Is the amount of information that must be remembered on this job fairly minimal?
11. *Stress:* Is there relatively little stress on this job?
12. *Boredom:* Are the chances of boredom on this job fairly small?

views attitudinal variables (such as satisfaction, intrinsic motivation, job involvement, and behavioral variables such as attendance and performance) as the most important outcomes of job design. The prescriptions of the motivational approach focus on increasing the complexity of jobs through such interventions as job enlargement, job enrichment, and the construction of jobs around sociotechnical systems.[47] Accordingly, a study of 213 different jobs found that the motivational attributes of jobs were positively related to the mental-ability requirements of workers in those jobs.[48]

An example of the motivational approach is Herzberg's Two-Factor theory, which argues that individuals are motivated more by intrinsic aspects of work such as the meaningfulness of the job content than by extrinsic characteristics such as pay.[49] Herzberg argued that the key to motivating employees was not through monetary incentives but through the redesign of jobs to make their work more meaningful.

A more complete model of how job design affects employee reactions is the "Job Characteristics Model" shown in Figure 6.8.[50] According to this model, jobs can be described in terms of five characteristics. *Skill variety* is the extent to which the job requires a variety of skills to be used to carry out the tasks. *Task identity* is the degree to which a job requires completing a "whole" piece of work from beginning to end. *Task significance* is the extent to which the job has an important impact on the lives of other people. *Autonomy* is the degree to which the job allows an individual to make decisions about the way the work will be carried out. *Feedback* is the extent to which a person receives clear information about the effectiveness of his or her performance from the work itself.

These five job characteristics determine the motivating potential of a job by affecting the three critical psychological states of "experienced meaningfulness," "responsibility," and "knowledge of results." According to the model, when the core job characteristics (and thus the critical psychological states) are high, individuals will have a high level of internal work motivation. This is expected to result in higher quantity and quality of work as well as higher levels of job satisfaction.

However, according to this model, the positive effects of job characteristics on motivational outcomes require that employees have adequate levels of satisfaction with the work environment (e.g., supervision, working conditions), that they have the necessary ability to perform the job, and that they have a need to grow (growth need strength). If employees lack these characteristics, then the positive motivational outcomes will not be observed, no matter how motivating the job characteristics are. One review of the job characteristics model did find some support for the idea that for those with high growth need strength, job characteristics were more positively related to motivational outcomes than for those with low growth need strength.[51]

Job-design interventions emphasizing the motivational approach tend to focus on increasing the motivating potential of jobs. Much of the work on job enlargement (broadening the types of tasks performed), job enrichment

FIGURE 6.8   The Job Characteristics Model

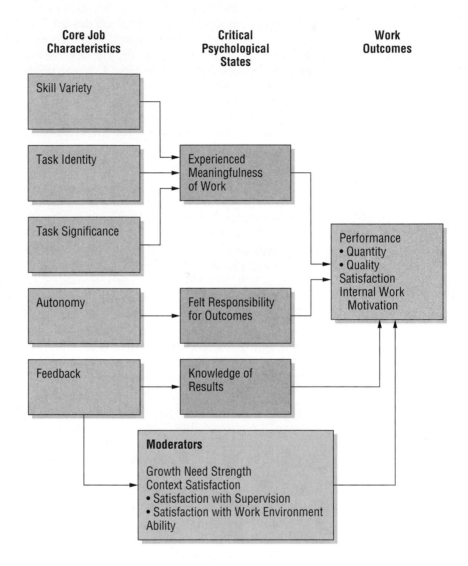

SOURCE: Figure 4.6 from Hackman & Oldman, *Work Design,* © 1980 Addison-Wesley Publishing Company. Reprinted by permission.

(adding more decision-making authority to jobs), and self-managing work teams has its roots in the motivational approach to job design. While most of the research on these interventions has demonstrated that they increase employee satisfaction and performance quality, these interventions do not consistently result in increased quantity of performance.

Mechanistic Approach

The mechanistic approach has its roots in classical industrial engineering. The focus of the mechanistic approach is on identifying the one best way to structure work that maximizes efficiency. This most often entails reducing the complexity of the work to provide more human resource efficiency and flexibility—that is, making the work so simple that anyone can quickly and easily be trained to perform it. This approach focuses on designing jobs around the concepts of task specialization, skill simplification, and repetition.

Scientific management was one of the earliest and best-known statements of the mechanistic approach.[52] According to this approach, productivity could be maximized by taking a scientific approach to the process of designing jobs. Scientific management first sought to identify the "one best way" to perform the job. This entailed performing time-and-motion studies to identify the most efficient movements for workers to make. Once the best way to perform the work is identified, workers should be selected based on their ability to do the job, they should be trained in the standard "one best way" to perform the job, and they should be offered monetary incentives to motivate them to work at their highest capacity.

The scientific management approach was built upon in later years, resulting in a mechanistic approach that calls for jobs to be designed so that they are very simple and so that they lack any significant meaningfulness. By designing jobs in this way, the organization reduces its need for high-ability individuals and thus becomes less dependent on individual workers. Individuals are easily replaceable—that is, a new employee can be trained to perform the job quickly and inexpensively.

Biological Approach

The biological approach to job design comes primarily from the sciences of biomechanics (i.e., the study of body movements), work physiology, and occupational medicine, and it is usually referred to as ergonomics. **Ergonomics** is concerned with examining the interface between individuals' physiological characteristics and the physical work environment. The goal of this approach is to minimize the physical strain on the worker by structuring the physical work environment around the way the human body works. It thereby focuses on outcomes such as physical fatigue, aches and pains, and health complaints.

The biological approach has been applied in redesigning equipment used in jobs that are physically demanding. Such redesign is often aimed at reducing the physical demands of certain jobs so that women can perform them. In addition, many biological interventions focus on redesigning machines and technology, such as adjusting the height of the computer keyboard to minimize occupational illnesses (e.g., carpal tunnel syndrome). The design of chairs and desks to fit posture requirements is very important in many office jobs and is another example of the biological approach to job

Technology & Structure

TECHNOLOGICAL SOLUTIONS TO HR PROBLEMS: ERGONOMICS AT TOYOTA

An example of the biological approach to job design is evidenced recently in the Japanese automobile industry. Historically, Japanese automakers have asked for employees to participate in decision making through quality circles. However, faced with an increasing shortage of skilled workers, increasing absenteeism and turnover, and employee desires for a high-quality work life, Japanese automakers are beginning to rethink their approach to job design.

One such change is to redesign the machinery that employees use in the assembly process. In the past, automobiles passed by an employee on a noisy chain-driven conveyor, and the employee would lean over, crouch down under, or reach into the car to attach the part where it belonged. However, at Toyota's high-tech Tahara No. 4 line, new electric vehicle carriers were installed to minimize the movements that an assembler would have to make that might put undue stress on their bodies. These new lines automatically adjust a car's height at every workstation to enable the employee to perform his or her job without undue stress.

According to the plant's general manager Hiromitsu Hayashida, the goal is to reduce the turnover of high-quality, expensively trained workers by making a comfortable working environment for them. How successful has this been? Toyota reports that during its first year of operation, not one employee quit Tahara's No. 4 line, compared with a typical turnover of 25 to 30 percent during a plant's first year of operations.

SOURCES: "Overhaul in Japan," *Business Week,* December 21, 1992, 80–84; A. Taylor, "How Toyota Copes with Hard Times," *Fortune,* January 25, 1993, 78–81.

design. An example of an application of the biological approach is given in the "Competing through Technology and Structure" box.

Perceptual/Motor Approach

The perceptual/motor approach to job design has its roots in the human-factors literature.[53] Whereas the biological approach focuses on physical capabilities and limitations, the perceptual/motor approach focuses on human mental capabilities and limitations. The goal is to design jobs in a way that ensures they do not exceed people's mental capabilities and limitations. This approach generally tries to improve reliability, safety, and user reactions by designing jobs in a way that reduces the information-processing requirements of the job. In designing jobs, one looks at the capabilities of the least capable worker and then constructs job requirements that an individual of that ability level could meet. Similar to the mechanistic approach, this approach generally has the effect of decreasing the job's cognitive demands.

Jobs such as air traffic controller, oil refinery operator, and quality-control inspector require a large amount of information processing. Many clerical and assembly-line jobs, on the other hand, require very little information processing. However, in designing all jobs, managers need to be aware of the information-processing requirements and ensure that these requirements do not exceed the capabilities of the least capable person who could potentially be performing the job.

Implications of Different Approaches for Job Design

A recent stream of research has aimed at understanding the trade-offs and implications of these different job design strategies. Many authors have called for redesigning jobs according to the motivational approach so that the work becomes more psychologically meaningful. However, one study examined how the various approaches to job design are related to a variety of work outcomes. Their results are summarized in Table 6.7. For example, in this study, job incumbents expressed higher satisfaction with jobs scoring highly on motivational approach. Also, jobs scoring high on the biological approach were ones for which incumbents expressed lower physical requirements. Finally, the motivational and mechanistic approaches were negatively related, suggesting that designing jobs to maximize efficiency very likely results in a lower motivational component to those jobs.

Another recent study demonstrated that enlarging clerical jobs made workers more satisfied, less bored, more proficient at catching errors, and better at providing customer service. However, these enlarged jobs also had costs, such as higher training requirements, higher basic-skill requirements, and higher compensation requirements based on job-evaluation compensable factors.[54] Again, it is important to recognize the trade-off between the motivational value of jobs and the efficiency with which the jobs are performed.

Finally, recent research has examined how job-design approaches relate to compensation. Starting from the assumption that job evaluation (the process of determining the worth of jobs to organizations) links job design and market forces, they examined the relationship between job-design approaches and both job-evaluation results and pay. They found that jobs high on the motivational approach had higher job-evaluation scores representing higher skill requirements and that these jobs had higher pay levels. Jobs high on the mechanistic and perceptual/motor dimensions had lower skill requirements and correspondingly lower wage rates. Finally, jobs high on the biological dimension had lower physical requirements and had a weak positive relationship to wage rates. Thus, it seems reasonable to conclude that jobs redesigned to increase the motivating potential result in higher costs in terms of ability requirements, training, and compensation.[55]

In summary, in designing jobs it is important to understand the trade-offs inherent in focusing on one particular approach to job design. Managers who seek to design jobs in a way that maximizes all the outcomes for job-holders and the organization need to be aware of these different approaches, understand the costs and benefits associated with each, and balance them appropriately to provide the organization with a competitive advantage.

TABLE 6.7   Summary of Outcomes from the Job-Design Approaches

Job Design Approach	Positive Outcomes	Negative Outcomes
Mechanistic	Decreased training time Higher utilization levels Lower likelihood of error Less change of mental overload and stress	Lower job satisfaction Lower motivation Higher absenteeism
Motivational	Higher job satisfaction Higher motivation Greater job involvement Higher job performance Lower absenteeism	Increased training time Lower utilization levels Greater likelihood of error Greater chance of mental overload and stress
Biological	Less physical effort Less physical fatigue Fewer health complaints Fewer medical incidents Lower absenteeism Higher job satisfaction	Higher financial costs because of changes in equipment or job environment
Perceptual/motor	Lower likelihood of error Lower likelihood of accidents Less chance of mental overload and stress Lower training time Higher utilization levels	Lower job satisfaction Lower motivation

SOURCE: Reprinted by permission of publisher, fom *Organizational Dynamics*, Winter/1987 ©1987. American Management Association, New York. All rights reserved.

SUMMARY

The analysis and design of work is one of the most important components to developing and maintaining a competitive advantage. Strategy implementation is virtually impossible without thorough attention devoted work-flow analysis, job analysis, and job design. Managers need to understand the entire work-flow process in their work unit to ensure that the process maximizes efficiency and effectiveness. To understand this work-flow process, managers also must have clear, detailed information about the jobs that exist in the work unit, and the way to gain this information is through the job-analysis process. Equipped with an understanding of the work-flow process and the existing job, managers can redesign jobs to ensure that the work unit is able to achieve its goals while individuals within the unit benefit on the various work-outcome dimensions such as motivation, satisfaction, safety, health, and achievement. This is one key to competitive advantage.

Discussion Questions

1. Assume you are the manager of a fast-food restaurant. What are the outputs of your work unit? What are the activities required to produce those outputs? What are the inputs?

2. Based on Question 1, consider the cashier's job. What are the outputs, activities and inputs for that job?

3. Consider the "job" of college student. Perform a job analysis on this job. What are the tasks required in the job? What are the knowledge, skills, and abilities necessary to perform those tasks? What environmental trends or shocks (e.g., computers) might change the job, and how would that change the skill requirements?

4. Discuss how the following trends are changing the skill requirements for managerial jobs in the United States: (a) increasing use of computers, (b) increasing international competition, (c) increasing work-family conflicts.

5. Why is it important for a manager to be able to conduct a job analysis? What are the negative outcomes that would result from not understanding the jobs of those reporting to the manager?

6. What are the trade-offs between the different approaches to job design? Which approach do you think should be weighted most heavily when designing jobs?

7. For the cashier job in Question 2, which approach to job design was most influential in designing that job? In the context of the total work-flow process of the restaurant, how would you redesign the job to more heavily emphasize each of the other approaches?

Notes

1. J. Galbraith and R. Kazanjian, *Strategy Implementation: Structure, Systems, and Process* (St. Paul, Minn.: West Publishing, 1986).

2. J. Barney, "Firm Resources and Sustained Competitive Advantage," *Journal of Management* 17 (1991): 99–120.

3. R. Schuler and S. Jackson, "Linking Competitive Strategies with Human Resource Management Practices," *Academy of Management Executive* 1 (1987): 207–219.

4. S. Lohr, "Making Cars the Volvo Way," *New York Times,* June 23, 1987, D1, D5.

5. J. Keefe and H. Katz, "Job Classification and Plant Performance in the Auto Industry," *Industrial Relations* 29 (1990): 111–118.

6. D. Ilgen and J. Hollenbeck, "The Structure of Work: Job Design and Roles," in *Handbook of Industrial & Organizational Psychology,* (2nd ed.), ed. M. Dunnette and L. Hough (Palo Alto: Consulting Psychologists Press, 1991): 165–208.

7. R. Harvey, "Job Analysis," in *Handbook of Industrial & Organizational Psychology,* (2nd ed.), ed. M. Dunnette and L. Hough, (Palo Alto: Consulting Psychologists Press, 1991): 71–164.

8. R. Griffin, *Task Design: An Integrative Approach* (Glenview, Ill.: Scott Foresman, 1982).

9. B. Brocka and M. S. Brocka," *Quality Management: Implementing the Best Ideas of the Masters,* (Homewood, Ill.: Business One Irwin, 1992).

10. R. Pritchard, D. Jones, P. Roth, K. Stuebing, and S. Ekeberg, "Effects of Group Feedback, Goal Setting, and Incentives on Organizational Productivity," *Journal of Applied Psychology* 73 (1988): 337—360.

11. D. Bowen and E. Lawler, "Total Quality-Oriented Human Resources Management," *Organizational Dynamics* (1992): 29–41.

12. M. Fefer, "Bill Gates' Next Challenge," *Fortune,* December 14, 1992, 30–41.

13. E. McCormick, "Job and task Analysis," in *Handbook of Industrial and Organizational Psychology,* ed. M. Dunnette, (Chicago: Rand McNalley, 1976): 651–696.

14. E. Primoff and S. Fine, "A History of Job Analysis," in *The Job Analysis Handbook for Business, Industry, and Government,* ed. S. Gael (New York: Wiley, 1988), 14–29.

15. W. Cascio, *Applied Psychology in Personnel Management,* 4th ed. (Englewood Cliffs, N.J.: Prentice-Hall, 1991).

16. P. Wright and K. Wexley, "How to Choose the Kind of Job Analysis You Really Need," *Personnel,* May 1985, 51–55.

17. R. Gatewood and H. Feild, *Human Resource Selection,* 2nd ed. (Hinsdale, Ill.: Dryden, 1990).

18. K. Murphy and J. Cleveland, *Performance Appraisal: An Organizational Perspective* (Boston: Allyn and Bacon, 1991).

19. I. Goldstein, *Training in Organizations* 3rd ed., (Pacific Grove, Cal.: Brooks/Cole, 1993).

20. R. Harvey, L. Friedman, M. Hakel and E. Cornelius, "Dimensionality of the Job Element Inventory (JEI): A Simplified Worker-Oriented Job-Analysis Questionnaire," *Journal of Applied Psychology* 73 (1988): 639–646.

21. J. Walker, *Human Resource Strategy* (New York: McGraw-Hill, 1992).

22. Harvey, "Job Analysis."

23. Wright and Wexley, "How to Choose the Kind of Job Analysis."

24. G. Hughes and E. Prien, "Evaluation of Task and Job Skill Linkage Judgments Used to Develop Test Specifications," *Personnel Psychology* 42 (1989): 283–292.

25. M. Campion, E. Pursell, and B. Brown, "Structured Interviewing for Personnel Selection," in *Applied Psychology in Business: A Manager's Handbook,* ed. J. Jones, B. Steffy, and D. Bray (Lexington, Mass.: Lexington Books, 1991).

26. G. Latham and K. Wexley, *Increasing Productivity through Performance Appraisal* (Boston: Addison-Wesley, 1981).

27. Goldstein, *Training in Organizations.*

28. E. Primhoff, *How to Prepare and Conduct Job Element Examinations* (Washington, DC: U.S. Government Printing Office, 1975).

29. E. Fleishman and M. Reilly, *Handbook of Human Abilities* (Palo Alto, Cal.: Consulting Psychologists Press, 1992).

30. E. Fleishman and M. Mumford, "Ability Requirements Scales," in *The Job Analysis Handbook for Business, Government, and Industry,* ed. S. Gael (New York: Wiley, 1988), 917–935.

31. R. Christal, *The United States Air Force Occupational Research Project* (AFHRL-TR-73-75) (Lackland AFB, Tex.: Air Force Human Resources Laboratory, Occupational Research Division, 1974).

32. G. Drauden, "Task Inventory Analysis in Industry and the Public Sector," in *The Job Analysis Handbook for Business, Government, and Industry,* ed. S. Gael (New York: Wiley, 1988), 157–172.

33. E. Levine, R. Ash and N. Bennett, "Exploratory Comparative Study of Four Job-Analysis Methods," *Journal of Applied Psychology* 65 (1980): 524–535.

34. E. McCormick and R. Jeannerette, "The Position Analysis Questionnaire," in *The Job Analysis Handbook for Business, Industry, and Government,* ed. S. Gael (New York: Wiley, 1988), 880–901.

35. *PAQ Newsletter* (August 1989).

36. A. O'Reilly, "Skill Requirements: Supervisor–Subordinate Conflict," *Personnel Psychology* 26 (1973): 75–80.

37. J. Hazel, J. Madden, and R. Christal, "Agreement between Worker–Supervisor Descriptions of the Worker's Job," *Journal of Industrial Psychology* 2 (1964): 71–79.

38. K. Wexley and S. Silverman, "An Examination of Differences between Managerial Effectiveness and Response Patterns on a Structured Job-Analysis Questionnaire," *Journal of Applied Psychology* 63 (1978): 646–649.

39. P. Conley and P. Sackett, "Effects of Using High- versus Low-Performing Job Incumbents as Sources of Job-Analysis Information," *Journal of Applied Psychology* 72 (1988): 434–437.

40. W. Mullins and W. Kimbrough, "Group Composition as a Determinant of Job-Analysis Outcomes," *Journal of Applied Psychology* 73 (1988): 657–664.

41. N. Hauenstein and R. Foti, "From Laboratory to Practice: Neglected Issues in Implementing Frame-of-Reference Rater Training," *Personnel Psychology* 42 (1989): 359–378.

42. N. Schmitt and S. Cohen, "Internal Analysis of Task Ratings by Job Incumbents," *Journal of Applied Psychology* 74 (1989): 96–104.

43. F. Landy and J. Vasey, "Job Analysis: The Composition of SME Samples," *Personnel Psychology* 44 (1991): 27–50.

44. B. Schneider and A. Konz, "Strategic Job Analysis," *Human Resource Management* 28 (1989): 51–63.

45. K. Cameron, S. Freeman, and A. Mishra, "Best Practices in White Collar Downsizing: Managing Contradictions," *The Executive* 5 (1991): 57–73.

46. M. Campion and P. Thayer, "Development and Field Evaluation of an Interdisciplinary Measure of Job Design," *Journal of Applied Psychology* 70 (1985): 29–34.

47. R. Griffin and G. McMahan, "Motivation through Job Design," in *OB: The State of the Science,* ed. J. Greenberg (Hillsdale, N.J.: Lawrence Earlbaum Associates, 1993).

48. M. Campion, "Ability Requirement Implications of Job Design: An Interdisciplinary Perspective," *Personnel Psychology* 42 (1989): 1–24.

49. F. Herzberg, "One More Time: How Do You Motivate Employees?" *Harvard Business Review* 65 (1987): 109–120.

50. R. Hackman and G. Oldham, *Work Redesign* (Boston: Addison-Wesley, 1980).

51. B. Loher, R. Noe, N. Moeller, and M. Fitzgerald, "A Meta-analysis of the Relation of Job Characteristics to Job Satisfaction," *Journal of Applied Psychology* 70 (1985): 280–289.

52. F. Taylor, *The Principles of Scientific Management* (New York: W. W. Norton, 1967). (Originally published in 1911 by Harper & Brothers.)

53. W. Howell, "Human Factors in the Workplace," in *Handbook of Industrial & Organizational Psychology,* 2nd ed., ed. M. Dunnette and L. Hough (Chicago: Rand-McNally, 1991), 2: 209–270.

54. M. Campion and C. McClelland, "Interdisciplinary Examination of the Costs and Benefits of Enlarged Jobs: A Job-Design Quasi-experiment," *Journal of Applied Psychology* 76 (1991): 186–198.

55. M. Campion and C. Berger, "Conceptual Integration and Empirical Test of Job Design and Compensation Relationships," *Personnel Psychology* 43 (1990): 525–553.

C A S E

WHIRLPOOL'S AUTOMATED PARTS DISTRIBUTION CENTER

Whirlpool Corporation, one of the world's leading manufacturers of household appliances, has a parts distribution center (PDC) located in LaPorte, Indiana. The PDC is a warehouse filled with the parts necessary for servicing malfunctioning Whirlpool appliances. When a service center in New Orleans, for example, runs low on parts, it submits an order to the PDC. Once received, the order is processed, and submitted to the warehouse area. Each item or set of items is listed on a three-by-six-inch card. A warehouse employee will receive a stack of cards, then travel around the warehouse on small trucks with trailers attached, find the parts listed on the cards, and place them in the trailers. Once an order is filled, it is transferred to the packing area, where it is packed, addressed, and mailed via either the postal service or a parcel service.

In an effort to streamline the process, the PDC's management decided to implement an automated system for processing orders. The facility would be retooled with conveyors running throughout it, minimizing the need for the small transportation vehicles. Three types of technology would be used to redesign the work process. First, hand-held terminals are small transportable computer terminals that provide the order information on a small screen slightly larger than the screen on a calculator. These terminals tell the employees which parts go with an order and allow the employee some ability to request additional information or to notify the central system of shortages. The "pick-to-light" system is a large area with numerous shelves with a number of bins holding smaller parts on each shelf. A light under a particular shelf lights up, indicating the number of parts in that bin that are needed. Finally, the carousel is an area where numerous bins are located on a moving carousel. The carousel is controlled by computers and rotates so that the bin holding required parts stops in front of the employee and a light comes on indicating the number of parts to pull from the bin.

QUESTIONS

1. Assume you are in charge of evaluating the change from a manual to an automated warehouse facility. What effects will this have on warehouse employee jobs?

2. How will the change affect the skills required of warehouse employees to perform the job?

3. How would you characterize the three types of jobs on the motivational dimension of job design? The mechanistic dimension?

4. What changes in work procedures might you recommend to increase one of the dimensions of job design?

PERFORMANCE MANAGEMENT

Objectives   *After reading this chapter, you should be able to:*

1. Identify the major determinants of individual performance.
2. Discuss the three general purposes of performance management.
3. Identify the five criteria for effective performance management systems.
4. Discuss the four approaches to performance management, the specific techniques used in each approach, and the way these approaches compare to the criteria for effective performance management systems.
5. Choose the most effective approach to performance measurement for a given situation.
6. Discuss the advantages and disadvantages of the different sources of performance information.
7. Choose the most effective source(s) for performance information for any situation.
8. Distinguish types of rating errors and explain how to minimize each in a performance evaluation.
9. Identify the characteristics of a performance measurement system that follows legal guidelines.
10. Conduct an effective performance feedback session.

Former Coach Cries Foul on Firing

The measurement and management of performance seldom receive the attention they deserve, given the potential risks involved in doing them poorly. Many companies do not pay much attention to the performance management process, and this lack of attention gets them into serious trouble.

For example, consider the situation of Earl Bruce, the former football coach at Ohio State University. Bruce had been hired to replace the successful, popular, and controversial former Buckeye coach Woody Hayes. However, on November 16, 1987, Ohio State University fired Bruce with two years remaining on his contract, causing many to question the university's decision, not the least of whom was Bruce himself. Four days later Bruce filed a breach-of-contract suit against the university, asking for $7.4 million in damages.

This might have surprised Bruce because during his time at OSU, Bruce had the highest winning percentage in the Big Ten. In addition, the April before his firing, he received a performance evaluation from Associate Athletic Director Bill Myles, signed by Athletic Director Rick Bay. The appraisal form listed 10 different areas of competence, and ratings on each dimension could range from 1 to 10. On that appraisal he received no rating lower than 8. Bruce threatened to sue the university for breach of contract. Obviously, the university, seeing that it might have a difficult time making the case that Bruce had been fired for poor performance with such a positive performance evaluation, was intent on settling the case out of court. Two weeks later, the suit was settled out of court for $471,000.

SOURCES: "Bruce, OSU Working out Coach's IOU," *Columbus Dispatch,* August 15, 1989, C1; and "Notebook" *Chicago Tribune,* November 22, 1989, C1.

INTRODUCTION

Organizations that seek to gain competitive advantage through their people must be able to manage the behavior and results of all employees. One of the most important challenges managers face is managing the performance of those over whom they have authority. Traditionally, HR people have considered the formal performance appraisal system as the primary means for managing employee performance. We take a very different view of the performance management process, however. We define **performance management** as the means through which managers ensure that employees' activities and outputs are congruent with the organization's goals. Performance management is central to gaining competitive advantage.

Our performance management system has three parts: defining performance, measuring performance, and feeding back performance information. First, a performance management system specifies which aspects of performance are relevant to the organization, primarily through **job analysis** (discussed in Chapter 6). Second, it measures those aspects of performance through **performance appraisal**, which is only one method for managing employee performance. Third, it provides feedback to employees through **performance feedback** sessions so that they can adjust their performance to the organization's goals. Performance feedback is also fulfilled through tying rewards to performance via the compensation system (e.g., merit increases or bonuses), a topic to be covered in Chapters 15 and 16.

In this chapter, we examine a variety of approaches to performance management. We begin with a model of the performance management process that helps us examine the system's purposes. Then we discuss the specific approaches to performance management and the strengths and weaknesses of each approach. We also discuss the various sources of performance information. The errors resulting from subjective assessments of performance are presented, as well as the means for reducing those errors. Then we discuss some effective components to performance feedback. Finally, we discuss the components of a legally defensible performance management system.

AN ORGANIZATIONAL MODEL OF PERFORMANCE MANAGEMENT

For many years, researchers in the field of HRM and industrial/organizational psychology focused on performance appraisal as a measurement technique.[1] The goal of these performance appraisal systems was to measure individual employee performance reliably and validly. This perspective, however, tended to ignore some very important influences on the performance management process. Thus, we begin this section by presenting the major purposes of performance management from an organizational rather than a measurement perspective. To do this, we need to understand the process of performance. Figure 7.1 depicts our process model of performance.

As the figure shows, individuals' attributes—their skills, abilities, and so on—are the raw materials of performance. For example, in a sales job, an organization wants someone who has knowledge of the products and good interpersonal skills. These raw materials are transformed into objective results through the employee's behavior. Employees can only exhibit behaviors if they have the necessary knowledge, skills, abilities, or other characteristics. Thus, employees with good product knowledge and interpersonal skills can talk about the advantage of various brands and can behave in a friendly, helpful manner (not that they necessarily display those behaviors, only that they *can* display them). On the other hand, employees with little product knowledge or interpersonal skills cannot effectively display those behaviors. The objective results are the measurable, tangible outputs of the work, and they are a consequence of the employee's or the work group's behavior. In our example, if a salesperson displays the correct behaviors, he or she will likely make a number of sales.

Another important component in our organizational model of the performance management system is the organization's strategy. The link between performance management and the organization's strategies and goals is often neglected. Chapter 2 pointed out that most companies pursue some type of strategy to attain their revenue, profit, and market-share goals. Divisions, departments, work groups, and individuals within the company must align their activities with these strategies and goals. If they are not aligned, then the likelihood of achieving the goals becomes small. How is this link made in organizations? Primarily by specifying what needs to be accomplished and what behaviors must be exhibited for the company's strategy to be implemented. This is one link that is being increasingly recognized

FIGURE 7.1   Model of Performance Management in Organizations

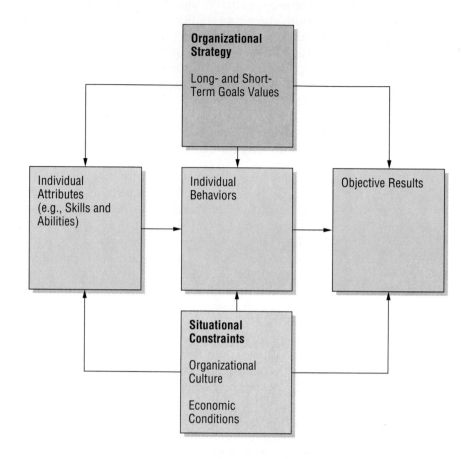

as necessary, through the increasing popularity of **performance planning and evaluation (PPE)** systems. PPE systems seek to tie the formal performance appraisal process to the company's strategies by specifying at the beginning of the evaluation period the types and level of performance that must be accomplished to achieve the strategy. Then at the end of the evaluation period, individuals and groups are evaluated based on how closely their actual performance met the performance plan. In an ideal world, performance management systems would ensure that all activities support the organization's strategic goals.

Finally, our model notes that situational constraints are always at work within the performance management system. As discussed previously, an employee may have the necessary skills and yet not exhibit the necessary behaviors. Sometimes the organizational culture discourages the employee from doing things that might be effective. Work-group norms often dictate what the group's members do and the results they produce. On the other hand, some people are simply not motivated to exhibit the right behaviors.

This often occurs if the employees do not believe that their behaviors will be rewarded with pay raises, promotions, and so forth. Finally, people may be performing effective behaviors, and yet the right results do not follow. For example, an outstanding salesperson may not have a large dollar volume because the economy is bad and people are simply not buying.

Thus, as you can see in Figure 7.1, employees must have certain attributes to perform a set of behaviors and achieve some results. To gain competitive advantage, the attributes, behaviors, and results must be tied to the company's strategy. It is also important to note that constraints exist within the work environment that often preclude employees from performing. Given this model of employee performance, we will next examine the purposes of performance management systems.

PURPOSES OF PERFORMANCE MANAGEMENT

The purposes of performance management systems are of three kinds: strategic, administrative, and developmental.

Strategic Purpose

First and foremost, a performance management system should link employee activities with the organization's goals. One of the primary ways strategies are implemented is through defining the results, behaviors, and, to some extent, employee characteristics that are necessary for carrying out that strategy, then developing measurement and feedback systems that will maximize the extent to which employees exhibit the characteristics, engage in the behaviors, and produce the results. To achieve this strategic purpose, the system must be flexible, because when goals and strategies change, the results, behaviors, and employee characteristics usually need to change correspondingly. However, performance management systems do not commonly achieve this purpose. As recently as 1985, a survey found that only 13 percent of the companies questioned were using their performance appraisal system to communicate company objectives.[2] In addition, a more recent survey of HR practitioners regarding the purposes of performance appraisal failed to include any questions about the extent to which the system is tied to the company's strategic objectives.[3] Most systems instead focus on administrative and developmental purposes.

Administrative Purpose

Organizations use performance management information (performance appraisals, in particular) in many administrative decisions: salary administration (pay raises), promotions, retention/termination, layoffs, and recognition of individual performance.[4] Despite the importance of these decisions, however, many managers, who are the source of the information, see the performance appraisal process only as a necessary evil they must go through to fulfill their job requirements. They feel uncomfortable evaluating others and feeding those evaluations back to the employees. Thus, they tend to rate everyone high, or at least rate them the same, and as a result, the performance appraisal information becomes relatively useless. For example, one manager stated, "There is really no getting around the fact that whenever I evaluate one of my people, I stop and think about the impact—the ramifications of my decisions on my relationship with the guy and his future here.... Call it being politically minded, or using managerial discretion, or fine-tuning the guy's ratings, but in the end, I've got to live with him, and I'm not going to rate a guy without thinking about the fallout."[5]

Developmental Purpose

A third purpose of performance management is to develop employees who are effective at their jobs. When employees are not performing as well as they should, performance management seeks to improve their performance. The feedback given during a performance evaluation process often pinpoints the employee's weaknesses. Ideally, however, the performance management system identifies not only the aspects of the employee's performance that are deficient but also the causes of these deficiencies—for example, a skill deficiency, a motivational problem, or some obstacle that is holding the employee back.

Managers are often uncomfortable confronting employees with their performance weaknesses. Such confrontations, although necessary to the effectiveness of the work group, often strain everyday working relationships. Giving high ratings to all employees enables a manager to minimize such conflicts, but then the developmental purpose of the performance management system is not fully achieved.[6]

The purposes of an effective performance management system are to link employee activities with the organization's strategic goals, furnish valid and useful information for making administrative decisions about employees, and provide employees with useful developmental feedback. Fulfilling these three purposes is central to gaining competitive advantage through human resources, and a vital step in performance management is to develop the measures by which performance will be evaluated. Thus, we next discuss the issues involved in developing and using different measures of performance.

PERFORMANCE MEASURES CRITERIA

In Chapter 6 we discussed how, through job analysis, one can analyze the job to determine exactly what constitutes effective performance. Once the company has determined, through job analysis and design, what kind of performance it expects from its employees, it needs to develop ways to measure that performance. This section presents the criteria, underlying job performance measures. Later sections discuss approaches to performance measurement, sources of information, and errors.

Although people differ about criteria to use to evaluate performance management systems, we believe that five stand out: strategic congruence, validity, reliability, acceptability, and specificity.

Strategic Congruence

Strategic congruence is the extent to which the performance management system elicits job performance that is congruent with the organization's strategy, goals, and culture. If a company emphasizes customer service, then its performance management system should assess how well its employees are serving the company's customer. Strategic congruence emphasizes the need for the performance management system to provide guidance so that employees can contribute to the organization's success. This requires systems flexible enough to adapt to changes in the company's strategic posture.

Most companies' appraisal systems remain constant over a long period of time and through a variety of strategic emphases. However, when a company's strategy changes, its employees' behavior needs to change, too.[7] The fact that they often do not change may account for why many managers see performance appraisal systems as having little impact on a firm's effectiveness.

Validity

Validity is the extent to which the performance measure assesses all the relevant—and only the relevant—aspects of performance. This is often referred to as "content validity." For a performance measure to be valid, it must not be deficient or contaminated. As you can see from Figure 7.2, one of the circles represents "true" job performance, that is, all of those aspects of performance relevant to being successful in the job. On the other hand, companies must use some measure of performance, such as a supervisory rating of performance on a set of dimensions or measures of the objective results on the job. Validity is concerned with maximizing the overlap between actual job performance and the measure of job performance.

A performance measure is deficient if it does not measure all aspects of performance (the purple portion of the job performance circle in the figure). An example is a system at a large university that assesses faculty members based more on research than teaching, thereby relatively ignoring a relevant aspect of performance.

A contaminated measure evaluates irrelevant aspects of performance or aspects that are not job related (see the purple portion of the performance measure circle in Figure 7.2). The performance measure should seek to minimize contamination, but its complete elimination is seldom possible. An example of a contaminated measure is the use of actual sales figures for

FIGURE 7.2   Contamination and Deficiency of a Job Performance Measure

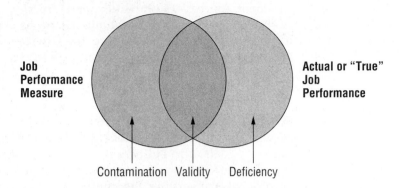

evaluating salespersons across very different regional territories. Often sales are highly dependent upon the territory (e.g., number of potential customers, number of competitors, economic conditions) rather than the actual performance of the salesperson. A salesperson who works harder and better than others might not have the highest sales totals because the territory simply does not have as much sales potential as others. Thus, to use these figures alone would be to use a measure that is strongly affected by things that are beyond the control of the individual employee.

Reliability

Reliability refers to the consistency of the performance measure. One important type of reliability is interrater reliability: the consistency among the individuals who evaluate the employee's performance. A performance measure has interrater reliability if two individuals give the same (or close to the same) evaluations of a person's job performance. With some measures, the extent to which all of the items rated are internally consistent is important (internal consistency reliability).

In addition, the measure should be reliable over time (test-retest reliability). A measure that results in drastically different ratings depending on the time at which the measures are taken lacks test-retest reliability. For example, if salespeople are evaluated based on their actual sales volume during a given month, it would be important to consider their consistency of monthly sales across time. What if an evaluator in a department store only examined sales during May? Employees in the lawn and garden department would have high sales volumes, but those in the men's clothing department would have somewhat low sales volumes. One needs to measure performance consistently across time.

If the measure is not reliable, it cannot be valid. For example, if there is no agreement about a person's job performance, how can a good decision (about a pay raise, a promotion, or a developmental need) be made about him or her? One evaluator may think a large pay raise is in order, the other may think pay should be cut. However, evidence seems to indicate that most subjective supervisory measures of job performance exhibit low reliability.[8]

Acceptability

Acceptability refers to whether the people who use the performance measure accept it. Many very elaborate performance measures are extremely valid and reliable, but they consume so much of managers' time that they refuse to use it. Alternatively, those being evaluated by a measure may not accept it. Either way, a system that is not accepted is almost worse than no measure at all. This points to the need to involve both managers and employees in the development of performance measures. Research has found that this increases the acceptability of the system.[9]

Specificity

Specificity is the extent to which the performance measure gives specific guidance to employees about what is expected of them and how they can meet these expectations. Specificity is relevant to both the strategic and developmental purposes of performance management. If a measure does not specify what an employee must do to help the company achieve its strategic goals, it becomes difficult for it to achieve its strategic purpose. Additionally, if the measure fails to point out an employee's performance problems, it is almost impossible for the employee to correct his or her performance.

APPROACHES TO MEASURING PERFORMANCE

The model of performance management presented in Figure 7.1 shows that one can manage performance by focusing on employee attributes, behaviors, or results. In addition, one could also measure performance in a relative way, making overall comparisons among individuals' performance. Finally, one could develop a performance measurement system that incorporates some variety of the above measures, as is recently evidenced by the TQM approach to measuring performance. Various techniques use a combination of these approaches. In this section, we explore these approaches to measuring and managing performance, discussing the techniques that are associated with each approach and evaluating these approaches against the criteria of strategic congruence, validity, reliability, acceptability, and specificity.

The Comparative Approach

The comparative approach to performance measurement consists of techniques that require the rater to compare an individual's performance with that of others. This approach usually uses some overall assessment of an individual's performance, or worth, and seeks to develop some ranking of the individuals within a given work group. At least three techniques fall under the comparative approach: ranking, forced distribution, and paired comparison.

Ranking.   *Ranking* is one of the techniques that arrives at an overall assessment of the individual's performance. Simple ranking requires managers to rank employees within their departments from highest to lowest (or best to worst). Alternation ranking, on the other hand, consists of a manager looking at a list of employees, deciding who is the best employee, and crossing that person's name off the list. From the remaining names, the manager decides who the worst employee is and crosses that name off the list—and so forth.

Ranking is one method of performance appraisal that has received some specific attention in the courts. In the *Albermarle v. Moody* case, the validation of the selection system was conducted using employee rankings as the measure of performance. The court actually stated, "There is no way of knowing precisely what criteria of job performance that supervisors were considering, whether each supervisor was considering the same criteria—or whether, indeed, any of the supervisors actually applied a focused and stable body of criteria of any kind."[10]

Forced Distribution.   The *forced distribution* method also uses a ranking format, but employees are ranked in groups. This technique requires the manager to put certain percentages of employees into predetermined categories (as depicted in Table 7.1). The example in Table 7.1 illustrates how Merck combines the performance of the division with individual performance to recommend the distributions of employees that should fall into each category. For example among poorly performing divisions (Not Acceptable), only 1 percent of employees should receive the highest rating (TF = Top 5%), whereas among top-performing divisions (EX = Exceptional) 8 percent of employees should receive the highest rating.

Again, this is a form of ranking, with the exception that employees are ranked into certain groups. A forced distribution was not the method discussed in the *Albermarle* case, but because of its similarity to ranking, one should also be cautious in evaluating the legal defensibility of this technique. However, it is also important to note that both rankings and forced distributions are effective ways of minimizing managers' tendency to provide uniformly high ratings for all employees.

Paired Comparison.   The *paired-comparison method* requires managers to compare every employee with every other employee in the work group, giving an employee a score of 1 every time he or she is considered the higher performer. Once all the pairs have been compared, the manager computes the number of times each employee received the favorable decision (i.e., counts up the points), and this becomes the employee's performance score.

The paired-comparison method tends to be rather time-consuming for managers and will become more so as organizations become flatter with an increased span of control. For example, a manager with 10 employees

TABLE 7.1

Proposed Guidelines for Targeted Distribution of Performance Ratings

Targeted employee rating distribution, by divisional performance

Performance Rating for Employees	Rating Type	Performance Rating for Divisions				
		EX Exceptional	WD With Distinction	HS High Standard	RI Room for Improvement	NA Not Acceptable
TF Top 5%	Relative	8%	6%	5%	2%	1%
TQ Top Quintile	Relative	20%	17%	15%	12%	10%
OU Outstanding **VG** Very Good **GD** Good	Absolute Absolute Absolute	71%	75%	75%	78%	79%
LF Lower 5% **NA** Not Acceptable	Relative Absolute	1%	2%	5%	8%	10%
PR Progressing		Not Applicable				

SOURCE: Reprinted with permission of The Conference Board, New York City.
* Data supplied by Merck & Co.; chart by Kevin J. Murphy, University of Rochester

must make 45 (i.e., 10(9)/2) different comparisons. However, if the group is increased to 15 employees, 105 comparisons must be made.

Evaluating the Comparative Approach.   The comparative approach to performance measurement provides an effective tool when the major purpose of the system is to differentiate employee performance. These techniques virtually eliminate problems of leniency, central tendency, and strictness. This is especially valuable if the results of the measures are to be used in making administrative decisions such as pay raises and promotions. In addition, they are relatively easy to develop and in most cases easy to use; thus, they are often considered acceptable by the users.

One problem with these techniques, however, is their common failure to be linked to the strategic goals of the organization. While raters can make their ratings based on the extent to which individuals' performance supports the strategy, this link is seldom made explicit. In addition, because of the subjective nature of the ratings, the actual validity and reliability depend on the raters themselves. Some firms seek to use multiple evaluators to reduce the biases of any individual, but most do not. At best one could conclude that their reliability and validity are modest.

Finally, these techniques lack specificity for feedback purposes. Based only on their relative rankings, individuals are completely unaware of what they must do differently in the future to improve their ranking. This puts a heavy burden on the manager to provide specific feedback beyond that of the rating instrument itself.

The Attribute Approach

The attribute approach to performance management focuses on the extent to which individuals have certain attributes (characteristics or traits) believed to be desirable for the company's success. The techniques that use this approach tend to define a set of traits—such as initiative, leadership, and competitiveness—and evaluate individuals on them.

Graphic Rating Scales. The most common form that the attribute approach to performance management takes is the *graphic rating scale.* Table 7.2 provides an example of a graphic rating scale Hamilton Jordan developed to evaluate cabinet members during President Jimmy Carter's administration. As you can see, a list of traits is followed by a 5-point (or some other number of points) rating scale. The manager considers one employee at a time, circling the number that signifies how much of that trait the individual has. Graphic rating scales can provide the rater with a number of different points (a "discrete" scale) or with a continuum along which the rater simply places a check mark (a "continuous" scale).

Graphic rating scales are easy to develop. The developer must simply brainstorm a list of traits or characteristics that he or she believes are necessary for effective job performance, or in some cases to develop generic phrases that describe aspects of that job performance (e.g., quantity of work, quality of work). In addition, most often these instruments can be (and often are) applied to widely diverse jobs.

The legal defensibility of graphic rating scales was questioned in the *Brito v. Zia* (1973) case. In this case, Spanish-speaking employees had been terminated as a result of their performance appraisals. These appraisals consisted of supervisors' rating subordinates on a number of work dimensions such as volume of work, quantity of work, job knowledge, dependability, and cooperation. The court criticized the subjective nature of these appraisals, and stated that the company should have presented empirical data demonstrating that the appraisal was significantly related to actual work behavior.

Mixed Standard Scales. *Mixed standard scales* were developed as a means of getting around some of the problems with graphic ratings scales. To create a mixed standard scale, one must define the relevant performance dimensions, then develop statements representing good, average, and poor performance along each dimension. These statements are then mixed with the statements from other dimensions on the actual rating instrument. An example of a mixed standard scale is presented in Table 7.3.

As you can see in Table 7.3, the rater is asked to complete the rating instrument by indicating whether the employee's performance is above (+), at (0), or below (−) the statement. A special scoring key is then used to score the employee's performance for each dimension. Thus, for example, if the employee's performance is above all three statements, he or she receives a seven. If the employee is below the good statement, at the average statement, and above the poor statement, a score of 4 is assessed. If the employee

TABLE 7.2

The Graphic Rating Scale Used to Evaluate Cabinet Members
in the Carter Administration

Staff Evaluation

Please answer each of the following questions about this person.

Office: *TIME Washington Bureau*

Name of Rater: *Robert Ajemian*
Bureau Chief

Name: *Jimmy Carter*

Salary: *$200,000*

Position: *President of the U.S.*

Duties: *Governing the nation as Chief of the Executive Branch, Commander in Chief of the armed forces, head of the Democratic Party*

Work Habits

1. On the average when does this person:
   arrive at work *before anybody else*
   leave work *before anybody else*

2. Pace of work:
   1   2   3   4   5   ⑥
   slow   fast

3. Level of effort:
   1   2   3   4   5   ⑥
   below capacity   full capacity

4. Quality of work:
   1   2   ③   4   5   6
   poor   good

5. What is he/she best at?
   (rank 1–5)
   _3_   Conceptualizing
   _2_   Planning
   _5_   Implementing
   _1_   Attending to detail
   _4_   Controlling quality

6. Does this person have the skills to do the job he/she was hired to do?
   yes ____
   no ____
   ? *not yet*

7. Would the slot filled by this person be better filled by someone else?
   yes ____
   no ____
   ? *not yet*

Personal Characteristics

8. How confident is this person? (circle one)
   x   x   x   x   x   ⊗   x
   self   confident   cocky
   doubting

9. How confident are you of this person's judgement?
   1   2   ③   4   5   6
   not confident   very confident

10. How mature is this person?
    1   2   3   4   5   ⑥
    immature   mature

11. How flexible is this person?
    1   ②   3   4   5   6
    rigid   flexible

12. How stable is this person?
    1   2   3   4   5   ⑥
    erratic   steady

13. How frequently does this person come up with new ideas?
    1   ②   3   4   5   6
    seldom   often

14. How open is this person to new ideas?
    1   2   3   4   5   ⑥
    closed   open

15. How bright is this person?
    1   2   3   4   ⑤   6
    average   very bright

16. What are this person's special talents?
    1. *tenacious belief in self*
    2. *antagonizing Congress*
    3. *can work with White House staff*

17. What is this person's range of information?
    1   2   3   4   5   ⑥
    narrow   broad

Interpersonal Relations

18. How would you characterize this person's impact on other people? (for example, hostile, smooth, aggressive, charming, etc.)
    1. *tranquilizing*
    2. *believable*
    3. *makes people think of Edward Kennedy*

19. How well does this person get along with:

Superiors	1	2	3	4	5	⑥
Peers	1	2	3	4	5	⑥
Subordinates	1	2	3	4	5	⑥
Outsiders	①	2	3	4	5	6

not well   very well

continued

TABLE 7.2

continued

20. In a public setting, how comfortable would you be having this person represent:

    You or your office   1 2 3 4 5 ⑥

    The President   1 2 ③ 4 5 6

       1=uncomfortable   6=comfortable

21. Rate this person's political skills.

    1   ②   3   4   5   6
    naive   savvy

Supervision and Direction

21. To what extent is this person focused on accomplishing the:

    Administration's goals   _40_%

    personal goals   _60_%

                       _100_%

23. How capable is this person at working toward implementing a decision with which he/she may not agree?

    ①   2   3   4   5   6
    reluctant   eager

24. How well does this person take direction?

    ①   2   3   4   5   6
    resists   readily

25. How much supervision does this person need?

    1   2   ③   4   5   6
    a lot   little

26. How readily does this person offer to help out by doing that which is not a part of his/her "job"?

    1   2   3   4   5   ⑥
    seldom   often

Summary

27. Can this person assume more responsibility

    yes   ___

    no   ___

    ?   _already has too much_

28. List this person's 3 major strengths and 3 major weaknesses.

    Strengths:

    1. _high sense of decency and moral_ _values_

    2. _identifies problems well_

    3. _rarely flops_

Weaknesses:

1. _dislikes admitting mistakes_

2. _substitutes pieties for programs_

3. _inability to cut loose from_ _subordinates_

29. List this person's 3 major accomplishments.

    1. _brought balanced approach to Middle_ _East_

    2. _aligned America more with forces of_ _change in the world_

    3. _visiting average Americans in their_ _homes_

30. List 3 things about this person that have disappointed you.

    1. _has no clear public philosophy_

    2. _attracted too little excellence to_ _government_

    3. _doesn't use power with confidence_

is below all three statements, he or she is given a rating of 1. This scoring is applied to all the dimensions to determine an overall performance score.

It is important to note that mixed standard scales were originally developed as trait-oriented scales. However, this same technique has recently been applied to instruments using behavioral rather than trait-oriented statements as a means of reducing rating errors in performance appraisal.[11]

Evaluating the Attribute Approach.   Managers need to be aware that attribute-based performance methods are the most popular methods in organizations. They are quite easy to develop and are generalizable across a variety of jobs, strategies, and organizations. In addition, if much attention is devoted to identifying those attributes relevant to job performance and carefully defining them on the rating instrument, they can be as reliable and valid as more elaborate measurement techniques.

TABLE 7.3   An Example of a Mixed Standard Scale

Three traits being assessed: Levels of performance in statements:
    Initiative (INTV)   High (H)
    Intelligence (INTG)   Medium (M)
    Relations with others (RWO)   Low (L)

Instructions: Please indicate next to each statement whether the employee's performance is above (+), equal to (0), or below (–) the statement.

INTV H	1. This employee is a real self–starter. The employee always takes the initiative and his/her superior never has to prod this individual.	+
INTG M	2. While perhaps this employee is not a genius, s/he is a lot more intelligent than many people I know.	+
RWO L	3. This employee has a tendency to get into unnecessary conflicts with other people.	0
INTV M	4. While generally this employee shows initiative, occasionally his/her superior must prod him/her to complete work.	+
INTG L	5. Although this employee is slower than some in understanding things, and may take a bit longer in learning new things, s/he is of average intelligence.	+
RWO H	6. This employee is on good terms with everyone. S/he can get along with people even when s/he does not agree with them.	–
INTV L	7. This employee has a bit of a tendency to sit around and wait for directions.	+
INTG H	8. This employee is extremely intelligent, and s/he learns very rapidly.	–
RWO M	9. This employee gets along with most people. Only very occasionally does s/he have conflicts with others on the job, and these are likely to be minor.	–

Scoring Key:

Statements			Score
High	Medium	Low	
+	+	+	7
0	+	+	6
–	+	+	5
–	0	+	4
–	–	+	3
–	–	0	2
–	–	–	1

Example Score from Ratings Above:

	Statements			Score
	High	Medium	Low	
Initiative	+	+	+	7
Intelligence	0	+	+	5
Relations with Others	–	–	0	2

However, these techniques fall short on several of the criteria for effective performance management. There is usually little strategic congruence between the techniques and the company's strategy. These methods are used because of the ease in developing them and because the same method (e.g., list of traits, comparisons) is generalizable across any organization and any strategy. In addition, these methods usually have very vague performance standards that are open to different interpretations by different raters. Because of this, different raters often provide extremely different ratings and rankings. The result is that both the validity and reliability of these methods are usually low.

Virtually none of these techniques provides any specific guidance on how an employee can support the company's goals or on what to do to correct performance deficiencies. In addition, when raters give feedback, these techniques tend to elicit defensiveness from employees. For example, how would you feel if you were told that on a 5-point scale, you were a 2 in maturity? Certainly you might feel somewhat defensive and unwilling to accept that judgment, as well as any additional feedback.

The Behavioral Approach

The behavioral approach to performance management attempts to define the behaviors an employee must exhibit to be effective in the job. The various techniques define those behaviors, then require managers to assess the extent to which employees exhibit them. We discuss five techniques that rely on the behavioral approach.

Critical Incidents.   The *critical incident* approach requires managers to keep a record of specific examples of effective and ineffective performance on the part of each employee. Here's an example of an incident described in the performance evaluation of an appliance repair person:

> *A customer called in about a refrigerator that was not cooling and was making a clicking noise every few minutes. The technician prediagnosed the cause of the problem and checked his truck for the necessary parts. When he found he did not have them, he checked the parts out from inventory so that the customer's refrigerator would be repaired on his first visit and the customer would be satisfied promptly.*

These incidents are used to give specific feedback to employees about what they do well and what they do poorly, and they can be tied to the company's strategy by focusing on incidents that best support that strategy. However, many managers resist having to keep a daily or weekly log of their employees' behavior. It is also often difficult to make comparisons among employees, since each incident is specific to that individual.

Behaviorally Anchored Rating Scales (BARS).   *Behaviorally anchored rating scales (BARS)* build on the critical incidents approach. They are designed to specifically define performance dimensions by developing behavioral anchors associated with different levels of performance.[12] An example of BARS is presented in Figure 7.3. As you can see, the performance dimension has a number of examples of behaviors that indicate specific levels of performance along the dimension.

To develop BARS, one first gathers a large number of critical incidents that represent effective and ineffective performance on the job. These incidents are classified into performance dimensions, and the ones that experts agree clearly represent a particular level of performance are used as behavioral examples (or anchors) to guide the rater. The manager's task is to consider an employee's performance along each dimension and determine where on the dimension the employee's performance fits using the behavioral anchors as guides. This rating becomes the employee's score for that dimension.

Behavioral anchors have advantages and disadvantages. One advantage is that they can increase interrater reliability by more specifically defining the performance dimension. A disadvantage is that they can bias information recall—that is, behavior that closely approximates the anchor is more easily recalled than other behavior. [13]

BARS are somewhat easy to use, and they are often readily accepted by both managers and employees. They also provide an excellent means for giving specific performance feedback to employees, and the performance dimensions or the behavioral anchors can be developed to tie into the company's strategy.

The major drawback of BARS is that they tend to be expensive and time-consuming. This presents a potential problem when a company's strategic focus shifts because substantial time then has to be spent developing BARS congruent with the new strategy. Research has also demonstrated that managers and their subordinates do not make much of a distinction between BARS and traits.[14]

Behavioral Observation Scales. A *behavioral observations scale* (BOS) is a variation of BARS. Like BARS, a BOS is developed from critical incidents.[15] However, a BOS differs from BARS in two basic ways. First, rather than discarding a large number of the behaviors that exemplify effective or ineffective performance, a BOS uses many of them to more specifically define all the behaviors necessary for effective performance (or that would be considered ineffective performance). Instead of using, say, four behaviors to define four levels of performance on a particular dimension, a BOS may use 15 behaviors. An example of a BOS is presented in Table 7.4.

A second difference is that rather than assessing which behavior best reflects an individual's performance, a BOS requires managers to rate the frequency with which the employee has exhibited each behavior during the rating period. These ratings are then averaged to compute an overall performance rating.

A BOS has some of the same advantages as a BARS, but it tends to consume more of the manager's time. It can be linked to a company's strategy, and it can be modified with any shift in strategic focus. The major drawback

FIGURE 7.3   Task-BARS Rating Dimension: Patrol Officer

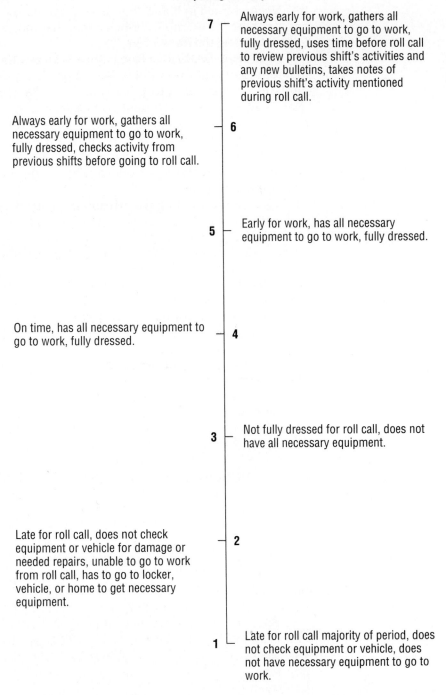

Preparing for Duty

7 — Always early for work, gathers all necessary equipment to go to work, fully dressed, uses time before roll call to review previous shift's activities and any new bulletins, takes notes of previous shift's activity mentioned during roll call.

Always early for work, gathers all necessary equipment to go to work, fully dressed, checks activity from previous shifts before going to roll call. — **6**

5 — Early for work, has all necessary equipment to go to work, fully dressed.

On time, has all necessary equipment to go to work, fully dressed. — **4**

3 — Not fully dressed for roll call, does not have all necessary equipment.

Late for roll call, does not check equipment or vehicle for damage or needed repairs, unable to go to work from roll call, has to go to locker, vehicle, or home to get necessary equipment. — **2**

1 — Late for roll call majority of period, does not check equipment or vehicle, does not have necessary equipment to go to work.

SOURCE: Adapted from R. Harvey, "Job Analysis," in *Handbook of Industrial and Organizational Psychology* ed. M. Dunnette and L. Hough (Palo Alto, Cal.: Consulting Psychologists Press, 1991), 138.

TABLE 7.4   An Example of a Behavioral Observation Scale (BOS) for Evaluating Job Performance

I. Overcoming Resistance to Change*

(1)   Describes the details of the change to subordinates.

  Almost Never   1   2   3   4   5   Almost Always

(2)   Explains why the change is necessary.

  Almost Never   1   2   3   4   5   Almost Always

(3)   Discusses how the change will affect the employee.

  Almost Never   1   2   3   4   5   Almost Always

(4)   Listens to the employee's concerns.

  Almost Never   1   2   3   4   5   Almost Always

(5)   Asks the employee for help in making the change work.

  Almost Never   1   2   3   4   5   Almost Always

(6)   If necessary, specifies the date for a follow-up meeting to respond to the employee's concerns.

  Almost Never   1   2   3   4   5   Almost Always

Total = _____

Below Adequate	Adequate	Full	Excellent	Superior*
6–10	11–15	16–20	21–25	26–30

SOURCE: G. Latham and K. Wexley, *Increasing Productivity through Performance Appraisal,* © 1981 Addison-Wesley Publishing Company. Reprinted by permission.
* Scores are set by management.

of a BOS is that it may require more information than most managers can process or remember. A BOS can have 80 or more behaviors, and the manager must remember how frequently an employee exhibited each of these behaviors over a 6- or 12-month rating period. This is taxing enough with regard to one employee, but managers often must rate ten or more employees.

In spite of these potential weaknesses, a direct comparison of BOS, BARS, and graphic rating scales found that both managers and employees prefer BOS for differentiating good from poor performers, maintaining objectivity, providing feedback, suggesting training needs, and being easy to use among managers and subordinates.[16]

Organizational Behavior Modification (OBM).   *Organizational behavior modification* entails managing the behavior of employees through a formal system of behavioral feedback and reinforcement. This system builds on the behaviorist view of motivation, which holds that individuals' future behavior is determined by past behaviors that have been positively reinforced. The techniques vary, but most of them have four components. First, they define a set of key behaviors necessary for job performance. Second, they use a measurement system to assess whether these behaviors are

FIGURE 7.4   Increases in Productivity for Housekeepers as a
Result of Behavior Management

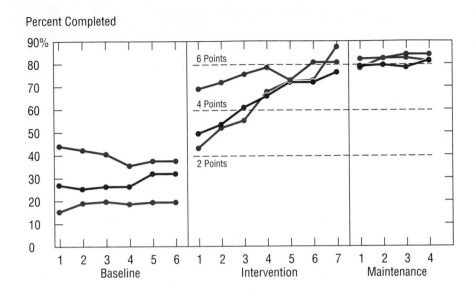

SOURCE: D. C. Anderson, C. Crowell, S. Sponsel, M. Clarke, and J. Spence, "Behavior Management in the Public Accommodations Industry: A Three-Project Demonstration," *Journal of Organizational Behavior Modification* 4 (1983): 57.

exhibited. Third, the manager or consultant informs employees of those behaviors, perhaps even setting goals for how often the employees should exhibit those behaviors. Finally, feedback and reinforcement are provided to employees.[17]

OBM techniques have been used in a variety of settings. One technique, referred to as "behavior management," was used to increase the performance of cleaning people in the hotel industry.[18] Housekeepers were asked to follow a 70-item behavioral checklist, checking off each behavior as they performed it. By providing feedback and reinforcement, management was able to increase housekeepers' performance, as shown in Figure 7.4. Similar results have been observed with respect to the frequency of safety behaviors in a processing plant.[19]

OBM techniques generally increase the frequency of the behaviors that they identify as leading to successful job performance. They provide specific guidance to employees about what is expected of them, and behaviors important to the company's strategy can be specified. These techniques are expensive to develop and maintain, however. Developing measurement systems (i.e., the means for observing the extent to which individuals are exhibiting behaviors) can be very labor intensive.

Assessment Centers.   Although assessment centers are usually used for selection and promotion decisions, they have also been used as a way of measuring managerial performance.[20] During an assessment center, individuals usually perform a number of simulated tasks, such as leaderless group discussions, in-baskets, and role playing. Assessors observe the individuals' behavior and evaluate their skill or potential as a manager.

The advantage of assessment centers is that they provide a somewhat objective measure of an individual's performance at managerial tasks. In addition, they provide specific performance feedback, and individualized developmental plans can be designed. For example, ARCO Oil & Gas Corporation sends its managers through assessment centers to identify their individual strengths and weaknesses and to create developmental action plans for each manager.

An interesting public-sector application of assessment centers is in the state government of North Carolina. Managers in the North Carolina state government can go through an assessment process to become "certified middle managers." This process includes an assessment center at the beginning of the certification program, from which an individualized developmental action plan is created. The developmental plan, implemented over approximately two years, consists of training programs and on-the-job developmental experiences. At the end of the two years, the manager attends the certification assessment center. Those who successfully meet the criteria set forth in the certification assessment center then become certified.

Assessment centers tend to be reliable, valid, and highly accepted. In addition, they provide specific information about an individual's strengths and weaknesses. They are expensive to conduct, however.[21] They also do not assess how managers actually perform their jobs on a daily basis, although they are accurate at measuring how well managers *can* perform their jobs.

Evaluation of the Behavioral Approach.   The behavioral approach can be very effective. It can link the company's strategy to the specific types of behavior necessary for implementing that strategy. It provides specific guidance and feedback for employees about the performance expected of them. Most of the techniques rely on in-depth job analysis, so the behaviors that are identified and measured are valid. Because those who will be using the system are involved in developing the measures, the acceptability is also often high. Finally, with a substantial investment in training raters, the techniques are reasonably reliable.

The major weaknesses have to do with the organizational context of the system. Although the behavioral approach can be closely tied to a company's strategy, the behaviors and measures must be constantly monitored and revised to ensure that they are still linked to the strategic focus. This approach also assumes that there is "one best way" to do the job and that the behaviors that constitute this best way can be identified. One study found that managers seek to control behaviors when they perceive a clear relationship between behaviors and results. When this link is not clear, they tend to rely on managing results.[22] The behavioral approach might be best suited to less complex jobs (where the best way to achieve results is somewhat clear) and least suited to complex jobs (where there are multiple ways, or behaviors, to achieve success).

The Results Approach.   The results approach focuses on managing the objective, measurable results of a job or work group. This approach assumes that subjectivity can be eliminated from the measurement process and that results are the closest indicator of one's contribution to organizational effectiveness.[23] We will examine two performance management systems that use results: management by objectives and the productivity measurement and evaluation system.

Management by Objectives (MBO).   *Management by objectives* is popular in both private and public organizations.[24] The original concept came from the accounting firm of Booz, Allen, and Hamilton and was called a "manager's letter." The process consisted of having all the subordinate managers write a letter to their superiors, detailing what their performance goals were for the coming year and how they planned to achieve them. Harold Smiddy applied and expanded this idea at General Electric in the 1950s, and Douglas McGregor has since developed it into a philosophy of management.[25]

In an MBO system, the top management team first defines the company's strategic goals for the coming year. These goals are passed on to the next layer of management, and these managers define the goals they must achieve for the company to achieve its goals. This goal-setting process cascades down the organization so that all managers are setting goals that help the company achieve its goals.[26] These goals are used as the standards by which an individual's performance is evaluated.[27]

MBO systems have three common components.[28] One, they require specific, difficult, objective goals. (An example of an MBO-based goal is presented in Table 7.5.) Two, the goals are not usually set unilaterally by management but with the managers' and subordinates' participation. Three, the manager gives objective feedback throughout the rating period to monitor progress toward the goals.

A recent review of the research on MBO has revealed two important findings regarding its effectiveness.[29] Of 70 studies examined, 68 showed productivity gains, while only 2 showed productivity losses, suggesting that MBO usually increases productivity. Also, productivity gains tend to be highest when there is substantial commitment to the MBO program from top management: an average increase of 56 percent when commitment was high, 33 percent when commitment was moderate, and 6 percent when commitment was low.

Clearly, MBO can have a very positive effect on an organization's performance. Considering the process through which goals are set (i.e., involvement of staff in setting objectives), it is also likely that MBO systems effectively link individual employee performance with the firm's strategic goals.

TABLE 7.5   An Example of a Management by Objectives (MBO)
Measure of Job Performance

PERFORMANCE OBJECTIVES

Position: T. J. Logan, General Sales and Marketing Manager, Kahala Products Division

Specific Objectives for the Year 1983	Results Obtained and Explanations
1. To achieve the sales growth of 14% to $9 million, as set out in detail in the sales budget (Reference PX 13, dated October 1, 1982). These sales to be achieved within the expense budget stipulated	1
2. To complete preparations for the launching of product X by April 1, 1983	2
3. To test market product Y in New England district during August–September 1983 and recommend further action by October 1, 1983	3
4. To insure that forward market analyses are carried out covering the Z product range and possible developments for that range, report to the Product Development Committee by July 1, 1983. Recommending lines for R&D effort on this range	4
5. Improve the speed of order analysis to achieve daily order summarizes by product group by March 1, 1983. Develop follow-up procedures to investigate variation in intake by product group	5
6. Draw up organization and manning proposals by October 6, 1983, to separate the sales organization of Z product range by July 1, 1984	6

SOURCE: Reprinted with the permission of The Free Press, a Division of Macmillan, Inc. from PAY: Employee Compensation and Incentive Plans by Thomas H. Patten, Jr. Copyright © 1977 by The Free Press.

Productivity Measurement and Evaluation System (ProMES).   The main goal of ProMES is to motivate employees to higher levels of productivity.[30] It is a means of measuring and feeding back productivity information to personnel.

ProMES consists of four steps. First, people in an organization identify the products, or the set of activities or objectives, the organization expects to accomplish. The organization's productivity depends on how well it produces these products. A product might be something like "quality of repair." Second, the staff define indicators of the products. Indicators are measures of how well the products are being generated by the organization. Quality of repair could be indicated by (1) return rate (percentage of items returned that did not function immediately after repair) and (2) percentage of quality-control inspections passed. Third, the staff establishes the contingencies between the amount of the indicators and the level of evaluation associated with that amount. Fourth, a feedback system is developed that provides employees and work groups with information about their specific level of performance on each of the indicators. An overall productivity score can be computed by summing the effectiveness scores across the various indicators.

Because this technique is somewhat new, it has been applied in only a few situations. However, research thus far strongly suggests it is effective in increasing productivity. (Figure 7.5 illustrates the productivity gains in the machine shop described previously.) The research also suggests the system is an effective feedback mechanism. However, users found it time-consuming to develop the initial system. Future research on ProMES needs to be conducted before drawing any firm conclusions, but the existing research indicates that this may be a useful performance management tool.

Evaluation of the Results Approach.   One advantage of the results approach is that it minimizes subjectivity, relying on objective, quantifiable indicators of performance. Thus, it is usually highly acceptable to both managers and employees. Another advantage is that it links an individual's results with the organization's strategies and goals.

A disadvantage is that objective measurements can be both contaminated and deficient—contaminated because they are affected by things that are not under the employee's control, such as economic recessions, and deficient because not all the important aspects of job performance are amenable to objective measurement. Another disadvantage of the results approach is that individuals may focus only on aspects of their performance that are measured, neglecting those that are not. One study found that objective performance goals led to higher performance but that they also led to less helping of coworkers.[31] A final disadvantage is that, though results measures provide objective feedback, the feedback may not help employees learn how they need to change their behavior to increase their performance. If baseball players are in a hitting slump, simply telling them that their batting average is .190 may not motivate them to raise it. Feedback focusing on the exact behavior (e.g., taking one's eye off the ball, dropping one's shoulder) that needs to be changed would be more helpful.[32]

The Total Quality Approach

Thus far we have examined the traditional approaches to measuring and evaluating employee performance. However, advocates of the total quality management (TQM) approach believe that most U.S. companies' perfor-

FIGURE 7.5   Increases in Productivity for Repair Shop Using ProMES Measures

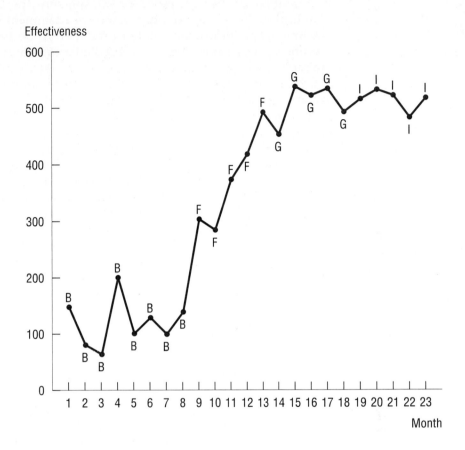

SOURCE: R. Pritchard, S. Jones, P. Roth, K. Stuebing, and S. Ekeberg, "The Evaluation of an Integrated Approach to Measuring Organizational Productivity," *Personnel Psychology* 42 (1989): 69–115.

mance management systems are incompatible with the quality philosophy for a number of reasons:

1. Most existing systems measure performance in terms of quantity, not quality.
2. Employees are held accountable for good or bad results to which they contribute but do not completely control.
3. Companies do not share the financial rewards of successes with employees according to how much they have contributed to them.
4. Rewards are not connected to business results.[33]

Sales, profit margins, and behavioral ratings are often collected by managers to evaluate employees' performance. However, according to TQM, these types of outcomes should not be used to evaluate employees' performance because they do not have complete control over them (i.e., they are contaminated). For example, for salespersons, performance evaluation (and salary increases) are often based on attainment of a sales quota. It is assumed that salespersons' abilities and motivation are directly responsible for their performance. However, TQM advocates argue that a larger determinant of whether a salesperson reaches the quota are "systems qualities," such as competitors' product price changes, and economic conditions, which are not under the salesperson's control. [34] Holding employees accountable for systems outcomes is believed to result in dysfunctional behavior, such as falsifying sales reports, budgets, expense accounts, and other performance measures, as well as lowering employees' motivation for continuous improvement.

TQM advocates suggest that the major focus of performance evaluations should be to provide employees with feedback about areas in which they can improve. Two types of feedback are necessary: (1) subjective feedback from managers, peers, and customers about the personal qualities of the employee and (2) objective feedback based on the work process itself using statistical quality-control methods. A good example of performance evaluation in a TQM environment is provided by Esoniq Corporation in the "Competing through Quality" box on page 263.

Subjective Performance Evaluation in TQM.   Performance feedback from managers, peers, and customers should be based on such dimensions as cooperation, attitude, initiative, and communication skills. Performance evaluation should include a discussion of the employee's career plans. TQM also strongly emphasizes that performance appraisal systems should avoid providing overall evaluations of employees (e.g., ratings such as excellent, good, poor). Categorizing employees is believed to encourage them to behave in ways that are expected based on their ratings. For example, "average" performers may not be motivated to improve their performance but rather may continue to perform at the expected level. Also, because employees do not have control over the quality of the system in which they work, employee performance evaluations should not be linked to compensation. Compensation rates should be based on prevailing market rates of pay, seniority, and business results, which are distributed equitably to all employees.

Objective Performance Evaluation in TQM.   Statistical process quality-control techniques are very important in TQM. These techniques provide employees with an objective tool to identify causes of problems and potential solutions. These techniques include process-flow analysis, cause-and-effect diagrams, Pareto charts, control charts, scattergrams, and histograms.[35] *Process-flow analysis* involves identifying each action and decision necessary to complete work, such as waiting on a customer or assembling a television set. Process-flow analysis is useful for identifying redundancy in processes that increase manufacturing or service time. Figure 7.6 shows a process-flow analysis for a company's internal recruiting process.

FIGURE 7.6 Process Flow Analysis

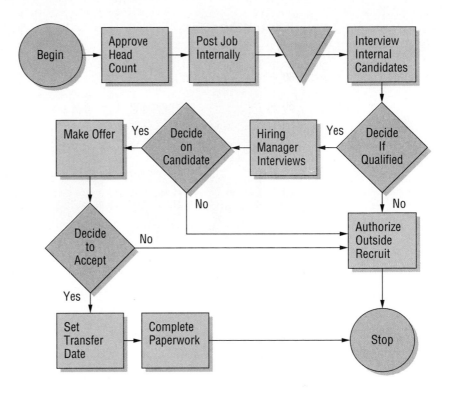

In *cause-and-effect diagrams,* events or causes that result in undesirable outcomes are identified. Employees try to identify all possible causes of a problem. The feasibility of the causes is not evaluated, and as a result, cause-and-effect diagrams produce a large list of possible causes.

A *Pareto chart* is used to highlight the most important cause of a problem. In a Pareto chart, causes are listed in decreasing order of importance, where importance is usually defined as the frequency with which that cause resulted in a problem. The assumption of Pareto analysis is that the majority of problems are the result of a small number of causes. Figure 7.7 shows a Pareto chart listing the reasons managers give for not selecting current employees for a job vacancy.

Control charts involve collecting data at multiple points in time. By collecting data at different times, employees can identify the different factors that contribute to an outcome and when they tend to occur. Figure 7.8 shows the percentage of employees hired internally for a company for each quarter between 1989 and 1991. Internal hiring increased dramatically dur-

FIGURE 7.7   Pareto Chart

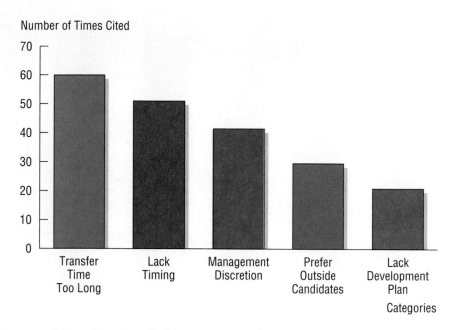

SOURCE: C. Carter, "Seven Basic Quality Tools," *HR Magazine,* January 1992, 83.

FIGURE 7.8   Control Chart

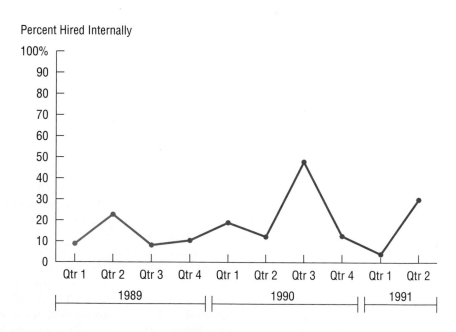

SOURCE: C. Carter, "Seven Basic Quality Tools," *HR Magazine,* January 1992, 82.

ing the third quarter of 1990. The use of control charts helps employees understand the number of internal candidates that can be expected to be hired each year. Also, the control chart shows that the amount of internal hiring conducted during this quarter is much larger than normal.

Histograms are used for displaying distributions of large sets of data. Data are grouped into a smaller number of categories or classes. Histograms are useful for understanding the amount of variance between an outcome and the expected value or average outcome. Figure 7.9 is a histogram showing the number of days it took a company to fill nonexempt job vacancies. The histogram shows that most nonexempt jobs took from 17 to 21 days to fill, and the amount of time to fill nonexempt jobs ranged from 1 to 33 days. If an HR manager relied simply on data from personnel files on the number of days it took to fill nonexempt positions, it would be extremely difficult to understand the variation and average tendency in the amount of time to fill the positions.

Scattergrams show the relationship between two variables, events, or different pieces of data. Scattergrams help employees determine whether the relationship between two variables or events is positive, negative, or zero. The scattergram in Figure 7.10 shows a negative relationship. The

FIGURE 7.9   Histogram

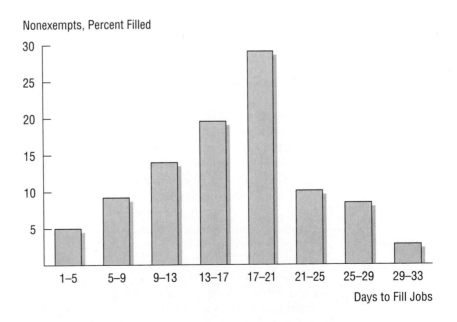

SOURCE: C. Carter, "Seven Basic Quality Tools," *HR Magazine,* January 1992, 83.

FIGURE 7.10   Scattergram

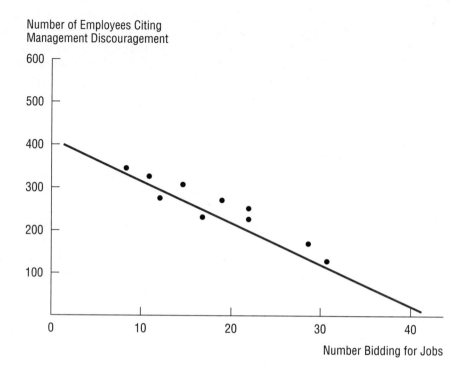

SOURCE: C. Carter, "Seven Basic Quality Tools," *HR Magazine,* January 1992, 83.

number of employees that bid for jobs increases when employees believe that managers are not discouraging them from bidding on jobs.

Evaluation of the TQM Approach.   The TQM approach relies primarily on a combination of the attribute and results approaches to performance measurement. However, traditional performance appraisal systems focus more on individual employee performance, while TQM adopts a systems-oriented focus.[36] Many companies may be unwilling to completely abandon their traditional performance management system because it serves as the basis for personnel selection validation, identification of training needs, or compensation decisions. Also, TQM advocates evaluation of personal traits (e.g., cooperation), which are difficult to relate to job performance unless the company has been structured into work teams.

Traditional performance management systems can, however, be changed to accommodate a total quality culture. For example, performance rating systems should include interpersonal skills that are related to

Quality

COMPETING THROUGH

THE TQM APPROACH TO PERFORMANCE MEASUREMENT AT ENSONIQ CORPORATION

Ensoniq Corporation manufactures electronic musical instruments, including synthesizers and keyboards, and it recently implemented a TQM system. It was founded in 1982 and has grown to an annual sales of approximately $25 million in 1989. The privately held company employs approximately 200 people.

Under its TQM approach to performance measurement, Ensoniq believes that performance reviews and compensation should not be linked. The wage and salary guide states that "the purpose of the performance reviews is to provide a dialogue between the employee and supervisor, whereby the employee's performance can be enhanced. The performance reviews are not used to determine the employee salary."

Employee performance reviews occur every four months. The reviews focus on the total effectiveness of employees in communications and leadership skills, adaptability, and initiative. Although this aspect of the performance review is somewhat qualitative, thus leaving room for favoritism, Ensoniq has not found this to be a problem, namely because salary discussions are not part of this process.

Employees also receive immediate and direct quantitative feedback from the system by using statistical quality-control methods. If a deviation from a product specification occurs in a manufacturing process, an investigation is initiated. If employees are responsible for the deviation, training, counseling, or reassignment may result. However, deviations from specifications (or performance problems) may also be the result of equipment malfunctions or defective supplies. Statistical quality-control methods help identify whether system components such as machine operation and supply quality, which may not be under the direct control of employees, need improvement.

SOURCE: R. S. Schuler and D. L. Harris, "Deming Quality Improvement: Implications for Human Resource Management as Illustrated in a Small Company," *Human Resource Planning* 14 (1991): 191–207; Ensoniq Personnel Policies handbook, effective November 10, 1989.

employees' jobs. Performance management systems that include objective outcomes (e.g., an MBO system) such as sales or service calls should allow for systems factors such as competitors' pricing and economic trends, which are not under employee control. Also, the TQM approach emphasizes that performance evaluation systems should measure quality and quantity of performance. The most important aspect of the TQM approach is its emphasis on feedback from peers, managers, and the work itself. The TQM approach emphasizes that employees need performance feedback more regularly than the traditional yearly performance appraisal. Continuous improvement in products and services can occur if managers interact with their employees daily and if employees use quality-control tools for problem solving, troubleshooting, and the development of new ideas.

TABLE 7.6

Evaluation of Approaches to Performance Measurement

	Criteria				
Approach	**Strategic**	**Validity**	**Reliability**	**Acceptability**	**Specificity**
Comparative	Poor, unless manager takes time to make link	Can be high if ratings are done carefully	Depends on rater, but usually no measure of agreement used	High; easy to develop and use	Very low
Attribute	Usually low; requires manager to make link	Usually low; can be fine if developed carefully	Usually low; can be improved by specific definitions of attributes	High; easy to develop and use	Very low
Behavioral	Can be quite high	Usually high; minimizes contamination and deficiency	Usually high	Moderate; difficult to develop, but accepted well for use	Very high
Results	Very high	Usually high; can be both contaminated and deficient	High; main problem can be test-retest— dependent upon timing of measure	High; usually developed with input from those to be evaluated	High regarding results, but low regarding behaviors necessary to achieve them
TQM	Very high	High, but can be both contaminated and deficient	High	High; usually developed with input from those to be evaluated	High regarding results, but low regarding behaviors necessary to achieve them

     In summary, organizations can take four approaches to measuring performance: comparative, attribute, behavior, and results. Table 7.6 summarizes the various approaches to measuring performance based on the criteria we set forth earlier and illustrates that each approach has strengths and weaknesses. As the TQM approach illustrates, often the most effective way of measuring performance is to rely on a combination of two or more alternatives. However, in most cases, the performance measures consist of some kind of ratings. These ratings must come from some source, and the next section will discuss the various sources of performance information.

CHOOSING A SOURCE FOR PERFORMANCE INFORMATION

Whatever approach to performance management is used, it is necessary to decide whom to use as the source of the performance measures. Each source has specific strengths and weaknesses. We discuss five primary sources: supervisors, peers, subordinates, customers, and self.

Supervisors

Supervisors are the most frequently used source of performance information. It is usually safe to assume that supervisors have extensive knowledge of the job requirements and that they have had adequate opportunity to observe their employees—in other words, that they have the ability to rate their employees. In addition, because the supervisor has something to gain from the employees' high performance and something to lose by low performance, they have the motivation to make accurate ratings.[37] Finally, feedback from supervisors is strongly related to performance.[38]

Problems with using supervisors as the source of performance information can occur in particular situations. In some jobs, for example, the supervisor does not have an adequate opportunity to observe the employee performing his or her job duties. For example, in outside sales jobs, the supervisor does not have the opportunity to see the salesperson at work most of the time. This usually requires that the manager occasionally spend a day accompanying the salesperson on sales calls. However, on those occasions the employee will be on his or her best behavior, so there is no assurance that performance that day accurately reflects performance when the manager is not around.

Also, some supervisors may be so biased against a particular employee that to use them as the sole source of information would result in less-than-accurate measures for that individual. Favoritism is a fact of organizational life, but it is one that must be minimized as much as possible in the performance management process.[39] Thus, the performance evaluation system should seek to minimize the opportunities for favoritism to affect ratings, and one way to do this is not to rely on only a supervisor's evaluation of an employee's performance.

Peers

Another source of performance information is the employee's coworkers. Peers are an excellent source of information in a job such as law enforcement, where the supervisor does not always have the opportunity to observe the employee. Peers have expert knowledge of job requirements, and they often have more of an opportunity to observe the employee in day-to-day activities. Peers also bring a different perspective to the evaluation process, which can be valuable in gaining an overall picture of the individual's performance. In fact, peers have been found to provide extremely valid assessments of performance in several different settings.[40]

One disadvantage of using peer ratings is the potential for friendship to bias ratings.[41] Little empirical evidence suggests that this is often a problem, however. Another disadvantage is that when the evaluations are made for administrative decisions, peers often find the situation of being both rater and ratee uncomfortable. When these ratings are used only for developmental purposes, however, peers react favorably.[42]

Subordinates

Subordinates are an especially valuable source of performance information when managers are being evaluated. Subordinates often have the best opportunity to evaluate how well a manager treats employees.

One problem with subordinate evaluations is that they give subordinates power over their managers, thus putting the manager in a difficult situation.[43] This can lead to managers' emphasizing employee satisfaction over productivity. However, this only happens when administrative decisions are made from these evaluations. As with peer evaluations, it is a good idea to use subordinate evaluations only for developmental purposes. To assure subordinates that they need not fear retribution from their managers, it is necessary to use anonymous evaluations and use at least three subordinates for each manager.

Self

Although self-ratings are not often used as the sole source of performance information, they can still be valuable.[44] Obviously, individuals have extensive opportunities to observe their own behavior, and they usually have access to information regarding their results on the job.

One problem with self-ratings, however, is a tendency toward inflated assessments. This stems from two sources. One, if the ratings are going to be used for administrative decisions (e.g., pay raises), it is in the employees' interests to inflate their ratings. Two, there is ample evidence in the social psychology literature that individuals attribute their poor performance to external causes, such as a coworker whom they think has not provided them with timely information. Although self-ratings are less inflated when supervisors provide frequent performance feedback, it is not advisable to use them for administrative purposes.[45] The best use of self-ratings is as a prelude to the performance feedback session to get employees thinking about their performance and to focus discussion on areas of disagreement.

Customers

As of May 1991, service industries employed 78 percent of all workers in the United States.[46] One writer has defined *services* this way: "Services is something which can be bought and sold but which you cannot drop on your foot."[47] Because of the unique nature of services—the product is produced and consumed on the spot—supervisors, peers, and subordinates often do not have the opportunity to observe employee behavior. Instead, the customer is often the only person present to observe the employee's performance and thus is the best source of performance information.

Many companies in service industries have moved toward customer evaluations of employee performance. Marriott Corporation provides a customer satisfaction card in every room and sends mail surveys to a random sample of customers after their stay in a Marriott hotel. Whirlpool's Consumer Services Division conducts both mail and telephone surveys of customers after factory service technicians have serviced their appliances. These surveys allow the company to evaluate an individual technician's customer-service behaviors while in the customer's home.

The weakness of customer surveys is that they are somewhat expensive. The printing, postage, phone, and labor can add up to hundreds of dollars for the evaluation of one individual. Thus, many companies conduct such evaluations only once a year for a short period of time.

In conclusion, the best source of performance information often depends on the particular job. One should choose the source or sources that provide the best opportunity to observe employee behavior and results. Table 7.7 summarizes this information for most jobs. Often, eliciting performance information from a variety of sources results in a performance management process that is accurate and effective. An example of this is the process used at Digital Equipment Corporation, discussed in the "Competing through Technology and Structure" box.

ERRORS IN PERFORMANCE MEASUREMENT

Research consistently reveals that humans have tremendous limitations in processing information. Because we are so limited, we often use "heuristics," or simplifying mechanisms, to make judgments, whether they are judgments about investments or about people.[48] These heuristics, which appear often in subjective measures of performance, can lead to rater errors.

Rater Errors

Similar to Me. "Similar to me" is the error we make when we judge those who are similar to us more highly than those who are not. Research has demonstrated that this effect is strong, and when similarity is based on

TABLE 7.7   Frequency of Observation for Various Sources of Performance Information

	Source				
	Supervisor	**Peers**	**Subordinates**	**Self**	**Customers**
Task					
Behavior	Occasional	Frequent	Rare	Always	Frequent
Results	Frequent	Frequent	Occasional	Frequent	Frequent
Interpersonal					
Behaviors	Occasional	Frequent	Frequent	Always	Frequent
Results	Occasional	Frequent	Frequent	Frequent	Frequent

SOURCE: Adapted from K. Murphy and J. Cleveland, *Performance Appraisal: An Organizational Perspective* (Boston: Allyn & Bacon, 1991).

demographic characteristics such as race or sex, it can result in discriminatory decisions.[49] Most of us tend to think of ourselves as effective, and so if others are like us—in race, gender, background, attitudes, or beliefs—we assume that they too are effective.

Contrast.   Contrast error occurs when we compare individuals with one another instead of against an objective standard. Consider a completely competent performer who works with a number of peers who are outstanding. If the competent employee receives lower-than-deserved ratings because of his or her outstanding colleagues, that is contrast error.

Distributional Errors.   Distributional errors are the result of a rater's tendency to use only one part of the rating scale. *Leniency* occurs when a rater assigns high (lenient) ratings to all employees. *Strictness* occurs when a manager gives low ratings to all employees—that is, holds all employees to unreasonably high standards. *Central tendency* reflects that a manager rates all employees in the middle of the scale. These errors pose two problems. First, they make it difficult to distinguish among employees rated by the same rater. Second, they create problems in comparing the performance of individuals rated by different raters. If one rater is lenient and the other is strict, the employees of the strict rater will receive significantly fewer rewards than those rated by the lenient rater.

Halo/Horns.   These errors both refer to a failure to distinguish among different aspects of performance. *Halo error* occurs when one positive performance aspect causes the rater to rate all other aspects of performance positively—for example, professors who are rated as outstanding researchers because they are known to be outstanding teachers. *Horns error* works in

Technology & Structure

TEAM APPRAISALS AT DIGITAL

Digital Equipment Corporation is one of the largest manufacturers of computer equipment in the world. Its manufacturing plants have been largely redesigned around a team-based concept, where work teams are in charge of managing themselves. These teams have started to change toward a participatory performance appraisal system.

The performance appraisal process in the Digital work groups can include input from self-appraisals and ratings from peers. The typical process takes approximately two to four weeks. It begins with the creation of the performance appraisal committee. This committee includes the person being evaluated, the chairperson (chosen by the person being evaluated), an internal management consultant, and two randomly selected team members. The person being evaluated then sends a list of his or her accomplishments and training for the past year. This information is used by committee members to provide input into the appraisal process. Within two weeks the chairperson sends this input to the person being evaluated. The evaluatee then writes his or her own

performance appraisal document, which is distributed to the committee for review. After a week, the committee meets to discuss the document. If no further information is needed, then a final rating is assigned, and the committee jointly sets goals for the next year. If further information is needed, then the committee can set a follow-up date for the next meeting.

Digital feels that the appraisal process has a number of advantages. Because team members have opportunities to observe one another, the ratings tend to be more accurate than traditional supervisory evaluations. In addition, because the responsibility for getting the appraisal done is on the employee's shoulders, these appraisals are seldom late. The process allows for timely feedback and participative goal setting for future performance, while grooming team members for future leadership roles.

The major disadvantage of the process is that it is time-consuming. However, given the positive reactions of employees to the process, the company feels that the process provides an extremely effective way to manage employee performance.

SOURCE: C. Norman and R. Zawacki, "Team Appraisals—Team Approach," *Personnel Journal,* September 1991, 101–103.

the opposite direction: one negative aspect results in the rater assigning low ratings to all the other aspects.

Halo and horns errors are a problem in that they preclude making the necessary distinctions between strong and weak performance. Halo error leads to employees believing that no aspects of their performance need improvement. Horns leads to employees becoming frustrated and defensive.

Reducing Rater Errors

Two approaches to reducing rating errors have been offered.[50] *Rater error training* attempts to make managers aware of rating errors and helps them develop strategies for minimizing those errors.[51] These programs consist of having the participants view videotaped vignettes designed to elicit rating errors such as "contrast." They then make their ratings and discuss how the error influenced the rating. Finally, they are given learning points regarding ways to avoid committing those errors. This approach has been shown to be effective for reducing errors, but there is also evidence that reducing rating errors can also result in reduced accuracy.[52]

Rater accuracy training, also called *frame-of-reference training*, attempts to emphasize the multidimensional nature of performance and thoroughly familiarize raters with the actual content of various performance dimensions. This involves providing examples of performance for each dimension and then discussing the actual or "correct" level of performance that the example represents.[53] Accuracy training does seem to increase accuracy, provided that the training allows practice in making ratings and offers feedback about their accuracy.[54]

PERFORMANCE FEEDBACK

Once the expected performance has been defined and the employees' performance has been measured, it is necessary to feed that performance information back to the employees so they can correct any deficiencies. The performance feedback process is complex and provokes anxiety for both the manager and the employee. Few of us feel comfortable sitting in judgment of others: The thought of confronting others with what we perceive to be their deficiencies causes most of us to shake in our shoes. If giving negative feedback is painful, receiving it can be excruciating—thus the importance of the performance feedback process.

Ways to Improve the Performance Feedback Process

If individuals are not made aware of how their performance is not meeting expectations, their performance will almost certainly not improve. In fact, it may get worse. An effective manager must possess the ability to provide specific performance feedback to employees in a way that elicits positive behavioral responses. The following process increases the potential for a successful performance feedback session.

Feedback Should Be Given Every Day, Not Once a Year.   There are two reasons for this. First, managers have a responsibility to correct performance deficiencies immediately on becoming aware of them. If performance is subpar in January, waiting until December to appraise the performance could mean an 11-month productivity loss. Second, a major determinant of how effectively a feedback session goes is the extent to which the subordinate is not surprised by the evaluation. An easy rule to follow is that employees should receive such frequent performance feedback that they already know almost exactly what their formal evaluation will be.

Ask the Employee to Rate His/Her Performance before the Session. Having employees complete a self-assessment before the feedback session can be very productive. It requires employees to think about their performance over the past rating period, and it encourages them to think about their weaknesses. Although self-ratings used for administrative decisions are often inflated, there is evidence that they may actually be lower than supervisors' ratings when done for developmental purposes. Another reason a self-assessment can be productive is that it can make the session go more smoothly by focusing discussion on areas where disagreement exists, resulting in a more efficient session. Finally, employees who have thought about past performance are more able to participate fully in the feedback session.

Encourage the Subordinate to Participate in the Session. Managers can take one of three approaches in performance feedback sessions. In the "tell-and-sell" approach, managers tell the employees how they have rated them and then justify these ratings. In the "tell-and-listen" approach, managers tell employees how they have rated them, then let the employees explain their side of the story. In the "problem-solving" approach, managers and employees work together to solve performance problems in an atmosphere of respect and encouragement. In spite of the research demonstrating the superiority of the problem-solving approach, most managers still rely on the tell-and-sell approach.[55]

When employees participate in the feedback session, they are consistently satisfied with the process.[56] One study found that, other than satisfaction with one's supervisor, participation was the single most important predictor of satisfaction with the feedback session.[57]

Recognize Effective Performance through Praise. One usually thinks of performance feedback sessions as focusing on the employee's performance problems. This should never be the case. The purpose of the session is to give accurate performance feedback, which entails recognizing effective performance as well as poor performance. Praising effective performance provides reinforcement for that behavior. It also adds credibility to the feedback by making it clear that the manager is not just identifying performance problems.

Focus on Solving Problems. A common mistake that managers make in providing performance feedback is to try to use the session as a chance to punish poor-performing employees by telling them how utterly lousy their performance is. This only reduces the employees' self-esteem and increases their defensiveness, neither of which will improve performance.

To improve poor performance, a manager must attempt to solve the problems causing it. This entails working with the employee to determine the actual cause and then agreeing how to solve it. For example, a salesperson's failure to meet a sales goal may be the result of lack of a proper sales pitch, lack of product knowledge, or stolen sales by another salesperson. Each of these causes requires a different solution. Without a problem-solving approach, however, the correct solution might never be identified.

Focus Feedback on Behavior or Results, Not on the Person. One of the most important things to do when giving negative feedback is to avoid questioning the employee's worth as a person. This is best accomplished by focusing the discussion on the employee's behaviors or results, not on the employee. To say, "You're screwing up! You're just not motivated!" will bring about more defensiveness and ill feelings than stating, "You did not meet the deadline that you agreed to because you spent too much time on another project."

Minimize Criticism. Obviously, if an individual's performance is below standard, some criticism must take place. However, an effective manager should resist the temptation to reel off a litany of offenses. Having been confronted with the performance problem, an employee often agrees that a change is in order. However, if the manager continues to come up with more and more examples of low performance, the employee may get defensive.

Agree to Specific Goals and Set a Date to Review Progress. The importance of goal setting cannot be overemphasized. It is one of the most effective motivators of performance.[58] Research has demonstrated that it results in increased satisfaction, motivation to improve, and performance improvement.[59] Besides setting goals the manager must also set a specific follow-up date to review the employee's performance toward the goal. This provides an added incentive for the employee to take the goal seriously and work toward achieving it.

DEVELOPING AND IMPLEMENTING A SYSTEM THAT FOLLOWS LEGAL GUIDELINES

We now discuss the legal issues and constraints affecting performance management. Because performance measures play a central role in such administrative decisions as promotions, pay raises, and discipline, employees who sue an organization over these decisions ultimately attack the measurement systems on which the decisions were made. Two types of cases have dominated: discrimination and unjust dismissal.

In discrimination suits, the plaintiff often alleges that the performance measurement system unjustly discriminated against the plaintiff because of race or gender. Many performance measure are subjective, and we have seen that individual biases can affect them, especially when those doing the measuring harbor racial or gender stereotypes.

In *Brito v. Zia,* the Supreme Court essentially equated performance measures with selection tests.[60] It ruled that the *Uniform Guidelines on Employee Selection Procedures* were applicable to evaluating the adequacy of a performance appraisal instrument. This ruling presents a challenge to those involved in developing performance measures, because a substantial body of research on race discrimination in performance rating has demonstrated that both white and black raters give higher ratings to members of their own racial group, even after rater training.[61] There is also evidence that the discriminatory biases in performance rating are worse when one group makes up a small percentage of the work group. When the vast majority of the group is male, females receive lower ratings; when the minority is male, males receive lower ratings.[62]

In the second type of suit, an unjust dismissal suit, the plaintiff claims that the dismissal was for reasons other than those the employer claims. For example, an employee who works for a defense contractor might blow the whistle on the company for defrauding the government. If the company fires the employee, claiming that the employee was performing poorly, he or she may argue that the firing was, in fact, because of blowing the whistle on the employer—in other words, that the dismissal was unjust. The court case will likely focus on the performance measurement system that was used as the basis for claiming the employee's performance was poor.

Because of the potential costs of discrimination and unjust dismissal suits, an organization needs to determine exactly what the courts consider a legally defensible performance management system. Based on two reviews of court decisions dealing with performance management systems, we offer the following characteristics of a system that will withstand legal scrutiny. [63]

1. The system should be developed by conducting a valid job analysis that ascertains the important aspects of job performance.

2. The system should be based on either behaviors or results; evaluations of ambiguous traits should be avoided.

3. Raters should be trained in how to use the system rather than simply given the materials and left to interpret how to conduct the appraisal.

4. There should be some form of review by upper-level managers of all the performance ratings, and there should be a system for employees to appeal what they consider to be an unfair evaluation.

5. The organization should provide some form of performance counseling or corrective guidance to help poor performers improve their performance before being dismissed.

SUMMARY

Measuring and managing performance is a challenging enterprise and one of the keys to gaining competitive advantage. Performance management systems serve strategic, administrative, and developmental purposes, and their importance cannot be overestimated. A performance measurement system should be evaluated against the criteria of strategic congruence, validity, reliability, acceptability, and specificity. Measured against these criteria, the comparative, attribute, behavioral, and results approaches have different strengths and weaknesses. The TQM approach holds great potential but is relatively new. Thus, deciding which approach and which source of performance information are the best depends on the job in question, and effective managers need to be aware of the issues involved in determining the best method or combination of methods for their particular situations. In addition, once performance has been measured, a major component of a manager's job is to feed that performance information back to employees in a way that results in improved performance rather than defensiveness and decreased motivation. Finally, because disciplinary action usually requires some performance documentation, managers must be sure that their performance management process—both the measures and feedback—will withstand a legal challenge.

Discussion Questions

1. What are examples of administrative decisions that might be made in managing the performance of professors? Developmental decisions?

2. What would you consider the strategy of your university (e.g., research, undergraduate teaching, graduate teaching, combination)? How might the performance management system for faculty members fulfill its strategic purpose of eliciting the types of behaviors and results required by this strategy?

3. If you were developing a performance measurement system for faculty members, what would be the types of attributes that you would seek to measure? Behaviors? Results?

4. What sources of performance information would you use to evaluate faculty members' performance?

5. The performance of students is usually evaluated with an overall results measure of grade point average. How is this measure contaminated? How is it deficient? What other measures might you use to more adequately evaluate student performance?

6. Think of the last time that you had a conflict with another person, either at work or school. Using the guidelines for performance feedback, how would you provide feedback to that person regarding his or her performance in a way that is effective?

Notes

1. K. Murphy and J. Cleveland, *Performance Appraisal: An Organizational Perspective* (Boston: Allyn & Bacon, 1991).

2. Commerce Clearing House, *Performance Appraisal: What Three Companies are Doing* (Chicago, Ill.: Commerce Clearing House, 1985).

3. J. Cleveland, K. Murphy, and R. Williams, "Multiple Uses of Performance Appraisal: Prevalence and Correlates," *Journal of Applied Psychology* 74 (1989): 130–135.

4. Ibid.

5. C. Longenecker, "Behind the Mask: The Politics of Employee Appraisal," *Academy of Management Executive* 1 (1987): 183.

6. M. Beer, "Note on Performance Appraisal," in *Readings in Human Resource Management,* ed. M. Beer and B. Spector, (New York: Free Press, 1985).

7. R. Schuler and S. Jackson, "Linking Competitive Strategies with Human Resource Practices," *Academy of Management Executive* 1 (1987): 207–219.

8. L. King, J. Hunter and F. Schmidt, "Halo in a Multidimensional Forced-Choice Performance Evaluation Scale," *Journal of Applied Psychology* 65 (1980): 507–516.

9. S. Silverman and K. Wexley, "Reactions of Employees to Performance Appraisal Interviews as a Function of their Participation in Rating Scale Development," *Personnel Psychology* 37 (1984): 703–710.

10. Albermarle Paper Company v. Moody, U.S. Supreme Court Nos. 74-389 and 74-428, 10 FEP Cases 1181 (1975).

11. F. Blanz and E. Ghiselli, "The Mixed Standard Scale: A New Rating System," *Personnel Psychology* 25 (1973): 185–199; K. Murphy and J. Constans, "Behavioral Anchors as a Source of Bias in Rating," *Journal of Applied Psychology* 72 (1987): 573–577.

12. P. Smith and L. Kendall, "Retranslation of Expectations: An Approach to the Construction of Unambiguous Anchors for Rating Scales," *Journal of Applied Psychology* 47 (1963): 149–155.

13. K. Murphy and J. Constans, "Behavioral Anchors as a Source of Bias in Rating," *Journal of Applied Psychology* 72 (1987): 573–577; M. Piotrowski, J. Barnes-Farrel, and F. Esrig, "Behaviorally Anchored Bias: A Replication and Extension of Murphy and Constans," *Journal of Applied Psychology* 74 (1989): 823–826.

14. U. Wiersma and G. Latham, "The Practicality of Behavioral Observation Scales, Behavioral Expectation Scales, and Trait Scales," *Personnel Psychology* 39 (1986): 619–628.

15. G. Latham and K. Wexley, *Increased Productivity through Performance Appraisal* (Boston: Addison-Wesley, 1981).

16. U. Wiersma and G. Latham, "The Practicality of Behavioral Observation Scales, Behavioral Expectation Scales, and Trait Scales," *Personnel Psychology* 39 (1986): 619–628.

17. D. C. Anderson, C. Crowell, J. Sucec, K. Gilligan, and M. Wikoff, "Behavior Management of Client Contacts in a Real Estate Brokerage: Getting Agents to Sell More," *Journal of Organizational Behavior Management* 4 (1983): 67–96.

18. D. C. Anderson, C. Crowell, S. Sponsel, M. Clarke, and J. Brence, "Behavior Management in the Public Accommodations Industry: A Three-Project Demonstration," *Journal of Organizational Behavior Modification* 4 (1983): 33–65.

19. J. Komaki, R. Collins, and P. Penn, "The Role of Performance Antecedents and Consequences in Work Motivation," *Journal of Applied Psychology* 67 (1982): 334–340.

20. Latham and Wexley, *Increasing Productivity through Performance Appraisal.*

21. W. Byham, "Assessment Centers for Spotting Future Managers," *Harvard Business Review* 48 (1970): 150–160.

22. S. Snell, "Control Theory in Strategic Human Resource Management: The Mediating Effect of Administrative Information," *Academy of Management Journal* 35 (1992): 292–327.

23. T. Patten, Jr., *A Manager's Guide to Performance Appraisal* (New York: Free Press, 1982).

24. M. O'Donnell and R. O'Donnell, "MBO—Is it Passe?" *Hospital and Health Services Administration* 28, no. 5 (1983): 46–58; T. Poister and G. Streib, "Management Tools in Government: Trends over the Past Decade," *Public Administration Review* 49 (1989): 240–248.

25. D. McGregor, "An Uneasy Look at Performance Appraisal," *Harvard Business Review* 35, no. 3 (1957): 89–94.

26. E. Locke and G. Latham, *A Theory of Goal Setting and Task Performance* (Englewood Cliffs, N.J.: Prentice-Hall, 1990).

27. S. Carroll and H. Tosi, *Management by Objectives* (New York: MacMillan, 1973).

28. G. Odiorne, *MBO II: A System of Managerial Leadership for the 80's* (Belmont, Cal.: Pitman Publishers, 1986).

29. R. Rodgers and J. Hunter, "Impact of Management by Objectives on Organizational Productivity," *Journal of Applied Psychology* 76 (1991): 322–326.

30. R. Pritchard, S. Jones, P. Roth, K. Stuebing, and S. Ekeberg, "The Evaluation of an Integrated Approach to Measuring Organizational Productivity," *Personnel Psychology* 42 (1989): 69–115.

31. P. Wright, J. George, S. Farnsworth, and G. McMahan, "Productivity and Prosocial Behavior: The Effects of Goals and Incentives on Spontaneous Helping," *Journal of Applied Psychology* (in press).

32. Latham and Wexley, *Increasing Productivity through Performance Appraisal.*

33. E. C. Huge, *Total Quality: An Executive's Guide for the 1990s* (Homewood, Ill.: Richard D. Irwin, 1990) see Chapter 5, "Measuring and Rewarding Performance," pps. 70–88; and W. E. Deming, *Out of Crisis* (Cambridge, Mass.: MIT Center for Advanced Engineering Study, 1986).

34. M. Caroselli, *Total Quality Transformations* (Amherst, Mass.: Human Resource Development Press, 1991); Huge, *Total Quality: An Executive's Guide for the 1990s.*

35. J. D. Cryer and R. B. Miller, *Statistics for Business: Data Analysis and Modeling* (Boston: PWS-Kent, 1991); C. Carter, "Seven Basic Quality Tools," *HR Magazine,* January 1992, 81–83.

36. D. E. Bowen and E. E. Lawler, III, "Total Quality-Oriented Human Resource Management," *Organizational Dynamics* 21 (1992): 29–41.

37. R. Heneman, K. Wexley, and M. Moore, "Performance Rating Accuracy: A Critical Review," *Journal of Business Research* 15 (1987): 431–448.

38. T. Becker and R. Klimoski, "A Field Study of the Relationship between the Organizational Feedback Environment and Performance," *Personnel Psychology* 42 (1989): 343–358.

39. L. Axline, "Performance Biased Evaluations," *Supervisory Management,* November 1991, 3.

40. K. Wexley and R. Klimoski, "Performance Appraisal: An Update," in *Research in Personnel and Human Resource Management,* vol. 2, K. Rowland and G. Ferris (Greenwich, Conn: JAI Press, 1984).

41. F. Landy and J. Farr, *The Measurement of Work Performance: Methods, Theory, and Applications* (New York: Academic Press, 1983).

42. G. McEvoy and P. Buller, "User Acceptance of Peer Appraisals in an Industrial Setting," *Personnel Psychology* 40 (1987): 785–797.

43. Murphy and Cleveland, *Performance Appraisal: An Organizational Perspective.*

44. J. Bernardin and L. Klatt, "Managerial Appraisal Systems: Has Practice Caught up with the State of the Art?" *Public Personnel Administrator,* November 1985, 79–86.

45. R. Steel and N. Ovalle, "Self-appraisal Based on Supervisor Feedback," *Personnel Psychology* 37 (1984): 667–685.

46. Bureau of Labor Statistics, *Employment and Earnings* (Washington, D.C.: U.S. Department of Labor, 1991).

47. E. Gummerson, "Lip Services—a Neglected Area of Service Marketing," *Journal of Services Marketing* 1 (1987): 1–29.

48. A. Tversky and D. Kahneman, "Availability: A Heuristic for Judging Frequency and Probability," *Cognitive Psychology* 5 (1973): 207–232.

49. K. Wexley and W. Nemeroff, "Effects of Racial Prejudice, Race of Applicant, and Biographical Similarity on Interviewer Evaluations of Job Applicants," *Journal of Social and Behavioral Sciences* 20 (1974): 66–78.

50. D. Smith, "Training Programs for Performance Appraisal: A Review," *Academy of Management Review* 11 (1986): 22–40.

51. G. Latham, K. Wexley, and E. Pursell, "Training Managers to Minimize Rating Errors in the Observation of Behavior," *Journal of Applied Psychology* 60 (1975): 550–555.

52. J. Bernardin and E. Pence, "Effects of Rater Training: Creating New Response Sets and Decreasing Accuracy," *Journal of Applied Psychology* 65 (1980): 60–66.

53. E. Pulakos, "A Comparison of Rater Training Programs: Error Training and Accuracy Training," *Journal of Applied Psychology* 69 (1984): 581–588.

54. W. Borman, "Job Behavior, Performance, and Effectiveness," in *Handbook of Industrial and Organizational Psychology* 2, ed. M. Dunnette and L. Hough (Palo Alto, Cal.: Consulting Psychologists Press, 1991), 271–326.

55. K. Wexley, V. Singh, and G. Yukl, "Subordinate Participation in Three Types of Appraisal Interviews," *Journal of Applied Psychology* 58 (1973): 54–57; K. Wexley, "Appraisal Interview," in *Performance Assessment*, ed. R. A. Berk (Baltimore: Johns Hopkins University Press, 1986), 167–185.

56. D. Cederblom, "The Performance Appraisal Interview: A Review, Implications, and Suggestions," *Academy of Management Review* 7 (1982): 219–227.

57. W. Giles and K. Mossholder, "Employee Reactions to Contextual and Session Components of Performance Appraisal," *Journal of Applied Psychology* 75 (1990): 371–377.

58. E. Locke and G. Latham, *A Theory of Goal Setting and Task Performance* (Englewood Cliffs, N.J.: Prentice-Hall, 1990).

59. H. Klein, S. Snell, and K. Wexley, "A Systems Model of the Performance Appraisal Interview Process," *Industrial Relations* 26 (1987): 267–280.

60. Brito v. Zia Co. 478 F.2d 1200 (10th. Cir. 1973).

61. K. Kraiger and J. Ford, "A Meta-Analysis of Ratee Race Effects in Performance Rating," *Journal of Applied Psychology* 70 (1985): 56–65.

62. P. Sackett, C. DuBois and A. Noe, "Tokenism in Performance Evaluation: The Effects of Work Groups Representation on Male-Female and White-Black Differences in Performance Ratings," *Journal of Applied Psychology* 76 (1991): 263–267.

63. G. Barrett and M. Kernan, "Performance Appraisal and Terminations: A Review of Court Decisions since Brito v. Zia with Implications for Personnel Practices," *Personnel Psychology* 40 (1987): 489–503; H. Feild and W. Holley, "The Relationship of Performance Appraisal System Characteristics to Verdicts in Selected Employment Discrimination Cases," *Academy of Management Journal* 25 (1982): 392–406.

C A S E

MANAGING EMPLOYEE PERFORMANCE

Peoples Natural Gas (PNG) is a regulated utility in the Pittsburgh area. The company has consistently maintained a pay-for-performance philosophy, yet despite this clearly stated policy, PNG found that the link between pay and performance was not at all clear among employees and managers. In 1988, PNG's Vice President of Human Resources Jim Flinn noted that managers and employees had been voicing a series of complaints about the existing performance appraisal and merit review processes.

PNG's executive leadership saw this as an excellent opportunity to enhance business performance through revamping the performance appraisal process, and they brought in a management consultant to aid in the process. The consultant first interviewed the executive team to get a sense of what the company's goals were for the performance appraisal system. In addition, interviews were conducted with 600 employees and managers. The results of these interviews revealed that (a) employees did not perceive a link between performance appraisals and the company or individual performance; (b) employees perceived that rewards such as merit increases and promotions were based on length of service rather than performance appraisal ratings; (c) performance appraisal had not been linked to developmental planning; (d) employees needed to actively participate in the performance appraisal process; and (e) managers were not universally effective in providing behavioral feedback and coaching employees.

QUESTIONS

1. Based on the chapter you just read, what recommendations do you have for developing a performance appraisal system that might best correct the problems with PNG's existing performance appraisal process?

2. How would you go about implementing this system at PNG? What types of obstacles might you face? What types of training programs will you have to provide?

SOURCE: K. Guinn and R. Corona, "Putting a Price on Performance," *Personnel Journal,* May 1991, 72–77.

WORK ATTITUDES AND JOB WITHDRAWAL

Objectives

After reading this chapter, you should be able to:

1. Explain what job satisfaction is and how it develops.
2. Describe various ways to measure job satisfaction and the benefits of conducting work attitude surveys.
3. Explain what job withdrawal is and how it relates to job satisfaction.
4. Describe the various manifestations of job withdrawal, such as behavior changes, physical withdrawal, psychological withdrawal, and employee health problems.
5. Describe where job dissatisfaction and withdrawal originate and potential ways to reduce them.

Violence and the U.S. Postal Service

Anthony Frank, the postmaster general of the United States, was concerned about work attitudes and the job satisfaction of his 750,000 postal employees. On November 16, 1991, he ordered a survey of all postal workers to learn about their hopes, their fears, and their views about their jobs. Many felt that Frank's concern came a little too late, however, since Thomas McIlvane, a dis-gruntled postal employee in Royal Oak, Michigan, had killed four workers and wounded five others the day before.

Although, McIlvane was no stranger to the law, having been dishonorably discharged from the marines for violent behavior, the Royal Oak incident was not simply the isolated act of a lone madman. Rather, the McIlvane incident was apparently part of a continuing pattern of violence among postal workers. Only a month before this, a postal worker in Ridgewood, New Jersey, killed his supervisor and two mail handlers. In 1989, a postal employee in Escondido, California, shot four colleagues at the post office in Orange Glen. In December 1988, a postal worker in New Orleans shot and wounded three other postal workers. All in all, there were 700 documented assaults between supervisors and subordinates at the U.S. Postal Service between 1986 and 1992.

What makes working for the U.S. Postal Service such a dissatisfying and stressful experience? Some have speculated that the bad times started when federal funding for the agency dried up in the mid-1980s. For the first time, the U.S. Postal Service had to turn a profit and therefore gain competitive advantage over private delivery systems like United Parcel Service. To generate that profit, it needed to move more mail faster than ever. Letter sorters worked with automated machines that required them to sort 60 letters a minute, an incredibly monotonous job that was monitored closely via computers that printed out reports anytime a worker made too many mistakes.

The postal service also hired many young college-educated supervisors to manage an older work force. Some long-tenured employees bristled under the new managers' paramilitary, autocratic management styles, which included the use of one-way mirrors to monitor mail theft. Finally, the postal service was downsizing, and many postal workers complained that workers were being "harassed" out of their jobs or unfairly dismissed. In the words of one Royal Oak worker: "Management pushes and pushes and pushes and doesn't know when to quit. They pushed the wrong guy too far."

SOURCES: D. Levin, "Ex-postal Worker Kills Three and Wounds 6 in Michigan," *The New York Times,* November 15, 1991, 6; M. Tolchin, "Concerned over Morale, Post Office Asking "Why?" *The New York Times,* November 15, 1991, 6; D. Levin, "Slayings at Michigan Post Office Spur a Review of All Employees," *The New York Times,* November 15, 1991, 8.

INTRODUCTION

Although violence in the workplace is a relatively uncommon phenomenon, it is one of many different negative consequences that can result from poor employee work attitudes and job dissatisfaction. More frequently occurring consequences include turnover, absenteeism, tardiness, reduced work effort, and theft. Many employers try to maintain high employee job satisfaction to avoid these negative consequences. Some believe that maintaining

FIGURE 8.1   An Overall Model of the Job Dissatisfaction/Job Withdrawal Process

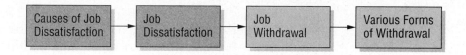

high job satisfaction is an important goal in and of itself—regardless of its impact on other outcomes. As one executive states, "I have over 500 people who spend over 60 percent of their waking hours in my plant five, six, sometimes seven days a week, and I don't know how much time traveling to and from work and thinking about their jobs. If they're basically unhappy with their work, then I am responsible for a helluva lot of human misery."[1]

The purpose of this chapter is to familiarize you with the causes and consequences of certain work attitudes, especially those related to the various forms of job withdrawal. Figure 8.1 depicts the model we will use to discuss these topics. The first section of the chapter focuses on job satisfaction—defining it, describing how it develops, and showing how to measure it. The second section focuses on job withdrawal, showing its different manifestations. We also discuss the relationships among various withdrawal reactions and the ways they relate to satisfaction. The third section focuses on factors in the workplace that cause dissatisfaction and job withdrawal and shows what human resource managers can do to improve attitudes and minimize employee withdrawal.

JOB SATISFACTION

Although there are many different work attitudes, job satisfaction is a central construct that has dominated the attention of both practitioners and social scientists. One can draw distinctions between other work attitudes (e.g., job involvement or organizational commitment) and job satisfaction, but research indicates there are strong associations between most work attitudes. Therefore, our treatment of work attitudes will focus specifically on overall job satisfaction and satisfaction with specific facets of the job.

Defining Job Satisfaction

The topic of job satisfaction has received a great deal of attention from social scientists. As far back as 1976, Edwin Locke estimated that there were over 3,000 articles or studies dealing with this topic.[2] More recent reviews show that this interest is still going strong.[3]

Following Locke, we define **job satisfaction** as a pleasurable feeling that "results from the perception that one's job fulfills or allows for the fulfillment of one's important job values." This definition reflects three important aspects of job satisfaction. First, job satisfaction is a function of values, defined as "what a person consciously or unconsciously desires to obtain." Second, different employees have different views of which values are *important*, and this is critical in determining the nature and degree of their job satisfaction. One person may value high pay above all else; another may value the opportunity to travel; another may value staying within a specific geographic region. The third important aspect of job satisfaction is *perception*. It is one's perception of one's present situation relative to one's values that matters. An individual's perceptions may not be a completely accurate reflection of reality, and different people may view the same situation differently.

In particular, people's perceptions are often strongly influenced by their frames of reference. A *frame of reference* is a standard point that serves as a comparison for other points and thus provides meaning. For example, an upper-level executive who offers a 6 percent salary increase to a lower-level manager might expect this to make the manager happy because inflation (the executive's frame of reference) is only 3 percent. The manager, on the other hand, might find the raise quite unsatisfactory because it is less than the 9 percent raise received by the manager's colleague, who does similar work (the manager's frame of reference). A person's frame of reference often reflects his or her average past experience.[4] It may also reflect his or her perceptions or other peoples' experience (i.e., his or her reference group).[5]

Thus, values, perceptions, and importance are the three components of job satisfaction. People will be satisfied with their jobs as long as they perceive that their jobs meet their important values. In some situations, we may be interested in an individual's overall level of job satisfaction, that is, how satisfied he or she is with the job as a whole. In other cases, we may be interested only in satisfaction related to a specific aspect of work, such as pay or supervision—in other words, "facets of satisfaction."

Measures of Job Satisfaction

Most attempts to measure job satisfaction rely on workers' self-reports. Some of these scales, such as the job descriptive index (JDI), emphasize various facets of work: pay, the work itself, supervision, coworkers. Table 8.1 presents several items from the JDI scale. Other scales emphasize overall satisfaction. Table 8.2 presents sample items from one of these measures. Finally, some scales avoid language altogether, relying on pictures. The faces scale shown in Figure 8.2 is an example.

There is a vast amount of data on the reliability and validity of these three scales.[6] There is also a wealth of data from companies that have used these scales in the past, which allows for comparisons across firms. Established scales are excellent places to begin if employers wish to assess the satisfaction levels of their employees. An employer would be foolish to "reinvent the wheel" by generating its own versions of measures of these broad constructs. For this reason, we will provide many items from widely used scales that measure the work attitudes that we discuss. These items,

TABLE 8.1   Sample Items from a Standardized Job Satisfaction Scale

Instructions: Think of your present work. What is it like most of the time? In the blank beside each word given below, write

<u>Y</u>   for "Yes" if it describes your work

<u>N</u>   for "No" if it does NOT describe your work

<u>?</u>   if you cannot decide

Work Itself	Pay	Promotion Opportunities
_____ Routine	_____ Less than I deserve	_____ Dead-end job
_____ Satisfying	_____ Highly paid	_____ Unfair policies
_____ Good	_____ Insecure	_____ Based on ability

Supervision	Coworkers
_____ Impolite	_____ Intelligent
_____ Praises good work	_____ Responsible
_____ Doesn't supervise enough	_____ Boring

SOURCE: W. K. Balzar, D. C. Smith, D. E. Kravitz, S. E. Lovell, K. B. Paul, B. A. Reilly and C. E. Reilly (1990). *User's Manual for the Job Descriptive Index (JDI) and the Job in General Scale (JIG)*. Bowling Green State University. Bowling Green, OH.

along with the citation, provide a starting point for companies that wish to incorporate such scales into their own company-specific surveys.

In some cases, organizations want to measure their employees' satisfaction with aspects of their work that are specific to that organization, (e.g., satisfaction with one particular health plan versus another). In these situations, the organization may need to create its own scales.

In any case, a systematic, ongoing program of survey research should be a prominent part of any human resource strategy for a number of reasons. First, it allows the company to monitor trends over time. Second, it provides a means of empirically assessing the impact of changes in policy (e.g., introduction of a new performance appraisal system) or personnel (e.g., introduction of a new CEO) on worker attitudes. Third, when these surveys incorporate standardized scales like the JDI, they often allow the company to compare itself with others in the same industry along these dimensions.

Yearly surveys also give employees a constructive outlet for voicing their concerns and frustrations. Employees' ability to handle dissatisfying work experiences is enhanced when they feel they have an opportunity to air their problems. Formalized opportunities to state complaints about one's work situation have been referred to as "voicing."[7] Research has shown that voicing provides employees an active, constructive outlet for their work frustrations.[8] For example, a study of nurses indicated that pro-

TABLE 8.2   Sample Items from a Standardized Scale that
Measures Overall Job Satisfaction

Instructions: Put a check beside the answer that you feel is most appropriate regarding your present job.

All in all, how satisfied are you with your job?

_____   Very satisfied

_____   Somewhat satisfied

_____   Not too satisfied

_____   Not at all satisfied

If a good friend of yours told you he or she was interested in working in a job like yours for your employer, would you recommend it to him or her?

_____   Strongly recommend this job

_____   Would have doubts about recommending this job

_____   Strongly advise against taking this job

Knowing what you know now, if you had to decide all over again to take the job you have now, what would you decide?

_____   Decide without hesitation to take the same job

_____   Would have some second thoughts about taking the same job

_____   Definitely decide not to take the same job

SOURCE: R. P. Quinn and G. L. Staines, *The 1977 Quality of Employment Survey* (Ann Arbor: Survey Research Center, Institute for Social Research, University of Michigan, 1979). Reprinted with permission.

viding such voicing mechanisms as an employee attitude survey and question and answer sessions between employees and management led to enhanced worker attitudes and less turnover.[9] Ongoing surveys, especially when combined with action plans to remedy areas of low satisfaction, convey the message that the company cares about the perceptions and feeling of its employees.

JOB WITHDRAWAL

Because most organizations are not in the "job satisfaction business," it is sometimes difficult to convince managers of the need to maintain high levels of job satisfaction. On top of this, research suggests that, for many jobs, there is not a strong and direct relationship between satisfaction and performance.[10] However, a number of highly disruptive behaviors and work outcomes are in fact related to satisfaction. Charles Hulin has argued that these behaviors can be categorized under the heading of a single construct that he refers to as **job withdrawal**.[11]

FIGURE 8.2 Example of a Simplified, Nonverbal Measure of Job Satisfaction

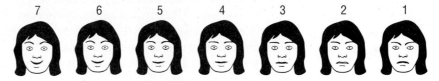

Job Satisfaction from the Faces Scale
Consider all aspects of your job. Circle the face that
best describes your feelings about your job in general.

SOURCE: The faces were adapted by permission of R. B. Dunham and J. B. Herman and published in the *Journal of Applied Psychology* 60 (1975): 629–631.

FIGURE 8.3 Adaptation of Hulin's 1991 Model of Job Withdrawal

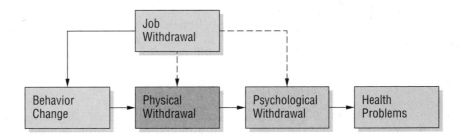

Solid line indicates progression.
Dotted line indicates selectivity.

Hulin defines *job withdrawal* as "a set of behaviors that dissatisfied individuals enact to avoid the work situation." Figure 8.3 shows an adaptation of Hulin's model in which the overall set of behaviors are grouped into four categories: behavior change, physical job withdrawal, psychological job withdrawal, and health problems; the last is a fourth category that can result if all the preceding behaviors fail to lead to a satisfactory resolution of the work problems.

We will present the various forms of withdrawal in a progression, as if individuals try the next category only if the preceding is either unsuccessful or impossible to implement. This theory of "progression of withdrawal" has a long history and many adherents.[12] Others have suggested that there is no tight progression, that any one of the categories can compensate for another and people choose the category that is most likely to redress the specific source of dissatisfaction.[13] Either way, the withdrawal behaviors are clearly related to one another, and they are all at least partially caused by job dissatisfaction.[14]

Behavior Change

One might expect that an employee's first response to dissatisfaction would be to try to change the conditions that generate the dissatisfaction. This can lead to supervisor-subordinate confrontation, perhaps even conflict, as dissatisfied workers try to bring about changes in policy or upper-level personnel. Where employees are unionized, it can lead to an increased number of grievances being filed.[15] Where employees are not unionized, dissatisfaction can lead to the formation of a union. Research indicates that there is a very strong relationship between dissatisfaction with economic aspects of work and unionization activity.[16]

Even in organizations without unions, employees can initiate change through *whistle-blowing*: taking grievances public by going to the media.[17] Employees can also sue their employers when the disputed policies relate to race, sex, safe working conditions, or any other aspect of employment regulated by state or federal laws. Such suits are costly, both financially and in terms of the firm's image, regardless of whether the firm wins or loses. Most employers would prefer to avoid litigation altogether, and keeping a majority of their employees happy is one means of achieving this.

Physical Job Withdrawal

If the job conditions cannot be changed, a dissatisfied worker may be able to solve his or her problem by leaving the job. This could take the form of an internal transfer if the dissatisfaction is job-specific (e.g., the result of an unfair supervisor or unpleasant working conditions). On the other hand, if the source of the dissatisfaction relates to organizationwide policies (e.g., lack of job security or below-market pay levels), organizational turnover is likely.

Voluntary turnover, which is strongly related to job satisfaction, is a costly and disruptive phenomenon for organizations. Hewlett-Packard, a high-technology firm, estimates that it spends $40,000 to replace one middle-level manager. Of course, replacement costs are not the only issue. Typically, only workers who have alternative employment opportunities consider leaving, and it is the best employees who often have the most opportunities. Thus, widespread dissatisfaction can cause dysfunctional turnover: the best employees moving on, the worst staying on and engaging in other forms of withdrawal behavior.[18] In the worst scenario, the better employees go to work for the company's competitors. Not only is all the time and money the organization invested in that employee lost, but the disgruntled employees may take sensitive information with them to their new jobs. As Martin Strasmore, consultant to Chase Manhattan Bank and Seimans notes, "All this downsizing is going to come back to haunt companies.... As soon as the economy turns around, many people are going to bolt from these companies."[19]

TABLE 8.3   Cost of Absenteeism to One Metropolitan School District

The number of personnel	1,400
Average absences per year	8.4
Total days lost	11,760
Cost of substitute personnel per day	$95.00

Total days lost × cost per day = 11,760 × 95.00 = $1,117,200

As we just noted, many employees who would prefer to quit their jobs have to stay on if they have no other employment opportunities. Another way of physically removing oneself from the dissatisfying work is to be absent.[20] Like turnover, absenteeism is disruptive and costly to an organization. Table 8.3 shows an example of the costs of absenteeism to one midsize metropolitan school district. Because the district has to pay for both the absent teacher (an average of $195 per day) and the substitute teacher (an average of $95 per day) on the day of the absence, the total cost to the school district can be enormous.[21] Cutting absenteeism rates in half could save literally millions of dollars.

Short of missing the whole day, a dissatisfied employee may be late for work. Although not as disruptive as absenteeism, tardiness can be costly, and tardiness is related to job satisfaction.[22] Tardiness can be especially costly when others depend on the tardy individual.

Psychological Withdrawal

When dissatisfied employees are unable to change their situation or remove themselves physically from their jobs, they may "psychologically disengage" themselves from their jobs. Although they are physically on the job, their minds may be somewhere else.

This psychological disengagement can take several forms. First, if the primary dissatisfaction has to do with the job itself, the employee may display a very low level of job involvement. **Job involvement** is the degree to which people identify themselves with their jobs. People who are uninvolved with their jobs consider their work an unimportant aspect of their lives. For them, performing well or poorly on the job does not really affect their self-concept, which makes them harder to motivate.[23] Over time, job dissatisfaction ultimately leads to low job involvement. Table 8.4 presents some items from a commonly used measure of job involvement.

A second form of psychological disengagement, which can occur when the dissatisfaction is with the employer as a whole, is a low level of organizational commitment. **Organizational commitment** is the degree to which an employee identifies with the organization and is willing to put forth effort on its behalf.[24] Individuals who have low organizational commitment

TABLE 8.4   Sample Items from a Standardized Job Involvement Scale

Instructions: Please consider each statement and circle the number that best represents the extent to which you agree or disagree with the statement.

The most important things that happen to me involve my work.

1	2	3	4	5
Strongly Disagree	Disagree	Uncertain	Agree	Strongly Agree

Sometimes I lie awake at night, thinking ahead to the next day's work.

1	2	3	4	5
Strongly Disagree	Disagree	Uncertain	Agree	Strongly Agree

You can measure a person pretty well by how good a job he or she does.

1	2	3	4	5
Strongly Disagree	Disagree	Uncertain	Agree	Strongly Agree

SOURCE: R. Kanungo, *Work Alienation,* Copyright 1982, Praeger Publishers, pp. 169–170. An imprint of Greenwood Publishing Group, Inc., Westport, CT. Reprinted with permission.

are often just waiting for the first good opportunity to quit their jobs. In other words, they have developed a strong intention to leave the organization. In the meantime, like individuals with low job involvement, they are often difficult to motivate. Like job involvement, organizational commitment is strongly related to job satisfaction. Table 8.5 presents some sample items from a widely used measure of organizational commitment. This measure also has items that assess the employee's intention to remain with the company, and these are presented as well.

Organizational commitment has been attracting a great deal of attention recently. Most employers feel that the staffing policies of the 1980s may have killed company loyalty in the 1990s. To cope with global competition, deregulation, hostile takeovers, and unprecedented levels of corporate debt, many companies were forced to slash their labor costs through massive layoffs. According to the Department of Commerce, 4.7 million workers who had held their jobs for more than three years have been dismissed since 1983. Between 1980 and 1989, General Motors eliminated over 150,000 workers. In 1992 alone, 375,000 workers were laid off. Figure 8.4 shows the number of people who lost work that year, by industry.[25] As Rudy Oswald, chief economist for the AFL-CIO, noted, "Workers have a right to be upset and angry. They have been bought and sold and have seen their friends and relations fired and laid off in large numbers. There is little bond between employers and workers anymore."[26]

Surveys of American workers support Oswald's claim. When asked, "Compared with ten years ago, are employees today more loyal or less loyal

TABLE 8.5   Sample Items from a Standardized Organizational Commitment Scale

Instructions: Please indicate the degree to which you agree or disagree with each of the statements using the following scale:

1	2	3	4	5
Strongly Disagree	Disagree	Uncertain	Agree	Strongly Agree

Identification:

I find that my values and the organization's values are very similar.

I really care about the fate of this organization.

I am proud to tell others that I work for this organization.

Effort:

This organization really inspires the best of me in the way of job performance.

I am willing to put forth a great deal of effort beyond that normally expected in order to help this organization be successful.

I feel very little loyalty to this organization (reverse coded).

Intention to Quit:

Deciding to work for this organization was a definite mistake on my part.

It would take very little change in my present circumstances to cause me to leave this organization.

There's not too much to be gained by sticking with this organization indefinitely.

SOURCE: R. T. Mowday, R. M. Steers, and L. W. Porter, "The Measurement of Organizational Commitment," *Journal of Vocational Behavior* 14 (1979): 224–227. Reprinted with permission of authors.

to their companies?" 63 percent said "less," only 22 percent said "more." Half of those responding said it was "likely" they would "change employers in the next five years." Thus, just as American businesses are trying to inculcate a new sense of worker participation and involvement, many of their employees are showing reduced levels of commitment and dependency. Moreover, as the "Competing through Globalization" box indicates, this low level of organizational commitment and job involvement among U.S. workers stands in stark contrast to some foreign competitors.

Health Problems

From a competitive advantage perspective, it is obvious that the presence of a large number of poorly involved, uncommitted workers who intend to quit at their first opportunity severely detracts from an organization's ability to survive. On the other hand, for the individuals involved, these attitudes may be quite adaptive. For example, we will define *stress* as an unpleasant emotional state resulting from a perceived threat to something one values. If a person is truly in a dissatisfying situation and can neither change it nor

FIGURE 8.4   Number of Individuals Laid Off between June 1, 1991, and
June 1, 1992, by Industry

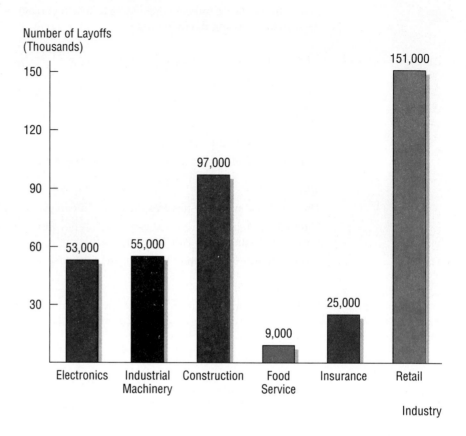

leave, psychological disengagement at least provides some degree of escape
from the stress. Without it, stress can translate into health problems.

Research has shown a strong link between work-related stress and mental disorders.[27] Indeed, stress-related mental disorders are the fastest-rising
category of occupational disease, and the number of lawsuits involving
organizations and stress-damaged employees is increasing at a rapid rate.
For example, after suffering a nervous breakdown, Richard Wilson won a
$3.5 million suit against his employer, Alco Standard Corporation.
Testimony in this case revealed that in an effort to get Wilson to quit, the
organization transferred him from a middle-level management position to a
janitorial position mopping up the employee cafeteria. Wilson, who had no
previous history of psychological disturbance "went bonkers," and the
court attributed his problems to his employer's actions.[28] This is not an isolated incident; in another case, an overworked advertising executive who
had a nervous breakdown successfully sued his employer.[29]

Stress has also been linked to physical disorders such as coronary heart
disease (CHD), one of the major causes of death in this country. As employ-

Globalization

THE LINK BETWEEN EMPLOYEE COMMITMENT AND COMPANY SUCCESS

The key to maintaining high levels of organizational commitment and job involvement among employees is giving them a sense of "joint fate" with the organization—that is, creating a perception the success or failure of the company as a whole is directly related to the employees' own outcomes in life. Once created, this perception drives employees to further their organization's interests in both large and small ways because they realize that this will pay off for them individually in the long run. In trying to compete internationally, U.S. companies must recognize that relative to some of their major foreign competitors, they trail badly on this one key indicator.

For example, 77 percent of Japanese workers surveyed strongly agreed with the statement "Your company's prosperity relates directly to improving your own quality of life." Only 28 percent of a matched sample of U.S. workers strongly agreed with the same state-

ment. Japanese companies actively try to cultivate a strong allegiance to the organization and hope that by doing so, they can reap the benefits of a dedicated set of experienced workers who intend to spend their entire life with their current employer.

This practice appears to translate into product quality differences between nations. Whereas 51 percent of American workers report being dissatisfied with the percentage of defective products produced on their jobs, the corresponding percentage of dissatisfied Japanese workers is only 31 percent. Clearly, to compete globally against the Japanese, U.S. companies intent on improving quality may first need to focus on the commitment and involvement of their employees. The only good news to report on this front is that some countries are even worse. In Italy, a scant 18 percent of manufacturing employees see any link between their organizations' prosperity and their own quality of life.

SOURCE: S. K. Paulson, W. H. Tomlinson, and J. Arai, "Global Differences in Quality Perceptions and Company Identity," *Human Resource Focus,* November 1992, 7.

ers are increasingly held liable for CHD, hypertension, and ulcers, the financial costs of stress are rising. Even when no lawsuits are filed, the costs can be high, since most employers pay for their employees' health insurance.

Job withdrawal takes on a variety of forms, and few of them are beneficial to the organization. Because organizations wish to avoid most forms of employee withdrawal, and because job satisfaction has such a strong effect on withdrawal, we will now focus on the causes of job dissatisfaction and some potential remedies.

SOURCES OF JOB DISSATISFACTION

Many aspects of organizational life can cause dissatisfaction among employees. Figure 8.5 presents the conceptual scheme we use to discuss these factors.[30] As this figure shows, organizational behavior can be thought of as the interaction of three separate systems: the *physical and technological*

FIGURE 8.5   Six Potential Sources of Job Dissatisfaction

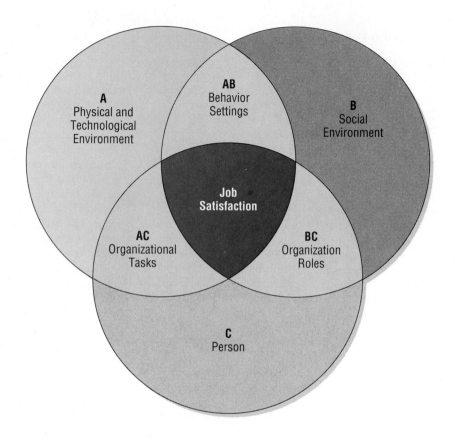

SOURCES: Adapted from J. E. McGrath, "Stress and Behavior in Organizations," in *Handbook of Industrial and Organizational Psychology*, ed. M. D. Dunnette (Chicago: Rand McNally, 1976), 1320–1365.

environment (A), in which behavior takes place; the *social environment* (B), in which interpersonal relationships among organizational members occur; and the *person* (C) whose job satisfaction is being looked at.

In addition to these three systems, dissatisfaction and stress can originate out of the overlapping areas shown in the figure. One of these, *behavioral settings* (AB), is at the intersection of the physical and technological environment and the social environment. The behavioral setting can be thought of as the physical surroundings as it relates to other people, including such factors as crowding or privacy. *Organizational tasks* (AC) is the intersection of the physical environment and the person. It is simply what the person's job is—that is, the formal function that he or she plays in carrying out the organization's mission. Tasks differ slightly from *roles* (BC), which occur at the intersection of the person and the social environment. Roles are the behavioral expectations that other people in the organization have for the person, including all the aspects of the task formally defined by the organization, but also many other things. These expectations develop over time through a negotiated process between the person and various other organizational members who have a stake in how the person performs the job.[31]

We now examine the various factors associated with each of the six sources of job dissatisfaction.

Physical and Technological Environment

Most workers react negatively to extreme physical environments. Extremes in temperatures can affect both job attitudes and job performance, and there are different optimal lighting requirements for different tasks. For example, perceived darkness correlates significantly with job dissatisfaction. Physical features of the environment, such as cleanliness, working outdoors, and health hazards, also affect job attitudes. Mail carriers with the U.S. Postal Service, for example, are certainly affected by their physical environment. This is reflected in the familiar motto that invokes "sleet, hail, and gloom of night." In addition to more psychological factors, such as complexity (discussed more fully below), physical features can often affect work attitudes.[32] The generally agreed upon unattractiveness of some jobs can be seen operationally in the fact that employers must often pay "compensating differentials" (i.e., extra pay) to workers whose tasks have unpleasant physical features. The notion of compensating differential will be discussed more fully in Chapter 16.

Technology and automation are typically employed to eliminate these aspects of the work, but these remedies are sometimes resisted by workers who fear they will be put out of work. For example, at the U.S. Postal Service, the powerful American Postal Workers Union has blocked many technological developments in order to minimize the loss of jobs. Many feel that lack of technological innovation is why the U.S. Postal Service cannot compete with private companies like United Parcel Service.[33]

Recent research on the physical features of the work environment has focused on less visible problems such as indoor air pollution. In fact, researchers have coined the term "sick building syndrome" (SBS) to refer to well-insulated physical structures with indoor air that contains excessive amounts of invisible pollutants. In today's office environment, fumes from copier machine liquids, carbonless paper, paint, rugs, synthetic draperies, wall paneling, and cleaning solvents—most of which contain traces of formaldehyde—are endlessly recycled. Also, in an effort to conserve energy, many firms turn off their air conditioning and heating systems on weekends, which allows mold and bacteria to grow and then spew forth into the work area on Monday morning.

In some cases, workers have taken matters into their own hands. In June 1988, 70 workers picketed the headquarters of the Environmental Protection Agency in Washington, D.C., charging that the contaminated air inside the building caused burning eyes, fatigue, dizziness, and breathing difficulty.

In California, a worker who claimed that formaldehyde fumes in a new office building caused him to lose consciousness and suffer permanent brain damage won $600,000 in a lawsuit.[34]

Social Environment

The two primary sets of people in an organization who affect job satisfaction are coworkers and supervisors. A person may be satisfied with his or her supervisor and coworkers for one of three reasons. First, the person may have many of the same values, attitudes, and philosophies that the coworkers and supervisors have. Most individuals find this very important. Indeed, many organizations try to foster a culture of shared values among employees. Even if one cannot generate a unifying culture throughout an entire organization, it is worth noting that increases in job satisfaction can be derived simply from congruence among supervisors and subordinates at one level.[35]

For example, after years of having a rather hierarchical and elitist structure, General Motors has recently tried to instill a more democratic corporate culture. Many of its moves are purely symbolic, such as shutting down the executive dining room on the 14th floor of GM headquarters. According to Executive Vice-President William Hogland, it used to be that "the big shooters went to the 14th floor, and the little people went someplace else." Other symbolic actions included dispensing with neckties on Fridays—a symbol that identified and separated former levels of employees. Although these kinds of changes hardly substitute for real business changes, they do have some value in reducing the "us versus them" divisions that can subvert cooperation and coordination across levels.[36]

Second, the person may be satisfied with his or her supervisor and coworkers because they provide social support. **Social support** means the degree to which the person is surrounded by other people who are sympathetic and caring. Considerable research indicates that social support is a strong predictor of job satisfaction, whether the support comes from supervisors or coworkers.[37]

Third, one's supervisor or coworkers may help the person attain some valued outcome. For example, a new employee may be uncertain about what goals to pursue or what paths to take to achieve those goals. This person will likely be satisfied with a supervisor or with coworkers who can help clarify those goals and paths.[38]

Because a supportive environment reduces dissatisfaction, many organizations foster team building both on and off the job (e.g., softball or bowling leagues). The idea is that group cohesiveness and support for individual group members will be increased through exposure and joint efforts. Although management certainly cannot ensure that each stressed employee develops friends, it can make it easier for employees to interact, a necessary condition for developing friendship and rapport.

For example, American Airlines teamed up with the Nature Conservancy environmental group to sponsor a "Teamwork for Nature" day in several U.S. cities. Employee teams reported for cleanup duty and helped by gathering litter, pulling weeds, and constructing fences. Some teams even worked on more elaborate projects such as installing irrigation systems or controlling erosion problems. Flight attendant Jacquiline Grant noted that "the nice thing about it is every employee group, regardless of their job description, can participate in their own way.... I think it has brought a lot of departments closer together."[39]

Behavior Settings

At the intersection of the physical and social environments, behavioral settings have two important and interrelated aspects: (1) *social density*, the number of people in an area divided by the number of square feet in the area, and (2) *privacy*, the freedom from external observation and interruption. Research with clerical workers shows that job satisfaction decreases as social density increases.[40] Social density is particularly problematic when it occurs in the absence of partitions or enclosures so that one is both crowded and lacks privacy. For example, one study found that neither crowding nor lack of partitions predicted satisfaction in office staff at a university. When crowding and lack of privacy occurred together though, dissatisfaction and turnover were exceptionally high.[41] However, as the "Competing through Technology and Structure" box indicates, with today's technology, even employees working in areas of low density (e.g., alone in their own office) can have their privacy invaded.

These findings have significant implications for organizations that have open office plans. An open office plan is a design scheme characterized by the absence of interior walls and partitions. In open office plans, all office personnel, from clerks to managers, are located in one large, open space. Advocates of the plan believe that open designs lead to increased work efficiency and communication and lower operating costs. Research suggests this is not the case, however, primarily because of problems with crowding and privacy. Research in companies that have moved away from open offices to more conventional offices shows that either decreasing social density or restoring partitions increases work satisfaction.[42] Other research shows that the egalitarian nature of open offices leads some categories of employees (managerial and professional) to resent the perceived loss of status conferred by personal offices.[43]

Person

Because both stress and dissatisfaction ultimately reside within the person, it is not surprising that many who have studied these outcomes have focused on individual differences. *Negative affectivity* is a term used to describe a dispositional dimension that reflects pervasive individual differences in satisfaction with any and all aspects of life. Individuals who are high in negative affectivity report higher levels of aversive mood states,

Technology & Structure

ETHICAL ISSUES WITH E-MAIL

In an effort to reduce waste, create more efficient communication among employees, and generally enhance their competitiveness, organizations are turning increasingly toward electronic means of communication. Since its inception in the early 1970s electronic mail (E-mail) has expanded to 10 million users today, and it is estimated that by the year 2000, 60 million users will be sending as many as 60 billion messages per year.

Given the speed with which this transition is taking place, it is not surprising to see organizations and employees struggling over issues of privacy and ownership. The Electronic Communications Privacy Act of 1986 does protect organizations and individuals from outside intrusions into their systems (much the same way that telephones are protected from wiretapping). However, no federal legislation protects individuals from internal snooping at the hands of suspicious supervisors or curious coworkers.

Clearly, prying through another person's E-mail is no more appropriate than reading their regular mail or rummaging around their desk. These kinds of privacy invasions under-

mine employee loyalty and trust. They also breed ill-will and suspicion. It could even drive employees away from using a more technologically efficient means of doing business, destroying any hope of gaining competitive advantage through this innovation.

Socially responsible organizations should not wait for legislation or litigation to prompt action on this issue but instead should act ethically and proactively to ward off potential future problems in this area. For example, firms should develop and communicate standardized policies regarding E-mail access and control. In terms of access, these documents should spell out (1) who has direct access to whose E-mail and (2) who must obtain the employee's consent prior to gaining access. These guidelines will differ for different industries, but in all cases they need to be justifiable in terms of "business necessity."

Employees may not always agree with the policies, but at least they are informed and can therefore base their actions on this knowledge rather than acting on a false presumption of privacy. These guidelines might even be communicated electronically on a regular basis to serve as a reminder.

SOURCE: R. Ulrich, "Respecting E-Mail Privacy," *Newsweek,* November 16, 1992, 10–11.

including anger, contempt, disgust, guilt, fear, and nervousness across all contexts (i.e., work *and* nonwork).[44]

People who are high in negative affectivity tend to focus extensively on the negative aspects of themselves and others. They are also more likely, in a given situation, to experience significantly higher levels of distress than others—which implies that some people bring dissatisfaction with them to work. These people may be relatively dissatisfied regardless of what steps the organization or the manager takes. Research has shown that negative affectivity in early adolescence is predictive of overall job dissatisfaction in adulthood. There were also significant relationships between work attitudes measured over a five-year period even for workers who changed employers and/or occupations.[45]

Although the causes of negative affectivity are not completely known, research that examined identical twins who were raised apart suggests that there may be a genetic component.[46] Thirty-four pairs of twins were measured for their general job satisfaction and their satisfaction with intrinsic and extrinsic aspects of the job. The researchers found a significant relationship between the ratings for each member of a pair, despite the fact that the twins were raised apart and worked at different jobs.

This suggests the importance of personnel selection as a way of raising overall levels of employee satisfaction. Although there is insufficient evidence on the predictive validity of negative affectivity scales used for this purpose, such evidence may be worth collecting. Moreover, interviews should assess the degree to which any job applicant has a history of chronic dissatisfaction with his or her employment. If applicants state that they were dissatisfied with their last six jobs, what makes the employer think they won't be dissatisfied with this one?

As we mentioned in our opening vignette about the shootings at the Royal Oak post office, Thomas McIlvane had a history of antisocial behavior, both in the military (from which he was dishonorably discharged) and in his local community (where he had a prominent police record). Apparently, the postal service had no formal system for doing background checks on job applicants. The day after the Royal Oak killings, however, Postmaster General Anthony Frank put such checks into place for all 750,000 U.S. postal workers.

Although the focus of this chapter is job dissatisfaction, one must recognize that dissatisfaction with other facets of life can spill over into the workplace. That is, a worker who is having problems with a spouse or family may attribute some of this negative affect to the job or organization.

Organizational Tasks

As a predictor of job dissatisfaction and stress, nothing surpasses the nature of the task itself.[47] Many aspects of a task have been linked to dissatisfaction, and several elaborate theories relating task characteristics to worker reactions have been formulated and extensively tested.[48] We discuss the three primary aspects of tasks that affect job satisfaction: the complexity of the task, the degree of physical strain and exertion on the job, and the value the employee puts on the task.

With a few exceptions, there is a strong positive relationship between task complexity and job satisfaction. That is, the boredom generated by simple, repetitive jobs that do not mentally challenge the worker leads to frustration and dissatisfaction.[49] This boredom can hinder performance on certain types of jobs. Airport security personnel, air traffic controllers, operators in nuclear power stations, medical technicians, and inspectors on production floors are all jobs that require vigilance. People with these jobs must continually monitor equipment and be prepared to respond to critical, but rarely occurring, events. The fact that the critical events occur so rarely often makes these jobs exceedingly boring, and this boredom can result in a lack of concentration. Lack of attention can lead to performance breakdowns with the worst consequences.

Interestingly, some research indicates that what are typically referred to as "disabilities" can often enhance performance on tasks requiring vigilance. Blind subjects do better than sighted people on auditory vigilance tasks, and deaf people do better than nondeaf people on visual vigilance tasks. It might be to an organization's benefit to hire the disabled for certain jobs that entail vigilance.[50]

The second primary aspect of a task that affects job satisfaction is the degree to which the job involves physical strain and exertion.[51] This aspect is sometimes overlooked at a time when automation has removed much of the physical strain associated with jobs. Indeed, the fact that technology has aimed to lessen work-related physical exertion indicates that it is almost universally considered undesirable. Nevertheless many jobs can still be characterized as physically demanding.

The third primary aspect is whether the object of the work promotes something that is valued by the worker. Over 1 million volunteer workers in the United States perform their jobs almost exclusively because of the meaning they attach to the work. Some of these jobs are even low in complexity and high in physical exertion. These volunteers view themselves as performing a worthwhile service, however, and this overrides the other two factors and contributes to high levels of satisfaction with the job. Similarly, several low-paying occupations (e.g., social services, religious orders) explicitly try to make up for pay deficiencies by appealing to the prospective employee's nonfinancial values. The Peace Corps, for example, attempts to recruit applicants by describing its work as "the toughest job you will ever love." Similar recruiting advertisements for Catholic priests mention that "the pay is low but the rewards are infinite."

One of the major interventions aimed at reducing job dissatisfaction is job enrichment, which explicitly focuses on the task as a source of dissatisfaction. **Job enrichment** is a term that refers to specific ways to add complexity and meaningfulness to a person's work. As the term suggests, this intervention is directed at jobs that are "impoverished" or boring because of their repetitive nature or low scope.

One approach to redesigning tasks, Hackman and Oldham's job characteristics theory, was previously discussed in Chapter 6. According to this theory, five core task characteristics affect work attitudes.

The first three, according to this theory, are (1) *skill variety*, that is, the number of different skills or activities needed to complete the task; (2) *task identity*, that is, the degree to which the person does a whole, identifiable piece of work (e.g., assembles a complete toaster as opposed to just attaching the left rear panel bolt); and, (3) *task significance*, that is, the degree to which the task has a meaningful impact on the lives of other people. According to the job characteristics theory, jobs that are high on variety, identity, and significance give the worker a sense that the work is meaningful.

For example, at Xerox, work was once structured along four large functional units including manufacturing, research, marketing, and finance.

Segmenting the work this way reduces the meaningfulness of many of the jobs. It also isolates workers from each other and distances them from customers. Thus, in 1992 CEO Paul Allaire restructured the organization into separate product divisions that each did its own manufacturing, research, marketing, and finance. Dan Cholish, a veteran Xerox engineer, was once a "one-dimensional" engineer, but now under the new system he has learned a little about manufacturing, finance, and marketing as he concentrates on customer needs. According to Cholish, "I've probably visited more customers in the last six months than I had in my last six years on my old assignment."[52]

Autonomy, that is, the degree to which the worker has the freedom and discretion necessary to plan how the work should be performed, is another critical feature of work, according to the job characteristics theory. Autonomy leads to a sense that the worker is responsible for the outcomes that result from the job. For example, at Motorola "total customer satisfaction" teams are given authority to make changes in production or any other work procedures, then given bonuses tied to improved defect rates or cycle times. One team used basic industrial engineering techniques to analyze inventory and ultimately reduced average levels of supply from seven weeks to four weeks—saving the company $2.4 million. These kinds of results often breed functional internal competition, since as one team member noted, "other workers were all jealous of our team." Internal competition can drive other teams to raise their standards of excellence, and greatly contribute to the organization's overall competitive advantage.[53]

Finally, the last critical aspect of work, according to the job characteristics theory, is *feedback,* that is, the degree to which the person gets direct and clear information on how well he or she is performing. Feedback is important because it helps the worker obtain knowledge of the results, which enhance both learning and motivation.[54] Feedback can often be enhanced by removing layers of "monitoring" management, instead making workers responsible for monitoring their own performance. For example, one of the more substantive changes in GM operating procedures associated with its cultural change discussed earlier was the elimination of 11,000 staffers at headquarters. According to one GM executive, these people were "the checkers who check the checkers," and their presence often undermined the quality-control initiative of those actually producing the product.[55]

All else being constant, jobs that are high on these five core characteristics lead to feelings of high job satisfaction and low job withdrawal, according to the job characteristics theory. Thus, building these factors into the work is one way of enhancing job satisfaction. This theory also holds that the link between job characteristics and outcomes is especially strong for individuals who are high in growth need strength, that is, the degree to which the person performing the job desires personal growth. Although it is not always successful in bringing about improved worker attitudes, job enrichment has often been successfully implemented.[56]

Another task-based intervention is **job rotation**. This is a process of systematically moving a single individual from one job to another over the course of time. Although employees may not feel capable of putting up with the dissatisfying aspects of a particular job indefinitely, they often feel they can do so temporarily. Job rotation can do more than simply spread out the dissatisfying aspects of a particular job. It can increase work complexity for employees and provide valuable cross-training in jobs so that employees eventually understand many different jobs. This makes for a more flexible work force and increases the workers' appreciation of the other tasks that have to be accomplished for the organization to complete its mission.[57]

Organizational Roles

Job dissatisfaction can occur at the intersection of the social environment and the person (BC), where organizational roles emerge. The person's role in the organization can be defined as the set of expected behaviors that both the person and other people who make up the social environment have for the person in that job. As we noted earlier, these expected behaviors include all the formal aspects of the job, and usually much more as well. That is, coworkers, supervisors, and clients or customers have expectations for the person that go beyond what is formally described as the person's job. Expectations have a large impact on how the person responds to the work.[58]

Three aspects of organizational roles stand out as significant influences on job satisfaction: role ambiguity, role conflict, and role overload.

Role ambiguity refers to the level of uncertainty about what the organization expects from the employee in terms of what to do or how to do it. Role ambiguity can also stem from a lack of information about the rewards and punishments associated with failing to do the right things or doing the right things in the wrong way.

A second source of dissatisfaction is *role conflict*: recognition of incompatible or contradictory demands by the person who occupies the role. Role conflict occurs in many different forms. For example, two or more people in the social environment may hold mutually exclusive expectations for the employee, or one person may hold two competing expectations, or the employee may be occupying more than one role at a time (and the roles have incompatible expectations). An employee who has a business trip scheduled during his or her child's first piano recital will feel torn between two roles that must be occupied simultaneously.

Dissatisfaction can also arise from *role overload,* a state in which too many expectations or demands are placed on the person (whereas *role underload* refers to the opposite problem). There can be both too much and too little task scope. Research on job stress has focused primarily on high-scope jobs (i.e., jobs that require the person to manage too many things). As the "Competing through Social Responsibility" box indicates, role overload seems to be an increasingly prevalent problem in today's organizations because of their emphasis on downsizing and cost-cutting. Table 8.6 shows some sample items from a scale that attempts to measure role-related problems.[59]

Because role problems rank just behind job problems in creating job dissatisfaction, interventions that aim directly at role elements have been cre-

TABLE 8.6   Sample Items from a Scale that Measures Role-Related Problems

Instructions: Rate the degree to which each of the following statements is true or false for your present job using the following scale:

1	2	3
False	Uncertain	True

Role Conflict:

Have to work under conflicting guidelines.

Have conflicting demands from people at work.

Have to do things you know should be done differently.

Role Ambiguity:

Doing work where you cannot always be certain of what is expected from you.

Doing work where you are not sure of how to divide your time properly.

Doing work where you don't know what has to be done to perform well.

Role Overload:

Working under continuous time pressure.

Working hard to meet deadlines.

Having too many things to do at one time.

SOURCE: T. J. Newton and A. Keenan, "Role Stress Reexamined: An Investigation of Role Stress Predictors," *Organizational Behavior and Human Decision Processes* 40 (1987): 346–368. Reprinted with permission from Academic Press.

ated. One such intervention, the "role analysis technique," shown in Figure 8.6, is designed to increase the communication and understanding of the various sets of role expectations that exist for a specific employee.[60]

In the **role analysis technique**, the role occupant and each member of the role occupant's role set (e.g., supervisors, coworkers, subordinates) are asked to write down what their expectations are for the role occupant. Then everybody is gathered together, and each person goes through his or her list. All the expectations are written out so that ambiguities can be removed and conflicts identified. Where there are conflicts, the group as a whole tries to decide how they should be resolved. When this is done throughout an organization, instances of overload and underload may be discovered, and role requirements may be traded off so that more balanced roles are developed. Relative to job enrichment, there has not been a great deal of research on role analysis technique. What little research is available suggests that this may be a useful means for reducing role pressures.

FIGURE 8.6   A Schematic Representation of Role Analysis Technique

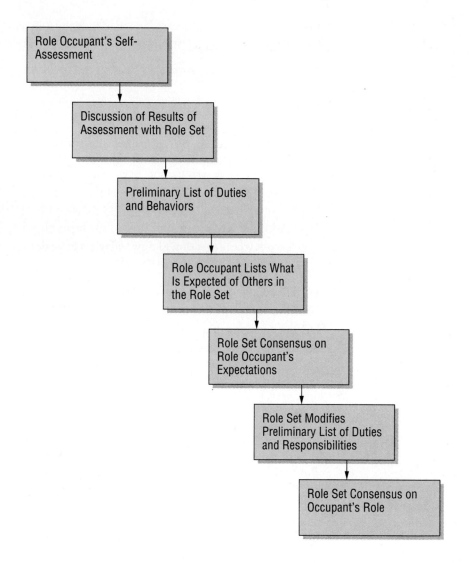

SUMMARY

In this chapter, we have defined and discussed job satisfaction, showing that it is a function of individuals' values and perceptions. We have also presented various ways to measure job satisfaction, and we argued that a system of annual attitude surveys should be a prominent part of any organizational human resource strategy. We defined and discussed job withdrawal and showed that job satisfaction is a major cause of many different forms of job withdrawal, including behavior change, physical withdrawal (e.g., turnover and absenteeism), psychological withdrawal (e.g., low job

Social Responsibility

COPING WITH THE RESULTS OF CORPORATE DOWNSIZING

Given the widespread layoffs associated with organizational downsizings, leveraged buyouts, and recession-induced cost-cutting, you might think that those who survived these purges were the lucky ones. Think again. Increasingly, managers at restructured organizations find that although the number of people working has decreased, the overall work load confronting the organization has remained unchanged.

For example, at U.S. Bank of Washington, Robert Kakiuchi used to work in a department staffed by 70 people. Now, after a merger and restructuring, that same department tries to provide almost the identical set of services with a staff of six. This salaried staff regularly works 14-hour shifts, six days a week to keep up with load. Not surprisingly, counselors at the bank's employee assistance program have noted an increase in stress-induced problems among employees, and their symptoms are not psychosomatic. The chemicals that the body generates when under stress (adrenaline and epinephrine) can be toxic under prolonged conditions. Eventually, they can affect the entire cardiovas-

cular system and bring on coronary heart disease. Indeed, the Japanese, who seem to be the role models for this trend, have a term for this: *karoshi*—death by overwork.

Part of an employer's social responsibility is to protect rather than exploit its workers, and many companies have worked hard to reduce work loads when they reduce staff. Tenneco CEO Michael Walsh notes that the key to their successful restructuring in 1991 was the elimination of "unproductive stress that arises out of bureaucracy and politics." Moreover, companies that unethically push their employees too far may find that this culture affects relationships with consumers as well. For example, some have speculated that the scandal at Sears auto-repair shops (where customers were charged for unnecessary or undelivered services) was attributable to unrealistic work demands and sales targets set by upper management. Even disregarding the $10 million fines, it is clear that this incident irreparably damaged the competitive advantage of this division of Sears.

SOURCE: A. B. Fisher, "Welcome to the World of Overwork," *Fortune*, November 30, 1992, 65–71.

involvement and low organizational commitment), and stress-related illnesses. Because most forms of job withdrawal lead to negative outcomes for the organization that detract from its competitive advantage, we closed this chapter by examining six different sources of job dissatisfaction and suggested some possible remedies.

Discussion Questions

1. Discuss the advantages of using published, standardized measures in employee attitude surveys. Are there any conditions when employers need to develop their own measures for such surveys? Where would one turn to learn about how to do this?

2. Describe the three constructs of job satisfaction, job involvement, and organizational commitment. When could an individual be high on one of these dimensions but low on two others? High on two of these dimensions but low on the third?

3. Organizational turnover is generally considered a negative outcome, and many organizations spend a great deal of time and money trying to reduce it. Can you think of some situations where an increase in turnover might be just what an organization needs? Given the difficulty of terminating employees, can you think of any organizational policies that might promote the retention of high-performing workers but promote voluntary turnover among low performers?

4. Three popular interventions for enhancing worker satisfaction are job enrichment, job rotation, and role analysis. What are the critical differences between these interventions, and under what conditions might one be preferable to the others?

5. If off-the-job stress and dissatisfaction begin to spill over and create on-the-job problems, what are the rights and responsibilities of the human resource manager in helping the employee to overcome these problems? Are intrusions into such areas an invasion of privacy, a benevolent and altruistic employer practice, or simply a prudent financial step taken to protect the firm's investment?

Notes

1. H. J. Reitz, *Behavior in Organizations* (Homewood, Ill.: Irwin-Dorsey, 1981), 202.

2. E. A. Locke, "The Nature and Causes of Job Dissatisfaction," in *The Handbook of Industrial and Organizational Psychology,* ed. M. D. Dunnette (Chicago: Rand McNally, 1976), 901–969.

3. M. T. Iaffaldono and P. M. Muchinsky, "Job Satisfaction and Job Performance: A Meta-Analysis," *Psychological Bulletin* 97 (1985): 251–273.

4. J. W. Thibaut and H. H. Kelly, *The Social Psychology of Groups* (New York: Wiley, 1959).

5. J. S. Adams and W. B. Rosenbaum, "The Relationship between Worker Productivity to Cognitive Dissonance about Wage Inequities," *Journal of Applied Psychology* 46 (1962): 161–164.

6. J. L. Price and C. W. Mueller, *Handbook of Organizational Measurement* (Marshfield, Mass.: Pitman Publishing, 1986).

7. A. O. Hirshman, *Exit Voice and Loyalty* (Cambridge, Mass.: Harvard University Press, 1970).

8. D. Farrell, "Exit, Voice, Loyalty and Neglect as Responses to Job Dissatisfaction: A Multidimensional Scaling Study," *Academy of Management Journal* 26 (1983): 596–607.

9. D. G. Spencer, "Employee Voice and Employee Retention," *Academy of Management Journal* 29 (1986): 488–502.

10. Iaffaldano and Muchinsky, "Job Satisfaction and Job Performance."

11. C. Hulin, "Adaption, Persistence and Commitment in Organizations," in *Handbook of Industrial and Organizational Psychology,* ed. M. D. Dunnette and L. M. Hough (Palo Alto, Cal.: Consulting Psychologists Press, 1991), 443–505.

12. D. W. Baruch, "Why They Terminate," *Journal of Consulting Psychology* 8 (1944): 35–46; J. G. Rosse, "Relations among Lateness, Absence and Turnover: Is There a Progression of Withdrawal?" *Human Relations* 41 (1988): 517–531.

13. Hulin, "Adaptation, Persistence, and Commitment in Organizations."

14. C. Hulin, M. Roznowski, and D. Hachiya, "Alternative Opportunities and Withdrawal Decisions," *Psychological Bulletin* 97 (1985): 233–250.

15. C. E. Labig and I. B. Helburn, "Union and Management Policy Influences on Grievance Initiation," *Journal of Labor Research* 7 (1986): 269–284.

16. C. Schreisheim, "Job Satisfaction, Attitudes towards Unions, and Voting in a Union Representation Election," *Journal of Applied Psychology* 63 (1978): 548–552.

17. M. P. Miceli and J. P. Near, "Characteristics of Organizational Climate and Perceived Wrongdoing Associated with Whistle-Blowing Decisions," *Personnel Psychology* 38 (1985): 525–544.

18. J. M. Carsten and P. E. Spector, "Unemployment, Job Satisfaction, and Employee Turnover: A Meta-analytic Test of the Muchinsky Model," *Journal of Applied Psychology* 72 (1987): 374–381; W. R. Wilhelm, "Helping Workers to Self-Manage their Careers," *Personnel Administrator* 28 (1983): 83–99; B. A. Gerhart, "Voluntary Turnover and Alternative Job Opportunities," *Journal of Applied Psychology* 75 (1990): 467–476; J. R. Hollenbeck and C. R. Williams, "Turnover Functionality versus Turnover Frequency: A Note on Work Attitudes and Organizational Effectiveness," *Journal of Applied Psychology* 71 (1987): 606–611.

19. S. Sherman, "A Brave New Darwinian Workplace," *Fortune,* January 25, 1993, 52.

20. R. D. Hackett and R. M. Guion, "A Re-evaluation of the Job Satisfaction-Absenteeism Relation," *Organizational Behavior and Human Decision Processes* 35 (1985): 340–381.

21. M. Iorio, "School District Fighting Teacher Absenteeism," *Lansing State Journal,* July 12, 1992, 1.

22. J. G. Rosse and H. E. Miller, "Relationship between Absenteeism and Other Employee Behaviors," in *New Approaches to Understanding, Measuring, and Managing Employee Absence,* ed. P. S. Goodman and R. S. Atkin (San Francisco: Jossey-Bass, 1984).

23. R. Kanungo, *Work Alienation* (New York: Praeger Publishers, 1982).

24. R. T. Mowday, R. M. Steers, and L. W. Porter, "The Measurement of Organizational Commitment," *Journal of Vocational Behavior* 14 (1979): 224–247.

25. J. Greenwald, "The Great American Layoffs," *Time,* July 20, 1992, 64–65.

26. J. Castro, "Where Did All the Gung-ho Go?" *Time,* September 11, 1989, 52–55.

27. C. Cooper and R. Payne, *Stress at Work* (London: John Wiley, 1978).

28. E. Lesly, "Good-bye Mr. Dithers: Abusive Bosses Are on the Run Thanks to Employees' Suits," *Business Week,* September 21, 1992, 52.

29. R. Poe, "Does Your Job Make You Sick?" *Across the Board* 9 (1987): 34–43.

30. J. E. McGarth, "Stress and Behavior in Organizations," in *Handbook of Industrial and Organizational Psychology,* ed. M. D. Dunnette (Chicago: Rand McNally, 1976).

31. D. R. Ilgen and J. R. Hollenbeck, "The Structure of Work: Job Design and Roles," in *Handbook of Industrial and Organizational Psychology,* 2nd ed., ed. M. D. Dunnette and L. M. Hough (San Diego, Cal.: Contemporary Psychology Press, in press).

32. G. B. Meese, M. I. Lewis, D. P. Wyon, and R. Kok, "A Laboratory Study of the Effects of Thermal Stress on the Performance of Factory Workers," *Ergonomics* 27 (1982): 19–43; D. G. Hayward, "Psychological Factors in the Use of Light and Lighting in Buildings," in *Designing for Human Behavior: Architecture and the Behavioral Sciences,* ed. J. Lang, C. Burnette, W. Moleski and D. Vachon (Stroudsburg, Penn.: Dowden, Hutchinson and Ross, 1974); G. R. Oldham and N. L. Rotchford, "Relationships between Office Characteristics and Employee Reactions: A Study of the Physical Environment," *Administrative Science Quarterly* 28 (1983): 542–556; E. F. Stone and H. G. Gueutal, "An Empirical Derivation of the Dimensions along which Characteristics of Jobs are Perceived," *Academy of Management Journal* 28 (1985): 376–396; S. J. Zacarro and E. F. Stone, "Incremental Validity of an Empirically Based Measure of Job Characteristics," *Journal of Applied Psychology* 73 (1988): 245–252.

33. S. B. Garland and M. Lewyn, "Can Tony Frank get Postal Workers to Cut Him Some Slack?" *Business Week,* August 27, 1990, 31.

34. A. Toufexis, "Got that Stuffy, Run-Down Feeling," *Time,* June 6, 1988, 75.

35. B. M. Meglino, E. C. Ravlin, and C. L. Adkins, "A Work Values Approach to Corporate Culture: A Field Test of the Value Congruence Process and its Relationship to Individual Outcomes," *Journal of Applied Psychology* 74 (1989): 424–433.

36. J. B. White, "GM's Overhaul of Corporate Culture Brings Results but Still Faces Hurdles," *The Wall Street Journal,* January 13, 1993, A3.

37. G. C. Ganster, M. R. Fusilier, and B. T. Mayes, "Role of Social Support in the Experience of Stress at Work," *Journal of Applied Psychology* 71 (1986): 102–111.

38. R. T. Keller, "A Test of the Path-Goal Theory of Leadership with Need for Clarity as a Moderator in Research and Development Organizations," *Journal of Applied Psychology* 74 (1989): 208–212.

39. J. Lawrence, "American Airlines: A Profile in Employee Involvement," *Personnel Journal,* August 1992, 63.

40. R. I. Sutton and A. Rafaeli, "Characteristics of Work Stations as Potential Occupational Stressors," *Academy of Management Journal* 30 (1987): 260–276.

41. G. R. Oldham and Y. Fried, "Employee Reactions to Workspace Characteristics," *Journal of Applied Psychology* 72 (1987): 75–84.

42. G. R. Oldham, "Effects of Change in Workspace Partitions and Spatial Density on Employee Reactions: A Quasi-Experiment," *Journal of Applied Psychology* 73 (1988): 253–260.

43. M. D. Zalesny and R. V. Farace, "Traditional versus Open Offices: A Comparison of Sociotechnical, Social Relations, and Symbolic Meaning Perspectives," *Academy of Management Journal* 30 (1987): 240–259.

44. D. Watson, L. A. Clark, and A. Tellegen, "Development and Validation of Brief Measures of Positive and Negative Affect: The PANAS Scales," *Journal of Personality and Social Psychology* 54 (1988): 1063–1070.

45. B. M. Staw, N. E. Bell, and J. A. Clausen, "The Dispositional Approach to Job Attitudes: A Lifetime Longitudinal Test," *Administrative Science Quarterly* 31 (1986): 56–78; B. M. Staw and J. Ross, "Stability in the Midst of Change: A Dispositional Approach to Job Attitudes," *Journal of Applied Psychology* 70 (1985): 469–480.

46. R. D. Arvey, T. J. Bouchard, N. L. Segal, and L. M. Abraham, "Job Satisfaction: Genetic and Environmental Components," *Journal of Applied Psychology* 74 (1989): 187–193.

47. B. A. Gerhart, "How Important Are Dispositional Factors as Determinants of Job Satisfaction? Implications for Job Design and Other Personnel Programs," *Journal of Applied Psychology* 72 (1987): 493–502.

48. Ilgen and Hollenbeck, "The Structure of Work."

49. L. W. Porter and R. M. Steers, "Organizational, Work and Personal Factors in Employee Absenteeism and Turnover," *Psychological Bulletin* 80 (1973): 151–176.

50. J. S. Warm and W. N. Dember, "Awake at the Switch," *Psychology Today,* April, 1986, 46–50.

51. Locke, "The Nature and Causes of Job Dissatisfaction."

52. L. Jones, "Xerox Is Rewriting the Book on Organization 'Architecture'," *Chicago Tribune,* December 29, 1992, 3-1, 3-2.

53. G. C. Hill and K. Yamada, "Motorola Illustrates How an Aged Giant Can Remain Vibrant," *The Wall Street Journal,* December 9, 1992, A1.

54. J. R. Hackman and G. R. Oldham, "Motivation through the Design of Work," *Organizational Behavior and Human Performance* 16 (1976): 250–279.

55. White, "GM's Overhaul of Corporate Culture."

56. Y. Fried and G. R. Ferris, "The Validity of the Job Characteristics Model: Some Neglected Issues," *Personnel Psychology* 40 (1987): 287–322.

57. R. W. Griffen, *Task Design: An Integrative Approach* (Glenview, Ill.: Scott, Foresman, 1982).

58. S. E. Jackson and R. S. Schuler, "A Meta-Analysis and Conceptual Critique of Research on Role Ambiguity and Role Conflict in Work Settings," *Organizational Behavior and Human Decision Processes* 36 (1985): 16–78.

59. T. J. Newton and R. S. Keenan, "Role Stress Reexamined: An Investigation of Role Stress Predictors," *Organizational Behavior and Human Decision Processes* 40 (1987): 346–368.

60. I. Dayal and J. M. Thomas, "Operation KPE: Developing a New Organization," *Journal of Applied Behavioral Sciences* 4 (1968): 473–506.

C A S E

THE BROKEN LINK: DECENTRALIZED AUTHORITY AND EMPLOYEE SATISFACTION

In 1990, Kentucky Fried Chicken (KFC) initiated a quality-improvement drive for its 2,000 company-owned restaurants. At the heart of this program was a corporate restructuring that attempted to get regional managers "closer to the customer" by decentralizing authority. Instead of getting enhanced worker satisfaction and improved quality, however, KFC got a bureaucratic mess. The chain's autonomous regional divisions failed to coordinate their efforts, and according to Edward Meagher, vice-president of the PepsiCo unit, "There was so much redundancy that the process became dysfunctional." For example, at one time, three different plans were being developed to improve service nationwide. Similar problems of "decentralization gone haywire" have been experienced by IBM, McDonnell Douglas, and General Dynamics.

Although enhanced job satisfaction can spring from decentralizing authority, organizations cannot lose sight of the fact that, eventually, all the inputs from different people have to be integrated. The need for this integration means that some degree of command and control needs to be retained at corporate headquarters.

QUESTIONS

1. What can organizations like KFC do to balance the need for promoting job satisfaction through autonomy yet still maintain centralized control?

2. Are there some organizational functions (manufacturing, marketing, human resource management, finance) that are easier to "push down" the hierarchy than others?

3. What type of safeguards can be built into corporate restructurings so that problems with duplication can be identified quickly and efficiently?

SOURCE: G. Fuchsberg, "Decentralized Management Can Have Its Drawbacks," *The Wall Street Journal*, December 9, 1992, B1.

DETROIT DIESEL CORPORATION: AN EVOLUTION OF TASKS AND ATTITUDES

Sitting around a table in one of the vendor conference rooms at Detroit Diesel, Jim Bachman, a Series 60 line trainer, and Jim Brown, UAW Local 163's shop chairman, recall an incident that highlights the extent of change in their plant. This example of shop floor activity illustrates to these two men, as well as to the 2,100 other hourly employees in the diesel engine plant, what it took to generate new employee attitudes toward both production quality and their jobs.

Through the efforts of employees and their union, the liner line was brought in house, into the Detroit Diesel plant. (A liner is a foundry cast part that fits into the engine block.) The union and company negotiated an agreement that provided for job classifications to allow liner technicians to do their own inspection and job setting. The operations on the new line included hardening the part in the furnace, rough boring the center, cutting grooves on a turning machine, grinding to obtain the correct overall diameter, using a honing machine to obtain the correct inside diameter, into which the pistons will fit, and inspecting the final product.

Unexpectedly, the new liner jobs raised some quality issues because of the complex job assignments and the many different machining operations employees needed to learn. At first, a high level of scrap was generated, so to help improve the situation, full-time hourly trainers were put in the area to assist, teach, and maintain a focus on quality. Jim Bachman is one of these trainers.

Soon after the liner technicians began their new jobs, one part of the work flow ran into a problem. As the liners came off the 100 percent gauge on the centerless grinder and moved on to the next operation, the liners were found to be slightly undersized. The problem clearly had gone undetected for some time, and when Bachman finally spotted the deviation, the liner techs discussed what to do. Within minutes, the line was shut down.

With production halted, area superintendent Jack Zibell was informed of the trouble. After an intense 30 minutes searching for the source of the problem, the liner techs, engineers, union quality reps, and area manager withdrew from their huddle. Everyone had agreed that an incorrectly set grinding wheel was the culprit. This was fixed quickly, and production was started up. However, employees began voicing their skepticism regarding what would happen to the more than 900 defective liners that were in the plant at that time. Comments like, "Management doesn't care about the quality; watch, they'll send those parts out," were heard by the superintendent, union officials, and other managers. Zibell and the others involved decided that this was the time to make it clear that shutting down the line was the right thing to do and that quality was a critical part of everyone's job. Management took the eight liner technicians involved in the line shutdown and had them find the 24 "worst case" liners. These were put into engines and submitted to the toughest quality test, the 200 hour check, in which the engines were placed under extreme conditions and run for 200 consecutive hours. To make sure that the employees knew this was taking place, each employee on the line was sent periodically to monitor the tests. When none of the "defective" liners failed, a second test of 100 hours was run in order to convince everyone that the defect had no impact on reliability.

Once the testing was complete, and even though not one of the liners had failed, the rest of the "defects" were scrapped because the potential for failure still existed. Employees were taken aback. This was not the "volume at all costs approach," but rather "quality at any cost." But even more dramatic to the liner techs was the fact that not once during the entire crisis had Zibell, the general superintendent, or Rob Tykal, the area manager, asked who had set up the faulty grinding wheel, nor had they attempted in any way to determine who was to "blame." Instead, Zibell, Tykal, and others were intent upon seeing that a group of engineers, liner techs, and union quality reps worked cooperatively to develop internal checks so that similar problems would not occur in the future anywhere on the line.

This approach to plant problems now typifies the expectations held for all employees, managers, and union members. Jobs and roles have changed. "Supervisors are expected to be coaches and part of the team," Jim Brown commented. Bachman agreed and added that "it used to be that people came in and did the same task, day in and day out. Now, people have multiple jobs and responsibilities. In my area, the liner group, people like to change jobs. They feel more important and better about themselves." Both men described what they see as more "pitching in and helping." In fact, one formal change in jobs came about when the union and management bargained a new contract that took forty-four manufacturing job classifications and reduced them to fourteen. In early 1993, they reduced these further when they rolled three of the existing fourteen into a single classification. "There is a lot less `it's not in my job classification!'" stated Brown. Not only have these changes affected the way problems are solved and the way jobs are done, but absenteeism has declined substantially while productivity, quality, and sales have all improved.

Detroit Diesel's Transformation

How did these changes come about at Detroit Diesel? It began over five years ago when Detroit Diesel's market share of diesel engines designed for the heavy duty truck market had fallen to an all time low of 3.3 percent. With 700 employees on layoff, high absenteeism rates, and skepticism about the long-term viability of the organization as GM moved to sell it, Roger Penske bought an initial 60 percent share (quickly increased to 80 percent) of the organization. Penske, who also owns and manages the Penske Racing Team, which recently won its ninth Indianapolis 500, came into the organization with the philosophy, "Effort Equals Results." As he says, "People ask me today about what's different at Detroit Diesel. I can tell you that the first thing is the spirit and teamwork."

Teamwork takes place at all levels, much of it demonstrated by the cooperative working relationship of the top-level managers and the union officials, including Jim Brown. Brown says he was skeptical at first. However, in a meeting, he and Penske both agreed to a 100 percent working partnership based on trust, which would continue unless one of the parties violated that trust. It was then that Brown began to believe they could make it work. The largest change from the *union* standpoint is the strong role the union now plays at Detroit Diesel.

During the past five years, virtually everyone's job has changed, and with new skills now necessary for high performance, constant training takes place. To support the employees with the kind of training necessary for a change of this magnitude, Detroit Diesel and UAW Local 163 jointly funded and built a world-class training and fitness center connected to the plant. Jim Brown commented that now "the union is a partner in running the business and is involved in all decision making. This has clearly changed my job."

To make sure that all employees share an understanding of the business side as well as a sense of why their jobs are important, Penske and Lud Koci, the president of Detroit Diesel, hold "Update Meetings" four times a year. With small groups of employees, this owner and his president present the corporate financial, marketing, and production information to their employees. They field questions, take suggestions, and make sure that the employees come away feeling like owners. The meetings run continually until all employees have been included. The increase in the company's market share to more than 26 percent and the projected 1993 increase in earnings have given employees, management, and the union something exciting to discuss. Shop chairman Brown commented that "the average employee in this plant probably knows as much about the business as the average executive in any other company."

A Continuing Process

Back on the liner line where this story started, liner technicians recently became aware of some problems with the liner material as it came in from the supplier foundry. As Jim Bachman described it, "We sent some employees out to the foundry that makes the liners so that we could get an understanding of what they have to do to deliver a good product to us. In turn, they came out to our shop to see what we were running into on a day-to-day basis." This kind of activity has helped the employees at Detroit Diesel understand the importance of what they can contribute to the final product, to product quality, and to the overall success of Detroit Diesel.

Currently, as the technology for a new flywheel housing line is being designed, the employees on the existing production line are being asked to show the engineers what is good about the design of the line they work on and what is bad. The joint design team's job is to design out the bad parts. Once again, employees will contribute all their job knowledge to assure that, as a team, the newly designed production line will use technology effectively to assure both product quality and ergonomically appropriate jobs. This is what Penske means when he says that "the one who puts out the most effort gets the best results."

DISCUSSION QUESTIONS

1. The Detroit Diesel case illustrates how the knowledge, skills, and abilities (KSAs) needed in a given class of jobs might change as the business strategy changes. What new KSAs in the liner technicians' jobs appear necessary because of the organizational need for high quality?

2. What types of training would be needed to support the change in job design described in the case?

3. Because the union and management have agreed to reduce the job classifications significantly, the content of each employee's job undoubtedly has been increased. What motivational impact would you expect from such a change?

4. Describe the current supervisory role at Detroit Diesel. What do you think the most critical skills for the production supervisors are?

5. What performance management techniques (discussed in Chapter 7) would be most effective in the situation described in the case? What balance between individual performance and group performance evaluation would you suggest?

6. Roger Penske has stated that "each employee in this firm is as important as any other." What elements of work life as described in the case suggest that Penske and his managers have followed through on this philosophy?

III

ACQUIRING HUMAN RESOURCES

Managing the internal and external environment, designing work processes, and measuring work outcomes are critical to company competitiveness. However, competitiveness is ultimately determined by the quality of the work force who provides services or develops products. The first steps toward ensuring that a company has a high-quality work force is recruiting and selecting employees. Managers also need to be aware of the skills and talents of the workforce and anticipate future human resource needs due to changes in technology, sales volume, product mix, or customer demands, as well as acquisitions or downsizing.

In Chapter 9, "Human Resource Planning," the role of human resource planning in relation to a company's business strat-

egy is described. We examine each step of the human resource planning process, which includes forecasting, goal setting, strategic choice, program implementation, and evaluation. The chapter shows how statistics can be used to predict human resource supply and demand. A key emphasis of the chapter is comparing the benefits and costs of different options that managers can use to deal with labor excesses and shortages, such as new hires, temporary workers, layoffs, and overtime work.

Chapter 10, "Job Choice and the Recruitment of Human Resources," provides an overview of the process by which individuals choose jobs and the role that recruitment plays in shaping these choices. The chapter emphasizes how human resource policies (such as internal versus external recruitment and employment-at-will policies), recruitment sources, and the characteristics and behavior of recruiters influence the type of individuals who will be interested in employment opportunities with an organization. The chapter highlights actions that managers can take during recruitment to assure that individuals who accept job offers meet their personal goals as well as help the company gain a competitive advantage.

Chapter 11, "Personnel Selection and Placement," familiarizes the manager with methods of minimizing errors in employee selection and placement. The chapter discusses five standards—validity, reliability, generalizability, utility, and legality—that selection methods should meet for the company to select employees who will help the company gain a competitive advantage. The chapter compares and evaluates selection methods such as ability tests, personality tests, work samples, and drug and honesty tests according to these standards. The implications of federal legislation such as the Americans with Disabilities Act and the Civil Rights Act of 1991 are highlighted.

HUMAN RESOURCE PLANNING

Objectives

After reading this chapter, you should be able to:

1. Discuss how to align a company's strategic direction with its human resource planning.
2. Determine the labor demand of workers in various job categories.
3. Determine the supply of labor, both internally and externally, for various job categories.
4. Discuss the advantages and disadvantages of various ways of eliminating a labor surplus or avoiding a labor shortage.
5. Evaluate the effectiveness of a human resource planning program.

A Tale of Two Labor Shortages

As we mentioned in the opening chapter of this book, significant changes in the supply of labor loom in the future of American business. The U.S. labor force is expected to grow just 1 percent through the 1990s, and most new entrants to the labor pool will be immigrants and minorities. Thus, employers in the United States are likely to face severe labor shortages that will drastically affect the way they do business.

The United States is not alone in facing destabilizing labor shortages, however. Japan may be even worse off. Although both nations face the same problem, the causes differ; more than likely, so will the solutions. An examination of these differences highlights the effects of general societal trends and culture on employers, particularly as these influences are mediated by labor markets.

In the United States, the cause of the labor shortage is not so much the number of "available bodies" as it is the skill levels of those who are available. Even during the recession of the early 1990s, when unemployment was high, many employers had difficulty finding applicants with the right levels of skills. According to surveys conducted by the National Association of Manufacturers, five of six applicants for manufacturing jobs were rejected because of gaps between their skills and the job's requirements. Of those rejected, two out of five were rejected specifically for lack of basic proficiency in reading and writing.

The U.S. response to this crisis has focused mainly on expanding the labor pool and upgrading the skills of the new, highly diverse entrants into the pool. The Aetna Institute for Corporate Education, founded by the Aetna Life and Casualty Corporation, is a $42 million response to this problem. The institute is housed in a building with hotel rooms and 56 classrooms, where a full-time faculty of 60 teach up to 400 "students" each day. It is the centerpiece of Aetna's ongoing reorganization scheme aimed at keeping the company competitive. The core of Aetna's plan involves rewriting all its job

descriptions to emphasize general competencies rather than job-specific skills. Individual employees are assessed on these competencies and then assigned to the institute to master whatever competencies they lack. The institute also helps employees develop competencies needed for upper-level jobs as part of a promotion-from-within policy.

Japan, on the other hand, has little or no problem with the skill levels of the current labor pool. For Japan, the issue is simply "a shortage of bodies." Fertility rates in Japan have been falling for 30 years, keeping the birth rate very low. In 1990, Japan's fertility rate reached 1.53, the lowest rate ever—in fact, a rate below the minimum needed to maintain population rates. Unlike the United States, where women, immigrants, and minorities move freely into the labor pool, Japan's cultural traditions preclude this. Instead, Japan hopes to solve the problem by replacing human labor with automation and robots.

The attitude toward women in the labor pool exemplifies the differences between the two cultures. Whereas U.S. companies are trying to lure more women into the labor market by developing more family-friendly policies, Japan is developing a program (*Akachan-no Kai*) aimed at inducing women to have more children. The ultimate effect of this program is to reduce rather than expand the role of women in the labor pool.

SOURCES: W. Johnston, "The Coming Labor Shortage," *Journal of Labor Research* 13 (1992): 5–10; R. Guest, "Desperately Seeking Students," *Far Eastern Economic Review* 155 (1992): 33–34; J. Smith, "How Businesses Search for Qualified Applicants," *Personnel Journal* 21 (1992): 1–2; A. Durity, "A Critical Role for Corporate Education," *Personnel* 68 (1992): 5–6; K. Goldstein, "Japan's Baby Bust," *Across the Board* 29 (1992): 58–59; J. Teresko, "Japan Today—Factory Automation," *Industry Week* 240 (1992): 33–42; A. Bernstein, "Do More Babies Mean Fewer Working Women?" *Business Week,* August 5, 1991, 49–50; Y. Nakamura, "Japan's Birthrate Sinks to Record Low," *Japan Times Weekly International Addition* 32 (1992): 1, 8.

INTRODUCTION

As this "tale of two labor shortages" illustrates, employers do not exist in a vacuum, and one of the major ways that societal trends and culture affect employers is through the labor market. Changes in the labor market create both constraints and opportunities for employers, and a company can respond to these challenges in many different ways. This variation creates another arena where organizations can gain a competitive advantage.

There are three keys to effectively utilizing labor markets to one's competitive advantage. First, companies must have a clear idea of their current level of human resources. In particular, they need to know the strengths and weaknesses of their present stock of employees. Second, they have to plan where they are going in the future and be aware how the present configuration of human resources relates to the configuration that will be needed in the future. Third, where there are discrepancies between the present configuration and the configuration required for the future, organizations need to have programs that will address these discrepancies.

This chapter examines human resource planning, which attempts to forecast and forestall these kinds of discrepancies. In the first half of the chapter, we examine the role of human resource planning in organizations and show its relationship to both overall business strategy and specific human resource strategies in the areas of personnel selection, training, and compensation. In the second half of the chapter, we lay out the actual steps that go into developing and implementing a human resource plan.

THE ROLE OF HUMAN RESOURCE PLANNING IN ORGANIZATIONS

As we have noted elsewhere, organizations are increasingly looking toward human resource policies as a means of gaining a competitive advantage in the marketplace. Achieving this requires a fundamental shift in the way human resource departments operate, and perhaps the most critical aspect of making this shift deals with human resource planning.

In the past, those working in human resources often had nonbusiness backgrounds, and in most cases this group served in a reactive mode, responding to requests and crises as they arose.[1]

To become a strategic partner in the company, however, human resource managers must fully appreciate the company's overall business strategy and determine how they can contribute to that strategy. This requires a forward-looking focus in which the human resource manager anticipates rather than reacts to problems and crises.

Properly implemented, human resource planning creates the kind of lead time necessary to ward off potential problems that might otherwise threaten the company's competitive position. In a dynamic environment, human resource planning may be the difference between companies that thrive and those that fail to survive. This is especially the case since—despite what would appear to be obvious benefits—only a small percentage of organizations actually engage in formal human resource planning.[2]

Relationship to Overall Business Strategy

As we noted in Chapter 2, companies might adopt many different types of competitive business strategies, and different strategies have different implications for those managing human resources. For example, Porter suggests that developing innovative products is one of the critical dimensions on which companies try to differentiate themselves from their competitors. That is, some companies attempt to be more creative than others and hope that this will lead to long-term success. Other companies compete, not by innovation, but by trying to be the lowest-cost producer or service provider, often through the use of more efficient mass-production technologies.

Choices the company's strategic business planners make regarding innovation versus cost have implications for strategic managers of human resources that cannot be ignored. Innovation-oriented firms require highly skilled human resources with long-term commitments to the firm. Moreover, since innovation entails experimentation and risk, these people need to be sustained through potentially long periods of low return on investment.[3] Companies focusing on a low-cost strategy, on the other hand, may need a large number of lower-wage employees who are willing to work at jobs that may be boring and provide few promotion opportunities.[4]

Human resource managers must be able to predict the kinds of problems that will arise in developing and maintaining these two different types of work forces. They should also develop a forward-looking plan to fend off these problems.

Relationship to Human Resource Subfunctions

Just as plans and strategies at the business level have implications for general human resource policies, general human resource policies have implications for the various human resource subfunctions. For example, we have divided the major sections of this book into chapters dealing with (1) assessing, (2) acquiring, (3) developing, and (4) compensating human resources, and these are often subdivisions within the overall human resource department of large organizations. All of these subfunctional areas are affected by business-level strategies.

For example, in terms of performance assessment, companies emphasizing innovation need to allow flexibility in how the work gets done in order to promote creativity. Hence, it is not surprising to find that companies that develop an innovation-oriented business strategy tend to evaluate employees in terms of work outcomes rather than work processes. In terms of acquiring and developing human resources, companies stressing innovation are more likely to promote from within and to provide training for future promotions than companies that are trying to minimize costs. Finally, in terms of compensation, innovation-oriented companies need to foster an air of experimentation and, hence, provide income security for employees by not basing compensation on short-term incentives. Low-cost, mass-production units, on the other hand, tend to employ highly structured piece-rate incentive plans to promote high productivity.[5]

If the human resource manager is not aware of the company's overall business strategy and its implications for human resources, it is impossible to predict what kind of challenges will face the human resources department. Failure to anticipate and prepare for challenges reduces the probability that they can be successfully met. Failure to plan eventually results in a human resource department that is constantly "putting out brushfires," initiating a vicious cycle where today's problems crowd out time for future planning, which in turn creates more problems. Given the central need for planning, we will lay out the steps involved in developing and implementing a human resource plan in the next section.

THE HUMAN RESOURCE PLANNING PROCESS

An overview of the human resource planning process is depicted in Figure 9.1. The process consists of forecasting, goal setting, strategic planning, program implementation, and program evaluation. We will discuss each of these stages in the next sections of this chapter. Throughout these sections, we will use a simplified running example of a small manufacturer of auto parts to illustrate the planning process.

Forecasting

The first step in the planning process is forecasting. In personnel **forecasting**, the human resource manager attempts to ascertain the supply and demand for various types of human resources. The primary goal is to predict areas within the organization where there will be future labor shortages or surpluses. Figure 9.2 shows that forecasts of labor demand and supply come together to generate predictions of labor shortages or surpluses.

FIGURE 9.1   A Five-Step Model of the Human Resource Planning Process

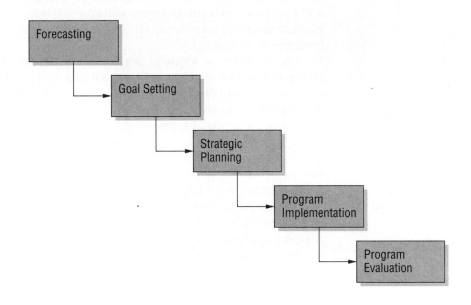

FIGURE 9.2   Combining Forecasts of Labor Demand and Labor Supply to Predict Impending Labor Surpluses and Shortages

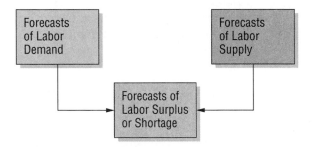

Forecasting, on either the supply or demand side, can be done using either statistical methods or judgmental methods. Statistical methods are excellent for capturing historic trends in a company's demand for labor, and under the right conditions they give predictions that are much more precise than those that could be achieved through subjective judgments of a human forecaster. On the other hand, many types of important events that might occur in the labor market have no historical precedent, and hence, statistical methods that work from historical trends are of little use. Rather, in these situations, one must rely on the pooled subjective judgments of experts, and their "best guesses" might be the only source from which to make inferences about the future. Typically, because of their complementary strengths and weaknesses, companies that do engage in human resource planning use a balanced approach that includes both statistical and judgmental components. We will examine both methods in the next sections.

Determining Labor Demand Statistically.   Typically, demand forecasts are developed around specific job categories or skill/ability areas relevant to the organization's current and future state. Two job categories that might be relevant to our small auto parts manufacturer would be (1) sales representatives and (2) production assemblers. If the plan were to be developed around skills and abilities, these two job categories might be represented by (1) skills in interpersonal relations and negotiating and (2) mechanical aptitude and physical dexterity.

Once the job categories or skills are identified, the planner needs to seek information that will help the planner predict whether the need for people with those skills or in that job category will increase or decrease in the future. Organizations differ in the sophistication with which such forecasts are derived. At the most sophisticated, an organization might have statistical models that predict labor demand for the next year given relatively objective statistics on leading indicators from the previous year. A **leading indicator** is an objective measure that accurately predicts future labor demand. For example, let's assume that our small parts manufacturer is located in the industrial Midwest and sells its product primarily to the Big Three automakers, where 50 percent of sales are to General Motors, 20 percent are to Ford, 20 percent are to Chrysler, and 10 percent are to auto parts distributors and repair shops.

Objective statistics on the Big Three automakers at one time period might accurately predict how much demand there will be for this company's product at a later time period. For example, since the auto parts manufacturer is a supplier, we might suspect, as shown in Figure 9.3, that inventory levels, sales levels, employment levels, and profits at the Big Three in one year might predict the demand for labor in the production assembler job category in the next year.

A **correlation coefficient** is a statistic that is particularly well suited to testing these kinds of suspicions. Because this statistic will also be relevant in later chapters (e.g., Chapter 11 on human resource selection), we will examine it in some detail here.

The correlation coefficient is a measure of the degree to which two sets of numbers are related. That is, it is a measure of similarity between two sets of numbers in terms of how they vary about their respective averages. For example, we might believe that the demand for labor in the production assembler job category in one year is related to the inventory levels of the Big Three automakers in the previous year. We could go back historically and find that each time inventories were above average, the demand for auto parts and, hence, the demand for production assemblers were below average.

The correlation coefficient expresses the strength of these kinds of relationships in numerical form, where a perfect positive relationship (i.e., as

FIGURE 9.3   Leading Indicators of the Demand for Labor for a
                  Hypothetical Auto Parts Manufacturer

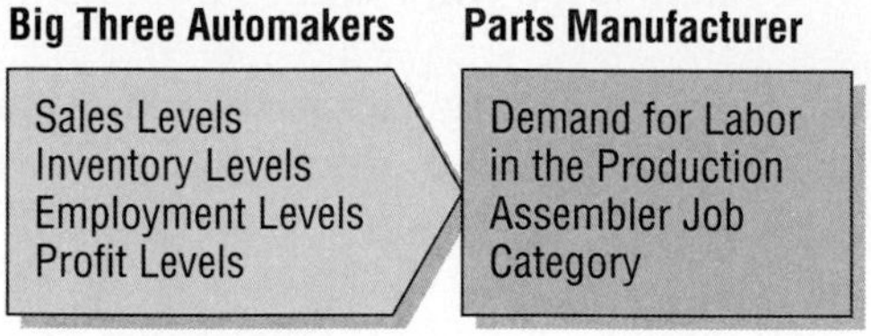

one set of numbers goes up, so does the other) equals +1.0, a perfect negative relationship (i.e., as one goes up, the other goes down) equals –1.0, and
no relationship equals .00.

Plotting the two sets of numbers on a two-dimensional graph often
helps one to appreciate the meaning of various levels of correlation, and
Figure 9.4 does this for values of +1.0, +.50, +.20, .00, and –.50. As you can
see, the sign of the correlation reveals whether the relationship is positive or
negative, and the absolute value of the correlation reveals the strength of
the relationship.

Let's assume that we discovered that over the last 15 years, the correlation between inventory levels and demand was –.50, the correlation between
sales levels and demand was +.50, the correlation between employment levels and demand was +.20, and finally the correlation between profit levels
and sales was .00. We would now know that the best two predictors of the
demand for labor are inventory levels and sales levels. We would also know
that employment levels are a modest predictor and that profit levels are
completely unrelated to the demand for labor.

With this knowledge in hand, we would do well to watch the inventory
levels, sales levels, and perhaps even employment levels at the Big Three
this year, since we now know these factors are "leading indicators," or predictors, of our demand for labor next year. If sales and employment levels
are down while inventories are up, we would forecast a reduction in our
demand for labor. If sales and employment levels are up while inventories
are down, we would forecast an increase in our demand for labor.

Finally, each of our three leading indicators does not need to be considered in isolation from the others. A **multiple correlation** can be obtained
that provides a quantitative measure of the relationship between these three
factors taken at once and our demand for labor. A multiple correlation is
just like a regular correlation in that it captures the degree of similarity
between two sets of numbers. However, in the case of the multiple correlation, one of the sets of numbers is derived by combining two or more variables and turning them into a single variable, which then can be correlated
with another single variable. For example, by using an equation like that
shown below, we can combine inventory levels (IL), sales levels (SL) and

FIGURE 9.4   Plots Associated with Various Levels of the Correlation Coefficient

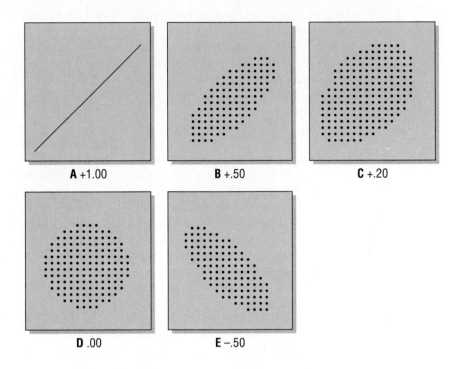

SOURCE: John A. Wagner, III and John R. Hollenbeck, *Management of Organizational Behavior*, © 1992, pp. 66, 90. Reprinted by permission of Prentice-Hall, Englewood Cliffs, New Jersey.

employment levels (EL) into one value (by weighing each and then adding them up) called our predicted demand for labor (PDL). This one value can then be correlated with the actual demand for labor (ADL), and this correlation would represent a multiple correlation between these three variables and ADL.

$$ADL = (PDL) = w_1 \, (IL) + w_2 \, (SL) + w_3 \, (EL) + Constant$$

A discussion of how the weights are chosen is beyond the scope of this text. (The interested reader can consult any good statistics text for a fuller discussion.) However, we will simply note that the method maximizes the correlation between ADL and PDL. This is generally accomplished by giving more weight to stronger predictors like IL and SL and less weight to weaker predictors like EL.

Determining Labor Demand Judgmentally.   Statistical planning models are useful when there is a long, stable history that can be used to reliably detect relationships among variables. However, these models almost always have to be complemented by subjective judgments of people who have expertise in the area. There are simply too many "once-in-a-lifetime" changes that have to be considered and that cannot be accurately captured in statistical models.

For example, our small-parts manufacturer might learn that the leadership at one of the Big Three automakers changed and that the new leadership plans on closing 21 plants over the next ten years. Because of the permanent plant closings, the company may decide to change its business strategy. That is, this company might decide to de-emphasize sales to the Big Three and expand sales to independent parts distributors and repair shops. This is an event that has no historical precedent, and hence, the company might want to consult all its best managers to get their opinions on exactly how much this change would affect the demand for labor in different job categories.

One decision-making technique that is particularly well suited to this type of forecasting is the **nominal group technique**, depicted in Figure 9.5. The key feature of this technique is that it separates the stage of idea generation from idea evaluation. Ideas are generated by people who work independently of each other. This reduces the chance that the group prematurely focuses on the first good idea to the exclusion of other ideas. It also minimizes the possibility that someone who has an idea hesitates to raise it out of fear of rejection. Only after a long list of ideas has been generated are they evaluated interactively by the whole group.

With today's networking technology, much of this interaction can take place through "electronic meetings" even though the individuals are geographically dispersed. For example, IBM has teams of people from different geographic areas interact over networked computers to discuss problems such as those encountered in this chapter. According to IBM executives, this allows the creation of teams with the best expertise on the issue without geographic or other travel-related constraints. Also, the anonymity of the computer often gets people who might otherwise be shy involved in the planning process.[6]

In the human resource planning context, for example, five business experts might convene and consider how the closing of 21 plants and the subsequent redirection of business strategy might impact the demand for labor in each job category. Each of these ideas might lead to a separate projection about the demand for labor in each job category. Once the ideas are expressed, the group as a whole can discuss each, identifying those that are most valid. Then, after identifying the five or six most important effects that the plant closings have on the demand for labor, each of the experts could privately make his or her own projection about the demand for labor in each category. The average of these could serve as the predicted demand for labor.

Such an analysis might indicate that the company would have a reduced demand in the production assembler job category but increased demand for individuals in the sales representative job category. This conclusion is reflected in the top portion of Figure 9.6.

FIGURE 9.5   The Nominal Group Technique

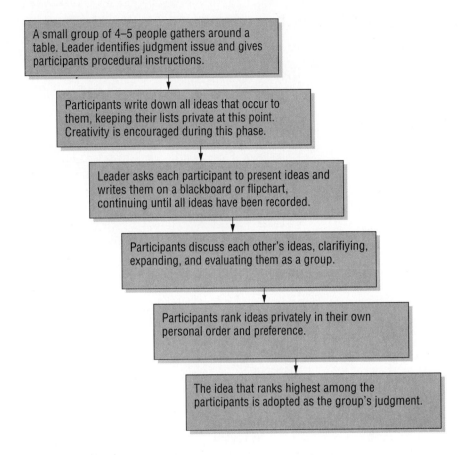

A small group of 4–5 people gathers around a table. Leader identifies judgment issue and gives participants procedural instructions.

Participants write down all ideas that occur to them, keeping their lists private at this point. Creativity is encouraged during this phase.

Leader asks each participant to present ideas and writes them on a blackboard or flipchart, continuing until all ideas have been recorded.

Participants discuss each other's ideas, clarifiying, expanding, and evaluating them as a group.

Participants rank ideas privately in their own personal order and preference.

The idea that ranks highest among the participants is adopted as the group's judgment.

SOURCE: J. A. Wagner and J. R. Hollenbeck, *Principles of Managing Organizational Behavior* (Englewood Cliffs, N.J.: Prentice-Hall, Inc. 1992): 501.

Determining Labor Supply Statistically.   Once a company has projected labor demand, it then needs to get an indicator of the firm's labor supply. Determining the internal labor supply calls for a detailed analysis of how many people are currently in various job categories (or who have specific skills) within the company. This analysis is then modified to reflect changes in the near future caused by retirements, promotions, transfers, voluntary turnovers, or terminations.

Determining the external supply of labor requires an analysis of the strengths and weaknesses of various sectors of the external labor market, and this increasingly involves international comparisons. Recent advances in telecommunications technology and aggressive efforts by foreign competitors to boost their educational systems have "put wings" on many jobs

FIGURE 9.6   Analysis of a Hypothetical Labor Shortage and Surplus

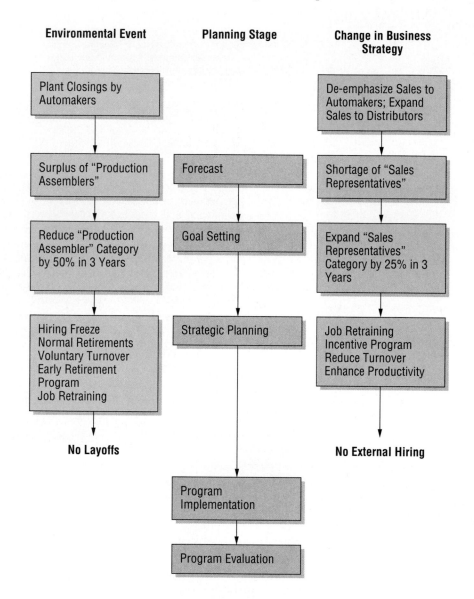

ranging from insurance claim processing to computer programming. For example, as we have noted earlier, Metropolitan Life Insurance has its medical claims analyzed in Ireland, where operating costs are about 35 percent less than in the United States. Typing mills in the Philippines are even more competitive, entering 10,000 characters for 50 cents. Those in China will do the same for a mere 20 cents. Clearly, the labor supplies of countries like China, India, Jamaica or those in Eastern Europe are creating an oversupply of labor for unskilled or low-skilled work. Despite the low cost of this

Globalization

COMPETING THROUGH

PRESTIGE, PRODUCTIVITY, AND ETHICS FIGURE INTO THE EQUATION

In the 1980s, many U.S. companies opening new plants located these enterprises overseas to take advantage of the relatively cheap supply of labor available in foreign countries. However, in the 1990s many non-U.S. firms have actually chosen to start up new ventures in the United States. For example, BMW, the world-renowned German luxury automaker, chose South Carolina as the site for its most recent new plant. Cie de Saint-Gobain, the giant French glass and buildings product maker, moved many of its operations out of Malaysia and into the United States. Finally, Hyundai Electronics Industries moved its corporate headquarters from South Korea to San Jose, California. Even though the U.S. labor market is considered a high-cost market relative to Mexico, Malaysia, or South Korea, other characteristics of the U.S. labor supply outweigh cost differences.

First, in some situations cost may not be the driving force in labor decisions, and the prestige of using U.S. workers relative to Mexican workers may compensate for cost differences. For example, with BMW, there was concern that many of their customers would not be willing to spend $50,000 for a car made in Mexico. This "image problem" was reinforced by the experiences of other German companies, such as Volkswagen AG, that reported quality-control problems in their Mexican plants. After weighing the advantages of cheap labor against

its needs for clean-room technology and advanced technological skills, the U.S. work force won out.

Second, productivity differences between the U.S. labor supply and others often make up for cost differences. For example, although the high average compensation of U.S. workers at Birmingham Steel ($55,000) would seem to make them easy prey for low-wage producers in Asia and South America, the higher productivity of the U.S. workers helps close the gap. High technology, when paired up with a small but skilled work force, decreases the percentage of total costs devoted to labor costs. As Birmingham Steel's chairman, James Todd, notes, "We don't care if their labor cost is zero, if productivity enhancements make our labor costs less than their transportation cost, we have them licked."

Finally, in some industries, companies find that the labor practices in some foreign countries are deplorable. For example, clothing manufacturer Levi Strauss found that many of its contractors in Bangladesh were routinely using unpaid child labor. On top of the ethical concerns, the company also had to consider the effect that such a practice might have on its brand identity among increasingly sensitive consumers. Thus, when examining the international labor supply, many companies find several reasons to opt for U.S. labor.

SOURCES: R. Keatley, "Luxury Automakers Consider Mexico: Its Low-Cost Labor versus Image Problem," *The Wall Street Journal*, December 16, 1992, A2; J. S. Lublin, "Firms Ship Unit Headquarters Abroad," *The Wall Street Journal*, December 9, 1992, B1; D. Milbank, "U.S. Productivity Gains Cut Costs, Close Gap with Low-Wage Overseas Firms," *The Wall Street Journal*, December 23, 1992, A2; J. Jones, "Exporting Jobs and Ethics," *Fortune*, October 5, 1992, 10.

source of labor, however, some foreign firms still find reasons for tapping the U.S. labor pool, as the "Competing through Globalization" box shows.

As in the case of labor demand, projections for labor supply can be derived from either historical statistical models or through judgmental techniques. One type of statistical procedure that can be employed for this

TABLE 9.1   A Hypothetical Transitional Matrix for an Auto Parts Manufacturer

Time 1990	Time 1993							
	(1)	(2)	(3)	(4)	(5)	(6)	(7)	(8)
(1) Sales Manager	.95							.05
(2) Sales Representative	.05	.60						.35
(3) Sales Apprentice		.20	.50					.30
(4) Assistant Plant Manager				.90	.05			.05
(5) Production Manager				.10	.75			.15
(6) Production Assembler					.10	.80		.10
(7) Clerical							.70	.30
(8) Not in Organization	.00	.20	.50	.00	.10	.20	.30	

purpose involves **transitional matrices**. Transitional matrices show the proportion (or number) of employees in different job categories at different times. Typically, these matrices show how people move in one year from one state (outside the organization) or job category to another state or job category.[7]

Table 9.1 shows a hypothetical transitional matrix for our parts manufacturer, focusing on seven job categories. Although these matrices look imposing at first, you will see that they are easy to read and use in determining the internal labor supply. A matrix like the one shown in Table 9.1 can be read in two ways. First, one can read the rows to answer the question, "Where did people in this job category in 1990 go by 1993." For example, 70 percent of those in the clerical job category (row 7) in 1990 were still in this job category in 1993, and the remaining 30 percent had left the organization. For the production assembler job category (row 6), 80 percent of those in this position in 1990 were still there in 1993. Of the remaining 20 percent, half (i.e., 10%) were promoted to the production manager job category, and the other half (i.e., 10%) left the organization. Finally, 75 percent of those in the production manager job category in 1990 were still there in 1993, while 10 percent were promoted to assistant plant manager and 15 percent left the organization.

Reading these kinds of matrices across rows makes it clear that there is a career progression within this firm from production assembler to production manager to assistant plant manager. Although we have not discussed rows 1 through 3, it might also be noted that there is a similar career progression from sales apprentice to sales representative to sales manager. In this organization, the clerical category is not part of any career progression. That is, this job category does not feed any other job categories listed in Table 9.1.

A transitional matrix can also be read from top to bottom (i.e., the columns) to answer the question "Where did the people in this job category in 1993 come from (i.e., Where were they in 1990)?" Again, starting with the clerical job (column 7), 70 percent of the 1993 clerical positions were filled by people who were also in this position in 1990 and that the remaining 30 percent were external hires (i.e., they were not part of the organization in 1990). In the production assembler job category (column 6), 80 percent of those occupying this job in 1993 occupied the same job in 1990, and the other 20 percent were external hires. Finally, the most diversely staffed job category seems to be production manager. Seventy-five percent of those in this position in 1993 held the same position in 1990. However, 10 percent were former production assemblers who were promoted, 5 percent were former assistant plant managers who were demoted, and 10 percent were external hires who were not with the company in 1990.

Matrices such as these are extremely useful for charting historical trends in the company's supply of labor. More importantly, if conditions remain somewhat constant, they can also be used to plan for the future. For example, if we believe that we are going to have a surplus of labor in the production assembler job category in the next three years, we note that by simply initiating a freeze on external hires, the ranks of this position will be depleted by 20 percent on their own.

Similarly, if we believed that we were going to have a labor shortage in the area of sales representatives, the matrix informs us that we may want to (1) decrease the amount of voluntary turnover in this position, since 35 percent of those in this category leave every three years; (2) speed the training of those in the sales apprentice job category so that they can be promoted more quickly than in the past; and/or (3) expand external recruitment of individuals for this job category, since the usual 20 percent of job incumbents drawn from this source may not be sufficient to meet future needs.

Determining Labor Supply Judgmentally.   As with labor demand, historical precedents for labor supply may not always be reliable indicators of future trends. Thus, statistical forecasts of labor supply also need to be complemented with judgmental methods.

The **Delphi technique** is a particularly good method for converting expert opinions on future labor supply into consensus-based forecasts to be used in human resource planning. The Delphi technique, shown in Figure 9.7, is similar to the nominal group technique discussed earlier, but it is different in one way—the group of experts never meets face-to-face. This saves money if these people are geographically dispersed, and it allows for more widespread participation than might be possible with the nominal group technique. As you will see, however, it can be more time-consuming.

Instead of interacting directly, the members of the group respond individually to certain questions in writing (e.g., "What is your projection for the supply of labor in this job category?"). The company might also request certain data. The individual responses are collected by a group leader, who then distributes the answers (along with any additional data requested) to

FIGURE 9.7   The Delphi Technique

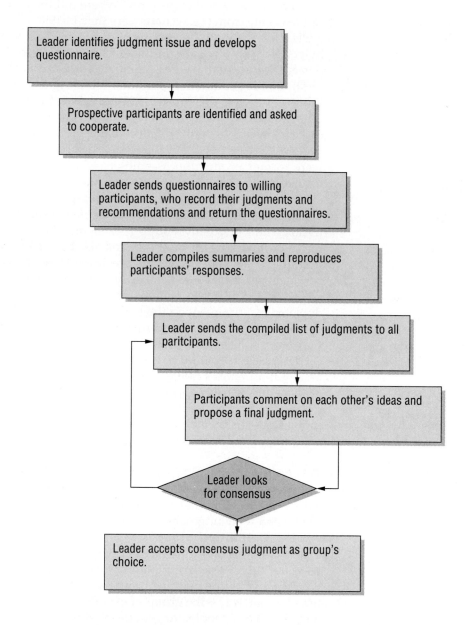

Leader identifies judgment issue and develops questionnaire.

Prospective participants are identified and asked to cooperate.

Leader sends questionnaires to willing participants, who record their judgments and recommendations and return the questionnaires.

Leader compiles summaries and reproduces participants' responses.

Leader sends the compiled list of judgments to all paritcipants.

Participants comment on each other's ideas and propose a final judgment.

Leader looks for consensus

Leader accepts consensus judgment as group's choice.

SOURCE: J. A. Wagner and J. R. Hollenbeck, *Principles of Managing Organizational Behavior* (Englewood Cliffs, N.J.: Prentice-Hall, Inc. 1992): 511.

other members of the group. The group members consider each other's positions then respond again to the original question. The procedure continues until the leader of the group perceives a consensus forming, and this consensus then becomes the projection for the supply of labor in the respective job category.

Determining Labor Surplus or Shortage.   Once forecasts for labor demand and supply are known, the planner can compare the figures to ascertain whether there will be a labor shortage or labor surplus for the respective job categories. As is evident in Figure 9.6, the results of such a comparison in our fictional company indicate that the changes in the product market and business strategy imply that there will be an oversupply of people in the production assembler job category but a shortage in the sales representative job category.

Goal Setting

The second step in the human resource planning process is goal setting. The purpose is to focus attention on the desired end state and to provide a benchmark for determining the relative success of a program aimed at redressing a pending labor shortage or surplus. The goals should come directly from the analysis of labor supply and demand and should include (1) a specific figure about what should happen with the job category or skill area and (2) a specific timetable for when results should be achieved.

The auto parts manufacturer, for instance, might set a goal to reduce the number of individuals in the production assembler job category by 50 percent over the next three years. Similarly, the firm might set a goal to increase the number of individuals in the sales representative job category by 25 percent over the next three years.

Strategic Choice

The third step in personnel planning is strategic choice. At this stage, the organization chooses from among the many different strategies available for redressing labor shortages or surpluses. Table 9.2 shows some of the options on the menu of a human resource planner seeking to reduce a labor surplus. Table 9.3 shows some of the options available to the same planner intent on avoiding a labor shortage.

This stage is critical because many options are available to the planner and they differ widely in their expense, speed, effectiveness, reliability, and, of course, amount of human suffering. The trade-offs are particularly salient when attempting to avert a labor surplus, since many of the faster solutions (layoffs, pay cuts, etc.) are high in human suffering, and most of the interventions that are low in human suffering (e.g., early retirement, natural attrition, retraining) tend to work slowly. For example, when Robert Crandall, CEO of American Airlines, announced the carrier's recent layoff of 600 employees, he noted, "This is not a happy day at American Airlines," and he alluded to the fact that this step might have been avoided if the company had done a better job in forecasting shifts in the industry that affected American's demand for labor.[8]

TABLE 9.2   Options for Reducing an Expected Labor Surplus

Option	Speed	Human Suffering
1. Layoffs	Fast	High
2. Pay reductions	Fast	High
3. Demotions	Fast	High
4. Transfers	Fast	Moderate
5. Work sharing	Fast	Moderate
6. Retirement	Slow	Low
7. Natural attrition	Slow	Low
8. Retraining	Slow	Low

TABLE 9.3   Options for Avoiding an Expected Labor Shortage

Option	Speed	Revocability
1. Overtime	Fast	High
2. Temporary employees	Fast	High
3. Subcontracting	Fast	High
4. Retrained transfers	Slow	High
5. Turnover reductions	Slow	Moderate
6. New external hires	Slow	Low

The strategies also differ in the way they trade off short-term and long-term problems. For example, although downsizing often has immediate positive effects (reduced operating costs, higher stock prices), the long-term effects are often negative. Zenith Electronics Corporation, for instance, cut its 1985 payroll in half (from 6,200 to 3,000) by 1990. But industry analysts say that the chronic downsizing left Zenith without the manufacturing capacity to meet demand for a hot new product—flat computer screens.[9]

Companies with sophisticated planning systems have an integrated approach to managing shortages and surpluses that attempts to minimize or eliminate the need for agonizing layoffs. These companies might try to buffer themselves from layoffs of permanent employees by using strategies that can be turned on and off rather painlessly. For example, a company may respond to a short-term labor shortage by increasing the amount of overtime worked by current employees and by increasing the use of temporary

Quality

A PERMANENT SOLUTION TO A TEMPORARY PROBLEM

Temporary employees are an attractive option to many firms because of the ease with which this source of labor can be turned off and on when the company is faced with uneven or cyclical demand for its products or services. In addition, since temporaries are usually not covered under the company's overall benefit plan, they are a less expensive source of labor relative to full-time, regular help. On the other hand, because of their lack of organization-specific experience and marginal commitment to the company, it is also a source of labor that troubles some employers concerned with quality. Some surveys indicate that the use of temporary employees damages service quality and the morale of full-time regular employees.

Banc One Wisconsin Corporation, however, has developed an innovative program for employing temporaries that allows it to take advantage of the positive features of this labor source while minimizing the negative side effects. Their program consolidates the use of one temporary agency that administers a temporary worker program "on-site" for the bank. In fact, the bank has even set up an office in its Milwaukee headquarters for the person who serves as the liaison between the bank and the temporary agency. The consolidation of this service saved the bank $100,000 in the first year and $140,000 in the second.

However, the most important impact of the program has been on the quality of service attributed to the new labor pool. Quality has improved for many reasons. First, by developing a pool of temporary workers trained specifically in the bank's policies and procedures, managers get workers with organization-specific experience (e.g., familiarity with the company's software). Thus, they can expect high-quality service from the temporaries without having to engage in lengthy orientations for each temporary employed. Second, after some time, the temporary employees become sensitive to the corporate culture at Banc One, with its emphasis on service quality. Indeed, many of the temporaries are eventually hired on as full-time regular staff. Finally, by alleviating what had been an ongoing, time-consuming problem for both managers and human resource staff, the new program freed up these individuals to focus on other innovative means to enhance service quality.

SOURCES: D. Burda, "Use of Nurse Temps Affects Staff Morale," *Modern Healthcare,* October 26, 1992, 52; J. E. Struve, "Making the Most of Temporary Workers," *Personnel Journal,* November 1991, 43–45.

employees hired from an outside agency. The company might also try to lease workers, a strategy that is becoming increasingly widespread among small employers.[10] Overtime, temporaries, and leased workers can then provide a buffer. If an economic downturn generates a labor surplus, the firm can simply eliminate overtime, temporaries, and leased workers and not have to lay off permanent employees. Moreover, as shown in the "Competing through Quality" box, the effective use of temporary employees can be instrumental in competing through quality in some service industries.

As another example, firms with a surplus of labor in one job category might be able to use those surplus employees to staff another area, provided there is enough lead time to train workers for new jobs. For example, during its downsizing process, Household International, a nationally recognized financial services firm, used a "displaced employee committee" to find internal positions for laid-off employees with good work records. During a restructuring that occurred between October and December 1990, this committee was successful in placing 75 percent of the displaced employees in positions ranging from filing clerk to assistant vice-president.[11] Similarly, when confronted with a recent slump in auto sales, Toyota Motor Company shifted 600 white-collar workers to assembly plants temporarily in an attempt to put these surplus employees to work.[12]

It is clear that the longer time a company has to prepare for the shortage or surplus, the more creatively it can respond, and the more options it has. If there is little or no advance warning, companies are compelled to institute layoffs and external hiring to handle unforeseen surpluses and shortages.

In our example of the auto parts manufacturer, the planner might make the following strategic choices in response to the impending labor surplus in the production assembler job category. First, the firm adopts a hiring freeze in this category. Second, based on past statistics that 10 percent of the employees in this category will retire or quit voluntarily over the next three years, while 10 percent are promoted out, the firm lets these natural processes reduce the surplus by 20 percent.

To reach the 50 percent goal, however, the firm might decide to initiate two new programs. First, an early retirement program that provides bonuses for those who retire early might be instituted. It is expected that 20 percent of those in this job category would voluntarily retire given this type of bonus incentive. Second, a job-retraining program that would develop the interpersonal and negotiation skills of former production assemblers could be created. Such a program could turn 10 percent of those currently in the production assembler job category into sales representatives within three years. Together, these two programs, along with the natural rate of retirement and turnover, should reduce the labor surplus without layoffs or pay cuts.

In response to the labor shortage in the sales representative job category, the first step has already been taken: The job-retraining program for production assemblers should add 10 percent to this job category. The second step might be to "stop the bleeding" by cutting the expected voluntary turnover in this category to 10 percent. A third goal could be to raise the productivity of those who stay by 5 percent, since increasing productivity allows one to get more out of the same number of people. Thus, the company might develop an incentive plan for sales representatives that (1) reduces turnover and (2) increases the productivity of the remaining employees. Thus, the company is able to reach the 25 percent expansion required in this job category without hiring any additional permanent employees.

Program Implementation

The programs developed in the strategic-choice stage of the process are then put into practice in the program-implementation stage. A critical aspect of program implementation is to make sure that some individual is held accountable for achieving the stated goals and has the necessary authority and resources to accomplish this goal. It is also important to have regular progress reports on the implementation to be sure that all programs are in place by specified times and have early effects that are somewhere in line with projections.

For example, if our auto parts manufacturer finds that, by the end of one year, no employees have taken advantage of the early retirement program, changes might have to be made to this program. Since no planner can predict with perfect accuracy how individuals might respond to a brand-new program such as this, quickly identifying failing programs can help save huge amounts of time and money. For example, the bonus provided to those who might retire early may be insufficient to get anyone to make such a major life change; therefore, planners may need to change the program or adopt a different approach.

Program Evaluation

The final step in the planning process is to evaluate the results. Of course, the most obvious evaluation is seeing whether the company has successfully avoided any potential labor shortages or surpluses. Although this bottom-line evaluation is critical, it is also important to go beyond it to see which of the specific parts of the planning process contributed to success or failure.

Thus, we might compare the forecasts of labor supply and demand to see whether our statistical models or experts were accurate in their predictions. Any inaccuracies need to be identified, and the models or experts need to be informed of these errors so that future forecasts can be more accurate. Maybe the forecast of the demand for production assemblers was too low because few of the plant closings predicted by the automakers actually occurred. The company might learn from this that pronouncements by the corporate boards of the organizations involved are not a reliable predictor of what those organizations actually do.

We might also inspect the programs to see whether they had the expected results. For example, we might find that the incentive program for sales representatives had the desired effects on turnover but only half the expected effect on productivity. Future attempts to use programs to increase productivity would need to be modified in light of such a result.

Finally, we might also examine the degree to which all the programs were properly implemented and carried out. For example, we may find that, despite its success in terms of converting production assemblers into sales representatives, the training program was initiated later than was intended. Future planning attempts involving this program would need to reflect that it was actually more successful than anticipated, since it got the desired results despite one-time implementation problems.

THE SPECIAL CASE OF AFFIRMATIVE ACTION PLANNING

We have argued that human resource planning is an important function that should be applied to an organization's entire labor force. It is also important to plan for various subgroups within the labor force. For example, affirmative action plans forecast and monitor the proportion of various protected group members, such as women or minorities, that are in various job categories or career tracks. As shown in the "Competing through Social Responsibility" box, because of the Americans with Disability Act and technological advances in "accommodation," affirmative action programs are increasingly focused on various segments of the disabled population.

The proportion of workers in these subgroups can then be compared to the proportion that each subgroup represents in the relevant labor market. This type of comparison is called a **work-force utilization review**. This process can be used to determine whether there are any subgroups whose proportion in the relevant labor market is substantially different from their proportion in the job category.

If such an analysis indicates that some group, for example, African Americans, makes up 35 percent or the relevant labor market for a job category, but that this same group constitutes only 5 percent of the actual incumbents in that job category in that organization, then this is evidence of underutilization. Underutilization could come about because of problems in selection. For example, in the auto parts manufacturer, if underutilization was present in the clerical job category, then this is a selection issue, since all clerical employees (as indicated in Table 9.1) were external hires.

Underutilization can also come about because of problems in internal movement, however. For example, whereas women may not be underutilized in the positions of sales apprentice or sales representative (i.e., 50 percent of the labor market is female and 50 percent of the sales apprentices and representatives are female), they may be underutilized in the next step of that career ladder—sales manager—where perhaps 0 percent of the sales managers are women.

This kind of review is critical for many different reasons. First, many firms adopt "voluntary affirmative action programs" to make sure underutilization does not occur. The motivation may be to promote diversity, that is, to help women and minorities access certain job categories or progress through certain career paths. Voluntary affirmative action programs could also be motivated by the desire to avoid lawsuits. As you should recall from the earlier chapter on legal issues, evidence for underutilization can be used to establish a prima facie case of discrimination under the new Civil Rights

Social Responsibility

COMPETING THROUGH

BREAKING DOWN BARRIERS IN THE WORKPLACE

Although the U.S. labor pool as a whole is expected to grow slowly over the next 15 years, one segment of that pool growing by 500,000 every year involves disabled workers. Many feel that the current demographic situation on the labor supply side provides a window of opportunity to employ disabled workers in ways that have never been attempted in the past. For example, McDonald's restaurants, after finding it more and more difficult to recruit teenage workers for its fast-food jobs, initiated a program to train and hire the mentally retarded and others with developmental disabilities. The program resulted in the employment of 3,000 people in 44 states and was celebrated in promotional advertisements, one of which won a major national marketing award.

Technological changes that have changed the way work is done have also boosted the employment opportunities for many disabled workers. For example, current technology allows the information encoded as a magnetic signal in a computer to be translated into speech (through a speech synthesizer), braille (through a hard-copy printer), or enlarged print right on the computer monitor. This kind of technology has forced companies to reconsider the impact that physical limitations like blindness can have on jobs that entail information that can be routed through a computer.

Despite gains on the technological front, however, the most difficult barriers to confront are the biases and stereotypes of current workers and managers. Most of these types of problems result not from malice but fear. Many who have not worked closely with the disabled in the past fear that they will not know how to act, and in not knowing what to do, appear foolish. This is particularly problematic for some older workers, who were often segregated from the disabled when they grew up. On the other hand, the last two generations of public school students have grown up with disabled classmates and feel more comfortable around the disabled. Training programs are available to help reduce the anxiety of those who might be initially uncomfortable around the disabled.

The payoff from programs that tap this underutilized segment of the labor pool can be high for many firms, and this is magnified with the passage of the Americans with Disabilities Act. Moreover, some companies find unexpected benefits to the rest of their work force after hiring the disabled. For example, one company that was having trouble getting workers adjusted to its new E-mail system made it clear that all memos sent to one blind co-worker had to go through the company's E-mail system. This way the message could be decoded through a speech synthesizer. This served as the needed catalyst to get virtually all the workers on the E-mail system, even when communicating to their nondisabled colleagues.

SOURCES: K. Teltsch, "Shrinking Labor Pool Opens Door to Millions of Disabled," *The New York Times,* December 5, 1990, C1; J. Anderson, "How Technology Brings Blind People into the Workplace: New Data Conversion Devices Have Opened Job Opportunities for This Willing but Underused Group," *Harvard Business Review* 67 (1989): 36–40.

Act. Thus, avoiding underutilization is particularly important to companies that may have trouble establishing the "business necessity" of their selection or promotion systems.

Second, companies might also engage in utilization reviews because they are legally required to do so. For example, if a company is a government contractor or subcontractor, Executive Order 11246 requires that such organizations maintain affirmative action programs. Also, affirmative action programs can be mandated by the courts as part of the settlement of discrimination complaints. Indeed, the new Civil Rights Act was largely supportive of these kind of **court-ordered affirmative action** plans.

Regardless of the motivation for adopting affirmative action planning programs, the steps required to execute such a plan are identical to the steps in the generic planning process discussed earlier in this chapter. That is, the company needs to assess current utilization patterns and then forecast how these are likely to change in the near future. If these analyses suggest that there is currently underutilization and if forecasts suggest that this problem is not likely to change, then the company may need to set goals and timetables for changing this situation. Certain strategic choices need to be made in the pursuit of these goals that might affect recruitment or selection practices, and then the success of these strategies has to be evaluated against the goals established earlier in the process.

SUMMARY

Effective human resource planning can be one of the most rewarding aspects of work in human resource management. Effective planning can enhance the success of the organization while minimizing the amount of human suffering resulting from poorly anticipated labor surpluses or shortages. The process itself need not be overly complex or sophisticated, and forecasts need not be perfect to be useful. Similarly, programs can take on many different forms and allow for creativity, and they do not have to work perfectly to be helpful. In light of these considerations, it is almost unethical for employers not to formally plan, and for certain employers, not having plans for members of various protected groups can be outright illegal. The statistics indicating that few organizations actually engage in formal planning are some of the most disheartening statistics in this field.

Discussion Questions

1. Discuss the effects that an impending labor shortage might have on the following three subfunctions of human resource management: selection and placement, training and career development, and compensation and benefits. Which subfunction might be most heavily impacted, and in what ways might these groups develop joint, cooperative programs to avert a labor shortage?

2. Discuss the costs and benefits associated with statistical versus judgmental forecasts for labor demand and labor supply. Under what conditions might either of

these techniques be infeasible? Under what conditions might both be feasible, but one more desirable than the other?

3. How should one decide on a time frame for human resource planning? What are the factors one would consider in adopting a one-to-three-year plan versus a five-to-ten-year plan?

4. In what way does human resource planning force line managers and staff professionals to work together? What are the distinctive competencies that each of these two groups brings to the human resource planning process, and why might the two sides not always see things the same way? What can be done to create effective teamwork among these groups?

5. Some companies have detailed affirmative action plans, complete with goals and timetables, for women and minorities, and yet have no formal human resource plan for the organization as a whole. Why might this be the case? If you were a human resource specialist interviewing with this company for an open position, what would this practice imply for the role of the human resource manager in that company?

Notes

1. J. Solomon, "People Power: Corporations Are Beginning to See Personnel Professionals as Strategic Managers of a Major Asset," *The Wall Street Journal*, March 9, 1990, 33.

2. J. T. Delaney, "Determinants of Formal Human Resource Planning in American Business," in *The Effective Use of Human Resources: A Symposium on New Research Approaches*, ed. D. J. B. Mitchell and J. Wildhorn (Los Angeles, Cal.: UCLA Institute of Industrial Relations Monograph and Research Series: 52).

3. S. E. Jackson, R. S. Schuler, and J. C. Rivero, "Organizational Characteristics as Predictors of Personnel Practices," *Personnel Psychology* 42 (1989): 727–786.

4. J. W. Dean and S. A. Snell, "Integrated Manufacturing and Job Design: Moderating Effects of Organizational Inertia," *Academy of Management Journal* 34 (1991): 776–804.

5. Jackson, et al., "Organizational Characteristics."

6. J. Batimo, "At These Shouting Matches, No One Says a Word," *Business Week*, June 11, 1990, 87.

7. D. W. Jarrell, *Human Resource Planning: A Business Planning Approach* (Englewood Cliffs, N.J.: Prentice-Hall, 1993).

8. B. O'Brian, "AMR's Unit Cuts Executive Ranks by 576 Employees," *The Wall Street Journal*, December 1, 1992, A6.

9. E. Lesley and L. Light, "When Layoffs Alone Don't Turn the Tide," *Business Week*, December 7, 1991, 100–101.

10. R. Resnick, "Leasing Workers," *Nation's Business*, November 1992, 21–25.

11. P. Stuart, "New Internal Jobs Found for Displaced Employees," *Personnel Journal*, August 1992, 50–53.

12. J. Rysart, "Some White-Collar Staff at Toyota to Shift to Plants," *The Wall Street Journal*, December 1, 1992, A8.

C A S E

CORPORATE STRATEGY AND HUMAN RESOURCE PLANNING

In 1992, Lockheed Corporation was a leader in the aerospace and electronics industry. However, as much as 70 percent of Lockheed's revenue at that time came from Department of Defense (DOD) contracts with the U.S. government. This was not good news. Because of the breakup of the Soviet Union, industry analysts in 1992 were forecasting that DOD procurement and funded research would drop from $117 million in 1990 to $68 million by 1995—a 42 percent reduction. Some analysts in 1992 were arguing that cost competitiveness and affordability would be the key to success in this industry as the same number of defense contractors vied for a reduced amount of business. Other analysts argued that a downsized military would be smaller but more technologically sophisticated, and hence companies that were the most innovative would survive.

Lockheed CEO Dan Tellep looked at this information and then had to make a difficult decision about the future of Lockheed. First, should Lockheed continue to pursue its current strategy and hope that its advanced technological capacities and history of superior performance would make it one of the few survivors of this current industry "shakedown"? Or should Lockheed change strategies by diversifying into civilian markets, where competing on price and affordability would be of most importance?

QUESTIONS

1. Assume you were the vice-president of Human Resources for Lockheed in 1992 and Tellep asked you for an analysis of the human resource implications of adopting one of these strategies over the other. What would be the major human resource challenges associated with either of these two strategies?

2. Assume that regardless of the strategy chosen, Tellep decided that Lockheed would need to reduce the size of its work force in 1995 by 40 percent, and he wished to do this in a way that strengthened the organization's ability to pursue its strategic mission. How would you devise the downsizing plan if Lockheed decided to compete on innovation? How would you devise it if Lockheed decided to compete on costs?

SOURCES: A. Barrett, "Friendly Fire," *Financial World,* January 21, 1992, 20–24; D. Hughes, "Affordable Systems to Drive Civil, Military Electronics," *Aviation Week and Space Technology* 137 (1992): 87–90; D. Fuqua, "The Implications of a Leaner but Technologically Meaner Military for Defense Contractors," *Production and Inventory Management Review* 11 (1992): 9–16.

10

JOB CHOICE AND THE RECRUITMENT OF HUMAN RESOURCES

Objectives   *After reading this chapter, you should be able to:*

1. Describe the features of jobs and organizations that most people view as critical when looking for work.
2. Describe the methods people use to process information about jobs and organizations and how this method is affected by individual differences.
3. Describe the various recruitment policies organizations adopt to make job vacancies more attractive.
4. List the various sources from which job applicants can be drawn, their relative advantages and disadvantages, and the methods for evaluating them.
5. Explain the role of the recruiter in the recruitment process, the limits he or she faces, and the opportunities available.

Urban Unemployment and Minority Teenagers

Alex Perez lives on the Lower East Side of New York City. He has had little success finding a job that interests him, and these days he has all but given up looking for work. Instead, he spends his time hanging out on city streets, and he is not alone. In major cities like Philadelphia, Chicago, and Detroit, fewer than 40 percent of people between 16 and 19 years of age are employed or even seeking employment. In Los Angeles and New York, only 20 percent of this age group work or seek work—a decrease of 13 percent since 1987.

In August 1991, Josephine Nieves, the commissioner of employment for New York City, noted that "we haven't begun to feel the real impact of this youth unemployment on the city. We are in for dire things if we have ever more kids on the street who have no knowledge of the working world." Nieve's warnings turned into reality ten months later in south-central Los Angeles, when the verdict in the Rodney King police brutality case sparked the worst inner-city riot in U.S. history.

One part of the teenage unemployment problem lies with the job-search process of these inexperienced individuals. Many teens have unrealistic expectations about the kind of work and salaries that are available for young, unskilled workers. Some of them shun work at low-paying courier jobs or fast-food restaurants, despite the fact that many employers like to see such experience listed on résumés. In addition, many youths have poor job-seeking skills. Many are afraid to go to job interviews, and those who do often dress in ways that convey the wrong impression (e.g., T-shirts and mirrored sunglasses).

The recruitment practices of employers are another part of the teenage unemployment problem,

however. Research on the recruiting practices of employers in inner cities suggests that strained race relations harm the labor market opportunities of minority youths. Employers in these areas often direct their recruiting at white neighborhoods and Catholic or magnet schools. Simultaneously, they avoid recruiting from sources that might reach minority youths, such as citywide newspapers and public agencies (like state employment services).

If an incident like the L.A. riot has not convinced employers of the need to expand their recruiting efforts to include minority youths, statistics from reports such as *Workforce 2000* drive the point home. As we mentioned in Chapter 1, by the year 2000, 59 percent of the entering work force will be non-white and female. The competitive positions of individual companies, and of the U.S. economy as a whole, depend on increasing the effectiveness of employer recruiting and individual decision making in choosing jobs.

SOURCES: P. Duke, "Urban Teen-agers, Who Often Live Isolated from the World of Work, Shun the Job Market," *The Wall Street Journal*, August 14, 1991, A10; K. Neckerman, "Hiring Strategies, Racial Bias and Inner-City Workers," *Social Problems* 38 (1991): 433–447.

INTRODUCTION

The purpose of this chapter is to familiarize you with the process by which individuals choose jobs and the role of personnel recruitment in shaping these choices. Figure 10.1 depicts the approach taken in this chapter, which focuses first on the job-choice process. Specifically, at the top of this figure,

FIGURE 10.1   Overview of the Individual Job Choice–Organizational Recruitment Process

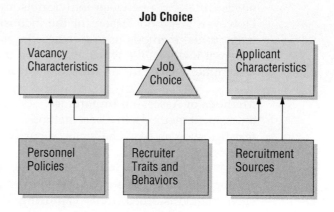

we show how an individual's job choice is a joint function of the applicant's characteristics and characteristics of the job and the organization being evaluated (which we describe with a single term, *vacancy characteristics*). We then look at three aspects of employer recruiting strategy, shown in the bottom half of the figure, that affect this process: (1) the way employer recruitment policies influence vacancy characteristics; (2) the way recruitment sources influence the kind of individuals who apply for a job; and (3) the way a recruiter influences the applicant's perception of the job and, perhaps, the applicant's self-perception. At the end of the chapter is a summary of the actions that employers can take during the recruitment process to ensure that individuals make job choices that further the goals of both the applicant and employer.

FACTORS THAT INFLUENCE JOB CHOICE

The job-choice process typically requires an individual to decide to accept one position in one organization over several others (or unemployment). This decision is a function of the characteristics of the person making the choice and the characteristics of the vacancies being considered. We will examine the important characteristics of vacancies and persons in the next two sections of this chapter.

Vacancy Characteristics

There has been a great deal of research on the affects of vacancy characteristics (i.e., job and organizational attributes) on job choice.[1] The findings vary widely and are too inconsistent to provide a single ranking of characteristics from most to least important. These findings are inconsistent for two reasons. First, work serves many different needs for an individual, and these needs differ both between individuals and within individuals over time. However, a second reason for the inconsistencies can be traced to differences in the methods used to assess importance in various studies. These different methods are worth examining because each is based on different assumptions about the usefulness of job applicants' self-reports.

Methods of Assessing Importance.   Some studies of job seekers use direct assessment methods. In direct methods, a person is given several job characteristics such as pay, challenge, security and asked simply to rank them in importance.

Other studies use indirect methods, where the importance of various vacancy characteristics is determined by looking at actual decisions. One such method is called **policy capturing**. Policy capturing is a technique by which one determines the importance of various factors in the decision process by determining the relationship between certain attribute levels and actual choices. That is, in policy capturing, one retrospectively determines what drove a person's decisions by contrasting the characteristics associated with the options chosen versus those not chosen.

In a typical policy-capturing study, vacancies are described to individuals along various dimensions (e.g., high in pay, low in challenge, highly secure), and then people are asked whether they would take the jobs. Table 10.1 shows the results of a hypothetical policy-capturing study, using six characteristics and ten jobs. Notice that Job 1 is high in pay, security, and location but low in challenge, advancement opportunities, and benefits. Job 2 is high in security, benefits, and location but low in challenge, pay, and advancement. If you cover up all the columns except pay and choice, you'll notice that every time pay is high, this person chooses that job (Jobs 1, 3, 4, 7, 9) and that every time pay is low, that job is not chosen (Jobs 2, 5, 6, 8, 10). If you do the same for benefits, you see that there are six times where the value of benefits (high or low) is different from the value for choice. This policy-capturing study suggests that pay is the most important characteristic for this person, and benefits the least important. Most policy-capturing investigations use correlations and regression analyses like those described in Chapter 9 to assess what features of the vacancy "predict" the individual's job choice.

The results from indirect methods, like policy capturing, sometimes differ from the results of studies in which people are directly asked what is important to them. This fact is worth noting because it implies that what people *say* is most important and what really *is* most important in their decisions are often different things.[2] This may be because when asked directly, people say what they think others want to hear rather than what they really feel. It could also be because some people lack insight into what truly drives their own decisions. Either way, you need to keep this in mind when interviewing and recruiting people so that you are not led astray by applicants' self-reports.

TABLE 10.1

Hypothetical Policy-Capturing Study

	Vacancy Characteristic						
	Challenge	Pay	Advancement	Security	Benefits	Location	Job Choice
Vacancy							
1	0	1	0	1	0	1	1
2	0	0	0	1	1	1	0
3	1	1	1	0	0	0	1
4	1	1	1	1	1	1	1
5	0	0	0	0	0	0	0
6	1	0	1	0	1	0	0
7	1	1	1	1	0	0	1
8	0	0	1	1	1	1	0
9	0	1	1	1	1	1	1
10	0	0	0	0	0	0	0
Sum of the difference between the vacancy characteristic and job choice	3	0	3	3	6	4	

For Vacancy Characteristics: 0 = low and 1 = high

Important Vacancy Characteristics.   Despite the variability in results arising from differing research methods and individual idiosyncracies, the findings from many of these studies overlap enough to enable us to single out perhaps a half-dozen characteristics that are almost always near the top.[3]

- *Pay level*—Pay is important because a person's job is typically the primary source of his or her income. Compared with other vacancy characteristics, pay is often ranked lower in studies that directly ask individuals for their preferences. However, studies that use indirect methods often find that pay is the most important vacancy characteristic.[4]

- *Challenge and responsibility*—For many people work plays a large role in establishing their personal identities. Hence, the challenge and level of responsibility of a job are often important characteristics affecting choice.[5] This seems to be especially true in studies employing direct methods of assessment, where people are explicitly asked what is important in a job.

- *Job security*—Security became a major concern among blue-collar workers in the late 1970s and early 1980s when many labor unions were making wage concessions in return for higher job–security provisions.[6]

Downsizing at all levels of companies in the late 1980s has also made this a growing concern among all types of workers today.

- *Advancement opportunities*—Having opportunities to advance within the organization is important to most people, especially applicants for managerial and professional vacancies.[7] Since promotion opportunities are often limited for staff professionals, some organizations provide dual career ladders (discussed in greater detail in Chapter 14) to create advancement opportunities for professionals.

- *Geographic location*—Some job applicants have strong preferences for where they want to work. An example is someone who needs to stay in (or move to) a particular area because his or her spouse works there. The increasing internationalization of many corporations has also forced many workers to assess just how far they are willing to go (literally) for their company. Many companies need employees to relocate in developing nations, which are considered "hardship posts." Employees' desires to avoid these locations force companies to pay a premium to attract workers to these areas.[8] Moreover, as the "Competing through Globalization" box shows, firms operating in even well-developed foreign locales are increasingly recruiting indigenous people to staff such positions.

- *Employee benefits*—Benefits are a large and ever-increasing expense for most employers, and they frequently figure heavily in published ratings of the "best companies to work for." Many applicants, however, find it hard to evaluate the relative values of different benefits packages. Indeed, studies indicate that even among current employees, many have little awareness of the benefits they receive or their value. Thus, it is not surprising that, relative to other vacancy characteristics, the importance of benefits is rather low.[9] Still, they are an important part of the decision-making process for some workers.

- *Additional job characteristics*—Clearly, the six characteristics just described are not the only things that might make a position attractive. There have been extensive surveys of people's work-related values, and a summary of the characteristics they measure is given in Table 10.2. Any of the characteristics listed there could be the key attribute of a vacancy for a particular individual. There have also been surveys of what are the best companies to work for, and these firms traditionally excel in one or more of the six areas described above or listed in Table 10.2. One widely acknowledged list of the 100 best companies to work for is shown in Table 10.3.

Characteristics of Individuals

Although vacancy characteristics figure heavily in a person's job choice, the person's own characteristics are also important. To help you understand how an individual's personal characteristics influence job choice, we first look at the process by which such decisions are made, then at some of the major differences that affect job choice.

Globalization

RECRUITING JAPANESE MANAGERS: IF YOU CAN'T BEAT THEM, HAVE THEM JOIN YOU

With more and more U.S. companies venturing into Japan each year, the need to find managers who can successfully lead such ventures has never been higher. Increasingly, companies expanding into this market have turned away from recruiting Americans for such posts, and instead have turned to hiring Japanese as top officers in their foreign subsidiaries. One reason for this is that U.S. companies find that it is too expensive to relocate American managers in Tokyo. The kind of life-style most American managers have come to expect is prohibitively expensive to maintain in Tokyo, and companies simply cannot continue to make up the difference in pay. In addition, few American managers have the necessary language skills, contacts, and cultural familiarity with this area to be fully successful there.

Recruiting Japanese managers for these subsidiaries, however, is no easy task either. Japanese executives have different priorities than many American managers, valuing the level of responsibility associated with the position more heavily than salary. It is important for Japanese managers to see that they will play a major role in the organization's overall mission. These managers also look for a commitment on the part of the employer to stay in Japan for the long haul and to provide the manager with the type of job security not typically associated with American corporations. Given Japan's high tax rate, companies must also be flexible in converting salary into noncash benefits such as company automobiles, vacations, or guaranteed loans. Finally, in some cases, the employer needs to recruit not only the manager, but his or her family, staff and mentor as well.

SOURCE: E. Surden, "Courting Local Talent—Hiring the Right Japanese Executive Could Put You in the Lead," *International Business* 4 (1991): 59–60; R. Smith, "In Search of Japanese Executives," *Personnel* 68 (1991): 11.

In our discussion, we attempt to integrate three different perspectives on job choice into a single model that proceeds in stages. This model, shown in Figure 10.2, suggests that a person deciding on a job goes through three stages: a noncompensatory decision stage, a compensatory decision stage leading to the development on an "implicit favorite," then, finally, a terminal stage in which all other jobs are compared with the implicit favorite.

FIGURE 10.2 A Three-Stage, Integrated Model of the Job-Choice Process

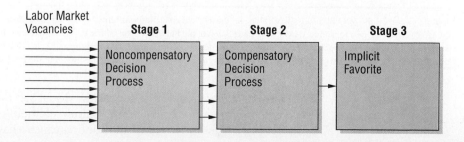

TABLE 10.2

Constructs Assessed by Major Surveys of Work-Related Values

Minnesota Importance Questionnaire	Work Values Inventory	Occupational Values	Job Values and Desires Questionnaire	Occupational Values Inventory
Ability utilization Achievement Activity	Achievement	Use special abilities		Preparation and ability
Advancement				Advancement
Authority		Exercise leadership	Leadership power	
Company policies and practices Compensation	Management Economic returns	Earn good money	Profit	Salary
Co-workers	Associates	Work with people		
Creativity	Creativity	Creative, original	Self-expression	
Independence[a] Moral values Recognition	Way of life		Fame	Personal goal
Responsibility[a] Security Social service	Independence Security Altruism	Free of supervision Secure future Helpful to others	Independence Social service	Security
Social status	Prestige	Social status, prestige	Status, esteem	Prestige
Supervision, human relations Supervision, technical	Supervisory relations			
Variety	Variety			
Working conditions	Surroundings Intellectual stimulation Esthetics	Provide adventure	Interesting experience	Interest and satisfaction

[a] Independence for the MIQ is "I could work alone on the job," whereas Responsibility is "I could make decisions on my own."

Noncompensatory Decision Processes.   Most job decision processes have both noncompensatory and compensatory elements. A **noncompensatory decision process** simply means that one vacancy characteristic is so impor-

TABLE 10.3   The 100 Best Companies to Work for in America

American Cast Iron Pipe (ACIPCO), Birmingham, Ala.

Advanced Micro Devices, Sunnyvale, Calif.

Alagasco (Alabama Gas), Birmingham

Anheuser-Busch, St. Louis

Apogee Enterprises, Minneapolis

Armstrong World Industries, Lancaster, Pa.

Avis, Garden City, N.Y.

Baptist Hospital of Miami, Miami

BE&K (construction), Birmingham, Ala.

Ben & Jerry's Homemade, Waterbury, Vt.

Beth Israel Hospital Boston, Boston

Leo Burnett, Chicago

Chaparral Steel, Midlothian, Texas

Compaq Computer, Houston

Cooper Tire & Rubber, Findlay, Ohio

Corning, Corning, N.Y.

Cray Research, Eagan, Minn.

Cummins Engine, Columbus, Ind.

Dayton Hudson, Minneapolis

Deere, Moline, Ill.

Delta Air Lines, Atlanta

Donnelly (glass), Holland, Mich.

Du Pont, Wilmington, Del.

A.G. Edwards, St. Louis

Erie Insurance Company, Erie, Pa.

Federal Express, Memphis

Fel-Pro, Skokie, Ill.

First Federal Bank of California, Santa Monica

H.B. Fuller Company, St. Paul, Minn.

General Mills, Minneapolis

Goldman, Sachs, New York

W. I. Gore & Associates, Newark, Del.

Great Plains Software, Fargo, N.D.

Hallmark Cards, Kansas City, Mo.

Haworth, Holland, Mich.

Herman Miller, Zeeland, Mich.

Hershey Foods, Hershey, Pa.

Hewitt Associates, Lincolnshire, Ill.

Hewlett-Packard, Palo Alto, Calif.

Honda of America Manufacturing, Marysville, Oh.

IBM, Armonk, N.Y.

Inland Steel Industries, Chicago

Intel, Santa Clara, Calif.

Johnson & Johnson, New Brunswick, N.J.

SC Johnson Wax, Racine, Wis.

Kellogg, Battle Creek, Mich.

Knight-Ridder, Miami

Lands' End, Dodgeville, Wis.

Lincoln Electric, Cleveland

Los Angeles Dodgers, Los Angeles

Lotus Development, Cambridge, Mass.

Lowe's Companies, North Wilkesboro, N.C.

Lyondell Petrochemical, Houston

3M, St. Paul, Minn.

McCormick, Hunt Valley, Md.

Marquette Electronics, Milwaukee

Mary Kay Cosmetics, Dallas

Merck, Whitehouse Station, N.J.

Methodist Hospital, Houston

Microsoft Corporation, Redmond, Wash.

J.P. Morgan & Co., New York

Morrison & Foerster, San Francisco

Moog, East Aurora, N.Y.

Motorola, Schaumburg, Ill.

Nissan Motor Manufacturing, Smyrna, Tenn.

Nordstrom, Seattle

Northwestern Mutual Life, Milwaukee

continued

SOURCE: From *100 Best Companies to Work for in America* by Robert Levering and Milton Moskowitz. Copyright © 1993 by Robert Levering and Milton Moskowitz. Used by permission of Doubleday, a division of Bantam Doubleday Dell Publishing Group, Inc.

TABLE 10.3   *continued*

Odetics, Anaheim, Calif.	Springs Industries, Fort Mill, S.C.
Patagonia, Ventura, Calif.	Steelcase, Grand Rapids, Mich.
J.C. Penney, Plano, Texas	Syntex Corporation, Palo Alto, Calif.
Physio-Control, Redmond, Wash.	Tandem Computers, Cupertino, Calif.
Pitney Bowes, Stanford, Conn.	TDIndustries, Dallas
Polaroid, Cambridge, Mass.	Tennant, Minneapolis
Preston Trucking, Preston, Md.	UNUM (insurance), Portland, Maine
Procter & Gamble, Cincinnati	USAA (insurance), San Antonio
Publix Super Markets, Lakeland, Fla.	US West, Englewood, Colo.
Quad/Graphics, Powaukee, Wis.	Valassis Inserts, Livonia, Mich.
Reader's Digest, Pleasantville, N.Y.	Viking Freight, San Jose, Calif.
REI (recreational equipment), Seattle	Wal-Mart Stores, Bentonville, Ark.
Rosenbluth International, Philadelphia	Wegmans, Rochester, N.Y.
SAS Institute, Cary, N.C.	Weyerhauser, Tacoma, Wash.
J.M. Smucker, Orrville, Ohio	Worthington Industries, Columbus, Ohio
Southwest Airlines, Dallas	Xerox, Stamford, Conn.
Springfield ReManufacturing, Springfield, Mo.	

tant to that person that any job vacancy that fails to meet the person's standard on that characteristic will not be considered—regardless of the job's standing on other dimensions.[10] In other words, "nothing can compensate" for the job's failing to live up to this one standard.

Table 10.4 shows three hypothetical job applicants and three hypothetical jobs. We will use these three people and these three jobs to illuminate several features of the job-choice process. First, we will note that each of the three uses at least one noncompensatory standard when hunting for a job. Person 1, a young unmarried worker, has noncompensatory standards regarding salary and advancement. This person will not consider any job that does not allow for advancement within the organization—regardless of the benefits or location. Person 2, the sole wage earner in a family with many children, has noncompensatory rules for salary and benefits but is flexible on location and advancement. Finally, Person 3, the spouse of a high-wage earner with lucrative benefits, needs to stay within a specific location but is less concerned with other job characteristics.

With thousands of different jobs open at any one time, simple, noncompensatory rules like these are effective in narrowing the number of jobs con-

TABLE 10.4 Three Hypothetical Job Applicants, Their Noncompensatory Standards, and the Characteristics of Three Jobs

Description of Person	Noncompensatory Standard	Description of Job
Person 1 Young, single	*Pay*: At least $35,000 *Benefits*: Uncritical *Advance*: Must promote from within *Location*: Uncritical	Job 1 *Pay*: $40,000 range *Benefits*: Full medical/pension *Advance*: Hires externally *Location*: Local positions
Person 2 Sole wage earner for large family	*Pay*: At least $40,000 *Benefits*: Full medical/pension *Advancement*: Uncritical *Location*: Uncritical	Job 2 *Pay*: $45,000 range *Benefits*: Limited *Advancement*: Promotes from within *Location*: Local positions
Person 3 Spouse of a high-wage earner	*Pay*: At least $30,000 *Benefits*: Uncritical *Advancement*: Uncritical *Location*: Must be local	Job 3 *Pay*: $50,000 range *Benefits*: Full medical/pension *Advancement*: Promotes from within *Location*: International locale

sidered. Research also tends to support the use of noncompensatory rules, at least during the early stages of looking for a job.[11]

When one examines the three job descriptions in Table 10.4, several facts become apparent. First, Person 1's second noncompensatory standard for advancement eliminates Job 1 from consideration. Even though the pay and benefits for this position are acceptable, these factors cannot compensate, in this person's mind, for the lack of advancement opportunities. Similarly, Job 2 is unacceptable to Person 2 because of its limited benefits package, and Job 3 is unacceptable to Person 3 because it entails an international assignment.

Compensatory Decision Processes. Once the job field has been narrowed using noncompensatory standards, individuals tend to engage in a more refined decision process that allows for compensatory relationships among factors. In other words, positive features on one dimension compensate for "acceptable, yet not outstanding" features on other dimensions. In this manner, the individual seeks to determine which of the various "acceptable" vacancies is most attractive.

One theory that is useful in understanding how this stage of the decision-making process works is **expectancy theory**.[12] According to expectancy theory, the attractiveness of any job is a function of three factors; valence, instrumentality, and expectancy.

Valence is the level of satisfaction the person expects to receive from a job that ranks high in some attribute. For example, the third column of Table 10.5 expands on Table 10.4 by providing the valences, expressed in points, of each of our three job seekers. Points are assigned to each dimension. The dimension with the most valence gets 4 points, the next most valent dimension gets 3 points, and so on. Notice that for Person 1, Job 1 has been eliminated using noncompensatory standards, so only Jobs 2 and 3 are analyzed in terms of valences. The table shows that although both pay and advancement are important for Person 1, advancement is a little more important than pay. Also, although location is not as critical as pay and advancement, location is slightly more important than benefits.

The second component of expectancy theory, **instrumentality**, is the perceived relationship between choosing a particular job and obtaining a desired outcome, such as high pay or lucrative benefits. The fourth column of Table 10.5 displays the instrumentalities for each of our three job seekers. These are expressed in terms of the perceived probability of receiving desirable levels of each outcome by choosing various jobs. So, Person 1 perceives a relatively high probability of receiving high pay by taking Job 2 (.9) but sees a relatively low probability of receiving lucrative benefits (.3). Since instrumentalities reflect perceptions and not necessarily reality, two different people can perceive different instrumentalities for the same job. In our example in Table 10.5, Person 3 sees a slightly higher probability of receiving desirable benefits by accepting Job 2 (.5) than does Person 1 (.3).

In expectancy theory, the relative attractiveness of a job is determined by combining valences and instrumentalities—specifically, by multiplying valences and instrumentalities, summing these for each job, and then declaring the job with the highest value the most attractive alternative. These calculations are shown in the fifth column of Table 10.5. Note that, according to this theory, Person 1 is most attracted to Job 2 (8.0). Person 3 is also most attracted to Job 2 (8.4). Person 2 is equally attracted to Job 1 and Job 3 (both at 7.3).

The final component of this theory of job choice is the construct for which the theory was named, **expectancy**, which is the perceived probability that a person can obtain a job. People may be highly attracted to certain jobs yet not try to pursue them if they believe there is little chance that they would be selected for them.

In expectancy theory, the motivation to try to obtain a job is a multiplicative function of the job's attractiveness and the person's expectancy. In other words, individuals multiply the overall attractiveness of the job and the perceived expectancy of obtaining the job (expressed as a probability ranging from .00 to 1.00). The sixth column of Table 10.5 shows the expectancies of the three job applicants in our running example, and the seventh column shows the product obtained by multiplying this expectancy times the attractiveness score derived in the fifth column.

TABLE 10.5

The Effect of Compensatory Decision-Making Processes on Three Job Applicants Looking at Three Jobs

Applicant	Job Vacancy	Valence Ratings	Instrumentalities for Each Job (0.9=High Probability)	Attractiveness of Job (Sum of Valence × Instrumentalities)	Expectancy	Motivation to Pursue Job (Attractiveness × Expectancy)
Person 1	Job 1	Pay—3 Benefits—1 Advancement—4 Location—2	Eliminated by noncompensatory standards			
	Job 2	Pay—3 Benefits—1 Advancement—4 Location—2	.9 .3 .8 .9	3 × .9 = 2.7 1 × .3 = 0.3 4 × .8 = 3.2 2 × .9 = 1.8 8.0	.8	8.0 × .8 = 6.40
	Job 3	Pay—3 Benefits—1 Advancement—4 Location–2	.8 .9 .8 .1	3 × .8 = 2.4 1 × .9 = 0.9 4 × .8 = 3.2 2 × .1 = 0.2 6.7	.9	6.7 × .9 = 6.03
Person 2	Job 1	Pay–4 Benefits–3 Advancement—2 Location—1	.8 .9 .3 .8	4 × .8 = 3.2 3 × .9 = 2.7 2 × .3 = 0.6 1 × .8 = 0.8 7.3	.8	7.3 × .8 = 5.84
	Job 2	Pay—4 Benefits—3 Advancement—2 Location—1	Eliminated by noncompensatory standards			
	Job 3	Pay—4 Benefits—3 Advancement—2 Location—1	.8 .8 .8 .1	4 x .8 = 3.2 3 × .8 = 2.4 2 × .8 = 1.6 1 × .1 = 0.1 7.3	.8	7.3 x 8 = 5.84
Person 3	Job 1	Pay—2 Benefits—1 Advancement—3 Location—4	.8 .8 .4 .8	2 × .8 = 1.6 1 × .8 = 0.8 3 × .4 = 1.2 4 × .8 = 3.2 6.8	.6	6.8 × .6 = 4.08
	Job 2	Pay—2 Benefits—1 Advancement—3 Location—4	.8 .5 .9 .9	2 × .8 = 1.6 1 × .5 = 0.5 3 × .9 = 2.7 4 × .9 = 3.6 8.4	.5	8.4 × .5 = 4.2
	Job 3	Pay—2 Benefits—1 Advancement—3 Location—4	Eliminated by noncompensatory standards			

Notice from this example that Person 3 generally holds lower expectancies for obtaining the various jobs than Persons 1 and 2. Indeed, although Person 3 is almost equally attracted to Job 2 as person 1 is, his or her lowered expectancy results in a much lower level of motivation to seek that job. Notice, too, that if expectancy approaches .00, the person will not be motivated to seek the job regardless of how attractive it is. Indeed, low expectancies seem to be one of the underlying problems for unemployed teenagers like Alex Perez, who was introduced in the vignette that opened this chapter.

Developing the Implicit Favorite.   Although noncompensatory decision-making processes are effective at eliminating a huge number of jobs from consideration, too many acceptable jobs are still left to consider using a time-consuming process such as expectancy theory for each one of them. For example, if the job field were narrowed down to ten acceptable jobs, this would imply a detailed expectancy analysis and comparison for 45 pairs of jobs (10 x 9/2).

Some researchers have speculated that job seekers use a complex compensatory process like that described by expectancy theory for a small number of jobs in order to arrive at an "implicit favorite."[13] This implicit favorite then becomes the standard to which all new vacancies are compared. Thus, if there are ten acceptable jobs, maybe only two or three of these will be analyzed in a compensatory fashion to arrive at the implicit favorite. The remaining seven or eight vacancies will then be compared only to the implicit favorite, not all the other possible jobs. This would reduce the number of detailed comparisons from 45 pairs to around 10 pairs of jobs.

Some researchers have also speculated that in conducting these comparisons, a decision maker is biased towards the initial implicit favorite.[14] In other words, that implicit favorite will only be replaced by a "new implicit favorite" if the new job is significantly better than the original. You might remember from Table 10.5 that the expectancy analysis for Person 2 suggested that Jobs 1 and 3 were equally attractive. According to the implicit-favorite provision, this suggests that the job that was evaluated first (Job 1) may have an edge over the job evaluated last (Job 3), even though the jobs are equally attractive according to expectancy theory.

Individual Differences in Decision-Making Processes.   Although the model laid out in Figure 10.2 is generic and could apply to all persons, in fact there are wide individual differences in the search processes people employ. Individuals with little experience in job hunting may employ only noncompensatory processes and accept the first job they find acceptable. Individuals with more experience (especially those with many bad experiences) may spend a huge amount of time analyzing in detail many jobs, yet still be reluctant to call off the search for new implicit favorites.

Individual differences in people's needs and values also come into play. Because of their different life situations, the three people in our example have wildly different rankings of what is most important in a job. These differences have obvious implications for their choices.

Individuals can also differ in their knowledge about themselves, various occupations, and industries or companies. John Crites has developed the concept of **vocational maturity** to capture these and other factors that make some individuals more effective in making job choices than others.[15] Figure 10.3 shows Crites's model of career maturity and the dimensions that constitute this model. The Adult Vocational Maturity Inventory was developed to assess individuals' standings on career maturity, and individuals' ratings on this scale have been found to relate to occupational success.[16]

THE ROLE OF HUMAN RESOURCE RECRUITMENT

Now that we have examined the job selection process from the job seeker's perspective, it is important to look at organizations' recruitment practices. Human resource recruitment refers to any organizational activity that is designed to affect (1) the number of people who apply for vacancies, (2) the type of people who apply for them, and/or (3) the likelihood that those applying for vacancies will accept positions if offered.[17] The goal of an organizational recruitment program is to ensure that when a vacancy occurs the organization has a number of reasonably qualified applicants (who would find the job acceptable) to choose from.

The goal of the recruiting, in other words, is not simply to generate large numbers of applicants. If these applicants are unqualified, the organization will incur great expense in personnel selection (discussed more fully in the next chapter), but few vacancies will actually be filled.

Neither is the goal of a personnel recruitment program to finely discriminate among reasonably qualified applicants. Recruiting new personnel and selecting new personnel are both complex processes. Each task is hard enough to accomplish successfully, even when one is well focused. Organizations explicitly trying to do both at the same time will probably not do either well.

Finally, the goal of human resource recruitment is not to trick applicants into accepting a job they would not find acceptable if they knew more about it. The biggest reason new employees quit jobs is unmet expectations.[18] Perhaps the biggest cause of unmet expectations is inflated job descriptions.

Because of strategic differences among companies (see Chapter 2), the importance assigned to recruitment may differ.[19] In general, however, all companies have to make decisions in three areas of recruiting: (1) personnel policies, which affect the kinds of jobs the company has to offer; (2) recruitment sources used to solicit applicants, which affects the kind of people who apply; and (3) the characteristics and behaviors of the recruiter, which affect the perceived fit between the applicant and the job. We will examine each of these in the remaining sections of this chapter.

FIGURE 10.3   A Model of Career Maturity

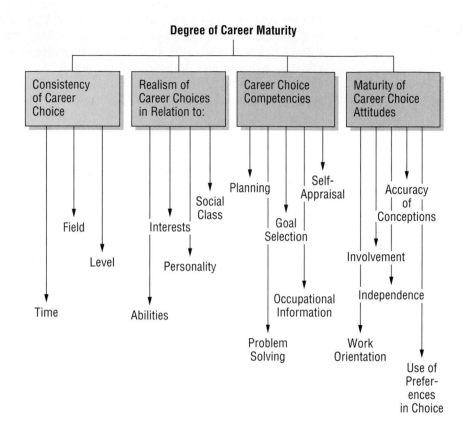

SOURCE: From John O. Crites, *Theory and Research Handbook, Career Maturity Inventory*, p. 6. Copyright © 1973 by McGraw-Hill, Inc. Reproduced by permission of the publisher, CTB/McGraw-Hill, Del Monte Research Park, Monterey, CA 93940. All rights reserved. Published in the U.S.A.

Personnel Policies

Personnel policies is a generic term we use to refer to organizational decisions that affect the nature of the vacancies for which people are recruited. If the research on recruitment makes one thing clear, it is that characteristics of the vacancy are more important than recruiters or recruiting sources when it comes to predicting job choice.[20]

For example, if we were to return to the three people and three jobs shown in Tables 10.4 and 10.5, we would see that in the absence of recruiter influence, one of the jobs (Job 2) has attracted two people (Persons 1 and 3), whereas the other two jobs have attracted only one person. Hence, because of these differences in the nature of the vacancy, the organization with a vacancy in Job 2 can be choosy in selecting a new employee. The organizations offering Jobs 1 and 3, however, need to compete for the one person (Person 2) who would be attracted to their vacancies.

In discussing the job-choice process, we isolated several job or organization characteristics most applicants deem desirable. Many of the personnel policies that can be used to affect job characteristics operate by affecting these specific features of the vacancy.

Internal versus External Recruiting.   One desirable feature of a vacancy, which we mentioned earlier, is that it provides ample opportunity for advancement and promotion. One organizational policy that affects this is the degree to which the company "promotes from within"—that is, recruits for upper-level vacancies internally rather than externally. Companies that promote from within often employ **job posting** programs: vacancies are publicized on bulletin boards, in company newsletters, or in memos.

We discuss internal versus external recruiting both here and in "Recruitment Sources" later in this chapter because this policy affects the nature of both the job and the individuals who apply. For now, we focus on the effects that promote-from-within policies have on job characteristics, noting that such policies make it clear to applicants that there are opportunities for advancement within the company. These opportunities spring not just from the first vacancy but from the vacancy created when a person in the company fills that vacancy. For example, in a company with three levels of management, a vacancy at the third level that is filled from within may "trickle down," creating a vacancy at the second level. This, in turn, creates a vacancy at the first level. When promotions are perceived to be based on merit, this can lead to a dynamic climate where people are highly motivated. Even opportunities for horizontal movement within the organization may be perceived as desirable from the applicant's perspective. Horizontal movement at least provides an opportunity to develop new skills or to escape from a poor initial job–person match.

Lead-the-Market Pay Strategies.   Because pay is an important job characteristic for almost all applicants, companies that take a "lead-the-market" approach to pay—that is, a policy of paying higher-than-current market wages—have a distinct advantage in recruiting. Pay can also be used to make up for a job's less desirable features—for example, paying higher wages to employees who have to work midnight shifts. These kinds of specific shift differentials or other forms of more generic "compensating differentials" will be discussed in more detail in later chapters that focus on compensation strategies. We merely note here that "lead" policies make any given vacancy appear more attractive to applicants.

It is worth noting that "lead-the-market" policies also put pressure on both the recruitment and selection systems to deliver the best employees. The only way a company can afford to pay higher wages is to have higher productivity, higher quality, greater innovation, or lower unit costs. Surprisingly, there is actually very little evidence that adopting such policies leads to such outcomes.[21]

Employment-at-Will Policies.   Employment-at-will policies state that either party in the employment relationship can terminate that relationship at any time, regardless of cause. Companies that do not have employment-at-will provisions typically have extensive **due process** policies. Due process policies formally lay out the steps an employee can take to appeal a termination decision. Recent court decisions have increasingly eroded employers' rights to terminate employees with impunity.[22] To protect themselves from wrongful discharge suits, employers have been encouraged to state explicitly, in all formal recruiting documentation, that the employment is "at will."

Some authors have gone so far as to suggest that all mention of due process should be eliminated from company handbooks, personnel manuals, and recruiting brochures.[23] Although this may have some legal advantages, job security is an important feature to many job applicants. Organizational recruiting materials that emphasize due process, rights of appeal, and grievance mechanisms send a message that job security is high; employment-at-will policies suggest the opposite. Research indicates that job applicants find companies with due process policies more attractive than companies with employment-at-will policies. Employment-at-will companies are only considered equally attractive to due process companies when the lack of job security is offset by higher-than-average compensation and benefits levels.[24]

Image Advertising.   Organizations often advertise specific vacancies (discussed later in "Recruitment Sources"). Sometimes, however, organizations advertise just to promote themselves as a good place to work in general. **Image advertising** is particularly important for companies in highly competitive labor markets that perceive themselves as having a bad image.[25]

We noted earlier that the challenge and responsibility of a job is an attractive characteristic for many people. Dow Chemical's $60 million television campaign in the early 1990s hammered home the message that "Dow lets you do great things." This message was clearly aimed at affecting the general public's view of the nature of the work at Dow. It was also an attempt to offset recurring negative publicity resulting from controversies surrounding the production of napalm (1970s), Agent Orange (1980s), and faulty breast implants (1990s).[26] This negative publicity sometimes affected Dow's ability to recruit on college campuses. In a similar fashion, the U.S. Army's "Be all that you can be" campaign pursued a similar objective. These advertisements focused on the challenge associated with army jobs. They also attempted to offset certain negative attributes of the work, such as the fact that, in some of its jobs at certain times, other people are systematically trying to kill you.

Because a vacancy's major characteristics play such a large role in job choice, the kinds of personnel policies just described clearly aid organizational recruitment efforts. This can be illustrated by returning to our running example from Tables 10.4 and 10.5. Currently, Job 1 is contending with

Job 3 to attract the one interested person (Person 2). If this company were to change its policy about hiring from within, all three applicants might rate it as the most attractive.

Almost any job characteristic can be used as an inducement to attract one set of people or another.[27] A company could emphasize flexible benefit plans, pleasant coworkers, shortened work weeks, on-site daycare, and literally hundreds of other job or organizational characteristics as part of the organization's personnel policies. Yet, as important as job characteristics are, it remains true that half the job-choice process has to do with the person making the choice. Organizations can influence the type of people both indirectly, by employing various sources of recruits, or directly, by having these people talk to organizational recruiters. We examine these two avenues in our next sections.

Recruitment Sources

The sources from which a company recruits potential employees are a critical aspect of its overall recruitment strategy. The total labor market is expansive; any single organization needs to draw from only a fraction of that total. The size and nature of the fraction that applies for an organization's vacancies will be affected by how (and to whom) the organization communicates its vacancies.[28] In the story that opened this chapter, many inner-city employers were failing to reach a vast number of minority youths because they were recruiting only at magnet and Catholic schools. These minority youths might have been reached by alternative recruiting methods, such as relying on state employment agencies or local newspapers. In this section, we examine the different sources from which recruits can be drawn, highlighting the advantages and disadvantages of each.

Internal versus External Sources. We discussed internal versus external sources of recruits earlier in this chapter and focused on the positive effects that internal recruiting can have on recruits' perceptions of job characteristics. We will now discuss this issue again, but with a focus on how using internal sources affects the kinds of people who are recruited.

In general, relying on internal sources offers a company several advantages.[29] First, it generates a sample of applicants who are well-known to the firm. Internal applicants have a history with the organization, so the company has much more information about them than can be learned from even the most intensive testing program. Second, these applicants are relatively knowledgeable about the company's vacancies, which minimizes the possibility of inflated expectations about the job. Third, it is generally cheaper and faster to fill vacancies internally.

With all these advantages, you may ask why any organization would ever employ external recruiting methods. There are several good reasons why organizations might decide to recruit externally.[30] First, for entry-level positions, and perhaps even for some specialized upper-level positions, there may not be any internal recruits from which to draw. Second, bringing in outsiders may expose the organization to new ideas or new ways of doing business. Using only internal recruitment can result in a work force whose members all think alike and who therefore may be poorly suited to innovation.[31] This would be a particular problem for a company in a dynamic environment that requires a flexible approach. Third, hiring externally may help the organization meet its goals for developing a work force that is diverse in terms of race or sex. Internal recruiting can lead to a homogeneous work force,[32] which can create legal problems because of underutilization of some protected groups.

For whatever reasons, it is a fact that few companies can or wish to recruit strictly from within. When turning to external sources, they encounter a wide and varied menu of options.

Direct Applicants and Referrals.   **Direct applicants** are people who apply for a vacancy without prompting from the organization. **Referrals** are people who are prompted to apply by someone within the organization. These two sources of recruits share some characteristics that make them excellent sources from which to draw.

First, many direct applicants are to some extent already "sold" on the organization. Most of them have done some homework and concluded that there is enough fit between themselves and the vacancy to warrant their submitting an application. This process is called "self-selection," and when it works effectively, it takes a great deal of pressure off the organization's recruiting and selection systems. A form of aided self-selection occurs with referrals too. Current employees (who are knowledgeable of both the vacancy and the person they are referring) do their homework and conclude that there is a fit between the person and the vacancy; they then sell the person on the job.

Although results from studies of recruitment sources are somewhat mixed, it should not be surprising to learn that direct applicants and walk-in candidates tend to show lower turnover and better work attitudes compared with candidates recruited from other sources (especially advertisements).[33] When one figures into these results the low costs of these sources, they clearly stand out as one of the best sources of new hires. Indeed, some employers even offer financial incentives to current employees for referring applicants who are accepted and perform acceptably on the job (e.g., stay 180 days).[34] The only problem with these sources, especially referrals, is that they tend to be relatively homogeneous in race and sex. If a company is underutilizing minority workers, using referrals from current employees may only exacerbate the problem.

Advertisements in Newspapers and Periodicals.   Advertisements to recruit personnel are ubiquitous, even though they typically generate less desirable recruits than direct applications or referrals, and at greater expense. However, since few employers can fill all their vacancies with direct applications and referrals, some form of advertising is usually needed. Moreover, an employer can take many steps to increase the effectiveness of this recruitment method.

The two most important questions to ask in designing a job advertisement are: (1) What do we need to say? and (2) To whom do we need to say it? With respect to the first question, many organizations fail to adequately communicate the specifics of the vacancy. Ideally, an employer using advertising as a recruitment method would attract the same kind of recruits that would result from direct applications and referrals. That is, persons reading the ad would get enough information to evaluate the job and its requirements, allowing them to make a well-informed judgment about the job and their own qualifications for it. This could mean running longer advertisements, which costs more. However, these additional costs should be evaluated against the costs of processing a huge number of applicants who are not reasonably qualified or who would not find the job acceptable once they learn more about it.

In terms of whom to reach with this message, the organization placing the advertisement has to decide which medium it will use. The classified section of local newspapers is the most common medium. It is a relatively inexpensive means of reaching a large number of people within a specified geographic area who are currently looking for work (or at least interested enough to be reading the classifieds). On the downside, this medium does not allow an organization to target skill levels very well. Typically, classified ads are read by many people who are either over- or underqualified for the position. Moreover, people who are not looking for work rarely read the classifieds, and thus, this is not the right medium for luring them away from their current employers. Specially targeted journals or periodicals may be better than general newspapers at reaching a specific part of the overall labor market. In addition, employers are increasingly using television—particularly cable television—as a reasonably priced way of reaching people who may or may not be actively looking for work.[35]

Public Employment Agencies.   The Social Security Act of 1935 requires that everyone receiving unemployment compensation be registered with a local state employment office. These state employment offices work with the United States Employment Service (USES) to try to ensure that unemployed individuals eventually get off state aid and back on employer payrolls. To accomplish this, agencies collect information from the unemployed about their skills and experiences. They also perform extensive testing using the General Aptitude Test Battery as an index of a variety of potential worker aptitudes (e.g., quantitative aptitude, mechanical aptitude, etc.).

Employers can register their job vacancies with their local state employment office, and the agency will attempt to find someone suitable using its computerized inventory of local unemployed individuals. The agency makes referrals to the organization at no charge, and these individuals can be interviewed or tested by the employer for potential vacancies. Because of certain legislative mandates, state unemployment offices often have specialized "desks" for minorities, handicapped individuals, and Vietnam-era veterans. Thus, this is an excellent source for employers who feel they are currently underutilizing any of these subgroups.

On the downside, some employers in the past have questioned whether some applicants referred by state employment services have a true desire to work. Any unemployed individual who wants to receive unemployment compensation *must* register—even those who may not really want to work. Since many minimum-wage jobs do not include health-care coverage, they are not as attractive as being unemployed when Medicaid (a federal program providing health-care coverage for the unemployed) is figured into the equation. Still, because of its low cost and potential screening capacity, this recruitment method can be a good source of applicants, especially when complemented by the firm's own internal screening mechanism (i.e., the employer's own work aptitude and motivation tests).

Private Employment Agencies.   Public employment agencies serve primarily the blue-collar labor market; private employment agencies perform much the same service for the white-collar labor market. Unlike public agencies, however, private employment agencies charge the organization for the referrals. Another difference between private and public employment agencies is that one doesn't have to be unemployed to use a private employment agency.

Because they are not subject to many of the legal mandates that public employment agencies face, private agencies can often be more selective in the development of their personnel inventories. Some private agencies have abused this freedom and have been found to be illegally discriminating against minorities. For example, the EEOC recently settled a suit against an agency called Interplace for $2 million. According to the EEOC, Interplace used a series of code terms such as "English as first" (indicating a preference for Caucasian employees), "Suite 30-40" (indicating a preference for younger workers), and "Don't talk to Maria" (indicating that Hispanics will not be considered) to assist employers in violating the provisions of the Civil Rights Act.[36]

Taken together, public employment agencies and law-abiding private employment agencies often serve as complementary sources that are especially helpful to small companies that need to fill vacancies quickly. As the "Competing through Social Responsibility" box shows, widespread layoffs among large organizations in the 1990s made these two types of agencies particularly good sources for older, experienced managerial workers who may have a great deal to offer small companies.

Executive Search Firms.   One special type of private employment agency is the so-called executive search firm (ESF). These agencies are often referred to as "headhunters" because, unlike the other sources we have examined, they operate almost exclusively with people who are currently employed. For example, when BMW sought to open its new U.S. plant, it used an executive search firm to help "liberate" Allen Kinzer and Edwin

COMPETING THROUGH

Social Responsibility

SMALL BUSINESS REAPS BENEFITS OF COMPANY LAYOFFS

The most recent recession has sometimes been referred to as the "white-collar recession" because so many of those laid off were in professional and managerial job categories at some of the larger Fortune 500 companies. These newly unemployed individuals are typically older than the usual job applicant, and many have been victims of age discrimination in their attempt to return to work. While some employers discriminate against this group, other companies—especially small businesses—have jumped at this rare opportunity to acquire experienced talent at bargain prices.

For many small businesses, several factors make hiring ex–big business executives and professionals enhance their competitive advantage. First, these managers can help small businesses organize and develop the structure necessary to grow beyond their current size. Second, former middle-level managers from large firms possess technical skills based on years of formal training paid for by their former employer. Third, many of these managers have developed contacts within their industry that immediately open up new markets or other opportunities for the small business that hires them.

For example, when Reidville Hydraulics needed help expanding, rather than recruiting a manager from another small business, they tapped Larry Becker, a laid-off executive from the Swedish multinational conglomerate, Axel Johnson AB. Becker offered his new company business planning, marketing, and other skills that the small company could never have developed internally.

Recruiting from this segment of the labor pool is not without risks, however. Some small businesses find that ex-executives from large companies have skills in delegation and internal politicking that have no place in a small, hands-on business. Also, small businesses require executives to fulfill multiple roles and do not allow for the same degree of specialization possible in large ones. Small businesses that can surmount these obstacles, however, often can secure the type of talent needed to grow into something other than small businesses.

SOURCE: J. S. Pouliot, "A Hiring Bonanza: Laid-off Managers," *Nation's Business,* November, 1992, 44; M. Selz, "Small Concerns: Tap Talent Pool of Ex-Managers," *The Wall Street Journal,* December 5, 1992, B1.

Buker from Honda. These two executives were vice-presidents for Honda's U.S. operations, and BMW was looking to recreate the success that Honda had by recruiting these individuals.[37]

Dealing with executive search firms is a sometimes sensitive process because executives may not want to advertise their availability for fear of their current employer's reaction. Thus, ESFs serve as an important confidentiality buffer between the employer and the recruit. Indeed, in the initial stages of recruiting, the two sides (employer and recruit) may be anonymous to each other.

ESFs are expensive to employ for both direct and indirect reasons. Directly, ESFs often charge one-third to one-half of the salary of the executive who is eventually placed. Indirectly, employers who use ESFs wind up having to lure people, not from unemployment, but from jobs that they may be quite satisfied with. A company in a growing industry may have to offer as much as 50 percent more than the executive's current pay to prompt him or her to take the new job.[38] It may also get involved in a costly bidding war for a specific person, which could mean providing a signing bonus. Indeed, the difficulty associated with trying to fill top positions externally provides yet another reason for adopting human resource policies that allow for internal recruitment at this level.

Colleges and Universities.   As most readers of this text are aware, all colleges and universities have their own placement services that seek to help their alumni obtain employment. Because newly minted college graduates make up a large part of the entry-level market for professional, technical, and managerial vacancies, many employers that hire in these job categories use such services. Organizations tend to focus especially on colleges that have strong reputations in areas for which they have critical needs (chemical engineering, public accounting, etc.).[39]

Many employers have found that to effectively compete for the best students, they need to do more than just sign prospective graduates up for interview slots. One of the best ways to establish a stronger presence on a campus is with a college internship program. For example, Dun & Bradstreet funds a summer intern program for minority MBA students and often hires these interns for full-time positions when they graduate.[40]

These kinds of programs allow an organization to get early access to potential applicants and to assess their capacities directly. For the interns, these programs, especially when the intern has some degree of autonomy, are a good way to clarify work-related needs and values.[41] The interns also get firsthand experience with the organization, which creates more realistic expectations. Internship programs promote the kinds of self-selection processes that enhance outcomes for both parties.

Internship programs do not need to be limited to college campuses, however. Some companies in inner-city areas work with local agencies to provide summer internships or jobs for teenage youths. Thus, while Alex Perez, from our opening story, was hanging out, Asalmah Muhammad, an 18-year-old from Brooklyn, was working with Mitsui Corporation as part of a summer jobs program. Not only did this experience provide Asalmah with his first structured work experience, it was also the first time he had ever spoken to a Japanese person. Programs like the one that placed Asalmah attest to the fact that joint government–private employer programs can at least make a dent in the teenage unemployment problem.[42]

On campus, another way of increasing one's presence is to participate in university job fairs. In general, a **job fair** is a place where many employers gather for a short time to meet large numbers of potential job applicants. Although job fairs can be held anywhere (e.g., at a hotel or convention center), campuses are ideal locations because of the large number of well-educated, yet unemployed, individuals who live there. Participation in job fairs is a rather inexpensive means of generating an on-campus presence, and it can even provide some one-on-one dialogue with potential recruits, the kind of dialogue that could not be achieved through less interactive media like news-

Technology & Structure

DATABASES POOL AVAILABLE TALENT

Although they have not been around long enough to be evaluated seriously, computerized recruitment databases are being created with increasing frequency. Indeed, in the last five years alone (1987 to 1992) there has been a fourfold increase in the number of firms offering such services. Most of them charge a small fee both to the recruits, who submit their names and résumés, and to the company that then searches the database. Information collected on recruits is usually standardized and includes name, address, educational background, work experience and goals, and perhaps desired salary.

Some databases specialize in African American or Hispanic job applicants. For example, Executive Telecom System Inc. has developed the Minority Graduate Database, which contains the electronic résumés of over 12,000 minority college graduates. Hispanic Business Inc. has developed a smaller database called HispanData with up to 5,000 minority résumés.

Relatively speaking, these kinds of databases are a fast and inexpensive means of obtaining potential recruits. The quality of the recruits obtained from computer databases is a question for future research. We could expect that this source is best for recruiting recent college graduates. Currently employed individuals might be reluctant to submit their names to databases that are this open to public scrutiny, and lower-level applicants may not be as familiar with this kind of technology.

SOURCE: A. Bargerstock, "Computer Databases: Windows to More Effective Recruitment," *Human Resource Professional* 4 (1991): 9–14; J. A. Breaugh, *Recruitment: Science and Practice* (Boston: PWS-Kent, 1992); R. Willis, "Recruitment: Playing the Database game," *Personnel* 67 (1990): 25–29; J. Koch, "Finding Qualified Hispanic Candidates," *Recruitment Today* 3 (1990): 35.

paper advertisements. On the other hand, a potential recruit attending a job fair may run into so many employers that his or her memory of any particular one may be weak without special effort on the part of the employer.

Finally, as the "Competing through Technology and Structure" box indicates, many of the advantages of a typical job fair can now be gained without ever getting recruiter and recruit in the same physical location. Computer recruitment databases allow employers to conduct searches that are widely distributed geographically, without ever leaving the home office.

Evaluating the Quality of a Source. Because there are few rules about the quality of a given source for a given vacancy, it is generally a good idea for employers to monitor the quality of all their recruitment sources. One means of accomplishing this is to develop and compare **yield ratios** for each source.[43] Yield ratios express the percentage of applicants who successfully move from one stage of the recruitment and selection process to the next. Comparing yield ratios for different sources helps determine which is best or most efficient for the type of vacancy being investigated. Data on cost per hire is also useful in establishing the efficiency of a given source.

TABLE 10.6   Hypothetical Yield Ratios for Five Different Recruitment Sources

	Recruiting Source				
	Local University	Renowned University	Employee Referrals	Newspaper Ad	Executive Search Firms
Resumes generated	200	400	50	500	20
Interview offers accepted	175	100	45	400	20
Yield ratio	87%	25%	90%	80%	100%
Judged acceptable	100	95	40	50	19
Yield ratio	57%	95%	89%	12%	95%
Accept employment offers	90	10	35	25	15
Yield ratio	90%	11%	88%	50%	79%
Cumulative yield ratio	90/200 45%	10/400 3%	35/50 70%	25/500 5%	15/20 75%
Cost	$30,000	$50,000	$15,000	$20,000	$90,000
Cost per hire	$333	$5,000	$428	$800	$6,000

Table 10.6 shows hypothetical yield ratios and cost-per-hire data for five different recruitment sources. For the job vacancies generated by this company, the best two sources of recruits are local universities and employee referral programs. Newspaper advertisements generate the largest number of recruits, but relatively few of these are qualified for the position. Recruiting at nationally renowned universities generates highly qualified applicants, but relatively few of them ultimately accept positions. Finally, executive search firms generate a small list of highly qualified and interested applicants, but this is an expensive source compared with other alternatives.

Recruiters

The last part of the model presented in Figure 10.1 that we will discuss is the recruiter. We discuss the recruiter this late in the chapter to reinforce our earlier observation that the recruiter often gets involved late in the process. In many cases, by the time a recruiter meets some applicants, they have already made up their minds about what they desire in a job and what the current job has to offer.

Also, in dual-purpose interviews (i.e., in which the recruiter is trying both to attract the candidate and to evaluate the candidate's appropriate-

FIGURE 10.4   Relative Impact of the Recruiter on Various
Recruitment Interview Outcomes

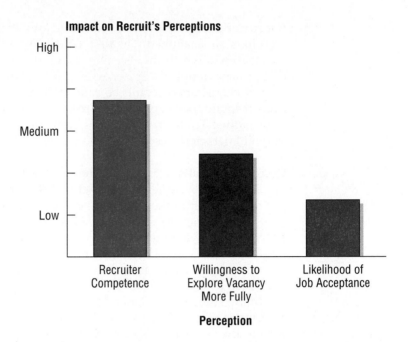

ness for the job), the applicant's anxiety in trying to make a good impression may have deleterious effects on his or her ability to evaluate information supplied by the recruiter.[44]

Finally, many applicants approach the recruiter with some degree of skepticism. Knowing that it is the recruiter's job to sell them on a vacancy, some applicants may discount what the recruiter says relative to what they have heard from other sources (e.g., friends, magazine articles, professors). For these and other reasons, recruiters' characteristics and behaviors seem to have little impact on applicants' job choices. Moreover, as shown in Figure 10.4, whatever impact a recruiter does have on an applicant lessens as one moves from reaction criteria (i.e., how the applicant felt about the recruiter) toward job-choice criteria (i.e., whether the applicant takes the job).[45]

We will discuss three recruiter attributes: (1) where he or she comes from in the organization—that is, functional area; (2) what the recruiter's personal traits are; and (3) what kinds of behaviors the recruiter engages in— particularly, how realistic he or she is in portraying a job's negative aspects.

Recruiter's Functional Area.   Most organizations must choose whether their recruiters are specialists in human resources or experts at particular jobs (e.g., supervisors or job incumbents). Some studies indicate that applicants find a job less attractive and the recruiter less credible when he or she is a personnel specialist.[46] This does not completely discount the role of personnel specialists in recruiting, but it does indicate that such specialists need to take extra steps to ensure that applicants perceive them as knowledgeable and credible.

Recruiter's Traits.   Two traits stand out when applicants' reaction to recruiters are examined. The first, which could be called "warmth," reflects the degree to which the recruiter seems to care about the applicant and is enthusiastic about his or her potential to contribute to the company. The second characteristic could be called "informativeness." In general, applicants respond more positively to recruiters who are perceived as warm and informative. These characteristics seem more important than such demographic characteristics as age, sex, or race.[47]

Recruiter's Realism.   Perhaps the most well-researched aspect of recruiting deals with the level of realism that the recruiter incorporates into his or her message. Since the recruiter's job is to attract candidates, there is some pressure to exaggerate the positive features of the vacancy while simultaneously downplaying the negative features. On the other hand, if the recruiter goes too far, the candidate can be misled and lured into taking the job under false pretenses. This can lead to a serious case of unmet expectations and, overall, to a high job-turnover rate.[48]

Many studies have looked at the capacity of "realistic job previews" to circumvent this problem and help minimize early job turnover. On the whole, the research suggests that the effect of realistic job previews on eventual turnover is weak and inconsistent.[49] Certainly, the idea that one can go overboard in selling a vacancy to a recruit—to the detriment of both the person and the organization—has merit. However, the belief that informing people about the negative characteristics of the job will "inoculate" them to such characteristics seems unwarranted based on the research conducted to date.

Thus, we return to the conclusion that the decisions an organization makes about personnel policies that directly affect the job's attributes (i.e., pay, security, advancement opportunities, and so on) will probably be more important than recruiter traits and behaviors in affecting job choice. If the job has characteristics that make it unsatisfying to most applicants, the recruiter can do little to solve this problem. Deceiving the applicant—even if it is possible—simply results in early job turnover, and explicitly telling the applicant of the job's negative aspects does not make these attributes go away.[50]

Enhancing Recruiter Impact.   Although research suggests that recruiters do not have much influence on job choice, this does not mean recruiters cannot have an impact. Most recruiters receive little training,[51] and recent research has attempted to find conditions in which recruiters do make a difference. Based on this research, an organization can take several steps to increase the impact that recruiters have on those they recruit.

First, recruiters can provide timely feedback. Applicants react very negatively to delays in feedback, often making unwarranted attributions for the

TABLE 10.7   Quotes from Recruits Who Were Repelled by Recruiters

One firm I didn't think of talking to initially, but they called me and asked me to talk with them. So I did, and then the recruiter was very, very rude. Yes, *very* rude, and I've run into that a couple of times (engineering graduate).

I had a very bad campus interview experience…the person who came was a last-minute fill-in…I think he had a couple of 'issues' and was very discourteous during the interview. He was one step away from yawning in my face…The other thing he did was that he kept making these (nothing illegal, mind you) but he kept making these references to the fact that I had been out of my undergraduate and first graduate programs for more than 10 years now… (MBA with 10 years experience).

_____ has a management training program which the recruiter had gone through [sic]. She was talking about the great presentational skills that _____ teaches you, and the woman was barely literate. She was embarrassing. If that was the best they could do, I did not want any part of them. Also, _____ and _____'s recruiters appeared to have real attitude problems. I also thought they were chauvinistic (arts undergraduate).

_____ had a set schedule for me which they deviated from regularly. Times overlapped, and one person kept me too long which pushed the whole day back. They almost seemed to be saying that it was my fault that I was late for the next one! I guess a lot of what they did just wasn't very professional. Even at the point when I was done, where most companies would have a cab pick you up, I was in the middle of a snowstorm in Chicago and they said, "You can get a cab downstairs." There weren't any cabs. I literally had to walk 12 or 14 blocks with my luggage, trying to find some way to get to the airport. They didn't book me a hotel for the night of the snowstorm so I had to sit in the airport for 8 hours trying to get another flight…they wouldn't even reimburse me for the additional plane fare (industrial relations graduate student).

The guy at the interview made a joke about how nice my nails were and how they were going to ruin them there due to all the tough work (engineering undergraduate).

SOURCE: S. L. Rynes, R. D. Bretz Jr., and B. Gerhart, "The Importance of Recruitment in Job Choice: A Different Way of Looking," *Personnel Psychology* 44 (1991): 487–521.

delays (e.g., the organization is uninterested in my application).[52] As we mentioned earlier in this chapter, people seem to develop an early initial favorite that all other offers must beat. This reinforces the need for timely responses in recruiting. The recruiter can fulfill this role by ensuring that all applicants get timely feedback and follow-up communications.

Second, recruiters need to avoid behaviors that might convey the wrong organizational impression. Table 10.7 lists some quotes from applicants who had extremely bad experiences with recruiters. The researchers concluded that "recruiters in our study were variously described as 'rude, boring, obnoxious, full of themselves, incompetent, barely literate jerks.'"[53] Clearly, these perceptions do not aid the recruitment process and cannot be allowed to occur. Independent exit interviews with recruits conducted by someone other than the recruiter are needed to ensure quality control in the field.

This is especially important since certain recruiter behaviors are illegal and can result in expensive lawsuits.

Third, recruiters can focus on inexperienced applicants, with whom they might be more influential. The perceptions of inexperienced applicants are more likely to be inaccurate or incomplete, and the needs and values of this set of people may be more amenable to change. For example, an inexperienced applicant who initially does not want to take an overseas assignment could be convinced that this would be an enjoyable adventure that would provide invaluable work experience. Although experienced applicants may be less easily influenced, they too may have inaccurate or incomplete perceptions of the job (e.g., what their supervisor or coworkers might be like, or special perks associated with one location or another). The recruiter can help fill in these blind spots and de-emphasize the amount of time spent on aspects of the job or organization that an experienced applicant might already know.

Fourth, as suggested earlier, the recruiter can avoid mixing personnel recruitment with personnel selection. The evidence (discussed more fully in the next chapter) on the relationship between the interviewer's assessments of a candidate and the candidate's success on the job is not very impressive. Recruiters should focus their limited time and talents on creating a reasonable pool of motivated applicants from whom selection decisions can be made. If a recruiter must perform both functions—attracting applicants and selecting recruits—then he or she should make it clear in the interview when the purpose of the interview has changed. If this is not done, applicants may focus more on themselves and their own self-presentations than on what the recruiter has to say about the vacancy.

Fifth, recruiting can be done in teams rather than by individuals. As we have seen, applicants tend to view line personnel (e.g., job incumbents and supervisors) as more credible than personnel specialists, so these kinds of recruiters should be part of any team. On the other hand, personnel specialists have knowledge that is not shared by line personnel (who perceive recruiting as a small part of their "real" job), and so they should be included as well. A recruiting team should include female and minority members to reinforce the message that the organization is an equal opportunity employer. It might also want to include both long-tenured and relatively new organizational members to give applicants a feel for both their near and perhaps distant future.

SUMMARY

This chapter focused on the process of recruiting people for job vacancies in an organization. The chapter introduced a model of the job-choice process suggesting that these decisions are determined primarily by the interaction between applicants' characteristics and the perceived characteristics of vacancies. On the one hand, this decision process was shown to have simple, noncompensatory aspects—that is, critical characteristics (e.g., lack of full medical benefits) of some jobs eliminate them immediately from consideration. We also suggested that later stages of the job-choice process include more complex compensatory processes, in which desirable features in one job characteristic (high pay) may offset undesirable features on other characteristics (low job security).

The role of an organizational recruitment program in affecting such choices was shown to have three components. First, through personnel policies, organizations can affect the attributes of the vacancies themselves by trying to ensure that they are desirable to qualified applicants (e.g., promote-from-within policies, due process provisions). Second, the organization can affect the nature of people who apply for positions by using different recruitment sources (e.g., recruiting from universities versus advertising in newspapers). Third, organizations can use recruiters to try to influence individuals' perceptions of jobs (e.g., eliminating misconceptions, clarifying uncertainties) or perceptions of themselves (e.g., changing their valences for various work outcomes).

Discussion Questions

1. In a previous chapter, we discussed the importance of conducting periodic attitude surveys among employees. Why might it also be a good idea to conduct attitude surveys of potential future employees (e.g., job applicants)? Discuss how one might best sample people for such a survey and the major questions one might ask.

2. Recruiting people for jobs that entail international assignments is becoming increasingly important for many companies. Where might one go to look for individuals interested in these types of assignments? How might recruiting practices aimed at these individuals differ from those one might apply to the "average" recruit?

3. Discuss the relative merits of internal versus external recruitment. What types of business strategies might best be supported by recruiting externally, and what types might call for internal recruitment? What factors might lead a firm to decide to switch from internal to external recruitment and vice versa?

4. Imagine that a company is experiencing a great deal of first-year turnover in a particular job category. Why might one need to examine either the recruitment sources for people in this job category or the recruiters responsible for staffing it?

5. Discuss the relative advantages and disadvantages of recruiting people who are currently unemployed versus those who are currently employed. How might employee referrals be useful in developing a pool of recruits who are already working for some other employer? What kind of incentives might a company use to enhance the frequency of employee referrals?

Notes

1. D. P. Schwab, S. L. Rynes, and R. J. Aldag, "Theories and Research on Job Search and Choice," in *Research in Personnel and Human Resources Management*, ed. G. Ferris and T. R. Mitchell (Greenwich, Conn.: JAI Press, 1987), 129–166.

2. K. J. Brookhouse, R. M. Guion, and M. E. Doherty, "Social Desirability Response Bias as One Source of the Discrepancy between Subjective Weights and Regression Weights," *Organizational Behavior and Human Decision Processes* 37 (1986): 316–328.

3. R. V. Dawis, "Vocational Interests, Values and Preferences," in *Handbook of Industrial and Organizational Psychology*, ed. M. D. Dunnette and L. M. Hough (Palo Alto, Cal.: Consulting Psychologists Press, 1991), 833–872.

4. H. J. Arnold and D. C. Feldman, "Social Desirability Response Bias in Self-report Choice Situations," *Academy of Management Journal* 24 (1981): 249–259.

5. D. T. Hall, *Careers in Organizations* (Pacific Palisades, Cal.: Goodyear Press, 1976).

6. R. Henderson, "Contract Concessions: Is the Past Prologue?", *Compensation and Benefits Review* 18 (1986): 17–30.

7. M. London and S. A. Stumpf, *Managing Careers* (Reading, Mass.: Addison-Wesley, 1982).

8. R. Winslow, "How Khartoum Won No. 1 Ranking as a Hardship Post," *The Wall Street Journal*, April 26, 1989, 1.

9. R. Levering, M. Moskowitz, and M. Katz, *The 100 Best Companies to Work for in America* (Reading, Mass.: Addison-Wesley, 1984); M. Wilson, G. B. Northcraft, and M. A. Neale, "The Perceived Value of Fringe Benefits," *Personnel Psychology* 38 (1985): 309–320; M. M. Harris and L. S. Fink, "A Field Study of Employment Opportunities: Does the Recruiter Make a Difference?", *Personnel Psychology* 40 (1987): 765–784.

10. L. G. Reynolds, *The Structure of Labor Markets* (New York: Harper and Row, 1951).

11. S. L. Rynes and H. E. Miller, "Recruiter and Job Influences on Candidates for Employment," *Journal of Applied Psychology* 68 (1983): 147–154.

12. V. H. Vroom, *Work and Motivation* (New York: Wiley, 1964).

13. P. O. Soelberg, "Unprogrammed Decision Making," *Industrial Management Review* 8 (1967): 19–29.

14. Ibid.

15. J. O. Crites, *Career Maturity Inventory* (Monterey, Cal.: McGraw-Hill, 1973).

16. D. I. Sheppard, "The Measurement of Vocational Maturity in Adults," *Journal of Vocational Behavior* 1 (1971): 399–406.

17. J. A. Breaugh, *Recruitment: Science and Practice* (Boston: PWS-Kent, 1992).

18. C. Hulin, "Adaptation, Persistence and Commitment in Organizations," in *Handbook of Industrial and Organizational Psychology*, ed. M. D. Dunnette and L. M. Hough (Palo Alto, Cal.: Consulting Psychologists Press, 1991), 445–505.

19. J. D. Olian and S. L. Rynes, "Organizational Staffing: Integrating Practice with Strategy," *Industrial Relations* 23 (1984): 170–183.

20. G. T. Milkovich and J. M. Newman, *Compensation* (Homewood, Ill.: Richard D. Irwin, 1990).

21. D. J. Koys, S. Briggs, and J. Grenig, "State Court Disparity on Employment-at-Will," *Personnel Psychology* 40 (1987): 565–577.

22. M. Leonard, "Challenges to the Termination-at-Will Doctrine," *Personnel Administrator* 28 (1983): 49–56.

23. C. Schowerer and B. Rosen, "Effects of Employment-at-Will Policies and Compensation Policies on Corporate Image and Job Pursuit Intentions," *Journal of Applied Psychology* 74 (1989): 653–656.

24. M. Magnus, "Recruitment Ads at Work," *Personnel Journal* 64 (1985): 42–63.

25. Breaugh, *Recruitment: Science and Practice*.

26. J. Bussey, "Dow Chemical Tries to Shed Tough Image and Court the Public," *The Wall Street Journal*, November 20, 1987, 1.

27. S. L. Rynes and A. E. Barber, "Applicant Attraction Strategies: An Organizational Perspective," *Academy of Management Review* 15 (1990): 286–310.

28. M. A. Conrad and S. D. Ashworth, "Recruiting Source Effectiveness: A Meta-analysis and Re-examination of Two Rival Hypotheses." (Paper presented at the annual meeting of the Society of Industrial/Organizational Psychology, Chicago, Ill., 1986).

29. Breaugh, *Recruitment: Science and Practice.*

30. Ibid.

31. R. S. Schuler and S. E. Jackson, "Linking Competitive Strategies with Human Resource Management Practices," *Academy of Management Executive* 1 (1987): 207–219.

32. S. E. Jackson, J. F. Brett, V. I. Sessa, and D. M. Cooper, "Some Differences Make a Difference: Individual Dissimilarity and group Heterogeneity as Correlates of Recruitment, Promotions, and Turnover," *Journal of Applied Psychology* 76 (1991): 675–689.

33. S. L. Rynes, "Recruitment, Job Choice, and Post-Hire Consequences: A Call for New Research Directions," in *Handbook of Industrial and Organizational Psychology*, ed. M. D. Dunnette and L. M. Hough (Palo Alto, Cal.: Consulting Psychologists Press, 1990), 400–444.

34. A. Halcrow, "Employers Are Your Best Recruiters," *Personnel Journal* 67 (1988): 42–49.

35. Breaugh, *Recruitment: Science and Practice.*

36. R. L. Brady, "Paying the Price for Discrimination," *HR Focus*, January 1993, 11.

37. J. Mitchell, "BMW Names 2 Honda Executives to Oversee New U.S. Assembly Plant," *The Wall Street Journal*, November 29, 1992, B4.

38. J. Greenwald, "Invasion of the Body Snatchers," *Time*, April 23, 1984, 41.

39. J. W. Boudreau and S. L. Rynes, "Role of Recruitment in Staffing Utility Analysis," *Journal of Applied Psychology* 70 (1985): 354–366.

40. L. Winter, "Employers Go to School on Minority Recruiting," *The Wall Street Journal*, December 15, 1992, B1.

41. M. S. Taylor, "Effects of College Internships on Individual Participants," *Journal of Applied Psychology* 73 (1988): 393–401.

42. Duke, "Urban Teenagers."

43. R. Hawk, *The Recruitment Function* (New York: American Management Association, 1967).

44. M. E. Harris, "Reconsidering the Employment Interview: A Review of Recent Literature and Suggestions for Future Research," *Personnel Psychology* 42 (1989): 691–726.

45. C. D. Fisher, D. R. Ilgen, and W. D. Hoyer, "Source Credibility, Information Favorability, and Job Offer Acceptance," *Academy of Management Journal* 22 (1979): 94–103; G. N. Powell, "Applicant Reactions to the Initial Employment Interview: Exploring Theoretical and Methodological Issues," *Personnel Psychology* 44 (1991): 67–83; N. Schmitt and B. W. Coyle, "Applicant Decisions in the Employment Interview," *Journal of Applied Psychology* 61 (1976): 184–192.

46. Harris and Fink, "A Field Study of Employment Opportunities"; M. S. Taylor and T. J. Bergman, "Organizational Recruitment Activities and Applicants' Reactions at Different Stages of the Recruitment Process," *Personnel Psychology* 40 (1984): 261–285; Fisher, Ilgen and Hoyer, "Source Credibility."

47. Rynes, "Recruitment, Job Choice, and Post-Hire Consequences."

48. J. P. Wanous, *Organizational Entry: Recruitment, Selection and Socialization of Newcomers* (Reading, Mass.: Addison-Wesley, 1980).

49. G. M. McEvoy and W. F. Cascio, "Strategies for Reducing Employee Turnover: A Meta-analysis," *Journal of Applied Psychology* 70 (1985): 342–353; S. L. Premack and J. P. Wanous, "A Meta-analysis of Realistic Job Preview Experiments," *Journal of Applied Psychology* 70 (1985): 706–719.

50. B. L. Dugoni and D. R. Ilgen, "Realistic Job Previews and the Adjustment of New Employees," *Academy of Management Journal* 24 (1981): 94–103.

51. R. W. Walters, "It's Time We Become Pros," *Journal of College Placement* 12 (1985): 30–33.

52. S. L. Rynes, R. D. Bretz, and B. Gerhart, "The Importance of Recruitment in Job Choice: A Different Way of Looking," *Personnel Psychology* 44 (1991): 487–522.

53. Ibid.

CAN SMALL BE BETTER FOR RECRUITING?

C A S E

John Chuang is the founder and CEO of MacTemps, a small temporary employee agency in Cambridge, Massachusetts. MacTemps currently has 70 full-time employees coordinating close to 800 temporary workers. Chuang has to compete for full-time employees against bigger, billion-dollar national agencies, and he finds that it is almost impossible to match these giants when it comes to salary and health plans. In addition, larger companies provide employees with stable career paths, where every couple of years, someone gets a promotion and a new title. This kind of internal movement is more difficult to promise in a company this small.

Yet there are also certain advantages that come with a smaller size, and Chuang is interested in exploiting these as far as possible. Assume that you were recently hired as the human resources specialist for MacTemps, and your job was to "out-recruit" the competition for the best talent.

QUESTIONS

1. How would you overcome some of the liabilities of small size to win over employees?

2. What features of your company's vacancies would you try to change to make them more attractive to potential recruits?

3. What nontraditional sources of recruits might you try to tap that might be missed by the larger companies?

SOURCE: J. Case, "The Best Small Companies to Work for in America, *Inc.*, November 1992, 89–103.

PERSONNEL SELECTION AND PLACEMENT

Objectives

After reading this chapter, you should be able to:

1. Establish the basic scientific properties of selection methods—reliability, validity, and generalizability.
2. Discuss how the particular characteristics of a job, organization, or applicant affect the utility of any test.
3. Appreciate the government's role in personnel selection decisions, particularly in the areas of constitutional law, federal laws, executive orders, and judicial precedent.
4. List the common methods used in selecting human resources.
5. Describe the degree to which each of the common methods used in selecting human resources meets the demands of reliability, validity, generalizability, utility, and legality.

Feeling Insecure in the Security Industry

John Padilla wanted to be a security guard. He applied to several different security companies in the state of New York. One company, OCS Security, rejected Padilla's application, but another, HSC Security, hired him and assigned him to Carle Place High School in Long Island. In July 1991, a mere two weeks after he was hired, Padilla fired 16 shots from a 9-millimeter gun into a car parked outside the school. Padilla killed two students and critically injured three others for no apparent reason. Had HSC Security bothered to check, they would have discovered that when he was hired, Padilla was on probation for two separate weapons and cocaine-possession convictions. HSC is now out of business. On the other hand, its former competitor, OSC Security, is still operating. As OSC human resource manager Brian Church notes, "Obviously, it's worth spending all the money we do on screening and training because we nixed John right away."

Unfortunately, tragedies such as this are hardly isolated incidents in this sector of the service economy. In January 1992, a Burns International Security Services guard set a fire at Hollywood's Universal Studios; the fire caused $25 million damage. That same month, a Pinkerton guard was arraigned for auto theft, having stolen cars from a county-owned car pool that he was supposed to protect; a Wells Fargo guard was found guilty of attempted murder in a robbery attempt on an armored car whose route he had once driven.

While the companies that hired these individuals attempt to weather the adverse publicity from these cases, another company, Guardsmark, has been singled out by industry watchers as the most quality conscious in the industry, based primarily on the company's personnel selection and placement procedures. Indeed, Guardsmark rejects 98 out of 100 applicants based on interviews, reference checks, and psychological tests. As Robert McCrie, editor of the industry's leading newsletter, notes, "My impression is that Guardsmark's screening and supervisory standards are better than the competition's."

SOURCES: R. Behar, "Thugs in Uniform," *Time*, March 9, 1992, 46–47.

INTRODUCTION

The incidents just described highlight the importance of hiring to an organization's competitive position. The competitive aspects of selection decisions become even more critical when firms hire from the same labor market. If one company systematically skims off the best applicants, the remaining companies must make do with what is left. For example, in the California labor market for security guards, 20 percent of the applicants have prior criminal convictions.[1] If half of the companies in this market are systematically screening and half are not, it is only a matter of time until those who fail to screen experience one problem or another.

The purpose of this chapter is to familiarize you with ways to minimize errors in employee selection and placement and, in doing so, to increase your company's competitive position. The chapter first focuses on five standards that should be met by any selection method. The chapter then evaluates several common selection methods according to those standards.

SELECTION METHOD STANDARDS

Personnel selection is the process by which companies decide who will or will not be allowed into their organization. Several generic standards should be met in any selection process. We focus on five: (1) reliability, (2) validity, (3) generalizability, (4) utility, and (5) legality. The first four of these standards build off each other: The preceding standard is often necessary but not sufficient for the one that follows. This is less the case with legal standards. However, a thorough understanding of the first four standards helps us understand the rationale underlying many of the legal standards.

Reliability

Much of the work in personnel selection involves measuring characteristics of people to determine who will be accepted for job openings. For example, we might be interested in applicants' physical characteristics (e.g., strength or endurance), their cognitive abilities (e.g., mathematics ability or verbal reasoning capacity), or aspects of their personality (e.g., their initiative or integrity). Whatever the specific focus, in the end we need to quantify people on these dimensions (i.e., assign numbers to them) so we can order them from high to low on the characteristic of interest. Once people are ordered in this way, we can then make decisions about whom to hire and whom to reject.

One of the key standards for any measuring device is its reliability. We define *reliability* as the degree to which a measure is free from random error.[2] If a measure of some supposedly stable characteristic such as intelligence is reliable, then the score a person receives based on that measure will be consistent over time and over different contexts.

True Scores and the Standard Error of Measurement. Most of the measuring done in personnel selection deals with complex characteristics like intelligence, integrity, and leadership ability. However, to appreciate some of the complexities in measuring people, we will consider something concrete in discussing these concepts: the measurement of height. For example, if we were measuring an applicant's height for a security guard position, we might start by using a 12-inch ruler. Let's say the first person we measure turns out to be 6 feet 1 and 2/16 inches tall. It would not be surprising to find out that someone else measuring the same guard an hour later found his height to be 6 feet and 12/16 inches. The same guard, measured by the original measurer the next day, might be 6 feet 1 and 6/16 inches tall. Table 11.1 shows the hypothetical results of a dozen different measurements of this one guard.

As Column 1 of this table makes clear, even though the guard's height is supposedly a stable characteristic, we get slightly different results each time he or she is assessed. Since the guard's "true height" is not changing, this shows us that each time the guard is assessed, we must be making slight

TABLE 11.1 Hypothetical Results from 12 Independent
Measures of One Person's Height

	(1) Height Measured with a Ruler	(2) True Height	(3) Error of Measurement	(4) Unsigned Error
1	6' 1 $\frac{2}{16}$"	6' 1"	+ $\frac{2}{16}$"	$\frac{2}{16}$"
2	6' 0 $\frac{12}{16}$"	6' 1"	− $\frac{4}{16}$"	$\frac{4}{16}$"
3	6' 1 $\frac{6}{16}$"	6' 1"	+ $\frac{6}{16}$"	$\frac{6}{16}$"
4	6' 1 $\frac{3}{16}$"	6' 1"	+ $\frac{3}{16}$"	$\frac{3}{16}$"
5	6' 0 $\frac{14}{16}$"	6' 1"	− $\frac{2}{16}$"	$\frac{2}{16}$"
6	6' 0 $\frac{10}{16}$"	6' 1"	− $\frac{6}{16}$"	$\frac{6}{16}$"
7	6' 1 $\frac{1}{16}$"	6' 1"	+ $\frac{1}{16}$"	$\frac{1}{16}$"
8	6' 1 $\frac{5}{16}$"	6' 1"	+ $\frac{5}{16}$"	$\frac{5}{16}$"
9	6' 0 $\frac{6}{16}$"	6' 1"	− $\frac{10}{16}$"	$\frac{10}{16}$"
10	6' 1 $\frac{4}{16}$"	6' 1"	+ $\frac{4}{16}$"	$\frac{4}{16}$"
11	6' 1 $\frac{5}{16}$"	6' 1"	+ $\frac{5}{16}$"	$\frac{5}{16}$"
12	6' 0 $\frac{12}{16}$"	6' 1"	− $\frac{4}{16}$"	$\frac{4}{16}$"
Average:	6' 1"	6' 1"	$\frac{0}{16}$"	$\frac{5}{16}$"

errors. Indeed, we can think of each of these 12 measurements as being composed of two parts: the guard's "true height" (which is unchanging) and the "error of measurement."

Table 11.1 breaks each of the 12 assessments into these two parts: true height (shown in column 2) and error of measurement (shown in column 3). So, for example, the first time we measured this person we obtained 6 feet 1 and $\frac{2}{16}$ inches. This measured height came about because the true height was 6 feet 1 inch, and there as a +$\frac{2}{16}$-inch error. The same person, measured the second time, was assessed at 6 feet and $\frac{12}{16}$ inches. This was obtained because the true height was still 6 feet 1 inch; however, this time the error was −$\frac{4}{16}$ inch.

At the bottom of these columns are the average true height and the average error of measurement. The average true height is 6 feet 1 inch, and the average error of measurement is zero. The latter turns out to be zero because the small positive and small negative errors cancel each other. However, Column 4, which displays the errors with the sign (positive or negative) removed, shows that on average, every time this guard is measured, there is an average error of plus or minus $\frac{5}{16}$ inch. This average unsigned error of measurement is referred to as the standard error of the measure.

If a measurement device were perfectly reliable, there would be no errors of measurement, and the standard error of the measure would be zero. If we used a measure of height that was not as reliable as a ruler—for example, guessing the guard's height after seeing him or her walk across the room—we might see a larger standard error of the measure (e.g., 2 inches). Thus, reliability refers to the measuring instrument (a ruler versus a visual guess) rather than to the characteristic itself.

Estimating Reliability. There is no direct way to capture the "true" reliability or the "true" standard error of the measure. We can estimate each of these, however. For example, *test-retest* estimates of reliability are obtained by simply finding the correlation (see Chapter 9 for a discussion of the correlation coefficient) between assessments taken at different times. *Split-half* estimates—used for assessments taken with paper-and-pencil methods (e.g., intelligence tests or personality questionnaires)—are obtained by cutting the test into halves (e.g., odd versus even items) and correlating the two halves.

Once we have obtained a reliability estimate, we can estimate the standard error of the measure using the following formula:

$$SE_m = s_x \sqrt{1 - r_{xx}}$$

where SE_m refers to the standard error of the measure, s_x is the standard deviation of characteristic x (e.g., height), and r_{xx} is the estimated reliability. (See Chapter 9 for a discussion of the standard deviation concept).

Standards for Reliability. Regardless of what characteristic we are measuring, we want highly reliable measures. But how high is high enough? Although there are many general rules for determining an acceptable level of reliability, it is best to keep in mind the kinds of decisions you make with the measure. Table 11.2 depicts two different scenarios of a manager choosing between two applicants for a mechanic's position and using a measurement of mechanical aptitude to aid in the decision. As the table makes clear, for some decisions a reliability of .70 may be sufficient. In Scenario 1, the applicants' scores are so far apart (15 points) relative to the standard error of the measure (5.48 points) that even with a .70 reliability, the manager can safely conclude that Job Applicant A has more mechanical aptitude than Job Applicant B.

In Scenario 2, on the other hand, the two applicants' scores are so close that even a reliability of .95 is insufficient to guarantee that person A's "true" mechanical aptitude is actually higher than person B's. That is, because the standard error of the measure (2.23 points) is larger than the difference between the two persons (1 point), if we tested these two people again, person B could easily obtain a higher score than person A. Under these conditions the manager needs to find some other basis for making the decision regarding these two applicants.

Although these scenarios suggest that no specific value of reliability is always "acceptable," they also drive home the point of why more reliability is better. Clearly, the more reliable the measure, the more likely it is that we will be able to base decisions on score differences that it reveals.

TABLE 11.2   Required Levels of Reliability for Two Different Decision Situations

Scenario 1

Test's reliability	=	.70
Test's standard deviation	=	10.00
Test's standard error of measurement	=	5.48
Job applicant A's test score	=	96
Job applicant B's test score	=	81

Scenario 2

Test's reliability	=	.95
Test's standard deviation	=	10.00
Test's standard error of measurement	=	2.23
Job applicant A's test score	=	90
Job applicant B's test score	=	89

Validity

We define validity as the extent to which performance on the measure is associated with performance on the job. A measure must be reliable if it is to have any validity. On the other hand, we can reliably measure many characteristics (e.g., height) that may have no relationship to whether someone can perform a job. For this reason, reliability is a necessary but insufficient condition for validity.

There are two primary methods for determining the validity of a selection method. One of these focuses on the relationship between scores on the selection measure and scores on some measure of job performance. The other focuses on the relationship between the content of the selection method (e.g., the nature of the items) and the content of the job.

Criterion-related Validation.   One method of establishing the validity of a selection method is to show that there is an empirical association between scores on the selection measure and scores for job performance. If there is a substantial correlation between test scores and job-performance scores, criterion-related validity has been established. This correlation is referred to as a *validity coefficient*.

Criterion-related validity studies come in two varieties: concurrent validation and predictive validation (see Figure 11.1). The easier type to perform is a concurrent validation study. An example would be administering a test to all the people currently in the job and then seeing how the incumbents' test scores correlate with measures of their performance on the job.

Predictive validation is more difficult because it seeks to establish an empirical relationship between tests scores taken prior to persons' being hired and their eventual performance on the job. Predictive validation

FIGURE 11.1   Graphic Depiction of Concurrent and Predictive Validation Designs

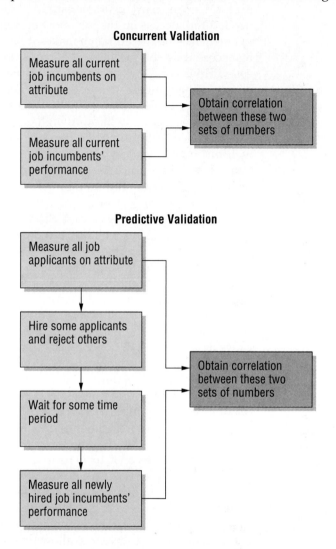

requires one to administer tests to job applicants, not current employees. In addition, one must wait for some time after test administration to see how a subset of those applicants (i.e., those who were actually hired) performed.

Despite the extra amount of effort and time, predictive validation is clearly superior to concurrent validation. First, job applicants (because they are seeking work) are typically more motivated to perform well on the tests than are current employees (who already have jobs). Second, current employees have learned many things on the job that job applicants have not yet have learned. Therefore, the correlation between test scores and job performance for current employees may not be the same as the correlation between test scores and job performance for less knowledgeable job applicants. Third, current employees tend to be homogeneous—that is, similar to each other on many characteristics.[3] Thus, on many of the characteristics needed for success on the job, most current employees will show *restriction in range*. This restricted range makes it hard to detect a relationship between test scores and job-performance scores because few of the current employees will be very low on the characteristic we are trying to validate. For example, if emotional stability is a characteristic required for the job of security guard, it is also quite likely that most guards who have amassed five or six years' experience will score high on this characteristic. Yet to validate a test, you need both high test scorers (who should subsequently perform well on the job) and low test scorers (who should perform poorly on the job). Thus, while concurrent studies can sometimes help one anticipate the results of predictive studies, they do not serve as substitutes.[4]

Limitations of Criterion-related Validation. Obviously, we would like our measures to be high in validity, but as with the reliability standard, we must also ask, how high is high enough? When trying to determine how much validity is enough, one typically has to turn to tests of statistical significance. A test of statistical significance answers the question, "How likely is it that a correlation of this size could have come about through luck or chance?"

Table 11.3 shows how big a correlation between a selection measure and a measure of job performance needs to be to achieve statistical significance at a level of .05 (i.e., there is only a 5 out of 100 chance that one could get a correlation this big by chance alone). While it is generally true that bigger correlations are better, the size of the sample on which the correlation is based plays a large role as well. If you tested only five people, a correlation of .70 is *not* big enough. With a sample of 100, on the other hand, a correlation of .20 *is* big enough. Since many of the selection methods we examine in the second half of this chapter generate correlations in the .20s and .30s, we often need samples of 80 to 90 people.[5] A validation study with a small sample (e.g., 20 people) is almost doomed to failure from the start.

Many companies are too small or too stable (i.e., do not generate a large number of openings each year) to use a criterion-related validation strategy. Indeed, even within large companies, many job categories do not generate enough openings each year to allow this type of validation.

Content Validation. When sample sizes are small, an alternative test-validation strategy, content validation, can be used. Content validation is performed by demonstrating that the items, questions, or problems posed by the test are a representative sample of the kinds of situations or problems that occur on the job.[6] A test that is content valid exposes the job applicant to situations that are likely to occur on the job, then tests whether the applicant currently has sufficient knowledge, skill, or ability to handle such situations.

For example, one general contracting firm that constructed tract housing needed to hire one construction superintendent.[7] This job involved organizing, supervising, and inspecting the work of many subcontractors involved in the construction process. The tests developed for this position

TABLE 11.3   Required Level of Correlation to Reach Statistical Significance as a Function of Sample Size

Sample Size	Required Correlation
5	.75
10	.58
20	.42
40	.30
80	.21
100	.19

attempted to mirror the job. One test was a scrambled subcontractor test, where the applicant had to take a random list of subcontractors (roofing, plumbing, electrical, fencing, concrete, etc.) and put them in the correct order that each should appear on the site. A second test measured construction-error recognition. In this test, the applicant went into a shed that was specially constructed to have 25 common and expensive errors (e.g., faulty wiring, upside-down windows, etc.) and record whatever problems he or she could detect. Because the content of these tests so closely parallels the content of the job, one can safely make inferences from one to the other.

Although criterion-related validity is established by empirical means, content validity is achieved primarily through a process of expert judgment. One means of quantifying the degree of content validity is to use the *content-validation ratio*. To calculate this ratio, a number of individuals considered experts on the job are assembled. These people review each test (or item) then categorize each test in terms of whether the skill or knowledge the test assesses is essential to the job. The content-validation ratio is then calculated from the following formula:

$$CVR = \frac{n_e - N/2}{N/2},$$

where n_e is the number of judges who rate the test "essential" and N is the number of judges. *CVR* equals 1.0 when all judges feel the test is essential, −1.0 when all judges feel it is nonessential. A *CVR* of .00 means there is complete disagreement on the degree to which the item is essential. Table 11.4 shows the level of *CVR* needed to achieve statistical significance as a function of the number of judges.[8]

Limitations of Content Validation.   The ability to use content validation in small sample settings makes it generally more applicable than criterion-related validation. However, content validation has two limitations.[9] First, one assumption behind content validation is that the person who is to be

TABLE 11.4   Required Level of Content Validation Ratio to Reach Statistical Significance as a Function of the Number of Judges

Number of Judges	Required Content Validation Ratio
5	.99
8	.75
10	.62
15	.49
30	.33

hired must have the knowledge, skills, or abilities at the time he or she is hired. Thus, it is not appropriate to use content validation in settings where the applicant is expected to learn the job in a formal training program conducted after selection.

Second, since subjective judgment plays such a large role in content validation, it is critical to minimize the amount of inference involved on the part of judges. Thus, the judges' ratings need to be made with respect to relatively concrete and observable behaviors (e.g., "applicant detects common construction errors" or "arranges optimal subcontractor schedules"). Content validation would be inappropriate for assessing more abstract characteristics such as intelligence, leadership capacity, or integrity.

Generalizability

Generalizability is defined as the degree to which the validity of a selection method established in one context extends to other contexts. There are three primary "contexts" over which we might like to generalize: different situations (i.e., jobs or organizations), different samples of people, and different time periods. Just as reliability is necessary but not sufficient for validity, validity is necessary but not sufficient for generalizability.

It was once believed, for example, that validity coefficients were *situationally specific*—that is, the level of correlation between test and performance varied as one went from one organization to another, even though the jobs studied seemed to be identical. Subsequent research has indicated that this is largely false. Rather, tests tend to show similar levels of correlation even across jobs that are only somewhat similar (at least for tests of intelligence or cognitive ability). Correlations with these kinds of tests do change as one goes across widely different kinds of jobs, however. Specifically, the more complex the job, the higher the validity of many tests.[10]

It was also believed that tests showed *differential subgroup validity*, which meant that the validity coefficient for any test–job performance pair was different for people of different races or sex. This belief was also refuted by subsequent research, and in general, one finds very similar levels of correlations across different groups of people.[11]

Because the evidence suggests that test validity often extends across situations and subgroups, validity generalization stands as an alternative for validating selection methods for companies that cannot employ criterion-related or content validation. *Validity generalization* is a three-step process. First, the company provides evidence from previous criterion-related validity studies conducted in other situations that shows that a specific test (e.g., a test of emotional stability) is a valid predictor for a specific job (security guard in a large company). Second, the company provides evidence from job analysis to document that the specific job (security guard in a small company) is similar in all major respects to the job validated elsewhere (in the large company). Finally, if the company can show that it uses a test that is the same as or similar to that used in the validated setting (i.e., the large company), then one can "generalize" the validity from the first context (large company) to the new context (small company).[12]

Although recent evidence supports the generalizability of many kinds of tests across situations and subgroups, it does not support the generalizability of tests across time. Indeed, it seems that the correlations tend to get smaller as the time interval lengthens. Although there is some controversy over the consistency of this downward pattern, the fact that the validities vary over time seems well accepted by researchers in this area.[13]

Utility

Utility is the degree to which the information provided by selection methods enhances the effectiveness of selecting personnel in real organizations.[14] In general, the more reliable, valid, and generalizable the selection method is, the more utility it will have. On the other hand, many characteristics of particular selection contexts enhance or detract from the usefulness of given selection methods, even when reliability, validity, and generalizability are held constant.

If we focus first on organizational issues, Figure 11.2 shows two different scenarios. Although the correlation between the test and job performance is the same for each company, the company in Scenario 2 derives much more utility from the test than the company in Scenario 1. That is, if one considers only the applicants who are selected, 60 percent of those selected by Company 1 turn out to be successful, versus 90 percent for Company 2. Because the *selection ratio*—that is, the percentage of people selected versus the total number of applicants—is lower for Company 2, Company 2 winds up selecting those with higher scores on the test and, thus, takes better advantage of the test–job performance relationship.

Three other organizational characteristics that affect the utility of a given test are the number of people selected, the rate of employee turnover, and the nature of employee turnover (in terms of performance differences between stayers and leavers). First, the greater the number of selection deci-

FIGURE 11.2   The Effect of the Selection Ratio on the Utility of
Any Test of a Given Validity

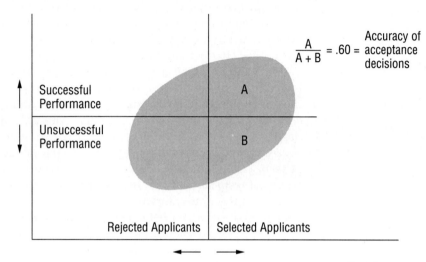

Scenario 1: Selection ratio = .50
Test validity = .50

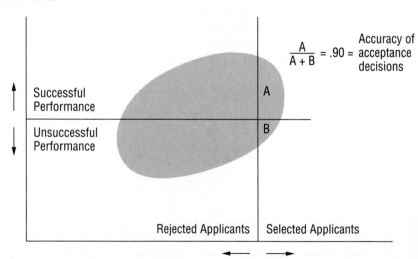

Scenario 2: Selection ratio = .90
Test validity = .50

sions for which a test can be used, the greater its utility. Clearly, researching, administering, and validating a test is hardly worth it if only one decision is made with the test. Second, if those selected with the test leave the organization after a very short period, there is less utility to testing than if those selected stay on the job for a long time. Third, if those who leave the job tend to be low performers rather than high performers, the utility of the test increases. Under these conditions, testing allows the company to replace low performers with individuals that the test indicates will be high performers.

There are also three characteristics of a job that affect the utility of a given test. First, the degree of difficulty of performing well on the job affects utility. For jobs that have high *base rates*—that is, the percentage of randomly hired people who could perform well is high—tests have little utility. Testing pays off primarily in contexts where it is difficult to find high performers.

Second, where the *economic consequences* to an organization of failure versus success on the job are great, testing has greater utility. For example, a test of sales ability might have greater utility for a company selling automobiles than for one selling candy. The sales difference between a "good" car salesperson and an average one might be $20,000 a month, versus a difference of perhaps $2,000 a month for a good versus an average candy seller.

Third, a given test's utility is influenced by a company's variable costs. *Variable costs* refer to any costs of doing business that increase as revenue increases. For example, hiring higher performers may require the company to raise salaries or benefits. Higher employee performance may also require the company to purchase more raw materials. Where any of these contingencies are in effect, the utility of any valid selection method (which results in hiring higher performers) decreases. Table 11.5 summarizes the conditions under which the utility of a test of any given reliability, validity, and generalizability is high versus low.[15] The "Competing through Technology" box illustrates just how large savings from rigorous selection standards can be in today's high-tech manufacturing companies.

Legality

The final standard that any selection method should adhere to is legality. All selection methods should conform to existing laws and existing legal precedents. Many of the issues related to selecting employees safely under U.S. law were discussed generically in Chapter 4. Our treatment there was a "top-down approach," where we started out with the U.S. Constitution and discussed the overall legal framework of the United States. Our focus here will take a "bottom-up approach," where we start with an angry person who feels unfairly treated and explore the many avenues that this person could take to rectify the problem.

For example, a 45-year-old Hispanic woman with a history of lower-back disability who was rejected for a job with a state agency in New York City that does contract work for the federal government could appeal this

TABLE 11.5   Summary of Conditions That Affect the Utility of a Test of Any Given Reliability, Validity, and Generalizability

Situation Where Testing Has Very High Utility	Situation Where Testing Has Very Low Utility
The cost of administering and scoring the test is low.	The cost of administering and scoring the test is high.
The organization can afford to accept only a small percentage of those who apply for jobs.	The organization needs to accept almost all of those who apply for jobs.
The test will be used to select a large number of people.	The test will be used to select a small number of people.
Those hired tend to stay on the job for a long time.	Those hired tend to quit the job after a short time.
Those who do quit the job tend to be low performers.	Those who quit the job tend to be high performers.
The job is one that few people can perform well.	The job is one that most people can perform well.
Performing well on the job has a major impact on the revenue generated by the company.	Performing well on the job has only a minor impact on the revenue generated by the company.
Performing well on the job has little impact on the variable costs of business.	Performing well on the job substantially increases the variable costs of business.

decision through litigation on at least 14 different grounds. After reading this section, you should be able to identify all the legal protections this person could invoke.[16] Having this knowledge yourself is critical, since many groups try to exploit employer fears in this area. For example, in 1992 a company called Handicapped Services in South Florida was charging employers $400 for copies of the government's free guidelines for the Americans with Disabilities Act.[17]

Constitutional Law.   As we noted in Chapter 4, the Constitution is directly involved in hiring when complaints are brought against employers under the Fourteenth Amendment. The Fourteenth Amendment regulates states and their agents and guarantees that no person shall be denied life, liberty, or property by the state without due process of law. Thus, a hiring decision made by a state agent (e.g., a state university) could be considered unconstitutional if it bore no reasonable relation to any legitimate purpose.

Constitutional law is used relatively sparingly in the context of personnel selection for three reasons. First, constitutional amendments are broad and therefore somewhat vague when applied to personnel selection.

Technology & Structure

HIGH SELECTION STANDARDS LOWER COSTS AT CARRIER CORPORATION

Many industrial experts view factories like Carrier Corporation's new compressor plant in Arkadelphia, Arkansas, as being the prototype for successful U.S. manufacturing in the year 2000. This "miniplant," built in the early 1990s, was designed to replace bigger plants constructed in the 1970s and 1980s, which generated high fixed costs and produced inflexible production lines. Obviously, what this new plant gave up in terms of physical size had to be made up with high-tech, automated engineering. Similarly, what the new factory gave up in terms of quantity of workers had to be offset by the quality of workers. At Carrier's new plant, responsiveness, flexibility, and being able to adjust are as critical for the personnel as they are for the automated machinery. To ensure the quality of its human resources, the selection process for new employees is a grueling six-week experience that results in a job for only 1 out of each 16 people who seek employment.

Getting a job at this Carrier plant starts with a standard intelligence test for job candidates, who must also be high school graduates. Only those scoring in the top 67 percent on this test advance to later stages. In the second stage of

this process, Carrier's managers closely check references with telephone contacts. The key to this stage is determining how well this person has worked with others in the past so that predictions can be made as to how well he or she would fit into the plant's "team-based" structure. Those who survive this stage are then interviewed by their potential team members.

Finally, for the few surviving applicants who make it this far, the last hurdle is a six-week course that meets for three hours, five nights a week. Most applicants must complete the course while still working at other jobs (since they have not been hired by Carrier yet and are unpaid for this time). The course focuses on applied mathematics, statistics, computer applications, and interpersonal relations. Graduates of this six-week course are rewarded with secure, well-paid jobs with good benefits. In return, Carrier has been rewarded with higher-quality compressors that are produced in half the time and at $35 less per unit when compared with those made at the plants that were replaced. In 1993, when annual production hits 750,000 units, this will represent a savings of over $25 million a year.

SOURCE: E. Norton, "Small Flexible Plants May Play Crucial Role in U.S. Manufacturing," *The Wall Street Journal*, January, 13, 1993, A2.

Second, constitutional complaints can only be brought up under grounds of differential treatment (see Chapter 4 for a review of this concept), and the person filing the complaint must show that the discrimination was intentional. Third, the Constitution regulates the actions only of government agencies and is therefore less widely applicable than existing legislation.

Federal Legislation. Three primary federal laws form the basis for a majority of the suits filed by job applicants. First, the Civil Rights Act of 1991 (discussed in Chapter 4), an extension of the Civil Rights Act of 1964, protects individuals from discrimination based on race, color, sex, religion, and national origin with respect to hiring (as well as compensation and working conditions). The 1991 act differs from the 1964 act in three important areas.

First, it codifies employers' explicit obligation to establish the business necessity of any neutral-appearing selection method that has had adverse impact on groups specified by the law. Second, it allows the individual filing the complaint to have a jury decide whether he or she may recover punitive damages (in addition to lost wages and benefits) for emotional injuries caused by the discrimination.[18] This can generate large settlements such as the one arrived at by Shoney Inc., where 18 African American employees were awarded $105 million to settle a racial discrimination suit.[19] Finally, it explicitly prevents the use of "race norming" as a means of giving preferential treatment to minority groups. The practice of race norming, and some recent controversy involving this practice, is explored in more detail in the "Competing through Social Responsibility" box.

The Age Discrimination in Employment Act of 1967 is also widely used in personnel selection. This act mirrors the Civil Rights Act of 1964 in its protections and, as amended in 1978, covers job applicants who are between the ages of 40 and 69. The act does not protect younger workers (thus, there is never a case for "reverse discrimination"), and like the most recent civil rights act, it allows for jury trials and punitive damages. This act makes almost all "mandatory retirement" programs illegal (i.e., company policies that dictate that everyone who reaches a set age must retire).

Litigation brought forward under this act surged by over 150 percent between 1991 and 1992 alone.[20] Two trends have combined to generate this increase: (1) the general aging of the work force and (2) recent attempts by organizations to downsize. Together, these trends have led to the displacement of many older workers who have brought age discrimination suits against their former employers. The list of companies being sued under this act is long and includes CBS Inc., McDonnell Douglas, Northwest Airlines, and Disneyland. Settlements can be expensive, and legal fees have to be paid win or lose. For example, Hazen Paper Company, whose case went all the way to the Supreme Court, spent almost as much ($500,000) in legal fees as it did in settlements ($600,000).[21]

Finally, the Americans with Disabilities Act of 1991 protects individuals with physical or mental disabilities (or with a history of the same). It extends the Vocational Rehabilitation Act of 1973, requiring employers to make "reasonable accommodations" to disabled individuals whose handicaps may prevent them from performing essential functions of the job as currently designed. "Reasonable accommodations" could include restructuring jobs, modifying work schedules, making facilities accessible, providing readers, or modifying equipment.

Employers need not make accommodations that cause "undue hardship." In other words, if the accommodation is "unduly costly, extensive, substantially disruptive, or fundamentally alters the nature of the job," the employer need not comply. Undue hardship can also be established if the employer can show that hiring the applicant will result in a direct threat to the safety of that person or others he or she encounters on the job despite

Social Responsibility

COMPETING THROUGH

THE CONTROVERSY SURROUNDING RACE NORMING

What should one do if a relatively valid predictor of future job success disqualifies members of some protected groups at a rate higher than other groups? This simple question is at the heart of recent controversies surrounding the issue of race norming. This issue was considered so important to ex-President George Bush that he was willing to veto the new Civil Rights Act of 1991 unless an explicit statement outlawing race norming was written into the act. With Bush out of the picture, however, some congressional leaders who were in favor of race norming are now considering amending this portion of the act. What is race norming and why is this concept so controversial?

In the area of selection testing, the term "norming" refers to the process whereby a distribution of scores on some test is obtained in order to develop standards for determining various cutoff points (e.g., the average score, the top 10th percentile score, etc.). This can be done for the whole sample or for subsamples of the entire sample (e.g., one can develop separate norms for males and females). When separate standards are developed for different groups based on race, this is called race norming.

Race norming is controversial because it is only applied where there are large differences in

test performance between races. In this context, this means that any given raw score will generate different percentile scores for members of different races. Since African Americans score lower as a group on many types of cognitive ability tests, race norming helps promote integration of the work force by adjusting their percentile scores upward. In addition, since it relies on hiring only the top scorers of each race, one derives many of the benefits of using valid selection techniques that are lost if one simply adopts quotas. Thus, it allows a company to both enhance its competitiveness and racially integrate the work force at the same time.

However, many non–African Americans feel that it achieves this goal at the expense of others who are penalized for being "stuck" in a high-performing group (e.g., Asians). Indeed, on one widely used test, the General Aptitude Test Battery, a score of 300 translates into a percentile score of 87 for African Americans, but only 47 for "Others." The current version of the Civil Rights Act makes race norming illegal. Some feel that this greatly complicates the ability of companies to both integrate the work force and use valid predictors in selection at the same time. Others feel this is essential to promoting competitiveness and preventing "reverse discrimination."

attempts at accommodation. This act also restricts many preemployment inquiries. For example, organizations cannot ask the job applicant whether he or she has a disability or require a medical examination prior to an offer of employment. Employers can ask if the applicant can perform essential job-related functions, however, and can make an offer of acceptance contingent on the results of a medical examination.

Before closing this section, we would like to remind you that hiring decisions are regulated at the state level also. We do not cover state laws in this text, but many states (like New York) and many large cities (like New York City) have laws or ordinances that parallel or extend the laws described here.

Executive Orders.   As noted in Chapter 4, the executive branch of the government also regulates hiring decisions through the use of executive orders. Executive Order 11246 parallels the protections provided by the Civil Rights Act of 1964 but goes beyond the 1964 act in two important ways. First, not only do the executive orders prohibit discrimination, they actually mandate that employers take affirmative action to hire qualified minority applicants. The executive orders also allow the government to suspend all business with a contractor while an investigation is being conducted (rather than waiting for an actual finding), which puts a great deal of pressure on employers to comply with these orders.

Executive orders are monitored by the Office of Federal Contract Compliance Programs (OFCCP), which issues guidelines (e.g., the *Affirmative Action Program Guidelines* published by the Bureau of National Affairs in 1983) to help companies comply. It should also be noted that state and municipal executive branches have similar powers; thus, governors and mayors can also have an impact on employers who do business with local government.[22]

Summary.   Returning to our example of the 45-year-old Hispanic woman who was rejected for a job with a government contractor in New York City, here are the remedies she could pursue. Since the employer is a state agent, she could (1) claim her Fourteenth Amendment rights were violated. She could also accuse the employer of (2) sex discrimination or (3) race discrimination based on the Civil Rights Act of 1991. She could (4) file a claim under the Americans with Disabilities Act because of her back problems. Since the employer is a government contractor, she could file a charge of discrimination with the OFCCP, based on either (5) sex or (6) race in line with Executive Order 11246. She could also file a claim with the New York State Division of Human Rights based on (7) age, (8) sex, (9) race, or (10) disability. Or she could file a claim based on (11) age, (12) sex, (13) race, or (14) disability under an executive order issued by the mayor of New York City. As this example shows, the scope of government involvement in hiring decisions is wide and complex.

TYPES OF SELECTION METHODS

The first half of this chapter laid out the five standards by which we can judge selection measures. In the second half of this chapter, we examine the common selection methods used in various organizations and discuss their advantages and disadvantages in terms of these standards.

Interviews

A selection interview has been defined as "a dialogue initiated by one or more persons to gather information and evaluate the qualifications of an applicant for employment."[23] The selection interview is the most widespread selection method employed in organizations.

Unfortunately, the long history of research on the employment interview suggests that, without proper care, it can be unreliable and low in validity.[24] It is simply not reasonable to think that unstructured, rambling conversations between interviewers and applicants will provide much information useful in predicting the job candidate's future success. Moreover, interviews are relatively costly because they require at least one person to interview another person, and these persons have to be brought to the same geographic location.

Finally, in terms of legality, the subjectivity embodied in the process often makes applicants upset, particularly if they fail to get a job after being asked apparently irrelevant questions like, "If you were a car, what kind of car would you be?" This only increases the probability that the applicants will take legal action against the company. The Supreme Court ruled in *Watson v. Fort Worth Bank and Trust* that subjective selection methods like the interview must be validated by traditional criterion-related or content-validation procedures.[25]

Increasing the Utility of Personnel Selection Interviews. Fortunately, more recent research has pointed to a number of concrete steps that one can employ to increase the utility of the personnel selection interview, and leading organizations are increasingly incorporating these steps into their selection programs. First, keep the interview structured, standardized, and focused on accomplishing a small number of goals. That is, plan to come out of each interview with quantitative ratings on a small number of dimensions that are observable (e.g., interpersonal style or ability to express oneself), and avoid ratings of abilities that may be better measured by tests (e.g., intelligence). In the words of one experienced interviewer for Johnson and Son Inc., "Gut feelings count, but the goal is controlled subjectivity."[26]

Second, ask questions that force the applicant to display the required knowledge or ability to execute behaviors on the spot. For example, *situational interview* questions, like the one used by Zales Jewelers (shown in Table 11.6), confront applicants with actual problems they might experience on the job and ask them to show how they would resolve the situation.[27]

It is also important to use multiple interviewers who are trained to avoid many of the subjective errors that can result when one human being is asked to rate another. That is, interviewers need to be made aware of their own biases, prejudices, and other personal features that may color their perceptions of others. This is facilitated by having many different people interview the candidate and then discuss him or her, so that interviewers' individual idiosyncrasies may be canceled out by those of their colleagues.[28] For example, at Levi Strauss, the human resource department makes sure women and minorities play a large role in interviewing job applicants to ensure their perspective is included.[29]

It is worth pointing out that employers are increasingly videotaping interviews, then sending the tapes (rather than the applicants) around from place to place. This is seen by some as a cost-effective means of allowing numerous raters to evaluate the candidate under standard conditions.[30]

TABLE 11.6   An Item from a Situational Interview Schedule
Used by a Retail Jewelry Chain

A customer comes into the store to pick up a watch he left for repair. The repair
was supposed to have been completed a week ago, but the watch is not back yet
from the repair shop. The customer becomes very angry. How would you handle
this situation?

1. Tell the customer it isn't back yet and ask him or her to check back with you later.

2. Apologize, tell the customer that you will check into the problem, and call him or
   her back later.

3. Put the customer at ease and call the repair shop while the customer waits.

SOURCE: Adapted from J. A. Wheeler and J. A. Gier, "Reliability and Validity of the Situational Interview
for a Sales Position," *Journal of Applied Psychology* 72 (1987): 484–487.

References and Biographical Data

Just as few employers would think of hiring someone without an interview,
nearly all employers also use some method for getting background information on applicants before an interview. This information can be solicited
from the people who know the candidate through reference checks. It can
also be solicited directly from the candidate through an application that
asks for biographical data.

The evidence on the reliability and validity of reference checks suggests
that these are, at best, weak predictors of future success on the job.[31] The
main reason for this low validity is that the evaluations supplied in most
reference letters are so positive that it is hard to differentiate applicants. As
Northwestern Bell's district manager of management employment notes,
"They all say, `This is the greatest individual the world has ever seen, the
next president, at least.'...It isn't always accurate."[32]

This problem with reference letters has two causes. First, the applicant
usually gets to choose who writes the letter and can thus choose only those
writers who think the highest of his or her abilities. Second, since letter writers can never be sure who will read the letters, they may fear that supplying
damaging information about someone could come back to haunt them. This
fear is well placed. Singer Diana Ross once circulated a letter that read, "If I
let an employee go, it's because either their work or their personal habits are
not acceptable to me. I do not recommend these people." She then listed
seven names. One of those on the list sued her for libel, and Ross avoided
legal reproach only by arriving at a costly out-of-court settlement. This is
hardly an isolated incident: Over 8,000 such suits have been filed since 1983.
In 72 percent of these cases, the recipient of the bad reference prevails, and
the average award is over $500,000 (the record is $1.9 million).[33]

The evidence on the utility of biographical information collected directly
from job applicants is much more positive, especially for certain occupa-

tional categories such as clerical and sales.[34] The low cost of obtaining such information significantly enhances its utility—especially when the information is used in conjunction with a well-designed follow-up interview.[35]

This information is typically assessed through long questionnaires employing multiple-choice formats, which are either mailed or distributed to groups. Some sample items from some of the major dimensions of life history assessed by these questionnaires are shown in Table 11.7.[36]

In terms of legal concerns, it should be noted that asking certain questions is illegal regardless of its impact. There is substantial variation from state-to-state on what constitutes a legal versus an illegal inquiry, and the reader should consult the Fair Employment Practices Commission in his or her home state to find out more.

Physical Ability Tests

Although automation and other advances in technology have eliminated or modified many physically demanding occupational tasks, a large number of jobs still require certain physical abilities. In these cases, tests of physical abilities may not only be relevant to predicting performance but relevant to predicting occupational injuries and disabilities as well.[37] There are seven classes of tests in this area, ones that evaluate (1) muscular tension, (2) muscular power, (3) muscular endurance, (4) cardiovascular endurance, (5) flexibility, (6) balance, and (7) coordination.[38]

The criterion-related validities for these kinds of tests for certain jobs is quite strong.[39] Unfortunately, these tests are likely to have an adverse impact on some disabled applicants and many female applicants, particularly the strength tests. For example, roughly two-thirds of all males score higher than the highest-scoring female on muscular tension tests.

There are two keys in deciding whether to use these kinds of tests. First, is the physical ability essential to performing the job and is this prominent in the job description? Neither the Civil Rights Act nor ADA requires employers to hire individuals who cannot perform essential job functions, and both accept a written job description as evidence of the essential functions of the job."[40] Second, is there a probability that failure to adequately perform the job would result in some risk to the safety or health of the applicant, coworkers, or clients? The "direct threat" clause of the ADA makes it clear that adverse impact against the disabled is warranted under such conditions.

Cognitive Ability Tests

Cognitive ability tests differentiate individuals on their mental rather than physical capacities. Cognitive ability has many different facets, although we will focus on three dominant ones.[41] "Verbal comprehension" refers to a person's capacity to understand and use written and spoken language. "Quantitative ability" concerns the speed and accuracy with which one can

TABLE 11.7   Sample Items from a Typical Biographical Information Questionnaire

1. What is your current employment status?
   a. Student with a full-time job
   b. Student with a part-time job
   c. Student, with no other employment
   d. Self-employed
   e. Unemployed
   f. Employed part-time
   g. Employed full-time
   h. Employed full-time, and also have a second job

2. What was your most enjoyable activity in college?
   a. I did not attend college
   b. Academic studies
   c. Athletics
   d. Social clubs
   e. Dramatics
   f. Student publications or radio
   g. College music
   h. Off-campus activities

3. At any time during the last five years, have you held a job in which other workers were directly responsible to you?
   a. No
   b. Yes, one person
   c. Yes, two to four people
   d. Yes, five to ten people
   e. More than ten people

4. Outside of balancing your checkbook, do you keep written records of what you spend?
   a. No, have never tried
   b. No, have tried but found it too time-consuming
   c. No, have tried but found it unnecessary
   d. No, have tried but quit for other reasons
   e. Yes

solve arithmetic problems of all kinds. "Reasoning ability," a broader concept, refers to a person's capacity to invent solutions to many diverse problems. Table 11.8 shows sample items from a cognitive ability test.

TABLE 11.8

Sample Items from Measures of Different Facets of Cognitive Ability

1. Verbal Ability   Which of the following words means most nearly *the same* as ABERRATION?

(a) conception   (b) discussion   (c) abhorrence

(d) deviation   (e) humiliation

Which of the following words means most nearly *the opposite* of AMICABLE?

(a) nauseous   (b) unfriendly   (c) obscene

(d) penetrating   (e) fondness

2. Quantitative Ability   Mrs. Jones deposits $700.00 in a bank that pays 3 percent interest per year. How much money will she have at the end of the year?

(a) $21.00   (b) $679.00   (c) $702.10

(d) $721.00   (e) $910.00

What is the value of r after it has been decreased by 16 2/3 percent?

(a) $1/6\ r$ (b) $1/3\ r$ (c) $5/6\ r$

(d) $6/7\ r$ (e) $7/6\ r$

3. Reasoning Ability   _____ is to prison as Smithsonian is to _____

(a) Alcatraz–Museum   (b) Guard–Washington, D.C. (c) Warden–Warhol

(d) Criminal–Washington, D.C. (e) Guard–Museum

Which design belongs in E—a, b, c, d, or e?

SOURCE: John A. Wagner, III and John R. Hollenbeck, *Management of Organizational Behavior* © 1992, pp. 66, 90. Reprinted by permission of Prentice Hall, Englewood Cliffs, N.J.

Some jobs require only one or two of these facets of cognitive ability. Under these conditions, maintaining the separation among the facets is appropriate. However, many jobs that are high in complexity require most, if not all, of the facets. In addition, there is generally a weak, but positive, relationship among the facets, and hence one often averages scores on all the facets to come up with one measure of cognitive ability. Highly reliable commercial tests measuring these kinds of abilities are widely available, and they are generally valid predictors of job performance. The validity of these kinds of tests is related to the complexity of the job, however, in that one sees higher criterion-related validation for complex jobs than for simple jobs. Still, the generalizability of these tests over many different jobs, along with their relatively low cost, makes them one of the best selection methods in terms of utility.[42]

One of the major drawbacks to these tests, however, is that they typically have adverse impact on blacks. In the past, the difference between the means for blacks and whites meant that an average black would score at the 16th percentile of the distribution of white scores.[43] Indeed, the notion of race norming alluded to earlier was born of the desire to use these high-utility tests in a manner that avoided adverse impact.

Fortunately, more recent data suggest that race differences in scores on cognitive ability tests have decreased significantly over the years. Figure 11.3 shows the results of a study that monitored trends in race differences on several tests of cognitive ability. The trend lines begin with children born in 1954, the year of the Supreme Court's decision in *Brown v. Board of Education*, and end with the scores for children born in 1970. Although differences persist, these have been cut in half in the intervening years.[44] If these trends were to continue at the same rate, one might find only negligible differences between the races on these kinds of tests for children born in the 1990s.

Personality Inventories

While ability tests attempt to categorize individuals relative to what they can do, personality measures tend to categorize individuals by what they are like. Two recent reviews of the personality literature independently arrived at five common aspects of personality.[45] We refer to these five major dimensions as (1) extroversion, (2) adjustment, (3) agreeableness, (4) conscientiousness, and (5) inquisitiveness. Table 11.9 lists each of these with a corresponding list of adjectives that fit each dimension.

Although it is possible to find reliable, commercially available measures of each of these traits, the evidence for their validity and generalizability is low. Only conscientiousness displays any validity across a number of different job categories, and here the correlations are in the .10s and low .20s. Extroversion is relevant to a few types of jobs such as sales and management, but here, too, the level of predictability is low. These tests sometimes perform better when used in conjunction with more traditional ability tests, but this is not always the case.[46]

Personality inventories also are more predictive when there are clear linkages between specific traits and specific characteristics of jobs, as opposed to blanket attempts to validate all traits for all jobs.[47] Although some have suggested that the use of these tests is increasing in the workplace, their relative lack of use has not produced a long history of litigation.[48]

Work Samples

Work-sample tests and job-performance tests attempt to simulate the job in miniaturized form—for example, a typing test for prospective clerical workers. An "in-basket test" is another example. In an in-basket test, job candidates are asked to respond to memos that typify the problems confronted

FIGURE 11.3 Yearly Trends in the Score Difference Between African American and White Students on Tests of Cognitive Ability

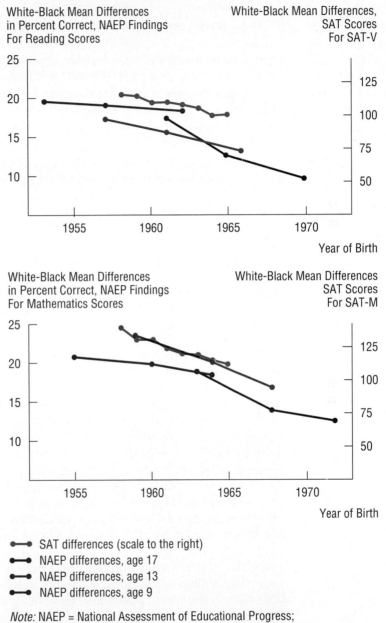

White-Black Mean Differences in Percent Correct, NAEP Findings For Reading Scores

White-Black Mean Differences, SAT Scores For SAT-V

Year of Birth

White-Black Mean Differences in Percent Correct, NAEP Findings For Mathematics Scores

White-Black Mean Differences SAT Scores For SAT-M

Year of Birth

● SAT differences (scale to the right)
● NAEP differences, age 17
● NAEP differences, age 13
● NAEP differences, age 9

Note: NAEP = National Assessment of Educational Progress; SAT = Scholastic Aptitude Test; V = Verbal; M = Mathematics

by those who already hold the job. The key in this and other forms of work-sample tests is the behavioral consistency between the requirements of the job and the requirements of the test.[49]

TABLE 11.9   The Five Major Dimensions of Personality Inventories

1. Extroversion	Sociable, gregarious, assertive, talkative, expressive
2. Adjustment	Emotionally stable, nondepressed, secure, content
3. Agreeableness	Courteous, trusting, good-natured, tolerant, cooperative, forgiving
4. Conscientiousness	Dependable, organized, persevering, thorough, achievement oriented
5. Inquisitiveness	Curious, imaginative, artistically sensitive, broad-minded, playful

Work-sample tests tend to be job specific—that is, tailored individually to each different job in each organization. On the positive side, this has resulted in tests that demonstrate a high degree of criterion-related validity. In addition, the obvious parallels between the test and the job make content validity high. In general, this reduces the likelihood that rejected applicants will challenge the procedure through litigation. What evidence is available also suggests that these tests are low in adverse impact.[50]

With all these advantages come two drawbacks. First, by their very nature the tests are job specific, so generalizability is low. Second, partly because a new test has to be developed for each job, and partly because of their nonstandardized formats, these tests are relatively expensive to develop. It is much more cost-effective to purchase a commercially available cognitive ability test that can be used for a number of different job categories within the company than to develop a test for each job. For this reason, some have rated the utility of cognitive ability tests higher than work-sample tests despite the latter's higher criterion-related validity.[51]

In the area of managerial selection, work-sample tests are typically the cornerstone in assessment centers. Generically, the term *assessment center* is used to describe a wide variety of specific selection programs that employ multiple selection methods to rate either applicants or job incumbents on their managerial potential. Someone attending an assessment center would typically experience work-sample tests such as an in-basket test and several tests of more general abilities and personality. Because they employ multiple selection methods, the criterion-related validity of assessment centers tends to be quite high. As the "Competing through Globalization" box indicates, the vast amount of information provided by assessment centers is especially critical when hiring managers in international locations. We will also discuss the use of assessment centers as career development exercises in Chapter 12.

Honesty Tests and Drug Tests

Many of the problems that confront society also exist within organizations, which has led to two new kinds of tests: theft tests and drug-use tests. Many companies used to employ polygraph tests, or lie detectors, to evaluate job

Globalization

PERSONNEL SELECTION AND CROSS-CULTURAL BARRIERS IN RUSSIA

Given the lack of familiarity of Westerners with Russian culture and business practices, it is almost impossible to find competent American managers for Russian subsidiaries. Yet, hiring a native Russian who can successfully perform the typical duties expected of a manager is also a formidable challenge.

The difficulty of accomplishing this feat is attributable to three factors. First, background checks and references are much more difficult to obtain for Russian applicants relative to what one might be accustomed to in the West. The personal and professional history of many potential applicants is inaccessible and often obscured by political and security institutions. Second, whereas graduates of Western business schools have all been exposed to similar curricula in accounting, finance, and human resources, there is little if any homogeneity in the education of Russian managers. For example, some Russian managers define profits as surplus cash (i.e., "We did not have any profits last year because we bought a new factory") and others treat cost reductions as profit. There is even less commonality when it comes to matters like pricing and marketing. Finally, although correcting hiring

mistakes in the United States by firing someone is not an easy matter, the situation is even more difficult in Russia, where employment security borders on being a religious right.

To ensure hiring the right manager in Russia, companies that succeed there typically employ many different types of tests. On the one hand, translated tests of general cognitive ability are critical to determine whether the individual has a sound educational background and is likely to be able to learn on the job. Translated personality inventories are also useful to determine whether the person has values that are compatible with running a business in a capitalistic system.

Since much of the business in Russia gets done through informal networks, however, these standardized tests are complemented by work-sample tests. The work-sample tests may require candidates to set up appointments with key officials, book hotel space, arrange for visas, secure official statistics, or obtain drafts of pending legislation. If the candidate is not sufficiently networked to execute these kinds of local tasks, then having the right abilities and personality traits may make little difference.

SOURCE: P. Lawrence and C. Vlachoutsicos, "Joint Ventures in Russia: Put the Locals in Charge," *Harvard Business Review*, January–February 1993, 44–54.

applicants, but this changed with the passage of the Polygraph Act in 1988. This act banned the use of polygraphs in employment screening for all private companies except for pharmaceutical companies and companies that supplied security guards for operations involved in health and safety.

Although the 1988 act eliminated polygraph testing, it did not eliminate the problem of theft by employees. As a result, the paper-and-pencil honesty testing industry was born. A mere one year after the Polygraph Act, 3.5 million such tests were administered to prospective American workers.[52]

Paper-and-pencil honesty tests typically ask applicants directly about their attitudes toward theft or their past experiences with theft. Some sample items are shown in Table 11.10. Given the recent development of these tests, there is not a great deal of independent evidence (i.e., evidence not generated by those who publish and sell the tests) on their reliability and

TABLE 11.10   Sample Items from a Typical Integrity Test

1. It's OK to take something from a company that is making too much profit.
2. Stealing is just a way of getting your fair share.
3. When a store overcharges its customers, it's OK to change price tags on merchandise.
4. If you could get into a movie without paying and not get caught, would you do it?
5. Is it OK to go around the law if you don't actually break it?

SOURCE: Reprinted with Permission, *Inc.* magazine February, 1992 © Copyright 1992 by Goldhirsh Group, Inc., 38 Commercial Wharf, Boston, Mass. 02110.

validity. This problem is compounded by the fact that it is difficult to come up with a criterion to use in validation studies of employee theft.

Some have asked whether these kinds of tests should be held to higher standards than traditional tests. Accusing someone of being a thief is a stronger assertion than suggesting that he or she is low on quantitative ability. Even the most liberal estimates of validity for these tests are insufficient to pass the "reasonable doubt" standard applied by the judicial system.[53] Moreover, when mistakes are made, these tend to falsely classify honest individuals as thieves rather than the other way around. Finally, any industry that grows as fast as the honesty test industry is subject to growing pains. One review of these tests noted the frequency of false or misleading claims found in the brochures published by many of the testing companies.[54] Although it is always a good rule to locally evaluate the reliability and validity of any selection method, this may be even more critical with honesty tests.

As with theft, there is a growing perception of the problems caused by drug use among employees. Indeed, 79 percent of Fortune 1000 chief executives cited substance abuse as a significant problem in their organizations, and 50 percent of medium and large organizations test applicants for drug use.[55] Because the physical properties of drugs are invariant and subject to highly rigorous chemical testing, the reliability and validity of drug tests are very high. This is especially the case when less expensive "screening tests" (e.g., immunoassay tests) are followed up with more expensive "confirmation tests" (e.g., gas chromatography tests).

The major controversies surrounding drug tests involve not their reliability and validity but whether they represent an invasion of privacy, an unreasonable search and seizure, or a violation of due process. Urinalysis and blood tests are invasive procedures, and accusing someone of drug use is a serious matter. As with honesty testing, there has not been a great deal of legislation or litigation in this area to date; however, one suspects that this might not be true in the future.

Employers considering the use of drug tests would be well advised to make sure that their drug-testing programs conform to some general rules.

First, these tests should be administered systematically to all applicants applying for the same job. Second, testing seems more defensible for jobs where there are safety hazards associated with failure to perform. Test results should be reported back to the applicant, who should be allowed an avenue of appeal (and perhaps retesting). Tests should be conducted in an environment that is as unintrusive as possible, and the results from those tests should be held in strict confidence. Finally, when testing current employees, the program should be part of a wider organizational program that provides rehabilitation counseling.[56]

SUMMARY

In this chapter, we examined the five critical standards with which all personnel selection methods should conform—that is, reliability, validity, generalizability, utility, and legality. We also looked at nine different selection methods currently used in organizations and evaluated each with respect to these five standards. Table 11.11, which presents a summary of these selection methods, can be used as a guide in deciding which test to use for a specific purpose.

Although we discussed each type of test individually, it is important to note in closing that there is no need to use only one type of test for any one job. Indeed, managerial assessment centers use many different forms of tests over a two- or three-day period to learn as much as possible about candidates for important executive positions. As a result, highly accurate predictions are often made, and the validity associated with the judicious use of multiple tests is higher than for tests used in isolation.

Discussion Questions

1. We examined nine different types of selection methods in this chapter. Assume that you were just rejected for a job based on one of these nine different methods. Obviously, you might be disappointed and angry regardless of what method was used to make this decision, but can you think of two or three methods that might leave you most distressed? In general, why might the acceptability of the test to applicants be an important standard to add to the five we discussed in this chapter?

2. Videotaping applicants in interviews is becoming an increasingly popular means of getting multiple assessments of that individual from different perspectives. Can you think of some reasons why videotaping interviews might also be useful in evaluating the interviewer? What would you look for in an interviewer if you were evaluating one on videotape?

3. Distinguish between concurrent and predictive validation designs, discussing why the latter is to be preferred over the former. Examine each of the nine selection methods discussed in this chapter and determine which of these would have their validity most and least affected by the type of validation design employed.

TABLE 11.11

A Summary Table Evaluating Personnel Selection Methods

Method	Reliability	Validity
Interviews	Low when unstructured and when assessing nonobservable traits	Low if unstructured and nonbehavioral
Reference checks	Low, especially when obtained from letters	Low because of lack of range in evaluations
Biographical information	High test-retest, especially for verifiable information	High criterion-related validity, but low in content validity
Physical ability tests	High	Moderate criterion-related validity; high content validity for some jobs
Cognitive ability tests	High	Moderate criterion-related validity; content validation inappropriate
Personality inventories	High	Low criterion-related validity for most traits; content validation inappropriate
Work-sample tests	High	High criterion and content validity
Honesty tests	Insufficient independent evidence	Insufficient independent evidence
Drug tests	High	High

4. Some have speculated that on top of increasing the validity of decisions, employing rigorous selection methods has symbolic value for organizations. What message is sent to applicants about the organization through hiring practices, and how might this message be reinforced by recruitment programs that occur before selection and training programs that occur after selection?

Notes

1. R. Behar, "Thugs in Uniform," *Time*, March 9, 1992, 46.

2. J. C. Nunnally, *Psychometric Theory* (New York: McGraw-Hill, 1978).

3. B. Schneider, "An Interactionist Perspective on Organizational Effectiveness," in *Organizational Effectiveness: A Comparison of Multiple Models*, ed. K. S. Cameron and D. A. Whetton (Orlando, Fla.: Academic Press, 1983), 27–54.

TABLE 11.11

continued

Generalizability	Utility	Legality
Low	Low, especially because of expense	Low, because of subjectivity and potential interviewer bias; also lack of validity makes job relatedness low
Low	Low, although not expensive to obtain	Those writing letters may be concerned with charges of libel
Usually job specific, but have been successfully developed for many job types	High; inexpensive way to collect vast amounts of potentially relevant data	May have adverse impact; thus often develop separate scoring keys based on sex or race
Low; only pertain to physically demanding jobs	Moderate for some physical jobs; may prevent expensive injuries/disability	Often has adverse impact on women and the disabled; need to establish job relatedness
High; predictive for most jobs, although best for complex jobs	High; low cost and wide application across diverse jobs in companies	Often has adverse impact on race, especially for African Americans, though decreasing over time
Low; few traits predictive for many jobs	Low, although inexpensive for jobs where specific traits are relevant	Low, because of cultural and sex differences on most traits, and low job relatedness in general
Usually job specific, but have been successfully developed for many job types	High, despite the relatively high cost to develop	High, because of low adverse impact and high job relatedness
Insufficient independent evidence	Insufficient independent evidence	Insufficient history of litigation, but will undergo scrutiny
High	Expensive, but may yield high payoffs for health-related costs	May be challenged on invasion-of-privacy grounds

4. N. Schmitt, R. Z. Gooding, R. A. Noe, and M. Kirsch, "Meta-Analysis of Validity Studies Published between 1964 and 1982 and the Investigation of Study Characteristics," *Personnel Psychology* 37 (1984): 407–422.

5. J. Cohen, *Statistical Power Analysis for the Behavioral Sciences* (New York: Academic Press, 1977).

6. C. H. Lawshe, "Inferences from Personnel Tests and Their Validity," *Journal of Applied Psychology* 70 (1985): 237–238.

7. D. D. Robinson, "Content-Oriented Personnel Selection in a Small Business Setting," *Personnel Psychology* 34 (1981): 77–87.

8. C. H. Lawshe, "A Quantitative Approach to Content Validity," *Personnel Psychology* 28 (1975): 563–575.

9. P. R. Sackett, "Assessment Centers and Content Validity: Some Neglected Issues," *Personnel Psychology* 40 (1987): 13–25.

10. F. L. Schmidt and J. E. Hunter, "The Future of Criterion-Related Validity," *Personnel Psychology* 33 (1980): 41–60; F. L. Schmidt, J. E. Hunter and K. Pearlman, "Task Differences as Moderators of Aptitude Test Validity: A Red Herring," *Journal of Applied Psychology* 66 (1982): 166–185; R. L. Gutenberg, R. D. Arvey, H. G. Osburn, and R. P. Jeanneret, "Moderating Effects of Decision-Making/Information Processing Dimensions on Test Validities," *Journal of Applied Psychology* 68 (1983): 600–608.

11. F. L. Schmidt, J. G. Berner and J. E. Hunter, "Racial Differences in Validity of Employment Tests: Reality or Illusion," *Journal of Applied Psychology* 58 (1974): 5–6.

12. Society for Industrial and Organizational Psychology, *Principles for the Validation and Use of Personnel Selection Procedures* (College Park, Md.: University of Maryland Press, 1987).

13. C. L. Hulin, R. A. Henry and S. L. Noon, "Adding a Dimension: Time as a Factor in the Generalizability of Predictive Relationships," *Psychological Bulletin* 107 (1990): 328–340; G. V. Barrett and R. A. Alexander, "A Re-examination of the Effects of Time on Validity Generalization: A Critique of Hulin, Henry and Noon," *Personnel Psychology* (in press).

14. J. W. Boudreau, "Utility Analysis for Decisions in Human Resource Management," in *Handbook for Industrial and Organizational Psychology*, ed. M. D. Dunnette and L. M. Hough (Palo Alto, Cal.: Consulting Psychologist Press, 1992).

15. J. W. Boudreau and C. J. Berger, "Decision-Theoretic Utility Analysis Applied to External Employee Movement," *Journal of Applied Psychology* 70 (1985): 581–612.

16. K. J. McCullough, *Selecting Employees Safely under the Law* (Englewood Cliffs, N.J.: Prentice-Hall, 1981).

17. T. L. O'Brian, "An Industry Emerges to Exploit the Disabilities Act," *The Wall Street Journal*, December 1, 1992, B2.

18. K. F. Ebert, "New Civil Rights Act Invites Litigation," *Personnel Law Update* 6 (1991): 3.

19. R. J. Smith, "Shoney's to Set Aside $105 Million in Pact to Settle Racial Case," *The Wall Street Journal*, November 4, 1992, G12.

20. J. Woo, "Ex-Workers Hit Back with Age-Bias Suits," *The Wall Street Journal*, December 8, 1992, B1.

21. P. M. Barrett, "How One Man's Fight for a Raise Became a Major Age-Bias Case," *The Wall Street Journal*, January 6, 1993, A1.

22. E. Thomas, "Assault on Affirmative Action," *Time*, February 25, 1985, 19–20.

23. R. L. Dipboye, *Selection Interviews: Process Perspectives* (Cincinnati, Oh.: South-Western Publishing, 1991).

24. J. E. Hunter and R. H. Hunter, "Validity and Utility of Alternative Predictors of Job Performance," *Psychological Bulletin* 96 (1984): 72–98.

25. Watson v. Fort Worth Bank and Trust, 108 Supreme Court 2791 (1988).

26. J. Solomon, "The New Job Interview: Show Thyself," *The Wall Street Journal*, December 4, 1989, B4.

27. J. A. Weekly and J. A. Geir, "Reliability and Validity of the Situational Interview for a Sales Position," *Journal of Applied Psychology* 72 (1987): 484–487.

28. G. Stasser and W. Titus, "Effects of Information Load and Percentage of Shared Information on the Dissemination of Unshared Information during Group Discussion,"*Journal of Personality and Social Psychology* 53 (1987): 81–93.

29. A. Cuneo, "Diverse by Design," *Business Week*, June 6, 1992, 72.

30. T. Libby, "Surviving the Group Interview," *Forbes*, March 24, 1986, 190; article in Dipboye, *Selection Interviews*, 210.

31. Hunter and Hunter, "Validity and Utility."

32. L. McDonnell, "Interviews and Tests Counting More as Past Employers Clam Up," *Minneapolis Tribune*, May 3, 1981.

33. J. B. Copeland, "Revenge of the Fired," *Newsweek*, February 16, 1987, 46–47.

34. Hunter and Hunter, "Validity and Utility"; R. R. Reilly and G. T. Chao, "Validity and Fairness of Some Alternative Employee Selection Procedures," *Personnel Psychology* 35 (1982): 1–62.

35. W. F. Cascio, "Accuracy of Verifiable Biographical Information Blank Responses," *Journal of Applied Psychology* 60 (1975): 767–769.

36. C. D. Anderson, J. L. Warner and C. C. Spencer, "Inflation Bias in Self-Assessment Examinations: Implications for Valid Employee Selection," *Journal of Applied Psychology* 69 (1984): 574–580.

37. J. R. Hollenbeck, D. R. Ilgen and S. M. Crampton, "Lower-Back Disability in Occupational Settings: A Human Resource Management View," *Personnel Psychology* (in press).

38. J. Hogan, "Structure of Physical Performance in Occupational Tasks," *Journal of Applied Psychology* 76 (1991): 495–507.

39. J. Hogan, "Physical Abilities," in *Handbook of Industrial and Organizational Psychology*, ed. M. D. Dunnette and L. M. Hough (Palo Alto, Cal.: Consulting Psychologists Press, 1991).

40. Americans with Disabilities Act of 1990, S. 933, Public Law 101-336 (1990).

41. Nunnally, *Psychometric Theory*.

42. L. S. Gottfredson, "The g Factor in Employment," *Journal of Vocational Behavior* 29 (1986): 293–296; Hunter and Hunter, "Validity and Utility"; Gutenberg et al., "Moderating Effects"; Schmidt, Berner and Hunter, "Racial Differences in Validity."

43. A. R. Jenson, "g: Artifact or Reality?" *Journal of Vocational Behavior* 29 (1986): 301–331.

44. L. V. Jones, "White-Black Achievement Differences: The Narrowing Gap," *American Psychologist* 39 (1984): 1207–1213.

45. M. R. Barrick and M. K. Mount, "The Big Five Personality Dimensions and Job Performance: A Meta-Analysis," *Personnel Psychology* 44 (1991): 1–26; L. M. Hough, N. K. Eaton, M. D. Dunnette, J. D. Camp and R. A. McCloy, "Criterion-Related Validities of Personality Constructs and the Effect of Response Distortion on Those zzz Validities," *Journal of Applied Psychology* 75 (1990): 467–476.

46. J. R. Hollenbeck, A. P. Brief, E. M. Whitener and K. E. Pauli, "An Empirical Note on the Interaction of Personality and Aptitude in Personnel Selection," *Journal of Management* 14 (1988): 441–450.

47. R. P. Tett, D. N. Jackson and M. Rothstein, "Personality Measures as Predictors of Job Performance: A Meta-Analytic Review," *Personnel Psychology* 44 (1991): 703–742.

48. S. Moses, "Personality Tests Come Back in I/O," *APA Monitor*, November 1991, 9.

49. P. F. Wernimont and J. P. Campbell, "Signs, Samples and Criteria," *Journal of Applied Psychology* 46 (1968): 417–419.

50. Hunter and Hunter, "Validity and Utility"; W. Cascio and N. Phillips, "Performance Testing: A Rose among Thorns?" *Journal of Applied Psychology* 32 (1979): 751–766; F. L. Schmidt, A. Greenthol, J. E. Hunter, J. Berner and F. Seaton, "Job Sample vs. Paper-and-Pencil Trade and Technical Tests: Adverse Impact and Examiner Attitudes," *Personnel Psychology* 30 (1977): 187–197.

51. Hunter and Hunter, "Validity and Utility."

52. C. Gorman, "Honestly, Can We Trust You?" *Time*, January 23, 1989, 44.

53. K. R. Murphy, "Detecting Infrequent Perception," *Journal of Applied Psychology* 72 (1987): 611–614.

54. P. R. Sackett, L. R. Burris and C. Callahan, "Integrity Testing for Personnel Selection: An Update," *Personnel Psychology* 42 (1989): 491–529.

55. M. Freudenheim, "Workers Substance Abuse Increasing, Survey Says," *The New York Times*, December 13, 1988, 2; J. P. Guthrie and J. D. Olian, "Drug and Alcohol Testing Programs: The Influence of Organizational Context and Objectives" (Paper presented at the Fourth Annual Conference of the Society for Industrial/Organizational Psychology, Boston, 1989).

56. K. R. Murphy, G. C. Thornton and D. H. Reynolds, "College Students' Attitudes toward Drug Testing Programs," *Personnel Psychology* 43 (1990): 615–631.

C A S E

PERSONNEL SELECTION IN TEAM ENVIRONMENTS

In the late 1980s and early 1990s, many companies, including Procter & Gamble, Motorola, Cummins Engine, Ford, ARCO, Kodak, and LTV turned to team-based structures to help increase quality and decrease costs. These organizations found that the selection of team members was a critical feature in the teams' ultimate success. They also discovered that the knowledge, skills, abilities, and traits that made someone a successful job incumbent working in isolation did not necessarily make that person a good team member.

As these companies gained experience with teams, they soon began to realize that there were also different types of teams and that the characteristics that made for a successful team member on one type of team did not translate to other types of teams. For example, there are "problem-solving teams" that meet every week for a few hours to discuss ways of improving quality or efficiency. This kind of team is different than a "self-managed production team" whose members work together all the time and are jointly responsible for all the production tasks associated with some recurrent or ongoing organizational activity. This type of team is different still from a "cross-functional, special-purpose team," which puts together specialists from different functional areas (production, engineering, marketing, human resources) to make a one-time decision or to work on a one-time special project.

QUESTIONS

1. Assume that you are a staffing specialist in one of these companies. What types of knowledge, skills, abilities, and traits would you recommend for people who work in teams versus those working alone?

2. What types of knowledge, skills, abilities and traits would you recommend for one type of team but not another?

3. What methods would you use to assess the knowledge, skills, abilities, and traits of prospective team members?

4. How would you assess the reliability and validity of these assessments?

NUCOR: SELECTING HIGH PERFORMERS

Tracy Shellabarger is comptroller of the Crawfordsville plant of Nucor Corporation, which produces steel. The Crawfordsville facility was built in 1988 and posed some unique employment issues. Tracy, in his Crawfordsville office in rural Indiana, described the human resources' implications for a start-up operation: "One of our major concerns was that potential employees would not be familiar with what it's like to work in a steel mill. Mills are very hot and loud. With sparks flying and the floor rumbling, there are people who will decide that they don't care about the pay. They conclude that it's frightening, and they're out of there."

Early in the plant start-up process, Nucor's management decided that newly hired employees would be sent to visit Nucor's and competitors' mills to provide a realistic preview of what it would be like to work in a steel mill. Some employees were even sent to Germany, which had the only plant at the time using the technology that Crawsfordsville was pioneering in the United States. The employees were at mills for two or three weeks. Not only did they observe, but after some training, they actually performed some of the jobs.

Shellabarger notes, "Probably the key to our success is communication. We told them about what they would see, discussed what they were seeing, and afterwards told them what they had seen. The technology they would experience in Crawfordsville was different in terms of scale, so that was explained carefully, too, in comparison to what they had seen."

One advantage Nucor had in recruiting in Crawfordsville was that they would be the highest-paying employer in the area. Tracy remembers, "At one Chamber of Commerce meeting I was asked if we were done recruiting for the mill. A few people explained their concern that we were taking their best employees. When we were recruiting for 40 jobs by newspaper advertisement and radio, we received approximately 750 applications."

Nucor's History

The history of Nucor is very different from those of large steel companies. In the early 1980s, most companies produced a wide range of steels, primarily from ore processed in blast furnaces. They found it difficult to compete with imports, usually from Japan, and had given up substantial market share to imports. The domestic share of the world's raw steel production declined from 19 to 11 percent by the early 1980s, and the large integrated steel firms, such as US Steel, were the hardest hit.

By the mid 1980s, large steel companies were restructuring, cutting capacity, dropping unprofitable lines, and trying to become responsive to the market. *The Wall Street Journal* stated that "the decline [in the steel industry] has resulted from such problems as high labor and energy costs in mining and processing iron ore, a lack of profits and capital to modernize plants, and conservative management that has hesitated to take risks."

While the industry giants were attempting to lobby the federal government for restrictive trade legislation, another steel company was taking a very different approach. Ken Iverson, chairman and CEO of Nucor Corporation, opposed import restrictions and thought that the steel industry in the United States had to change. He spearheaded technological changes at Nucor and also developed a joint venture with the Japanese. Nucor appears to have a four-year technological lead on competitors; it is the largest mini-mill company and is currently the ninth largest steel producer in the United States. Sales in 1991 were $1.4 billion. Expansions planned for 1993 and 1994 are expected to boost Nucor's share of the domestic sheet-steel market from 6 percent to 10 percent, making Nucor the fourth largest steelmaker in the United States.

Nucor uses the mini-mill concept, which is an alternative to the traditional integrated mill. Mini-mills use electric arc furnaces and create a narrow product line from scrap steel. The technology is cheaper, less complex, and more efficient than the integrated mill. Mini-mills tend to be located in areas where labor is cheap, frequently nonunionized, and the customer is close.

The 800,000 ton $265 million mini-mill built in Crawfordsville was different in that it was the first mini-mill to implement an untested German technology that produced flat rolled steel. Flat rolled steel, which was 52 percent of the U.S. market, was the largest market for steel products. Flat rolled steel is thin sheet steel that is used in car bodies, refrigerators, and other products. Crawfordsville is now running at 125 percent of capacity, with a $45 per ton cost advantage over almost every integrated steel company in the United States.

Nucor's Philosophy of Management

Iverson describes a homegrown philosophy of management that has been successful. Nucor uses few management layers (4 compared with the more traditional 9 to 11 common in the industry). Staffing is minimal;

the corporate office in Charlotte, North Carolina, has 22 staff people. Each of the fifteen plants has a general manager. Operations are strongly decentralized, with each division designated a profit center.

The Nucor culture is termed egalitarian by Iverson. Everyone gets the same vacations, holidays, and health care programs. Nucor has no mission statement or job descriptions. Iverson says, "I think the reason is that job descriptions tell you what you cannot do. I don't want to limit people that way."

The emphasis at Nucor is on earning a good living and ensuring job security. Standards for both quality and output are set for groups of 25 to 30 people, who are responsible for completing a task from start to finish, such as making good billet tons or finish tons. If the goal is exceeded, employees are paid a weekly bonus that can run 150 percent of base pay.

Although base pay is considerably less than steel industry standards, the bonus allows workers a far higher earning potential than that at most other plants. If a bonus is earned it is paid weekly so employees clearly see the connection between effort and reward. There is a profit-sharing plan in which 10 percent of all pre-tax earnings is returned to employees. Even a five-minute absence from work may result in forfeiture of a bonus for the week, and few employees are absent, since they are not paid for an absence of less than three days.

The work groups are responsible for decisions about work. Iverson claims managers can make bad decisions, and workers should tell them if that is the case. Communication moves both up and down the hierarchy, with responsibility pushed down to the lowest possible level. When there is a performance issue within the group, the group identifies the problem and solves it.

There have been no layoffs in twenty years at Nucor. If business is slow, plants may work only three or four days a week, and the workers' pay drops. There is also a program called "Share the Pain." During the slow periods, a foreman's pay can drop 20 to 25 percent, department heads' pay drops 35 to 40 percent, and officers' pay drops 65 to 70 percent.

The Crawfordsville Mill

Of the nearly 445 people who work in the Crawfordsville mill, approximately 225 work on steel production, and 115 have maintenance jobs. The remainder are people in such areas as sales, finance, clerical, and guard positions. Although there are approximately 63 different jobs for those who work in steel production and 16 jobs for those in maintenance, there are no formal job descriptions. Cross training ensures that employees do not stand idle when there is down time in a particular job.

Vincent Schiavoni, hot mill manager, describes the selection process when Crawfordsville was hiring: "We [managers] had to decide how to approach this enormous job on our own—almost all of us had come from mills and did not have any human resources experience. We brainstormed a game plan with the general manager. We were all there when people came in to apply. We wanted to ensure that people filled out their applications themselves and we saw how people presented themselves. There was a short test given assessing basic math skills. In groups of two or three, we prescreened the applications."

When people were asked back for an interview, they met a manager and two foremen. Mechanical skill was considered critical. Shellabarger notes that "in the rural areas where our mills are located, potential employees have likely grown up around farms and so are used to working with equipment." Schiavoni mentioned that background and experience, for example, in reconstructing cars and motorcycles, were considered important.

Schiavoni noted that Nucor was not interested in steel knowledge. After all, the technology was completely new, so no one was familiar with it. "When someone admitted they didn't know anything about steel, but were eager to learn, I knew that was the person we wanted. For a person to move to the next step, he had to have the strong approval of at least two of us, and most often, all three of us would be very positive."

For applicants that met the requirements, the next step was an interview by a psychologist to determine whether the applicant was interested and capable of participating on a team and whether he or she would be motivated by the bonus system of Nucor.

The final decisions on the candidates were made by the team of managers and foremen that interviewed the candidates. Schiavoni notes, "I was pleased by the process. Although it was very time consuming at a

SOURCES:
"Business Briefs: Nucor Corp.," *The Wall Street Journal*, July 8, 1993, B4; F. C. Barnes, in J. M. Higgins and J. W. Vincze, *Strategic Management: Text and Cases.* (Fort Worth, TX: Dryden Press, 1993); "Empowering Employees," *Chief Executive*, March/April 1989, 44–49; "Hot Steel and Good Common Sense," *Management Review*, August 1992, 25–27; T. P. Pare, "Big Threat to Big Steel's Future," *Fortune*, July 15, 1991, 106–108; T. M. Rohan, *Industry Week*, January 21, 1991, 26–28; R. Wrubel, "Ghost of Andy Carnegie?" *Financial World*, September 29, 1992, 50–52.

point when we were all busy with a lot of issues related to start-up, we knew the time invested would be worth it for the future. We knew the success of the plant was just as dependent of the attitudes and abilities of the people as it was on the new technology.

"I was pleased that there was a high level of agreement between the psychologist and managers on the candidates. Also, people warned us that there would be high turnover the first year, but we had virtually none. The little turnover we've experienced is related to personal, not job-related, problems of employees and low performance." Shellabarger adds that "the production bonus strongly motivates the great majority of our employees. Although the bonus is posted weekly, they can figure out their results at the end of each day."

There is very little hiring now because of the no-layoff policy of Nucor. Employees are, however, reassigned. For example, Shellabarger says, "Although we have two strand tenders per shift, we believe that we need only one. We'll move the second strand tenders to other areas of the mill where we are adding galvanizing and a second casting line."

DISCUSSION QUESTIONS

1. What do you think are the critical recruiting and selection processes that have contributed to Nucor's success?

2. How does the employment process match the Nucor way of doing business?

3. How could you demonstrate that Nucor's employee selection process was valid, legal, and benefited the company?

3. What were the advantages and/or disadvantages for employees who visited other mills before Crawfordsville was completed?

4. Do you believe that the recruiting and selection strategies used at Crawfordsville would work equally well in nonmanufacturing environments? Why or why not?

DEVELOPING HUMAN RESOURCES

In Part IV we extend the discussion of the work force begun in Part III. Critical to a company's competitiveness is not only attracting competent workers but retaining them. The four competitive challenges—quality, technological and structural, global, and social—are key issues in employee training, development, and career management. To be successful, companies must ensure that employees have the appropriate skills to work productively in teams, with new technology, in international settings, and with people from different ethnic, racial, gender, and cultural backgrounds.

Chapter 12, "Training," discusses the components of effective training systems. The manager's role in determining employees' readiness for training, creating a positive learning environment, and

ensuring that training is used on the job is emphasized. Presentational, hands-on, and group training methods are discussed.

We begin Chapter 13, "Employee Development," by considering managers' and employees' roles in companies that use work teams. The use of assessment, job experiences, formal courses, and interpersonal relationships to develop employees is emphasized. Current issues in employee development, including cross-cultural preparation and managing workforce diversity, are highlighted to show how companies deal with social and global challenges.

Chapter 14, "Career Management," describes companies' and employees' responsibilities in managing careers. The developmental needs of employees in different career stages are discussed. A key focus of the chapter is the elements of a career-planning system that can help employees identify career goals and prepare action plans to meet their goals.

Several issues related to the competitive challenges are discussed—work and family conflict, plateauing, and outplacement strategies.

TRAINING

Objectives   *After reading this chapter, you should be able to:*

1. Discuss how training can help companies gain a competitive advantage.
2. Describe the role of the manager in identifying training needs, training goals, and supporting the application of training on the job.
3. Conduct a needs assessment to determine whether training is necessary.
4. Evaluate and create conditions to ensure employees' readiness for training.
5. Discuss the strengths and weaknesses of presentation, hands-on, and group training methods.
6. Select the appropriate training method based on the training objectives.
7. Design a training environment to maximize learning.
8. Conduct a cost-benefit analysis of a training program.
9. Choose appropriate training outcomes and evaluation design to determine training-program effectiveness.

*Using Training
to Gain a
Competitive
Advantage*

In 1990 Federal Express won the Malcolm Baldrige National Quality Award largely because of its ability to measure customer satisfaction. Every day the company measures how well the day's work met customer-service indicators related to on-time delivery, damaged packages, lost packages, and nine other "service-quality indicators." Training plays an important role in Federal Express's goal to be the number one overnight express carrier in the world. The company spends 3 percent of its total expenses, or about $225 million a year, on training. About 900 of the company's 91,000 employees work in training functions. Besides mandated training for pilots, Federal Express uses an interactive video network to deliver job training to 45,000 customer-contact employees, couriers, and ground operations people around the world. An electronic university network delivers college courses using personal computers. A Leadership Institute is designed to help managers understand the company's culture and philosophy. A Quality Academy teaches numerous quality processes and tools. Customer-service personnel take five weeks of training before they begin work. Knowledge of what customers want and detailed job knowledge are seen by Chairman Frederick Smith as critical for the success of FedEx. Smith says, "You could never justify the costs of our FXTV network or our interactive video training system. But if you ask me, those would be among the top ten highest payoff projects we've ever done at Federal Express."

SOURCE: P. A. Galagan, "Training Delivers Results to Federal Express," *Training and Development Journal,* December 27, 1991, 33.

INTRODUCTION

The situation at Federal Express illustrates how training can be used by companies to gain a competitive advantage. Typically, U.S. companies have not used training for this purpose. U.S. employers spend approximately $30 billion, or 1 to 2 percent of their payroll, on formal training activities.[1] Lack of investment in training is an often-cited reason why U.S. companies are losing market share to foreign competition. For example, on average, U.S. firms spend about $2,600 per worker per year on training, while Japanese firms spend about $6,500 per worker per year.[2] However, Federal Express, Solectron, Andersen Consulting, and other U.S. firms believe that training plays an important role in increasing productivity and competitiveness. As a result, they invest from 3 to 5 percent of their payroll in training.[3] For example, to achieve its quality objectives, Xerox has spent $125 million on training, in addition to the 2.5 percent of revenue it spends on training each year. The investment in quality training has paid off handsomely, since the company has regained market share from the Japanese in the copier market. Motorola provides each employee with about three and a half to five days of training per year.[4]

Why do these companies and many others believe that investment in training will help them gain a competitive advantage? In Chapter 1, we proposed that companies can gain a competitive advantage if they successfully deal with quality, global, technology and structural, and social challenges. Training can:

- Increase employees' knowledge of foreign competitors and cultures, which is critical for success in foreign markets.

- Help ensure that employees have the basic skills to work with new technology such as robots and computer-assisted manufacturing processes.

- Help employees understand how to work effectively in teams to contribute to product and service quality.

- Ensure that the company's culture emphasizes innovation, creativity, and learning.

- Ensure employment security by providing new ways for employees to contribute to the company when their job changes, their interests change, or their skills become obsolete.

- Prepare employees to accept and work more effectively with each other, particularly with minorities and women.[5]

HIGH-LEVERAGE TRAINING STRATEGY: A SYSTEMATIC APPROACH

Many companies have begun to reconfigure their training function in order to gain competitive advantage. This type of training practice, referred to as **high-leverage training**, is linked to strategic business goals and objectives, is supported by top management, relies on an instructional design model to ensure the quality of training and to contain costs, and is compared or benchmarked to programs in other organizations.[6] High-leverage training practices help create working conditions that encourage continuous learning. Continuous learning is critical for companies to be competitive in a marketplace in which customer needs, quality standards, and product specifications are constantly changing, new competitors are entering the marketplace, and new technologies that render manufacturing processes and service-delivery systems obsolete become readily available.

In general, **training** refers to a planned effort by a company to facilitate the learning of job-related knowledge, skills, or behavior by employees.[7] The goal of training efforts is for employees to master the specific knowledge, skill, or ability emphasized in a specific training program and to apply it in their day-to-day activities. However, for companies that use high-leverage training to gain a competitive advantage, training can also help to create a learning organization.

A **learning organization** is one whose employees are continuously attempting to learn new things and apply what they learn to improve product or service quality. Improvements do not stop when the formal training process is completed.[8] When training is viewed from the high-leverage perspective, employees see that critical thinking and evaluation of process and services is given more than faint praise. **Continuous learning** is expected from employees and is rewarded. Continuous learning requires employees to understand the relationship between their jobs, their work units and the company and to be familiar with the company's business goals.[9] Employees are expected to teach and learn from other employees. Managers take an active role in identifying training needs and helping to ensure that employees use training in their work.

One example of continuous learning is Johnsonville Foods, where a personal development fund was established for each employee.[10] Each employee receives $100 to spend every year on any type of development activity. The development experience does not have to be work related; the only requirement is that it encourages the person to think. Johnsonville also provides personal development workshops and a library resource center where employees can check out materials on a variety of topics. Many of the learning experiences at Johnsonville are experiential. For example, employees may serve on task forces or write business and marketing plans. The reward system reinforces the continuous learning philosophy. Twice each year employees receive a portion of the company's profits, the amount based on individual job performance, performance as a team member, and personal growth and development. The "Competing through Technology and Structure" box discusses how another company promotes continuous learning among employees.

In this chapter, we emphasize the conditions through which training practices can help companies gain competitive advantage and the role that the manager can play in contributing to a high-leverage training effort.

DESIGNING EFFECTIVE TRAINING SYSTEMS

One of the key characteristics of training systems that contribute to competitiveness is that they are designed according to the instructional design process.[11] **Instructional design process** refers to a systematic approach for developing training programs. Table 12.1 presents the components of the instructional design process. This process emphasizes that effective training practices involve more than just choosing the most popular and colorful training method.

Needs Assessment

The first step in the instructional design process is to conduct a needs assessment. Figure 12.1 summarizes the needs assessment process.

A needs assessment helps determine whether training is necessary. There are many different "pressure points" that may suggest that training is necessary: performance problems, new technology, internal or external customer requests for training, job redesign, new legislation, changes in customer preferences, new products, or employees' lack of basic skills. It is important to note that by themselves these "pressure points" do not guaran-

Technology & Structure

COMPETING THROUGH

TRAINING VERSUS LEARNING AT ESSO

Esso Resources Canada, an oil-producing facility with 450 employees, changed its traditional training system to match the company's new high-involvement team work environment. Crucial to changing the training system was distinguishing training from learning. *Training* was defined as the process of providing employees with the knowledge and skills needed to work safely and to meet government regulations and business needs. *Learning* was defined as a skill or knowledge that helped increase employees' ability to do a job more effectively and design improvements in the job. Employees from each of the job families were given the responsibility of analyzing their jobs to determine essential training needs. Employees were responsible for determining the contents of learning. To help employees and teams decide learning and training the company provided them with several tools:

- A learning guide that explained needs assessment and the learning process.

- A learning-style instrument designed to help employees understand how they learn best.

- A learning journal that discusses how to apply learning on the job.

- A learning resource guide that provides employees with a list of books, workshops, and videotapes.

Employees are responsible for communicating learning activities to their managers. At least once a year employees review their learning activities with their supervisors. Results of the new training system are encouraging. Employees spend an average of five days per year on learning activities. The costs for no-shows at training programs have decreased more than 50 percent.

SOURCE: C. W. Nemeth and M. B. Hiebert, "Two Roads to High Involvement," *Training and Development*, June 1991, 55–56.

tee that training is the correct solution. For example, a delivery truck driver who hooks up the supply line of a mild anesthetic to the supply line of a hospital's oxygen system may make this mistake for a number of reasons, including a lack of knowledge about the appropriate line hookup for anesthetic (a training problem), anger over a salary increase that was recently denied by the driver's manager, or a lack of attention to the job's details because of a substance abuse problem. One of the goals of needs assessment is to determine whether the "pressure points" can be successfully addressed by training.

Needs assessment typically involves organizational analysis, person analysis, and task analysis.[12] **Organizational analysis** involves determining the appropriateness of training, given the company's business strategy, its resources available for training, and support by managers and peers for training activities. **Person analysis** involves: (1) determining whether performance deficiencies result from a lack of knowledge, skill, or ability (a

TABLE 12.1   Components of Instructional Design

1. Needs assessment
   - Organizational analysis
   - Person analysis
   - Task analysis
2. Ensure employees' "readiness" to learn
   - Attitudes and motivation
   - Basic skills
3. Create a learning environment
   - Identify learning objective and training outcomes
   - Meaningful material
   - Practice
   - Feedback
   - Observe others
   - Administer and coordinate program
4. Ensure transfer of training
   - Self-management strategies
   - Peer and manager support
5. Select training method
   - Presentational techniques
   - Hands-on techniques
   - Group techniques
6. Evaluate training
   - Identify training outcomes and evaluation design
   - Cost-benefit analysis

---

training issue) or from a motivational or work-design problem; (2) identifying who needs training; and (3) determining employees' readiness for training. **Task analysis** includes identifying the important tasks and knowledge, skill, and behaviors that need to be emphasized in training. Because organizational and person analysis are concerned with identifying whether training is the correct solution to a problem, it is important to conduct these analyses prior to devoting managers' and technical experts' time to identifying tasks, knowledge, skills, and abilities that should be included in a training program—that is, before conducting a task analysis.

Organizational Analysis.   Managers need to consider three factors before choosing training as the solution to any pressure point: support of managers and peers for training activities, the company's strategic direction, and the training resources available.

FIGURE 12.1   The Needs Assessment Process

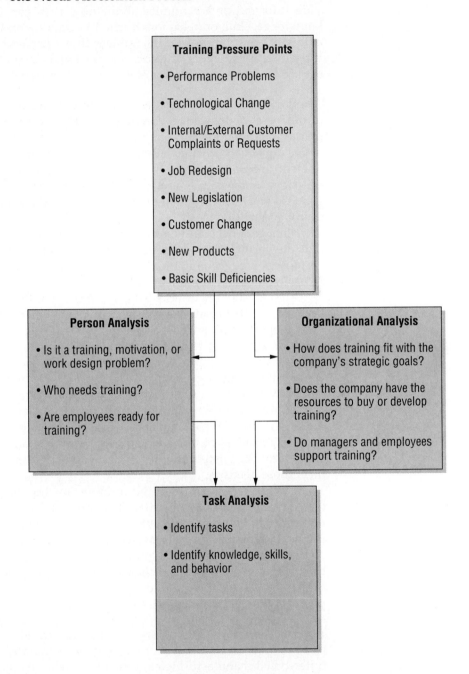

Support of Managers and Peers for Training Activities.   A number of studies have found that peer and manager support for training is critical. The key factors to success are a positive attitude among peers and managers about participation in training activities, managers' and peers' willingness to provide information to trainees about how they can more effectively use knowledge, skill, or behaviors learned in training on the job, and the availability of opportunities for the trainees to use training content in their job.[13] If peers' and managers' attitudes and behaviors are not supportive, employees are not likely to apply training content to their jobs.

Training and Company Strategy.   In Chapter 2, we discussed the importance of business strategy for a company to gain a competitive advantage. The plan or goal that the company chooses to achieve strategic objectives has a major impact on whether resources (money, trainers' time, program development) should be devoted to addressing a training pressure point. Table 12.2 describes four business strategies—concentration, internal growth, external growth, and disinvestment—and highlights the implications of each for training practices.[14]

Managers need to identify the prevailing business strategy to ensure that they are allocating enough of their budget to training activities, that employees are receiving training on relevant topics, and that employees are receiving the right amount of training.[15]

A good example of how business strategy influences training practices is Travelers Corporation, a leading provider of group health, life, and casualty/property insurance to large companies. Travelers' strategic objective is to become the number one provider of financial services in the United States.[16] To achieve this goal, all employees must be trained to use data-processing technology, and managers need to learn how to manage in a company in which data-processing technology makes more information available at the lower levels of the organization and in which products are more tailored to the customers' needs. In the past, managers at Travelers were expected to be product experts; now managers must know how to determine the customers' needs and identify financial experts who can meet those needs.

At Travelers, the role of the training function has changed to support the company's strategic objective. The training function supports the corporate strategy of automation not only by developing and administering programs designed to improve employees' computer literacy but also by using computer-based instructional systems such as interactive video tailored to the computer demands of each job. A new management development program has been implemented to educate managers about how to share power and serve as a resource for employees.

Training Resources.   It is necessary to identify whether the company has the budget, time, and expertise for training. For example, if it is installing computer-based manufacturing equipment in one of its plants, it has three possible strategies for dealing with the need to have computer-literate employees. First, the company can decide that given its staff expertise and budget, it can use internal consultants to train all affected employees. Second, the company may decide that it is more cost-effective to identify

TABLE 12.2

Implications of Business Strategy for Training

Strategy	Emphasis	How Achieved	Key Issues	Training Implications
Concentration	•Increase market share •Reduce operating costs •Create or maintain market niche	•Improve product quality •Productivity improvement or technical process innovation •Customize products or services	•Skill currency •Development of existing work force	•Team building •Cross-training •Specialized programs •Interpersonal skill training •On-the-job training
Internal Growth	•Market development •Product development •Innovation •Joint ventures	•Market existing products/add distribution channels •Global market expansion •Modify existing products •Create new or different products •Expansion through joint ownership	•Creating new jobs and tasks •Innovation	•Support or promote high-quality communication of product value •Cultural training •Help in development of organizational culture that values creative thinking and analysis •Technical competence in jobs •Manager training in feedback and communication •Conflict negotiation skills
External growth (Acquisition)	•Horizontal integration •Vertical integration •Concentric diversification	•Acquire firms operating at same stage in product market chain (new market access) •Acquire business that can supply or buy products •Acquire firms that have nothing in common with acquiring firm	•Integration •Redundancy •Restructuring	•Determine capabilities of employees in acquired firms •Integrate training systems •Methods and procedures of combined firms •Team building
Disinvestment	•Retrenchment •Turnaround •Divestiture •Liquidation	•Cost reduction •Asset reduction •Revenue generation •Redefine goals •Sell off all assets	•Efficiency	•Motivation, goal setting, time management, stress management, cross-training •Leadership training •Interpersonal communications •Outplacement assistance •Job-search skills training

employees who are computer literate by using tests and work samples to reassign employees who do not have computer skills. Choosing this strategy suggests that the company has decided to devote resources to selection and placement rather than training. Third, because it lacks time or expertise, the company may decide to purchase training from a consultant.

If a company decides to purchase a training program from a consultant, an important consideration is to select one who will deliver a high-quality product. Managers need to carefully evaluate consultants before selecting one.[17] First, managers should identify consultants who can provide the services the company desires. Many companies do this by distributing a request for proposals to prospective consultants and advertising for consulting services in professional magazines. The request for proposals invites consultants to submit written bids. A request for proposals contains information such as the types of services the company is interested in receiving, the number of employees who need to be trained, and limits on funding for the project. The request for proposals makes the process of choosing a consultant easier because it eliminates having to review consultants who cannot provide the services outlined in the proposal. Also, the request for proposals provides a standard set of criteria against which all consultants will be identified.

Once a qualified consultant has been identified, managers should check the consultant's reputation by contacting prior clients and professional organizations (such as the American Society for Training and Development). The consultant's experience should be evaluated (e.g., What industry has the consultant's work focused on?). Managers should carefully consider the services, materials, and fees that are outlined in the consulting contract. For example, it is not uncommon for training materials, manuals, and handouts to remain the property of the consultant. If the company wishes to use these materials for training at a later date, it would have to pay additional fees to the consultant.

Person Analysis.   Person analysis helps the manager identify whether training is appropriate and which employees need training. In certain situations, such as the introduction of a new technology or service, all employees may need training. However, when managers, customers, or employees identify a problem (usually as a result of a performance deficiency), it is often unclear whether training is the solution. Managers should consider the questions shown in Table 12.3 when deciding whether performance deficiencies can be corrected by training.[18]

From the organization's perspective, training should be considered if any of the following is true:

1. The performance discrepancy has the potential to cost the company a significant amount of money from lost productivity or customers.

TABLE 12.3 Questions to Ask in Deciding Whether Performance Problems Can be Corrected by Training

1. What is the performance discrepancy?
    - What is the difference between what employees are doing and what they should be doing?
    - What is not being accomplished that is causing problems?
2. Is the performance discrepancy important?
    - What does it cost the company?
    - What happens if the discrepancy is not corrected?
3. Is the performance discrepancy caused by a basic skills problem (reading, computation, writing) or a knowledge problem?
    - Could the employees perform if they were required to do so?
    - Are the employees' skills or knowledge deficient?
4. If the performance discrepancy is not caused by a problem in skills or knowledge, why are employees not performing up to standards?
    - Is it caused by a performance obstacle such as incorrect tools, equipment, or materials? Are good employees punished by being given more work or harder work?
    - Are poor performers rewarded in some way?
    - Are performance expectations clear?
5. If the performance discrepancy is caused by a skills or knowledge problem, how can that be solved?
    - Can the job be changed so that employees' present knowledge and skill levels are satisfactory?
    - Can job aids be provided to compensate for the lack of knowledge or skills?
    - Can the employees learn the knowledge or skills required for effective performance?
    - Should employees be reassigned to another job and new employees hired?
6. Have the employees received prior training in the skills or knowledge that appear to be deficient?
    - Is the training program deficient in some way?
    - Do employees use the skills and knowledge often?
    - Have they demonstrated the skills or knowledge in the past?
7. What is the most effective course of action to correct the performance discrepancy in terms of the company's goals and objectives?

SOURCE: Adapted from R. F. Mager and D. Pipe, *Analyzing Performance Problems*, 2nd ed. (Belmont, Cal.: Pittman Learning, 1984), and A. P. Carnevale, L. J. Gainer, and A. S. Meltzer, *Workplace Basics Training Manual* (San Francisco: Jossey-Bass, 1990).

2. Employees do not know how to perform correctly. They received little or no previous instruction, or the training they received was faulty.

3. Employees cannot demonstrate the correct knowledge or behavior. Previous training was conducted, but they have not used the knowledge or skills in their work until recently.

4. Performance expectations are clear, there are no obstacles to performance (such as faulty tools or equipment), and nonperformers are not rewarded in some way (for example, if employees are dissatisfied with their compensation they may work only according to the specific terms of a labor agreement).

5. Other options such as job aids, redeployment of employees, and job redesign are too expensive or unrealistic.

6. Training will best suit the long-term interests of the firm.

Task Analysis.   Task analysis results in a description of work activities, including tasks performed by the employee and the knowledge, skills, and abilities required to successfully complete the tasks. A task is a statement of an employee's work activity in a specific job. A task analysis involves:

1. Selecting the job(s) to be analyzed.

2. Developing a preliminary list of tasks performed on the job by interviewing and observing expert employees and their managers and talking with others who have performed a task analysis.

3. Verifying the importance of the tasks for the job through task inventories or expert committees composed of managers, employees, and other persons ("subject matter experts"). Table 12.4 presents a sample task-analysis questionnaire.

4. Identifying the knowledge, skills, or abilities necessary to successfully perform each task using interviews and questionnaires. For training purposes, information concerning how difficult it is to learn the knowledge, skill, or ability is important, as well as whether the knowledge, skill, or ability is expected to be acquired by the employee before taking the job.[19]

Ensuring Employees' Readiness for Training

The second step in the instructional design process is to evaluate whether employees are ready to learn. Although managers are not often trainers, they can play an important role in the training process. How? One way is to ensure that employees are motivated to learn. **Motivation to learn** is the desire of the trainee to learn the content of the training program.[20] A number of research studies have shown that motivation is related to knowledge gain, behavior change, or skill acquisition in training programs.[21] Managers need to ensure that employees' motivation to learn is as high as possible. They can do this by ensuring employees' self-efficacy; understanding the

TABLE 12.4   Sample Task Statement Questionnaire

Task Statement Questionnaire

Name

Position

Date

Please rate each of the task statements according to three factors, the *importance* of the task for effective performance, how *frequently* the task is performed, and the degree of *difficulty* required to become effective in the task. Use the following scales in making your ratings.

Importance

4 = Task is critical for effective performance

3 = Task is important but not critical for effective performance

2 = Task is of some importance for effective performance

1 = Task is of no importance for task performance

0 = Task is not performed

Frequency

4 = Task is performed once a day

3 = Task is performed once a week

2 = Task is performed once every few months

1 = Task is performed once or twice a year

0 = Task is not performed

Difficulty

4 = Effective performance on the task requires extensive prior experience and/or training (12–18 months or longer)

3 = Effective performance on this task requires minimal prior experience and training (6–12 months)

2 = Effective performance on the task requires a brief period of prior training and experience (1–6 months)

1 = Effective performance on the task does not require specific prior training and/or experience

0 = This task is not performed

Task	Importance	Difficulty	Frequency
1. Ensuring maintenance on equipment, tools, and safety controls			
2. Monitoring employee performance			
3. Scheduling employees			
4. Using statistical software on the computer			
5. Monitoring changes made in processes using statistical methods			

benefits of training; being aware of training needs, career interests, and goals; understanding work environment characteristics; and ensuring employees' basic skills levels.

Self-efficacy. **Self-efficacy** is the employees' belief that they can successfully learn the content of the training program. The training environment is potentially threatening to many employees who may not have extensive educational experience or who have little experience in the particular area emphasized by the training program. For example, training employees to use equipment for computer-based manufacturing represents a potential threat, especially if employees are intimidated by new technologies and do not have confidence in their ability to master the skills needed to use a computer. Research has demonstrated that self-efficacy is related to performance in training programs.[22] Managers can increase employees' self-efficacy level by:

1. Letting employees know that the purpose of training is to try to improve performance rather than to identify areas in which employees are incompetent.

2. Providing as much information as possible about the training program and purpose of training prior to the actual training.

3. Showing employees the training success of their peers who are now in similar jobs.

Understanding the Benefits of Training. Employees' motivation to learn can be enhanced by communicating to them the potential job-related, personal, and career benefits they may receive as a result of attending the training program. These benefits may include learning a more efficient way to perform a process or procedure, establishing contacts with other employees in the firm (e.g., networking), or increasing opportunities to pursue different career paths. The communication from the manager about potential benefits should be realistic. Unmet expectations about training programs have been shown to adversely affect motivation to learn.[23]

Awareness of Training Needs, Career Interests, and Goals. To be motivated to learn in training programs, employees must be aware of their skill strengths and weaknesses and of the link between the training program and improvement of their weaknesses.[24] Managers should make sure that employees understand why they are asked to attend training programs, and they should communicate the link between training and improvement of skill weaknesses or knowledge deficiencies. This can be accomplished by sharing performance-appraisal information with the employee, holding career development discussions, or having the employee complete a self-evaluation of his or her skill strengths and weaknesses and career interests and goals.

Work Environment Characteristics.   Employees' perceptions of two characteristics of the work environment—situational constraints and social support—are critical determinants of motivation to learn. **Situational constraints** include lack of proper tools and equipment, materials and supplies, budgetary support, and time. **Social support** refers to managers' and peers' willingness to provide feedback and reinforcement.[25]

To ensure that the work environment enhances trainees' motivation to learn, managers need to:

1. Provide materials, time, job-related information, and other work aids necessary for employees to use new skills or behavior before participating in training programs.
2. Speak positively about the company's training programs to employees.
3. Let employees know they are doing a good job when they are using content training in their work.
4. Encourage work-group members to involve each other in trying to use new skills on the job by soliciting feedback and sharing training experiences and situations in which training content was helpful.
5. Provide employees with time and opportunities to practice and apply new skills or behaviors to their work.

Basic Skills.   Employees' motivation to learn in training activities can also be influenced by the degree to which they have the reading, writing, and communication skills needed to understand the content of training programs, in other words, **basic skills**. Recent forecasts of the skill levels of the U.S. work force indicate that managers will likely encounter employees who lack these skills.[26] Companies are beginning to take actions to combat employees' basic skill deficiencies. A recent survey of U.S. businesses suggests that about 25 percent of companies with at least 100 employees provide some type of remedial training to their employees. Training in writing skills, reading skills, basic math, and English as a second language is most prevalent.[27]

Managers need to conduct a literacy audit to determine employees' basic skill levels. Table 12.5 shows the activities involved in conducting a literacy audit.

Research suggests that training programs must include certain characteristics to be effective.[28] For example, the purpose of training must be explained to trainees. Basic skill instruction should be integrated into the training program. Tasks, work contexts, materials, and procedures taken from the job for which employees are being trained need to be used in the training program. The content of the training program should build on employees' current knowledge.

A good example of how these characteristics are incorporated into a training program is the electronics technicians training program developed by the Ford Foundation.[29] Before the start of the program, students are

TABLE 12.5   Performing a Literacy Audit

Step 1.   Observe employees to determine the basic skills they need to be successful in their job. Note the materials the employee uses on the job, the tasks performed, and the reading, writing, and computations completed by the employee.

Step 2.   Collect all materials that are written and read on the job and identify computations that must be performed to determine the necessary level of basic skill proficiency. Materials include bills, memos, and forms such as inventory lists and requisition sheets.

Step 3.   Interview employees to determine the basic skills they believe are needed to do the job. Consider the basic skill requirements of the job yourself.

Step 4.   Determine whether employees have the basic skills needed to successfully perform the job. Combine the information gathered by observing and interviewing employees and evaluating materials they use on their jobs. Write a description of each job in terms of reading, writing, and computation skills needed to perform successfully.

Step 5.   Develop or buy tests that ask questions relating specifically to the employee's job. Ask employees to complete the tests.

Step 6.   Compare test results with the description of the basic skills required for the job (from step 5). If the level of employees' reading, writing, and computation skills does not match the basic skills required by the job, then a basic skills problem exists.

SOURCE: U.S. Department of Education, U.S. Department of Labor. *The Bottom Line: Basic Skills in the Workplace* (Washington, D.C., 1988) 14–15.

given information about electronic technician jobs. Students are told that they will learn how to think about operating, maintaining, and repairing electrical equipment they are familiar with such as flashlights, curling irons, and table lamps. These appliances were selected because they are useful for introducing basic electronic concepts and procedures.

A book that covers the basic literacy skills needed to read training and job-related material in electronics is provided to trainees. The exercises and worksheets provided in the book help the trainee master "reading-to-do" and "reading-to-learn" skills that have been identified as required in the majority of jobs.[30] "Reading-to-do" involves searching for and reading information in manuals, books, or charts (e.g., looking up information such as repair specifications in a technical manual or scanning tables and graphs to locate information). "Reading-to-learn" involves reading information to apply it in the future, such as reading instructions on how to use a piece of equipment (e.g., paraphrasing and summarizing information).

Besides learning reading skills related to electronics, trainees study how electronics is used in the flashlights and table lamps. Also, the textbook introduces students to mathematical concepts and their applications, including scientific notation (which is needed to understand waves that appear on an oscilloscope). This training program has been successful in preparing competent electronics technicians for entry-level positions.

Lack of basic reading skills may impede learning. Managers should evaluate the readability of the material to ensure that its reading level does not exceed that required by the job. *Readability* refers to the difficulty level of written materials.[31] A readability assessment usually involves analysis of sentence length and word difficulty. If the reading level of trainees does not match the reading level needed for the training materials, three options are available. First, managers should determine whether it is feasible to use video or on-the-job training, which involves learning by watching and practicing rather than by reading. Second, employees who do not possess the necessary reading level should be identified through reading tests and reassigned to other positions more congruent with their skill levels. Third, managers should determine whether the job can be redesigned to accommodate employees' reading levels. The third option is certainly most costly and least practical. Therefore, managers need to either consider alternative training systems or screen employees for jobs and training opportunities on the basis of reading, computation, writing, and other basic skill requirements. The "Competing through Social Responsibility" box describes the efforts of some companies to boost their employees' basic skill levels.

Create a Learning Environment

Learning involves a permanent change in behavior. For employees to acquire knowledge and skills in the training program and apply this information in their jobs, the training program needs to include specific learning principles. Educational and industrial psychologists and instructional design specialists have identified several conditions under which employees learn best.[32]

Employees Need to Know Why They Should Learn.   Employees learn best when they understand the purpose and expected outcome of training activities. **Training objectives** based on the training needs analysis help employees understand why they need training. A good training objective has three components:

1. A statement of what the employee is expected to do (performance).
2. A statement of the quality or level of performance that is acceptable (criterion).
3. A statement of the conditions under which the trainee is expected to perform the desired outcome (conditions).

A training objective for a customer-service training program for retail salespersons might be: "After training the employee will be able to express concern [performance] to all irate customers by a brief (fewer than ten words) apology, only after the customer has stopped talking [criteria] and no matter how upset the customer is [conditions]." These objectives are also useful

Social Responsibility

COMPETING THROUGH

BASIC SKILLS RECEIVE BOOST FROM CONCERNED COMPANIES

A number of companies are beginning to improve their competitiveness by attacking literacy problems through training. The Brenlin Group, an Ohio metalworking manufacturing holding company with 4,200 employees, has learning centers at company work sites. These learning centers include self-paced, computer-aided instruction designed to bring employees to a minimum eighth-grade reading and math level. Three years after the learning centers were opened, the company experienced lower turnover, increased sales dollars per employee, and increased employee involvement.

Magnavox Electronic Systems Company, a hi-tech manufacturer of satellite communications and navigational equipment located in Torrance, California, found that 52 percent of hourly employees were functionally illiterate in reading and 36 percent were illiterate in basic math. The company developed several classes designed to improve employees' deficiencies. These classes included two English-as-a-second-language classes for foreign-born employees, a language class for English-speaking employees, and a math and communications skills class. The courses used documents, tables, and calculations that employees actually used on the job. The program results were impressive. Reading skills for the students who completed the program improved 15 percent, math skills 21 percent. The average monthly efficiency of employees who completed the program increased 45 percent.

Methodist Medical Center of Illinois offers courses in reading, English, and math. The program is offered to employees during work time. Employees in housekeeping, food service, linens, and supply processing and delivery are participating in the program. Instructors use items the students are familiar with to improve literacy levels. For example, employees learn how to use a calculator while learning numbers. Supervisors report that the most notable change resulting from the program is employees' improved confidence in themselves and their ability to perform their jobs. Supervisors also report the quality of employees' written assignments (e.g., schedules, documents, worksheets) has improved.

SOURCE: L. Solovy-Pratt and R. M. Vicary, "A Hospital's Perspective for Illiteracy," *Training and Development,* November 1992, 60–61; D. J. Ford, "The Magnavox Experience," *Training and Development,* November 1992, 55–57; Bureau of National Affairs, "Department of Labor's LIFT Awards Recognize Successful Training Programs," *Employee Relations Weekly* 10 (1992): 1116.

for identifying the types of training outcomes that should be measured to evaluate training-program effectiveness.

Employees Need to Use Their Own Experiences as a Basis for Learning. Employees are more likely to learn when the training is linked to their current job experiences and tasks, that is, meaningful to them. To enhance the meaningfulness of training, the material should be presented using concepts, terms, and examples familiar to trainees. For example, in the retail salesperson customer-service program, the meaningfulness of the material will be helped by using scenarios of unhappy customers actually encountered by salespersons in stores.

Employees Need to Have Opportunities to Practice. Practice involves having the employee demonstrate the knowledge, skill, or behavior emphasized in the training objectives under the conditions and performance standards specified by the objective. For practice to be effective, it needs to actively involve the trainee, include overlearning (repeated practice), take the appropriate amount of time, and include the appropriate unit of learning (i.e., amount of material).

Learning will not occur if employees practice only by talking about what they are expected to do. For example, using the objective for the customer-service course just discussed, practice would involve having trainees participate in role playing with unhappy customers (customers upset with poor service, poor merchandise, or exchange policies). Trainees need to continue to practice even if they have been able to perform the objective several times (overlearning). Overlearning helps the trainee become more comfortable using new knowledge and skills and increases the length of time the trainee will retain the knowledge, skill, or behavior.

It is also important to consider whether to have only one practice session or to use multiple practice sessions. Distributed practice sessions have been shown to result in more efficient learning of skills than continuous practice.[33] With factual information, the less meaningful the material and the greater its length or difficulty, the better distributed practice sessions are for learning.[34]

A final issue related to practice is how much of the training should be practiced at one time. One option is that all tasks or objectives should be practiced at the same time (whole practice). Another option is that an objective or task should be practiced individually as soon as each is introduced in the training program (part practice). It is probably best to employ both whole and part practice in a training session. Trainees should have the opportunity to practice individual skills or behaviors. If the skills or behaviors introduced in training are related to one another, the trainee should demonstrate all of them in a practice session after they are practiced individually. For example, one of the objectives of the customer-service training for retail salespersons is learning how to deal with an unhappy customer. Salespersons likely have to learn three key behaviors: (1) greeting disgruntled customers, (2) understanding their complaints, and then (3) identifying and taking appropriate action. Practice sessions should be held for each of the three behaviors (part practice). Then, another practice session should be held so that trainees can practice all three skills together (whole practice). If trainees were only given the opportunity to practice the behaviors individually, it is unlikely that they would be able to deal with an unhappy customer.

Employees Need Feedback. Employees need information about how well they are meeting the training objectives. To be effective, feedback should focus on specific behaviors and be provided as soon as possible after the trainees' behavior.[35] Also, positive trainee behavior should be verbally praised or reinforced. One of the most powerful tools is the use of videotape in practice sessions. Trainers should view the videotape with trainees, provide specific information about how behaviors need to be modified, and praise trainee behaviors that meet objectives.

Employees Learn by Observing Others.   According to social learning theory, people learn by observing and imitating the actions of significant others. This idea has recently been applied to training in a process known as *behavior-modeling training*, which uses models to get trainees' attention and to demonstrate the skills or behaviors that trainees need to learn. For the model to be effective, the desired behaviors or skills need to be clearly specified, and the model should have characteristics (such as age, position) similar to the target audience.[36] After observing the model, trainees should have the opportunity to reproduce the skills or behavior shown by the model in practice sessions.

Employees Need the Training Program to Be Properly Coordinated and Arranged.   Coordinating the training program involves activities before, during, and after the program. Good coordination ensures that trainees are not distracted by events (such as an uncomfortable room or poorly organized materials) that could interfere with learning. Activities before the program include communicating to trainees the purpose of the program, the place it will be held, the name of a person to contact if they have questions, and any preprogram work they are supposed to complete. Books, speakers, handouts, and videotapes need to be prepared. Any necessary arrangements to secure rooms and equipment (such as VCRs) should be made. The physical arrangement of the training room should complement the training technique. For example, it would be difficult for a team-building session to be effective if the seats in a room cannot be moved for group activities. If visual aids will be used, all trainees should be able to see them. It is important to make sure that the room is physically comfortable (adequate lighting and ventilation). Trainees should be informed of starting and finishing times, break times, and location of bathrooms. Distractions (such as phone messages) need to be kept to a minimum. If trainees will be asked to evaluate the program or take tests to determine what they have learned, time should be allotted for this activity at the end of the program. Following the program, any credits or recording of the names of trainees who completed the program should be done. Handouts and other training materials should be stored or returned to the consultant. The end of the program is also a good time for the manager to consider how the program could be improved if it will be offered again.

Ensure Transfer of Training

For training programs to be successful, trainees must use training in their work. **Transfer of training**—the use of knowledge, skills, and behaviors learned in the training environment on the job—is influenced by trainee characteristics, the extent to which the training program is designed to make learning possible, and the work environment.[37]

We previously discussed the factors that influence employees' readiness for training. These factors also influence the transfer of training to the job. How can transfer of training be enhanced? A number of activities may be useful: self-management, manager involvement, and developing networks.

Training programs should prepare employees to manage their use of new skills and behaviors on the job.[38] Specifically, within the training program, trainees should be given the opportunity to set goals for using skills or behaviors on the job, identify conditions under which they might fail to use them, identify the positive and negative consequences of using them, and monitor their use of them. Also, trainees need to understand that it is natural to encounter difficulty in trying to use skills on the job. Relapses into old behavior and skill patterns does not mean that trainees should give up. Finally, because peers and supervisors on the job may be unable to provide rewards for using new behaviors or provide feedback automatically, trainees need to create their own reward system and ask peers and managers for feedback.

One way to get managers involved in training is through action planning. Trainees should complete an action plan with their manager that lists the steps the trainee will take to apply the newly learned skills and knowledge on the job. Another way to get managers to support training activities is to use the managers as trainers. This means that the managers must take a course before their employees do. If training the managers to be trainers is not possible, special sessions could be held to explain the purpose of the training and explain the role they can play in transferring training to the job. The managers' responsibilities should be clearly specified—as they were in one retail chain described in the "Competing through Quality" box.

Transfer of training can also be enhanced by creating a support network among the trainees.[39] For example, interviews with trainees could be used to develop a newsletter that features trainees who were successful in using new skills. Monthly meetings of trainees to discuss the problems and successes in using new skills on the job may also aid in transfer of training.

Training Methods

A number of different methods can be used to help employees acquire new knowledge, skills, and behaviors. Survey results suggest that videotapes, lectures, one-on-one instruction, and role-playing are the most frequently used training methods. Technology is having a major impact on the delivery of training programs. Advances in personal computers now permit the use of multimedia training presentations in which sound, animation, photographs, and video can be integrated into the delivery of a training program. For example, each classroom at Dow Chemical's training center has Macintosh computers, video projectors, laserdisc players, VCRs, response keypads for

Quality

TRAINING IS THE KEY TO CUSTOMER SERVICE AT REVCO

Superior customer service is one of the major objectives of most companies' total quality programs. Revco D.S., a large Ohio-based drugstore chain, identified three behaviors that were critical for creating a good customer-service environment. The behaviors include greeting customers when they entered the store, asking customers if they needed assistance when they observed them looking for a product, and making eye contact with customers when they spoke to them.

Their approach to customer-service training, although simple, emphasized how managers' involvement and support for training

can ensure its success. Each store manager was given a training guide. The guide described the three customer-service behaviors and emphasized that managers were responsible for observing and coaching employees to ensure that they were using the behaviors. A five-minute video prepared by the CEO explaining his enthusiasm for the program was distributed to all stores. To evaluate the effectiveness of the program, Revco sent "secret shoppers" into the stores to check on employees' use of the three customer behaviors. The shoppers reported that employees demonstrated the three behaviors over 90 percent of the time.

SOURCE: G. M. Piskurich, "Service Training Made Simple," *Training and Development*, January 1991, 37–38.

students, and CD-ROM players used for the development of videodiscs. However, having state-of-the-art instructional technology should not be the guiding force in choosing a training method. The specific instructional method used should be based on the training objectives. Instructional methods can be crudely grouped into three broad categories: presentation techniques, hands-on techniques, and group-building techniques.[40] The "Competing through Globalization" box discusses how to apply these methods in an international setting.

Presentation techniques.   Presentation techniques include traditional classroom instruction, video teleconferencing, and audiovisual techniques, which are ideal for presenting new facts, information, different philosophies, or alternative problem-solving solutions or processes.

Classroom Instruction.   Classroom instruction typically involves having the trainer lecture a group. In many cases, the lecture is supplemented with question-and-answer periods, discussion, or case studies. Classroom instruction remains a popular training method despite new technologies such as interactive video and computer-assisted instruction. Traditional classroom instruction is one of the least expensive, least time-consuming ways to present information on a specific topic to a large number of trainees. Also, the more active participation, job-related examples, and exercises that the instructor can build into traditional classroom instruction, the more likely trainees will learn and use the information presented on the job.

Globalization

COMPETING THROUGH

COMPANIES TAKE GLOBAL VIEW OF TRAINING

U.S. companies are taking advantage of business opportunities around the world. Along with these opportunities comes the need for companies to train expatriates and foreign nationals (employees from the host country) in a wide variety of skills, including language skills and computer skills. U.S. companies must carefully consider whether the training methods they use in domestic facilities are appropriate for overseas operations. American trainers believe that experiential, hands-on training methods are most effective. However, for employees of other cultures, hands-on methods may be counter to cultural norms. For example, Asian and Arab employees prefer observing trainers demonstrate skills rather than participating in role playing. The use of interactive video as a training strategy is inappropriate in Japan and other societies where people prefer to learn and work in teams.

Johnson Wax's team-building course has not been delivered at the company's Brazil facilities. Because Brazil's culture strongly emphasizes teamwork, asking employees to take a team-building course would be insulting. To avoid the problems associated with trying to adapt training programs to the cultures of different countries, Agvet, a division of Merck and Company, Inc., which produces livestock and agricultural products, develops most of its training programs in the United States, but they are delivered in different ways. For example, to train salespersons in each subsidiary, Agvet will often train a line manager to deliver the training. Line managers are able to adapt the training course to meet the norms of the local culture.

SOURCE: M. J. Marquardt and D. W. Engel, *Global Human Resources* (Englewood Cliffs, N.J., 1993) and B. Gerber, "A Global Approach to Training," *Training*, September 1989, 42–47.

Video Teleconferencing.   Video teleconferencing is used by geographically dispersed companies to quickly provide information about new policies or procedures to field locations.[41] Video teleconferencing usually includes a telephone link so that trainees viewing the presentation can call in questions and comments to the trainer. Also, satellite networks allow companies to link up with industry-specific and educational courses for which employees receive college credit and job certification. IBM, Digital Equipment, and Eastman Kodak are among the many firms that subscribe to the National Technological University, which broadcasts courses throughout the United States that technical employees need to obtain advanced degrees in engineering.[42]

An advantage of video teleconferencing is that the company can save on travel costs. It also gives employees in geographically dispersed sites the opportunity to receive training from experts who would not otherwise be available to visit each location.

The major disadvantage of teleconferencing is the lack of interaction between the trainer and the audience. That's why a communications link between employees and the trainer is so important. Also, on-site instructors or facilitators should be available to answer questions and moderate question-and-answer sessions.

Audiovisual Techniques. Audiovisual instruction includes overheads, slides, and video. Video is the most popular instructional method.[43] It has been used for improving communications skills, interviewing skills, and customer-service skills and for illustrating how procedures (e.g., welding) should be followed. Video is, however, rarely used alone. It is usually used in conjunction with lectures to show trainees "real-life" experiences and examples. Video is also a major component of behavior modeling and interactive video instruction.

The use of video in training has a number of advantages. First, the trainer has the option to review, slow down, or speed up the lesson, which gives the trainer flexibility in customizing the session depending on the expertise of the trainees. Second, trainees can be exposed to equipment, problems, and events that cannot be easily demonstrated, such as equipment malfunctions, angry customers, or emergencies. Third, trainees are provided with consistent instruction. Program content is not affected by the interests and goals of a particular trainer. Fourth, videotaping trainees allows them to see and hear their own performance without the interpretation of the trainer. As a result, trainees cannot attribute poor performance to the bias of external evaluators such as the trainer or peers.

Hands-on Techniques. **Hands-on techniques** include on-the-job training, simulations, business games and case studies, behavior modeling, and interactive video. These methods are ideal for developing specific skills, understanding how skills and behaviors can be transferred to the job, experiencing all aspects of completing a task, or dealing with interpersonal issues that arise on the job.

On-the-Job Training (OJT). Companies spend between $90 billion and $180 billion annually on informal on-the-job training compared with $30 billion on formal off-the-job training.[44] OJT can be useful for training newly hired employees, upgrading the skills of experienced employees when new technology is introduced, cross-training employees within a department or work unit, and orienting transferred or promoted employees to their new jobs. The basic philosophy of OJT is that employees learn through observing peers or managers performing the job and trying to imitate their behavior.

OJT takes various forms, including apprenticeships and self-directed training programs. Regardless of the specific type, effective OJT programs include the following characteristics:

1. A policy statement that describes the purpose of OJT and emphasizes the company's support for it.
2. A clear specification of who is accountable for conducting OJT. If managers conduct OJT, this is mentioned in their job descriptions and is part of their performance evaluation.

TABLE 12.6   Principles of Structured On-the-Job Training

Preparing for Instruction

1. Break down the job into important steps.
2. Prepare the necessary equipment, material, supplies.
3. Decide how much time you will devote to OJT and when you expect the employee to be competent in skill areas.

Actual Instruction

1. Demonstrate to the employee how to perform the task.
2. Explain the key points or behaviors involved in the task.
3. Demonstrate to the employee how to perform the task again.
4. Let the employee try to perform one or more parts of the task.
5. Help the employee perform the whole job.
6. Let the employee perform the whole job. Praise correct performance and provide specific feedback concerning necessary improvements. Allow time for additional practice.
7. Let the employee work on his or her own to complete the task.

SOURCE: Adapted from W. J. Rothwell and H. C. Kazanas, "Planned OJT Is Productive OJT," *Training and Development Journal,* October 1990, 53–55 and K. N. Wexley and G. P. Latham, *Developing and Training Human Resources in Organizations,* 2nd ed. (New York: Harper Collins, 1991).

3. A thorough review of OJT practices (program content, types of jobs, length of program, cost savings) at other companies in similar industries.
4. Training of managers and peers in the principles of structured OJT (see Table 12.6).
5. Availability of lesson plans, checklists, procedure manuals, training manuals, learning contracts, and progress report forms for use by employees who conduct OJT.
6. Evaluation of employees' levels of basic skills (reading, computation, writing) before OJT.[45]

Self-directed learning involves having employees take responsibility for all aspects of learning—when it is conducted and who will be involved. For example, at Corning Glass, new engineering graduates participate in an OJT program called SMART (self-managed, awareness, responsibility, and technical competence).[46] Each employee is responsible for seeking the answers to a set of questions (e.g., "Under what conditions would a statistician be involved in the design of engineering experiments?") by visiting plants and research facilities and meeting with technical engineering experts and managers. After employees complete the questions, they are evaluated by a committee of peers who have already completed the SMART program. Evaluations have shown that the program cuts employees' start-up time in their new jobs from six weeks to three weeks. It is effective for a number of reasons. It encourages active involvement of the new employees in learning and allows flexibility in finding time for training. It has a peer-review evaluation component that motivates employees to complete the questions correctly. And, as a result of participating in the program, employees make contacts throughout the company and gain a better understanding of the technical and personal resources available within the company.

Apprenticeship is a work-study training method with both on-the-job training and classroom training.[47] To qualify as a registered apprenticeship program under state or federal guidelines, at least 144 hours of classroom instruction and 2,000 hours, or one year, of on-the-job experience is required.[48] Apprenticeships can be sponsored by individual companies or by groups of companies cooperating with a union. The majority of apprenticeship programs are in the skilled trades such as plumbing, carpentry, electrical work, and bricklaying.

One of the major advantages of an apprenticeship program is that learners have the opportunity to earn pay while they learn. This is important because the programs can last for several years. (Learners' wages increase automatically as their skills improve.) Also, apprenticeships are usually effective learning experiences because they involve learning why and how a task is performed in classroom instruction provided by local trade schools, high schools, or community colleges. OJT involves assisting a certified tradesperson (a journeyman) at the work site.

One disadvantage of apprenticeship programs is that minorities' and women's access to these programs has been restricted because of unions' and employers' choice of men for entry-level jobs.[49] Another is that there is no guarantee jobs will be available when the program is completed.

Simulations.   A simulation is a training method that represents a real-life situation, with trainees' decisions resulting in outcomes that mirror what would happen if the trainee were on the job. Simulations, which allow trainees to see the impact of their decisions in an artificial, risk-free environment, are used to teach production and process skills as well as management and interpersonal skills.

Simulators replicate the physical equipment that employees use on the job. For example, at Motorola's Programmable Automation Literacy lab, employees who may never have worked with a computer or robot learn to operate them.[50] Before entering the lab, employees are given a two-hour introduction to factory automation, which introduces new concepts, vocabulary, and computer-assisted manufacturing. The simulator allows trainees to become familiar with the equipment by designing a product (a personalized memo holder). Also, trainees do not have to be afraid of the impact of wrong decisions; errors are not as costly as they would be if the trainees were using the equipment on an actual production line. Success in simple exercises with the robot and computer increase their confidence that they can work successfully in an automated manufacturing environment.

Business Games and Case Studies.   Situations that trainees study and discuss (case studies) and business games in which trainees must gather information, analyze it, and make decisions are primarily used for management skill development. Games stimulate learning because participants are actively involved and they mimic the competitive nature of business. The types of decisions that participants make in games include all aspects of management practice: labor relations (agreement in contract negotiations), marketing (the price to charge for a new product), or finance (financing the purchase of new technology). For example, Market Share, part of a marketing management course at Nynex Corporation, requires participants to use strategic thinking such as competitive analysis to increase market share.[51] The playing board is divided into different segments representing the information industry (e.g., cable, radio). Teams of two or three players compete to gain market share by determining where the team will allocate its efforts and challenge opponents' market share.

Looking Glass© is another simulation designed to develop teamwork and individual management skills.[52] In this program, participants are assigned different roles in a glass company. On the basis of memos and correspondence, each participant interacts with other members of the management team over the course of six hours. Participants' behavior and interactions in solving the problems described in correspondence are recorded and evaluated. At the conclusion of the simulation, participants are given feedback regarding their performance.

Behavior Modeling.   Research suggests that behavior modeling is one of the most effective techniques for teaching interpersonal skills.[53] Each training session, which typically lasts four hours, focuses on one interpersonal skill such as coaching or communicating ideas. Each session includes a presentation of the rationale behind the key behaviors, a videotape of a model performing the key behaviors, practice opportunities using role playing, evaluation of a model's performance in the videotape, and a planning session devoted to understanding how the key behaviors can be used on the job. In the practice sessions, trainees are provided with feedback regarding how closely their behavior matches the key behaviors demonstrated by the model. The role playing and modeled performance are based on actual incidents in the employment setting in which the trainee needs to demonstrate success.

Interactive Video.   Interactive video combines the advantages of video and computer-based instruction. Instruction is provided one-on-one to trainees via a monitor connected to a keyboard. Trainees use the keyboard or touch the monitor to interact with the program. Interactive video is used to teach technical procedures and interpersonal skills. For example, Federal Express's 25-disc interactive video curriculum includes courses related to customer etiquette, defensive driving, and delivery procedures.[54] As Federal Express discovered, interactive video has many advantages. First, training is individualized. Employees control what aspects of the training program they want to view. They can skip ahead where they feel competent, or they can review topics. Second, employees receive immediate feedback concerning their performance. Third, training is more convenient for both employers and employees. Regardless of employees' work schedules, they can have access to the equipment, which is located at their work site. From the employer's standpoint, the high cost of developing interactive video programs and purchasing the equipment is offset by the reduction in instructor costs and travel costs related to a central training location. At Federal Express, interactive video has made it possible to train 35,000 customer-contact employees in 650 locations nationwide, saving the company millions of dollars. Without interactive video, it would have been impossible for Federal Express to deliver consistent high-quality training. The main disadvantage of interactive video is the high cost of developing the courseware. This may be a particular problem for courses in which frequent updates are necessary.[55]

Group-Building Techniques.   **Group-building techniques** such as wilderness training help trainees share ideas and experiences, build group identity, understand the dynamics of interpersonal relationships, and get to know their own strengths and weaknesses and those of their coworkers. Group techniques focus on helping teams increase their skills for effective teamwork. A number of different training techniques are available to improve work group or team performance, to establish a new team, or to improve interactions among different teams. All involve examination of feelings, perceptions, and beliefs about the functioning of the team, discussion, and development of plans to apply what was learned in training to the team's performance in the work setting.

Adventure Learning.   Adventure learning focuses on the development of teamwork and leadership skills using structured outdoor activities.[56] Adventure learning appears to be best suited for developing skills related to group effectiveness such as self-awareness, problem solving, conflict management, and risk taking. Adventure learning may involve strenuous, challenging physical activities such as dogsledding or mountain climbing. Adventure learning can also use structured individual and group outdoor activities such as wall climbing, rope courses, trust falls (in which each trainee stands on a table and falls backwards into the arms of fellow group members), climbing ladders, and traveling from one tower to another using a device attached to a wire that connects the two towers. For adventure-learning programs to be successful, the exercises should be related to the types of skills that participants are expected to develop. Also, after the exercises a skilled facilitator should lead a discussion about what happened in the exercise, what was learned, how what happened in the exercise relates to the job situation, and how to set goals and apply what was learned on the job.[57]

Does adventure learning work? Rigorous evaluations of the impact of adventure learning on productivity or performance have not been conducted. However, former participants often report that they gained a greater understanding of themselves and the ways they interact with their coworkers. One of the keys to the success of an adventure learning program may be the insistence that whole work groups participate together so that group dynamics that inhibit effectiveness can emerge and be discussed.

Team Training. Team training involves coordinating the performance of individuals who work together to achieve a common goal. Team training is an important issue when information must be shared and individuals affect the overall performance of the group. For example, in the military as well as the private sector (e.g., nuclear power plants, commercial airlines), much of the work is performed by crews, groups, or teams. Successful performance depends on coordination of individual activities to make decisions, team performance, and readiness to deal with potentially dangerous situations (e.g., an overheating nuclear reactor). Team-training sessions usually involve presentation and hands-on techniques. Research suggests that teams that are effective in training develop procedures to identify and resolve errors, coordinate information gathering, and reinforce each other.[58]

Evaluating Training Programs

Training Outcomes. Examining the outcomes of a program helps evaluate its effectiveness. These outcomes should be related to the program objectives (discussed above), which help trainees understand the purpose of the program. **Training outcomes** can be classified into four broad categories: reactions, learning, behavior, and results.[59] A number of methods are useful for collecting training outcomes: surveys; observations; peer, manager, or self-ratings; focus groups; and personnel records.

Reaction outcomes relate to what trainees' thought of the program, including the facilities, trainers, and content. Trainees are asked to complete a brief survey at the conclusion of the program. Reactions are the most frequently used method of evaluating training. Reactions are useful for identifying what trainees thought was successful and what inhibited learning.

Learning outcomes are used to determine the extent to which trainees are familiar with principles, facts, techniques, skills, or processes presented in the training program. Typically, tests are used to assess learning. However, if the training technique used was a hands-on approach, trainees' performance in role playing or simulations may be used to evaluate learning. Both reaction and learning outcomes are usually collected before the trainees leave the training site. As a result, these measures do not help determine the extent to which the trainees actually use the training content in their jobs (transfer of training).

Behavior outcomes are used to determine the extent to which the trainees' behavior changes on the job as a result of participation in the program. Behavioral assessment typically involves having trainees' managers or peers provide ratings of job performance or the frequency with which the trainee exhibits behaviors that were emphasized in the training program.

Results outcomes are used to determine the payoff the training program has had for the company. Examples of results outcomes include reduced costs related to employee turnover or accidents, increased production, and improvements in product quality or customer service.

Behavior and results outcomes can be used to determine transfer of training, that is, the extent to which training has resulted in a change in behavior or has influenced objective measures of firm effectiveness.

Which training outcome measure is best? The answer depends on the training objectives. For example, if the instructional objectives identified business-related outcomes such as increased customer service or product quality, then results outcomes should be included in the evaluation.

Reasons for Evaluating Training.   Many companies are beginning to invest millions of dollars in training programs to help gain a competitive advantage. Firms with high-leverage training practices not only invest large sums of money into developing and administering training programs but also evaluate training programs. Why should training programs be evaluated?

1. To determine whether the program is meeting objectives, is enhancing learning, and is resulting in transfer of training to the job.
2. To determine whether trainees believe that the content and administration of the program (e.g., schedule, accommodations, trainers, materials) were satisfactory.
3. To determine the financial benefits and costs of the program.
4. To compare the costs and benefits of different training programs to choose the best program.

Evaluation Designs.   A number of different evaluation designs can be applied to training programs.

Pretest/Posttest with Comparison Group.   In this method a group of employees who receive training and a group who do not are compared. Outcome measures are collected from both groups before and after training. If improvement is greater for the training group than the comparison group, this provides evidence that training is responsible for the change.

Pretest/Posttest.   This method is similar to the pretest/posttest comparison group design but has one major difference: No comparison group is used. The lack of a comparison group makes it difficult to rule out the effects of business conditions or other factors as explanations for changes. This design is often used by companies that want to evaluate a training program but are uncomfortable with excluding certain employees or that only intend to train a small group of employees.

Posttest Only.   In this method, only training outcomes are collected. This design can be strengthened by adding a comparison group (which helps to rule out alternative explanations for changes). The posttest-only design is appropriate when trainees (and the comparison group, if one is used) can be expected to have similar levels of knowledge, behavior, or results outcomes (e.g., same number of sales, equal awareness of how to close a sale) prior to training.

Time Series. In the time-series method, training outcomes are collected at periodic intervals before and after training. (In the other evaluation designs we have discussed, training outcomes are collected only once before and after training.) A comparison group can also be used with a time-series design. One advantage of the time-series design is that it allows an analysis of the stability of training outcomes over time. This type of design is frequently used to evaluate training programs that focus on improving readily observable outcomes such as accident rates, productivity, or absenteeism that vary over time. For example, a time-series design was used to evaluate the extent to which a training program helped improve the number of safe work behaviors in a food manufacturing plant.[60] Observations of safe work behavior were taken over 25 weeks. Training directed at increasing the number of safe behaviors was introduced after approximately five weeks. The number of safe acts observed varied across the observation period. However, the number of safe behaviors increased after the training program was conducted and remained stable across the observation period.

There is no one appropriate evaluation design. Several factors need to be considered in choosing an evaluation design:[61]

- The size of the training program.
- Purpose of training.
- Implications if a training program does not work.
- Company norms regarding evaluation.
- Costs of designing and conducting an evaluation.
- The need for speed in obtaining program effectiveness information.

For example, if a manager is interested in determining how much employees' communications skills have changed as a result of participating in a behavior-modeling training program, a pretest-posttest comparison group design is necessary. Trainees should be randomly assigned to training and no-training conditions. These evaluation design features give the manager a high degree of confidence that any communication skill change is the result of participating in the training program.[62] This type of evaluation design is also necessary if the manager wants to compare the effectiveness of two training programs.

Evaluation designs without pretesting or comparison groups are most appropriate in situations where the manager is interested in identifying if a specific level of performance has been achieved (for example, are employees who participated in behavior-modeling training able to adequately communicate their ideas?) In this situation the manager is not interested in determining how much change has occurred.

National Cash Register's (NCR) training evaluation strategy is a good example of how company norms regarding evaluation and the purpose of training influence the type of training evaluation design chosen.[63] NCR views training as an effective method for developing human resources. The education department checks whether a program was well designed and conducted based on how trainees rated the course, how much trainees learned, and whether trainees are using the skills in their job. Training programs are expected to provide a good return on investment; that is, they are expected to contribute to the profitability of the company.

For training courses whose financial payoff can be identified, NCR tries to determine the contribution that training makes to the bottom line by identifying how much money the company is making or saving because employees are now performing their jobs the way they were taught in training. Financial indicators are readily available for sales and engineering employees at NCR. As a result, training programs conducted with these two groups of employees often involve rigorous evaluation designs (e.g., posttest designs with comparison groups) that help determine whether training is responsible for positive changes in financial indicators. For example, a sales course produced a 200 percent increase in sales with no significant difference in the number of sales calls made by the trained sales group in comparison with the untrained sales group (comparison group). Similarly, a training course designed to teach technical procedures to field engineers who repair NCR computers at customers' sites had a positive impact on the bottom line. The benchmark for the average site visit was expected to be about 50 minutes. Data collected from 700 on-site service calls following the training showed that engineers who completed the course met the benchmark time. Engineers who did not take the course spent an average of 1 hour and 40 minutes on-site.

Although NCR continues to struggle with the issue of how to measure the return on investment for interpersonal skills training programs such as leadership training, it has made major gains in showing how training can contribute to competitive advantage.

Cost-Benefit Analysis.   **Cost-benefit analysis** is the process of determining the economic benefits of a training program using accounting methods. Determining the economic benefits of training involves determining training costs and benefits. Training cost information is important for several reasons:

1. To understand total expenditures for training, including direct and indirect costs.

2. To compare the costs of alternative training programs.

3. To evaluate the proportion of money spent on training development, administration, and evaluation, as well as to compare monies spent on training for different groups of employees (exempt versus nonexempt, for example).

4. To control costs.[64]

Determining Costs.   Training costs include direct and indirect costs.[65] *Direct costs* include salaries and benefits for all employees involved in training, including trainees, instructors, consultants, and employees who design the program; program material and supplies; equipment or classroom rentals or purchases; and travel costs. *Indirect costs* are not related directly to the design, development, or delivery of the training program. They include general office supplies, facilities, equipment, and related expenses; travel and expenses not directly billed to one program; training department management and staff salaries not related to any one program; and administrative and staff support salaries.

One method for comparing costs of alternative training programs is the resource requirements model.[66] The resource requirements model compares equipment, facilities, personnel, and materials costs across different stages of the training process (training design, implementation, needs assessment, development, and evaluation). Use of the resource requirements model can help determine overall differences in costs between training programs. Also, costs incurred at different stages of the training process can be compared across programs.

Determining Benefits.   To identify the potential benefits of training, the company must review the original reasons that the training was conducted. For example, training may have been conducted to reduce production costs or overtime costs or to increase the amount of repeat business. A number of methods may be helpful in identifying the benefits of training:

1. Technical, academic, and practitioner literature summarizes the benefits that have been shown to relate to a specific training program.

2. Pilot training programs assess the benefits on a small group of trainees before a company commits more resources.

3. Observance of successful job performers can help a company determine what successful job performers do differently from unsuccessful job performers.[67]

Cost-Benefit Analysis.   A cost-benefit analysis is best explained by an example.[68] A wood plant produced panels contractors used as building materials. The plant employed 300 workers, 48 supervisors, 7 shift superintendents, and a plant manager. The business had three problems. First, 2 percent of the wood panels produced each day were rejected because of poor quality. Second, the production area was experiencing poor housekeeping, such as improperly stacked finished panels that would fall on employees. Third, the number of preventable accidents was higher than the industry average. To correct these problems, supervisors were trained in performance management and interpersonal skills related to quality problems and poor work habits of employees and in rewarding employees for performance improvement. The supervisors, shift superintendents, and plant manager attended training. Training was conducted in a hotel close to the plant. The training program was purchased from a consultant and used videotape. Also, the instructor for the program was a consultant. Costs were determined as follows:

Direct Costs

Instructor	$ 0
In-house instructor (12 days @ $125 per day)	1,500
Fringe benefits (25% of salary)	375
Travel expenses	0
Materials ($60 × 56 trainees)	3,360
Classroom space and audiovisual equipment (12 days @ $50 per day)	600
Refreshments ($4 per day × 3 days × 56 trainees)	672
Total direct costs	$ 6,507

Indirect Costs

Training management	$ 0
Clerical and administrative salaries	750
Fringe benefits (25% of salary)	187
Postage, shipping, and telephone	0
Pre- and posttraining learning materials ($4 × 56 trainees)	224
Total indirect costs	$ 1,161

Development Costs

Fee for program purchase	$ 3,600
Instructor training	
Registration fee	1,400
Travel and lodging	975
Salary	625
Benefits (25% of salary)	156
Total development costs	$ 6,756

Overhead Costs

General organizational support, top management time (10% of direct, indirect, and development costs)	$ 1,443
Total overhead costs	$ 1,443

Compensation for Trainees

Trainees' salaries and benefits (based on time away from job)	$16,969
Total training costs	$32,836
Cost per trainee	$ 587

The benefits of the training were identified by considering why training was conducted (quality of panels, housekeeping, accidents). The benefits were determined as follows:

Operational Results Area	How Measured	Results before Training	Results after Training	Differences (+ or -)	Expressed in Dollars
Quality of panels	Percent rejected	2 percent rejected— 1,440 panels per day	1.5 percent rejected— 1,080 panels per day	.5 percent— 360 panels	$720 per day $172,800 per year
Housekeeping	Visual inspection using 20-item checklist	10 defects (average)	2 defects (average)	8 defects	Not measurable in $
Preventable accidents	Number of accidents	24 per year	16 per year	8 per year	$48,000 per year
	Direct cost of accidents	$144,000 per year	$96,000 per year	$48,000 per year	

$$\text{ROI} = \frac{\text{Return}}{\text{Investment}} = \frac{\text{Operational results}}{\text{Training costs}} = \frac{\$220,800}{\$32,836} = 6.7$$

Total savings: $220,800

SOURCE: Adapted from D. G. Robinson and J. Robinson, "Training for Impact," *Training & Development Journal*, August 1989, 30–42.

It is important to recognize that other more sophisticated methods are available for determining the dollar value of training. For example, utility analysis assesses the dollar value of training based on estimates of the difference in job performance between trained and untrained employees, the number of individuals trained, the length of time a training program is expected to influence performance, and a measure of the variability in job performance in the untrained group of employees.[69] These methods require the use of a pretest/posttest design with a comparison group.

SPECIAL ISSUES

Legal Issues

A number of training situations can make an employer vulnerable to legal actions, including:[70]

- *Employee injury during a training activity*—On-the-job training and simulations often involve the use of work tools and equipment that could cause injury if incorrectly used (e.g., welder, printing press). Managers should ensure that employees are warned of potential dangers from incorrectly using equipment and that safety equipment is used. Adventure learning experiences demand a high level of physical fitness. As a result, employees should be asked to sign injury waivers or provide proof of a recent physical exam before being allowed to participate in these activities.

- *Employee or other injury outside the classroom*—Managers should ensure that trainees have the necessary level of competence in knowledge, skills, and behaviors before they are allowed to operate equipment or interact with customers.

- *Breach of confidentiality or defamation*—Managers should ensure that information placed in employees' files regarding performance in training activities is accurate. Also, before discussing an employees' performance in training with other employees or using training performance information for promotion or salary decisions, managers should tell employees that training performance will be used in that manner.

- *Reproducing and using copyrighted material in training classes without permission*—The use of videotapes, learning aids, manuals, and other copyrighted materials in training classes without requesting permission from the developer of the material is illegal. Managers should ensure that all training materials are purchased from the vendor or consultant who developed them or that permission to reproduce materials have been obtained.

The exclusion of minorities and women from training programs is illegal.[71] Nonetheless, a recent study conducted by the U.S. Labor Department found that training experiences necessary for promotion are not as available to women and minorities.[72] Managers must ensure that women and minorities are not denied access to training through communicating available training opportunities to all employees.

A recent court case suggests that information that is revealed during training sessions makes companies vulnerable to discrimination claims. At Lucky Food Stores, a California supermarket chain, notes taken during a diversity training program were used as evidence of discrimination. As part of the training program, supervisors were asked to close their eyes and imagine a successful manager. Many of the supervisors verbally stated that they imagined a white male. Other supervisors made comments about their stereotypes regarding women and minorities such as, "Women cry more" and "Black women are more aggressive." These comments were found in a file of notes taken by a company official who attended the training program. Lucky Food Stores argued that the notes were not evidence of discrimination but used by the trainer to show that employees have a biased perception of a good employee. The plaintiff in the court case argued that the company conducted the diversity training sessions only to avoid an investigation by the Equal Employment Opportunity Commission. Before the court could reach a decision on whether the company was guilty of racial discrimination, a settlement was reached in the case. The settlement requires Lucky Food Stores to establish training programs to identify and promote minorities to management jobs.

Training and Pay Systems

Training is increasingly being linked to employees' compensation through the use of skill-based pay systems. (We discuss the characteristics of skill-based pay systems in greater detail in Chapter 15, "Pay Structure Decisions".) In skill-based pay systems employees' pay is based primarily on the knowledge and skills they possess rather than the knowledge or skills necessary to successfully perform their current job.

Skill-based pay systems have several implications for training systems. Since pay is directly tied to the amount of knowledge or skill employees have obtained, employees will be motivated to attend training programs. This means that the volume of training conducted, as well as training costs, will increase. Skill-based pay systems require continual evaluation of employees' skills and knowledge to ensure that employees are competent in the skills acquired in training programs.

SUMMARY

Technological innovations, new product markets, and a diverse work force have increased the need for companies to reexamine how their training practices contribute to learning. In this chapter we discussed a systematic approach to training, including needs assessment, design of the learning environment, consideration of employee readiness for training, and transfer-of-training issues. We reviewed numerous training methods and stressed that the key to successful training was to choose a method that would best accomplish the objectives of training. We also emphasized how training can contribute to effectiveness through establishing a link with the company's strategic direction and demonstrating through cost-benefit analysis how training contributes to profitability. Training is no longer a haphazard activity. The importance of a systematic approach to training is critical for a company to successfully compete and remain profitable.

Discussion Questions

1. Noetron, a retail electronic store, recently invested a large amount of money to train sales staff to improve customer service. The skills emphasized in the program include how to greet customers, determine their needs, and demonstrate product conveniences. The company wants to know whether the program is effective. What outcomes should they collect? What type of evaluation design should they use?

2. "Melinda," bellowed Toran, "I've got a problem and you've got to solve it. I can't get people in this plant to work together as a team. As if I don't have enough trouble with the competition and delinquent accounts, now I have to put up with running a zoo. It's your responsibility to see that the staff gets along with each other. I want a human relations training proposal on my desk by Monday." How would you determine the need for human relations training? How would you determine whether you actually had a training problem? What else could be responsible?

3. Assume you are general manager of a small seafood company. Most of the training that takes place is unstructured and occurs on the job. Currently, more-senior fish cleaners are responsible for teaching new employees how to perform the job. Your company has been profitable, but recently wholesale fish dealers who buy your product have been complaining about the poor quality of your fresh fish. For example, some fillets have not had all the scales removed and abdomen parts remain attached to the fillets. You have decided to change the on-the-job training received by the fish cleaners. How will you modify the on-the-job training to improve the quality of the product delivered to the wholesalers?

4. A training needs analysis indicates that managers' productivity is inhibited because they are reluctant to delegate tasks to their subordinates. Suppose you had to decide between using adventure learning or interactive video for your training program. What are the strengths and weaknesses of each technique? Which would you choose? Why? What factors would influence your decision?

5. To improve product quality, a company is introducing a computer-assisted manufacturing process into one of its assembly plants. The new technology is likely to result in substantial modification of jobs. Employees will also be required to learn statistical process-control techniques. The new technology and push for quality will require employees to attend numerous training sessions. Over 50 percent of the employees who will be affected by the new technology completed their formal education over ten years ago. Only about 5 percent of the company's employees have used the tuition reimbursement benefit. What should management do to maximize employees readiness for training?

6. A training course was offered for maintenance employees in which trainees were supposed to learn how to repair and operate a new, complex electronics system. On the job, maintenance employees were typically told about a symptom experienced by the machine operator and were asked to locate the trouble. During training, the trainer would pose various problems for the maintenance employees to solve. He would point out a component on an electrical diagram and ask, "What would happen if this component was faulty?" Trainees would then trace the circuitry on a blueprint to uncover the symptoms that would appear as a result of the problem. You are receiving complaints about poor troubleshooting from maintenance foremen who supervise employees who have completed the program. The trainees are highly motivated and have the necessary prerequisites. What is the problem with the training course? What recommendations do you have for fixing this course?

Notes

1. A. P. Carnevale, L. J. Gainer, and J. Villet, *Training in America: The Organization and Strategic Role of Training*, (San Francisco: Jossey-Bass, 1990).

2. *Chicago Tribune,* June 14, 1992, Sec. 1, p. 18.

3. R. Henkoff, "Companies That Train Best," *Fortune,* March 22, 1993, 62–64, 68, 73–75.

4. Carnevale, Gainer and Villet, *Training in America.*

5. I. L. Goldstein and P. Gilliam, "Training Systems Issues in the Year 2000," *American Psychologist* 45 (1990): 134–143.

6. A. P. Carnevale, "America and the New Economy," *Training and Development Journal,* November 1990, 31–52.

7. K. N. Wexley and G. P. Latham, *Developing and Training Human Resources in Organizations* 2nd ed. (New York: Harper Collins, 1991).

8. D. Senge, "The Learning Organization Made Plain and Simple," *Training and Development Journal,* October 1991, 37–44.

9. J. M. Rosow and R. Zager, *Training: The Competitive Edge* (San Francisco: Jossey-Bass, 1988).

10. L. Honold, "The Power of Learning at Johnsonville Foods," *Training* 5, April 1991, 54–58.

11. I. L. Goldstein, *Training in Organizations* (Monterey, Cal.: Brooks/Cole, 1990).

12. Wexley and Latham, *Developing and Training Human Resources in Organizations.*

13. J. Z. Rouillier and I. L. Goldstein, "Determinants of the Climate for Transfer of Training." (Presented at Society of Industrial/Organizational Psychology meetings, St. Louis, Mo., 1991.); J. S. Russell, J. R. Terborg, and M. L. Powers, "Organizational Performance and Organizational Level Training and Support," *Personnel Psychology* 38 (1985): 849–863; H. Baumgartel, G. J. Sullivan, and L. E. Dunn, "How Organizational Climate and Personality Affect the Pay-off from Advanced Management Training Sessions," *Kansas Business Review* 5 (1978): 1–10.

14. Carnevale, Gainer, and Villet, *Training in America;* L. J. Gainer, "Making the Competitive Connection: Strategic Management and Training (ASTD Special Report)," *Training and Development Journal,* September 1989, s1–s30.

15. Carnevale, Gainer, and Villet, *Training in America.*

16. J. V. Hickey, "The Travelers Corporation: Expanding Computer Literacy in the Organization," in *Successful Training Strategies,* ed. J. Casner-Lotto and Associates (San Francisco: Jossey-Bass, 1988), 19–34.

17. B. Gerber, "How to Buy Training Programs," *Training,* June 1989, 59–68.

18. R. F. Mager and P. Pipe, *Analyzing Performance Problems: Or You Really Oughta Wanna,* 2nd ed. (Belmont, Cal.: Pittman Learning, 1984); A. P. Carnevale, L. J. Gainer, and A. S. Meltzer, *Workplace Basics Training Manual* (San Francisco: Jossey-Bass, 1990).

19. Ibid; I. Goldstein, "Training in Organizations," in *Handbook of Industrial/Organizational Psychology,* 2nd ed., ed. M. D. Dunnette and L. M. Hough (Palo Alto, Cal.: Consulting Psychologists Press, 1991), 2: 507–619.

20. R. A. Noe, "Trainees' Attributes and Attitudes: Neglected Influences on Training Effectiveness," *Academy of Management Review* 11 (1986): 736–749.

21. T. T. Baldwin, R. T. Magjuka, and B. T. Loher, "The Perils of Participation: Effects of Choice on Trainee Motivation and Learning," *Personnel Psychology* 44 (1991): 51–66; S. I. Tannenbaum, J. E. Mathieu, E. Salas, and J. A. Cannon-Bowers, "Meeting Trainees' Expectations: The Influence of Training Fulfillment on the Development of Commitment, Self-Efficacy, and Motivation," *Journal of Applied Psychology* 76 (1991): 759–769.

22. M. E. Gist, C. Schwoerer and B. Rosen, "Effects of Alternative Training Methods on Self-Efficacy and Performance in Computer Software Training," *Journal of Applied Psychology* 74 (1989): 884–891.

23. W. D. Hicks and R. J. Klimoski, "Entry into Training Programs and Its Effects on Training Outcomes: A Field Experiment," *Academy of Management Journal* 30 (1987): 542–552.

24. R. A. Noe and N. Schmitt, "The Influence of Trainee Attitudes on Training Effectiveness: Test of a Model," *Personnel Psychology* 39 (1986): 497–523.

25. L. H. Peters, E. J. O'Connor, and J. R. Eulberg, "Situational Constraints: Sources, Consequences, and Future Considerations," in *Research in Personnel and Human Resource Management,* ed. K. M. Rowland and G. R. Ferris (Greenwich, Conn.: JAI Press, 1985), 3: 79–114; E. J. O'Connor, L. H. Peters, A. Pooyan, J. Weekley, B. Frank, and B. Erenkranz, "Situational Constraints Effects on Performance, Affective Reactions, and Turnover: A Field Replication and Extension," *Journal of Applied Psychology* 69 (1984): 663–672; D. J. Cohen, "What Motivates Trainees?" *Training and Development Journal,* November 1990, 91–93; Russell, Terborg, and Power, "Organizational Performance and Organizational Level Training and Support."

26. Carnevale, "America and the New Economy."

27. C. Lee, "Who Gets Trained in What?" *Training,* October 1991, 47–59.

28. J. M. Rosow and R. Zager, *Training: The Competitive Edge* (San Francisco: Jossey-Bass, 1988), Chapter 7, "Designing Training Programs to Train Functional Illiterates for New Technology."

29. Ibid.

30. Carnevale, Gainer, and Meltzer, *Workplace Basics Training Manual.*

31. D. R. Torrence and J. A. Torrence, "Training in the Face of Illiteracy," *Training and Development Journal,* August 1987, 44–49.

32. C. E. Schneier, "Training and Development Programs: What Learning Theory and Research Have to Offer," *Personnel Journal,* April 1974, 288–293; M. Knowles, "Adult Learning," in *Training and Development Handbook,* 3rd ed., ed. R. L. Craig (New York: McGraw-Hill, 1987): 168–179; R. Zemke and S. Zemke, "30 Things We Know for Sure about Adult Learning," *Training,* June 1981, 45–52; B. J. Smith and B. L. Delahaye, *How to Be an Effective Trainer,* 2nd ed. (New York: Wiley, 1987).

33. W. McGehee and P. W. Thayer, *Training in Business and Industry* (New York: Wiley, 1961).

34. Wexley and Latham, *Developing and Training Human Resources in Organizations.*

35. Ibid.

36. A. Bandura, *Social Foundations of Thought and Action* (Englewood Cliffs, N.J.: Prentice-Hall, 1986); P. J. Decker and B. R. Nathan, *Behavior Modeling Training: Principles and Application* (New York: Prager, 1985).

37. T. T. Baldwin and J. K. Ford, "Transfer of Training: A Review and Directions for Future Research," *Personnel Psychology* 41 (1988): 63–105.

38. R. D. Marx, "Relapse Prevention for Managerial Training: A Model for Maintenance of Behavior Change," *Academy of Management Review* 7 (1982): 433–441; G. P. Latham and C. A. Frayne, "Self-management Training for Increasing Job Attendance: A Follow-up and Replication," *Journal of Applied Psychology* 74 (1989): 411–416.

39. C. M. Petrini (ed.), "Bringing It Back to Work," *Training and Development Journal,* December 1990, 15–21.

40. Lee, "Who Gets Trained in What?"; W. Hannum, *The Application of Emerging Training Technology* (San Diego, Cal.: University Associates, 1990); B. Filipczak, "Make Room for Training," *Training,* October 1991, 76–82; Carnevale, Gainer, and Meltzer, *Workplace Basics Training Manual.*

41. Hannum, *The Application of Emerging Training Technology.*

42. Rosow and Zager, *Training: The Competitive Edge.*

43. Lee, "Who Gets Trained in What?"

44. A. P. Carnevale, "The Learning Enterprise," *Training and Development Journal,* February 1989, 26–37.

45. W. J. Rothwell and H. C. Kanzanas, "Planned OJT Is Productive OJT," *Training and Development Journal*, October 1990, 53–56.

46. D. B. Youst and L. Lipsett, "New Job Immersion without Drowning," *Training and Development Journal*, February 1989, 73–75. G. M. Piskurich, *Self-Directed Learning* (San Francisco: Jossey-Bass, 1993).

47. R. W. Glover, *Apprenticeship Lessons from Abroad* (Columbus, Oh.: National Center for Research in Vocational Education, 1986).

48. Commerce Clearing House, Inc., *Orientation-Training* (Chicago, Ill.: Personnel Practices Communications, Commerce Clearing House, 1981) 501–905.

49. Eldredge v. Carpenters *JATC* (1981). 27 Fair Employment Practices. *Bureau of National Affairs*, 479.

50. A. F. Cheng, "Hands-on Learning at Motorola," *Training and Development Journal*, October 1990, 34–35.

51. A. Richter, "Board Games for Managers," *Training and Development Journal*, July 1990, 95–97.

52. M. W. McCall, Jr., and M. M. Lombardo, "Using Simulation for Leadership and Management Research," *Management Science* 28 (1982): 533–549.

53. G. P. Latham and L. M. Saari, "Application of Social Learning Theory to Training Supervisors through Behavior Modeling," *Journal of Applied Psychology* 64 (1979): 239–246.

54. D. Filipowski, "How Federal Express Makes Your Package Its Most Important," *Personnel Journal*, February 1992, 40–46.

55. Hannum, *The Application of Emerging Training Technology*.

56. R. J. Wagner, T. T. Baldwin, and C. C. Rowland, "Outdoor Training: Revolution or Fad?" *Training and Development Journal*, March 1991, 51–57.

57. P. F. Buller, J. R. Cragun, and G. M. McEvoy, "Getting the Most Out of Outdoor Training," *Training and Development Journal*, March 1991, 58–61.

58. R. L. Oser, A. McCallum, E. Salas, and B. B. Morgan, Jr., "Toward a Definition of Teamwork: An Analysis of Critical Team Behaviors," Technical Report 89-004 (Orlando, Fla.: Naval Training Research Center, 1989).

59. D. L. Kirkpatrick, "Evaluation of Training," in *Training and Development Handbook,* 2nd ed., ed. R. L. Craig (New York: McGraw Hill, 1976), 18-1–18-27.

60. J. Komaki, K. D. Bardwick, and L. R. Scott, "A Behavioral Approach to Occupational Safety: Pinpointing and Reinforcing Safe Performance in a Food Manufacturing Plant," *Journal of Applied Psychology* 63 (1978): 434–445.

61. A. P. Carnevale and E. R. Schulz, "Return on Investment: Accounting for Training," *Training and Development Journal*, July 1990, S1–S32; P. R. Sackett and E. J. Mullen, "Beyond Formal Experimental Design: Toward an Expanded View of the Training Evaluation Process," *Personnel Psychology* (in press); S. I. Tannenbaum and S. B. Woods, "Determining a Strategy for Evaluating Training: Operating within Organizational Constraints," *Human Resource Planning* 15 (1992): 63–81; R. D. Arvey, S. E. Maxwell, and E. Salas, "The Relative Power of Training Evaluation Designs under Different Cost Configurations," *Journal of Applied Psychology* 77 (1992): 155–160.

62. D. A. Grove and C. O. Ostroff, "Program Evaluation," in *Developing Human Resources*, ed. K. N. Wexley (Washington, DC: BNA Books, 1991), 185–219.

63. B. Filipczak, "The Business of Training at NCR," *Training*, February 1992, 55–60.

64. Carnevale and Schulz, "Return on Investment: Accounting for Training."

65. Ibid; G. Kearsley, *Costs, Benefits, and Productivity in Training Systems* (Boston: Addison-Wesley, 1982).

66. Ibid.

67. D. G. Robinson and J. Robinson, "Training for Impact," *Training and Development Journal,* August 1989, 30–42.

68. Ibid.

69. J. E. Matheiu and R. L. Leonard, "Applying Utility Analysis to a Training Program in Supervisory Skills: A Time-Based Approach," *Academy of Management Journal* 30 (1987): 316–335; F. L. Schmidt, J. E. Hunter, and K. Pearlman, "Assessing the Economic Impact of Personnel Programs on Work-Force Productivity," *Personnel Psychology* 35 (1982): 333–347; J. W. Boudreau, "Economic Considerations in Estimating the Utility of Human Resource Productivity Programs," *Personnel Psychology* 36 (1983): 551–576.

70. J. K. McAfee and L. S. Cote, "Avoid Having Your Day in Court," *Training and Development Journal,* April 1985, 56–60.

71. J. S. Russell, "A Review of Fair Employment Cases in the Field of Training," *Personnel Psychology* 37 (1984): 261–276.

72. U.S. Department of Labor, *A Report on the Glass Ceiling Initiative* (Washington, DC: U.S. Department of Labor, 1991).

73. Bureau of National Affairs, "Female Grocery Employees Prevail in Sex-Bias Suit against Lucky Stores," *BNAs Employee Relations Weekly* 10 (1992): 927–938; Stender v. Lucky Stores Inc., DC NCalifornia, No. c-88-1467, 8/18/92.

C A S E

MAINTENANCE TRAINING AT GENERAL MILLS

The Lodi, California, General Mills plant produces cereals, cake mixes, and frostings. The facility includes processing, distribution, and power-generation operations. Maintenance employees work in either mechanical or electrical/electronic maintenance. They are all required to be competent in certain core competencies (electrical, mechanical, welding). A few employees with advanced electronic skills are needed to troubleshoot and repair electronic boards.

Equipment in the facility is continually replaced as new technology becomes available. These changes mean that maintenance personnel must know how to troubleshoot, maintain, and repair a wide variety of equipment. The plant recently initiated a new maintenance training system with several goals. These goals include ensuring that all maintenance employees have learned the core competencies and can apply them, and using the most cost-effective training approach.

QUESTIONS

1. How should the core competencies that the maintenance employees need be determined?

2. What training method(s) do you think would be most cost-effective in this situation?

SOURCE: J. R. Hanlin and N. J. Johns, "Championship Training," *Training and Development,* February 1991, 56–62.

13

EMPLOYEE DEVELOPMENT

Objectives   *After reading this chapter, you should be able to:*

1. Discuss the work roles that employees, managers, and executives need to assume for companies to gain a competitive advantage.
2. Discuss how organizational characteristics influence a company's choice of development activities.
3. Discuss how psychological assessment can be used for employee development.
4. Develop a formal mentoring program.
5. For any given job, make suggestions regarding how job experiences can be used for skill development.
6. Develop a program to prepare employees for international job assignments.
7. Propose activities that companies should engage in to effectively manage a diverse work force.

Management Development Continues at GTE Despite Restructuring

In recent years, GTE Corporation, a major player in the telecommunications business, has had many reasons for cutting back on its management development activities. Some of its businesses have experienced slow growth, and the company merged with Contel Corporation. Although the merger made GTE, with 162,000 employees, the largest U.S.-based local telephone company, considerable resources had to be devoted to restructuring the company, including downsizing some units and transferring and outplacing employees.

Despite these problems, GTE has continued its management development efforts. Approximately 3 percent of GTE's managers and professionals have accepted reassignments designed to give them exposure to both regulated and unregulated businesses that GTE is involved in. The reassignments can involve moving supervisors to facilities that provide them with increased responsibility, moving professionals to cross-functional jobs designed to improve their breadth of knowledge and experience, or moving executives from one operating group to another. Over half of upper management changes jobs every two years (what the company calls "management churn"). Relocations and transfers sends a signal to employees that GTE believes they have additional con-

tributions to make to the company. Besides the growth experiences related to relocations and transfers, the reassignments often include higher salary and status.

GTE believes that management development has helped it deal successfully with the changes brought about through the development of new businesses and the merger with Contel. Because GTE believes that it is important to develop managerial talent from within, management development will continue to play a major role for the company.

SOURCE: N. C. Tompkins, "GTE Managers on the Move," *Personnel Journal,* August 1992, 86–91.

INTRODUCTION

As the example of GTE illustrates, management development is a key component of a company's employee development efforts. Traditionally, development has focused on management-level employees, while line employees received training designed to improve a specific set of skills needed for their current job. However, with the greater use of work teams and greater involvement of employees in all aspects of business, development is becoming increasingly important for all employees. **Development** refers to the acquisition of knowledge, skills, and behaviors that improve employees' ability to meet changes in job requirements and in client and customer demands. It involves learning that is not necessarily related to the employee's current job.[1] Whereas training usually focuses on employees' current jobs, development helps prepare them for a variety of jobs in the company and increases their ability to move into jobs that may not yet exist.[2]

Why is employee development important? Employee development is a necessary component of a company's efforts to improve quality, to meet the challenges of global competition and social change, and to incorporate technological advances and changes in work design. Increased globalization of product markets compels companies to help their employees understand cultures and customs that affect business practices. For high-involvement companies and work teams to be successful, their employees need strong interpersonal skills. Employees must also be able to perform roles tradition-ally reserved for managers. Legislation (such as the Civil Rights Act of 1991), labor market forces, and a company's social responsibility dictate that employers provide women and minorities with access to development activities that will prepare them for managerial positions. Companies must help employees overcome stereotypes and attitudes that inhibit the innova-tive contributions that can come from a work force made up of employees with diverse ethnic, racial, and cultural backgrounds. The "Competing through Quality" box shows how one hospital develops its employees as part of its total quality program.

We begin this chapter by discussing the work roles that employees, managers, and executives need to assume for their companies to gain a competitive advantage. Then, we identify the organizational characteristics that influence companies' involvement in and approaches to employee development. Four approaches—education, assessment, job experiences, and interpersonal relationships—used to develop employees, managers, and executives are presented. We show the types of skills, knowledge, and behaviors that are strengthened by each development method. We conclude with a discussion of current development issues, including ways to prepare employees to be successful in culturally diverse work environments both in the United States and abroad, joint union-management development efforts, and succession planning.

THE WORK ROLES OF EMPLOYEES, MANAGERS, AND EXECUTIVES

Before we discuss the different approaches used in employee development, it is important to understand the roles that employees, managers, and exec-utives are expected to play in their jobs. As you will learn, employees' and managers' work roles differ in traditional and high-involvement work environments.

Employees' Work Roles

Traditionally, the employee's role was to perform tasks and administer ser-vices according to the manager's directions. Employees were discouraged from becoming involved in improving the quality of the product or ser-vices. This was considered the responsibility of engineers and other special-ists in the company's quality-control unit. However, with the movement toward high-involvement companies using the team concept, employees today are performing many management roles (e.g., hiring, scheduling work, interacting with customers and vendors). For example, Eaton's Belmond, Iowa, plant, which manufactures engine valves for automobiles and trucks, recently started to implement the team concept.[3] Before the implementation of work teams, the manufacturing was done on an assem-

Quality

BAPTIST MEMORIAL HOSPITAL DEVELOPS TOTAL QUALITY COUNCIL— AND ITS EMPLOYEES

Baptist Memorial Hospital (BMH) is a 1,500-bed hospital in Memphis, Tennessee. As part of the hospital's total quality program a number of committees were formed. A Total Quality Council including presidents and directors from medical, health services, administrative, and quality review services was formed. Three major committees report to the Total Quality Council. The department quality-improvement committee deals with quality issues related to a specific hospital department. The interdisciplinary quality-improvement committee reports on multidepartment quality issues. The satisfaction-assessment committee reports on quality issues identified by feedback from patients, employees, and vendors. Six Key Process Teams (KPTs) addressing bedside care, diagnostic reports, accounts receivable, admissions, discharges, and general aesthetics have been formed. These teams have been successful in reducing costs. For example, one KPT identified and corrected a problem with room charges for obstetrics patients. Patients and insurance companies were confused by the room charge process. Patients who arrived in the evening were charged a partial rate for the first day of their stay but were not charged for the last day of their stay. The KPT corrected the problem by charging the normal room rate for the first day regardless of the time of the patient's arrival at the hospital but charging nothing for the last day of the patient's stay. This saved the hospital approximately $230,000 per year.

In addition to actively involving all employees through committees, BMH added a quality component to its management development process. Groups of four or five managers are assigned to work with a "coach" (a manager more experienced in total quality management) on a one-to-one basis. BMH chose an individualized development approach because the hospital recognized that managers had different levels of expertise in quality management. The coach helps the manager understand the process of implementing quality management in the work unit. The quality management implementation process involves three phases: the champion phase (the manager learns to develop customer/supplier agreement with subordinates), the model phase (the manager develops customer/supplier agreements with other departments), and the mentor phase (the manager assists employees in developing customer supplier agreements with direct customers).

SOURCE: M. Boyd and C. Haraway, "Total Quality at Baptist Memorial Hospital," *Journal for Quality and Participation,* January/February 1991, 60–66.

bly line. Now, different groups or cells of employees work on separate aspects of the manufacturing process. There are three different "cells," each with different responsibilities. All cell members know how to run the other operations within the cell. They rotate responsibilities every two hours. Each cell has a leader responsible for many of the duties usually done by the supervisor (e.g., completing requisition slips for new parts and purchase orders, reading blueprints for new orders, scheduling).

For teams to be effective, several conditions must exist. First, the members must understand and agree with the team goals and objectives. Second, team members must understand and accept their roles. The roles may include advising, promoting, organizing budgets and schedules, and developing new ideas.[4] For example, team members need to agree on who will be responsible for gathering and sharing information with other team members (adviser role). Third, team members need to agree on the procedures for accomplishing work. Last, team members need to have strong relationship skills (e.g., communication and conflict resolution skills). The "Competing through Technology and Structure" box illustrates the importance of developing individual employee skills in a redesigned work environment.

Managers' Work Roles

Research suggests that managers in traditional work environments are expected to do the following:[5]

- *Manage individual performance*—motivate employees to change performance, provide performance feedback, and monitor training activities.
- *Develop employees*—explain work assignments, provide technical expertise.
- *Plan and allocate resources*—translate strategic plans into work assignments, establish target dates for projects.
- *Coordinate interdependent groups*—persuade other units to provide products or resources needed by the work group, understand the goals and plans of other units.
- *Manage group performance*—define areas of responsibility, meet with other managers to discuss effects of changes in the work unit on their groups.
- *Monitor the business environment*—develop and maintain relationships with clients and customers, participate in task forces to identify new business opportunities.
- *Represent one's work unit*—develop relationships with other managers, communicate the needs of the work group to other units, provide information on work-group status to other groups.

Regardless of the company level they are at, all managers are expected to serve as a spokesperson to other work units, managers, and vendors (i.e., represent the work unit). The amount of time managers devote to some of these roles varies according to how high in the company the manager is. Line managers spend more time managing individual performance and developing employees than mid-level managers or executives. The most important roles for mid-level managers and executives are planning and allocating resources and coordinating interdependent groups. Executives also spend more of their time monitoring the business environment by analyzing market trends, developing relationships with clients, and overseeing sales and marketing activities.

The roles and duties of managers in high-involvement companies are shown in Table 13.1. The managers' role is to create the conditions necessary

Technology & Structure

EMPLOYEE SKILLS BENEFIT BOTH SOUTHWEST INDUSTRIES AND ITS WORKERS

Southwest Industries is an aerospace engineering company that reorganized its work force into teams to improve quality and reduce costs. The overall organizational structure was flattened by reducing the number of levels of supervision between top management and line employees from seven to four. Four strategic business groups were formed: two manufacturing teams, a support team, and an administrative team. The reorganization into teams has been quite successful. Total shipments increased 30 percent from the previous year while lead time decreased 30 percent and inventory dropped 40 percent. Production costs also decreased by 40 percent from previous levels. What is responsible for the success of the restructuring?

The reorganization into teams produced a decentralization of authority. Key manufacturing decisions are now made by the experts —the technicians. For example, frame manufacturing teams reduced machinery maintenance time. Before the teams were implemented, the machine operators focused on running, not maintaining, the equipment. With maintenance and operations a team responsibility, the team members corrected the problems. The machines are now operated with no breakdowns between scheduled maintenance periods. The teams also give employees a sense of ownership and pride in their work. The work redesign was accompanied by the introduction of a new skill-based pay system. The new pay system rewards employees according to their knowledge of team functions and skills. The movement to work teams also resulted in a change in how quality was viewed by the company. Quality is now a major corporate goal. Quality is now viewed as an important element of the entire manufacturing process. A just-in-time (JIT) manufacturing philosophy was adopted. JIT relies on employees to eliminate waste and reduce costs associated with idle inventory. This means that team members are constantly concerned with identifying their customers, determining their needs, and investigating how customer needs can be filled more efficiently and effectively.

SOURCE: R. M. Robinson, S. L. Oswald, K. S. Swinehart, and J. Thomas, "Southwest Industries: Creating High-Performance Teams for High-Technology Production," *Planning Review,* November–December 1991, 10–14, 47.

to ensure team success. These include managing alignment, coordination, decision processes, continuous learning, creativity, and maintaining trust.[6]

To manage successfully in a team environment, managers need to develop "people skills," including negotiation, sensitivity, coaching, conflict-resolution, and communication skills. A lack of people skills has been shown to be related to managers' failure to advance in their careers.[7]

Executives' Work Roles

"Executive" typically refers to the chairperson of the board, the chief operating officers, the vice-presidents, and the heads of business units and divisions. Executives are responsible for creating a context for company change,

TABLE 13.1   Manager's Roles in a Work-Team Environment

Manager's Role	Key Duties
Alignment	• Clarify team goals and company goals. • Help employees manage their objectives. • Scan organization environment for useful information for the team.
Coordination	• Ensure team is meeting internal and external customer needs. • Ensure team meets its quantity and quality objectives. • Help team resolve problems with other teams. • Ensure uniformity in interpretation of policies and procedures.
Decision process	• Facilitate team decision making. • Help team use effective decision-making processes (deal with conflict, statistical process control).
Continuous learning	• Help team identify training needs. • Help team become effective at on-the-job training. • Create environment that encourages learning.
Creating and maintaining trust	• Ensure each team member is responsible for his or her work load and customers. • Treat all team members with respect. • Listen and respond honestly to team ideas.

building employees' commitment and sense of ownership, and achieving a balance between the company's current performance and innovation. A 1988 survey of Fortune 500 companies found that leadership, implementation of business strategies, and management of organizational change are the most important topics in executive education programs. Programs directed at developing executives' understanding of global business issues are another important part of executive development.[8]

Executive education programs typically involve action learning.[9] Executives may meet with customers or work on real problems facing the company. In either case, they are required to offer solutions to customers' needs or business problems. Table 13.2 presents an example of an executive education program. Such programs include team-building exercises (such as adventure learning, discussed in Chapter 12), the opportunity to receive feedback regarding management style, and discussion with clients and customers about the strengths and weaknesses of the company's products and services.

TABLE 13.2

Emhart Corporation's "Global Competitiveness" Effective Education Program

Overall Needs	Program Concept	Program Objectives	Subject Matter
• To broaden and strengthen Emhart's key management resources • To provide a continuing forum for management interchange and the exchange of ideas/experiences to build working relationships and foster teamwork • To review and reinforce the knowledge and skills required for success	• A 5-½ day Executive Education Program to provide: —The practical competencies necessary to successfully compete in the world marketplace —A global business perspective essential to success in a world business environment • A program design that requires: —The interchange of ideas and information among executives —Cross-divisional/functional cooperation and coordination —The application of new competencies to the development of individual and business action plans	• Assist Emhart in making the transition from a successful domestic company to a successful global competitor • Encourage the development of a global perspective in managing Emhart and each business unit • Foster an understanding of key factors in the external environment and their implications for Emhart • Assess Emhart's global competitive position and recommend actions to further develop and improve this position • Review and reinforce competencies required for the effective management of a competitive global enterprise and encourage on-the-job application • Provide a continuing forum for management interchange, building working relationships across divisions, establishing networks, sharing experiences and developing teamwork	• The Nature and Value of a Global Perspective • The World in the Year 2000 • Global Competitive Trends • The Dynamics of Global Trade • Global Sourcing, Design and Manufacturing • Cultural Differences • Global Markets/ Marketing • Operational Issues in a Global Business • Global Competitiveness: Critical Success Factors • Conclusions and Implications

S O U R C E : From *Executive Development* by J. F. Bolt. Copyright © 1989 by Ballinger Publishing Company. Reprinted by permission of HarperCollins Publishers Inc.

ORGANIZATIONAL CHARACTERISTICS THAT INFLUENCE EMPLOYEE DEVELOPMENT

Employee development programs are influenced by several organization characteristics: the organization's degree of integration of business units; its global presence; its business conditions; its staffing strategy; its human resource planning; its extent of unionization; and manager, employee, and human resource staff involvement in development.[10]

Integration of Business Units

The degree to which a company's units or businesses are integrated affects the kind of development activity that takes place. In a highly integrated business, employees need to understand other units, services, and products in the company. Development activities likely include opportunities to move to other business units (job rotation) to gain an understanding of the whole business. In planning their management development programs, companies with high levels of integration need to determine the skills and competencies that all managers need to be successful.

Global Presence

As we noted in Chapter 1, the development of global product and service markets is one of the many challenges U.S. companies face today. Many companies, such as GE, GM and IBM, have had international operations for a number of years. Other companies, such as Medtronics, which makes heart valves, have only recently begun to expand their operations overseas. For companies with global operations, developmental issues include preparing employees for overseas assignments, using temporary and international assignments to develop employees, and determining whether development will be conducted and coordinated from a central U.S. facility (such as IBM's education center, located at the company's headquarters in Armonk, New York) or will be the responsibility of each satellite.

Business Conditions

Business conditions create specific human resource requirements.[11] For companies in an unstable business environment—characterized by mergers, acquisitions, or disinvestment of businesses—employee development activities may be abandoned, left up to the discretion of managers, or become more short-term (such as only offering training courses to correct skill deficiencies rather than preparing them for new assignments). These programs emphasize the development of skills and characteristics (e.g., how to deal with change) that are needed regardless of the structure the company takes. Employee development may not even occur as a result of a planned effort. Employees who remain with a company following a merger, acquisition, or disinvestment usually find that their job now has different responsibilities requiring new skills. For employees in companies experiencing growth— that is, an increased demand for their product and services—there may be many new opportunities for lateral job moves and promotions resulting from the expansion of sales, marketing, and manufacturing operations or from the start-up of new business units. These employees are usually excited about participating in development activities because new positions often offer higher salaries and more challenging tasks.

During periods when companies are trying to revitalize and redirect their business, earnings are often flat. As a result, fewer incentives for development such as promotions and salary increases may be available. In many cases, companies downsize their work forces as a way of cutting costs. Development activities under these conditions focus on ensuring that employees are available to fill the positions vacated by retirement or turnover. Development also involves helping employees avoid skill obsolescence.

Staffing Strategy

Two aspects of a company's staffing strategy influence development: the criteria used to make promotion and assignment decisions (**assignment flow**) and the places where the company prefers to obtain the human resources to fill open positions (**supply flow**).[12] Companies vary on the extent to which they make promotion and job assignment decisions based on individual performance or on group or business-unit performance. They also vary on the extent to which their staffing needs are met by relying on current employees (internal labor market) or on employees from competitors and recent entrants into the labor market, such as college graduates (external labor market). Figure 13.1 displays the two dimensions of staffing strategy. The interaction between assignment and supply flow results in four distinct types of companies: fortresses, baseball teams, clubs, and academies. Each company type places a different emphasis on development activities. For example, some companies (such as medical research companies) emphasize innovation and creativity. These types of companies are labeled "baseball teams." Because it may be difficult to develop skills related to innovation and creativity, they tend to handle staffing needs by luring employees away from competitors or by hiring graduating students with specialized skills.

The recent restructuring of IBM demonstrates how employee development practices can be affected by business strategy. IBM, historically the dominant firm in the computer industry, has been viewed as an "academy" because of its large investment in employee training and development (e.g., providing 40 hours of training for each manager per year) and its exclusive reliance on the internal labor market for its staffing needs.[13] It is also well-known for rewarding individual performance, particularly of its salespersons. However, because of the company's inability to get its new computers to the market quickly and its failure to meet its customers' demands for hardware and software that was compatible with other computer systems, in 1992 IBM experienced the first deficit in its history. As a result, the company decentralized its operations. It now operates as 13 separate manufacturing, development, and marketing businesses (e.g., the Enterprise Systems division, which manufactures mainframes; the Technology Products division, which manufactures computer chips and electronics; and the IBM North America division, which markets products in North America).

The divisions are free to compete with one another and to form partnerships. Divisions are also free to develop their own human resource prac-

FIGURE 13.1   Implications of Staffing Strategy for Employee Development

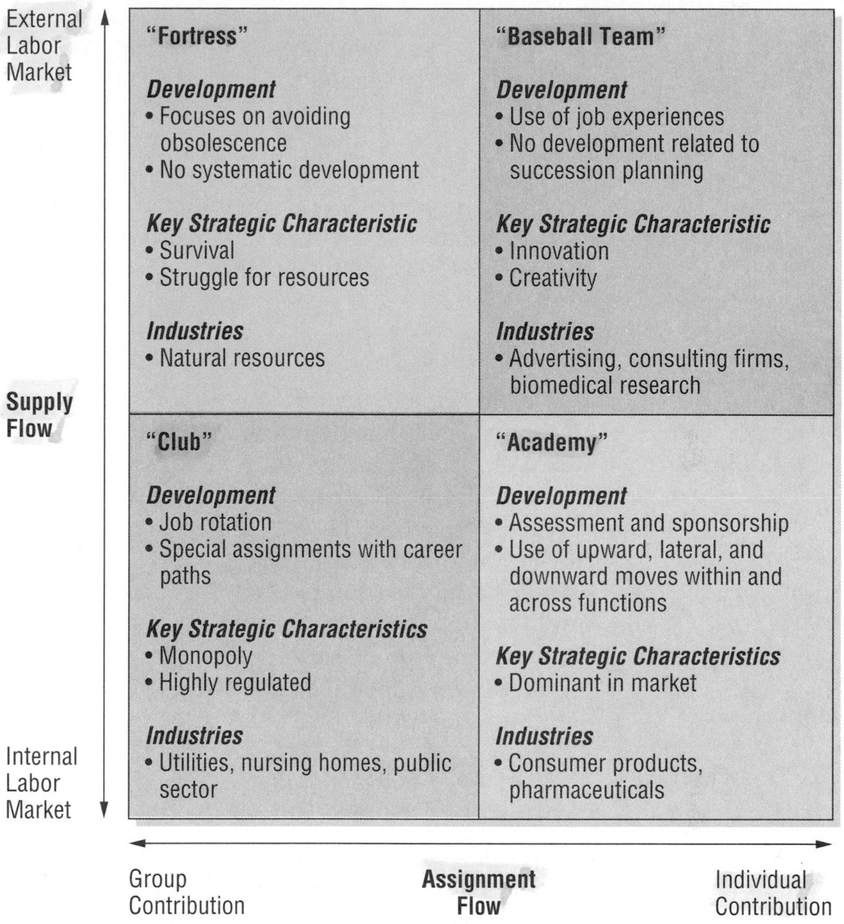

External Labor Market ↑

Supply Flow

Internal Labor Market ↓

"Fortress"

Development
• Focuses on avoiding obsolescence
• No systematic development

Key Strategic Characteristic
• Survival
• Struggle for resources

Industries
• Natural resources

"Baseball Team"

Development
• Use of job experiences
• No development related to succession planning

Key Strategic Characteristic
• Innovation
• Creativity

Industries
• Advertising, consulting firms, biomedical research

"Club"

Development
• Job rotation
• Special assignments with career paths

Key Strategic Characteristics
• Monopoly
• Highly regulated

Industries
• Utilities, nursing homes, public sector

"Academy"

Development
• Assessment and sponsorship
• Use of upward, lateral, and downward moves within and across functions

Key Strategic Characteristics
• Dominant in market

Industries
• Consumer products, pharmaceuticals

Group Contribution ←—— **Assignment Flow** ——→ Individual Contribution

SOURCE: Adapted from J. A. Sonnenfeld and M. A. Peiperi "Staffing Policy as a Strategic Response: A Typology of Career Systems," *Academy of Management Review* 13 (1988): 588–600.

tices. IBM's human resource function, which used to be in charge of employee and management development, has been spun off as a subsidiary called Workforce Solutions. The manufacturing and development divisions now buy services from Workforce Solutions and from other companies. Because IBM is moving from an academy-style staffing strategy to a baseball team strategy (recruiting talent from the external labor market rather than developing internal talent), it may decrease its investment and involvement in employee development.

Human Resource Planning

As we discussed in Chapter 9, human resource planning includes the identification, analysis, forecasting, and planning of changes needed in the human resources area to help the company meet changing business conditions.[14] Human resource planning allows the company to anticipate the movement of human resources in the company because of turnover, transfers, retirements, or promotions. Human resource plans can help identify where employees with certain types of skills are needed in the company. Development activities can be initiated to prepare employees for increased responsibilities in their current job, promotions, lateral moves, transfers, and downward job opportunities that are predicted by the human resource plan.

Unionization

Employee unions' interest in employee development has resulted in joint union-management programs designed to help employees prepare for new jobs. When companies begin retraining and productivity-improvement efforts without involving unions, the efforts are likely to fail. The unions may see the programs as just another attempt to make employees work harder without getting to share any of the productivity gains. Joint union-management programs ensure that all parties (unions, management, employees) understand the development goals and are committed to making the changes necessary for the company to make profits and for employees to both keep their jobs and share in any increased profits.

Manager, Employee, and Human Resource Staff Involvement in Development

How often—and how well—a company's employee development program is used is affected by the degree to which managers, employees, and specialized development staff are involved in the process. Complete ownership of employee development by a staff of human resource specialists may result in a wide range of classroom-based development opportunities (e.g., seminars). However, job-based development experiences may remain limited because the managers who make job and task assignments may not think employee development is a high priority.

If line managers are aware of what development activity can achieve, such as reducing the time it takes to fill open positions, they will be more willing to become involved in it. They will also become more involved in the development process if they are rewarded for participating. At Xerox, performance evaluations are directly related to pay increases.[15] Part of a manager's performance appraisal examines the actions the manager has taken to promote and develop women and minorities (e.g., moving women and minorities into pivotal jobs that provide them the experience needed to become senior managers).

An emerging trend in development is that employees must initiate the development process by contacting their manager or the human resource department.[16] Companies will support developmental activities (such as tuition reimbursement, providing developmental planning) but give employees the responsibility for expressing an interest in development activities.

APPROACHES TO EMPLOYEE DEVELOPMENT

Companies use four approaches to develop employees: formal education, assessment, job experiences, and interpersonal relationships.[17]

Formal Education

Formal education programs include off-site and on-site programs designed specifically for the company's employees, short courses offered by consultants or universities, executive MBA programs, and university programs in which participants actually live at the university while taking classes. These programs may involve lectures by business experts, business games and simulations, adventure learning, and meetings with customers. Many companies (e.g., Motorola, IBM, GE, Metropolitan Financial, Dow) have training and development centers that offer one- or two-day seminars as well as weeklong programs. There are usually separate education programs offered for supervisors, middle managers, and executives. Special programs for particular jobs (such as engineer) are also offered—for example, Honeywell's course, "Personal Computers in Manufacturing Operations." Companies may also include personal development courses as part of their education programs (e.g., American Medical Systems, a division of Pfizer, offers courses in stress management and preretirement planning).

For example, at General Electric's Management Development Institute in Crotonville, New York, courses in manufacturing and sales, marketing, and advanced management training are offered.[18] Tuition ranges from $800 for a half-week conference to $14,000 for a four-week executive development course. Tuition is paid for by the employee's business unit. The curriculum consists of the following components:

- *Corporate Entry Leadership Conferences I and II*—New hires learn about global competition and GE's values and are asked to examine their personal values. Three years after attending this program, the employees return for a program on total business competitiveness. They are given real projects to work on and have to agree to make changes in their business units.

- *New Manager Development Program*—New managers learn how to manage at GE. The program has special emphasis on teaching people skills to be used in hiring, appraising, and building work teams.

- *Senior Functional Program*—Senior functional managers attend programs on leadership development in their specific functional areas (e.g., marketing, finance). Managers work on real business problems as part of the program.
- *Executive Programs*—Executive programs include adventure learning and projects. In one program, the head of a business unit presents an unresolved business problem that teams of managers must solve. The managers interview customers and competitors and collect background information on which they base their recommendations.
- *Officer Workshops*—In these workshops, the CEO and the company officers meet to try to solve companywide issues.

Most companies consider the primary purpose of education programs to be providing the employee with job-specific skills.[19] Unfortunately, there has been little research on the effectiveness of formal education programs. In a study of Harvard University's Advanced Management Program, participants reported that they had acquired valuable knowledge from the program (e.g., how globalization affects a company's structure). They said the program helped them gain a broader perspective on issues facing their company, increased their self-confidence, and helped them learn new ways of thinking and looking at problems.[20]

Assessment

Assessment involves collecting information and providing feedback to employees about their behavior, communication style, or skills.[21] The employees, their peers, managers, and customers may be asked to provide information. Assessment is most frequently used to identify employees with managerial potential and to measure current managers' strengths and weaknesses. Assessment is also used to identify managers with the potential to move into higher-level executive positions, and it can be used with work teams to identify the strengths and weaknesses of individual team members and the decision processes or communication styles that inhibit the team's productivity.

Companies vary in the methods and the sources of information they use in developmental assessment. Many companies provide employees with performance-appraisal information. Companies with more sophisticated development systems use psychological tests to measure employees' skills, personality types, and communication styles. Self, peer, and manager's ratings of employees' interpersonal style and behavior may also be collected. Following are several popular assessment tools.

Myers-Briggs Type Indicator®.   **Myers-Briggs Type Indicator (MBTI)** is the most popular psychological test for employee development. As many as 2 million people take the MBTI in the United States each year. The test consists of more than 100 questions about how the person feels or prefers to behave in different situations (e.g., "Are you usually a good 'mixer' or rather quiet and reserved?"). The MBTI is based on the work of Carl Jung, a psychologist who believed that differences in individuals' behavior resulted from decision-making, interpersonal communication, and information-gathering preferences. The MBTI identifies individuals' preferences for energy (introversion versus extroversion), information gathering (sensing versus intuition), decision making (thinking versus feeling), and life-style (judging versus perceiving).[23] The *energy* dimension determines where individuals gain interpersonal strength and vitality. Extroverts (E) gain energy through interpersonal relationships. Introverts (I) gain energy by focusing on personal thoughts and feelings. The *information-gathering* preference relates to the actions individuals take when making decisions. Individuals with a Sensing (S) preference tend to gather facts and details. Intuitives (I) tend to focus less on facts and more on possibilities and relationships between ideas. *Decision-making style* preferences differ based on the amount of consideration the person gives to others' feelings in making a decision. Individuals with a Thinking (T) preference tend to be very objective in making decisions. Individuals with a Feeling (F) preference tend to evaluate the impact of potential decisions on others and be more subjective in making a decision. The *life-style* preference reflects an individual's tendency to be flexible and adaptable. Individuals with a Judging (J) preference focus on goals, establish deadlines, and prefer to be conclusive. Individuals with a Perceiving (P) preference tend to enjoy surprises, like to change decisions, and dislike deadlines.

Sixteen unique personality types result from the combination of the four MBTI preferences. The 16 different personality types are shown in Table 13.3. Each person has developed strengths and weaknesses as a result of using his or her preferences. For example, individuals who are Introverted, Sensing, Thinking, and Judging (known as ISTJs) tend to be serious, quiet, practical, orderly, and logical. These persons have the ability to organize tasks, be decisive, and follow through on plans and goals. ISTJs have several weaknesses because they have not used the opposite preferences—Extroversion, Intuition, Feeling, and Perceiving. Potential weaknesses for ISTJs include problems dealing with unexpected opportunities, appearing too task oriented or impersonal to colleagues, and making quick decisions.

The MBTI is used for understanding such things as communication, motivation, teamwork, work styles, and leadership. For example, it can be used by salespersons or executives who want to become more effective at interpersonal communication by learning things about their own personality styles and the way they are perceived by others. The MBTI can help develop teams by matching team members with assignments that allow them to capitalize on their preferences and helping employees understand how the different preferences of team members can lead to useful problem solving.[24] For example, employees with an Intuitive preference can be assigned brainstorming tasks. Employees with a Sensing preference can be given the responsibility of evaluating ideas.

Research on the validity, reliability, and effectiveness of the MBTI is inconclusive.[25] People who take the MBTI find it a positive experience and

TABLE 13.3

Sixteen Personality Types Used in the Myers-Briggs Type Indicator

	Sensing Types (S)		Intuitive Types (N)	
	Thinking (T)	**Feeling (F)**	**Feeling (F)**	**Thinking (T)**
Introverts (I)				
Judging (J)	**ISTJ** Serious, quiet, earn success by concentration and thoroughness. Practical, orderly, matter-of-fact, logical, realistic and dependable. Take responsibility.	**ISFJ** Quiet, friendly, responsible and conscientious. Work devotedly to meet their obligations. Thorough, painstaking, accurate. Loyal, considerate.	**INFJ** Succeed by perseverance, originality and desire to do whatever is needed or wanted. Quietly forceful, conscientious, concerned for others. Respected for their firm principles.	**INTJ** Usually have original minds and great drive for their own ideas and purposes. Skeptical, critical, independent, determined, often stubborn.
Perceiving (P)	**ISTP** Cool onlookers—quiet, reserved and analytical. Usually interested in impersonal principles, how and why mechanical things work. Flashes of original humor.	**ISFP** Retiring, quietly friendly, sensitive, kind, modest about their abilities. Shun disagreements. Loyal followers. Often relaxed about getting things done.	**INFP** Care about learning, ideas, language and independent projects of their own. Tend to undertake too much, then somehow get it done. Friendly, but often too absorbed.	**INTP** Quiet, reserved, impersonal. Enjoy theoretical or scientific subjects. Usually interested mainly in ideas, little liking for parties or small talk. Sharply defined interests.
Extroverts (E)				
Perceiving (P)	**ESTP** Matter-of-fact, do not worry or hurry, enjoy whatever comes along. May be a bit blunt or insensitive. Best with real things that can be taken apart or put together.	**ESFP** Outgoing, easygoing, accepting, friendly, make things more fun for others by their enjoyment. Like sports and making things. Find remembering facts easier than mastering theories.	**ENFP** Warmly enthusiastic, high-spirited, ingenious, imaginative. Able to do almost anything that interests them. Quick with a solution and to help with a problem.	**ENTP** Quick, ingenious, good at many things. May argue either side of a question for fun. Resourceful in solving challenging problems, but may neglect routine assignments.
Judging (J)	**ESTJ** Practical, realistic, matter-of-fact, with a natural head for business or mechanics. Not interested in subjects they see no use for. Like to organize and run activities.	**ESFJ** Warm-hearted, talkative, popular, conscientious, born cooperators. Need harmony. Work best with encouragement. Little interest in abstract thinking or technical subjects.	**ENFJ** Responsive and responsible. Generally feel real concern for what others think or want. Sociable, popular. Sensitive to praise and criticism.	**ENTJ** Hearty, frank, decisive, leaders. Usually good in anything that requires reasoning and intelligent talk. May sometimes be more positive than their experience in an area warrants.

say it helps them change their behavior. MBTI scores appear to be related to one's occupation. Analysis of managers' MBTI scores in the United States, England, Latin America and Japan suggests that a large majority of all managers have certain personality types (ISTJ, INTJ, ESTJ, or ENTJ). However, MBTI scores are not necessarily stable over time. Studies in which the MBTI was administered at two different times found that as few as 24 percent of those who took the test were classified as the same type the second time.

The MBTI is a valuable tool for understanding communication styles and the ways people prefer to interact with others. Because it does not measure how well employees perform their preferred functions, it should not be used to appraise performance or evaluate employees' promotion potential. Furthermore, MBTI types should not be viewed as unchangeable personality patterns.

Assessment Center.   The **assessment center** is a process in which multiple raters (also known as assessors) evaluate employees' performance on a number of exercises.[26] The exercises may include leaderless group discussions, interviews, and role plays. From 6 to 12 employees usually participate at one time. An assessment center is usually held at an off-site location such as a conference center. The exercises are designed to measure employees' administrative and interpersonal skills. Skills that are typically measured include leadership, oral communication, written communication, judgment, organizational ability, and stress tolerance.

The assessors are usually managers from the organization who have been trained to identify behaviors related to the skills that will be assessed. Typically, each assessor is assigned to observe and record one or two employees' behavior in each exercise. The assessors review their notes and rate the employee's level of skills (for example, 5 = high level of leadership skills, 1 = low level of leadership skills). After all employees have completed the exercises, the assessors meet to discuss their observations of each employee. They compare their ratings and try to agree on each employee's rating for each of the skills.

Assessment centers are primarily used to identify employees with management potential. Research suggests that assessment center ratings are related to performance, salary level, and career advancement.[27] Assessment centers are also useful for development purposes, because employees who participate in the process receive feedback regarding their skill strengths and weaknesses. In some organizations, such as Eastman Kodak, training courses and development activities related to the skills evaluated in the assessment center are available to employees.[28]

Benchmarks.   Benchmarks© is an instrument designed to measure the factors that are important to being a successful manager. The items measured by Benchmarks are based on research that examines the lessons executives learn at critical events in their careers.[29] This includes items that measure managers' skills in dealing with subordinates, acquiring resources, and cre-

TABLE 13.4   Skills and Perspectives Related to Managerial Success

Resourcefulness	Can think strategically, engage in flexible problem-solving behavior, and work effectively with higher management.
Doing whatever it takes	Has perseverance and focus in the face of obstacles.
Being a quick study	Quickly masters new technical and business knowledge.
Building and mending relationships	Knows how to build and maintain working relationships with coworkers and external parties.
Leading subordinates	Delegates to subordinates effectively, broadens their opportunities, and acts with fairness towards them.
Compassion and sensitivity	Shows genuine interest in others and sensitivity to subordinates' needs.
Straightforwardness and composure	Is honorable and steadfast.
Setting a developmental climate	Provides a challenging climate to encourage subordinates' development.
Confronting problem subordinates	Acts decisively and with fairness when dealing with problem subordinates.
Team orientation	Accomplishes tasks through managing others.
Balance between personal life and work	Balances work priorities with personal life so that neither is neglected.
Decisiveness	Prefers quick and approximate actions to slow and precise ones in many management situations.
Self-awareness	Has an accurate picture of strengths and weaknesses and is willing to improve.
Hiring talented staff	Hires talented people for his/her team.
Putting people at ease	Displays warmth and a good sense of humor.
Acting with flexibility	Can behave in ways that are often seen as opposites.

SOURCE: Adapted from C. D. McCauley, M. M. Lombardo, and C. J. Usher, "Diagnosing Management Development Needs: An Instrument Based on How Managers Develop," *Journal of Management* 15 (1989): 389–403.

ating a productive work climate. Table 13.4 depicts the 16 skills and perspectives believed to be important for becoming a successful manager. These skills and perspectives have been shown to be related to performance evaluations, bosses' ratings of promotability, and actual promotions received.[30] To get a complete picture of managers' skills, the managers' supervisors, their peers, and the managers themselves all complete the instrument. A summary report presenting the self-ratings and ratings by others is provided to the manager, along with information about how the ratings compare with those of other managers. A development guide with examples of experiences that enhance each of the skills and how successful managers use the skills is also available.

Performance Appraisals.   These can be useful for employee development under certain conditions.[31] The appraisal system must provide specific information to employees about their performance problems and ways they can improve their performance. This includes providing a clear understanding of the differences between current performance and expected performance, identifying the causes of the performance discrepancy, and developing action plans to improve performance. Managers must be trained in providing performance feedback and must provide that feedback daily. Managers also need to monitor employees' progress in carrying out the action plan. Using self-, peer, and manager evaluations can provide employees with multiple perspectives on their performance and development needs.

Regardless of the assessment method used, the information must be shared with the employee for development to occur. Along with the assessment information, the employee needs suggestions for correcting skill weaknesses and using skills already learned. These suggestions might be to participate in training courses or develop skills through new job experiences. Based on the assessment information and available development opportunities, employees should develop an action plan to guide their self-improvement efforts.

Job Experiences

Most employee development occurs through job experiences.[32] In the example at the beginning of this chapter, GTE was shown to rely heavily on job experiences for developing managers. A major assumption of using job experiences for employee development is that development is most likely to occur when there is a mismatch between the employee's skills and past experiences and the skills required for the job. To be successful in their jobs, employees must stretch their skills—that is, they are forced to learn new skills, apply their skills and knowledge in a new way, and master new experiences.[33]

Most of what we know about development through job experiences comes from a series of studies conducted by the Center for Creative Leadership.[34] Executives were asked to identify key events in their careers that made a difference in their managerial styles and the lessons they learned from these experiences. The key events included those involving the job assignment (e.g., fix a failing operation), those involving interpersonal relationships (e.g., getting along with supervisors), and the specific type of transition required (e.g., situations in which the executive did not have the necessary background). The job demands and what employees learned from them are shown in Table 13.5. Although the research on development through job experiences has focused on executives and managers, line employees can also learn from job experiences. As we noted earlier, for

TABLE 13.5   Examples of What Employees Learn from Job Demands

Job Demand	What to Learn
Dealing with jobs that have more responsibility and tasks	• How to deal with clients, customers, or markets • How to manage time and others • How to deal with pressure
Handling job transitions	• How to handle new responsibilities • How to prove yourself to others
Creating change	• How to solve problems created by persons who used to have the job • How to make key decisions that will affect other people, product development, or service delivery
Coping with situations outside the chain of command	• How to influence peers and boss • How to influence key people over whom you have no direct authority • How to understand competitive markets
Working without advice and support	• How to bargain for scarce resources to get job done • How to pursue a solution to a problem that managers and peers do not support • How to influence managers

a work team to be successful, its members now need the kinds of skills that only managers were once thought to need (e.g., dealing directly with customers, analyzing data to determine product quality, resolving conflict among team members). Besides the development that occurs when a team is formed, employees can further develop their skills by switching work roles within the team.

Figure 13.2 shows the various ways that job experiences can be used for employee development. These include enlarging the current job, job rotation, transfers, promotions and downward moves.

Enlarging the Current Job.   Employees can develop in their current job by adding challenges or new responsibilities. This could include such activities as temporary project assignments, switching roles within a work team, or researching new ways to serve clients and customers.

Job Rotation.   **Job rotation** involves providing employees with a series of job assignments in various functional areas of the company or movement among jobs in a single functional area or department.[35] For example, at McDonnell Douglas the job-rotation program in finance is within the finance function because employees need to understand all aspects of budgeting. Greyhound Financial Corporation has a job-rotation program for high-

FIGURE 13.2 How Job Experiences Are Used for Employee Development

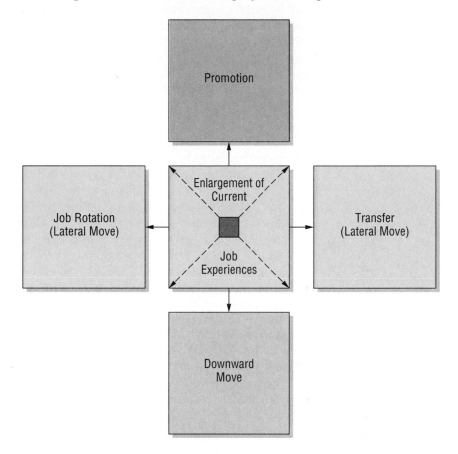

potential executive managers, a program known as "muscle-building."[36] Managers are put in departments where they will have to perform tasks different from those they have performed in the past. They maintain their titles and compensation levels while moving through the assignments, which vary in terms of status. The length of time employees spend in each job varies depending on the assignment's purpose. In the Greyhound program, assignments last two years.

A new approach to job rotation is for two companies to exchange employees. First Chicago National Bank and Kodak participated in an employee exchange program so that the two companies could better understand each other's business and how to improve the services provided.[37] For example, an employee from First Chicago helped the business imaging division of Kodak identify applications for compact disc technology. The Kodak employee helped First Chicago understand areas within the bank that could benefit from imaging technology.

Job rotation helps employees gain an overall appreciation of the company's goals, increases their understanding of different company functions, develops a network of contacts, and improves their problem-solving and decision-making skills.[38] A potential problem with job rotation is that employees do not receive challenging assignments because they do not have enough time to understand the work unit. Another potential problem is that employees find it very difficult to specialize in specific functions because they gain a general overview in their training.

Transfers, Promotions, and Downward Moves.   Upward, lateral, and downward mobility is available for development purposes in most companies.[39] In a **transfer**, an employee is given a different job assignment in a different area of the company. Transfers do not necessarily involve increased job responsibilities or increased compensation. They are likely lateral moves (a move to a job with similar responsibilities). **Promotions** are advancements into positions with greater challenges, more responsibility, and more authority than in the previous job. Promotions usually include pay increases.

Transfers may involve relocation within the United States or to another country. They can be stressful not only because the employee's work role changes, but if the employee has a family, the employees' spouse must find new employment and the family has to join a new community. Transfers disrupt employees' daily lives, interpersonal relationships, and work habits.[40] They have to find new housing, shopping, health-care, and leisure facilities, and they may be many miles from the emotional support of friends and family. They also have to learn a new set of work norms and procedures, develop interpersonal relationships with their new managers and peers, and they are expected to be as productive in their new jobs as they were in their old jobs even though they may know very little about the products, services, processes, or employees for which they are responsible.

Because transfers can be anxiety provoking, many companies have difficulty getting employees to accept them. Research has identified the employee characteristics associated with a willingness to accept transfers:[41] high career ambitions, a belief that one's future with the company is promising, and a belief that accepting a transfer is necessary for success in the company. Employees who are not married and not active in the community are more willing to accept transfers. Among married employees, the spouse's willingness to move is the most important influence on whether employees will accept a transfer.

A **downward move** occurs when an employee is given a reduced level of responsibility and authority.[42] This may involve a move to another position at the same level, but with less authority and responsibility (lateral demotion), a temporary cross-functional move, or a demotion because of poor performance. Temporary cross-functional moves to lower-level positions, which give employees experience working in different functional areas, are most frequently used for employee development. For example, engineers who want to move into management often take lower-level positions (e.g., shift supervisor) to develop their management skills.

Because of the psychological and tangible rewards of promotions (e.g., an increased feeling of self-worth, high salary, and higher status in the company), employees are more willing to accept promotions than they are to accept lateral or downward moves. Promotions are more readily available when a company is profitable and growing. When a company is restructuring and/or is experiencing stable or declining profits, especially if a large number of employees are interested in promotions and the company tends to rely on the external labor market to staff higher-level positions, promotion opportunities may be limited.[43]

Unfortunately, many employees have difficulty associating transfers and downward moves with development. They see them as punishments rather than as opportunities to develop skills that will help them achieve long-term success with the company. Many employees decide to leave a company rather than accept a transfer. Companies need to successfully manage transfers not only because of the costs of replacing employees but because of the costs directly associated with them. For example, GTE spends approximately $60 million a year on home purchases and other relocation costs such as temporary housing and relocation allowances.[44] One of the challenges companies face is learning how to use transfers and downward moves as development opportunities—convincing employees that accepting these opportunities will result in long-term benefits for them.

To ensure that employees accept transfers, promotions, and downward moves as development opportunities, companies can provide the following:[45]

- Information about the content, the challenges, and the potential benefits of the new job.

- Involvement in the transfer decision by sending the employees to preview the new locations and giving them information about the community and other employment opportunities.

- Clear performance objectives and early feedback about their job performance.

- A host at the new location, someone who will help them adjust to the new community and workplace.

- Information about how the job opportunity will affect their income, taxes, mortgage payments, and other expenses.

- Reimbursement and assistance in selling, purchasing, and renting a place to live.

- An orientation program for the new location and job.

- Guarantee that the new job experiences will support the employees' career plans.

Interpersonal Relationships

Employees can also develop skills and increase their knowledge about the company and its customers by interacting with a more-experienced organizational member.

Mentoring.   A **mentor** is an experienced, productive senior employee who helps develop a less-experienced employee (the protégé). Most mentoring relationships develop informally as a result of interests or values shared by the mentor and protégé. They can also develop as part of a planned company effort to bring together successful senior employees with less-experienced employees. One of the limitations of formal mentoring programs is that the mentors may not be able to provide counseling and coaching in a relationship that has been artificially created.[46]

One of the major advantages of formalized mentoring programs is that they ensure access to mentors for all employees, regardless of gender or race. An additional advantage is that the participants in the mentoring relationship know what is expected of them.[47] Table 13.6 presents the characteristics of a successful formal mentoring program.

Benefits of Mentoring Relationships.   Both mentors and protégés can benefit from a mentoring relationship.[48] Research suggests that mentors provide career and psychosocial support to their protégés. Career support includes coaching, protection, sponsorship, and providing challenging assignments, exposure, and visibility. Psychosocial support includes serving as a friend and a role model, providing positive regard and acceptance, and providing an outlet for the protégé to talk about anxieties and fears. Additional benefits for the protégé include higher rates of promotion, higher salaries, and greater organizational influence.

Mentoring relationships provide opportunities for mentors to develop their interpersonal skills and increase their feelings of self-esteem and worth to the organization. For individuals in technical fields such as engineering or health services, the protégé may help them gain knowledge about important new scientific developments in their field (and therefore prevent them from becoming technically obsolete).

Purposes of Mentoring Programs.   Mentor programs are used to socialize new employees, to increase the likelihood of skill transfer from training to the work setting, and to provide opportunities for women and minorities to gain the exposure and skills needed to move into managerial positions. As an illustration, consider the National Association of Secondary School Principals' two-day simulation designed to improve school administrators' interpersonal and administrative skills. Program participants are matched with mentors, who observe their behavior in the simulation. Following the simulation, mentors give their protégés feedback about their behavior in the simulation. The mentors and protégés also discuss the protégés' development goals, and they agree on a development plan. The mentors are experienced, successful school administrators. As part of the simulation, mentors and protégés are required to meet formally three months after the simulation to discuss the progress the protégés have made on their development plans. In many cases, the mentors and protégés also meet informally.

In the United States, women and minorities are underrepresented in managerial positions. Also, for women in managerial positions, their salary

TABLE 13.6   Characteristics of a Successful Formal Mentoring Program

1. Mentor and protégé participation is voluntary. Relationship can be ended at any time without fear of punishment.

2. Mentor-protégé matching process does not limit the ability of informal relationships to develop. For example, a mentor pool can be established to allow protégés to choose from a variety of qualified mentors.

3. Mentors are chosen on the basis of their past record in developing employees, willingness to serve as a mentor, and evidence of positive coaching, communications, and listening skills.

4. The purpose of the program is clearly understood. Projects and activities that the mentor and protégé are expected to complete are specified.

5. The length of the program is specified. Mentor and protégés are encouraged to pursue the relationship beyond the formal time period.

6. A minimum level of contact between the mentor and protégé is specified.

7. Protégés are encouraged to contact one another to discuss problems and share successes.

8. The mentor program is evaluated. Interviews with mentors and protégés are used to obtain immediate feedback regarding specific areas of dissatisfaction. Surveys are used to gather more detailed information regarding benefits received from participating in the program.

9. Employee development is rewarded, which sends a signal to managers that mentoring and other development activities are worth their time and effort.

progression and career progression lags behind male managers.[49] One reason is that they often do not receive the same development opportunities that men do. Women and minorities often find it difficult to find mentors because of their lack of access to the "old boy network," managers' preference to interact with other managers of similar status rather than with line employees, and intentional exclusion by managers who have negative stereotypes about women's and minorities' abilities, motivation, and job preferences.[50] Potential mentors may view minorities and women as a threat to their job security because they believe affirmative action plans give those groups preferential treatment.

As part of their approach to managing a diverse work force, many companies are using mentoring programs to ensure that women and minorities gain the skills and visibility needed to move into managerial positions. For example, at Pacific Bell, a task force was appointed to study why there were relatively few promotions of minority managers and few structured programs to help managers improve their skills.[51] The task force found that support from an older mentor at some time in a manager's career was necessary for career advancement and skill development. As a result, Pacific Bell devised a development program for minority managers. Besides working with their immediate supervisors to develop career goals, trainees work with executive mentors who are at least two levels above the trainees. The mentors have input into the development plan and meet frequently with the trainees. Pacific Bell received an award from the Department of Labor for its commitment to equal employment opportunity.

CURRENT ISSUES IN EMPLOYEE DEVELOPMENT

Cross-Cultural Preparation

Cross-cultural preparation involves educating employees and their families who are given an assignment in a foreign country. To successfully conduct business in the global marketplace, employees must understand the business practices and the cultural norms of different countries. In the United States, we emphasize timeliness and efficiency in conducting business; to assume that other countries do the same can result in embarrassment and lost business. Table 13.7 gives examples of business practices and cultural norms from Middle Eastern, Latin American, and Asian countries. As you can see, punctuality and timeliness may very well offend persons from many other countries.

To prepare employees for international assignments, companies need to provide cross-cultural education. Most U.S. companies send employees overseas without any preparation. As a result, the number of employees who return home before completing their assignments is higher for U.S. companies than for European and Japanese companies.[52] U.S. companies lose more than $2 billion a year as a result of failed overseas assignments.

To be successful in overseas assignments, expatriates (employees on foreign assignments) need to be:

1. Competent in their area of expertise.
2. Able to communicate verbally and nonverbally in the host country.
3. Flexible, tolerant of ambiguity, and sensitive to cultural differences.
4. Motivated to succeed and willing to learn about the host country's culture, language, and customs.
5. Supported by family.[53]

One reason for the high failure rate of U.S. expatriates is that companies place more emphasis on developing employees' technical skills than on preparing them to work in other cultures. Research suggests that the comfort of an expatriate's spouse and family is the most important determinant of whether the employee will complete the assignment.[54]

The key to a successful foreign assignment appears to be a combination of training and career management for the employee and his or her family. Foreign assignments involve three phases: predeparture, on-site, and repatriation (i.e., preparing to return home). Training is necessary in all three phases.

TABLE 13.7   Business Practices and Cultural Norms of Other Countries

Middle Easterners	Latin America: Mexico, Central, and South America	Asians: Japan, China, India, and Pacific Basin
• Decisions are not made by correspondence or telephone. • Being on time for appointments or keeping appointments is unusual. • First business visits are leisurely. It is considered rude for visiting business person to try to talk business during the initial meeting with the host. • Do not eat with the left hand. The left hand is for private matters. • A visitor must be careful not to admire anything the host owns, because the host may feel obliged to give it to the admirer.	• Pace in Latin America is traditionally slow especially when negotiations are underway. • Brazilians do not like quick, infrequent visits. • Deals are never concluded over the phone or by letter but in person. • Latin Americans are late according to North American standards but expect North Americans to be on time. • Pleasantries are always exchanged before conducting business. • The work one does is directly related to social class.	• Saving face and achieving harmony are important factors in business negotiations. • Never put a Japanese in a position where he must admit failure. • Avoid direct communication about money. • Third-party introductions are important. • In communication, sentences are frequently unfinished so that the person can conclude in their own mind. • A premium is placed on long-term relations with customers and suppliers. • Japanese tend to resist pressure on deadline or delivery dates.

SOURCE: Adapted from P. R. Harris and R. T. Moran, *Managing Cultural Differences,* 3rd ed. (Houston: Gulf Publishing, 1991).

Predeparture Phase. In the predeparture phase, employees need to receive language training and an orientation in the new country's culture and customs. It is critical that the family be included in the orientation programs.[55] Expatriates and their families need information about housing, schools, recreation, shopping, and health-care facilities in the area where they will live. Expatriates also need to discuss with their managers how the foreign assignment fits into the expatriates' career plans and what type of position the expatriate can expect upon return.

On-Site Phase. On-site training involves continued orientation to the host country and its customs and cultures through formal programs or through a mentoring relationship. Expatriates and their families may be paired with an employee from the host country who helps them understand the new, unfamiliar work environment and community.[56]

Repatriation Phase.   The repatriation phase prepares expatriates for return. Expatriates and their families are likely to experience high levels of stress and anxiety when they return because of the changes that have occurred since their departure. This shock can be reduced by providing expatriates with company newsletters and community newspapers and by ensuring that they receive personal and work-related mail from the United States while they are on foreign assignment. It is also not uncommon for employees and their families to have to readjust to a lower standard of living in the United States than they had in the foreign country, where they may have enjoyed maid service, limousine service, private schools, and clubs. Salary and other compensation arrangements should be worked out well before employees return from overseas assignments.

Aside from reentry shock, many expatriates decide to leave the company because the assignment they are given upon returning to the United States has less responsibility, challenge, and status than the foreign assignment.[57] As noted earlier, career planning discussions need to be held before the employees leave the United States to ensure that they understand the positions they will be eligible for upon repatriation. GE Medical Systems' approach to its global work force is explained in the "Competing through Globalization" box.

Cross-cultural training methods include lecture presentations that expatriates and their families attend on the customs and culture of the host country. Experiential exercises, such as miniculture experiences, allow expatriates to spend time with a family in the United States from the ethnic group of the host country. Research suggests that the degree of difference between the United States and the host country (cultural novelty), the amount of interaction with host country citizens and host nationals (interaction), and the familiarity with new job tasks and work environment (job novelty) all influence the type of cross-cultural training method used.[58] Experiential training methods are most effective (and most needed) in assignments with a high level of cultural and job novelty that require a high level of interpersonal interaction with host nationals.

Managing Work-Force Diversity

The goal of diversity training is to eliminate values, stereotypes, and managerial practices that inhibit employees' personal development and therefore allow employees to contribute to organizational goals regardless of their race, sexual orientation, gender, family status, religious orientation, or cultural background.[59] Traditionally, companies have been concerned with ensuring that women and minorities were adequately represented in the labor force. **Managing diversity** involves creating an environment that allows all employees to contribute to organizational goals and experience personal growth. This requires the company to develop employees so that

Globalization

GE MEDICAL SYSTEMS HELP EMPLOYEES "GO GLOBAL"

GE Medical Systems (GEMS) based in Milwaukee, Wisconsin, sells and services X-ray, CAT-scan, magnetic resonance, nuclear medicine, and ultrasound systems. GEMS has manufacturing facilities in Milwaukee, Paris, Tokyo, Italy, and Spain. Non-U.S. business revenue has increased from 13 percent in 1985 to 40 percent in 1992.

GEMS' success in the global marketplace is a direct result of the company's multifaceted approach to cross-cultural preparation. The Global Leadership Program involved more than 200 managers from all facilities. As part of the program, each manager was part of a multicultural project team that worked on developing solutions to global business issues. The managers also participated in adventure learning training. To be successful in the adventure learning exercises, managers had to learn to communicate with team members who spoke different languages. The managers also had the opportunity to learn about different cultures by meeting with team members in their host countries to discuss the team project. The host team member shared the unique aspects of their culture with their peers.

GEMS also has an extensive program to prepare employees who are scheduled for international assignments (expatriates). Employees receive predeparture counseling, culture and language training, and individualized education plans for school-age children. Employees who have completed an international assignment in the same country serve as mentors for the expatriates. They answer questions about living conditions, customs, and culture, based on their experiences. Expatriates are also assigned to a peer mentor when they arrive in the host country. Peer mentors help employees and their families adjust to work and the new surroundings.

GEMS also provides cross-cultural and language training for employees who work in the United States but have frequent contact with businesses in foreign countries. These employees receive training addressing how U.S. culture is viewed by persons from other countries. Former expatriates serve as instructors. This type of training is necessary because GEMS employees frequently interact with employees from Tokyo and Paris facilities via videoconferencing.

SOURCE: P. Stuart, "Global Outlook Brings Good Things to GE Medical," *Personnel Journal,* June 1992, 138–143.

they are comfortable in working with others from a wide variety of ethnic, racial, and religious backgrounds.

Managing Diversity through Adherence to Legislation.   One approach to managing diversity is through affirmative action policies and by making sure that human resource practices meet standards of equal employment opportunity laws.[60] This approach rarely results in changes in employees' values, stereotypes, and behaviors that inhibit productivity and personal development. Figure 13.3 shows the cycle of disillusionment resulting from managing diversity by relying solely on adherence to employment laws. The cycle begins when the company realizes it must change policies regarding women and minorities because of legal pressure or a discrepancy between the number of women and minorities in the work force and the number

FIGURE 13.3   Cycle of Disillusionment Resulting from Managing Diversity through Adherence to Legislation

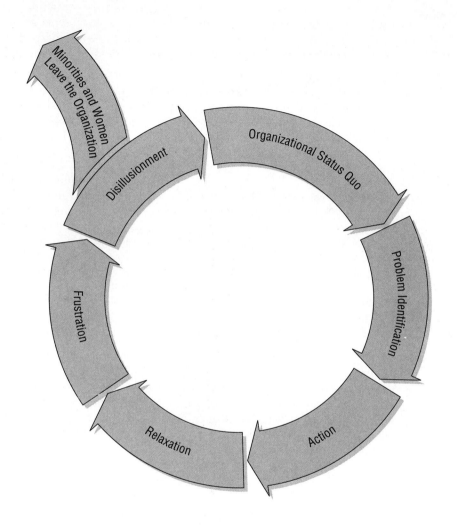

SOURCE: Reprinted with the permission of HRMagazine published by the Society for Human Resource Management, Alexandria VA.

available in the labor market. To address these concerns, a greater number of women and minorities are hired by the company. Managers see little need for additional action because women and minority employment rates reflect their availability in the labor market. However, as women and minorities gain experience in the company, they likely become frustrated. Managers and coworkers may avoid providing coaching or performance feedback to women and minorities because they are uncomfortable interacting with individuals from different ethnic or racial backgrounds. Coworkers may express beliefs that women and minorities are employed only because they received special treatment (e.g., hiring standards were lowered).[61] As a result of their frustration, women and minorities may form support groups to voice their concerns to management. Because of the work atmosphere, women and minorities fail to fully utilize their skills and may leave the company.

The point of this discussion is not to suggest that companies should be reluctant to engage in affirmative action or pursue equal opportunity employment practices. However, affirmative action without additional supporting strategies does not deal with issues of assimilating women and minorities into the work force. To successfully manage a diverse work force, companies need to ensure that:

- Employees understand how their values and stereotypes influence their behavior toward others of different gender, ethnic, racial, or religious backgrounds.
- Employees gain an appreciation of cultural differences among employees.
- Behaviors that isolate or intimidate minority group members change.

This can be accomplished through specific training activities.

Managing Diversity through Attitude and Behavior Change.   Diversity training programs differ according to whether attitude or behavior change is emphasized.[62] Attitude change programs focus on increasing employees' awareness of differences in cultural and ethnic backgrounds, physical characteristics (e.g., disabilities), and personal characteristics that influence behavior toward others. The assumption underlying these programs is that, by increasing their awareness of stereotypes and beliefs, employees will be able to avoid negative stereotypes when interacting with employees of different backgrounds. The programs help employees consider the similarities and differences between cultural groups, examine their attitudes toward affirmative action, or analyze their beliefs about why minority employees are successful or unsuccessful in their jobs. Many of these programs use videotapes and experiential exercises to increase employees' awareness of the negative emotional and performance effects of stereotypes, values, and behaviors on minority group members. For example, 3M conducts workshops in which managers are asked to assess their attitudes towards stereotypical statements about race, age, and gender.[63] The participants select two stereotypes they hold and consider how these stereotypes affect their ability to manage. One of the most popular video training packages, Copeland Griggs Productions' "Valuing Diversity Training Program," involves three days of training that focuses on managing differences, diversity in the workplace, and cross-cultural communications.

Behavior change programs focus on changing the organizational policies and individual behaviors that inhibit employees' personal growth and productivity. These programs identify incidents that discourage employees from working up to their potential. Groups of employees are asked to identify specific promotion opportunities, sponsorship, training opportunities, or performance management practices that they believe were handled unfairly. Their views regarding how well the work environment and management practices value employee differences and provide equal opportunity may also be collected. Specific training programs are developed to address the issues presented in the focus groups. At Honeywell Corporation, diversity training involves four strategies:

1. Increasing managers' understanding and commitment to diversity.
2. Promoting a fair work environment that values diversity.
3. Developing the skills and talents of all employees.
4. Helping employees reduce barriers to personal and professional development.[64]

For attitude and behavioral change programs to be successful, managers should be evaluated on performance objectives related to managing diversity (e.g., development of female and minority employees).

The "Competing through Social Responsibility" box shows how United Parcel Service helps its employees manage diversity.

Joint Union-Management Programs

To be more competitive, U.S. industries that have lost considerable market share to foreign competition (e.g., the auto industry) have developed joint union-management training. Both labor and management have been forced to accept new roles: Employees need to become involved in business planning and strategic decision making, and management needs to learn how to share power and allow worker participation in decision making.

The initial goal of these programs was to help displaced employees find new jobs by providing skill training and outplacement assistance. Currently, **joint union-management programs** provide a wide range of services designed to help employees prepare for workplace changes resulting from new technology and restructuring. Both the employers and the unions contribute money for the administration of the programs and both oversee the programs' operation. The United Auto Workers–Ford Education Development and Training Program includes the following:

- *Life/Education Planning Program*—Helps employees determine their career needs and interests and links them with resources in the community.

- *Education and Training Assistance Plan*—Assists employees in identifying appropriate courses at colleges and universities and provides tuition reimbursement.

- *Skills Enhancement Program*—Provides counseling and assistance related to adult basic education, high school completion, general education development, and English as a second language.

- *College and University Options Program*—Makes both degree and nondegree college and technical training more accessible for employees. Provides workshops for employees, on-site course registration, classes

COMPETING THROUGH

Social Responsibility

UPS CARRIES DIVERSITY TRAINING TO GREAT LENGTHS

Since 1968, United Parcel Service (UPS) has used the Community Internship Program for preparing managers for dealing with a diverse work force. Upper and mid-level managers are taken off their regular job for one month and placed in communities or situations they would not likely encounter on the job. The assignments have included serving meals to the homeless, helping migrant workers build houses and schools, or working to rid inner-city neighborhoods of drugs. Managers who are accustomed to a well-organized work day are placed in situations where they have to react to crises every day. About 800 managers have completed these internships. The program costs UPS approximately $10,000 for each intern. Since about 40 managers go through the program each year, it costs UPS $400,000 per year. However, UPS feels that the program benefits for the managers and the communities they work in outweigh the costs. UPS's rationale for the program is that managers are better able to manage a diverse

work force because these experiences help them see how much they have in common with persons from different backgrounds. The managers also learn the frustrations that women and minorities feel in trying to deal with a social system that is designed for persons who are successful. For example, at an internship in McAllen, Texas, the managers discovered that poor sanitation and contaminated drinking water were responsible for many health problems diagnosed at a local health clinic. The managers proposed new sanitation methods and purification process to clean up the water supplied to migrant workers in the area.

Participation in the program is not voluntary. Initially, the program was for managers who refused to work constructively with minority employees. The program is now viewed by managers as an important part of their development plan. Many who have participated in the program have received better job assignments within the company.

SOURCE: B. Filipczak, "25 Years of Diversity at UPS," *Training,* August 1992, 42–46.

at times that are convenient to employees, and credits for college-level knowledge.

- *Targeted Education, Training, or Counseling Projects*—Provide projects that are related to the specific educational or counseling needs of a specific location or segment of the work force.
- *Successful Retirement Planning Program*—Provides preretirement planning to employees and their spouses.
- *Financial Education Program*—Covers topics such as personal financial planning, investment and insurance, wills, and trusts.[65]

Another type of joint labor-management program involves educating both employees and managers regarding business issues. For example, in the UAW-GM Paid Education Leave Program (PEL), employees and managers attend classes taught by university faculty. The classes stress (1) the changes taking place in the auto industry (e.g., new technology, foreign competitors), (2) the need for labor-management cooperation, (3) an understanding of the influence of government regulation on the auto industry, and (4) an understanding of strategic planning and change.[66] Employees and managers believe that the greatest benefit of the program is that, by providing them with an awareness and knowledge of the key issues facing the auto industry, it helps them to do a better job.

Succession Planning

Succession planning primarily involves the identification and tracking of "high-potential employees." High-potential employees are those the company believes are capable of being successful in higher-level managerial positions such as general manager of a strategic business unit, functional director (e.g., director of marketing), or the chief executive officer (CEO).[67] High-potential employees typically participate in fast-track development programs that involve education, executive mentoring and coaching, and rotation through job assignments.[68] Job assignments are based on the successful career paths of the managers the high-potential employees are being prepared to replace. High-potential employees may also receive special assignments, such as making presentations and serving on committees and task forces. The objectives of fast-track development programs are:

- Developing future managers for mid-manager to executive positions.
- Providing companies with a competitive advantage in attracting and recruiting talented employees.
- Helping retain managerial talent within the company.[69]

Research suggests that the development of high-potential employees involves three stages.[70] A large pool of employees may initially be identified as high-potential employees, but the numbers are reduced over time because of turnover, poor performance, or a personal choice not to strive for a higher-level position. In Stage I, high-potential employees are selected: Those who have completed elite academic programs (e.g., an MBA at Stanford) or who have been outstanding performers are identified. Psychological tests such as assessment centers may also be used.

In Stage II, high-potential employees receive development experiences. Those who succeed are the ones who continue to demonstrate good performance. A willingness to make sacrifices for the company is also necessary (e.g., accepting new assignments or relocating to a new geographic location). Good oral and written communication skills, an ease in interpersonal relationships, and a talent for leadership are a must. In what is known as a tournament model of job transitions, high-potential employees who meet the expectations of their senior managers in this stage are given the opportunity to advance into the next stage of the process.[71] Employees who do not meet the expectations are ineligible for higher-level managerial positions in the company.

To reach Stage III, high-potential employees usually have to be seen by top management as fitting into the company's culture and having the personality characteristics needed to successfully represent the company. These employees have the potential to occupy the company's top positions. In Stage III, the CEO becomes actively involved in developing the employees, who are exposed to the company's key personnel and are given a greater understanding of the company's culture. It is important to note that the development of high-potential employees is a slow process. Reaching Stage III may take 15 to 20 years.

Developing Managers with Dysfunctional Behaviors

A number of studies have identified managerial behaviors that can cause an otherwise competent manager to be ineffective. These behaviors include insensitivity to others, inability to be a team player, arrogance, and poor conflict-management skills.[72] For example, a skilled manager who is interpersonally abrasive, aggressive, and an autocratic leader may find it difficult to motivate subordinates, alienate internal and external customers, and have trouble getting their ideas accepted by their superiors. These managers are in jeopardy of losing their jobs because of the dysfunctional behaviors. Typically, a combination of assessment, training, and counseling are used to help managers change the dysfunctional behavior.

One example of a program designed specifically to develop managers with dysfunctional behavior is the Individual Coaching for Effectiveness (ICE) program.[73] Although the effectiveness of these types of programs needs to be further investigated, research conducted to date suggests that managers' participation in these programs result in skill improvement and reduced likelihood of termination.[74] The ICE program includes diagnosis, coaching, and support activities. The program is tailored to the manager's needs. Clinical, counseling, or industrial/organizational psychologists are involved in all phases of the ICE program. They conduct the diagnosis, coach and counsel the manager, and develop action plans for implementing new skills on the job.

The first step in the ICE program, diagnosis, involves collecting information about the manager's personality, skills, and interests. Interviews with the manager, his or her supervisor, and colleagues and psychological tests are used to collect this information. This information is used to determine whether the manager can actually change the dysfunctional behavior. For example, personality traits such as extreme defensiveness may make it difficult for the manager to change his or her behavior. If it is determined that the manager can benefit from the program, then specific developmental objectives tailored to the manager's needs are set. The manager and his or her supervisor are typically involved in this process.

The coaching phase of the program first involves presenting the manager with information about the targeted skills or behavior. This may include information about principles of effective communication or teamwork, tolerance of individual differences in the workplace, or conducting effective meetings. The second step is for the manager to participate in behavior-modeling training (discussed in Chapter 12). The manager also receives psychological counseling to overcome beliefs that may inhibit learning the desired behavior.

The support phase of the program involves creating conditions to ensure that the manager is able to use the new behaviors and skills acquired in the ICE program on the job. The supervisor is asked to provide feedback to the manager and the psychologist about progress made in using the new skills and behavior. The psychologist and manager identify situations in which the manager may tend to rely on dysfunctional behavior. The coach and manager also develop action plans that outline how the manager should try to use new behavior in daily work activities.

SUMMARY

Technological, product-market, and labor-market changes dictate that companies become actively involved in developing their employees. This chapter began by presenting the roles in which employees, managers, and executives need to be successful so that companies can gain a competitive advantage. In high-involvement work environments, employees are expected to perform roles previously reserved for managers. The changes in roles mean that all employees need to develop people skills. Development can occur through education, job experiences, interpersonal relationships, and assessments of employees' knowledge, skills, attitudes, and behaviors. Companies' involvement in development activities varies according to the business conditions, the company's staffing strategy, and other organizational characteristics. Regardless of the organization's characteristics, most have to prepare employees to work in diverse cultures, both in the United States and abroad. Employers also need to become involved in succession planning: preparing employees for managerial openings resulting from turnover, retirements, or promotions.

Discussion Questions

1. How would you expect the development activities of a company that is dominant in its product market to differ from those of a company that emphasizes research and development?

2. What do you think is the most important organizational characteristic that influences employee development? Why?

3. The vice-president of Engineering of a small manufacturing company gives you the assignment of preparing three engineers for a six-month assignment in Tokyo, Japan. Two of the engineers are married. One of the married engineers has a daughter in high school. What suggestions would you have to increase the probability that these engineers will be successful?

4. How could assessment be used to create a productive work team?

5. What skills, attitudes, or values do you think should be emphasized in development programs designed to prepare managers to manage a diverse work force? If

you were asked to develop a four-hour workshop for managers, what content and activities would you include?

6. Your boss is interested in hiring a consultant to help identify new managers from current employees. She asks you to outline the type of assessment program you believe would do the best job of identifying employees who will be successful managers. What will you tell her?

7. Many employees are unwilling to relocate geographically because they like their current community, and spouses and children prefer not to move. How could an employee's current job be changed to develop his or her leadership skills?

Notes

1. M. London, *Managing the Training Enterprise* (San Francisco: Jossey-Bass, 1989).

2. R. W. Pace, P. C. Smith, and G. E. Mills, *Human Resource Development* (Englewood Cliffs, N.J.: Prentice-Hall, 1991); W. Fitzgerald, "Training versus Development," *Training and Development Journal*, May 1992, 81–84.

3. M. Berg, "Eaton's Self-managed Workteams." (Plan B paper submitted in partial fulfillment of the requirements for the MAIR degree, Industrial Relations Center, University of Minnesota, 1992.)

4. D. F. Van Eynde, "High Impact Team Building Made Easy," *HR Horizons*, Spring, 1992, 37–41; J. R. Hackman, ed., *Groups that Work and Those that Don't: Creating Conditions for Effective Teamwork* (San Francisco: Jossey-Bass, 1990); D. McCann and C. Margerison, "Managing High-Performance Teams," *Training and Development Journal*, November 1989, 53–60.

5. A. I. Kraut, P. R. Pedigo, D. D. McKenna, and M. D. Dunnette, "The Role of the Manager: What's Really Important in Different Managerial Jobs," *Academy of Management Executive* 4 (1988): 36–48; F. Luthans, "Successful vs. Effective Real Managers," *Academy of Management Executive* 2 (1988): 127–132; H. Mintzberg, *The Nature of Managerial Work* (New York: Harper & Row, 1973).

6. B. Gerber, "From Manager into Coach," *Training*, February 1992, 25–31; C. Carr, "Managing Self-managed Workers," *Training and Development Journal*, September 1991, 37–42.

7. P. Kizilos, "Fixing Fatal Flaws," *Training*, September 1991, 66–70; F. S. Hall, "Dysfunctional Managers: The Next Human Resource Challenge," *Organizational Dynamics*, August 1991, 48–57.

8. J. Bolt, *Executive Development* (New York: Harper Business, 1989); H. S. Jonas, R. E. Fry, and S. Srivasta, "The Office of the CEO: Understanding the Executive Experience," *Academy of Management Executive* 4 (1990): 36–48; J. Noel and R. Charam, "GE Brings Global Thinking to Light," *Training and Development Journal*, July 1992, 29–33.

9. B. O'Reilly, "How Execs Learn Now," *Fortune*, April 5, 1993.

10. R. J. Campbell, "HR Development Strategies," in *Developing Human Resources*, ed. K. N. Wexley (Washington, D.C.: BNA Books, 1991), 5-1–5-34; J. K. Berry, "Linking Management Development to Business Strategy," *Training and Development Journal*, August 1990, 20–22.

11. M. London, "Organizational Support for Employees' Career Motivation: A Guide to Human Resource Strategies in Changing Business Conditions," *Human Resource Planning* 11, no. 1 (1988): 23–32.

12. J. A. Sonnenfeld and M. A. Peiperl, "Staffing Policy as a Strategic Response: A Typology of Career Systems," *Academy of Management Review* 13 (1988): 588–600.

13. D. Kirkpatrick, "Breaking up IBM," *Fortune*, July 27, 1992, 44–58.

14. V. R. Ceriello and C. Freeman, *Human Resource Management Systems: Strategies, Tactics, and Techniques* (Lexington, Mass.: Lexington Books, 1991).

15. V. Sessa, "Managing Diversity at the Xerox Corporation: Balanced Workforce Goals and Caucus Groups," in *Diversity in the Workplace: Human Resource Initiatives,* ed. S. E. Jackson & Associates (New York: The Guilford Press, 1992), 37–64.

16. D. T. Jaffe and C. D. Scott, "Career Development for Empowerment in a Changing Work World," in *New Directions in Career Planning and the Workplace,* ed. J. M. Kummerow (Palo Alto, Cal.: Consulting Psychologist Press, 1991): 33–60.

17. Campbell, "HR Development Strategies"; M. A. Sheppeck and C. A. Rhodes, "Management Development: Revised Thinking in Light of New Events of Strategic Importance," *Human Resource Planning* 11, 159–172; B. Keys and J. Wolf, "Management Education: Current Issues and Emerging Trends," *Journal of Management* 14 (1988): 205–229; L. M. Saari, T. R. Johnson, S. D. McLaughlin, and D. Zimmerle, "A Survey of Management Training and Education Practices in U.S. Companies," *Personnel Psychology* 41 (1988): 731–744.

18. T. A. Stewart, "GE Keeps Those Ideas Coming," *Fortune,* August 12, 1991, 41–49; N. M. Tichy, "GE's Crotonville: A Staging Ground for a Corporate Revolution," *The Executive* 3 (1989): 99–106.

19. Ibid.

20. G. P. Hollenbeck, "What Did You Learn in School? Studies of a University Executive Program," *Human Resource Planning* 14 (1991): 247–260.

21. A. Howard and D. W. Bray, *Managerial Lives in Transition: Advancing Age and Changing Times* (New York: Guilford, 1988); Bolt, *Executive Development*; J. R. Hinrichs and G. P. Hollenbeck, "Leadership Development," in *Developing Human Resources,* ed. K. N. Wexley (Washington, D.C.: BNA Books, 1991), 5-221–5-237.

22. D. Druckman and R. A. Bjork, eds, *In the Mind's Eye: Enhancing Human Performance* (Washington, DC: National Academy Press, 1991): R. Zemke, "Second Thoughts about the MBTI," *Training,* April 1992, 43–47.

23. S. K. Hirsch, *MBTI Team Member's Guide* (Palo Alto, Cal.: Consulting Psychologists Press, 1992); A. L. Hammer, *Introduction to Type and Careers* (Palo Alto, Cal.: Consulting Psychologists Press, 1993).

24. A. Thorne and H. Gough, *Portraits of Type* (Palo Alto, Cal.: Consulting Psychologists Press, 1991).

25. Druckman and Bjork, *In the Mind's Eye*; M. H. McCaulley, "The Myers-Briggs Type Indicator and Leadership," in *Measures of Leadership,* ed. K. E. Clark and M. B. Clark (West Orange, N.J.: Leadership Library of America, 1990), 381–418.

26. L. F. Schoenfeldt and J. A. Steger, "Identification and Development of Management Talent," in *Research in Personnel and Human Resource Management,* ed. K. N. Rowland and G. Ferris (Greenwich, Conn.: JAI Press, 1989), 7: 151–181.

27. B. B. Gaugler, D. B. Rosenthal, G. C. Thornton, III, and C. Bentson, "Meta-analysis of Assessment Center Validity," *Journal of Applied Psychology* 72 (1987): 493–511; D. W. Bray, R. J. Campbell, and D. L. Grant, *Formative Years in Business: A Long-Term AT&T Study of Managerial Lives* (New York: Wiley, 1974).

28. G. C. Thornton, III and W. C. Byham, *Assessment Centers and Managerial Performance* (New York: Academic Press, 1982).

29. C. D. McCauley and M. M. Lombardo, "Benchmarks: An Instrument for Diagnosing Managerial Strengths and Weaknesses," in *Measures of Leadership,* ed. K. E. Clark and M. B. Clark (West Orange, N.J.: Leadership Library of America, 1990), 535–545.

30. C. D. McCauley, M. M. Lombardo, and C. J. Usher, "Diagnosing Management Development Needs: An Instrument Based on How Managers Develop," *Journal of Management* 15 (1989): 389–403.

31. S. B. Silverman, "Individual Development through Performance Appraisal," in *Developing Human Resources,* ed. K. N. Wexley (Washington, D.C.: BNA Books, 1991), 5-120–5-151.

32. M. W. McCall, Jr., M. M. Lombardo, and A. M. Morrison, *Lessons of Experience* (Lexington, Mass.: Lexington Books, 1988).

33. R. S. Snell, "Congenial Ways of Learning: So Near Yet So Far," *Journal of Management Development* 9 (1990): 17–23.

34. McCall, Lombardo, and Morrison, *Lessons of Experience*; M. W. McCall, "Developing Executives through Work Experiences," *Human Resource Planning* 11 (1988): 1–11; M. N. Ruderman, P. J. Ohlott, and C. D. McCauley, "Assessing Opportunities for Leadership Development," in *Measures of Leadership,* ed. K. E. Clark and M. B. Clark (West Orange, N.J.: Leadership Library of America, 1990), 547–562.

35. K. N. Wexley and G. P. Latham, *Developing and Training Human Resources in Organizations,* 2nd ed. (New York: Harper Collins, 1991).

36. Management Development Report, Winter 1988/1989 (Alexandria, Virg.: American Society for Training and Development, 1988/1989); G. B. Northcraft, T. L. Griffith, and C. E. Shalley, "Building Top Management Muscle in a Slow Growth Environment: How Different Is Better at Greyhound Financial Corporation," *The Executive* 6 (1992): 32–41.

37. D. Gunsch, "Customer Service Focus Prompts Employee Exchange," *Personnel Journal,* October 1992, 32–38.

38. M. London, *Developing Managers* (San Francisco: Jossey-Bass, 1985); M. London, *Managing the Training Enterprise* (San Francisco: Jossey-Bass, 1989).

39. D. C. Feldman, *Managing Careers in Organizations* (Glenview, Ill.: Scott-Foresman, 1988).

40. J. M. Brett, L. K. Stroh, and A. H. Reilly, "Job Transfer" in *International Review of Industrial and Organizational Psychology: 1992,* ed. C. L. Cooper and I. T. Robinson (Chichester, England: John Wiley and Sons, 1992); D. C. Feldman and J. M. Brett, "Coping with New Jobs: A Comparative Study of New Hires and Job Changers," *Academy of Management Journal* 26 (1983): 258–272; J. M. Brett, "Job Transfer and Well-being," *Journal of Applied Psychology* 67 (1992): 450–463.

41. R. A. Noe, B. D. Steffy, and A. E. Barber, "An Investigation of the Factors Influencing Employees' Willingness to Accept Mobility Opportunities," *Personnel Psychology* 41 (1988): 559–580; S. Gould and L. E. Penley, "A Study of the Correlates of Willingness to Relocate," *Academy of Management Journal* 28 (1984): 472–478; J. Landau and T. H. Hammer, "Clerical Employees' Perceptions of Intraorganizational Career Opportunities," *Academy of Management Journal* 29 (1986): 385–405; R. P. Duncan and C. C. Perruci, "Dual Occupation Families and Migration," *American Sociological Review* 41 (1976): 252–261; J. M. Brett and A. H. Reilly, "On the Road Again: Predicting the Job Transfer Design," *Journal of Applied Psychology* 73 (1988): 614–620.

42. D. T. Hall and L. A. Isabella, "Downward Moves and Career Development," *Organizational Dynamics* 14 (1985): 5–23.

43. H. D. Dewirst, "Career Patterns: Mobility, Specialization, and Related Career Issues," in *Contemporary Career Development Issues,* ed. R. F. Morrison and J. Adams (Hillsdale, N.J.: Lawrence Erlbaum, 1991): 73–108.

44. Tomkins, "GTE Managers on the Move."

45. F. J. Minor, L. A. Slade, and R. A. Myers, "Career Transitions in Changing Times," in *Contemporary Career Development Issues,* ed. R. F. Morrison and J. Adams (Hillsdale, N.J.: Lawrence Erlbaum, 1991): 109–120; C. C. Pinder and K. G. Schroeder, "Time to Proficiency Following Job Transfers," *Academy of Management Journal* 30 (1987): 336–353.

46. K. E. Kram, *Mentoring at Work: Developmental Relationships in Organizational Life* (Glenview, Ill.: Scott-Foresman, 1985); L. L. Phillips-Jones, "Establishing a Formalized Mentoring Program," *Training and Development Journal* 2 (1983): 38–42; K. Kram, "Phases of the Mentoring Relationship," *Academy of Management Journal* 26 (1983): 608–625; G. T. Chao, P. M. Walz and P. D. Gardner, "Formal and Informal Mentorships: A Comparison of Mentoring Functions and Contrasts with Nonmentored Counterparts," *Personnel Psychology* 45 (1992): 619–636.

47. A. H. Geiger, "Measures for Mentors," *Training and Development Journal,* February 1992, 65–67.

48. G. F. Dreher and R. A. Ash, "A Comparative Study of Mentoring among Men and Women in Managerial, Professional, and Technical Positions," *Journal of Applied Psychology* 75 (1990): 539–546; J. L. Wilbur, "Does Mentoring Breed Success?" *Training and Development Journal* 41 (1987): 38–41; R. A. Noe, "Mentoring Relationships for Employee Development," in *Applying Psychology in Business: The Handbook for Managers and Human Resource Professionals,* ed. J. W. Jones, B. D. Steffy, and D. W. Bray (Lexington, Mass.: Lexington Books, 1991), 475–482; M. M. Fagh and K. Ayers, Jr., "Police Mentors," *FBI Law Enforcement Bulletin,* January 1985, 8–13; K. Kram, "Phases of the Mentor Relationships," *Academy of Management Journal* 26 (1983): 608–625; R. A. Noe, "An Investigation of the Determinants of Successful Assigned Mentoring Relationships," *Personnel Psychology* 41 (1988): 457–479.

49. L. K. Stroh, J. M. Brett, and A. H. Reilly, "All the Right Stuff: A Comparison of Female and Male Managers' Career Progression," *Journal of Applied Psychology* 77, 251–260.

50. U.S. Department of Labor, *A Report on the Glass Ceiling Initiative* (Washington, DC: U.S. Government Printing Office, 1991); R. A. Noe, "Women and Mentoring: A Review and Research Agenda," *Academy of Management Review* 13 (1988): 65–78; B. R. Ragins and J. L. Cotton, "Easier Said Than Done: Gender Differences in Perceived Barriers to Gaining a Mentor," *Academy of Management Journal* 34 (1991): 939–951.

51. L. Roberson and N. C. Gutierrez, "Beyond Good Faith: Commitment to Recruiting Management Diversity at Pacific Bell," in *Diversity in the Workplace,* ed. S. Jackson & Associates (New York: The Guilford Press, 1992), 65–88.

52. R. L. Tung, "Selection and Training of Personnel for Overseas Assignments," *Columbia Journal of World Business* 16 (1981): 18–78.

53. S. Ronen, "Training the International Assignee," in *Training and Development in Organizations,* ed. I. L. Goldstein (San Francisco: Jossey-Bass, 1989), 417–453.

54. J. S. Black and J. K. Stephens, "The Influence of the Spouse on American Expatriate Adjustment and Intent to Stay in Pacific Rim Overseas Assignments," *Journal of Management* 15 (1989): 529–544.

55. E. Dunbar and A. Katcher, "Preparing Managers for Foreign Assignments," *Training and Development Journal,* September 1990, 45–47.

56. P. R. Harris and R. T. Moran, *Managing Cultural Differences* (Houston: Gulf Publishing, 1991).

57. Ibid.

58. J. S. Black and M. Mendenhall, "A Practical but Theory-Based Framework for Selecting Cross-Cultural Training Methods," in *Readings and Cases in International Human Resource Management,* ed. M. Mendenhall and G. Oddou (Boston: PWS-Kent, 1991): 177–204.

59. S. E. Jackson and Associates, *Diversity in the Workplace: Human Resource Initiatives* (New York: Guilford Press, 1992).

60. R. R. Thomas, "Managing Diversity: A Conceptual Framework," in *Diversity in the Workplace,* ed. S. E. Jackson & Associates (San Francisco: Jossey-Bass, 1992), 306–318.

61. M. E. Heilman, C. J. Block, and J. A. Lucas, "Presumed Incompetent? Stigmatization and Affirmative Action Efforts," *Journal of Applied Psychology* 77, 536–544.

62. B. Gerber, "Managing Diversity," *Training,* July 1990, 23–30.

63. C. M. Solomon, "The Corporate Response to Workforce Diversity," *Personnel Journal,* August 1989, 43–53. A. Morrison, *The New Leaders: Guidelines on Leadership Diversity in America,* (San Francisco: Jossey-Boss, 1992).

64. Ibid.

65. E. S. Tomasko and K. K. Dickinson, "The UAW-Ford Education Development and Training Program," in *Joint Training Programs,* ed. L. A. Ferman, M. Hoyman, J. Cutcher-Gershenfeld, and E. J. Savoie (Ithaca, N.Y.: ILR Press, 1991), 71–94.

66. S. J. Schurman, M. K. Hugentoble, and H. Stack, "Lessons from the UAW-GM Paid Education Leave Program," in *Joint Training Programs,* ed. L. A. Ferman, M. Hoyman, J. Cutcher-Gershenfeld, and E. J. Savoie (Ithaca, N.Y.: ILR Press, 1991), 71–94.

67. C. B. Derr, C. Jones, and E. L. Toomey, "Managing High-Potential Employees: Current Practices in Thirty-three U.S. Corporations," *Human Resource Management* 27 (1988): 273–290.

68. H. S. Feild and S. G. Harris, "Entry-Level, Fast-Track Management Development Programs: Developmental tactics and Perceived Program Effectiveness," *Human Resource Planning* 14 (1991): 261–273.

69. Ibid.

70. Derr, Jones and Toomey, "Managing High-Potential Employees."

71. J. E. Rosenbaum, "Tournament Mobility: Career Patterns in a Corporation," *Administrative Sciences Quarterly* 24 (1979): 220–241.

72. M. W. McCall, Jr. and M. M. Lombardo, "Off the Track: Why and How Successful Executives Get Derailed," Technical Report No. 21 (Greensboro, N.C.: Center for Creative Leadership, 1983).

73. L. W. Hellervik, J. F. Hazucha and R. J. Schneider, "Behavior Change: Models, Methods, and a Review of Evidence," in *Handbook of Industrial and Organizational Psychology,* 2nd ed., ed. M. D. Dunnette and L. M. Hough (Palo Alto, Cal.: Consulting Psychologists Press, 1992), 13: 823–899.

74. D. B. Peterson, "Measuring and Evaluating Change in Executive and Managerial Development." (Paper presented at the annual conference of the Society for Industrial and Organizational Psychology, Miami, Florida, 1990.)

KEEPING PACE WITH WORK-FORCE DIVERSITY

C A S E

Continental Insurance was interested in building a corporate culture to support the company's mission, business direction, and commitment to employee development. The CEO's awareness of the changing characteristics of the work force led the company to study the ethnic, gender, and racial characteristics of new hires and of employees who were promoted and left the company. The study revealed an imbalance of male, female, and minorities in Continental's employment groups. Executive, middle-manager, and manager positions were almost entirely occupied by white males, while women and minorities dominated the professional, technical, and nonexempt positions.

QUESTIONS

1. Discuss what Continental might do from an employee development perspective to help women and minorities move into management positions.

2. If Continental was interested in using a mentoring program to provide women and minorities with the exposure and visibility to top managers, how should the mentoring program be designed?

SOURCE: Bureau of National Affairs *Workforce Strategies* 3, no. 12 (December 21, 1992), WS71–WS76.

14

CAREER MANAGEMENT

Objectives   *After reading this chapter, you should be able to:*

1. Identify the reasons why companies need to help employees manage their careers.
2. Explain the issues employees experience in their career development and what companies can do to help them deal with these issues.
3. Design a career-planning system.
4. Effectively perform the manager's role in career planning.
5. Design an effective socialization program for new employees.
6. Develop policies designed to help employees deal with work and family conflict.
7. Design layoff and outplacement strategies that reduce the negative effects on displaced workers and remaining employees.

Three Employees'
Career Concerns*

Jeff Doe, an international sales manager, works in the medical device industry. The company he works for has grown rapidly in the last five years and is now the leading manufacturer of heart pacemakers. Most of the competition comes from Asian companies that sell pacemakers at lower prices. Jeff finds his job rewarding, but it requires him to travel extensively to Asia. His trips, which average four to six weeks, are seriously interfering with his family life. Jeff's wife has to care for their two small children by herself. Jeff may be forced to change employers because the company does not recognize his problem. For example, it limits Jeff's personal, reimbursable phone calls to 30 minutes each week while he is in Asia.

Sophia Martinez works for a Fortune 500 company that manufactures adhesives. She has been working in the same department for ten years. She has had three promotions. She has mastered her current job responsibilities. She still likes what she is doing, but she is frustrated because there are no new learning opportunities in her job. Much of the time she has no energy for work. She feels she has been passed over and ignored by management. She sometimes thinks of herself as a failure and believes her managers and coworkers also see her that way.

Toran Joinner is the engineering manager for a small, family-owned company that produces hot and cold breakfast cereals. Over the last 20 years the company's sales have doubled every 5 years. Because of rapid market growth, the company has almost continuously been expanding its manufacturing operations. Toran has been in his position for four years. He thinks he has no career path. He has asked for feedback and suggestions for career development but has never received any concrete answers. He would like to be vice-president of manufacturing operations some day, but he is confused as to what he should do to prepare for this position. The company has an extensive personal development plan but no career development system. He is frustrated because it appears that the company awards the few available promotions based on seniority rather than on performance. He thinks the company may be stretched too thin.

Jeff, Sophia, and Toran are all experiencing concerns related to their careers. Their experiences are similar to those of many employees in U.S. companies. Jeff's concerns have to do with conflicts between his work and nonwork roles and his need for the company to be more sensitive to the relationship between work and family. Sophia thinks she is "stuck" in her position. She is experiencing what is known as career plateauing. Toran needs the company to provide him with information regarding how he can reach his career goal: becoming vice-president of manufacturing operations.

---

* The career concerns described are based on interviews conducted with employees from three different companies. The names are fictitious.

INTRODUCTION

Jeff's, Sophia's, and Toran's career concerns are a direct consequence of the competitive challenges discussed in Chapter 1. These challenges have important implications for how employees and companies manage careers.

For example, in Chapter 1 we discussed several changes in the characteristics of the work force that have important implications for the management of careers[1]. The greater involvement of dual-career and single-parent families in the work force and increased job responsibility mean that companies have to become more sensitive to the potential conflict between employees' work and nonwork roles (Jeff's career concern). This involves developing policies on work and family issues. The age of the work force is increasing. One implication of the aging work force is that companies need to be sensitive to the motivational and reward needs of older employees. Changes in employees' values suggest that employees may be less interested in promotions, salary increases, status, or power—traditional indicators of career success—and more interested in employment that is congruent with their own values; that is, they want psychological success. Psychological success is related to the achievement of personal goals such as recognition, family success, or job performance.

The trend toward flatter organizational structures means that career success can no longer be defined in terms of promotions because few will be available. Companies have to help employees understand that other types of development activities (discussed in Chapter 13), such as job rotation and lateral moves, are signs of career success, not failure. Flatter organizational structures also increase the likelihood that many employees will plateau. To combat plateauing (Sophia's career concern) companies have to take actions to ensure that employees receive challenging assignments with increased responsibilities. To succeed in a volatile and competitive business environment, companies have reduced their commitment to remain in specific businesses. As a result, employees need to ensure that their skills are current in case they should lose their jobs.

Rapid changes in technology and a trend toward giving employees more responsibility has made work both more rewarding and more demanding. Because of the need to meet customers' needs, both employees and companies may neglect career-planning issues (Toran's career concerns). The failure to engage in career planning has negative results for both the company and its employees. From the company's perspective, the failure to help employees plan their careers can result in a shortage of employees to fill open positions. From the employee's perspective, the lack of career planning can result in frustration and feelings of not being valued by the company. As we will see in this chapter, companies, managers, and employees need to take actions to ensure that career planning occurs.

Companies need to help employees manage their careers to maximize their career motivation. Career motivation has three aspects: career resilience, career insight, and career identity.[2] *Career resilience* is the extent to which employees are able to cope with problems that affect their work.

Career insight is how much employees know about their interests, their skill strengths and weaknesses, and the ways these perceptions relate to their career goals. *Career identity* is the degree to which employees define their personal value according to their work.

Companies can only be innovative and adaptable to the degree that their employees have career motivation. Employees who have high career resilience are able to respond to obstacles in the work environment and adapt to unexpected events (such as changes in work processes or customer demands). They are willing to develop new ways to use their skills to cope with obstacles and unexpected events. Employees with high career insight set career goals and participate in development activities that help them reach those goals. They tend to take actions that keep their skills from becoming obsolete. Employees with high career identity are committed to the company; they are willing to do whatever it takes (e.g., work long hours) to complete projects and meet customer demands. They also take pride in working for the company and are active in professional and trade organizations.

Jeff's, Sophia's, and Toran's career concerns illustrate the wide range of career development issues that companies must help employees deal with to maximize their motivation, satisfaction, and productivity. The first step in successfully managing careers is to understand what a "career" is. This chapter begins with a discussion of the concept of a career. Next, we present a model of career development that highlights the developmental challenges employees face and what companies can do to help employees meet these challenges. We examine career-planning systems and the roles employees, managers, and companies play in these systems. Finally, we examine a number of current career development issues, including orientation, job loss, plateauing, and work and family conflict.

THE CAREER CONCEPT

What Is a Career?

A career can be viewed a number of ways.[3] It can be viewed as a sequence of positions held within an occupation. For example, a university faculty member can hold assistant, associate, and full professor positions. A career can also be viewed in the context of mobility within an organization. For example, an engineer may begin her career as a staff engineer. As her expertise, experience, and performance increase, she may move through advisory engineering, senior engineering, and senior technical positions. A career can also be viewed as a characteristic of the employee. Each employee's career consists of different jobs, positions, and experiences.

Viewing a career as the property of an occupation or an organization is probably shortsighted for two reasons.[4] First, employees do not always spend their entire careers within one occupation or company. Second, employees' career interests are not stable. Statistics indicate that employees today change careers more frequently than ever before.[5] For example, many engineering employees ultimately work at managerial positions that use very little of their technical training. Before becoming an internal human resource consultant for Northwest Airlines, Sylvia Miller was a schoolteacher, then she was a flight attendant, and then she went to school for an advanced degree in human resource management![6]

We consider a **career** to be "the pattern of work-related experiences that span the course of a person's life."[7] Work experiences include positions, job experiences, and tasks. Work experiences are influenced by employees' values, needs, and feelings. Employees' career needs vary depending on their stage of career development and their biological age. As a result, it is important for managers to understand the career development process and the differences in employees' needs and interests at each stage of development.

A Model of Career Development

Career development is the process by which employees progress through a series of stages, each characterized by a different set of developmental tasks, activities, and relationships.[8] It is important to point out that there are several different career development models, and the research literature does not agree which model is best. We discuss three kinds of models. The **life-cycle models** suggest that employees face certain developmental tasks over the course of their careers—that they move through distinct life or career stages. The **organization-based models** also suggest that careers proceed through a series of stages, but these models suggest that career development involves employees' learning to perform certain activities. Each stage involves changes in activities and relationships with peers and managers. A third kind of model, the **directional pattern model**, describes how employees view their careers.[9] It suggests that employees make decisions about how quickly they want to progress through the career stages and at what point they want to return to an earlier career stage. For example, some employees plan on staying in a job or occupation their entire lives and have well-thought-out plans for moving within the occupation. These employees have a linear concept of their careers. Other employees view their careers as a spiral. They work within a certain job or occupation for a time, then take a job in an entirely different area. A good example are management consultants. They often work within one company on a particular project for a number of years, but once the project is completed, they move on to a different company with an entirely different project.

Table 14.1 presents a career development model that incorporates the important contributions that each of these models makes to understanding careers. As the table shows, researchers generally recognize four career stages: exploration, establishment, maintenance, and disengagement. Each career stage is characterized by developmental tasks, activities, and relationships. Research suggests that employees' current career stage influences their needs, attitudes, and job behaviors. For example, one study found that salespersons in the exploration career stage tended to change jobs and

TABLE 14.1

A Model of Career Development

	Career Stage			
	Exploration	**Establishment**	**Maintenance**	**Disengagement**
Developmental Tasks	Identify interests, skills, fit between self and work	Advancement, growth, security, develop life-style	Hold on to accomplishments, update skills	Retirement planning, change balance between work and nonwork
Activity	Helping Learning Following directions	Independent contributor	Training Sponsorship Policymaker	Phase out of work
Relationship to other employees	Apprentice	Colleague	Mentor	Sponsor
Age	Less than 30	30–45	45–60	60+
Years on job	Less than 2 years	2–10 years	More than 10 years	More than 10 years

accept promotions more frequently than salespersons in the other career stages. Another study found that the degree to which employees identify with their job is affected more by the job's characteristics (e.g., variety of tasks, responsibility for task completion) in early career stages than in later career stages.[10]

As Table 14.1 shows, an employee's age and length of time on the job are believed to be good signals of the employee's career stage. However, relying strictly on these two characteristics would lead to erroneous conclusions about the employee's career needs. For example, many changes that older employees make in their careers involve "recycling" back to an earlier career stage.[11] Recycling involves changing one's major work activity after having been established in a specific field. Recycling is accompanied by a reexploration of values, skills, and interests, and potential employment opportunities. It is also not uncommon for employees who are considering changes in their careers to conduct informational interviews with managers and other employees who hold jobs in functional areas they believe may be congruent with their interests and abilities. For example, Sam Lifshus, a 93-year-old, has experienced recycling.[12] He is a nursing assistant at Memorial Hospital in Hollywood, California. He is a retired furrier and auctioneer. He started his medical career at age 92. To prepare himself for his medical career, Sam took classes through a senior-citizen employment program. Another person's experience with recycling is highlighted in the "Competing through Globalization" box.

Globalization

EX-PROFESSOR LEARNS JAPANESE AND MANUFACTURING AT FUJITSU

Many individuals are recycling out of old careers and into new ones. Steven Miller, a professor at Carnegie Melon University in Pittsburgh who studied manufacturing and factory automation, decided to give up his academic position for a chance to manage manufacturing operations. He accepted a job with Fujitsu Ltd. in Oyama, Japan. Fujitsu offered him a training period in Japan and the top American manager's position in a Richardson, Texas, facility, where he will manage a telecommunications factory similar to the one he trained at in Japan. During his training, Miller spent half of each day studying Japanese and the rest on the factory floor, learning from employees and helping them with assembly work. The most important things he learned were not technical but the organization of employees. For example, the Oyama factory averages more than ten suggestions from each of its 3,800 employees per year. Every idea is considered by management. Miller believes that a major difference between American and Japanese facilities is that American facilities tend to view change as a special activity requiring outsiders, such as consultants, in order to be successful. In Japan, learning and doing is part of the daily factory routine, so change is more easily accepted.

One of Miller's challenges is how to create a learning environment at the Texas facility. Another challenge is that he is going to have to overcome the tendency of Japanese companies to allow Americans to hold high-level managerial positions but to reduce their power by appointing a Japanese executive to handle relations with headquarters. Also, American managers are often excluded from important business decisions.

SOURCE: "Learning by Doing: A U.S. Professor Takes an Unusual Course in a Japanese Factory", *The Wall Street Journal*, March 30, 1992, 1.

Exploration Stage.   In the exploration stage, individuals attempt to identify the type of work that interests them. They consider their interests, values, and work preferences, and they seek information about jobs, careers, and occupations from coworkers, friends, and family members. Once they identify the type of work or occupation that interests them, individuals can begin pursuing the needed education or training. Typically, exploration occurs in the mid-teens to early-to-late twenties (while the individual is still a student in high school, college, or technical school). Exploration continues when the individual starts a new job. In most cases, employees who are new to a job are not prepared to take on work tasks and roles without help and direction from others. In many jobs, the new employee is considered an apprentice. From the company's perspective, orientation and socialization activities are necessary to help new employees get as comfortable as possible with their new jobs and coworkers so they can begin to contribute to the company's goals.

Establishment Stage.   In the establishment stage, individuals find their place in the company, make an independent contribution, achieve more responsibility and financial success, and establish a desirable life-style. Employees at this stage are interested in being viewed as a contributor to the company's success. They learn how the company views their contributions from informal interactions with peers and managers and from formal feedback received through the performance-appraisal system. For employees in this stage, the company needs to develop policies that help balance work and nonwork roles. Also, employees in this stage need to become more actively involved in career-planning activities.

Maintenance Stage.   In the maintenance stage, the individual is concerned with keeping skills up-to-date and being perceived by others as someone who is still contributing to the company. Individuals in the maintenance stage have many years of job experience, much job knowledge, and an in-depth understanding of how the company expects business to be conducted. Employees in the maintenance stage can be valuable trainers or mentors for new employees. They are usually asked to review or develop company policies or goals. Their opinions about work processes, problems, and important issues that the work unit is facing may be solicited. From the company's perspective, a major issue is how to keep employees in the maintenance stage from plateauing. Also, the company needs to ensure that the employees' skills do not become obsolete.

Disengagement Stage.   In the disengagement stage, individuals prepare for a change in the balance between work and nonwork activities. When we think of disengagement, we typically think of older employees electing to retire and concentrate entirely on nonwork activities such as sports, hobbies, traveling, or volunteer work. However, for many employees, the disengagement stage does not mean a complete reduction in work hours. Rather, many decide to remain with the company but work reduced hours, perhaps serving as a consultant. Also, regardless of age, employees may elect to leave a company to change occupations or jobs. Some may be forced to leave the company because of downsizing or mergers. Employees who leave the company often recycle back to the exploration stage. They need information about potential new career areas, and they have to reconsider their career interests and skill strengths. From the company's perspective, the major career management activities in the disengagement stage are retirement planning and outplacement.

As the previous discussion illustrates, employees bring a range of career development issues to the workplace. Besides developing policies and programs that will help employees deal with their career development issues (in order to maximize their level of career motivation), companies need to identify employees' career development needs. A career planning system can help employees, managers, and the company identify career development needs.

CAREER-PLANNING SYSTEMS

Career planning is the process through which employees:

- Become aware of interests, values, strengths, and weaknesses.
- Obtain information about job opportunities within the company.
- Identify career goals.
- Establish action plans to achieve career goals.[13]

Career-planning systems benefit both employees and the company.[14] Career planning helps employees develop their interests and skills. It can also result in higher levels of employee satisfaction because it can help employees identify and move to jobs that are congruent with their goals and plans. From the company's perspective, career-planning systems reduce the time needed to fill job openings, they aid in succession planning (preparing employees for openings resulting from turnover or retirement), they identify employees with managerial talent, and they provide all employees with the opportunity to identify their career goals and develop plans for reaching those goals.

Components of Career-Planning Systems

Companies' career-planning systems vary in the level of sophistication and the emphasis they place on the different components of the process. However, all career-planning systems include the components shown in Figure 14.1.

Self-Assessment. Self-assessment helps employees determine their career interests, values, aptitudes, and behavioral tendencies. It often involves the use of psychological tests such as the Strong-Campbell Interest Inventory and the Self-Directed Search. The former helps employees identify their occupational and job interests; the latter identifies employees' preferences for working in different type of environments (e.g., sales, counseling, landscaping). Tests may also help employees identify the relative value they place on work and leisure activities. Career counselors are often used to assist employees in the self-assessment process and interpret the results of psychological tests.

For example, a man who had served as a branch manager at Wells Fargo Bank for 14 years enjoyed both working with computers and researching program-development issues.[15] He was experiencing difficulty in choosing whether to pursue further work experiences with computers or enter a new career in developing software applications. Psychological tests he completed as part of the company's career-assessment program confirmed that he had strong interests in research and development. As a result, he began his own software design company.

FIGURE 14.1   The Career-Planning Process

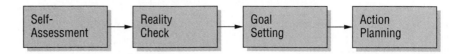

Reality Check.   Employees receive information about how the company evaluates their skills and knowledge and where they fit into the company's plans (e.g., potential promotion opportunities, lateral moves). Usually, this information is provided by the employee's manager as part of the performance-appraisal process. It is not uncommon in well-developed career-planning systems for the manager to hold separate performance appraisals and career development discussions. For example, in Coca-Cola U.S.A.'s career-planning system, employees and managers have a separate meeting after the annual performance review to discuss the employee's career interests, strengths, and possible development activities.[16]

Goal Setting.   Employees determine their short- and long-term career goals during this phase of the career-planning process. These goals usually relate to desired positions (e.g., to become sales manager within three years), level of skill application (e.g., to use one's budgeting skills to improve the unit's cash-flow problems), work setting (e.g., to move to corporate marketing within two years), or skill acquisition (e.g., to learn how to use the company's human resource information system). These goals are usually discussed with the manager and written into a development plan. A development plan is shown in Figure 14.2.

Action Planning.   During this phase, employees determine how they will achieve their short- and long-term career goals. Action plans may involve enrolling in training courses and seminars, conducting informational interviews, or applying for job openings within the company.

Role of Employees, Managers, and Company in Career Planning

Employees, their managers, and the companies share the responsibility for career planning.[17]

Employee's Role.   A **psychological contract** is the expectations that employers and employees have about each other. Traditionally, the psychological contract emphasized that the company would provide continued employment and advancement opportunities if the employee remained with the company and maintained a high level of job performance. However, because of the technological and structural, and social competitive challenges we discussed in the chapter introduction, the psychological con-

FIGURE 14.2   A Career Development Plan

Development Needs—Current Position
Specific knowledge and skills needed to
improve or maintain satisfactory performance:

Development Needs—Future Position
Specific knowledge and skills to get ready for next position:

Target Job:

Development Activities
Manager and employee will work together to implement the following actions:

Development Objectives
Behavior or results demonstrating development needs are being met:

Results

Date:

Employee's Signature:

Manager's Signature:

tract between employees and companies has changed. Companies are unable to offer job security and advancement opportunities. Employees are more interested in work that offers challenge, variety, and opportunities to be creative. Employees remain interested in having job security, although they realize that lifetime employment with one company is unrealistic.

The new psychological contract suggests that employees can increase their value to their current employer (and increase their employment opportunities) by taking responsibility for career planning.[18] Companies with well-developed career-planning systems expect employees to take responsibility for their own career planning. For example, British Petroleum Exploration's employees are provided with a personal-development-planning guidebook that leads them through assessment, goal setting, development planning, and action planning.[19] Participation in the program is voluntary. The employees must also approach their manager to initiate career-related discussion as part of the personal-development-planning process.

Regardless of how sophisticated the company's career-planning system is, employees should take several career-planning actions.[20] They should:

- Take the initiative to ask for feedback from managers and peers regarding their skill strengths and weaknesses.
- Identify their stage of career development and development needs.
- Gain exposure to a range of learning opportunities (e.g., sales assignments, product-design assignments, administrative assignments).
- Interact with employees from different work groups inside and outside the company (e.g., professional associations, task forces).

Manager's Role.   Regardless of the type of formal career-planning system in place at the company, managers play a key role in the career-planning process. In most cases, employees look to their managers for career advice. Why? Because managers typically evaluate employees' readiness for job mobility (e.g., promotions). Also, managers are often the primary source of information about position openings, training courses, and other developmental opportunities. Unfortunately, many managers avoid becoming involved in career-planning activities with employees because they do not feel qualified to answer employees' career-related questions, they have limited time for helping employees deal with career issues, and they do not have the interpersonal skills needed to fully understand career issues.[21]

To help employees deal with career issues, managers need to be effective in four roles: coach, appraiser, adviser, and referral agent.[22] To understand these roles, consider the case of José, who works in the oil and chemical industry. José is an industrial hygienist at a chemical plant, where safety is critical. He is unhappy about what he thinks is a lack of career development at the company. As a result, he is considering leaving the company. José has been at a refinery in Texas the past year, but he wants to move back to Utah for family reasons. He was denied a lateral move to a plant in Utah. He made the request at a time when the company was downsizing and seeking voluntary retirements. The company understands that José wants to return to Utah, but it does not feel he is ready for another move. José considers his career stunted, and he thinks that the company does not care about him. Although he is unhappy, his performance is acceptable.

How can José's manager help him deal with this career issue to avoid losing a solid performer? José and his manager need to sit down and discuss his career. Table 14.2 presents the type of results that a manager should try to achieve in a career discussion. José's manager needs to clarify José's

TABLE 14.2   Characteristics of Successful Career Discussions

- Manager gains an awareness of employee's work-related goals and interests.
- Manager and employee agree on the next developmental steps.
- Employee understands how the manager views his or her performance, developmental needs, and options.
- Manager and employee agree on how the employee's needs can be met on the current job.
- Manager identifies resources to help the employee accomplish the goals agreed upon in the career discussion.

SOURCE: Adapted from F. L. Otte and P. G. Hutcheson, *Helping Employees Manage Careers* (Englewood Cliffs, N.J.: Prentice-Hall, 1992): 57–58.

career concerns (coaching role). The manager also needs to make sure that José understands that although his job performance is acceptable, the company believes he needs to gain more experience at the Texas facility (appraiser role). Third, José's manager needs to discuss with José what can be done now to help him feel better about his job and the company and help him understand how the Texas refinery position fits into the larger picture of his career development (adviser role). José and his manager should discuss and agree on a timetable for his next possible move (which could be to a position in Utah). The manager may give José advice concerning the correct timing for requesting a transfer, given the company's financial situation. Finally, José's manager should let him know about career counseling or other career-planning resources available within the company (role of referral agent).

Company's Role.   Companies are responsible for providing employees with the resources needed to be successful in career planning. These resources include:

- Career workshops (seminars on such topics as the way the career-planning system works, self-assessment, and goal setting).
- Career centers or information systems (places or databases where employees can find information about job openings and training programs).
- Career-planning workbooks (printed guides that direct employees through a series of exercises, discussions, and guidelines related to career planning).
- Career counseling (advice from a professionally trained counselor who specializes in working with employees seeking assistance with career issues).
- Career paths (planning job sequences, identification of skills needed for advancement within and across job families, e.g., technical jobs to management jobs).

The company also needs to monitor the career-planning system to ensure that managers and employees are using the system as intended and to evaluate whether the system is helping the company meets its objectives (e.g., shortening the time it takes to fill positions).

At 3M, career management, which involves a number of activities, is supported by a network of resources throughout the company.[23] Activities include a performance-appraisal and development process designed to facilitate communication between employees and managers, who work together to develop plans for performance and career development. The company also has a career-resources center, which provides reference materials, publications, and books regarding career-planning issues and development opportunities within the company. Employees can discuss career issues with trained counselors and explore interests, values, and work-environment preferences through psychological testing. The Career Resources Department at 3M offers seminars on topics such as self-assessment, interviewing techniques, and managers' roles in career development. The company also provides help in placing employees who have lost their jobs because of transfers, downsizing, health problems, or disabilities. Finally, 3M has two information bases devoted to career issues. The Job Information System is a computer-based system that allows employees to nominate themselves for job openings. Through the Internal Search System, managers can use the human resource information system to identify employees who match job requirements. Data regarding employees' job history, location, performance rating, and career interests can be obtained from this system.

CAREER DEVELOPMENT ISSUES

This section of the chapter discusses several important career development issues that companies need to address. These issues include the socialization and orientation of new employees, career plateauing, dual career paths, skill obsolescence, balancing work and family, job loss, and retirement.

Socialization and Orientation

Organizational socialization is the process by which new employees are transformed into effective members of the company. Socialization involves three phases:[24]

Anticipatory Socialization.   Anticipatory socialization occurs before the individual joins the company. Individuals develop expectations about the company, job, working conditions, and interpersonal relationships through interactions with representatives of the company (e.g., recruiters, prospective peers, and managers) during the selection process. Potential employees need to be provided with realistic information about the job, working conditions, company, and location (a realistic job preview) to ensure that they develop appropriate expectations. Unmet expectations resulting from the selection process have been shown to be related to employee turnover.[25]

Encounter.   No matter how realistic the information they were provided during interviews and site visits, individuals beginning a new job will experience shock and surprise.[26] Employees need to become familiar with job tasks, receive appropriate training, and understand company practices and procedures. Challenging work and cooperative and helpful managers and peers have been shown to enhance employees' learning a new job.[27] Employees also need to develop interpersonal relationships with peers, managers, and other employees they interact with in the company.

Settling In.   In the settling-in phase, employees begin to feel comfortable with their job demands and social relationships. They begin to work on resolving work conflicts (e.g., too much work to do, conflicting demands of the job) and conflicts between work and nonwork activities. Employees are interested in the company's evaluation of their performance and in learning about potential career opportunities within the company.

Employees need to complete all three phases of the socialization process to fully contribute to the company. For example, employees who do not feel they have established good working relationships with coworkers will likely spend time and energy worrying about relationships with other employees rather than being concerned with product development or customer service. Employees who experience successful socialization are more motivated, more committed to the company, and more satisfied with their jobs.[28]

Orientation programs play an important role in socializing employees. **Orientation** involves familiarizing new employees with company rules, policies, and procedures. Too often, orientation programs consist of completing payroll forms and reviewing personnel policies with managers or human resource representatives. New employees have little opportunity to ask questions or interact with peers and their managers. The characteristics of effective socialization programs are listed in Table 14.3. An important characteristic of effective orientation programs is that peers, managers, and senior coworkers are actively involved in helping new employees adjust to the work group.[29]

Before being assigned to their plant locations, new engineers at Pillsbury, for example, have a one-year headquarters assignment.[30] They are provided with a mentor (a senior engineer), who helps them understand the technical engineering resources available within the company. The mentor also helps them become familiar with the community and deal with relocation issues. New engineers attend seminars in which engineers from different divisions (e.g., frozen foods) explain the role of engineering. New employees also have the opportunity to meet "key players" in engineering management at Pillsbury.

Similarly, new employees and their managers are actively involved in the new orientation program at Corning Glass.[31] Corning Glass was experiencing turnover among its high-potential new employees. Employees were

TABLE 14.3   Characteristics of Effective Orientation Programs

- Employees are encouraged to ask questions.
- Program includes information on both technical and social aspects of the job.
- Orientation is the responsibility of the new employee's manager.
- Debasing and embarrassing new employees is avoided.
- Formal and informal interactions with managers and peers occur.
- Programs involve relocation assistance (e.g., house hunting, information session on the community for employees and their spouses).
- Employees are provided information about the company's products, services, and customers.

leaving the company because they felt the company had a sink-or-swim attitude toward new hires. As a result, Corning designed a new orientation process. The major features of the orientation process include:

- *Manager preparation*—Hiring managers are given guidelines and checklists that specify the steps they should take before and after the arrival of new employees.
- *Guided self-learning*—Managers are encouraged to spend the first two weeks orienting new employees to the job and the company rather than focusing on their regular job duties. Each new employee is provided with a workbook that requires him or her to learn about the company's customers, suppliers, objectives, and culture. It is up to the employee to decide how to complete the workbook questions (e.g., interviews, visits to the company resource center). The manager and employee jointly review the answers to the workbook questions. If the employee needs more information, the learning period is extended.
- *Organization acculturation*—During their first three months, employees attend seminars on Corning's philosophy, culture, and values.

Retention data suggest that the orientation program is a success. It has resulted in 25 to 35 percent increase in retention of new employees in comparison with employees who did not take the new program.

Career Plateauing

An employee is considered **plateaued** if the likelihood of receiving future job assignments with increased responsibility is low. Employees in mid-career are most likely to plateau. Plateauing is not necessarily a bad thing for the employee or the company. A plateaued employee may not desire increased job responsibilities. Also, as the example of Sophia at the beginning of the chapter illustrates, job performance may meet the minimum acceptable standards. Plateauing becomes dysfunctional when the employee feels stuck in a job that offers no potential for personal growth. Such frustration results in poor job attitude, increased absenteeism, and poor job performance.[32]

Employees can plateau for several reasons:[33]

- Lack of training.
- Low need for achievement.
- Unfair pay decisions or dissatisfaction with pay raises.
- Confusion about job responsibilities.
- Slow company growth resulting in reduced development opportunities.

Managers can help plateaued employees in a number of ways. First, they need to help employees understand that being "stuck" in a position is not necessarily the employee's fault (e.g., it could be the result of a hiring freeze). Second, managers should provide performance feedback to employees, especially to unproductive ones. Third, managers should encourage employees to become involved in developmental opportunities, including training courses, job exchanges, and short-term assignments in which the employees can use their expertise outside their departments. Participating in development opportunities may prepare employees for more challenging assignments in their current job or may qualify them for new positions within the company. Managers should also encourage plateaued employees to seek career counseling to help them understand why they are plateaued and their options for dealing with the problem. Employees should be encouraged to "reality-test" the solutions they believe will solve their plateauing through discussions with their manager, coworkers, and human resource manager.

Dual Career Paths

A **career path** is a sequence of job positions involving similar types of work and skills that employees move through in the company.[34] An important issue for companies that employ professional employees such as engineers and scientists is how to ensure that they feel they are valued. Many companies' career paths are structured such that the only way engineers and scientists (individual contributors) can advance and be financially rewarded is by moving into managerial positions. Figure 14.3 shows an example of a traditional career path for scientists and managers. Advancement opportunities within a technical career path are limited. Also, managerial career paths may be more highly compensated than technical career paths. A career-path system such as is shown in Figure 14.3 can have negative consequences for the company. Scientists may elect to leave the company because of lower status, less salary, and fewer advancement opportunities than managers. Also, if scientists want to gain status and additional salary, they must choose to become managers.

Many companies are developing multiple or dual career-path systems to give scientists and other individual contributors additional career oppor-

FIGURE 14.3   Traditional Career Path for Scientists and Managers

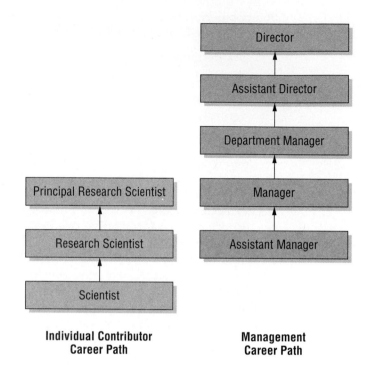

tunities. A **dual career-path system** gives employees the opportunity to remain in a technical career path or move into a management career path.[35] Figure 14.4 shows a dual career-path system. Scientists have the opportunity to move into three different career paths: a scientific path and two management paths. It is assumed that because employees can earn comparable salaries and have similar advancement opportunities in either path, they will choose the path that best matches their interests and skills. British Petroleum recently restructured to allow employees to pursue a dual career path (see the "Competing through Technology and Structure" box).

Effective career paths have several characteristics:[36]

- Salary, status, and incentives for technical employees compare favorably with those of managers.
- Individual contributors' base salary may be lower than managers', but they are given opportunities to increase their total compensation through bonuses (e.g., for patents and developing new products).
- The individual contributor career path is not used to satisfy poor performers who have no managerial potential. The career path is for employees with outstanding technical skills.

FIGURE 14.4   Example of a Dual Career-Path System

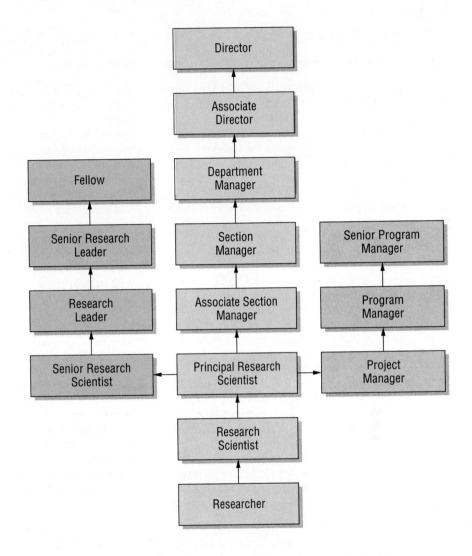

SOURCE: Z. B. Leibowitz, B. L. Kaye and C. Farren, "Multiple Career Paths," *Training and Development Journal*, October 1992, 31–35.

- Individual contributors are given the opportunity to choose their career path. The company provides assessment resources (such as psychological tests and developmental feedback, discussed in Chapter 13). Assessment information gives employees the opportunity to see how similar their interests, work values, and skill strengths are to employees in technical and managerial positions.

Technology & Structure

COMPETING THROUGH

BRITISH PETROLEUM DISCOVERS THE BENEFITS OF A DUAL CAREER-PATH SYSTEM

British Petroleum Exploration (BPX), the unit of British Petroleum that locates and develops oil and gas reserves, has 10,000 employees. An attitude survey in 1989 revealed that employees felt they had no influence in the company and their productivity was inhibited by paperwork. As a result, BPX was involved in an organizational transformation designed to create a culture of personal responsibility. Part of the organizational transformation was to challenge the assumption that the only way to be successful at BPX was to choose the management career track. Individual contributors (such as engineers and scientists) could only move so high in the company without assuming managerial responsibility. After individual contributors reached the top job in the career path, they had two choices: stop progressing upward or leave the company.

BPX decided to develop a dual career-path system. One path would be for managers and the other for individual contributors. The paths are comparable in terms of responsibility, rewards, and influence. Managers, individual contributors, and human resource staff all participated in the development of the career-path system. The first step in the process was the development of descriptions of skills and performance levels that applied to managerial and individual contributor positions. Skill matrices were developed for the two career paths. Each skill matrix describes the skills needed for each position within the career path. The skills needed to switch to the other career path are also described. The skills matrices were distributed to all employees so they were aware of the skills they needed in their current jobs and the skills they needed to change jobs. Employees can move from the individual contributor to the managerial career path based on their performance, qualifications, and business needs. The skills matrices are integrated with performance appraisal, reward, and training systems. For example, the skills matrices were used as a source of information for BPX's development program. The matrices were used to determine what performance improvement, training, or experience the employee needs to meet current job responsibilities and prepare for his or her next career move.

BPX believes that innovation is enhanced by providing employees with career paths that reward individual contributors as well as management contributors. Also, BPX believes that it will be easier to recruit and keep talented scientists and engineers because the dual career path demonstrates the company's interest in satisfying employees' career interests.

SOURCE: M. Moravec and R. Tucker, "Transforming Organizations for Good," *HR Magazine*, October 1991, 74–76 and R. Tucker, M. Moravec, and K. Ideus, "Designing a Dual Career Track System," *Training and Development Journal*, June 1991, 55–58.

Skills Obsolescence

Obsolescence is a reduction in an employee's competence resulting from a lack of knowledge of new work processes, techniques, and technologies that have developed since the employee completed his or her education.[37] Avoiding skills obsolescence has traditionally been a concern of employees in technical and professional occupations such as engineering and medicine. However, rapid technological change affects all aspects of business from manufacturing to administration, and therefore all employees are at risk of becoming obsolete. If employees' skills become obsolete, both the employee and the company suffer. The company will be unable to provide new products and services to customers, losing their competitive advantage. The employee will not be valued by the company. For example, the secretary who fails to keep up with developments in word-processing software (e.g., merging text with figures, tables, charts, and pictures) will soon be unable to produce state-of-the-art documents for his or her internal customer, the advertising manager. The advertising manager's clients may view the company's material as outdated and therefore give their advertising business to a competitor. The secretary's value to the company will be reduced and he or she will likely be an outplacement candidate.

What can be done to avoid skills obsolescence? As we mentioned in the chapter on training, many companies are combating skills obsolescence by encouraging employees to attend courses, seminars, and programs, and to consider how to do their jobs better on a daily basis. This is part of a continuous learning philosophy. Obsolescence can also be avoided by:[38]

- Providing employees with the opportunity to exchange information and ideas.
- Giving employees challenging job assignments early in their careers.
- Providing job assignments that challenge employees and require them to "stretch" their skills.
- Providing rewards for updating behaviors (such as taking courses), suggestions, and customer-service and product innovations.
- Allowing employees to attend professional conferences, subscribe to professional journals and magazines, or enroll in university, technical school, or community center courses at low cost or no cost.

Balancing Work and Family

Families with a working husband, homemaker wife, and two or more children account for only 7 percent of American families. The increasing number of two-career couples and single heads of households creates a challenge for companies. Companies have to carefully consider how to manage employees who are concerned with simultaneously meeting the needs of work and family. Work and family roles are likely to conflict because employees are forced to take several different roles (e.g., parent, spouse, employee) in a number of different environments (e.g., workplace, home, and community). Research suggests that dual-career families, single-parent families, and families with children under the age of five are likely to experience the most work and family conflict.[39] Recent legislation will help alleviate work-family conflicts that occur when employees have to care for infants or deal with family illness. As we mentioned in Chapter 4, the Family and Medical Leave Act (FMLA) provides for up to 12 weeks of unpaid leave for parents with new infants or newly adopted children. The FMLA also covers employees who must take a leave of absence from work to care for a family member who is ill or to deal with a personal illness. Companies are required to provide the employee with health-care benefits during their leave of absence.

At the beginning of this chapter, Jeff, the international sales manager, was frustrated with his company's lack of accommodation to his needs to talk more frequently with his family while he was overseas. Feelings of frustration are only one outcome of work and family conflict. Such conflict has also been found to be related to increased health risks, decreased productivity, tardiness, turnover, and poor mental health.[40] It is also important to recognize that work-family conflict even applies to employees who do not have children or spouses. All employees have nonwork roles and activities that may conflict with work.

Types of Work-Family Conflict.   Three types of work-family conflict have been identified: time-based conflict, strain-based conflict, and behavior-based conflict.[41]

Time-based conflict occurs when the demands of work and family interfere with each other. For example, jobs that demand late evenings at the office, overtime work, or out-of-town travel conflict with family activities and team-sport schedules. **Strain-based conflict** results from the stress of work and family roles. For example, a newborn child deprives parents of sleep; as a result, it is difficult for them to concentrate at work. **Behavior-based conflict** occurs when employees' behavior in work roles is not appropriate for their behavior in family roles. For example, managers' work demands that they be logical, impartial, and authoritarian. At the same time, these same managers are expected to be warm, emotional, and friendly in their relationships with their family members.

Company Policies to Accommodate Work and Family

Many companies are beginning to respond to work and family issues by developing policies designed to reduce the potential for work-family conflict. These policies emphasize the communication of realistic information about the demands of jobs and careers, flexibility in where and when work is performed, and support services such as child-care and elder-care programs. Research suggests that company policies that help employees manage work and family conflicts enhance employees' job performance, reduce costs associated with disability leave, and reduce turnover and absenteeism.[42]

Communicating Information about Work and Family Policies and Job Demands.   Employees need to be made aware of the time demands and the stress related to jobs within the company. This information helps employees choose career opportunities that match the importance they place on work. Employees also need to be aware of the company's work and family practices, such as flexible benefits related to dependent care and leave policies.

TABLE 14.4   Alternative Work Schedules and Work Arrangements

	Where	When
Traditional	Work at place of employment	5 days 40 hours per week
Flextime	Work at place of employment	Work 40 hours but have choice when to start and end work. May require work during certain core hours.
Compressed work week	Work at place of employment	4 days 10 hour workdays
Temporary work	Work at place of employment	Work on as-needed basis.
Job sharing	Work at place of employment	Split 5-day, 40-hour workweek with other employee.
Part-time work	Work at place of employment	Less than 8 hours a day or 5 days a week.
Shift work	Work at place of employment	Morning, afternoon or overnight shifts on rotating basis.
Work at home	Work at home	Varies, could be 5 days, 40 hours per week.

Flexibility in Work Arrangements and Work Schedules.   A key way to deal with work-family conflicts is to provide employees with more flexibility about when work is performed (work schedules) and where it is performed (work arrangements). Work and family conflict can be reduced by increasing the amount of control that employees have over work and family demands.[43] As we discussed in Chapter 5, one way many firms have provided employees with additional control is through alternative work schedules involving flextime or part-time work. Table 14.4 presents examples of alternative work arrangements and work schedules. These work arrangements provide employees with more control over their work schedule, giving them time to deal with family demands (e.g., paying bills, caring for infants and small children) and avoid the difficulties of commuting. Alternative work arrangements reduces stress and absenteeism. Home-based work is dominated by individuals in educational, professional, business, repair, and social-service occupations. The major difficulties posed by alternative work schedules and work arrangements include communication problems (employees may be at different locations and on different work schedules), a lack of necessary supplies and equipment, and family interruptions.[44]

Support Services.   Companies need to provide three support services: manager training, child care, and elder care. Many employees are concerned about using flexible work arrangements and schedules because they fear that managers will view them as uninterested in their careers, and accuse them of "shirking" their job responsibilities. They fear that managers may not provide them with development opportunities and will evaluate their performance less favorably. Companies need to train managers to understand that employees' use of work-family policies should not be punished. The more supportive the manager is (e.g., a willingness to discuss family-related problems), the less work-family conflict employees will experience.[45]

Almost two-thirds of all women with children younger than 14 are in the work force. Companies can help these employees deal with child-care demands in a number of ways. The child-care services companies most frequently provide are help in identifying child-care resources and flexible benefit plans that allow employees to pay for child care with pretax dollars. (Flexible benefit plans are discussed in Chapter 17.) Child-care services need to be flexible to meet the needs of a diverse work force. A single parent may need more assistance than an employee with a spouse who works part-time. Employees with young infants may want to choose parental leave, part-time work, or work at home. Unfortunately, only 5 percent of midsize to large companies provide any type of child-care assistance.[46] The lack of child care likely has the greatest impact on low-income parents, who may have to choose between working or staying home with their children.

A growing concern for many employees is how to care for aging parents—that is, elder care. At least 20 percent of all employees currently care for a parent. The care of elderly persons will only increase in importance in the United States because 21 percent of the U.S. population will be 65 or over by the year 2000. The stresses of elder care result in outcomes similar to those of parents with children: absenteeism, work interruptions, and lack of energy. Elder care may be even more demanding than child care if the elder has a debilitating disease such as Alzheimer's. Companies are beginning to offer employees insurance programs to defray elder-care costs (e.g., nursing home expenses).[47]

A good example of a company with policies to help employees manage work and family conflicts is Marriott Corporation. Marriott, one of the largest employers in the nation, is a leader in quality-of-life issues.[48] Of its 260,000 employees, over 50 percent are women; more than one-third of Marriott's employees have children under 12. Based on a nationwide employee survey, Marriott developed a number of work and family policies:

- *Child-care choice*—A professional child-care referral service designed to assist employees locate affordable child care.

- *Child-care discount program*—Child-care centers have agreed to offer a 10 percent discount or to waive registration fees for Marriott employees.

- *Family-care spending account*—This allows employees to use pretax dollars to pay for child or elder care.

- *Elder care*—The company provides seminars about the care available for aging family members.

- *The "Balance"*—This quarterly newsletter provides information on work and family issues.

- *Child development center*—An on-site daycare facility at Marriott Headquarters provides day care and activities for 60 children.

In addition to these programs, a training module for managers is being considered. Marriott's director of work and family life believes that a key message to communicate to employees is that helping employees balance work and family is a legitimate business issue.

One of the most controversial ideas for alleviating work-family conflict is creating separate career tracks for career-primary and career-family women.[49] Because of childbearing and child-raising responsibility, the cost of employing women is greater than the cost of employing men. To reduce these costs, companies might consider providing more flexible employment relationships for women who want to combine career and family (career-family women). Use of this strategy to alleviate work and family conflict would involve identifying early in the women's career, whether they are career-family women or career-primary women (women for whom career is the top priority). Career-family women would be provided with high-quality child care and flexible work schedules. As a result of these accommodations, career-family women's pay will be lower than career-primary women's. Career-family women are trading career growth and compensation for freedom from job pressures. For career-primary women, companies should ensure that they are given the same opportunities for development and advancement as talented men.

These ideas may also apply to men. The basic issue is whether employees' advancement opportunities and compensation should differ depending on the type of trade-offs they are willing to make regarding work and family. Keep in mind that there are several negative outcomes of this strategy. Forcing women (or men) to be permanently tracked or labeled as career-primary or career-family, reinforces negative stereotypes concerning the commitment and productivity of employees with families. Permanently tracking or labeling employees as career-primary or career-family assumes that the degree of work-family conflict remains constant during the employees' careers. Forcing employees to remain in a career track that might be unsuitable means the company is not effectively using employees to gain a competitive advantage. Finally, employees will likely resent having to identify a career track based on their family status, resulting in dissatisfaction and turnover. Providing alternative work arrangements and schedules and support services are a more effective strategy for helping employees cope with work-family conflict than labeling or tracking employees.

Job Loss

Corporate restructuring, downsizing, mergers, acquisitions, and takeovers have resulted in many production workers, engineers, and managers losing their jobs. Layoffs, however, can have a positive benefit for the company.[50] Costs can be reduced, and stock prices frequently go up because the layoff is viewed as a signal that the company is getting "back to basics." During severe economic downturns, layoffs can help the company survive. However, anticipated cost savings may not occur if the company is forced to replace laid-off employees with more expensive consultants, the company incurs costs resulting from the need to train remaining employees to complete the work of displaced workers, and business units decide to replace expertise previously provided by employees from corporate headquarters by hiring new employees.[51]

Layoffs can also be costly. Companies that lay employees off can experience lowered job commitment, distrust of management, and difficulties recruiting new employees.[52] Job loss also causes stress and disrupts the lives of the laid-off employees.

Companies should try to avoid laying off employees. Companies should identify employees who are critical for the operation of the business. The jobs of these employees should be protected except during the most severe economic conditions. This can be done through changes in staffing strategies such as the use of "buffers" (i.e., using overtime work and hiring temporary employees during short-term business upturns or to meet special customer needs).[53] If economic conditions sour, the company can reduce overtime and end temporary assignments without sacrificing full-time employees' jobs. Another way to avoid layoffs is to determine whether employees who have been targeted for layoffs can be transferred to other jobs, a process known as *inplacement*. If layoffs are still unavoidable, companies need to provide outplacement services, which help prepare employees for losing their jobs and reduce the potential negative effects of layoffs. Outplacement services should provide:[54]

- Advance warning and explanation for layoff.
- Psychological, financial, and career counseling.
- Assessment of skills and interests.
- Job campaign services such as resume-writing assistance and interview training.
- Job banks where job leads are posted and out-of-town newspapers, phones, and books regarding different occupations and geographic areas are available.

Employees in upper-level managerial and professional positions typically receive more personalized outplacement services (e.g., office space, private secretary) than employees in lower-level positions.[55] Outplacement also involves training managers how to conduct termination meetings with employees. Table 14.5 presents guidelines for managers to follow in conducting termination meetings. Providing counseling for laid-off employees is critical because employees first have to deal with the shock of the layoff and their feelings of anger, guilt, disbelief, and blame before they can begin searching for a new job.

Typically, companies devote more resources to outplacing employees who have lost their jobs than to employees who remain. However, company success will be determined by the productivity of the survivors. Research

TABLE 14.5   Guidelines for Termination Meetings with Employees

1. Planning
- Alert outplacement firm that termination will occur (if appropriate).
- Prepare severance and benefit packages.
- Prepare public statement regarding terminations.
- Prepare statement for employees unaffected by terminations.
- Have telephone numbers available for medical or security emergencies.

2. Timing
- Terminations should not occur on Friday afternoon, very late on any day, or before a holiday. Terminate employees early in the week so employees can receive counseling and outplacement assistance.

3. Place
- Usually occurs in employee's office.
- May need HR representative present to explain severance and outplacement package.
- In sensitive cases where severe emotional reaction is expected, third party is also needed.

4. Length
- Meeting should be short and to the point. Termination should occur within the first two minutes. Remainder of time should be spent on explaining separation benefits and allowing employee to express feelings.

5. Approach
- Provide straightforward explanation, stating reasons for termination.
- Statement should be made that the decision to terminate was made by management and is irreversible.
- Do not discuss your feelings, needs, or problems.

6. Benefits
- Written statement of salary continuation, benefits continuation, outplacement support (e.g., office arrangements, counseling) and other terms and conditions should be provided and discussed with the employee.

SOURCE: Adapted from R. J. Lee, "Outplacement Counseling for the Terminated Manager," in *Applying Psychology in Business*, ed. J. W. Jones, B. D. Steffy and D. W. Bray (Lexington, Mass.: Lexington Books, 1991), 489–508.

suggests that the attitudes and productivity of employees who remain with the company are influenced by their beliefs regarding the fairness of the lay-off and the changes in their working conditions.[56] For example, survivors are more likely to view layoffs as fair if employees are asked to cut costs to avoid layoffs, and if the factors used to decide whom to lay off (e.g., performance, seniority) are applied to all employees. Survivors need to be trained to deal with increased work-load and job responsibilities that will result from the consolidation and loss of jobs. The company also needs to provide survivors with realistic information about their future with the company.

Retirement

Retirement involves leaving a job and work role and making a transition into life without work. For some employees, retirement involves making a transition out of their current job and company and seeking full- or part-time employment elsewhere. Research suggests that issues regarding retirement will increase in importance in the near future. By the year 2000, over 22 percent of the U.S. population will be over 65 years of age. Recent changes in the Social Security system and an increase in the mandatory retirement age from 65 to 70 suggest that employees may elect to work longer (see the "Competing through Social Responsibility" box). However, over half of all employees retire before age 63, and 80 percent leave by the time they are 70. This may be because employees accept companies' offers of early retirement packages, which usually include generous financial benefits. The aging work force and the use of early retirement programs to shrink companies' work forces have two implications. First, companies must take steps to prepare employees for retirement. Second, companies must be careful that early retirement programs do not unfairly discriminate against older employees.

Preretirement Socialization.   **Preretirement socialization** is the process of helping employees prepare for exit from work. It encourages employees to learn about retirement life, plan for adequate financial, housing, and health-care resources, and form accurate expectations about retirement. Employees' satisfaction with life after retirement is influenced by their health, their feelings about their jobs, and their level of optimism. Employees who attend preretirement socialization programs have fewer financial and psychological problems and experience greater satisfaction with retirement compared with employees who do not attend these programs. These programs typically address the following topics:[57]

- Psychological aspects of retirement, such as developing personal interests and activities.
- Housing, including a consideration of transportation, living costs, and proximity to medical care.
- Health during retirement; nutrition and exercise.
- Financial planning, insurance, and investments.
- Estate planning.
- Collecting benefits from company pension plans and Social Security.

Social Responsibility

OLDER WORKERS' CAREER POSSIBILITIES EXPAND

Demographic changes in the labor force have influenced several companies to hire older workers and retirees. Days Inn of America, The Travelers Corporation, and B&Q plc are three companies that have used older employees and retirees to gain a competitive advantage. Days Inn, the hotel chain, began hiring older workers (defined as those 50 and older) as reservation agents in 1986 because of difficulties in recruiting younger workers. Days Inns reservation facility, located in Atlanta and Knoxville, is a 24-hour-a-day operation that handles 20,000 phone calls a day. Days Inn compared the costs and benefits of hiring older versus younger workers. It found that older workers stayed on the job longer than younger workers. This resulted in average savings of recruiting and training costs of $1,100 per employee. Also, older employees generated more revenues by booking more reservations than younger employees.

The Travelers Corporation, an insurance and financial services company, established a job bank for its retirees. Over 700 retirees are involved in the program. They fill positions ranging from unskilled data-entry positions to professional positions. The Travelers compared the costs of their retiree program to the cost of hiring temporary employees through an employment agency. The company found that use of the job bank resulted in $871,000 savings in employment agency fees and sales tax. The use of former employees as temporary employees reduces the length of time employees need to learn about the company before becoming productive in their jobs.

B&Q plc, a British hardware chain, was experiencing high turnover, recruitment problems, and lack of product knowledge among its employees. To determine whether older employees could help the company solve these problems, a new store was staffed entirely with employees over 50 years old. A study comparing this store to five similar company stores revealed that turnover was markedly lower at the store staffed by the older workers. Older workers were absent 39 percent less than younger workers in other stores. Theft and damage to inventory was less than half the average of the other five stores.

SOURCE: "Days Inn Hits Gold in Older Workers", *Augusta Chronicle*, (Georgia), December 1, 1991; "An Old Story," *Across the Board*, November 1991, 35–40; and results of a study by The Commonwealth Fund released on May 21, 1991, at the annual meeting of the National Council on Aging: "New Findings Show Why Employing Workers over 50 Makes Good Financial Sense for Companies." Available from The Commonwealth Fund, New York, NY 10021-2692.

Many companies also use alternative work arrangements to help employees make the transition into retirement. Polaroid has two creative plans.[58] "Rehearsal retirement" allows employees considering retirement to try it out. If they do not like it, they can return to their former jobs. Another program, "tapering off," allows employees to exit the company gradually by working shorter workweeks.

Although formal preretirement socialization programs are primarily for employees who are considering retirement, employees who are not close to retirement age should begin to prepare for retirement. Financial planning and insurance is necessary to ensure that employees will have income levels and health care necessary to live comfortably during retirement.

Early Retirement Programs.   Early retirement programs offer employees financial benefits to leave the company. These programs are usually part of the company's strategy to reduce labor costs without having to lay off employees. Financial benefits usually include a lump sum of money and a percentage of salary based on years of service. These benefits can be quite attractive to employees, particularly those with long tenure with the company. Eligibility for early retirement is usually based on age and years of service. For example, GTE Telephone Operations–North Area invites employees to consider retirement when the sum of their age and years of service approaches 76.[59] Early retirement programs have two major problems. First, one of the dangers of these programs is that employees with expertise, who would be difficult to replace, elect to leave the company. Older employees may also believe that early retirement programs are discriminatory. To avoid costly litigation, companies need to make sure that early retirement programs:[60]

- Are part of the employee benefit plan.
- Justify age-related distinctions for eligibility for early retirement.
- Allow employees to voluntarily choose early retirement.

Eligibility requirements should not be based on stereotypes about ability and skill decrements that occur with age. Research suggests that small declines in specific abilities and skills related to age have little effect on job performance.[61] Employees' decisions are considered voluntary if they have the opportunity to refuse to participate, they are given complete information about the plan, and they are given a reasonable amount of time to make their decisions.

SUMMARY

This chapter focused on career management. It began with a discussion of the competitive challenges that influence career management. Based on life-cycle, organizational, and directional-pattern perspectives of careers, a career development model was introduced. It suggested that employees face different developmental tasks, depending on their career stage (exploration, establishment, maintenance, disengagement). The actions that companies can take to help employees deal with these developmental tasks were highlighted.

The career-planning process consists of assessment, reality check, goal setting, and action planning. For career planning to be successful, employees, managers, and the company must all be actively involved. Finally, current career development issues including orientation and socialization, plateauing, dual career ladders, skill obsolescence, balancing work and family, job loss, and retirement were presented. Specific practices of companies that have been successful in dealing with these issues were emphasized.

Discussion Questions

1. What are the advantages of involving the employee, manager, and coworkers in the socialization process?

2. What stage of career development are you in? What career concerns are most important to you? Are these concerns consistent with any one of the development models presented in the chapter?

3. Discuss the implications that the career development model presented in the chapter may have for planning training and development activities.

4. Why should companies be interested in helping employees plan their careers? What benefits can companies gain? What are the risks?

5. Discuss how plateaued employees can be reenergized to achieve personal growth and contribute to the company's productivity.

6. Discuss the advantages and disadvantages of having separate career tracks for employees based on the importance they place on work and nonwork/family activities.

Notes

1. M. London and M. M. Greller, "Demographic Trends and Vocational Behavior: A Twenty-Year Retrospective and Agenda for the 1990s," *Journal of Vocational Behavior* 38 (1991): 125–164; M. M. Greller and D. M. Nee, *From Baby Boom to Baby Bust: How Business Can Meet the Demographic Challenge* (Reading, Mass.: Addison-Wesley, 1989); D. T. Hall and J. Richter, "Balancing Work Life and Home Life: What Can Organizations Do to Help?" *Academy of Management Executive* 11 (1988): 213–223.

2. M. London and E. M. Mane, *Career Management and Survival in the Workplace* (San Francisco: Jossey-Bass, 1987); M. London, "Toward a Theory of Career Motivation," *Academy of Management Review* 8 (1983): 620–630.

3. J. H. Greenhaus, *Career Management* (Chicago: The Dryden Press, 1987).

4. D. T. Hall, *Careers in Organizations* (Pacific Palisades, Cal.: Goodyear Publishing, 1976); M. B. Arthur, D. T. Hall and B. S. Lawrence, *Handbook of Career Theory* (New York: Cambridge University Press, 1989).

5. B. P. Grossman and R. S. Blitzer, "Choreographing Careers," *Training and Development* January 1992, 67–69.

6. Personal conversation with Sylvia Miller, HR consultant, Northwest Airlines, Inc, December 1991.

7. Greenhaus, *Career Management*.

8. Ibid.

9. D. E. Super, *The Psychology of Careers* (New York: Harper & Row, 1957); G. Dalton, P. Thompson and R. Price, "The Four Stages of Professional Careers," *Organizational Dynamics*, Summer 1972, 19–42; M. J. Driver, "Career Concepts—a New Approach to Career Research," in *Career Issues in Human Resource Management*, ed. R. Katz (Englewood Cliffs, N.J.: Prentice-Hall, 1982), 23–34.

10. J. W. Slocum and W. L. Cron, "Job Attitudes and Performance during Three Career Stages," *Journal of Vocational Behavior* 26 (1985): 126–145; S. Rabinowitz and D. T. Hall, "Changing Correlates of Job Involvement," *Journal of Vocational Behavior* 18 (1981): 138–144.

11. F. L. Otte and P. G. Hutcheson, *Helping Employees Manage Careers* (Englewood Cliffs, N.J.: Prentice-Hall, 1992).

12. D. Lade, "Man Starts New Job at Age 93," *Sun-Sentinel* (Fort Lauderdale, Florida), June 13, 1991.

13. D. C. Feldman, *Managing Careers in Organizations* (Glenview, Ill.: Scott-Foresman, 1988).

14. J. E. Russell, "Career Development Interventions in Organizations," *Journal of Vocational Behavior* 38 (1991): 237–287; T. C. Gutteridge, "Organizational Career Development Systems: The State of the Practice," in *Career Development in Organizations*, ed. D. T. Hall & Associates (San Francisco: Jossey-Bass, 1986), 50–94.

15. Consulting Psychologists Press, "Wells Fargo Helps Employees Change Careers," *Strong Forum* 8, no. 1 (1991): 1.

16. L. Slavenski, "Career Development: A Systems Approach," *Training and Development Journal* February, 1987: 56–60.

17. F. J. Miner, "Computer Applications in Career Development Planning," in *Career Development in Organizations*, ed. D. T. Hall & Associates (San Francisco: Jossey-Bass, 1986), 202–235.

18. D. T. Jaffe and C. D. Scott, "Career Development for Empowerment in a Changing Work World," in *New Directions in Career Planning and the Workplace*, ed. J. M. Kumerow (Palo Alto, Cal.: Consulting Psychologists Press, 1991), 33–59.

19. K. Labich, "Take Control of Your Career," *Fortune*, November 18, 1991, 87–96; R. Tucker and M. Moravec, "Do-It-Yourself Career Development," *Training*, February 1992, 48–52.

20. S. Sherman, "A Brave New Darwinian Workplace," *Fortune*, January 25, 1993, 50–56.

21. B. M. Moses and B. J. Chakins, "The Manager as Career Counselor," *Training and Development Journal*, July 1989, 60–65.

22. Z. B. Leibowitz, C. Farren and B. L. Kaye, *Designing Career Development Systems* (San Francisco: Jossey-Bass, 1986).

23. Information provided by Susan Runkel, Management Resource Planning Specialist, 3M, December 1991.

24. D. C. Feldman, "A Contingency Theory of Socialization," *Administrative Science Quarterly* 21 (1976): 433–452; D. C. Feldman, "A Socialization Process that Helps New Recruits Succeed," *Personnel* 57 (1980): 11–23; J. P. Wanous, A. E. Reichers and S. D. Malik, "Organizational Socialization and Group Development: Toward an Integrative Perspective," *Academy of Management Review* 9 (1984): 670–683.

25. J. P. Wanous, *Organizational Entry* (Reading, Mass.: Addison-Wesley, 1980).

26. M. R. Louis, "Surprise and Sense Making: What Newcomers Experience in Entering Unfamiliar Organizational Settings," *Administrative Science Quarterly* 25 (1980): 226–251.

27. R. F. Morrison and T. M. Brantner, "What Enhances or Inhibits Learning a New Job? A Basic Career Issue," *Journal of Applied Psychology* 77 (1992): 926–940.

28. Feldman, *Managing Careers in Organizations*.

29. Ibid; D. Reed-Mendenhall and C. W. Millard, "Orientation: A Training and Development Too," *Personnel Administrator* 25, no. 8 (1980): 42–44; M. R. Louis, B. Z. Posner and G. H. Powell, "The Availability and Helpfulness of Socialization Practices," *Personnel Psychology* 36 (1983): 857–866.

30. Pillsbury engineering orientation program.

31. D. B. Youst and L. Lipsett, "New Job Immersion Without Drowning," *Training and Development*, February, (1989): 73–75.

32. D. C. Feldman and B. A. Weitz, "Career Plateaus Reconsidered," *Journal of Management* 14 (1988): 69–80; Feldman, *Managing Careers in Organizations*; J. P. Near, "A Discriminant Analysis of Plateaued versus Nonplateaued Employees," *Journal of Vocational Behavior* 26 (1985): 177–188; S. K. Stout, J. Slocum, Jr. and W. L. Cron, "Dynamics of the Career Plateauing Process," *Journal of Vocational Behavior* 22 (1988): 74–91.

33. Feldman and Weitz, "Career Plateaus Revisited"; B. Rosen and T. H. Jerdee, "Managing Older Working Careers," in *Research in Personnel and Human Resource Management*, ed. F. R. Ferris and F. M. Rowland (Greenwich, Conn.: JAI Press, 1988), 6: 3774.

34. Greenhaus, *Career Management*.

35. H. D. Dewirst, "Career Patterns: Mobility, Specialization, and Related Career Issues," in *Contemporary Career Development Issues*, ed. R. F. Morrison and J. Adams (Hillsdale, N.J.: Lawrence Erlbaum, 1991), 73–107.

36. Z. B. Leibowitz, B. L. Kaye and C. Farren, "Multiple Career Paths," *Training and Development Journal*, October 1992, 31–35.

37. S. S. Dubin, "Maintaining Competence through Updating," in *Maintaining Professional Competence*, ed. S. L. Willis and S. S. Dubin (San Francisco: Jossey-Bass, 1990), 9–43.

38. J. A. Fossum, R. D. Arvey, C. A. Paradise and N. E. Robbins, "Modeling the Skills Obsolescence Process: A Psychological/Economic Integration," *Academy of Management Review* 11 (1986): 362–374; S. W. J. Kozlowski and B. M. Hults, "An Exploration of Climates for Technical Updating and Performance," *Personnel Psychology* 40 (1988): 539–564.

39. C. Lee, "Balancing Work and Family," *Training*, September 1991, 23–28; D. E. Super, "Life Career Roles: Self-realization in Work and Leisure," in *Career Development in Organizations*, ed. D. T. Hall (San Francisco: Jossey-Bass, 1986), 95–119; P. Voydanoff, "Work Role Characteristics, Family Structure Demands, and Work/Family Conflict," *Journal of Marriage and the Family* 50 (1988): 749–762; R. F. Kelly and P. Voydanoff, "Work/Family Role Strain among Employed Parents," *Family Relations* 34 (1985): 367–374.

40. J. H. Greenhaus and N. Beutell, "Sources of Conflict between Work and Family Roles," *Academy of Management Review* 10 (1985): 76–88; J. H. Pleck, *Working Wives/Working Husbands* (Newbury Park, Cal.: Sage Publications, 1985); Kelly and Voydanoff, "Work Family Role Strain."

41. Greenhaus and Beutell, "Sources of Conflict between Work and Family Roles."

42. J. H. Greenhaus, "The Intersection of Work and Family Roles: Individual, Interpersonal, and Organizational Issues," in *Work and Family*, ed. E. B. Godsmith (Newbury Park, Cal.: Sage Publications, 1987), 23–44; Bureau of National Affairs, "Measuring Results: Cost-Benefit Analyses of Work and Family Programs," *Employee Relations Weekly* (Washington, D.C.: Bureau of National Affairs, 1993).

43. L. E. Duxbury and C. A. Higgins, "Gender Differences in Work-Family Conflict," *Journal of Applied Psychology* 76 (1991): 60–74.

44. J. L. Pierce, J. W. Newstrom, R. B. Dunham and P. E. Barber, *Alternative Work Schedules* (Boston: Allyn and Bacon, 1989); F. W. Horvath, "Work at Home: New Findings from the Current Population Survey," *Monthly Labor Review* 109, no. 11 (1986): 31–35; J. R. King, "Working at Home Has Yet to Work Out," *The Wall Street Journal*, December 22, 1989, B1–B2.

45. F. S. Rodgers and C. Rodgers, "Business and the Facts of Family Life," *Harvard Business Review*, November–December 1989, 121–129; S. J. Goff, M. K. Mount and R. L. Jamison, "Employer Support Child Care, Work/Family Conflict, and Absenteeism: A Field Study," *Personnel Psychology* 43 (1990): 793–809.

46. U.S. Department of Labor, *Childcare: A Workforce Issue* (Washington, D.C.: U.S. Department of Labor, 1988); M. L. Sher and G. Brown, "What to Do with Jenny," *Personnel Administrator* 34 (1989): 31–41; D. J. Petersen and D. Massengill, "Child Care Programs Benefit Employers Too," *Personnel* 65 (1988): 58–62; E. E. Kossek, "Diversity in Child-Care Assistance Needs: Employee Problems, Preferences, and Work-Related Outcomes," *Personnel Psychology* 43 (1990): 769–791; N. R. Fritz, "Someone to Watch over Them," *Personnel* 65 (1988): 4–5.

47. R. S. Azarnoff and Scharlach, "Can Employees Carry the Elder-Care Burden?" *Personnel Journal*, September 1988, 60–67; American Association of Retired Persons, *The Aging Workforce* (Washington, D.C.: American Association of Retired Persons, 1990); J. L. Lefkovich, "Business Responds to Elder-Care Needs," *HR Magazine*, June 1992, 103–108.

48. C. M. Solomon, "Marriott's Family Matters," *Personnel Journal* 70 (1991): 40–42.

49. F. N. Schwartz, "Management Women and the New Facts of Family Life," *Harvard Business Review*, January–February 1989, 65–76.

50. V. Brownstein, "Though Some Jobs Are Gone for Good, Employment Will Rise Again," *Fortune*, November 18, 1991, 29–34; J. C. Latack, "Organizational Restructuring and Career Management: From Outplacement and Survival to Inplacement," in *Research in Personnel and Human Resource Management*, ed. G. R. Ferris and K. M. Rowland (Greenwich, Conn.: JAI Press, 1990), 109–139.

51. W. F. Cascio, "Downsizing: What Do We Know? What Have We Learned?" *Academy of Management Executive* 7, no. 1 (1993): 95–104.

52. J. Brockner, "The Effects of Work Layoffs on Survivors: Research, Theory, and Practice," in *Research in Organizational Behavior*, ed. B. M. Staw and L. L. Cummings (Hillsdale, N.J.: Lawrence Erlbaum, 1988), 10: 45–95; L. Greenhalgh, A. T. Lawrence and R. I. Sutton, "Determinants of Workforce Reduction Strategies in Declining Organizations," *Academy of Management Review* 13 (1988): 241–254.

53. J. F. Bolt, "Job Security: Its Time Has Come," *Harvard Business Review*, November–December 1983, 115–123; M. Messmer, "Right Sizing Reshapes Staffing Strategies," *HR Magazine*, October 1991, 60–62.

54. J. C. Latack and J. B. Dozier, "After the Ax Falls: Job Loss as Career Transition," *Academy of Management Review* 11 (1986): 375–392; J. Brockner, "Managing the Effects of Layoffs on Survivors," *California Management Review*, Winter (1992): 9–28; S. L. Guinn, "Outplacement Programs: Separating Myth from Reality," *Training and Development Journal* 42 (1988): 48–49; D. R. Simon, "Outplacement: Matching Needs, Matching Services," *Training and Development Journal* 42 (1988): 52–57.

55. E. B. Picolino, "Outplacement: The View from HR," *Personnel*, March 1988, 24–27.

56. Brockner, "Managing the Effects of Layoffs on Survivors."

57. A. L. Kamouri and J. C. Cavanaugh, "The Impact of Preretirement Education Programs on Workers' Preretirement Socialization," *Journal of Occupational Behavior* 7 (1986): 245–256; N. Schmitt and J. T. McCune, "The Relationship between Job Attitudes and the Decision to Retire," *Academy of Management Review* 24 (1981): 795–802; N. Schmitt, B. W. Coyle, J. Rauschenberger and J. K. White, "Comparison of Early Retirees and Non-retirees," *Personnel Psychology* 32 (1981): 327–340; T. A. Beehr, "The Process of Retirement," *Personnel Psychology* 39 (1986): 31–55; S. M. Comrie, "Teach Employees to Approach Retirement as a New Career," *Personnel Journal* 64, no. 8 (1985): 106–108.

58. "Retirees Get a Dry Run before Taking the Plunge," *Personnel Management Policies and Practices* 35, no. 15 (1987): 3–4.

59. R. E. Hill and P. C. Dwyer, "Grooming Workers for Early Retirement," *HR Magazine*, September 1990, 59–63.

60. M. L. Colusi, P. B. Rosen and S. J. Herrin, "Is Your Early Retirement Package Courting Disaster?" *Personnel Journal*, August 1988, 60–67.

61. Rosen and Jerdee, "Managing Older Workers' Careers."

C A S E

CAREER OPPORTUNITIES AFFECT MORALE AND PERFORMANCE

Delco Systems Operations, a business unit of Delco Electronics, was experiencing a number of problems with its clerical staff. Employees in clerk and senior clerk positions felt that their work was not recognized. Many employees felt that the job title "clerk" was demeaning. The type of work that the clerical staff performed often did not match the job description for these positions. Clerical employees are not involved in career planning. An analysis of the clerk's jobs suggested that four separate types of jobs existed:

- *Group 1*—Spent almost 75 percent of their time using word-processing equipment to enter text.
- *Group 2*—Spent most of their time answering questions regarding personal computer software (e.g, spreadsheets, word-processing applications).
- *Group 3*—Primarily coordinated projects on an ongoing basis, gathered and analyzed sales and administrative cost data, and wrote reports.
- *Group 4*—Handled multiple tasks: word processing, answering telephones, greeting visitors.

QUESTION

1. **Top management believes that to improve the morale of the clerical staff and reduce turnover, the career opportunities for clerical staff need to be improved. What should Delco do to enhance the career opportunities of the clerical staff?**

SOURCE: W. Eigen, "Transform Office Jobs into Careers," *Personnel Journal*, October 1991, 102–109.

TRAINING IS OUR COMPETITIVE ADVANTAGE: ARTHUR ANDERSEN AND ANDERSEN CONSULTING

Arthur Andersen Worldwide Organization is the world's third-largest accounting and consulting organization, with 1992 revenues of $5.6 billion. In 1989, the company was restructured into two business units, Arthur Andersen (which provides corporate specialty services and audit, business, and tax advisory services) and Andersen Consulting (which aids clients in the application of the integration of information-based technologies for competitive advantage, strategic planning, and change management). The two business units share many support services, including training. Together they invest approximately 5.5 percent of their combined annual revenues, which amounts to more than $300 million, in the development and training of their employees. This amount is significantly higher than the U.S corporate average.

Lawrence Weinbach, managing partner and chief executive of the firm, says, "Education gives us our competitive edge. Anybody can hire smart people. It's what you do with them that makes the difference. In a professional service organization, all you have to sell are your people's abilities, so we invest in that." Andersen clearly hires its share of smart people. It recruits bright college graduates aggressively in such fields as accounting, computer science, engineering, and communications. However, unlike in many organizations, the company does not expect that these recent graduates will be "up and running" on the job immediately. They are trained extensively in the culture and methods of what many employees call "The Firm" (not to be confused with any recent movies or novels by that title).

How did this emphasis on training as a competitive advantage begin at Arthur Andersen? Over 80 years ago, the company founder, Arthur Andersen, decided that the accountants he hired for audit and tax season work would do a higher quality job if he not only made them year-round employees but provided them with training as well. Recently, Steven M. Hronec commented that, "as a partner, I expect training to be very responsive to our changing marketplace. Our client's needs are changing, and I expect training to be able to be done very quickly, very focused, and in a way that responds to these changes."

The Andersen Training Function

Unlike most U.S. companies, Andersen provides the most intensive training for new employees at the start of the career ladder. Virtually all new staff recruits, from countries across the globe, receive three weeks of professional education. The primary training site in the United States is the Center for Professional Education in St. Charles, Illinois. Additionally, however, Andersen has training sites in the Netherlands and in Spain.

The initial training is common for all employees, for the most part. Andersen has developed standard methodologies and approaches to problem solving that allow Andersen personnel from any country to work together to develop unique, effective solutions designed to fit individual business challenges. Herbert W. Desch, managing partner of the Professional Education Division (PED) and the organization's chief training officer, notes, "Individual brilliance is not as important as the ability to share different ideas and a variety of potential solutions through a worldwide team approach. As a global organization, we believe that clients ought to be able to get the same level of quality service from any of our offices. When you train for a worldwide culture and teach consistent methodologies for approaching complex tasks, you have a better chance of providing consistent quality while reaching solutions tailored to an individual client's needs." The global perspective is very much a part of the Andersen training process. Alan Malby, a manager with Andersen Consulting's London office, believes that the cultural mix of trainees at the St. Charles facility leads to a international team spirit "which is particularly of benefit as projects get larger and people from other offices are drafted to complete complex projects."

Each person, new or experienced, in the Andersen organization of 48,000 professionals receives an average of 138 hours of training each year. Roughly one-third of the training takes place at the St. Charles center—a 151-acre campus, where new recruits participate in rigorous training sessions, working up to 12 hours per day. The St. Charles training center also offers hundreds of special "schools" or courses that provide continual professional development for the company's experienced personnel. Most courses are taught by people from line operations. "In our culture it's an honor to teach," says Desch. Training sessions include topics in basic auditing, tax law, and state of the art client/server technology specifically designed for the Andersen Consulting professionals.

The Andersen Professional Education Division handles training design and development, provides training support, and does curriculum planning. It uses several technologies to deliver training, including video conferencing, digital interactive (DVI), CD-ROM, and desktop computers. Desch estimates that the division is one of the largest employers of instructional designers and technologists in the United States. To shorten the time between the recognition of new training needs and design and delivery of the actual training, PED has begun to use teams (called "group technology cells," similar to those used in manufacturing) made up of subject matter experts, educational experts, and graphic artists to bring new training programs to the staff quickly.

Training Responsiveness to Client Needs

The speed of training in new technologies and tax law changes provides Andersen with professionals who are up-to-date. A current example of this process is the aggressive training now under way in the area of client/server networks (networks of desktop computers now used by about 70 percent of Andersen Consulting's new business). "Anticipating a market shift, we rolled out our first client/server training in just five months. Andersen Consulting has more than 3,000 professionals, and we'll have an additional 6,000 professionals, proficient in these applications by 1993." Desch predicts that the company will have as many as 24,000 consulting professionals skilled in client/server solutions by the end of 1994.

More training, however, does not always mean better performance; therefore, Andersen's training staff monitors progress towards training objectives. Evaluation reports go to the partners. Every unit in the company that uses training must account for it, and all training is evaluated at least at the level of participants' reactions to the material and process. One recent program on state and local tax law was evaluated fully, to determine effects on revenue and quantity of work. The evaluation showed that tax professionals who took the training had more billable hours than those who did not take the course.

Individual Career Development

From the perspective of Andersen's people, the training function provides many elements of what is needed for successful career development. As one recent recruit states, "To succeed, you need the desire and the opportunity. At Andersen Consulting, the opportunities for success match my ambitions. The winning attitude, the well-defined career opportunities, and the practical training I've found here push my potential to the limit. I believe in succeeding on my own merit.... I also think it's smart to have help."

During an individual's first five years as a consultant, he/she will receive nearly 800 hours of formal training, an investment in human resources worth approximately $32,000. At the individual level, the emphasis is to provide both formal classroom training along with carefully chosen on-the-job experiences. Early job assignments cross business and technical areas, allowing new staff to discover interests and abilities. Training is used to support staff as they move up in levels of responsibility and as they broaden their skills. Opportunities for growth are constantly made available as people move from staff consultant to senior consultant, to manager, and, potentially, to associate partner and partner.

The Andersen Worldwide Organization considers itself an established team, which takes great pride in the skills and abilities of its members. Part of the culture reinforced by training and work teams is the ability to pull from many resources to complete a job effectively. One junior staff member notes that "working with and as a team is extremely important here. If you challenge yourself as an individual and pull together as a team, you can get any job accomplished." This sense of team membership is extended through the use of a counselor (or mentor) program for new employees. An executive level member of the organization is immediately assigned to each new hire. This "counselor" serves as a sounding board throughout the individuals career—offering advice on how best to achieve goals, providing performance feedback, and just listening.

The Andersen companies clearly believe that the skills of their people are the lifeblood of their organization. Here, training is not just a first-year proposition. The firm has developed lifelong training, tailored to the individual's interests and to the needs of his or her clients. Although the emphasis may change from basic skills to advanced technical training, the goal remains to achieve superior performance.

Patricia A. Galagan, "Training Keeps the Cutting Edge Sharp for the Andersen Companies." *Training and Development Journal*, January 1993, 30–35; Andersen Consulting, *Your Career and Professional Development*, Arthur Andersen & Co., S.C., 1991; "Training Counts," *New Accountant*, September 1991.

DISCUSSION QUESTIONS

1. In what ways has Arthur Andersen & Co. used the training function to meet its competitive challenges? Why is training so important to the success of this organization?

2. As a new recruit to either side of the Andersen businesses, what would your expectations be regarding career development opportunities? How might this play a role in the success of their recruiting programs?

3. Evaluate the counselor (or mentor) program concept that Arthur Andersen uses with new entry level employees. What benefits may be associated with such a program?

4. It is stated in the case that during initial training sessions, work days may be as long as 12 hours. In many of the large accounting/consulting firms, long work days are the norm. What does this communicate about corporate culture in these firms? What personal characteristics might fit such a culture? What costs and benefits may be associated with this practice?

5. Andersen executives believe that assuring culturally diverse groups of trainees in their programs leads to more effective international business efforts. In what ways can this practice enhance their international operations?

6. Why is the practice of evaluating and justifying training programs important to the credibility of, and management support for, the Andersen professional development programs?

COMPENSATING HUMAN RESOURCES

In the preceding parts of the book, we have seen that the employment relationship is based on an exchange between employees and companies. Employees use their skills and knowledge to help the company reach productivity and quality goals and develop innovative products and services. To gain a competitive advantage, companies have to provide employees with a safe working environment, training and development opportunities, work design that maximizes employee satisfaction and productivity, and policies that help employees balance work and non-work activities.

Compensation and benefits also play an important role in motivating employees, rewarding them for their contributions, and attracting new employees to join the company. Part V discusses three

components of compensation and benefits. Chapter 15, "Pay Structure Decisions," describes different approaches for establishing pay rates for jobs. Employees often evaluate the acceptability of their pay by comparing it with what other employees earn both inside and outside the company. The chapter discusses pay surveys and job evaluation, two methods managers should use to determine the value of jobs. The chapter also discusses the importance of labor market and produce forces in determining the company's compensation strategy, new types of pay structures (such as skill-based pay), and the similarities and differences between U.S. and other countries' pay structures.

Chapter 16, "Recognizing Individual Contributions with Pay," focuses on how to recognize the contributions that individual employees make to the success of the company. Agency theory, reinforcement theory, and expectancy theory are described and used to explain the potential influence of reward programs on employees' performance. Merit pay, profit sharing, gainsharing programs, and executive pay are discussed. The link between the company's business strategy and the program chosen to reward individuals is emphasized.

In Chapter 17, "Employee Benefits," attention is shifted from cash to noncash compensation, such as health care, paid time off, and retirement programs. The cost of benefits, particularly health care benefits, has risen dramatically in the last 20 years. As a result, the chapter emphasizes how companies might control benefit costs while ensuring that the quality of their work force is not compromised. The chapter discusses the major provisions of benefit programs, the reasons for increased benefit costs, and legal constraints that affect how benefit programs are designed and administered. The importance of effectively communicating the value of benefits to employees is emphasized. Benefit plans for U.S. employees are compared with those for employees in other countries.

15

PAY STRUCTURE DECISIONS

Objectives

After reading this chapter, you should be able to:

1. List the major decision areas and concepts in employee compensation management.
2. Describe the major administrative tools used to manage employee compensation.
3. Explain the importance of competitive labor-market and product-market forces in compensation decisions.
4. Explain the importance of process issues such as communication in compensation management.
5. Describe new developments in the design of pay structures.
6. Explain where the United States stands from an international perspective on pay issues.
7. Explain the reasons for the controversy over executive pay.
8. Describe the regulatory framework for employee compensation.

Reducing Employment to Cut Labor Costs

International Business Machines has reduced employment from a peak of 403,000 in 1986 to 301,500 in 1992, and projects a decrease to 225,000 in 1994. General Motors plans to cut employment by 74,000 by the mid-1990s. Compaq Computer, GTE Corporation, and Du Pont have also conducted or plan to carry out significant work-force reductions. More than 85 percent of the Fortune 1000 companies downsized white-collar employment between 1987 and 1991. Why?

First, employees are expensive. Employment expenses account for 30 to 80 percent of general and administrative costs in most companies. Therefore, to sell automobiles, computers, or telecommunications services at a competitive price, employment costs, relative to those of competing companies, need to be kept under control. When demand for products declines, pressure to cut employment costs increases further. Second, companies like General Electric have sought to reduce bureaucracy and enhance the timeliness and quality of decisions at a time of constant change by cutting what were deemed unnecessary levels of management and by broadening the responsibilities of managers who remain.

Still, cost control and reducing bureaucracy are not the only considerations in managing employee compensation. As Chapter 10 suggests, employee compensation levels must be high enough to attract and retain employees of sufficient quantity and quality. Employees must also believe they are paid well enough to compensate for the added responsibility (and perhaps stress) that comes with "doing more with less." Indeed, many organizations have reduced employee compensation costs by keeping employment as low as possible, while giving the employees who remain the opportunity for very high pay if they and the organization perform well.

In addition, as discussed in Chapter 14, the reactions of employees left behind after employment reductions may depend on how fairly the pain is shared in the organization. Employees may question the fairness of layoffs, pay freezes, and pay cuts if top executives are simultaneously earning record compensation. Critics suggest that giving multimillion-dollar paychecks to executives while employees lose their jobs is to human resource management what "Imelda Marcos's 3,000 pairs of shoes were to the Philippines." Clearly, pay decisions can generate strong reactions.

SOURCES: S. Drake, "Building a New Corporate Order," *Human Resource Executive*, 20; Bureau of National Affairs, "Computer Firms Announce Cutbacks," *Daily Labor Report*, October 9, 1992, A12; L. Hooper, "IBM Will Raise Number of Jobs It Plans to Trim," *The Wall Street Journal*, February 11, 1993, A3; W. F. Cascio, "Downsizing: What Do We Know? What Have We Learned?" *Academy of Management Executive* 7 (1993): 95–104; Bureau of National Affairs, "More Employers Rewarding Workers Based on Performance Criteria, Survey Shows," *Daily Labor Report*, September 3, 1992, A12; S. Lohr, "Amid Layoffs and the Recession, Executives' Pay is under Scrutiny," *New York Times*, January 20, 1992, D1ff. F. Flaherty, "Big Blue Will Make Deep Cuts—But Precisely Where?" *New York Times*, August 1, 1993, Sec. 3, p. 2.

INTRODUCTION

The preceding discussion suggests that pay, or employee compensation, is a central part of the employment relationship. From the employees' point of view, policies having to do with wages, salaries, and other earnings have a major impact on their overall income and thus their standard of living. Both the level of pay and how fair it seems compared with others' pay is important. Pay is also often considered a sign of status and success. Employees attach great importance to pay decisions when they evaluate their relationship with the organization. Therefore, pay decisions must be carefully managed and communicated.

From the employer's point of view, pay is a powerful tool for furthering the organization's strategic goals. First, pay has a major impact on employee attitudes and behaviors. It influences the kind of employees who are attracted to (and remain with) the organization, and it can be a powerful tool for aligning current employees' interests with those of the broader organization. Second, employee compensation is typically a significant organizational cost and thus requires close scrutiny.

Pay decisions can be broken into two major areas: **pay structure** and individual pay. In this chapter, we focus on pay structure, which in turn entails a consideration of pay level and job structure. **Pay level** is defined here as the average pay (including wages, salaries, bonuses) of jobs in an organization. (Benefits could also be included, but these are discussed separately in Chapter 17.) **Job structure** refers to the relative pay of jobs in an organization. Consider the same two jobs in two different organizations. In Organization 1, jobs A and B are paid an annual average compensation of $40,000 and $60,000, respectively. In Organization 2, the pay rates are $45,000 and $55,000, respectively. Organizations 1 and 2 have the same pay level ($50,000), but the job structures (relative rates of pay) differ.

Both pay level and job structure are characteristics of organizations and reflect decisions about jobs rather than about individual employees. In other words, this chapter's focus is on why and how organizations attach pay policies to jobs. In the next chapter, we look within jobs to discuss the different approaches that can be used to determine the pay of individual employees as well as the advantages and disadvantages of these different approaches.

Why is the focus on jobs in developing a pay structure? As the number of employees in an organization increases, so too does the number of human resource management decisions. In determining compensation, for example, each employee must be assigned a rate of pay that is acceptable in terms of external, internal, and individual equity (defined later) and in terms of the employer's cost. Although each employee is unique and thus requires some degree of individualized treatment, standardizing the treatment of similar employees (e.g., those with similar jobs) can help greatly to make compensation administration and decision making more manageable and more equitable. Thus, pay policies are often attached to particular jobs rather than tailored entirely to individual employees.

EQUITY THEORY AND FAIRNESS

In discussing the consequences of pay decisions, it is useful to keep in mind that employees often evaluate their pay relative to that of other employees. Equity theory suggests that people evaluate the fairness of their situations by comparing them with those of other people.[1] According to the theory, a person (*P*) compares his or her own ratio of perceived outcomes *O* (e.g., pay, benefits, working conditions) to perceived inputs, *I* (e.g., effort, ability, experience) to the ratio of a comparison other (*O*).

$$O_p/I_p <, >, \text{ or } = O_O/I_O?$$

If *P*'s ratio (O_p/I_p) is smaller than the comparison other's ratio (O_o/I_o), underreward inequity results. If *P*'s ratio is larger, overreward inequity results, although evidence suggests that this type of inequity is less likely to occur and less likely to be sustained because *P* may rationalize the situation by reevaluating his or her outcomes less favorably or inputs (i.e., self-worth) more favorably.[2]

The consequences of *P*'s comparisons depend on whether equity is perceived. If equity is perceived, no change is expected in *P*'s attitudes or behavior. In contrast, perceived inequity may cause *P* to restore equity. Some ways of restoring equity are counterproductive, including: (1) reducing one's own inputs (e.g., not working as hard), (2) increasing one's outcomes (e.g., theft), (3) leaving the situation that generates perceived inequity (e.g., leaving the organization or refusing to work or cooperate with employees who are perceived as overrewarded).

Equity theory's main implication for managing employee compensation is that to an important extent, employees evaluate their pay by comparing it with what others get paid, and their work attitudes and behaviors are influenced by such comparisons. Another implication is that employee *perceptions* are what determine their evaluation. The fact that management believes its employees are paid well compared with those of other companies does not necessarily translate into employees' beliefs. Employees may have different information or make different comparisons than management.

Three types of employee social comparisons of pay are especially relevant in making pay-level and job-structure decisions (see Table 15.1). First, *external* pay comparisons focus on what employees in other organizations are paid for doing the same general job. Such comparisons are likely to influence the decisions of applicants to accept job offers as well as the attitudes and decisions of employees about whether to stay with an organization or take a job elsewhere (see Chapters 8 and 10). The organization's choice of pay level influences its employees' external pay comparisons and their consequences. A market pay survey is the major administrative tool organizations use in choosing a pay level.

Second, *internal* pay comparisons focus on what employees within the same organization, but in different jobs, are paid. Employees make comparisons with lower-level jobs, jobs at the same level (but perhaps in different skill areas or product divisions), and jobs at higher levels. Indeed, the opening vignette discussed comparisons between employees in lower-paying jobs and those in the executive suite. These comparisons may influence general attitudes of employees; their willingness to transfer to other jobs within the organization; their willingness to accept promotions; their

TABLE 15.1

Pay Structure Concepts and Consequences

Pay Structure Decision Area	Administrative Tool	Focus of Employee Pay Comparisons	Consequences of Equity Perceptions
Pay level	Market pay surveys	External	External employee movement (attraction and retention of quality employees); labor costs; employee attitudes
Job structure	Job evaluation	Internal	Internal employee movement (promotion, transfer, job rotation); cooperation between employees; employee attitudes

inclination to cooperate across jobs, functional areas, or product groups; and their commitment to the organization. The organization's choice of job structure influences its employees' internal comparisons and their consequences. Job evaluation is the major administrative tool organizations use to design job structures.

Third, employees make internal pay comparisons with others performing the same job. Such comparisons are most relevant to the following chapter, which focuses on using pay to recognize individual contributions and differences.

We now turn to ways to choose and develop pay levels and pay structures, the consequences of such choices, and the ways two administrative tools, market pay surveys and job evaluation, help in making pay decisions.

DEVELOPING PAY LEVELS

Market Pressures

Any organization faces two important competitive market challenges in deciding what to pay its employees: product-market competition and labor-market competition.

Product-Market Competition. First, organizations must compete effectively in the product market. In other words, they must be able to sell their goods and services at a quantity and price that will bring a sufficient return on their investment. Organizations compete on multiple dimensions (e.g., quality, service), and price is one of the most important dimensions. An important influence on price is the cost of production.

An organization that has higher labor costs than its product-market competitors will have to charge higher average prices for products of similar quality. Thus, for example, if labor costs are 30 percent of revenues at Company A and Company B, but Company A has labor costs that are 20 percent higher than those of Company B, we would expect Company A to have product prices that are higher by (.30 x .20) = 6 percent. At some point, the higher price charged by Company A will contribute to a loss of its business to competing companies with lower prices (like Company B). One study, for example, found that in 1991 the wage and benefit cost to produce a small car was approximately $1,700 for Ford Motor, $1,800 for Chrysler, and $2,400 for General Motors.[3] Thus, if all other costs were equal, General Motors would have to sell the same quality car for $600 to $700 more than would Ford or Chrysler.

Therefore, *product-market competition* places an *upper bound* on labor costs and compensation. This upper bound is more constrictive when labor costs are a larger share of total costs and when demand for the product is affected by changes in price (i.e., demand is *elastic*). Although costs are only one part of the competitive equation (productivity is just as important), higher costs may result in a loss of business. In the absence of clear evidence on productivity differences, costs need to be closely monitored.

What components make up labor costs? A major component is the average cost per employee. This is made up of both direct payments (such as wages, salaries, and bonuses) and indirect payments (such as health insurance, Social Security, unemployment compensation, and so forth). A second major component of labor cost is the staffing level (i.e., number of employees). Not surprisingly, financially troubled organizations often seek to cut costs by focusing on one or both components. Staff reductions, hiring freezes, wages and salary freezes, and sharing benefits costs with employees are several ways of enhancing the organization's competitive position in the product market.

Labor-Market Competition.   A second important competitive market challenge is *labor-market competition*. Essentially, labor-market competition is the amount an organization must pay to compete against other companies that hire similar employees. These labor-market competitors typically include not only companies that have similar products but also those in different product markets that hire similar types of employees. If an organization is not competitive in the labor market, it will fail to attract and retain employees of sufficient numbers and quality. For example, even if a computer manufacturer offers newly graduated electrical engineers the same pay as other computer manufacturers, if automobile manufacturers and other labor-market competitors offer salaries $5,000 higher, the computer company may not be able to hire enough qualified electrical engineers. Labor-market competition places a *lower bound* on pay levels.

Employees as a Resource

Because organizations have to compete in the labor market, they should consider their employees not just as a cost but as a resource in which the organization has invested and from which it expects valuable returns. Although controlling costs has a direct effect on an organization's ability to compete in the product market, the organization's competitive position can be compromised if costs are kept low at the expense of employee productivity and quality. Having higher labor costs than your competitors is not necessarily bad if you also have the best and most effective work force, one that produces more products of better quality.

Pay policies and programs are one of the most important human resource tools for encouraging desired employee behaviors and discouraging undesired behaviors. Therefore, they must be evaluated, not just in terms of costs, but in terms of what sort of returns they generate—how they attract, retain, and motivate a high-quality work force. For example, if the average revenue per employee in Company A is 20 percent higher than in Company B, it may not be important that the average pay in Company A is 10 percent higher than in Company B.

Deciding What to Pay

Although organizations face important external labor- and product-market pressures in setting their pay levels, a range of discretion remains.[4] How large the range is depends on the particular competitive environment the organization faces. Where the range is broad, an important strategic decision is whether to pay above, at, or below the market average. The advantage of paying above the market average is the ability to attract and retain the top talent available, which can translate into a highly effective and productive work force. The disadvantage, however, is the added cost.

So, under what circumstances do the benefits of higher pay outweigh the higher costs? According to **efficiency wage theory**, one circumstance is when organizations have technologies or structures that depend on highly skilled employees. For example, organizations that emphasize decentralized decision making may need higher-caliber employees. Another circumstance where higher pay may be warranted is when an organization has difficulties observing and monitoring its employees' performance. It may therefore wish to provide an above-market pay rate to ensure their incentive to put forth maximum effort. The theory is that employees who are paid more than they would be paid elsewhere will be reluctant to "shirk" (i.e., not work hard) because they wish to retain their good job.[5]

Market Pay Surveys

As mentioned in Chapter 1, total quality management emphasizes the key importance of *benchmarking*, a procedure in which an organization compares its own practices against those of the competition. This notion is relevant in compensation management. Benchmarking against product-market and labor-market competitors is typically accomplished through the use of one or more pay surveys, which provide information on going rates of pay among competing organizations.

The use of pay surveys requires answers to several important questions:[6]

1. Which employers should be included in the survey? Ideally, they would be the key labor market and product market competitors.

2. Which jobs are included in the survey? Because only a sample of jobs is ordinarily used, care must be taken that the jobs are representative in terms of level, functional area, and product market. Also, the job content must be sufficiently similar.

3. If multiple surveys are used, how are all the rates of pay weighted and combined? Organizations often have to weight and combine pay rates because different surveys are often tailored toward particular employee groups (labor markets) or product markets. The organization must decide how much relative weight to give to its labor- and product-market competitors in setting pay.

Several factors come into play when deciding how to combine surveys.[7] Product-market comparisons that focus on labor costs are likely to deserve greater weight when (1) labor costs represent a large share of total costs, (2) product demand is elastic (i.e., it changes in response to product price changes), (3) the supply of labor is inelastic, and (4) employee skills are specific to the product market (and will remain so). In contrast, labor-market comparisons may be more important when (1) attracting and retaining qualified employees is difficult and (2) the costs (administrative, disruption, etc.) of recruiting replacements are high.

As this discussion suggests, knowing what other organizations are paying is only one part of the story. It is also necessary to know what those organizations are getting in return for their investment in employees. To find that out, some organizations examine ratios such as revenues/employees and revenues/labor cost. The first ratio includes the staffing component of employee cost but not the average cost per employee. The second ratio, however, includes both. Note that comparing these ratios across organizations requires caution. For example, different industries rely on different resources (e.g., labor and capital). So, comparing the ratio of revenues to labor costs of a petroleum company (capital intensive, high ratio) to a bank (labor intensive, low ratio) would be like comparing apples and oranges. But within industries, such comparisons can be useful. Besides revenues, other return-on-investment data might include product quality, customer satisfaction, and potential work-force quality (e.g., average education levels).

Rate Ranges.   As the preceding discussion suggests, obtaining a single "going rate" of market pay is a complex task that involves a number of subjective decisions—it is both an art and a science. Once a market rate has been chosen, how is it incorporated into the pay structure? Typically—especially for white-collar jobs—it is used for setting the midpoint of pay-rate ranges

TABLE 15.2   Frequency and Size of Rate Ranges, Selected Jobs

Job	Percentage Using Rate Ranges[a]	Percentage by which Highest-Paid Worker Exceeded Lowest-Paid Worker in Same Job and Establishment (Where Rate Range Is Used)
Computer systems analyst	99%	30%
Computer programmer	95	32
Drafter	86	30
Forklift operator	38	15
Truck driver, tractor trailer	30	14

SOURCE: Bureau of Labor Statistics, *Monthly Labor Review,* December 1984 and March 1985.

[a] Cases in which there are at least two employees in the job.

for either jobs or pay grades (discussed next). Market-survey data are also often collected on minimum and maximum rates of pay as well. The use of ranges permits a company to recognize differences in employee performance, seniority, training, and so forth in setting individual pay (discussed in the next chapter). For some blue-collar jobs, however, particularly those covered by collective-bargaining contracts, there may be a single rate of pay for all employees within the job.

Table 15.2 presents some selected Bureau of Labor Statistics data on the use of rate ranges and their size. Note that the professional and technical occupations (computer systems analyst, computer programmer, drafter) almost always make use of rate ranges, whereas the blue-collar jobs (truck driver, forklift operator) often work under single-rate arrangements. Even where rate ranges exist, the difference in pay between the lowest- and highest-paid workers is smaller for the blue-collar positions. The less frequent use of ranges and the smaller pay differences probably reflect both the influence of unionization, which often strives for equal pay within jobs, and the fact that performance differences are of greater consequence at higher job levels.

Key Jobs and Nonkey Jobs.   In using pay surveys, it is necessary to make a distinction between two general types of jobs: **key jobs** (or benchmark jobs) and **nonkey jobs**. Key jobs have relatively stable content and—perhaps most important—are common to many organizations. Therefore, it is possible to obtain market pay survey data on them. Note, however, that to avoid too much of an administrative burden, organizations may not gather market pay data on all such jobs. In contrast to key jobs, nonkey jobs are, to an important extent, unique to organizations; thus, by definition, they cannot be directly valued or compared through the use of market surveys. Therefore, they are treated differently in the pay-setting process.

DEVELOPING A JOB STRUCTURE

Although external comparisons of the sort we have been discussing are important, employees also evaluate their pay using internal comparisons. So, for example, a vice-president of marketing may expect to be paid roughly the same amount as a vice-president of information systems because they are at the same organizational level, with similar levels of responsibility and similar impacts on the organization's performance. A job structure can be defined as the relative worth of various jobs in the organization, based on these types of internal comparisons. We now turn to a discussion of how such decisions are made.

Job Evaluation

One typical way of measuring job worth is to perform an administrative procedure called **job evaluation**. A job-evaluation system is composed of **compensable factors** and a weighting scheme based on the importance of each compensable factor to the organization. Simply stated, compensable factors are the characteristics of jobs that an organization values and chooses to pay for. These characteristics include job complexity, working conditions, required education, required experience, responsibility, and so on. Most job-evaluation systems use several compensable factors. Job analysis (discussed in Chapter 6) provides basic descriptive information on job attributes, and the job-evaluation process assigns a value to these compensable factors.

Scores can be generated in a variety of ways, but they typically include input from a number of people. A job-evaluation committee is commonly used to generate ratings. Although there are numerous ways to evaluate jobs, the most widely used is the point-factor system, which yields job-evaluation points for each compensable factor.[8]

The Point-Factor System.   After generating scores for each compensable factor on each job, job evaluators often apply a weighting scheme to account for the differing importance of the compensable factors to the organization. Weights can be generated in two ways. First, a priori weights can be assigned, which means factors are weighted using expert judgments about the importance of each compensable factor. Second, weights can be derived empirically based on how important each factor seems to be in determining pay in the labor market. (Statistical methods such as multiple regression can be used for this purpose.) For the sake of simplicity, we assume in the fol-

TABLE 15.3   Example of a Three-Factor Job-Evaluation System

| | Compensable Factors | | | |
Job Title	Experience	Education	Complexity	Total
Computer operator	40	30	40	110
Computer programmer	40	50	65	155
Systems analyst	65	60	85	210

lowing example that equal a priori weights are chosen, which means that the scores on the compensable factors can be simply summed.

Table 15.3 shows an example of a three-factor job-evaluation system applied to three jobs. Note that the jobs differ in the levels of experience, education, and complexity required. Summing the scores on the three compensable factors provides an internally oriented assessment of relative job worth in the organization. In a sense, the computer programmer job is worth 41 percent (155/110 – 1) more than the computer operator job, and the systems analyst job is worth 91 percent (210/110 – 1) more than the computer operator job. Whatever pay level is chosen (based on benchmarking and competitive strategy), we would expect the pay differentials to be somewhat similar to these percentages. The internal job-evaluation and external survey-based measures of worth can, however, diverge.

Developing a Pay Structure

In the example provided in Table 15.4, there are 15 jobs, 10 of which are key jobs. For these key jobs, both pay-survey and job-evaluation data are available. For the five nonkey jobs, by definition, no survey data are available, only job-evaluation information. Note that, for simplicity's sake, we work with data from only two pay surveys and we use a weighted average that gives twice as much weight to survey 1. Also, our example works with a single structure. Many organizations have multiple structures that correspond to different job families (e.g., clerical, technical, professional) or product divisions.

How are the data in Table 15.4 combined to develop a pay structure? First, it is important to note that both internal and external comparisons must be considered in making compensation decisions. However, because the pay structures suggested by internal and external comparisons do not necessarily converge, employers must carefully balance them. Studies suggest that employers may differ significantly in the degree to which they place priority on internal- or external-comparison data in developing pay structures.[9]

TABLE 15.4   Job Evaluation and Pay Survey Data

Job	Key Job?	Job Title	Job Evaluation	Survey #1 (S1)	Survey #2 (S2)	Survey Composite (2/3*S1+1/3*S2)
A	y	Computer operator	110	$1,750	$1,505	$1,668
B	y	Engineering tech I	115	$1,918	$1,659	$1,832
C	y	Computer programmer	155	$2,536	$2,251	$2,441
D	n	Engineering tech II	165			
E	n	Compensation analyst	170			
F	y	Accountant	190	$3,142	$2,695	$2,993
G	y	Systems analyst	210	$3,717	$3,351	$3,595
H	n	Computer programmer —senior	225			
I	y	Director of personnel	245	$4,332	$3,918	$4,194
J	y	Accountant—senior	255	$4,526	$3,713	$4,255
K	y	Systems analyst—senior	270	$5,103	$4,915	$5,040
L	y	Industrial engineer	275	$4,779	$4,169	$4,576
M	n	Chief accountant	315			
N	y	Senior engineer	320	$6,110	$5,715	$5,978
O	n	Senior scientist	330			

SOURCE: Adapted from S. Rynes, B. Gerhart, G. T. Milkovich, and J. Boudreau, *Current Compensation Professional Institute* (Scottsdale, Ariz.: American Compensation Association, 1988).

At least three pay-setting approaches, which differ according to their relative emphasis on external or internal comparisons, can be identified.[10]

Market Survey Data.   The approach with the greatest emphasis on external comparisons (i.e., market-survey data) is achieved by directly basing pay on market surveys that cover as many key jobs as possible. For example, the rate of pay for job A in Table 15.5 would be $1,668; for job B, $1,832; and for job C, $2,441. For nonkey jobs (jobs D, E, H, M, and O), however, pay-survey information is not available, and one must proceed differently. Basically, one develops a market **pay-policy line** based on the key jobs (for which there are both job-evaluation and market-pay-survey data available). As Figure 15.1 shows, the data can be plotted with a line of best fit estimated. This line can be generated using a statistical procedure (regression analysis)*. Doing so yields the following equation: –$575 + $19.73 × Job evaluation points. In other words, the predicted monthly salary (based on fitting a line to the key job data) is obtained by plugging the number of job-

---

* Regression analysis minimizes the squared distances of the data points from the policy line.

TABLE 15.5   Pay Midpoints under Different Approaches

Job	Key Job?	Job Title	Job Evaluation	Pay Midpoints (1) Survey+Policy	(2) Policy	(3) Grades
A	y	Computer Operator	110	$1,668	$1,595	$1,891
B	y	Engineering Tech I	115	$1,832	$1,694	$1,891
C	y	Computer Programmer	155	$2,441	$2,483	$2,878
D	n	Engineering Tech II	165	$2,681	$2,681	$2,878
E	n	Compensation Analyst	170	$2,779	$2,779	$2,878
F	y	Accountant	190	$2,993	$3,174	$2,878
G	y	Systems Analyst	210	$3,595	$3,568	$3,864
H	n	Computer Programmer—Senior	225	$3,864	$3,864	$3,864
I	y	Director of Personnel	245	$4,194	$4,259	$3,864
J	y	Accountant—Senior	255	$4,255	$4,456	$4,851
K	y	Systems Analyst—Senior	270	$5,040	$4,752	$4,851
L	y	Industrial Engineer	275	$4,576	$4,851	$4,851
M	n	Chief Accountant	315	$5,640	$5,640	$5,837
N	y	Senior Engineer	320	$5,978	$5,739	$5,837
O	n	Senior Scientist	330	$5,936	$5,936	$5,837

SOURCE: Adapted from S. Rynes, B. Gerhart, G. T. Milkovich, and J. Boudreau, *Current Compensation Professional Institute* (Scottsdale, Ariz.: American Compensation Association, 1988).

evaluation points into this equation. Thus, for example, job D, a nonkey job, would have a predicted monthly salary of –$575 + $19.73 × 165 = $2,681.

As Figure 15.1 also indicates, it is not necessary to fit a straight line to the job-evaluation and pay-survey data. In some cases, a pay structure that provides increasing monetary rewards to higher-level jobs may be more consistent with the organization's goals or with the external market. For example, nonlinearity may be more appropriate if higher-level jobs are especially valuable to organizations and the talent to perform such jobs is rare. The curvilinear function in Figure 15.1 is described by the following equation:

Natural logarithm of pay = $6.84 + .006 × Job-evaluation points.

Pay-Policy Line.   A second pay-setting approach that combines information from external and internal comparisons is to use the pay-policy line to derive pay rates for both key and nonkey jobs. This approach differs from the first approach in that actual market rates are no longer used for key jobs. This introduces a greater degree of internal consistency into the structure because the pay of all the jobs is directly linked to the number of job-evaluation points.

FIGURE 15.1   Pay Policy Lines, Linear and Natural Logarithmic Functions

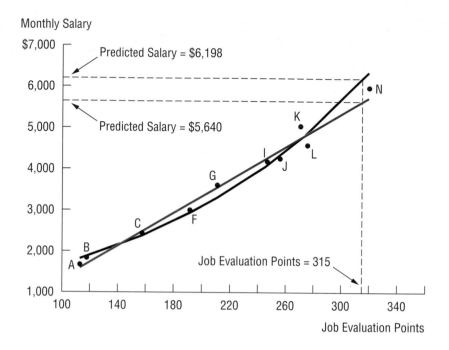

Pay Grades.   A third approach is to group jobs into a smaller number of pay classes or **pay grades**. Table 15.6 (see also Table 15.5, last column), for example, demonstrates one possibility: a five-grade structure. Each job within a grade would be assigned the same midpoint, minimum, and maximum. The advantage of this approach is that the administrative burden of setting separate rates of pay for hundreds (even thousands) of different jobs is reduced. It also permits greater flexibility in moving employees from job to job without raising concerns about, for example, going from a job having 230 job-evaluation points to a job with 215 job-evaluation points. What might look like a demotion in a completely job-based system is often a non-issue in a grade-based system. Note that the **range spread** (the distance between the minimum and maximum) is larger at higher levels, in recognition of the fact that performance differences are likely to have more impact on the organization at higher job levels (see Figure 15.2).

The disadvantage of using grades is that some jobs will be underpaid and others overpaid. For example, job C and job F both fall within the same grade. The midpoint for job C under a grade system is $2,878 per month, or about $400 more than under the two alternative pay-setting approaches. Obviously, this will contribute to higher labor costs and potential difficulties in competing in the product market. Unless there is an expected return to this increased cost, the approach is questionable. Job F, on the other hand,

TABLE 15.6   Sample Pay-Grade Structure

	Job-Evaluation Points		Monthly Pay Rate		
Pay Grade	Minimum	Maximum	Minimum	Midpoint	Maximum
1	100	150	$1,513	$1,891	$2,270
2	150	200	$2,302	$2,878	$3,453
3	200	250	$3,092	$3,864	$4,637
4	250	300	$3,881	$4,851	$5,821
5	300	350	$4,670	$5,837	$7,005

FIGURE 15.2   Sample Pay-Grade Structure

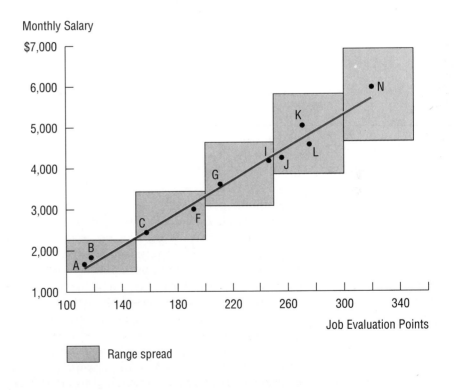

is paid between $100 and $300 less per month under the grades system than it would be otherwise. Therefore, the company may find it more difficult to compete in the labor market.

Conflicts between Market Pay Surveys and Job Evaluation

An examination of Table 15.5 suggests that the relative worth of jobs is quite similar overall, whether based on job-evaluation or pay-survey data. However, some inconsistencies typically arise, and these are usually indicated by jobs whose average survey pay is either below or above the pay-policy line by a significant amount. The closest case in Table 15.5 is job L, for which the average pay falls below the policy line. One possible explanation is that a relatively plentiful supply of people in the labor market are capable of performing this job, so the pay needed to attract and retain them is lower than would be expected given the job-evaluation points. Another kind of inconsistency occurs when market surveys show that a job is paid higher than the policy line (e.g., job K). Again, this may be a reflection of relative supply and demand, in this case resulting in pay being driven higher.

How are conflicts between external and internal comparisons resolved, and what are the consequences? The example of the vice-presidents of marketing and information processing may help illustrate the type of choice faced. The marketing VP job may receive the same number of job-evaluation points, but market-survey data may indicate that it typically pays less than the information processing VP job, perhaps because of tighter supply for the latter. Does the organization pay based on the market survey (external comparison) or on the job-evaluation points (internal comparison)?

Emphasizing the internal comparison would suggest paying the two VPs the same. In doing so, however, either the VP of marketing would be "overpaid" or the VP of information processing would be "underpaid." The former drives up labor costs (product-market problems); the latter may make it difficult to attract and retain a quality VP of information processing (labor-market problems).

Another consideration has to do with the strategy of the organization. In some organizations (e.g., Pepsi, Nike), the marketing function is critical to success. Thus, even though the market for marketing VPs is lower than that for information processing VPs, an organization may choose to be a pay leader for the marketing position (e.g., pay at the 90th percentile) but only meet the market for the information systems position (e.g., pay at the 50th percentile). In other words, designing a pay structure requires careful consideration of which positions are most central to dealing with critical environmental challenges and opportunities in reaching the organization's goals.[11]

What about emphasizing external comparisons? Two potential problems arise. First, the VP of marketing may be dissatisfied because he or she expects a job of similar rank and responsibility to be paid similarly. Second, it becomes difficult to rotate people through different VP positions (e.g., as a training and development tool), because going to the marketing VP position might appear as a demotion to the VP of information processing.

There is no one right solution to such dilemmas. Each organization must decide which objectives are most essential and choose the appropriate strategy. However, there seems to be a growing sentiment that external comparisons deserve greater weight because organizations are finding it increasingly difficult to ignore market competitive pressures.[12]

Monitoring Compensation Costs

Pay structure influences compensation costs in a number of ways. Most obviously, the pay level at which the structure is pegged has an influence on these costs. However, this is only part of the story. The pay structure represents the organization's intended policy, but actual practice may not coincide with it. Take, for example, the pay-grade structure presented earlier. The midpoint for grade 1 is $1,891, and the midpoint for grade 2 is $2,878. Now, consider the data on a group of individual employees, which is presented in Table 15.7. One frequently used index of the correspondence between actual and intended pay is the **compa-ratio**, computed as follows:

Compa-ratio = Actual average pay for grade/pay midpoint for grade

The compa-ratio provides a direct assessment of the degree to which actual pay is consistent with the pay policy. A compa-ratio less than one suggests that actual pay is lagging behind the policy, whereas a compa-ratio greater than one indicates that pay (and costs) exceeds that of the policy. Although there may be good reasons for compa-ratios to differ from one, managers should also consider whether the pay structure is allowing costs to get out of control.

THE IMPORTANCE OF PROCESS: COMMUNICATION AND PARTICIPATION ISSUES

Compensation management has been criticized for following the simplistic belief that "if the right technology can be developed, the right answers will be found."[13] In reality, however, any given pay decision is rarely obvious to the diverse groups that make up organizations, regardless of the decision's technical merit or basis in theory. Of course, it is important when changing pay practices to decide which program or combination of programs makes most sense, but it also matters *how* such decisions are made and how they are communicated.[14]

Participation

Employee participation in compensation decision making can take many forms. For example, employees may serve on task forces that are charged with recommending and designing a pay program. They may also be asked to help communicate and explain its rationale. This is particularly true in the case of job evaluation, as well as many of the programs discussed in the next chapter. To date, for what are perhaps obvious reasons, employee participation in pay-level decisions remains fairly rare.

It is important to distinguish between participation by those affected by policies and those who must actually implement the policies. Managers are in the latter group (and often in the former group at the same time). As in other areas of human resource management, line managers are typically the

TABLE 15.7   Compa-Ratios for Two Grades

Employee	Job	Pay	Midpoint	Compa-Ratio
	Grade 1			
1	Engineering Tech I	$2,000	$1,891	1.06
2	Computer Programmer	$1,800	$1,891	.95
3	Engineering Tech I	$2,200	$1,891	1.16
4	Engineering Tech I	$2,100	$1,891	1.11
				1.07
	Grade 2			
5	Computer Programmer	$3,400	$2,878	1.18
6	Accountant	$3,300	$2,878	1.14
7	Accountant	$3,200	$2,878	1.11
				1.15

people who are responsible for making policies work. Their intimate involvement in any change to existing pay practices is, of course, necessary.

Communication

An old philosophical question is: "If a tree falls in the forest and no one is there to hear it, does it make a sound?" In compensation management, an analogous question arises. If a new or improved pay program is a great idea in theory but no one understands how it works or why it is a great idea, is it really a great idea? The answer is probably no. For example, if an organization thinks that changing product-market pressures necessitate lower pay levels for the organization to compete, is it likely that employees will also see the need for this "obvious" solution? Probably not.

A dramatic example of the importance of communication was found in a study of how an organization communicated pay cuts to its employees and the effects on theft rates and perceived equity.[15] Two organization units received 15 percent across-the-board pay cuts. A third unit received no pay cut and served as a control group. The reasons for the pay cuts were communicated in different ways to the two pay-cut groups. In the "adequate explanation" pay-cut group, management provided a significant amount of information to explain its reasons for the pay cut and also expressed significant remorse. In contrast, the "inadequate explanation" group received much less information and no indication of remorse. The control group received no pay cut (and thus no explanation).

The control group and the two pay-cut groups began with the same theft rates and equity perceptions. After the pay cut, the theft rate was 54 percent higher in the adequate explanation group than in the control group.

But in the "inadequate explanation" condition, the theft rate was 141 percent higher than in the control group. In this case, communication had a large, independent effect on employees' attitudes and behaviors.

Communication is likely to have other important effects. We know, for example, that not only actual pay but the comparison standard influences employee attitudes.[16] Under two-tier wage plans, employees doing the same jobs are paid two different rates, depending on when they were hired. Moreover, the lower-paid employees do not ordinarily move into the higher-paying tier. Common sense might suggest that the lower-paid employees would be less satisfied. Not necessarily. In fact, a study by Peter Capelli and Peter Sherer found that the lower-paid employees were more satisfied on average.[17] Apparently, those in the lower tier used different (lower) comparison standards than those in the higher tier. The lower-tier employees compared their jobs to unemployment or lower-paying jobs they had managed to avoid. As a result, they were more satisfied, despite being paid less money for the same work. This finding does not mean that two-tier wage plans are necessarily a good idea. Indeed, they seem to be diminishing in number. Rather, consistent with equity theory, it shows that the way employees compare their pay with other jobs matters, and managers need to take this into consideration.

Managers play the most crucial communication role because of their day-to-day interactions with their employees. Therefore, they must be prepared to explain why the pay structure is designed as it is, and to judge whether employee concerns about the structure need to be addressed with changes to the structure. One common issue is deciding when a job needs to be reclassified because of substantial changes in its content. If an employee takes on more responsibility, he or she will often ask the manager for assistance in making the case for increased pay for the job.

CURRENT CHALLENGES

Problems with Job-based Pay Structures[18]

The approach taken in this chapter, that of defining pay structures in terms of jobs and their associated responsibilities, remains the most widely used in practice. However, job-based pay structures have a number of potential limitations.[19] First, they may encourage bureaucracy. The job description sets out specific tasks and activities for which the incumbent is responsible and, by implication, those for which the incumbent is not responsible. Although this facilitates performance evaluation and control by the manager, it can also encourage a lack of flexibility and a lack of initiative on the part of employees: "Why should I do that? It's not in my job description." Second, the structure's hierarchical nature reinforces a top-down decision-making and information flow and status differentials, which do not lend themselves to taking advantage of the skills and knowledge of those closest to production. Third, the bureaucracy required to generate and update job

TABLE 15.8   Example of Pay Bands

Traditional Structure		Banded Structure	
Grade	**Title**	**Band**	**Title**
14	Senior Accountant	6	Senior Accountant
12	Accountant III		
10	Accountant II	5	Accountant
8	Accountant I		

SOURCE: P. LeBlanc, *Perspectives in Total Compensation* 3, no. 3 (March 1992): 1–6. Used with permission of the National Practice Director, Sibson & Company, Inc.

descriptions and job evaluations can become a barrier to change because wholesale changes to job descriptions can involve a tremendous amount of time and cost. Fourth, the job-based pay structure may not reward desired behaviors, particularly in a rapidly changing environment where the knowledge, skills, and abilities needed yesterday may not be very helpful today and tomorrow. Fifth, the emphasis on job levels and status differentials encourages promotion-seeking behavior but may discourage lateral employee movement because employees are reluctant to accept jobs that are not promotions or that appear to be steps down.

Responses to Problems with Job-based Pay Structures

Delayering and Banding.   In response to the problems caused by job-based pay structures, some organizations are **delayering**, or reducing the number of job levels. For example, General Electric replaced its 29 pay grades with 5 grades. Pay grades 8 through 11, for instance, were combined into one pay band ranging from $33,000 to $74,000, giving GE considerably more flexibility in job assignments and in assigning merit increases.[20] In the automobile industry, Saturn, the new division of General Motors, has only a few job classifications, in sharp contrast to other U.S. automobile manufacturers, which average 67, but very similar to Japanese manufacturers, which average 12. Table 15.8 shows how banding might work for a small sample of jobs.[21]

One possible consequence of delayering and banding is a reduced opportunity for promotion. Therefore, organizations need to consider what they will offer employees instead. Continuous training, greater responsibility, and pay tied to seniority or performance are some of the approaches being used (see the "Competing through Technology and Structure" box).[22] In addition, to the extent that there are separate ranges within bands, the new structure may not represent as dramatic a change as it might appear. These distinctions can easily become just as entrenched as they were under the old system.

Technology & Structure

SKILL-BASED PAY AND EMPOWERMENT AT GENERAL ELECTRIC APPLIANCES

Shoshanna Zuboff, author of *In the Age of the Smart Machine,* argues that in organizations of the future, success will depend on management's ability to create an environment that fosters the capacity to improve and innovate. To do so, the fundamental focus of management will need to shift from the principle of control to the principle of continuous learning. Many organizations have found that changes in the pay structure are essential to achieving this refocusing. The General Electric plant in Bayamon, Puerto Rico, makes surge protectors that protect power stations and power lines from lightning strikes. The facility employs 172 hourly workers, 15 salaried "advisers," and the plant manager. There are no supervisors. A more traditional operation would have about twice as many salaried employees. The need for supervisors and white-collar staff is less because much of the decision making has been turned over to employee teams that meet weekly. Each team is responsible for a part of the plant's operation such as receiving, assembly, or shipping. The advisers assist the teams only when they need help. To provide employees with the skills and knowledge neces-sary to support this change in organization structure, the pay structure is designed to pay for learning and skill acquisition. Hourly workers change jobs every six months so that they understand each job and how it affects the other parts of the plant. In return, they are rewarded with a "triple-scoop" compensation plan that pays for skill, knowledge, and business performance. Workers receive a 25-cents-per-hour pay increase the first time they go through each of the 4 six-month rotations. In addition, they can almost double their pay by "declaring a major" and becoming an expert in an area such as machine maintenance or quality control. Further pay increases can be achieved by completing courses in English, business practices, and other areas. Pay is also linked to skills by virtue of the fact that promotions are based on skills rather than seniority. Finally, by meeting goals for plant performance and individual attendance, bonuses of over $200 per quarter are also possible. According to GE, the work force is 20 percent more productive than any equivalent plant, and productivity is expected to increase by another 20 percent in the upcoming year.

SOURCE: T. A. Stewart, "The Search for the Organization of Tomorrow," *Fortune*, May 18, 1992, 93ff.

Paying the Person: Pay for Skill and Knowledge.   A second response to job-based pay-structure problems has been to move away from linking pay to jobs and toward building structures based on individual characteristics such as skill or knowledge.[23] The basic idea is that if you want employees to learn more skills and become more flexible in the jobs they perform, you should pay them to do it. (See Chapter 12 for a discussion of the implications of skill-based pay systems on training.) According to Gerald Ledford, however, it is "a fundamental departure" because employees are now "paid for the skills they are capable of using, not for the job they are performing at a particular point in time."[24]

Skill-based pay systems seem to fit well with the increased breadth and depth of skill that changing technology continues to bring.[25] For example, in a production environment, workers might be expected not only to operate machines but also to take responsibility for maintenance and troubleshooting, quality control, even modifying computer programs.[26] Toyota concluded years ago that "none of the specialists [e.g., quality inspectors, many managers, and foremen] beyond the assembly worker was actually adding any value to the car. What's more…assembly workers could probably do most of the functions of specialists much better because of their direct acquaintance with conditions on the line."[27]

In other words, an important potential advantage of skill-based pay is its contribution to increased worker flexibility, which in turn facilitates the decentralization of decision making to those who are most knowledgeable. It also provides the opportunity for leaner staffing levels because employee turnover or absenteeism can now be covered by current employees who are multiskilled.[28] In addition, multiskilled employees are important in cases where different products require different manufacturing processes or where supply shortages or other problems call for adaptive or flexible responses—characteristics typical, for example, of many newer so-called advanced manufacturing environments (e.g., flexible manufacturing, just-in-time systems).[29] More generally, it has been suggested that skill-based plans also contribute to a climate of learning and adaptability and give employees a broader view of how the organization functions. Both changes should contribute to better use of employees' know-how and ideas.

Of course, skill-based approaches also have potential disadvantages.[30] First, although the plan will likely enhance skill acquisition, the organization may find it a challenge to use the new skills effectively. If it has not been carefully planned, it may find itself with large new labor costs but little payoff. In other words, if skills change, work design must change as quickly to take full advantage. Second, if pay growth is based entirely on skills, problems may arise if employees "top out" by acquiring all the skills too quickly, leaving no room for further pay growth. (Of course, this problem can also afflict job-based systems.) Third, and somewhat ironically, skill-based plans may generate a large bureaucracy—usually a criticism of job-based systems. Training programs need to be developed. Skills must be described, measured, and assigned monetary values. Certification tests must be developed to determine whether an employee has acquired a certain skill. Finally, as if the challenges in obtaining market rates under a job-based system were not enough, there is almost no body of knowledge regarding how to price combinations of skills (versus jobs) in the marketplace. Obtaining comparison data from other organizations will be difficult until skill-based plans become more widely used.

Can the U.S. Labor Force Compete?

We often hear that U.S. labor costs are simply too high to allow U.S. companies to compete effectively with companies in other countries. The average hourly labor costs of manufacturing production in the United States and in other advanced industrialized and newly industrialized countries are given in the following table for 1985 and 1990.[31]

	1985	1990
Industrialized		
United States	$13.01	$14.77
Germany	$ 9.57	$21.53
Japan	$ 6.43	$12.64
Newly Industrialized		
Mexico	$ 1.60	$ 1.80
Hong Kong	$ 1.73	$ 3.20
Korea	$ 1.25	$ 3.82

Based solely on a cost approach, it would perhaps make sense to try to shift many types of production from the United States to other countries, particularly the newly industrialized countries. Would this be a good idea? Not necessarily. There are several factors to consider.

Instability of Country Difference in Labor Costs.   First, note that relative labor costs are very unstable over time. For example, in 1985, U.S. labor costs were (13.01/9.57), or 36 percent greater than those of (West) Germany. But by 1990, the situation was reversed, with (West) German labor costs exceeding those of the United States by (21.53/14.77), or 46 percent. Did German employers suddenly become more generous, while U.S. employers clamped down on pay growth? Not exactly. Because all our figures are expressed in U.S. dollars, changes in currency exchange rates have a very important influence on such comparisons, and these exchange rates often fluctuate significantly from year to year. For example, in 1985, when German labor costs were 74 percent of those in the United States, the U.S. dollar was worth 2.94 German marks. But in 1990, the U.S. dollar was worth 1.62 German marks. If the exchange rate in 1990 were still 1 to 2.94, the average German hourly wage in U.S. dollars would be $11.80, or about 80 percent of the U.S. average. In any event, relative to countries like Germany, U.S. labor costs are now a bargain.

Skill Levels.   Second, the quality and productivity of national labor forces can vary dramatically. This is an especially important consideration when comparisons are drawn between labor costs in industrialized countries like the United States and developing countries like Mexico. For example, in 1986, the high school enrollment in Organization for Economic Cooperation and Development (OECD) countries (United States, Western Europe, Japan, Canada, Australia) was 93 percent of those who were the relevant age, compared with 40 percent in developing countries like Mexico, Hong Kong, and

Korea. Similarly, for college enrollment, the figures in 1986 were 39 percent in the OECD countries versus 7 percent in the developing countries. Thus, lower labor costs may simply reflect the lower average skill level of the work force. As a consequence, certain types of skilled labor are often not available in low-labor-cost countries.

Productivity.   Third, and most directly relevant, is the question of comparative productivity. Unfortunately, such comparisons are very difficult. However, as a very crude measure, one can consider the gross domestic product (or total output of the economy) per person, adjusted for differences in purchasing power. On this measure, the United States remains the highest in the world. In 1990, these figures were:[32]

U.S.	$21,449
Germany	$18,291
Japan	$17,634

The corresponding figures for the newly industrialized countries would be dramatically lower.

Nonlabor Considerations.   Fourth, any consideration of where to locate production cannot be based on labor considerations alone. For example, although the average hourly labor cost in Country A may be $15 versus $10 in Country B, if labor costs are 30 percent of total operating costs and nonlabor operating costs are roughly the same, then the total operating costs might be $65 (50 + 15) in Country A and $60 (50 + 10) in Country B. Thus, although labor costs in Country B are 33 percent less, total operating costs are only 7.7 percent less. This may not be enough to compensate for differences in skills and productivity, transportation costs, taxes, and so on. Further, the direct labor component of many products, particularly high-tech products (e.g., electronic components) may often be 5 percent or less. Thus, the effect on product price competitiveness may be insignificant.[33]

In fact, an increasing number of organizations have decided that it is more important to focus on nonlabor-related factors in deciding where to locate production (see the "Competing through Globalization" box).[34] Product development speed may be greater when manufacturing is physically close to the design group. Quick response to customers (e.g., making a custom replacement product) is difficult when production facilities are on the other side of the world. Inventory levels can be dramatically reduced through the use of manufacturing methods like just-in-time production. But, suppliers need to be in close physical proximity. Table 15.9 provides some examples of companies that have moved work back to the United States.

Overhead Costs.   Finally, although U.S. labor costs are lower than in Western European countries (e.g., Germany), some evidence suggests that the United States actually has higher overhead costs than Western Europe

COMPETING THROUGH

Globalization

QUALITY AND MARKET PROXIMITY ALSO AFFECT PLANT LOCATIONS IN GLOBAL CAR INDUSTRY

The Bayerische Motoren Werke AG (BMW) 325 series takes about 8 seconds to go from 0 to 60 miles per hour, and starting in 1995, it will be built not just in Germany, but also in a new $400 million plant in Spartanburg, South Carolina. BMW spent three and a half years considering 250 possible sites in Europe, Asia, and North America. Why did BMW choose South Carolina? One reason was a desire to avoid Germany's high labor costs. According to *Business Week*, "BMW doesn't think it can compete anymore from a domestic base that has the shortest workweek, longest vacations, and highest business taxes in the industrial world." Bernd Pischetsrieder, head of manufacturing for BMW, said that overall labor cost in Spartanburg is expected to be 30 percent less than in Germany. He noted that BMW planned to pay the prevailing rate in the Spartanburg area of about $10 per hour, which is less than the $16 average hourly rate in the U.S. automobile industry.

Still, as noted in Chapter 3, labor costs (and taxes) were not the only considerations. Mexico, where automobile industry workers earn $10 to $20 per day, was not chosen. A key factor considered by BMW in choosing Spartanburg is

that the United States is the single largest automobile market, and South Carolina has a strong infrastructure (good highways, airport, and proximity to an ocean port) to facilitate distribution of cars in the U.S. market and to other countries. Finally, competitiveness in the luxury automobile market demands a high-quality product. Buyers parting with $30,000 or more for an automobile have high expectations. Thus, a high-quality work force is needed. Although labor costs in Mexico are lower, and many of its plants have very good quality records, some manufacturers have experienced quality difficulties there, making for some reluctance among companies that compete on quality like BMW (and Daimler-Benz, manufacturer of Mercedes) to invest heavily in Mexico instead of the United States. In fact, in April 1993, Mercedes-Benz announced that it would invest $300 million in a U.S. assembly plant that will build a new sport utility vehicle beginning in 1997. Most of the vehicles will be built for export. To some extent, luxury manufacturers may also worry that customers will not be convinced that a Mexican-made version is of the same quality as a German or U.S.-made version, regardless of the actual quality.

SOURCE: F. Protzman, "BMW Details Plans to Build Cars in South Carolina," *New York Times,* June 24, 1992, D4; "The Exodus of German Industry is Under Way," *Business Week,* May 25, 1992, 42–43; R. Keatley, "Luxury-Auto Makers Consider Mexico: Its Low-Cost Labor vs. Image Perception," *The Wall Street Journal,* November 27, 1992, A4; E. Lapham, "U.S. Plant Key Part of the New Mercedes," *Automotive News,* April 12, 1993, 1ff.

(and Japan). For example, a Boston University study reports the following percentages of overhead costs/manufacturing costs:[35]

	1990
Japan	18%
Western Europe	21%
United States	26%

TABLE 15.9   Some Companies That Have Moved Work Back to the United States

Company	Product	Previous Source	Where It's Made Now
ADDS (part of AT&T)	Computer Terminal	Asia	Hauppauge, New York
American Tourister	Softside luggage	Asia	Jacksonville, Florida
Chicago Pneumatic Tool	Impact wrench	Joint venture in Japan	Utica, New York
Espirit	30% of women's apparel	Asia	California and the Southeast
GE Fanuc Automation	Programmable logic controller	Japan	Charlottesville, Virginia
Modicon (part of Daimler-Benz)	Module for programmable logic controller	Hong Kong	Andover, Massachusetts
Nicole Miller	Apparel	Hong Kong	New York City and eastern Pennsylvania
Tandy	Desktop computer	South Korea	Fort Worth, Texas
Texas Instruments	Hand-held calculator	Asia	Lubbock, Texas
Xerox	Replaceable cartridge for desktop copiers	Japan	Webster, New York

SOURCE: Organization for Economic Cooperation and Development. Used with permission of *Fortune*, © 1991 Time Inc. All rights reserved.

These data may suggest the need for further work by U.S. companies in boosting the productivity of white-collar employees, which has increased at a slower rate than blue-collar productivity.

Executive Pay

The issue of executive pay has been given widespread attention in the press. On the one hand, the issue has received more coverage than it deserves because there are very few top executives and their compensation accounts for only a very small share of an organization's total labor costs. On the other hand, top executives have a disproportionate ability to influence organization performance, so decisions about their compensation are critical. Top executives also help set the tone or culture of the organization. If, for example, the top executive's pay seems unrelated to the organization's performance, staying high even when business is poor, employees may not understand why some of their pay should be at risk and depend on how the organization is performing.

TABLE 15.10   Average Salaries of Top Managers and Other Selected Occupations

	Number	Average earnings (1991)
Managing Directors at Major Wall Street Firms[a]	1,200	$1,100,000
Senior Managers at Large Companies[b]	8,000	664,000
Professional Athletes[c]	2,500	627,000
Partners at Major Law Firms[d]	12,200	445,000
Doctors[e]	400,000	170,000

SOURCE: M. J. Mandel, "Who'll Get the Lion's Share of Wealth in the '90s? The Lions." Reprinted from June 8, 1992 issue of *Business Week* by special permission, copyright © 1992 by McGraw-Hill, Inc.
[a]Median compensation
[b]Includes long-term compensation
[c]Baseball, football and basketball
[d]Average profits per partner in 1990
[e]Excluding residents

How much do executives make, and how does it compare with some other high-paid occupations? Table 15.10 provides some data. The average 1991 earnings of senior executives at large companies was $664,000, which is actually less than the pay of managing directors at major Wall Street companies, about the same as professional athletes, and somewhat more than top lawyers. As such, one could argue that the compensation levels of senior managers is not out of line, especially given their impact on the success of organizations and the economy as a whole.

So, why has there been so much criticism of executive pay? First, looking beyond the averages reveals some very highly paid executives. For example, in 1990, the chief executives of Time Warner and Reebok International received $99.6 million and $33.3 million, respectively. In 1991, Anthony O'Reilly, chief executive of H.J. Heinz Company, received $75.1 million in salary, bonus, and stock options. Typically, pay of this magnitude reflects participation in a stock plan (see Chapter 16) rather than salary or short-term bonuses. (Anthony O'Reilly states his compensation, mostly in stock, should be considered relative to his performance over a 10-year, not a 1-year period. During these 10 years, the company's stock value increased 733 percent.)[36] Second, U.S. top executives are the highest paid in the world (Table 15.11). The fact that the differential between top-executive pay and that of an average manufacturing worker is so much higher in the United States has been described as creating a "trust gap"—that is, in employees' minds, a "frame of mind that mistrusts senior management's intentions, doubts its competence, and resents its self-congratulatory pay." The issue becomes even more salient at a time when so many of the same companies with high executive pay are simultaneously engaging in layoffs or other forms of employment reduction. Employees might ask: "If the company needs to cut costs, why

TABLE 15.11   Total Remuneration of Chief Executive Officers in Selected Countries

Country	1992 CEO Total Remuneration	1992 CEO Purchasing Power (U.S. = 100)	1991 CEO/Manufacturing Employee Total Remuneration Multiple
United States	$752,400	100%	25
France	$479,800	45%	16
Japan	$390,700	31%	11
Germany	$390,900	47%	10

SOURCE: Used with permission of Towers Perrin, "1991 Worldwide Remuneration" and "1992 Worldwide Remuneration" (New York: Towers Perrin, © Copyright 1991 and 1992). Note: Data based on companies with at least $250 million in sales; total remuneration includes salary, bonus, company contributions, perquisites, and long-term incentives.

not cut executive pay rather than our jobs?"[37] As suggested by the analogy to Imelda Marcos's shoes in the opening of this chapter, the issue is one of perceived fairness in difficult economic times. Third, and perhaps more important than *how much* top executives are paid is *how* they are paid. This is an issue we return to in the next chapter. The "Competing through Social Responsibility" box describes how one company addresses these issues.

GOVERNMENT REGULATION OF EMPLOYEE COMPENSATION

Equal Employment Opportunity

Equal Employment Opportunity (EEO) regulation (e.g., Title VII, Civil Rights Act of 1964) prohibits sex- or race-based differences in employment outcomes such as, unless justified by business necessity (e.g., pay differences stemming from differences in job performance). In addition to regulatory pressures, organizations must be prepared to deal with changing labor-market and demographic realities. At least two trends are directly relevant in discussing EEO. First, the labor-force participation rate of women has risen from 37.7 percent in 1960 to 57.7 percent in 1989. Second, between 1980 and 1990, the white population grew by 6.0 percent; the nonwhite population grew by 25.3 percent. The percentage of white males in organizations will probably continue to decline, which means that attention to EEO issues in compensation will be that much more important.

Is there equality of treatment in pay determination? Typically, the popular press focuses on raw earnings ratios. For example, in 1988, among year-round, full-time workers, the percentage of female-to-male average

Social Responsibility

EXECUTIVE PAY AT BEN & JERRY'S ICE CREAM

Peter Drucker, a well-known management writer, has suggested that executive pay should not exceed the pay of the lowest-paid worker in the company by more than a certain multiple. At Ben & Jerry's Ice Cream, such a policy is in place. The salaries of their top executives, Ben Cohen and Jerry Greenfield, are not permitted to exceed a 7:1 ratio compared to the lowest-paid employee. Moreover, the board of directors has capped executive salaries at $100,000. Elizabeth Lonergan, acting human resource director at Ben & Jerry's, argues in a recent issue of *Human Resource Executive* that "you have to have a trust gap at companies where the top people earn 300 times more than the employees." Ben & Jerry's revenues have grown from less than $2 million in 1983 to about $100 million in 1991, making it one of

Vermont's ten largest companies. Its ice cream was described by *Time* magazine as "the best ice cream in the world." The company believes that adherence to its social mission has played an important part in its prosperity. Its compensation philosophy of linked prosperity is consistent with its social mission. An important goal is to enhance the quality of life for its workers. Thus, when the company is able to increase the pay of its lowest-paid workers from $8 per hour to $8.25 per hour, the pay of its top executives can also increase, but not before then. Chief Executive Officer Ben Cohen hopes to bring all employees to the point where they can afford to buy a house. The cap on executive pay helps focus the company on what it feels is its responsibility for its employees' quality of life.

SOURCE: J. J. Laabs, "Ben & Jerry's Caring Capitalism," *Personnel Journal,* November 1992, 50–57; E. Raimy, "Reversal of Fortune," *Human Resource Executive,* June 1992, 46ff.

earnings was .65, and the percentage of black-to-white earnings was .75. These percentages have generally risen over the last two to three decades, but significant race and sex differences in pay clearly remain.[38]

The usefulness of raw percentages is limited, however, because some portion of earnings differences arises from differences in legitimate factors: education, labor-market experience, and occupation. Adjusting for such differences reduces earnings differences based on race and sex, but significant differences remain. With few exceptions, such adjustments rarely account for any more than one-half of the earnings differential.[39]

What aspects of pay determination are responsible for such differences? In the case of women, it is suggested that their work is undervalued. Another explanation rests on the "crowding" hypothesis, which argues that women were historically restricted to entering a small number of occupations. As a result, the supply of workers far exceeded demand, resulting in lower pay for such occupations. If so, market surveys would only perpetuate the situation.

Comparable worth (or pay equity) is a public policy that advocates remedies for any undervaluation of women's jobs. The idea is to obtain equal pay, not just for jobs of equal content (already mandated by the Equal

Pay Act of 1963), but for jobs of equal value or worth. Typically, job evaluation is used to measure worth. Table 15.12, which is based on state of Washington data from one of the first comparable-worth cases, suggests that measures of worth based on internal comparisons (job evaluation) and external comparisons (market surveys) can be compared. In this case, many disagreements between the two measures appear. Internal comparisons suggest that women's jobs are underpaid, whereas external comparisons are less supportive of this argument. For example, although the licensed practical nurse job receives 173 job-evaluation points and the truck driver position receives 97 points, the market rate (and thus the state of Washington employer rate) for the truck driver position is $1,286 per month versus only $1,030 per month for the nurse. The truck driver is paid 127 percent more than the pay-policy line would predict, whereas the nurse is paid only 75 percent of the pay-policy line prediction.

One potential problem with using job evaluation to establish worth independent of the market is that job-evaluation procedures were never designed for this purpose.[40] Rather, as demonstrated earlier, their major use is in helping to capture the market-pay policy and then applying that to nonkey jobs for which market data are not available. In other words, job evaluation has typically been used to help apply the market-pay policy, quite the opposite of replacing the market in pay-setting.

As with any regulation, there are also concerns that EEO regulation obstructs market forces, which, according to economic theory, provide the most efficient means of pricing and allocating people to jobs. In theory, moving away from a reliance on market forces would result in some jobs being paid too much and others too little, leading to an oversupply of workers for the former, an undersupply for the latter. In addition, some empirical evidence suggests that a comparable-worth policy would not have much impact on the relative earnings of women in the private sector.[41] One limitation of such a policy is that it targets single employers, ignoring the fact that men and women tend to work for different employers.[42] To the extent that segregation by employer contributes to pay differences between men and women, comparable worth would not be effective. In other words, to the extent that sex-based pay differences are the result of men and women working in different organizations with different pay levels, such policies will have little impact.

Perhaps most important, despite potential problems with market rates, the courts have consistently ruled that using the going market rates of pay is an acceptable defense in comparable-worth litigation suits.[43] The rationale is that organizations face competitive labor and product markets. Paying less or more than the market rate will put the organization at a competitive disadvantage. Thus, there is no comparable-worth legal mandate in the U.S. private sector. On the other hand, as of 1989, 20 states had begun or completed comparable-worth adjustments to public-sector employees pay.[44] In addition, the Canadian province of Ontario recently mandated comparable worth in both the private and public sector.

Another line of inquiry has focused on pinpointing the point at which women's pay falls behind that of men. Some evidence indicates that women

TABLE 15.12 Job-Evaluation Points, Monthly Prevailing Market-Pay Rates, and Proportion Female Incumbents in Job

Benchmark Title	Evaluation Points	Monthly Prevailing[a] Rates	Prevailing Rate as Percentage of Predicted[b]	Percentage of Female Incumbents
Warehouse worker	97	$1,286	109.1%	15.4%
Truck driver	97	1,493	126.6	13.6
Laundry worker	105	884	73.2	80.3
Telephone operator	118	887	71.6	95.7
Retail sales clerk	121	921	74.3	100.0
Data entry operator	125	1,017	82.1	96.5
Intermediate clerk typist	129	968	76.3	96.7
Highway engineering tech	133	1,401	110.4	11.1
Word processing equipment operator	138	1,082	83.2	98.3
Correctional officer	173	1,436	105.0	9.3
Licensed practical nurse	173	1,030	75.3	89.5
Automotive mechanic	175	1,646	120.4	0.0
Maintenance carpenter	197	1,707	118.9	2.3
Secretary	197	1,122	78.1	98.5
Administrative assistant	226	1,334	90.6	95.1
Chemist	277	1,885	116.0	20.0
Civil engineer	287	1,885	116.0	0.0
Highway engineer 3	345	1,980	110.4	3.0
Registered nurse	348	1,368	76.3	92.2
Librarian 3	353	1,625	90.6	84.6
Senior architect	362	2,240	121.8	16.7
Senior computer system analyst	384	2,080	113.1	17.8
Personnel representative	410	1,956	101.2	45.6
Physician	861	3,857	128.0	13.6

SOURCE: Reprinted with permission of *Public Personnel Management*, published by the International Personnel Management Association.

[a]Prevailing market rate as of July 1, 1980. Midpoint of job range set equal to this amount.

[b]Predicted salary is based on regression of prevailing market rate on job-evaluation points $2.43 \times$ job-evaluation points + 936.19, r = .77.

lose ground at the time they are hired and actually do better once they are employed for some time.[45] One interpretation is that when actual job performance (rather than the limited general qualification information available on applicants) is used in decisions, women may be less likely to encounter unequal treatment. If so, more attention needs to be devoted to ensuring fair treatment of applicants and new employees.[46]

It is likely, however, that organizations will differ in terms of where any women's earnings disadvantage arises. For example, advancement opportunities for women and other protected groups may be hindered by unequal access to the "old boy" or informal network. This, in turn, may be reflected in lower rates of pay. Mentoring programs have been suggested as one means of improving access. Indeed, one recent study found that mentoring was successful, having a significant positive effect on the pay of both men and women, with women receiving a greater payoff in percentage terms than men.[47]

Minimum Wage, Overtime, and Prevailing Wage Laws

The 1938 **Fair Labor Standards Act (FLSA)** establishes a minimum wage for jobs that was raised from $3.80 per hour in 1991 to the current $4.25 per hour. The FLSA was amended in 1990 to permit a subminimum training wage equal to the greater of $3.35 per hour or 85 percent of the **minimum wage**, which employers are permitted to pay most employees under the age of 20 for a period of up to 90 days. Approximately 5.7 million U.S. workers work for the minimum wage.[48]

The FLSA also requires that employees be paid at a rate of one and a half times their hourly rate for each hour of overtime worked beyond 40 hours in a week. The hourly rate includes not only the base wage but also other components such as bonuses and piece-rate payments. The FLSA requires overtime pay for any hours beyond 40 in a week that an employer "suffers or permits" the employee to perform, regardless of whether the work is done at the workplace or whether the employer explicitly asked or expected the employee to do it.[49] If the employer knows the employee is working overtime but neither moves to stop it nor pays time and a half, a violation of the FLSA may have occurred. Recently, a department store was the target of a lawsuit that claimed employees were "encouraged" to, among other things, write thank you notes to customers outside of scheduled work hours but were not compensated for this work. Although the company denied encouraging this off-the-clock work, it recently reached an out-of-court settlement to pay between $15 million and $30 million in back pay (plus legal fees of $7.5 million) to approximately 85,000 sales representatives it employed between 1987 and 1990.[50]

Executive, professional, administrative, and outside sales occupations are *exempt* from FLSA coverage. *Nonexempt* occupations are covered and include most hourly jobs. One estimate is that just over 20 percent of employees fall into the exempt category.[51] Exempt status depends on job responsibilities and salary, and the standards can be fairly complicated. For example, seven criteria, including whether two or more people are supervised and whether there is authority to hire and fire, are used to determine whether and employee is an executive. The Wage and Hour Division, Employment Standards Administration, U.S. Department of Labor, and its local offices can provide further information on these definitions.

Two other pieces of legislation are the 1931 Davis-Bacon Act and the 1936 Walsh-Healy Public Contracts Act, both of which require federal contractors to pay employees no less than the prevailing wages in the area. Davis-Bacon covers construction contractors receiving federal money of more than $2,000. Typically, prevailing wages have been based on relevant union contracts, partly because only 30 percent of the local labor force is required to be used in establishing the prevailing rate. Walsh-Healy covers all government contractors receiving $10,000 or more in federal funds.

SUMMARY

In this chapter, we have discussed the nature of the pay structure and its component parts, the pay level, and the job structure. Equity theory suggests that social comparisons are an important influence on how employees evaluate their pay. Employees make external comparisons between their pay and the pay they believe is received by employees in other organizations. Such comparisons may have consequences for employee attitudes and retention. Employees also make internal comparisons between what they receive and what they perceive others within the organization are paid. These types of comparisons may have consequences for internal movement, cooperation, and attitudes (e.g., organization commitment). Such comparisons play an important role in the controversy over executive pay, as illustrated by the focus of critics on the ratio of executive pay to that of lower-paid workers.

Pay benchmarking surveys and job evaluation are two administrative tools widely used in managing the pay-level and job-structure components of the pay structure, which influence employee social comparisons. Pay surveys also permit organizations to benchmark their labor costs against other organizations. Globalization is increasing the need for organizations to be competitive in both their labor costs and productivity.

The nature of pay structures is undergoing a fundamental change in many organizations. One change is the move to fewer pay levels to reduce labor costs and bureaucracy. Second, some employers are shifting from paying employees for narrow jobs to giving them broader responsibilities and paying them to learn the necessary skills.

Finally, a theme that runs through this chapter and the next is the importance of process in managing employee compensation. How a new program is designed, decided on, implemented, and communicated is perhaps just as important as its core characteristics.

Discussion Questions

1. You have been asked to evaluate whether your organization's current pay structure makes sense in view of what competing organizations are paying. How would you determine what organizations to compare your organization to? Why might your organization's pay structure differ from those in competing organizations? What are the potential consequences of having a pay structure that is "out of line" relative to your competitors?

2. Top management has decided that the organization is too bureaucratic and has too many layers of jobs to compete effectively. You have been asked to suggest innovative alternatives to the traditional "job-based" approach to employee compensation and to list the advantages and disadvantages of these new approaches.

3. If major changes of the type mentioned in question 2 are to be made, what types of so-called process issues need to be considered? Of what relevance is equity theory in helping understand how employees might react to changes in the pay structure?

4. Are executive pay levels unreasonable? Why or why not?

5. Your company plans to build a new manufacturing plant but is undecided where to locate it. What factors would you consider in making a decision about which country (or state) to build the plant in?

6. You have been asked to evaluate whether the pay structure is fair to women and minorities. How would you go about answering this question?

Notes

1. J. S. Adams, "Inequity in Social Exchange," in *Advances in Experimental Social Psychology*, ed. L. Berkowitz (New York: Academic Press, 1965); P. S. Goodman, "An Examination of Referents Used in the Evaluation of Pay," *Organizational Behavior and Human Performance* 12 (1974): 170–195.

2. J. B. Miner, *Theories of Organizational Behavior* (Hinsdale, Ill.: Dryden Press, 1980).

3. Steve Lohr, "Ford and Chrysler Outpace Japanese in Reducing Costs," *New York Times* (1992): D1.

4. B. Gerhart and G. T. Milkovich, "Organizational Differences in Managerial Compensation and Financial Performance," *Academy of Management Journal* 33 (1990): 663–691; E. L. Groshen, "Why Do Wages Vary among Employers?" *Economic Review* 24 (1988): 19–38.

5. G. A. Akerlof, "Gift Exchange and Efficiency-Wage Theory: Four Views," *American Economic Review* 74 (1984): 79–83; J. L. Yellen, "Efficiency Wage Models of Unemployment," *American Economic Review* 74 (1984): 200–205.

6. S. L. Rynes and G. T. Milkovich, "Wage Surveys: Dispelling Some Myths about the 'Market Wage'," *Personnel Psychology* 39 (1986): 71–90.

7. B. Gerhart and G. T. Milkovich, "Employee Compensation: Research and Practice," in *Handbook of Industrial and Organizational Psychology*, vol. 3, 2nd ed, ed. M. D. Dunnette and L. M. Hough (Palo Alto, Cal.: Consulting Psychologists Press, 1992).

8. G. T. Milkovich and J. Newman, *Compensation* (Homewood, Ill.: BPI/Irwin, 1990).

9. B. Gerhart, G. T. Milkovich and B. Murray, "Pay, Performance, and Participation," in *Research Frontiers in Industrial Relations and Human Resources*, ed. D. Lewin, O. S. Mitchell and P. D. Sherer (Madison, Wisc.: IRRA, 1992).

10. C. H. Fay, "External Pay Relationships," in *Compensation and Benefits*, ed. L. R. Gomez-Mejia (Washington, D.C.: Bureau of National Affairs, 1989).

11. J. P. Pfeffer and A. Davis-Blake, "Understanding Organizational Wage Structures: A Resource Dependence Approach," *Academy of Management Journal* 30 (1987): 437–455.

12. Levine (1987); E. E. Lawler, "What's Wrong with Point-Factor Job Evaluation," *Compensation and Benefits Review* 18, no. 2 (1986): 20–28.

13. E. E. Lawler III, *Pay and Organizational Development* (Reading, Mass.: Addison-Wesley, 1981).

14. R. Folger and M. A. Konovsky, "Effects of Procedural and Distributive Justice on Reactions to Pay Raise Decisions," *Academy of Management Journal* 32 (1989): 115–130. Gerhart, Milkovich, and Murray (forthcoming); J. Greenberg, "Determinants of Perceived Fairness of Performance Evaluations," *Journal of Applied Psychology* 71 (1986): 340–342; H. G. Heneman III, "Pay Satisfaction," *Research in Personnel and Human Resource Management* 3 (1985): 115–139.

15. J. Greenberg, "Employee Theft as a Reaction to Underpayment of Inequity: The Hidden Cost of Pay Cuts," *Journal of Applied Psychology* 75 (1990): 561–568.

16. Adams, "Inequity in Social Exchange"; C. J. Berger, C. A. Olson and J. W. Boudreau, "The Effect of Unionism on Job Satisfaction: The Role of Work-Related Values and Perceived Rewards," *Organizational Behavior and Human Performance* 32 (1983): 284–324; P. Capelli and P. D. Sherer, "Assessing Worker Attitudes under a Two-Tier Wage Plan," *Industrial and Labor Relations Review* 43 (1990): 225–244; R. W. Rice, S. M. Phillips and D. B. McFarlin, "Multiple Discrepancies and Pay Satisfaction," *Journal of Applied Psychology* 75 (1990): 386–393.

17. Capelli and Sherer, "Assessing Worker Attitudes."

18. This section draws freely on B. Gerhart and R. D. Bretz, "Employee Compensation in Advanced Manufacturing Technology," in *Human Factors in Advanced Manufacturing*, ed. W. Karwowski and G. Salvendy (New York: Wiley [forthcoming]).

19. R. M. Kanter, *When Giants Learn to Dance* (New York: Simon and Schuster, 1989); E. E. Lawler III, *Strategic Pay* (San Francisco: Jossey-Bass, 1990).

20. "Farewell, Fast Track," *Business Week*, 192–200, December 10, 1990.

21. J. P. Womack, D. T. Jones and D. Roos, *The Machine that Changed the World* (New York: MacMillan, 1990).

22. "Farewell, Fast Track."

23. Lawler, *Strategic Pay*; G. Ledford, "3 Cases on Skill-Based Pay: An Overview," *Compensation and Benefits Review*, March–April 1991, 11–23.

24. Ledford, "3 Cases," 199.

25. P. S. Adler, "Managing Flexible Automation," *California Management Review* 30, no. 3 (1988): 34–56; T. Cummings and M. Blumberg, "Advanced Manufacturing Technology and Work Design," in *The Human Side of Advanced Manufacturing Technology*, ed. T. D. Wall, C. W. Clegg and N. J. Kemp (Chichester, Great Britain: John Wiley & Sons, 1987); Y. P. Gupta, "Human Aspects of Flexible Manufacturing Systems," *Production and Inventory Management Journal* 30, no. 2 (1989): 30–36; R. E. Walton and G. I. Susman, "People Policies for the New Machines," *Harvard Business Review* 87, no. 2 (1987): 98–106; Womack, et al., *The Machine That Changed the World*.

26. T. D. Wall, J. M. Corbett, R. Martin, C. W. Clegg and P. R. Jackson, "Advanced Manufacturing Technology, Work Design, and Performance: A Change Study," *Journal of Applied Psychology* 75 (1990): 691–697.

27. Womack, et al, *The Machine That Changed the World*, 56.

28. Lawler, *Strategic Pay*.

29. Ibid.; Gerhart and Bretz, "Employee Compensation."

30. N. Gupta, D. Jenkins and W. Curington, "Paying for Knowledge: Myths and Realities," *National Productivity Review*, Spring 1986, 107–123; Lawler, *Strategic Pay*; Gerhart and Milkovich, "Employee Compensation."

31. *Daily Labor Report*, January 7, 1992.

32. *New York Times*, March 8, 1992, p. E5. Original data from Organization for Economic Cooperation and Development. Per person gross domestic product in 1990 using purchasing power parity rates.

33. E. Faltermayer, "U.S. Companies Come Back Home," *Fortune*, December 30, 1991, 106ff.

34. Ibid.

35. T. Peterson, "Can Corporate America Get Out from under Its Overhead?" *Business Week*, May 18, 1992, 102.

36. "What, Me Overpaid?" CEOs Fight Back," *Business Week*, May 4, 1992, 142ff.

37. A. Farnham, "The Trust Gap," *Fortune*, December 4, 1989, 56ff.

38. P. Ryscavage and P. Henle, "Earnings Inequality in the 1980s," *Monthly Labor Review* 113, no. 12 (1990): 3–16; F. D. Blau and M. A. Beller, "Trends in Earnings Differentials by Gender, 1971–1981," *Industrial and Labor Relations Review* 41 (1988): 513–529; L. A. Carlson and C. Swartz, "The Earnings of Women and Ethnic Minorities, 1959–1979," *Industrial and Labor Relations Review* 41 (1988): 530–546; M. W. Horrigan and J. P. Markey, "Recent Gains in Women's Earnings: Better Pay or Longer Hours?" *Monthly Labor Review* 113, no. 7 (June 1990): 11–17.

39. B. Gerhart, "Gender Differences in Current and Starting Salaries: The Role of Performance, College Major, and Job Title," *Industrial and Labor Relations Review* 43 (1990): 418–433; G. G. Cain, "The Economic Analysis of Labor-Market Discrimination: A Survey," in *Handbook of Labor Economics*, ed. O. Ashenfelter and R. Layard (New York: North-Holland, 1986), 694–785.

40. D. P. Schwab, "Job Evaluation and Pay-Setting: Concepts and Practices," in *Comparable Worth: Issues and Alternatives*, ed. E. R. Livernash (Washington, D.C.: Equal Employment Advisory Council, 1980).

41. B. Gerhart and N. El Cheikh, "Earnings and Percentage Female: A Longitudinal Study," *Industrial Relations* 30 (1991): 62–78; R. S. Smith, "Comparable Worth: Limited Coverage and the Exacerbation of Inequality," *Industrial and Labor Relations Review* 61 (1988): 227–239.

42. W. T. Bielby and J. N. Baron, "Men and Women at Work: Sex Segregation and Statistical Discrimination," *American Journal of Sociology* 91 (1986): 759–799.

43. S. L. Rynes and G. T. Milkovich, "Wage Surveys: Dispelling Some Myths about the 'Market Wage'," *Personnel Psychology* 39 (1986): 71–90; G. T. Milkovich and J. Newman, *Compensation* (Homewood, Ill.: BPI/Irwin, 1990).

44. Ibid.

45. Gerhart, "Gender Differences in Current and Starting Salaries"; B. Gerhart and G. T. Milkovich, "Salaries, Salary Growth, and Promotions of Men and Women in a Large, Private Firm," in *Pay Equity: Empirical Inquiries*, ed. R. Michael, H. Hartmann, and B. O'Farrell (Washington, D.C.: National Academy Press, 1989).

46. Gerhart, "Gender Differences in Current and Starting Salaries"; B. Gerhart and S. Rynes, "Determinants and Consequences of Salary Negotiations by Graduating Male and Female MBAs," *Journal of Applied Psychology* 76 (1991): 256–262.

47. D. J. Brass, "Men's and Women's Networks: A Study of Interaction Patterns and Influence in an Organization," *Academy of Management Journal* 28 (1985): 327–343; B. Rosen, M. E. Templeton and K. Kirchline, "First Few Years on the Job: Women in Management," *Business Horizons* 24, no. 12 (1981): 26–29; K. Cannings and C. Montmarquette, "Managerial Momentum: A Simultaneous Model of the Career Progress of Male and Female Managers," *Industrial and Labor Relations Review* 44 (1991): 212–228; R. A. Noe, "Women and Mentoring: A Review and Research Agenda," *Academy of Management Review* 13 (1988): 65–78; G. F. Dreher and R. A. Ash, "A Comparative Study of Mentoring among Men and Women in Managerial, Professional, and Technical Positions," *Journal of Applied Psychology* 75 (1990): 539–546.

48. K. G. Salwen, "Business Groups Prepare to Square Off against Clinton on Minimum Wage Issue," *The Wall Street Journal*, February 8, 1993, A2.

49. A. W. Sherman, Jr. and G. W. Bohlander, *Managing Human Resources* (Cincinnati: South-Western Publishing, 1992), 334.

50. G. A. Patterson, "Nordstrom Inc. Sets Back-Pay Accord on Suit Alleging 'Off-the-Clock' Work," *The Wall Street Journal*, January 12, 1993, A2.

51. R. I. Henderson, *Compensation Management: Rewarding Performance* (Englewood Cliffs, N.J.: Prentice-Hall, 1989), 56.

REWARDING EMPLOYEES ON THE SLOW TRACK

Edgar S. Woolard, Jr., chief executive officer at Du Pont, held 20 different jobs in 32 years in the course of climbing the corporate ladder. But employment reductions, including the "pruning" of middle management, may mean that this sort of rapid upward mobility may be a thing of the past. Indeed, at many companies, the delayering of middle-management levels may indicate a long-term structural change rather than a temporary response to a short-run economic slowdown. In the past, the most important way for an employee to earn more was to be promoted quickly. But, delayering and banding (combining pay levels into a smaller number) means fewer management levels at many companies and, therefore, less opportunity for promotion. A *Business Week* cover story bid "Farewell to the Fast Track" and described the new employment system's reduced opportunity for promotion as the "slow track."

QUESTIONS

1. Is *Business Week* correct?

2. Are there fewer opportunities to reward high-performing managers with promotions? If so, how can high performers be rewarded? Consider both monetary and nonmonetary rewards.

SOURCE: "Farewell, Fast Track," *Business Week*, December 10, 1990, 192–200.

16

RECOGNIZING INDIVIDUAL CONTRIBUTIONS WITH PAY

Objectives   *After reading this chapter, you should be able to:*

1. Describe the fundamental pay programs for recognizing individual employees' contributions to the organization's success.
2. List the advantages and disadvantages of the pay programs.
3. List the major factors to consider in matching the pay strategy to the organization's strategy.
4. Explain the importance of process issues such as communication in compensation management.
5. Describe how U.S. pay practices compare with those of other countries.

Sears Discontinues Incentive Pay in Auto Centers

A headline in the June 23, 1992, edition of the *New York Times* read "Sears's Auto Centers to Halt Commissions." Sears, Roebuck & Company had just been charged with fraud because of the alleged overcharging of customers for automobile repairs in New Jersey and California. In an undercover investigation by the California Department of Consumer Affairs, 38 visits to 27 Sears automobile repair shops had resulted in 34 cases of unnecessary service and repair recommendations, some of the unnecessary repairs costing as much as $550. How had this occurred? According to the *New York Times*, Edward A. Brennan, the chairman of Sears, "conceded that the incentive compensation program and sales goals created an environment where mistakes occurred." On the same day, *The Wall Street Journal* reported that employees' pay in the automotive repair shops was based "solely on the amount of repairs customers authorize[d]," but that Sears would be replacing its compensation program with one that focused on "quality."

SOURCES: L. M. Fisher, "Sears Auto Centers to Halt Commissions," *New York Times,* June 23, 1992, D1; G. A. Patterson, "Sear's Brennan Accepts Blame for Auto Flap," *The Wall Street Journal,* June 23, 1992, B1ff.

INTRODUCTION

This set of unfortunate events provides a good illustration of the power of an employee compensation system to motivate employee behavior. The problem is that the compensation system's power is sometimes misdirected, so that it motivates the wrong behaviors.

In the preceding chapter, we focused on setting pay for jobs. In this chapter, we focus on using pay to recognize and reward the contributions of individual employees to the organization's success. With important exceptions (e.g., single-rate systems found in some union settings), employees working at the same job for the same organization do not receive the same rates of pay. Instead, differences in performance (individual, group, or organization), seniority, skills, and so forth are used as a basis for differentiating pay between employees.[1]

A number of key questions arise in evaluating different programs for recognizing individual contributions. First, what are the costs of the program? Second, what is the expected return (e.g., in terms of influences on attitudes and behaviors) from such investments? Third, does the program fit with the organization's human resource strategy and its overall business strategy?

Organizations have a relatively large degree of discretion in making individual pay decisions, especially compared to the pay-level decisions discussed in the previous chapter. The same organizational pay level (or "compensation pie") can be distributed ("sliced") among employees in many different ways. Whether each employee's share is based on individual performance, profits, seniority, or other factors, the size of the pie (and thus the cost to the organization) can remain the same.

Regardless of cost differences, different individual pay programs can have very different consequences for productivity and return on investment. Indeed, a study of individual pay and pay-level practices at roughly 150 organizations found not only that the largest differences between organizations had to do with individual pay practices but that these differences resulted in different levels of profitability.[2]

How Does Pay Influence Individual Employees?

Pay plans are typically used to energize, direct, or control employee behavior. Equity theory, described in the previous chapter, is relevant here as well. Most employees compare their own pay with that of others, especially those in the same job. Perceptions of inequity may cause employees to take actions to restore equity. Unfortunately, some of these actions (e.g., quitting or lack of cooperation) may not be helpful to the organization.

Three additional theories also help explain compensation's effects: reinforcement, expectancy, and agency theories.

Reinforcement Theory. Thorndike's Law of Effect states that a response followed by a reward is more likely to recur in the future. The implication for compensation management is that high employee performance followed by a monetary reward will make future high performance more likely. By the same token, high performance not followed by a reward will make it less likely in the future. The theory emphasizes the importance of a person's actual experience of a reward.

Expectancy Theory. Although expectancy theory also focuses on the link between rewards and behaviors, it emphasizes expected (rather than experienced) rewards. In other words, it focuses on the effects of incentives. Behaviors (e.g., job performance) can be described as a function of ability and motivation. As described in Chapter 11, motivation is hypothesized to be a function of expectancy, instrumentality, and valence perceptions. Compensation systems differ according to their impact on these motivational components. Generally speaking, the main factor is instrumentality: the perceived link between behaviors and pay. Valence of pay outcomes should remain the same under different pay systems. Expectancy perceptions often have more to do with job design and training than pay systems.*

Agency Theory. This theory focuses on the divergent interests and goals of the organization's stakeholders and the ways that employee compensation can be used to align these interests and goals. Agency theory is an important explanatory tool in economics and finance but has been relatively neglected in human resource management, despite being highly relevant to understanding employee compensation. Therefore, we cover it in some depth.

An important characteristic of the modern corporation is the separation of ownership from management (or control). Unlike the early stages of capitalism, where owner and manager were often the same, today, with

---

*A possible exception would be skill-based pay, which directly influences employee training and thus expectancy perceptions.

some exceptions (mostly smaller companies), most stockholders are far removed from the day-to-day operation of companies. Although this separation has important advantages, it also creates agency costs—the interests of the **principals** (i.e., owners) and their **agents** (i.e., managers) may no longer converge.* What is best for the agent, or manager, may not be best for the owner.

Three types of agency costs arise in managerial compensation.[3] First, although shareholders seek to maximize their wealth, management may be spending money on things such as perquisites (e.g., "superfluous" corporate jets) or "empire building" (acquisitions that do not add value to the company but may enhance the manager's prestige or pay.) Second, managers and shareholders may differ in their attitudes toward risk. Shareholders can diversify their investments (and thus their risks) more easily than managers (whose only source of income may be their job), so managers are typically more averse to risk. They may be less likely to pursue projects or acquisitions with high potential payoff. It also suggests a preference on the part of managers for relatively little risk in their pay (e.g., high emphasis on base salary, low emphasis on uncertain bonuses or incentives). Indeed, research shows that managerial compensation in manager-controlled firms is more often designed in this manner.[4] Third, decision-making horizons may differ. For example, if managers change companies more than owners change ownership, managers may be more likely to maximize short-run performance (and pay), perhaps at the expense of long-term success.

Agency theory is also of value in the analysis and design of nonmanagers' compensation. In this case, the divergence of interests may exist between managers (now in the role of principals) and their employees (who take on the role of agents).

In designing either managerial or nonmanagerial compensation, the key question is, "How can such agency costs be minimized?" Agency theory says that the principal must choose a contracting scheme that helps align the interests of the agent with the principal's own interests (i.e., reduces agency costs). These contracts can be classified as either behavior

---

*The advantage of such separation is that it permits owners (principals) to freely transfer (stock) ownership without disrupting the operations of the firm because their agents (e.g., professional managers) have taken over the control function. The ability to transfer ownership allows shareholders to diversify their portfolios (and thus their risk). A second advantage is that different people can specialize and focus on what they do best (work to their relative advantage). So, some people will work strictly as entrepreneurs, others will have more success as managers. A third advantage is that such a system improves the mobility of financial capital, thus helping meet the large capital requirements of modern corporations. For further discussion, see E. F. Fama and M. C. Jensen, "Separation of Ownership and Control," *Journal of Law and Economics* 26 (1983): 301–325; R. E. Hoskisson, M. A. Hitt, T. A. Turk and B. B. Tyler, "Balancing Corporate Strategy and Executive Compensation: Agency Theory and Corporate Governance," *Research in Personnel and Human Resources* 7 (1989): 25–57.

oriented (e.g., merit pay) or outcome oriented (e.g., stock options, profit sharing, commissions).[5]

At first blush, outcome-oriented contracts seem to be the obvious solution. If profits are high, compensation goes up. If profits go down, compensation goes down. The interests of "the company" and employees are aligned. An important drawback, however, is that such contracts increase the agent's risk. And, because agents are averse to risk, they may require higher pay (a compensating wage differential) to make up for it.[6]

Behavior-based contracts, on the other hand, do not transfer risk to the agent and thus do not require a compensating wage differential. However, the principal must be able to monitor with little cost what the agent has done. Otherwise, the principal must either invest in monitoring and information or structure the contract so that pay is linked at least partly to outcomes.[7]

Which type of contract should an organization use? It depends partly on the following factors:[8]

Risk Aversion.   Risk aversion among agents makes outcome-oriented contracts less likely.

Outcome Uncertainty.   Profit is an example of an outcome. Agents are less willing to have their pay linked to profits to the extent that there is a risk of low profits. They would therefore prefer a behavior-oriented contract.

Job Programmability.   As jobs become less programmable (and more difficult to monitor), outcome-oriented contracts become more likely. Programmable, or routine, jobs entail performing the same tasks in a predictable and structured way. Job programmability is of particular interest because of the increasing complexity of organizations and technology. Under such circumstances, monitoring is more difficult, making behavior-based contracts less likely. Indeed, evidence suggests that research-and-development-oriented organizations, where work is highly complex and technical (and monitoring difficult), do indeed rely more heavily on outcome-oriented arrangements such as profit sharing and stock plans.[9] In addition, pay level is higher in such organizations, consistent with the idea that risk borne by employees must be compensated with higher pay.

Measurable Job Outcomes.   When outcomes are more measurable, outcome-oriented contracts are more likely.

Ability to Pay.   Outcome-oriented contracts contribute to higher compensation costs because of the risk premium.

Tradition.   A tradition or custom of using (or not using) outcome-oriented contracts will make such contracts more (or less) likely.

In summary, the reinforcement, expectancy, and agency theories all focus on the fact that behavior-reward contingencies can shape behaviors.

However, agency theory is of particular value in compensation management because of its emphasis on the risk-reward trade-off, an issue that needs close attention when companies consider variable pay plans, which can carry significant risk.

Influences on Labor-Force Composition

Traditionally, using pay to recognize individual contributions has been thought of as a way to influence the behaviors and attitudes of current employees, whereas pay level and benefits have been seen as a way to influence so-called membership behaviors: decisions about whether to join or remain with the organization. However, there is increasing recognition that individual pay programs may also have an effect on the nature and composition of an organization's work force.[10] For example, it is possible that an organization that links pay to performance may attract more high performers than an organization that does not link the two. There may be a similar effect with respect to job retention.[11]

Continuing the analysis, perhaps organizations that link pay to individual performance are more likely to attract individualistic employees, while organizations relying more heavily on team rewards are more likely to attract more team-oriented employees. Although there is no concrete evidence of this yet, it has been found that different pay systems attract people with different personality traits and values.[12] The implication is that the design of compensation programs needs to be carefully coordinated with the business and human resource strategy.

PROGRAMS

In compensating employees, an organization does not have to choose one program over another. Instead, a combination of programs is often the best solution. For example, one program may foster teamwork and cooperation but not enough individual initiative. Another may do the opposite. Used in conjunction, a balance may be attained.[13]

Table 16.1 provides an overview of the programs for recognizing individual contributions. Each program shares a focus on paying for performance. The programs differ according to four design features: (1) payment method, (2) frequency of payout, (3) ways of measuring performance, and (4) choice of which employees are covered. In a perhaps more speculative vein, the table also suggests the *potential* consequences of such programs for (1) performance motivation of employees, (2) attraction of employees, (3) organization culture, and (4) costs. Finally, there are three contingencies that may influence whether each pay program fits the situation:

TABLE 16.1

Programs for Recognizing Individual Contributions

	Incentive Pay	Merit Pay	Gainsharing	Profit Sharing	Ownership
Design Features					
Payment method	Bonus	Changes in base pay	Bonus	Bonus	Equity changes
Frequency of payout	Weekly	Annually	Monthly or quarterly	Semiannually or annually	When stock sold
Performance measures	Output, productivity, sales	Supervisor's appraisal	Production or controllable costs	Profit	Stock value
Coverage	Direct labor	All employees	Production or service unit	Total organization	Total organization
Consequences					
Performance motivation	Clear performance reward connection	Little relationship between pay and performance	Some impact in small units	Little pay-performance relationship	Very little pay-performance relationship
Attraction	Pays higher performers more	Over time pays better performers more	Helps with all employees	Helps with all employees	Can help lock in employees
Culture	Divides work force, adversarial	Competition within work groups	Supports cooperation, problem solving	Knowledge of business	Sense of ownership
Costs	Maintenance high	Requires well-developed performance-appraisal system	Ongoing maintenance needed operating costs variable	Relates costs to ability to pay	Cost not variable with performance
Contingencies					
Organization Structure	Many independent jobs	Helped by measurable jobs and work units	Fits small stand-alone work units	Fits any company	Fits most companies
Management style	Control	Some participation desirable	Fits participation	Works best with participation	Works best with participation
Type of work	Stable, individual easily measurable	Individual unless group appraisals done	All types	All types	All types

SOURCE: Adapted from E. E. Lawler, III, "Pay for Performance: A Strategic Analysis," in *Compensation and Benefits*, ed. L.R. Gomez-Mejia (Washington, D.C.: Bureau of National Affairs, 1989).

(1) organization structure, (2) management style, and (3) type of work. We now discuss the different programs and some of their potential consequences in more depth.

Merit Pay

In merit pay programs annual pay increases are usually linked to performance-appraisal ratings (see Chapter 7). Some type of merit pay program exists in almost all organizations (although evidence on merit pay effectiveness is surprisingly scarce).[14] Indeed, given the pervasiveness of merit pay programs, we devote a good deal of attention to them here.

Basic Features.   Many merit pay programs work off of a **merit increase grid**. As Table 16.2 indicates, both the size and frequency of pay increases are determined by two factors. The first factor is the individual's performance rating (because better performers should receive higher pay). The second factor is position in range (i.e., an individual's compa-ratio). So, for example, an employee with a performance rating of EX and a compa-ratio of 120 would receive a pay increase of 9 to 11 percent. By comparison, an employee with a performance rating of EX and a compa-ratio of 85 would receive an increase of 13 to 15 percent.* One reason for factoring in the compa-ratio is to control compensation costs and maintain the integrity of the pay structure. If a person with a compa-ratio of 120 received a merit increase of 13 to 15 percent, he or she would soon exceed the pay-range maximum. Not factoring in the compa-ratio would also result in uncontrolled growth of compensation costs for employees who continue to perform the same job year after year. Instead, some organizations think in terms of assessing where the employee's pay is now and where it should be, given a particular performance level. Consider Table 16.3. An employee who consistently performs at the EX level should be paid at 115 to 125 percent of the market (i.e., a compa-ratio of 115 to 125). To the extent that the employee is far from that pay level, larger pay increases are necessary to move the employee to the correct position. On the other hand, if the employee is already at that pay level, smaller pay increases will be needed. The main objective in the latter case would be to provide pay increases that are sufficient to maintain the employee at the targeted compa-ratio.

In controlling compensation costs, another factor that requires close attention is the distribution of performance ratings (see Chapter 7). In many organizations, 60 to 70 percent of employees fall into the top two (out of four to five) performance-rating categories.[15] This means tremendous growth in compensation costs because most employees will eventually be above the midpoint of the pay range, resulting in compa-ratios well over

---

*Note that the general magnitude of increases in such a table is influenced by inflation rates. Thus, the percentage increases in such a grid would have been considerably lower in the late 1980s and early 1990s.

TABLE 16.2 Example of Merit Increase Grid from Merck Co., Inc.

1986 Salary Planning Guideline

Suggested Merit Increase Percentage

Performance Rating	Compa-Ratio 80.00–95.00	Compa-Ratio 95.01–110.00	Compa-Ratio 110.01–120.00	Compa-Ratio 120.01–125.00
EX Exceptional within Merck	13%–15%	12%–14%	9%–11%	to maximum of range
WD Merck Standard with Distinction	9%–11%	8%–10%	7%–9%	—
HS High Merck Standard	7%–9%	6%–8%	—	—
RI Merck Standard Room for Improvement	5%–7%	—	—	—
NA Not Adequate for Merck	—	—	—	—

Suggested Timing Since Last Increase

Performance Rating	Compa-Ratio 80.00–95.00	Compa-Ratio 95.01–110.00	Compa-Ratio 110.01–120.00	Compa-Ratio 120.01–125.00
EX Exceptional within Merck	12–13 months	12–14 months	14–15 months	—
WD Merck Standard with Distinction	12–14 months	12–14 months	14–16 months	—
HS High Merck Standard	13–14 months	13–15 months	—	—
RI Merck Standard Room for Improvement	13–14 months	—	—	—
NA Not Adequate for Merck	—	—	—	—

SOURCE: K. J. Murphy, "Merck & Co., Inc., (B)" Boston: Harvard Business School, case 491-006. Copyright © 1990 by the President & Fellows of Harvard College. Reprinted with permission.

100. To avoid this, some organizations provide guidelines regarding the percentage of employees who should fall into each performance category, usually limiting the percentage that can be placed in the top two categories. These guidelines are enforced differently, ranging from true guidelines to strict forced-distribution requirements.

In general, merit pay programs have the following characteristics. First, there is a focus on identifying individual differences in performance. These are assumed to reflect differences in ability or motivation. By implication, system constraints on performance are not seen as significant. Second, the

TABLE 16.3   Compa-Ratio Targets and Performance Ratings

Performance Rating	Compa-Ratio Target
EX Exceptional within Merck	115–125
WD Merck Standard with Distinction	100–120
HS High Merck Standard	90–110
RI Merck Standard Room for Improvement	80–95
NA Not Adequate for Merck	none

SOURCE: K. J. Murphy, "Merck & Co., Inc., (B)" Boston: Harvard Business School, case 491-006. Copyright © 1990 by the President & Fellows of Harvard College. Reprinted with permission.

majority of information on individual performance is collected from the immediate supervisor. Peer and subordinate ratings are rare, and where they do exist, they tend to receive less weight than supervisory ratings.[16] Third, there is a policy of linking pay increases to performance-appraisal results.[17] Fourth, the feedback under such systems tends to occur infrequently, often once per year at the formal performance review session. Fifth, the flow of feedback tends to be largely unidirectional, from supervisor to subordinate.

Criticisms of Traditional Merit Pay Programs.   Criticisms of this process have been raised. Deming, for example, argues that it is unfair to rate individual performance because "apparent differences between people arise almost entirely from the system that they work in, not from the people themselves."[18] Examples of system factors include coworkers, the job, materials, equipment, customers, management, supervision, and environmental conditions. These are believed to be largely outside the worker's control, instead falling under management's responsibility. Deming argues that the performance rating is essentially "the result of a lottery."[19]

Deming also argues that the individual focus of merit pay discourages teamwork: "Everyone propels himself forward, or tries to, for his own good, on his own life preserver. The organization is the loser."[20] As an example, if people in the purchasing department are evaluated based on the number of contracts negotiated, they may have little interest in materials quality, even though manufacturing is having quality problems.

Deming's solution is to eliminate the link between individual performance and pay. This approach reflects a desire to move away from recognizing individual contributions. What are the consequences of such a move? It is possible that fewer employees with individual-achievement orientations would be attracted to and remain with the organization. One study of job retention found that the relationship between pay growth and individual performance over time was weaker at higher performance levels. As a consequence, the organization lost a disproportionate share of its top performers.[21] In other words, too little emphasis on individual performance may leave the organization with average and low performers.

Thus, although Deming's concerns about too much emphasis on individual performance are well taken, one must be careful not to replace one set of problems with another. Instead, there needs to be an appropriate balance between individual and group objectives. At the very least, ranking and forced-distribution performance-rating systems need to be considered with caution, lest they contribute to behavior that is too individualistic and competitive.

Another criticism of merit pay programs is the way they measure performance. If the performance measure is not perceived as being fair and accurate, the entire merit pay program can break down. One potential impediment to accuracy is the almost exclusive reliance on the supervisor for providing performance ratings, even though peers and subordinates often have as good or better information on a person's performance.

In general, process issues appear to be very important in administering merit pay. In any situation where rewards are distributed, employees appear to assess fairness along two dimensions: distributive (based on how much they receive) and procedural (what process was used to decide how much).[22] Some of the most important aspects of procedural fairness or justice appear in Table 16.4. These items suggest that employees desire clear and consistent performance standards and opportunities to provide input, discuss their performance, and appeal any decision they believe to be incorrect.

The final, and perhaps most basic, criticism of merit pay is that it does not really exist. High performers are not paid significantly more than mediocre or even poor performers in most cases.[23] For example, in the late 1980s and early 1990s, merit increase budgets often did not exceed 4 to 5 percent. Thus, high performers might receive 6 percent raises versus 3.5 to 4 percent raises for average performers. On a salary of $40,000 per year, the difference in take-home pay would not be more than about $300 per year, or about $6 per week. Critics of merit pay point out that this difference is probably not significant enough to influence employee behaviors or attitudes.

Of course, small differences in pay can accumulate into large differences over time.* For example, over the course of a 30-year career, an initial annual salary difference of $740 with equal merit increases thereafter of 7 percent would accumulate into a career salary advantage of $75,738.[24] Whether employees think in these terms is open to question, however. But even if they do not, nothing prevents an organization from developing a communication program that makes clear to employees that what may appear to be small differences in pay can add up to large differences over time. It should also be kept in mind that merit ratings are often closely linked to promotions, which in turn are closely linked to salary. Thus, even in merit pay settings where performance differences are not recognized in the short run, high performers are likely to have significantly higher career earnings.

---

*The present value of the salary advantage would be $29,489 (based on a discount rate of 5 percent).

TABLE 16.4   Aspects of Procedural Justice in Pay Raise Decisions

Indicate the extent to which your supervisor did each of the following:

1. Was honest and ethical in dealing with you.
2. Gave you an opportunity to express your side.
3. Used consistent standards in evaluating your performance.
4. Considered your views regarding your performance.
5. Gave you feedback that helped you learn how well you were doing.
6. Was completely candid and frank with you.
7. Showed a real interest in trying to be fair.
8. Became thoroughly familiar with your performance.
9. Took into account factors beyond your control.
10. Got input from you before a recommendation.
11. Made clear what was expected of you.

Indicate how much of an opportunity existed, after the last raise decision, for you to do each of the following things:

12. Make an appeal about the size of a raise.
13. Express your feelings to your supervisor about the salary decision.
14. Discuss, with your supervisor, how your performance was evaluated.
15. Develop, with your supervisor, an action plan for future performance.

SOURCE: R. Folger, and M. A. Konovsky, "Effects of Procedural and Distributive Justice on Reactions to Pay Raise Decisions," *Academy of Management Journal* 32 (1989): 115.

Individual Incentives

Like merit pay, individual incentives reward individual performance, but with two important differences. First, payments are not rolled into base pay. They must be continuously earned and re-earned. Second, performance is usually measured as physical output (e.g., number of water faucets produced) rather than by subjective ratings. Individual incentives have the potential to significantly increase performance. Locke and his colleagues found that monetary incentives increased production output by a median of 30 percent—more than any other motivational device studied.[25]

Nevertheless, individual incentives are relatively rare for a variety of reasons.[26] First, most jobs (e.g., those of managers and professionals) have no physical output measure. Instead, they involve what might be described as "knowledge work." Second, there are many potential administrative problems (e.g., setting and maintaining acceptable standards) that often prove to be intractable. Third, individual incentives may do such a good job of motivating employees that they do whatever they get paid for and nothing else (see opening vignette). Fourth, as the name implies, individual incentives typically do not fit well with a team approach. Fifth, they may be inconsistent with the goals of acquiring multiple skills and proactive problem solving. Learning new skills often requires employees to slow or stop production. If the employees are paid based on production volume, they may not want to slow down or stop. Sixth, some incentive plans reward output volume at the expense of quality.

Therefore, although individual incentives carry potential advantages, they are not likely to contribute to a flexible, proactive, problem-solving work force. In addition, such programs may not be particularly helpful in the pursuit of total quality management objectives.

Profit Sharing and Ownership

Profit Sharing. At the other end of the individual–group continuum are profit sharing and stock ownership plans. Under **profit sharing**, payments are based on a measure of organization performance (profits), and the payments do not become part of the base salary. Profit sharing has two potential advantages. First, it may encourage employees to think more like owners, taking a broad view of what needs to be done to make the organization more effective. Thus, the sort of narrow self-interest encouraged by individual incentive plans (and perhaps also by merit pay) is presumably less of an issue. Instead, increased cooperation and citizenship are expected. Second, because payments do not become part of base pay, labor costs are automatically reduced during difficult economic times, and wealth is shared during good times. Consequently, organizations may not need to rely on layoffs as much to reduce costs during tough times.[27]

As an example, Union Carbide's plan for the 14,000 employees in its U.S. chemical and plastics division froze base salaries, but if return on capital exceeded 8 percent, employees could get lump-sum payments of up to 15.4 percent of base. Larry Doyle, vice-president of human resources, pointed out that Union Carbide secretaries consequently got to the point where they were "not bashful about nudging managers to stay at a Holiday Inn instead of a more expensive Hyatt."[28] Profit sharing has been used at several well-known companies, including Hewlett-Packard, USX, Ford, General Motors (GM), Alcoa, Caterpillar, Monsanto, and AT&T. Like Union Carbide, a number of these companies (e.g., AT&T, Monsanto) replaced some portion of base salary with the potential to earn shares of the profits. In other words, there is not only an upside potential but a downside risk as well.[29]

Does profit sharing contribute to better organization performance? The evidence is not yet clear. Although one review finds consistent support for a correlation between profit-sharing payments and profits, questions have been raised about the direction of causality.[30] For example, both Ford and GM have had profit-sharing plans in their contracts with the United Auto Workers (UAW) since 1984. The average profit-sharing payment at Ford has been $13,225 per worker versus an average of $1,837 per worker at GM because Ford has been more profitable.[31] Given that the profit-sharing plans are similar, it seems unlikely they caused Ford to be more profitable. Rather, it would appear that profits were higher at Ford for other reasons, resulting in higher profit-sharing payments.

This example also helps illustrate the fundamental drawback of profit sharing. Why should automobile workers at GM receive profit-sharing payments that are only one-seventh the size received by those doing the same type of work at Ford? Is it because Ford UAW members performed seven times better than their counterparts at GM? Probably not. Rather, workers are likely to view top-management decisions regarding products, engineering, pricing, and marketing as more important. As a result, with the exception of top (and perhaps some middle) managers, most employees are unlikely to see a very strong connection between what they do and what they earn under profit sharing. This means that performance motivation is likely to change very little under profit sharing. Consistent with expectancy theory, motivation depends on a strong link between behaviors and valued consequences such as pay (instrumentality perceptions).

Another factor that reduces the motivational impact of profit-sharing plans is that most plans are of the *deferred* type. In 1989, 16 percent of full-time employees in medium and large private establishments participated in profit-sharing plans, but only 1 percent of employees overall (i.e., 6.3 percent of those in profit-sharing plans) were in cash plans where profits were paid to employees during the current time period.[32]

Not only may profit sharing fail to increase performance motivation, but employees may also react very negatively when they learn that such plans do not pay out during business downturns.[33] First, they may not feel they are to blame because they have been performing their jobs well. Other factors are beyond their control, so why should they be penalized? Second, what seems like a "small" amount of risked pay for a manager earning $80,000 per year can be very painful to someone earning $15,000 or $20,000.

Consider the case of the Du Pont Fibers Division, which in 1989 implemented a plan that linked a portion of employees' pay to division profits.[34] After the plan's implementation, employees' base salary was about 4 percent lower than similar employees in other divisions, unless 100 percent of the profit goal (a 4 percent increase over the previous year's profits) was reached. Thus, there was what might be called "downside risk." However, there was also considerable upside opportunity: If 100 percent of the profit goal was exceeded, employees would earn more than similar employees in other divisions. For example, if the division reached 150 percent of the profit goal (i.e., 6 percent growth in profits), employees would receive 12 percent more than comparable employees in other divisions.

How did the plan work? In 1989, it worked fine. The profit goal was exceeded, and employees earned slightly more than employees in other divisions. In 1990, however, profits were down 26 percent from 1989, and the profit goal was not met. Employees received no profit-sharing bonus. Instead, they earned 4 percent less than comparable employees in other divisions. Profit sharing was no longer seen as a very good idea. Du Pont management responded to employee concerns by eliminating the plan and returning to a system of fixed base salaries with no variable (or risk) component. This outcome is perhaps not surprising from an agency theory perspective, which suggests that employees must somehow be compensated before they will be willing to assume increased risk.

One solution some organizations choose is to design plans that have upside but not downside risk. In such cases, when a profit-sharing plan is introduced, base pay is not reduced. Thus, when profits are high, employees share in the gain, but when profits are low, they are not penalized. Such plans largely eliminate what is purported to be a major advantage of profit sharing: reducing labor costs during business downturns. During business upturns, labor costs will increase. Given that the performance benefits of such plans are suspect, an organization runs the risk under such plans of increasing its labor costs with little return on its investment.

In summary, although profit sharing may be useful as one component of a compensation system (e.g., to enhance identification with broad organizational goals), it may need to be complemented with other pay programs that more closely link pay to outcomes that individuals or teams can control (or "own"). In addition, profit sharing runs the danger of contributing to employee resistance and higher labor costs, depending on how it is designed.

Ownership. Employee ownership is similar to profit sharing in some key respects, such as encouraging employees to focus on the success of the organization as a whole. In fact, with ownership, this focus may be even stronger. Also, like profit sharing, ownership may not result in motivation for very high individual performance. And, because employees may not realize any financial gain until they actually sell their stock (typically upon leaving the organization), the link between pay and performance may be even less obvious than under profit sharing. Thus, from a reinforcement theory standpoint (with its emphasis on actually experiencing rewards), performance motivation may be especially low.

One way of achieving employee ownership is through **stock options**, which give employees the opportunity to buy stock at a fixed price. As an example, say that the employees receive options to purchase stock at $10 per share in 1995, and the stock price reaches $30 per share in 2000. They have the option of purchasing stock (i.e., "exercising" their stock options) at $10 per share in 2000, thus making a tidy return on investment if the shares are then sold. If the stock price goes down to $8 per share in the year 2000, however, there will be no financial gain. Therefore, employees—like those described in the "Competing through Technology and Structure" box—are encouraged to act in ways that will benefit the organization.

Stock options have typically been reserved for executives. More recently, there seems to be a trend toward pushing eligibility farther down in the organization.[35] In fact, some companies (e.g., Pepsi-Cola, Hewlett-Packard) now grant stock options to all employees. Some studies suggest that organization performance is higher when a greater percentage of top- and middle-level managers are eligible for long-term incentives such as stock options, which is consistent with agency theory's focus on the problem of encouraging managers to think like owners.[36] However, it is not clear

COMPETING THROUGH

Technology & Structure

STOCK OPTIONS AND SILICON VALLEY

According to the Small Business Administration, companies with fewer than 20 employees created 4 million jobs between 1988 and 1990. In contrast, companies with over 100 employees lost 1.2 million jobs during the same period. Among small companies, high-technology small companies, in particular, are probably considered most important to U.S. competitiveness. Some of the compensation practices in these high-tech companies might themselves be described as "high tech" and bear closer examination.

Alisa Baker, writing in *The Wall Street Journal*, has referred to stock options as "a perk that built Silicon Valley." High-technology start-up companies (e.g., computer hardware and software, telecommunications) like those in Silicon Valley typically offer very modest salary and benefits for two reasons. First, small start-up companies are often cash poor and need to conserve what cash they have for investment in plants and equipment. They may not be able to afford to take on additional fixed salary and benefits costs. Second, start-up companies wish to encourage risk taking, innovation, and experimentation to develop new technologies and products, which in turn, will produce company growth. Further, in a high-technology start-up, an additional problem arises—the owners may find it difficult to monitor or judge the performance of employees working on new and complex technologies. Therefore, agency theory

suggests that there will be a greater use of outcome-oriented contracts (e.g., stock options) and less use of behavior-oriented contracts. Employees are not evaluated on particular behaviors or actions taken in the short run. Rather, their fortunes are tied to those of the company. So, if the company grows and becomes very profitable, employees share in the success.

Microsoft founder Bill Gates, with a net worth of about $7 billion, is considered the richest man in the United States, thanks in large part to Microsoft stock's 1,200 percent increase in value since being first offered to the public. But, Mr. Gates is not alone in sharing the fruits of Microsoft's amazing growth. Well before going public, Gates gave employees the opportunity to buy stock at $1 per share. When the company did go public in March 1986, the stock was at $25.75 a share. A year later it reached $90. These and later employees also benefitted from three stock splits since 1989. Microsoft admits to 500 millionaire employees, while other estimates run as high as 2,200 employee millionaires. A similar story can be found at Apple, where Baker notes that "everyone from secretaries to the 26-year-old founder became a millionaire." These and other employees in Silicon Valley "traded off traditional employee benefits and salary for a shot at the gold," and they got it.

SOURCE: A. J. Baker, "Stock Options—A Perk that Built Silicon Valley," *The Wall Street Journal*, June 23, 1993, A20; T, Egan, "They Came for the Dream, Not the Pay. Then Stock Options Made them Rich," *New York Times*, June 28, 1992, Section 3, p 1.

whether these findings would hold up for lower-level employees, who may see much less opportunity to influence overall organization performance.

Employee stock ownership plans (ESOPs), under which employers provide employees with stock in the company, are the most common form of employee ownership (see Table 16.5 for examples), with the number of employees in such plans increasing from 4 million in 1980 to 10 million in 1989.[37] ESOPs raise a number of unique issues. On the negative side, they

TABLE 16.5   Examples of Companies with Employee Stock Ownership Plans

By Size of Employee Holdings		By Size of Company	
Company	Employee Stake[a]	Company	Employee Stake[a]
Morgan Stanley	57%	Exxon	9%
Stone & Webster	52	AT&T	11
Oregon Steel Mills	47	Procter & Gamble	25
Grumman	43	Amoco	6
Rockwell International	41	Chevron	16
Century Telephone	39	Bellsouth	7
Topps	37	General Motors	9
Herman Miller	35	GTE	9
Kroger	34	Atlantic Richfield	9
McDonnell Douglas	33	Abbott Labs	7

SOURCE: A. Bernstein, "Joe Sixpack's Grip on Corporate America," *Business Week,* July 15, 1991, 108.
[a]Includes holdings in pension funds, savings plans, and ESOPs. Ranked by market value.

can carry significant risk for employees. An ESOP must, by law, invest at least 51 percent of assets in its company's stock, resulting in less diversification of investment risk and, in some cases, no diversification. Consequently, when employees buy out companies in poor financial condition to save their jobs, or when the ESOP is used to fund pensions, employees risk serious financial difficulties if the company does poorly.[38] This is not just a concern for employees, because, as agency theory suggests, employees may require higher pay to offset increased risks of this sort.

ESOPs can be attractive to organizations because they have tax and financing advantages and can serve as a takeover defense (under the assumption that employee owners will be "friendly" to management). ESOPs give employees the right to vote their securities (if registered on a national exchange).[39] As such, some degree of participation in a select number of decisions is mandatory, but overall participation in decision making appears to vary significantly across organizations with ESOPs. Some studies suggest that the positive effects of ownership are larger in cases where employees have greater participation,[40] perhaps because the "employee-owner comes to psychologically experience his/her ownership in the organization."[41]

Finally, what are the monetary costs of ownership plans? This question seems to have received surprisingly little attention in the past. As noted in our later discussion of managerial and executive pay, the accounting treatment of stock options is currently being reconsidered. Briefly, one can compare the issuing of stock options to the government's printing money. The more money that is printed, the less valuable the dollar becomes (resulting in inflation). Similarly, if stock, either in the form of options or ESOPs, is

TABLE 16.6   Reported Positive Effects of Gainsharing Programs

	Percentage of Managers Who Mentioned Effect
Improved performance of employees	14.9%
Change in employees' attitudes, job interest	14.9
Increased productivity environment	11.9
Reduction in scrap, rework, and waste	11.9
Better use of material, supplies, and equipment	11.9
Cost savings suggestions	10.5
Improved process or procedures	9.0
Better product quality	7.5

SOURCE: T. Rollins, "Productivity-Based Group Incentive Plans: Powerful, But Use with Caution," *Compensation and Benefits Review*, May–June 1989, 39–50.

distributed, but the real value of the company remains the same, then the value of a share of stock is reduced.*

Gainsharing, Group Incentives, and Team Awards

Gainsharing.   **Gainsharing** programs offer a means of sharing productivity gains with employees. Although sometimes confused with profit-sharing plans, gainsharing differs in two key respects. First, instead of using an organization-level performance measure (profits), the programs measure group or plant performance, which are likely to be seen as more controllable by employees. Second, payouts are distributed more frequently and not deferred. In a sense, gainsharing programs represent an effort to pull out the best features of organization-oriented plans like profit sharing and individual-oriented plans like merit pay and individual incentives. Like profit sharing, gainsharing encourages pursuit of broader goals than individual-oriented plans do. But, unlike profit sharing, gainsharing can motivate employees much as individual plans do because of the nature of the performance measure and the frequency of payouts. Indeed, studies indicate that gainsharing has a positive impact on performance.[42] Table 16.6 shows some of the positive effects reported by organizations using gainsharing plans.

---

*One study found that the value of shares was reduced annually by an amount roughly equal to 2.2 percent of pretax profits (R. Richardson and J. Barnes, Working Paper, London School of Economics, 1990, cited in "Unseen Apples and Small Carrots," *The Economist*, April 13, 1991, 75).

TABLE 16.7   Example of Gainsharing (Scanlon plan)

Single Ratio Scanlon Monthly Report

1. Sales	$1,100,000
2. Less sales returns, allowances, discounts	25,000
3. Net Sales	1,075,000
4. Add: increase in inventory (at cost or selling price)	125,000
5. Value of production	1,200,000
6. Allowed payroll costs (20% of value of production)	240,000
7. Actual payroll costs	210,000
8. Bonus pool	30,000
9. Company share (50%)	15,000
Subtotal	15,000
10. Reserve for deficit months (25%)	3,750
11. Employee share—immediate distribution	11,250

SOURCE: Reprinted with permission, p. 57 from *Gainsharing: Plans for Improving Performance,* by Brian Graham-Moore and Timothy L. Ross. Copyright © 1990 by the Bureau of National Affairs, Inc., Washington, D.C. 20037.

Table 16.7 provides an example of how one type of gainsharing, a Scanlon plan (developed in the 1930s by Joseph N. Scanlon, president of a local union at Empire Steel and Tin Plant in Mansfield, Ohio), works. The Scanlon plan provides a monetary bonus to employees (and the organization) if the ratio of labor costs to the sales value of production is kept below a certain standard, $240,000 (20 percent of $1.2 million) in this example. Because actual labor costs were $210,000, there is a savings of $30,000. The organization receives 50 percent of the savings, and the employees receive the other 50 percent, although part of the employees' share is set aside in the event that actual labor costs exceed the standard in upcoming months.

Gainsharing plans like the Scanlon plan often encompass more than just a monetary component. As Table 16.8 indicates, there is often a strong emphasis on taking advantage of employee know-how to improve the production process through regular meetings, teams, suggestion systems, and other activities. In a related issue, a number of recommendations have been made about the organization conditions that should be in place for gainsharing to be successful. Commonly mentioned factors include (1) management commitment, (2) a need to change or a strong commitment to continuous improvement, (3) management's acceptance and encouragement of employee input, (4) high levels of cooperation and interaction, (5) employment security, (6) information sharing on productivity and costs, (7) goal setting, (8) commitment of all involved parties to the process of change and improvement,

TABLE 16.8   Gainsharing Support Activities

Activity	Number of Responses[a]	Percentage of Organizations Using Activity (N=57)
Periodic meetings	41	72%
Problem-solving teams	34	60
Newsletter	31	54
Training program	31	54
Steering committee	29	51
Suggestion system	27	47
Auditing	19	33
Other	6	11

SOURCE: Reprinted with permission of The Conference Board, New York City.
[a]Note: Respondents reported multiple activities.

and (9) agreement on a performance standard and calculation that is understandable, seen as fair, and closely related to managerial objectives.[43]

Group Incentives and Team Awards.   Whereas gainsharing plans are often plantwide, group incentives and team awards typically pertain to a smaller work group.[44] Group incentives (like individual incentives) tend to measure performance in terms of physical output, whereas team award plans may use a broader range of performance measures (e.g., cost savings, successful completion of product design, meeting deadlines). As with individual incentive plans, these plans have a number of potential drawbacks. Competition between individuals may be reduced, but it may be replaced by competition between groups or teams. Also, as with any incentive plan, a standard-setting process must be developed that is seen as fair by employees, and these standards must not exclude important dimensions such as quality.

Mixed Plans and Strategy Examples

As the preceding discussion indicates, every pay program has advantages and disadvantages. Therefore, rather than choosing one program, some companies find it useful to design a mix of pay programs, one that has just the right chemistry for the situation at hand. (See the "Competing through Quality" box for an example.) Relying exclusively on merit pay or individual incentives may result in high levels of work motivation but unacceptable levels of individualistic and competitive behavior and too little concern for broader plant or organization goals. Relying too heavily on profit sharing and gainsharing plans may improve the degree of cooperation and con-

Quality

BONUSES AND COMMUNICATIONS AT HERMAN MILLER

Herman Miller, a furniture manufacturer, has been using a pay plan since 1950 that combines elements of gainsharing and profit sharing. Quarterly bonuses are based on company profits, market share, and efficiency in using noncash assets. Quality is also heavily emphasized, with measures of customer service and product-quality surveys. In addition, employees have the opportunity to enhance efficiency and quality through a suggestion system. However, the company does not offer individual rewards for suggestions. Rather, the rewards go to all employees in the form of quarterly bonuses that result from the positive effect of the suggestions on the performance measures. The philosophy is to discourage internal competition and idea hoarding and instead reinforce the idea that any good suggestion will need a group effort to be successful. Communication is another key element of the pay plan. Employees receive videos each month that provide a description of the bonus calculations and rationale. The videos also show top executives discussing the business environment and the company's operational and marketing strategies for competing effectively. Like the quarterly bonus plan, this information encourages employees to think in terms of making the total business a success.

SOURCE: "Benchmarking HR: Measuring up to the Leaders," *HR Executive,* June 1992, 23–40.

cern for the welfare of the entire plant or organization, but it may reduce individual work motivation to unacceptable levels. However, a particular mix of merit pay, gainsharing, and profit sharing could contribute to acceptable performance on all these performance dimensions.

As an example, consider the Merck pay plan shown in Table 16.9. Notice how it differs from the plan shown earlier (Table 16.2). Instead of pay being based solely on individual performance, division performance is also considered. Thus, the number of employees permitted to receive the top performance rating (TF) is 8 percent in exceptional (EX) divisions but only 1 percent in unacceptable (NA) divisions. Because pay increases are tied to performance ratings, employees in better-performing divisions receive larger pay increases. Because their pay increases depend on both individual and division performance, they should be encouraged to balance narrow individual goals and broader division-level goals in cases where the two do not completely correspond.

MANAGERIAL AND EXECUTIVE PAY

Because of their significant ability to influence organization performance, top managers and executives are a strategically important group whose compensation warrants special attention. In the previous chapter, we dis-

TABLE 16.9

Pay Increase Guidelines Incorporating Individual and Division Performance at Merck & Co., Inc.

Proposed Guideline for Targeted Distribution of Performance Ratings

Performance Rating for Employee	Rating Type	Targeted Employee Rating Distribution, by Divisional Performance				
		Performance Rating for Division:				
		EX Exceptional	WD With Distinction	HS High Standard	RI Room for Improvement	NA Not Acceptable
TF Top 5%	Relative	8%	6%	5%	2%	1%
TQ Top Quintile	Relative	20%	17%	15%	12%	10%
OU Outstanding	Absolute					
VG Very Good	Absolute	71%	75%	75%	78%	79%
GD Good	Absolute					
LF Lower 5%	Relative	1%	2%	5%	8%	10%
NA Not Acceptable	Absolute					
PR Progressing		Not Applicable				

SOURCE: K. J. Murphy, "Merck & Co., Inc., (B)" Boston: Harvard Business School, case 491-007. Copyright © 1990 by the President & Fellows of Harvard College. Reprinted with permission.

cussed how much this group is paid. Here, we focus on the issue of how their pay is determined.

Each year, *Business Week* publishes a list of top executives who did the most for their pay and those who did the least. The latter group has been the impetus for much of the attention to executive pay. The problem seems to be that in some companies, top-executive pay is high every year, regardless of profitability or stock market performance. One study, for example, found that CEO pay changes by $3.25 for every $1,000 change in shareholder wealth. This relationship was interpreted to mean that "the compensation of top executives is virtually independent of corporate performance."[45]

How can executive pay be linked to organization performance? From an agency theory perspective, the goal of owners (shareholders) is to encourage the agents (managers and executives) to act in the best interests of the owners. This may mean less emphasis on noncontingent pay, such as base salary, and more emphasis on outcome-oriented "contracts" that make some portion of executive pay contingent on the organization's profitability or stock performance.[46] Among middle- and top-level managers, it is common to use both short-term bonus and long-term incentive plans to encourage the pursuit of both short- and long-term organization performance objectives. Indeed, in the *Business Week* survey of over 300 companies, the average base salary plus short-term bonus of $1.1 million accounts for less than one-half of average total executive compensation of $2.5 million. The remaining $1.4 million includes stock options and other forms of long-term

TABLE 16.10 Funding Methods for Executive Bonus Pools

Aluminum Co. of America	15% of total cash dividends
Ashland Oil	6% of after-tax net income
Boeing Co.	6% of before-tax net income
Bristol-Meyers	Lesser of 6% of before-tax net income or 8% of after-tax net income
Du Pont	20% of after-tax net income in excess of 6% of stockholders' equity
Goodyear Tire & Rubber	10% of after-tax net income in excess of consolidated book value of outstanding capital stock
ITT Corp.	12% of after-tax net income in excess of 6% of stockholders' equity
International Paper	8% of after-tax net income in excess of 6% of stockholders' equity
Rockwell International	2% of the first $100 million of before-tax net income plus 3% of the next $50 million of before-tax net income plus 4% of the next $25 million of before-tax net income plus 5% of the balance
Unocal Corp.	3% of after-tax net income in excess of 6% of stockholders' equity

SOURCE: Reprinted by permission of *The Wall Street Journal,* © 1990 Dow Jones & Company, Inc. All rights reserved worldwide.

compensation. Table 16.10 provides some examples of how the sizes of short-term bonus pools are determined. In addition, a decision must be made regarding how the pool is distributed to managers covered by the plan. In many cases, such distributions are based on individual performance. Long-term incentives typically depend on stock market performance (price appreciation and sometimes dividend payouts). The stock options plan discussed earlier is one such example.

To what extent do organizations use such pay-for-performance plans, and what are their consequences? A recent study suggests that organizations vary substantially in the extent to which they use both long-term and short-term incentive programs. The study further found that greater use of such plans among top- and middle-level managers was associated with higher subsequent levels of profitability.* As Table 16.11 indicates, greater reliance on short-term bonuses and long-term incentives (relative to base

---

*Of course, the effectiveness of any bonus or long-term incentive program depends on its design. Many questions have been raised, for example, regarding the way stock options are actually used in some organizations. See Graef Crystal's book, *In Search of Excess: The Overcompensation of American Executives* (New York: W. W. Norton, 1991).

TABLE 16.11   The Relationship between Managerial Pay and
Organization Return on Assets

		Predicted Return on Assets	
Bonus/Base Ratio	**Long-Term Incentive Eligibility**	**%**	**$a**
10%	28%	5.2%	$250 million
20%	28%	5.6%	$269 million
10%	48%	5.9%	$283 million
20%	48%	7.1%	$341 million

SOURCE: B. Gerhart and G. T. Milkovich, "Organizational Differences in Managerial Compensation and
Financial Performance," *Academy of Management Journal* 33 (1990): 663–691.
aBased on the assets of the average Fortune 500 company in 1990.

pay) resulted in substantial improvements in return on assets.[47]

Finally, executive pay has been receiving increasing attention from regulators. The Securities and Exchange Commission (SEC) recently considered a number of changes to the rules governing executive pay, including proposals to (1) require companies to more clearly report executive compensation levels and the company's performance relative to that of competitors over a five-year period, (2) give stockholders more direct input regarding executive-pay decisions, and (3) change the accounting treatment of stock options such that their cost would be reflected as a charge against earnings (i.e., an expense), consistent with the accounting treatment of other forms of employee compensation.[48] Proposal 1 was adopted.[49] Proposal 2 was not adopted, although the SEC did make it easier for shareholders to communicate with one another about shareholder meetings. Proposal 3 was also not adopted, but the Financial Accounting Standards Board (FASB) did subsequently adopt a rule requiring companies to show the granting of stock options as an expense beginning in 1997. A major difficulty in treating stock options as an expense is that their value is not known at the time they are granted because it depends on future stock appreciation. Only an estimate can be made. Nevertheless, the FASB ruling will require companies to make such estimates because previously stock options were essentially "free" to companies even though the options can have tremendous value to those receiving them.

PROCESS AND CONTEXT ISSUES

In Chapter 15, we discussed the importance of process issues such as communication and employee participation. Significant differences in how such issues are handled can be found both across and within organizations, suggesting that organizations have considerable discretion in this aspect of compensation management.[50] As such, it represents another strategic opportunity to distinguish one's organization from the competition.

Employee Participation in Decision Making

Consider, for example, employee participation in decision making and its potential consequences. Involvement in the design and implementation of pay policies has been linked to higher pay satisfaction and job satisfaction, presumably because employees have a better understanding of and greater commitment to the policy when they are involved.[51] The "Competing through Social Responsibility" box describes one company's success in involving employees.

What about the effects on productivity? Agency theory provides some insight. The delegation of decision making by a principal to an agent creates agency costs, because employees may not act in the best interests of top management. In addition, the more agents there are, the higher the monitoring costs.[52] Together, these suggest that delegation of decision making can be very costly.

On the other hand, agency theory suggests that monitoring would be less costly and more effective if performed by employees because they have knowledge about the workplace and behavior of fellow employees that managers do not have. As such, the right compensation system might encourage self-monitoring and peer monitoring.[53]

Researchers have suggested that two general factors are critical to encouraging such monitoring: monetary incentives (outcome-oriented contracts in agency theory) and an environment that fosters trust and cooperation. This environment, in turn, is a function of employment security, group cohesiveness, and individual rights for employees—in other words, respect for and commitment to employees.[54]

Communication

Another important process issue is communication. Earlier, we spoke of its importance in the administration of merit pay, both from the perspective of procedural fairness and as a means of obtaining the maximum impact from a merit pay program. More generally, a change in any part of the compensation system is likely to give rise to employee concerns. Rumors and assumptions based on poor or incomplete information are always an issue in administering compensation, partly because of its importance to employee economic security and well-being. Therefore, in making any changes, it is crucial to determine how best to communicate reasons for the changes to employees. Some organizations now rely heavily on videotaped messages from the chief executive officer to communicate the rationale for major changes. Brochures that include scenarios for typical employees are also used, as are focus-group sessions where small groups of employees are interviewed to obtain feedback about concerns that can be addressed in later communication programs.

Social Responsibility

COMPETING THROUGH

EMPOWERING EMPLOYEES TO DESIGN THEIR OWN INCENTIVE PROGRAMS

"At C&S Wholesale Grocers, Inc., pay for performance begins and ends with the employee." According to Mitch Davis, vice-president of people affairs, "We'll pay incentives to any employee who helps us figure out how to do it." The company's empowerment of employees to develop incentive plans began about four years ago when self-managed teams in a warehouse designed a plan that would pay each team member equally according to the team's performance on productivity and quality goals. Since then, employees from a variety of departments, including accounts payable and human resources, have designed incentive plans to help improve their performance. Teams design the plan and set their own standards with input from the human resource and finance staffs. As a result, about 75 percent of the 1,000 employees are covered by some type of incentive plan. Although standards are often set too high or too low initially, this is not seen as a problem. It is recognized that business conditions and goals are always changing, so flexibility is necessary. The company reports that employee-designed incentive plans have helped reduce product damage by 50 percent. The company's productivity is twice the industry average and it has one-fifth fewer supervisors than its competitors.

SOURCE: "Benchmarking HR: Measuring up to the Leaders," *HR Executive*, June 1992, 23–40.

Pay and Process: Intertwined Effects

The preceding discussion treats process issues such as participation as factors that may facilitate the success of pay programs. At least one commentator, however, has described an even more important role for process factors in determining employee performance:

> *Worker participation apparently helps make alternative compensation plans…work better—and also has beneficial effects of its own…It appears that changing the way workers are treated may boost productivity more than changing the way they are paid.*[55]

This suggestion raises a broader question: How important are pay decisions, per se, relative to other human resource practices? Although it may not be terribly useful to attempt to disentangle closely intertwined programs, it is important to reinforce the notion that human resource programs, even those as powerful as compensation systems, do not work alone. Consider gainsharing programs. As described earlier, pay is often only one component of such programs (see Table 16.8). How important are the nonpay components?[56] On the one hand, there is ample evidence that gainsharing programs that rely almost exclusively on the monetary component can have substantial effects on productivity.[57] On the other hand, a study of an automotive parts plant found that adding a participation component (monthly meetings with management to discuss the gainsharing plan and ways to increase productivity) to a gainsharing pay incentive plan raised productivity. In a related study, employees were asked about the factors that motivated them to engage in active participation (e.g., suggestion systems). Employees reported that the desire to earn a monetary bonus was much less important than a number of nonpay factors, particularly the desire for influence and control in how their work was done.[58] A third study reported that productivity and profitability were both enhanced by the addition of employee participation in decisions, beyond the improvement derived from monetary incentives such as gainsharing.[59]

ORGANIZATION STRATEGY AND COMPENSATION STRATEGY: A QUESTION OF FIT

Although much of our focus has been on the general, or average, effects of different pay programs, it is also useful to think in terms of matching pay strategies to organization strategies. To use an example from medicine, using the same medical treatment regardless of the symptoms and diagnosis would be foolish. In choosing a pay strategy, one must consider how effectively it will further the organization's overall business strategy. Consider again the findings reported in Table 16.11. The average effect of moving from a pay strategy with below-average variability in pay to one with above-average variability is an increase in return on assets of almost 2 points (from 5.2 percent to 7.1 percent). But in some organizations, the increase could be smaller. In fact, greater variability in pay could contribute to a lower return on assets in some organizations. In other organizations, greater variability in pay could contribute to increases in return on assets of greater than 2 points. Obviously, being able to tell where variable pay works and where it does not could have substantial consequences.

In Chapter 2, we discussed the Miles and Snow typology of organization strategies. Briefly, "defenders" are organizations that focus more on efficiency and cost control and less on new-product or market development. In contrast, "prospector" organizations constantly search for new product and market opportunities. "Analyzer" firms are in between, integrating aspects of defender and prospector organizations. How should compensation strategies differ according to whether an organization follows a defender or a prospector strategy?

Table 16.12 provides some suggested matches. Basically, a prospector organization's emphasis on innovation, risk taking, and growth is linked to a pay strategy that shares risk with employees but also provides them with the opportunity for high future earnings by having them share in whatever success the organization has. This means relatively low levels of fixed compensation in the short run but the use of bonuses and stock options, for example, that can pay off handsomely in the long run. Stock options have been described as the pay program "that built Silicon Valley," having been used by companies such as Apple, Sun Microsystems, and others.[60] When such companies become successful, everyone from top managers to secretaries can become millionaires if they own stock. Prospector organizations

TABLE 16.12   Matching Organization Strategy and Pay Strategy

Pay Strategy Dimensions	Business Unit Strategy	
	Defenders	Prospectors
Risk Sharing (Variable Pay)	Low	High
Time Orientation	Short-term	Long-term
Pay Level (short run)	Above market	Below market
Pay Level (long-run potential)	Above market	Above market
Benefits Level	Above market	Below market
Centralization of Pay Decisions	Centralized	Decentralized
Pay Unit of Analysis	Job	Skills

SOURCE: Adapted from L. R. Gomez-Mejia and D. B. Balkin, *Compensation, Organizational Strategy, and Firm Performance* (Cincinnati: South-Western, 1992), Appendix 4b.

are also thought to benefit from a less bureaucratic orientation, in the sense of having more decentralization and flexibility in pay decisions and in recognizing individual skills, rather than being constrained by job or grade-classification systems. On the other hand, defender organizations are thought to require a very different set of pay practices by virtue of their lower rate of growth, more stable work force, and greater need for consistency and standardization in pay decisions.

INTERNATIONAL COMPARISONS

We noted in the previous chapter that the productivity of the U.S. labor force probably remains among the best (and perhaps is the best) in the world. However, there are two important caveats to consider. First, although current levels of productivity are important, future productivity and competitiveness depend on productivity *growth*. On this dimension, the United States has not done as well in recent decades. For example, between 1960 and 1987, Japan's output per hour grew at 7.7 percent, versus 2.8 percent in the United States. Second, the productivity data we have discussed thus far reflect national averages. However, there are significant differences among industries and organizations, which are often of greater interest to managers and employees who have very specific competitive challenges. One of the most publicized cases is that of the automobile industry. The U.S. and Canadian share of world motor-vehicle production has fallen from over 70 percent in 1955 to approximately 25 percent in the late 1980s. The share of the U.S. domestic motor-vehicle market held by U.S. manufacturers has

TABLE 16.13   Some Comparisons between U.S. and Japanese
Pay and Employment Practices

	Japan	United States
Percentage of work force in teams	69%	17%
Suggestions per employee	62	.4
Job classifications	12	67
Training for new production workers (hours)	380	46
Use of job rotation (4 point scale, 0 = none 4 = frequent)	3	.9

SOURCE: Reprinted with permission of J. P. Womack, D. T. Jones and D. Roos, *The Machine That Changed the World* (New York: MacMillan, 1990), 92.

fallen from nearly 100 percent in 1955 to just over 60 percent by the late 1980s.[61] Why?

One answer has to do with productivity differences. The average Japanese plant requires fewer assembly hours per vehicle (17 versus 25) and one-third less physical space, and carries a dramatically lower inventory (0.2 days versus 2.9 days). Moreover, the Japanese plants demonstrate that such efficiency does not have to come at the expense of quality. In fact, their quality (e.g., defects per 100 vehicles) is 25 percent higher than that of U.S. manufacturers. Finally, Japanese producers achieve all of this despite having lower labor costs.[62]

What explains the high productivity in Japanese automobile plants? One element is their greater level of automation. However, much importance has also been attached to the nature of Japanese management.[63] As Table 16.13 indicates, the Japanese make greater use of teams, have more suggestions per employee, fewer job classes, more training for new production workers, and much greater use of job rotation. What are the possible consequences of such differences? Focusing on employee compensation, the smaller number of job classes (and associated pay rates) may help explain the greater flexibility in rotating employees across jobs. Second, employment stability (a type of benefit) is also significantly greater.[64] Third, the use of bonuses linked to profits is common. Manufacturing production workers in Japan receive, on average, 26 percent of their direct annual pay in the form of bonuses. In contrast, U.S. production workers receive an average of 0.5 percent of their pay in the form of bonuses.[65] Combined with the organization of work into teams and the other practices, this may contribute to less of the individualistic focus about which Deming has raised concerns. Although U.S. companies can learn much from other countries, they should keep in mind that lifting only bits and pieces of an employee relations system can be risky.[66] The practices in Japan, for example, may reinforce and support one another. Leave a key ingredient out of the recipe, and it is not clear how the dish will turn out.

SUMMARY

Our focus in this chapter has been on the design and administration of programs that recognize individual contributions to the organization's success. These programs vary as to whether they link pay to individual, group, or organization performance. Often, it is not so much a choice of one program or the other as it is a choice between different combinations of programs that seek to balance individual, group, and organization objectives.

Wages, bonuses, and other types of pay have an important influence on an employee's standard of living. This carries at least two important implications. First, pay can be a powerful motivator. An effective pay strategy can have a substantial positive impact on an organization's success. Conversely, as the opening vignette to this chapter suggests, a poorly conceived pay strategy can have detrimental effects. Second, the importance of pay means that employees care a great deal about the fairness of the pay process. A recurring theme is that pay programs must be explained and administered in such a way that employees understand their underlying rationale and believe it is fair.

The fact that organizations differ in their business and human resource strategies suggests that the most effective compensation strategy will differ from one organization to another. Although benchmarking programs against the competition is informative, what is successful in some organizations may not be a good idea for others. The same point holds in international comparisons. While it is true, for example, that Japan has had a high rate of productivity growth and therefore its human resource practices warrant close study, a practice that works well in Japan may not transfer successfully to organizations in the United States.

Discussion Questions

1. To compete more effectively, your organization is considering a profit sharing plan to increase employee effort and to encourage employees to think like owners. What are the potential advantages and disadvantages of such a plan? Would the profit sharing plan have the same impact on all types of employees? What alternative pay programs should be considered?

2. Gainsharing plans have often been used in manufacturing settings but can also be applied in service organizations. Discuss how performance standards could be developed for gainsharing plans in hospitals, banks, insurance companies, and so forth.

3. The opening vignette to the chapter described an incentive plan that had unintended consequences and was discontinued. Would you have eliminated the plan? Are there any modifications that could have been made to salvage the incentive plan?

4. Your organization has two business units. One unit is a long established manufacturer of a product that competes on price and has not been subject to many
technological innovations. The other business unit is just being started. It has no
products yet, but it is working on developing a new technology for testing the
effects of drugs on people via simulation instead of through lengthy clinical trials. Would you recommend that the two business units have the same pay programs for recognizing individual contributions? Why or why not?

5. Compare the U.S. and Japanese approaches to recognizing individual contributions with the pay system. Would any of the Japanese practices be of help in U.S.
organizations? What cautions should be raised when considering importing
practices from other countries?

Notes

1. We draw freely in this chapter on several recent literature reviews: B. Gerhart and G. T.
Milkovich, "Employee Compensation: Research and Practice," in *Handbook of Industrial and
Organizational Psychology* vol. 3, 2nd ed., ed. M. D. Dunnette and L. M. Hough (Palo Alto,
Cal.: Consulting Psychologists Press, 1992); B. Gerhart, G. T. Milkovich and B. Murray,
"Pay, Performance, and Participation," in *Research Frontiers in Industrial Relations and
Human Resources*, ed. D. Lewin, O. S. Mitchell, and P. D. Sherer (Madison, Wisc.: IRRA,
1992); B. Gerhart and R. D. Bretz, "Employee Compensation in Advanced Manufacturing
Technology," in *Human Factors in Advanced Manufacturing*, ed. W. Karwowski and G.
Salvendy (New York: Wiley, [forthcoming]).

2. B. Gerhart and G. T. Milkovich, "Organizational Differences in Managerial Compensation
and Financial Performance," *Academy of Management Journal* 33 (1990): 663–691.

3. R. A. Lambert and D. F. Larcker, "Executive Compensation, Corporate Decision Making,
and Shareholder Wealth," in *Executive Compensation*, ed. F. Foulkes (Boston: Harvard
Business School Press, 1989), 287–309.

4. L. R. Gomez-Mejia, H. Tosi and T. Hinkin, "Managerial Control, Performance, and
Executive Compensation," *Academy of Management Journal* 30 (1987): 51–70; H. L. Tosi, Jr.,
and L. R. Gomez-Mejia, "The Decoupling of CEO Pay and Performance: An Agency
Theory Perspective," *Administrative Science Quarterly* 34 (1989): 169–189.

5. K. M. Eisenhardt, "Agency Theory: An Assessment and Review," *Academy of Management
Review* 14 (1989): 57–74.

6. Ibid.; Hoskisson et al, "Balancing Corporate Strategy."

7. Eisenhardt, "Agency Theory."

8. E. J. Conlon and J. M. Parks, "Effects of Monitoring and Tradition on Compensation
Arrangements: An Experiment with Principal-Agent Dyads," *Academy of Management
Journal* 33 (1990): 603–622; K. M. Eisenhardt, "Agency- and Institutional-Theory
Explanations: The Case of Retail Sales Compensation," *Academy of Management Journal* 31
(1988): 488–511; Eisenhardt, "Agency Theory"; Gerhart and Milkovich, "Employee
Compensation."

9. G. T. Milkovich, J. Hannon and B. Gerhart, "The Effects of Research and Development
Intensity on Managerial Compensation in Large Organizations," *Journal of High Technology
Management Research* 2 (1991): 133–150.

10. G. T. Milkovich and A. K. Wigdor, *Pay for Performance* (Washington, D.C.: National
Academy Press, 1991); Gerhart and Milkovich, "Employee Compensation."

11. B. Gerhart, "Voluntary Turnover, Job Performance, Salary Growth, and Labor Market
Conditions," (Cornell University: Center for Advanced Human Resource Studies,
Working Paper, No. 90-12).

12. R. D. Bretz, R. A. Ash and G. F. Dreher, "Do People Make the Place? An Examination of the Attraction-Selection-Attrition Hypothesis," *Personnel Psychology* 42 (1989): 561–581; T. A. Judge and R. D. Bretz, "Effect of Values on Job Choice Decisions," *Journal of Applied Psychology* 77 (1992): 261–271.

13. A. Majchrzak, *The Human Side of Factory Automation* (San Francisco: Jossey-Bass, 1988); E. E. Lawler, III, *Strategic Pay* (San Francisco: Jossey-Bass, 1990); Gerhart and Milkovich, "Employee Compensation."

14. R. D. Bretz, G. T. Milkovich and W. Read, "The Current State of Performance Appraisal Research and Practice," *Journal of Management* 18 (1992): 321–352; R. L. Heneman, "Merit Pay Research," *Research in Personnel and Human Resource Management* 8 (1990): 203–263; Milkovich and Wigdor, *Pay for Performance.*

15. Bretz, Milkovich, and Read, op cit.

16. Ibid.

17. Ibid.

18. W. E. Deming, *Out of the Crisis* (Cambridge, Mass.: Center for Advanced Engineering Study, Massachusetts Institute of Technology, 1986), 110.

19. Ibid.

20. Ibid.

21. Gerhart, "Voluntary Turnover."

22. R. Folger and M. A. Konovsky, "Effects of Procedural and Distributive Justice on Reactions to Pay Raise Decisions," *Academy of Management Journal* 32 (1989): 115–130; J. Greenberg, "Determinants of Perceived Fairness of Performance Evaluations," *Journal of Applied Psychology* 71 (1986): 340–342.

23. E. E. Lawler, III, "Pay for Performance: A Strategic Analysis," in *Compensation and Benefits*, ed. L. R. Gomez-Mejia (Washington, D.C.: Bureau of National Affairs, 1989); A. M. Konrad and J. Pfeffer, "Do You Get What You Deserve? Factors Affecting the Relationship between Productivity and Pay," *Administrative Science Quarterly* 35 (1990): 258–285; J. L. Medoff and K. G. Abraham, "Are Those Paid More Really More Productive? The Case of Experience," *Journal of Human Resources* 16 (1981): 186–216; K. S. Teel, "Are Merit Raises Really Based on Merit?" *Personnel Journal* 65, no. 3 (1986): 88–95.

24. B. Gerhart and S. Rynes, "Determinants and Consequences of Salary Negotiations by Graduating Male and Female MBAs," *Journal of Applied Psychology*, 1991.

25. E. A. Locke, D. B. Feren, V. M. McCaleb, K. N. Shaw and A. T. Denny, "The Relative Effectiveness of Four Methods of Motivating Employee Performance," in *Changes in Working Life*, ed. K. D. Duncan, M. M. Gruenberg and D. Wallis (New York: Wiley, 1980), 363–388.

26. Gerhart and Milkovich, "Employee Compensation."

27. This ideas has been referred to as the "share economy." See M. L. Weitzman, "The Simple Macroeconomics of Profit Sharing," *American Economic Review* 75 (1985): 937–953. For supportive empirical evidence, see the following studies: J. Chelius and R. S. Smith, "Profit Sharing and Employment Stability," *Industrial and Labor Relations Review* 43 (1990): 256S–273S; B. Gerhart, "Employment Stability under Different Managerial Compensation Systems," (Cornell University: Center for Advanced Human Resource Studies, Working Paper 91-02); D. L. Kruse, "Profit Sharing and Employment Variability: Microeconomic Evidence on the Weitzman Theory," *Industrial and Labor Relations Review* 44 (1991): 437–453.

28. "How You'll Be Paid in the 1990s," *Fortune*, April 9, 1990, 11.

29. "Watching the Bottom Line Instead of the Clock," *Business Week*, November 7, 1988; "Another Day, Another Dollar Needs Another Look," *Personnel* 68, January 1991: 9–13; "Saturn: An Outpost of Change in GM's Steadfast Universe," *New York Times*, March 17, 1991, sec. 4, p. 4; C. O'Dell *People, Performance, and Pay* (Houston, Tx: American Productivity Center, 1987) The Conference Board; *Variable Pay: New Performance Rewards,*

Research Bulletin No. 246 (New York: The Conference Board, 1990); Bureau of National Affairs, *Changing Pay Practices: New Developments in Employee Compensation* (Washington, D.C.: Bureau of National Affairs, 1988); Bureau of National Affairs, *Nontraditional Incentive Pay Programs*, Personnel Policies Forum Survey, No. 148 (Washington, D.C.: Bureau of National Affairs, 1991); M. L. Weitzman and D. L. Kruse, "Profit Sharing and Productivity," in *Paying for Productivity*, ed. A. S. Blinder (Washington, D.C.: Brookings Institution, 1990).

30. Gerhart and Milkovich, "Employee Compensation".

31. Bureau of National Affairs, *Employee Relations Weekly*, November 5, 1990, 8: 1358.

32. E. M. Coates, III, "Profit Sharing Today: Plans and Provisions," *Monthly Labor Review*, April 1991, 19–25.

33. American Management Association, *CompFlash*, April 1991, 3. General Motors' Saturn division has also recently scaled back its reliance on profit sharing because of lower-than-expected profits.

34. American Management Association, *CompFlash*, April 1991, 3.

35. "Executive Compensation: Taking Stock," *Personnel* 67, December 1990, 7–8; "Another Day, Another Dollar," 9–13.

36. Gerhart and Milkovich, "Organizational Differences in Managerial Compensation."

37. "Taking Stock of Employee Ownership Plans," *USA Today*, May 30, 1989, 3B.

38. "Employees Left Holding the Bag," *Fortune*, May 20, 1991, 83–93; Conte and Svejnar, "The Performance Effects of Employee Ownership Plans."

39. M. A. Conte and J. Svejnar, "The Performance Effects of Employee Ownership Plans," in *Paying for Productivity*, ed. A. S. Blinder (Washington, D.C.: The Brookings Institution, 1990), 245–294.

40. Ibid.; T. H. Hammer, "New Developments in Profit Sharing, Gainsharing, and Employee Ownership," in *Productivity in Organizations*, ed. J. P. Campbell, R. J. Campbell, & Associates (San Francisco: Jossey-Bass, 1988); K. J. Klein, "Employee Stock Ownership and Employee Attitudes: A Test of Three Models," *Journal of Applied Psychology* 72 (1987): 319–332.

41. J. L. Pierce, S. Rubenfeld and S. Morgan, "Employee Ownership: A Conceptual Model of Process and Effects," *Academy of Management Review* 16 (1991): 121–144.

42. L. Hatcher and T. L. Ross, "From Individual Incentives to an Organization-wide Gainsharing Plan: Effects on Teamwork and Product Quality," *Journal of Organizational Behavior* 12 (1991): 169–183; R. T. Kaufman, "The Effects of Improshare on Productivity," *Industrial and Labor Relations Review* 45 (1992): 311–322; M. H. Schuster, "The Scanlon Plan: A Longitudinal Analysis," *Journal of Applied Behavioral Science* 20 (1984): 23–28; J. A. Wagner, III, P. Rubin and T. J. Callahan, "Incentive Payment and Nonmanagerial Productivity: An Interrupted Time Series Analysis of Magnitude and Trend," *Organizational Behavior and Human Decision Processes* 42 (1988): 47–74.

43. T. L. Ross and R. A. Ross, "Gainsharing: Sharing Improved Performance," in *The Compensation Handbook*, 3rd ed., ed. M. L. Rock and L. A. Berger (New York: McGraw-Hill, 1991).

44. T. M. Welbourne and L. R. Gomez-Mejia, "Team Incentives in the Workplace," in *The Compensation Handbook*, 3rd ed., ed. M. L. Rock and L. A. Berger (New York: McGraw-Hill, 1991).

45. M. C. Jensen and K. J. Murphy, "Performance Pay and Top-Management Incentives," *Journal of Political Economy* 98 (1990): 225–264.

46. M. C. Jensen and K. J. Murphy, "CEO Incentives—It's Not How Much You Pay, but How," *Harvard Business Review* 68 (May–June 1990): 138–153.

47. Gerhart and Milkovich, "Organizational Differences in Managerial Compensation."

48. American Management Association, "Under Scrutiny by Regulatory Agencies: Stock Option Grants," *CompFlash*, July 1992; F. S. Worthy, "The Battle of the Bean Counters," *Fortune*, June 1, 1992, 117ff; A. Saker, "Bill Takes Aim at Stealth Compensation," *Ithaca Journal*, February 2, 1993, 8A; A. L. Cowan, "Stock Option Accounting Is Planned," *New York Times*, April 8, 1993, D1ff.

49. R. D. Hershey, Jr., "SEC Acts on Behalf of Stockholders," *New York Times*, June 24, 1992, D1.

50. J. Cutcher-Gershenfeld, "The Impact on Economic Performance of a Transformation in Workplace Relations," *Industrial and Labor Relations Review* 44 (1991): 241–260; Irene Goll, "Environment, Corporate Ideology, and Involvement Programs," *Industrial Relations* 30 (1991): 138–149.

51. L. R. Gomez-Mejia and D. B. Balkin, *Compensation, Organizational Strategy, and Firm Performance* (Cincinnati: South-Western, 1992); G. D. Jenkins and E. E. Lawler, III, "Impact of Employee Participation in Pay Plan Development," *Organizational Behavior and Human Performance* 28 (1981): 111–128.

52. D. I. Levine and L. D. Tyson, "Participation, Productivity, and the Firm's Environment," in *Paying for Productivity*, ed. A. S. Blinder (Washington, D.C.: The Brookings Institution, 1990).

53. M. C. Jensen and W. H. Meckling, "Rights and Production Functions: An Application to Labor-Managed Firms and Codetermination," *Journal of Business* 52 (1979): 469–506; Levine and Tyson, "Participation, Productivity, and the Firm's Environment."

54. Ibid.

55. A. S. Blinder, *Paying for Productivity* (Washington, D.C.: The Brookings Institution, 1990).

56. Hammer, "New Developments in Profit Sharing"; Milkovich and Wigdor, *Pay for Performance*; D. J. B. Mitchell, D. Lewin and E. E. Lawler, III, "Alternative Pay Systems, Firm Performance and Productivity," in *Paying for Productivity*, ed. A. S. Blinder (Washington, D.C.: The Brookings Institution, 1990).

57. Kaufman, "The Effects of Improshare on Productivity"; M. H. Schuster, "The Scanlon Plan: A Longitudinal Analysis," *Journal of Applied Behavioral Science* 20 (1984): 23–28; J. A. Wagner, III, P. Rubin and T. J. Callahan, "Incentive Payment and Nonmanagerial Productivity: An Interrupted Time Series Analysis of Magnitude and Trend," *Organizational Behavior and Human Decision Processes* 42 (1988): 47–74.

58. C. R. Gowen, III and S. A. Jennings, "The Effects of Changes in Participation and Group Size on Gainsharing Success: A Case Study," *Journal of Organizational Behavior Management* 11 (1991): 147–169.

59. L. Hatcher, T. L. Ross and D. Collins, "Attributions for Participation and Nonparticipation in Gainsharing-Plan Involvement Systems," *Group and Organization Studies* 16 (1991): 25–43; Mitchell et al., "Alternative Pay Systems".

60. A. J. Baker, "Stock Options—A Perk that Built Silicon Valley," *The Wall Street Journal*, A20.

61. J. P. Womack, D. T. Jones and D. Roos, *The Machine that Changed the World* (New York: MacMillan, 1990).

62. Ibid., 92 and 98; P. Capdevielle, "International Comparisons of Hourly Compensation Costs," *Monthly Labor Review* 112 (June 1989): 10–12; Fluctuations in currency exchange rates make such comparisons difficult. However, over the years, hourly compensation costs (including benefits) have been lower in Japan. For evidence on the automobile industry, see "Ford and Chrysler Outpace Japanese in Reducing Costs," *New York Times*, June 18, 1992, D1ff.

63. Womack et al., *The Machine that Changed the World*, 98.

64. Ibid.

65. M. Hashimoto, "Employment and Wage Systems in Japan and Their Implications for Productivity," in *Paying for Productivity*, ed. A. S. Blinder (Washington, D.C.: The Brookings Institution, 1990), 257.

66. Morishima, "Information Sharing and Collective Bargaining in Japan: Effects on Wage Negotiation," *Industrial and Labor Relations Review* 44 (1991): 469–485.

C A S E

INCENTIVE PAY FOR DOCTORS

At U.S. Healthcare, Inc., a health maintenance organization (HMO), physicians' pay is linked in part to how well they score on patients' responses to questionnaires. Examples of questions include (1) How easy is it to make appointments for checkups? (2) How long is the waiting time in the doctor's office? (3) How much personal concern does the doctor show patients? Some doctors like the system because it gives them a clear message about how to excel and rewards them for doing so. Others, however, are not convinced incentive pay is a good idea. One criticism is that patient surveys of quality may give too much weight to "fringe issues" such as how friendly the receptionist is or whether the doctor was on time, instead of more important matters such as whether the patient received the correct care or treatment. Another concern is that individual incentive or merit pay systems disrupt the ability of doctors to work together as colleagues. One Massachusetts-based HMO tried a system where staff doctors received different bonuses depending on whether the section heads rated their work as "exemplary." The result? One doctor described "doctors almost getting into fistfights over what amounted to a $500 bonus."

QUESTIONS

1. Is incentive or merit pay for physicians a good idea?
2. How can such incentives be designed to achieve the best health care?
3. What are the most appropriate ways to measure the quality of health care?

SOURCE: G. Anders, "More Managed Health-Care Systems Use Incentive Pay to Reward 'Best' Doctors," *The Wall Street Journal*, January 25, 1993, B1ff.

EMPLOYEE BENEFITS

Objectives

After reading this chapter, you should be able to:

1. Discuss the growth in benefits costs and the underlying reasons for that growth.
2. Explain the major provisions of employee benefits programs.
3. Describe the effects of benefits management on cost and work-force quality.
4. Explain how employee benefits in the United States compare with those in other countries.
5. Explain the importance of effectively communicating the nature and value of benefits to employees.
6. Describe the regulatory constraints that affect the way employee benefits are designed and administered.

Social Responsibility or Financial Solvency?

In 1988, John W. McGann informed his employer, H & H Music Company of Houston, that he had the AIDS virus. McGann had health insurance through H & H Music Company. Nevertheless, because of the anticipated high costs of McGann's future medical treatment, the company subsequently cut his maximum medical benefit from $1 million to $5,000. The company was able to do so because its health insurance plan was self-insured, meaning that the company used its own assets to cover the insurance claims of its employees. The Supreme Court ruled that under the Employee Retirement Income Security Act, self-insured plans are allowed to reduce or terminate benefit levels in response to cost-control concerns. Approximately one-half of all U.S. employees are covered by self-insured health insurance plans and thus face similar risks if they develop a costly disease such as AIDS, cancer, or Alzheimer's. Further, because an insurance company often handles the paperwork under self-insured plans, most employees probably do not recognize this risk.

Why would an employer take an action so harmful to its employees? Employers, especially small ones, argue that the costs of providing coverage for even one such seriously ill person could put them out of business. Why, then, do employers not shift from self-insurance to coverage through insurance companies where risks are pooled and borne by the insurance company? Many employers have moved to self-insured plans, according to testimony before Congress, because of "the desperation they face in coping with current health-care market forces and rising costs." Finally, although the American Medical Association and others argued that what happened to McGann was

bad law and bad policy, the Bush administration Labor Department pointed out that with 35 million American workers already without health insurance, preventing employers from reducing or terminating benefits to reduce their costs would exacerbate the problem by making employers less willing to offer health insurance if they cannot protect themselves against the risk of large future insurance costs.

As this example indicates, one of the main challenges in managing employee benefits is how to be a socially responsible employer while keeping benefits costs from reaching levels that threaten the employer's ability to compete or even survive. Although medical benefits have become an area of particular concern, challenges exist across the benefits spectrum. Just as important, however, are the reactions of employees to the benefits program and the way it is administered. As such, managing benefits has some important parallels to managing compensation.

SOURCE: *Daily Labor Report*, December 2, 1992, A-13; R. Pear, "U.S. Is to Argue Employers Can Cut Health Insurance," *New York Times*, October 16, 1992, p. 1+; Bureau of National Affairs, "Congress Urged to Amend Pension Law to Prevent Reductions in Health Coverage," *Daily Labor Report*, December 2, 1992, A-11 to A-13.

INTRODUCTION

If one thinks of benefits as a part of total employee compensation, many of the concepts discussed in the two previous chapters on employee compensation apply here as well. This means, for example, that both cost and behavioral objectives are important. In 1990, the cost of benefits added an average of 38.4 percent to every dollar of payroll, thus accounting for about

28 percent of the total employee compensation package. Controlling labor costs is not possible without controlling benefits costs. When Ford Motor Company pays $529 in health-care costs per car produced, its ability to sell automobiles at a competitive price is reduced.[1] On the behavioral side, benefits seem to influence whether potential employees come to work for a company, whether they stay, when they retire—perhaps even how they perform (although the empirical evidence, especially on the latter point, is surprisingly limited). Broadly speaking, then, the labor cost and behavioral consequences of benefits once again suggest that organizations need to compete effectively in both product and labor markets.

Although it makes sense to think of benefits as part of total compensation, benefits have unique aspects. First, there is the question of legal compliance. Although direct compensation is subject to government regulation, the scope and impact of regulation on benefits is far greater. Some benefits, such as Social Security, are mandated by law. Others, although not mandated, are subject to significant regulation or must meet certain criteria to achieve the most favorable tax treatment; these include pensions and savings plans. The heavy involvement of government in benefits decisions reflects the central role benefits play in maintaining economic security.

A second unique aspect of benefits is that organizations so typically offer them that they have come to be institutionalized. Providing medical benefits of some sort has become almost obligatory for many employers. A large employer that did not offer such benefits to its full-time employees would be highly unusual, and the employer might well have trouble attracting and retaining a quality work force.

A third unique aspect of benefits, compared with other forms of compensation, is their complexity. It is relatively easy to understand the value of a dollar as part of a salary, but not as part of a benefits package. The advantages and disadvantages of different types of medical coverage, pension provisions, disability insurance, and so forth are often difficult to grasp, and their value (beyond a general sense that they are good to have) is rarely as clear as the value of one's salary. Most fundamentally, employees may not even be aware of the benefits available to them; and if they are aware, they may not understand how to use them. When employers spend large sums of money on benefits but employees do not understand the benefits or attach much value to them, the return on employers' benefits investment will be fairly dismal.[2]

REASONS FOR BENEFITS GROWTH

In thinking about benefits as part of total compensation, a basic question arises: Why do employers choose to channel a significant portion of the compensation dollar away from cash (wages and salaries) into benefits? Economic theory tells us that people prefer a dollar in cash over a dollar's worth of any specific commodity because the cash can be used to purchase

FIGURE 17.1   Growth of Employee Benefits, Percentage of Wages and Salaries

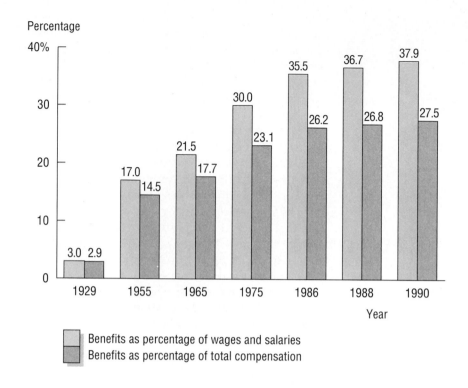

SOURCE: U.S. Chamber of Commerce Research Center, *Employee Benefits 1990* (Washington, D.C.: U.S. Chamber of Commerce, 1991).

the commodity or something else.[3] Thus, cash is less restrictive. Several factors, however, have contributed to less emphasis on cash and more on benefits in compensation. To understand these factors, it is useful to examine the growth in benefits over time and the underlying reasons for that growth.

Figure 17.1 gives an indication of the overall growth in benefits. Note that in 1929, on the eve of the Great Depression, benefits added an average of only 3 percent to every dollar of payroll. By 1955, this figure had grown to 17 percent, and it continued to grow steadily until the 1980s, when benefits growth leveled off at about 38 percent for every payroll dollar.

Many factors contributed to this tremendous growth.[4] First, during the 1930s several new laws were passed as part of Franklin Roosevelt's New Deal, a legislative program aimed at buffering people from the devastating effects of the Great Depression. The Social Security Act and other legislation established legally required benefits (such as the Social Security retirement system) and modified the tax structure in such a way as to effectively make other benefits, such as workers' compensation (for work-related injuries) and unemployment insurance, mandatory. Second, wage and price controls

TABLE 17.1   Example of Marginal Tax Rates

	Employee 1 Salary = $15,000		Employee 2 Salary = $45,000	
	Nominal Tax Rate	Effective Tax Rate	Nominal Tax Rate	Effective Tax Rate
Federal	15.0%	15.0%	28.0%	28.0%
State (New York)	7.9%	6.7%	7.9%	5.7%
City (New York)	4.3%	3.7%	4.4%	3.2%
Social Security	6.2%	6.2%	6.2%	6.2%
Medicare	1.5%	1.5%	1.5%	1.5%
Total tax rate		33.0%		44.5%

Note: State and city taxes are deductible on the federal tax return, reducing their effective tax rate.

instituted during World War II, combined with labor-market shortages, forced employers to think of new ways to attract and retain employees. Because benefits were not covered by wage controls, employers channeled more resources in this direction. Once institutionalized, such benefits tended to remain even after wage and price controls were lifted.

Third, the tax treatment of benefits programs is often more favorable for employees than the tax treatment of wages and salaries, meaning that a dollar spent on benefits has the potential to generate more value for the employees than the same dollar spent on wages and salaries. The **marginal tax rate** is the percentage of additional earnings that goes to taxes. Consider the two hypothetical employees in Table 17.1 and the effect on their take-home pay of a $1,000 increase in salary. The total effective marginal tax rate is higher for higher-paid employees and also varies according to state and city. (New York State and New York City are among the highest.) A $1,000 annual raise for the employee earning $15,000 would result in an annual increase in take-home pay of $670 ($1,000 x [1 − .33]). For the employee earning $45,000 per year, the increase in net pay from a $1,000 increase would be $550 ($1,000 × [1 − .45]). In contrast, an extra $1,000 put into benefits would lead to an increase for both employees of $1,000 in "take-home benefits."

Employers, too, realize tax advantages from certain types of benefits. Although both cash compensation and most benefits are deductible as operating expenses, employers (like employees) pay Social Security tax on salaries below a certain amount ($57,600 in 1993) and Medicare tax on salaries up to $135,000, as well as other taxes like workers' compensation and unemployment compensation. However, no such taxes are paid on most employee benefits. The bottom line is that the employer may be able to provide more value to employees by spending the extra $1,000 on benefits instead of salary.

The tax advantage of benefits also takes another form. Deferring compensation until retirement allows the employee to receive cash, but at a time (retirement) when the employee's tax rate is sometimes lower because of a lower income level. More important, perhaps, is that investment returns on the deferred money typically accumulate tax free, resulting in much faster growth of the investment.

A fourth factor that has influenced benefits growth is the cost advantage that groups typically realize over individuals. Organizations that represent large groups of employees can purchase insurance (or self-insure) at a lower rate because of economies of scale, which spread fixed costs over more employees to reduce the cost per person. Insurance risks can be more easily pooled in large groups, and large groups can also achieve greater bargaining power in dealing with insurance carriers or medical providers.

The final factor influencing the growth of benefits was the growth of organized labor from the 1930s through the 1950s. This growth was partly a result of another piece of New Deal legislation, the National Labor Relations Act, which greatly enhanced trade unions' ability to organize workers and negotiate contracts with employers. Benefits were often a key negotiation objective. (Indeed, they still are. It is estimated that more than one-half of workers who struck in 1991 did so over health-care coverage issues.)[5] Unions were able to successfully pursue their members' interests in benefits, particularly when tax advantages provided an incentive for employers to shift money from cash to benefits. For unions, a new benefit such as medical coverage was a tangible success that could have more impact on prospective union members than a wage increase of equivalent value, which might have amounted to only a cent or two per hour. Also, many nonunion employers responded to the threat of unionization by implementing the same benefits for their own employees, thus contributing to benefits growth.

BENEFITS PROGRAMS

Most benefits fall into one of the following categories: social insurance, private group insurance, retirement, and pay for time not worked.[6] Table 17.2, based on Bureau of Labor Statistics (BLS) data, provides an overview of the prevalence of specific benefits programs.

Social Insurance (Legally Required)

Social Security.   Among the most important provisions of the Social Security Act of 1935 was the establishment of old-age insurance and unemployment insurance. The act was later amended to add survivors insurance (1939), disability insurance (1956), hospital insurance (Medicare, part A, 1965), and supplementary medical insurance (Medicare, part B, 1965) for the elderly. Together, these provisions constitute the federal Old Age,

TABLE 17.2 Percentage of Full-Time Workers Who Participate in Selected Benefit Programs

	Medium and Large Private Establishments[a] Full time 1989	Small Private Establishments[b] Full time 1990
Medical care	92%	69%
Dental care	66	30
Sickness and accident insurance	43	26
Long-term disability insurance	45	19
Paid sick leave	68	47
All retirement[c]	81	42
Defined benefit pension	63	20
wholly employer financed	60	19
partly employer financed	3	1
Defined contribution	48	31
Retirement	36	28
wholly employer financed[d]	14	16
partly employer financed	22	11
Life insurance	94	64
wholly employer financed	82	53
partly employer financed	12	19
Paid leave		
holidays	97	84
vacation	97	88
maternity leave	3	2
paternity leave	1	—[e]
Unpaid		
maternity leave	37	17
paternity leave	18	8

SOURCES: *Employee Benefit Notes*, April 1992. BLS Survey Shows High Rate of Benefit Participation among Public Employees (Washington, D.C.: Employee Benefit Research Institute), original data from U.S. Government Printing Office, 1988 and 1992; *Employee Benefits in Medium and Large Establishments*, 1989 (Washington, D.C.: U.S. Government Printing Office, 1990); *Employee Benefits in Small Private Establishments*, 1990 (Washington, D.C.: U.S. Government Printing Office, 1991).
[a]These data represent 32 million full-time employees in private nonagricultural establishments with 100 or more employees in the District of Columbia and in all states except Alaska and Hawaii.
[b]These data represent 32 million full-time employees in private nonagricultural establishments with fewer than 100 employees. The survey was composed primarily of small independent businesses, although about 25 percent of respondents were small establishments that were part of larger enterprises.
[c]Includes defined benefit pension plans and defined contribution retirement plans. The total is less than the sum of the individual items because many employees participated in both types of plans.
[d]Employees participating in two or more plans were counted as participants in wholly employer-financed plans only if all plans were noncontributory.
[e]Less than 0.5 percent.

Survivors, Disability, and Health Insurance (OASDHI) program. Over 90 percent of U.S. employees are covered by the program, the main exceptions being railroad and federal, state, and local government employees, who often have their own plans. Note, however, that an individual employee must meet certain eligibility requirements to receive benefits. To be fully insured typically requires 40 quarters of covered employment and minimum earnings of $540 (in 1991) per quarter (or $2,160 per year). However, the eligibility rules for survivors and disability benefits are somewhat different.

Social Security retirement (old-age insurance) benefits for fully insured workers begin at age 65 (full benefits) or age 62 (at a permanent reduction in benefits). Although the amount of the benefit depends on one's earnings history, benefits go up very little after a certain level; thus, high earners help subsidize benefit payments to low earners. Cost-of-living increases are provided each year that the consumer price index increases.

An important attribute of the Social Security retirement benefit is that it is free from state tax in about one-half of the states and entirely free from federal tax. However, the federal tax code has an earnings test for those who are still earning wages. In 1991, beneficiaries under age 65 were allowed to make $7,080; those between 65 and 69 were allowed to make $9,720. If these amounts are exceeded, the Social Security benefit is reduced $1 for every $2 in excess earnings for those under age 65 and $1 for every $3 for those 65 to 69. Those age 70 or older face no penalty. These provisions are important because of their effects on the work decisions of those between 62 and 70. The earnings test increases a person's incentive to retire (otherwise full Social Security benefits are not received), and if he or she continues to work, the incentive to work part-time rather than full-time increases.

How are retirement and other benefits financed? Both employers and employees are assessed a payroll tax. In 1993, each paid a tax of 7.65 percent (a total of 15.3 percent) on the first $57,600 of the employee's earnings. Of the 7.65 percent, 6.2 percent funds OASDHI, and 1.45 percent funds Medicare (part A). In addition, beginning in 1993, the 1.45 percent Medicare tax is assessed on earnings up to $135,000.

What are the behavioral consequences of Social Security benefits? Because they are legally mandated, employers do not have discretion in designing this aspect of their benefits programs. However, Social Security does affect employees' retirement decisions. The eligibility age for benefits and the tax penalty for earnings above a certain level contribute to an outflow of employees once they reach their middle 60s. If, as some have suggested, pay rises with age more quickly than productivity does late in employees' careers, these retirements are a positive outcome for employers. Indeed, in recent years, many employers have relied heavily on early retirement incentives to reduce employment. On the other hand, when older employees leave, they take with them a great deal of experience and expertise.

Unemployment Insurance. Established by the 1935 Social Security Act, this program has four major objectives: (1) to offset lost income during involuntary unemployment; (2) to help unemployed workers find new jobs, (3) to provide an incentive for employers to stabilize employment, and (4) to preserve investments in worker skills by providing income during short-term layoffs (which allows them to return to their employer rather than start over with another employer).

The unemployment insurance program is financed largely through federal and state taxes on employers. Although, strictly speaking, the decision to establish the program is left to each state, the Social Security Act created a tax incentive structure that quickly led every state to establish a program. The federal tax rate is currently 0.8 percent. The state tax rate varies, the minimum being 5.4 percent on the first $7,000 of wages. Many states have a higher rate or impose the tax on a greater share of earnings.

A very important feature of the unemployment insurance program is that no state imposes the same tax on every employer. Instead, the size of the tax depends on the employer's **experience rating**. Employers that have a history of laying off a large share of their work forces pay higher taxes than those who do not. In some states, an employer that has had very few layoffs may pay no state tax. In contrast, an employer with a poor experience rating could pay a tax as high as 5 to 10 percent, depending on the state.[7]

Unemployed workers are eligible for benefits if they (1) have a prior attachment to the work force (often 52 weeks or 4 quarters of work at a minimum level of pay), (2) are available for work, (3) are actively seeking work (including registering at the local unemployment office), and (4) were not discharged for cause (e.g., willful misconduct), did not quit voluntarily, and are not out of work because of a labor dispute.

Benefits also vary by state, but they are typically about 50 percent of a person's earnings and last for 26 weeks. Extended benefits for up to 13 weeks are also available in states with a sustained unemployment rate above 6.5 percent. Emergency extended benefits are also sometimes funded by Congress.[8] All states have minimum and maximum weekly benefit levels. In contrast to Social Security retirement benefits, unemployment benefits are taxed as ordinary income.

Because unemployment insurance is, in effect, legally required, management's discretion is limited here, too. Management's main task is to keep its experience rating low by avoiding unnecessary work-force reductions (by relying, for example, on the sorts of actions described in Chapter 14).

Workers' Compensation. Prior to enactment of these laws, workers suffering work-related injuries or diseases could receive compensation only by suing for damages. Moreover, the common law (see Chapter 4) defenses available to employers meant that such lawsuits were not usually successful. In contrast, workers' compensation laws cover job-related injuries and death.[9] These laws operate under a principle of no-fault liability, meaning that an employee does not need to establish gross negligence by the employer. In return, employers receive immunity from lawsuits. (One exception is the employer who intentionally contributes to a dangerous workplace.) Employees are not covered when injuries are self-inflicted or stem from intoxication or "willful disregard of safety rules."[10] Approximately 90 percent of all U.S. workers are covered by state workers' compensation laws, although again there are differences among states, with coverage ranging from 70 percent to over 95 percent.

Workers' compensation benefits fall into four major categories: (1) disability income, (2) medical care, (3) death benefits, and (4) rehabilitative services.

Disability income is typically two-thirds of predisability earnings, although each state has its own minimum and maximum. In contrast to unemployment insurance benefits, disability benefits are tax free. The system is financed differently by different states, some having a single state fund, most allowing employers to purchase coverage from private insurance companies. Self-funding by employers is also permitted in most states. The cost to the employer is based on three factors. The first factor is the nature of the occupations and the risk attached to each. Premiums for low-risk occupations may be less than 1 percent of payroll; the cost for some of the most hazardous occupations may be as high as 100 percent of payroll. The second factor is the state where work is located. Wyoming pays a worker $2,612 for the loss of a thumb and $5,690 for loss of an eye; in contrast, Connecticut pays $63,755 for the loss of a thumb and $157,685 for the loss of an eye.[11] The third factor is the employer's experience rating.

The cost of the workers' compensation system to U.S. employers has grown dramatically, from just over $30 billion in 1986 to over $60 billion in 1992, leading to an increased focus on ways of controlling workers' compensation costs.[12] The experience rating system again provides an incentive for employers to make their workplaces safer. Dramatic injuries (e.g., losing a finger or hand) are less prevalent than minor ones, such as sprains and strains. Back strain is the most prevalent injury (31 percent of all injuries), costing an average of $24,000 per claim.[13] Many actions can be taken to reduce workplace injuries, such as work redesign, training, and so forth.[14] Some of these changes can be fairly simple (e.g., permitting workers to sit instead of having them bend over). It is also important to hold managers accountable (e.g., in their performance evaluations) for making workplaces safer and getting employees back to work promptly following an injury. With the recent passage of the Americans with Disabilities Act, employers are under even greater pressure to deal effectively and fairly with workplace injuries. See the discussion in Chapter 5 on safety awareness programs for some of the ways employers and employees are working to make the workplace safer.

Private Group Insurance

As we pointed out earlier, group insurance rates are typically lower than individual rates because of economies of scale, the ability to pool risks, and the greater bargaining power of a group. This cost advantage, together with tax considerations and a concern for employee security, helps explain the prevalence of employer-sponsored insurance plans. We discuss three major types: medical insurance, life insurance, and long-term disability. Note that these programs are not legally required. Rather, they are offered at the discretion of employers.

Medical and Life Insurance.   Not surprisingly, public opinion surveys indicate that medical benefits are by far the most important benefit to the average person.[15] As Table 17.2 indicates, most full-time employees, particularly in medium and large companies, are provided with such benefits by their employers. Three basic types of medical expenses are typically covered: hospital expenses, surgical expenses, and physicians' visits. Other benefits that employers may offer include dental care, vision care, birthing centers, and prescription drug programs. Perhaps the most important issue in benefits management is the challenge of providing quality medical benefits while controlling rapidly escalating costs, a subject we return to in a later section.

The **Consolidated Omnibus Budget Reconciliation Act (COBRA)** of 1985 requires employers to permit employees to extend their health insurance coverage at group rates for up to 36 months following a "qualifying event" such as termination (except for gross misconduct), a reduction in hours that leads to the loss of health insurance, death, and other events. The beneficiary (whether the employee, spouse, or dependent) must have access to the same services as employees who have not lost their health insurance. Note that the beneficiaries do not receive the coverage for free. Rather, they receive the advantage of purchasing coverage at the group rather than the individual rate.

Table 17.2 indicates that most employers provide life insurance and fund it without employee contributions. Increasingly, employers are extending coverage to employees who have retired.

Disability Insurance.   Two basic types of disability coverage exist.[16] As Table 17.2 indicates, about 43 percent of employees in medium and large companies are covered by short-term disability plans (also known as sickness and accident insurance), and about 45 percent are covered by long-term disability plans. Short-term plans typically provide benefits for six months or less, at which point long-term plans take over, potentially covering the person for life. The salary replacement rate is typically between 50 and 70 percent, although short-term plans are sometimes higher. There are often caps on the amount that can be paid each month. Federal income taxation of disability benefits depends on the funding method. Where employee contributions completely fund the plan, there is no federal tax. Benefits based on employer contributions are taxed. Finally, disability benefits, especially long-term ones, need to be coordinated with other programs, such as Social Security disability benefits.

Retirement

Earlier we discussed the old-age insurance part of Social Security, a legally required source of retirement income. Although this remains the largest single component of the elderly's overall retirement income (38 percent), the combination of private pensions (17 percent) and earnings from assets (i.e., savings and other investments like stock) account for an even larger share (25 percent).*

Employers have no legal obligation to offer private retirement plans, but most do. As we note later, if a private retirement plan is provided, it must meet certain standards set forth by the Employee Retirement Income Security Act.

Defined Benefit.   The most common type of retirement plan, *defined benefit,* guarantees ("defines") a specified retirement benefit level to employees based typically on a combination of years of service and age as well as on the employee's earnings level (usually the five highest earnings years). For instance, an organization might guarantee a monthly pension payment of $1,500 to an employee retiring at age 65 with 30 years of service and an average salary over the final 5 years of $40,000. As Table 17.2 indicates, 63 percent of full-time employees in large and medium companies and 20 percent in small companies were covered by such plans in 1989 and 1990, respectively. This translates into about 28 percent of employees (versus companies) being covered by these plans. (The smaller percentage of employees covered relative to companies stems from the fact that most people are employed by small companies.) Other research indicates that 85 percent of salaried employees in large (mostly Fortune 100) companies were covered under defined benefit plans in 1990. The replacement ratio (pension payment/final salary) ranges from about 21 percent for a worker aged 55 with 30 years of service who earned $35,000 in his or her last year to about 36 percent for a 65-year-old worker with 40 years of service who earned the same amount. With Social Security added in, the ratio for the 65-year-old worker increases to about 77 percent.[17]

---

*The remainder of the elderly's income comes from earnings (17%) and other (3%). *Employee Benefits Notes*, July 1992, pp. 1–3. Original data from: Susan Grad, *Income of the Population 55 or older 1988*. U.S. Department of Health and Human Services, Social Security Administration, Publication 13-11871 (Washington, D.C.: Government Printing Office, 1988).

Defined benefit plans insulate employees from investment risk, which is borne by the company. In the event of severe financial difficulties that force the company to terminate or reduce employee pension benefits, the **Pension Benefit Guaranty Corporation (PBGC)** provides some protection of benefits. Established by the **Employee Retirement Income Security Act (ERISA) of 1974**, the PBGC guarantees a basic benefit, not necessarily complete pension benefit replacement, for employees who were eligible for pensions at the time of termination. In 1991, the maximum monthly benefit was limited to the lesser of $1/12$ of an employee's annual gross income during a PBGC-defined period, or $2,250. The PBGC is funded by a contribution in 1991 of $16 per plan participant, which can increase up to $34 to the degree that a plan is underfunded. Since its creation, the PBGC has provided benefits for roughly 375,000 workers and retirees who would have otherwise lost their pension benefits, with 85 percent receiving what their full benefit would have been.[18]

A number of companies have seriously underfunded defined benefit pension plans. As of early 1993, General Motors had $51 billion in pension plan obligations, but only $39 billion in assets, a shortfall of $12 billion. Other companies with significant underfunding have included Chrysler ($4 billion), LTV ($3 billion), and Bethlehem Steel ($1.9 billion).[19] It may be that companies negotiating labor contracts have been guilty of promising to improve pension benefits rather than wages, in the hope that in the future they would have the money to pay employees that they did not have at the time. Ultimately, if the companies cannot meet these obligations, the PBGC will be left with the responsibility. Consequently, concern about the future solvency of the PBGC is growing.[20]

A relatively recent phenomenon is voluntary termination of defined benefit plans by employers for reasons other than financial difficulties. Between 1982 and 1985, in particular, the investment growth of pensions assets far exceeded the growth in defined pension benefit obligations. As of 1991, more than $20 billion was transferred from pension funds to corporate treasuries through such terminations. Terminations require that the company set aside sufficient monies to meet all benefit obligations, but excess assets can go to the company, making money available for capital investment, stockholder dividends, and so forth. This practice, however, has raised a debate whether the money should go to the organization or to the employees for whom the investments had been originally earmarked. Partly as a consequence of this practice, Congress modified its tax policies in 1988 and 1990 to discourage such terminations.[21]

Defined Contribution.   Unlike defined benefit plans, *defined contribution* plans do not promise a specific benefit level for employees upon retirement. Rather, an individual account is set up for each employee with a guaranteed size of contribution. The advantage of such plans for employers is that they shift investment risk to employees and present fewer administrative challenges because there is no need to calculate payments based on age and service and no need to make payments to the PBGC.[22] As Table 17.2 indicates,

48 percent of large companies and 31 percent of small companies have such plans. Note that in small companies defined contribution plans are actually more prevalent than defined benefit plans, perhaps because of employers' desire to avoid long-term obligations or perhaps because small companies, which tend to be younger, tend to adopt defined contribution plans. Many companies have both defined benefit and defined contribution plans.

There are a wide variety of defined contribution plans, a few of which are briefly described here. One of the simplest is a *money purchase plan*, under which an employer specifies a level of annual contribution (e.g., 10 percent of salary). At retirement age, the employee is entitled to the contributions plus the investment returns. The term "money purchase" stems from the fact that employees often use the money to purchase an annuity rather than taking it as a lump sum. Profit-sharing plans and employee stock ownership plans are also often used as retirement vehicles. Both permit contributions (cash and stock, respectively) to vary from year to year, thus allowing employers to avoid fixed obligations that may be burdensome in difficult financial times. **Section 401(k) plans** (named after the tax code section) permit employees to defer compensation on a pretax basis. Annual contributions in 1991 were limited to $8,475 and are adjusted each year according to the consumer price index.[23]

Defined contribution plans put the responsibility for wise investing squarely on the shoulders of the employee. (See the "Competing through Social Responsibility" box.) These investment decisions will become more critical because 401(k) plans alone are expected to provide as much as 50 percent of total retirement income by the year 2012 (up from about 15 percent in 1992).[24] Several factors affect the amount of income that will be available to an employee upon retirement. First, the earlier the age at which investments are made, the longer the period returns can accumulate. As Figure 17.2 shows, an annual investment of $3,000 made between ages 21 and 29 will be worth much more at age 65 than a similar investment made between 31 and 39. Second, different investments have different historical rates of return. Between 1946 and 1990, the average annual return was 11.4 percent for stocks, 5.1 percent for bonds, and 5.3 percent for cash (e.g., bank savings accounts).[25] As Figure 17.2 shows, based on the historical rates of return, an investment in a mix of 60 percent stock, 30 percent bonds, and 10 percent cash between the ages of 21 and 29 would be worth almost four times as much at age 65 as would the same amount invested in a bank savings account. A third consideration is the need to counteract investment risk by diversification. Thus, although stocks have the greatest rate of return, investment experts often choose a mix of stock, bonds, and cash, as shown in Figure 17.2, to reduce investment risk. Younger investors may wish to have more stock, while those closer to retirement age typically have less stock in their portfolios.

Funding, Communication, and Vesting Requirements.   ERISA does not require organizations to have pension plans, but those that are set up must meet certain requirements. In addition to the termination provisions dis-

Social Responsibility

GENERAL ELECTRIC'S 401(k) RETIREMENT PLAN

As employers shift more money toward defined contribution plans like 401(k)s and less toward traditional defined benefit plans, the nature of its social responsibility to employees changes and the responsibility of employees for their own retirement well-being increases. Although most larger employers still have defined benefit plans, many are shifting more of the retirement package to 401(k)s. Many smaller employers offer only 401(k)s. The employer no longer promises a specified pension payment to employees upon retirement. Instead, the employee is responsible for taking advantage of the opportunity to shift a portion of pretax salary into the 401(k) account. Usually, the employer matches some portion of the contribution.

In addition to deciding how much to set aside for retirement, a second new employee responsibility is to decide how to invest the money. This responsibility is all the more important because unlike defined benefit plans, 401(k)s are not insured by the federal Pension Benefit Guaranty Corporation. Fortunately, more companies are recognizing the need to design plans that reduce investment risk to employees and increase their ease of use. One basic principle of investing is that putting all one's eggs in one investment basket is risky. Therefore, whereas in the past, an employee may have been able to invest only in the stock of its employer, more companies are moving toward meeting the U.S. Department of Labor's recommendation that at least three investment choices (in addition to company stock) be provided.

At GE, the average employee allocates 401(k) monies as follows: GE common stock (36%), long-term interest mutual fund (29%), short-term interest fund (10%), common stock mutual fund (9%), money market mutual fund (5%), and U.S. Savings Bonds (4%). The average annual return of this portfolio over the past three years has been 13 percent. GE matches 50 cents for every dollar contributed by employees up to 6 percent of salary (and up to 7 percent after three years). In other words, an employee with a salary of $50,000 contributing $3,000 would receive an additional $1,500 contribution from GE. Approximately 80 percent of GE employees participate in the 401(k) plan. GE enhances employee investment flexibility not only by offering multiple investment choices but also by permitting employees to change the amount of their contribution at any time, changing investment funds up to once a month, and by providing an automated voice response system that provides account updates and permits fund allocation changes using the phone keys.

SOURCE: T. P. Pare, "Is Your 401(k) Plan Good Enough?" *Fortune*, December 28, 1992, 78–83.

cussed earlier, plans must meet certain guidelines on management and funding. For example, employers are required to make yearly contributions that are sufficient to cover future obligations. (As noted previously, not all do so.) ERISA also specifies a number of reporting and disclosure requirements involving the IRS, the Department of Labor, and employees.[26] Employees, for example, must receive within 90 days after entering a plan a **summary plan description (SPD)** that describes the plan's funding, eligibility requirements, risks, and so forth. Upon request, an employer must also make available to an employee an individual benefit statement, which describes the

FIGURE 17.2   The Relationship of Retirement Savings to Age when Savings Begins and Type of Investment Portfolio

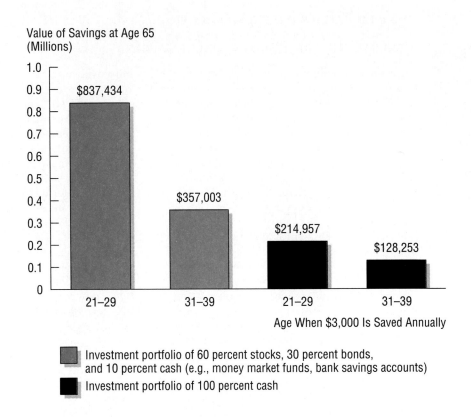

Value of Savings at Age 65 (Millions)

Age When $3,000 Is Saved Annually

Investment portfolio of 60 percent stocks, 30 percent bonds, and 10 percent cash (e.g., money market funds, bank savings accounts)

Investment portfolio of 100 percent cash

employee's vested and unvested benefits. Obviously, employers may wish to provide such information on a regular basis anyway as a means of increasing the understanding and value employees attach to their benefits.

ERISA guarantees employees that when they become participants in a pension plan and work a specified minimum number of years, they earn a right to a pension upon retirement. These are referred to as **vesting rights**.[27] A vested employee has the right to his or her pension at retirement age, regardless of whether that employee remains with the employer until that time. Employee contributions to their own plans are always completely vested. The vesting of employer-funded pension benefits must take place under one of two schedules.* First, employers may choose to vest employ-

---

*These are the two choices relevant to the majority of employers. However, so-called "top-heavy plans" where pension benefits for "key" (e.g., highly paid top managers) exceed a certain share of total pension benefits require faster vesting for nonkey employees. On the other hand, multiemployer pension plans need not provide vesting until after ten years of employment. See Beam and McFadden, *Employee Benefits*.

ees after five years. Until that time, employers can provide zero vesting if they choose. Second, employers may vest employees over a three-to-seven-year period, with at least 20 percent vesting in the third year and each year thereafter. These two schedules represent minimum requirements; employers are free to vest employees more quickly.

These requirements were put in place to prevent companies from terminating employees before they have reached retirement age or before they reach their length-of-service requirements in order to avoid paying pension benefits. It should also be noted that transferring employees or laying them off as a means of avoiding pension obligations is not legal either, even if such actions are motivated partly by business necessity.[28] On the other hand, employers are free to choose whichever of the two vesting schedules is most advantageous. For example, an employer that experiences high quit rates during the fourth and fifth years of employment may wish to choose five-year vesting as a way of minimizing pension costs.

The typical pension is designed to discourage employee turnover. Even if an employee's pension benefit is vested, it is usually smaller if the employee changes employers, mainly because the size of the benefit depends on earnings in the final years with an employer. Consider an employee who earns $30,000 after 20 years and $60,000 after 40 years.[29] The employer pays an annual retirement benefit equal to 1.5 percent of final earnings times the number of years of service. If the employee stays with the employer for 40 years, the annual benefit level upon retirement would be $36,000 (.015 × $60,000 × 40). If, instead, the employee changes employers after 20 years (and has the same earnings progression), the retirement benefit from the first employer would be $9,000 (.015 × $30,000 × 20). The annual benefit from the second employer would be $18,000 (.015 × $60,000 × 20). Therefore, staying with one employer for 40 years would yield an annual retirement benefit of $36,000, versus a combined annual retirement benefit of $27,000 ($9,000 + $18,000) if the employee changes employers once.

Of course, in recent years, many employers have sought to reduce their work forces, so they use pensions for an opposite purpose—to encourage employees to leave. One method is to adjust years-of-service credit upward for employees willing to retire, resulting in a higher retirement benefit for them (and less monetary incentive to work). These work-force reductions may also be one indication of a broader trend toward employees becoming less likely to spend their entire careers with a single employer. On one hand, if more mobility across employers becomes necessary or desirable, the current pension system's incentives against (or penalties for) mobility may require modification. On the other hand, perhaps increased employee mobility will reinforce the continued trend toward defined contribution plans (e.g., 401(k)'s), which have greater portability (ease of transfer of funds) across employers.

International Comparisons.   About 45 percent of the U.S. private-sector labor force is covered by pension plans, compared with 100 percent in France, 92 percent in Switzerland, 42 percent in Germany, and 39 percent in

FIGURE 17.3   Legally Mandated Vacation Days in Various Countries (for employees with one year of service)

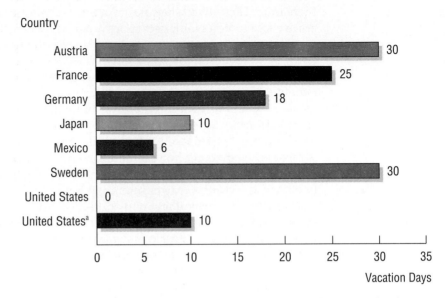

ᵃTypical practice among large employers—not legally mandated

SOURCE: Adapted from K. Matthes, "In Pursuit of Leisure: Employees Want More Time Off," *HRFocus*, May 1992, 1.

Japan. Among those covered by pensions, U.S. workers are significantly less likely to be covered by defined benefit plans (28 percent) than Japanese workers (100 percent) or German workers (90 percent).

Pay for Time not Worked

At first blush, paid vacation, holidays, sick leave, and so forth may not seem to make economic sense. The employer pays the employee for time not spent working, receiving no tangible production value in return. Therefore, some employers may see little direct advantage. Perhaps for this reason, a minimum number of vacation days is mandated by law in Western Europe. As many as 30 days of vacation is not uncommon for relatively new employees in Europe (see Figure 17.3). By contrast, there is no legal minimum in the United States, but ten days is typical for large companies. U.S. workers must typically be with an employer for 20 to 25 years before they receive as much paid vacation as their Western European counterparts. In both the United States and Western Europe, around ten paid holidays is typical, regardless of length of service.[30]

Although there is a cost to providing time off with pay, an organization would probably have some difficulty attracting and retaining employees if it did not offer a competitive vacation package. In fact, some companies (e.g., in Silicon Valley) have found it necessary to go a step further and offer benefits such as sabbaticals to keep their top technical people from leaving. (Another hoped-for benefit of a sabbatical is that the employee will return revitalized with some innovative ideas to pursue.)

Family benefits that include employer-supported child care, flexible work practices, and family leave are a developing area in benefits plans (see Chapter 5). Family leave has received much attention, and the **Family and Medical Leave Act** was signed into law by President Clinton in February 1993. Prior to the act, only about 40 percent of all working women were eligible for guaranteed, unpaid, job-protected maternity leave. The act requires organizations with 50 or more employees within a 75-mile radius to provide as much as 12 weeks of unpaid leave after childbirth or adoption; to care for a seriously ill child, spouse, or parent; or for an employee's own serious illness.[31] Employees are guaranteed the same or a comparable job on their return to work. Employees with less than one year of service or who work under 25 hours per week are not covered.

Supporters of the act believe it will help U.S. workers reduce conflicts between their work and family responsibilities. Many employers had already taken steps to deal with this issue, partly to help attract and retain key employees. As noted by one source, only "about 4 percent of American families fit the stereotypical image of a father who works outside the home and a mother who stays home and takes care of the children."[32]

The United States still offers significantly less unpaid leave than most Western European countries and Japan. Moreover, *paid* family leave remains rare in the United States (fewer than 5 percent are eligible for paid leave, despite some state laws), in even sharper contrast to Western Europe and Japan, where it is typically mandated by law (see Chapter 5).[33] Until the passage of the Americans with Disabilities Act, the only applicable law was the **Pregnancy Discrimination Act of 1978**, which requires employers that offer disability plans to treat pregnancy as they would any other disability.

Sick leave programs often provide full salary replacement for a limited period of time, usually not exceeding 26 weeks. The amount of sick leave is often based on length of service, accumulating with service (e.g., one day per month). Sick leave policies need to be carefully structured to avoid providing employees with the wrong incentives. For example, if sick leave days disappear at the end of the year (rather than accumulate), a "use it or lose it" mentality may develop among employees, contributing to greater absenteeism. Organizations have developed a number of measures to counter this.[34] Some allow sick days to accumulate, then pay employees for the number of sick days when they retire or resign. Employers may also attempt to communicate to their employees that accumulated sick leave is better saved to use as a bridge to long-term disability, because the replacement rate (i.e., the ratio of sick leave or disability payments to normal salary) for the former is typically higher. Sick leave payments may equal 100 percent of usual salary, whereas the replacement ratio for long-term disability might be 50 percent, so the more sick leave accumulated, the longer an employee can avoid dropping to 50 percent of usual pay when he or she is unable to work.

MANAGING BENEFITS: EMPLOYER OBJECTIVES AND STRATEGIES

Although the regulatory environment places some important constraints on benefits decisions, employers retain significant discretion and need to evaluate the payoff of such decisions. As discussed earlier, however, this evaluation needs to recognize that employees have come to expect certain things from employers. Employers who do not meet these expectations run the risk of violating what has been called an "implicit contract" between the employer and its workers. If employees believe their employers feel little commitment to their welfare, they can hardly be expected to commit themselves to the company's success.

Clearly, there is much room for progress in the evaluation of benefits decisions. Despite some of the obvious reasons for benefits—group discounts, regulation, and minimizing compensation-related taxes—organizations do not do as well as they could in spelling out what they want their benefits package to achieve and evaluating how well they are succeeding. Research suggests that most organizations do not have written benefits objectives.[35] Obviously, without clear objectives to measure progress, evaluation is difficult (and less likely to occur). Table 17.3 provides an example of one organization's written benefits objectives.

Surveys/Benchmarking

As with cash compensation, an important element of benefits management is knowing what the competition is doing. Survey information on benefits packages is available from private consultants, and somewhat less regularly from the Bureau of Labor Statistics (BLS).[36] BLS data of the sort that appear in Table 17.2 and the more detailed information on programs and provisions available from consultants are useful in designing competitive benefits packages. To compete effectively in the product market, cost information is also necessary. A widely used source is the annual survey conducted by the U.S. Chamber of Commerce, which provides information on benefits costs for specific categories as well as breakdowns by industry and organization size. Table 17.4 provides an excerpt of some of these data for 1990.

TABLE 17.3   One Company's Written Benefits Objectives

- To establish and maintain an employee benefit program that is based primarily on the employees' needs for leisure time and on protection against the risks of old age, loss of health and loss of life.
- To establish and maintain an employee benefit program that complements the efforts of employees on their own behalf.
- To evaluate the employee benefit plan annually for its effect on employee morale and productivity, giving consideration to turnover, unfilled positions, attendance, employees' complaints and employees' opinions.
- To compare the employee benefit plan annually with that of other leading companies in the same field and to maintain a benefit plan with an overall level of benefits based on cost per employee that falls within the second quintile of these companies.
- To maintain a level of benefits for nonunion employees that represents the same level of expenditures per employee as for union employees.
- To determine annually the cost of new, changed and existing programs as a percentage of salaries and wages and to maintain this percentage as much as possible.
- To self-fund benefits to the extent that a long-run cost savings can be expected for the firm and catastrophic losses can be avoided.
- To coordinate all benefits with social insurance programs to which the company makes payments.
- To provide benefits on a noncontributory basis, except for dependent coverage for which employees should pay a portion of the cost.
- To maintain continual communications with all employees concerning benefit programs.

SOURCE: Used with permission: *Employee Benefits,* 3rd Edition, Burton T. Beam, Jr., and John J. McFadden, © 1992 by Dearborn Financial Publishing, Inc. Published by Dearborn Financial Publishing, Inc./Chicago. All rights reserved.

Cost Control

In thinking about cost-control strategies, it is useful to consider several factors. First, the larger the cost of a benefit category, the greater the opportunity for savings. Second, the growth trajectory of the benefit category is also important. Even if costs are currently acceptable, the rate of growth may result in serious costs in the future. Third, cost-containment efforts can only work to the extent that the employer has significant discretion in choosing how much to spend in a benefit category. Much of the cost of legally required benefits (e.g., Social Security) is relatively fixed, which constrains cost-reduction efforts. Even with legally required benefits, however, employers can take actions to limit costs because of "experience ratings,"

TABLE 17.4   Employee Benefits in 1990 by Category and Cost

	Percentage of Payroll	Percentage of Benefits Cost	Cost in Dollars	Change in Percentage of Payroll from 1980
Legally required	8.8%	22.9%	$2,842	–1.1%
FICA and Railroad Retirement Tax	6.9	18.0	2,228	
Retirement and savings plans	5.5	14.3	1,776	–20.3%[a]
Life insurance and death benefit	0.5	1.3	161	
Medical and related	9.9	25.8	3,197	86.8%[b]
Current employees	8.9	23.2	2,874	
Retirees	1.0	2.6	323	
Paid rest periods	2.4	6.3	775	–31.4%
Payments for time not worked	10.5	27.3	3,391	6.1%
Miscellaneous	0.8	2.1	258	
Totals	38.4%	100.0%	$12,402	

SOURCE: U.S. Chamber of Commerce Research Center, *Employee Benefits* (Washington, D.C.: U.S. Chamber of Commerce, 1991).
[a]Estimate—1980 and 1990 data not exactly comparable.
[b]Estimate—1980 and 1990 data not exactly comparable. Data on only health and dental insurance component shows an increase of 44 percent between 1980 and 1990.

which impose higher taxes on employers with high rates of unemployment or workers' compensation claims.

As should be evident from Table 17.4, one benefit, "Medical and related," stands out as a target for cost control because its costs are large and growing rapidly, and there are relatively few regulatory constraints.

Controlling Medical Expenses.   In the United States, health-care expenditures have gone from 5.3 percent of the gross national product ($27 billion) in 1960 to over 12 percent ($666 billion) in 1990.[37] As Table 17.5 indicates, the United States spends more on health care than any other country in the world. Why have medical benefits grown at such a rapid pace? No simple answer is possible, but a host of factors have been suggested, including technological advances, increasing malpractice suits, lack of cost-control incentives because of third-party payers, and a lack of competition among health-care providers.[38]

Americans might be willing to accept the highest health-care costs in the world if they believed they were receiving superior care. However, several public opinion surveys suggest fairly widespread dissatisfaction with

TABLE 17.5

Health-Care Costs and Outcomes in Various Countries

1990 Data	Life Expectancy Male/Female	Infant Mortality Rate[a]	Per Capita Health Expenditures[b]	Health Expenditures as a Percentage of GDP	Doctors per 1,000 People	Average Days Inpatient Care[c]
Japan	75.9/81.8[c]	4.6[c]	$1,171	6.5%	1.6[d]	51.4
Canada	73.0/79.7[e]	7.2[c]	$1,730	9.0%	2.2	13.0
Britain	72.8/78.4[c]	7.9	$974	6.2%	1.4[c]	14.8
France	72.7/80.9	7.2	$1,543	8.9%	2.6[c]	12.8
Italy	72.6/79.1[c]	8.5	$1,234	7.7%	1.3[c]	11.7
Germany	72.6/79.0[c]	7.5[c]	$1,487	8.1%	3.0[c]	16.2
United States	72.1/79.0	9.2	$2,566	12.4%	2.3	9.2

SOURCE: Organization for Economic Cooperation and Development, Used with permission of *Fortune*, © 1992 Time, Inc. All rights reserved.
[a]Per 1,000 live births.
[b]Adjusted for purchasing power, 1990 U.S. dollars.
[c]1989.
[d]1988.
[e]1986.

the current system.[39] For example, 85 percent of Americans believe the U.S. health-care system is either "fair" or "poor." The most frequently mentioned major concerns are cost (49 percent), quality (36 percent), and access and availability (12 percent). Other data are also used to criticize the American health-care system. One widely reported statistic is that 33 million Americans are uninsured.[40] Other data (perhaps related) indicate that the United States compares poorly to other countries on measures of life expectancy and infant mortality (see Table 17.5).

Unlike workers in most Western European countries, who have nationalized health systems, the majority (152 million) of Americans receiving health insurance get it through their employers.[41] Not surprisingly, then, many of the efforts at controlling costs and increasing quality and coverage have been undertaken by employers. These efforts, broadly referred to as *managed care*, fall into the following major categories: (1) plan design, (2) use of alternative providers, (3) use of alternative funding methods, (4) claims review, (5) education and prevention, and (6) external cost-control systems.[42] Examples appear in Table 17.6.

One trend in plan design has been to shift costs to employees through the use of deductibles, coinsurance, exclusions and limitations, and maximum benefits. Table 17.7 provides an example of a plan that relies on such features. Another trend has been to focus on reducing, rather than shifting, costs through such activities as preadmission testing and second sur-

TABLE 17.6   Ways Employers Use Managed Care to Control Health-Care Costs

Plan Design
Cost shifting to employees
  Deductibles
  Coinsurance
  Exclusions and limitations
  Maximum benefits
Cost Reduction
  Preadmission testing
  Second surgical opinions
  Coordination of benefits
  Alternatives to hospital stays (e.g., home health care)

Alternative Providers
Health maintenance organizations (HMOs)
Preferred provider organizations (PPOs)

Alternative Funding Methods
Self-funding

Claims Review

Health Education and Preventive Care
Wellness programs
Employee assistance programs (EAPs)

Encouragement of External Control Systems
National Council on Health Planning and Development
Employer coalitions

SOURCE: Adapted from B. T. Beam, Jr. and J. J. McFadden, *Employee Benefits*, 3rd ed. (Chicago: Dearborn Financial Publishing, 1992).

gical opinions. The use of alternative providers like **health maintenance organizations (HMOs)** and **preferred provider organizations (PPOs)** has also increased. HMOs differ from more traditional providers by focusing on preventive care and outpatient treatment, requiring employees to use only HMO services, and providing benefits on a prepaid basis. Many HMOs pay physicians and other health-care workers on a flat salary basis instead of using the traditional fee-for-service system, under which a physician's pay may depend on the number of patients seen. Paying on a salary basis is intended to reduce incentives for physicians to schedule more patient visits or medical procedures than might be necessary. PPOs

TABLE 17.7

Example of a Company Medical Plan

MediChoice Options

	Medical Plan/Basic Option	**Preferred Provider Option**	**HMO Option**
Employee contributions (monthly)	None	$8.00 (employee only) $16.00 (employee + 1) $24.00 (employee + 2)	None
Deductibles (annual)	$300 (individual) $500 (family)	$100 (individual) $200 (family)	None
Employee annual out-of-pocket expense limit (after deductible)	$2500 (individual) $5000 (family)	$1000 (individual) $2000 (family)	N/A
Lifetime Maximum	$500,000	$1,000,000	N/A

Coverage:

Preadmission tests		
Second surgical opinions	Expenses covered at 100% of reasonable and customary charge levels subject to deductibles	Covered in full
Outpatient/Ambulatory surgery		
Home health care		
Hospice care		

Hospital room and board	Expenses covered at 80% of reasonable and customary charge levels after deductible	Expenses covered at 90% of reasonable and customary charge levels after deductible	Covered in full except for $3.00 physician visit copayment
Inpatient hospital services			
Surgical fees (inpatient)			
Diagnostic tests			
Physician visits (when medically necessary)			
Inpatient substance abuse treatment			

Psychiatric care	Expenses covered at 50% of reasonable and customary charge levels subject to deductibles	Covered in full except for $8.00 copayment for outpatient drug abuse treatment
Chiropractic care		
Outpatient substance abuse treatment		

Routine physical exams	Not covered	Covered in full
Well baby care		
Immunizations		

continued

SOURCE: Reprinted with Permission, "Employee Benefits and Services," by Robert M. McCaffery, from *Compensation and Benefits*, pp. 3–112 and 3–113, edited by Luis R. Gomez-Mejia. Copyright © 1989 by the Bureau of National Affairs Inc., Washington D.C. 20037.

TABLE 17.7

continued

MediChoice Options

	Medical Plan/Basic Option	Preferred Provider Option	HMO Option
Special Conditions		Specified reductions in benefits for non-compliance with precertification and concurrent review requirements and second-surgical opinion provisions. No coverage for nonemergency weekend hospital admissions.	Coverage is coordinated through a specific group of doctors, hospitals, and medical services associated with the HMO.

are essentially groups of health-care providers who contract with employers, insurance companies, and so forth to provide health care at a reduced fee. They differ from HMOs in that they do not provide benefits on a prepaid basis and employees often are not required to use the preferred providers. Instead, employers may provide incentives for employees to choose, for example, a physician who participates in the plan. In general, PPOs seem to be less expensive than traditional delivery systems but more expensive than HMOs.[43] Another trend in employers' attempts to control costs has been to vary required employee contributions based on the employee's health and risk factors rather than charging each employee the same premium. As Table 17.8 indicates, employees even receive refunds under some conditions. The "Competing through Quality" box describes how one major corporation has used HMOs to rein in health-care costs.

Given the public's general dissatisfaction with our country's health-care system, employer-initiated changes may not be enough. Some type of national health insurance plan is strongly favored by 25 percent and favored by 54 percent of Americans. Only 4 percent strongly oppose such a system. Many top corporate executives also see a national health-care system as a solution to their problems. One survey of chief financial officers, for example, found that 33 percent favored such a system. A survey of chief executives from the largest U.S. companies found that 91 percent believed "a fundamental change or complete rebuilding of the health-care system is needed," although national health insurance was seen more as an option for the future.[44]

National health care would probably reduce employer costs, and it would clearly be much less expensive for employers than some other proposals. Employer-based health insurance plans and so-called pay or play proposals, where an employer either provides health insurance or con-

TABLE 17.8   The Effects of Health and Risk Factors on Employees'
Health Insurance Premiums

Type of Employee	Rate
Worker covered by spouse's insurance plan	$240 paid *to employee*
Single nonsmoker who passes wellness checkup and chooses lowest benefit plan	$84 premium[a]
A married smoker with an uninsured spouse and children who fails wellness checkup and chooses highest benefit plan	$1,080 premium
An early retiree with no dependents and 20 years of service who passes the wellness test and chooses the lowest benefit plan	$156 premium[a]
An early retiree with 10 years of service who fails the wellness checkup, has an uninsured spouse, and chooses the highest benefit plan	$2,292 premium

SOURCE: G. Kramon, "Medical Insurers Vary Fees to Aid Healthier People: Trend to Halt Subsidies," *New York Times*, March 24, 1991, sec. 1, p. 1. Original data based on plan used by Baker Hughes, Inc., a Houston-based oilfield services company.
[a]Employees also receive a $100 rebate to use in purchasing other health-care services.

tributes a portion of its payroll to a public insurance plan, would increase employers' costs as much as $86 billion and $45 billion, respectively.[45]

As this book goes to press, the Clinton Administration's health care plan has not been finalized, but certain features appear likely. First, every American citizen and other legal U.S. resident would be covered. Second, most people would obtain health insurance through regional purchasing cooperatives or "health alliances" that would negotiate contracts with HMOs and other health care providers. Third, the health alliances would collect money from employees and employers to fund the coverage of employed persons through what the Clinton Administration calls a "wage-based premium," and what others call a payroll tax. This might be 7 percent for employers and 2 percent for employees. For some large employers that currently spend much more on health care, the plan may be attractive. Among other employers (e.g. small businesses) the plan may not be well received. Premiums for persons without jobs would be paid by the federal government.

Staffing Responses to Control Benefit Cost Growth.   Employers may change staffing practices to control benefits costs. First, because benefits costs are fixed (in that they do not usually go up with hours worked), the benefits cost per hour can be reduced by having employees work more hours. However, there are drawbacks to having employees work more hours. The Fair Labor Standards Act (FLSA) requires that nonexempt employees be paid time-and-a-half for hours in excess of 40 per week. Yet

Quality

MANAGED COMPETITION AT XEROX

To control the growth in its costs while maintaining high quality health care for its employees, Xerox, headquartered in Rochester, New York, has implemented the first managed competition system of any Fortune 500 company. It has begun setting the level of its contribution to employee health-care costs on the basis of the most efficient health maintenance organization (HMO) in each geographic area in which it operates. Competition among multiple HMOs in each locale is the cornerstone of the plan. If an employee wants health-care coverage that is more costly than the local "benchmark" (most efficient) HMO, the employee must pay the difference. The system provides an incentive for employees to realize a savings if they choose the more efficient plans and makes them pay extra for choosing less efficient health-care providers.

Xerox has taken pains to ensure that the health-care providers in each area meet high quality standards. In 1990, when the managed competition began to take shape, only 94 out of 160 HMOs serving Xerox at the time were selected to remain as providers. Since then, others have been approved, raising the total to 185. Health-care quality is monitored on an ongoing basis. Overall customer satisfaction ranges from 70 percent at the lowest-rated HMO to 95 percent for the highest-rated. Employees are also asked whether their doctors ask them the right questions during examinations.

What have the results of the new managed competition plan been? While maintaining quality, the growth in costs has been reduced significantly. In previous years, Xerox's health-care costs grew at about a 20 percent annual rate. In contrast, costs of the 59 percent of Xerox employees in HMOs rose 15 percent in 1992 and are expected to rise by 9 percent in 1993. Better still, cost increases for the 23 percent of Xerox employees covered by the benchmark HMOs were less than 8 percent in 1992 and are expected to be only 5.5 percent in 1993.

SOURCE: E. Faltermayer, "Yes, the Market Can Curb Health Costs," *Fortune*, December 28, 1992, 84–87.

the decline in U.S. work hours tapered off in the late 1940s; work hours have actually gone up since then. It is estimated that Americans were working the equivalent of one month longer in 1987 than they were in 1969.[46] Increased benefits were identified as one of the major reasons for this.

A second possible effect of FLSA regulations (though this is more speculative) is that organizations will try to have their employees classified as exempt whenever possible. The growth in the number of salaried workers (many of whom are exempt) may also reflect an effort by organizations to limit the benefits cost per hour without having to pay overtime. A third potential effect is the growth in part-time employment and the use of temporary workers, which may be a response to rising benefits costs.[47] As Table 17.9 indicates, part-time workers are much less likely to receive benefits than full-time workers. Benefits for temporary workers are also usually quite limited. (See, however, the "Competing through Technology and Structure" box, which paints a different picture of one company.)

TABLE 17.9   Benefits for Full-time versus Part-time Employees

	Percentage of Firms Providing Benefit	
	Part-Time Employees	**Full-Time Employees**
Benefit		
Health	22%	99%
Retirement	32%	85%
Vacation	33%	98%

SOURCE: U.S. Chamber of Commerce Research Center, *Employee Benefits 1990* (Washington, D.C.: U.S. Chamber of Commerce, 1991).

Nature of the Work Force

Although general considerations such as cost control and "protection against the risks of old age, loss of health and life" (see Table 17.3) are important, employers must also consider the specific demographic composition and preferences of their current work forces in designing their benefits packages.

At a broad level, basic demographic factors such as age and sex can have important consequences for the types of benefits employees want. For example, an older work force is more likely to be concerned about (and use) medical coverage, life insurance, and pensions. A work force with a high percentage of women of childbearing age may care more about disability leave. Young, unmarried men and women often have less interest in benefits generally, preferring higher wages and salaries.

Although some general conclusions about employee preferences can be drawn based on demographics, more finely tuned assessments of employee benefit preferences need to be done. One approach is to use marketing research methods to assess employees' preferences the same way consumers' demands for products and services are assessed.[48] Methods include personal interviews, focus groups, and questionnaires. Relevant questions might include the following:

- What benefits are most important to you?
- If you could choose one new benefit, what would it be?
- If you were given x dollars for benefits, how would you spend it?

As with surveys generally, care must be taken not to raise employee expectations regarding future changes. If the employer is not prepared to act on the employees' input, surveying may do more harm than good.

The preceding discussion may imply that the current makeup of the work force is a given, but such is not the case. As discussed earlier, the ben-

Technology & Structure

BENEFITS FOR PART-TIMERS AT STARBUCKS COFFEE COMPANY

An important structural change is the increasing number of part-time jobs in many U.S. organizations. Still, most employers treat employees in such jobs differently from full-time employees. One major difference is that employers typically offer a much less attractive benefits package to part-timers. Starbucks Coffee Company is an exception. The company runs "143 espresso-bar-cum-coffee-emporiums" in the Pacific Northwest and Chicago and plans to expand soon to Denver and Washington, D.C. It offers health insurance (including vision and dental) after 90 days to all employees who work 20 hours or more per week. Employees also participate in a 401(k) savings plan after a year and in a stock option plan if they work from April 1 to the end of the year.

Howard Schultz, chief executive officer, believed from the start that his employees, nearly two-thirds of whom are part-timers, would be "crucial" to the company's continued success as it grew from 11 stores five years ago to its current size. Schultz said he realized that "the most competitive advantage we would have was our people." With around three-quarters of its workers working at retail counters, interacting regularly with customers, it was important that employees feel good about the company because the company competes on two dimensions: its coffee and its customer service. Schultz decided that both

social responsibility and good business sense pointed toward offering part-timers a full array of benefits. His sense of social responsibility may stem partly from the fact that he spent most of his youth in New York City housing projects and experienced the type of financial insecurity that benefits can help prevent.

From a business perspective, Schultz argues that beyond improving customer service, offering benefits also reduces hiring costs and increases employee retention. He points out that the annual employee turnover rate at Starbucks is 60 percent, compared with 150 percent to 300 percent in the retail industry as a whole and a whopping 400 percent in the fast-food industry in particular. Starbucks calculates the cost of hiring an employee to be $550. If so, while a competitor with a 300 percent turnover rate would have to hire three people (3 × $550 = $1,650 in costs) per job per year, Starbucks would need to spend only $330 (.6 × $550) per year to keep the same job filled. Corey Rosen of the National Center for Employee Ownership, a nonprofit group, suggests that "most companies that have many part-timers don't look at the overall picture." They focus on the savings from not offering benefits but overlook the costs of such a policy. In addition, "The prevailing wisdom...is that part-timers won't stay [and] it then becomes self-fulfilling."

SOURCES: D. Gunsch, "Benefits Leverage Hiring and Retention Efforts," *Personnel Journal*, November 1992, 91–97; B. P. Noble, "Benefits? For Part-Timers?" *New York Times*, August 16, 1992, sec. 3, p. 23.

efits package may have an important influence on the composition of the work force. For example, a benefits package that has strong medical benefits and pensions may be particularly attractive to older people or those with families. An attractive pension plan may be a way to attract workers who wish to make a long-term commitment to an organization. Where turnover costs are high, this type of strategy may have some appeal. On the other hand, a company that has very lucrative health-care benefits may attract

TABLE 17.10   Employee Perceptions versus Actual Cost and Market Value of
Employer Contributions to Employee Medical Insurance

	Employer Contribution			Market Value[a]		
	Actual	Employee Perception	Ratio	Actual	Employee Perception	Ratio
Coverage						
Individual	$34	$23	68%	$61	$37	61%
Family	$64	$24	38%	$138	$43	31%

SOURCE: Adapted from M. Wilson, G. F. Northcraft and M. A. Neale, "The Perceived Value of Fringe Benefits," *Personnel Psychology* 38 (1985): 309–320.

Note: Dollar values in table represent means across three different insurance carriers for individual coverage and three different carriers for family coverage.

[a]Defined as the amount a nonemployee would have to pay to obtain same level of coverage.

and retain people with high health-care costs. Sick leave provisions may also affect the composition of the work force. Organizations need to think about the signals their benefits packages send and the implications of these signals for the work-force composition.

Communicating with Employees

Effective communication of benefits information to employees is critical if employers are to have any hope of realizing sufficient returns on their benefits investments. Research makes it clear that current employees and job applicants often have a very poor idea of what benefits provisions are already in place and the cost or market value of those benefits. One study asked employees to estimate both the amount contributed by the employer to their medical insurance and what it would cost the employees to provide their own health insurance. Table 17.10 shows that employees significantly underestimated both the cost and market value of their medical benefits. In the case of family coverage, employees estimated that the employer contributed $24, only 38 percent of the employer's actual contribution. This employer was receiving a very poor return on its benefits investment: $0.38 for every $1.00 spent.[49]

The situation with job applicants is no better. One study of MBAs found that 46 percent believed that benefits added 15 percent or less on top of direct payroll. Not surprisingly, perhaps, benefits was dead last on the MBAs' priority list in making job choices.[50] Another study of undergraduate business majors found similar results, with benefits ranked 15th (out of 18) in importance in evaluating jobs. These results must be interpreted with caution, however. Some research suggests that job attributes can be ranked low in importance, not because they are unimportant per se, but because all employers are perceived to be about the same on that attribute. If some employers offered noticeably poorer benefits, the importance of benefits could become much greater.

Organizations can take action to help remedy the problem of applicants' and employees' lack of knowledge about benefits. One study found that employees' awareness of benefits information was significantly increased through several media, including memoranda, question-and-answer meetings, and detailed brochures. The increased awareness, in turn, contributed to significant increases in benefits satisfaction. Another study suggests, however, that increased employee knowledge of benefits can have a positive or negative effect, depending on the nature of the benefits package. For example, there was a negative, or inverse, correlation between cost to the employee and benefits satisfaction overall, but the correlation was more strongly negative among employees with greater knowledge of their benefits.[51] The implication is that employees will be least satisfied with their benefits if their cost is high and they are well informed.

One thing an employer should consider with respect to written benefits communication is that over 27 million employees in the United States may be functionally illiterate. Of course, there are many alternative ways to communicate benefits information (see Table 17.11). Nevertheless, most organizations spend less than $10 per year per employee to communicate information about benefits, and almost all of this is spent on written communication rather than on more personalized or "innovative" approaches such as benefits fairs, videos, and so forth. Considering that organizations spend an average of $12,402 per worker per year on benefits, together with the complex nature of many benefits and the poor understanding of most employees, the typical communication effort seems woefully inadequate.[52] Organizations are spending less than $1 to communicate every $1,000 in benefits.

Flexible, or Cafeteria-Style, Benefit Plans

Rather than a single standard benefits package for all employees, flexible benefit plans permit employees to choose the types and amounts of benefits they want for themselves. Plans vary according to such things as whether minimum levels of certain benefits (e.g., health-care coverage) are prescribed and whether employees can receive money for having chosen a "light" benefits package (or have to pay extra for more benefits). One example is vacation, where some plans permit employees to give up vacation days for more salary or, alternatively, purchase extra vacation days through a salary reduction.

What are the potential advantages of such plans?[53] In the best case, almost all of the objectives discussed previously can be positively influenced. First, employees can gain a greater awareness and appreciation of what the employer provides them, particularly with plans that give employees a lump sum to allocate to benefits. Second, by permitting employee

TABLE 17.11   Benefits Communication Techniques

Word of mouth	Booklets
Employee meetings	Computerized statements
Manuals	Letters to employees
Paycheck inserts	Posters
Annual reports	Check stubs
Personal counseling	Benefits fairs
Interactive computers	Annual benefits review
Television and video tapes	Slide presentations
Benefit quizzes	Telephone hot lines

SOURCE: Reprinted with permission from "An Evaluation of Benefit Communication Strategy," by M.C. Giallourakis and G.S. Taylor, which appeared in the December 1991 issue, *Employee Benefits Journal,* published by the International Foundation of Employee Benefit Plans, Brookfield, Wisc.

choice, there should be a better match between the benefits package and the employee's preferences. This, in turn, should improve employee attitudes and retention.[54] Third, employers may achieve overall cost reductions in their benefits programs. Cafeteria plans can be thought of as similar to defined contribution plans, whereas traditional plans are more like defined benefit plans. The employer can control the size of the contribution under the former, but not under the latter, because the cost and utilization of benefits is beyond the employer's control. Costs can also be controlled by designing the choices so that employees have an incentive to choose more efficient options. For example, in the case of the medical flex-plan depicted in Table 17.7, employees who do not wish to take advantage of the (presumably more cost-effective) HMO have to pay significant deductibles and other costs under the alternative plans.

One drawback of cafeteria-style plans is their administrative cost, especially in the initial design and start-up stages. However, software packages and standardized flex-plans developed by consultants offer some help in this regard. Another possible drawback to these plans is adverse selection. Employees are most likely to choose benefits that they expect to need the most. Someone in need of dental work would choose as much dental coverage as possible. As a result, employer costs can increase significantly as each employee chooses benefits based on their value to him or her. Another result of adverse selection is the difficulty in estimating what benefits costs will be under such a plan, especially in small companies. Adverse selection can be controlled, however, by placing limitations on coverage amounts, pricing benefits that are subject to adverse selection higher, or using a limited set of packaged options, which prevents employees from choosing too many benefits options that would be susceptible to adverse selection.

Flexible Spending Accounts. A flexible spending account permits pretax contributions to an employee account that can be drawn on to pay for uncovered health-care expenses (e.g., deductible or coinsurance payments). A separate account of up to $5,000 per year is permitted for pretax contributions to cover dependent-care expenses. The federal tax code requires that funds in the health-care and dependent-care accounts be earmarked in advance and spent during the plan year. Remaining funds revert to the employer.[55] Therefore, the accounts work best to the extent that employees have predictable expenses. The major advantage of such plans is the increase in take-home pay that results from pretax payment of health and dependent-care expenses. Consider again the hypothetical employee with annual earnings of $45,000 and an effective total marginal tax rate of 45 percent from Table 17.1. The take-home pay from an additional $10,000 in salary with and without a flexible dependent-care account is:

	No Flexible Spending Care Account	Flexible Spending Care Account
Salary portion	$10,000	$10,000
Pretax dependent-care contribution	–$ 0	–$ 5,000
Taxable salary	$10,000	$ 5,000
Tax (45 percent)	–$ 4,500	–$ 2,250
After-tax cost of dependent care	–$ 5,000	–$ 0
Take-home pay	$ 500	$ 2,750

Therefore, the use of a flexible spending account saves the employee $2,250 per year.

GENERAL REGULATORY ISSUES

Although we have already discussed a number of regulatory issues, some additional ones require attention.

Nondiscrimination Rules and Qualified Plans

As a general rule, all benefits packages must meet certain rules to be classified as qualified plans.[56] What are the advantages of a qualified plan? Basically, it receives more favorable tax treatment than a nonqualified plan. In the case of a qualified retirement plan, for example, these tax advantages include (1) an immediate tax deduction for employers for their contributions to retirement funds, (2) no tax liability for the employee at the time of the employer deduction, and (3) investment returns (e.g., from stocks, bonds, money markets) on the retirement funds that accumulate tax free.[57]

What rules must be satisfied for a plan to obtain qualified status? Each benefit area has different rules. It would be impossible to describe the various rules here, but some general observations are possible. Taking pensions as an example again, vesting requirements must be met. More generally, qualified plans must meet so-called *nondiscrimination rules*. Basically, this means that a benefit cannot discriminate in favor of "highly compensated employees." One rationale behind such rules is that the tax benefits of qualified benefits plans (and the corresponding loss of tax revenues for the U.S. government) should not go disproportionately to the wealthy.[58] Rather, the favorable tax treatment is designed to encourage employers to provide important benefits to a broad spectrum of employees. The nondiscrimination rules discourage owners or top managers from adopting plans that benefit them exclusively.

Sex, Age, and Disability

Beyond the Pregnancy Discrimination Act's requirements that were discussed earlier in the chapter, a second area of concern for employers in assuring legal treatment of men and women in the benefits area has to do with pension benefits. Women tend to live longer than men, meaning that pension benefits for women are more costly, all else being equal. However, in its 1978 *Manhart* ruling, the Supreme Court declared it illegal for employers to require women to contribute more to a defined benefit plan than men: Title VII protects individuals, and not all women outlive all men.[59]

Two major age-related issues have received attention under the Age Discrimination in Employment Act (ADEA) and later amendments such as the Older Workers Benefit Protection Act (OWBPA). First, employers must take care not to discriminate against workers over age 40 in the provision of pay or benefits. As one example, employers cannot generally cease accrual (i.e., stop the growth) of retirement benefits at some age (e.g., 65) as a way of pressuring older employees to retire.[60] Second, early retirement incentive programs need to meet the following standards to avoid legal liability: (1) the employee is not coerced to accept the incentive and retire, (2) accurate information is provided regarding options, and (3) the employee is given adequate time (i.e., not pressured) to make a decision.

Employers also have to comply with the Americans with Disabilities Act (ADA), which went into effect in 1992. The ADA, for example, specifies that employees with disabilities must have "equal access to whatever health insurance coverage the employer provides other employees." However, the act also notes that the terms and conditions of health insurance can be based on risk factors as long as this is not a subterfuge for denying the benefit to those with disabilities. Employers with risk-based programs in place would be in a stronger position, however, than employers who make changes after hiring employees with disabilities.[61]

TABLE 17.12   Retiree Benefits and New Accounting Rules

Retiree Health Care Costs	Before FASB 106	After FASB 106
Total costs	$8 million	$33 million
As percentage of payroll	1.9%	5.5%
As percentage of pretax profits	2.5%	8.5%
Cost per active employee (eligible for retiree medical coverage)	$647	$1,945

SOURCE: Used with permission of *Employee Benefit Plan Review* magazine, published monthly by Charles D. Spencer & Associates, Inc., Chicago. Respondents were 72 companies who currently provide health benefits to about 1.5 million active employees and 500,000 retirees.

Retiree Health-Care Accounting Changes

Financial Accounting Statement (FAS) 106, issued by the Financial Accounting Standards Board, became effective in 1993. This new rule states that any benefits (excluding pensions) provided after retirement (the major one being health care) can no longer be funded on a pay-as-you-go basis. Rather, they must be paid on an accrual basis, and companies must begin to enter these future cost obligations on their financial statements.[62] As Table 17.12 indicates, the effect on financial statements is rather dramatic. AT&T, a company with a large retiree population, reported that the initial effect of adopting FAS 106 would be a reduction in net income of between $5.5 and $7.5 billion. General Motors (GM) announced that it would take a $20.8 million reduction in net income, resulting in a total loss of $23.5 billion in 1992, the largest loss in corporate history.[63]

As a result of increasing retiree health-care costs, there is a widespread movement among companies to control costs. GM announced that it would require 190,000 white-collar employees and retirees to pay insurance premiums for the first time in its history, with projected savings of $40 million.[64] Copayments and deductibles will also be increased. In a survey of over 1,000 companies that offer retiree health-care benefits, 7 percent had actually ended retiree health-care benefits or planned to do so within the next two years.[65] Furthermore, 65 percent had implemented (or planned to implement) benefit reductions, and 47 percent had increased (or planned to increase) required contributions from retirees. Obviously, such changes hit the elderly hard, especially those with relatively fixed incomes. Not surprisingly, legal challenges are under way. The need to balance the interests of shareholders, current employees, and retirees in this area will be one of the most difficult challenges facing managers in the future.

Taken together, retiree medical care and pension liabilities (discussed earlier), can have a very large effect on the company's financial health. In fact, Standard & Poor's (S&P) reacted to GM's announcement by downgrading GM's debt from A-minus to BBB-plus. This means that S&P is warning investors that GM has become a more risky company. As a result, GM will find it more costly to raise capital. S&P warned that the cash needed by GM each year to cover "its massive benefits obligations will be a substantial drain on the company's financial resources—and therefore a significant competitive disadvantage—for the foreseeable future."[66]

SUMMARY

Effective management of employee benefits is an important means by which organizations successfully compete. Benefits costs are substantial and continue to grow rapidly in some areas, most notably health care. Control of such costs is necessary to compete in the product market. At the same time, employers must offer a benefits package that permits them to compete in the labor market. Beyond investing more money in benefits, this attraction and retention of quality employees can be helped by better communication of the value of the benefits package and by allowing employees to tailor benefits to their own needs through flexible benefits plans.

Employers continue to be a major source of economic security for employees, often providing health insurance, retirement benefits, and so forth. Changes to benefits can have a tremendous impact on employees and retirees. Therefore, employers carry a significant social responsibility in making benefits decisions. At the same time, employees need to be aware that they will increasingly become responsible for their own economic security. Health-care benefit design is changing to encourage employees to be more informed consumers, and retirement benefits will depend more and more on the financial investment decisions employees make on their own behalf.

Discussion Questions

1. The opening vignette described how a company sharply reduced its maximum coverage for an employee after it found out he had the AIDS virus. Should companies be permitted to take this sort of action? Where does the social responsibility of employers end, and where does it need to make a profit begin?

2. Your company, like many others, is experiencing double-digit percentage increases in health care costs. What suggestions can you offer that may help reduce the rate of cost increases?

3. Why is communication so important in the employee benefits area? What sorts of programs can a company use to communicate more effectively? What are the potential positive consequences of more effective benefits communication?

4. What are the potential advantages of flexible benefits and flexible spending accounts? Are there any potential drawbacks?

5. Although benefits account for a large share of employee compensation, many feel there is little evidence on whether an employer receives an adequate return on the benefits investment. One suggestion has been to link benefits to individual, group, or organization performance. Explain why you would or would not recommend this strategy to an organization.

Notes

1. K. Jackson, "Accounting Change Forces Ford to Post Loss in Billions," *Automotive News*, December 21, 1992, 6.

2. H. W. Hennessey, "Using Employee Benefits to Gain a Competitive Advantage," *Benefits Quarterly*, 5, no. 1 (1989): 51–57; B. Gerhart and G. T. Milkovich, "Employee Compensation: Research and Practice," in *Handbook of Industrial and Organizational Psychology*, vol. 3, 2nd ed., ed. M. D. Dunnette and L. M. Hough (Palo Alto, Cal.: Consulting Psychologists Press, 1992).

3. R. G. Ehrenberg and R. S. Smith, *Modern Labor Economics* (Glenview, Ill.: Scott, Foresman and Company, 1988).

4. B. T. Beam, Jr. and J. J. McFadden, *Employee Benefits* (Chicago: Dearborn Financial Publishing, 1992).

5. Bureau of National Affairs, "Most Workers Who Struck in 1990 Did So Over Health Coverage, AFL-CIO Says," *Daily Labor Report*, August 20, 1991, A12.

6. The organization and description in this section draws heavily on Beam and McFadden, *Employee Benefits*.

7. J. A. Penczak, "Unemployment Benefit Plans," in *Employee Benefits Handbook*, 3rd ed., ed. J. D. Mamorsky (Boston: Warren, Gorham, & Lamont, 1992).

8. D. Runner, "Changes in Unemployment Insurance Legislation in 1992," *Monthly Labor Review* 116 (January 1993): 56–59.

9. J. V. Nackley, *Primer on Workers' Compensation* (Washington, D.C.: Bureau of National Affairs, 1989).

10. Beam and McFadden, *Employee Benefits*, 59.

11. Nackley, *Primer on Workers' Compensation*.

12. M. D. Fefer, "What to Do About Workers' Comp," *Fortune*, June 29, 1992, 80ff.

13. Ibid.

14. J. R. Hollenbeck, D. R. Ilgen and S. M. Crampton, "Lower Back Disability in Occupational Settings: A Review of the Literature from a Human Resource Management View," *Personnel Psychology* 45 (1992): 247–278.

15. Gallup-collected data are summarized in: Employee Benefit Research Institute, "Health-Care Reform: Trade-offs and Implications," *EBRI Issue Brief*, No. 125 (Washington, D.C.: Employee Benefit Research Institute, April 1992).

16. Beam and McFadden, *Employee Benefits*.

17. L. M. Dailey and J. A. Turner, "Private Pension Coverage in Nine Countries," *Monthly Labor Review*, May 1992, 40–43; Hewitt Associates, *Salaried Employee Benefits Provided by Major Employers in 1990* (Lincolnshire, Ill: Hewitt Associates, 1990); W. J. Wiatrowski, "New Survey Data on Pension Benefits," *Monthly Labor Review*, August 1991, 8–21.

18. Beam and McFadden, *Employee Benefits*; J. B. Lockhart, "Securing the Pension Promise," *Labor Law Journal*, April 1991, 195–200.

19. A. R. Karr, "Risk to Retirees Rises as Firms Fail to Fund Pensions They Offer," *The Wall Street Journal*, February 4, 1993, A1ff.

20. J. Gerth, "U.S. Pension Agency in Deep Trouble, Economists Warn," *New York Times*, December 20, 1992, 1ff.

21. M. J. Alderson and J. L. VanDerhei, "Disturbing the Balance in Corporate Pension Policy: The Case of Excess Asset Reversion Legislation," *Benefits Quarterly* 7, no. 3 (1991): 38–51.

22. R. M. McCaffery, "Employee Benefits and Services," in *Compensation and Benefits*, ed. L. R. Gomez-Mejia (Washington, D.C.: Bureau of National Affairs, 1989).

23. F. G. Sieller, "Cash or Deferred Arrangements: Section 401(k) Plans," in *Employee Benefits Handbook*, 3rd ed., ed. J. D. Mamorsky (Boston: Warren, Gorham, and Lamont, 1992).

24. T. P. Pare, "Is Your 401(k) Plan Good Enough?" *Fortune*, December 28, 1992, 78ff.

25. J. Fierman, "How Secure is Your Nest Egg?" *Fortune*, August 12, 1991, 50–54.

26. Beam and McFadden, *Employee Benefits*.

27. B. J. Coleman, *Primer on Employee Retirement Income Security Act*, 3rd ed. (Washington, D.C.: Bureau of National Affairs, 1989).

28. Continental Can Company v. Gavalik. Summary in *Daily Labor Report*. (1987, December 8). Supreme Court lets stand Third Circuit ruling that pension avoidance scheme is ERISA violation. No. 234, p. A-14.

29. D. A. DeCenzo and S. J. Holoviak, *Employee Benefits* (Englewood Cliffs, N.J.: Prentice-Hall, 1990).

30. U.S. data on paid holidays are from Hewitt Associates, *Salaried Employee Benefits Provided by Major U.S. Employers* (Lincolnshire, Ill.: Hewitt Associates, 1990); European data are from Commerce Clearing House, *Doing Business in Europe* (New York: Commerce Clearing House, 1990).

31. Employee Benefit Research Institute, "The Employer's Role in Helping Working Families," *Employee Benefit Notes*, November 1991, 3–5; "Most Small Businesses Appear Prepared to Cope with New Family Leave Rules," *The Wall Street Journal*, February 8, 1993, B1ff.

32. "The Employer's Role in Helping Working Families," *Employee Benefit Notes*, November 1991, 3–5. For examples of child-care arrangements in some well-known companies (e.g., AT&T, Apple, Exxon, IBM, Merck) see "A Look at Child-Care Benefits," *USA Today* (March 14, 1989), 4B.

33. Bureau of National Affairs, *101 Key Statistics on Work and Family for the 1990s* (Washington, D.C.: Bureau of National Affairs, 1989), 29.

34. D. A. DeCenzo and S. J. Holoviak, *Employee Benefits* (Englewood Cliffs, N.J.: Prentice-Hall, 1990).

35. Hennessey, "Using Employee Benefits to Gain a Competitive Advantage."

36. For example, Hewitt Associates, *Salaried Employee Benefits*; Bureau of Labor Statistics, *Employee Benefits in State and Local Governments, 1990* (Washington, D.C.: U.S. Government Printing Office, 1992); Bureau of Labor Statistics, *Employee Benefits in Medium and Large Establishments, 1989* (Washington, D.C.: U.S. Government Printing Office, 1990); Bureau of Labor Statistics, *Employee Benefits in Small Private Establishments, 1990* (Washington, D.C.: U.S. Government Printing Office, 1991).

37. U.S. Department of Health and Human Services, Health Care Financing Administration, *Source Book of Health Insurance Data*, 1991; U.S. Chamber of Commerce Research Center, *Employee Benefits* (Washington, D.C.: U.S. Chamber of Commerce, 1991).

38. Beam and McFadden, *Employee Benefits*.

39. Employee Benefit Research Institute/Gallup Poll, *Public Attitudes on Health Insurance, 1991*, EBRI Report No. G-26 (Washington, D.C.: Employee Benefit Research Institute, 1991).

40. Employee Benefit Research Institute, "Health Care Reform: Trade-offs and Implications," *EBRI Issue Brief*, No. 125, April 1992.

41. Employee Benefit Research Institute, "Health Care Reform."

42. Beam and McFadden, *Employee Benefits*.

43. Ibid.

44. Employee Benefit Research Institute/The Gallup Organization, Inc., *Public Attitudes on National Health Insurance*; "Business Execs Split on Ways to Solve Crisis," (1992, April). *HRFocus*, April 1992, 6; P. J. Hilts, "Corporate Chiefs See Need for U.S. Health-Care Action," *New York Times*, April 8, 1991, D1ff.

45. Employee Benefit Research Institute, "Health-Care Reform."

46. J. Schor, *The Overworked American: The Unexpected Decline of Leisure* (New York: Basic Books, 1991); For a critique of Schor's research, see A. Feuerstein, "A Critique of the 'Overworked American,'" Unpublished manuscript, ILR, Cornell University, 1992.

47. G. Mangum, D. Mayall and K. Nelson, "The Temporary Help Industry: A Response to the Dual Internal Labor Market," *Industrial and Labor Relations Review* 38 (1985): 599–611; M. Montgomery, "On the Determinants of Employer Demand for Part-Time Workers," *Review of Economics and Statistics* 70 (1988): 112–117; F. A. Scott, M. C. Berger and D. A. Black, "Effects of the Tax Treatment of Fringe Benefits on Labor-Market Segmentation," *Industrial and Labor Relations Review* 42 (1989): 216–229. Some conflicting evidence on part-time workers, however, is provided by C. Tilly, "Reasons for the Continued Growth in Part-Time Employment," *Monthly Labor Review* 114, no. 3 (1991): 10–18.

48. Beam and McFadden, *Employee Benefits*.

49. M. Wilson, G. B. Northcraft and M. A. Neale, "The Perceived Value of Fringe Benefits," *Personnel Psychology* 38 (1985): 309–320. Similar results were found in other studies reviewed by H. W. Hennessey, P. L. Perrewe and W. A. Hochwarter, "Impact of Benefit Awareness on Employee and Organizational Outcomes: A Longitudinal Field Experiment," *Benefits Quarterly* 8, no. 2 (1992): 90–96.

50. R. Huseman, J. Hatfield and R. Robinson, "The MBA and Fringe Benefits," *Personnel Administrator* 23, no. 7 (1978): 57–60. See summary in H. W. Hennessey, Jr., "Using Employee Benefits to Gain a Competitive Advantage," *Benefits Quarterly* 5, no. 1 (1989): 51–57.

51. Hennessey et al., "Impact of Benefit Awareness." The same study found no impact of the increased awareness and benefits satisfaction on overall job satisfaction; G. F. Dreher, R. A. Ash and R. D. Bretz, "Benefit Coverage and Employee Cost: Critical Factors in Explaining Compensation Satisfaction," *Personnel Psychology* 41 (1988): 237–254.

52. M. C. Giallourakis and G. S. Taylor, "An Evaluation of Benefit Communication Strategy," *Employee Benefits Journal* 15, no. 4 (1991): 14–18; U.S. Chamber of Commerce, *Employee Benefits*.

53. Beam and McFadden, *Employee Benefits*.

54. For supportive evidence, see A. E. Barber, R. B. Dunham and R. A. Formisano, "The Impact of Flexible Benefits on Employee Satisfaction: A Field Study," *Personnel Psychology* 45 (1992): 55–75; E. E. Lawler, *Pay and Organizational Development* (Reading, Mass.: Addison-Wesley, 1981).

55. P. Biggins, "Flexible/Cafeteria Plans," in *Employee Benefits Handbook*, 3rd ed., ed. J. D. Mamorsky (Boston: Warren, Gorham and Lamont, 1992).

56. For a description of these rules, see M. M. Sarli, "Nondiscrimination Rules for Qualified Plans: The General Test," *Compensation and Benefits Review* 23, no. 5 (September–October 1991): 56–67.

57. Beam and McFadden, *Employee Benefits*, 359.

58. Beam and McFadden, *Employee Benefits*, 355.

59. Los Angeles Dept. of Water & Power v. Manhart. 435 US SCt 702 (1978), 16 EPD, 8250.

60. S. K. Hoffman, "Discrimination Litigation Relating to Employee Benefits," *Labor Law Journal*, June 1992, 362–381.

61. Ibid., 375.

62. Ibid.

63. W. A. Reimert, "Accounting for Retiree Health Benefits," *Compensation and Benefits Review* 23, no. 5 (September–October, 1991): 49–55; D. P. Levin, "20.8 Billion G.M. Charge for Benefits," *New York Times*, February 2, 1993, D4.

64. Bureau of National Affairs, "GM to Require 190,000 White-Collar Workers, Retirees to Pay Insurance Premiums for First Time," *Daily Labor Report*, August 26, 1992, A10.

65. S. LaRock, "FAS 106: Some Firms Bite Retiree Bullet, Others Delay Adopting Accounting Rule," *Employee Benefit Plan Review*, May 1992, 16–20.

66. J. B. White, "GM's Pension, Medical Cost Liabilities Cause S & P to Downgrade Firm's Debt," *The Wall Street Journal*, February 4, 1993, A2ff.

C A S E

ARE THE RETIREMENT YEARS THE GOLDEN YEARS?

Clark Garrecht, an Eastern Airlines pilot who was earning about $100,000 per year, was looking forward to spending retirement playing golf and traveling abroad. But he did not plan on Continental Airlines Holdings, Eastern's parent company, filing for bankruptcy. At age 59, after 24 years with the company earning a sizable income, Garrecht found himself having trouble paying his bills. His defined benefit pension payment will not be the $2,600 he had counted on. Instead, it will be $2,250 per month, the maximum guaranteed by the federal Pension Benefit Guaranty Corporation. The $300,000 in his defined contribution retirement plan was temporarily frozen because of Eastern's liquidity problems and the bankruptcy. He also lost his company-paid $90,000 life insurance policy, his low-cost airline flights to anywhere, and five years of medical coverage—which can easily run into thousands of dollars a year.

QUESTIONS

1. **How can these sorts of threats to employees' economic security be avoided?**

2. **Are events like this part of a growing trend toward less economic security for employees?**

3. **To what extent do factors such as globalization and more intense competition in product markets make such changes inevitable?**

4. **What can companies do? What can employees do? Is there a role for government?**

SOURCE: J. Fierman, "How Secure is Your Nest Egg?" *Fortune*, August 12, 1991, 50ff.

BUDGET RENT-A-CAR AND INTERNATIONAL

In the corporate offices in Lisle, Illinois, Jack McEnery, the corporate vice-president of training and compensation, and Sylvia McGeachie, vice-president of human resources for Europe, the Middle East, and Africa, were discussing the implementation of the new incentive plan. The plans appeared to be developing smoothly, and both were pleased by the progress they had made in resolving various administrative issues. It was, however, clear from the discussion that neither previous practice nor theory was available to guide their actions. Most organizations have only recently begun to cope with the ambiguous issues that are being discussed by McEnery and McGeachie.

Suddenly, McGeachie became quiet and thoughtful and then said, "You know, Jack, France mandated compulsory profit sharing in 1967 for companies operating within France. This is going to impact our incentive plan. Are we going to factor in this required compensation before the incentives are determined? We certainly don't want to pay for both. That would mean, in effect, a double bonus for managers."

In France, the Law of 1967 enacted mandatory, private profit sharing. Any employer with more than 100 employees must establish a profit-sharing plan within a prescribed framework. The total employees' share in profits is determined at the end of each year. The minimum requirement is that the profit-sharing formula applies to the excess, if any, of the after-tax profit minus 5 percent of invested capital. Allocation is made on the basis of salary. Typically, the profit sharing is distributed in the form of company shares, with a restriction that employees cannot cash these shares for five years.

Budget's incentive plan was designed to support a global strategy that would reward salaried employees for achieving corporate goals. If 70 percent of the corporate goals regarding profitability are reached, there is a payout to all exempt employees. The amount is based both on profit and on the salary grade of the exempt employee. No base pay is at risk; however, considerable additional compensation may be possible when profit goals are achieved. For example, a manager may receive 25 percent of his/her salary immediately and 25 percent after three years. A vice president may receive 40 percent of his/her salary via an immediate payout and an equivalent amount in three years. Twenty percent of the payout relates to the level of total corporate profitability, another 20 percent relates to regional profitability, and 60 percent depends on the achievement of local goals (in this case, France).

Budget's intention was to align pay practices with business strategy and also compensate employees internationally in a fair, comparable manner. The philosophy was that of "think globally, but act locally." Since France had mandated profit sharing, however, several issues occurred to McEnery and McGeachie as they discussed the incentive plan.

Budget's History

Budget was founded in 1958 by Morris Mirkin and Jules Lederer in a Los Angeles storefront. They began renting Chevys at $4 a day and $.04 a mile. In the mid 1960s, Budget began international operations when it opened operations in Canada and Puerto Rico. Expansion into Great Britain occurred a few years later.

As of 1993, Budget Rent-a-Car is the third largest company in the car rental industry. There are approximately 3,200 locations worldwide (about half are owned by licensees). Sales in 1992 were $2.4 billion, with half of the sales accounted for by licensees. There are 160,000 vehicles available for rent worldwide.

Issues in Compensation

During a continuation of their discussion, McEnery asked McGeachie, "Do you think that with the mandated profit-sharing process in France we can create a sufficiently motivating environment with Budget's incentive plan? I think it is important that we avoid underpayment since that will be frustrating and may be perceived as unfair by employees. On the other hand, overpayment is both inappropriate for Budget and possibly de-motivating. Why, after all, if you already get a high reward for moderate effort make an extraordinary effort?"

"I agree," McGeachie responded, "but I think that if we ensure that the rewards are high enough beyond the legal requirements, motivation will be strong. We must try to ensure in France that approximately the same level of pay related to profit is at risk as in other countries. It is my perception after working a great deal with the French that although historically the government has had a socialistic orientation, there would be few differences among the French managers in how they would react to incentives as compared with other Europeans. French managers have become cosmopolitan in understanding the trends of business across

Europe, and incentive compensation is a very important issue right now. We must discuss the issue with our people in France, but I think in this area, at least, we will see similar reactions and motivation."

After some consideration, McEnery suggested, "So we have to consider the factors that might interfere with the level of the reward." "That's right," said McGeachie, "and one critical issue to consider is the income tax rate of the French. Although the income tax also funds health care coverage and pensions, it is very high. There is a rapidly sliding scale based on income, with no deductions allowed except for dependents. For instance, the income tax rate is 50 percent at the American equivalent of approximately $52,000. The same incentive amount will equate to less reward in France as compared with the United States because of taxes."

"Let me play devil's advocate," said McEnery, "and suggest that while pay is a concern of the company and employee, the income tax rate is the concern of the citizen and the government of a country." (Some compensation specialists believe that the analysis should be pretax; otherwise, every time a government changes the tax structure, the compensation structure of organizations would need revision.)

The discussion was continued later with the marketing manager in France, Bertrand Guidard. Guidard stated, "Employee reactions to incentives will depend, in France, on the level of the employee. Higher-level employees are very concerned about profitability in France since they recognize this relates to the future of Budget in France as well as to their bonus. The incentive plan is very motivating for managers, although I don't believe that lower level employees are motivated by the idea of possible incentives. We need an incentive plan, although it has to be possible to reach."

Conclusions

In international compensation, there are two forces that must be considered simultaneously. First, there must be a global vision that allows an organization to formulate a business strategy that crosses national bor-

SOURCES:
"The Quality Imperative—
What It Takes to Win in
the Global Economy,"
Business Week, October 25,
1991 (whole issue); D. J.
Carey and P. D. Howes,
"Developing a Global Pay
Program," *Journal of
International Compensation
and Benefits,* 1, no. 1 (1992):
30–34; F. K. Hahn,
"Shaping Compensation
Packages in Global
Companies," *Journal of
Compensation and Benefits,*
November/December,
1991, 11–16; J. S. Hyman
and R. G. Kantor, "The
Globalization of
Compensation," *Journal of
International Compensation
and Benefits,* 1, no. 1 (1992):
25–29; M. J. Marquardt and
D. W. Engel, *Global Human
Resource Development,*
(Englewood Cliffs, N.J.:
Prentice-Hall, 1993).

ders. Many argue that a single marketplace has been created by competitiveness of global operations. Particularly in a service organization, the ability to attract and retain customers is critical. The emphasis on quality in service has become a monumental concern. Poor service may send more customers to your global competition than price or quality.

The second consideration is the impact of local conditions. Culture, and even operations of an international organization, will vary across borders. Therefore, an international compensation decision involves the reinforcement of global strategy but also must recognize and reward differences in cultural approaches. Communication is critical about both basic compensation philosophy and the way goals are set, measured, and rewarded.

The management of human resources may be the key to global success. Compensation strategies therefore need to reinforce the concept of service delivery. The incentive plan described for Budget was designed to maintain the motivation and satisfaction of management employees, as well as to ensure the company's competitive ability to attract and retain the best employees.

DISCUSSION QUESTIONS

1. What do you think Budget should do about the incentive plan in France?
2. Do you think that compensation decisions should be made pre- or post-tax? Defend your position.
3. What should "think globally, act locally" mean when implementing an incentive plan such as Budget's?
4. Put yourself in the position of a manager for Budget. How do you reconcile the issue of government-mandated profit sharing versus additional incentives designed by Budget? Would compensation be likely to affect your behavior or other managers' behavior in different ways?

VI

SPECIAL TOPICS IN HUMAN RESOURCE MANAGEMENT

In the previous parts of the book we have discussed how work design, performance management, staffing and selection, training and development, and compensation practices can help companies meet the global, quality, technological and structure, and social competitive challenges. We have also emphasized the important environmental factors (e.g., strategy, legal) that influence the effectiveness of human resource management practices. Most companies have individual or collective expertise available for dealing with environmental issues and human resource practices.

In Part VI, we discuss two specialized areas of human resource management. Labor and management relations are of primary concern to those companies whose employees are represented by a union. Also, although many tech-

nological advances in microcomputer hardware and software have occurred in the past decade, many companies are just beginning to use human resource information systems for tracking, reporting, and decision making.

Chapter 18, "Collective Bargaining and Labor Relations," discusses the change, in many cases, from an adversarial to a cooperative relationship between labor and management. The chapter also discusses union structure and membership, the organizing process, contract negotiation, and the relationship between labor relations and company effectiveness.

Chapter 19, "Human Resource Information Systems," provides an easy-to-understand yet up-to-date overview of hardware and databases for human resource management. The factors that managers should consider in choosing hardware are emphasized. Because managers will increasingly be in charge of selecting hardware or software applications, the steps in the development of a human resource information system (including vendor selection) are also discussed. A key focus of the chapter is software applications that can help improve the efficiency and effectiveness of human resource planning, performance management, training, career management, and compensation and benefits administration.

18

COLLECTIVE BARGAINING AND LABOR RELATIONS

Objectives   *After reading this chapter, you should be able to:*

1. Describe what is meant by collective bargaining and labor relations.
2. Identify the labor relations goals of management, labor unions, and society.
3. Explain the legal environment's impact on labor relations.
4. Describe the major labor–management interactions: organizing, contract negotiations, and contract administration.
5. Describe the new, less adversarial approaches to labor–management relations.
6. Explain how changes in competitive challenges (e.g., product-market competition and globalization) are influencing labor–management interactions.
7. Explain how labor relations in the public sector differ from labor relations in the private sector.

Conflict and Cooperation: GM and the UAW

The main issue in the August 1992 strike at the General Motors fabricating plant in Lordstown, Ohio, was job security. GM planned to close part of the plant and send work out to subcontractors, which would have resulted in 240 unionized tool-and-die workers' losing their jobs. The immediate impact of the strike was a shutdown of automobile production at GM's Saturn plant due to lack of parts. Because of the car's popularity, Saturn dealers were already having trouble satisfying customer demand. According to Donald Hudler, vice-president of Saturn sales, "Yesterday, our retailers were crying for cars. Today, they're just crying." The union's clear message was: "We're not going to sit back and not protect ourselves for the future. ...Hopefully, this [strike] will set a trend

665

and get a message to GM that our people want to work and if our contract is violated, we won't stand for it."

By September 5, the dispute had not been settled, the strike was continuing, and another nine GM plants had been forced to halt production, idling over 42,000 workers, because of a lack of parts from the struck Lordstown plant. A day later, GM agreed to postpone closing the part of the plant it had planned and find new jobs for the workers when it did close it. The strike ended, but GM lost production of 24,415 automobiles, and it now realized that its plan to eliminate 80,000 North American jobs by 1996 was likely to encounter significant opposition from the United Auto Workers (UAW).

SOURCES: L. Pinto and P. Frame, "Dark Side of Lean: Ohio Strike Halts Tenn," *Automotive News*, August 31, 1992, 4; *New York Times*, September 5, 1992, 33; L. Pinto, "Lordstown Is Omen for '93," *Automotive News*, September 7, 1992, 1.

INTRODUCTION

These events at GM illustrate both the important role of labor relations in running a business and the influence of competitive challenges on the nature of labor relations. Increased competition in the automobile market has forced GM to rethink the way its business is organized and managed, including its labor relations. To be more competitive, GM has decided it must become a smaller and more efficient producer of automobiles. It plans to substantially reduce its work force, which includes many UAW workers. GM is also attempting to shift its production to use less expensive labor. This includes setting up production facilities in places like Mexico and subcontracting work to nonunion U.S. facilities. However, the UAW will fight to protect its members' wages and employment. GM's and the UAW's conflicting objectives become readily apparent during a strike.

A strike (withholding labor) is a key union bargaining tool, and it is effective to the extent that is imposes costs on the company—in the example, lost sales. Strikes also impose costs on workers, however. In the short term, workers lose their income; in the longer term, they may be replaced by other workers, or their jobs may disappear altogether if the strike costs the company too many customers. For GM, another potential cost is that it may have more difficulty (and may have to expend more resources) in closing down facilities or subcontracting work as a means of improving productivity. If so, both employment and sales could suffer in the long run.

Still, as is often the case with labor–management relationships, the relationship between GM and the UAW is complex, and focusing exclusively on what happened at Lordstown would be to focus on only one aspect of the relationship. Indeed, one reason the strike received so much attention is that it affected production of the Saturn, which has been a highly successful product for GM. Ironically, a major reason for Saturn's success has probably been the innovative labor–management relations that GM and the UAW have worked together to develop. Compared with most GM plants, employees at Saturn work under more flexible work rules, have greater participation in decisions, and work more closely with management to produce an automobile that effectively competes in both cost and quality. As with most union–management relationships, conflict and cooperation are part of the relationship between GM and the UAW.

THE LABOR RELATIONS FRAMEWORK

John Dunlop, former secretary of labor and a leading industrial relations scholar, suggested in *Industrial Relations Systems* in 1958 that such a system consists of four elements: (1) an environmental context (technology, market pressures, and the legal framework, especially as it affects bargaining power); (2) participants, including employees and their unions, managements, and the government; (3) a "web of rules" (i.e., rules of the game) that describe the process by which labor and management interact and resolve disagreements (e.g., the steps followed in settling contract grievances), and (4) ideology.[1] For the industrial relations system to operate properly, the three participants must, to some degree, have a common ideology (e.g., acceptance of the capitalist system) and must accept the roles of the other participants. Acceptance does not translate into convergence of interests, however. To the contrary, some degree of worker–management conflict is inevitable because, although the interests of the two parties overlap, they also diverge in key respects (e.g., how to divide the economic profits).[2]

Therefore, according to Dunlop and other U.S. scholars of like mind, an effective industrial relations system does not eliminate conflict. Rather, it provides institutions (and a "web of rules") that resolve conflict in a way that minimizes its costs to management, employees, and society. The collective-bargaining system is one such institution, as are related mechanisms such as mediation, arbitration, and participation in decision making. These ideas formed the basis for the development in the 1940s of schools and departments of industrial and labor relations to train labor relations professionals who, working in both union and management positions, would have the skills to minimize costly forms of conflict such as strikes (which were reaching record levels at the time) and maximize integrative (win-win) solutions to such disagreements.[3]

A more recent industrial relations model, developed by Harry Katz and Thomas Kochan, is particularly helpful in laying out the types of decisions managements and unions make in their interactions and the consequences of such decisions for attainment of goals in areas such as wages and benefits, job security, and the rights and responsibilities of unions and managements.[4] According to Katz and Kochan, these choices occur at three levels.

First, at the *strategic* level, management makes basic choices such as whether to work with its union(s) or to devote its efforts to developing nonunion operations. Environmental factors (or competitive challenges) offer both constraints and opportunities in implementing strategies. For example, if public opinion toward labor unions becomes negative during a particular time period, some employers may see that as an opportunity to rid themselves of unions, whereas other employers may seek to develop a better working relationship with their unions. Similarly, increased competition may dictate the need to increase productivity or reduce labor costs, but whether this is accomplished by shifting work to nonunion facilities or by working with unions to become more competitive is a strategic choice that management faces.

Although management has often been the initiator of change in recent years, unions face a similar choice between fighting changes to the status quo and being open to new labor–management relationships (e.g., less adversarial forms of participation in decision making, such as labor–management teams). The "Competing through Technology and Structure" box describes one union's initiative that benefitted both the union and the company.

Katz and Kochan suggest that labor and management choices at the strategic level in turn affect the labor–management interaction at a second level, the *functional level,* where contract negotiations and union organizing occur, and at the final, *workplace level,* the arena in which the contract is administered. In the opening vignette, GM's strategic-level choice to cut costs and increase productivity, combined with the UAW's strategic choice to take a stand on subcontracting at Lordstown, contributed to conflict (a strike) at the workplace level over the administration of the contract. Although the relationships between labor and management at each of the three levels are somewhat interdependent, the relationship at the three levels may also differ. For example, while management may have a strategy of building an effective relationship with its unions at the strategic level, there may be significant day-to-day conflicts over work rules, grievances, and so forth at any given facility or bargaining unit.

The labor relations framework depicted in Figure 18.1 incorporates many of the ideas discussed so far, including the important role of the environment (i.e., the competitive challenges); union, management, and societal goals; and a separation of union–management interactions into categories (union organizing, contract negotiation, contract administration) that can have important influences on one another but may also be analyzed somewhat independently. The model also highlights the important role that relative bargaining power plays in influencing goals, union–management interactions, and the degree to which each party achieves its goals. Relative bargaining power, in turn, is significantly influenced by the competitive environment (i.e., legal, social, quality, technology/structure, and globalization competitive challenges) and the size and depth of union membership.[5]

We now describe the components of this model in greater depth. The remainder of the chapter is organized into the following sections: the goals and strategies of society, unions, and managements; union structure

Technology & Structure

COMPETING THROUGH

PROACTIVE CHANGES AT UNION CAMP PAPER

Mark Wilson, president of the United Paperworkers International Union Local 407, points out that the union had "seen people come into this country eatin' our lunch in cars and textiles. We decided we're going to adapt before we lose paper." The response to foreign competition has taken a number of forms at the Union Camp paper plant in Savannah, Georgia. Six local unions put together work teams to develop new, more efficient work rules. The unions also helped Union Camp install a new, more efficient papermaking machine that is managed in a way that breaks with past practice. Two of the three daily work shifts on the machine are run without supervisors. Instead, teams of workers have complete responsibility. Each member of the team is trained to do more than one type of job, and the teams select their own members (based on competence, not seniority). Resistance from both managers and workers to such changes is often significant. Wilson received many phone calls from union members around the country warning him not to let management take advantage of the union. However, the plant, which was losing money in the mid-1980s and was in danger of shutting down, remains open, and union members have jobs, suggesting that both the union and the company have come out ahead.

SOURCE: P. Nulty, "Look What the Unions Want Now," *Fortune*, February 8, 1993, 128ff. Used with permission of *Fortune*, © 1993 Time Inc. All rights reserved.

(including union administration and membership); the legal framework, perhaps the key aspect of the competitive environment for labor relations; union and management interactions (organizing, contract negotiation, contract administration); and goal attainment. Environmental factors (other than legal) and bargaining power are discussed in the context of these sections. In addition, two special topics, international comparisons and public sector labor relations, are discussed.

GOALS AND STRATEGIES

Society

In one sense, labor unions, with their emphasis on group action, do not fit well with the individualistic orientation of U.S. capitalism. However, industrial relations scholars such as Beatrice and Sidney Webb and John R. Commons argued in the late 1800s and early 1900s that individual workers' bargaining power was far smaller than that of employers, who were likely to have more financial resources and the ability to easily replace workers.[6] Effective institutions for worker representation (e.g., labor unions) were therefore seen as a way to make bargaining power more equal.

FIGURE 18.1   A Labor Relations Framework

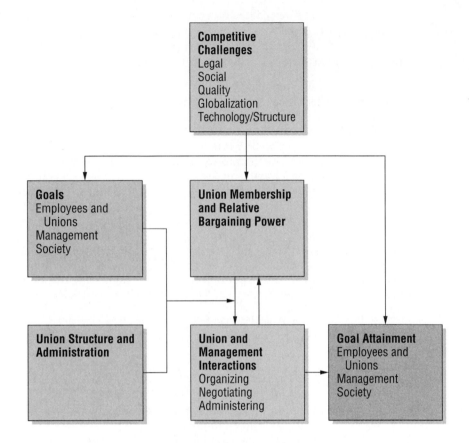

Labor unions' major benefit to society is the institutionalization of industrial conflict, which is therefore resolved in the least costly way. Thus, although disagreements between management and labor continue, it is better to resolve disputes through discussion (collective bargaining) than by battling in the streets. As an influential group of industrial relations scholars put it in describing the future of advanced industrial relations around the world: "Class warfare will be forgotten. The battles will be in the corridors instead of the streets, and memos will flow instead of blood."[7] In this sense, collective bargaining not only has the potential to reduce economic losses caused by strikes but may also contribute to societal stability. For this reason, industrial relations scholars have often viewed labor unions as an essential component of a democratic society.[8] These were some of the beliefs that contributed to the enactment of the National Labor Relations Act (NLRA) in 1935, which sought to provide an environment conducive to collective bargaining and has since regulated labor and management activities and interactions.

Although an industrial relations system based on collective bargaining has drawbacks, so too do the alternatives. Unilateral control by management sacrifices workers' rights. Extensive involvement of government and the courts can result in conflict resolution that is expensive, slow, and imposed by someone (e.g., a judge) with much less firsthand knowledge of the circumstances than either labor or management.

Management

One of management's most basic decisions is whether to encourage or discourage the unionization of its employees. It may discourage unions because it fears higher wage and benefit costs, the disruptions caused by strikes, and an adversarial relationship with its employees or, more generally, greater constraints placed on its decision-making flexibility and discretion. Historically, management has used two basic strategies to avoid unionization.[9] It may seek to provide employment terms and conditions that employees will perceive as sufficiently attractive and equitable so that they see little gain from union representation. Or it may aggressively oppose union representation, even where there is significant employee interest. Use of the latter strategy has increased significantly during the last 20 to 30 years.

If management voluntarily recognizes a union or if employees are already represented by a union, the focus is shifted from dealing with employees as individuals to employees as a group. Still, certain basic management objectives remain: controlling labor costs and increasing productivity (by keeping wages and benefits in check) and maintaining management prerogatives in important areas such as staffing levels and work rules. Of course, management always has the option of trying to decertify a union (i.e., encourage employees to vote out the union in a **decertification** election) if it believes that the majority of employees no longer wish to be represented by the union.

Labor Unions

Labor unions seek, through collective action, to give workers a formal and independent voice in setting the terms and conditions of their work. Table 18.1 shows typical provisions negotiated by unions in collective-bargaining contracts. Labor unions attempt to represent their members' interests in these decisions.

A major goal of labor unions is bargaining effectiveness, because with it comes the power and influence to make the employees' voice heard and to effect changes in the workplace.[10] As the opening to this chapter suggests, the right to strike is one important component of bargaining power. In turn, the success of a strike (actual or threatened) depends on the relative magnitude of the costs imposed on management versus those imposed on the union. A critical factor is the size of union membership. More members

TABLE 18.1

Typical Provisions in Collective-Bargaining Contracts

Establishment and Administration of the Agreement

Bargaining unit and plant supplements

Contract duration and reopening and renegotiation provisions

Union security and the checkoff

Special bargaining committees

Grievance procedures

Arbitration and mediation

Strikes and lockouts

Contract enforcement

Functions, Rights, and Responsibilities

Management rights clauses

Plant removal

Subcontracting

Union activities on company time and premises

Union–management cooperation

Regulation of technological change

Advance notice and consultation

Wage Determination and Administration

General provisions

Rate structure and wage differentials

Allowances

Incentive systems and production bonus plans

Production standards and time studies

Job classification and job evaluation

Individual wage adjustments

General wage adjustments during the contract period

Job or Income Security

Hiring and transfer arrangements

Employment and income guarantees

Reporting and call-in pay

Supplemental unemployment benefit plans

Regulation of overtime, shift work, etc.

Reduction of hours to forestall layoffs

Layoff procedures; seniority; recall

Worksharing in lieu of layoff

Attrition arrangements

Promotion practices

Training and retraining

Relocation allowances

Severance pay and layoff benefit plans

Special funds and study committees

Plant Operations

Work and shop rules

Rest periods and other in-plant time allowances

Safety and health

Plant committees

Hours of work and premium pay practices

Shift operations

Hazardous work

Discipline and discharge

Paid and Unpaid Leave

Vacations and holidays

Sick leave

Funeral and personal leave

Military leave and jury duty

Employee Benefit Plans

Health and insurance plans

Pension plans

Profit-sharing, stock purchase, and thrift plans

Bonus plans

Special Groups

Apprentices and learners

Handicapped and older workers

Women

Veterans

Union representatives

Nondiscrimination clauses

SOURCE: T. A. Kochan, *Collective Bargaining and Industrial Relations* (Homewood, Ill.: Richard D. Irwin, 1980), 29. Original data from: J. W. Bloch, "Union Contracts–A New Series of Studies," *Monthly Labor Review* 87 (October 1964): 1184–1185.

translate into a greater ability to halt or disrupt production and also into greater financial resources for continuing a strike in the face of lost wages.

UNION STRUCTURE, ADMINISTRATION, AND MEMBERSHIP

A necessary step in discussing labor–management interactions is a basic knowledge of how labor and management are organized and how they function. Management has been described throughout this book. We now focus on labor unions.

National and International Unions

Most union members belong to a national or international union. Most national unions are composed of multiple local units, and most are affiliated with the American Federation of Labor and Congress of Industrial Organizations (AFL-CIO).

The largest AFL-CIO-affiliated national unions are listed in Table 18.2. (The National Education Association, with 2 million members, is not affiliated with the AFL-CIO.) An important characteristic of a union is whether it is a *craft* or *industrial* union. The electrical workers' and carpenters' unions are craft unions, meaning that the members all have a particular skill or occupation. Craft unions often are responsible for training their members (through apprenticeships) and for supplying craft workers to employers. Requests for carpenters, for example, would come to the union hiring hall, which would decide which carpenters to send out. Thus, craft workers may work for many employers over time, their constant link being to the union. A craft union's bargaining power depends greatly on the control it can exercise over the supply of its workers.

In contrast, industrial unions are made up of members who are linked by their work in a particular industry (such as steelworkers and autoworkers). Typically they represent many different occupations. Membership in the union is a result of working for a particular employer in the industry. Changing employers is less common than it is among craft workers, and employees who change employers remains members of the same union only if they happen to move to other employers covered by that union. Whereas a craft union may restrict the number of, say, carpenters in order to maintain higher wages, industrial unions try to organize as many employees in as wide a range of skills as possible.

TABLE 18.2   AFL-CIO-affiliated Labor Unions with 100,000 or More Members in 1989 and 1991

	Number of Members	
Organization	1989	1991
Teamsters	1,161,000	1,400,000
State, County, Municipal (AFSCME)	1,090,000	1,200,000
Food and Commercial Workers (UFCW)	999,000	977,000
Automobile, Aerospace, and Agricultural (UAW)	917,000	840,000
Service Employees (SEIU)	762,000	881,000
Electrical Workers (IBEW)	744,000	730,000
Carpenters	613,000	494,000
Teachers (AFT)	544,000	573,000
Machinists	517,000	534,000
Communication Workers	492,000	492,000
Steelworkers	481,000	459,000
Laborers	406,000	406,000
Operating Engineers	330,000	330,000
Hotel, Restaurant Employees	278,000	269,000
Plumbing and Pipefitting	220,000	220,000
Postal Workers	213,000	228,000
Paperworkers	210,000	202,000
Letter Carriers	201,000	210,000
Clothing and Textile Workers (ACTWU)	180,000	154,000
Electronic, Electrical, and Salaried	171,000	160,000
Government Employees (AFGE)	156,000	151,000
Garment Workers (ILGWU)	153,000	143,000
Fire Fighters	142,000	151,000
Retail, Wholesale Department	137,000	128,000
Painters	128,000	124,000
Graphic Communications	124,000	113,000
Ironworkers	111,000	101,000
Sheet Metal Workers	108,000	108,000
Bakery, Confectionery, and Tobacco	103,000	101,000

SOURCES: Reprinted with permission from J. A. Fossum, *Labor Relations*, 5th ed. (Homewood, Ill.: Richard D. Irwin, 1992); and "AFL-CIO-affiliated Labor Unions," from *Directory of U.S. Labor Organizations*, 1992–1993 edition. Copyright © 1992 by the Bureau of National Affairs, Inc., Washington, D.C. 20037.

Local Unions

Even when a national union plays the most critical role in negotiating terms of a collective-bargaining contract, negotiation occurs at the local level as well over work rules and other issues that are locally determined. In addition, administration of the contract is largely carried out at the local union level. Consequently, the bulk of day-to-day interaction between labor and management takes place at the local union level.

The local of an industrial-based union may correspond to a single large facility or to a number of small facilities. In a craft-oriented union, the local may cover a city or a region. The local union typically elects officers (e.g., president, vice-president, treasurer). Responsibility for contract negotiation may rest with the officers, or a bargaining committee may be formed for this purpose. Typically, the national union provides assistance, ranging from background data about other settlements and technical advice to sending a representative to lead the negotiations.

Individual members' participation in local union meetings includes the election of union officials and strike votes. However, most union contact is with the shop steward, who is responsible for ensuring that the terms of the collective-bargaining contract are enforced. The shop steward represents employees in contract grievances. Another union position, the business representative, performs some of the same functions, especially where the union deals with multiple employers, as is often the case with craft unions.

American Federation of Labor and Congress of Industrial Organizations (AFL-CIO)

The AFL-CIO is, not a labor union, but rather an association that seeks to advance the shared interests of its member unions at the national level, much like the Chamber of Commerce or the National Association of Manufacturers do for their member employers. As Figure 18.2 indicates, there are approximately 90 affiliated national unions and 60,000 locals. An important responsibility of the AFL-CIO is to represent labor's interests in public-policy issues such as civil rights, economic policy, safety, and occupational health. It also provides information and analysis that member unions can use in their activities: organizing new members, negotiating new contracts, and administering contracts.

Union Security

The survival and security of a union depends on its ability to ensure a regular flow of new members and member dues to support the services it provides. Therefore, unions typically place high priority on negotiating two contract provisions with an employer that are critical to a union's security or viability

FIGURE 18.2   Structure of the American Federation of Labor and Congress of Industrial Organizations (AFL-CIO), 1991

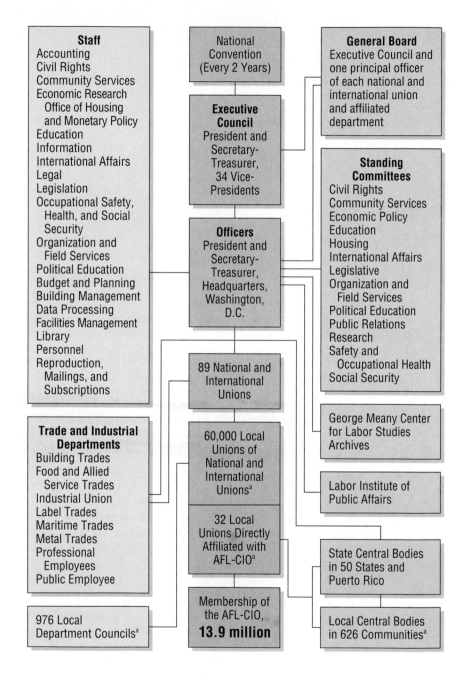

SOURCES: J. A. Fossum, *Labor Relations*, 5th ed. (Homewood, Ill: Richard D. Irwin, 1992), 118. Updated with data from C. D. Gifford, *Directory of U.S. Labor Organizations*, 1992–93 (Washington, D.C.: Bureau of National Affairs, 1992).
[a]1989 data.

checkoff provisions and union membership or contribution. First, under a **checkoff** provision, the employer, on behalf of the union, automatically deducts union dues from employees' paychecks.

A second union security provision focuses on the flow of new members (and their dues). The strongest union security arrangement is a **closed shop**, under which a person must be a union member (and thus pay dues) before being hired. A closed shop is, however, illegal under the NLRA. A **union shop** requires a person to join the union within a certain amount of time (30 days) after beginning employment. An **agency shop** is similar to a union shop but does not require union membership, only that dues be paid. **Maintenance of membership** rules do not require union membership but do require that employees who choose to join must remain members for a certain period of time (e.g., the length of the contract).

Under the 1947 Taft-Hartley Act (an amendment to the NLRA), states may pass so-called **right-to-work laws**, which make union shops, maintenance of membership, and agency shops illegal. The idea behind such laws is that compulsory union membership (or making employees pay union dues) infringes on the employee's right to freedom of association. From the union perspective, a big concern is "free riders," employees who benefit from union activities without belonging to a union. By law, all members of a bargaining unit, whether union members or not, must be represented by the union. If the union is required to offer service to all bargaining unit members, even those who are not union members, it may lose its financial viability.

Union Membership and Bargaining Power

At the strategic level, management and unions meet head-on over the issue of union organizing. Increasingly, employers are actively resisting unionization in an attempt to control costs and maintain their flexibility. Unions, on the other hand, must organize new members and hold on to their current members to have the kind of bargaining power and financial resources needed to achieve their goals in future organizing, and to negotiate and administer contracts with management. For this reason we now discuss trends in union membership and possible explanations for those trends.

Since the 1950s, union membership has consistently declined as a percentage of employment; it now stands at 16 percent of all employment and 12 percent of private-sector employment.[11] As Figure 18.3 indicates, this decline shows no indication of reversing (or even slowing down). If the trend continues, private-sector membership in unions may fall below 5 percent in the foreseeable future.[12]

What factors explain the decline in union membership? Several have been identified.[13]

Structural Changes in the Economy.   At the risk of oversimplifying, one might say that unions have traditionally been strongest in urban workplaces (especially those outside the South) that employ middle-age workers in blue-collar jobs. However, much recent job growth has occurred among women and youth in the service sector of the economy. Although

FIGURE 18.3   Union Membership in the United States as a Percentage of Employment

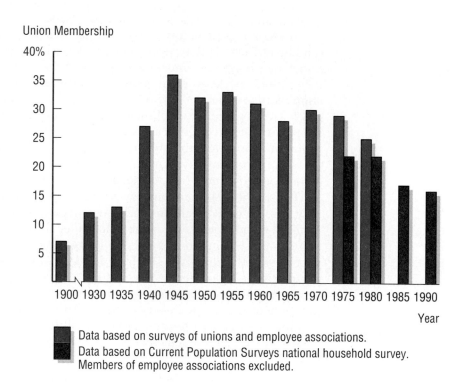

Union Membership

Data based on surveys of unions and employee associations.
Data based on Current Population Surveys national household survey.
Members of employee associations excluded.

SOURCES: C. Chang and C. Sorrentino, "Union Membership in 12 Countries," *Monthly Labor Review* 114, no. 12 (1991): 46–53; L. Troy and N. Sheflin, *Union Sourcebook* (West Orange, N.J.: Industrial Relations Data and Information Services, 1985); Bureau of Labor Statistics, *Handbook of Labor Statistics* (Washington, D.C., 1992).

unionizing such groups is possible, unions have so far not had much success organizing these groups in the private sector. Despite the importance of structural changes in the economy, studies show that they account for no more than one-quarter of the overall union membership decline.[14] Also, Canada, which has been undergoing similar structural changes, has experienced growth in union membership since the early 1960s. It is now 33 percent of employment, compared with 16 percent in the United States.

Increased Employer Resistance.   Almost one-half of large employers in a survey reported that their most important labor goal was to be union-free. This contrasts sharply with 30 years ago, when one observer wrote that "many tough bargainers [among employers] prefer the union to a situation where there is no union. Most of the employers in rubber, basic steel and the automobile industry fall in this category." The idea then was that an effective union could help assess and communicate the interests of employees to management, thus helping management make better decisions. But product-market pressures, such as foreign competition, have contributed to increasing employer resistance of unions. These changes in the competitive environment have contributed to a change in management's perspective and goals.[15]

Over 30 years ago, unions were often able to organize entire industries. For example, the UAW organized all four major producers in the automobile industry (GM, Ford, Chrysler, and American Motors). The UAW usually sought and achieved the same union–management contract at each company. As a consequence, a negotiated wage increase in the industry could be passed on to the consumer in the form of higher prices. No company was undercut by its competitors because the labor cost of all major producers in the industry was determined by the same union–management contract, and the American public had little option but to buy American-made cars.* However, the onset of foreign competition in the automobile market changed the competitive situation as well as the UAW's ability to organize the industry.[16] U.S. automakers were slow to recognize and respond to the competitive threat from foreign producers, resulting in a loss of market share and employment.

Competitive threats have contributed to increased employer resistance to union-organizing and, in some cases, to an increased emphasis on ridding themselves of existing unions. Unionized workers receive, on average, 10 percent higher pay (excluding benefits) than their nonunion counterparts. Many employers have decided that they can no longer compete with these higher labor costs, and union membership has suffered as a result.[17] One measure of increased employer resistance is the dramatic increase in the late 1960s in the number of unfair employer labor practices (i.e., violations of sections of the NLRA such as section 8(a)(3), which prohibits firing employees for union organizing, discussed later) even though the number of elections held did not change much (see Figure 18.4). The use of remedies such as back pay for workers also grew, but the costs to employers of such penalties does not appear to have been sufficient to prevent the growth in employer unfair labor practices. Not surprisingly, the union victory rate in representation elections has decreased from almost 59 percent in 1960 to about 47 percent in 1991. Since 1980, the number of elections has declined by more than 50 percent. Moreover, decertification elections have gone from about 4 percent of elections in 1960 to about 18 percent of elections in 1991.[18]

At a personal level, some managers may face serious consequences if a union successfully organizes a new set of workers or mounts a serious organizing drive. One study indicated that 8 percent of the plant managers in

---

*Different employers could face the same contract provisions for one of two reasons: (1) They could be part of an agreement between a union and multiple employers. (2) So-called pattern bargaining, in which the first labor–management contract in an industry set the pattern that other employers followed, may have occurred.

FIGURE 18.4   Employer Resistance to Union Organizing

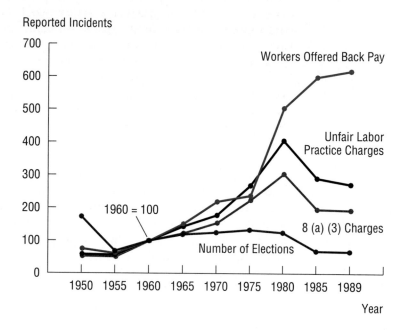

SOURCE: Adapted and updated from R. B. Freeman and J. L. Medoff, *What Do Unions Do?* (New York: Basic Books, 1984). Data for 1985 and 1989 from NLRB annual reports.

Note: 8(a)(3) charges refer to the section of the NLRA that makes it an unfair employer labor practice to discriminate against (e.g., fire) employees who engage in union activities such as union organizing.

companies with organizing drives were fired, and 10 percent of those in companies where the union was successful were fired (compared with 2 percent in a control group).[19] Furthermore, only 3 percent of the plant managers facing an organizing drive were promoted, and none of those ending up with a union contract were promoted (compared with 21 percent of the managers in the control group). Therefore, managers are often under intense pressure to oppose unionization attempts.

Substitution with HRM.   A major study of the human resource management strategies and practices among large, nonunion employers found that union avoidance was often an important employee relations objective.[20] Top management's values in such companies drive specific policies such as promotion from within, an influential personnel/human resource department, and above-average pay and benefits. These policies, in turn, contribute to a number of desirable outcomes such as flexibility, positive employee attitudes, and responsive and committed employees, which ultimately lead to higher productivity and better employee relations. In other words, employers attempt to remain nonunion by offering most of the things a union can offer, and then some, while still maintaining a productivity advantage over their competitors. Of course, one aspect of union representation that employers cannot duplicate is the independent employee voice that a union provides.

Substitution by Government Regulation.   Since the 1960s, regulation of many employment areas has increased, including equal employment opportunity, pensions, and worker displacement. Combined with existing regulations, this increase may result in fewer areas in which unions can provide worker rights or protection beyond those specified by law. Yet, Western European countries generally have more regulations *and* higher levels of union membership than the United States.[21]

Worker Views.   Industrial relations scholars have long argued that the absence in the United States of a history of feudalism and of strong class distinctions found in Western Europe have contributed to a more pragmatic, business-oriented (versus class-conscious) unionism. Although this may help explain the somewhat lower level of union membership in the United States, its relevance in explaining the downward trend is not clear.

Union Actions.   In some ways, unions have hurt their own cause. First, corruption in unions such as the Teamsters may have had a detrimental effect. Second, questions have been raised about how well unions have adapted to recent changes in the economic structure. Employee groups and economic sectors with the fastest growth rates tend to have the lowest rates of unionization.[22] Women are less likely to be in unions than men (12.6 percent versus 19.3 percent), and service-sector industries such as finance, insurance, and real estate have a much lower union representation (2.5 percent) than does manufacturing (20.6 percent). The South is also less heavily organized than the rest of the country (9.2 percent versus 19.2 percent).

LEGAL FRAMEWORK

Although the competitive challenges have a major impact on labor relations, the legal framework of collective bargaining is an especially critical determinant of union membership and relative bargaining power and, therefore, of the degree to which employers, employees, and society are successful in achieving their goals. The legal framework also constrains union structure and administration and the manner in which unions and employers interact. Perhaps the most dramatic example of labor law's influence is the 1935 passage of the Wagner Act (also known as the National Labor Relations Act, or NLRA) which actively supported collecting bargaining, rather than impeding it. As a result, union membership nearly tripled, from 3 million in 1933 (7.7 percent of all employment) to 8.8 million (19.2 percent of employment) by 1939.[23] With increased membership came greater union bargaining power and, consequently, more success in achieving union goals.

Before the 1930s, the legal system was generally hostile to unions. The courts generally viewed unions as coercive organizations that hindered free trade. Unions' focus on collective voice and collective action (e.g., strikes, boycotts) did not fit well with the American emphasis on capitalism, individualism, freedom of contract, and property rights.[24]

The Great Depression of the 1930s, however, shifted public attitudes toward business and the free-enterprise system. Unemployment rates as high as 25 percent and a 30 percent drop in the gross national product between 1929 and 1933 focused attention on employee rights and on the shortcomings of the system as it existed then. The nation was in a crisis, and President Franklin Roosevelt responded with dramatic action: the New Deal. On the labor front, the 1935 NLRA ushered in a new era of public policy for labor unions, enshrining collective bargaining as the preferred mechanism for settling labor–management disputes.

The introduction to the NLRA states:

> It is in the national interest of the United States to maintain full production in its economy. Industrial strife among employees, employers, and labor organizations interferes with full production and is contrary to our national interest. Experience has shown that labor disputes can be lessened if the parties involved recognize the legitimate rights of each in their relations with one another. To establish these rights under the law, Congress enacted the National Labor Relations Act. Its purpose is to define and protect the rights of employees and employers, to encourage collective bargaining, and to eliminate certain practices on the part of labor and management that are harmful to the general welfare.[25]

The rights of employees are set out in section 7 of the act, including the "right to self-organization, to form, join, or assist labor organizations, to bargain collectively through representatives of their own choosing, and to engage in other concerted activities for the purpose of collective bargaining. The act also gives employees the right to refrain from any or all of such activities except [in cases] requiring membership in a labor organization as a condition of employment."[26]

Examples of protected activities include:

- Union organizing.
- Joining a union, whether it is recognized by the employer or not.
- Going out on strike to secure better working conditions.
- Refraining from activity on behalf of the union.[27]

Unfair Labor Practices–Employers

The NLRA prohibits certain activities by both employers and labor unions. Unfair labor practices by employers are listed in Section 8(a) of the NLRA. Section 8(a)(1) prohibits employers from interfering with, restraining, or

TABLE 18.3   Examples of Employer Unfair Labor Practices

- Threatening employees with loss of their jobs or benefits if they join or vote for a union.

- Threatening to close down a plant if organized by a union.

- Questioning employees about their union membership or activities in a manner that restrains or coerces them.

- Spying or pretending to spy on union meetings.

- Granting wage increases that are timed to discourage employees from forming or joining a union.

- Taking an active part in organizing a union or committee to represent employees.

- Providing preferential treatment or aid to one of several unions trying to organize employees.

- Discharging employees for urging other employees to join a union or refusing to hire applicants because they are union members.

- Refusing to reinstate workers when job openings occur because the workers participated in a lawful strike.

- Ending operation at one plant and opening the same operation at another plant with new employees because employees at the first plant joined a union.

- Demoting or firing employees for filing an unfair labor practice or for testifying at an NLRB hearing.

- Refusing to meet with employees' representatives because the employees are on strike.

- Refusing to supply the employees' representative with cost and other data concerning a group insurance plan covering employees.

- Announcing a wage increase without consulting the employees' representative.

- Failing to bargain about the effects of a decision to close one of employer's plants.

SOURCE: National Labor Relations Board, *A Guide to Basic Law and Procedures under the National Labor Relations Act* (Washington, D.C.: U.S. Government Printing Office, 1991).

coercing employees in exercising their rights to join or assist a labor organization or to refrain from such activities. Section 8(a)(2) prohibits employer domination of or interference with the formation or activities of a labor union. Section 8(a)(3) prohibits discrimination in any aspect of employment that attempts to encourage or discourage union-related activity. Section 8(a)(4) prohibits discrimination against employees for providing testimony relevant to enforcement of the NLRA. Section 8(a)(5) prohibits employers from refusing to bargain collectively with a labor organization that has standing under the act. Examples of employer unfair labor practices are listed in Table 18.3.

Unfair Labor Practices–Labor Unions

Originally, the NLRA did not list any union unfair labor practices. These were added through the 1947 **Taft-Hartley Act**. The 1959 **Landrum-Griffin Act** further regulated unions' actions and their internal affairs (e.g., finan-

TABLE 18.4   Examples of Union Unfair Labor Practices

- Mass picketing in such numbers that nonstriking employees are physically barred from entering the plant.

- Acts of force or violence on the picket line, or in connection with a strike.

- Threats to employees of bodily injury or that they will lose their jobs unless they support the union's activities.

- Fining or expelling members for crossing a picket line that is unlawful.

- Fining or expelling members for filing unfair labor practices or testifying before the NLRB.

- Insisting during contract negotiations that the employer agree to accept working conditions that will be determined by a group to which it does not belong.

- Fining or expelling union members for the way they apply the bargaining contract while carrying out their supervisory responsibilities.

- Causing an employer to discharge employees because they spoke out against a contract proposed by the union.

- Making a contract that requires an employer to hire only members of the union or employees "satisfactory" to the union.

- Insisting on the inclusion of illegal provisions in a contract.

- Terminating an existing contract and striking for a new one without notifying the employer, the Federal Mediation and Conciliation Service, and the state mediation service (where one exists).

- Attempting to compel a beer distributor to recognize a union, the union prevents the distributor from obtaining beer at a brewery by inducing the brewery's employees to refuse to fill the distributor's orders.

- Picketing an employer to force it to stop doing business with another employer who has refused to recognize the union (a "secondary boycott").

SOURCE: National Labor Relations Board, *A Guide to Basic Law and Procedures under the National Labor Relations Act* (Washington, D.C.: U.S. Government Printing Office, 1991).

cial disclosure, conduct of elections). Section 8(b)(1)(a) of the NLRA states that a labor organization is not to "restrain or coerce employees in the exercise of the rights guaranteed in section 7" (described earlier). Table 18.4 provides examples of union unfair labor practices.

Enforcement

Enforcement of the NLRA rests with the National Labor Relations Board (NLRB), which is composed of a five-member board, the general counsel, and 33 regional offices. The basis for the NLRA is the commerce clause of the U.S. Constitution. Therefore, the NLRB's jurisdiction is limited to employers whose operations affect commerce generally and interstate commerce in particular. In practice, only purely local firms are likely to fall outside the NLRB's jurisdiction. Specific jurisdictional standards (nearly 20) that vary by industry are applied. Two examples of businesses that are covered (and the 1990 standards): retail businesses that had more than

$500,000 in annual business and newspapers that had more than $200,000 in annual business.

The NLRB's two major functions are to conduct and certify representation elections and prevent unfair labor practices. In both realms, it does not initiate action. Rather, it responds to requests for action. The NLRB's role in representation elections is discussed in the next section. Here, we discuss unfair labor practices.

Unfair labor practice cases begin with the filing of a charge, which is investigated by a regional office. A charge must be filed within six months of the alleged unfair practice, and copies must be served on all parties (registered mail is recommended). If the NLRB finds the charge to have merit and issues a complaint, there are two possible actions. It may defer to a grievance procedure agreed on by the employer and union. Otherwise, a hearing is held before an administrative law judge. The judge makes a recommendation, which can be appealed by either party. The NLRB has the authority to issue cease-and-desist orders to halt unfair labor practices. It can also order reinstatement of employees, with or without back pay. Note, however, that the NLRA is not a criminal statute, and punitive damages are not available. If an employer or union refuses to comply with an NLRB order, the board has the authority to petition the U.S. Court of Appeals. The court can choose to enforce the order, remand it to the NLRB for modification, change it, or set it aside altogether.

UNION AND MANAGEMENT INTERACTIONS: ORGANIZING

To this point, we have discussed macro trends in union membership. Here, we shift our focus to the more micro questions of why individual employees join unions and how the organizing process works at the workplace level.

Why Do Employees Join Unions?

Virtually every model of the decision to join a union focuses on two questions.[28] First, is there a gap between the pay, benefits, and other conditions of employment that employees actually receive versus what they believe they should receive? Second, if such a gap exists and is sufficiently large to motivate employees to try to remedy the situation, is union membership seen as the most effective or instrumental means of change? The outcome of an election campaign hinges on how the majority of employees answer these two questions.

The Process and Legal Framework of Organizing

The NLRB is responsible for ensuring that the organizing process follows certain steps. At the most general level, the NLRB holds a union representation election if at least 30 percent of employees in the bargaining unit sign authorization cards, which indicate their interest in holding an election. If over 50 percent of the employees sign authorization cards, the union may request that the employer voluntarily recognize it. If fewer than 50 percent of the employees sign, or if the employer refuses to recognize the union voluntarily, the NLRB conducts a secret-ballot election. The union is certified by the NLRB as the exclusive representative of employees if over 50 percent of employees vote for the union. If more than one union appears on the ballot and neither gains a simple majority, a runoff election is held. Once a union has been certified as the exclusive representative of a group of employees, no additional elections are permitted for one year. After the negotiation of a contract, an election cannot be held for the contract's duration or for three years, whichever comes first. The parties to the contract may agree not to hold an election for longer than three years, but an outside party cannot be barred for more than three years.

As mentioned previously, union members' right to be represented by leaders of their own choosing was expanded under the Taft-Hartley Act to include the right to vote an existing union out—that is, to decertify it. The process follows the same steps as a representation election. A decertification election is not permitted when a contract is in effect. Research indicates that when decertification elections are held, unions typically do not fare well, losing nearly 75 percent of the time during the late 1980s. Moreover, the number of such elections has increased from roughly 5 percent of all elections in the 1950s and 1960s to 15 to 20 percent from 1982 to 1990.[29]

The NLRB also is responsible for determining the appropriate bargaining unit and the employees who are eligible to participate in organizing activities. A unit may cover employees in one facility or multiple facilities within a single employer, or the unit may cover multiple employers. In general, employees on the payroll just prior to the ordering of an election are eligible to vote, although this rule is modified in some cases where, for example, employment in the industry is irregular. Most employees who are on strike and who have been replaced by other employees are eligible to vote in an election (e.g., a decertification election) that occurs within 12 months of the onset of the strike.

The following types of employees cannot be included in bargaining units: agricultural laborers, independent contractors, supervisors, and managers. Beyond this, the NLRB attempts to group together employees who have a community of interest in their wages, hours, and working conditions. In many cases, this grouping will be sharply contested, with management and the union jockeying to include or exclude certain employee subgroups in the hope of influencing the outcome of the election.

Representation Elections: Management and Union Strategies and Tactics

Tables 18.5 and 18.6 list common campaign issues that arise during most representation elections. Unions attempt to persuade employees that their wages, benefits, treatment by employers, and opportunity to influence

TABLE 18.5   Prevalence of Certain Union Issues in Representation Elections

Union Issues	Percentage of Campaigns
Union will prevent unfairness, set up grievance procedure/ seniority system	82%
Union will improve unsatisfactory wages	79
Union strength will provide employees with voice in wages, working conditions	79
Union, not outsider, bargains for what employees want	73
Union has obtained gains elsewhere	70
Union will improve unsatisfactory sick leave/insurance	64
Dues/initiation fees are reasonable	64
Union will improve unsatisfactory vacations/holidays	61
Union will improve unsatisfactory pensions	61
Employer promises/good treatment may not be continued without union	61
Employees choose union leaders	55
Employer will seek to persuade/frighten employees to vote against union	55
No strike without vote	55
Union will improve unsatisfactory working conditions	52
Employees have legal right to engage in union activity	52

SOURCES: J. A. Fossum, *Labor Relations*, 5th ed. (Homewood, Ill.: Richard D. Irwin), 149. Original data adapted from J. G. Getman, S. B. Goldberg and J. B. Herman, *Union Representation Elections: Law and Reality* (New York: Russell Sage Foundation, 1976), Table 4–3.

workplace decisions are not sufficient and that the union will be effective in obtaining improvements. Management emphasizes that it has provided a good package of wages, benefits, and so on. It also argues that, whereas a union is unlikely to provide improvements in such areas, it will likely impose certain costs on employees, such as union dues and the income loss resulting from strikes.

As Table 18.7 indicates, employers use a variety of methods to oppose unions in organizing campaigns, some of which may go beyond what the law permits, especially in the eyes of union organizers. This perception is supported by our earlier discussion, which noted a significant increase in employer unfair labor practices since the late 1960s (see Figure 18.4).

Why would employers increasingly break the law? Fossum suggests that the consequences (e.g., back pay and reinstatement of workers) of doing so are "slight."[30] His review of various studies suggests that discrimination against employees involved in union organizing decreases union–

TABLE 18.6   Prevalence of Certain Management Issues in Representation Elections

Management Issues	Percentage of Campaigns
Improvements not dependent on unionization	85%
Wages good, equal to/better than under union contract	82
Financial costs of union dues outweigh gains	79
Union is outsider	79
Get facts before deciding, employer will provide facts and accept employee decision	76
If union wins, strike may follow	70
Loss of benefits may follow union win	67
Strikers will lose wages, lose more than gain	67
Unions not concerned with employee welfare	67
Strike may lead to loss of jobs	64
Employer has treated employees fairly/well	60
Employees should be certain to vote	54

SOURCES: J. A. Fossum, *Labor Relations*, 5th ed. (Homewood, Ill.: Richard D. Irwin), 149. Original data adapted from J. G. Getman, S. B. Goldberg and J. B. Herman, *Union Representation Elections: Law and Reality* (New York: Russell Sage Foundation, 1976), Table 4–2.

organizing success significantly and that the cost of back pay to union activists reinstated in their jobs is far smaller than the costs that would be incurred if the union managed to organize and gain better wages, benefits, and so forth.

Still, the NLRB attempts to maintain a noncoercive atmosphere under which employees feel they can exercise free choice. It will set aside an election if it believes that either the union or the employer has created "an atmosphere of confusion or fear of reprisals."[31] Examples of conduct that may lead to an election result being set aside include:

- Threats of loss of jobs or benefits by an employer or union to influence votes or organizing activities.
- A grant of benefits or a promise of benefits as a means of influencing votes or organizing activities.
- An employer or union making campaign speeches to assembled groups of employees on company time less than 24 hours before an election.
- The actual use or threat of physical force or violence to influence votes or organizing activities.[32]

In response to organizing difficulties, the union movement has tried alternative approaches. **Associate union membership** is not linked to an employee's workplace and does not provide representation in collective

TABLE 18.7   Percentage of Firms Using Various Methods to Oppose
Union Organizing Campaigns

Survey of Employers	
Consultants used	41%
Unfair labor practice charges filed against employer	24
Survey of Union Organizers	
Consultants/lawyers used	70
Unfair labor practices by employer	
Charges filed	36
Discharges or discriminatory layoffs	42[a]
Company leaflets	80
Company letters	91
Captive audience speech	91[b]
Supervisor meetings with small groups of employees	92
Supervisor intensity in opposing union	
Low	14
Moderate	34
High	51

SOURCE: R. B. Freeman and M. M. Kleiner, "Employer Behavior in the Face of Union Organizing Drives," *Industrial and Labor Relations Review* 43, no. 4 (April 1990), pp. 351–365. © Cornell University.
[a] This percentage is larger than the figure for charges filed because it includes cases in which no unfair labor practice charge was actually filed against the employer.
[b] Refers to management's requiring employees to attend a session on company time at which the disadvantages of union membership are emphasized.

bargaining. Instead, the union provides other services, such as discounts on health and life insurance or credit cards.[33] In return, the union receives membership dues and a broader base of support for its activities. Associate membership may be attractive to employees who wish to join a union but cannot because their workplace is not organized by a union.

Corporate campaigns seek to bring public, financial, or political pressure on employers during the organizing (and negotiating) process.[34] For example, the Building and Construction Trades Department of the AFL-CIO successfully lobbied Congress to eliminate $100 million in tax breaks for a Toyota truck plant in Kentucky until Toyota agreed to use union construction workers and pay union wages.[35] The Amalgamated Clothing and Textile Workers Union (ACTWU) corporate campaign against J.P. Stevens during the late 1970s was one of the first and best known. The ACTWU organized a boycott of J.P. Stevens products and threatened to withdraw its pension funds from financial institutions where J.P. Stevens officers acted as directors. J.P. Stevens subsequently agreed to a contract with the ACTWU.[36]

UNION AND MANAGEMENT INTERACTION: CONTRACT NEGOTIATION

The majority of contract negotiations take place between unions and employers that have been through the process before. In most cases, management has come to accept the union as an organization that it must work with. But when the union has just been certified and is negotiating its first contract, the situation can be very different. In fact, unions are unable to negotiate a first contract between 27 and 37 percent of the cases.[37]

Labor–management contracts differ in their *bargaining structures*, that is, the range of employees and employers that are covered. As Table 18.8 indicates, the contracts differ, first, according to whether narrow (craft) or broad (industrial) employee interests are covered. Second, they differ according to whether they cover multiple employers or multiple plants within a single employer.* Different structures have different implications for bargaining power and the number of interests that must be incorporated in reaching an agreement.

The Negotiation Process

Richard Walton and Robert McKersie suggested that labor–management negotiations could be broken into four subprocesses: distributive bargaining, integrative bargaining, attitudinal structuring, and intraorganizational bargaining.[38] **Distributive bargaining** focuses on dividing a fixed economic pie between the two sides. A wage increase, for example, means that the union gets a larger share of the pie, management a smaller share. It is a win-lose situation. **Integrative bargaining** has a win-win focus; it seeks solutions beneficial to both sides. So, if management needs to reduce labor costs, it could reach an agreement with the union to avoid layoffs in return for the union agreeing to changes in work rules that might enhance productivity.

Attitudinal structuring refers to the relationship and trust between labor and management negotiators. Where the relationship is poor, it may be difficult for the two sides to engage in integrative bargaining because there is little trust that the other side will carry out its part of the deal. For example, the union may be reluctant to agree to productivity-enhancing work-rule changes to enhance job security if, in the past, it has made similar concessions but believes that management did not stick to its assurance of greater job security. Thus, the long-term relationship between the two parties can have a very important impact on negotiations and their outcomes.

Intraorganizational bargaining reminds us that labor–management negotiations involve more than just two parties. Within management, and to an even greater extent within the union, different factions can have con-

---

*A single employer may have multiple plants, some union, some nonunion.

TABLE 18.8   Types and Examples of Bargaining Structures

Multiemployer (Centralized)	Single employer — Multiplant	Single employer —Single Plant (Decentralized)
Craft Union (Narrow)		
Construction trades	Airline	Craft union in small manufacturing plant
Interstate trucking	Teachers	
Longshoring	Police	Hospital
Hospital association	Firefighters	
	Railroad	
Industrial or Multiskill Union (Broad)		
Coal mining (underground)	Automobiles	Industrial union in small manufacturing plant
Basic steel (pre-1986)	Steel (post 1986)	
Hotel association	Farm equipment	
	State government	
	Textile	

SOURCE: H. C. Katz and T. A. Kochan, *An Introduction to Collective Bargaining and Industrial Relations* (New York: McGraw-Hill, 1992). Used with permission of McGraw-Hill.

flicting objectives. High-seniority workers, who are least likely to be laid off, may be more willing to accept a contract that has layoffs (especially if there is also a significant pay increase for those whose jobs are not at risk). Less-senior workers would likely feel very differently. Thus, negotiators and union leaders must simultaneously satisfy both the management side and their own internal constituencies. If they do not, they risk the union membership's rejecting the contract, or they risk being voted out of office in the next election. Management, too, is unlikely to be of one mind about how to approach negotiations. Some will focus more on long-term employee relations, others will focus on cost control, and still others will focus on what effect the contract will have on stockholders.

Management's Preparation for Negotiations

Clearly, the outcome of contract negotiations can have important consequences for labor costs and labor productivity, and, therefore, for the company's ability to compete in the product market. Adapting Fossum's discussion, we can divide management preparation into the following seven areas, most of which have counterparts on the union side.[39]

1. *Establishing interdepartment contract objectives*—The employer's industrial relations department needs to meet with the accounting, finance, pro-

duction, marketing, and other departments and set contract goals that will permit each department to meet its responsibilities. As an example, finance may suggest a cost figure above which a contract settlement would seriously damage the company's financial health. The bargaining team needs to be constructed to take these various interests into account.

2. *Reviewing the old contract*—This step focuses on identifying provisions of the contract that might cause difficulties by hindering the company's productivity or flexibility or by leading to significant disagreements between management and the union.

3. *Preparing and analyzing data*—Information on labor costs and the productivity of competitors, as well as data the union may emphasize, needs to be prepared and analyzed. The union data might include cost-of-living changes and agreements reached by other unions that could serve as a target. Data on employee demographics and seniority are relevant for establishing the costs of such benefits as pensions, health insurance, and paid vacations. Finally, management needs to know how much it would be hurt by a strike. How long will its inventory allow it to keep meeting customer orders? To what extent are other companies positioned to step in and offer replacement products? How difficult would it be to find replacement workers if the company decides to continue operations during a strike?

4. *Anticipating union demands*—Recalling grievances over the previous contract, having ongoing discussions with union leaders, and becoming aware of settlements at other companies are ways of anticipating likely union demands and developing potential counterproposals.

5. *Establishing the cost of possible contract provisions*—Wages have not only a direct influence on labor costs but often an indirect effect on benefit costs (e.g., Social Security, paid vacation). Recall that benefits add 35 to 40 cents to every dollar's worth of wages. Also, wage or benefit increases that seem manageable in the first year of a contract can accumulate to less manageable levels over time.

6. *Preparing for a strike*—If management intends to operate during a strike, it may need to line up replacement workers, increase its security, and figure out how to deal with incidents on the picket line and elsewhere. If management does not intend to operate during a strike (or if the company will not be operating at normal levels), it needs to alert suppliers and customers and consider possible ways to avoid the loss of their business. This could even entail purchasing a competitor's product in order to have something to sell to customers.

7. *Determining strategy and logistics*—Decisions must be made about the amount of authority the negotiating team will have. What concessions can it make on its own, and which ones require it to check with top management? On which issues can it compromise, and on which can it not? Decisions regarding meeting places and times must also be made.

Negotiation Stages and Tactics

Negotiations go through various stages.[40] In the early stages, many more people are often present than in later stages. On the union side, this may give all the various internal interest groups a chance to participate and voice their goals. This, in turn, helps send a message to management about what the union feels it must do to satisfy its members, and it may also help the union achieve greater solidarity. Union negotiators often present an extensive list of proposals at this stage, partly to satisfy their constituents and partly to provide themselves with issues on which they can show flexibility later in the process. Management may or may not present proposals of its own; sometimes it prefers to react to the union's proposals.

During the middle stages, each side must make a series of decisions, even though the outcome is uncertain. How important is each issue to the other side? How likely is it that disagreement on particular issues will result in a strike? When and to what extent should one side signal its willingness to compromise on its position?

In the final stage, pressure for an agreement increases as the deadline for a strike approaches. Public negotiations may be only part of the process. Negotiators from each side may have one-on-one meetings or small-group meetings where public-relations pressures are reduced. In addition, a neutral third party may become involved, someone who can act as a go-between or facilitator. In some cases, the only way for the parties to convince each other of their resolve (or to convince their own constituents of the other party's resolve) is to allow an impasse to occur.

A variety of books are available that suggest how to avoid impasses by using mutual gains or integrative bargaining tactics. For example, *Getting to Yes,* by Roger Fisher and William Ury, describes four basic principles:

1. Separate the people from the problem;
2. Focus on interests, not positions;
3. Generate a variety of possibilities before deciding what to do; and
4. Insist that the results be based on some objective standard.

Bargaining Power, Impasses, and Impasse Resolution

Employers' and unions' conflicting goals are resolved through the negotiation process just described. An important determinant of the outcome of this process is the relative bargaining power of each party, which can be defined as the "ability of one party to achieve its goals when faced with opposition from some other party to the bargaining process."[41] In collective bargaining, an important element of power is the relative ability of each party to withstand a strike. Although strikes are rare, the threat of a strike often looms large in labor–management negotiations. The relative ability to take a strike, whether one occurs or not, is an important determinant of bargaining power and, therefore, of bargaining outcomes.

Management's Willingness to Take a Strike

Management's willingness to take a strike comes down to two questions:

1. *Can the company remain profitable over the long run if it agrees to the union's demands?* The answer is more likely to be yes to the extent that higher labor costs can be passed on to consumers without losing business. This, in turn, is most likely when (1) the price increase is small because labor costs are a small fraction of total costs or (2) there is little price competition in the industry. Low price competition can result from regulated prices, from competition based on quality (rather than price), or from the union's organizing all or most of the employers in the industry, which eliminates labor costs as a price factor.

   Unions share part of management's concern with long-term competitiveness because a decline in competitiveness can translate into a decline in employment levels. On the other hand, the majority of union members may prefer to have higher wages, despite employment declines, particularly if a minority of the members (those with low seniority) suffer more employment loss and the majority keep their employment with higher wages.

2. *Can the company continue to operate in the short run despite a strike?* Although "hanging tough" on its bargaining goals may pay off for management in the long run, the short-run concern is the loss of revenues and profits from production being disrupted. In the example that opened this chapter, GM knew it needed to reduce labor costs in the long run in order to be competitive, but the short-run cost was a strike that disrupted the sales of what may have been its hottest seller, the Saturn. The cost to strikers is a loss of wages and possibly a permanent loss of jobs.

   Under what conditions is management most able to take a strike? The following factors are important:[42]

1. *Product demand*—Management is less able to afford a strike when the demand for its product is strong because that is when more revenue and profits are lost.

2. *Product perishability*—Farm workers at harvest time, truckers transporting perishable food, airline employees at peak travel periods—a strike by these kinds of employees will result in permanent losses of revenue, thus increasing the cost of the strike to management.

3. *Technology*—An organization that is capital intensive (versus labor intensive) is less dependent on its employees and more likely to be able to use supervisors or others as replacements. Telephone companies are typically able to operate through strikes, even though installing new equipment or services and repair work may take significantly longer than usual.

4. *Availability of replacement workers*—When jobs are scarce, replacement workers are more available and perhaps more willing to cross picket lines. Using replacement workers to operate during a strike raises the

stakes considerably for strikers who may be permanently replaced.[43] Most strikers are not entitled to reinstatement until there are job openings for which they qualify. If replacements were hired, such openings may not occur for some time (if at all). Labor Secretary Robert Reich and the Clinton administration have asked Congress to reconsider legislation that would prohibit the permanent replacement of striking workers.

5. *Multiple production sites and staggered contracts*—Multiple sites and staggered contracts permit employers to shift production from the struck facility to facilities that, even if unionized, have contracts that expire at different times (so they are not able to strike at the same time).

6. *Integrated facilities*—When one facility produces something that other facilities need for their products, the employer is less able to take a strike because the disruption to production goes beyond that single facility. The UAW strike at the Lordstown plant, which completely shut down production at Saturn, is a good example. The just-in-time production system, which provides very little stockpiling of parts, further weakens management's ability to take a strike.

7. *Lack of substitutes for the product*—A strike is more costly to the employer if customers have a readily available alternative source from which to purchase the goods or services the company provides.

Bargaining outcomes also depend on the nature of the bargaining process and relationship, which includes the types of tactics used and the history of labor relations. The vast majority of labor–management negotiations do not result in a strike, because a strike is typically not in the best interests of either party. Furthermore, both the union and management usually realize that if they wish to interact effectively in the future, the experience of a strike can be difficult to overcome. When strikes do occur, the conduct of each party during the strike can also have a lasting effect on labor–management relations. Violence by either side or threatening employees with job loss by hiring replacements can make future relations difficult.

Impasse-Resolution Procedures: Alternatives to Strikes

Given the substantial costs of strikes to both parties, procedures that resolve conflicts without strikes have arisen in both the private and public sectors. Because many public-sector employees do not have the right to strike, alternatives are particularly important in that arena.

Three often-used impasse-resolution procedures are mediation, fact finding, and arbitration. All of them rely on the intervention of a neutral third party, most typically provided by the Federal Mediation and Conciliation Service (FMCS), which must be notified 30 days prior to a planned change in contract terms (including a strike). **Mediation** is the least formal but most widely used of the procedures (in both the public and private sectors). One survey found it was used by nearly 40 percent of all large private-sector bargaining units.[44] A mediator has no formal authority but, rather, acts as a facilitator and go-between in negotiations.

A **fact finder**, most commonly used in the public sector, typically reports on the reasons for the dispute, the views and arguments of both sides, and (in some cases) a recommended settlement, which the parties are free to decline. That these recommendations are made public may give rise to public pressure for a settlement. Even if a fact finder's settlement is not accepted, the hope is that he or she will identify or frame issues in such a way as to facilitate an agreement. Sometimes, for the simple reason that fact-finding takes time, the parties reach a settlement during the interim.

The most formal form of outside intervention is **arbitration**, under which a solution is actually chosen by an arbitrator (or arbitration board). In some instances, the arbitrator can fashion his or her own solution (*conventional* arbitration). In other cases, the arbitrator must choose either the management's or union's final offer (*final offer* arbitration) on either the contract as a whole or on an issue-by-issue basis. Traditionally, arbitrating the enforcement or interpretation of contract terms (rights arbitration) has been widely accepted, whereas arbitrating the actual writing or setting of contract terms (interest arbitration, our focus here) has been reserved for special circumstances. These include some public-sector negotiations, where strikes may be especially costly (e.g., police, firefighters) and a very few private-sector situations, where strikes have been especially debilitating to both sides (e.g., the steel industry in the 1970s).[45] One reason for avoiding greater use of interest arbitration is a strong belief that the parties closest to the situation (unions and management, not an arbitrator) are in the best position to effectively resolve their conflicts.

UNION AND MANAGEMENT INTERACTIONS: CONTRACT ADMINISTRATION

Grievance Procedure

Although the negotiation process (and the occasional resulting strike) receive the most publicity, the negotiation process typically occurs only about every three years, whereas contract administration goes on day after day, year after year. The two processes—negotiation and administration—are linked, of course. Vague or incomplete contract language developed in the negotiation process can make administration of the contract difficult. Such difficulties can, in turn, create conflict that can spill over into the next negotiation process.[46] Furthermore, events during the negotiation process—strikes, the use of replacement workers, or violence by either side—can lead to management and labor difficulties in working successfully under a contract.

A key influence on successful contract administration is the grievance procedure for resolving labor–management disputes over the interpretation and execution of the contract. During World War II, the War Labor Board helped institutionalize the use of arbitration as an alternative to strikes to settle disputes that arose during the term of the contract. The soon-to-follow Taft-Hartley Act further reinforced this preference. Today, the great majority of grievance procedures have binding arbitration as a final step, and only a minority of strikes occur during the term of a contract (most occur during the negotiation stage). Strikes during the term of a contract can be especially disruptive because they are more unpredictable than strikes during the negotiation phase, which occur only at regular intervals.

Beyond its ability to reduce strikes, a grievance procedure can be judged using three criteria.[47] First, how well are day-to-day contract questions resolved? Time delays and heavy use of the procedure may indicate problems. Second, how well does the grievance procedure adapt to changing circumstances? For example, if the company's business turns downward and the company needs to cut costs, how clear are the provisions relating to subcontracting of work, layoffs, and so forth? Third, in multiunit contracts, how well does the grievance procedure permit local contract issues (e.g., work rules) to be included and resolved?

From the employees' perspective, the grievance procedure is the key to fair treatment in the workplace, and its effectiveness rests both on the degree to which employees feel they can use it without fear of recrimination and whether they believe their case will be carried forward strongly enough by their union representative. The **duty of fair representation** is mandated by the NLRA and requires that all bargaining-unit members, whether union members or not, have equal access to and representation by the union in the grievance procedure. Too many grievances may indicate a problem, but so may too few. A very low grievance rate may suggest a fear of filing a grievance, a belief that the system is not effective, or a belief that representation is not adequate.

As Table 18.9 suggests, most grievance procedures have several steps prior to arbitration. Moreover, the majority of grievances are settled during the earlier steps of the process, which is desirable both to reduce time delays and avoid the costs of arbitration. If the grievance does reach arbitration, the arbitrator makes the final ruling in the matter. A series of Supreme Court decisions in 1960, commonly known as the Steelworkers Trilogy, established that the courts should essentially refrain from reviewing the merits of arbitrators' decisions and, instead, limit judicial review to the question of whether the issue was subject to arbitration under the contract.[48] Furthermore, unless the contract explicitly states that an issue is not subject to arbitration, it will be assumed that arbitration is an appropriate means of deciding the issue. Giving further strength to the role of arbitration is the NLRB's general policy of deferring to arbitration.

What types of issues most commonly reach arbitration? Data from the FMCS on a total of 5,934 grievances in 1988 show that discharge and disciplinary issues topped the list with 2,654 cases.[49] Other frequent issues: the use of seniority in promotion, layoffs, and transfers (500 cases), work assignments and scheduling (423 cases), distribution of overtime or use of compulsory overtime (156 cases), and subcontracting (137 cases).

TABLE 18.9   Steps in a Typical Grievance Procedure

Employee-initiated Grievance

Step 1

a. Employee discusses grievance or problem orally with supervisor.

b. Union steward and employee may discuss problem orally with supervisor.

c. Union steward and employee decide (1) whether problem has been resolved or (2) if not resolved, whether a contract violation has occurred.

Step 2

a. Grievance is put in writing and submitted to production superintendent or other designated line manager.

b. Steward and management representative meet and discuss grievance. Management's response is put in writing. A member of the industrial relations staff may be consulted at this stage.

Step 3

a. Grievance is appealed to top line management and industrial relations staff representatives. Additional local or international union officers may become involved in discussions. Decision is put in writing.

Step 4

a. Union decides on whether to appeal unresolved grievance to arbitration according to procedures specified in its constitution and/or bylaws.

b. Grievance is appealed to arbitration for binding decision.

Discharge Grievance

a. Procedure may begin at step 2 or step 3.

b. Time limits between steps may be shorter to expedite the process.

Union or Group Grievance

a. Union representative initiates grievance at step 1 or step 2 on behalf of affected class of workers or union representatives.

SOURCE: T. A. Kochan, *Collective Bargaining and Industrial Relations* (Homewood, Ill.: Richard D. Irwin, 1980), 395.

What criteria do arbitrators use to reach a decision? In the most common case—discharge or discipline—the following due process questions are important:[50]

1. *Did the employee know what the rule or expectation was and what the consequences of not adhering to it were?*

2. *Was the rule applied in a consistent and predictable way?* In other words, are all employees treated the same?

3. *Are facts collected in a fair and systematic manner?* An important element of this principle is detailed record keeping. Both employee actions (e.g.,

tardiness) and management's response (verbal or written warnings) should be carefully documented.

4. *Does the employee have the right to question the facts and present a defense?* An example in a union setting is a hearing with a shop steward present.

5. *Does the employee have the right to appeal a decision?* An example is recourse to an impartial third party, such as an arbitrator.

6. *Is there progressive discipline?* Except perhaps for severe cases, an arbitrator will typically look for evidence that an employee was alerted as early as possible that his or her behavior was inappropriate and the employee was given a chance to change prior to some form of severe discipline, such as discharge.

7. *Are there unique mitigating circumstances?* Although discipline must be consistent, individuals differ in terms of their prior service, performance, and discipline record. All of these factors may need to be considered.

New Labor–Management Strategies

Jack Barbash has described the nature of the traditional relationship between labor and management (during both the negotiation and administration phases) as follows:

> *Bargaining is a love-hate, cooperation-conflict relationship. The parties have a common interest in maximizing the total revenue which finances their respective returns. But they take on adversarial postures in debating how the revenue shall be divided as between wages and profits. It is the adversarial posture which has historically set the tone of the relationship.*[51]

Although there have always been exceptions to the adversarial approach, there are signs of a more general transformation to less adversarial workplace relations (at least where the union's role is accepted by management).[52] This transformation has two basic objectives: (1) to increase the involvement of individuals and work groups in overcoming adversarial relations and increasing employee commitment, motivation, and problem solving and (2) to reorganize work so that work rules are minimized and flexibility in managing people is maximized. These objectives are especially important for companies that need to be able to shift production quickly in response to changes in markets and customer demands (e.g., steel minimills). The specific programs aimed at achieving these objectives include employee involvement in decision making, self-managing employee teams, labor–management problem-solving teams, broadly defined jobs, and sharing of business information with employees.[53]

Union resistance to such programs has often been substantial, precisely because the programs seek to change the nature of workplace relations and the role that unions play. Union leaders have often feared that such programs will weaken unions' role as an independent representative of employee interests. Indeed, according to the NLRA, to "dominate or interfere with the formation or administration of any labor organization or contribute financial or other support to it" is an unfair labor practice. An example of a prohibited practice is "taking an active part in organizing a union or committee to represent employees."[54]

One case that has received much attention is that of Electromation, a small electrical parts manufacturer. In 1992 the NLRB ruled that the company had violated the NLRA by setting up worker–management committees (typically about six workers and one or two managers) to solve problems having to do with absenteeism and pay scales.[55] The original complaint was filed by the Teamsters union, which was trying to organize the (nonunion) company and felt that the committees were, in effect, illegally competing with them to be workers' representatives. Similarly, Polaroid recently dissolved an employee committee that had been in existence for over 40 years in response to the U.S. Labor Department's claim that it violated the NLRA. The primary functions of the employee committee had been to represent employees in grievances and to advise senior management on issues such as pay and company rules and regulations. In a third case, the NLRB ruled in 1993 that seven worker-management safety committees at DuPont Co. were illegal under the NLRB because they were dominated by management. The committee members were chosen by management and their decisions were subject to the approval of the management members of the committees. Finally, the committees made decisions about issues that were mandatory subjects of bargaining with the employees' elected representative—the chemical workers union.[56] The impact of such cases will be felt both in nonunion companies as union organizers move to fill the worker-representation vacuum, and in unionized companies as managements find they must deal more directly and effectively with their unions. (The Detroit Diesel Video Case at the end of Part II provides an example of the latter.)

Although there are legal concerns to address, some evidence suggests that these new approaches to labor relations can contribute significantly to an organization's effectiveness. One study, for example, compared the features of traditional and transformational approaches to labor relations at Xerox.[57] As Table 18.10 indicates, the transformational approach was characterized by better conflict resolution, more shop-floor cooperation, and greater worker autonomy and feedback in decision making. Furthermore, compared with the traditional approach, transformational labor relations were found to be associated with lower costs, better product quality, and higher productivity (see the "Competing through Social Responsibility" box).

LABOR RELATIONS OUTCOMES

The effectiveness of labor relations can be evaluated from management, labor, and societal perspectives. Management seeks to control costs and enhance productivity and quality. Labor unions seek to raise wages and benefits and exercise control over how employees spend their time at work

TABLE 18.10 Patterns in Labor–Management Relations Using Traditional and Transformational Approaches

	Pattern	
Dimension	Traditional	Transformational
Conflict resolution		
Frequency of conflicts	High	Low
Speed of conflict resolution	Slow	Fast
Informal resolution of grievances	Low	High
Third and fourth step grievances	High	Low
Shop-floor cooperation		
Formal problem-solving groups (e.g., quality, reducing scrap, employment security)	Low	High
Informal problem-solving activity	Low	High
Worker autonomy and feedback		
Formal autonomous work groups	Low	High
Informal worker autonomous activity	Low	High
Worker-initiated changes in work design	Low	High
Feedback on cost, quality, and schedule	Low	High

SOURCE: Adapted from J. Cutcher-Gershenfeld, "The Impact of Economic Performance of a Transformation in Workplace Relations," *Industrial and Labor Relations Review* 44 (1991): 241–260.

(e.g., through work rules). Each of the three parties typically seeks to avoid forms of conflict (e.g., strikes) that impose significant costs on everyone. In this section, we examine several outcomes.

Strikes

Table 18.11 presents data on strikes in the United States that involved 1,000 employees or more. Because strikes are more likely in large units, the lack of data on smaller units is probably not a major concern, although such data would, of course, raise the figure on the estimated time lost to strikes.* Although strikes impose significant costs on union members, employers, and society, it is clear from Table 18.11 that strikes are the exception rather than the rule. Very little working time is lost to strikes in the United States, and their frequency today is quite low by historical standards. Does this mean that

---

*For example, in the 1960s, this estimate is 12 percent using data on strikes involving 1,000 or more employees versus 17 percent for all strikes.

Social Responsibility

A NEW MODEL OF UNION–MANAGEMENT COOPERATION AT MAGMA COPPER

When J. Burgess Winter left his previous company to assume the position of president and chief executive officer at Magma Copper Company in 1988, he realized immediately where he would have to focus his efforts—labor relations, which "were, in a word, abysmal." There was a long history of animosity in labor relations. For example, even as Winter was taking on his new role, both sides were preparing for a strike. "The company brought in sleeping trailers and soup kitchens and prepared to hire replacement workers." At the same time, violence began to erupt—bombs were found in the company's mine and shots were fired at Winter's home. Although a settlement was reached, Winter described the atmosphere as "horrible, just dreadful…we couldn't conduct our daily business properly."

The first step toward change was when Winter informed Marsh Campbell, vice-president of human resources, that he wanted to end the adversarial relationship and build on the workers' expertise to help turn the company around. Campbell noted that this was "music to my ears. I'd always wanted to take this kind of [cooperative] approach ever since the days I studied labor relations in college." Campbell discussed the idea with Bob Guadiana, the district director of the United Steelworkers of America, the company's largest union. Guadiana agreed that they should pursue the idea.

The first step was two days of off-site meetings between 17 senior union and management officials and a third-party facilitator. Although things began slowly, eventually both sides vented their frustrations and "the ice began to melt" as the two sides focused on their mutual interests. The group drafted a document that spelled out what the new union–management relationship should be like, and the group designated itself the Joint Union–Management Cooperation Committee (JUMCC). The JUMCC would oversee implementation of the changes, which included (1) two-day team-building workshops for all employees in mixed

union–management groups—Winter opened and closed each workshop himself; (2) leadership training for the company's 300 supervisors to teach them how to be a different type of supervisor—a facilitator, coach, and resource person; (3) assignment of worker–management teams responsible for major productivity challenges. Perhaps the most dramatic payoff was a breakthrough by a union–management team that showed the company a way to operate a mine at a profit rather than closing it. Productivity in the mine eventually rose to 60 to 70 percent higher than the previous best, and the new approach, which included new methods and more flexible work rules, was implemented at other mines.

Most recently, Magma signed a new contract with its ten unions that is innovative in several ways: (1) the contract length is 15 years versus the usual 3 years, reducing uncertainty about labor relations on both sides; (2) it guarantees no work stoppages for 8 years; (3) it uses joint union–management teams to resolve contact disputes; if they cannot agree, the issue goes to an arbitration panel whose decisions are binding; (4) the contract was signed eight months early by using a new bargaining process. Instead of the union and management separately developing proposals and then haggling over them, contract proposals were developed jointly by five union–management teams.

Since 1988, Magma Copper's productivity has increased 43 percent and its operating costs have decreased from 78 cents per pound of copper to 68 cents (while the price of copper hovers around $1 per pound). Winter predicts that operating costs will drop to 58 cents per pound within three years, placing Magma with the very best in the industry, despite what he describes as their lower-grade ore. "None of this would have been possible, Mr. Winter emphasizes, without the farsightedness of the unions and the involvement of employees." Just as important, according to union leaders, was the impetus for change in labor relations that came from the chief executive officer of the company.

SOURCE: Reprinted with permission from *Industry Week,* March 16, 1992. Copyright Penton Publishing, Inc., Cleveland, Ohio.

TABLE 18.11   Work Stoppages Involving 1,000 Workers or More

Year	Stoppages	Percentage of Total Working Time
1950	424	0.26%
1955	363	0.16
1960	222	0.09
1965	268	0.10
1970	381	0.29
1975	235	0.09
1980	187	0.09
1985	54	0.03
1990	44	0.02
1991	40	0.02

SOURCE: Reprinted with permission from *Daily Labor Report*, no. 23, pp. B1–B3 (Feb. 5, 1992). Copyright 1992 by the Bureau of National Affairs, Inc. (800–372–1033).

the industrial relations system is working well? Not necessarily. Some would view the low number of strikes as another sign of labor's weakness.

Wages and Benefits

In 1989, private-sector unionized workers received, on average, wages that were 21 percent higher than their nonunion counterparts; benefits were 78 percent higher. Total compensation was 35 percent higher for union-covered employees.[58] Note, however, that these are raw differences. To assess the net effect of unions on wages more accurately, adjustments must be made. We now briefly highlight a few of these.

The union–nonunion wage gap is likely to be overestimated to the extent that unions can more easily organize workers who are already highly paid or who are more productive. The gap is likely to be underestimated to the extent that nonunion employers raise wages and benefits in response to the perceived "union threat" in the hope that their employees will then have less interest in union representation. When these and other factors are taken into account, the net union advantage in wages, though still substantial, is reduced to about 10 percent. The union benefits advantage is also reduced, but it remains larger than the union wage effect, and the union effect on total compensation is therefore larger than the wage effect alone.[59]

Beyond differences in pay and benefits, unions typically influence the way pay (and promotions) are determined. Whereas management often seeks to deal with employees as individuals, emphasizing performance differences in pay and promotion decisions, unions seek to build group solidarity and avoid the possibly arbitrary treatment of employees. To do so, unions focus on equal pay for equal work: Any differences between employees in pay or promotions, they say, should be based on seniority (an objective measure) rather than on performance (a subjective measure susceptible to favoritism). It is very common in union settings for there to be a single rate of pay for all employees in a particular job classification.

Productivity

There has been much debate regarding the effects of unions on productivity.[60] Unions are believed to decrease productivity in at least three ways: (1) the union pay advantage causes employers to use less labor and more capital per worker than they would otherwise, which reduces efficiency across society; (2) union contract provisions may limit permissible work loads, restrict the tasks that particular workers are allowed to perform, and require employers to use more employees for certain jobs than they otherwise would; and (3) strikes, slowdowns, and working-to-rule (i.e., slowing down production by following every workplace rule to an extreme) result in lost production.[61] The "Competing through Globalization" box describes how Ford and the UAW learned from Japan how to overcome these barriers to productivity.

On the other hand, unions can have positive effects on productivity. Employees, whether members of a union or not, communicate to management regarding how good a job it is doing by either the "exit" or "voice" mechanisms. "Exit" refers to simply leaving the company to work for a better employer. "Voice" refers to communicating one's concerns to management without necessarily leaving the employer. Unions are believed to increase the operation and effectiveness of the voice mechanism.[62] This, in turn, is likely to reduce employee turnover and its associated costs. A second way that unions can increase productivity is (perhaps ironically) through their emphasis on the use of seniority in pay, promotion, and layoff decisions. Although management typically prefers to rely more heavily on performance in such decisions, using seniority has a potentially important advantage—namely, it reduces competition among workers. As a result, workers may be less reluctant to share their knowledge with less-senior workers because they do not have to worry about less-senior workers taking their jobs. Finally, the introduction of a union may have a "shock effect" on management, pressuring it into tightening standards and accountability and paying greater heed to employee input in the design and management of production.[63]

Although there is evidence that unions have both positive and negative effects on productivity, most studies have found that union workers are more productive than nonunion workers. Nevertheless, it is generally recognized that most of the findings on this issue are open to a number of alternative explanations, making any clear conclusions difficult. For example, if unions raise productivity, why has union representation of employees declined over time, even within industries?[64] A related concern is that unionized establishments are more likely to survive where there is some

Globalization

COMPETING THROUGH

LABOR–MANAGEMENT COOPERATION AT FORD MOTOR COMPANY

Foreign automobile producers, particularly the Japanese, have made significant inroads into the U.S. market, cutting into what was formerly the domain of General Motors, Ford, Chrysler (and earlier, American Motors). From 1978 to 1982, Ford's annual motor vehicle sales dropped 47 percent. A major reason was the Japanese advantage in productivity and quality. Of late, American producers, particularly Ford and Chrysler, have managed to narrow the productivity and quality gaps. Ford needs one-half as many workers per vehicle today as it did in the late 1970s. This increase in productivity seems to be paying off, as Ford's market share in the United States has gone from 21 percent in January 1992 to 23.5 percent in January 1993. At the same time, the Japanese market share during the same period dropped from 30 percent to 27 percent.

A major factor in Ford's increased productivity has been the development of a better relationship with its workers, represented by the United Auto Workers (UAW). Management made a greater effort to increase employee involvement. Former Ford chairman Phillip Caldwell made numerous visits to plants in the early 1980s to ask the rank and file for ideas on how to improve. Caldwell noted that "it's stupid to deny yourself the intellectual capability and constructive attitude of tens of thousands of workers."

The Walton Hills plant outside of Cleveland, Ohio, is an example of how change came about in one plant. UAW Local 420 used to prided itself on its tough approach to management, going out on strike once, for example, because there were no doors on the restrooms. Its labor contract contained some of the most expensive work rules in the company. The "walking millwright rule" required that a millwright accompany forklift drivers whenever machinery was moved. Another rule permitted workers to finish their work day and leave after three to four hours if they produced their quota of parts. It was Ford's least productive plant.

In 1980, the UAW was informed that the plant would be closed. Local UAW president Joseph D'Amico said that he "opened [his] eyes and saw what reality was." The UAW asked for a chance to save the plant and subsequently negotiated an elimination of work rules that was projected to save Ford $15 million annually. Not everyone was enthusiastic about the idea. Some UAW members set fire to copies of the proposed agreement. But it eventually passed with 88 percent support among the membership. Subsequently, Ford sponsored a trip of Ford executives and UAW officials to visit automobile plants in Japan. D'Amico says that his observations in Japan persuaded him that "the Japanese didn't work harder; they simply did a better job working together. I learned the best way to accomplish anything is to talk."

inherent productivity advantage unrelated to unionism that actually offsets a negative impact of unionism. If so, these establishments would be overrepresented, whereas establishments that did not survive the negative impact of unions would be underrepresented. Consequently, any negative impact of unions on productivity would be underestimated.

Profits and Stock Performance

Even if unions do raise productivity, a company's profits and stock performance may still suffer if unions raise costs (e.g., wages) or decrease investment by a greater amount. Recent studies found that unions have a "large" negative effect on profits. Similarly, one recent study finds that each dollar of unexpected increase in collectively bargained labor costs results in a dollar reduction in shareholder wealth. Other research suggests that investment in research and development is lower in unionized firms.[65] These research findings describe the average effects of unions. The consequences of more innovative union–management relationships for profits and stock performance are less clear.

THE INTERNATIONAL CONTEXT

As Table 18.12 indicates, the United States has more union members than any Western European country or Japan. On the other hand, aside from France, the United States has the lowest unionization rate (union density). Why? One explanation is that the United States does not have a history of feudalism, as Western Europe does. Nor does it have the deep class-based divisions in society that resulted from feudalism. Labor and social democratic political parties are commonplace in Western Europe, and they are major players in the political process. Furthermore, the labor movement in Western Europe is broader than that in the United States. It extends not just to the workplace but—through its own or closely related political parties—directly into the national political process.

An examination of trends in union membership around the world suggests that the situation in the United States is somewhat unique. To be sure, the United States is not the only country to experience a decline in the unionization rate. To some extent, then, a common set of factors probably contributes to the decline (e.g., structural changes in the world economy). On the other hand, there are some substantial differences. "Factionalism and mutual animosities" between unions in France and major legislative changes in the United Kingdom during the 1980s are two examples. In the United States, deregulation of the trucking and airline industries contributed to an intensification of competition. Combined with the fact that the union wage premium in the United States is substantially larger than in other advanced industrialized countries, it is not surprising that management opposition would be higher in the United States than elsewhere.[66] This, in turn, may help explain why the decline in union density has been especially steep in the United States.

It seems likely that, with the growing globalization of markets, labor costs and productivity will continue to be key challenges. The European Community's movement toward a common market and the ongoing North American Free Trade Agreement discussions among the United States, Canada, and Mexico both suggest that goods, services, and production will

TABLE 18.12   Union Membership, Density Ratios, and Changes in
Density Ratios in Eight Countries

Country	Union Membership, 1989 (thousands)	Density Ratio 1989 (percent)	Percentage Point Change in Density Ratio, 1980–1989	Percentage Change in Density Ratio, 1980–1989
United States	16,960	16%	–6	–27
Canada	2,536	33	0[b]	0[b]
Japan	12,227	26	–5	–16
France	1,970	11	–8	–42
Germany	8,082	33	–3	–8
Italy	6,930	47	–6	–11
Sweden	3,415	84	+4	+5
United Kingdom	9,214	41[a]	–10	–20

SOURCE: C. Chang and C. Sorrentino, "Union Membership in 12 Countries," *Monthly Labor Review* 114, no. 12 (1991): 46–53.

Note: Density ratio = Union membership as a percentage of total civilian employment.

[a] Based on 1988 data.

[b] Estimate—Canadian data not directly comparable.

continue to move more freely across international borders. Whereas vast differences in wages, benefits, and other costs of doing business (e.g., regulation) exist, there will be a tendency to move to areas that are less costly, unless skills are unavailable or productivity is significantly lower there. For example, Morton Bahr, president of the Communication Workers of America, claims that AT&T has already begun to close U.S. manufacturing plants where workers earn $9 per hour and is moving jobs to Mexico, where workers earn 90 cents per hour. Without tariffs on goods and services flowing from Mexico to the United States, such moves may be more attractive to employers. Unless labor unions can increase their productivity sufficiently or organize new production facilities, membership is likely to continue to decline.

In addition to membership, the United States differs from Western Europe in the degree of formal worker participation in decision making. Works' councils (joint labor–management decision-making institutions at the enterprise level) and worker representation on supervisory boards of directors (codetermination) are mandated by law in countries such as Germany. The Scandinavian countries, Austria, and Luxembourg have similar legislation. German works' councils make decisions about changes in work or the work environment, discipline, pay systems, safety, and other human resource issues. The works' councils exist, in part, because collective bargaining agreements in countries such as Germany tend to be oriented much more toward industrywide or regional issues, with less emphasis on local issues. The degree of codetermination on supervisory boards depends on the size and industry of the company. For example, in German organizations having more than 2,000 employees, one-half of board members must be worker representatives. (However, the chairman of the board, a management representative, can cast a tie-breaking vote.) In contrast, worker representation on boards of directors in the United States is still rare.[67]

THE PUBLIC SECTOR

Unlike the private sector, union membership in the public sector grew in the 1960s and 1970s and remained fairly stable through the 1980s. As of 1988, 36.5 percent of government employees were union members, and 43.4 percent of all government employees were covered by a collective-bargaining contract.[68] Like the NLRA in the private sector, changes in the legal framework contributed significantly to union growth in the public sector. One early step was the enactment in Wisconsin of collective-bargaining legislation in 1959 for its state employees.[69] Executive Order 10988 provided collective-bargaining rights for federal employees in 1962. By the end of the 1960s, most states had passed similar laws. The Civil Service Reform Act of 1978, Title VII, later established the Federal Labor Relations Authority (modeled after the NLRB). Many states have similar administrative agencies to administer their own laws.

An interesting aspect of public-sector union growth is that much of it has occurred in the service industry and among white-collar employees—groups that have traditionally been viewed as difficult to organize. The American Federation of State, County, and Municipal Employees (AFSCME), with over 1 million members by the mid-1980s, had about 400,000 members in health care, 100,000 clerical, and 110,000 professional and technical employees.[70]

In contrast to the private sector, strikes are illegal at the federal level of the public sector and in most states. At the local level, all states prohibit strikes by police (Hawaii is a partial exception) and firefighters (Idaho is the exception). Teachers and state employees are somewhat more likely to have the right to strike, depending on the state. Legal or not, strikes nonetheless do occur in the public sector. In 1991, of the 40 strikes involving 1,000 or more workers, 7 were in the public sector. Of these, one involved state workers and six (five in education) involved local government workers. An examination of strikes in smaller work units also suggests that the majority of work stoppages are at local levels, usually involving teachers or other school employees.[71]

SUMMARY

Labor unions seek to represent the interests of their members in the workplace. Although this may further the cause of industrial democracy, management often finds that unions increase labor costs while setting limits on the company's flexibility and discretion in decision making. As a result, the company may witness a diminished ability to compete effectively in a global economy. Not surprisingly, management in nonunion companies often feels compelled to actively resist the unionization of its employees. This, together with a host of economic, legal, and other factors, has contributed to union losses in membership and bargaining power. There are some indications, however, that managements and unions are seeking new, more effective ways of working together to enhance competitiveness while giving employees a voice in how workplace decisions are made.

Discussion Questions

1. Why do employees join unions?

2. What has been the trend in union membership in the United States, and what are the underlying reasons for the trend?

3. What are the consequences for management and owners of having a union represent employees?

4. What are the general provisions of the National Labor Relations Act, and how does it affect labor–management interactions?

5. What are the features of traditional and nontraditional labor relations? What are the potential advantages of the "new" nontraditional approaches to labor relations?

6. How does the U.S. industrial and labor relations system compare with systems in other countries such as those in Western Europe?

Notes

1. J. T. Dunlop, *Industrial Relations Systems* (New York: Holt, 1958).

2. C. Kerr, "Industrial Conflict and Its Mediation," *American Journal of Sociology* 60 (1954): 230–245.

3. In 1946, roughly 1.5 percent of working time was lost to strikes. This compares to 0.3 percent of working time lost in the following period, 1950–1979. See A. M. Glassman and T. G. Cummings, *Industrial Relations: A Multidimensional View* (Glenview, Ill.: Scott, Foresman, 1985), 64; W. H. Holley, Jr. and K. M. Jennings, *The Labor Relations Process* (Chicago: Dryden Press, 1984), 207.

4. T. A. Kochan, *Collective Bargaining and Industrial Relations* (Homewood, Ill.: Richard D. Irwin, 1980), 25; H. C. Katz and T. A. Kochan, *An Introduction to Collective Bargaining and Industrial Relations* (New York: McGraw-Hill, 1992), 10.

5. Katz and Kochan, *An Introduction to Collective Bargaining*.

6. S. Webb and B. Webb, *Industrial Democracy* (London: Longmans, Green, 1987); J. R. Commons, *Institutional Economics* (New York: Macmillan, 1934).

7. C. Kerr, J. T. Dunlop, F. Harbison and C. Myers, "Industrialism and World Society," *Harvard Business Review*, February 1961, 113–126.

8. T. A. Kochan and K. R. Wever, "American Unions and the Future of Worker Representation," in *The State of the Unions*, ed. G. Strauss et al. (Madison, Wis.: Industrial Relations Research Association, 1991).

9. Katz and Kochan, *An Introduction to Collective Bargaining*.

10. J. Barbash, *The Elements of Industrial Relations* (Madison, Wis.: University of Wisconsin Press, 1984).

11. Bureau of National Affairs, "Proportion of Union Members Declines to Low of 15.8 Percent," *Daily Labor Report*, February 9, 1993, B3-B7.

12. B. T. Hirsch, *Labor Unions and the Economic Performance of Firms* (Kalamazoo, Mich.: W. E. Upjohn Institute, 1991); R. B. Freeman, "Contraction and Expansion: The Divergence of Private Sector and Public Sector Unionism in the United States," *Journal of Economic Perspectives* 2 (1988): 63–88; G. N. Chaison and D. G. Dhavale, "A Note on the Severity of the Decline in Union Organizing Activity," *Industrial and Labor Relations Review* 43 (1990): 366–373.

13. Katz and Kochan, *An Introduction to Collective Bargaining*. They, in turn, build on work by J. Fiorito and C. L. Maranto, "The Contemporary Decline of Union Strength," *Contemporary Policy Issues*, 3 (1987): 12–27.

14. G. N. Chaison and J. Rose, "The Macrodeterminants of Union Growth and Decline," in *The State of the Unions*, ed. G. Strauss et al. (Madison, Wis.: Industrial Relations Research Association, 1991).

15. T. A. Kochan, R. B. McKersie and J. Chalykoff, "The Effects of Corporate Strategy and Workplace Innovations in Union Representation," *Industrial and Labor Relations Review* 39 (1986): 487–501; Chaison and Rose," The Macrodeterminants of Union Growth;" J. Barbash, *Practice of Unionism* (New York: Harper, 1956), 210; W. N. Cooke and D. G. Meyer, "Structural and Market Predictors of Corporate Labor Relations Strategies," *Industrial and Labor Relations Review* 43 (1990): 280–293; T. A. Kochan and P. Capelli, "The Transformation of the Industrial Relations and Personnel Function," in *Internal Labor Markets*, ed. P. Osterman (Cambridge, Mass.: MIT Press, 1984).

16. Kochan and Capelli, "The Transformation of the Industrial Relations and Personnel Function."

17. S. B. Jarrell and T. D. Stanley, "A Meta-Analysis of the Union–Nonunion Wage Gap," *Industrial and Labor Relations Review* 44 (1990): 54–67; P. D. Lineneman, M. L. Wachter and W. H. Carter, "Evaluating the Evidence on Union Employment and Wages," *Industrial and Labor Relations Review* 44 (1990): 34–53.

18. National Labor Relations Board, *A Guide to Basic Law and Procedures under the National Labor Relations Act* (Washington, D.C.: U.S. Government Printing Office, 1991).

19. R. B. Freeman and M. M. Kleiner, "Employer Behavior in the Face of Union Organizing Drives," *Industrial and Labor Relations Review* 43 (1990): 351–365.

20. F. K. Foulkes, "Large Nonunionized Employers," in *U.S. Industrial Relations 1950–1980: A Critical Assessment*," ed. J. Steiber et al. (Madison, Wis.: Industrial Relations Research Association, 1981).

21. Katz and Kochan, *An Introduction to Collective Bargaining*.

22. E. E. Herman, J. L. Schwarz and A. Kuhn, *Collective Bargaining and Labor Relations* (Englewood Cliffs, N.J.: Prentice-Hall, 1992), 32. Note that the percentage of employed workers increased less quickly because employment grew 18 percent during the same period.

23. Ibid., 33.

24. Kochan, *Collective Bargaining and Industrial Relations*, 61.

25. National Labor Relations Board. *A Guide to Basic Law and Procedures under the National Labor Relations Act* (Washington, D.C.: U.S. Government Printing Office, 1991).

26. Ibid.

27. Ibid.

28. H. N. Wheeler and J. A. McClendon, "The Individual Decision to Unionize," in *The State of the Unions*, ed. G. Strauss et al. (Madison, Wis.: Industrial Relations Research Association, 1991).

29. NLRB annual reports.

30. J. A. Fossum, *Labor Relations*, 5th ed. (Homewood, Ill.: Richard D. Irwin, 1992), 149.

31. National Labor Relations Board, *A Guide to Basic Law*, 17.

32. Ibid.

33. Herman et al., *Collective Bargaining*; P. Jarley and J. Fiorito, "Associate Membership: Unionism or Consumerism?" *Industrial and Labor Relations Review* 43 (1990): 209–224.

34. Katz and Kochan, *An Introduction to Collective Bargaining*; R. L. Rose, "Unions Hit Corporate Campaign Trail," *The Wall Street Journal*, March 8, 1993, B1.

35. P. Jarley and C. L. Maranto, "Union Corporate Campaigns: An Assessment," *Industrial and Labor Relations Review*, 44 (1990): 505–524.

36. Katz and Kochan, *An Introduction to Collective Bargaining*.

37. Chaison and Rose, "The Macrodeterminants of Union Growth."

38. R. E. Walton and R. B. McKersie, *A Behavioral Theory of Negotiations* (New York: McGraw-Hill, 1965).

39. Fossum, *Labor Relations*, 262; see also C. S. Loughran, *Negotiating a Labor Contract: A Management Handbook*, 2nd ed. (Washington, D.C.: Bureau of National Affairs, 1990).

40. C. M. Steven, *Strategy and Collective Bargaining Negotiations* (New York: McGraw-Hill, 1963); Katz and Kochan, *An Introduction to Collective Bargaining*.

41. Kochan, *Collective Bargaining and Industrial Relations*.

42. Fossum, *Labor Relations*, 183–184.

43. A. Bernstein, "You Can't Bargain with a Striker Whose Job is No More," *Business Week*, August 5, 1991, 27.

44. Kochan, *Collective Bargaining and Industrial Relations*, 272.

45. Herman et al., *Collective Bargaining*.

46. Katz and Kochan, *An Introduction to Collective Bargaining*.

47. Kochan, *Collective Bargaining and Industrial Relations*, 386.

48. United Steelworkers v. American Manufacturing Co., 363 U.S. 564 (1960); United Steelworkers v. Warrior Gulf and Navigation Co., 363 U.S. 574 (1960); United Steelworkers v. Enterprise Wheel and Car Corp., 363 U.S. 593 (1960).

49. Original data from: U.S. Federal Mediation and Conciliation Service, Forty-first Annual Report, Fiscal Year 1988 (Washington, D.C.: U.S. Government Printing Office, 1988). Summarized in Fossum, *Labor Relations*, 465–466.

50. J. R. Redecker, *Employee Discipline: Policies and Practices* (Washington, D.C.: Bureau of National Affairs, 1989).

51. Barbash, *The Elements of Industrial Relations*, 6.

52. T. A. Kochan, H. C. Katz and R. B. McKersie, *The Transformation of American Industrial Relations* (New York: Basic Books, 1986), Chapter 6.

53. J. B. Arthur, "The Link between Business Strategy and Industrial Relations Systems in American Steel Minimills," *Industrial and Labor Relations Review* 45 (1992): 588–506; M. Schuster, "Union–Management Cooperation," in *Employee and Labor Relations*, ed. J. A. Fossum (Washington, D.C.: Bureau of National Affairs, 1990).

54. National Labor Relations Board, *A Guide to Basic Law*.

55. A. Bernstein, "Putting a Damper on that Old Team Spirit," *Business Week*, May 4, 1992, 60.

56. Bureau of National Affairs, "Polaroid Dissolves Employee Committee in Response to Labor Department Ruling," *Daily Labor Report*, June 23, 1992, A-3. K. G. Salwen, "DuPont is Told It Must Disband Nonunion Panels," *The Wall Street Journal*, June 7, 1993, A-2.

57. J. Cutcher-Gershenfeld, "The Impact of Economic Performance of a Transformation in Workplace Relations," *Industrial and Labor Relations Review* 44 (1991): 241–260.

58. Herman et al., *Collective Bargaining,* 274–275. In the union sector, total compensation was $18.25 ($12.11 in wages, $6.14 in benefits). In the nonunion sector, total compensation was $13.48 ($10.03 in wages, $3.45 in benefits).

59. Jarrell and Stanley, "A Meta-Analysis of the Union–Nonunion Wage Gap;" R. B. Freeman and J. Medoff, *What Do Unions Do?* (New York: Basic Books, 1984).

60. J. T. Addison and B. T. Hirsch, "Union Effects on Productivity, Profits, and Growth: Has the Long Run Arrived?" *Journal of Labor Economics* 7 (1989): 72–105.

61. R. B. Freeman and J. L. Medoff, "The Two Faces of Unionism," *Public Interest* 57 (Fall 1979): 69–93.

62. Ibid.

63. S. Slichter, J. Healy and E. R. Livernash, *The Impact of Collective Bargaining on Management* (Washington, D.C.: The Brookings Institution, 1960); Freeman and Medoff, "The Two Faces of Unionism."

64. Freeman and Medoff, "What Do Unions Do?;" Herman et al., *Collective Bargaining;* Addison and Hirsch, "Union Effects on Productivity;" Katz and Kochan, *An Introduction to Collective Bargaining;* Lineneman et al., "Evaluating the Evidence."

65. Addison and Hirsch, "Union Effects on Productivity." See also B. T. Hirsch, *Labor Unions and the Economic Performance of Firms* (Kalamazoo, Mich.: W. E. Upjohn Institute, 1991); J. M. Abowd, "The Effect of Wage Bargains on the Stock Market Value of the Firm," *American Economic Review* 79 (1989): 774–800; Hirsch, *Labor Unions.*

66. C. Chang and C. Sorrentino, "Union Membership in 12 Countries," *Monthly Labor Review* 114, no. 12 (1991): 46–53; D. G. Blanchflower and R. B. Freeman, "Going Different Ways: Unionism in the U.S. and Other Advanced O.E.C.D. Countries," (Symposium on the Future Role of Unions, Industry, and Government in Industrial Relations. University of Minnesota.) Cited in Chaison and Rose, "The Macrodeterminants of Union Growth," 23.

67. J. P. Begin and E. F. Beal, *The Practice of Collective Bargaining* (Homewood, Ill.: Richard D. Irwin, 1989); T. H. Hammer, S. C. Currall and R. N. Stern, "Worker Representation on Boards of Directors: A Study of Competing Roles," *Industrial and Labor Relations Review* 44 (1991): 661–680; Katz and Kochan, *An Introduction to Collective Bargaining;* Ibid; H. Gunter and G. Leminsky, "The Federal Republic of Germany," in *Labor in the Twentieth Century,* ed. J. T. Dunlop and W. Galenson (New York: Academic Press, 1978), 149–196.

68. Herman et al., *Collective Bargaining,* 348.

69. J. F. Burton and T. Thomason, "The Extent of Collective Bargaining in the Public Sector," in *Public Sector Bargaining,* ed. B. Aaron, J. M. Najita and J. L. Stern (Washington, D.C.: Bureau of National Affairs, 1988).

70. Herman et al., *Collective Bargaining,* 351.

71. Fossum, *Labor Relations,* 474, 479; Bureau of National Affairs, "Work Stoppages," *Daily Labor Report,* February 5, 1992, B1–B3.

UNITED AIRLINES GETS TOUGH ON UNIONS

In what was described by *The Wall Street Journal* as "playing hardball with labor unions in an attempt to lower costs," Stephen M. Wolf, chairman of United Airlines, announced that United would not take delivery of more than $2 billion worth of planes from Boeing Company that had been scheduled for 1994 and 1995. United also suggested that it may abandon unprofitable short-distance routes and use Southwest, a nonunion and low-cost airline, to feed passengers into its major routes. United could lease its planes to help Southwest do this. Presumably, subcontracting routes to Southwest and not taking delivery of new planes (for possible expansion) would result in eventual employment cutbacks at United.

Wolf has asked the three major unions—flight attendants, machinists, and pilots—for productivity increases that would come from changes in work rules (e.g., having flight attendants and pilots fly more hours) and from employees paying about 5 percent of the cost of their medical benefits. The flight attendants' and machinists' unions have refused to accept such changes, while the pilots' union is considering the proposal.

Wolf stated that management's proposal to the union—to accept work-rule and medical-payment changes—was "not brutalizing anybody... It's not a management decision; it's a marketplace decision." Wolf may have been referring to the fact that all the major airlines have had to retrench and lay off employees since the 1980s because the passenger-capacity and fare system built up then is too expensive at the current level of passenger traffic and airline competition. One exception is Southwest, a relatively new carrier that has successfully competed against the more established airlines and grown rapidly, even in difficult economic times, by maintaining low costs and "getting the most out of its workers."

QUESTIONS:

1. Would you agree that United is "playing hardball" with its labor unions? If so, do you agree with its strategy?
2. If you were Wolf, would you pursue the same labor relations strategy?
3. If you were a member of the attendants', machinists', or pilots' unions, how would you react to United's labor relations strategy?
4. Is the labor relations strategy being pursued by Wolf in the best interests of United? Of its customers? Of its employees? What are the alternatives?

SOURCE: A. Salpukas, "United Air Gets Tough on Unions," *New York Times*, March 19, 1993, C1–C2.

19

HUMAN RESOURCE INFORMATION SYSTEMS

Objectives

After reading this chapter, you should be able to:

1. Use computer technology to help a company gain a competitive advantage.
2. Describe the types of computer applications used to manage human resources.
3. Select and/or evaluate hardware and databases being used in human resource information systems.
4. Develop a security and privacy policy for databases, software, and computer systems.
5. Manage the process of developing or purchasing a human resource information system.
6. Discuss how human resource applications are useful for staffing, human resource planning, training and career development, and compensation and benefits.

Tellabs, Inc.

In 1986, Tellabs Inc., a developer of digital telecommunications equipment, decided to change from traditional manufacturing methods to a manufacturing system that used quality management techniques. The goal of the company's total quality management approach was a zero-defect rate in the company's products and at each step of the manufacturing process. The total quality approach required that the company develop the capability to quickly identify and fix problems.

Tellabs was making slow progress toward meeting quality goals. There were several reasons for this. One of the difficulties was that many jobs were not carried out properly because employees did not have the necessary skills. The mismatch between employees' skills and those required by the jobs occurred because managers could not easily access information about employees' skills. Another problem was that all 1,050 of Tellab's employees had not yet completed the company's quality training curriculum, and it was difficult for managers to identify which employees had the skills necessary to meet customers' quality standards.

The company was using traditional methods for managing human resource information. Payroll was administered by an outside vendor, and all employee data (absenteeism rates, performance ratings, skill inventory, etc.) were stored in individual employee files. Obtaining a summary of these data was impossible. If managers wanted to access skill inventories of employees (to determine appropriate jobs for them or to review their training needs), they had to review each employee's file.

SOURCE: M. Michaels, "Computer-Based Human Resource Planning and Management," in *Applying Psychology in Business*, ed. J. Jones, B. Steffy, and D. Bray (New York: Lexington Books, 1991), 446–451.

INTRODUCTION

Tellabs's difficulty in gaining access to the human resource information it needed to institute total quality management is not unique. Traditionally, human resource information has been stored in paper files. These files provide a snapshot of each employee's work, salary, performance, and educational history. To use this information for decision making, managers had to spend many hours reviewing files. Compiling, summarizing, and inventorying this information was a big problem.

As we noted in Chapter 1, technological advances in microcomputers have resulted in the development of software applications and electronic databases that make it easier for human resources to be efficiently and effectively managed. **Human resource information systems (HRISs)** include software programs and computers (mainframe and personal computers) that deal with the entry, maintenance, updating, and use of human resource information. HRISs include hardware, software, data, procedures, peripheral devices (such as printers), and customers or users.[1]

The purpose of HRISs is to provide users, or the customers of the system, with information. Customers include human resource professionals who work in the various functional areas (such as staffing or compensation), executives, and line managers. The uses of human resource information vary. Customers use HRISs to make strategic decisions (e.g., in human resource planning), to avoid litigation (e.g., identifying the underutilization of women and minorities), to evaluate policies or practices (e.g., tracking tuition reimbursement costs), or to support the daily operations of the company (e.g., making sure employees' hours are properly recorded).

In previous parts of this book, we discussed how companies should acquire, develop, and reward human resources to gain a competitive advantage. In this chapter, we show how companies use computer technology in acquiring, developing, and rewarding human resources. We begin the chapter with a discussion of the historical evolution of HRISs, types of computer applications, and the ways HRISs contribute to a company's competitive objectives. Next, we introduce the reader to databases and hardware used in HRISs, relevant security issues, and the steps necessary in developing an HRIS. The chapter concludes with a discussion of HRIS applications in staffing, human resource planning, performance management, training and career development, and compensation and benefits.

HISTORICAL EVOLUTION OF HRISs

The growth of HRISs has been strongly influenced by the growth of computer technology and by government regulations.[2] In the 1960s, a company's information about hiring, firing, promoting, transferring, and paying its employees resided in paper files. It was difficult to use this information for planning or decision making because one had to go through each file by hand and find the needed information. Applications related to human resource management were written primarily for expensive, large, **mainframe computers** that required the users to be experts in computer technology. Mainframe computers have large storage capacity and can quickly perform complex mathematical calculations. Today, however, the software related to human resources can be used on personal computers, and it does not require extensive computer experience to use it.

During the 1970s, mainframe computers became more widely available. They were used to assist with the calculation of cost data such as accounts receivable or inventory control. Because payroll costs were one of the most important costs that companies were concerned with, computers were first used to track and administer payroll.

The explosion of computer technology in the late 1970s and throughout the 1980s lowered the cost of mainframe systems, of personal computers with the same storage capabilities and data-manipulation speed as mainframes, and of software applications targeted specifically for human resource management. Thus, even smaller companies were able to afford human resource information systems.

Along with the increasing availability and lowered costs of computers came the realization that they could be put to wider use. New applications allowed companies to use the information not only for routine storage and retrieval but to track trends and forecast future needs.

A company gains several advantages by automating its human resource functions:

1. The company can store, retrieve, and process employee information electronically, eliminating manual record keeping and paperwork.

2. The system can consolidate, sort, analyze, compare, and report information immediately in a form that HR staff and managers can use for decision making.

3. Decision makers can track and monitor trends and other information needed for calculations, "what-if" analysis, and strategic, long-range forecasting.[3]

TYPES OF COMPUTER APPLICATIONS IN HUMAN RESOURCE MANAGEMENT

Among the hundreds of computer applications available today, three types have been used in human resource management: transaction processing, reporting, and tracking; decision support systems; and expert systems.[4]

Transaction Processing, Reporting, and Tracking

Transaction processing refers to computations and calculations used to review and document human resource decisions and practices. This includes documenting employee relocation, payroll expenses, and training course enrollments. This type of application helps companies comply with regulations such as federal laws or track adherence to company policies. For example, the Equal Employment Opportunity Act (1991) requires employers with 50 or more employees to provide the government (in the EEO-1 report) with information regarding employees' race and gender by job category.

Decision Support Systems

Decision support systems are designed to help managers solve problems. They usually include a "what-if" feature, which allows users to see how outcomes change when the assumptions or the data change. The systems are useful, for example, in helping companies determine the number of new hires they need based on different turnover rates or the availability of employees with technical skills given a change in customer or product demands.

Expert Systems

Expert systems have three elements:

- A knowledge base that contains facts, figures, and rules about a specific subject.

- A decision-making capability that, imitating an expert's reasoning ability, draws conclusions from those facts and figures to solve problems and answer questions.

- A user interface that gathers and gives information to the person using the system.

Expert systems are designed to simulate the decision-making process of human experts. The system recommends actions that the user can take based on the information the user provides. The recommended actions are those that a human expert would take in a situation with similar characteristics.

The use of expert systems in human resource management is relatively new. Some companies use them to help employees decide how to allocate monies for benefits or to help managers schedule and determine the labor requirements of projects.

Mrs. Fields Cookies uses expert systems in its interviewing process.[5] Job applicants answer a series of questions about the type of work they desire and their educational and work experiences. Depending on their answers, the computer generates additional questions. For example, if an applicant responds positively to the computer's question regarding a desire for temporary work, the computer asks the applicant how long he or she plans to stay if hired on a temporary basis. Standardizing the administration and wording of the interview questions ensures that job candidates are asked only legally allowed questions. The computer also probes for contradictions, such as overlapping dates of employment for previous jobs. The computer assigns points to particular answers, but it does not decide who will be hired. The manager gets a printed report of scores, answers to questions, and other information that might be useful (e.g., that a teenager who wants to work nights may be too young for night work).

Table 19.1 illustrates how each type of computer application can be used to help companies reach competitive objectives related to costs, quality, and innovation.

DATABASES AND HARDWARE FOR HRISs

What is a Database?

A **database** refers to the set of topics on which an HRIS collects and maintains information.[6] Databases contain several data files (topics), which are made up of employee information (records) containing data fields. A **data field** is an element or type of information such as employee name, social security number, or job classification.

The most popular database structure is known as a relational database.[7] In a **relational database**, information is stored in separate files, which look like tables. These files can be linked by common elements (fields) such as name, identification number, or location. This contrasts with the traditional file structure, in which all data associated with an employee was kept in only one file. In the relational database shown in Figure 19.1, employee personal information is located in one file and salary information in another, but both topics of information can be accessed via the employees' Social Security Number.

Users of relational databases have the ability to file and retrieve information according to any field or multiple fields across different tables or

TABLE 19.1   Relationship between Competitive Objectives and Computer Applications

HR Competitive Objectives	Types of Computer Applications		
	Transaction Processing/ Reporting/Tracking Systems	Decision Support Systems	Expert Systems
Cost Leadership: People Working Harder	• Reduces paper handling • Standardizes entry and reporting • Increases processing accuracy • Increases report turnaround • Early warning of goal deviations	• Increases chance of innovation for HR cost controls	• Decreases need for HR experts • Helps spread database and training costs over entire work force
Quality/ Customer Satisfaction: People Working Smarter	• Increases time for HR quality initiatives • Enables custom reports and data entry • Increases awareness of HR information and can lead to its improvement	• Increases chance of innovations for HR quality/customer satisfaction	• Enables line employees to make HR decisions informed by HR expertise • Increases customizing of HR programs • Increases line satisfaction with/ understanding of HR
Innovation: People Working with Vision	• Increases time for HR innovation • Awareness of goal deviations sparks discoveries	• Powerful support for discovery • Shortens discovery process • Fast testing, reporting and documentation of new finds	• Increases time for HR innovation • Line understanding of HR sparks collaboration and discovery

SOURCE: From R. Broderick and J. W. Boudreau, "Human Resource Management, Information Technology, and the Competitive Edge," *Academy of Management Executive* 6 (1992): 7–17.

databases. Relational databases have helped advance HRISs, because they provide an easy way to organize data. Also, the number of data fields that can be kept for any employee using a relational database is limitless. The ability to join or merge data from several different tables or to view only a

FIGURE 19.1　　Example of a Relational Database

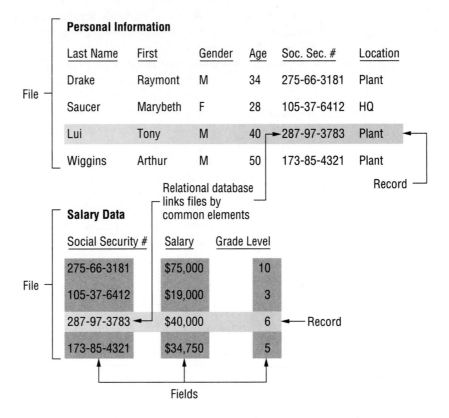

subset of data is especially useful in human resource management. Databases that have been developed to track employee benefit costs, training courses, and compensation, for example, contain separate pieces of employee information that can be accessed and merged as desired by the user. Relational technology also allows databases to be established in several different locations. Users in one plant or division location can access data from any other company location. Consider an oil company. Human resources data—such as the names, salaries, and skills of employees working on an oil rig in the Gulf of Mexico—can be stored at company headquarters. Databases at the oil-rig site itself might contain employee name, safety equipment issued, and appropriate skill certification. Headquarters and oil-rig managers can access information on each database as needed.

Choosing Hardware

Hardware refers to all equipment used in the computer system. Before you choose hardware, you need to identify what applications (software, programs) you need the hardware for. The particular applications you need will dictate the amount of memory, the speed, the networking capabilities, and the storage requirements for the personal computer you acquire. For example, many computers with an older (and slower) 80286 microprocessor chip may not be able to run multiple applications such as *Windows* (an operating system) and a word-processing program (typical software used today on personal computers).

Besides the computer itself, you need to determine which peripherals are needed. A **peripheral** is an input, output, or secondary storage device such as printer, scanner, or disk drive that is external to the computer. Most human resource applications require the printing of reports and other documents. Printers vary in terms of print quality, color, speed, and ability to reproduce graphics and to use various fonts. Many human resource applications now available allow printed information to be directly entered into the computer's database through the use of scanners and optical character recognition software. Scanners can read both straight text (such as surveys and résumés) and tabular information (such as spreadsheets and job-application forms). Optical character recognition software translates the text into language the computer can understand (ASCII).

Mainframe Computers

Although personal computers have the memory and processing capability to handle many applications that previously could be handled only by mainframe computers, mainframes continue to be used for human resource applications.[8] Traditionally, payroll has been done on mainframe computers. But mainframe vendors are beginning to develop personal-computer-based human resource applications that can be linked with payroll systems. With the development of new storage devices, mainframe computers now have tremendous storage capabilities. For large companies, the sheer number of employees means that human resource information needs to be stored on a mainframe computer. Mainframe computers at different sites are also better able to handle the processing needed to allow many users to use databases and applications simultaneously. The speed of mainframes makes it possible to simultaneously update databases in real time. This means that as updates (changes, additions) are made to one database, the same changes are made simultaneously in all databases that contain the data field. For example, if an employee terminates employment, not only must compensation databases be adjusted, but databases related to employee benefits, staffing, and human resource planning must be adjusted as well.

Personal Computers

Advances in microprocessors, memory, networks, and software environments have resulted in the increased use of personal computers for human resource applications.[9] Calculations can now be performed on personal computers with the same efficiency and speed as on mainframe computers. Data for every employee can be stored on them, and employee databases and application software can be shared among personal computers. Perhaps the most important reason personal computers are being increasingly used to manage human resources is the development of software environments that make it easier to use them.

Microprocessors.   Microprocessors are the tiny chips inside personal computers that allow computations and other types of data manipulation to be performed. The latest generation of microprocessors for IBM and IBM-based machines include the 80486 and 80586 microprocessors. Most HR applications need a personal computer with at least a '386 microprocessor, and the '486 and '586 microprocessors significantly shorten the time it takes to perform calculations. Larger databases need faster processors to perform calculations. **Math coprocessors** allow the personal computer to perform high-speed calculations.[10]

Memory.   Most human resource applications will run on personal computers that have a standard 640 kilobytes of random access memory (RAM) and 80 to 100 megabytes on a hard drive. *Random access memory* is memory that the computer uses to read or access programs. A kilobyte is 1,000 bytes (a *byte* is the amount of storage space required to represent a single letter or number.) Software that compresses the hard-drive storage space needed for files is now available (e.g., Stacker®). These applications free up additional storage space on the hard drive.

Networks.   Networks—personal computers connected to one another or to a mainframe computer with cabling—allow users to share data sets, files, software, printers, and data storage devices.[11] The computers may be located in the same room or in different locations. A **local area network** is a network that is confined to the same physical location, such as a classroom or an office building. Figure 19.2 shows a local area network. Networks have stimulated the development of client-server system architecture. In this type of system, files and software applications are stored on one mainframe or personal computer, known as a "file server."[12] The other computers (the "clients") can access the file server and borrow data sets and software applications. Networks have several uses.

   For example, suppose labor-contract negotiations between union and management representatives from transportation and health-care industries have occurred in an electronic meeting room. Each negotiator is provided with a personal computer. The personal computers are linked to each other through a local area network. The network capability provides several advantages. An encyclopedia of all information relevant to the negotiations, such as proposals and letters of agreement, is stored on the file server. Entire documents or parts of them (such as the current labor contract) can be shared electronically by the negotiators. Terms and conditions of the contract that are agreed on by all parties can be quickly entered into the contract and saved for future reference on the file server. Copies of the contract can be more quickly prepared for approval by the union membership.[13]

FIGURE 19.2   A Local Area Network

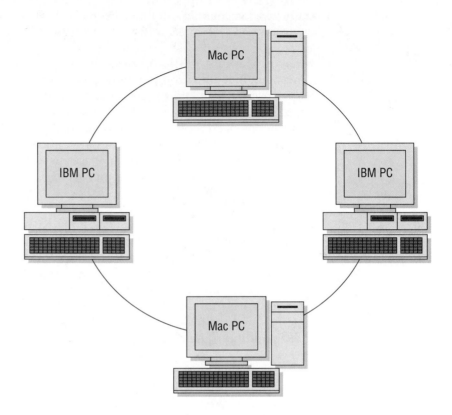

The major advantage of networking is that employees can communicate with one another by sharing data and software. Networking allows companies to develop electronic mail (E-mail). **E-mail** allows computer users to send messages and files directly to one another. E-mail is also useful for communicating with customers. E-mail allows employees to leave detailed messages for one another rather than have to wait to talk over the telephone. For example, Beckwith Machinery, a heavy-equipment dealer in Pittsburgh, has found that E-mail helps work shifts communicate more effectively with each other. Before the company installed E-mail, shifts were often unsure about what jobs were completed and what they should be working on. Through E-mail, employees completing a shift can leave a detailed description of the work that needs to be done.[14]

As we noted earlier in the chapter, employers have traditionally computerized the payroll function. Payroll databases contain information not only about an employee's salary but about hours worked, job function, location, taxes, and demographic data such as race, age, and gender. With networking capabilities, demographic data can be accessed for entirely different functions, such as EEO-1 reports. This suggests another important advantage of networks: They help eliminate data redundancy. A final advantage is that networks can play a security role. The network can be set up so that "clients" can access databases and software stored on the file server only if they have the correct security password.

Software Environments.   A software environment is an application that enables the user to more easily interact with the software. For example, Apple Macintosh computers have a built-in graphical user interface that allows the user to communicate with the computer through graphic representations on the screen rather than by memorizing keystroke sequences. This makes application programs easier to learn and allows the user to move back and forth between applications (for example, between a word-processing program and a spreadsheet). IBM-based personal computer users can now also communicate through graphics rather than through computer commands. *Windows,* a software program introduced by Microsoft Corporation, allows users of IBM and IBM-compatible personal computers that use the DOS operating system to work in a graphical rather than computer command environment.

Security and Privacy Issues: Databases, Hardware, and Software

Major security and privacy concerns include determinations about what types of employee information should be stored on the system (such as salary information), who has physical access to computer hardware and data, and who can access and modify databases.[15] Table 19.2 summarizes the steps that should be taken to secure an HRIS.

Every data field included in the human resources database should be there for a clear business reason. For example, managers should question the reason for including information regarding employees' religious beliefs or political affiliations. Managers should periodically audit employee databases and remove outdated, irrelevant, or inaccurate information.

One of the major advantages of human resource information systems is also a potential liability. Employees have access to information that can be useful for decision making. However, most of that information (e.g., salary information, financial account information, personal information) needs to remain private. Various laws regulate the extent to which employees, company representatives, and parties outside the company can have access to the information in employee records. Therefore, managers should be aware of the privacy legislation in their state. In Minnesota, for example, employees have the right to see the information in their personnel files that deals with warnings, discipline, performance evaluation, and attendance.

Companies also need to develop policies regarding the disclosure of information to government agencies, credit companies, and marketing orga-

TABLE 19.2   Steps That Companies Should Take to Secure HRIS

1. Train all users how to securely use and handle the equipment, data, and software.
2. Train employees to "sign off" personal computers after they are through using them.
3. Do not allow passwords to be shared. Change passwords frequently.
4. Run software through a virus-detection program before using it on the system.
5. Ensure that backup copies, data files, software, and printouts are used only by authorized users.
6. Make backup copies of data files and programs.
7. Ensure that all software and mainframe applications include an audit trail (a record of the changes and transactions that occur in a system, including when and who performed the changes).
8. Use edit controls (such as passwords) to limit employees' access to data files and data fields.

SOURCE: Adapted from L. E. Adams, "Securing Your HRIS in a Microcomputer Environment," *HR Magazine*, February 1992, 56–61.

nizations. The most difficult questions relating to information disclosure involve information provided to other companies about former employees. Managers must be careful not to provide information that could be judged slanderous by the courts.

Protecting the information system against unauthorized access is important because employees can often use personal computers to link up with mainframe computers where confidential information is stored. Most software packages provide features such as passwords that limit employees' ability to view and change specific types of data. Unauthorized copying of software by employees may violate copyright laws and could subject the company to severe legal penalties.

Another area of concern is computer viruses. A **virus** is a destructive, unauthorized computer code that someone has intentionally built into a piece of hardware or software. Viruses can erase data stored in memory or cause pictures or diagrams to appear on computer monitors, thereby keeping the computer's operating system from functioning. Viruses usually enter computer systems either on purpose (e.g., a disgruntled employee) or because naive users have entered a data set or application from a separate storage medium (such as a contaminated floppy disk). To protect against viruses, a virus-detection program should be installed on all computers. These programs identify and destroy viruses before they can cause damage. All software applications and disks should be examined by the virus-protection program, particularly if they are from sources outside the company.

STEPS IN THE DEVELOPMENT OF AN HRIS

System development can mean developing an entire information system for the human resource department or simply implementing an application for a specific human resource function (such as applicant tracking or training administration). A project team should be used to guide system development. The team should be composed of employees with technical expertise (e.g., information systems experts) and employees who have knowledge of the functional area in question.

Typically, the development of a human resource information system involves four stages: analysis, system design, implementation, and evaluation.[16]

Analysis

The analysis step is similar to the needs analysis process used in training. The goal is to determine users' data and report needs. To do that, the following questions need to be asked:

- Is the project feasible, considering the resources and technical expertise available?
- What are the goals and scope of the project?
- How are data generated and exchanged within the functional area or division that is considering developing the system?
- What is the information generated by the area used for?
- What data should be included in the system?
- What processes are used to meet the needs of internal and external customers?

A number of techniques are used to answer these questions. **Data-flow diagrams** show the flow of data among departments. (Figure 19.3 shows a data-flow diagram for payroll data.) This figure shows the steps in producing a paycheck. Information about the employee and department are sent to the general account. The payroll check is issued based on a payment voucher that is generated from the general accounting ledger. **Data-entity relationship diagrams** show the types of data used within a business function and the relationship among the different types of data. In **scenario analysis**, simulations of real-world issues are presented to data end-users. The end-users are asked to indicate how an information system could help address their particular situations and what data should be maintained to deal with those situations. *Surveys and focus groups* collect information about the data collected, used, and stored in a functional area, as well as information about time and data-processing requirements. Users may be asked to evaluate the importance, frequency, and criticality of automating specific tasks within a functional area. (e.g., How critical is it to have an applicant tracking system that maintains data on applicants' previous work experi-

FIGURE 19.3   A Data-Flow Diagram for Payroll Data

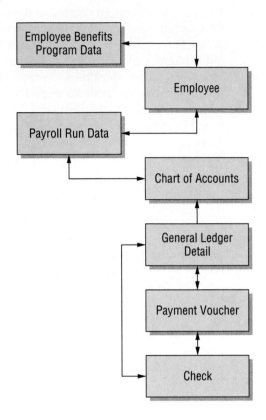

ence?) *Cost-benefit analyses* compare the costs of completing tasks with and without an automated system or software application. For example, the analysis should include the costs in terms of people, time, materials and dollars; the anticipated costs of software and hardware; and labor, time, and material expenses.[17]

System Design

In this step, the goals are to design data structure and content based on the needs analysis, to develop software that will meet the storage and processing requirements of the data, and to choose the hardware necessary for operating the software application.

The decision to purchase software or a system or develop it in-house depends on several factors.[18] Table 19.3 shows the factors that need to be considered when making the buy-versus-build decision. Hardware costs will be the same whether the system is purchased or developed in-house. In-house development of the program needed to run the system is typically more expensive unless the company has programmers available for devel-

TABLE 19.3   Purchase versus In-house Development of Computer Systems or Software

1. Does the company have programmers who are capable of developing the system or software application?
2. Can the purchased software or system meet the company's needs?
3. Can the software or system interact with current systems and software applications?
4. Does the company have the resources to provide training, technical support, and file maintenance, and to develop system and user documentation?

opment. The cost of the project should be estimated by comparing the price of a commercially developed system to the programming costs of a system developed in-house.

Managers also need to consider how soon the system or software application will become outdated. The design of commercially developed systems and software often is too generic to fit company needs. As a result, it will soon be obsolete. A system developed in-house will match the company needs and can be modified to meet future needs. A final consideration is whether the company has the resources to provide users with training, documentation, and technical support. If users are not provided with appropriate support, the system will not be used. Most commercial developers of systems and software applications provide support as part of the cost of the project.

Many companies lack the expertise to design software applications related to human resource management. As a result, they rely on vendors to provide hardware and software products. Prospective vendors can be found in software catalog, at trade shows, through advertisements in industry publications, and through the recommendations of managers and human resource professionals in other companies. Companies often develop a "request for proposal," which is sent to prospective vendors. This identifies what the company hopes and needs to achieve with the application, how much it can spend, what it expects from the vendor in the way of maintenance and training, and how the vendor should submit a proposal (including a contact person and a proposal deadline). There are at least two reasons to use a request for proposal in choosing a vendor. First, it forces the company to consider the goals and requirements of the application. Second, it reduces the time that would otherwise be devoted to personally communicating the company's needs to competing vendors.

A list of potential vendors is generated by evaluating the proposals. The next step in vendor selection is to evaluate the technical and functional aspects of each vendor's products.[19] This involves an on-site demonstration by the vendor, hands-on use of the application by the company, and an evaluation of the match between the vendor's application and the hardware and other systems the company is already using. Vendor evaluation should also include evaluating the training the vendor will provide to users within

TABLE 19.4   Characteristics of User-Friendly Software

- Easy to access
- Uses icons or menus for choices (limits memorizing commands)
- Guides users through mistakes
- Contains self-explanatory error messages
- Has a data dictionary
- Checks semantics and syntax
- Offers windows, scrolling, highlighting, pointers, and similar features
- Offers a tutorial or other instructional aid
- Allows for downloading to and uploading from microcomputers
- Allows translation from one microcomputer platform to another (i.e., IBM to Mac, if necessary)

SOURCE: Adapted from V. R. Ceriello and C. Freeman, *Human Resource Management Systems* (New York: Lexington Press, 1991).

the company, the quality of the technical and user documentation, and the vendor's product service and warranty. Table 19.4 presents some characteristics that make software easier to use. Managers should ensure that the software they are considering buying has these characteristics. Finally, it is important to determine whether the vendor is committed to the products and services they offer, because if their business changes direction, the product purchased may not receive adequate support and updating.

Once a vendor has been selected, a contract needs to be negotiated and signed. It should stipulate the schedule for implementing the application, maintenance schedules, licensing and copyright agreements, payment schedules, quantity and types of documentation provided, and descriptions of the training and support the vendor will provide.

Implementation

The most important step in the system-development process is ensuring that employees, managers, and other parties who have an interest in the system will use it. As Table 19.5 shows, expectations for system performance vary among employees. State-of-the art human resource applications make it easier for managers and employees to perform their jobs. However, employees and managers may resist using a new application if it requires them to change the way they are accustomed to working. Such resistance can be reduced by:

- Providing users with information about the advantages of the new application or information system.
- Training users to use the new application.

TABLE 19.5 Employee Group Expectations about Human Resource Information Systems and Software Applications

Employee Group	Expectations
Technical experts	Is the system technically sophisticated? Is the system enjoyable to maintain? Is the technical documentation appropriate?
Human resource user (manager, specialists)	Is the system easy to use? Is the system well documented? Does the system provide timely, valuable, and accurate information?
Manager	Does the system provide accurate and timely reports? Does the system aid in managing employees? Does the system help generate a profit? Does the system reduce expenses?
Employees	Is the information generated by the system accurate? Will personal information be kept confidential? Does the system help me improve the quality or efficiency of products or services I provide to customers? Is the system easy to use?

SOURCE: Adapted from M. J. Kavanagh, H. G. Gueutal, and S. I. Tannenbaum, *Human Resource Information Systems: Development and Applications* (Boston: PWS-Kent, 1990).

- Gradually phasing the new system in by conducting **parallel testing** (allowing both the old and the new systems to operate in order to compare their accuracy and usefulness).
- Allowing users to experiment with the new system.
- Soliciting users' involvement in needs analysis and vendor evaluation (users groups).
- Providing easily accessible technical support (e.g., a telephone hot line).
- Providing easy-to-understand system documentation.
- Soliciting and acting on users' feedback.

Evaluation

The effectiveness of an HRIS can be evaluated by showing the cost and time savings realized by implementing the system, the improvements in decision making (e.g., better-qualified job candidates), and the improvements in customer service.[20] For example, a new system at Chevron called EPIC (Emphasizing People at Chevron) has reduced both the amount of data gathering the human resources staff has to do, and the number of printed policy statements and handbooks.[21] By using the HRIS, employees receive detailed information about human resource policies.

HRIS APPLICATIONS

At the beginning of this chapter, we discussed Tellabs' difficulty using human resource information to support its total quality management effort. To better use its available human resource information, Tellabs purchased a microcomputer-based HRIS. The system is used to manage benefits, to report information (including, for example, that required by law, in areas such as equal employment opportunity, occupational safety and health, and immigration), and to track hirings, absenteeism, performance evaluation, and employees' skills. The system also provides managers with information about employees' skills and training courses they have completed.

Today, nearly 1,000 personal-computer-based human resource applications are available.[22] Because of the wide variety, several publications that deal exclusively with human resource management (for example, *HR Magazine*, *Personnel Journal*) devote one issue a year to reviewing software applications. We review the HRIS applications available in the areas of staffing, human resource planning, performance management, training and career development, and compensation and benefits in the following sections.

Staffing Applications

Common HRIS applications used in the area of staffing include applicant tracking, recruitment-practices tracking, help in meeting equal employment opportunity reporting requirements, and help in maintaining databases of employee information.

Applicant Recruiting and Tracking.   Applicant tracking helps a company maintain its information on job candidates and identify suitable candidates for particular positions. An effective applicant-tracking system:

1. Retrieves applications by name, Social Security number, or other identifiers.
2. Tracks all the events in the application process (e.g., interviews, tests).
3. Allows the user to determine how long an application has remained active.
4. Contains the information needed to meet equal employment opportunity reporting requirements, such as name, gender, race, and date of application.
5. Tracks data entry (allows for entry of only essential applicant information).
6. Simplifies the recruiter's function (provides basic data needed to schedule interviews, generate reports, and reduce the list of job candidates).
7. Allows an evaluation of recruiting strategy to be made—e.g., by identifying which sources of advertising bring in the best candidates or the cost-effectiveness of visiting various college campuses.
8. Permits customization (allows additional types of data to be added to the file, such as test results or job offers).

9. Increases the applicant pool (potential job candidates can be identified and tracked earlier; qualified candidates can be tracked after a position is filled).

10. Increases selection criteria by allowing simultaneous searches based on several types of criteria, such as skills, work history, and educational background).[23]

Equal Employment Opportunity and Affirmative Action Reporting Requirements. To comply with equal employment opportunity requirements, companies have to provide reports to the federal government. The most common is the EEO-1 report, which shows the number of employees by race and gender within nine job categories (e.g., professional, office and clerical, craft workers). A section of an EEO report is shown in Figure 19.4. The EEO-1 report is usually submitted annually to the Equal Employment Opportunity Commission. All government contractors and any employers who have been found to engage in illegal hiring practices are also required to file affirmative action reports. To complete either kind of report, employers need to:

1. Describe the work force by job category and job classification.

2. Evaluate the adverse impact of employment practices on representatives of protected classes (e.g., women and minorities) in the work force.

3. Determine the availability for jobs of qualified members of protected classes.

4. Evaluate the company's utilization of qualified protected class members.

5. Describe the company's goals and timetables for implementing equal employment opportunity or affirmative action initiatives.

6. Monitor those initiatives.[24]

Because of EEO and affirmative action reporting requirements, employers need to keep track of job candidates' and employees' race and gender and the percentages of women and minorities in the internal and external work force by job category. Collecting this information into databases makes it easier to track affirmative action and EEO-related statistics. Many software packages are available that generate the necessary EEO and affirmative action reports. (One of the most popular is *ABRA 2000 Human Resource System.*)

Developing a Master Employee Database. Companies usually keep data about employees in one large file. Information in the master employee database can be used for many purposes: administering payroll, tracking compensation and benefit costs, human resource planning, and meeting EEO reporting requirements. The master employee database usually includes information such as the employee's name, Social Security number, job status (full- or part-time), hiring date, position, title, rate of pay, citizenship status, job history, job location, mailing address, birth date, and emergency contacts.

FIGURE 19.4   Section D—Employment Data of EEO-1 Report

Number of Employees		Male						Female					
	Overall Total	White	Black	Hispanic	Asian	American Indian		White	Black	Hispanic	Asian	American Indian	
	A	B	C	D	E	F		A	B	C	D	E	F	G
Officials and Managers	1												
Professionals	2												
Technicians	3												
Sales Workers	4												
Office and Clerical	5												
Craft Workers (Skilled)	6												
Operatives (Semiskilled)	7												
Laborers (Unskilled)	8												
Service Workers	9												
Total	10												
Total employment reported in previous EEO-1 report	11												

Formal on-the-job training	White Collar	12												
	Production	13												

SOURCE: Adapted from V. R. Ceriello, *Human Resource Management* (New York: Lexington Books, 1991), 420.

Using Staffing Applications for Decision Making.   Information related to applicant recruiting and tracking can help managers make recruiting practices more efficient and productive. For example, managers can evaluate the yield of recruiting sources. Those sources that produce the greatest number of applicants who are offered and accept positions are targeted for subsequent recruiting efforts, and low-yield sources are abandoned. Managers can also determine which recruiters are providing the most successful employees. EEO reporting and adverse-impact analyses can help managers evaluate the extent to which women and minority employees are gaining access to managerial and other highly compensated and valued positions in the company.

At Nike, the sports shoe company, recruitment has become less costly and time-consuming because the company uses an applicant-tracking system.[25] Before the automated system was implemented, job applicants had to submit a separate résumé for each job they were interested in. The old system also lacked the capability to process and store data from unsolicited job applications. Most of the 35,000 unsolicited applications Nike received were thrown away. Using *Resumix,* an applicant-tracking program, the company now enters every résumé it receives into the system. *Resumix* also gives managers the ability to cross-reference résumés. Using *Resumix,* Nike has lowered the time and cost of employee recruitment. The company is running fewer newspaper ads, and the ads are more general, generating a greater variety of candidates. *Resumix* has also reduced the time needed to fill positions.

Human Resource Planning Applications

Two principal computer applications are related to human resource planning: succession planning and forecasting.[26] *Succession planning* ensures that the company has employees who are prepared to move into positions that become available because of retirement, promotion, transfers, terminations, or expansion of the business. The "Competing through Technology and Structure" box discusses succession planning at AT&T. *Forecasting* includes predicting the number of employees who have certain skills and the number of qualified individuals in the labor market.

Because human resource planning involves company-specific calculations involved in determining future employee turnover, growth rates, and promotion patterns, human resource planning applications usually require more customization than applications for other human resource functions. They usually contain several data files, including a starting-population file, exit-rate file, growth-rate file, and promotion patterns. The starting-population file lists employees by job classification within each job family. These file lists usually include all active, regular, full-time employees. However, starting-population files may include only specific populations of employees. Starting-population data that may be used include job grade, gender, race/ethnicity, age, service, training, and experience information. Starting-population lists that are limited to specific

Technology & Structure

SUCCESSION PLANNING AT AT&T

AT&T recently purchased a new PC-based succession-planning system that is linked to other staffing and development systems worldwide. This system helps AT&T gain a competitive advantage by linking its management development needs to its global strategic plans and by ensuring that companywide skills are identified and developed as needed. Succession-planning systems are usually data intensive. For succession planning to be effective, decision makers need a large amount of information about the managers' skills and the requirements of leadership positions. What contributed to the effectiveness of AT&T's PC-based succession planning system?

- *Ready availability of extensive information on employees and positions*—Two databases were linked in this system. One database has information on job incumbents and successors and on key leadership positions. Information about managers is stored in the other database, which includes data on job history, assessments of strengths and weaknesses, career and development needs, training taken and planned, and skills and functional expertise (such as language proficiency).

- *Link to other systems*—To assure efficiency, the succession-planning system had to be able to use data from other human resource information systems. Basic biographical personnel data and employee demographic information can be downloaded from the corporate HRIS to the succession-planning system. Data from the executive strategic staffing system identifies high-potential employees.

- *Flexibility of the system to change*—The succession-planning system selected has the capacity for creating new data fields, varying lengths of data elements, and storing limitless sets of data in tables. It has a succession ripple feature that automatically identifies in advance the affects of a candidate moving to another position, permitting "what-if" modeling during the selection process. It allows the user to identify the readiness of each candidate in the selection pool. Candidates are identified both by codes reflecting their readiness and by the specific requirements they lack for succession.

- *Report-writing capabilities*—The report-writing feature permits the user to create a variety of report formats, link data from different databases, save and catalog reports, and create graphics that illustrate data relationships.

SOURCE: V. J. Brush and R. Nardoni, "Integrated Data Supports AT&T's Succession Planning," *Personnel Journal* 71 (1992): 103–109.

populations of employees are used to identify the mobility patterns of these employee groups. Exit-rate data include promotion patterns, training completion rates, turnover rates, and hiring rates. Growth-rate data include the percentage increase in the number of employees within the job or demographic characteristic (e.g., females) of interest. Promotion patterns include the rate of movement into and out of each position.

Information regarding starting population and exit and growth rates is useful for conducting work-force profile analysis and work-force dynamics analysis.[27]

Work-Force Profile Analysis.   To determine future labor supply and demand, it is necessary to identify the characteristics of the current work force, a process known as a *work-force profile review*. The HRIS can be used to generate reports that provide information regarding employee demographics (such as age), the number of employees in each job classification, and the interaction between demographics and company characteristics (e.g., the average age of employees within each job classification or division of the company).

Work-Force Dynamics Analysis.   A **work-force dynamics analysis** involves analyzing employee movement over time. Promotion, demotion, transfer, and turnover data are used. Employee movement data can also be used to forecast the effects of layoffs or hiring on the future work force. Work-force dynamics analysis provides the following kinds of information:

1. Number of new hires, transfers, and promotions by job classification or department.
2. The total number of promotions, or the number of promotions from a specific job to another job or from one division to another division.
3. The number of employees the company will need in the future.
4. The number of employees who will be available to fill future job openings.

Using Human Resource Planning Applications for Decision Making. The work-force profile review provides managers with information regarding:

1. Divisions or departments that have the greatest concentration of employees who are nearing retirement age.
2. Job classifications in which there are too few employees who are ready for promotion.
3. Job classifications in which there are few women or minorities.
4. Job classifications or departments that have large groups of employees who lack basic skills.

An example of a human resource planning application is Cyborg Systems Workforce Planning module.[28] This application, which can be run on either a mainframe or a personal computer, retains data on employees' skills and work experience, education, job history, and termination and separation. It permits integration with payroll applications so that data can be shared between the databases. It reports on the number of people hired, terminated, transferred, and promoted by pay class. It also reports on the net change and percentage change in hiring, termination, or transfers during each business cycle, month, or other time frame chosen by the user.

Managers can use information about employee movement, skills, and job openings to make decisions about where employees should be deployed to help the company successfully execute its business strategy.

Performance-Management Applications

Employees' performance ratings, disciplinary actions, and work-rule violations can be stored in electronic databases. Personal computers are also increasingly being used for monitoring the actual performance and productivity of service employees.[29] For example, at a General Electric customer-service center, agents answer over 14,000 telephone inquiries per day. The agents' calls are recorded and reviewed to help the agent improve customer service. American Airlines also monitors the telephone calls that come into its reservation centers. Managers can hear what the agents tell customers and see what agents enter on their personal computer screens. One of the disadvantages of monitoring is that employees sometimes find it demoralizing, degrading, and stressful. To avoid the potential negative effect of performance monitoring, managers must communicate why employees are being monitored. Nonmanagement employees also need to be involved in monitoring and coaching less-experienced employees. Legislation regarding computer monitoring may occur in the future. Both the U.S. House and Senate have recently considered legislation designed to protect employees' rights from being violated by computer monitoring (The Privacy for Consumers and Workers Act).

Using Performance-Management Applications for Decision Making.
Performance-management applications are available to help managers tailor performance-rating systems to jobs and assist the manager in identifying solutions to performance problems.[30] Software is available to help the manager customize performance-rating forms for each job. The manager determines the performance standard for each job and rates each employee according to the appropriate standards. The manager receives a report summarizing the employees' strengths and weaknesses. The report also provides information regarding how different the employee's performance was from the established standard.

Performance-diagnosis applications ask the manager for information about performance problems (e.g., has the employee been trained in the skills that caused the performance problem?) and the work environment (e.g., does the employee work under time pressure?). The software analyzes the information and provides the manager with solutions to consider in dealing with the performance problem.

Training and Career Development Applications

Training applications have primarily been used to track information related to training administration (e.g., course enrollments, tuition reimbursement summaries, and training costs), employee skills, and employees' training activities. Important database elements for training administration include training courses completed, certified skills, and educational experience. Georgia Power uses a database system that tracks internal training classes, available classroom space, instructor availability, costs, and the salaries of training class members.[31] Figure 19.5 illustrates a screen showing training

FIGURE 19.5   Example of a Training Budget Screen

```
   ■   Cost Center: Accounting
   ■   Total Budget: 4500

                       Budget    Expenditure    Variance

      Course           3500         1000          2500

      Accommodation     600           00           600

      Meals             300           00           300

      Travel            100           00           100

      Total            4500         1000          3500
```

SOURCE: Adapted from Spectrum Human Resource Systems Corporation, "TD/2000: Training and Development System: Sample Screens and Reports" (Denver, Colorado).

costs for an accounting department. Cost information can be used by managers to determine which departments are exceeding their training budgets. This information can be used to reallocate training dollars during the next budget period. Databases are also available that provide professional employees, such as engineers and lawyers, with access to summaries of journal articles, legal cases, and books to help these employees keep up-to-date.[32]

Career development applications assess the employees' career interests, work values, and career goals. The computer provides employees with information about positions in the company that meet their interests and values. Company information systems may also have career development plans for each employee. These may include information such as skill strengths, projected training and development needs, target positions, and ratings of readiness for managerial or other positions.

Using Training and Career Development Applications for Decision Making.   Managers can use skills inventories to ensure that they are getting the maximum benefit out of their training budget. Using skills inventories, managers can determine which employees need training and can suggest training programs to them that are appropriate for their job and skill levels. Skill inventories are also useful for identifying employees who are qualified for promotions and transfers. Finally, they can also be useful for helping managers to quickly build employee teams with the necessary skills to respond to customer needs, product changes, international assignments, or work problems.

Career development applications can help managers improve the effectiveness of their career development discussions with employees. They also help employees determine their interests, goals, and work values, which is often a difficult and uncomfortable task for managers. By having employees complete a self-assessment of interests, goals, and values, managers and employees can have a more efficient and effective career development discussion that focuses on developing career plans and helping employees progress toward their career goals.

Career development applications also can help managers advise employees on available development opportunities (e.g., new jobs). For example, as we mentioned in Chapter 14, 3M has an internal-search system that helps managers identify qualified internal candidates for job openings, and a job-information system that provides employees with access to information about internal job openings and the opportunity to nominate themselves for job openings.[33]

Compensation and Benefits Applications

Applications in compensation and benefits include payroll, job evaluation, salary surveys, salary planning, international compensation, and benefits management.

Payroll. Meeting a payroll involves calculating and reporting federal, state, and local taxes; computing gross pay, deductions, and net pay for each pay period; arranging for transfer of monies into appropriate accounts; distributing payments and records to employees; and reporting dollars allocated to payroll and benefits to the accounting function. Several issues have to be considered in designing or choosing a payroll system. The company must decide whether payroll will be administered in-house or by a service bureau. The company must also decide the extent of integration between payroll and other human resource information systems.

In many companies, payroll is done by a **service bureau**, a company that provides payroll services to other organizations. One of the advantages of a service bureau is that it ensures that the company's payroll meets federal, state, and local laws. It also provides a level of computer expertise that may be unavailable within the company. Many service bureaus have developed other human resource applications that integrate with their payroll systems. A problem arises when a company wants to use human resource applications that have not been developed by the service bureau. The service bureau may be unable or unwilling to integrate its payroll system with other applications.

Besides deciding whether to have its payroll done by a service bureau, managers have to decide whether payroll will be integrated with other human resource data systems. In an **integrated payroll system**, the information in the payroll system is shared with other databases. In most companies, payroll is not linked to other human resource information systems. However, the trend is toward integrated systems because of the reduced costs resulting from sharing databases. Another advantage of an integrated payroll is that it cuts down on the storage of redundant information, thus speeding up the computer's computing time. Tesseract Corporation's payroll system is completely integrated with both its human resource manager and its benefits systems. Information needed for salary planning and compliance with government regulations can be shared between the systems. The integration of payroll with other systems raises important security issues because access to payroll data needs to be restricted to certain employees.

Job Evaluation.   Job evaluation involves determining the worth of each job and establishing pay rates. In computerized job evaluation, jobs are given points, and the relative worth of each job is determined by the total number of points.[34] Managers and employees complete surveys that ask them to rate their jobs' level of problem solving, interaction with customers, and other important compensable factors. The survey data are entered into the computer. A summary of the survey responses is generated and checked for accuracy (e.g., jobs high in complexity should also have high ratings of required job knowledge). The computer calculates a point value to assign each job to a salary grade.

Salary Surveys.   Salary surveys are sent to competing companies to gain information about compensation rates, pay levels, or pay structures. The information gathered may include salary ranges, average salary of job incumbents, and total compensation of job incumbents. Software designed specifically for this purpose collects, records, analyzes, and generates reports comparing company salary ranges to those of competitors.

Salary Planning.   Salary planning anticipates changes in employees' salaries because of seniority or performance. Salary-planning applications calculate merit-increase budgets and allocate salary increases based on merit or seniority. They also allow users to see what effect changes in the amount of money devoted to merit, seniority, or cost-of-living wage increases would have on compensation budgets. Figure 19.6 illustrates a screen from a software application showing the current salary for several positions and the anticipated salaries based on the company's compensation strategy.

Home Box Office (HBO) has a proactive approach toward compensation.[35] The company believes that all employees should understand their salary, why it was assigned and what type of merit increase they can expect. Merit increases are based on performance ratings. The HRIS staff helps the

FIGURE 19.6   Example of a Screen from a Payroll Application

Salary Analysis

Job Title	Annual Salary	Plan—Annual Salary
Accountant	28,750.35	28,900.00
Executive	84,975.80	87,235.12
Retail Clerk	16,000.00	17,115.00
Project Leader	23,450.00	24,555.00
Maintenance Engineer	18,025.48	19,750.35
Secretary, Senior	20,640.56	24,005.80

SOURCE: Adapted from Cyborg Systems, Inc., Advertisement for The Solution Series (Chicago: Cyborg Systems Inc., 1992).

human resource department administer the performance reviews. HRIS staff provides an evaluation report for each employee. The report includes the employee's current salary and performance evaluations from previous years. The HRIS staff also assists in the bonus-administration program, converting each employee's performance ratings into a bonus rating, developing calculation worksheets, entering data, and providing a wide range of reports that are needed to determine the amount of money available for merit raises. One of the HRIS products related to the bonus system is a report that estimates and calculates bonuses for employees and confirms the approved bonus.

International Compensation.   These applications perform U.S. and foreign tax calculations necessary to determine the costs of international assignments. Many international compensation applications can also calculate salary levels and cost-of-living differentials between U.S. and international cities.

Benefits Management.   Benefits can be classified into three types: time benefits (e.g., sick leave, parental leave), risk benefits (various forms of health and long-term disability insurance that help employees and their families in case of injury or death), and security benefits (retirement and savings programs).[36] Benefits management includes tracking coverage for employees and former employees, producing reports on changes in benefits coverage, and determining employee eligibility for benefit plans. Software is available to help administer flexible benefits programs, pensions, retirement planning, and defined benefit and defined contribution plans. These applications can track the employee's enrollment in each part of the benefit plan, track claims, communicate premium costs to employees, calculate taxes, and determine employee eligibility for coverage. For example, Siemens Corporation uses a flexible benefit software application that allows employees from all forty Siemens companies to enroll in and inquire about their benefits plans by using a touchtone telephone.[37] HRIS benefits applications can reduce the time it takes to process changes in employees' benefit plans. They also allow employers to track current benefit expenses and project future benefits costs. The "Competing through Quality" box shows how TRW's HRIS helped with its new flexible benefits plan.

HRIS benefits applications can also help companies comply with federal legislation regarding benefits. For example, the Comprehensive Omnibus Budget Reconciliation Act (COBRA) requires companies to offer health benefits to terminated and retired employees. The company must ensure that all eligible former employees and their dependents have been notified of their option of continuing health benefits; it must also track who accepts and who declines coverage and determine when COBRA coverage has expired.[38] Software is available that automates the record–keeping and reporting requirements necessary to comply with COBRA.

Using Compensation and Benefits Applications for Decision Making. These software applications provide graphical depictions of pay ranges and salary lines. They allow managers to quickly see the effects of changes in compensation rates and policies. Compensation and benefits applications can be useful for determining the impact of different percentages of pay increases on total compensation costs. Managers can use job-evaluation data to determine which jobs are over- or underpaid in comparison with other jobs in the company. Hypothetical pay ranges can be constructed based on different compensation strategies. For example, the costs of a "lead the market" strategy can be determined before the company decides on this compensation approach.

Managers can also use compensation information to make adjustments in an individual employee's compensation. For example, managers can determine whether employee performance ratings are related to merit increases and can identify the employee's position within the pay range.

Benefits applications are useful for evaluating the costs of changes in benefits availability and how changes in the characteristics of the employee population (such as age or gender) may affect benefits costs. The implications of different types of early retirement programs on benefits costs can also be considered before a program is offered.

Quality

TECHNOLOGY MEETS TOTAL QUALITY MANAGEMENT AT TRW

TRW's Space and Defense unit has had flexible benefits since 1974. In 1989, the company adopted a new flexible benefits plan. As part of the plan to communicate the new benefits plan to employees, a computer program was created that allowed employees to investigate various benefit plans and enrollment options. After employees made their choices, the program printed out completed enrollment forms that were sent to the benefits department. A temporary staff had to be hired to process the large amount of paperwork. Enrollment forms were received, checked, sorted, batched, sent to data entry, keypunched, returned, and filed. The process was slow and prone to error.

An important concept in the total quality management approach to systems development is process reengineering. *Process reengineering* involves identifying where processes can be improved and then adding technology where it best fits. The benefits-enrollment process was examined in order to eliminate unnecessary work and speed the process up. A small data file of the employee's plan selection and dependent information was added to the program. This created paperless benefits enrollment. The improved benefits enrollment process eliminated nine steps, resulting in the employee's data being moved directly to a computer file, bypassing the long paper flow. After the data are entered into the company's mainframe computer, a confirmation statement of each employee's choices is printed. With the more efficient enrollment process, employees receive their confirmation statement in days rather than weeks, as was the case in prior years. As a result of employees' enrolling through the "direct" method, the error rate was reduced by two-thirds.

SOURCE: From V. E. Krebs, "Total Quality and Information Technology: An HRIS Mandate for the 90s," *The Review* 70 (1991): 14–20.

SUMMARY

In this chapter, we examined the role of human resource information systems in organizations. As we noted in Chapter 1, one of the major competitive challenges that companies face is how to harness technology to gain a competitive advantage. One way is through the use of human resource information systems. These provide managers with access to human resource information that they can use for decision making, planning, or tracking costs. We discussed the basic aspects of these systems that managers need to be aware of, including hardware and databases, security issues, and system development. We also discussed how HRIS applications are being used to more effectively manage staffing, human resource planning, performance management, training and career development, and compensation and benefits functions.

Discussion Questions

1. Your company is replacing its large mainframe computer with several smaller computers in an effort to decentralize information systems. Employees through-

out the company will have access to personal computers that will be networked to each other. The personal computers will also have access to databases and applications stored in the larger computers. Employees will have access to software applications and databases related to compensation, staffing, and résumés. Your boss asks you to meet with her to discuss security issues related to the new computer system. What will you tell her?

2. The Americans with Disabilities Act (ADA) requires employers to accommodate qualified disabled employees so they can perform essential job functions. What data fields need to be included in an employee master database to help the company comply with ADA? What about a job-applicant database?

3. What skills and positions should be represented on a vendor-evaluation project team?

4. How can a human resource information system help companies reach total quality goals?

5. You have just purchased a new word-processing application for clerical employees. The employees are satisfied with their current word-processing package, but you believe the new package produces better graphics and is easier to use. What can you do to ensure that the employees use the new applications?

6. How could a self-managed work team that manufacturers televisions benefit from training software?

Notes

1. N. J. Beutell and A. J. Walker, "HR Information Systems," in *Managing HR in the Information Age*, ed. R. S. Schuler (Washington, D.C.: Bureau of National Affairs, 1991), 6-167–6-203.

2. M. J. Kavanagh, H. G. Gueutal and S. I. Tannenbaum, *Human Resource Information Systems: Development and Application* (Boston: PWS-Kent, 1990); V. R. Ceriello and C. Freeman, *Human Resource Management Systems* (Lexington, Mass.: Lexington Books, 1991).

3. Bureau of National Affairs, *Personnel Management* (Washington, D.C.: The Bureau of National Affairs, 1990), 251:501–251:604.

4. R. Broderick and J. W. Boudreau, "Human Resource Management, Information Technology, and the Competitive Edge," *Academy of Management Executive* 6 (1992): 7–17; J. J. Lawler, "Computer-Mediated Information Processing and Decision Making in Human Resource Management," in *Research in Personnel and Human Resources Management*, ed. G. Ferris and K. Rowland (Greenwich, Conn.: JAI Press, 1992), 10:301–344.

5. D. E. Kirrane and P. R. Kirrane, "Managing by Expert Systems," *HR Magazine*, March 1990, 37–39.

6. Ceriello and Freeman, *Human Resource Management Systems*.

7. J. Frazee and A. Briscoe, "Relational Technology: A Strategic Weapon for the 1990s," *The Review*, Spring 1990, 6–12; R. Henson, "Computer Databases Built for HR," *HRMagazine*, April 1990, 59–61.

8. R. Brookler, "What Hardware Means to the HRIS," *Personnel Journal*, May 1992, 122–127.

9. Ibid.; S. E. O'Connell, "The HR Automation Budget," *HR Magazine*, July 1992, 31–32.

10. University of Minnesota Information Services, *Computer and Information Services Newsletter*, no. 12 (1992): 267.

11. T. M. Moulton, "Implementing an HR Local Area Network," *HR Magazine*, October 1992, 29–30.

12. T. L. Hunter, "How Client/Server Is Reshaping the HRIS," *Personnel Journal,* July 1992, 38–46; B. Pollack, "Provide Exciting Opportunities for HRIS Function," *The Review,* Spring 1990, 15–41.

13. B. C. Herniter, E. Carmel and J. F. Nunamaker, Jr., "Computers Improve the Efficiency of the Negotiations Process," *Personnel Journal,* April 1993, 93–99.

14. R. Hotch, "How to Stay in Touch over the Network," *Nation's Business,* July 1992, 60.

15. B. Leonard, "Open and Shut HRIS," *Personnel Journal,* July 1991, 59–62.

16. D. Horsfield, "Before the First Data Is Keyed," *Computers in Personnel,* Winter 1988, 51–54.

17. L. Quillen, "Human Resources Computerization: A Dollars-and-Cents Approach," *Personnel Journal,* July 1989, 74–77.

18. J. J. Brennan, "Personal Computers in Human Resources," *The Review,* February 1992, 8–13.

19. G. TenEyck, "Software Purchase: A to Z," *Personnel Journal,* October 1990, 73–79; V. R. Ceriello, "How Do You Choose a Vendor?" *Personnel Journal,* December 1984, 32–38.

20. T. R. V. Davis, "Information Technology and White-Collar Productivity," *Academy of Management Executive* 5 (1991): 55–67.

21. J. F. Stright, "Managing a Culture of Change," *The Review,* February/March 1991, 16–21.

22. R. B. Frantzreb, ed., *The 1993 Personnel Software Census* (Roseville, Cal.: Advanced Personnel Systems, 1993).

23. P. Anthony, "Track Applicants, Track Costs," *Personnel Journal,* April 1990, 75–81; L. Stevens, "Resume Scanning Simplifies Tracking," *Personnel Journal,* April 1993, 77–79.

24. Ceriello and Freeman, *Human Resource Management Systems.*

25. J. Cohan, "Nike Uses Resumix to Stay Ahead in the Recruitment Game," *Personnel Journal,* November 1992, 9 (supplement).

26. S. E. Forrer and Z. B. Leibowitz, *Using Computers in Human Resources* (San Francisco: Jossey-Bass, 1991); Ceriello and Freeman, *Human Resource Management Systems.*

27. Kavanaugh et al., *Human Resource Information Systems.*

28. Cyborg Systems Inc., Advertising brochure titled "The Solution Series" (1992).

29. G. Bylinsky, "How Companies Spy on Employees," *Fortune,* November 4, 1991, 131–140.

30. Forrer and Leibowitz, *Using Computers in Human Resources.*

31. Ibid.

32. L. Granick, A. Y. Dessaint and G. R. VandenBos, "How Information Systems Can Help Build Professional Competence," in *Maintaining Professional Competence,* ed. S. L. Willis and S. S. Dubin (San Francisco: Jossey-Bass, 1990), 278–305.

33. Personal Communication, Susan Runkel, Career Resources, April 18, 1992.

34. F. H. Wagner, "The Nuts and Bolts of Computer-Assisted Job Evaluation," *The Review,* October/November 1991, 16–22.

35. M. Coleman–Carlone, "HBO's Program for Merit Pay," *Personnel Journal,* May 1990, 86–90.

36. Ceriello and Freeman, *Human Resource Management Systems.*

37. H. Glatzer, "Top Secret—Maybe," *Human Resource Executive* 7 (1993): 26–29.

38. Kavanagh et al., *Human Resource Information Systems.*

C A S E

THE SEARCH FOR A NEW PAYROLL SYSTEM AT MEDTRONIC, INC.

Medtronic Inc. is a leading medical device company that produces cardiac pace-makers and heart valves. Medtronic has over 7,000 employees in the United States and 2,300 overseas. Medtronic generated $1.2 billion in revenues for fiscal 1992. The current payroll system was installed in 1985. Since 1985, the payroll system has been supported in-house. The system runs on a large mainframe computer. It has met minimal performance requirements, though at considerable cost ($219,000 in programming support, $216,000 in operational costs, and $353,000 in department costs). Because the maintenance and enhancement costs will continue to escalate, the current payroll system needs to be replaced.

From a strategic perspective, the payroll and HRIS functions want:

- Fully functional software that will meet future needs and government requirements.

- A system that will allow payroll and HR functions to more quickly adapt to changes in the company's business plans.

- A common, intergrated HR/payroll database.

- Complete access to data input and reporting by HR/payroll staff and line managers.

- A cost-effective alternative to business units not currently at headquarters.

QUESTIONS

1. What process should Medtronic use to develop a new payroll system?
2. If you were on the project team in charge of evaluating payroll system vendors, what would you want vendors to show you in their demonstrations to convince you to purchase their systems?

SOURCE: Based on a personal conversation with Ron Hanscome, HRIS Manager, Medtronic, Inc., February 15, 1993.

SATURN CORPORATION AND THE UAW: A TEST OF LABOR'S PARTNERSHIP WITH MANAGEMENT

V I D E O   C A S E

In early 1993, Michael Bennett, the local union president at Saturn Corporation, found himself facing three different opposition slates in his campaign to remain as President of United Auto Workers Local 1853. Mr. Bennett was a supporter of the highly publicized cooperative Saturn partnership, which a number of labor relations experts called a model for U.S. industry. His support had remained strong in spite of criticism both from a minority of Saturn workers and from several UAW officials. Were he to lose the election, Mr. Bennett was concerned that Saturn workers might rapidly return to a more traditional, adversarial relationship with management. A Saturn spokesman said the company would stay out of the election. "We're in strong support of the partnership between Saturn and the UAW, but as for the election, that's a local UAW issue," he commented.

The issues behind this hotly contested election were many and help to shed some light on the dynamics within cooperative labor-management relationships at the plant level. However, the history of Saturn Corporation and its labor-management relationship must be considered to put the local union election in context.

A Brief History of Saturn's Development

Like the other members of the Big Three in the U.S. auto industry, since the late 1970s, General Motors had been losing ground steadily to high-quality small Japanese imports. Although the U.S. auto industry had been working to improve product quality and design, the companies found it virtually impossible to gain market share on the Japanese, who maintained a rapid pace of design and quality improvements.

By 1984, Roger Smith, then chairman of GM, was well into a search for an innovative strategic move. A team of 99 GM managers and UAW officials, chosen from across the United States, was given the mission to study GM divisions and other top-performing, internationally successful corporations to create a new type of organization—one that would build a successful small car. The goal was to produce a vehicle better than Honda's Accord or Toyota's Camry.

The "Group of 99" was insistent that Saturn Corporation be formed as a separate subsidiary so that it would have the freedom not only to create a culture of its own but also to break any and all rules that constrained its parent company. To help GM's finances substantially, Saturn had to slash costs, boost quality, and improve the relationships that traditionally existed among workers, their union, and management.

Although 1985 marked the formal start-up of Saturn, production did not begin until 1990. In the interim, a joint committee of managers and union officials shared equal responsibility for site selection, organizational design, product decisions, and hiring. As part of this process, a "living" agreement (one with no expiration date, that is intended to be modified when needed) was bargained by the union and management. Among other things, it reduced work classifications (therefore increasing the flexibility to deploy workers) and guaranteed job security. Saturn would have one classification for production workers and five for skilled trades. Additionally, everyone would be put on salary, part of which eventually would be determined by productivity and quality level.

By early 1988, as the production and assembly plants were being constructed in Spring Hill, Tennessee, Saturn representatives began visiting GM plants and UAW local halls searching for workers. Under the partnership agreement, all Saturn employees were to be selected from current UAW members drawn from 136 GM locations in 34 states. The Saturn recruiters told current and laid-off workers who were interested to be prepared to shed old habits and to work as a team. All blue- and white-collar applicants had to be approved by a Saturn panel drawn from both union members and management.

For most Saturn managers, the joint recruitment and selection process was the first time UAW local leadership had real input into a "management" process. It was a new experience for most workers, too. Eric Smith came to Saturn from an Oldsmobile plant in Lansing, Michigan. "I like the idea of working with my brains, not just my hands," said the line worker. For Delbert Arkin, Saturn offered a way of escaping restrictive work rules that prevented him from making simple repairs to the machine he ran 40 to 60 hours a week. The decision to go to Saturn was not always easy, however, because employees gave up their former plant seniority when they transferred to the Spring Hill plant.

Saturn's Performance

In June 1990, with start-up costs of roughly $3.5 billion, full production of the Saturn automobile began. Early reports were that customers were delighted with their new cars; however, some quality problems arose, including a worse than average defect rate. Additionally, two recalls occurred. As Saturn moved into a new model year, improvements were made to correct problems, and quality improved markedly. However, production in January 1991 was seriously lagging behind expectations. Saturn delayed the opening of 30 dealerships and made payments to more than 58 established dealerships to compensate them for the lack of cars.

In the 1991 model year, Saturn built just 50,000 cars, one-third the original projection and well below capacity of 240,000. However, in the same year, Saturn sold, on the average, more cars per dealer than any other manufacturer, including Honda, which had been the leader for two years. The 1992 results were similar. A 1992 J.D. Power survey showed that Saturn owners recommended their car to people more often than owners of any other car. The low level of production, however, kept Saturn from breaking even, and the pressure for improved production affected the labor relations in the Saturn facilities.

By the end of 1992, productivity was at 90 percent of capacity. In 1993, Saturn's results reached a new height when total monthly sales for February surpassed those of the Honda Accord. Projections for 1993 showed Saturn reaching break even by midyear. The company announced the hiring of 1,000 new employees for a third shift, a move they hoped would eliminate some of the stress for the work force and improve the production figures.

Although Saturn's recent productivity, sales, and customer satisfaction figures suggest the new venture is moving toward profitability, an August 1993 recall of 352,000 vehicles to fix a wiring system defect could seriously damage Saturn's reputation for quality and customer service. Saturn hopes to avoid potential negative impact on customers' quality perceptions by acting quickly to correct the problem.

The Labor-Management Relationship

Obviously, from its inception, Saturn has been designed and run as a radical experiment. The company is managed under a unique union-management partnership agreement, which gives workers a voice in all planning and operating decisions. UAW Local 1853, frequently in the person of President Michael E. Bennett, participates in all decisions, including pricing, capital expenditures, and dealer operations. "It's as different as it could be," says R. Timothy Epps, vice-president of people systems at Saturn, as he compares the Saturn experience to his years in other organizations. "We're committed to an entirely different set of beliefs. One is to have UAW involvement in all aspects of the business. The other crucial principle is that we believe that those people affected by a decision should be involved in the decision."

Cooperation between organized labor and management is not a new concept, but few firms have pushed it as far as Saturn has. At each managerial level—from the president to team line managers—and within all staff functions, a UAW counterpart shares decision making equally with Saturn managers. The top decision-making group, the Strategic Action Committee (SAC), does long-range planning and makes the policy and product decisions. This committee includes the president of Saturn, Richard "Skip" LeFauve, his union counterpart, Michael Bennett, several vice-presidents, and a representative of the international office of the UAW.

The history of Saturn and the partnership agreement only sound utopian, however. As both management and union officials readily admit, they have found it difficult to eliminate the familiar confrontational approach in favor of a spirit of constructive cooperation. Local President Bennett admits that it took him a long time to develop the trust in management that was necessary to continue to make the system work. Early on, both parties tested the other to see how power sharing would really work.

Bennett gives much of the credit for the partnership's current success to CEO LeFauve. "It takes leadership [from] the CEO and vice-presidents to maintain the integrity of this thing," he says. This does not mean that the union and management never disagree. "There is conflict, but it's managed differently," Bennett says. "It's not adversarial. It's more advocacy in terms of finding a better solution or better options."

One example of the type of conflict that occurs was the October 1991 worker slowdown to protest a decline in quality, at a point when management was critically concerned with lagging production. The workers were concerned that increased production goals would result in a slide in quality that they were working hard to stabilize and improve. As a new version of the contract was negotiated, management conceded that Saturn's slow production start was in large part its own fault. Therefore, when the new contract was settled, the production goal was eased, and the plan to tie pay to productivity was postponed until production had risen to an acceptable level.

At the shop floor level, labor-management relations differ substantially from those found in a traditional auto plant. Because Saturn uses a semiautonomous work team approach, there are no supervisors, and each team has a jointly appointed work team counselor. Above this level, people called *work-unit module advisers* serve as troubleshooters for the teams within each business unit. Although the union continues to play a strong role, it is a decision-making role, not just a reactive, adversarial role activated only when conflict occurs.

Organizational and Union "Growing Pains"

Although Saturn has continued to see a strong demand for its cars, the GM subsidiary has had to struggle to break even, resulting in a situation that has included high amounts of overtime and pressure to cut costs and boost productivity. Currently, most employees are alternating days to nights from one week to the next, while working 50-hour weeks, although this should decrease when the third shift is in place.

The work hours have, in part at least, increased the dissent heard in the plant regarding the local union election. Opposition to Mike Bennett has criticized his being too distant from the workers. Mr. Bennett agrees that he spends less time on the floor than other union leaders, but he suggests that this is due to the large number of issues for which he is responsible. "Part of my problem is visibility," he states.

Other issues that have received coverage during the campaign include whether union representatives should continue to be appointed by Bennett or whether more should be elected by the membership. The rotating work schedules have caused dissatisfaction, and some union members suggest that a more adversarial approach might put an end to this practice. However, Bennett has responded that "you don't have the luxury of fighting all the time while people steal your jobs away overseas.... The days of table-pounding grievance handlers are over," he said in a letter to members. "Union leaders must win arguments as advocates, not adversaries." The question the union election will answer is whether the members at Saturn believe that Bennett is a strong enough advocate for them, as well as for Saturn.

SOURCES:
L. Armstrong, "Here Comes GM's Saturn," *Business Week*, April 9, 1990, 56–62; B. Geber, "Saturn's Grand Experiment," *Training*, June 1992, 27–35; C. M. Solomon, "Behind the Wheel at Saturn," *Personnel Journal*, June 1991, 72–74; N. Templin, "Union Election at GM's Saturn to Test Labor's Partnership with Management," *The Wall Street Journal*, March 24, 1993, A4; O. Suris, "Recall by Saturn Could Tarnish its Reputation," *The Wall Street Journal*, August 11, 1993, A3, A7.

DISCUSSION QUESTIONS

1. Describe the elements of the human resource and labor relations system at Saturn Corporation that provide a competitive advantage.

2. What is the role of a union in an organization such as Saturn Corporation? If in fact decision making is truly shared, is a union needed?

3. What arguments exist against an arrangement such as Saturn's partnership? Is such a system in the best interests of the employees? List arguments for and against a shared partnership arrangement.

4. What skills would managers and union leaders need to develop to successfully make such a cooperative, shared system work? Would these skills be needed on the shop floor, too?

5. Compare Saturn's labor-management relationship with what you know about the relationship at Detroit Diesel Corporation (Part II's Video Case). How are they similar? What different elements are at work?

6. Bennett draws a distinction between the union as "adversary" and the union as "advocate." What is the difference?

GLOSSARY

Acceptability   The extent to which a performance measure is deemed to be satisfactory or adequate by those who use it.

Action steps   The part of a written affirmative plan that specifies what an employer plans to do to reduce underutilization of protected groups.

Agency shop   A union security provision that requires an employee to pay union membership dues but not to join the union.

Agent   In agency theory, a manager, or one who acts on behalf of an owner (principal); in human resources management, may refer to an employee.

Arbitration   A procedure for resolving collective-bargaining impasses by which an arbitrator chooses a solution to the dispute.

Assessment center   A process in which multiple raters evaluate employees' performance on a number of exercises.

Assessment   Collecting information and providing feedback to employees about their behavior, communication style, or skills.

Assignment flow   The criteria used to make promotion and assignment decisions.

Associate union membership   A form of union membership by which the union receives dues in exchange for services (e.g., health insurance, credit cards) but does not provide representation in collective bargaining.

Attitudinal structuring   The aspect of the labor-management negotiation process that refers to the relationship and level of trust between the negotiators.

Basic skills   Reading, writing, and communication skills needed to understand the content of a training program.

Behavior-based conflict   A type of work-family conflict that occurs when employees' behavior in work roles is not appropriate for their behavior in family roles.

Benchmarking   The process of finding examples of excellent products, services, or systems.

Bona fide occupational qualification (BFOQ)   A job qualification based on race, sex, religion, and so on that an employer asserts is a necessary qualification for the job.

Career   The pattern of work-related experiences that span the course of a person's life.

Career development   The process by which employees progress through a series of stages, each characterized by a different set of developmental tasks, activities, and relationships.

Career path   A sequence of job positions involving similar types of work and skills that employees move through in a company.

Career planning   A process by which employees become aware of interests, values, strengths, and weaknesses; obtain information about job opportunities within their company; identify career goals; and establish action plans to achieve career goals.

Checkoff   A union contract provision that requires an employer to deduct union dues from employees' paychecks.

Closed shop   A union security provision requiring a person to be a union member before being hired.

Compa-ratio   An index of the correspondence between actual and intended pay.

Compensable factors   The characteristics of jobs that an organization values and chooses to pay for.

Competitive advantage   A company's ability to make products or offer services that are valued by customers more than those of competing firms.

Competitiveness   A company's ability to maintain and gain market share in its industry.

Compressed workweek   A 40-hour workweek composed of four 10-hour days.

Concurrent validation   A criterion-related validity study in which a test is administered to all the people currently in a job and then comparing how the incumbents' scores correlate with measures of their performance on the job.

Consolidated Omnibus Budget Reconciliation Act (COBRA)   The 1985 act that requires employers to permit employees to extend their health insurance coverage at group rates for up to 36 months following a qualifying event, such as layoff.

Content validation   A test-validation strategy performed by demonstrating that the items, questions, or problems posed by a test are a representative sample of the kinds of situations or problems that occur on the job.

Continuous learning   The requirement that employees understand the relationships between their jobs, their work units, and the company.

Corporate campaigns   Union activities designed to exert public, financial, or political pressure on employers during the union-organizing process.

Correlation coefficient   A statistic that measures the degree to which two sets of numbers are related to each other.

Cost-benefit analysis   The process of determining the economic benefits of a training program using accounting methods.

Court-ordered affirmative action   Affirmative action plans mandated by the courts as part of the settlement of discrimination complaints.

Criterion-related validity   A method of establishing the validity of a personnel selection method by showing a substantial correlation between test scores and job-performance scores.

Cross-cultural preparation   The process of educating employees and their families who are given an assignment in a foreign country.

Data field   In human resource information systems (HRISs), an element or type of information in an employee record, such as employee name, Social Security number, or job classification.

Data-entry relationship diagrams   A technique used in the analysis stage of the development of a human resource information system that shows the type of data used in a business function and the relationship among data.

Data-flow diagram   A technique used in the analysis stage of the development of a human resource information system to show the flow of data among departments.

Database   The set of topics on which a human resource information system collects and maintains information.

Decertification   The process by which employees vote no longer to be represented by their union.

Delayering   Reducing the number of job levels within an organization.

Delphi technique   A forecasting technique in which individuals respond to questions in writing, the responses are gathered by a group leader and distributed to members of the group, then the group members respond again to the original questions; the procedure continues until a consensus is formed.

Development   The acquisition of knowledge, skills, and behaviors that improve an employee's ability to meet changes in job requirements and in client and customer demands.

Direct applicants   People who apply for a job vacancy without prompting from the organization.

Directional pattern model   A career development model in which employees make decisions about how quickly they want to progress through career stages and at what point they want to return to an earlier career stage.

Disparate impact   A theory of discrimination based on facially neutral employment practices that disproportionately exclude a protected group from employment opportunities.

Disparate treatment   A theory of discrimination based on different treatment given to individuals because of their race, color, religion, sex, national origin, age, or disability status.

Distributive bargaining   The part of the labor-management negotiation process that focuses on dividing a fixed economic "pie."

Downward move   A job change involving a reduction in an employee's level of responsibility and authority.

Dual career-path system   A career-path system that enables employees to remain in technical or scientific careers but earn salaries and have advancement opportunities comparable to those in management careers.

Due process   Policies by which a company formally lays out the steps an employee can take to appeal a termination decision.

Duty of fair representation   The National Labor Relations Act requirement that all bargaining-unit members have equal access to and representation by the union in contract negotiation and administration (e.g., grievance procedures).

E-mail   A computer networking tool that allows computer users to send messages and files directly to one another and to communicate electronically with customers.

Efficiency wage theory   A wage paid that influences the productivity of a worker.

Employee assistance programs (EAPs)   Employer programs that attempt to ameliorate problems encountered by workers who are drug dependent, alcoholic, or psychologically troubled.

Employee Retirement Income Security Act of 1974 (ERISA)   The act that increased the fiduciary responsibilities of pension plan trustees, established vesting rights and portability provisions, and established the Pension Benefit Guaranty Corporation (PBGC).

Employee stock ownership plan (ESOP)   An employee ownership plan that provides employers certain tax and financial advantages when stock is granted to employees.

Employee wellness programs   Preventive programs that attempt to promote good health among employees who are not necessarily having current health problems.

Employment-at-will doctrine   The doctrine that, in the absence of a specific contract, either an employer or employee could sever an employment relationship at any time.

Empowerment   Giving employees responsibility and authority to make decisions regarding all aspects of product development or customer service.

Equal employment opportunity   The government's attempt to ensure that all individuals have an equal opportunity for employment, regardless of race, color, religion, sex, or national origin.

Ergonomics   The interface between individuals' physiological characteristics and the physical work environment.

Exercising of authority   One of Harrison's cultural factors; it stifles risk taking, innovation, and entrepreneurship by penalizing initiative.

Expectancy   The perceived probability that a person can obtain a given job.

Expectancy theory   The theory that says that the attractiveness of any job is a function of valence, instrumentality, and expectancy.

Experience rating   A rating that determines the size of an employer's unemployment and workers' compensation taxes, based on that employer's history of laying off employees and its injury rates.

External analysis   Examining the organization's operating environment to identify strategic opportunities and threats.

Fact finder   A person who reports on the reasons for a labor-management dispute, the views and arguments of both sides, and a nonbinding recommendation for settling the dispute.

Fair Labor Standards Act (FLSA)   The 1938 law that established the minimum wage and overtime pay.

Family and Medical Leave Act   The 1993 act that requires employers with 50 or more employees to provide up to 12 weeks of unpaid leave after childbirth or adoption; to care for a seriously ill child, spouse, or parent; or for an employee's own serious illness.

Financial Accounting Statement (FAS) 106   The rule issued by the Financial Accounting Standards Board in 1993 requiring companies to fund benefits provided after retirement on an accrual rather than a pay-as-you-go basis

and to enter these future cost obligations on their financial statements.

Flextime   A nontraditional work schedule that allows an employee to work flexible hours around a required core time.

Forecasting   The attempts to determine the supply of and demand for various types of human resources to predict areas within the organization where there will be future labor shortages or surpluses.

Formal education programs   Employee development programs, including short courses offered by consultants or universities, executive MBA programs, and university programs.

Four-fifths rule   A rule that states that an employment test has disparate impact if the hiring rate for a minority group is less than four-fifths, or 80 percent, of the hiring rate for the majority group.

Gainsharing   A form of group compensation based on group or plant performance (rather than organizationwide profits) that does not become part of the employee's base salary.

General duty clause   The provision of the Occupational Health and Safety Act that states that an employer has an overall obligation to furnish employees with a place of employment free from recognized hazards.

Generalizability   The degree to which the validity of a selection method established in one context extends to other contexts.

Goals   What an organization hopes to achieve in the medium- to long-term future.

Goals and timetables   The part of a written affirmative action plan that specifies the percentage of women and minorities that an employer seeks to have in each job group and the date by which that percentage is to be attained.

Group-building techniques   Techniques that help trainees share ideas and experiences, build group identity, understand the dynamics of interpersonal relationships, and get to know their own strengths and weaknesses and those of their coworkers.

Hands-on techniques   Training methods that provide direct experience; for example, on-the-job training, simulations, business games and case studies, behavior modeling, and interactive video.

Hardware   All equipment used in a computer system.

Hawthorne Studies   Studies conducted at a Western Electric plant in 1927 suggesting that increases in employee productivity can be realized if employees are treated in a positive manner.

Health maintenance organization (HMO)   A health-care plan that provides benefits on a prepaid basis for employees who are required to use only HMO medical service providers.

High-leverage training   Training practice that links training to strategic business goals, has top management support, relies on an instructional design model, and is benchmarked to programs in other organizations.

Host country   The country in which the parent-country organization seeks to locate or has already located a facility.

Host-country nationals (HCNs)   Employees born and raised in a host country.

Human resource information systems (HRISs)   The software programs and computers that deal with the entry, maintenance, updating, and use of human resource information.

Image advertising   Advertising organizations use to promote themselves as a good place to work.

Individualism/collectivism   One of Hofstede's cultural dimensions; describes the strength of the relation between an individual and other individuals in a society.

Instructional design process   A systematic approach for developing training programs.

Instrumentality   The perceived relationship between choosing a particular job and obtaining a desired outcome.

Integrated payroll system   A payroll system whose information is shared with other databases.

Integrative bargaining   The part of the labor-management negotiation process that seeks solutions beneficial to both sides.

Internal analysis   The process of examining an organization's strengths and weaknesses.

Intraorganizational bargaining   The part of the labor-management negotiation process that focuses on the conflicting objectives of factions within labor and management.

ISO 9000   A series of quality assurance standards developed by the International Organization for Standardization in Switzerland, ISO 9000 certification is becoming a requirement for doing business in the European Community, Austria, Finland, Iceland, Liechtenstein, Norway, Sweden, Switzerland, Australia, Japan, South America, and Africa.

Job analysis   The process of getting detailed information about jobs.

Job description   A list of the tasks, duties, and responsibilities that a job entails.

Job design   The process of defining the way work will be performed and the tasks that will be required in a given job.

Job enrichment   Ways to add complexity and meaningfulness to a person's work.

Job evaluation   An administrative procedure used to measure job worth.

Job fair   A place where employers gather, often at a university, for a short time to meet large numbers of potential job applicants.

Job involvement   The degree to which people identify themselves with their jobs.

Job posting   Programs companies adopt to promote from within, such as publicizing vacancies on bulletin boards, in company newsletters, or in memos.

Job redesign   Changing the tasks or the way work is performed in an existing job.

Job rotation   1. A process of systematically moving a single individual from one job to another over the course of time. 2. Providing employees with a series of job assignments in various functional areas of the company or movement among jobs in a single functional area or department.

Job satisfaction   A pleasurable feeling that results from the perception that one's job fulfills or allows for the fulfillment of one's important job values.

Job specification   A list of the knowledge, skills, abilities, and other characteristics that an individual must have to perform a job.

Job structure   The relative pay of jobs in an organization.

Job withdrawal   A set of behaviors that dissatisfied individuals enact to avoid the work situation.

Joint union-management programs   Programs funded by both employers and unions designed to help employees prepare for workplace changes resulting from new technology and restructuring.

Key jobs   Benchmark jobs, used in pay surveys, that have relatively stable content and are common to many organizations.

Landrum-Griffin Act   The 1959 act that regulated unions' actions and their internal affairs (e.g., financial disclosure and conduct of elections).

Leading indicator   An objective measure that accurately predicts future labor demand.

Learning organization An organization whose employees are continuously attempting to learn new things and apply what they learn to improve product or service quality.

Life-cycle model A career development model in which employees face certain developmental tasks over the course of their careers—that they move through distinct life or career stages.

Local area network A network that is confined to one physical location.

Long-term–short-term orientation One of Hofstede's cultural dimensions; describes how a culture balances immediate benefits with future rewards.

Mainframe computer A computer with large storage capacity that can quickly perform mathematical calculations. These computers can simultaneously serve a large number of users. Access to these computers is through terminals.

Maintenance of membership Union rules requiring members to remain members for a certain period of time (e.g., the length of the union contract).

Malcolm Baldrige National Quality Award An award established in 1987 to promote quality awareness, to recognize quality achievements of U.S. companies, and to publicize successful quality strategies.

Managing diversity The process of creating an environment that allows all employees to contribute to organizational goals and experience personal growth.

Marginal tax rate The percentage of an additional dollar of earnings that goes to taxes.

Masculinity-femininity One of Hofstede's cultural dimensions; describes the division of roles between the sexes within a society.

Math coprocessor A microprocessor that allows a personal computer to perform high-speed calculations.

Mediation A procedure for resolving collective-bargaining impasses by which a mediator with no formal authority acts as a facilitator and go-between in the negotiations.

Mentor An experienced, productive senior employee who helps develop a less-experienced employee.

Merit increase grid A grid that combines an employee's performance rating with that employee's position in a pay range to determine the size and frequency of his or her pay increases.

Minimum wage The lowest amount that employers are legally allowed to pay; the 1990 amendment of the Fair Labor Standards Act permits a subminimum wage to workers under the age of 20 for a period of up to 90 days.

Mission A statement of an organization's reason for being by specifying the customers served, the needs satisfied, and the technology used.

Motivation to learn The desire of the trainee to learn the content of a training program.

Multiple correlation A quantitative measure of the relationship between two or more variables that have been turned into a single variable and a third, single variable.

Myers-Briggs Type Indicator (MBTI) The MBTI is a psychological test used for team building and leadership development which identifies employees' preferences for energy, information gathering, decision making, and life-style.

Nominal group technique A forecasting technique in which people working independently generate ideas that are then evaluated by the entire group.

Noncompensatory decision process A job applicant's decision process in which one vacancy characteristic is so important to the applicant that any vacancy that fails to meet the applicant's standard on that characteristic will not be considered.

Nonkey jobs Jobs that are unique to organizations and that cannot be directly valued or compared through the use of market surveys.

Obsolescence A reduction in an employee's competence resulting from a lack of knowledge of new work processes, techniques, and technologies that have developed since the employee completed his or her education.

Occupational Safety and Health Act of 1970 (OSHA) The law that authorizes the federal government to establish and enforce occupational safety and health standards for all places of employment affecting interstate commerce.

Organization-based model A career development model in which careers proceed through a series of stages and that career development involves employees' learning to perform certain activities.

Organizational analysis A process for determining the appropriateness of training.

Organizational commitment The degree to which an employee identifies with the organization and is willing to put forth effort on its behalf.

Organizational socialization The process by which new employees are transformed into effective members of a company.

Orientation Familiarizing new employees with company rules, policies, and procedures.

Parallel testing The use of both old and new human resource information systems simultaneously to compare their accuracy and usefulness.

Parent country The country in which a company's corporate headquarters is located.

Parent-country nationals (PCNs) Employees who were born and live in a parent country.

Pattern or practice A theory of discrimination that allows plaintiffs to show that an employer intended to discriminate by showing a statistical disparity between the work force and a relevant comparison group and that the disparity is the result of some discriminatory motive.

Pay grade Jobs of similar worth or content grouped together for pay administration purposes.

Pay level The average pay, including wages, salaries, and bonuses, of jobs in an organization.

Pay policy line A mathematical expression that describes the relationship between a job's pay and its job evaluation points.

Pay structure The relative pay of different jobs (job structure) and how much they are paid (pay level).

Pension Benefit Guaranty Corporation (PBGC) The agency that guarantees to pay employees a basic retirement benefit in the event that financial difficulties force a company to terminate or reduce employee pension benefits.

Performance appraisal The process through which an organization gets information on how well an employee is doing his or her job.

Performance feedback The process of providing employees with information regarding their performance effectiveness.

Performance management The means through which managers ensure that employees' activities and outputs are congruent with the organization's goals.

Performance planning and evaluation (PPE) Any system that seeks to tie the formal performance appraisal process to the company's strategies by specifying at the beginning of the evaluation period the types and level of performance that must be accomplished in order to achieve the strategy.

Peripheral An input, output, or secondary storage device such as a printer or scanner that is external to a computer itself.

Person analysis A process for determining whether employees need training, who needs training, and whether employees are ready for training.

Personnel selection The process by which companies decide who will or will not be allowed into their organization.

Plateauing A career development stage in which the likelihood is low that the employee will receive future job assignments with increased responsibility.

Policy capturing A technique by which one determines the importance of various factors in the decision process by determining the relationship between certain attribute levels and actual choices.

Power distance One of Hofstede's cultural dimensions; concerns how a culture deals with hierarchical power relationships and the unequal distribution of power.

Predictive validation A criterion-related validity study that seeks to establish an empirical relationship between applicants' test scores and their eventual performance on the job.

Preferred provider organization (PPO) A group of health-care providers who contract with employers, insurance companies, and so forth to provide health care at a reduced fee.

Pregnancy Discrimination Act of 1978 The law that requires employers that offer disability plans to treat pregnancy as they would any other disability.

Preretirement socialization The process of helping employees prepare for exit from work.

Principal In agency theory, the owner of a business; in human resource management, may refer to a manager.

Profit sharing A group compensation plan in which payments are based on a measure of organization performance (profits) and do not become part of the employees' base salary.

Promotion Advances into positions with greater challenge, more responsibility, and more authority than the employee's previous job.

Psychological contract The expectations that employers and employees have about each other.

Radius of trust One of Harrison's cultural factors; refers to the identification that individuals feel with others in society.

Range spread The distance between the minimum and maximum amounts in a pay grade.

Recruitment The process of seeking applicants for potential employment.

Referrals People who are prompted to apply for a job by someone within the organization.

Relational database A database structure that stores information in separate files that can be linked by common elements.

Reliability   The consistency of a performance measure; the degree to which a performance measure is free from random error.

Retirement   Leaving a job and work role and making a transition into life without work.

Right-to-work laws   State laws that make union shops, maintenance of membership, and agency shops illegal.

Rigor of the ethical system   One of Harrison's cultural factors; refers to the degree of social justice in a culture.

Role analysis technique   A method that enables a role occupant and other members of the role occupant's role set to specify and examine their expectations for the role occupant.

Role behaviors   Behaviors that are required of an individual in his or her role as a job holder in a social work environment.

Safety awareness programs   Employer programs that attempt to instill symbolic and substantive changes in the organization's emphasis on safety.

Scenario analysis   A technique used in the analysis stage of the development of a human resource information system, in which end-users are asked to indicate how an information system could help them deal with business situations that are presented to them.

Scientific Management   A human resource management theory developed in 1911 that emphasized identifying employees who had the appropriate skills and abilities to perform certain tasks, providing wage incentives to employees for increased productivity, providing employees with rest breaks, and carefully studying jobs to identify the best method for performing a job.

Section 401(k) plan   A retirement plan named after the tax code provision that allows employees to defer compensation on a pretax basis.

Selection   The process by which an organization attempts to identify applicants with the necessary knowledge, skills, abilities, and other characteristics that will help it achieve its goals.

Self-directed learning   A program in which employees take responsibility for all aspects of learning.

Self-efficacy   The employees' belief that they can successfully learn the content of a training program.

Service bureau   A company that provides payroll services to other organizations.

Situational constraints   Factors in the work environment that affect a trainee's motivation to learn.

Skill-based pay   Pay based on the skills employees acquire and are capable of using.

Social support   1. The degree to which a person is surrounded by other people who are sympathetic and caring. 2. The willingness of managers and peers to provide a trainee with feedback and reinforcement.

Specificity   The extent to which a performance measure gives detailed guidance to employees about what is expected of them and how they can meet these expectations.

Standard deviation rule   A rule used to analyze employment tests to determine disparate impact; it uses the difference between the expected representation for minority groups and the actual representation to determine whether the difference between the two is greater than would occur by chance.

Standard error of the measure   The average unsigned error of measurement in a series of measurements of the same element.

Stock option   An employee ownership plan that gives employees the opportunity to buy the company's stock at a previously fixed price.

Strain-based conflict   A type of work-family conflict that results from the stress of work and family roles.

Strategic choice   The organization's strategy; the ways an organization will attempt to fulfill its mission and achieve its long-term goals.

Strategic congruence   The extent to which the performance management system elicits job performance that is consistent with the organization's strategy, goals, and culture.

Strategic human resource management   A pattern of planned human resource deployments and activities intended to enable an organization to achieve its goals.

Strategy formulation   The process of deciding on a strategic direction by defining a company's mission and goals, its external opportunities and threats, and its internal strengths and weaknesses.

Strategy implementation   The process of devising structures and allocating resources to enact the strategy a company has chosen.

Succession planning   The identification and tracking of high-potential employees capable of filling higher-level managerial positions.

Summary plan description   A reporting requirement of the Employee Retirement Income Security Act (ERISA) that obligates employers to describe the plan's funding, eligibility requirements, risks, and so forth, within 90 days after an employee has entered the plan.

Supply flow   The places where a company prefers to obtain the human resources to fill open positions.

Taft-Hartley Act   The 1947 act that outlined unfair union labor practices.

Task analysis   The process of identifying the tasks, knowledge, skill, and behaviors that need to be emphasized in training.

Theory Y management   A management philosophy that suggested that employees will contribute to company goals if they are given the opportunity to participate in decisions concerning their job and to take responsibility for their work.

Third country   A country other than a host or parent country.

Third-country nationals (TCNs)   Employees born in a country other than a parent or host country.

Time-based conflict   A type of work-family conflict that occurs when the demands of work and family interfere with each other.

Total quality management   A cooperative form of doing business that relies on the talents and capabilities of both labor and management to continually improve quality and productivity.

Training   A planned effort to facilitate the learning of job-related knowledge, skills, and behavior by employees.

Training objectives   Statement of what the employee is expected to do, the quality or level of performance, and conditions under which the trainee is expected to perform.

Training outcomes   A way to evaluate the effectiveness of a training program based on trainee reactions, learning, behavior, and results.

Transfer   The movement of an employee to a different job assignment in a different area of the company.

Transfer of training   The use of knowledge, skills, and behaviors learned in training on the job.

Transitional matrix   A statistical procedure that shows the proportion (or number) of employees in different job categories at different times.

Transnational process   The extent to which a company's planning and decision-making processes include representatives and ideas from a variety of cultures.

Transnational representation   Reflects the multinational composition of a company's managers.

Transnational scope   A company's ability to make HR decisions from an international perspective.

Uncertainty avoidance   One of Hofstede's cultural dimensions; describes how cultures seek to deal with an unpredictable future.

Union shop   A union security provision that requires a person to join the union within a certain amount of time after being hired.

Utility   The degree to which the information provided by selection methods enhances the effectiveness of selecting personnel in real organizations.

Utilization analysis   The part of a written affirmative action plan that compares the race, sex, and ethnic composition of an employer's work force with that of the available labor supply.

Valence   The level of satisfaction a job applicant expects to receive from a job that ranks high in some attribute.

Validity   The extent to which a performance measure assesses all the relevant—and only the relevant—aspects of job performance.

Vesting right   The right an employee gains after meeting minimum years of service requirements to receive his or her pension at retirement age, regardless of whether that employee remains with the employer until that time.

Virus   A destructive, unauthorized code that someone has intentionally built into a piece of hardware or software.

Vocational maturity   Factors such as knowledge about themselves, various occupations, and industries or companies that make some individuals more effective in making job choices than others.

Work, innovation, saving, and profit   One of Harrison's cultural factors; it values rationality, education, and an orientation toward the future.

Work-flow design   The process of analyzing the tasks necessary for the production of a product or service and allocating these tasks to particular work units or individuals.

Work-force dynamics analysis   An analysis of employee movement (e.g., promotion, demotion, transfer, and turnover) over time.

Work-force utilization review   A comparison of the proportion of workers in protected subgroups with the proportion that each subgroup represents in the relevant labor market.

Yield ratios   The percentage of applicants who successfully move from one stage of the recruitment and selection process to the next.

NAME AND COMPANY INDEX

A

Abbott Labs, 597
Abernathy, J., 118n
Abowd, J. M., 712n
Abraham, K. G., 612n
Abraham, L. M., 306n
Adams, J. S., 304n, 576n
Adams, L. E., 726n
Addison, J. T., 712n
ADDS (AT&T), 568
Adkins, C. L., 305n
Adler, J., 158n
Adler, N., 97, 108n, 113n
Adler, P. S., 577n
Advanced Micro Devices, 349
Aetna Institute for Corporate
    Education, 316
Aetna Life and Casualty
    Corporation, 316
A.G. Edwards, 349
Agvet, 439
Akerlof, G. A., 576n
Alagasco (Alabama Gas), 349
Alcan Aluminum Ltd., 102
Alcoa, 593
Alco Standard Corporation, 290
Aldag, R. J., 371n
Alderson, M. J., 654n
Alexander, R. A., 76n, 406n
Allaire, Paul, 299
Allen, Robert E., 54
Allied Signal, 60
Allstate, 144–145
Aluminum Co. of America, 603
Amalgamated Clothing and Textile
    Workers Union (ACTWU), 689
American Airlines, 187, 294–295, 331,
    738
American Association of Retired
    Persons, 534n
American Business Collaboration for
    Quality Dependent Care, 181
American Cast Iron Pipe (ACIPCO),
    349
American Federation of Labor and
    Congress of Industrial
    Organizations (AFL-CIO),
    673–676, 679
American Federation of State,
    County, and Municipal
    Employees (AFSCME), 708

American Management Association,
    613n, 614n
American Medical Systems, 471
American Motors, 679
American Postal Workers Union,
    293
American Society for Training and
    Development, 18, 426
American Tourister, 568
American West Airlines, 181
Amoco Corporation, 50, 54, 597
Anders, G., 615n
Andersen Consulting, 418, 536–539
Anderson, C. D., 407n
Anderson, D. C., 252n, 275n
Anderson, J., 337n
Anheuser-Busch, 349
Anthony, P., 746n
Apogee Enterprises, 349
Appenzeller, Timothy, 117
Apple Computer, 29, 62, 596
Arai, J., 291n
ARCO Oil & Gas Corporation, 253,
    408
Armstrong, L., 752n
Armstrong World Industries, 349
Arnold, H. J., 372n
Arthur, J. B., 711n
Arthur, M. B., 531n
Arthur Andersen, 536–539
Arthur Andersen Worldwide
    Organization, 536–539
Arvey, R. D., 306n, 406n, 457n, 533n
Ash, R. A., 230n, 498n, 579n, 612n,
    656n
Ashenfelter, O., 578n
Ashland Oil, 603
Ashworth, S. D., 373n
AST, 61, 78
AT&T, 54, 181, 593, 597, 652, 707,
    736
Atchison, T. J., 39n
Atkinson, W., 165n
Atlantic Richfield, 597
Automatic Data Processing, 178
Avis, 349
Avon Products Incorporated, 23
Axel Johnson AB, 363
Axline, L., 276n
Ayers, K., Jr., 498n
Azarnoff, R. S., 534n

B

B&Q plc, 529
Bachman, Jim, 308, 311
Bahr, Morton, 707
Bailey, B., 36n
Baker, Alisa, 596, 596n, 614n
Baker Hughes, Inc., 174, 643n
Bakke, David, 123
Baldwin, T. T., 455n, 456n, 457n
Balkin, D. B., 76n, 608n, 614n
Balzar, W. K., 283n
Banc One Wisconsin Corporation,
    333
Bandura, A., 456n
Bank of America, 80
Banres, J., 598n
Baptist Hospital of Miami, 349
Baptist Memorial Hospital
    (Memphis), 462
Barbash, J., 699, 710n
Barber, A. E., 185n, 373n, 497n, 656n
Barber, P. E., 533n
Bardwick, K. D., 457n
Bargerstock, A., 365n
Barnes, F. C., 413n
Barnes-Farrel, J., 275n
Barney, J., 75n, 229n
Baron, J. N., 578n
Barrett, A., 340n
Barrett, G. V., 277n, 406n
Barrett, P. M., 153n, 406n
Barrick, M. R., 407n
Bartholomew, S., 113n
Baruch, D. W., 304n
Bates, Dorothy, 151
Batimo, J., 339n
Batten, T., 77n
Baumgartel, H., 455n
Bay, Rick, 234
BE&K, 349
Beach, D. E., 2n
Beal, E. F., 712n
Beam, Burton T., Jr., 637n, 640n, 654n
Bechtel, 60
Becker, Larry, 363
Becker, T., 276n
Beckwith Machinery, 724
Becton Dickinson, 29
Beehr, T. A., 534n
Beer, M., 275n
Begin, J. P., 712n

Behar, R., 376n, 404n
Bell, N. E., 306n
Beller, M. A., 578n
Bellsouth, 597
Ben & Jerry's Homemade Ice Cream, 349, 571
Bennett, Michael E., 748, 750–752
Bennett, N., 230n
Bentson, C., 496n
Berg, M., 495n
Berger, C. J., 231n, 406n, 577n
Berger, M. C., 656n
Bergman, T. J., 373n
Bernardin, J., 276n, 277n
Berner, J. G., 406n, 407n
Bernstein, A., 317n, 597n, 711n
Berry, J. K., 495n
Beth Israel Hospital Boston, 349
Bethlehem Steel, 629
Beutell, N. J., 533n, 745n
Bielby, W. T., 578n
Biggins, P., 656n
Birmingham Steel, 327
Bjork, R. A., 496n
Black, D. A., 656n
Black, J. S., 114n, 498n
Blair, G., 107n
Blake, S., 23n, 38n
Blanchflower, D. G., 712n
Blanz, F., 275n
Blau, F. D., 578n
Blinder, A. S., 614n
Blitzer, R. S., 531n
Bloc, L., 174n
Bloch, J. W., 672n
Block, C. J., 498n
Blumberg, M., 577n
BMW, 102, 327, 362–363, 567
Boeing Company, 603, 712n
Bohlander, G. W., 579n
Bolt, J. F., 466n, 495n, 534n
Booz, Allen, and Hamilton, 254
Borman, W., 277n
Bosco, James, 178
Bossidy, Lawrence, 60
Bouchard, T. J., 306n
Boudreau, J. W., 373n, 406n, 458n, 554n, 555n, 577n, 720n, 745n
Bowen, D. E., 230, 276n
Boyd, David, 155
Boyd, M., 462n
Brady, R. L., 373n
Brandt, E., 37n
Brantner, T. M., 532n
Brass, D. J., 579n
Bray, D. W., 496n
Breaugh, J. A., 365n, 372n

Brence, J., 275n
Brenlin Group, 434
Brennan, Edward A., 581
Brennan, J. J., 746n
Brett, J. F., 373n
Brett, J. M., 497n, 498n
Bretz, R. D., 369n, 374n, 577n, 611n, 612n, 656n
Brief, A. P., 407n
Briggs, S., 372n
Briscoe, A., 745n
Bristol-Meyers, 603
British Petroleum Exploration (BPX), 512, 520
Brocka, B., 10n, 230n
Brocka, M. S., 230n
Brocka, M. Z., 10n
Brockner, J., 534n
Broderick, R., 720n, 745n
Brookhouse, K. J., 372n
Brookler, R., 745n
Broscheit, K., 184n
Brown, B., 230n
Brown, G., 534n
Brown, Jim, 308–311
Brownstein, V., 534n
Bruce, Earl, 233–234
Brush, V. J., 736n
Bryan, L., 184n
Budget Rent-a-Car, 658–660
Buker, Edwin, 363
Buller, P. F., 267n, 457n
Bundy, Sandra, 145–146
Burck, C., 69n
Burda, D., 333n
Bureau of Business Practices, 12n, 13n, 37
Bureau of National Affairs, 434n, 458n, 500n, 533n, 544n, 613n
Burger King, 163–164
Burke, J. W., 37n
Burns International Security Services, 376
Burris, L. R., 407n
Burton, Arthur, 146
Burton, J. F., 712n
Bush, George, 122, 391
Bussey, J., 372n
Butler, M. C., 112n
Byham, W. C., 275n, 496n
Bylinsky, G., 746n

C
C&S Wholesale Grocers, Inc., 606
Cain, G. G., 578n
Caldwell, Phillip, 68, 705
California Edison, 174

Callahan, C., 407n
Callahan, T. J., 613n, 614n
Calonius, E., 77n
Cameron, K., 231n
Camp, J. D., 407n
Campbell, J. P., 407n
Campbell, Marsh, 702
Campbell, R. J., 495n, 496n
Campbell Soup Company, 168
Campion, M., 230n, 231n
Cannings, K., 579n
Cannon-Bowers, J. A., 455n
Capdevielle, P., 614n
Capelli, Peter, 561, 577n, 710n
Carey, D. J., 661n
Carlson, L. A., 578n
Carmel, E., 746n
Carnegie Melon University, 507
Carnevale, A. P., 20n, 37n, 427n, 454n, 455n, 456n, 457n
Caroselli, M., 276n
Carr, C., 495n
Carrier Corporation, 140, 204, 389
Carroll, S., 276n
Carsten, J. M., 304n
Carter, C., 259–263n, 276n
Carter, W. H., 710n
Cascio, W. F., 39n, 230n, 373n, 407n, 534n, 544n
Case, J., 374n
Castelli, J., 191n
Castro, J., 305n
Caterpillar, 593
Caudron, S., 37n, 174n
Cavanaugh, G. F., 38n
Cavanaugh, J. C., 534n
CBS Inc., 390
Cederblom, D., 277n
Center for Creative Leadership, 477
Center for Public Resources, 38n
Century Telephone, 597
Ceriello, V. R., 496n, 730n, 734n, 745n, 746n
Chaison, G. N., 710n
Chakins, B. J., 532n
Chalykoff, J., 710n
Champion International, 174
Chang, C., 678n, 707n, 712n
Chao, G. T., 154n, 407n, 498n
Chaparral Steel, 1, 2, 349
Charam, R., 495n
Chase Manhattan Bank, 80, 286
Chelius, J., 612n
Cheng, A. F., 457n
Chevron, 31, 597, 731
Chicago Pneumatic Tool, 568
Choate, P., 38n

Cholish, Dan, 299
Christal, R., 230n, 231n
Chrysler Motors Corporation, 54, 61, 548, 629, 679
Chuang, John, 374
Church, Brian, 376
Cie de Saint-Gobain, 103, 327
Citicorp, 80
Clark, L. A., 306n
Clarke, M., 252n, 275n
Clausen, J. A., 306n
Clegg, C. W., 577n
Cleveland, J., 230n, 268n, 274n
Clinton, Bill, 122, 130, 181
Coates, E. M., III, 613n
Coca-Cola U.S.A., 510
Cohan, J., 746n
Cohen, Ben, 571
Cohen, D. J., 456n
Cohen, J., 405n
Cohen, S., 231n
Coleman, B. J., 655n
Coleman-Carlone, M., 746n
Collins, D., 185n, 614n
Collins, R., 275n
Colusi, M. L., 535n
Commerce Clearinghouse, 16, 38n, 274n, 457n
Commission of the European Communities, 93n
Commons, John R., 669, 709n
Commonwealth Fund, 529n
Communication Workers of America, 707
Compaq Computer Corporation, 62, 67, 77, 78, 349, 543
Comrie, S. M., 534n
Conference Board, The, 600n
Conley, P., 231n
Conlon, E. J., 611n
Conrad, M. A., 373n
Conrad, P., 113n
Constans, J., 275n
Conte, M. A., 613n
Contel Corporation, 459–460
Continental Airlines Holdings, 657
Continental Insurance, 499
Control Data Corporation, 174, 177
Cooke, W. N., 710n
Cooper, C., 305n
Cooper, D. M., 373n
Cooper, M., 185n
Cooper Tire & Rubber, 349
Copeland, J. B., 184n, 407n
Copeland, L., 114n
Copeland Griggs Productions, 489

Corbett, J. M., 577n
Cornelius, E., 230n
Corning Glass, 60, 349, 441, 515–516
Corona, R., 278n
Cote, L. S., 458n
Cotton, J. L., 498n
Cowan, A. L., 614n
Cox, T. H., 23n, 38n
Coyle, B. W., 373n, 534n
Cragun, J. R., 457n
Crampton, S. M., 166n, 184n, 407n, 654n
Crandall, Robert, 331
Cray Research, 62, 349
Crites, John O., 355, 356n, 372n
Cron, W. L., 532n, 533n
Cronshaw, S., 76n
Crosby, Philip, 9, 10
Crowell, C., 252n, 275n
Cryer, J. D., 276n
Crystal, Graef, 603n
Cummings, T. G., 577n, 709n
Cummins Engine, 349, 408
Cuneo, A., 406n
Curington, W., 578n
Currall, S. C., 712n
Cutcher-Gershenfeld, J., 614n, 701n, 711n
Cyborg Systems Inc., 742n, 746n

D
Daft, R. L., 36n
Dailey, L. M., 654n
Dainoff, M. J., 158n
Dalton, G., 531n
D'Amico, Joseph, 705
Daniel Industries, 91–92
Danner, Raymond, 155
Davis, Mitch, 606
Davis, T. R. V., 746n
Davis-Blake, A., 577n
Dawis, R. V., 348n, 372n
Dayal, I., 307n
Days Inn of America, 529
Dayton Hudson, 349
Dean, J. W., 39n, 75n, 76n, 113n, 339n
DeCenzo, D. A., 655n
Decker, P. J., 456n
Deere, 349
Delahaye, B. L., 456n
Delaney, J. T., 339n
Delco Electronics, 535
Delco Systems Operations, 535
Dell, 61, 78
Delta Airlines, 187, 349
Delta Wire, 68

Dember, W. N., 306n
Deming, W. Edwards, 9, 10, 276n, 590, 612n
Denny, A. T., 612n
Derr, C. B., 499n
Desch, Herbert W., 537–538
Dessaint, A. Y., 746n
Detroit Diesel, 308–311
Dewirst, H. D., 497n, 533n
Dhavale, D. G., 710n
Dickinson, K. K., 499n
Digital Equipment Corporation, 23, 269, 439
Dipboye, R. L., 406n
Disneyland, 390
Dodson, R. L., 37n
Doherty, M. E., 372n
Donnelly, 349
Dow Chemical, 54, 358, 437, 471
Dowling, P. J., 112n, 114n
Doyle, Larry, 593
Dozier, J. B., 534n
Drake, S., 544n
Drauden, G., 230n
Dreher, G. F., 498n, 579n, 612n, 656n
Driver, M. J., 531n
Drucker, Peter, 571
Druckman, D., 496n
Dubin, S. S., 533n, 746n
DuBois, C., 277n
Dugoni, B. L., 374n
Duhon, D. L., 184n
Duke, P., 342n, 373n
Duke Power Company, 142–143, 195–196
Dumaine, B. D., 38n, 39n
Dun & Bradstreet, 364
Dunbar, E., 114n, 498n
Duncan, R. P., 497n
Dunham, R. B., 185n, 285n, 533n, 656n
Dunlop, J. T., 709n
Dunn, L. E., 455n
Dunnette, M. D., 407n, 495n
Du Pont, 349, 543, 579, 603, 700
Du Pont Fibers Division, 594
Durity, A., 317n
Duxbury, L. E., 533n
Dwyer, P. C., 535n

E
Eastern Airlines, 657
Eastman Kodak, 439, 475
Eaton, N. K., 407n
Ebert, K. F., 406n
Edwards, E. L., 184n

Egan, T., 596n
Ehrenberg, R. G., 654n
Eigen, W., 535n
Eisenhardt, K. M., 611n
Ekeberg, S., 201n, 230n, 257n, 276n
El Cheikh, N., 578n
Emhart Corporation, 466
Employee Benefit Research Institute, 655n
Engel, D. W., 439n, 661n
Ensoniq Corporation, 264
Epps, R. Timothy, 750
Erenkranz, B., 456n
Erfurt, J. C., 173n, 184n
Erie Insurance Company, 349
Espirit, 568
Esrig, F., 275n
Esso Resources Canada, 421
Eulberg, J. R., 456n
Executive Telecom System Inc., 365
Exxon, 597

F

Fabriacatore, J. M., 114n
Fagh, M. M., 498n
Faltermayer, E., 578n, 644n
Fama, E. F., 584n
Farace, R. V., 306n
Farnham, A., 578n
Farnsworth, S., 276n
Farr, J., 276n
Farrell, D., 304n
Farren, C., 519n, 532n, 533n
Fay, C. H., 577n
Federal Express, 349, 417–418, 444
Federal Labor Relations Authority, 708
Federal Mediation and Conciliation Service (FMCS), 695, 697
Fefer, M. D., 230n, 654n
Feig, J., 107n
Feild, H. S., 230n, 277n, 499n
Feldman, D. C., 372n, 497n, 532n, 533n
Fel-Pro, 349
Feren, D. B., 612n
Ferris, G. R., 76n, 306n
Ferro Corporation, 6
Feuerstein, A., 656n
Fielding, J. E., 184n
Fierman, J., 655n, 657n
Filipczak, B., 456n, 457n, 491n
Filipowski, D., 36n, 457n
Fine, S., 230n
Fink, L. S., 372n
Fiorito, J., 710n, 711n

First Chicago National Bank, 479
First Federal Bank of California, 349
Fisher, A. B., 301n
Fisher, C. D., 58n, 373n
Fisher, K. F., 37n
Fisher, L. M., 582n
Fisher, Robert, 693
Fitzgerald, M., 231n
Fitzgerald, W., 495n
Fleishman, E. A., 214n, 230n
Flinn, Jim, 278
Folger, R., 577n, 592n, 612n
Foote, A., 173n, 184n
Ford, D. J., 434n
Ford, J. K., 277n, 456n
Ford Motor Company, 9, 43–44, 408, 548, 593–594, 619, 679, 705
Forker, L. B., 10n, 37n
Formisano, R. A., 656n
Forrer, S. E., 39n, 746n
Forward, G. E., 2n
Fossum, J. A., 533n, 674n, 676n, 687n, 688n, 711n
Foti, R., 231n
Foulkes, F. K., 710n
Frank, Anthony, 279, 297
Frank, B., 456n
Frantzreb, R. B., 746n
Frayne, C. A., 456n
Frazee, J., 745n
Freeman, C., 496n, 730n, 745n
Freeman, R. B., 680n, 689n, 710n, 712n
Freeman, S., 231n
Freudenheim, M., 408n
Fried, Y., 306n
Friedman, D. E., 185n
Friedman, J., 153n
Friedman, L., 230n
Fritz, N. R., 534n
Fry, R. E., 495n
Fuchsberg, G., 307n
Fujitsu, 507
Fuqua, D., 340n
Fusilier, M. R., 305n

G

Gainer, L. J., 20n, 37n, 427n, 454n
Gainey, James, 146
Galagan, P. A., 418n, 539n
Galbraith, J., 76n, 229n
Ganster, G. C., 305n
Gardner, P. D., 498n
Garland, S. B., 305n
Garrecht, Clark, 657
Gates, Bill, 596

Gatewood, R., 230n
Gaugler, B. B., 496n
Geber, B., 752n
GE Fanuc Automation, 568
Geiger, A. H., 498n
Geir, J. A., 406n
GE Medical Systems, 487
General Accounting Office, 37n
General Dynamics, 307
General Electric, 6, 169, 254, 467, 471, 544, 562, 631, 738
General Mills, 349, 458
General Motors, 43–44, 66, 97, 197, 288, 294, 299, 467, 471, 543, 548, 593–594, 597, 629, 631, 652–653, 679
George, J., 276n
Georgia Power, 738
Gerber, B., 37n, 38n, 455n, 495n, 499n
Gerhart, B., 305n, 306n, 369n, 374n, 554n, 555n, 576n, 577n, 578n, 604n, 611n, 612n
Gerth, J., 654n
Getman, J. G., 687n, 688n
Ghiselli, E., 275n
Giallourakis, M. C., 649n, 656n
Gier, J. A., 394n
Gifford, C. D., 676n
Giles, W., 277n
Gillette Company, 8
Gilliam, P., 455n
Gilligan, K., 275n
Gilmore, J. B., 185n
Gist, M. E., 455n
Glassman, A. M., 709n
Glatzer, H., 746n
Glover, R. W., 457n
Goff, S. J., 533n
Goldberg, S. B., 687n, 688n
Golden, K., 51n, 76n
Goldman, Sachs, 349
Goldstein, I. L., 230n, 455n
Goldstein, K., 317n
Goll, Irene, 614n
Gomez-Mejia, L. R., 36n, 76n, 577n, 608n, 611n, 613n, 614n
Gooding, R. Z., 405n
Goodman, P. S., 576n
Goodyear Tire & Rubber, 603
Gordon, E. E., 37n
Gorman, C., 407n
Gottfredson, L. S., 407n
Gough, H., 496n
Gould, S., 497n
Gowen, C. R., III, 614n
Grad, Susan, 628n

Graham-Moore, Brian, 599n
Granick, L., 746n
Grant, D. L., 496n
Grant, Jacquiline, 295
Gray, D. A., 2n
Gray, R., 154n
Great Plains Software, 349
Greenberg, J., 571, 577n, 612n
Greenhalgh, L., 534n
Greenhaus, J. H., 531n, 533n
Greenthol, A., 407n
Greenwald, J., 305n, 373n
Greller, M. M., 531n
Grenig, J., 372n
Greyhound Financial Corporation, 478–479
Griffin, R., 229n, 231n, 306n
Griffith, T. L., 497n
Griggs, L., 114n
Grimaldi, J. V., 183n
Groshen, E. L., 576n
Grossman, B. P., 531n
Grove, D. A., 457n
Grumman, 597
GTE Corporation, 459–460, 481, 543, 597
GTE Telephone Operations-North Area, 530
Guadiana, Bob, 702
Guardsmark, 376
Guest, R., 317n
Gueutal, H. G., 39n, 305n, 731n, 745n
Guidard, Bertrand, 660
Guinn, K., 278n
Guinn, S. L., 185n, 534n
Guion, R. M., 305n, 372n
Guitierrez, N. C., 498n
Gummerson, E., 277n
Gunsch, D., 497n, 646n
Gunter, H., 712n
Gupta, N., 578n
Gupta, U., 154n
Gupta, Y. P., 577n
Gutenberg, R. L., 406n
Guthrie, J. P., 408n
Gutteridge, T. C., 532n

H
H & H Music Company, 617
Hachiya, D., 304n
Hackett, R. D., 305n
Hackman, J. R., 224n, 231n, 306n, 495n
Hahn, F. K., 661n
Hakel, M., 230n
Halcrow, A., 373n

Hall, D. T., 38n, 372n, 497n, 531n, 532n
Hall, F. S., 495n
Hallmark Cards, 349
Hallock, R. G., 184n
Hammer, A. L., 496n
Hammer, T. H., 497n, 613n, 712n
Handicapped Services, 388
Hanlin, J. R., 458n
Hannon, J., 611n
Hannum, W., 456n
Hanscome, Ron, 747n
Hanson, D., 184n
Hanson, W. C., 38n
Haraway, C., 462n
Harbison, F., 709n
Harrigan, Susan, 157–158
Harris, D. L., 264n
Harris, M. M., 372n
Harris, P. R., 485n, 498n
Harris, S. G., 499n
Harrison, J. S., 36n, 37n, 76n
Harrison, Lawrence, 87–89, 113n
Harvard University, 472
Harvey, R., 229n, 230n, 250n
Hashimoto, M., 615n
Hatcher, L., 613n, 614n
Hatfield, J., 656n
Hauenstein, N., 231n
Hawk, R., 373n
Haworth, 349
Hayes, Woody, 233
Hayward, D. G., 305n
Hazel, J., 231n
Hazen Paper Company, 126, 390
Hazucha, J. F., 499n
Hazzard, L., 165n
H.B. Fuller Company, 349
Healy, J., 712n
Heilman, M. E., 498n
Heirich, M. A., 173n, 184n
Helburn, I. B., 304n
Hellervik, L. W., 499n
Helms, Harry, 117
Henderson, D. K., 191n
Henderson, R., 372n
Henderson, R. I., 579n
Heneman, H. G., III, 577n
Heneman, R. L., 276n, 612n
Henkoff, R., 455n
Henle, P., 578n
Hennessey, H. W., Jr., 654n, 656n
Henry, R. A., 406n
Henson, R., 745n
Herbstman, H., 184n
Herman, E. E., 710n

Herman, J. B., 285n, 687n, 688n
Herman Miller, 349, 597, 601
Herniter, B. C., 746n
Herrin, S. J., 535n
Hershey, R. D., Jr., 614n
Hershey Foods, 174, 349
Herzberg, F., 223, 231n
Hewitt Associates, 349, 654n, 655n
Hewlett-Packard, 60, 286, 349, 593, 595
Hickey, J. V., 455n
Hicks, W. D., 455n
Hiebert, M. B., 421n
Higgins, C. A., 533n
Higgins, J. M., 413n
Hill, Anita, 145
Hill, C., 75n
Hill, G. C., 306n
Hill, R. E., 535n
Hilts, P. J., 655n
Hinkin, T., 611n
Hinrichs, J. R., 496n
Hiromitsu, Hayashida, 226
Hirsch, B. T., 710n, 712n
Hirsch, S. K., 496n
Hirshman, A. O., 304n
Hispanic Business Inc., 365
Hitchcock, J. E., 191n
Hitt, A., 36n
Hitt, M. A., 37n, 76n, 584n
H.J. Heinz Company, 569
Hochwarter, W. A., 656n
Hoffman, S. K., 656n
Hofstede, Geert, 84–87, 86n, 88n, 113n
Hogan, J., 407n
Hogland, William, 294
Holland, R., 154n
Hollenbeck, G. P., 496n
Hollenbeck, J. R., 166n, 184n, 229n, 305n, 323n, 325n, 330n, 397n, 407n, 654n
Holley, W. H., Jr., 277n, 709n
Hollingsworth, J. A., 185n
Holmes, A., 185n
Holoviak, S. J., 655n
Home Box Office (HBO), 741–742
Honda Motor Company, 67, 363
Honda of America Manufacturing, 349
Honeywell, 24, 471, 490
Honold, L., 455n
Hooper, L., 544n
Hopkins, Elizabeth, 138
Horrigan, M. W., 578n
Horsfield, D., 746n

Horvath, F. W., 533n
Hoskisson, R. E., 36n, 37n, 76n, 584n, 611n
Hotch, R., 746n
Hough, L. M., 407n
Howard, A., 496n
Howell, W., 231n
Howes, P. D., 661n
Hoyer, W. D., 373n
Hronec, Steven M., 536
HSC Security, 375
Huber, V., 76n
Hudson Institute, 145
Huge, E. C., 276n
Hugentoble, M. K., 499n
Hughes, D., 340n
Hughes, G., 230n
Hulin, Charles L., 284–285, 304n 372n, 406n
Hults, B. M., 533n
Hunter, J. E., 154n, 275n, 276n, 406n, 407n, 458n
Hunter, R. H., 154n, 406n
Hunter, T. L., 746n
Huseman, R., 656n
Hutcheson, P. G., 513n, 532n
Hyman, J. S., 661n
Hyundai Electronics Industries, 327

I
Iacocca, Lee, 61
Iaffaldono, M. T., 304n
IBM, 5, 13, 62, 65, 72, 73, 77, 181, 307, 324, 349, 439, 467–469, 543
IBM Enterprise Systems, 468
IBM North America, 468
IBM Technology Products, 468
IBP, 158
Ideus, K., 520n
Ilgen, D. R., 166n, 184n, 229n, 305n, 373n, 374n, 407n
Ilgen, G. R., 654n
Industrial Innovations, 165
Inland Steel Industries, 349
Intel, 349
International Organization for Standardization, 10
International Paper, 603
Interplace, 362
Iorio, M., 305n
Isabella, L. A., 497n
ITT Corp., 603
Iverson, Ken, 410–411

J
Jaben, J., 182n

Jablonski, J. R., 10n, 37n
Jackofsky, E., 76n
Jackson, D. N., 407n
Jackson, D. S., 158n
Jackson, Delbert, 145
Jackson, E. C., 183n
Jackson, K., 654n
Jackson, P. R., 577n
Jackson, S. E., 76n, 229n, 275n, 306n, 339n, 373n
Jackson, S. L., 37n
Jackson, Susan F., 58n
Jaffe, C. A., 191n
Jaffe, D. T., 496n, 532n
Jamison, R. L., 533n
Jarley, P., 711n
Jarrell, D. W., 339n
Jarrell, S. B., 710n
J.C. Penney, 350
Jeanneret, R. P., 231n, 406n
Jenkins, D., 578n
Jenkins, G. D., 614n
Jennings, K. M., 709n
Jennings, S. A., 614n
Jensen, M. C., 584n, 613n, 614n
Jenson, A. R., 407n
J.M. Smucker, 350
John Morell, 158
Johns, N. J., 458n
Johnson & Johnson, 26, 60, 174, 181, 349
Johnson, J., 185
Johnson, Lyndon, 122, 125, 130
Johnson, R. B., 22n
Johnson, S., 184n
Johnson, T. R., 496n
Johnsonville Foods, 420
Johnson Wax, 439
Johnston, W. B., 16n, 19n, 76n, 113n, 317n
Jonas, H. S., 495n
Jones, C. J., 499n
Jones, D. T., 577n, 609n, 614n
Jones, G., 75n, 77n
Jones, J., 327n
Jones, L., 306n
Jones, L. V., 407n
Jones, S., 201n, 230n
Jones, S., 257n, 276n
Jordan, Hamilton, 244
J.P. Morgan, 80, 349
J.P. Stevens, 689
Judge, T. A., 612n
Jung, Carl, 473
Junglebutt, A., 37n
Juran, Joseph, 9, 10

K
Kahneman, D., 277n
Kakiuchi, Robert, 301
Kamouri, A. L., 534n
Kanter, R. M., 112n, 577n
Kantor, R. G., 661n
Kanungo, R., 288n, 305n
Kanzanas, H. C., 441n, 457n
Karr, A. R., 146n, 654n
Kassouf, Thomas, 204
Katcher, A., 498n
Katz, H. C., 229n, 691n, 709n, 711n
Katz, M., 372n
Kaufman, R. T., 613n
Kavanaugh, M. J., 39n, 731n, 745n
Kaye, B. L., 519n, 532n, 533n
Kazanjian, R., 76n, 229n
Kearns, David, 11
Kearsley, G., 457n
Keatley, R., 102n, 327n, 567n
Keefe, J., 229n
Keehn, J., 38n
Keenan, A., 302n
Keenan, R. S., 306n
Kelleher, Herb, 187–189, 191
Keller, R. T., 305n
Kellogg, 349
Kelly, H. H., 304n
Kelly, R. F., 533n
Kemp, N. J., 577n
Kendall, L., 275n
Kentucky Fried Chicken, 307
Kernan, M., 277n
Kerr, C., 709n
Kerr, J., 76n
Keys, B., 496n
Kimbrough, W., 231n
Kinesis Corporation, 165
King, J. R., 533n
King, L., 275n
King, Dr. Martin Luther, Jr., 125
King, R., 184n
King, Rodney, 342
Kingston Technology, 69
Kinnear, James, 171
Kinzer, Allen, 362
Kirchline, K., 579n
Kirkpatrick, D. L., 457n, 495n
Kirrane, D. E., 745n
Kirrane, P. R., 745n
Kirsch, I. S., 37n
Kirsch, M., 405n
Kizilos, P., 495n
Klatt, L., 276n
Klein, H., 277n
Klein, K. J., 613n

Kleiner, M. M., 689n
Klimoski, R. J., 276n, 455n
Knight-Ridder, 349
Knowles, M., 456n
Koch, J., 365n
Kochan, T. A., 672n, 691n, 698n, 709n, 710n
Koci, Lud, 310
Kodak, 408, 479
Kok, R., 305n
Komaki, J., 275n, 457n
Konovsky, M. A., 577n, 592n, 612n
Konrad, A. M., 612n
Konz, A., 76n, 231n
Kossek, E. E., 180, 185n, 534n
Koys, D. J., 372n
Kozlowski, S. W. J., 533n
Kraar, L., 36n
Kraiger, K., 277n
Kram, K. E., 498n
Kramon, G., 643n
Kraut, A. I., 495n
Kravitz, D. E., 283n
Krebs, V. E., 744n
Kroger, 597
Krone, Kevin, 189
Kruse, D. L., 612n, 613n
Kuhn, A., 710n
Kummerow, J. M., 37n

L
Laabs, J. J., 8n, 28n, 571n
Labate, J., 183n
Labich, K., 532n
Labig, C. E., 304n
Lade, D., 532n
Lambert, R. A., 611n
Landau, J., 497n
Lands' End, 349
Landy, F. J., 36n, 231n, 276n
Lapham, E., 567n
Larcker, D. F., 611n
LaRock, S., 657n
Latack, J. C., 534n
Latham, G. P., 230n, 251n, 275n, 276n, 277n, 441n, 455n, 456n, 457n, 497n
Lawler, E. E., III, 230n, 276n, 577n, 587n, 612n, 614n, 656n
Lawler, J. J., 745n
Lawrence, A. T., 534n
Lawrence, B. S., 531n
Lawrence, J., 306n
Lawrence, P., 401n
Lawshe, C. H., 405n
Layard, R., 578n

Lazar, E., 115n
Lederer, Jules, 659
Ledford, G., 577n
Ledford, Gerald, 562
Ledvinka, James, 38n, 114n, 119, 120n, 153n
Lee, C., 38n, 456n, 533n
Lee, R. J., 527n
LeFauve, Richard "Skip," 751
Lefkovich, J. L., 534n
Leibowitz, Z. B., 39n, 519n, 532n, 533n, 746n
Leminsky, G., 712n
Leo Burnett, 349
Leonard, B., 746n
Leonard, M., 372n
Leonard, R. L., 458n
Lesley, E., 339n
Lesly, E., 305n
Levering, R., 349–350n, 372n
Levin, D. P., 280n, 657n
Levine, D. I., 614n
Levine, E., 230n
Levi Strauss, 27–29, 327, 393
Lewin, D., 614n
Lewis, M. I., 305n
Lewyn, M., 305n
Libby, T., 406n
Lifshus, Sam, 506
Light, L., 339n
Lincoln Electric, 349
Lineneman, P. D., 710n
Linger, P., 38n
Lipsett, L., 457n, 533n
Livernash, E. R., 712n
Locke, Edwin, 276n, 277n, 281, 304n, 592, 612n
Lockheed Corporation, 340
Loden, M., 38n
Loher, B. T., 231n, 455n
Lohr, Steve, 229n, 544n, 576n
Lombardo, M. M., 457n, 476n, 496n, 497n, 499n
London, M., 372n, 495n, 497n, 531n
Lonergan, Elizabeth, 571
Longenecker, C., 275n
Lopez, J., 77n
Los Angeles Dodgers, 349
Lotus Development, 349
Loughran, C. S., 711n
Louis, M. R., 532n
Lovell, S. E., 283n
Lowe's Companies, 349
LTV, 408, 629
Lublin, J. S., 155n, 327n
Lucas, J. A., 498n

Lucky Food Sores, 452
Luthans, F., 495n
Lutz, Robert A., 54
Lyondell Petrochemical, 349

M
McAfee, J. K., 458n
McCaffery, Robert M., 641–642, 654n
McCaleb, V. M., 612n
McCall, M. W., Jr., 457n, 497n, 499n
McCallum, A., 457n
McCann, D., 39n, 495n
McCauley, C. D., 476n, 496n, 497n
McCaulley, M. H., 496n
McClean Credit Union, 125
McClelland, C., 231n
McClendon, J. A., 710n
McCloy, R. A., 407n
McCormick, E., 230n, 231n, 349
McCrie, Robert, 376
McCullough, K. J., 406n
McCune, J. T., 534n
McDonald's, 337
McDonnell, L., 406n
McDonnell Douglas, 137, 307, 390, 478, 597
McEnery, Jack, 658–660
McEvoy, G. M., 276n, 373n, 457n
McFadden, John J., 637n, 640n, 654n
McFarlin, D. B., 577n
McGann, John W., 617
McGarth, J. E., 292n, 305n
McGarvey, M., 184n
McGeachie, Sylvia, 658–660
McGehee, M., 456n
McGregor, Douglas, 254, 275n
McIlvane, Thomas, 279, 297
McKenna, D. D., 495n
McKennon, Keith R., 54
McKersie, Robert, 690, 710n, 711n
McLaughlin, S. D., 496n
McMahan, G., 75n, 77n, 231n, 276n
MacTemps, 374
Madden, J., 231n
Mager, R. F., 427n, 455n
Magjuka, R. T., 455n
Magma Copper Company, 702
Magnavox Electronic Systems Company, 434
Magnus, M., 372n
Main, J., 37n
Majchrzak, A., 612n
Malby, Alan, 537
Malik, S. D., 532n
Mallory, M., 158n
Mandel, M. J., 569n

Mane, E. M., 531n
Mangan, J. F., 184n
Mangum, G., 656n
Maranto, C. L., 710n, 711n
March, J. G., 183n
Marciariello, J. A., 37n
Margerison, C., 39n, 495n
Markey, J. P., 578n
Markus, T., 184n
Marquardt, M. J., 439n, 661n
Marquette Electronics, 349
Marriott Corporation, 267, 524–525
Marsh, B., 154n
Marshall, Betty J., 155
Martin, J., 51n
Martin, R., 577n
Marx, R. D., 456n
Mary Kay Cosmetics, 349
Mason, J. C., 185n
Massengill, D., 534n
Mathieu, J. E., 455n, 458n
Matthes, K., 634
Mauner, E. H., 185n
Mautz, J., 165n
Maxwell, Hamish, 54
Maxwell, S. E., 457n
Mayall, D., 656n
Mayes, B. T., 305n
Meagher, Edward, 307
Meckling, W. H., 614n
Medoff, J. L., 612n, 680n, 712n
Medtronic Inc., 467, 747
Meese, G. B., 305n
Meglino, B. M., 305n
Meltzer, A. S., 20n, 37n, 427n,
    455n
Mendenhall, M., 114n, 498n
Mercedes-Benz, 567
Merck & Co., 242, 243n, 349, 589, 590,
    602
Messmer, M., 534n
Methodist Hospital (Houston), 349
Methodist Medical Center of Illinois,
    434
Metropolitan Financial, 471
Metropolitan Life Insurance, 51, 91,
    326
Meyer, D. G., 710n
Meyer, H., 113n
Miceli, M. P., 304n
Michaels, M., 716n
Microsoft Corporation, 202, 349
Milbank, D., 102n, 327n
Miles, R., 62, 75n, 76n, 607
Milkovich, G. T., 76n, 372n, 554n,
    555n, 576n, 577n, 578n, 604n,
    611n, 654n

Millard, C. W., 532n
Miller, H. E., 305n, 372n
Miller, K., 38n
Miller, R. B., 276n
Miller, Steven, 507
Miller, Sylvia, 505, 531n
Mills, G. E., 495n
Mims, Forrest, III, 117
Miner, F. J., 532n
Miner, J. B., 576n
Minor, F. J., 497n
Mintzberg, H., 77n, 495n
Mirkin, Morris, 659
Misa, K. F., 114n
Mishra, A., 231n
Mitchell, D. J. B., 614n
Mitchell, J., 44n, 373n
Mitsui Corporation, 364
Moberg, D., 38n
Modicon (Daimler-Benz), 568
Moeller, N., 231n
Monsanto, 593
Montgomery, M., 656n
Montmarquette, C., 579n
Moog, 349
Moore, M., 276n
Moran, R. T., 485n, 498n
Moran, Stahl, & Boyer, Inc., 114n
Moravec, M., 520n, 532n
Morgan, B. B., Jr., 457n
Morgan, R. R., 37n
Morgan, S., 613n
Morgan Stanley, 597
Morishima, 615n
Morrison & Foerster, 349
Morrison, A. M., 497n, 499n
Morrison, R. F., 532n
Morrow, Robert M., 54
Moses, B. M., 532n
Moses, S., 407n
Moskowitz, M., 349–350n, 372n
Mossholder, K., 277n
Motorola, 24, 299, 349, 408, 418, 442,
    471
Moulton, T. M., 745n
Mount, M. K., 407n, 533n
Mowday, R. T., 289n, 305n
Mrs. Fields Cookies, 719
Muchinsky, P. M., 304n
Mueller, C. W., 304n
Muhammad, Asalmah, 364
Mulcany, C., 184n
Mullen, E. J., 457n
Mullins, W., 231n
Mumford, M. D., 214n, 230n
Murphy, K. R., 230n, 268n, 274n,
    275n, 407n, 408n

Murphy, Kevin J., 243n, 589n, 590n,
    602n, 613n
Murray, B., 577n, 611n
Murray, C., 154n
Myers, C., 709n
Myers, Isabel Briggs, 474n
Myers, R. A., 497n
Myles, Bill, 234

N
Nackley, J. V., 654n
Nakamura, Y., 317n
Nardoni, R., 736n
Nathan, B. R., 456n
National Association of
    Manufacturers, 38n, 675
National Association of Secondary
    School Principals, 482
National Cash Register, 447–448
National Center for Employee
    Ownership, 646
National Center on Education and
    the Economy, 38n
National Education Association, 673
National Labor Relations Board,
    683n, 684n, 708, 710n, 711n
National Semiconductor, 115
National Semiconductor, Israel, 115
National Technological University,
    439
Nature Conservancy, 294
Neale, M. A., 372n, 647n, 656n
Near, J. P., 304n, 533n
Neckermn, K., 342n
Nee, D. M., 531n
Neikirk, W., 196n
Nelson, K., 656n
Nemeroff, W., 277n
Nemeth, C. W., 421n
Newman, J. M., 372n, 576n, 578n
Newsday, 157
Newstrom, J. W., 185n, 533n
Newton, T. J., 302n, 306n
Nicole Miller, 568
Nieves, Josephine, 341
Nike, 735
Nissan, 44, 349
Nixon, Richard M., 130
Noah, T., 154n
Noble, B. P., 646n
Noe, A., 277n
Noe, R. A., 231n, 405n, 450n, 455n,
    456n, 497n, 498n, 579n
Noel, J., 495n
Noer, D. M., 105n
Noon, S. L., 406n
Nordstrom, 349

Norman, C., 269n
North Carolina State, 253
Northcraft, G. B., 372n, 497n, 647n, 656n
Northwest Airlines, 390
Northwestern Mutual Life, 349
Norton, E., 140n, 204n, 389n
Norton, R., 112n
Norton-Holmes, Eleanor, 132
Novak, J. F., 185n
Nucor Corporation, 409–413
Nulty, P., 669n
Nunamaker, J. F., Jr., 746n
Nunnally, J. C., 404n
Nynex Corporation, 443

O
Oberg, Alcestis, 117
O'Brian, B., 339n
O'Brian, T. L., 154n, 406n
O'Connell, S. E., 745n
O'Connor, E. J., 456n
OCS Security, 375
Oddou, G. R., 114n
O'Dell, C., 612n
Odetics, 350
Odiorne, G., 276n
O'Donnell, M., 275n
O'Donnell, R., 275n
Organization for Economic Cooperation and Development, 639n
Ohio State University, 233–234
Ohlott, P. J., 497n
Oldham, G. R., 224n, 231n, 305n, 306n
O'Leary-Kelly, A., 154n
Olian, J. D., 76n, 372n, 408n
Olsen, K., 113n
Olson, C. A., 577n
O'Mara, J., 22n
Oregon Steel Mills, 597
O'Reilly, Anthony, 231n, 569
O'Reilly, B., 37n, 81n, 113n, 495n
Osburn, H. G., 406n
Oser, R. L., 457n
Ostroff, C. O., 457n
Oswald, Rudy, 288
Oswald, S. L., 464n
Otte, F. L., 513n, 532n
Ovalle, N., 276n

P
Pace, R. W., 495n
Pacer Systems, 69
Pacific Bell, 483–484
Pacific Gas and Electric (PG&E), 22

Pacific National Bank, 174
Packer, A., 16n, 76n, 113n
Padilla, John, 375
Paetzold, R., 154n
Paradise, C. A., 533n
Pare, T. P., 413n, 631n, 655n
Parks, J. M., 611n
Parliman, G. C., 184n
Pascale, R., 77n
Pastin, M., 38n
Patagonia, 350
Patten, Thomas H., Jr., 255n, 275n
Patterson, G. A., 579n, 582
Paul, K. B., 283n
Pauli, K. E., 407n
Paulson, S. K., 291n
Payne, R., 305n
Pear, R., 154n
Pearlman, K., 406n, 458n
Pedigo, P. R., 495n
Peiper, R., 113n
Peiperl, M. A., 469n, 495n
Pence, E., 277n
Penczak, J. A., 654n
Penley, L. E., 497n
Penn, P., 275n
Pension Benefit Guaranty Corporation (PBGC), 629
Penske, Roger, 310, 311
Penske Racing Team, 310
People Express, 53, 54
Peoples Natural Gas, 278
Pepperidge Farm, 158
PepsiCo, 307
Pepsi-Cola, 595
Perrewe, P. L., 656n
Perruci, C. C., 497n
Personick, M. E., 183n
Peters, L. H., 456n
Peters, T., 30n, 39n
Petersen, D. J., 534n
Peterson, D. B., 499n
Peterson, Don, 44
Peterson, T., 578n
Petrini, C. M., 456n
Pfeffer, J. P., 577n, 612n
Pfeiffer, Eckhard, 78
Pfizer, 471
Pflaum, B. B., 184n
Philip Morris Companies Inc., 54
Phillips, N., 407n
Phillips, S. M., 577n
Phillips-Jones, L. L., 498n
Physio-Control, 350
Picolino, E. B., 534n
Piel, Jonathon, 117
Pieper, R., 94n, 113n

Pierce, J. L., 185n, 533n, 613n
Pinder, C. C., 497n
Pinkerton, 376
Piotrowski, M., 275n
Pipe, D., 427n
Pipe, P., 455n
Pirerchia, P. V., 184n
Pischetsrieder, Bernd, 567
Piskurich, G. M., 438n
Pitney Bowes, 350
Pleck, J. H., 533n
Poe, R., 305n
Poister, T., 275n
Polaroid, 350, 529, 700
Pollack, B., 746n
Ponitcell, J., 37n
Pooyan, A., 456n
Porter, L. W., 289n, 305n, 306n, 318
Porter, Michael, 61, 75n, 76n
Posner, B. Z., 532n
Postage Meter Inc., 39
Pouliot, J. S., 363n
Powell, G. H., 532n
Powell, G. N., 373n
Powers, M. L., 455n
Premack, S. L., 373n
Preston Trucking, 350
Price, J. L., 304n
Price, R., 531n
Prien, G., 230n
Primoff, E. S., 212n, 230n
Principal Financial Group, The, 151
Pritchard, R., 201n, 230n, 257n, 276n
Procter & Gamble, 24, 350, 408, 597
Protzman, F., 567n
Publix Super Markets, 350
Pulakos, E., 277n
Pulley, B., 156n
Pursell, E., 230n, 277n

Q
Quad/Graphics, 350
Quarterdeck Office Systems, 51
Quick, J. C., 2n, 191n
Quillen, L., 746n
Quinn, J., 75n, 77n
Quinn, R. P., 284n

R
Rabinowitz, S., 532n
Rafaeli, A., 306n
Ragins, B. R., 498n
Raimy, E., 571n
Ramanujam, V., 51n, 76n
Rauschenberger, J., 534n
Ravlin, E. C., 305n
Read, W., 612n

Reader's Digest, 350
Reagan, Ronald, 11, 122
Reber, R. A., 184n
Redecker, J. R., 711n
Reed-Mendenhall, D., 532n
REI, 350
Reich, Robert, 695
Reichers, A. E., 532n
Reidville Hydraulics, 363
Reilley, R., 154n
Reilly, A. H., 497n, 498n
Reilly, B. A., 283n
Reilly, C. E., 283n
Reilly, M., 230n
Reilly, R. R., 407n
Reimert, W. A., 657n
Reitz, H. J., 304n
Reliable Cartage, 175
Rennie, Jack, 69
Resnick, R., 339n
Revco D. S., 438
Reynolds, C., 110n
Reynolds, D. H., 408n
Reynolds, L., 158n
Reynolds, L. G., 372n
Rhoades, Ann, 189
Rhodes, C. A., 496n
Rice, R. W., 577n
Richardson, F. H., 54
Richardson, R., 598n
Richter, A., 457n
Richter, J., 38n, 531n
Ricklees, R., 38n
Rivero, J. C., 339n
Robbins, N. E., 533n
Roberson, L., 498n
Roberts, Leonard, 155
Robinson, D. D., 405n
Robinson, D. G., 451n, 458n
Robinson, J., 451n, 458n
Robinson, R., 656n
Robinson, R. M., 464n
Rockwell International, 597, 603
Rodgers, C., 533n
Rodgers, F. S., 533n
Rodgers, R., 276n
Rogers, Fran, 181
Rohan, T. M., 413n
Rokeach, M., 113n
Rollins, T., 598n
Ronen, S., 498n
Roos, D., 577n, 609n, 614n
Roosevelt, Franklin, 620, 682
Rose, J., 710n, 711n
Rose, R. L., 711n
Rosen, B., 372n, 455n, 579n

Rosen, Corey, 646
Rosen, P. B., 535n
Rosenbaum, J. E., 499n
Rosenbaum, W. B., 304n
Rosenbluth International, 350
Rosener, J. B., 38n
Rosenthal, D. B., 496n
Rosow, J. M., 455n
Ross, Diana, 394
Ross, J., 306n
Ross, R. A., 613n
Ross, T. L., 599n, 613n, 614n
Rosse, J. G., 304n, 305n
Rotchford, N. L., 305n
Roth, P., 201n, 230n, 257n, 276n
Rothstein, M., 407n
Rothwell, W. J., 441n, 457n
Roughton, J., 184
Rouillier, J. Z., 455n
Rowland, C. C., 457n
Rowland, K., 76n
Roznowski, M., 304n
Rubbermaid, 27
Rubenfeld, S., 613n
Rubin, P., 613n, 614n
Rubio, L., 113n
Ruderman, M. N., 497n
Runkel, Susan, 532n, 746n
Runner, D., 654n
Russell, J. E., 532n
Russell, J. S., 455n, 458n
Rynes, S. L., 76n, 369n, 371n, 372n,
    373n, 374n, 554n, 555n, 576n,
    578n, 612
Rysart, J., 339n
Ryscavage, P., 578n

S
Saari, L. M., 457n, 496n
Sackett, P. R., 231n, 277n, 405n, 407n,
    457n
Saker, A., 614n
Salas, E., 455n, 457n
Salpukas, A., 713n
Salwen, K. G., 579n, 711n
Samsung Group, 79
Sanger, D. E., 171n
Santora, J. E., 174n
Sarli, M. M., 656n
Sartain, Libby, 190
SAS Institute, 350
Sathe, V., 113n
Saturn Corporation, 562, 748–752
Saveri, A., 37n
Sawyer, K., 184n
Scanlon, Joseph N., 599

Scardello, V., 114n
Scarpello, V. G., 38n
Schares, G., 113n
Scharlach, 534n
Schein, V. A., 185n
Schiavoni, Vincent, 412
Schlesinger, L., 76n
Schmidt, F. L., 275n, 406n, 407n, 458n
Schmitt, N., 231n, 373n, 405n, 456n,
    534n
Schneider, B., 76n, 231n, 404n
Schneider, R. J., 499n
Schneier, C. E., 456n
Schoenfeldt, L. F., 58n, 496n
Schor, J., 656n
Schowerer, C., 372n
Schreisheim, C., 304n
Schroeder, K. G., 497n
Schuch, R., 184n
Schuler, R. S., 58n, 76n, 77n, 113n,
    114n, 229n, 264n, 275n, 306n,
    339n, 373n
Schultz, Howard, 646
Schulz, E. R., 457n
Schurman, S. J., 499n
Schuster, M. H., 613n, 614n
Schwab, Armand, Jr., 117
Schwab, D. P., 371n, 578n
Schwartz, F. N., 534n
Schwarz, J. L., 710n
Schwoerer, C., 455n
Scientific American, 117
SC Johnson Wax, 349
Scott, C. D., 496n, 532n
Scott, F. A., 656n
Scott, L. R., 457n
Sears, Roebuck & Company, 67, 301,
    581–582
Seaton, F., 407n
Segal, N. L., 306n
Segal, T., 181n
S. E. Jackson and Associates, 114n,
    498n
Selz, M., 363n
Senge, D., 455n
Senge, P., 77n
Sessa, V. I., 373n, 496n
Shalley, C. E., 497n
Shapiro, D., 184n
Shaw, Ben, 58n
Shaw, K. N., 612n
Sheflin, N., 678n
Shellabarger, Tracy, 409, 413
Shellenbarger, S., 177n, 178n, 181n,
    185n
Shell Oil Company, 54

Sheppard, D. I., 372n
Sheppeck, M. A., 496n
Sher, M. L., 534n
Sherer, P. D., 561, 577n
Sherman, A. W., Jr., 579n
Sherman, S., 305n, 532n
Shlaes, A., 95n
Shoney's Inc., 155, 390
Sieller, F. G., 654n
Siemens Corporation, 743
Silverman, S. B., 231n, 275n, 497n
Simison, R. L., 183n
Simon, D. R., 534n
Simon, H. A., 183n
Simonds, R. H., 183n
Singh, V., 277n
Slade, L. A., 497n
Slavenski, L., 532n
Slichter, S., 712n
Slocum, J. W., 532n, 533n
Smiddy, Harold, 254
Smith, B. J., 456n
Smith, D., 277n
Smith, E., 174n
Smith, Frederick, 418
Smith, G., 76n
Smith, J., 184n, 317n
Smith, K., 171n
Smith, P., 275n
Smith, P. C., 495n
Smith, R., 347n
Smith, R. J., 406n
Smith, Roger, 748
Smith, R. S., 578n, 612n, 654n
Snell, R. S., 497n
Snell, S. A., 39n, 75n, 76n, 77n, 113n,
    275n, 277n, 339n
Snow, C., 62, 75n, 76n, 77n, 607
Society for Human Resource
    Management, 16
Society for Industrial and
    Organizational Psychology,
    406n
Soelberg, P. O., 372n
Solectron, 418
Solo, S., 171n
Solomon, C. M., 38n, 499n, 534n,
    752n
Solomon, J., 77n, 154n, 339n, 406n
Solovy-Pratt, L., 434n
Solow, R., 114n
Sonnenfeld, J. A., 469n, 495n
Sony Corporation, 174
Sorrentino, C., 678n, 707n, 712n
Southwest Airlines, 71, 187–191, 350,
    712–713
Southwest Industries, 464

Spector, P. E., 304n
Spectrum Human Resources Systems
    Corporation, 739n
Spence, J., 252n
Spencer, C. C., 407n
Spencer, D. G., 304n
Spillane, J. F., 37n
Sponsel, S., 252n, 275n
Springfield ReManufacturing, 350
Springs Industries, 350
Srivasta, S., 495n
Stack, H., 499n
Staines, G. L., 284n
Stanley, T. D., 710n
Starbucks Coffee Company, 646
Stasser, G., 406n
Staw, B. M., 306n
Steel, R., 276n
Steelcase, 350
Steers, R. M., 289n, 305n, 306n
Steffy, B. D., 497n
Steger, J. A., 496n
Stephens, J. K., 498n
Stern, R. N., 712n
Stetzer, E., 184n
Steven, C. M., 711n
Stevens, L., 746n
Stewart, T. A., 36n, 37n, 60n, 77n,
    496n
Stone & Webster, 597
Stone, E. F., 305n
Stout, S. K., 533n
Strasmore, Martin, 286
Streib, G., 275n
Strickland, A., 76n
Strickler, G., 153n
Stright, J. F., 39n, 746n
Stroh, L. K., 497n, 498n
Struve, J. E., 333n
Stuart, P., 339n, 487n
Stuebing, K., 201n, 230n, 257n,
    276n
Stumpf, S. A., 372n
Sucec, J., 275n
Sullivan, G. J., 455n
Sullivan, S. E., 185n
Sun, David, 69
Super, D. E., 531n, 533n
Surden, E., 347n
Suris, O., 752n
Susman, G. I., 577n
Sutton, R. I., 306n, 534n
Svejnar, J., 613n
Swain, Lawrence, 146
Swartz, C., 578n
Swinehart, K. S., 464n
Syntex Corporation, 350

T
Tadjer-Winkler, R., 184n
Taguchi, Genichi, 10
Tandem Computers, 350
Tandy, 568
Tannenbaum, S. I., 39n, 455n, 457n,
    731n, 745n
Taylor, A., 44n, 76n, 226n
Taylor, F. W., 36n, 231n
Taylor, G. S., 649n, 656n
Taylor, M. S., 373n
TDIndustries, 350
Teagarden, M. B., 112n
Teel, K. S., 612n
Teitelbaum, R. S., 191n
Tellabs Inc., 715–716, 732
Tellegen, A., 306n
Tellep, Dan, 340
Teltsch, K., 337n
Tempiin, N., 752n
Templeton, M. E., 579n
Templin, N., 44n, 77n
TenEyck, G., 746n
Tennant, 350
Tenneco, 303
Terborg, J. R., 455n
Teresko, J., 317n
Tesseract Corporation, 741
Tett, R. P., 407n
Texaco, 171
Texas Instruments, 568
Thayer, P. W., 231n, 456n
Thibaut, J. W., 304n
Thomas, Clarence, 132, 145
Thomas, E., 406n
Thomas, J., 464n
Thomas, J. M., 307n
Thomas, R. R., 498n
Thomason, T., 712n
Thompson, A., 76n
Thompson, P., 531n
Thompson's Computer Electronics,
    165
Thornburg, L., 73n
Thorne, A., 496n
Thornton, G. C., III, 408n, 496n
3M, 349, 489, 514
Tichy, N. M., 496n
Tilley, D., 37n
Tilly, C., 656n
Time-Warner, 181
Titus, W., 406n
Todd, James, 327
Tolchin, M., 280n
Tomasko, E. S., 499n
Tomlinson, W. H., 291n
Tompkins, N. C, 460n

Toomey, E. L., 499n
Topps, 597
Torrence, D. R., 456n
Torrence, J. A., 456n
Tosi, H. L., Jr., 276n, 611n
Toufexis, A., 305n
Towers Perrin, 5, 36n, 38n, 96n, 112n, 113n, 570n
Toyota, 44, 226, 334, 564, 689
Trans World Airlines, 146
Travelers Corporation, 424, 529
Troy, L., 678n
TRW, 744
Tsui, A.S., 36n
Tucker, R., 520n, 532n
Tucker, S., 151n
Tung, R., 114n
Tung, R. L., 37n, 498n
Tungsram, 6
Turk, T. A., 584n
Turner, J. A., 654n
Turque, W., 184
Turrif, T. W., 168n, 184n
Tversky, A., 277n
TWA, 187
Tykal, Rob, 309
Tyler, B. B., 584n
Tyson, L. D., 614n

U
U-Haul International, 174
Ulrich, D., 36n, 54n, 77n
Ulrich, R., 296n
Union Camp, 669
Union Carbide, 593
United Airlines, 712–713
United Auto Workers (UAW), 66, 593–594, 705, 748–752
United Parcel Service, 491
United Steelworkers of America, 163, 702
University of Minnesota Information Services, 745n
Unocal Corp., 603
UNUM, 350
Urban, J., 118n
Ury, William, 693
USAA, 350
U.S. Bank of Washington, 303
U.S. Bureau of Labor Statistics, 7n, 15n, 17n, 37n, 277n, 551n
U.S. Chamber of Commerce Research Center, 620n, 638n, 645n, 655n
U.S. Department of Commerce, 37n
U.S. Department of Health and Human Services, 655n

U.S. Department of Labor, 38n, 432n, 458n, 498n, 534n
U.S. Federal Mediation and Conciliation Service, 711n
U.S. Government Printing Office, 623n
U.S. Healthcare, Inc., 615
Usher, C. J., 476n, 496n
U.S. Postal Service, 279–280, 293, 297
US West, 350
USX Corporation, 118

V
Valassis Inserts, 350
VandenBos, G. R., 746n
VanDerhei, J. L., 654n
Van Eynde, D. F., 495n
Vasey, J., 231n
Velasquez, M., 38n
Verespec, M. A., 184n
Vicary, R. M., 434n
Viking Freight, 350
Villet, J., 454n
Vincze, J. W., 413n
Vinson, Michelle, 147
Vlachoutsicos, C., 401n
Volkswagen AG, 327
Volvo, 197
Von Glinow, M. A., 112n
Voydanoff, P., 533n
Vroom, V. H., 372n

W
Wachter, M. L., 710n
Wagner, E., 154n
Wagner, F. H., 746n
Wagner, J. A., III, 323n, 325n, 330n, 397n, 613n, 614n
Wagner, R. J., 457n
Walker, A. J., 745n
Walker, B. A., 38n
Walker, George, 68
Walker, J., 77n, 230n
Wall, T. D., 577n
Wallin, J. A., 184n
Wal-Mart Stores, 350
Walsh, Michael, 303
Walters, R. W., 374n
Walton, Richard, 577n, 690, 711n
Walz, P. M., 498n
Wang, 24
Wanous, J. P., 373n, 532n
Warm, J. S., 306n
Warner, J. L., 407n
Watson, D., 306n
Weaver, D. A., 184n

Webb, B., 669, 709n
Webb, S., 669, 709n
Weekley, J., 456n
Weekly, J. A., 406n
Wegmans, 350
Weinbach, Lawrence, 536
Weitz, B. A., 533n
Weitzman, M. L., 612n, 613n
Welbourne, T. M., 613n
Wells Fargo, 376
Wernimont, P. F., 407n
Wester, J., 38n
Western Electric, 4
Wever, K. R., 709n
Wexley, K. N., 209n, 211n, 230n, 231n, 251n, 275n, 276n, 277n, 441n, 455n
Weyerhauser Corporation, 70, 350
Wheeler, H. N., 710n
Wheeler, J. A., 394n
Whirlpool, 72, 196, 232, 267
White, J. B., 305n, 657n
White, J. K., 534n
Whitener, E. M., 407n
Whitestone, D., 76n
Wiatrowski, W. J., 654n
Wiebe, F. A., 185n
Wiersema, M. F., 36n
Wiersma, U., 275n
Wigdor, A. K., 611n
W.I. Gore & Associates, 349
Wikoff, M., 275n
Wilbur, J. L., 498n
Wilhelm, W. R., 304n
Williams, C. R., 305n
Williams, Lynn, 163
Williams, R., 274n
Willis, R., 365n
Wilson, M., 372n, 647n, 656n
Wilson, Mark, 669
Wilson, Richard, 290
Winokur, L. A., 146n
Winslow, R., 372n
Winter, J. Burgess, 702
Winter, L., 373n
Wolf, J., 496n
Wolf, Stephen M., 712–713
Womack, J. P., 577n, 609n, 614n
Woo, J., 153n, 406n
Woodman, R., 77n
Woods, S. B., 457n
Woolard, Edgar S., Jr., 579
Wooldridge, B., 38n
Woolsey, C., 174n
Work/Family Directions Inc., 181
Workforce Solutions, 73, 469
Worthington Industries, 350

Worthy, F. S., 614n
Wright, L., 184n
Wright, P., 75n, 76n, 77n, 209n, 211n, 230n, 276n
Wrightsman, G., 165n
Wrubel, R., 413n
Wynter, L., 154n
Wyon, D. P., 305n

X
Xerox, 11, 29, 298–299, 350, 418, 470, 568, 644

Y
Yamada, K., 306n
Yates, R., 90n, 113n
Yellen, J. L., 576n
Yeung, A., 54n, 77n
Youngblood, S., 76n
Youst, D. B., 457n, 533n
Yukl, G., 277n

Z
Zacarro, S. J., 305n
Zager, R., 455n, 456n

Zales Jewelers, 393–394
Zalesny, M. D., 306n
Zawacki, R., 269n
Zemke, R., 456n, 474n, 496n
Zemke, S., 456n
Zengerle, P., 118n
Zenith Electronics Corporation, 332
Zibell, Jack, 308–309
Zimmerle, D., 496n
Zuniga, J., 118n
Zytec Corporation, 13

SUBJECT INDEX

A

ABRA 2000 Human Resource
    System, 733
Absenteeism, 287
  and child care, 180
Action steps, 134
ADA. *See* Americans with
    Disabilities Act
ADEA. *See* Age Discrimination in
    Employment Act of 1967
Administrative linkage, 50
Adventure learning, 444
Advertising, 358–459
Affirmative action, 148–149, 336–
    338
  and employee development,
    487–489
  and information systems, 733
  and Vietnam veterans, 127
AFL-CIO, 673–676, 679
AFSCME (American Federation of
    State, County, and Municipal
    Employees), 708
Age discrimination, 126
Age Discrimination in Employment
    Act (ADEA) of 1967, 124, 126,
    651
  and personnel selection, 390–391
Agency shop, 677
Agency theory, 583
Agents, 584
Albermarle Paper v. Moody, 142, 242
American Federation of Labor and
    Congress of Industrial
    Organizations (AFL-CIO),
    673–676, 679
American Federation of State,
    County, and Municipal
    Employees (AFSCME), 708
Americans with Disabilities Act
    (ADA), 24–25, 124, 128–129
  and employee benefits, 651
  and personnel selection, 390
  and reasonable accommodation,
    149–152, 390
  and social responsibility, 337
Apprenticeships, 442
Arbitration, 696
Assessment, 472
Assessment center, 253–254, **475**

Assignment flow, 468
Associate union membership, 688
Attitudinal structuring, 690
Audiovisual aids, 440
Autonomy, 223–224
  and job dissatisfaction, 299

B

Bakke v. California Board of Regents,
    123
Baldrige award. *See* Malcolm
    Baldrige National Quality
    Award
Bargaining power, 677–681
BARS. *See* Behaviorally anchored
    rating scales
Basic skills, 431
Behaviorally anchored rating scales
    (BARS), 248–249
  sample of, 250
Behavioral observations scale (BOS),
    249–251
  sample of, 251
Behavior-based conflict, 522
Behavior modeling, 443
Benchmarking, 9
Benchmarks™, 475–477
Benefits programs
  cafeteria-style, 648–650
  disability insurance, 625–626
  medical and life insurance, 627–
    628
  retirement plans, 628–634
  social insurance, 622–626
  time off with pay, 634–636
  unemployment insurance, 625
  workers' compensation, 625–626
Bona fide occupational
    qualification (BFOQ), 137
BOS. *See* Behavioral observations
    scale
Britain
  health care costs in, 639
  unions in, 707
Brito v. Zia, 244, 273
Bundy v. Jackson, 145–146

C

Canada
  health care costs in, 639

  unions in, 707
Career, 505. *See also* Career
    development; Career planning
Career development, 505–508,
    514–531
  and dual careers, 517–520
  and family issues, 521–525
  and information systems, 738–740
  and job loss, 525–528
  plateaus of, 516–517
  and retirement, 528–530
  and skills obsolescence, 520–521
  and socialization, 514–516
  stages of, 507–508
Career path, 517
Career planning, 509–514
  company's role in, 513–514
  components of, 509–510
  employee's role in, 510–512
  manager's role in, 512–513
  and self-assessment, 509
Cause-and-effect diagrams, 259
Checkoff, 677
Child care, 180, 181
  in EEC, 93
  and work schedules, 522–525
Civil Rights Act (CRA)
  of 1866, 123–125
  of 1871, 123–125
  of 1991, 25, 124, 127–128, 389, 391
  and pay structure, 570–574
Classroom instruction, 438
Closed shop, 677
COBRA, 627
Cognitive ability tests, 395–399
Collective bargaining, 668. *See also*
    Labor relations
  contract, 672
Compa-ratio, 559
  and merit increase grid, 589
  and performance ratings, 590
Compensable factors, 552
Compensation. *See* Benefits
    programs; Pay; Pay programs;
    Pay structure
Competition, global, 6–8
Competitive advantage, 2
Competitiveness, 2
Compressed workweek, 176–177,
    523

Computers, 721–726. *See also* Information systems, human resources (HRISs)

Consolidated Omnibus Budget Reconciliation Act (COBRA), 627

Constitution, U.S., 120–123
amendments to, 119, 123
and personnel selection, 388–389

Continuous learning, 419

Contract negotiation, 690–696. *See also* Labor relations

Control charts, 259–260
sample of, 261

Copyright ethics, 452

Corporate campaigns, 689

Correlation coefficient, 321, 323

Cost-benefit analysis, 448–451

Court-ordered affirmative action, 338

CRA. *See* Civil Rights Act

Critical incidents, 248

Cross-cultural preparation, 484–486

CTDs (cumulative trauma disorders), 157–158

Cultural diversity
and communication, 108
and employee development, 484–486
and expatriates, 103–111
and international HRM, 84–90
managing, 21–24

Culture
Harrison's views of, 87–89
Hofstede's views of, 84–87
implications of for HRM, 89–90

Cumulative trauma disorders (CTDs), 157–158

Customers
and employee performance, 267
and HR management, 69–74
and quality, 9

D

Database, 719
master employee, 733

Data-entity relationship diagrams, 727

Data field, 719

Data-flow diagrams, 727

Death by overwork (*karoshi*), 171

Decertification, 671

Defendant's rebuttal
in disparate impact, 141–142
in disparate treatment, 136–137

Delayering, 562

Delphi technique, 329–330

Development, 59, 460

Direct applicants, 360

Directional pattern model, 505

Disability insurance, 625–628

Disabled workers. *See* Human resources

Discharge, 172–175

Discipline, 172–175

Discrimination
age, 126
and benefits plans, 650–651
and pregnant women, 124, 129, 635
reverse, 123, 148–149
sexual, 118
at Shoney's Inc., 155
theories of, 135–145
and workers with disabilities, 128–129, 651–652

Disparate impact, 136, 138–139
at Carrier Corporation, 140

Disparate treatment, 135, 138

Distributive bargaining, 690

Downsizing, 301
and job loss, 525–528

Downward move, 480–481

Drug testing, 402–403

Dual career-path system, 518

Due process, 172–175, 358

Duty of fair representation, 697

E

EAPs (employee assistance programs), 167–170

Economic systems, 94–97

Economy, structure of, 14–18

Education
and employee development, 471–472
and human capital, 90–92

EEC. *See* European Economic Community

EEO-1 report, 733, 734

EEOC (Equal Employment Opportunity Commission), 119, 131–133

Efficiency wage theory, 549

Elder care, 180–181
and retirement, 528–530
and work schedules, 522–525

E-mail, 724
ethics, 296

Emergent strategies, 67–68

Employee assistance programs (EAPs), 167–170

Employee benefits. *See also* Benefits programs

growth of, 619–622
and information systems, 740–744
managing, 636–650
and unionized workers, 703–704
and workers with disabilities, 651
and work schedules, 646

Employee development
approaches to, 471–481
assessment of, 472–477
cross-cultural, 484–486
and diversity, 486–490
and dysfunctional managers, 493–494
and education, 471–472
and globalization, 467
and job experiences, 477–481
and organizational characteristics, 466–471
and relationships, interpersonal, 481–484
and succession planning, 492–493
and union-management programs, 490–492
and work roles, 461–465

Employee performance. *See* Performance management

Employee relations. *See also* Labor relations
family care policies, 180–182
and health, 165–172
and safety, 159–165
and working conditions, 172–182

Employee Retirement Income Security Act (ERISA) of 1974, 629

Employees. *See* Employee development; Employee relations; Human resources; Labor force; Performance management; Personnel selection

Employee stock ownership plans (ESOPs), 596

Employee wellness programs (EWPs), 168, 170–174

Employers, 100 best, 349–350

Employment-at-will doctrine, 173, 358

Empowerment, 28

Equal employment opportunity, 123
and constitutional amendments, 123
current issues, 145–152
and discrimination, 135–145
enforcement of, 131–134
and executive orders, 130

and information systems, 733
and legislation, 119–122, 123–131
and pay structure, 124, 570–574
regulatory model of, 119–120
Equal Employment Opportunity
Commission (EEOC), 119,
131–133
Equal Pay Act of 1963, 124, 125
Equity theory, 545–547
Ergonomics, 225, 226
ERISA (Employee Retirement
Income Security Act), 629
ESOPs (employee stock option
plans), 596
Ethics, 25–26
of cheap labor, 327
copyright, 452
E-mail, 296
European Economic Community
(EEC), 82
social rights in, 92–93
EWPs (employee wellness
programs), 168, 170–174
Executive branch, of U.S.
government, 121–122
Executive Order 10988, 708
Executive Order 11246, 124, 130, 392
Executive Order 11478, 130
Executive orders, 130, 133–134, 392
Executive pay, 568–570, 571, 601–
604
Exercising of authority, 87
Expatriate(s), 97
compensating, 109–111
and employee development,
484–486
managing, 103–111
reacculturation of, 111, 486
Expectancy, 352
Expectancy theory, 352, 583
Experience rating, 625
External analysis, 48

F
Fact finder, 696
Fair Labor Standards Act (FLSA),
125, **574**
Family and Medical Leave Act, 124,
130, 181–182, 521–522, **635**
Family care policies, 180–182
FAS (Financial Accounting
Statement), 106, 652
Federal Labor Relations Authority
(FLRA), 708
Federal Mediation and Conciliation
Service (FMCS), 695

Feedback, 223–224
and employee development,
270–272, 477
and job dissatisfaction, 299
on performance, 270–272
on training, 435–436
Financial Accounting Statement
(FAS) 106, 652
Fleishman Job Analysis System
(FJAS), 211, 212–214
Flextime, 177–178, 523
Forced distribution, 242, 243
Forecasting, 319–331
Formal education programs, 471
Four-fifth's rule, 139
Fourteenth Amendment, 123, 124,
388
France
health care costs in, 639
unions in, 707

G
Gainsharing, 587, 598–600
Games, for training, 443
General Aptitude Test Battery
(GATB), 149, 150, 216, 361
General duty clause, 160
Germany
health care costs in, 639
and human capital, 90–91
legal system in, 92
unification of, 82
unions in, 707
Global issues. *See also* Globalization
competition, 6–8
cultural diversity, 84–90
economic systems, 94–97
education, 90–92
employees, managing, 97–111
European Economic Community,
82, 93
expatriates, 103–111
German unification, 82
human capital, 90–92
North American Free Trade
Agreement, 83–84
political systems, 92
Soviet bloc, 94
Soviet Union disintegration, 83
Globalization. *See also* Global issues
and cultural diversity, 487
and education, 466
and employee commitment, 291
and employee development, 467
and employee training, 439
and ethics of cheap labor, 327

and Gillette Company, 8
and HRM, 6–8, 79–115
and human capital shortage, 51
Japanese management, 90, 347, 507
and labor relations, 705, 706–708
and labor supply, 325–331
and market proximity, 567
and sexual harassment, 146
Soviet Union, personnel selection
in, 401
and stress, Japanese-type, 171
Goals, 48, 134
setting, 510
Graphic rating scales, 244
sample of, 245–246
Grievance procedure, 696–699
Griggs v. Duke Power, 138, 141,
142–143
Group-building techniques, 444

H
Halo error, 268–269
Hands-on techniques, 440
Hardware, 721
Harrison's cultural factors, 87–89
Hawthorne studies, 4
Hazelwood School District v. United
States, 143–144
Health
in EEC, 93
and employee, 165–172
and job withdrawal, 289–291
Health care
costs, 639
and managing medical expenses,
638–643
Health maintenance organizations
(HMOs), 640
Herzberg's Two-Factor Theory, 223
High-leverage training, 419
Histograms, 261
sample of, 261
Hofstede's cultural dimensions,
84–87
Hopkins v. Price Waterhouse, 127, 138
Horns error, 268–269
Host country, 97
Host-country nationals (HCNs), 97
HRISs (human resource information
systems), 29–31, 716
HRM. *See* Human resource
management
Hulin's model of job withdrawal,
284–291
Human capital. *See* Human
resources; Labor force

Human resource information systems (HRISs), 29–31, **716.** *See also* Information systems, human resources
Human resource management (HRM). *See also* Strategic management
and benefits issues, 617–661
and career management, 501–540
competitive challenges to, 1–8, 6–31
and employee development, 459–500
and employee performance, 233–277
and employee relations, 157–186
and employee training, 417–458
and equal employment opportunity, 145–156
global issues in, 1–8
history of, 3–6
and information systems, 715–753
and job analysis, 204, 220
and job choice, 341–355
and job design, 220–228
and labor relations, 666–713
legal environment of, 117–156
pay issues, 543–616
and personnel selection, 375–416
planning, 315–340
recruitment, 355–370
and social challenges, 14–26
strategic, 43–78
and technology challenges, 26–31
and work attitudes, 279–312
Human resource planning
and affirmative action, 336–338
and business strategy, 318
and employee development, 470
and goal setting, 331
and labor demand, 321–324
process of, 319–331
strategic choice, 331–334
subfunctions, 318–319
Human resources. *See also* Labor force; Personnel selection
acquiring, 33–34
and benefits, 60–61
compensating, 34
developing, 34
with disabilities, 93, 149–152, 651–652
and feedback, 270–272, 477
health of, 165–172
and incentives, 60–61
and injuries, 452
and legal issues, 119

management of, 97–111
and pay, 60–61
and performance management, 59–60
planning, 315–316
recruitment of, 59
rights of, 160–161
selection of, 59
shortages of, 51, 315–317
skills of, 15–20, 26–27
temporary, 523, 333, 374
training of, 59
and values, 20–21
and violence, 279–280
work roles of, 461–463

I
Image advertising, 358
Incentive pay, 587, 592–593, 600
Individual Coaching for Effectiveness (ICE), 493–494
Individualism/collectivism, 85, 88
Information systems, human resources (HRISs)
applications, 718–720
and computers, 718–720, 721–726
developing, 727–731
history of, 717–719
Innovation, 87
Instructional design process, 420, 422
Instrumentality, 352
Insurance. *See* Benefits programs
Integrated payroll system, 741
Integrative bargaining, 690
Integrative linkage, 52–53
Interactive video, 443–444
Internal analysis, 48
Interviews, 392–394
Intraorganizational bargaining, 690
Ireland, human capital in, 51, 91
ISO 9000 (International Organization for Standardization 9000), **10–11**
Italy
health care costs in, 639
unions in, 707

J
Japan
health care costs in, 639
labor shortages in, 315–316
management in, 90, 347, 507
pay practice in, 609
stress in, 171
unions in, 707

Job
characteristic theory, 298–300
choice, 345–346
descriptive index, 282–283
element rating scale, 212
hazards, 163–164
loss, 290, 525–528
security, 25, 345–346
sharing, 178–180, 523
structure, 552–559
vacancy, 343–346
Job analysis, 57–59
and HR managers, 205–206
information required for, 207–210, 218–220
and line managers, 206
manager's guide to, 216–220
methods of, 210–216
Job choice
compensatory decision process, 351–354
implicit favorite, 354
and 100 best companies to work for, 349–350
and personal characteristics, 346–355
and vacancy characteristics, 343–346
Job description, 207
sample of, 208
Job descriptive index, 282–283
Job design, 57–59
biological approach to, 222, 225–226, 228
implications of, 227
mechanistic approach to, 221, 225, 228
motivational approach to, 220–224, 228
perceptual/motor approach to, 222, 226–227, 228
Job dissatisfaction
and autonomy, 289
and behavior settings, 295
and organizational roles, 300–302
and organizational tasks, 297–300
and personality, 295
and physical and technological environment, 293–300
and social environment, 294–295
sources of, 291–302
Job enrichment, 298
Job evaluation, 552
Job fair, 364
Job involvement, 287
Job posting, 357

Job rating scales
  involvement, 288
  organizational commitment, 289
  role-rating, 302
  satisfaction, 283, 284
Job redesign, 220
Job rotation, 299–300, 478–480
Job satisfaction, 281
  defining, 281–282
  measures of, 282–284
  rating tools for, 283, 284, 288, 289,
    302
Job specification, 207
Job structure, 545
Job withdrawal, 284
  and behavior change, 286
  and health problems, 289–291
  Hulin's model of, 284–291
  physical, 286–287
  psychological, 287–289
**Joint union-management programs,
  490**–492
Judicial branch, of U.S. government,
  122

K
Karoshi (death by overwork), 171
Key jobs, 551
KSAO. *See* Job specification

L
Labor costs
  comparative, 95, 565, 608–610
  and North American Free Trade
    Agreement, 83
Labor demand, 321–324, 332
Labor force. *See also* Human capital;
  Human resources
  age distribution in, 15
  and benefits plans, 645–647
  composition of, 14
  new entrants to, 16
  and pay structure, 586
  skills of, 15–20
  U.S., and pay, 564–570, 608–610
Labor-market competition, 548
Labor relations. *See also* Employee
    relations
  bargaining power, 677–681
  business strategy, 61
  contract administration, 696–700
  contract negotiation, 690–696
  and globalization, 706–708
  goals, 669–673
  grievance procedure, 696–699
  legal framework, 681–685

and National Labor Relations
    Board, 684–689
  organizing, 685–689
  and productivity, 704–706
  strategies, 699–700
  strikes, 694–696, 701–703
  unfair, 682–683
  union structure, 669–673
Labor supply, 325–331, 332
  and cheap-labor ethics, 327
Labor unions. *See* Labor relations
Landrum-Griffin Act, 683
Layoffs, 290, 525–528
Leading indicator, 321
Learning organization, 419
Legal cases
  Albermarle Paper v. Moody, 142, 242
  Bakke v. California Board of Regents,
    123
  Brito v. Zia, 244, 273
  Bundy v. Jackson, 145–146
  Griggs v. Duke Power, 138, 141,
    142–143
  *Hazelwood School District v. United
    States*, 143–144
  Hopkins v. Price Waterhouse, 127, 138
  Lorance v. AT&T Technologies, 127,
    132
  Martin v. Wilks, 127, 149
  McDonnell Douglas Corp. v. Green,
    137, 144
  Meritor Savings Bank v. Vinson, 147
  Patterson v. McClean Credit Union,
    125, 127
  UAW v. Johnson Controls, Inc., 137
  Wards Cove Packing Co. v. Antonio,
    122, 127, 141
Legal environment, 24–25. *See also*
    Affirmative action; Constitution,
    U.S.; Discrimination; Equal
    employment opportunity; Legal
    cases; government acts by name
    (e.g., Civil Rights Act)
  and HRM, 92, 117–156
  and performance management,
    270–272
  of personnel selection, 387–392
  of training, 451–453
  U.S., 119–130
Legislative branch, of U.S.
    government, 121
  and personnel selection, 389–392
Life-cycle model, 505
Life insurance, 627–628. *See also*
    Benefits programs
Literacy audit, 431–432

Local area network, 723
**Long-term-short-term orientation,
  87**
Lorance v. AT&T Technologies, 127,
  132

M
Mainframe computers, 717
Maintenance of membership, 677
**Malcolm Baldrige National Quality
  Award, 11**–12
  and Reagan, Ronald, 11
  at Zytec Corporation, 13
Management by objectives (MBO),
  254–255
Managing diversity, 486–490
Managing employees. *See* Human
  resources; Performance
  management
Maquiladora plants, 83, 100
Marginal tax rate, 621
Martin v. Wilks, 127, 149
Masculinity-femininity, 86
Math coprocessor, 723
MBO (management by objectives),
  254–255
MBTI (Myers-Briggs Type Indicator),
  472–475
McDonnell Douglas Corp. v. Green,
  137, 144
Mediation, 695
Medical insurance, 627–628. *See also*
    Benefits programs
Medical plan, sample of, 641–642
Medicare, 622–624
Mentor, 482
Mentoring, 482–484
Merit increase grid, 588
  sample of, 589
Meritor Savings Bank v. Vinson, 147
Merit pay, 587, 588–591
Minimum wage, 574
Mission, 48
Mixed-motive cases, 138
Mixed standard scales, 244–246
  sample of, 247
Motivation to learn, 428
Multinationals, U.S., employees of,
  81
Multiple correlation, 322
**Myers-Briggs Type Indicator
  (MBTI), 472**–475

N
NAFTA (North American Free Trade
    Agreement), 83–84

National Institute for Occupational
   Safety and Health
   (NIOSH), 159
National Labor Relations Act
   (NLRA), 670, 681–685
National Labor Relations Board
   (NLRB), 684–689
Needs assessment, 420–428
Negative effectivity, 295–297
Networks, 723
NIOSH (National Institute for
   Occupational Safety and
   Health), 159
Nominal group technique, 324
Noncompensatory decision process,
   347
Nonkey jobs, 551
North American Free Trade
   Agreement (NAFTA), 83–84

O
Obsolescence, 520–521
Occupational Safety and Health Act
   of 1970 (OSHA), 159–163
Office of Federal Contract
   Compliance Procedures
   (OFCCP), 133–134
Old Age, Survivors, Disability, and
   Health Insurance
   (OASDHI), 624
100 best U.S. employers, 349–350
One-way linkage, 50
On-the-job training (OJT), 440–441
Organizational analysis, 421
Organizational behavior
   modification (OBM), 251–253
Organizational commitment,
   287–289
   scale of, 289
Organizational socialization, 514
Organization-based model, 505
Orientation, 515–516
OSHA (Occupational Safety and
   Health Act), 159

P
Paired comparison, 242–243
PAQ (Position Analysis
   Questionnaire), 215–216, 217
Parallel testing, 731
Parent country, 97
Parent-country nationals (PCNs), 97
Pareto chart, 259
   sample of, 260
Part-time employment, 178–180
   as alternative practice, 523
   and employee benefits, 646

Pattern or practice, 136, 143–144
Patterson v. McClean Credit Union,
   125, 127
Pay. See also Pay structure
   comparisons, international,
      608–610
   influence on individuals, 583–586
   and information systems, 740–744
   and labor force, 583–586
   managerial and executive, 601–604
   process issues, 604–607
   programs, 586–601
   rate ranges, 550–551
   strategy, 607–608
   for time off, 634–636
   and unionized workers, 703–704
Pay grades, 556–557
Pay level, 545
   developing, 547–552
   and job choice, 345
Pay-policy line, 554
Pay programs
   gainsharing, 587, 598–600
   incentives, group, 600
   incentives, individual, 587, 592
   merit pay, 587, 588–591
   profit sharing, 587, 593–595
   stock ownership, 587, 595–597
Pay structure, 545
   and Civil Rights Act, 570–574
   and communication, 560–561, 605
   and compensation costs,
      monitoring, 559
   developing, 553–557
   employee participation in, 559–560,
      605
   and equal employment
      opportunity, 570–574
   equity theory of, 545–547
   executive pay, 568–570
   and government regulation,
      570–574
   job-based, 561–564
   and job structure, 552–559
   and market pressures, 547–548
   market survey data, 549–552,
      554–555
   and pay grades, 556–557
   and pay levels, 547–552
   and U.S. labor force, 564–568
   and wage laws, 574–575
Pension Benefit Guaranty
   Corporation (PBGC), 629
Pension benefits, 651–652. See also
   Employee benefits; Retirement
Performance appraisal, 234, 477
Performance feedback, 234, 270–272

Performance management, 59,
   234–236, 427
   and feedback, 270–272
   and information sources, 263–267
   legal issues of, 272–273
   and measurement, 238–241
   organizational model of, 235–237
   purposes of, 237–238
Performance measurement, 265
   and compa-ratio, 590
   methods, 244–270
   at Peoples Natural Gas, 278
Performance planning and
   evaluation (PPE), 236
Peripheral, 722
Personality inventories, 398
Person analysis, 421
Personnel policies, 356–359
Personnel selection. See also
   Personnel selection methods
   and age discrimination, 390–391
   legal issues of, 387–392
   at Nucor Corporation, 409–413
   and workers with disabilities, 390
Personnel selection methods
   cognitive ability tests, 395–398, 404
   drug tests, 402–403, 404
   generalizability of, 384–385, 405
   honesty tests, 400–402, 404
   interviews, 392–394, 404
   legal issues of, 387–392, 405
   personality inventories, 398, 400,
      404
   physical ability tests, 395, 404
   references and biographical data,
      394–395, 396, 404
   reliability of, 377–379, 404
   types of, 392–403
   utility of, 385–386, 405
   validity of, 380–384, 404
   work samples, 398–400, 404
Plaintiff's burden
   in disparate impact, 139–141
   in disparate treatment, 135–136
Plaintiff's rebuttal
   in disparate impact, 142
   in disparate treatment, 137–138
Plant Closing Act of 1988, 176
Plateaued, 516
Policy capturing, 344
Polygraph Act, 401
Polygraph tests, 400–402
Position Analysis Questionnaire
   (PAQ), 215–216, 217
Power distance, 85
Preferred provider organizations
   (PPOs), 640

Pregnancy Discrimination Act of 1978, 635
Pregnancy Discrimination Act of 1979, 124, 129
Preretirement socialization, 528
Principals, 584
Process-flow analysis charts, 258–259
Profit, 87
Profit sharing, 587, **593–595**
ProMES (productivity measurement and evaluation system), 200
samples of, 201, 257
Promotions, 480–481
Psychological contract, 510

Q
Quality
at Allied Signal, 60
and Baldrige award, 13
and bonuses, 601
and competition, international, 8–14
and competition, managed, 644
at Ensoniq Corporation, 264
and information systems, 744
and productivity, 102
and temporary employees, 333
and TQM, 60, 264, 462
and training, 438
and work-flow design, 204
at Zytec Corporation, 13

R
Race norming, 391
Radius of trust, 87
Range spread, 556
Ranking, 242
Rater accuracy training, 269
Rater error training, 269
Reasonable accommodation, 149–152, 390
Reconstruction Civil Rights Acts, 123–125
Recruiters, 366–377
Recruitment, 59. *See also* Human resources; Personnel selection; Personnel selection methods; Recruitment sources
Recruitment sources
advertising, 360–361
applicants and referrals, 360
colleges and universities, 364–365
evaluating quality of, 365–366
executive search firms, 362–364
internal/external, 359–360
private employment agencies, 362, 374

public employment agencies, 361–362
recruiters, 366–370
Reference checks, 392–394
Referrals, 360
Rehabilitation Act of 1973, 124
Reinforcement theory, 583
Relational database, 719
sample of, 721
Reliability, 240–241
estimation of, 379
of personnel selection methods, 377–379
standards of, 379–380
Retirement, 528–530, 628–634
Retrenchment, 65–66
Reverse discrimination, 123, 148–149
Right-to-work laws, 677
Rigor of the ethical system, 87
Role analysis technique, 301, 302
Role behaviors, 63

S
Safety, in the workplace, 159–165
Safety awareness programs, 163–166
Salary. *See* Pay; Pay programs; Pay structure
Saving, 87
Scattergrams, 261–262
sample of, 262
Scenario analysis, 727
Scientific Management, 3, 225
Section 401(k) plans, 630, 631
Self-assessment, 509
Self-directed learning, 441
Self-efficacy, 430
Service bureau, 740
Sexual harassment, 145–148
EEOC definition of, 147
overseas, 146
Shift work, 523
Simulations, training, 442–443
Situational constraints, 431
Skill-based pay, 562
Skills
of employees, 15–20
obsolescence, 520–521
and pay structures, 562–563
requirements, 26–27
training, 431–433
variety, 223–224
Social insurance, 622–626. *See also* Benefits programs
Socialism, 94, 95
Social responsibility
and basic skills training, 434

child and elder care, 181
and corporate downsizing, 301
and cultural diversity, 22, 491
in the EEC, 93
empowerment and pay, 606
and executive pay, 571
and 401(k) plans, 631
hiring laid-off employees, 363
and labor relations, 702
older worker opportunity, 529
at Pacific Gas and Electric, 22
at Principal Financial Group, 151
race norming, 391
and small businesses, 69, 363
and workers with disabilities, 151, 337
Social Security Act of 1935, 361, 622, 624
Social support, 294, 431
Soviet Union
disintegration of, 83
personnel selection in, 401
Specificity, 241
Standard deviation rule, 139–141
Stock options, 595
Stock ownership, 587, 595–597
Strain-based conflict, 522
Strategic choice, 49
Strategic congruence, 239
Strategic human resource management, 46
Strategic management, 45–48, 61–62
and customer orientation, 69–74
directional, 64–67
emergent, 67–68
and formulation of strategy, 48–55
and implementation of strategy, 55–68
at People Express, 53–55
and retrenchment, 65–66
and staffing, 468–469
and training, 425
Strategy formulation, 46
Strategy implementation, 46, 55–68
Stress, 289–291
and death by overwork, 171
Strikes, 694–696, 701–703
Subject-matter experts (SMEs), 210, 213–215, 216
Succession planning, 492–493
Summary plan description (SPD), 631
Supply flow, 468
Support services, 523–525
Supreme Court, U.S., 122
and Clarence Thomas hearings, 145
Sweden, unions in, 707

T

Taft-Hartley Act, 683

Task analysis, 422
  inventory, 214–215
Tax rates
  comparative, 96
  marginal, 621–622
Technology and structure
  and cumulative trauma disorders,
      165
  and disparate impact, 140
  dual career-path system, 520
  E-mail ethics, 296
  and ergonomics at Toyota, 226
  and hiring standards, 389
  and information systems, 736
  and keyboard designs, 165
  at Levi Strauss & Company, 28
  and personnel selection, 389
  and recruitment databases, 365
  and socialism, 94
  and stock options, 596
  and teamwork, 28, 269, 464
  training vs. learning, 421
  and unions, 669
  and Workforce Solutions (IBM), 73
Temporary work, 523
Theory Y management, 4
Third country, 97
Third-country nationals (TCNs), 97
Thirteenth Amendment, 123, 124
  and discrimination theories,
      135–145
Thorndike's Law of Effect, 583
Time-based conflict, 522
Timetables, 134
Title VII (of Civil Rights Act), 124,
    125–126, 132
Total quality management (TQM),
    9, 256–264
  at Carrier Corporation, 204
  at Ensoniq Corporation, 263
  at Southwest Airlines, 187–191
Training, 59. *See also* Training
    systems
  at Arthur Andersen, 536–540
  and business strategy, 425

  and globalization, 439
  high-leverage, 419–420
  and information systems, 738–740
  and learning environment, 433–436
  legal issues of, 451–453
  needs assessment, 420–428
  systems, 420–451
  team, 445
Training objectives, 433
Training outcomes, 445
Training systems
  and cost-benefit analysis, 448–451
  and employee readiness, 428–433
  evaluating, 445–451
  group-building techniques,
      444–445
  hands-on techniques, 440–441
  and learning environment, 433–436
  needs assessment, 420–423
  presentation techniques, 438–440
  self-directed learning, 441–444
  and skill-based pay, 453
Transfer, 480–481
Transfer of training, 436–437
Transitional matrices, 328–329
Transnational process, 101
Transnational representation, 101
Transnational scope, 101
Two-way linkage, 52

U

UAW v. Johnson Controls, Inc., 137
Uncertainty avoidance, 86
Unemployment insurance, 625
*Uniform Guidelines on Employee
    Selection Procedures,* 133, 273
Unions, 61. *See also* Labor relations
  and employee development,
      490–492
Union shop, 677
United Auto Workers (UAW), 66,
    679, 705. *See also* Labor relations
  and Saturn Corporation, 748–753
Utilization analysis, 133–134

V

Valence, 352

Validity, 239
  in personnel selection, 239–240,
      380–385
Vesting rights, 632
Video teleconferencing, 439
Vietnam Era Veteran's Readjustment
    Act of 1974, 127
Virus, 726
Vocational maturity, 355
  model of, 356
Vocational Rehabilitation Act of
    1973, 126–127

W

Wages. *See* Pay; Pay programs; Pay
    structure
Wards Cove Packing Co. v. Antonio,
    122, 127, 141
Women
  discrimination against, 129
  in workforce, 573
  as working mothers, 177
  and work schedules, 525
Work, 87
Work attitudes
  at Detroit Deisel, 308–311
  job dissatisfaction, 291–302
  job satisfaction, 281–284
  job withdrawal, 284–291
Workers' compensation, 625–626. *See
    also* Benefits programs
Work-family conflicts, 521–525
Work-flow analysis, 199–204
Work-flow design, 199
Work-force dynamics analysis, 737
Work-force utilization review, 336
Work schedules, 523
  and child care, 522–525
  flextime, 177–178, 523
  nontraditional, 176–178
Work value survey, 348

Y

Yield ratios, 365

1